THE CAMBRIDGE HISTORY OF
IRELAND

The eighteenth and nineteenth centuries were an era of continuity as well as change. Though properly portrayed as the era of 'Protestant Ascendancy' it embraces two phases – the eighteenth century when that ascendancy was at its peak; and the nineteenth century when the Protestant elite sustained a determined rearguard defence in the face of the emergence of modern Catholic nationalism. Employing a chronology that is not bound by traditional datelines, this volume moves beyond the familiar political narrative to engage with the economy, society, population, emigration, religion, language, state formation, culture, art and architecture, and the Irish abroad. It provides new and original interpretations of a critical phase in the emergence of a modern Ireland that, while focused firmly on the island and its traditions, moves beyond the nationalist narrative of the twentieth century to provide a history of late early modern Ireland for the twenty-first century.

JAMES KELLY is Professor of History at Dublin City University. He is a member of the Irish Manuscripts Commission, and President of the Irish Economic and Social History Society. His publications include *That Damn'd Thing Called Honour: Duelling in Ireland, 1750-1860* (1995); *Henry Flood: Patriots and Politics in Eighteenth-Century Ireland* (1998); *Poynings' Law and the Making of Law in Ireland, 1660-1800* (2007); and, as editor (with Martyn Powell), *Clubs and Societies in Eighteenth-Century Ireland* (2010); (with Mary Ann Lyons), *The Proclamations of Ireland, 1660-1820* (5 vols. 2014), and (with Elizabeth FitzPatrick) *Food and Drink in Ireland* (2016). His book *Sport in Ireland, 1600-1840* (2014) won the special commendation prize offered by the National University of Ireland in 2016.

THE CAMBRIDGE HISTORY OF
IRELAND

GENERAL EDITOR

THOMAS BARTLETT, professor emeritus of Irish history,
University of Aberdeen

This authoritative, accessible and engaging four-volume history vividly presents the Irish story – or stories – from c.600 to the present, within its broader Atlantic, European, imperial and global contexts. While the volumes benefit from a strong political narrative framework, they are distinctive also in including essays that address the full range of social, economic, religious, linguistic, military, cultural, artistic and gender history, and in challenging traditional chronological boundaries in a manner that offers new perspectives and insights. Each volume examines Ireland's development within a distinct period, and offers a complete and rounded picture of Irish life, while remaining sensitive to the unique Irish experience. Bringing together an international team of experts, this landmark history both reflects recent developments in the field and sets the agenda for future study.

VOLUMES IN THE SERIES

VOLUME I
600–1550
EDITED BY BRENDAN SMITH

VOLUME II
1550–1730
EDITED BY JANE OHLMEYER

VOLUME III
1730–1880
EDITED BY JAMES KELLY

VOLUME IV
1880 to the Present
EDITED BY THOMAS BARTLETT

THE CAMBRIDGE HISTORY OF
IRELAND

*

VOLUME III
1730–1880

*

Edited by
JAMES KELLY
Dublin City University

CAMBRIDGE
UNIVERSITY PRESS

CAMBRIDGE
UNIVERSITY PRESS

University Printing House, Cambridge CB2 8BS, United Kingdom

One Liberty Plaza, 20th Floor, New York, NY 10006, USA

477 Williamstown Road, Port Melbourne, VIC 3207, Australia

314–321, 3rd Floor, Plot 3, Splendor Forum, Jasola District Centre, New Delhi – 110025, India

79 Anson Road, #06-04/06, Singapore 079906

Cambridge University Press is part of the University of Cambridge.

It furthers the University's mission by disseminating knowledge in the pursuit of education, learning, and research at the highest international levels of excellence.

www.cambridge.org
Information on this title: www.cambridge.org/9781107115200
DOI: 10.1017/9781316335680

First published 2018
Paperback edition first published 2020

Printed in the United Kingdom by TJ International, Padstow, Cornwall

A catalogue record for this publication is available from the British Library.

ISBN – 4-Volume Set 978-1-107-16729-2 Hardback
ISBN – Volume I 978-1-107-11067-0 Hardback
ISBN – Volume II 978-1-107-11763-1 Hardback
ISBN – Volume III 978-1-107-11520-0 Hardback
ISBN – Volume IV 978-1-107-11354-1 Hardback
ISBN – Set 978-1-316-61783-0 Paperback
ISBN – Volume I 978-1-107-52756-0 Paperback
ISBN – Volume II 978-1-107-54046-0 Paperback
ISBN – Volume III 978-1-107-53559-6 Paperback
ISBN – Volume IV 978-1-107-53415-5 Paperback

Contents

Introduction: Interpreting Late Early Modern Ireland   *1*

JAMES KELLY

PART I
POLITICS

1 · Irish Jacobitism, 1691–1790   *23*

VINCENT MORLEY

2 · The Politics of Protestant Ascendancy, 1730–1790   *48*

JAMES KELLY

3 · Ireland during the Revolutionary and Napoleonic
Wars, 1791–1815   *74*

THOMAS BARTLETT

4 · The Impact of O'Connell, 1815–1850   *102*

PATRICK M. GEOGHEGAN

Contents

Contents

Contents

Illustrations

Figures

Tables

Maps

Contributors

TOBY BARNARD, Fellow Emeritus, Hertford College, Oxford University.

COLIN BARR, Senior Lecturer, School of Divinity, History and Philosophy, University of Aberdeen.

THOMAS BARTLETT, Professor Emeritus, School of Divinity, History and Philosophy, University of Aberdeen.

ANDY BIELENBERG, Senior Lecturer, School of History, University College Cork.

MICHAEL BROWN, Professor of Irish, Scottish and Enlightenment History, University of Aberdeen.

SARAH-ANNE BUCKLEY, Lecturer, Department of History, NUI Galway.

CHRISTINE CASEY, Associate Professor in Architectural History, Department of History of Art, Trinity College Dublin.

LIAM CHAMBERS, Senior Lecturer and Head of Department of History, Mary Immaculate College, Limerick.

MAURA CRONIN, Senior Lecturer, Department of History, Mary Immaculate College, Limerick.

BARRY CROSBIE, Assistant Professor, Department of Literature and Cultural Studies, The Education University of Hong Kong.

VIRGINIA CROSSMAN, Professor of Modern Irish History, Department of History, Philosophy and Religion, Oxford Brookes University.

DAVID DICKSON, Professor of Modern History, Department of History, Trinity College Dublin.

AIDAN DOYLE, Lecturer, Roinn na NuaGhaeilge, University College Cork.

PATRICK M. GEOGHEGAN, Professor in Modern History, Department of History, Trinity College Dublin.

PETER GRAY, Professor of Modern Irish History, School of History, Anthropology, Philosophy and Politics, Queen's University Belfast.

PATRICK GRIFFIN, Madden-Hennebry Professor of History and Department Chair, Department of History, University of Notre Dame.

BRIAN GURRIN, Post-doctoral Research Fellow at Ulster University.

ANDREW R. HOLMES, Lecturer in History, School of History, Anthropology, Philosophy and Politics, Queen's University Belfast.

DOUGLAS KANTER, Associate Professor of History, Florida Atlantic University.

JAMES KELLY, Professor of History, School of History and Geography, Dublin City University.

KEVIN KENNY, Professor of History, Boston College

IAN McBRIDE, Foster Professor of Irish History, Hertford College, Oxford University.

VINCENT MORLEY, independent scholar.

LESA NÍ MHUNGHAILE, Lecturer, Roinn na Gaeilge, NUI Galway.

THOMAS O'CONNOR, Senior Lecturer, History Department, Maynooth University.

CIARAN O'NEILL, Ussher Assistant Professor, Department of History, Trinity College Dublin.

MARTYN J. POWELL, Professor of History, and Head of Department, Department of History and Welsh History, University of Aberystwyth.

General Acknowledgements

As General Editor of the Cambridge History of Ireland, I wish to express my gratitude to all those who assisted in bringing these four volumes to publication. My fellow editors, Brendan Smith, Jane Ohlmeyer and James Kelly have been unstinting with their time and unwavering in their determination to bring their respective volumes to completion as expeditiously as possible. John Cunningham offered vital editorial support at key points in this process. The team at Cambridge University Press, headed by Liz Friend-Smith, supported initially by Amanda George and latterly by Claire Sissen and Bethany Thomas, has been at all times enthusiastic about the project. It has been a great pleasure working with them. My thanks to the often unsung archivists whose documentary collections were freely drawn upon by the contributors in all volumes, to those who helped source images, and to those who drew the informative maps. Lastly, my warmest thanks to all the contributors who gave freely of their expertise in writing their chapters, and for their patience in awaiting publication of their efforts.

Thomas Bartlett, MRIA
General Editor, The Cambridge History of Ireland

Acknowledgements

The preparation of this volume could not have taken place without the good will and support of many people. It is a pleasure in this context to thank the contributors individually and collectively for their endeavour, and enthusiasm for the project. This has greatly assisted with the creation and construction of the volume. I wish also to thank my fellow-editors, Professor Tom Bartlett, Professor Jane Ohlmeyer and Professor Brendan Smith, for their fellowship and collegiality, and for their guidance and advice. Thanks are also extended to Dr John Cunningham for the administrative assistance he provided which has assisted with coordination and preparation during the planning and editing of this volume.

Since no work of history can ever be undertaken, still less completed, without access to the sources in manuscript, print and digital form, it is appropriate that the editor acknowledge the many libraries, librarians and library assistants who have helped in myriad ways to make this work possible. I wish, particularly, to thank Mary Broderick of the National Library for her assistance. A more specific gratitude and acknowledgement is extended to the owners, custodians, trustees and keepers of the manuscripts cited in this work that were consulted in the Archdiocese of Sydney archives; Archives du Collège des Irlandais, Paris; Archives du Ministère des Affaires Étrangères, Paris; Archives of San Clemente, Rome; Archivo della Sacra Congregozione della Dottrina dell Fide, Rome; the Bodleian Library, Oxford University; Borthwick Institute, York; the British Library, London; Cambridge University Library; Cashel Diocesan Archives, Cashel; Christ Church, Oxford University; Dublin City Archives; Dublin Diocesan Archives; Lambeth Palace Library, London; Linenhall Library, Belfast; The National Archives (at Kew); the National Archives of Ireland, Dublin; the National Library of Ireland, Dublin; the National Library of Scotland, Edinburgh; the National Library of Wales, Aberystwyth; Nottingham University Library; Pontifical Irish College, Rome; the Presbyterian Historical Society of Ireland Library and

Archives, Belfast; the Public Record Office of Northern Ireland, Belfast; Royal Archives, Windsor; Royal Irish Academy, Dublin; St Mary's Seminary and University Archives, Baltimore; St. Pauls-without-the-Walls, Rome; Somerset Record Office, Taunton; and W.L. Clements Library, Ann Arbor, Michigan. Acknowledgement is offered in respect of the illustrations in the tables of illustrations and figures above.

James Kelly
Dublin City University

Abbreviations

AAI	*Art and architecture of Ireland*, A. Carpenter gen. ed., 5 vols. (New Haven: Yale University Press, 2014)
AAS	Archives of the Archdiocese of Sydney
Add. MS	Additional Manuscript
AICP	Archives du Collège des Irlandais, Paris
BL	British Library
Bodl.	Bodleian Library, Oxford
b.	born
c.	*circa*
CP	Cullen papers
dep.	deposit
d.	died
DDA	Dublin Diocesan Archives
DSE	Dublin Stock Exchange
edn	edition
GDP	gross domestic product
HO	Home Office
HMC	Historical Manuscripts Commission
HMSO	Her Majesty's Stationery Office
IAA	Irish Architectural Archive
IIP	Independent Irish Party
IRB	Irish Republican Brotherhood
ITS	Irish Texts Society
MP	Member of Parliament
MS(S)	Manuscript(s)
NAI	National Archives of Ireland
NGI	National Gallery of Ireland
NLI	National Library of Ireland

NLS	National Library of Scotland
n.d.	no date
NKP	New Kirby papers
NPG	National Portrait Gallery
n.s.	new series
ODNB	*Oxford Dictionary of National Biography* (60 vols., Oxford, 2004)
PG	*Pennsylvania Gazette*
PICRA	Pontifical Irish College, Rome, Archives
PRONI	Public Record Office of Northern Ireland
RDS	Royal Dublin Society
RIA	Royal Irish Academy
SP	State Papers
TCD	Trinity College Dublin
TNA	The National Archives, Public Record Office
UCC	University College Cork
UCD	University College Dublin
UVF	Ulster Volunteer Force
WSC	Wide Street Commission

General Introduction

The aims of this four-volume History of Ireland are quite straightforward. First, we seek to offer students, and the general reader, a detailed survey, based on the latest research, of the history of the island from early medieval times to the present. As with other Cambridge histories, a chronological approach, in the main, has been adopted, and there is a strong narrative spine to the four volumes. However, the periods covered in each volume are not the traditional ones and we hope that this may have the effect of forcing a re-evaluation of the familiar periodisation of Irish history and of the understanding it has tended to inspire. A single twist of the historical kaleidoscope can suggest – even reveal – new patterns, beginnings and endings. As well, among the one hundred or so chapters spread over the four volumes, there are many that adopt a reflective tone as well as strike a discursive note. There are also a number that tackle topics that have hitherto not found their way into the existing survey literature. Second, we have sought at all times to locate the history of Ireland in its broader context, whether European, Atlantic or, latterly, global. Ireland may be an island, but the people of the island for centuries have been dispersed throughout the world, with significant concentrations in certain countries, with the result that the history of Ireland and the history of the Irish people have never been coterminous. Lastly, the editors of the individual volumes – Brendan Smith, Jane Ohlmeyer, James Kelly and myself – have enlisted contributors who have, as well as a capacity for innovative historical research, demonstrated a talent for writing lucid prose. For history to have a social purpose – or indeed any point – it must be accessible, and in these volumes we have endeavoured to ensure that this is the case: readers will judge with what success.

Thomas Bartlett, MRIA
General Editor, The Cambridge History of Ireland

MAP 1. Map of Ireland.

Introduction: Interpreting Late Early Modern Ireland

JAMES KELLY

The history of the eighteenth and nineteenth centuries in Ireland poses a variety of hermeneutical challenges. While this period was traditionally depicted by those of the Catholic and nationalist tradition as an era when a foreign minority Protestant elite oppressed the native (Catholic) majority, the historical and historiographical perspectives of those in the Protestant tradition were disposed to be more positive. Though these readings are now anachronistic, they continue to register in popular discourse and, to a degree, among those who take their historical understanding from an engagement with material culture (art and architecture particularly). As a result, any attempt to interpret the eighteenth and nineteenth centuries must come to terms with the fact that the collective memory is anchored in atavistic attitudes as well as in a formative historiography that long mirrored the ethno-religious division that shaped the era. Guided by these considerations, this introduction seeks, using the narratives generated by a variety of English and German visitors, in the first instance to highlight the depth and nature of the divisions that existed and with which historians of the period must engage. Second, it seeks by briefly surveying the major trends over a century and a half to locate the volume and its content in its historiographical context.

'Improvement' versus 'Contentment'

Writing in 1780, in his little-read 'tour through Ireland', Philip Luckombe (1730–1803) commented approvingly that over the course of 'ninety years' the 'island' which, for many centuries, was 'a continual field of blood … has made … a vast progress … in almost every thing'.[1] Though there is nothing

---

1 P. Luckombe, *A Tour through Ireland: in several entertaining Letters wherein the Present State of that Kingdom is considered and the most noted Cities, Towns, Seats, Rivers, Buildings etc are described, interspersed with observations on manners, customs, antiquities, curiosities, and Natural History of that Country* (London: Lowndes, 1780), p. x; for Luckombe see *ODNB, sub nomine.*

1

in Luckombe's travelogue to suggest that he was as deferential as his better-known contemporary, Arthur Young, to the Anglo-Irish elite his admiration of 'elegant seats', 'well planted' villages, 'handsome' Protestant churches and 'a fine fertile and populous country' echoed their preoccupation with 'improvement' and 'industry'. This climaxed, in Luckombe's wordy narrative, with his lyrical description of the 'genteel, sensible and friendly' inhabitants of Lurgan, County Armagh – 'one of the prettiest little market-towns in the north of this kingdom' – and his endorsement of their lifestyle: 'from the similarity of … the language, manners, and dispositions of its inhabitants to those of the English, [it] ha[s] for many years acquired the name of Little England, and an Englishman at Lurgan … will think himself in his own country'.[2]

If there are few more explicit illustrations of the benefits of an anglicised vision of 'improvement' for Ireland, its more general merits were indicated by another travel writer. James Hall (of Walthamstow, Essex) observed *en passant* in his account of his tour of Ireland in 1812 that 'the man' who makes 'some new and useful improvement' like 'a happy adventurer at sea, discovers, as it were an unknown land, and imports an additional trade to his own country'.[3] And, commenting upon what might advantageously be done in Ireland, Hall recommended that the landed proprietors who sought 'to rouse tenants to industry, and better their condition' should follow the example of their enlightened peers (he elsewhere instanced John Foster of Collon, County Louth, as a model) and 'give tolerably long leases, on condition that, year after year, the tenants improve certain portions of their farm, describing such improvements minutely, and making these *a sine qua non* to the continuance of the lease'.[4] He did not add that this was the practice in England. But the 'pleasure' he too took from the 'neat, cleanly habitations' he observed in Ulster was in such stark contrast to the 'wretched' mud cabins and swarms of ragged beggars he (and others) observed elsewhere that they epitomised the benefits that must flow if the population forswore indolence, and directed their energies to the maintenance of 'decent and comfortable' cottages, with 'neat and useful' gardens populated 'with … good vegetables', and adorned with 'a few humble flowers and shrubs' – in other words, embraced the

2 Luckombe, *A Tour through Ireland*, pp. 314–15.
3 J. Hall, *Tour through Ireland: particularly the Interior and least known parts*, 2 vols. (London: R.P. Moore, 1813), vol. ii, p. 209.
4 Ibid., pp. 219–20, 293–4; for Foster see A.P.W. Malcomson, *John Foster (1740–1828): the politics of improvement and prosperity* (Dublin: Four Courts Press, 2011).

culture of improvement as it was practised in England.[5] It also supported the conclusion, advanced by John Bernard Trotter, who toured the island in the 1810s, that it was in Ireland's interest to accede to a dependent relationship with Great Britain. 'I consider their [the Irish nation's] happiness and prosperity to be inseparably linked with England's friendship! It is that rational independence at home, under the British government, which Flanders long enjoyed under Austria, and Norway under Denmark ... The wild and detestable phantom of mistaken liberty ought not to delude them [the Irish people] ... They are a nation more suited to set and execute, than to govern and plan.'[6] Though Trotter did not offer this observation in support of the Anglo-Irish Union, about which he possessed well-conceived reservations, his conviction that it was in Ireland's interest to accept a dependent relationship with Great Britain sat easily with his view of 'the vast advantages of English improvement'.[7]

Support for a legislative union was the most striking political manifestation of the shared sense of belonging binding Protestants in Britain and Ireland of which the common commitment to improvement was a still longer standing economic and cultural expression.[8] The most notable organisational expressions of improvement in operation in Ireland were the Dublin Society, established in 1731, and the Linen Board, established twenty years earlier.[9] Indicatively, both were funded by parliament, and while it is the case that the commercial success of the linen industry was not dependent on the Board, the fact that the Dublin Society offered 'instruction in physics, chemistry, mineralogy, botany, zoology, architecture, sculpture, drawing, etching all free of charge' in 1820 when Heinrich Meidlinger, a German merchant, visited the country attests to its cultural range and improving zeal.[10] A no less striking attestation, chronicled *in extenso* in Arthur Young's *Tour of Ireland, 1776–79,* is

5 Hall, *Tour through Ireland*, vol. II, p. 212; J.B. Trotter, *Walks through Ireland in the years 1812, 1814 and 1817* (London: Richard Phillips, 1819), pp. 16, 17.

6 Trotter, *Walks through Ireland*, p. 597. Trotter was the Irish-born private secretary to the British foreign secretary, Charles James Fox: see *ODNB, sub nomine.*

7 Trotter, *Walks through Ireland*, pp. 295, 404–5.

8 D. Kanter, *The making of British Unionism, 1740–1848: politics, government, and the Anglo-Irish constitutional relationship* (Dublin: Four Courts Press, 2009); T.C. Barnard, *Improving Ireland? Projectors, prophets and profiteers, 1641–1786* (Dublin: Four Courts Press, 2008).

9 H.D. Gribbon, 'The Irish Linen Board, 1711–1828' in L.M. Cullen and T.C. Smout (eds.), *Comparative aspects of Scottish and Irish economic and social history* (Edinburgh: John Donald, 1977), pp. 77–87; K. Bright, *The Royal Dublin Society, 1815–1845* (Dublin: Four Courts Press, 2004).

10 'Travel account of Heinrich Meidlinger, 1820–27' in E. Bourke (ed.), *'Poor green Erin': German travel writers' narratives on Ireland from before the 1798 Rising to after the Great Famine,* 2nd edn (Frankfurt: Peter Lang, 2013), pp. 96–7.

provided by the sheer number of landowners who pursued improved methods of husbandry, but the enclosure of the countryside, the development of industrial villages, the construction of elegant new residences and the laying out of bespoke demesnes were equally indicative.[11] This is not to suggest, as the instances in which travellers sat at a 'dining table laden down to the point of superabundance' in 'dilapidated', 'large country residence[s]' bear witness, that improvement was pursued by all of the landed elite.[12] But there are still stronger signs to suggest that resistance was keener among the populace, not only because they were disinclined to be told what to do by a landed elite towards whom they were at best ambivalent, but also because they did not buy into a world-view that prioritised 'industry'.[13]

Divining the attitude of the 'peasant' from the travel literature is challenging given the identification of a majority of authors with the then dominant improving culture, but a search can pay dividends. The accounts provided by travellers of 'well-watered and cultivated' landscapes 'abound[ing] in bleaching-greens', and houses and cottages 'with an orchard and snug garden' in east Ulster certainly suggest that the vision of 'opulence and comfort' that epitomised improvement was embraced by those who worked the land there.[14] The 'excellent cultivation of land, good farmhouses, woods, orchards, fine and well-inclosed fields and meadows, respectable cottages [and] well-conditioned cattle' that John Trotter observed in the vicinity of Doneraile, County Cork illustrate also that 'English improvement' was not confined to Ulster moreover.[15] 'The great farmers' of Leinster and Munster who prospered from the 'great prices for the produce of land' during the 1790s and the early nineteenth century presumably pursued a comparable course, though they accorded less effort to its visible expression than they did to expanding their holdings, husbanding wealth and staking their children.[16] The cottagers, small farmers and cottiers, whose number were on the rise, were certainly less than enthusiastic. Though its regional concentration cautions against

---

11 B.J. Graham and L.J. Proudfoot (eds.), *Urban improvement in provincial Ireland, 1700–1840* (Dublin: Group for the Study of Irish Historic Settlement, 1994); J.G. Lockhart, 'Planned villages in Scotland and Ireland 1700–1850' in T.M. Devine and D. Dickson (eds.), *Ireland and Scotland: parallels and contrasts* (Edinburgh: John Donald, 1983), pp. 132–43; V. Costello, *Irish demesne landscapes, 1660–1740* (Dublin: Four Courts Press, 2016).

12 'Travel account of Friedrich Hering, 1806–07' in Bourke (ed.), *German travel writers' narratives on Ireland*, p. 80.

13 See the observations in 'Travel account of Karl Gottlob Küttner, 1783–4' in Bourke (ed.), *German travel writers' narratives on Ireland*, pp. 23–5.

14 Hall, *Tour through Ireland*, vol. II, p. 212.

15 Trotter, *Walks through Ireland*, p. 295.

16 Ibid., p. 16.

assuming that they were representative, the fact that the Whiteboys targeted the enclosure of the countryside in the 1760s suggests that there were many in the expanding ranks of smallholders who were actively hostile to improvement because it collided with traditional ways.[17] There is no Irish equivalent to John Clare, the rural poet, who articulated the concerns of those at the sharp end of the improving initiatives pursued in the English east midlands. For this reason the perspectives the more curious travellers provide into the lives and economies of the Irish peasants, suggesting not only that they were not 'lazy'[18] but that they pursued a model of existence that was rational, and happier than that enjoyed by their English equivalents, provide a valuable counter-perspective to the normative focus on poverty and the potato.

James Hall is particularly intriguing in this respect. While no less disposed than others of his ilk to conclude from the 'unimproved or neglected state of agriculture' and the 'irregular … cabins or cottages scattered over the country' that they provided few of 'the elegancies of life or hardly allow us to think that their inhabitants enjoy the common accommodations of it', Hall perceived that the people lived a life of contentment:

> When we see how the cabins are peopled, the swarms of children at their play; the rows of young people of both sexes in the fields with their shovels, turning up the soil, and depositing their favourite food, the potatoes, or casting up the turf from the bogs for fuel; when we see them returning from their chapels, and loitering away the afternoon of the day of rest in companies, or enduring a greater portion of fatigue at their sports than that of their ordinary labour through the week; we see that the people are sociable … they are equal, and most of them are happy.[19]

And concluding that the relaxed lifestyle pursued by Ireland's rural dwellers was preferable to the 'tyranny' to which those who resided 'in commercial cities' in England were subjected, Hall observed that 'the multiplied cares and toils which attach themselves to our complicated way of life' meant not only that family life there was less emotionally fulfilling (especially for children) but also that 'the people' sacrificed 'the duties and gratifications of social life' to 'the mammon of unrighteousness'.[20] It is an arresting, and rarely articulated,

---

17 J.S. Donnelly, 'The Whiteboys, 1761–65', *Irish Historical Studies*, 21 (1978–9), 20–55.
18 Writing in 1806–7, Johan Friedrich Hering, an army surgeon stationed at Dunmore, noticed 'how laboriously the people here work the land', though he acknowledged this was a consequence of the primitiveness of their tools: Bourke (ed.), *German travel writers' narratives on Ireland*, pp. 79–80.
19 Hall, *Tour through Ireland*, vol. ii, pp. 290–1.
20 Ibid., p. 291.

perspective, but it received conditional contemporary endorsement from John Trotter, who maintained that the 'fortitude and humility' with which 'the poor Irishman' bore his lot was indicative of contentment,[21] and from Karl Küttner's avowal a generation earlier that the average Irish peasant was not just 'much happier than any of us' but habitually disposed to be so because he was not motivated 'to go to the slightest trouble to improve his situation' for the simple reason that because 'his neighbours live like him' he was not disposed to envy, or, it can be added, emulation.[22]

These are contestable opinions to be sure. Yet the acknowledgement that the peasantry were content because they had access to a foodstuff that not only permitted households to meet their own immediate calorific needs but also provided them with a surplus sufficient (as various travellers could personally attest) to share with visitors, with beggars and, should the need arise, with less fortunate neighbours is noteworthy. It constituted a quite different vision of society than the competitive economy that reified industry and improvement.[23]

The monotony of 'an eternally unchangeable meal of potatoes' did not pass travellers by un-noted,[24] but as Hall's brief reference to sporting activity and others to music and dance attest, there was a recognition too that the peasantry possessed a rich social and cultural life, and that the absence of burdensome financial hurdles allowed young couples to set up home and to generate their own (large) families without too much calculation.[25]

It was not a lifestyle that many visitors, even those who identified its merits, wished to assume, as its disadvantages patently outweighed its advantages. This reality was largely hidden from view when the country experienced the so-called 'gap in famines' that spanned the second half of the eighteenth century and the first fifteen years of the nineteenth.[26] Moreover, it was not to endure, as the famine fever observed by John Trotter in 1817 and the acute distress encountered by Thomas Reid in 1822 attest; and the intensifying economic crisis in the ensuing quarter century, culminating in the Great

21 Trotter, *Walks through Ireland*, p. 17
22 'Travel account of Karl Gottlob Küttner, 1783', p. 24.
23 Hall, *Tour through Ireland*, vol. II, p. 283; N. Ó Ciosáin, *Ireland in official print culture 1800–1850: a new reading of the Poor Inquiry* (Oxford: Oxford University Press, 2014), chapter 5.
24 'Travel account of Anton Schutte, 1845' in Bourke (ed.), *German travel writers' narratives on Ireland*, p. 505.
25 Hall, *Tour through Ireland*, vol. II, p. 290; Kelly, below pp. 502–8.
26 D. Dickson, 'The gap in famines: a useful myth' in E.M. Crawford (ed.), *Famine: the Irish experience: subsistence crises and famines in Ireland* (Edinburgh: John Donald, 1989), pp. 96–111. It can be noted that the MP for Carlisle, J.C. Curwen, who visited in 1813, apprehended a calamity if the potato failed: *Observations on the state of Ireland*, 2 vols. (London: Baldwin, Cradock and Joy, 1818), vol. II, p. 121.

Famine, demonstrated with devastating effect.[27] By the same token the benign image of 'industry' and 'improvement' cultivated by generations of advocates ignored its negative consequences – its disruptive impact on the economies of the poor, and the ensuing instances of agrarian and food protest.[28]

William of Orange or James II

The antipathetic positions identifiable in the attitudes of the ruling elite in Ireland and (their differences on political points notwithstanding) their equivalents in Great Britain on the one part and the populace of Ireland on the other to economic growth were compounded by comparable differences in attitude to the prevailing political system and constitutional arrangements. Karl Küttner, for example, was profoundly struck by the depth of the cleavage when he was informed of the divided reaction to reports that a French expeditionary force was spotted on the Munster coast in June 1779:

> The people who have estates around here gave a blood curdling description of the anxieties they suffered. The fear of an islander who is not used to seeing enemies in his country, and who knows that all invasions are combined with disorder and excesses, is understandable as such. But that was not the main concern, but rather the greatest fear they had was of the Catholics who outnumbered the Protestants in the district by far. An impoverished, uncouth and forlorn populace had got it into their heads that, as soon as their co-religionists the French had seized hold of the coastal region, the Irish would have their ancient rights restored and would receive back the lands lost by their ancestors. Therefore the first thing that was expected of these Catholic Irish in the event of a French landing was that they would attack the Protestants, manhandle them, and plunder all the wealthy country seats.[29]

Küttner's account of the 'consternation' caused by so-called 'sham invasion' is not unique.[30] It does, however, highlight the endurance of the divisions forged

---

27 Trotter, *Walks through Ireland*, pp. 272–3, 278, 299–300, 313, 330–1, 342, 371–3, 453–4, 531; T. Reid, *Travels in Ireland in 1822* (London: Longman, Hurst and Orme, 1823), pp. 264, 276–82, 309; J. Mokyr, *Why Ireland starved: a quantitative and analytical history of the Irish economy 1800–1850* (London: Allen and Unwin, 1985).

28 T.M. Devine, 'Unrest and stability in rural Ireland and Scotland 1760–1840' in P. Roebuck and R. Mitchison (eds.), *Economy and society in Scotland and Ireland, 1500–1939* (Edinburgh: John Donald, [1988]), pp. 126–39; J. Kelly, *Food rioting in Ireland in the eighteenth and nineteenth centuries: the 'moral economy' and the Irish crowd* (Dublin: Four Courts Press, 2017).

29 'Travel account of Karl Gottlob Küttner, 1783', pp. 27–8.

30 J. Kelly, '"Disappointing the boundless ambitions of France": Irish Protestants and the fear of invasion, 1661–1815', *Studia Hibernica*, 37 (2011), 85–7; S. Conway, *The British Isles and the War of American Independence* (Oxford: Oxford University Press, 2000), pp. 196–9.

in the crucible of conflict in the 1680s and 1690s, which are further attested by the same author's account of the fact that both communities had different royal heroes: 'William III is held in especially high regard [by Protestants], and the nation has erected a pyramid [*sic*] in his honour ... not far from the Drogheda where he crossed the Boyne, and defeated his father-in-law ... The Catholics despise him ... heartily, and look upon James II as a saint.'[31] Consistent with the exclusion of Jacobitism from the public sphere, it is difficult to locate positive reference to James II in the printed record of either the eighteenth or the nineteenth century. By comparison, reverential references to William III abound and his prominence in the material as well as visual culture of the age is no less complete. Indeed, as indicated by Küttner's allusion to the obelisk erected in the Boyne Valley in the 1730s, there were a number of royal monuments in symbolically significant locations. The most iconic, because it was the focal point of the state-sponsored commemoration every 4 November (William's birthday), was Grinling Gibbons' equestrian statue of the king outside the houses of parliament on College Green, Dublin. A proliferation of pottery, glass and other visual images, made possible by the development of techniques of mass production, ensured the image was available to all in the nineteenth century, but the cult of William of which they are expressions was anticipated in the eighteenth century by the practice of toasting 'the Glorious and immortal memory', which suited the contemporary passion for sociable dining and the related preference for affirming political identity by drinking toasts to political heroes.[32]

This was not the full extent of Protestant identity forging, moreover. Building on foundations put in place since the Restoration, the 1730s and 1740s witnessed a palpable quickening in the pulse of official and popular idealisation of the Hanoverian monarchy equivalent to that fostered in Georgian Britain. Its most emblematical feature was not royal imagery, though portraits and statues of George I and II were prominently located in Dublin and Cork, but the proliferation of occasions when a positive image of the monarchy was fostered by state, municipal, corporate and landed interests by means of entertainments that, inter alia, involved the ringing of bells, lighting bonfires

31 'Travel account of Karl Gottlob Küttner, 1783', p. 21.
32 R. Usher, *Protestant Dublin, 1660–1760: architecture and iconography* (Basingstoke: Palgrave, 2012); J. Kelly, 'The Glorious and immortal memory: commemoration and Protestant identity in Ireland 1660–1800', *Proceedings of the Royal Irish Academy*, 94c (1994), 25–52; J. Kelly, 'The consumption and sociable use of alcohol in eighteenth-century Ireland', *Proceedings of the Royal Irish Academy*, 115c (2015), 249–54; M.J. Powell, 'Political toasting in eighteenth-century Ireland', *History*, 91 (2006), 508–29.

and fireworks, public illuminations, and the provision of barrels of beer, hogsheads of wine and roast oxen to inculcate positive associations.[33] The impact of these occasions on the Protestant population is attested by the ease with which popular loyalism negotiated the challenge posed to the 'Glorious memory' by Patriot commemorative practices during the 1770s and 1780s, and the still more subversive revolutionary commemorative calendar of political radicals in the 1790s, since it was the combination of devotion to the memory of William of Orange, respect for the Protestant succession and the harnessing of the extant tradition of popular loyalism, developed around the anniversary of battles fought between 1688 and 1691, that served to make popular loyalism such a potent force in the nineteenth century.[34] The claim, published by the *Kerry Evening Post*, that there were 160,000 Orange Lodges and 270,000 'Orangemen' in the country in 1831 may have little connection with reality, given that the Orange Order was then an 'unlawful association'. But the figures accurately reflect the Order's attraction to the by then combined forces of Protestantism and Presbyterianism, and the appeal of a tradition that melded established patterns of demonstration (assembly, marching, toasting) with the rhetoric and ideology of uncompromising 'Protestant Ascendancy' that was developed in the 1780s and 1790s.[35]

By comparison, having been effectively excluded from the public sphere by 1710,[36] the inability of Irish Jacobitism to sustain a defiant presence in the public realm once the authorities had policed out of existence the practice of commemorating the Pretender's birthday (10 June) forced Jacobites into the shadows.[37] Indicatively, positive references to James II, James III (the 'Old Pretender') and sundry other Jacobites are only encountered in Gaelic

---

33 H. Smith, *Georgian monarchy: politics and culture 1714–1760* (Cambridge: Cambridge University Press, 2006), pp. 132–5; Kelly, 'The Glorious and immortal memory', pp. 36–8; Usher, *Protestant Dublin, 1660–1760*, chapter 3.

34 A. Blackstock, *Loyalism in Britain and Ireland, 1793–1839* (Woodbridge: The Boydell Press, 2007); J. Hill, 'Loyal societies in Ireland, 1690–1790' in J. Kelly and M. Powell (eds.), *Clubs and societies in eighteenth-century Ireland* (Dublin: Four Courts Press, 2010), pp. 181–202; A. Blackstock, 'Loyalty and the monarchy in Ireland, c.1660–c.1840' in A. Blackstock and F. O'Gorman (eds.), *Loyalism and the formation of the British world, 1775–1914* (Woodbridge: The Boydell Press, 2014), pp. 95–101; J. Kelly, *Sir Richard Musgrave, 1746–1818: ultra-Protestant ideologue* (Dublin: Four Courts Press, 2009).

35 *Kerry Evening Post*, 13 April 1831; A. Blackstock, 'The trajectories of loyalty and loyalism in Ireland, 1793–1849' in Blackstock and O'Gorman (eds.), *Loyalism and the formation of the British world, 1775–1914*, pp. 103–24.

36 J. Kelly, 'Regulating print: the state and the control of print in eighteenth-century Ireland', *Eighteenth-Century Ireland*, 23 (2008), 146–50.

37 P. Fagan, 'The Dublin Catholic mob, 1700–1750', *Eighteenth-Century Ireland*, 4 (1989), 124–5; É. Ó Ciardha, *Ireland and the Jacobite cause, 1685–1766: a fatal attachment* (Dublin: Four Courts Press, 2002); Kelly, 'The Glorious and immortal memory', pp. 32–3.

poetry, which circulated in manuscript.[38] Occasional acts of defiance, such as raising a toast to James III in public, demonstrate that Jacobitism persisted. But the power and authority of the Protestant state was so overwhelming that the likelihood of Jacobitism seriously testing, and still less undermining, the foundations of Protestant authority – a real possibility for at least a quarter century after the strategic withdrawal negotiated at Limerick in 1691 – continued to diminish.[39] It was not that a majority of members of the Irish Protestant interest ever felt sufficiently secure to believe that they could relax their guard. There were some, to be sure, who had concluded by the 1770s that the Penal Laws against Catholics were redundant, but those like the lord chancellor, John FitzGibbon, who maintained in 1793 in the debate on admitting Catholics to the franchise (of which they had been deprived in 1728) that the Penal Laws were 'dictated by self-defence and self-preservation' spoke for the many who remained unconvinced.[40] Thirty year earlier, such a step could not have been contemplated. In 1764, during the first of what was an irregular but defining sequence of regional agrarian protests, the Church of Ireland dean, William Henry, wrote to the archbishop of Canterbury, Thomas Secker, to alert him to 'the secret springs and schemes' of the Whiteboys; their purpose, he pronounced ominously, was to advance 'the interest of Popery', and they had done so to such effect 'that unless some effectual remedys were applyed in time, we should have the tragedy of 1641 acted over again upon the first rupture with France and Spain, and officers sent by those powers to head the Papists'.[41] Henry's fears were misplaced, but the captivating power that the attentively cultivated memory of 1641 had on Protestant consciousness through the eighteenth and nineteenth centuries was a critical factor in valorising those in their ranks who were 'distinguished for [their] warm zeal for the Protestant religion, the British interest, and a steady adherence to [Glorious] Revolution principles'.[42]

The commitment to 'the British and Protestant interest' in which Henry zealously laboured (his term) during his lifetime dovetailed with the

---

38 V. Morley, *The popular mind in eighteenth-century Ireland* (Cork: Cork University Press, 2017), pp. 64–5, 72, 121–2, 274–5 and *passim*.

39 Kelly, 'The Glorious and immortal memory', p. 40; Kelly, ' "Disappointing the boundless ambitions of France" ', pp. 51–70.

40 J. Kelly (ed.), *Proceedings of the Irish House of Lords 1771–1800*, 3 vols. (Dublin: Irish Manuscripts Commission, 2008), vol. II, p. 267.

41 Henry to Secker, 29 Dec. 1764 in R.G. Ingram (ed.), ' "Popish cut-throats against us": Papists, Protestants and the problem of allegiance in eighteenth-century Ireland' in M. Barber et al. (eds.), *From the Reformation to the Permissive Society: a miscellany*, Church of England Record Society 18 (Woodbridge: The Boydell Press, 2010), p. 178.

42 Ibid.

commitment to improvement that he expressed in the attention he gave the 'colony of Protestants' that he 'had the comfort of planting in the [Church of Ireland] dioceses of Killala and Ac[h]onry'.[43] It was, of course, fundamentally incompatible with the world-view of the Catholic population, which, as a partial survey of households conducted in 1731 indicated, may have comprised as much as 90 per cent of the population of the province of Connacht where Killala and Achonry were located. The demographic ratios were less polarised elsewhere but, other than Ulster, where the number of taxable households that were identified as 'Protestant' (meaning occupied by members of the Church of Ireland, the Presbyterian Church or a minority Dissenter communion) exceeded the number that were 'Papist', Catholics outnumbered Protestants by more than four to one.[44] Moreover, their advantage was growing, as the demographic expansion that was a motor of economic activity until it was brought to a crashing halt by the Great Famine was disproportionately among those who were dependent on the land.[45] More consequently, perhaps, it was increasingly driven by those who were prepared, by reason of their reliance on the potato and its suitability to Ireland's climatic conditions, to live on smallholdings. The implications of this for the social structure were not lost on those who described the island in word pictures during the eighteenth and nineteenth centuries, since other than the 'extreme poverty' of which the ubiquitous 'low mud cabins', the 'hideous beggars' and 'ragged people' were unavoidable evidence, the matter to which they returned time and again was the modest size of the 'social class, which is England's strength: the yeomanry, proprietor occupiers … wealthy leaseholders', 'gentleman farmers', 'merchants and manufacturers'.[46] The implications of this for the polity were more opaque because, no more than those historians who were trained to believe that literature was not a usable source,[47] travel writers were ill equipped to assess the *mentalité* of the peasantry other than indirectly (as exemplified by the quotation from Karl Küttner provided above[48]) or by reliance on their own observations. The results may have been the anticipated

---

43 Henry to Secker, 20 Nov., 23 Sept. 1765 in Ingram (ed.), ' "Popish cut-throats against us" ', pp. 174, 185.
44 S.J. Connolly, *Religion, law and power: the making of Protestant Ireland 1660–1760* (Oxford: Oxford University Press, 1992), pp. 144–7.
45 See Gurrin, Chapter 8 below.
46 'Travel account of Johann Friedrich Hering, 1806–07', 'Travel account of Casper Voght, 1810–12' in Bourke (ed.), *German travel writers' narratives on Ireland*, pp. 49, 68–9, 78–9; Luckombe, *A tour through Ireland*, p. 19.
47 See T. Dunne, *The writer as witness: literature as historical evidence* (Cork: Cork University Press, 1987).
48 See p. 7.

mélange of prejudice and *cliché*, but there are those like James Hall and John Trotter who challenged not only received opinions at the time, but also certain historiographical perspectives. The lesson is that contrary views must be considered in any attempt to provide a balanced perspective on a society that was so acutely polarised between those who embraced the culture of improvement and those who did not, between those who cultivated allegiance to the Protestant succession and those who wanted it overthrown, and between the 'rich and mighty [who] possess[ed] massive tracts of land and those who work[ed] it [and] live[d] in extreme poverty'.[49] Kasper Vogts, a prison reformer from Hamburg with thirty years of experience interacting with 'poor people', is another visitor whose perspective is also deserving of notice. He was persuaded by the 'similarity' he observed between the circumstances of tenant farmers in Ireland and the peasantry of 'some provinces of pre-revolutionary France' when he visited in 1794 to observe that 'no other nation is as ripe for revolution'. Itemising 'the religion, the poverty, the light diet, the insolence of the nobility, [and] the impossibility of obtaining justice from them', he concluded that 'dissatisfaction is so great' as a result of such 'prohibitive' and 'extortionate' imposts as the hearth tax and the tithe that, were they to receive the opportunity, 'the people would gladly unite with the French'.[50]

The Historiographical Context

Because Vogts' interpretation of the state of Ireland in the 1790s is not far removed from that of the elements of the United Irishmen that were then developing a revolutionary strategy, its value as a guide should not be understated.[51] It is notable that it fits more easily into a narrative of eighteenth- and nineteenth-century Irish history that accommodates 'the popular mind', as defined by Vincent Morley (Chapter 1), than it does a viewpoint which conceives of the eighteenth century as a stable polity.[52] There are, of course, other definitions, and other attempts to identify and describe the 'popular mind', notably R.B. McDowell's classic inquiries into Anglophone 'public opinion' in the late eighteenth century, which fits more easily with the latter

---

49 'Travel account of Karl Gottlob Küttner, 1783', pp. 23–5.
50 'Travel account of Casper Voght, 1795', pp. 57–8, 63.
51 M. Elliott, *Partners in revolution: the United Irishmen and France* (New Haven: Yale University Press, 1982); J. Quinn, 'The United Irishmen and social reform', *Irish Historical Studies*, 31 (1998), 188–201.
52 See Morley, Chapter 1 below.

perception.[53] What is clear, as the contrasting societal attitudes to improvement and the state sketched out above indicate, is that this was a society where political, religious and social differences ran deep. Indeed, they may have run deeper in Ireland than was the case in other *ancien régime* European societies. If this is so, revealing though it may be to locate Ireland within Europe's *ancien régime*, it must inevitably be incomplete if it elides the particular characteristics that define the unique history of the polity.[54] Similar reservations may be expressed with reference to anatomies of the population, whether conceived on the grand scale exemplified by Toby Barnard's magisterial reconstruction of Irish Protestantism over more than a century, or Robert Whan's more compact attempt to do likewise for the less socially diverse world of Ulster Presbyterianism over a shorter time-span. They sustain a view of Ireland that permits it to be seen as comparable in the case of the former to provincial England and in the case of the latter to lowland Scotland. And yet the difficulties both authors encounter in reconstructing the 'lower classes' within their chosen communities highlight the methodological limitations of this approach. It is certainly difficult to conceive how an 'anatomy' of the Catholic population, which was predominantly 'lower class', could successfully negotiate the severe evidential challenges it must encounter, and, by implication, if such an approach possesses the capacity to solve the interpretative problems that contemporary travel accounts highlight.[55] They will certainly not be solved by locating the kingdom of Ireland within the framework of a composite monarchy, or by any of the models of state building (whether the fiscal-military state of the eighteenth century or the bureaucratic institutional state of the nineteenth), though – like the *ancien régime* approach, and recent transnational exploration of 'the Irish in Europe' (see Chapter 21) – these do serve further to reveal the limits of the traditional nationalist narratives by locating the island within an international context, which is the object of Part v of this volume.[56]

---

53 R.B. McDowell, *Irish public opinion 1750–1800* (London: Faber and Faber, 1943).

54 The most influential such analysis is Connolly, *Religion, law and power*.

55 T. Barnard, *A new anatomy of Ireland: the Irish Protestants, 1649–1770* (New Haven: Yale University Press, 2003); R. Whan, *The Presbyterians of Ulster, 1680–1730* (Woodbridge: The Boydell Press, 2013).

56 D. Hayton, J. Kelly and J. Bergin (eds.), *The eighteenth-century composite state: representative institutions in Ireland and Europe, 1689–1800* (Basingstoke: Palgrave, 2010); C.I. McGrath, *Ireland and Empire, 1692–1770* (London: Pickering, 2012); C.I. McGrath and C. Fauske (eds.), *Money, power and print: inter disciplinary studies on the financial revolution in the British Isles* (Newark: University of Delaware Press, 2008); A. Graham and P. Walsh (eds.), *The British fiscal-military states 1660–c.1783* (London: Routledge, 2016); see Crossman, Chapter 20 below.

One could go on, but the point is already made. It is profoundly difficult to provide a balanced interpretation of any age or era, still less one with a disputed historiography. Yet one must endeavour, by identifying and embracing the diversity of interests, to demonstrate how they related to each other, even where they barely interacted, or, as was the case in the eighteenth century, one was so successful in occluding the other that it can be a challenge even to locate evidence. There is the implication of the fact that the primary archive – and as such the evidential spine with which historians interested in the era must engage – was assembled at the behest of the state. It is fashionable, in certain circles, to argue that the limits of this (English) archive can be made good by appealing to the corpus of Irish-language material, and recent work utilising its primary component – Gaelic poetry – has demonstrated its potential in divining the popular mind, but it has less to offer on economic, social, gender, intellectual, recreational and other aspects of Irish society with which historians seek also to engage and, inter alia, address here. A more profitable way of proceeding must be to interrogate all extant evidential seams – manuscripts in all languages, artefacts in all forms, landscapes of all kinds, and so on – wherever they can be shown to be historically purposeful, to read against the grain and, not least given their historiographical legacy, to transcend traditional confessional, ideological and linguistic barriers because reliance on one is as likely as not to limit rather than to maximise the potential to advance historical understanding.

It would be helpful in realising this aspiration if the trajectory of the historiography of the era were better understood, for though it offers no guarantee that we will not pursue exclusive fields of inquiry, construct closed narratives or follow modish trends to no great effect, it is integral to disciplinary awareness that can only be beneficial. It is not possible here to do other than provide an outline, but even a sketch will help to contextualise the contents of this volume. In keeping with the contested environment in which it took place, the first attempts at presenting a history of eighteenth- and, to a lesser extent, nineteenth-century Ireland emanated with individuals who sought to promote a particular political message. Thus Henry Grattan junior's five-volume monument to his father, which contains a wealth of original documentation on the operation of the Irish executive in the last quarter of the eighteenth century, and the Catholic question during the first two decades after the Act of Union, was ushered into print between 1839 and 1846 with the object of supporting the emerging case for its repeal. Meanwhile, R.R. Madden's even larger act of recovery of the United Irishmen laid the foundations for their prominence in a nationalist historiography that dovetailed with the historical agenda of the Young Ireland movement.[57] By comparison, if one excepts a two-volume selection of the letters of John Beresford and a volume in Lord Castlereagh's correspondence, the mainstream political narrative of the eighteenth-century Irish parliament was largely dependent for illumination on the shafts of light cast in the biographies and collections of correspondence of English statesmen.[58] The prevailing approach in sum was either incidental or *engagé*, and this is how it was to continue. Indeed, if anything, this approach became still more entrenched, as the striking methodological and archival advances that one can identify with Ranke and the opening of major state archives (the Public Record Office of Ireland was established in 1867) continued to be subordinated in the second half of the nineteenth century to the production of narratives that mirrored the politics of their authors on the major political issues of the day. Thus Home Rulers contrived successfully to apotheosise the eighteen years between 1782 and 1800 as 'Grattan's parliament' and to deny the legitimacy of the Act of Union.[59] Unionists, by contrast, played down the history of the legislature in favour of the Act of Union, and they had allies in those like James Anthony Froude whose object was to demonstrate how unsuited the Irish were to the challenge of government.[60] Meanwhile, those of an assertively nationalist disposition fostered an image of Wolfe Tone and Robert Emmet that echoed their sacrificial version of nationalism, while the plethora of Catholic ordinands, perceiving the missionary potential of history, produced a version of the Penal Laws and Catholic endurance that elevated their message over the reality.[61] The result was a hollowed out version of the eighteenth century that – the Penal Laws, the politics of patriotism, 'Grattan's parliament' and the United Irishmen apart – was presented as something of an interlude between the seventeenth

57 H. Grattan, *Memoirs of the life and times of the right hon. Henry Grattan*, 5 vols. (London: Henry Colburn, 1839–46); R.R. Madden, *The United Irishmen: their lives and times*, 2nd edn, 4 vols. (Dublin: James Duffy, 1858–60); J. Quinn, *Young Ireland and the writing of Irish history* (Dublin: UCD Press, 2015), pp. 84–7.

58 W. Beresford (ed.), *The correspondence of John Beresford*, 2 vols. (London: Woodfall and Kinder, 1854); H. Vane (ed.), *Memoirs and correspondence of Viscount Castlereagh*, 4 vols. (London: Henry Colburn, 1849); C.S. Parker, *Sir Robert Peel: . . . his private correspondence*, 3 vols. (London: John Murray, 1891–3); C. Ross (ed.), *Correspondence of Charles, Marquess of Cornwallis*, 3 vols. (London: John Murray, 1859).

59 J. Kelly, *Henry Grattan* (Dundalk: Historical Association of Ireland, 1993); G. O'Brien, *Anglo-Irish politics in the age of Grattan and Pitt* (Dublin: Irish Academic Press, 1983); J.G. Swift MacNeill, *How the Union was carried* (London: Kegan Paul, 1887).

60 J.A. Froude, *The English in Ireland in the eighteenth century*, 3 vols. (London: Longmans, Green and Co., 1872–4); T. Dunbar Ingram, *A history of the Legislative Union of Great Britain and Ireland* (London: Macmillan, 1887).

61 M. Elliott, *Robert Emmett: the making of a legend* (London: Profile, 2003).

century and the present, and compelling only in so far as it related to current concerns. This selective approach continued into the early nineteenth century. This was, to be sure, of little interest historically to the consolidating unionist interest, though they upheld the value of the Act of Union in works that were more obviously political than historical, while nationalists, again depending on their hue, focused on the Catholic emancipation, on repeal and, inspired by John Mitchell's *ferocious polemic*, on the Great Famine.[62]

While one can locate parallels with the earlier contrasting attitudes to improvement and the state in these narratives, the history that was produced in Ireland compared poorly with what was being presented in those jurisdictions where the foundations of the modern academic discipline were being laid.[63] As a result, instead of building on the partial (in every sense of the term) but evidentially admirable histories of J.A. Froude, W.E.H. Lecky and T. Dunbar Ingram, and fostering an approach to historical inquiry that was less ideologically partisan, the opposite happened.[64] One of the reasons for this, Ciaran Brady has pointed out, was that the infrastructure required to support academic historical inquiry in Ireland was deficient by comparison not only with those jurisdictions that were in the vanguard globally, but also with polities of comparable size – Scotland most notably.[65] Furthermore, the public at large was disinclined to engage dispassionately with the past, because the past was hardly any less deeply contested than the present, with the result that when the Irish Revolution of the early twentieth century was over, and nationalism and unionism had achieved ascendancy in their respective jurisdictions by the early 1920s, they provided a context for the consolidation of the incompatible readings of the eighteenth and nineteenth centuries that had emerged during the preceding decades. The most significant new works in that respect in so far as the nationalist narrative of the eighteenth

62 A. Jackson, 'Unionist history', in C. Brady (ed.), *'Interpreting Irish history: the debate on historical revisionism, 1938–1994* (Dublin: Irish Academic Press, 1994), pp. 253–68; J. Mitchel, *The last conquest of Ireland (perhaps)* (New York: Lynch, Cole and Meehan, 1873).

63 One may instance the history of education as an illustration, which was well in arrear of developments in Germany: see J. Kelly and S. Hegarty, 'Writing the history of Irish education' in Kelly and Hegarty (eds.), *Schools and schooling, 1650–2000* (Dublin: Four Courts Press, 2017), pp. 18–22.

64 C. Brady, *James Anthony Froude: an intellectual biography* (Oxford: Oxford University Press, 2014), p. 266; J. Kelly, 'The historiography of the Act of Union' in M. Brown, P.M. Geoghegan and J. Kelly (eds.), *The Irish Act of Union, 1800: bicentennial essays* (Dublin: Irish Academic Press, 2003), pp. 5–36; W.E.H. Lecky, *History of Ireland in the eighteenth century*, 5 vols. (London: Longmans, Green and Co., 1896).

65 C. Brady, 'Arrested development: competing histories and the formation of the Irish historical profession 1801–1938' in T. Frank and F. Hadler (eds.), *Disputed territories and shared pasts: overlapping national histories in modern Europe* (Basingstoke: Palgrave, 2010), pp. 277–8.

century was concerned were George O'Brien's *An economic history of Ireland in the eighteenth century* (1918) and Daniel Corkery's *The hidden Ireland: a study of Gaelic Munster* (1924), which between them provided powerful, ideological readings that reduced complex historical issues to a simple but compelling hermeneutic of suppression, oppression and victimhood.[66] Neither author was a trained historian but these and allied works provided a historical interpretation that complemented the historical, religious and linguistic vision that the nation's political leadership sought to disseminate. It was inherently ahistorical, however, both because it was evidentially selective, and because it was out of line with the source-based approach in the ascendant in the halls of academia in Great Britain, and with the pioneering inclusive social history that distinguished the *Annales* school in France. It was inevitable, as a result, that it elicited a riposte from those who perceived that a less ideologically compromised history was required.

The story of the emergence of what its most influential exponents – T.W. Moody and R.D. Edwards – termed 'scientific history' does not need retelling.[67] Their most enduring achievement was the construction of a disciplinary infrastructure. Their most significant historiographical monument is the *New history of Ireland*, which was published in nine volumes between 1976 and 2005. The lengthy period that elapsed between the commissioning of the contributions and the publication of the individual volumes had a profound influence on the content to this undertaking, which can reasonably be described as a monument to Irish 'revisionist' history. Yet the most striking achievement of the volumes (vols. IV, V and VI) that engage with the eighteenth and nineteenth centuries is the comprehensive political narrative they provide. It may be that this narrative is accomplished more successfully in volume V (which engages with the period 1801–70) than volume IV (which deals with the long eighteenth century, 1691–1800) because the latter had a richer quantity of monograph research on which to draw. This notwithstanding, volume IV was a considerable achievement, and the presence of strong chapters on the economy (by L.M. Cullen), on Irish language and literature (by Brian Ó Cuív), on the visual arts (Anne Crookshank) and on music (Brian

---

66 G. O'Brien, *An economic history of Ireland in the eighteenth century* (London: Maunsel, 1918); D. Corkery, *The hidden Ireland: a study of Gaelic Munster in the eighteenth century* (Dublin: T.H. Gill, 1924).

67 C. Brady, ' "Constructive and instrumental": the dilemma of Ireland's first "new historians"' in Brady (ed.), *Interpreting Irish history: the debate on historical revisionism, 1938–1994*, pp. 3–7; R. Bourke, 'Historiography' in R. Bourke and I. McBride, *The Princeton history of modern Ireland* (Princeton: Princeton University Press, 2016), pp. 271–91.

Boydell) attests to a conceptual openness for which 'revisionism' is seldom credited.[68] Be that as it may, the political narrative that provides the spine for volume V: *Ireland under the Union, I (1801–70)* and volume VI: *Ireland under the Union, II (1870–1921)* is more authoritative because they were more up to date and firmly grounded in the surviving archive.[69]

As is the case with its companion volumes, the object of volume III in *The Cambridge history of Ireland* is neither to replicate nor to replace *A new history of Ireland*, but to reflect the state of the historiography in the present. To this end, the volume aspires, while engaging with the familiar, to offer fresh perspectives not only by providing new and up-to-date accounts of established subjects but also by engaging with recent and emerging trends to provide a fuller perspective on this period of a century and half, while acknowledging the historiographical tradition of which it is a part. It seeks, as this suggests, to offer a more complete and integrated reading of the eighteenth and the nineteenth centuries, by displacing the binary reading explicit in how the period was conceived of by those who lived it, and presented by those who wrote the formative (ideological) interpretations in the nineteenth and early twentieth centuries. This re-imagining is assisted by the fact that this volume, like the others in the series, is not bound by fixed and firm chronological signposts that continue to demarcate political history. This has particular pertinence for the Act of Union, which was so long the fulcrum round which the narrative of eighteenth- and nineteenth-century history pivoted. This was appropriate when the narrative of Irish history answered to the dominant political ideologies and religions that defined the *Zeitgeist*. Indeed, the case in its favour was compelling when the dominant issue was government. K.T. Hoppen's luminous recent analysis bears witness to its enduring significance, but, it possesses less organisational import in a more broadly conceptualised narrative.[70]

What is apparent in the political and social realm is that the eighteenth and nineteenth centuries witnessed two parallel processes – one bound up with the manner in which the 'Protestant interest' in the eighteenth century exercised its ascendancy over a weakened Catholic polity; the other with the

---

68 T.W. Moody and W.E. Vaughan (eds.), *A new history of Ireland*, vol. IV: *Eighteenth-century Ireland, 1691–1800* (Oxford: Oxford University Press, 1986).

69 W.E. Vaughan (ed.), *A new history of Ireland*, vol. V: *Ireland under the Union, I, 1801–70* (Oxford: Oxford University Press, 1989); W.E. Vaughan (ed.), *A new history of Ireland*, vol. VI: *Ireland under the Union, II, 1870–1921* (Oxford: Oxford University Press, 1996).

70 K. Theodore Hoppen, *Governing Hibernia: British politicians and Ireland, 1800–1921* (Oxford: Oxford University Press, 2016).

attenuation of that ascendancy in the nineteenth century in the face of an increasingly assertive Catholic populace. The turning point can be located in the 1790s for it was then that the combination of London's insistence that Protestants 'forgo their exclusive pre-eminence' and the surge in insurgency, which prompted their acquiescence in an Anglo-Irish union, placed the once commanding 'ascendancy' on the defensive and permitted the once marginalised Catholic population over time to seize the political initiative.[71] If, as this implies, the Act of Union can be conceived of as a strategic retreat, it proved well judged in the short term. It seemed to vindicate the argument of those who maintained that Great Britain had 'made a compact with the Protestant party of Ireland only' since the resulting union facilitated those committed to the preservation of 'Protestant Ascendancy' in Britain and Ireland not only to resist the further admission of Catholics to the political process for three decades, but also to mount a stout rearguard defence of their position in Ireland by embracing the once alienated Presbyterian community and by adopting modes of political behaviour that mirrored the emerging mass politics that defined the era and beyond.[72]

They did so, moreover, in the teeth of an increasingly organised Catholic population. Effectively neutralised as a threat to Protestant ascendancy in the eighteenth century by the Penal Laws and the development of a security strategy that deterred rebellion, they were able, their poetry suggests, to sustain a measure of intellectual resistance, while the Catholic faith served equally well as a religiously inspiring force. As a result, once the small but canny Catholic elite, which was quick to recognise that a Jacobite restoration was a chimera, secured the repeal of some of the Penal Laws beginning in the 1770s, they contrived to utilise the space thereby provided, and a rare capacity for political organisation to produce out of 'peasant blood and popular sentiment – a genuinely Irish kind of democracy'.[73] This might not have happened in the absence of Daniel O'Connell – in the words of the German political radical Jakob Venedy, 'the very epitome of Irishness, the clearest expression of the Irish national character' – but, once it had happened, the political context changed forever.[74] The impact of the transformation that O'Connell wrought to the body politic over two decades was interrupted by the Great Famine,

---

71 J. Kelly, 'The origins of the Act of Union: an examination of unionist opinion in Britain and Ireland, 1650–1800', *Irish Historical Studies*, 25 (1987), 260–3.

72 Trotter, *Walks through Ireland*, p. 360.

73 'Travel account of Jakob Venedy, 1843' in Bourke (ed.), *German travel writers' narratives on Ireland*, p. 454.

74 Ibid., p. 434.

but the trend in favour of greater Catholic influence was almost certainly fixed. And so, regardless of whether one chooses to configure the era spanning a century and a half as 'the fall and rise of the Irish nation' or the acme and decline of Protestant ascendancy, as various historians and commentators have done to date, the struggle for political power and ideology provides the unifying narrative spine to the history of the eighteenth and nineteenth centuries (Parts I, III and VI).[75] There were other forces at play while this was taking place, of course. The failure of the economy to keep pace with the needs of the populace (Chapters 6 and 7) ensured not only that there was major emigration before as well as after the Great Famine (Chapters 8, 21, 22, 25), but also that the population lived and functioned in an environment that was sometimes inherently threatening. Further, the social system, social attitudes, and modes of organisation and behaviour, family life, even the language people spoke were changing (Part IV). These issues, individually and severally, are as crucial to this effort to provide a history of this era as the more familiar political narrative. It is not possible, as was once the case, to subordinate all of these to one interpretative theme in keeping with the fact that history is inherently a dialogue between the past and the present. What follows provides a perspective from the present on a crucial phase of Irish history that continues to echo in new as well as familiar ways.

---

75 See T. Bartlett, *The fall and rise of the Irish nation: the Catholic question 1690–1830* (Dublin: Gill & Macmillan, 1992).

PART I

*

POLITICS

Irish Jacobitism, 1691–1790

VINCENT MORLEY

Introduction

Irish Jacobitism has been likened to Samuel Beckett's *Waiting for Godot*: a drama in which nothing happens, twice. This is amusing, but to base an assessment of the ideology's significance on its failure to inspire spontaneous rebellions in 1715 and 1745 would be to discount its role in shaping the political culture of the Catholic community for most of the eighteenth century, in driving recruitment to Irish regiments in the armies of France and Spain during the first half of the century, and in forestalling an accommodation between the Catholic Church and the British state until after the death of James Francis Stuart ('James III' to Jacobites) in 1766. Furthermore, as the vernacular literature of the period was pervaded with Jacobite sentiment, elements of the ideology continued to influence Irish popular culture well into the nineteenth century (Illustration 1).

The roots of Irish loyalty to the house of Stuart can be traced to the beginning of the seventeenth century when James VI and I was acknowledged as legitimate king of Ireland by the native learned class.[1] Fearghal Óg Mac an Bhaird and Eochaidh Ó hEodhasa were professional poets linked to native lords who had been in rebellion against Elizabeth I, but both men extolled the first Stuart monarch in verse: Mac an Bhaird asked rhetorically if anyone could behold the three crowns in James' charter without pleasure, and Ó hEodhasa compared the Scottish king's accession to the dispersal of mists by a radiant sun.[2] The Stuarts traced their descent from the kings of Dál Riada who expanded their territory from Antrim into Argyllshire in the fifth century – a

---

1 See B. Ó Buachalla, 'James our true king: the ideology of Irish royalism in the seventeenth century' in D.G. Boyce, R. Eccleshall and V. Geoghegan (eds.), *Political thought in Ireland since the seventeenth century* (London: Routledge, 1993), pp. 7–35.
2 L. McKenna (ed.), *Aithdioghluim dána*, 2 vols. (London: Irish Texts Society, 1939), vol. 1, p. 177; P.A. Breatnach, 'Metamorphosis 1603', *Éigse*, 17 (1977–8), 174, 176.

1. Prince James Francis Edward Stuart (1688–1766), the only son of James II and Mary of Modena, was recognised by many Irish Jacobites as James III. He was popularly known as the 'Old Pretender'. Mezzotint by John Simon, *c*.1700–25 (National Portrait Gallery).

circumstance that allowed Irish authors to portray the new royal house as a Milesian dynasty. About 1634, Geoffrey Keating argued in his influential manuscript history, *Foras feasa ar Éirinn*, that the coronations of James I and his successor, Charles I, at Westminster Abbey had fulfilled an old prophecy that Milesian monarchs would rule wherever the *lia Fáil* (stone of destiny) was situated.[3] The importance of the Stuarts' Milesian ancestry in securing the loyalty of the Old Irish was also stressed by John Lynch in his history of Ireland, published in 1662.[4] It is revealing that Sir Phelim O'Neill, leader of the 1641 rebellion in Ulster, considered it advisable to claim that he was acting 'by authority from His Majesty out of England', while prominent insurgents in other parts of Ireland also pretended to be acting pursuant to royal commissions.[5] Similarly, the oath of association adopted by the Confederate Catholics contained a pledge to defend the person and prerogatives of Charles I.[6] Yet popular sentiment may have been more varied than this suggests. When a new style of polemical verse in colloquial Irish emerged around the middle of the seventeenth century, it gave amateur authors from a middle-ranking social layer a literary voice for the first time: the attitudes they expressed towards the crown ranged from the frank hostility of 'An síogaí Rómánach', a popular northern composition of uncertain authorship, to the warm enthusiasm of Éamonn Mac Cárthaigh, a Munster author who looked forward to seeing Irish military exiles escort Charles II and James, Duke of York (the future James II), home to their kingdoms.[7]

The Restoration settlement proved to be a disappointment for many former landowners but the experience of Puritan rule during the interregnum had strengthened royalist sentiment in the Catholic community as a whole. When members of the gentry signed a 'remonstrance' in 1662 asserting their loyalty to Charles II and repudiating the idea that the papacy had any temporal power in Ireland, the resulting controversy threatened to reopen earlier divisions among Catholics. Their differences were more nuanced than they had been in the 1640s, however: if a national congregation of clergy declined to endorse the remonstrance in 1666, its members adopted an alternative 'protestation of loyalty' affirming the allegiance of Catholics to the crown 'in all civil and temporal affairs'.[8] In 1685, the tensions inherent in the divided temporal and spiritual loyalties of the Catholic population were eased, if not

---

3 G. Keating, *Foras feasa ar Éirinn*, ed. D. Comyn, vol. I (London: Irish Texts Society, 1902), p. 208.

4 'Gratianus Lucius' [John Lynch], *Cambrensis eversus*, 3 vols., ed. M. Kelly (Dublin: Celtic Society, 1851), vol. III, p. 52.

5 N. Canny, *Making Ireland British 1580–1650* (Oxford: Oxford University Press, 2001), pp. 471–2, 537.

6 'Philopater Irenaeus' [John Callaghan], *Vindiciarum Catholicorum Hiberniae* (Paris: Camusat and Le Petit, 1650), chapter 1, p. 6.

7 C. O'Rahilly (ed.), *Five seventeenth-century political poems* (Dublin: Dublin Institute for Advanced Studies, 1952), pp. 21, 99–100.

8 V. Morley, 'Peter Walsh' in J. McGuire and J. Quinn (eds.), *Dictionary of Irish Biography*, 9 vols. (Cambridge: Cambridge University Press, 2009), vol. IX, pp. 756–60.

wholly resolved, by the accession of a Catholic monarch. The Irish literature of the period records the sense of elation produced by the more inclusive policies adopted under James II, with the appearance of Irish-speaking
judges on the bench and Irish-speaking sentries in the army being celebrated
in verse by Dáibhí Ó Bruadair and Diarmaid mac Sheáin Bhuí Mac Cárthaigh
respectively.[9] According to a contemporary account, when the king landed in
Ireland in March 1689 he was cheered by the populace on his journey from
Kinsale to Dublin 'as if he had been an angel from heaven'.[10] James' success in
putting an army of some 36,000 men into the field testifies to the enthusiasm
of Catholic Ireland for his cause, but his precipitate flight after the Battle of
the Boyne exposed him to harsh criticism: an anonymous song of the period
described the defeated monarch as 'rí meata do ghlac na ritréada' ('a cow-
ardly king who took to retreat').[11] Expressing frustration at James' lukewarm
support for Irish interests, another anonymous song claimed that the king's
shoes were mismatched: while one was of Irish manufacture the other was
English.[12] Criticism such as this co-existed with respect for a monarch who was
perceived to have lost his throne because of his religion. Seán Ó Neachtain, a
Dublin-based schoolteacher, praised James II in an elegy for Mary of Modena,
the late king's widow, who died in 1718:

> 'Measg naomh agus ógh, tá'n dís so budh gnódh,
> sliocht Mhíleadh go h-ísioll, fá dhaoírse 'n a n-deóigh.[13]

> (Among saints and virgins are this couple who were noble, the
> descendants of Milesius are humbled and in bondage after them.)

The Williamite revolution is presented here as a severe blow to the native
population. Yet the generally creditable performance of a hastily raised and
poorly equipped Irish army allowed some pride to be salvaged from the
defeat: a third anonymous song of the period acclaimed Patrick Sarsfield as
a hero who snatched victory from King William's hand by destroying a siege
train as it approached Limerick city. The popularity of this song is clear from

9 J.C. MacErlean (ed.), *Duanaire Dháibhidh Uí Bhruadair*, 3 vols. (London: Irish Texts
   Society, 1917), vol. III, pp. 88, 96.
10 J.T. Gilbert (ed.), *A Jacobite narrative of the war in Ireland, 1688–1691* (Dublin: Joseph
   Dollard, 1892), p. 46.
11 B. Ó Buachalla (ed.), *Nua-dhuanaire*, 3 vols. (Dublin: Dublin Institute for Advanced
   Studies, 1976), vol. II, p. 2.
12 B. Ó Buachalla, 'Briseadh na Bóinne', *Éigse*, 23 (1989), 89.
13 J. Hardiman (ed.), *Irish minstrelsy, or bardic remains of Ireland*, 2 vols. (London: J. Robins,
   1831), vol. II, p. 18.

the fact that its air was included in a published collection of the 'most celebrated' Irish tunes in 1724.[14]

The 'Wild Geese'

The flow of Irish Jacobites to the continent began in 1690 when 5,000 untrained recruits were transferred to France in exchange for a French force sent to stiffen resistance to William III. When the war in Ireland ended, most Jacobites who were still in arms chose to be evacuated under the terms of the articles of Limerick. By one estimate, the number of Irish soldiers in France stood at 18,000 in 1692: some 6,000 were serving in the French army while a further 12,000 continued to serve James II, whose army-in-exile was maintained by French subsidies. After the peace of Ryswick (1697), the Irish corps were reduced to eight regiments of infantry and one of cavalry, numbering 6,000 men, all of which were incorporated into the French army.[15] Some of these units were transferred to the service of the Bourbon claimant during the War of Spanish Succession, but when the War of Austrian Succession began in 1740 the Irish brigade in the French service still stood at five regiments of infantry (then designated Bulkeley's, Dillon's, Clare's, Berwick's and Rothe's) and one of cavalry (Fitzjames'). At the same date, three Irish regiments (Hibernia, Irlanda and Ultonia), all of infantry, were in the service of Spain. The members of these corps were known to contemporaries as 'wild geese'. An early instance of the expression occurs in a Jacobite *aisling* by Conchúr Ó Briain, parish priest of Castlelyons, County Cork, in which 'géanna fiáine' were reported to be haunting harbours and enquiring about ships bound for Spain; if the attribution is correct, this poem cannot date from any later than 1720, the year of Ó Briain's death.[16] The phrase also became current in English at an early date: William King, Church of Ireland archbishop of Dublin, referred to 'a sort of people called the Wild Geese' and 'the vermin commonly called Wild Geese' in two letters written during 1722.[17] As Ó Briain had done, King applied the term to men who had already

---

14 For the text, see T. Ó Concheanainn (ed.), *Nua-dhuanaire*, 3 vols. (Dublin: Dublin Institute for Advanced Studies, 1981), vol. III, pp. 2–3. For the music and background, see J. and W. Neal, *A collection of the most celebrated Irish tunes*, ed. N. Carolan (Dublin: Irish Traditional Music Archive, 2010), pp. 80, 98–100.

15 G. Rowlands, *An army in exile: Louis XIV and the Irish forces of James II in France, 1691–1698* (London: Royal Stuart Society, 2001), pp. 6, 18.

16 R. Ó Foghludha (ed.), *Carn Tighearnaigh.i. an tAthair Conchubhar Ó Briain, D.D.* (Dublin: Oifig an tSoláthair, 1938), p. 10.

17 É. Ó Ciardha, *Ireland and the Jacobite cause, 1685–1766: a fatal attachment* (Dublin: Four Courts Press, 2002), pp. 200, 202.

enlisted in a foreign service but had not yet left Ireland. The expression was certainly in common use by 1724 when the collection of tunes mentioned above included an air entitled 'Gye fiane', an anglicised spelling of the variant plural form 'géidhe fiáine'.[18] In 1726, a Dublin newspaper reported that a ship had been seized near Cork 'for transporting men for the Pretender or some other foreign service who are called Wild Geese'.[19] Given that the wild goose is a migratory species, use of the term carried a clear implication that the military exiles would return from overseas in due course.

The peace of Utrecht (1713) was followed by an upsurge in clandestine recruitment to fill the depleted ranks of the Irish regiments. Hopes raised by the death of Queen Anne and the Scottish rising of 1715 are also likely to have stimulated interest. Recruiting agents commonly assured recruits that they were entering the service of the Stuart pretender and would soon return to Ireland. State papers record the arguments used by one such agent in 1715:

> some of the Inlisted then objected that they fear'd they were to goe and serve the ffrench King, or to goe to Newfoundland. Luke Ford then assured them that they should serve none but King James the Third, and that he was affraid the King would be in his March for England before they could reach him, that he was sure they should return before the End of Harvest and should not fight till they return'd.[20]

The authorities were sufficiently alarmed to issue a proclamation against 'such traiterous and unlawful practices' in 1714 and to reinforce the message with a printed letter addressed to justices of the peace.[21] Although it was known in official circles that the Stuart pretender no longer maintained a military force and that any recruits attracted by Jacobite propaganda would find themselves serving the king of France or Spain, the use to which the Irish regiments might be put remained a source of concern. As Archbishop King wrote in 1714, 'if there should be any opportunity, they will be ready and trained to serve the interests of the chevalier'.[22] Archbishop Hugh Boulter of Armagh made a similar observation in 1730, writing that 'all the recruits raised here for France or Spain are generally considered as persons that may

---

18 Neal, *A collection of the most celebrated Irish tunes*, pp. 78, 96–7.
19 P. Fagan, *An Irish bishop in penal times: the chequered career of Sylvester Lloyd OFM, 1680–1747* (Dublin: Four Courts Press, 1993), p. 83.
20 The National Archives, PRO, SP 63/373, f. 34 *verso*. See also, B. Ó Buachalla, *Aisling Ghéar: na Stíobhartaigh agus an t-aos léinn 1603–1788* (Dublin: An Clóchomhar, 1996), pp. 334–42.
21 J. Kelly and M.A. Lyons (eds.), *The Proclamations of Ireland 1660–1820*, 5 vols. (Dublin: Irish Manuscripts Commission, 2014), vol. II, pp. 690–2.
22 Ó Ciardha, *Ireland and the Jacobite cause*, p. 142. The 'chevalier' was James III.

some time or another pay a visit to this country as enemies'.[23] The potential for such a development is apparent from the letters sent by James III to six Irish-born generals in the French service in March 1722, requesting them to assemble officers for conveyance to England in support of a planned Jacobite rising that proved to be abortive.[24] Although France had been an ally of Great Britain since 1716, the Stuart pretender remained confident that he could rely on the loyalty and discretion of the highest-ranking Irish officers in the French service. A revealing expression of the feelings of one such officer is contained in the letter Brigadier William O'Shaughnessy addressed to James III on the occasion of his promotion to the rank of *maréchal de camp* (major-general) in 1734:

> Sir, It is my duty to inform your Majesty, that in the last promotion of Generall officers made by the court of france, I was declared Marechal de Camps. It has been hitherto your Royall Pleasure, to honour me with a degree above that, which I have had in the french service and I hope your Majesty, will doe me the same honour on this occasion, by granting me the Patent of lieuftenant Generall. That honour would be infinitely more dear to me, if it furnished me an occasion of shedding the last drop of my blood for your Majestys service.[25]

A commission from James III was of no practical benefit to an officer who was pursuing a career in the French army; it might even have been an impediment. O'Shaughnessy's request must therefore be seen as a declaration of political commitment. Similarly, when Charles O'Brien, 6th Viscount Clare, was promoted to the rank of *maréchal de France* (field marshal) in 1757, he wrote at once to James III and expressed the hope that 'I may, in this new station, be happy enough to be useful to your Majesty's service and cause.'[26] A commitment to Jacobitism extended to the rank and file of the Irish regiments. In 1728, at a time when Great Britain and France were still allied, Aodh Buí Mac Cruitín, then serving as a private soldier in the Clare regiment, composed a poem for his comrades-in-arms in which he imagined a successful invasion of England and the execution of George II.[27] This cannot be dismissed as a mere literary fantasy: in July 1745, several hundred volunteers

23 Ibid., p. 259. See also, J. Kelly, '"Disappointing the boundless ambition of France": Irish Protestants and the fear of invasion, 1661–1815', *Studia Hibernica*, 37 (2011), 27–105.
24 P. Fagan (ed.), *Ireland in the Stuart papers*, 2 vols. (Dublin: Four Courts Press, 1995), vol. I, pp. 31–2.
25 Royal Archives, Windsor, Stuart papers 175/77.
26 Fagan, *Ireland in the Stuart papers*, vol. II, p. 206.
27 V. Morley, 'Hugh MacCurtin: an Irish poet in the French army', *Eighteenth-Century Ireland*, 8 (1993), 49–58.

from the Irish regiments embarked in a French privateer with the intention of accompanying Prince Charles Edward to Scotland.[28] In the event, their vessel was damaged in an engagement and was forced to return to France. Even so, the Jacobite army defeated at Culloden included more than 400 men from Irish regiments who reached Scotland after the rising began, and the number of Irishmen intercepted at sea by the Royal Navy was greater still.[29] Several Irish officers from the Spanish regiments also expressed a desire to serve in Scotland during the rebellion.[30]

In Ireland itself, the 'wild geese' were accorded a prominent place in vernacular literature, and consequently in popular culture, for most of the eighteenth century. Literary sources indicate that they were seen by their compatriots as members of an army-in-exile. For example, Toirealach (Terencio) Ó Néill, whose ancestors were lords of the Fews in County Armagh, left Ireland about 1709 and rose to be lieutenant-colonel of the Hibernia regiment in the Spanish service; but Séamas Dall Mac Cuarta, a blind poet from County Louth, addressed a poem to the officer some seventeen years after his departure – that is to say, about the time of the Anglo-Spanish War of 1727 – urging him to return with an invading army.[31] Likewise, Seán de Hóra, a County Clare blacksmith, composed a Jacobite *aisling* around the time of the 1745 rising in Scotland in which he anticipated the imminent arrival in Ireland of Viscount Clare, an officer who had commanded his family's regiment since 1720.[32] These poets showed a familiarity with the careers of distinguished figures who were connected with their own districts, but many of the literary references to military exiles cannot be explained by traditional deference towards local gentry families. For example, the return of Lord Clare was anticipated in an anonymous northern song which also toasted the health of Felipe V and cannot therefore have been composed any later than 1746, the year of the Spanish king's death.[33] Clare remained a focus of literary attention throughout his long and successful military career. At the beginning of

---

28 D. Szechi, *The Jacobites: Britain and Europe 1688–1788* (Manchester: Manchester University Press, 1994), pp. 97–8; J. Black, *Culloden and the '45* (Stroud: Alan Sutton, 1993), p. 67.

29 J.C. O'Callaghan, *History of the Irish Brigades in the service of France* (Glasgow: Cameron and Ferguson, 1870), p. 453.

30 Fagan (ed.), *Ireland in the Stuart papers*, vol. II, pp. 39–40.

31 S. Ó Gallchóir, 'Filíocht Shéamais Daill Mhic Cuarta' (MA thesis, St Patrick's College, Maynooth, 1967), p. 52. For details of Ó Néill's career, see T. Ó Fiaich (ed.), *Art Mac Cumhaigh: Dánta* (Dublin: An Clóchomhar, 1973), p. 162.

32 B. Mac Cumhghaill (ed.), *Seán de Hóra* (Dublin: Oifig an tSoláthair, 1956), p. 49.

33 É. Ó Muirgheasa (ed.), *Dhá chéad de cheoltaibh Uladh* (Dublin: Oifig an tSoláthair, 1934), p. 20.

the Seven Years War, he was again praised in song by the Limerick-born poet
Tadhg Gaelach Ó Súilleabháin, along with some less eminent officers:

> Tá an dragan d'fhuil Iarla an Iarthair ársa,
> an Carathach cliarach, Triath na Blarnan,
> Gallasoniere is Tiarna 'n Chláir dhil
>   'na gcinndíon Gaíol fé bhánbhrat sróil.[34]

> (The warrior of the race of the veteran western earl, MacCarthy of
> the followers – the lord of Blarney, Galissonière and dear Lord Clare,
> are protecting commanders of Gaels under a white silken banner.)

Apart from Lord Clare, who was born in France, two Irishmen are mentioned
in the above passage. The first reference is to Ulick Burke, a son of the 9th Earl
of Clanricarde and a colonel in the French service; Burke had previously written to the Stuart pretender offering to raise a rebellion in Connacht if arms for
6,000 men were landed there.[35] The second reference is to Robert McCarthy,
heir to the forfeited titles 'Earl of Clancarty', 'Viscount Muskerry' and 'Baron of
Blarney', who resigned a commission in the Royal Navy in 1741 and tendered his
services to James III. The poet's admiration for Britain's continental enemies is
also evident in the above quotation: the Marquis de la Galissonière commanded
the French fleet that defeated Admiral John Byng off Minorca in 1756.

While it endured, the Anglo-French alliance facilitated discrete recruitment in Ireland for the French service. This practice was controversial, but
recruiting parties were allowed to visit the country on occasion and the rank
and file of the Irish regiments in France remained substantially Irish until the
War of Austrian Succession. Based on a study of regimental muster rolls,
it has been calculated that Irishmen still accounted for 67 per cent of the
troops in the Irish regiments in 1737 but that this figure had fallen to 30 per
cent by the end of the war.[36] The peace of Aix-la-Chapelle (1748) left Anglo-
French tensions unresolved and the practice of allowing French regiments
to recruit in Ireland was not resumed. Indeed, there was some traffic in the
opposite direction, and it was claimed in the Irish House of Lords that the
return of 'great numbers' of Irish-born veterans from France was tending

---

34 Ú. Nic Éinrí (ed.), *An cantaire siúlach: Tadhg Gaelach* (Dingle: An Sagart, 2001), p. 134.

35 Fagan (ed.), *Ireland in the Stuart papers*, vol. I, pp. 262–5.

36 C. J. Ó Conaill, 'The Irish regiments in France: an overview of the presence of Irish soldiers in French service, 1716–1791' in E. Maher and G. Neville (eds.), *France–Ireland: anatomy of a relationship* (Franfurt am Main: Peter Lang, 2004), p. 334.

'to endanger his Majesty's government and the peace of the kingdom'.[37] By 1763, at the end of the Seven Years War, the proportion of Irishmen in the ranks of the French regiments was as low as 11 per cent.[38] It was more difficult still for Spanish regiments to procure recruits from Ireland, given the chronic tensions between Spain and Great Britain; unsurprisingly, the proportion of Irishmen in the Spanish regiments declined at an earlier date. As with the French regiments, however, their officer corps remained largely Irish: as late as 1768, for example, only a handful of non-Irish officers were serving in the Irlanda regiment.[39] Dismay at the failure of the 1745 rising in Scotland and the inconclusive outcome of the War of Austrian Succession may have discouraged recruitment, although the literary sources in Irish provide little evidence of disillusionment. Even the death of Lord Clare in 1761 failed to extinguish hopes that an Irish commander would return at the head of an invading army: when Count Alexander O'Reilly, an Irish-born veteran of the Hibernia regiment, was appointed to command a Spanish expedition against Algiers in 1775, a Jacobite song composed in County Cork identified Ireland as the intended target and predicted that the Irish would shortly be freed as the Israelites had once been rescued from Egyptian bondage.[40]

The Catholic Clergy

The alignment of the Catholic Church with Jacobitism can be said to date from the accession of James II when Pope Innocent XI acknowledged the king's right to nominate bishops. Only three bishops were appointed to Irish dioceses on James' nomination before the Williamite revolution but he continued to exercise his right in exile and had nominated a further ten bishops by 1697. However, an Irish act (9 William III, c. 1) of that year required all Catholic bishops to leave the country by 1 May 1698 and no further episcopal appointments were made before James died in 1701. His son was then recognised as *de jure* monarch by Pope Clement XI, but in view of the vulnerable position of the Irish church it was not considered opportune to fill any vacant sees until 1707 when seven bishops were appointed on the nomination of

37 P. Fagan, *Divided loyalties: the question of the oath for Irish Catholics in the eighteenth century* (Dublin: Four Courts Press, 1997), p. 94.
38 Ó Conaill, 'The Irish regiments in France', p. 334.
39 Ó. Recio Morales, *Ireland and the Spanish Empire, 1600–1825* (Dublin: Four Courts Press, 2010), p. 195.
40 V. Morley (ed.), *Washington i gceannas a ríochta: Cogadh Mheiriceá i Litríocht na Gaeilge* (Dublin: Coiscéim, 2005), p. 11.

James III. Political tensions rose in 1708 when the Stuart pretender attempted to land in Scotland, and a year later the Irish parliament passed an act (8 Anne, c. 3) requiring all priests to abjure the Pretender by 25 March 1710 on pain of transportation. Fears that this act would be strictly enforced may explain the appointment of five bishops without a Stuart nomination in the period between 1711 and 1713. Complaints to Rome by James III elicited assurances that his right of nomination would be respected in future, although the procedure was modified. Thereafter, two papal briefs were issued on the appointment of a bishop: one for the Stuart claimant which mentioned his nomination, and a second for the bishop in which this reference was omitted. It was hoped that this precaution would reduce the risk of Irish prelates being treated as Jacobite agents should their papers fall into the hands of the civil authorities. This arrangement continued without further interruption until the death of James III in 1766, by which time more than a hundred bishops had been appointed to Irish sees.[41]

The political sympathies of the lower clergy can be gauged from the fact that fewer than forty priests in all of Ireland took the oath of abjuration in accordance with the act of 1709. Priests could plausibly claim that it was impossible for them to affirm that they were taking the oath 'heartily, willingly and truly' in view of the penalty prescribed for non-jurors, but the principal difficulty lay in the requirement to swear that the heir of James II 'hath not any right or title whatsoever to the crown of this realm'. William O'Daly, parish priest of Kilfenora, County Clare, expressed his revulsion at the prospect of his fellow priests taking the oath in significant numbers:

> Mo scíos, mo lagar, mo scartacha im chlí breoite,
> an tíoradh trasna so ar eaglais chríoch Fódla,
> gan díon dá maithibh 's gach teallaire mí-eolach
> ag scríobh gurb d'Anna is ceart sealbh na dtrí gcoróineach.[42]

> (My woe, my weakness, the innards of my body are ailing, this general scorching of the church of Ireland's land, with no shelter for its dignitaries and every ignorant upstart writing that possession of the three crowns is Anne's by right.)

The effect of O'Daly's verse on any priests who may have been wavering cannot be known, but he was appointed bishop of Kilfenora in 1722. The career of Sylvester Lloyd, a Franciscan and a convert from the established

---

41 C. Giblin, 'The Stuart nomination of Irish bishops 1687–1765', *Irish Ecclesiastical Record*, 105 (1966), 35–47.

42 V. Morley (ed.), *Aodh Buí Mac Cruitín* (Dublin: Field Day Publications, 2012), p. 61.

church, also benefited from his commitment to the Stuart cause. Writing from Dublin in 1726, Lloyd furnished Colonel Daniel O'Brien, the Pretender's representative in Paris, with details of the regional distribution and strength of military garrisons in Ireland.[43] When Thomas Nugent, the 4th Earl of Westmeath and one of the small number of Catholic peers, promoted a 'humble address' from the 'Roman Catholics of the Kingdom of Ireland' to George II on the occasion of his accession in 1727, the initiative was denounced by Lloyd, who drafted a set of 'queries' that characterised the address as 'vile and nauseous flattery'.[44] He may also have been the author of a long poem in English that satirised the signatories – a group which included four peers along with a number of lawyers and merchants.[45] Lloyd's political zeal was rewarded in 1728 when he was appointed bishop of Killaloe; in a congratulatory letter, James III hoped that 'the new dignity will enable you the more to be useful to religion and my service'.[46] Not every bishop was a convinced Jacobite, of course, but no priest who harboured ambitions for a mitre could afford to offend the Stuart court. Moreover, many bishops saw it as their religious duty to promote the cause of the legitimate monarch. In 1733, James Dunne, who later became bishop of Ossory, assured James III that 'Your Majesty's cause is the cause of God; whoever serves well the one must serve the other.'[47] On learning of his nomination as bishop of Kildare in 1734, Stephen Dowdall conveyed his thanks to the exiled monarch who had been 'pleased to command my service', assuring him that he would 'instruct the peoples committed to my care in the duty and loyalty due to Your Majesty and your royal family'.[48] Having seen the exiled Duke of Ormond at Avignon in 1741, Bishop Michael McDonagh of Kilmore wrote to James' secretary of state, expressing the hope that Ormond would 'soon have an opportunity with many more to show their zeal and vigour in restoring the Royal family to their just right'.[49] As late as 1756, Bishop Anthony Blake of Ardagh assured James III that he would 'deem it an indispensable point of my duty to promote on all occasions your interest'.[50]

---

43 Fagan (ed.), *Ireland in the Stuart papers*, vol. I, pp. 87–90.
44 Fagan, *An Irish bishop in penal times*, p. 101.
45 I. McBride, 'Catholic politics in the penal era: Father Sylvester Lloyd and the Delvin address of 1727' in J. Bergin, E. Magennis, L. Ní Mhungaile and P. Walsh (eds.), *New perspectives on the Penal Laws* (Dublin: Eighteenth-Century Ireland Society, 2011), pp. 115–47.
46 Fagan (ed.), *Ireland in the Stuart papers*, vol. I, p. 126.
47 Ibid., p. 185.
48 Ibid., p. 197.
49 Ibid., p. 322.
50 Ibid., vol. II, pp. 196–7.

In view of the close links between the Holy See and the Stuart court, which was based in Rome from 1719, it is not surprising to find members of the clergy among the authors of Jacobite verse. Compositions from the early decades of the eighteenth century by Conchúr Ó Briain and William O'Daly have already been mentioned, and priests remained conspicuous among the authors of political verse until the middle decades of the century. In 1757, Uilliam English, a member of the Augustinian community in Cork city, celebrated Austrian victories over Frederick II of Prussia, a British ally, by directing scatological abuse at George II in a Jacobite song:

> An eol díbhse 'dhaoine i bhFonn Fáil
> Seoirse go cloíte, 's i lomghá?
> > Aiteas mo chroí 'stigh
> > mar theagmhaigh a bhríste,
> 's ná glanfadh an taoide a thiompán.[51]

> (Do you know, O people in the land of Ireland, that George is crushed and in dire need? It's a joy to my heart within, what happened to his breeches, and the tide wouldn't clean his fundament!)

Similarly, Liam Ó hIarlaithe, a priest from Ballyvourney in west Cork, celebrated the death of George II in 1760 in a poem which also predicted that the Seven Years War would end with a Stuart restoration.[52] By this time, however, the church had begun to reassess its policy.

In 1757, Archbishop Michael O'Reilly of Armagh and five other bishops – all but one of them his suffragans – prepared a draft pastoral letter that proposed to instruct priests to offer prayers for George II at Sunday Mass.[53] The draft was rejected by the bishops of the other ecclesiastical provinces, although not before its text had become public. When it was discussed by clergy in Dublin, Thomas Burke, the provincial of the Dominicans, observed that 'any priest who read the text from the altar, or prayed for George II and his family as the primate wished, would take his life in his hands'.[54] The controversy abated following the death of Archbishop O'Reilly in 1758, at which time Bishop John O'Brien of Cloyne advised the Stuart court that the signatories of the letter had been thrown into 'great confusion', adding that this proceeded from concern that the failed initiative would 'exclude them from a certain succession

---

51 Ú. Nic Éinrí (ed.), *Canfar an dán: Uilliam English agus a chairde* (Dingle: An Sagart, 2003), p. 144.
52 D. Ó Muirithe (ed.), *Cois an Ghaorthaidh* (Dublin: An Clóchomhar, 1987), p. 17.
53 Fagan, *Divided loyalties*, p. 121.
54 Ó Buachalla, *Aisling Ghéar*, p. 643.

lately opened by the death of their chief'.[55] In the event, James III looked outside the province of Armagh for a successor and nominated the reliable Anthony Blake of Ardagh. Writing to the Pretender in 1759, the new primate expressed his hope that 'you may comfort us once with your longed-for return to your native soil'.[56] In the same year, the outspoken Stuart loyalist Thomas Burke was appointed bishop of Ossory. These nominations must be seen as rearguard actions, however, and the pressure for an accommodation with the reigning dynasty did not abate. When government appointed Friday, 12 March 1762, as an official day of fasting and prayer, a letter from Archbishop Richard Lincoln of Dublin reminded congregations of Christ's injunction to 'give unto Caesar what belongeth to Caesar' and urged them to 'offer up your prayers for the spiritual happiness of his gracious Majesty King George the Third'.[57] It was a straw in the wind for clerical supporters of the house of Stuart.

Jacobite Literature

The prospect of securing either military commissions in mainland Europe or ecclesiastical preferment in Ireland is unlikely to have determined the allegiance of more than a small minority of the Catholic community. Many more people must have been exposed to the literature of the period, which was suffused with Jacobitism. In the nature of things, it is impossible to quantify the importance of cultural factors in shaping political attitudes, yet the ubiquity of Jacobite sentiment in vernacular song and verse – and the absence of a countervailing loyalist voice in Irish – leaves no room to doubt that the literature both reflected and sustained popular support for the Stuart cause. Jacobite compositions were as diverse in form as they were pervasive, and range from elegies composed in a high linguistic register by accomplished poets to anonymous songs couched in colloquial speech. It is possible, none the less, to detect a gradual shift from more cultivated to more demotic forms. As the century advanced, Jacobite verse was increasingly written in accentual metres suitable for singing: by the 1740s, such lyrics were commonly set to popular airs. Some Jacobite compositions from around the middle of the century have secured permanent places in the Irish song tradition: notable examples include 'Mo ghille mear' ('My lively laddie') by Seán Clárach Mac Dónaill and 'Rosc catha na Mumhan' ('The battle-cry of Munster') by Piaras

---

55 Fagan (ed.), *Ireland in the Stuart papers*, vol. ii, p. 222.
56 Ibid., p. 239.
57 *Pue's Occurrences*, 13 March 1762 quoted in J. Brady (ed.), 'Catholics and Catholicism in the eighteenth century press', *Archivium Hibernicum*, 16 (1951), 104.

Mac Gearailt. This popularisation of form was complemented by a gradual democratisation of content as the focus of later authors shifted from the restoration of the pre-1691 *ancien régime* to the overthrow of the new establishment that emerged from the Williamite settlement.

The production of Jacobite literature was not uniform, either geographically or chronologically. The bulk of the extant material originated either in Munster or, to a lesser extent, in the Ulster–Leinster border region, in keeping with the presence of scribal networks in the areas concerned. Literary evidence is patchier elsewhere, but there is no reason to assume that the political culture of districts in which scribes were active was exceptional. For example, the following verse is taken from an anonymous song that was orally transmitted in counties Donegal and Tyrone before it was collected in the early years of the twentieth century:

> Tá Séarlas óg ag triall thar sáile,
> > Beidh siad leis-sean cúpla gárda,
> Beidh siad leis-sean Franncaigh is Spáinnigh,
> > Agus bainfidh siad rinnc' a's éir'cighibh.[58]

> (Young Charles is voyaging over the sea, there'll be a few guards with him, there'll be Frenchmen and Spaniards with him, and they'll make the heretics dance.)

Much of the literature was composed at times of optimism engendered by the prospect of war after long periods of peace, by British military reverses, or by rumours of imminent invasion. Hopes of a Stuart restoration were high during the War of Spanish Succession and again around 1715; they declined during the period of the Anglo-French alliance but revived as international tensions increased in the years before the outbreak of the War of Austrian Succession. The 1745 rising prompted a flood of Jacobite compositions; its failure may have had less effect on perceptions in Ireland than the fact that Prince Charles' small army advanced into the heart of England and shook the Hanoverian establishment. In any event, French victories in the opening phase of the Seven Years War were greeted by a fresh outpouring of Jacobite verse.

Jacobite compositions from the 1690s and the early decades of the eighteenth century tended to be aristocratic in tone and commonly deplored the death, expropriation or exile of prominent Jacobites. Works in this vein include Séamas Dall Mac Cuarta's elegy for Colonel Sorley McDonnell, killed

---

58 É. Ó Muirgheasa (ed.), *Céad de cheoltaibh Uladh* (Dublin: M.H. Mac Giolla agus a Mhac, 1915), p. 151.

at the head of his regiment in the battle of Aughrim; Diarmaid mac Sheáin Bhuí Mac Cárthaigh's elegy for Justin McCarthy, Viscount Mountcashel, who died in France in 1694; Aodh Buí Mac Cruitín's elegies for the brothers Daniel and Charles O'Brien, 4th and 5th Viscounts Clare, who died of injuries received in the battles of Marsaglia (1693) and Ramillies (1706) respectively; Liam Rua Mac Coitir's elegy for Sir James Cotter, who was hanged in controversial circumstances in 1720; and Eoghan Mac Cárthaigh's elegy for Donagh MacCarthy, Earl of Clancarty, who died at Hamburg in 1734.[59] Yet this emphasis on leading members of the native gentry never monopolised the literature, and other themes that ultimately proved to be more enduring were present from the beginning. Aogán Ó Rathaille, a County Kerry poet who died in 1729, frequently lamented the downfall of the MacCarthys – 'na flatha fá raibh mo shean roimh éag do Chríost' ('the princes to whom my ancestors were subject before the death of Christ') as he memorably described them – but his grievances against the post-Revolution establishment were not restricted to the attainder of well-known Jacobites.[60] In a poem beginning 'monuarsa an Chárthfhuil tráite tréithlag' ('my grief that the MacCarthys are spent and exhausted'), he regretted that Ireland was now a country without a native ruling class ('tír gan triath de ghrianfhuil Éibhir'); but he also wrote that it was a country without justice for the poor ('tír gan chothrom do bhochtaibh'), a country in which the Catholic Church had been suppressed ('tír gan eaglais chneasta ná cléirigh'), and a country that had been subjugated by English-speakers ('tír do briseadh le foireann an Bhéarla').[61] Ó Rathaille was an early exponent of the allegorical *aisling*, arguably the best-known genre of Jacobite literature in Irish. In the *aisling*, the poet typically encounters a spirit-woman at an isolated location. In most Jacobite *aislingí*, the woman identifies herself as Ireland and reassures a despondent poet that the Stuart pretender will shortly arrive at the head of an army, but in some compositions the roles are reversed and the poet lifts the spirits of a grieving woman with the news of a recent British defeat. The *aisling* was a familiar literary genre that served as an effective means of

---

59 S. Ó Gallchóir (ed.), *Séamas Dall Mac Cuarta: dánta* (Dublin: An Clóchomhar, 1971), pp. 63–9; T. Ó Donnchadha (ed.), *Amhráin Dhiarmada mac Seáin Bhuidhe Mac Cárrthaigh* (Dublin: M.H. Mac Goill agus a Mhac, 1916), pp. 14–25; Morley, *Aodh Buí Mac Cruitín*, pp. 3, 17–21; R. Ó Foghludha (ed.), *Cois na Cora* (Dublin: Oifig Díolta Foillseacháin Rialtais, 1937), pp. 29–41; R. Ó Foghludha, *Eoghan an Mhéirín* (Dublin: Oifig Díolta Foillseacháin Rialtais, 1937), pp. 44–51.
60 B. Ó Buachalla (ed.), *Aogán Ó Rathaille* (Dublin: Field Day Publications, 2007), p. 43.
61 Ibid., p. 13.

communicating political messages to a largely illiterate population – a function it would retain until the nineteenth century.[62]

When the ideology expressed in Jacobite literature is assessed, three main themes can be identified: namely, faith, king and country. In his lament for Sorley MacDonnell who fell at Aughrim, Mac Cuarta wrote that the deceased had fought:

> Fá aon chreideamh Phádraig is ar ghrá mhic na hóighe,
> le fírinne dár náisiún is do shásamh na córa
>
> (For the only faith of Saint Patrick and from love of the Virgin's
> Son, with fidelity to our nation and to vindicate the right)

These lines were written in the immediate aftermath of the Williamite revolution, but John Lloyd, a Limerick schoolmaster, was still emphasising the importance of ethnicity, legitimacy and religion in a Jacobite song composed three generations later:

> Is fada treibh Ghael ghroí ghlais – an gasra gliadh –
> gan reachta, gan rí dílis, gan Aifreann na gcliar.[63]
>
> (Long has the tribe of vigorous Gael Glas – the fighting band – been
> without laws, without a proper king, without the Mass of the clergy.)

Whenever Irish authors envisaged a Stuart restoration, they invariably associated it with the re-establishment of Catholicism: 'beidh dlighe na Rómha i ngnás go mór' ('the law of Rome will be much in fashion'); 'beidh a gcealla ag an Eaglais fhíre' ('the true church will possess their churchyards'); 'beidh cléir go seasamhach, talamhach, tóiceach' ('clergy will be established, propertied, endowed'); and 'oird bhinne is cléirigh ina ndúchas' ('melodious liturgies and clerics in their patrimony').[64] The Stuart pretender was commonly portrayed as a Gael of impeccably Milesian descent: 'an duine ba ghile ar shliocht chine Scoit trí huaire' ('the most splendid, thrice over, among the progeny of Scot's race'); 'taoiseach na nGaoidheal nglan' ('the chieftain of the pure Gaels'); 'an réx de shaorshliocht cheap Ghaoidheal' ('the king from the noble lineage of

---

62 For three *aislingí* in which Daniel O'Connell is praised, see D. Ó Muirithe (ed.), *An tamhrán macarónach* (Dublin: An Clóchomhar, 1980), pp. 103–7.

63 Nic Éinrí, *Canfar an Dán*, p. 159. Gael Glas, a forebear of Milesius, was the eponymous ancestor of the Gaels.

64 R. Ó Foghludha (ed.), *Éigse na Máighe* (Dublin: Oifig Díolta Foilseachán Rialtais, 1952), p. 112; M. Comer Bruen and D. Ó hÓgáin (eds.), *An Mangaire Súgach* (Dublin: Coiscéim, 1996), p. 112; B. Ó Cróinín (ed.), *Piaras Mac Gearailt: a shaol agus a shaothar* (Dingle: An Sagart, 2015), p. 163; Ó Muirithe, *Cois an Ghaorthaidh*, p. 13.

Gael's stock'); 'réx ceart na Féinne' ('the proper king of the *Fianna*'); and 'ráib leabhair léidmheach d'árd-fhuil Mhilésius' ('the lithe, daring champion from the noble blood of Milesius').[65] Alongside these confessional and dynastic loyalties, Ireland's status as an ancient kingdom was asserted. Far from being an appanage of the crown of England, the country had a crown of its own – one of three that rightfully belonged to the house of Stuart: 'ag cailliúint a thrí gcorónach' ('forfeiting his three crowns'); 'go nglacathar thu i dtrí chróinnibh' ('may you be received into three crowns'); 'réidhfidh ar trí choróiníbh' ('he'll settle for three crowns'); 'ná hiarrfaidh acht trí chróinní' ('who will only demand three crowns'); and 'seilbh trí gcoróin ag an leon ná habraim' ('possession of three crowns held by the lion I won't name').[66]

Publication of Jacobite material in Ireland would have exposed the author and printer to prosecution for seditious libel, but emigrant authors enjoyed greater freedom. The most important example of a Jacobite text published abroad is James MacGeoghegan's *Histoire de l'Irlande ancienne et moderne* which appeared at Paris in three volumes between 1758 and 1763.[67] A former military chaplain, MacGeoghegan dedicated his history to Irish troops in the service of France. His representation of Irish history reflected the perspective of the vernacular literature: no other nation had displayed such loyalty to the true faith in the face of persecution ('nulle autre nation n'a conservé le dépôt de la foi, depuis deux siècles de persécution, avec autant de fermeté & de courage'); the Old Irish had readily acknowledged the Milesian ancestry of the first Stuart monarch ('ils le regardoient comme un Prince qui leur devoit l'origine') and recognised this as a legitimate title to the crown of Ireland ('titre valable à la Couronne d'Irlande'); while Ireland itself had already been an ancient kingdom at the time of the English invasion ('cette Isle étoit décorée de ce titre longtemps avant que les Anglois y fussent connus').[68]

Even a cursory comparison of Irish literature with that of Highland Scotland helps to highlight the distinctive features of Irish Jacobitism. Jacobite authors in Scotland gave a wide berth to religious controversy that could only

---

65 Ó Buachalla, *Aogán Ó Rathaille*, p. 34; Ó Foghludha, *Carn Tighearnaigh*, p. 19; Ú. Nic Éinrí and M. Spillane (eds.), *Seán Ó Tuama ó Chromadh an tsubhachais* (Dublin: Coiscéim, 2012), p. 113; R. Ó Foghludha (ed.), *Ar bruach na Coille Muaire* (Dublin: Oifig an tSoláthair, 1939), p. 41; Mac Cumhghaill, *Seán de Hóra*, p. 35.

66 E. Ó hAnluain (ed.), *Seon Ó hUaithnín* (Dublin: An Clóchomhar, 1973), p. 37; Ó Foghludha, *Carn Tighearnaigh*, p. 28; Nic Éinrí and Spillane, *Seán Ó Tuama*, p. 122; Ó Foghludha, *Cois na Cora*, p. 26; Comer Bruen and Ó hÓgáin, *An Mangaire Súgach*, p. 110.

67 L'Abbé MacGeoghegan, *Histoire de l'Irlande ancienne et moderne*, 3 vols. (Paris: Antoine Boudet, 1758–63); V. Geoghegan, 'A Jacobite history: the Abbé MacGeoghegan's *History of Ireland*', *Eighteenth-Century Ireland*, 6 (1991), 37–55.

68 MacGeoghegan, *Histoire de l'Irlande*, vol. I, p. 262; vol. III, p. 637; vol. II, p. 367.

sow dissension among a confessionally mixed community; in Scotland, the religious card was played by Whigs.[69] Furthermore, the national dimension was much weaker in the Highlands: there were no Scottish equivalents of the many allegorical representations of Ireland, while Scotland's position within a larger British polity was acknowledged from an early date.[70] In contrast to the Irish, Scottish Jacobites stressed the prerogatives of the crown and the principle of indefeasible hereditary right. Iain Ruadh Stiùbhart, who fought for the French at Fontenoy and commanded a regiment in Prince Charles' army, saw his Gaelic-speaking audience as part of a wider British population that was being punished for their disloyalty:

> Is amhuil bha Breatunn fo bhròn
> > O'n a thréig iad a' chòir 's an Rìgh;
> Ghabh flaitheas ruinn corruich ro-mhór,
> > Crom an donais! chaidh 'n seòrsa an diasg![71]

(Thus has Britain been sorrowful since they abandoned justice and their king; heaven conceived an immense anger against us, damn it! the race has drained away!)

Yet Scottish authors also displayed a confidence in the military potential of their countrymen that is absent from Irish literature. Alasdair Mac Mhaighstir Alasdair MacDhòmhnaill, who later served as a captain in the Jacobite army during the 1745 Rebellion, assured Prince Charles that a powerful army would rally to his standard as soon as he landed:

> Tha muir is tìr co-rèidh dhuit
> Mur dèan thu fèin a searg:
> Dòirtidh iad 'nan ceudaibh
> 'Nan laomaibh tiugha treuna
> À Briotainn is à Èirinn
> Mu d' standard brèidgheal dearg:
> A' ghaisridh sgaiteach ghuineach rìoghail,
> Chreuchdach fhìor-luath gharg.[72]

(Sea and land are equally ready for you, unless you blight them yourself; they will rush in their hundreds, in dense, powerful bands from Britain and

69 V. Morley, 'Idé-eolaíocht an tSeacaibíteachais in Éirinn agus in Albain', *Oghma*, 9 (1997), 14–24.
70 V. Morley, 'The idea of Britain in eighteenth-century Ireland and Scotland', *Studia Hibernica*, 33 (2004–5), 101–24.
71 J. Lorne Campbell (ed.), *Highland songs of the Forty-five* (Edinburgh: Scottish Gaelic Texts Society, 1984), p. 188.
72 D.S. Thomson (ed.), *Alasdair Mac Mhaighstir Alasdair: Selected Poems* (Edinburgh: Scottish Gaelic Texts Society, 1996), p. 106.

Ireland, about your white-striped crimson standard – the active,
keen, royal, wounding, truly swift and ferocious troops.)

In contrast, the section of the Irish population that was most sympathetic to Jacobitism was disarmed, leaderless and acutely aware of its impotence. Whenever Irish authors envisaged the arrival of Prince Charles Edward, they assumed he would be accompanied by an army:

Casfaidh na héanlaith, dá ngairmtear géanna,
    in arm go gléasta gan spás puinn
i gcabhair le Séarlas, an cathbhile is tréine
    dar sheasaimh ó d'éagadar cnámha Fhinn.[73]

(The birds that are called 'geese' will return, armed and equipped without much delay, assisting Charles, the mightiest champion to have lived since the death of Fionn's people.)

No invasion of Ireland, however successful, could have effected a Stuart restoration. Geography dictated that an army could march on London from Edinburgh, but not from Dublin, and this strategic reality ensured that Ireland would never play more than a diversionary role in Jacobite plans.

The Jacobite Twilight

When Pope Clement XIII declined to recognise Prince Charles Edward as *de jure* monarch on the death of James III in 1766, the Catholic Church in Ireland was at last free to acknowledge the legitimacy of George III's title to the crown. Within two years, reports appeared in the press of prayers being offered for the royal family at Sunday Mass in some dioceses.[74] By 1767, an initiative was already in train to devise a new oath of allegiance that could be taken by Catholics. Frederick Augustus Hervey, the Church of Ireland bishop of Derry, took the lead in consulting leading churchmen and a Catholic Committee which numbered Charles O'Conor and Dr John Curry among a membership drawn from landed, professional and commercial interests.[75] Early indications were that Rome's change of policy towards the Stuarts, coming in the aftermath of Britain's comprehensive victory over the Bourbon powers in the Seven Years War, had extinguished any

73 Nic Éinrí, *Canfar an Dán*, p. 112.
74 *Finn's Leinster Journal*, 9 Jan. 1768 and *Freeman's Journal*, 6 Feb. 1768, quoted in Brady, *Catholics and Catholicism*, pp. 129–30.
75 Fagan, *Divided loyalties*, pp. 125–56.

lingering loyalty to Jacobitism among Catholics of means. Two contrasting entries in Charles O'Conor's diary indicate that he revised his views at an early date. On 22 September 1745, five days after Prince Charles entered Edinburgh in triumph, O'Conor wrote:

> Mac Mic Rígh Sémuis anos a n-Albain ag buaidhirt na dtrí ríoghacht. Níl fhios nach amhlaidh as férr.[76]

> (The son of King James' son now in Scotland, disturbing the three kingdoms. One doesn't know that it isn't for the best.)

This is not a ringing endorsement of the Scottish rising, but the double negative suggests an openness to the possibility of a Jacobite victory and a cautious optimism that such an outcome might produce a change for the better. However, in a second entry dated 14 February 1746, O'Conor concluded that the collapse of the rebellion marked the definitive failure of the Jacobite project:

> An Stibhardach do dhíbeirt astech go Gaodhaltacht na hAlban a mesg na sleibhte, agus an chuid as mó dhá mhuintir do imthecht uadha. Ag sin drithle dédhionach do choindil taoi dol as re trí fichitt bliadhain, mur dtoirmiosgan Dia.[77]

> (The Stuart being driven into the Scottish Highlands among the mountains, and most of his people leaving him. That's the last flicker of a candle that has been going out for three score years, unless God prevents it.)

The process of drafting a suitable oath of allegiance for Catholics was protracted, but the principal difficulty lay in its repudiation of the temporal powers of the papacy rather than in its abjuration of the Stuarts. In 1774, the Irish parliament passed an 'act to enable his Majesty's subjects of whatever persuasion to testify their allegiance to him' (13 & 14 Geo. III, c. 35). Surprisingly, perhaps, the act sparked a lively controversy within the Catholic community, and the arguments advanced by supporters of the oath leave little doubt that the opposition was largely inspired by residual Jacobite sentiment.[78] Referring to Prince Charles Edward, Patrick Molloy, a prominent member of the Catholic clergy in Kilkenny, asked rhetorically, 'what could we expect from this same *pretended Messiah*? The *redemption*

---

76 S. Ní Chinnéide (ed.), 'Dhá leabhar nótaí le Séarlas Ó Conchubhair', *Galvia*, 1 (1954), 39.
77 Ibid.
78 V. Morley, 'Catholic disaffection and the oath of allegiance of 1774' in J. Kelly, J. McCafferty and C.I. McGrath (eds.), *People, politics and power: essays on Irish history 1660–1850* (Dublin: UCD Press, 2009), pp. 122–42.

of Israel! Nonsense! – Its utter destruction, perhaps.'[79] Similarly, Arthur O'Leary, a Capuchin priest based in Cork city, argued that 'all we expect from him is the liberty to *fast and pray*; this we enjoy without his mediation, and it would be madness to forfeit it'.[80] Reports of groups of Catholics taking the oath in open court began to appear in the press from the middle of 1775, and although only 1,500 persons did so under the terms of the 1774 Act, large numbers subscribed once the Catholic Relief Act of 1778 (17 & 18 Geo. III, c. 49) exempted jurors from restrictions on the leasing and inheritance of land.[81]

If the withdrawal of papal recognition from the Stuart pretender allowed many Catholics of substance to swear allegiance to George III with an easy conscience, authors from humbler social backgrounds were still ready to assert Charles Edward's title to the crown. At some date between 1767 and 1771, the County Armagh poet Art Mac Cumhaigh imagined a heated debate between a ruined pre-Reformation church at Faughart, County Louth, and a newly built Protestant church at Forkhill, County Armagh, in which the former addressed its modern rival as follows:

> Is ar fheartaibh Mhic Dé nár mhairidh tú i gcéim
> Nó go gcuiridh Rí Séarlus brón ort.[82]

> (And by the miracles of God's Son may you not live in pomp,
> but may King Charles cast you into sorrow.)

Similarly, the Pretender's royal title was acknowledged in an anonymous song associated with the Whiteboy agitation that disturbed much of east Munster and south Leinster during the 1760s and 1770s:

> is buacach na blátha go fuadrach ag fásadh,
> ar dhualladh na mbánta gan mhilleadh,
> le huaill 's le háthas na mBuachaillí Bána,
> faoi thuairim Rí Seárlas go dtiocfadh.[83]

> (Sprightly are the flowers that are vigorously growing, unspoilt on the
> sward of the meadows, with the halloos and delight of the Whiteboys
> at the thought that King Charles will come.)

---

79 Ibid., p. 133.
80 Ibid., p. 135.
81 Fagan, *Divided loyalties*, pp. 176–88.
82 É. Ó Muirgheasa (ed.), *Dánta diadha Uladh* (Dublin: Oifig Díolta Foillseacháin Rialtais, 1936), p. 10.
83 Ó Buachalla, *Aisling Ghéar*, p. 634.

The Whiteboys' sporting of white cockades and their playing of the Scottish Jacobite air 'The white cockade' have been noted and discounted by the movement's historian.[84] But if the agitation was inspired by economic grievances, the vernacular literature indicates that the political culture of the social layers involved in the movement remained strongly Jacobite. Another anonymous song noted the defection of the Catholic clergy but continued to hope that the established order might be overthrown by the 'wild geese' and the Stuart pretender:

> Ca ngeabhadh faoilchoin síghe na ngaoith-leas do bhíos fo'n spéir 'san aoidhche?
> Ar chualadh sgeul chlainn Luiteir mhéith ag iarraidh ar ccléir do ghuidhe leo!
> Iompadh gach naon de threibh Mhilesius go cruadh chum Dé le hintin,
> go mbuadh Dia ccéim a ccruaing a ccéin le trúpaidh Gaedhal ar Stiobhairt.[85]

> (Where would they be going, the fairy warriors [Whiteboys] of the airy raths who stray abroad at night? Have you heard the story of Luther's plump race asking our clergy to pray for them! Let everyone of the Milesian race turn earnestly to God with fervour, so that God might win their status in a distant clash with the Irish troops of our Stuart.)

Before long, frankly anti-clerical sentiments were being expressed in Irish-language literature even as the once common figure of the priest-poet became an endangered species. While it is impossible to demonstrate cause and effect, these developments have been attributed to the realignment of the Catholic clergy with a political and social establishment that was still viewed with hostility by much of the laity.[86] Political verse composed during the American revolutionary war confirms the continuing prevalence of Jacobite sentiment among sections of the populace. Tomás Ó Míocháin, a County Clare schoolmaster, predicted that the conflict would end with a Stuart restoration:

> D'éis an chluiche seo Éire ligfear
> dá céile dlitheach ceart díleas,
> an féinne fuinneamhach faobhrach fuilingeach
> Séarlas soineanta Stíobhart.[87]

> (After this contest Ireland will be left to her legitimate, true, proper spouse, the energetic, keen, tenacious warrior, Charles Stuart the serene.)

---

84 J.S. Donnelly, 'The Whiteboy movement, 1761–5', *Irish Historical Studies*, 21 (1978), 29.
85 The song entitled 'Clann Shadhbha agus Shaidhbhín', Royal Irish Academy MS. 23 E 12, p. 409.
86 Ó Buachalla, *Aisling Ghéar*, pp. 638–47.
87 Morley (ed.), *Washington i gceannas a ríochta*, p. 21.

Likewise, Prince Charles Edward was referred to as 'Carolus Rex' in works from the same period by Ceallachán Mac Cárthaigh and Eoghan Rua Ó Súilleabháin, authors from counties Cork and Kerry respectively.[88]

The death of Charles Edward Stuart in 1788 marked the effective end of the Stuart cause. Although his younger brother Henry Benedict Stuart – the 'Duke of York' to Jacobites – survived, he pursued a clerical career after the failure of the 1745 rebellion and rose to be cardinal bishop of Frascati, near Rome. Charles Edward was lamented in verse by Seán Ó Muláin, a teacher from Cork city who would later write republican verse. Ó Muláin's political trajectory was not unique: Micheál Óg Ó Longáin was another prolific poet from County Cork who made the transition from Jacobitism to republicanism between the 1780s and the 1790s.[89] At the opposite end of Ireland, an anonymous song collected from the oral tradition in County Donegal demonstrates that republican ideas could be reconciled with an older loyalty to the house of Stuart. Republican France was held up as an example in the first verse of the song:

> Ó éirigidh suas a thogha na bhfear
> 'gus cuirigidh píce ar bharr gach cleith,
> leagaigidh síos iad lucht a droch-chroidhe,
> agus cuirigidh dlighe na Frainc' ar bun.[90]

> (O rise up you finest of men and fix a pike head on the top of every shaft, strike down the evil-hearted ones and establish French law.)

However, the second verse contained an assurance that the Duke of York had a sizeable army at his disposal ('tá arm go leor ag Duke of York'); from the context, this can only refer to Henry Benedict Stuart. Similarly, a document discovered on a suspected member of the Defenders when he was admitted to Cavan gaol in June 1795 expressed the hope that 'the duke of York will save us' alongside a more conventional republican hope that 'French Defenders will uphold the cause and Irish Defenders will pull down the British laws.'[91] It seems likely that the Cardinal Duke of York held a dual appeal for disaffected Catholics in the 1790s: in view of his royal descent and his high ecclesiastical office, the last member of the house of Stuart posed a simultaneous challenge to the legitimacy of the reigning monarch and the established church.

---

88 Ibid., pp. 88 and 102.
89 For relevant compositions by Ó Muláin and Ó Longáin, see V. Morley, 'The continuity of disaffection in eighteenth-century Ireland', *Eighteenth-Century Ireland*, 22 (2007), 198–201.
90 Ó Muirgheasa, *Céad de cheoltaibh Uladh*, p. 152.
91 T. Bartlett, 'Defenders and Defenderism in 1795', *Irish Historical Studies*, 24 (1985), 388–9.

Conclusion

All hope of a Stuart restoration vanished with the death of Prince Charles Edward, but Irish Jacobitism – unlike its Scottish equivalent – encompassed religious, dynastic and national loyalties. Deeply embedded in popular culture, the ideology's religious and national elements survived the extinction of the house of Stuart. Originally a counter-revolutionary movement that aimed to restore the *ancien régime* overthrown at Aughrim, Jacobitism raised a standard around which the substantial section of Irish society that was hostile to the post-1691 establishment could rally; in doing so, it effectively prevented the popular legitimation of the reigning dynasty that might otherwise have occurred with the passage of time. Moreover, the aspirations of its adherents gradually shifted from the recovery of forfeited estates to the expulsion of the Anglo-Irish gentry and the disestablishment of the Anglican church. When the Stuart succession failed, former Jacobites who still hoped to see the overthrow of the existing political and religious order had little alternative but to embrace a new ideology – a development made easier by the fact that they had long regarded France as the most likely agent of Ireland's deliverance.

2

The Politics of Protestant Ascendancy, 1730–1790

JAMES KELLY

The authority of the Protestant interest in Ireland was as its zenith during the six decades 1730 to 1790. Having overcome the challenge they experienced during the reign of James II and the military confrontation that followed his deposition in 1688, they were assisted to consolidate their emerging political, social and economic ascendancy by the decision to entrust the task of making law for Ireland to an Irish Protestant parliament. It took some time for MPs and peers in parliament to develop a *modus operandi* with the Irish executive, which was answerable in the first instance to the King (or Queen) and ministers in London, but this composite monarchy was put on a solid political footing when parliament and executive concluded an arrangement – the so-called 'compromise' of 1695 – whereby, in return for an undertaking to raise the revenue required for the administration and defence of the kingdom, peers and MPs were permitted to initiate legislation in the form of heads of bills, and leading members of the House of Commons were encouraged to take an active part in the practical arts of parliamentary management.[1] The process by which this outcome was brought about was neither uneventful nor uncomplicated. But by 1730 the near eclipse of the Irish Privy Council as a source of law had combined with the system of parliamentary management that had evolved since the 1690s to produce a more streamlined, and efficient, arrangement whereby an individual undertook the responsibility – hence the usage of the label 'undertaker' to describe this person.[2] Henry Boyle (1684–1764) performed this role for two decades until the early 1750s, when factional rivalries precipitated the first serious period of political instability since the Wood's halfpence crisis of the mid-1720s. The undertaker system survived the Money Bill dispute, 1753–6, not least because

---

1 C.I. McGrath, *The making of the eighteenth-century Irish constitution: government, parliament and the revenue, 1692–1714* (Dublin: Four Courts Press, 2000), pp. 73–117; J. Kelly, *Poynings' Law and the making of law in Ireland, 1660–1800* (Dublin: Four Courts Press, 2007), chapter 1.
2 See Volume II, McGrath, Chapter 5 and Hayton, Chapter 6.

of the continuing refusal of lords lieutenant to reside in Ireland for the duration of their time in office, but the episode raised serious doubts in the minds of British ministers as to the suitability of the arrangement. No less significantly, the invocation by Boyle and his allies of the rhetoric of patriotism had an enduring legacy.

The emergence of an explicitly Patriot voice in the House of Commons was less significant than changing conceptions of empire and the serendipity of personality in causing George, Lord Townshend to bring the curtain down on the undertaker system between 1769 and 1772. Moreover, its termination accented emerging trends. Traditionally, the development of a strong Patriot interest in the House of Commons has been ascribed to a generational shift in the membership of the House of Commons. This was not inconsequential. But the expansion of the public sphere, the conflation of Townshend's efforts to strengthen the authority of the Irish executive, and the impact, first, of John Wilkes' defiance of the political elite at Westminster, and, second, of the American colonists' resistance to the efforts of the crown to make them bear the cost of their defence were inspirational. Because this was largely confined to the popular political realm prior to the commencement of the American War of Independence in 1775 it has attracted less attention than it merits. Furthermore, it is improbable it would have prompted an attempt to restructure the commercial and constitutional connection that bound Britain and Ireland but for the leadership and direction provided by the energised Patriot interest in the House of Commons, the indecision of the Irish administration, and the loss of confidence of the British government. The Volunteers, a civilian militia established during the American War of Independence to defend Ireland, were the most striking manifestation of the ensuing convergence of popular and elite politics, without which neither free trade nor legislative independence would have been achieved. For many of those from the 'middling sort' for whom the manner of their achievement was a revelation of the potential of a more inclusive political system, the priority, once commercial and constitutional reform had been attained, was to reform the parliamentary and representative system. To this end, a campaign aimed at widening the representative base of the Irish parliament was pursued in 1783–5, initially under the umbrella of the Volunteers. However, divisions within their ranks on its merits dovetailed with deeper reservations about admitting Catholics to the political process, to enable those of a more conservative mind-set to take charge of the Irish administration. They were not strong enough to undo the recent constitutional and commercial changes, despite an imaginative attempt spearheaded by William Pitt in 1785, but they remained in control and were able thereby to ensure that the political orchestra responded to their baton. As a result, it was apparent by the end of the 1780s that legislative independence represented less of a new era in the history of the Anglo-Irish nexus than a new phase in the administration of the dependent kingdom of Ireland that satisfied neither conservatives nor liberals.

The Floruit and Eclipse of the Undertaker System, 1730–1772

The death in October 1729 of William Conolly (b. 1662), who was the dominant presence in Irish politics during the reign of George I (1714–27), and the first 'undertaker' or chief manager of government business in the House of Commons, hastened a generational shift in Irish politics.[3] The instinctive response of the Conolly interest to the 'speaker's' death was to retain possession of the suite of positions – the speakership of the House of Commons and the chief commissionership of the revenue most notably – from which, along with the office of lord justice, the 'undertaker' derived his authority.[4] The role was assumed initially by Sir Ralph Gore (1675? –1733), who succeeded Conolly as Speaker, and to whom there was 'general deference', but his death in February 1733 hastened the fragmentation of the Conolly interest. Its preferred successor was Marmaduke Coghill (1673–1739), an able and experienced 'man of business', but he did not possess the requisite temperament or personality. Besides, he did not have the support of the lord lieutenant, Lionel Sackville, 1st Duke of Dorset. Persuaded that Henry Boyle, MP for County Cork, was a better candidate, vice-regal support proved decisive and Boyle achieved what was a long-standing ambition when he was elected Speaker in October 1733. His identification in 1734 as 'the properest person' to serve as a lords justice (in company with the lord chancellor and primate of the Church of Ireland) in the absence of the lord lieutenant, who was intent on returning to England during the long interval between meetings of parliament, was a further demonstration of trust, and Dorset took encouragement from the response of the political class. 'The Whigs are now more united than they have been since the death of Mr Conolly', he confided to the Duke

---

3 P. Walsh, *The making of the Irish Protestant Ascendancy: the life of William Conolly, 1662–1729* (Woodbridge: The Boydell Press, 2010).
4 D. Hayton, 'The beginnings of the undertaker system' in T. Bartlett and D.W. Hayton (eds.), *Penal era and golden age: essays in Irish history, 1690–1800* (Belfast: Ulster Historical Foundation, 1979), pp. 32–54.

of Newcastle.[5] Dorset's confidence in Boyle was justified, for though relations between the two men were not warm during the final three years of the lord lieutenant's first term as viceroy of Ireland, the fact that 'all things go on quietly', as the baron of the court of Exchequer, John Wainwright, observed in 1736, was a welcome contrast to the eventfulness and contention that characterised the 1720s.[6] (Illustration 2)

Though some at least of the credit for Boyle's calming impact can reasonably be attributed to the support he received from successive lords lieutenant – the Duke of Dorset, 1731–37, the 3rd Duke of Devonshire, 1737–45, and the Earl of Chesterfield, 1746–7 – his unassuming manner and unpretentious conduct belied a calculating political mind and a steely ambition.[7] Like Conolly before him, Boyle contrived to retain the necessary room to manoeuvre by making it known to the incumbent lord lieutenant that his support could not be assumed. He worked closely with Dublin Castle to ensure that the financial legislation upon which the government of the kingdom was dependent was ushered onto the statute book with few complications, but was less forthcoming on matters that were politically controversial even when this discommoded the Irish administration. These episodes were not sufficiently commonplace or serious to undermine a relationship that was mutually advantageous, since his failure in 1733–4 to support the attempt by government to repeal the 1704 sacramental test provision that barred Protestant Dissenters from a raft of official positions, and measures aimed at preventing the smuggling of wool to France in 1741–2, were not impelled by populism.

Boyle's intellectual and geographical horizon was firmly fixed on Ireland. In contrast to the Earl of Bessborough, the leader of the Ponsonby interest, who cultivated political connections in England, Boyle prioritised the domestic concerns of the country gentlemen with which he identified, and upon whom he relied. Because of his position as Speaker of the House of Commons for more than twenty years, as a lords justice (on fifteen occasions), and as commissioner of the revenue between 1735 and 1739, and the influence he wielded with a succession of lords lieutenant, he was ideally positioned

---

5 Dorset to Newcastle, 22 Feb. 1733/4, Lansdowne papers, MS 1235 ff. 28–9, BL.
6 Wainwright to Dodington, 14 May 1736 in HMC, *Reports on various collections, vi: Eyre Matcham MSS* (London: HMSO, 1909), p. 67.
7 Unless otherwise noted, the following account of Henry Boyle draws on A.P.W. Malcomson, 'Lord Shannon' in E. Hewitt (ed.), *Lord Shannon's letters to his son* (Belfast: Public Record Office of Northern Ireland (henceforth PRONI), 1982), pp. xxiii–lxxix; E. Magennis, *The Irish political system, 1740–1765: the golden age of the undertakers* (Dublin: Four Courts Press, 2000).

His Excellency Henry Boyle

2. Henry Boyle, 1st Earl of Shannon (1682–1764), Speaker of the Irish House of Commons, 1733–56, was the dominant politician and the most effective parliamentary 'undertaker' of his generation. Mezzotint by John Brooks (probably 1750s) (National Portrait Gallery).

to ensure that the fruits of influence – place, pension and position – were dispensed in the directions he wanted and into the possession of those he favoured. Yet it would be wrong to suggest that Boyle presided over an essentially venal nexus of factions. If the trust reposed in him by the Irish administration depended on his ability to steer essential financial legislation through the Commons chamber, the support he garnered from MPs in connections other than his own, and from the influential ranks of those who proudly described themselves as 'independent country gentlemen', was dependent on his endorsement of a legislative programme that embraced the economics of improvement and the politics of Protestant security.[8]

In statistical terms, an average of nineteen bills received the royal assent in Ireland during the twelve sessions that Boyle was Speaker of the House of Commons. Though slightly in excess of the average registered during the seven sessions chaired by William Conolly, the total is less consequential than – financial legislation apart – the proportion of measures devoted to the support of the linen industry, canal and road development and the promotion of tillage.[9] Similarly, the readiness with which MPs endorsed measures aimed at tightening loopholes in the corpus of 'penal' legislation, at supporting the edifice of Protestant Ascendancy, and at responding to the perceived threat, internal and external, posed by the majority Catholic population and their Jacobite and French fellow travellers, could not have occurred without Boyle's support.[10] It also points to the fact that he shared the feeling of vulnerability that bound the Protestant interest in Ireland at this point, and that he made an important contribution to the forging of a broad consensus which ensured the Anglo-Irish connection and attachment to the Hanoverian succession remained strong. It was not that MPs were pliant or disposed to eschew assertion, but 'easy sessions' were normative because the undertaker system effectually defused tensions and differences between the executive and parliament. As the Duke of Devonshire noted in 1741: 'there are great divisions among those who compose the government interest, [but] each is for appearing to have the principal share in what is done'.[11] As a result, the Earl of Chesterfield

8 E. Magennis, 'Henry Boyle' in J. McGuire and J. Quinn (eds.), *Dictionary of Irish Biography*, 9 vols. (Cambridge: Cambridge University Press, 2009), vol. 1, pp. 718–20.

9 Kelly, *Poynings' Law*, p. 242, table 6; Irish Legislation database, at www.qub.ac.uk/ild/.

10 J. Kelly, 'Sustaining a confessional state: the Irish parliament and Catholicism' in D.W. Hayton, J. Kelly and J. Bergin (eds.), *The eighteenth-century composite state* (Basingstoke: Palgrave, 2010), pp. 55–63; J. Kelly, ' "Disappointing the boundless ambitions of France": Irish Protestants and the fear of invasion, 1661–1815', *Studia Hibernica*, 37 (2011), 51–77.

11 Devonshire to Newcastle, 11, 17 Nov. 1741, Lansdowne MS 1235 ff. 30–1, BL.

reported reassuringly at the height of the Jacobite rebellion scare in 1745, 'I have here a loving and lovely parliament that gives me no other trouble than that of gently restraining some improper marks of zeal for the king and some improper compliments to myself.'[12]

It is helpful to keep this in mind as, beginning in the late 1740s, significant fissures appeared in the undertaker system. Boyle was alert to this, as he had successfully contrived to mitigate their impact during the 1730s and 1740s. His most notable action to this end was to vacate his seat on the revenue board in 1739 in favour of Brabazon Ponsonby, 1st Earl of Bessborough (1679–1758).[13] This strategy bought him some time, but the marriage of two of Bessborough's sons to daughters of the Duke of Devonshire in 1739 and 1743, and the appointment of William Ponsonby as chief secretary, heightened the underlying rivalry that defined their relationship. This had developed to such a pitch by 1747 that the then lord lieutenant, Earl Harrington, apprehended that a difference over patronage 'threatened an open breach, the consequences of which must have been very prejudicial to his majesty's service by throwing our parliamentary affairs here into confusion'.[14] This did not come to pass, and the manner in which the political elite closed ranks, first to isolate Charles Lucas and ultimately to force him into exile when he threatened to bring his brand of confrontational politics from the Dublin municipal arena into the political mainstream, suggested that the system was robust enough to handle any shock.[15] This might have been the case if the personages at the head of the Irish administration had proceeded with appropriate discretion. A crucial moment was reached in 1750, when the 'old bitch', which was the Dublin mob's unflattering description of Harrington, was forced out of office and a new team that combined experience in the persona of the 1st Duke of Dorset, and youth in Lord George Sackville, his chief secretary, assumed the reins of power.[16] Had Dorset been guided by the same pragmatic considerations that determined his actions in 1733, he might have averted confrontation, but he permitted the running to be made by Sackville and the ambitious primate

12 Chesterfield to Pelham, 29 Oct. 1745, Newcastle of Clumber papers, NeC 1535, Nottingham University Library.
13 J. Kelly, 'The Ponsonby family' in Multi-text project in Irish history: history of early-modern Ireland at http://multitext.ucc.ie/d/The_Ponsonby_Family (accessed Dec. 2015).
14 Harrington to Pelham, 12 March 1747 in *Eighteenth-century Irish official papers in Great Britain*, ed. A.P.W. Malcomson, 2 vols. (Belfast: PRONI [1973]–1990), vol. 1, p. 71.
15 S. Murphy, 'The Lucas affair: a study of municipal and electoral politics in Dublin, 1742–9', MA thesis, UCD, 1981, *passim*.
16 Fox to Pelham, 28 May 1750, Newcastle of Clumber papers, NeC 1213, Nottingham University Library.

Archbishop George Stone, who had concluded that the influence that Boyle had accrued at the expense of the executive was detrimental to the interests of English government in Ireland. With the Ponsonbys eager to assume the undertaker role, there was a potential alternative to Henry Boyle, and the lord lieutenant and chief secretary were sufficiently enamoured of the idea for Boyle to conclude not only that he was not trusted, but also that he was destined to be dispensed with once the Ponsonbys and the Irish administration put together a working majority in the House of Commons.

Henry Boyle regarded this prospect with mounting disquiet. He elaborated on his concerns in a rare letter to the prime minister, Henry Pelham: 'the union and harmony with which the King's business has been carried on here for several years past, which by a diligent application of near twenty years I had happily effected, is now in danger of being interrupted and disturb'd to answer the private views of a very few'.[17] The 1751–2 session was particularly difficult. 'There has been', Edward Barry, the MP for Charleville, reported to the Earl of Orrery in March, 'an open quarrel since the beginning of the session between the Speaker and the Primate, and a coldness, to give it a mild expression, between him and the Castle.'[18] Boyle refused to turn his back on twenty years of service or to 'quit his friends while they supported him', but with the question now being asked 'whether the Speaker is to stand or fall', he concluded that he was left with little alternative, consistent with his honour, but to take a stand. He did so with some confidence, moreover, because a majority of those who took his side let it be known that they did not want to 'be governed by the Primate and an English party'.[19] This was to impose an overly partisan, albeit rhetorically attractive, interpretation on events. The point at issue, George Stone countered, referring to the power Henry Boyle wielded in the late 1740s, was whether a lord lieutenant 'should have the principal or, indeed, any share in the direction of public affairs'.[20] As 'a staunch whig',[21] Boyle was reluctant to reduce matters to such simple sloganising, but he was acutely aware that the issue of the influence he possessed provided him and his allies, who were drawn to the emerging Patriot impulse, with a

---

17 Boyle to Pelham, 13 June 1753, Newcastle of Clumber papers, NeC 1573, Nottingham University Library.
18 Barry to Orrery, 4 March 1752 in *The Orrery letters*, ed. Countess of Cork and Orrery, 2 vols. (London, 1903), vol. ii, p. 103.
19 Ibid., pp. 103–5.
20 Stone to Pelham, 26 May 1752, Newcastle of Clumber papers, NeC 1571/1–2, Nottingham University Library.
21 Draft of John Ryder to Dudley Ryder, [Feb. 1754] in *Eighteenth-century Irish official papers*, ed. Malcomson, vol. ii, p. 52.

standard around which they could gather, without as well as within parliament. Moreover, Boyle was shrewd enough to choose his ground carefully,
and when he determined to draw a line in the sand in 1753 he did so not on
the main money bill, but on the subordinate matter of the allocation of the
surplus in the Irish exchequer.[22] The point at issue was whether royal consent
was required before the money could be expended. Boyle opposed a provision to that effect and his strategy was vindicated when, on 18 December,
against a backdrop of heightened public anxiety, he prevailed, 122 votes to 117,
in the crucial division, as Sackville reported from Dublin:

> The question was represented as a struggle of Ireland against England, and
> there was not a common fellow in the streets that was not made to believe
> that if we had carried the question all the money was to be sent the next
> day to England and that in the future parliaments were to be no longer held
> in Ireland. This notice was so encouraged that the mob was with some dif-
> ficulty prevented from breaking into the House during the debate, and we
> heard of nothing but Ireland forever when the door open'd.[23]

His tactical triumph over his opponents notwithstanding, Boyle had, his
critics pointed out, not only openly defied the lord lieutenant's attempt to
'maintain ... the authority and dignity of the crown' but also animated 'the old
distinction of English and Irish interest[s]' that had fallen into disuse subsequent
to his assumption of the role of undertaker.[24] He had as a result put his own
position at risk. His dismissal from the chancellorship of the exchequer in 1754
meant that his defiance did not pass unpunished, but the combination of an
unprecedented display of public support, orchestrated by a network of newly
established Patriot clubs, and the unwillingness of the government to intervene ensured that his hold on the speakership of the House of Commons was
not challenged.[25] Indeed, since he was publicly championed 'as the protector
of the libertys of Ireland', the British government, now headed by the 1st Duke
of Newcastle, concluded that they would only make matters worse by siding
openly with the Irish administration. This decision effectively sealed the fate of
Dorset, Sackville and Primate Stone, who was subjected to an unprecedented

---

22 The standard account of these events is D. O'Donovan, 'The Money Bill dispute of
   1753' in Bartlett and Hayton (eds.), *Penal era and golden age*, pp. 55–87.
23 Sackville to Pelham, 18 Dec. 1753, Newcastle of Clumber papers, NeC 1583, Nottingham
   University Library.
24 Sackville to Pelham, 2 May 1752, Newcastle of Clumber papers, NeC 1567/1,
   Nottingham University Library.
25 B. Harris, 'The Patriot clubs of the 1750s' in J. Kelly and M.J. Powell (eds.), *Clubs and
   societies in eighteenth-century Ireland* (Dublin: Four Courts Press, 2010), pp. 224–43.

campaign of vilification in the Patriot press.[26] It was an extraordinary turn of events, and matters were never to be the same again. The emergence of an identifiable Patriot political connection in the House of Commons was one of the more enduring legacies of the Money Bill dispute,[27] but the more immediate, prompted by the brokering of a resolution to the dispute by Dorset's successor, the Marquis of Hartington, in 1756, was the departure of Henry Boyle from the speakership. Boyle did not retire from political life; he remained active until his death in 1764, but his was no longer the commanding presence of old. The fact that his successor as Speaker of the House of Commons was John Ponsonby indicated that the undertaker system had survived the crisis.

There is no historiographical consensus on the position of the undertaker system in the wake of the Money Bill dispute. R.E. Burns has suggested that the system emerged from the dispute stronger than ever.[28] It can certainly be argued, based on the abandonment of the attempt pursued by the Duke of Bedford, following his assumption of the lord lieutenancy in 1757, 'to govern … without a party' and the sequence of short duration incumbents until Townshend's appointment in 1767, that Dublin Castle was more dependent on the managerial skills of the leaders of the main connections.[29] However, the fact that nobody was as dominant during these years as Henry Boyle was at his peak weakens that argument. Many individuals and faction leaders were willing to work with Dublin Castle to be sure, but the fact that they did so in an overtly self-interested manner reinforced the negative image of the system as venal if not corrupt. Moreover, ministers and opinion formers in England viewed it with an increasingly critical eye. They may, as Patriot voices in Ireland avowed, have arrived at the wrong conclusion in the mid-1750s when they interpreted the actions of Boyle and his 'country friends' and the thrust of the resolutions approved at meetings of Patriot clubs as evidence that the kingdom sought 'independency'.[30] Boyle and others explicitly

26 Sackville to Pelham, 18 Oct. 1753, Newcastle of Clumber papers, NeC 1577/1, Nottingham University Library; J.R. Hill, '"Allegories, fictions, and feigned representations": decoding the Money Bill dispute, 1752–56', *Eighteenth-Century Ireland*, 21 (2006), 66–88.
27 J. Kelly, 'Patriot politics 1750–91' in A. Jackson (ed.), *The Oxford handbook of modern Irish history* (Oxford: Oxford University Press, 2014), pp. 479–96.
28 R.E. Burns, *Irish parliamentary politics in the eighteenth century*, 2 vols. (Washington: Catholic University of America Press, 1989–90), vol. ii, pp. 321–4.
29 Ibid.; Fox to Digby, 21 Nov. 1757 in Earl of Ilchester, *Henry Fox, first Lord Holland*, 2 vols. (London: John Murray, 1920), vol. ii, p. 83.
30 Barry to Orrery, 4 March 1752 in *The Orrery Letters*, vol. ii, p. 103; Boyle to Pelham, 13 June 1752, Newcastle of Clumber papers, NeC 1573, Nottingham University Library; Gordon to [Newcastle], [Sept. 1756], Newcastle papers, Add. MS 32874, ff. 33–5, British Library (henceforth BL).

denied that this was their intention, but the conclusion that the leaders of Irish factions were 'so infatuated with a vain popularity etc. that there is no depending on them' meant, inevitably, that they were increasingly perceived as unreliable.[31] This did not prompt any developed initiatives, but it did elicit a variety of propositions, informed by the conclusion that Boyle had wielded too much power. One suggestion, actively canvassed by the Duke of Bedford in order to reduce the power of 'party' leaders in Ireland, was that control of the administration of the kingdom should be entrusted in the absence of the lord lieutenant to 'a lord deputy … free from all Irish connection'.[32] Another was 'the continued residence of the lord lieutenant'. Neither was implemented, though the conviction that, whenever a suitable 'opportunity' presented, it should be grasped 'to put an end to the absurd system' of undertaking encouraged the Grenville government to decide in principle in February 1765, a few months after Boyle's death, that future lords lieutenant should reside in Ireland, and bring to an end the pattern of temporary residence dating back to 1701.[33] The increasing activity of the small but vocal Patriot interest in the House of Commons – their number augmented in the general election that followed George III's accession to the throne in 1760 – was also a consideration. Guided by Edmund Sexten Pery, Henry Flood and Charles Lucas, the Patriots pursued a range of policy changes in support of their goal of a pattern of government more in keeping with the principles of the Glorious Revolution. However, despite their best efforts to limit the pensions list, to place the militia on a statutory footing, to provide for general elections every seven years and to animate major constitutional issues, the fact that the undertaker system survived unaltered suggested it was set fair to continue for many more years when George, Lord Townshend was appointed lord lieutenant in August 1767. In fact, he was to surprise all and bring the curtain down on the system.

Lord Townshend did not come to Ireland with a plan or instructions either to reform or to restructure the system of government.[34] He was, however, convinced of the importance of placing imperial administration

---

31 Thomas Pakenham's essay on Ireland, 4 Sept. 1755, Chatsworth papers, T/3158/852, PRONI.
32 Bedford to Pitt, 4 Jan. 1758, Lansdowne MS 1235 ff. 45–7, BL.
33 Sedgwick to Weston, 8 Jan. 1765 in HMC, *10th report appendix 1: C.F. Weston Underwood MSS* (London: Eyre and Spottiswoode, 1885), pp. 380–1; J. Kelly, 'Residential and non-residential lords lieutenants: the viceroyalty, 1703–90' in P. Gray and O. Purdue (eds.), *The Irish lord lieutenancy, c. 1541–1922* (Dublin: UCD Press, 2012), pp. 66–96.
34 This follows T. Bartlett, 'The Townshend viceroyalty, 1767–72' in Bartlett and Hayton (eds.), *Penal era and golden age*, pp. 88–112.

on a sounder footing as a result of the sizeable territorial accretions to the British Empire that resulted from its triumph over France in the Seven Years War ('The Great War for Empire'). Furthermore, as an experienced soldier, he was acutely aware of the need for additional military man-power, and temperamentally disinclined to pander to either the affec-tations, the ambitions or the avarice of politicians. There were enough straws in the wind to have caused the leaders of the main Irish political interests – Patriots as well as undertakers – to conclude in advance of his arrival that Townshend was a figure of more substance than his imme-diate predecessors. Yet the combination of self-interest and hubris that informed their actions, and the inadequate direction provided by their nominal leader, Speaker John Ponsonby, lulled them into a false sense of complacency. They were encouraged in this stance by Townshend's acqui-escence to the demand for legislation in 1768 providing for a general elec-tion every eight years. But the failure of the Irish parliament in 1768 to approve the augmentation of the Irish army establishment to 15,000 men (which was a ministerial priority), and its decision in 1769 to reject the Privy Council money bill, which was required, consistent with the provi-sions of Poynings' Law, to permit the convening of a new parliament, was perceived as defiance of royal authority, and Townshend responded accordingly. Following the precedent set by Lord Sydney in 1692 he pro-rogued the House of Commons.[35] This was a radical step, and it unleashed a torrent of public criticism as the increasingly politicised public linked Townshend's intervention with other unpalatably 'arbitrary' actions they identified in the broader Atlantic world of which they were increasingly conscious.[36] Their response was comparable to that of the English Whigs to their exclusion from power following George III's accession to the throne; to that of the reform-minded to the refusal to accept that John Wilkes was a legitimately elected member of the Westminster parliament; and to the American colonists' response to the attempts to compel them to agree to additional taxation to pay for the administration of the Empire. Moreover, they were not without inspirational advocates. Encouraged by Junius, the penetrating English commentator, to believe that Townshend was 'the creature of Lord Bute' (the despised first prime minister of George III), and that, in the words of the peers who protested the prorogation, he

35 Kelly, *Poynings' Law*, pp. 253–5.
36 *Baratariana: a select Collection of Fugitive Political Pieces, published during the Administration of Lord Townshend in Ireland*, 3rd edn (Dublin, 1777), letters 2 and 4.

was 'actuated only by the most arbitrary caprice, to the detriment of his majesty's interests, to the injury of this oppressed country, and to the unspeakable vexation of persons of every condition', they vowed to resist.[37] Townshend, meanwhile, set about forging a Commons majority, and he did so with greater success than the Duke of Dorset in 1752–4. He was assisted, to be sure, by differences between the leaders of the main factions and between them and the Patriots, and by their broader tactical *naïveté* in the face of a resolute and determined adversary.[38] Moreover, though it was not always promptly provided, Townshend could count on the backing of 'the ministry'. As a result, when he convened a meeting of parliament in the spring of 1771, it was he and not his opponents who emerged victorious. He did not have the 'numbers' in every division, but he did prevail in those that mattered, and when John Ponsonby chose to resign the speakership rather than deliver a complimentary address to the King approving of Townshend's conduct, the gap between Ponsonby's management of affairs and the more adept Boyle was plain to see. The popular press initially applauded Ponsonby's action as 'proof of his disinterestedness and true patriotism' and, lamenting 'the late gigantic strides of ministerial power among us', bemoaned the fact that 'it is our misfortune to live in an age in which oppression and corruption make up the shameful and destructive ... measures of the administration'.[39] This was egregiously to exaggerate the order of the change that was taking place, but it did herald the end of an era – an era in which the Protestant landed elite had exercised more direct influence on the administration and making of law for the kingdom of Ireland than the legal and political structures agreed in the early 1690s anticipated. This outcome was assisted by if not predicated upon the unwillingness of successive lords lieutenant to reside in Ireland for the duration of their appointment. The fact that Townshend's successors had no choice in this matter changed the nature of the office, but the fact that it overlapped with the emergence of a more vocal public and a demand for a more inclusive political system meant that lords lieutenant would encounter larger and different problems, which they did not prove equally competent in managing.

37 *The Letters of Junius*, ed. J. Cannon (Oxford: Oxford University Press, 1978), p. 166; House of Lords protest, 26 Dec. 1769 in *A collection of the protests of the House of Lords* (Dublin: J. Milliken, 1772).

38 T. Bartlett, 'Opposition in late eighteenth-century Ireland: the case of the Townshend viceroyalty', *Irish Historical Studies*, 22 (1981–2), 66–87; Allan to Townshend, 29 Nov. 1770, Townshend papers, MS 730/42, National Archives of Ireland.

39 *Limerick Chronicle*, 11 March 1771, 23 May 1771.

Public Opinion, and the Politics of Free Trade and Legislative Independence, 1772–1782

The termination of the undertaker system of parliamentary management, and the assumption by Dublin Castle of the responsibility of ensuring the administration had the numbers in the House of Commons both to progress legislation and to avoid embarrassment, accelerated the political realignment already in train that paved the way for the emergence in the late 1770s of a vigorous Patriot voice in parliament. This took time to realise, as the impact of the loss or withdrawal of key figures (Charles Lucas died in 1771; Edmond Sexten Pery succeeded John Ponsonby as Speaker also in 1771; Henry Flood embarked on a prolonged negotiation that resulted in his assumption of government office in 1775) diminished their parliamentary impact for a time. Equally significantly, Townshend's successor, Simon, Earl Harcourt, and his chief secretary, Sir John Blaquiere, proved an effective team, and they were able with the assistance of a number of ambitious men and interests to ensure the administration of the kingdom of Ireland remained on an even keel during the four years, 1772–6, when they were at the helm. The Patriots might have made more of an impression had they coordinated and concerted their approach, but they remained a loose coalition of individual voices rather than a coherent connection. They targeted 'the great national grievance' of that moment – 'the increasing deficiency and [budget] debt' – but they 'differ[ed] widely as to the means of redressing' these 'evils'.[40] Moreover, apart from Sir Edward Newenham, whose dismissal from his 'employment' in the revenue by Lord Townshend was presented as 'barefaced ... vengeance', there were few in their ranks committed to bridging the gap that separated parliamentary and popular politics.[41] As the ostensible heir to Lucas' mantle, Newenham was as predisposed as his predecessor to use print to get his point across, with this difference; whereas Lucas had prioritised the pamphlet to advance his case in support of the principles of the ancient constitution he believed had been diluted by the accretion by the crown of influence, Newenham's preferred medium was the newspaper, and his benchmark was his idealised perception of the Glorious Revolution. He also preferred to write behind the shelter of a pseudonym (Brutus most notably). In any event, he sought,

---

40 Diary of a journey through England, Wales and Ireland made by Rev. J. Burrowes, 1773, т/3551, PRONI.

41 J. Kelly, *Sir Edward Newenham, MP, 1734–1814: defender of the Protestant constitution* (Dublin: Four Courts Press, 2004), pp. 74–8; *Limerick Chronicle*, 22 June 1772.

consistent with Patriot conviction, not only to uphold the traditions of religion (Protestantism) and liberty that bound the ranks of the Protestant elite in Ireland to Great Britain, but also confidently to assert their entitlement to precisely the same rights.[42]

In specific terms, liberal activists in the early 1770s built on the pattern of agitation that was pursued in the 1760s when Charles Lucas identified limiting the duration of parliament as 'essentially necessary for the preservation of the national constitution'. Informed by Lucas' observation shortly before his death that it was 'the interest and duty of all bodies of electors, at all times, to watch over the conduct of their chosen delegates', the priority object in the early 1770s was to identity electoral candidates who would agree to be guided by the electorate. Lucas signalled the importance of this in 1771; Newenham and his allies identified it as a political goal.[43] Their efforts were facilitated by a further expansion in the public sphere as, building on the foundations laid by the *Freeman's Journal* following its establishment in 1763, there was a surge in the number of newspapers with a reformist agenda. It would be an exaggeration to claim that they shaped political discourse, but the observation in the address to the public featured in the founding issue of the *Dublin Evening Journal* in 1778, that 'every effort of administration seems bent towards establishing a favourite scheme of despotism', was indicative of the fact that the Irish administration was on the back foot in the public sphere for most of the 1770s and early 1780s.[44]

The *Dublin Evening Journal*'s pronouncement may have been no less of a misrepresentation than earlier assertions that Townshend was guided by 'arbitrary' intent, but it echoed the increasingly confrontational tone of political discourse. The many contributions penned in the 1760s and 1770s debating what it meant to be 'a patriot' and how to distinguish between a 'true patriot' and a 'mock' or 'pseudo patriot' might seem recondite, but they were more than word games to those who shared the conclusion, arrived at by Humphrey Search, the anonymous contributor whose verbal prolixity rivalled

---

42 I. McBride, 'The common name of Irishman: Protestantism and patriotism in eighteenth-century Ireland' in T. Claydon and I. McBride (eds.), *Protestantism and national identity: Britain and Ireland, c.1650–c.1850* (Cambridge: Cambridge University Press, 1998), p. 260.

43 Lucas' answer to the guild of shoemakers, *Freeman's Journal*, 21 Jan. 1766; Lucas' answer to the address of the grand jury of the city of Dublin: *Limerick Chronicle*, 23 May 1771; Kelly, *Sir Edward Newenham*, pp. 84–5, 108–9.

44 *Dublin Evening Journal*, 3 Feb. 1778; J. Kelly, 'Political publishing, 1700–1800' in R. Gillespie and A. Hadfield (eds.), *The Oxford history of the Irish book*, vol. III: *1550–1800* (Oxford: Oxford University Press, 2005), pp. 215–33.

Edward Newenham, that 'it was the want of patriotism that caused the late prorogation'.[45] This was doubtful history, but it appealed to readers of the *Freeman's Journal* (1763–), the *Hibernian Journal* (1771–), the *Limerick Chronicle* (1768? –), the *Dublin Evening Journal* (1778–), the progenitor of the *Dublin Evening Post*, and other titles which teemed with such sentiment. It also echoed with the section of the public that attended debating clubs – such as the Society of Free Citizens (Dublin), the Athenian Academy for Free Debate (Dublin) and the Free Debating Society (Limerick) – that accelerated popular politicisation by promoting public awareness of current political and allied issues.[46]

The inability of those who plied a reform agenda to persuade more than a handful of candidates in advance of the 1776 general election to subscribe to a 'test' undertaking to consult and to be guided by the wishes of their constituents indicates that the rhetoric of patriotism and reform had less purchase within the political mainstream than its advocates assumed. Yet the identification of MPs as 'patriots' or 'true patriots' in the public and private lists that were a feature of the political landscape at this time is evidence of the realignment that was underway.[47] It is necessary to make this point because of the enduring tendency to attribute the transformation of the political mood that defines the late 1770s to the reverberations of the outbreak of hostilities in Britain's American colonies.[48] There is no denying that the American War of Independence provided Patriot MPs with a cause that was more compelling than the issues – the proposed tax on the landed rentals of non-resident landowners (the 'absentee tax') or the newspaper stamp tax – that excited controversy in Ireland in 1773–4, or that there was empathy in Ireland for the colonists' cause. Despite this, the Harcourt administration was successful in securing parliamentary approval for the deployment of troops from the Irish army establishment to the rebellious colonies in North America. However, the fact that the sinuous Harcourt had to have extensive recourse to patronage to ensure he had the votes to negotiate the short summer sitting in 1776

---

45 *Freeman's Journal*, 17 April 1773. He is referring to 1769.

46 M.J. Powell, 'The Society of Free Citizens and other popular political clubs, 1749–89' in Kelly and Powell (eds.), *Clubs and societies in eighteenth-century Ireland*, pp. 245–55; *Limerick Chronicle*, 13, 23 Nov. 1772; *Dublin Evening Journal*, 21.

47 J. Kelly, 'Parliamentary reform in Irish politics, 1760–90' in D. Dickson et al. (eds.), *The United Irishmen: republicanism, radicalism and rebellion* (Dublin: Lilliput Press, 1993), pp. 76–8; J. Kelly (ed.), 'Review of the House of Commons, 1774', *Eighteenth-Century Ireland*, 18 (2004), 163–210; *Freeman's Journal*, 2 April, 2 July 1774.

48 See V. Morley, *Irish opinion and the American Revolution, 1760–1783* (Cambridge: Cambridge University Press, 2002); S. Conway, *The British Isles and the War of American Independence* (Oxford: Oxford University Press, 2000); M.R. O'Connell, *Irish politics and social conflict in the age of the American Revolution* (Philadelphia: University of Pennsylvania Press, 1965).

when this approval was secured meant that the future might be even more trying.

Harcourt's resort to patronage is explicable, as a comparison of the size of the Patriot interest in the House of Commons divisions before and after the 1776 election reveals that their ranks had grown from about 50 to about 70.[49] This was hardly sufficient to register more than a respectable minority in a house of 300 members. But the ostensibly modest character of this numerical growth was boosted by the inclusion in their ranks of Henry Grattan and John Forbes, who were to prove two of the Patriots' most important and influential voices. Though Grattan's superior oratorical skills soon propelled him to the forefront of what was to prove an intimidatingly powerful phalanx, its effectiveness was magnified by the weaknesses of the administration. Like Harcourt, whom he succeeded as lord lieutenant in December 1776, John Hobart, the 2nd Earl of Buckinghamshire, possessed diplomatic experience, but his political instincts were less finely tuned, and his understanding of the position, and of men and measures, less developed. Furthermore, his choice of chief secretary was disastrous. Richard Heron, or 'Richard Wigblock' as he was unflatteringly termed in Ireland, possessed neither the debating skill nor the political nous now required of a chief secretary, and that distinguished the more successful holders of that office. As a result, the administration experienced problems in the House of Commons from the outset. To compound matters, instead of surrounding himself with dependable men of business and cultivating the leaders of the main interests, who traditionally provided the foundation of the administration's majority, he constructed a looser coalition and depended for guidance on a small number of *intimes*. This was not a recipe for stable government in good times; it was still more hazardous when times were challenging, for though the administration negotiated the 1777–8 session without serious difficulty, the negative impact of the embargo imposed in 1776 on the export of provisions to the American colonies contributed to 'the general decay of our trade and manufacture' reported in August 1778. This focused attention on the array of mercantilist restrictions that subordinated the kingdom's commerce to that of Great Britain.[50] Resented as much as a symbol of the kingdom's dependency as a cause of economic difficulty, the perception that the kingdom's economic travails would be eased if these restrictions were lifted encouraged ministers in London to respond

---

49 D. Lammey, 'The growth of the "Patriot opposition" in Ireland during the 1770s', *Parliamentary History*, 7:2 (1988), 273.

50 St George to Hardwicke, 10 Aug. 1778, Hardwicke papers, Add. MS 35615 f. 16, BL.

positively to exigent calls in Ireland for relief. Hopes were raised when four measures removing the barriers in the way of Irish participation in the colonial trade were presented to the Westminster parliament in 1778, but the withdrawal of the entitlement to import directly in the face of determined pressure from British commercial and manufacturing interests proved a bitter pill. Unwilling simply to accede to what one contemporary denominated the 'addition of insult to oppression', public opinion was galvanised by the resulting anger, and by further dis-improvement in the economic environment during 1778–9, to follow the example of the American colonists and to resolve neither to import nor to consume British-produced goods.[51]

The inauguration, beginning in the summer of 1778, of a non-consumption campaign was a transformational moment as it brought what was until then a political campaign for rights into the expanding realm of consumption, and drew an increasingly politicised public, women as well as men, from the margins closer to the political centre. This process was facilitated, to be sure, by the accelerated formation of militia corps known as Volunteers, as the Protestant population responded in time-honoured fashion to the security challenges posed by the need to send troops on the Irish military establishment to America; and, once France entered the war in 1778 on the side of the Americans, by the fear of a French invasion.[52] In keeping with precedent, and the fundamentally loyalist impulse that fuelled this response at the outset, many of the corps were constituted from, or around, existing loyal clubs and societies; some, such as the Boyne, Aughrim and Culloden clubs in County Cork, echoed previous emergencies in 1756, 1745 and 1715.[53] The problem the administration encountered was that, having spurned the invitation to establish a state militia (because they did not have the resources or foresight), the Volunteers operated outside of their control. This was not a problem with respect to a majority of traditional 'true blue' clubs, but as the number of Volunteers rose from some 8,000 in February 1779 to some 20,000 three months later, en route to 40,000 in September, the outlook of the membership became palpably more assertive. From the perspective of devotees of the venerable Whig concept of the 'citizen soldier', or the

---

51 *Letters from an Ulster land agent, 1774–1785*, ed. W.H. Crawford (Belfast: PRONI, 1976), p. 24.

52 For this and what follows see Neal Garnham, *The militia in eighteenth-century Ireland* (Woodbridge: The Boydell Press, 2012); P. Higgins, *A nation of politicians: gender, patriotism and political culture in late eighteenth-century Ireland* (Madison: University of Wisconsin Press, 2010); Kelly, 'Disappointing the boundless ambitions of France', pp. 82–9.

53 *Dublin Evening Journal*, 18 April, 4 July 1778.

more recent insight which highlights the contemporary perception of them as the epitome of manly virtue, this was a welcome development. Political activists like James Napper Tandy in Dublin, who confidently believed that it was time to realise the ideals of the ancient constitution and to achieve the equality of rights that was their birth right, sought without hesitation to rally the Volunteers to the cause of commercial reform, or 'free trade' as it was labelled. Experienced observers, particularly those of a conservative hue for whom the stability of the Anglo-Irish connection was their political lodestar, apprehended 'danger' from the politicisation of the Volunteers, and their worst fears came close to realisation on the assembly of MPs in October for the 1779–80 session. Two events stood out. The first, on 4 November, which was the anniversary of William of Orange's birthday, featured an assembly of thousands of Volunteers on College Green bearing placards demanding 'free trade or else'; the second, on 16 November, was even more explicitly political, as the Volunteers that gathered on this occasion did so in support of Henry Grattan's initiative to increase the pressure on the administration by limiting the money parliament was prepared to vote. Since MPs had previously approved an amendment to the address to the lord lieutenant seeking 'free trade', it was clear that the worst-case scenario for any administration, and for the security of the Anglo-Irish nexus, was about to come to pass – the administration was no longer in control of the House of Commons. Bowing to the inevitable, and implicitly admitting that a legislative union (which he had discreetly investigated) was an impossibility, the prime minister in December authorised the commercial reforms that permitted Irish merchants and shippers access to the Empire on the same terms as their British equivalents, and the repeal of the infamous restrictions authorised in 1698 on the export of Irish woollens.[54]

Like their peers in Great Britain, Irish upholders of the subordination of the kingdom of Ireland perceived the surrender of parliament to the will of 'the people' with profound unease. Having failed in their attempts to convince the prime minister to recall Buckinghamshire, fears that Ireland would seek to emulate the American colonists and pursue independence inevitably surfaced. Such concerns seemed well founded when, in the spring of 1780, Henry Grattan raised the constitutional points of Poynings' Law and the Declaratory Act, and spoke openly of legislative independence. Though the agitation of this matter at this time may have given the impression that

---

54 J. Kelly, 'The origins of the Act of Union: an examination of unionist opinion in Britain and Ireland, 1650–1800', *Irish Historical Studies*, 25 (1987), 251–4.

the Patriots in parliament had taken the lead on this sensitive matter, this was not the case. Impelled by the Volunteers, who, John Forbes reported in February, are 'determined … not to quit the field till their constitution is returned to them', the Patriot MPs were lagging behind public opinion.[55] There is no reason to conclude that a united Patriot front would have been any more successful at this moment, but the suspicion with which many political moderates perceived the politicisation of the Volunteers and the agitation of constitutional issues was sufficient to suggest that the Patriots in parliament were not sufficiently resolute to press the matter to a successful resolution on their own.

Following the adjournment of parliament in September 1780 and the replacement of the unpopular and incompetent Buckinghamshire in December with the more credible (and politically adept) Frederick Howard, 8th Earl of Carlisle, discipline was gradually restored to the ranks of the Castle phalanx. Carlisle's recommendation that Henry Flood should be dismissed from office for non-cooperation heartened those who looked to Dublin Castle for leadership, and who aspired to restore the political initiative to parliament. In truth, most exaggerated the extent to which it had been lost, as the paucity of public resolutions demanding constitutional reform in the summer of 1781 attests, but the perception of Carlisle's very able chief secretary, William Eden, that the 'aristocratic part' of the constitution had been 'undermined' ran deep, and it assisted him as he pursued the task of restoring discipline to Castle ranks.[56] Moreover, he could not simply dismiss the expectations of those who believed constitutional reform must be advantageous to the kingdom. The lack of a consensus on how best to proceed, manifest in the House of Commons in the first part of the 1781–2 session, suggests that, if the matter had been left to MPs and peers, no reforms would have ensued, but this is not what happened. Impatient at the lack of progress, the Volunteers of Ulster assumed the initiative, convened a delegate assembly at Dungannon, County Tyrone, in February 1782, and approved a suite of resolutions (many of which were drafted by the leaders of the Patriot interest in parliament) calling on Volunteer corps throughout the country to pronounce in support of a number of constitutional reforms. This was not sufficient on its own to guarantee success, but it did generate momentum behind the demand and emboldened the Patriot leadership, so that when the collapse of the government of Lord North in March brought the Rockingham Whigs to

55 Forbes to Shelburne, 4 Feb. 1780, Bowood papers, B33 ff. 13–20, BL.
56 Quoted in Conway, *The British Isles and the War of American Independence*, p. 214.

power, both Grattan, as the effective leader of the Patriots in the House of Commons, and Lord Charlemont, the commander in chief of the Volunteers, capitalised on the good relations they enjoyed with the Whigs to push the matter towards a resolution. Grattan's role in this respect was critical. It was he who proposed the amendment to the address to the lord lieutenant on 16 April 1782 that effectively drowned out the sounds emanating from government signalling their preference for a 'negotiated compact' that defined the respective rights and responsibilities of the two kingdoms. As a result, the 'settlement' that brought the 'constitution of 1782' into being was lop-sided in favour of Ireland. As well as the repeal of the Declaratory Act (1720), which meant that the Westminster parliament could no longer legislate for Ireland, and the modification of Poynings' Law, which deprived the Privy Council of the entitlement to respite and amend Irish legislation, the Irish House of Lords regained the appellate jurisdiction it had lost in 1720.

The Meaning of Legislative Independence, 1782–1790

The euphoria that gripped Ireland on the removal in 1782 of the constitutional binds that had limited the Irish parliament's capacity to legislate was demonstrated by the decision of the House of Commons to authorise a payment of £50,000 to Henry Grattan. This single action served, as intended, to liberate Grattan from financial worry, and ostensibly to free him to focus on realising the vision of which he had spoken on 16 April of transforming Ireland from 'a Protestant settlement' into an 'Irish nation'.[57] This was not to be, however, for no sooner had the reforms that defined 'legislative independence' been authorised than a small coterie of individuals, led by Henry Flood, alleged that the changes that had been authorised could be rescinded because the Westminster legislature had not renounced its claim to make law for Ireland. This contention excited a strong reaction from those on all sides of the Irish Sea whose fondest wish was to put the recent years of disharmony to one side, but Flood's arguments echoed strongly with a minority, who were sufficiently resolute to convince ministers that there would be no return to normalcy until their concerns were met.

The formal recognition of the right of the Irish parliament to make law for Ireland in the spring of 1783 signalled the end of the so-called 'renunciation'

57 *The Speeches of Henry Grattan*, 4 vols. (London, 1822), vol. 1, p. 102.

crisis of 1782–3, but as well as an enduring legacy of distrust – symbolised by the depiction of Grattan as the 'little Patriot' when the 'crisis' was at its height – it hastened the break-up of the grand consensus of popular and political opinion that had united behind the demand for legislative independence in the spring of 1782.[58] This was inevitable, of course, as individuals and interests that had previously maintained a close relationship with the Irish administration sought to rebuild trust, and others, unhappy at the collapse of the boundaries between parliamentary and popular politics, were encouraged by the imminent conclusion of war in North America to disengage from the Volunteers. The administration miscalculated when it embarked prematurely in the second half of 1782 on an ill-conceived attempt to replace the Volunteers with provincial regiments of fencibles, but though this was unsuccessful it demonstrated that the Volunteers would no longer be deferred to, and, by extension, that they would not be able in the future to wield the influence they had done so effectively in 1779–80 and 1782. This was a matter of profound consequence because whereas moderate Patriots were disposed to conclude that no further major change was required, this was not true of those political activists and Volunteers from the 'middling sort' for whom parliamentary reform was a logical and necessary next step.

In keeping with the pattern of politicisation that was accented during the heady days of the late 1770s and the 1780s, the impetus for the campaign to reform the representative system came initially from Ulster. It was initiated by an assembly of delegates of more than 300 Volunteer corps at Dungannon in June 1782 which pronounced in support of 'the more equal representation of the people'. Uncertainty as to how best to proceed dovetailed with the 'renunciation crisis' to interrupt matters for a year when another Ulster initiative, driven this time by a smaller delegate meeting in Lisburn on 1 July 1783, resulted in the establishment of a committee of correspondence to solicit expert opinion from Britain as well as Ireland. Choosing for good reason to ignore the advice of Lord Charlemont that 'the measure alone should be recommended without specifying any mode whatsoever', the Ulster Volunteers approved a programme embracing annual parliaments, the abolition of decayed and depopulated boroughs, a secret ballot, shorter elections, and the extension of the franchise to all propertied Protestant males. This was a radical programme, and it would have been still more so had those who

---

58 P.J. Jupp, 'Earl Temple's viceroyalty and the question of renunciation', *Irish Historical Studies*, 17 (1972–3), 299–317; *Freeman's Journal*, 7 Dec. 1782.

had drunk deeply of the cup of toleration that had taken strong hold of the Volunteer rank and file since 1778 had their way and secured full support for the extension of the franchise to Roman Catholics. More cautious counsels prevailed, however, with the result that the matter was still unresolved when delegates from corps from all four provinces gathered in a Grand National Convention in Dublin in November. This was to prove a crucial moment. Having contrived successfully in comparable circumstances in 1779 and in 1782 to compel parliament to bend to their will, the expectation of the warmest advocates of parliamentary reform was that history would be repeated and that the Volunteers would prevail once more. It was not to be. Having failed to arrive in advance at an agreed position on Catholic enfranchisement, the delegates provided their opponents with a weapon with which to bring the Convention into disrepute, and the re-energised Irish administration, headed by a new lord lieutenant, the under-rated Lord Northington, which was under instruction to frustrate reform at all costs, rose to the challenge. This course of events did not prevent the Convention rallying behind a plan of reform shorn of several of the radical propositions that the more committed reformers desired, but it was too late and insufficient. Faced by the combined opposition of the Irish administration and the serried ranks of those borough magnates who were unwilling either to share or to cede control of the House of Commons to those they refused to believe possessed the necessary attributes to govern, MPs imperiously refused to be dictated to by an armed body and the reform bill was lost by 158 votes to 49.[59]

The rejection of reform, by such a decisive margin, was a turning point in the history of the Volunteers and in the relationship of parliament and the politicised population. In an attempt to rescue parliamentary reform from oblivion, both moderates and radicals vainly pursued the issue through 1784 into the spring of 1785. The majority of the Protestant elite in Ireland required little persuasion that a more inclusive legislature was contrary to their ascendancy, while the Irish administration was convinced that it must exacerbate the task of maintaining a stable Anglo-Irish connection. There was, in reality, little evidence beyond the pronouncements of a small section of the popular press that separation had any champions, though the surge in popular protest that accompanied the rejection of parliamentary reform for a second time in March 1784, and a number of other popular measures to assist hard-pressed manufacturers, encouraged the administration to adopt

59 Kelly, 'Parliamentary reform in Irish politics, 1760–90', pp. 78–81.

an increasingly hard-line stance.[60] Crackdowns on the 'liberty of the press' in 1784 and a warning to the Volunteers that proscription was a real possibility in 1785 certainly served to cow opposition; the withdrawal of the already depleted Volunteers from politics saved them from proscription but the price was increasing irrelevance.

Though the government in London and its strong-willed lieutenants in Ireland greeted these developments and the restoration of calm that accompanied the eclipse of radical reform in 1784 as another step on the return to normalcy, the reality was that they were ill at ease at what was perceived as the alarmingly loose nature of the Anglo-Irish connection. Had they taken a more detached view of affairs they might have taken heart from the manner in which, building on the foundations put in place by Lord Northington in 1783, the Duke of Rutland further strengthened the authority of the administration and their command of the House of Commons. This was not sufficient to allay unease however, and, persuaded that an innovative commercial union would link the two islands in mutual interest, the prime minister, William Pitt, conceived of a scheme of eleven, rising to twenty, propositions aimed at binding the two island kingdoms in a commercial and financial embrace.[61] It was an initiative of unusual precocity, but it was also ill timed. Convinced that Pitt was, in the words of Lord Charlemont, embarked on 'an insidious attack upon the constitution of Ireland', the largely rudderless Patriots were galvanised into action, and they were able, with the assistance of the English Whigs who were desperate to give Pitt a bloody nose, to rally sufficient support to discourage the prime minister from proceeding with the scheme.[62]

This outcome was embarrassing both for the prime minister and for the Irish administration. It inflicted no permanent damage, however. Indeed, the fact that the Irish parliament embarked in the same year, 1785, on a pattern of annual sittings that was to produce more legislation in sixteen sessions than in the preceding thirty-six attests to the legislative industry of the assembly once the legislative shackles that had long bound it were removed. Yet, paradoxically, it was often also extremely uneventful. Commenting on the 1788 session, the Speaker of the House of Commons John Foster observed: 'I never remember one so quiet or in which the business of government went on so

---

60 J. Kelly, 'Mathew Carey's Irish apprenticeship: editing the *Volunteers Journal*, 1783–84', *Eire-Ireland*, 49:3&4 (2014), 201–43.

61 J. Kelly, *Prelude to Union: Anglo-Irish politics in the 1780s* (Cork: Cork University Press, 1992).

62 Charlemont to Joy, 3 March 1789, Joy papers, MS 11/12, Linenhall Library.

smooth and rapid.'[63] It was not like this every year, but it is a measure of the dominance exerted by the Irish administration that it could afford to *volte face* on sensitive issues such as tithe reform, which it did in 1787–8, when it realised that to do otherwise would have caused difficulties with one or both houses of parliament.[64] The problem with this was that it was storing up resentments among those precluded from access to the legislature. It may be, given the inactivity of the Catholic Committee in the mid and late 1780s, and the quietude of the middle-class activists for whom parliamentary reform was a *sine qua non*, that their reticence was perceived by those in power as acceptance of existing arrangements when they were not even acquiescent.

Conclusion

There were certainly sufficient straws in the wind by the late 1780s to indicate that, by refusing to embrace the 'middling sort' in the representative system, and even to consider its relationship with the executive, the Irish parliament functioned in a manner not entirely different from that in which it had functioned sixty years previously. Yet the political world was much more uncertain in 1790 than it was in 1730. In 1730, it was embarking on an era whose major episodes – the Money Bill dispute, 1753–6, the termination of undertaking, 1769–71, and the commercial and constitutional crises of 1779–82 – were separated by longer periods of stability. This era was approaching its end as the 1780s drew to a conclusion, for while it would be misleading to suggest that anybody anticipated then that the abolition of the Irish parliament would be accomplished within a decade, it was already being talked about.[65] More importantly, there were clear and distinct signs of unhappiness among many of the 'middling sort' both with the operation of government, with the conservative tenor of legislation, and with the political impotence of patriotism.[66] Indeed, the latter was thoroughly out-gunned and out-argued by the proponents of Protestant Ascendancy in the formative debate on the Protestant constitution in church and state in 1786–8.[67]

---

63 Foster to Sheffield, 15 March 1788, Additional Sheffield papers, T/3465/36, PRONI.
64 J. Kelly, 'The genesis of Protestant Ascendancy: the Rightboy disturbances of the 1780s and their impact upon Protestant opinion' in G. O'Brien (ed.), *Parliament, politics and people: essays in eighteenth-century Irish history* (Dublin: Irish Academic Press, 1989), pp. 93–127.
65 Kelly, 'The origins of the Act of Union', pp. 257–9.
66 *Ramsey's Waterford Chronicle*, 11 March 1788, 2 Oct. 1789.
67 Kelly, 'The genesis of Protestant Ascendancy', pp. 93–127.

There was no prophesising the future then, but a perspicacious reader of events might have concluded that there were sufficient pointers to suggest not only that the stability then obtaining was not destined long to endure but also, when the demand for significant change was animated in the 1790s, that the Protestant elite would no longer enjoy the unchallenged political ascendancy that aptly describes its position between 1730 and 1790.

3

Ireland during the Revolutionary and Napoleonic Wars, 1791–1815

THOMAS BARTLETT

Introduction

Over the centuries, wars conducted in Ireland, or waged abroad, have had a decisive impact in shaping the course of Irish history, and none more so than the Revolutionary and Napoleonic wars that lasted continuously from 1793 to 1815. It was, for example, against the backdrop of these wars that the twin ideologies of republican separatism and unionism, polar opposites in Irish politics, first emerged to set the agenda for the next hundred years, and more, of Anglo-Irish and intra-Irish relations. Again, sectarian feuding, agrarian insurgency and armed rebellion – the three often, and quite erroneously, conflated in the official mind as 'disaffection' – defined these years, and by 1815 the first two at least had seemingly become embedded in Irish life. In 1790, around 10,000 troops had been stationed in Ireland; by the wars' end a force of over 33,000 was considered barely adequate. As well, the 'Catholic Question' – i.e. whether Irish Catholics should enjoy political rights – under the threat of war with France in 1793, became a key matter for Irish and British governments, and it was to remain so for the next thirty years. Lastly, and often overlooked, there was the impact of all-out, or even 'total', war on Irish society and economy. Wartime boom followed by post-war bust left the Irish economy stricken and led quickly to the widespread immiseration of a growing rural population that was increasingly 'at risk'. All in all, the period of the Revolutionary and Napoleonic wars can be viewed as the crucible of modern Ireland.

Mobilisation for War

We may consider first the material impact of the wars. It was evident from the outbreak of hostilities in February 1793 that the coming conflict would be no ordinary, *ancien régime*-style, limited war. Within a matter of months fifty-six regiments had been added to the British army, with no fewer than twenty-two raised in Ireland: by 1801, 469,000 men had been mobilised. In 1794 one third of the British army became Irish – and Irish Catholic – a proportion that continued, and was sometimes exceeded, throughout the nineteenth century.[1] The figures for the Royal Navy are no less striking: from 17,000 men in 1792, the navy increased to 85,000 in 1801, of which some 40 per cent of landsmen – the lowest grade in the navy – were Irish; the Irish percentage for all grades amounted to 20 and 25 per cent.[2]

Until 1793, Irish Catholic military recruitment was prohibited, at least officially, though it is clear that this ban was very often breached. In that year, the passing of a Catholic Relief Act in Ireland (revealingly, a few weeks after France's declaration of war) made Irish Catholics eligible to hold most commissions in the armed forces (though only in Ireland) and this relaxation was taken as a green light for the open enlistment of Irish recruits. A massive recruitment campaign of Irish Catholics into the British army and the Royal Navy was quickly underway and continued, more or less, until 1815. The formation of an Irish Militia, again in 1793, was intended to assist in this process of mass recruitment. This essentially new formation was county-based, was soon some 20,000 strong, and would have an overwhelmingly Catholic rank and file with a Protestant (Church of Ireland or Presbyterian) officer corps. The Irish Militia was initially designed for home defence in the coming struggle – it would free up regular soldiers to serve abroad – but from an early date it was regarded as a possible, and then a vital, source of recruits for the regular regiments. There were serious disturbances in 1793 when the Irish Militia was first mobilised, and Dublin Castle would always remain suspicious of its loyalty, especially after clear evidence of (limited) infiltration of its ranks by subversives was uncovered in 1797, and in view of its (allegedly) poor performance against a French incursion in 1798. So far as the Castle was concerned, the obvious solution was to use the Irish Militia as a nursery for the regular army, and large numbers and sometimes entire companies were enlisted or 'volunteered' for service abroad. By 1805, some 5,000 militiamen a year were entering the regulars. In 1811, in the teeth of Catholic opposition, for the Militia was seen as a Catholic force, a Militia Interchange Act was passed in order to facilitate the exchange of Irish Militia regiments for English Militia

1 J.E. Cookson, *The British armed nation, 1793–1815* (Oxford: Oxford University Press, 1997), pp. 95, 126, 254n; L. Colley, *Britons: forging the nation, 1707–1837* (New Haven: Yale University Press, 1992), pp. 284–9.
2 J. Ross Dancy, *The myth of the press gang* (Woodbridge: The Boydell Press, 2015), p. 165 and *passim*.

regiments and to promote the enlistment of the members of the Irish Militia into the regular British army.[3] Within a short period of time, some 10,000 member of the Irish Militia were despatched annually to England, or further afield, and were replaced by English Militia.

Overall, it has been estimated that Ireland, with a population of between 4 and 5 million in the 1790s sent at least 150,000 recruits to the British armed forces during the Revolutionary and Napoleonic wars.[4] It is no exaggeration to say that, without Irish recruits, the British army's onslaught on the French, Spanish and Dutch West Indian islands from 1793 to 1801 would not have been possible, if only because it was Irish recruits that replenished the ranks of the fallen: 89,900 private soldiers served in this theatre between these years, most of them shipping out of Cork, and some 43,000 died, almost all from tropical diseases.[5] Indeed, it has even been claimed that it was the huge number of Irish recruits during these wars that later permitted the British army to fight Napoleon without resort to conscription.[6] And as is well known, Wellington's successful Peninsula campaigns from 1808 on simply could not have taken place without Irish recruits. By 1813, he was in command of an army in Spain of some 73,000 men, of whom a large proportion were evidently Irish, and it was Wellington's Irish troops who were credited with victory in the climactic battle of the Napoleonic wars.[7] Home Office minister Lord Sidmouth conceded that it was 'the supply of troops derived from Ireland [that] turn'd the scale on the 18th of June at Waterloo'.[8]

Nor was Ireland's contribution to the defeat of revolutionary France and the downfall of Napoleon confined to recruits. In matters of finance, Ireland was important to the British war effort, and in the supply of provisions for the armed forces the island was to prove vital. Funding for soldiers – regulars, militiamen, Yeomanry – on the Irish establishment not surprisingly soared as

---

3 A report to Dublin Castle in July 1811 had it that the purpose of the Militia Interchange Act was 'to disarm the Catholics and leave them to the bayonets of the English': Home Office Papers (hereafter HO 100/164/ff. 229–30, The National Archives (henceforth TNA). Earlier, in May 1811, Pole had noted 'that the Catholics, both the laity and the clergy are in alarm, considering it [Militia interchange] a political device to weaken their party by removing a strength on which they have much dependence': Pole to Ryder, 27 May 1811, HO 100/163 f. 319, TNA.

4 D.A. Chart, 'The Irish levies during the Great French War', *English Historical Review*, 32 (1917), 497–516.

5 R. Knight, *Britain against Napoleon: the organization of victory* (London: Allen Lane, 2013), pp. 75–6.

6 K. Linch, *Britain and Wellington's army: recruitment, society and tradition, 1807–15* (Basingstoke: Palgrave, 2011), p. 16.

7 R. Holmes, *Soldiers* (London: Allen Lane, 2012), p. 284.

8 Sidmouth to Whitworth, 24 June 1815, HO 100/184 f. 204, TNA.

the numbers recruited and paid for by Ireland surged: the cost of the armed forces in Ireland was £544,000 in 1792; this rose steeply to £5,400,000 in 1800, and peaked at £6,200,000 in 1804 before falling back to £4,000,000 in 1815 as the war was drawing to an end.[9] Such outlays were unsustainable and Ireland came near to bankruptcy in 1797 through the scale of her outpourings to pay for troops and for other war-related expenses. British government nervousness at the parlous state of Irish finances was a factor in the quest for a legislative Union, for the bags of cash conveyed to the Irish government in the late 1790s both to bail it out and to enable it to make necessary payments were an added argument in favour of a legislative take-over.

Finance was important, but provisions for the armed forces of the crown were vital. The Cork region dominated the supply of provisions to both the army and the navy, and the area met the enormous demand for beef, pork, butter, oats and beer. Cork merchants and Munster graziers prospered, and so too did cattle dealers throughout Ireland: in 1811 around 45,000 cattle were shipped across the Irish Sea.[10] It was a similar story with the export of horses. Overall, it has been estimated that graziers' incomes rose 1 to 2 per cent per annum during the wars. But if their incomes rose, such emphatically was not the case with subsistence farmers or cottiers – those who needed land for food and rent. Increasingly, they found themselves in competition for land they had intended for cultivation but which was now destined for cattle grazing. Moreover, a series of poor harvests in 1799–1800, due largely to unseasonable rain and cold weather, produced a poor return for the struggling tenant, and a growing population put added pressure on diminishing resources. Food prices rose steeply, caused by poor harvests, the demands of the military and probably a certain amount of forestalling by large producers. The result was a smothered – and sometimes quite open – species of class war in the Irish countryside from the mid-1790s on in which cattle were houghed, i.e. had their hamstrings sliced, 'strangers', i.e. anyone from outside the neighbourhood, were flogged and warned off, and wagons or barges carrying grain were on occasion seized by hungry crowds. Finally, wartime demand for deadstock (beef), livestock (cattle, horses), drystock (biscuit) and even wet stock (pork), allied to robust population growth, led to growing subdivision

---

9 'A concise view of the charge of the military establishment of Ireland … [1598–1821]', MS 999/308/3/18, National Archives of Ireland (henceforth NAI).

10 See D. Dickson, *Old World colony: Cork and South Munster, 1630–1830* (Cork: Cork University Press, 2005), pp. 369–96; Knight, *Britain against Napoleon*, p. 167. In January 1809 some 50,000 pairs of shoes were shipped from Cork to the British army in Portugal: HO 100/151 f. 27, TNA.

of holdings at the lower end of the rural Irish social pyramid, and, with this, a necessary dependence on the prolific, if fickle, potato. It is from the period of the 'French' wars that the malign configuration of the Irish population structure, one that was to collapse in catastrophe in the 1840s, can be dated. As early as 1807 one alarmed observer was describing how, in Tipperary, population growth was 'exceeding every estimate which has been made of it' and noting that the people 'live upon potatoes which require no great industry to cultivate and spend all their leisure time at wakes, funerals and drinking houses'.[11] By the wars' end, a large and a growing proportion of the Irish rural population found itself increasingly at risk, and to no cause more pertinent than the impact of the wars themselves. The political fallout from the wars was no less dramatic.

Politicisation

It has been customary to date the birth of the republican project that was to engulf Ireland in the 1790s to the setting up of the Society of United Irishmen in Belfast in October 1791.[12] However, for decades before this date government officials in both Dublin and London had easily been persuaded to see a separatist impulse behind the most innocuous political developments. Thus the Money Bill dispute of the 1750s was held by some to be directed at the Anglo-Irish connection, and during the Volunteer excitement of the period of the American War (1778–83) there were those who, with rather more reason, feared that the link might ultimately be threatened by the Volunteers' demands. When in the 1780s those same Volunteers turned their attention to reform of the Irish parliament, their action was quickly denounced as an assault on the connection. Irish reformers, announced the lord lieutenant, the Duke of Rutland, in 1785, 'drink the French king on their knees and their declared purpose is a separation from England and the establishment of the Roman Catholic religion'.[13] Similarly, in the mid-1780s the rural disturbances carried out by the Rightboys, despite all evidence to the contrary, sparked

---

11 J. Cooke to Sir A. Wellesley, 7 June 1807, Wellesley transcripts, T/2627/3/2/181, PRONI.
12 For what follows see N.J. Curtin, *The United Irishmen: popular politics in Ulster and Dublin, 1791–1798* (Oxford: Oxford University Press, 1994); K. Whelan, *The Tree of Liberty: radicalism, Catholicism and the construction of Irish identity, 1760–1800* (Cork: Cork University Press, 1997); J. Smyth, *The men of no property: Irish radicals and popular politics in the late eighteenth century* (Basingstoke: Macmillan, 1992).
13 Quoted in T. Bartlett, *The fall and rise of the Irish nation: the Catholic question, 1690–1830* (Dublin: Gill & Macmillan, 1992), p. 110.

alarms and fears for the connection, and even for the safety of the established church. Unease was in fact the predominant note in Anglo-Irish relations throughout the eighteenth century, and it did not take much to bring it to full-blown anxiety. Indeed, after the American colonies had fought their way out of the British Empire in 1783, anxiety for the future of Britain's overseas possessions, Ireland among them, became pervasive. Hence, when in October 1791 a group of mostly Presbyterian and Church of Ireland reformers – Samuel Neilson, Samuel McTier, Thomas Russell and Theobald Wolfe Tone among them – inspired by the French Revolution, came together in Belfast to found a society to seek parliamentary reform, the authorities immediately damned their society's stated objective as merely a blind, or a trap for the unwary. The United Irishmen, they claimed, aimed at nothing less than an Irish republic, separate and distinct from Britain, and almost certainly linked to France.

In point of fact, Theobald Wolfe Tone, a Dublin-based barrister, who was to play a leading role in the setting up of the Society of United Irishmen in Belfast, and a month later in Dublin, had already in a letter to his friend Russell set out his political creed that 'the bane of Irish prosperity is the influence of England' and that separation 'would be a regeneration of this country'. However, for reasons of prudence he had sought to keep his opinions to himself and a few trusted friends. The authorities, however, had quickly obtained a copy of Tone's letter, and John FitzGibbon, attorney general and later lord chancellor, thereafter rarely resisted an opportunity to quote from it as proof that the United Irishmen were from the beginning a separatist conspiracy and were never just a society that sought parliamentary reform.

In his pamphlet *An argument on behalf of the Catholics of Ireland* (Dublin, 1791) Tone dissected with forensic brilliance the reasons for earlier reform failures; he had drawn appropriate lessons from the French Revolution, and he had detailed how parliamentary reform could be achieved in Ireland through the unity of Catholic, Protestant and Dissenter. For those who feared the admission of Irish Catholics to the body politic, Tone pointed to the example of France, where French Catholics had apparently spearheaded the revolution. If French Catholics could act as citizens, even elect Protestants to the National Assembly in Paris, then, incontestably, Irish Catholics could be trusted with liberty too. Divisions between Catholic and Protestant in Ireland, he maintained, had been artificially kept up in the interest of a foreign government intent on keeping Ireland 'the prey of England, the laughing stock of the knaves who plunder us'. Dazzled by admiration for the great events afoot in revolutionary France – monarchy overthrown, a republic installed, the separation of church and state, a ringing declaration of the Rights of

Man, and, not least, the Catholic Church apparently laid low – Tone and his friends were supremely confident that they would be successful in their quest for reform in Ireland.

It is just possible that Pitt's government, and especially his foreign minister, Lord Grenville, might have been content simply to monitor the activities of the Society of United Irishmen in Belfast and Dublin, had not further developments in Britain and in France brought home to them the unprecedented challenge that monarchical government everywhere was about to face. In November 1791, barely a month after the Belfast Society of United Irishmen had been established, the radical reformer Thomas Hardy set up the London Corresponding Society. Even before then, however, similar reform societies had been set up in northern England and in Scotland: all were founded in admiration of the French Revolution; all proclaimed a reform agenda; and all were viewed with deep suspicion by Pitt's government.

Then, on 18 November 1792, a dinner celebrating both the French Revolution and the French victory at Valmy over the Prussians was held at White's Hotel in Paris. Those attending numbered around 100 and were later dubbed the 'British Club', though there were many other nationalities present. The dinner was presided over by the most famous radical of his day, Thomas Paine, celebrated for his contribution to the American cause in 1776 and, more recently, for his trenchant reply to Edmund Burke's scathing attack on the French Revolution. In an atmosphere of exuberant, intoxicating conviviality, some diners proposed to convey an address to the National Convention congratulating it on its work, and celebrating the Revolution. The address was duly presented some ten days later, and was received with great enthusiasm by the Convention: significantly, of the fifty who signed it, there were no fewer than sixteen Irishmen, including Lord Edward FitzGerald, and John and Henry Sheares (all three destined to die violently in the summer of 1798), along with some who had served in the Irish regiments in French service and some who were seminarians at the Irish College in Paris. A British spy, Captain George Monro, kept Pitt's foreign secretary, Lord Grenville, well informed of these transactions.

The implications of this dinner and the subsequent address were unmistakeable, for a pattern had now emerged of transnational radicalism or republicanism, both deeply influenced by events in France and both deeply inimical to British interests. United Irish radical reformers in Dublin and Belfast, Irish and British republicans in London and Paris, and French revolutionaries were making common cause. The issues at the heart of the Burke–Paine pamphlet war of 1790 would surely soon lead to a real war between Britain and France, while the French revolutionary decree offering support to nations wishing to be free had to set alarm bells ringing concerning Ireland. Hence the urgency shown by Pitt and Dundas to offer generous and far-reaching concessions to Irish Catholics in 1793, for these boons were seen as a vital way to keep them detached from Irish, French and British republicans, as well as to fasten them to Britain's side in the coming struggle.[14]

At around the same time that the so-called 'British Club' was meeting in White's Hotel in Paris, to celebrate all things revolutionary, and the United Irishmen in Belfast were propagating the cause of reform in their newspaper, the *Northern Star*, in Dublin, the lord lieutenant Lord Westmorland, under ever-increasing pressure to deliver on Catholic concessions,[15] reported to London that in counties Down, Louth and Armagh there existed 'almost a state of war'.[16] He was referring to the sectarian conflict between Catholics and Protestants (mostly Church of Ireland) that had raged intensely in these counties over the preceding months.

The roots of this sectarian insurgency went back many decades, but in the 1780s communal relations in south Ulster, for reasons that are not yet altogether clear, deteriorated both rapidly and decisively. The structure of the linen industry in the counties of Antrim, Armagh, Tyrone and Down, with its linen weavers acting as independent, one might even say self-employed, workers, played a part and was frequently cited as a cause. Linen drapers paid cash to linen weavers for their work and this cash permitted the weavers, mostly young people, to set up for themselves. Removed thereby from the control of parent, landlord or clergyman, it was more or less inevitable, so the contemporary argument ran, that mayhem ('intoxication and riot') would ensue. The linen industry was also a magnet for outsiders, and as the population of County Armagh, and adjacent areas, began to swell this led to increased competition for available farm holdings. Given the region's unhappy history from the early seventeenth century, it is not surprising that rivalry for scarce resources should have taken on a distinct sectarian colouring. In addition, recent Catholic assertiveness, or insolence, was frequently alleged as producing a Protestant backlash. Some Catholics, for example, had been admitted to the ranks of the Volunteers and were thereby permitted to carry arms. Bearing arms had ever been a hugely valued Protestant monopoly

14 M. Ferradou, 'Histoire d'un "festin patriotique" à l'hôtel White (18 novembre 1792)', *Annales Historique de la Révolution Française* 382 (2015), 123–43. My thanks to Mathieu Ferradou for permitting me to read his work in advance of publication.
15 See below, pp. 92–3.
16 Westmorland to Pitt, 13 Nov. 1792, Chatham papers, 30/8/331 ff. 90–1, TNA.

(probably more prized than the franchise itself), and hence its loss was hugely resented. In and of themselves, however, the Volunteers had already proved a destabilising force in Ulster society, for they had not hesitated to threaten the political establishment with their arms. And of course, as the prospect of Catholic relief gained traction in the 1770s and late 1780s, with British ministers apparently now cherishing the Catholic, Protestants living in central and east Ulster, areas that had retained a vivid historical memory stretching back to the Catholic rebellion of 1641, grew alarmed.

By the mid-1780s, Catholic Defenders and Protestant Peep of Day Boys confronted each other throughout south Ulster on a regular basis, at communal amusements such as cockfights or at fairs and markets, or even at arranged battles. In general, however, while blood was spilled, few lives were lost in these confrontations, for both sides tended to act with circumspection where violence was concerned. There were, however, unmistakeable signs that more serious trouble was brewing. Thus, while there had been two deaths from affray, with no executions between 1784 and 1788, there were no fewer than nine deaths from disturbances between 1788 and 1791, along with seven executions in 1790–1 alone.[17] The most notorious, and certainly the most gruesome, murders took place in Forkhill, County Armagh on 28 January 1791.

That day, a party of men, deemed Defenders, broke into the home of Alexander Barkley, a recently arrived Protestant schoolmaster into what had hitherto been a Catholic backwater. They proceeded to cut out his tongue and that of his wife and that of his wife's brother. They also cut off her thumb and four fingers of one hand. The men both survived, but Mrs Barkley died from her injuries. The murder and the mutilations were profoundly shocking and were not soon forgotten. Ten years later, in his tendentious account of the rebellions in Ireland, Sir Richard Musgrave singled out these atrocities for special mention, even though by that date he had many others to detail.[18]

Sectarian murder committed in Forkhill, the Society of United Irishmen founded in Belfast, and a raucous republican dinner held in Paris, were all linked or twisted together, and not just in time. They all occurred against the backdrop of a looming war with France, a war that threatened to be

---

17 D. Miller, 'The Armagh Troubles, 1784–95' in S. Clark and J. Donnelly (eds.), *Irish peasants: violence and political unrest 1780–1914* (Manchester: Manchester University Press, 1984), p. 168.
18 R. Musgrave, *Memoirs of the different rebellions in Ireland from the arrival of the English . . .*, 2nd edn (Dublin: Milliken, 1801), p. 61; Kyla Madden, *Forkhill Protestants, Forkhill Catholics 1787–1858* (Liverpool: Liverpool University Press, 2005), pp. 3–6.

radically different from any fought before, and, in turn, that war would give added urgency to the pressing question of concessions for Irish Catholics. Together, these developments meant that, for the foreseeable future, matters of defence, invasion, insurgency, security, subversion, disaffection and, not least, Catholic emancipation would jostle each other and vie for dominance on the Irish political agenda. In other words, the Irish Question of the nineteenth century was about to be defined.

Insurgency

The United Irishmen were committed to a reform of the Irish parliament and they were confident that this could be achieved through an alliance with the Catholics of Ireland, and through the deployment of the means by which the so-called 'Constitution of 1782' had allegedly been achieved. What this meant in practice was that all denominations in Ireland, particularly Irish Catholics, were urged to put past differences behind them – in effect, to turn away from that 'blood-stained field', Irish history itself – and embrace the new dispensation for humankind that had opened with the Revolution in France. Hence, in July 1792 Wolfe Tone would become secretary to the Catholic Committee in Dublin, as well as taking a prominent role in the Dublin Society of United Irishmen and composing some of their addresses. More broadly, the United Irishmen would publish a new newspaper, the *Northern Star*, which would tell the 'truth' about events in France (in their view wholly misrepresented in the government prints), would keep readers informed on events in the fledgling republic of the United States (again woefully neglected), and would, of course, miss no opportunity to propagate the creed of the Society: every man a citizen. They would also seek to revitalise the Volunteers from the slumber into which they had fallen since the heady days of 1778–82; and inevitably a reform convention, on the model of the celebrated Dungannon Convention of 1782, would be summoned immediately. Confident that history was both on the move, and on their side, the United Irishmen anticipated few difficulties in achieving their ends.

To the authorities in both London and Dublin, the United Irishmen were identified from the beginning as an existential threat to the Anglo-Irish connection. Tone's incautious letter extolling separatism as his 'ultimate solution' to the Irish problem was conclusive in this respect. But even without this 'proof' of their real intent, neither the Irish nor the British government was prepared under any circumstances to countenance parliamentary reform along the lines called for by the United Irishmen. At the very least, the Society's unabashed admiration for France rendered its members suspect to the authorities, and then downright treasonous after the outbreak of war in February 1793. Hence the editors of the *Northern Star* were subject to legal harassment throughout 1792, the Volunteers themselves were banned in March 1793 (it had probably been a mistake for the United Irishmen to rename them the 'National Guard' and to try to ignite them with the cry 'Citizen-soldiers, to arms!'), and lastly, in August 1793, the summoning of representative conventions was outlawed. In addition, a substantial Catholic Relief Act, planned to keep the Catholics within the (British) government's embrace, was passed in April 1793. One by one, the chosen pathways to reform were relentlessly shut down or closed off.

With the outbreak of war came the realisation that Ireland was a probable target of French aggression, for, while the French revolutionaries might have emphatically renounced the old ways of governance and diplomacy, they could not as easily ignore the long-held view of French strategists that Ireland was the weakest link in Britain's defences. William Duckett, Irish-born former seminarian in Paris, *convive* at the White's Hotel dinner, and now full-time revolutionary, was the first French agent to visit Ireland with a view to ascertaining its readiness for French intervention. Colonel Eleazer Oswald was next to arrive, in June 1793. He was an American enthusiast for the French Revolution and he too had attended the dinner at White's Hotel. The reports of both men were inconclusive. Then, in April 1794, the Revd William Jackson arrived in Dublin. Unluckily for him, he was accompanied on his journey from France, through England and on to Ireland by one of Pitt's agents, and when enough incriminating evidence had been gathered, Jackson was arrested. Wolfe Tone had been in contact with Jackson in Dublin and had prepared a briefing statement or memorandum for him on the likely reaction in Ireland to a French incursion. To write such a document was of course treasonable in a time of war, but because authorship could not be fully proved against Tone, he entered into an agreement with the authorities by which, in return for revealing what he knew of the United Irish plans, he would be allowed to exile himself to the United States. (Jackson was not so lucky: found guilty at his trial in April 1795, he committed suicide in the dock.) Meanwhile, pursuant to the treasonable correspondence with the United Irishmen that had emerged with Jackson's arrest, the Society was suppressed in May 1794.

At this point, it is commonly claimed, the United Irishmen, shut out of constitutional means through which to pursue their aims, went underground, emerging in 1795 as an oath-bound secret society that looked to

French assistance as the only way to achieve them. And, since the French authorities had no interest at all in parliamentary reform, the United Irishmen had, in effect, no choice but to seek a republic in Ireland, and separation from England: nothing less could induce the French to intervene militarily. Moreover, because the French preferred to help those who would help themselves, the United Irishmen had no option but to turn to the Defenders, who, by 1795, were engaged in an active insurgency in a broad swathe of counties across south Ulster, north Leinster and north Connacht.

Quite what lay behind Defenderism and the Defenders was something of a mystery to Dublin Castle: 'We know not the bottom or design or extent of the insurrection', confessed under secretary Cooke in February 1793.[19] Savage repression had little effect: the next month he claimed that some fifty Defenders had been killed and one hundred captured, and a few weeks after that the *Freeman's Journal* reported that the death sentence had been pronounced on twenty-one Defenders at Dundalk, County Louth.[20] Despite these harsh measures, the Defenders had continued to spread from county to county. On paper at least, this agrarian secret society offered the urban radicals in the United Irishmen a ready-made military force to boost their revolutionary credentials and to impress the French government with their commitment to a republic to be achieved by force of arms. In the event, Theobald Wolfe Tone, following a short period of exile in the United States, took himself off to France. He landed there in February 1796: his mission, agreed in advance with fellow United Irishmen Thomas Russell and Thomas Addis Emmet, was to conjure up a French military force to invade Ireland.

It may be doubted if the alleged division between a constitutional and a military phase of the Society of United Irishmen is all that convincing. A number of the leaders were separatists from the start, and the repression offered by Dublin Castle and the military authorities from an early date was scarcely calculated to persuade reformers that their goals could be achieved by peaceful means. Thus General Richard Whyte, in military command of Belfast in March 1793, believing that his situation there was 'pretty similar to my late friend Gen[era]l Gage at Boston ... daily threatened by the malcontents with a Bunker's Hill and a Lexington', thought to get his retaliation in first and turned his troops loose on the radicals of that town. They had dared to exhibit pictures of Mirabeau and Benjamin Franklin, and a fiddler

---

19 Cooke to Nepean, 8 Feb. 1793, HO 100/39 f. 82, TNA.
20 *Freeman's Journal*, 16–18 April 1793: this report may not have meant that twenty-one Defenders were in fact executed.

had played 'a rascally, outlandish, disloyal tune' (the *Ça Ira*, a French revolutionary song) to taunt his men. Many windows, and a few heads, were broken before 'his charming boys' were called off.[21] It was a modest foretaste of the military mayhem that would ensue later in the decade.

There was never any prospect at all of parliamentary reform being granted: the outbreak of war had ruled it out definitively, but even before then, as the 'peaceful' decade of the 1780s had revealed, it could not be countenanced. In 1793 the British government could just about control the Irish parliament, and the Irish parliament could just about control Ireland: parliamentary reform would put both in jeopardy. A military 'turn' for the United Irishmen had to have been on the cards from their foundation.

Allying with the Defenders, however, incurred numerous risks for the United Irishmen, for the Defenders appeared to be everything that the United Irishmen were not. The Defenders were rural, the United Irishmen were, mostly, urban; the Defenders were 'poor, ignorant labouring men', the United Irishmen were socially removed from them;[22] the Defenders were aggressively sectarian, the United Irishmen offered a secular vision of the future; the Defenders defined themselves by their willingness to inflict violence and sustain casualties, the United Irishmen showed little stomach for either – so far. And yet, the United Irishmen believed that these risks were worth incurring, for an association with the Defenders gave them in theory a force of rural insurgents who could fight alongside the French when they arrived. And certainly the French authorities were familiar with the Defender phenomenon: it was one of the topics on which they pressed Tone for information during his discussions at the French ministry of war concerning a possible French expedition to Ireland.[23]

By a fortunate coincidence, Tone arrived in France just when a debate was under way among French strategists as to how best to damage England (Britain hardly figured). The French revolutionary authorities were adamant

---

21 Whyte to [Cooke?], 8 April 1793, HO 100/46 ff. 59–60, TNA; Whyte to Hobart, 29 March 1793, HO 100/43 ff. 152–4, TNA.

22 This did not mean that the Defenders were unaware of what was going on in the world. Westmorland commented that the Defenders were filled with 'an expectation of change' and held a 'general belief that the French were the friends of the poor'. He was moved to ponder 'how such people in such uncultivated places could be made acquainted with these ideas': Westmorland to Dundas, 8 June 1793, HO 100/40 f. 21, TNA. Two years later, the newly arrived lord lieutenant, Earl Camden, reported that there is 'too general an expectation among the common people of some good that they are to derive from fraternity' and that they are 'ready to join the French in the event of an expected invasion': Camden to Portland, 28 May 1795, HO 100/57 ff. 336–42, TNA.

23 M. Elliott, *Theobald Wolfe Tone: prophet of Irish independence* (New Haven: Yale University Press, 1989), pp. 291–2.

that 'Pitt's gold' lay behind the Vendée uprising, and his support for the ill-fated Quiberon Bay landings of June 1795 by French royalist counter-revolutionaries caused equal outrage. How fitting to pay back Pitt and England by encouraging an uprising in Ireland, England's Vendée. General Lazare Hoche was very much in favour of such an action; he had fought in the vicious Vendéean civil war, indeed he was credited with suppressing the rebels, and he was on record since 1793 as being in favour of a revenge campaign against England to be conducted in Ireland.

Throughout 1796, Tone, by now an officer in the French army, argued and explained where necessary, and cajoled and hustled when required, in order to move forward the planned expedition to Ireland. Eventually, after interminable delays, in December 1796 a French war fleet carrying some 14,000 soldiers sailed from Brest and made its way to Bantry Bay in south-west Ireland. Faced with mountainous seas off Ireland no landing was possible, and the invasion fleet was eventually forced to limp back to France, *re infecta*.

The abortive French descent on Bantry Bay was, in retrospect, a turning point in the military history of the 1790s. The British Admiralty had flatly refused to believe that the French navy, in view of its troubles during the Revolution, still retained the capacity to carry out an amphibious landing abroad. The expedition to Bantry Bay had settled that question, and new measures were swiftly put in place to ensure that another French naval breakout from Brest could not happen. Again, while Dublin Castle had been well aware that the United Irishmen had been very active in suborning members of the armed forces of the crown, particularly Irish militiamen, until the French expedition little had been done about it. That was to change after Bantry Bay. Similarly, while it had been known for some time that subversives in Ulster had been active in swearing in thousands of members, once again no systematic counter-insurgency campaign had been mounted against them. That, too, was to change after the shock of the abortive French expedition. As for the United Irishmen, they had had a major propaganda boost with a French fleet in Bantry Bay. They had often bragged that they were 'partners in revolution' with the French, and their boastings had been often scoffed at. Bantry Bay had been the perfect riposte, and the lesson to be drawn was clear: the French had come once; they would certainly come again.[24]

And yet, in the long run, the failed French landing proved a disaster for the United Irishmen, and in the months after January 1797 they endured a further

---

24 The classic account is M. Elliott, *Partners in Revolution: the United Irishmen and France* (New Haven: Yale University Press, 1982).

series of reverses. New naval protocols were put in place to keep the French fleet blockaded in the Atlantic ports and a purge was carried out among the armed forces in Ireland to ensure that if the French did return they would not be joined by disaffected members of the armed forces. Following a series of courts martial in the summer of 1797, around twenty soldiers (including four soldiers of the Monaghan Militia at Blaris Camp, County Antrim, who were long remembered)[25] were shot for treachery (i.e. being sworn United Irishmen), with numerous others flogged and/or sentenced to serve abroad for life. But especially, following the poor showing of Ulster during the emergency prompted by the French fleet's arrival off the coast of west Cork, the fateful decision was taken to disarm the would-be rebels in that province. Camden's embarrassing admission during the crisis that he had had to retain a large force in Ulster to police a threatened native insurgency rather than despatch it to the south-west of Ireland to confront a foreign enemy was crucial to this decision. Ulster was now to be dragooned and, armed with new powers under the 1796 Insurrection Act, the army's generals were exhorted to go well beyond what even that draconian law permitted, and to treat all Ulster, and eventually all Ireland, as enemy territory.

General Thomas Knox, on counter-insurgency duties in mid-Ulster in March 1797, gave as his opinion that 'laws, though ever so strict, will not do. Severe military execution alone will recover the arms from the hands of the rebels', and he declared that, because of the abortive French invasion, 'the spirit of rebellion has wonderfully increased in the north within these last 8 weeks'. He then put forward what he called his 'shocking remedy ... to quieten the province. I look upon Ulster to be a La Vendée and [believe] that it will not be brought into subjection but by the same means adopted by the [French] republicans in power – namely spreading devastation through the most disaffected parts.'[26] Accordingly, throughout 1797 and on into 1798, the United Irish organisation that had for years been continously swearing in members and drilling them in a military fashion came under relentless and ruthless attack in Ulster and elsewhere. Numerous arrests were made, with house-burnings, torture, shootings and floggings all routinely carried out by the military in an attempt to ensure that, should the French return, there would be little or no support for them in Ireland.

25 Col. J. Bagot, of the Kildare Militia, reported on 3 Oct. 1806 that one of the toasts drunk by subversives in Antrim was to 'the four boys at Blair's moor [*sic*] that fear God and not men': HO 100/138 f. 158, TNA.
26 T. Knox to Duke of Abercorn, 21 March 1797, Abercorn papers, T/2541/1B3/6/10, PRONI.

In their determination to destroy the United Irish movement in Ulster, the authorities did not shy away from playing the sectarian card. Sectarian rioting and feuding between those 'disunited Irishmen' – the Defenders and the Peep of Day Boys – had continued unabated in east and mid-Ulster after 1793, but in general Dublin Castle had not taken sides and had instead urged local magistrates to deal robustly and even-handedly with culprits who appeared before them. However by 1795, and certainly by 1796, it was evident to Camden's advisers such as John Beresford, the chief commissioner of the Revenue Board, and Lord Clare, the lord chancellor, that, so far had the situation on the ground deteriorated in Ulster, a policy of 'arming the Protestants who can be depended upon' was called for.[27] Already in September 1795, the Orange Order had been formed in Armagh out of a number of local loyalist associations such as the Boyne Society and the Peep of Day Boys, and it spread rapidly, with parades taking place on 12 July 1796 at various venues in Armagh, and elsewhere. General Knox encouraged them and, while on duty in Tyrone, sought to take advantage of them. 'As to the Orangemen, we have rather a difficult card to play', he explained in August 1796. 'They must not be entirely discountenanced, on the contrary we must in certain degree uphold them for, with all their licentiousness, on them must we rely for the preservation of our lives and properties should critical times occur.'[28]

A further boost for loyalism came in late August 1796 with the formation of an Irish Yeomanry. Throughout the summer of that year Camden's letters and despatches described in detail how insurgency had worsened. On 24 August he regaled the Duke of Portland in the Home Office in London with 'various accounts from the county of Antrim [that] state the planting of the tree of liberty, the celebration of French victories by bonfires and the open audacity of stopping [mail-coach] passengers to shout for the French'. He also related how little confidence he had in the loyalty of a number of regiments of Irish Militia and how he had come under pressure from local landlords, equally suspicious of the Militia's reliability, to authorise a new military formation, a Yeomanry, 'for their *own* [sic] and for the protection of the country'.[29] Portland, though nervous of anything that had the appearance of the recently banned Volunteers, accepted Camden's suggestion.[30]

---

27 J. Beresford to Lord Auckland, 4 Sept. 1796 in W. Beresford (ed.), *The correspondence of the Rt. Hon. John Beresford*, 2 vols. (London: Woodfall and Kinder, 1854), vol. II, p. 129; Clare to Camden, 7 Sept. 1796, Camden papers, T/2627/4/201, PRONI.

28 Gen. Knox to Cooke, 13 Aug. 1796, Rebellion papers, 620/24/106, NAI.

29 Camden to Portland, 24 Aug. 1796, HO 100/62 ff. 190–4, TNA.

30 Portland to Camden, 29 Aug. 1796, HO 100/62 ff. 200–3, TNA.

The military thinking behind the Yeomanry was quite simple: they were to be deployed in their own areas to pursue local wrongdoers and subversives so that regular soldiers could be freed up for service abroad or despatched to confront the French should they effect a landing in Ireland. But the formation of the Yeomanry was also designed to give confidence to those Protestants who were hostile to the United Irish conspiracy, who were disturbed at the apparent inaction against its leaders and who were fearful at what appeared to be the inexorable rise of Irish Catholics. From the beginning, the Yeomanry was strongly Protestant in composition, with a marked Orange hue about it, and it came to be regarded as an almost direct counterpart to the 'Catholic' Irish Militia, with whom it frequently engaged in sectarian fighting.

Armed with new laws (the Insurrection Act, Gunpowder Act), equipped with new forces (the Irish Yeomanry, the Scottish Fencibles), and well briefed on the progress of the United Irish plans through a panoply of agents and informers, Dublin Castle through 1797 and 1798 turned the tide against the United Irishmen and their rural allies. In March 1798, pursuant to information received, almost the entire Leinster leadership of the United Irishmen was arrested in Dublin; in May, Lord Edward FitzGerald, military leader of the United Irishmen, was shot and captured, and he died from his wounds in early June; shortly after, his successors, the Sheares brothers, Henry and John, were arrested, and they were tried, convicted and executed in July 1798.

By then a full-scale rising had broken out, not, as had been anticipated or feared, in Dublin, but in the counties around the capital, and especially in County Wexford where an initial rebel victory at Oulart (May 27) had electrified the south-east and drawn thousands into the movement. However, after a number of victories, the insurgents, almost all Catholic though often with Protestant leaders, found themselves hemmed in by the armed forces of the crown and were finally routed at Vinegar Hill, outside Enniscorthy, County Wexford on 21 June 1798. A much smaller rising took place in County Antrim on 6 June, and then another, a week later, in County Down, but, deprived of an initial victory, without coordination and heavily outnumbered, the rebels, mostly Presbyterian though with some Catholics in their ranks, were easily scattered. A landing by a small French force under General Humbert at Killala, County Mayo on 22 August 1798 could do nothing to alter that overall verdict of rebel failure, and the year ended with a series of trials (following his court martial, Theobald Wolfe Tone died of a self-inflicted wound in November), executions and banishments. Altogether perhaps 25,000 rebels had died, and with them around 600 soldiers. A further casualty was to be the Irish parliament; on learning that rebellion had broken out in Ireland, Pitt had determined that this was the opportunity he needed to push for a Union of the two parliaments.

The rebellion had only been a few days old when an alarmed Camden described the reaction among his advisers to the fighting. Recalling that the 'mistake of America' was to react too slowly, he called for military reinforcements at once, but then cautioned:

> Savage cruelties, party and religious prejudice has literally made the Protestant part of the country mad. The army partake of the fury. It is scarcely possible to restrain the violence of my own immediate friends and advisers within any justifiable bounds. They are prepared for extirpation and any appearance of lenity on the part of government raises a flame which runs like wildfire through the street and over the country.[31]

Camden's fears of a bloodbath were justified, as reports of massacres of prisoners and grisly sectarian atrocities (inter alia, 350 insurgents intent on surrender slaughtered by Sir James Duff's men at Curragh, County Kildare: over 100 Protestants burned alive at Scullabogue, County Wexford) poured into the Castle. Camden was replaced as lord lieutenant in June by Lord Cornwallis and he too tried to restrain crown forces from regarding every man in a brown coat as a rebel, but with as little success as his predecessor: he was soon lamenting the 'numberless murders committed by our people' (similar, in his eyes, to American loyalists) and putting the blame for these, perhaps unfairly, on the Irish Yeomanry, who 'take the lead in rapine and murder'.[32]

The extreme violence witnessed during the 1798 rebellion, and during the run-up to it, bears comparison with that perpetrated in the Vendée and later in Spain. As in these theatres, irregular combatants were simply not recognised as legitimate fighters and therefore the usual restraints on soldiers' conduct could be abandoned. Thus, General Humbert and his French soldiers, on their surrender at Ballinamuck, County Longford, were granted the status of prisoners of war and were well treated. In marked contrast, their Irish allies were immediately attacked, with scores more executed on the road from Ballinamuck to Killala, a distance of around 90 miles. For example, Major Acheson, from Carrick on Shannon, County Leitrim, coolly reported to his superior that he had executed nineteen prisoners there in one day and that he had in custody 113 more still to be punished.[33]

---

31 Camden to Pitt, 29 May 1798, Chatham papers 30/8/326 f. 303, TNA. On 8 June he warned Pitt about the danger of 'depopulation' caused by religious furies in Ireland: Camden to Pitt, 7 June 1798, Chatham papers 30/8/326 ff. 414–5, TNA.
32 Quoted in Bartlett, *Fall and rise*, p. 240.
33 Major Acheson to —, 17 Sept. 1798, Military reports, MIC 67/143, PRONI.

In this fevered atmosphere, in which calls for revenge rang out and demands were made for retaliation and retribution, the Union passed. Despite Pitt's honeyed words at the time promising an impartial legislature in London, soberly and calmly addressing Irish problems, and adjudicating on them in a fair-minded way, it was always likely that the prejudices of the past, now mightily reinforced and gallingly refreshed by the scarifying experiences of the 1790s, and of the 1798 rebellion in particular, would triumph over a more generous policy. True, in the first few years after Union there was an attempt, however halting, to govern Ireland on 'Union principles' (i.e. ruling out the bad old ways of the 1790s), but whatever slim chance there was that such a policy might be pursued was fatally undermined by that aftershock of the 1798 rebellion, viz. the rebellion headed by Robert Emmet in July 1803. Emmet's rebellion – little more than a bloody riot in Thomas Street – was easily squashed but it shook British rule in Ireland and caused the abandonment of those 'Union principles' that had briefly underlain it.

Union and the Catholic Question

At the time of the passing of the Catholic Relief Act of 1793, most observers had assumed, and very many Irish Protestants had feared, that, once the vote in the county constituencies had been conceded to Irish Catholics, the right to sit in parliament could not be far behind. Henry Grattan and Edmund Burke, both 'friends' to the Catholic cause, certainly believed this to be the case. They congratulated each other that 'the Catholics have gotten everything [for] . . . they have gotten the greater part in possession and the remainder in a certain and approaching reversion'.[34] The leaders of the Catholics themselves also thought so, for the Catholic Committee, its work considered done, was speedily wound up, and its servants, among them the headlong enthusiast for the French Revolution Theobald Wolfe Tone, in effect stood down.[35] Even those opposed to Catholic claims seemed resigned to a further and rapid Catholic advance deeper into the Protestant redoubt of the constitution. John Foster, Speaker of the Irish Commons, and a noted opponent of concessions for Catholics, flatly refused to accept that the right to sit in parliament would long be withheld from Catholics and he posed the question, 'upon what ground can you say men are fit to be electors and unfit to be

34 H. Grattan to E. Burke, 25 March 1793 in H. Grattan (ed.), *Memoirs of the life and times of Henry Grattan*, 5 vols. (Dublin: H. Colburn, 1839–46), vol. v, p. 558.
35 Bartlett, *Fall and rise*, p. 186.

elected?'[36] After all, once the circle of the constitution had been comprehensively breached, there seemed to be no obvious line between exercising the franchise and taking a seat in parliament if elected. And yet, as is well known, over thirty years were to elapse before 'Catholic emancipation' – as the concession on seats in parliament was quickly known – was conceded, or taken. How can this puzzle be unravelled?

It seems clear that Prime Minister William Pitt and his chief cabinet ally, Henry Dundas, were resolved not to yield this final concession to Catholics in 1793, or later, because they wanted to hold something substantial in reserve should the prospect of an Anglo-Irish legislative union open up. Union had been on Pitt's mind for some time and in various letters to confidants he had indicated that it was his preferred solution to the problem of Anglo-Irish relations. However, while Pitt was well aware that there was no immediate prospect of a proposal for Union gaining the assent of the Irish parliament, he also knew that the threat or promise of seats for Catholics in a united parliament could be both a vital stick and a tempting carrot at some future, more favourable, moment. And that moment might not be that far off, for one result of conceding the franchise to Catholics was that Union was now spoken of openly. Already Westmorland, the (admittedly excitable) Irish lord lieutenant, had revealed that, even where votes for Catholics were concerned, 'the Protestants frequently declare that they will have an Union rather than give the franchise to the Catholics, and the Catholics that they will have an Union rather than submit to their present state of degradation'. He sagely advised Pitt to consider how 'the violence of both parties might be turned on this occasion to the advantage of England'.[37] It is from 1793 and the Catholic Relief Act of that year that a pro-Union lobby, with John FitzGibbon, later Lord Clare, at its head, can be identified.

It was because Pitt regarded a legislative union as the 'ultimate solution' (his words) to Anglo-Irish problems that he firmly ruled out any attempt at extending the concessions of 1793 so as to include Catholic eligibility to sit in the Irish parliament.[38] Hence, when in early 1795 Earl Fitzwilliam, the newly appointed and very headstrong lord lieutenant, proposed granting that very concession, Pitt had no option but to recommend his withdrawal. Fitzwilliam's sponsorship of Catholic emancipation brought about his downfall. Catholic emancipation was simply too valuable to be thrown away on Irish Catholics.

---

36 Westmorland to Pitt, 13 Nov. 1792, Chatham papers 30/8/331 f. 90, TNA.
37 Westmorland to Pitt, 13 Nov. 1792, Chatham papers 30/8/331 f. 90, TNA.
38 Pitt to Dundas, 8 Nov. 1792, Pitt papers, W.L. Clements Library, Ann Arbor, Michigan.

Pitt's opportunity came with the rebellion of 1798.[39] By then, Pitt had become convinced that the British government could not long control the Irish parliament and, as well, that the Irish parliament could not control Ireland. He was equally persuaded that strategic necessity – the effective prosecution of the war with revolutionary France – required the end of the separate Irish parliament.[40] Accordingly, even before the rebellion was crushed, plans were drawn up to put a full stop to the Irish parliament's existence. For their part, Irish Catholics were given to understand by the lord lieutenant, Lord Cornwallis, appointed in June 1798, that Union would be followed by emancipation.

Catholic Ireland welcomed the prospect of Union.[41] Certainly, the Catholic hierarchy to a man was in support; on occasion the bishops' enthusiasm for the end of the Irish parliament threatened to get out of hand, and Dublin Castle was moved to urge restraint on them lest Protestant feelings were inflamed, and Protestant suspicions about secret deals were aroused. The only significant Catholic opposition came from Daniel O'Connell, an up-and-coming barrister, who declared at a public meeting in Dublin in January 1800 that he would prefer the reintroduction of the Penal Laws to the loss of the Irish parliament. But his was, in effect, a lone voice for, just as in 1793 it was widely assumed that electing and getting elected to parliament were intimately linked, so too in 1800 it was almost a given that emancipation would follow Union, that Union without emancipation made little sense. And yet, once again, the expected concession did not materialise. George III ruled it out of the question, and soon after the passing of the Irish Act of Union, Pitt, Dundas, Cornwallis and his chief secretary, Lord Castlereagh, with others, resigned office. Evidently, despite all the glowing rhetoric about inclusion, access and impartiality that had accompanied its passing, in the end the Union was to be simply a Protestant Union, with consequences that were to dog its acceptance, and threaten its legitimacy throughout the nineteenth century and beyond.

Catholic emancipation met with determined and successful resistance for decades after 1801. A Protestant Union and a Protestant Empire were to be maintained at all costs, and this meant total resistance to Catholic claims, for Catholic emancipation was seen simply as code both for Irish republican separatism and for Catholic ascendancy. By 1815 Catholic emancipation was

---

39 Bartlett, *Fall and rise*, pp. 245–67.
40 On this point see W. Doyle, 'The Union in a European context', *Transactions of the Royal Historical Society*, sixth series, 10 (2001), 167–80.
41 'The great body of the people in general, and of the Catholics in particular, are decidedly for it [Union]': Cornwallis to Ross, 7 Nov. 1799 in C. Ross (ed.), *The correspondence of Charles, first Marquis Cornwallis*, 3 vols. (London: John Murray, 1859), vol. III, p. 143.

evidently much further away from achievement than it had been even ten years earlier. The king's hostility to Catholic Relief had been unshakeable, and the resolute and determined efforts of his ministers in London and servants in Dublin – notably Sir Robert Peel as chief secretary – to frustrate Irish Catholic ambitions carried the day. Admittedly, Irish Catholics had helped defeat their own cause, for they had proved adept at alienating potential friends and at sowing discord among themselves.

Between 1805, when the first post-Union campaign for emancipation was begun, and 1815, when the French wars ended, Catholic divisions over strategy, over siding with William Pitt or running with Charles James Fox, over whether or not to petition, over whether or not to accept 'securities', over the suggestion of state salaries for priests, and, not least, whether or not to cooperate fully with their fellow Catholics in England, did the Irish Catholic cause great damage.[42] W. W. Pole, chief secretary to the Duke of Richmond, commented cheerfully in 1812 that he saw no need to act against the Catholics as they seemed infinitely capable of ruining matters themselves without any assistance from him. As he put it, with rather more accuracy than elegance: to date, 'they [the Catholics] have bitched their own thing most completely'.[43]

By 1815 emancipation was firmly ruled out in British and Irish government circles as being nothing less than another term for separatism and sectarian triumph. The Catholic leader Daniel O'Connell and his allies, wrote Richmond in 1813, seek to end the English connection and they believe firmly that 'Ireland could support itself as a separate nation.' In the same year, Redesdale, a former lord chancellor of Ireland, averred that O'Connell cared nothing for emancipation and that he was simply 'an Irish republican' who sought to break the connection with England. This belief or perception, when allied to the high level of violence, especially sectarian violence, in the Irish countryside, strengthened the conviction that the entire post-Union campaign for Catholic emancipation was nothing less than a continuation of the republican conspiracy of the 1790s. Catholic emancipation, therefore, because it was seen as nothing less than a vehicle for both Irish separatism and Catholic ascendancy, had to be resisted at whatever cost.

---

42 Bartlett, *Fall and rise*, pp. 269–311: 'Securities' were demands that a British government, in the event of Catholic emancipation being granted, would have some say, up to a veto, over the appointment of Irish Catholic bishops.
43 W.W. Pole to Richmond, 11 Jan. 1812, Richmond papers, MS 60, NLI.

The State of Ireland in the Early Nineteenth Century

In March 1808, William Smith, a magistrate in Clonmel, County Tipperary, described the area surrounding the town, to a distance of 16 miles, as 'The Theatre of Disorder'. In truth, in the first two decades of the nineteenth century, the term could have been applied to almost the entire island of Ireland. Violence, whether political, sectarian or agrarian – or a combination of all three – was a key feature from north to south, with reports of murder, arson, mutilation, flogging, abduction, assault and intimidation regularly featuring in the in-tray of those English administrators tasked with governing Ireland. In addition, observers noted what they felt was the inherent Irish love of fighting for the sake of it: 'Paddy is easily persuaded to partake of this amusement.'[44]

Thus, between 1802 and 1805 there was a recurrence of Whiteboy activity in south-east Tipperary, a feature of which was an onslaught on wealthy farmers, graziers mostly, by landless labourers, unable to rent land because of high prices for cattle.[45] At least twelve murders were recorded. Between July and September 1806 various official digests of outrages listed ears cut off, houses burned, burglary, horses maimed, individuals flogged or 'carded' – their backs scored with a plank studded with nails – weapons stolen, all of which were on occasion perpetrated by men 'wearing white shirts or white kerchiefs'.[46] In that year, and in 1807, there were frequent reports of meetings held by 'people styling themselves Defenders' in County Antrim, and 'Threshers', considered similar in outlook to Defenders,[47] were discovered in Armagh, Cavan, Leitrim, Longford and Mayo (they assembled wearing straw hats, 'one of the usual badges of the Defenders', or 'dressed in a sort of white shirt over their coats').[48] By 1808, a new agrarian insurgency was under way

---

44 W. Smith to E.B. Littlehales, 15 March 1808, HO 100/14 ff. 132–6, TNA.
45 P. Roberts, 'Caravats and Shanavests: Whiteboyism and faction fighting in east Munster, 1802–11' in Clark and Donnelly (eds.), *Irish peasants*, pp. 64–101.
46 'Report on persons in custody', [July 1806], 'A list of persons scourged', 29 Sept. 1806, HO 100/136 ff. 69–74; HO 100/138 f. 109, TNA.
47 'Defenders varied from the Threshers in the western part of Ireland for they carried on their business more slyly and safer from being censured by the law, for they omitted that part of the obligation which related to pulling down the tithes and taxes of the clergy of all denominations': 'Information', 6 Aug. 1807, HO 100/142 f. 181, TNA.
48 'Defenderism in the North', Dec. 1806, HO 100/136 ff. 435–63, TNA; Maj. Campbell to W. Elliot, 18 Oct. 1806, HO 100/138 f. 313, TNA; Bedford to Spencer, 30 Dec. 1806, HO 100/136 ff. 472–5, TNA; Foster to Sheffield, 8 Dec. 1806, Additional Sheffield papers, T/ 3725/26, PRONI.

as Shanavests and Caravats battled with each other in Munster, their contest, their historian has claimed, 'a product of the wartime agricultural boom'.[49] They were still fighting in 1814.[50] A prominent feature of the essentially class-based dispute between Caravats and Shanavests was the abduction of the daughters of the latter by members of the former gang, so as to obtain a handsome dowry. William Bagwell, a magistrate in Tipperary, claimed that 'no farmer now able to give his daughter fifty pounds or upwards can venture to keep her in his house'. Around fifty young women may have been kidnapped in the Tipperary-Waterford area between 1800 and 1815.[51] In addition, sectarian brawling between units of the Yeomanry and the Irish Militia, while not unknown in the late 1790s, became regular occurrences in the post-Union period: for example, when the King's County Militia encountered the Omagh Yeomanry at Omagh, County Tyrone in August 1809, a riot ensued. Two yeomen were killed and another badly wounded. It was reported that the militiamen were wearing green ribbons and they had attacked the yeomen, crying 'they would pull down the Orange ribbons'.[52] There were numerous reports of disaffection among the Militia. Brigade Major Halpin claimed in 1808 that the men in the Limerick and Tipperary Militias were 'all rebels', and Sylvester Buck, on infiltrating the Westmeath Militia in 1807, uncovered a conspiracy involving fifty 'brothers' who met regularly in a Sligo tavern: 'if a Protestant [entered] in the company, the trigger finger was to be pulled'.[53]

By 1809, as the debates on Catholic emancipation grew ever more heated, and resistance to it ever more determined, the threat of extreme and extensive sectarian violence grew more and more acute throughout Ireland. In February of that year, Sir Richard Musgrave revealed details of a 'treasonable conspiracy' among the Catholics of Munster, 'the main object of which is

---

49 Roberts, 'Caravats and Shanavests', p. 81. Thomas Prendergast, a major in the Tipperary Militia and a magistrate, claimed that the Caravat–Shanavest feuding was merely a cover 'for the purpose of training people in use of arms and acting together': Prendergast to General Houston, [April 1808], HO 100/147 ff. 150–8, TNA.

50 D. Delany to Peel, 14 Aug. 1814, HO 100/180 f. 131, TNA.

51 Bagwell to —, 4 Feb. 1809, HO 100/153 f. 148, TNA.

52 J. Stewart to E.B. Littlehales, 12 Aug. 1809, HO 100/153 ff. 366–8, TNA. In July 1810, the Lough Allen [Leitrim] Yeomanry 'were set upon one by one' and unmercifully beaten by a large crowd of locals who were heard to shout that 'there is not a Protestant they meet alone but they will cut to pieces': W. Slack to Pole, 25 July 1810, HO 100/159 f. 61, TNA.

53 'Papers and informations concerning S. Buck's allegations of disaffection in the Westmeath Regiment of Militia', Aug.–Sept. 1807, HO 100/142 ff. 59–60, 164–9, TNA. Buck had to be sent on leave following his 'discoveries' as he had 'altogether exhausted his constitution in associating and drinking with the villains'.

an universal extermination of Protestants of every description'. Alarmingly, he claimed that the plot 'was conducted with much more secrecy than that which took place in 1798'.[54] Admittedly, Musgrave was a noted hothead, but his was still an influential voice in English Tory circles.[55] In December 1813, Whitworth, the lord lieutenant, pointing to 'the rooted and rancorous hatred of government' among Catholics, called for the reintroduction of the Insurrection Act, in his view most unwisely repealed ten years earlier. 'Ireland is not to be governed as England is', he argued; 'the character and spirit of the governed are completely different.'[56] By that date, Ribbonism, another Catholic conspiracy on the model of Defenderism, had spread widely.

Ribbonism was first mentioned in 1810 by General Hart when he reported disturbances in Donegal between Orange yeomen and Roman Catholics, who '[style] themselves king's defenders or Ribbonmen'. A year later he was claiming that the 'animosity between the Ribbandmen [sic] and the Orangemen was hardly to be credited'.[57] Ribbonism expanded throughout west Ulster, and beyond, in the next few years: in 1813 Ribbonmen paraded near Newry 'in regular military order proclaiming twenty pounds for an Orangeman or a Protestant';[58] in 1815 it was alleged that 10,000 Ribbonmen drawn from counties Tyrone, Donegal and Derry had assembled at a fair at Donemana, near Strabane, County Tyrone, that they were active as well in Leitrim and Antrim, and that there was even – rumour had it – a Grand Ribbon Committee that met regularly in Dublin.[59] Ribbonism was a direct offshoot of Defenderism, sharing many of the same oaths and catechisms with the 1790s movement, and it excited the same dread and apprehension among elite observers. The growth of Ribbonism, with members allegedly swearing an oath 'to destroy

---

54 Musgrave to the Agar, 25 Feb. 1809, Normanton papers, T/3719/C/43/32, PRONI.
55 J.J. Sack, *From Jacobite to Conservative: reaction and orthodoxy in Britain, c1760–1832* (Cambridge: Cambridge University Press, 1993), pp. 96–8; J. Kelly, *Sir Richard Musgrave: ultra-Protestant ideologue* (Dublin: Four Courts Press, 2009).
56 Whitworth to Sidmouth, 13 Dec. 1813, 21 Apr. 1814, HO 100/175 ff. 163–8, HO 100/177 f. 397, TNA.
57 General G.V. Hart to Abercorn, 12 Aug. 1810, Abercorn papers, T/2541/1B3/16/10, PRONI; Hart to Lieut. MacManus, 18 June 1811, HO 100/163 ff. 386–8, TNA. Hart conceded that it might be a good idea to ban Orange processions but only 'provided it was so done as not entirely to extinguish a spirit that, well directed, I understand, has formerly been of use and in some portion of which still to exist there may be no harm and perhaps some safety'.
58 G. Atkinson to Peel, 9 Oct. 1813, HO 100/173 f.136, TNA.
59 G. Hill to Peel, 2 Sept. 1815, HO 100/185 ff. 99–100, TNA; 'Petition of the Protestant inhabitants of Ballinamore, County Leitrim', 5 Nov. 1815, HO 100/187 f. 341, TNA; Peel to Hill, 16 Jan. 1814, HO 100/176 f. 380, TNA.

heretics, not one excepted', coincided with the spread of the prophecies of Pastorini.[60]

In July 1814, Richard Cuppaidge, a magistrate in Athlone, County Westmeath, reported that he had captured 'a fellow called Dowlan' among whose papers was a tract showing that 'Pastorini's exposition of the Revelation [*sic*] has been well disseminated through (and well understood by) the people of the country.'[61] This was a reference to the commentary on the Book of Revelation by Bishop Charles Walmsley, pen-name Signor Pastorini, first published in 1790, but many times since reprinted and circulated in tract or pamphlet form.[62] In this work, Walmsley or Pastorini forecast the end of Protestantism in Ireland in either the year 1821 or 1825. Prophecy of this sort was quite common in Ireland; the United Irishmen had published tracts revealing that the Revolution in France had been predicted a hundred years before it happened, and in 1810 Littlehales in Dublin Castle detailed how

> Skully spoke of a prophecy which he saw 30 years ago which mentioned most of the late great events ... the principal streets [of London] would be covered with dead bodies and that in Ireland soon after a great commotion would take place and that the lord lieutenant would fall by the hand of the son of an Irish lord and that afterwards she would be independent and free.[63]

Pastorini's dire prophecies of the imminent end of Protestantism fitted in well with such apocalyptic utterances, and they were to gain wide currency, eventually underlying the Rockite disturbances of the 1820s.[64]

The pervasive sectarian violence in the period 1800–15, the frequent uncovering of murder plots and republican conspiracies, the apparently anarchic nature of rural crime and the frequent panic-stricken cries for help from beleaguered Protestants (who allegedly awoke 'each morning [to] the sad intimation of a robbery, the torture of a neighbour, the destruction of a house or an unfortunate victim sacrificed to brutality')[65] led inexorably to the conclusion that 'an honest despotic government would be the fittest government for Ireland', for 'the prevailing religion of Ireland operates as an impediment

---

60 'Ribbonmen's oath from County Leitrim', Feb. 1812, HO 100/166 f. 234, TNA.

61 Cuppaidge to Gregory, 12 July 1814, HO 100/179 f. 139, TNA.

62 J.S. Donnelly, 'Pastorini and Captain Rock: millenarianism and sectarianism in the Rockite movement of 1821–4' in Clark and Donnelly (eds.), *Irish peasants*, pp. 102–39

63 Littlehales to Beckett, 22 June 1810, HO 100/158 ff. 247–62, TNA. 'Skully' was almost certainly Denys Scully, the Catholic pamphleteer.

64 J. Donnelly Jr, *Captain Rock: the Irish agrarian rebellion of 1821–4* (Madison: University of Wisconsin Press, 2009).

65 E.V. Fitzgerald, Limerick, to Gregory, 17 Sept. 1815, HO 100/185 f. 209, TNA.

rather than an aid to the ends of civil government'.[66] There could therefore be no question of Catholic emancipation.

The end of the war with Napoleonic France brought no improvement, but only added dangers, in the security situation in Ireland. Recognising the risks that peace might bring, Henry Goulburn, undersecretary for war, a few weeks before Napoleon's abdication, helpfully offered Peel 600 former prisoners of the French who had been freed on parole: barred from fighting on the continent, these men from the 55th and 69th regiments could yet prove serviceable in Ireland where they would be 'at full liberty to cut the throats of rebels or Catholics'.[67] Others feared that the speedy ending of army and navy contracts for provisions could lead to disturbances. Peel, however, dismissed these anxieties. Irish unrest, unlike English, was not fuelled by want, but was caused by 'sheer wickedness and depravity', and he believed that an economic recession 'would rather tend to diminish than increase it'.[68] Again, there were real concerns that the demobbed soldiers might make use of their weapon training: already one alarmed observer had commented on the precision of the 'nocturnal parades' of the disaffected and on 'their steadiness in platoon firing'.[69] At the war's end, a plan was immediately drawn up to encourage the enlistment of men in the Irish Militia into the regular army: to disembody them and send them home, it was argued, 'could raise the level of licentiousness in certain districts'.[70]

Then, in November 1815, William Baker, a magistrate, was shot dead at Thomastown, County Tipperary, a murder that engendered something akin to panic among the Munster gentry. His killing, noted a fellow magistrate, was 'a forfeit that almost every active magistrate of this country must pay to the savage brutality of the lower orders of it'.[71] A reward of £5,000 was offered for information on the shooting.[72] Not surprisingly, in view of the on-going, seemingly intractable, violence in rural Ireland – the Baker murder was one of

---

66 Peel to Gregory, 15 March, 25 Dec. 1816 in C.S. Parker (ed.), *Sir Robert Peel from his private papers*, 2 vols. (London: John Murray, 1891), vol. I, pp. 215, 236–7.

67 H. Goulburn to Peel, 18 March 1814, Peel papers, Add. MS 40235, BL. They could also be used in North America 'to assist in keeping the Yankees out of Canada'.

68 Peel to Beckett, 5 Dec. 1816 in Parker (ed.), *Peel papers*, vol. I, p. 235.

69 Castlemaine to Peel, 25 Oct. 1813, HO 100/173 f. 292, TNA.

70 Whitworth to Sidmouth, 26 March 1816, HO 100/16 ff. 353–60, TNA.

71 R. Creaghe to [Peel?], 28 Nov. 1815, HO 100/187 f. 395, TNA. Baker had apparently caused outrage by refusing to sign a petition pleading for leniency for a Clonmel woman, Mrs Hussey, under sentence of transportation to New South Wales for having firearms.

72 Admiral Hallowell to General Clinton, 14 Dec. 1815, Clinton papers, MS 10,214(5), NLI is the source for the extraordinary reward money.

ten in Tipperary alone that year[73] – a decision was made to keep up a force of some 33,000 soldiers in Ireland, though General Hewett, the commander in chief, warned that even this number would scarcely be sufficient.[74] On seeing this figure, Sidmouth, at the Home Office in London, protested: 'It is a mortifying consideration that when the danger from foreign enemies has ceased and that of rebellion cannot be said to exist, there should still be a necessity of keeping up an immense military force in Ireland.'[75] He had, however, no alternative but to agree, for Whitworth had already impressed upon him that 'this government [in Ireland] must in fact be considered as a military government and to be effectual must be made a very strong one'. Whitworth also claimed that the lower orders in Ireland were similar to the French lower orders and that the same means used there, presumably in the Vendée, were needed to keep them under control.[76] Out of 'total war' had come 'total resistance'.

73 A. Jacob to Atty-Genl Saurin, 30 Nov. 1815, HO 100/187 ff. 413–14, TNA.
74 Hewett to Peel, 23 Oct. 1815, HO 100/187 f. 359, TNA.
75 Sidmouth to Whitworth, 8 Dec. 1815, HO 100/188 ff. 66–7, TNA.
76 Whitworth to Sidmouth, 16 June 1814, HO 100/178 f. 261, TNA.

4

The Impact of O'Connell, 1815–1850

PATRICK M. GEOGHEGAN

Introduction

'Was O'Connell necessary?'[1] This question was posed by a British historian a number of years ago and it is worth revisiting in any attempt to assess the impact of O'Connell on Irish and British politics in the first half of the nineteenth century. To his admirers, O'Connell was the man who pioneered mass politicisation and laid the foundations for modern participatory democracy; to his detractors he was the man who brought the priests into Irish politics, while at the same time suffocating the Irish language, and coarsening political discourse. By the end of the nineteenth century some historians were in no doubt that O'Connell had done more to hinder than to help the causes he championed. W.E.H. Lecky concluded his major study of *Leaders of public opinion in Ireland* by suggesting that it was debatable whether O'Connell's life was a blessing or a curse for Ireland.[2] In part, this was because O'Connell was blamed for directly contributing to the polarisation of Irish politics along sectarian lines, first by the manner in which he pursued Catholic emancipation, and then for the way he organised the repeal movement. Friedrich Engels dismissed O'Connell as a 'cunning old lawyer' and wondered how much might have been achieved 'if a sensible man possessed O'Connell's popularity, or if O'Connell had a little more understanding and a little less egotism and vanity'.[3] For W.B. Yeats, O'Connell was 'the Great Comedian', the crowd-pleasing rhetorician staging a theatre of political melodrama, and he has been described by Paul Bew more recently as 'more concerned with provoking an

---

1 B. Aspinwall, 'Was O'Connell necessary? Sir Joseph Dillon, Scotland, and the movement for Catholic emancipation' in D.M. Loades (ed.), *The end of strife* (Edinburgh: T. and T. Clark, 1984).
2 W.E.H. Lecky, *Leaders of public opinion in Ireland*, 2 vols. (London: Longmans, Green and Co., 1903), vol. II, conclusion.
3 *Karl Marx, Frederick Engels: collected works* (New York: International Publishers, 1975), vol. III, p. 389.

immediate popular response than with personal integrity or long-term consequences, whole-heartedly professing Catholic piety in public while seducing housemaids in private without any sense of incongruity, not because he was insincere but because he didn't understand sincerity'.[4]

This chapter explores the impact of O'Connell from the moment in 1815 when he became the champion of Irish Catholic nationalism following the killing of John D'Esterre in a duel, to shortly after his death in the middle of the Great Famine. Five themes will be explored. The first is O'Connell's mobilisation of mass popular politics, initially with his campaign for emancipation in the 1820s. An unintended consequence of this campaign was the conflation of nationalism with Catholicism in the minds of the Protestant minority, despite O'Connell's best efforts to create a wider coalition in favour of both emancipation and repeal of the Union. The second issue addressed is O'Connell's impact on British politics in the 1830s in the House of Commons, and his campaign for justice for Ireland. Third, the chapter will locate O'Connell in an international context by examining O'Connell's contribution to the development of European Catholicism, American anti-slavery, and the idea of peaceful, mass politics. The fourth theme is the impact of the failed campaign for repeal he pursued in the 1840s. Finally, the chapter will assess the legacy of O'Connell's campaigns on Irish politics, the extent to which he contributed to polarisation along sectarian lines (and the extent to which any campaign for full civil rights made this inevitable). Alongside O'Connell's many triumphs, most notably the inauguration of mass peaceful politics, are the implications of bringing the priest into Irish political life, and the tensions this created. Also notable are the later criticisms of O'Connell for failing to develop a form of nationalism that was neither Gaelic nor fully independent, often summarised by reference to his comments on the Irish language but which were more nuanced than is generally acknowledged. The rejection of 'old Ireland' values in the 1840s will also be explored, culminating in the failed rebellion of 1848, and in the rejection of the O'Connellite approach to politics by subsequent generations.

Repoliticising the Irish Nation

The rise of O'Connell, and his domination of political debate in the first half of the nineteenth century, is better understood if it is located in the context of

4 P. Bew and P. Maume, 'The great advocate', *Dublin Review of Books*, 8 (Winter 2008) (www.drb.ie/essays/the-great-advocate), accessed 1 June 2016.

what preceded it. O'Connell's achievement was to repoliticise the 'Catholic nation' that was broken down and defeated, suffocated by government policies and a series of reversals and setbacks since the mid-1790s. O'Connell succeeded partly through force of personality, and partly by adopting innovative strategies to advance his causes; the result was that he re-energised a people that was listless. This was the true impact of O'Connell, a Promethean figure who harnessed his talents as an orator, an organiser and a leader, to inspire, cajole, embarrass, provoke and command.

O'Connell believed that the years 1782–1800 were 'the only period of Irish history' – a glorious time of prosperity and growth, when Ireland had her own parliament and a measure of political independence.[5] In his later years this period would be memorialised as 'Grattan's parliament', a misleading and inaccurate term, but one that reflected O'Connell's view of that time. O'Connell never wavered in his belief that this was a moment of great progress, until the British government deliberately provoked the 1798 rebellion.[6] He was convinced this was done as a way of crushing the United Irishmen, and abolishing the Irish parliament by illegal and unconstitutional means. This was a misreading of the past but, deliberate or not, it allowed O'Connell to frame the debate for an Irish parliament in binary terms: an Irish parliament meant a restoration of liberties, prosperity and peace; rule from London meant repression, austerity and conflict.

This was O'Connell's view from the very start of his political career. O'Connell's maiden political intervention on 15 January 1800 was a speech in opposition to the Union, and it framed his political principles for the rest of his career. It became an article of faith, affirming and reaffirming the essential rightness of his cause, based on his reading of the recent past. Indeed, O'Connell liked to boast that the speech was 'the text-book of his political career', and that you would learn anything you needed about his beliefs by studying it.[7] Its key feature was O'Connell's mythologising of the period of legislative independence, and his claim that Irish Catholics would prefer 'the re-enactment of the penal code in all its pristine horrors ... [to] the lesser and more sufferable evil' of a Union. He insisted he would rather trust in 'the

5 Taking the phrase from Grattan himself, see Grattan to O'Connell, 3 Jan. 1819 in *The correspondence of Daniel O'Connell*, ed. M.R. O'Connell, 8 vols. (Shannon and Dublin: Irish University Press (vols. I–III); Stationery Office (vol. IV); Blackwater (vols. V–VIII), 1972–80), vol. II, p. 186.
6 P. Geoghegan, 'Daniel O'Connell and the Irish Act of Union' in J. Kelly, J. McCafferty and C.I. McGrath (eds.), *People, politics and power: essays on Irish history, 1660–1850* (Dublin: UCD Press, 2009), pp. 175–6.
7 Ibid.

justice of his brethren, the Protestants of Ireland, who have already liberated him, than lay his country at the feet of foreigners'.[8] The reality – as O'Connell must have known – was that the Protestant parliament had attempted to resist the limited grant of civil rights to Catholics (including the right to vote, and to enter the professions) in 1792–3, and that it had been obliged to accede by a British government anxious to secure Catholic loyalty at the start of a long conflict with revolutionary France. But in politics a certain amount of self-deception is necessary, and O'Connell constructed a narrative that united the Irish against a common external adversary.

What the period 1782–1800 did witness was the extraordinary politicisation of the Irish nation. Grattan never declared on 16 April 1782, the day on which the Irish parliament approved a resolution calling for constitutional reform, that Ireland had become a nation, but it was a subsequent rewriting of the past that reflected a greater truth.[9] Legislative independence – no matter how limited it was in reality – led to a reawakening of Irish political confidence. And the impact of the American and French revolutions on Irish politics was immense. The politicisation of Ireland in the 1790s was transformative, and it was encapsulated in Wolfe Tone's suggestion that the name Irishman should become the common name for Catholic, Protestant and Dissenter.[10] It was as much an act of claiming the name 'Irish' for those who were not Catholic, as it was the inclusion of Catholics within the United Irish political project, and it kick-started a period of extraordinary political activity. That activity came to an end with a series of defeats: first the crushing of the 1798 rebellion, and the unleashing of terror across the country to suppress radicalism; and second, the passing of the Act of Union in 1800 to eradicate the political self-confidence that had been achieved since 1782.

By comparison, the period 1801 to 1815 was an era of depoliticisation, as successive British governments tried to use the new Union framework as a way of tranquilising the country, and to depress any attempts to rally or raise resistance to the new structures. Recent work has shown that ministers had no clear idea of how to govern Ireland in the wake of the Union.[11] Some

---

8 *The life and speeches of Daniel O'Connell M.P.*, ed. J. O'Connell, 2 vols. (Dublin: J. Duffy, 1846), vol. 1, p. 9.
9 See R. Koebner, 'The early speeches of Henry Grattan', *Bulletin of the Institute of Historical Research*, 30 (1957), 102–14; G. O'Brien, 'The Grattan mystique', *Eighteenth-Century Ireland*, 1 (1986), 177–94; W.J. McCormack, 'Vision and revision in the study of eighteenth-century Irish parliamentary rhetoric', *Eighteenth-Century Ireland*, 2 (1987), 7–35.
10 T. Bartlett, *Ireland: a history* (Cambridge: Cambridge University Press, 2010), p. 213.
11 S. O'Reilly, 'Completing the Union: the politics of implementation in Ireland, 1801–1815', PhD thesis, Trinity College Dublin, 2014.

lord lieutenants like the Duke of Bedford, 1806–7, wanted to 'complete the Union'; others believed that all the key work had been done and that all that was required was to keep a firm grip on the people. The Duke of Richmond, who headed the Irish executive from 1807 to 1813, represented 'a return to the traditional policy of coercive and repressive approaches to keeping Ireland in check' and aggressively pursued anti-Catholic strategies. The overall result was that Catholic hopes that had been raised by the Union were set back, and there was an increasing sense that Catholic rights would continue to be subordinated to the rhetoric of Protestant Ascendancy. This was the period when, O'Connell believed, a culture of defeat had taken hold of the Irish people, when you could identify a Catholic on the street by 'his subdued and slavish look and gait'.[12] So O'Connell was determined to rally the people, confident that victories that could not be achieved on fields of battle could be achieved on other fields. O'Connell used the courtrooms as his personal arena, challenging and rebuking Ascendancy judges, insulting his opponents, and even, on one notorious occasion, threatening to horse-whip the attorney general in open court.[13] O'Connell's verbal aggression was not just an expression of temperament, it was a political tactic. It was a deliberate way of showing that Catholics could be equal, that they could address and confront their opponents on equal terms. This drew attention and comment. In a famous sketch of O'Connell, published in 1825, it was observed that he carried his umbrella as if it was a pike, marching to the Four Courts as if he was marching into battle.[14] Even O'Connell's decision to purchase a house on Merrion Square, which he could hardly afford, made a political point. By being the first Catholic to move into the square he was asserting his equality with the (Protestant) elite who lived there.

O'Connell's career as a lawyer laid the foundation for his success as a politician. It established his reputation as 'The Counsellor', the person who saved lives in almost impossible situations, and forged an aura that carried over to his other pursuits. His courtroom exploits empowered O'Connell to stand forth as the defender of his people, allowing him to sympathise with causes, while simultaneously opposing them politically. The best example is the agrarian agitation of the 1820s. O'Connell's willingness to act for various Whiteboys and Rockites charged with serious offences, including rape and

---

12 *Correspondence of Daniel O'Connell, the Liberator*, ed. W.J. Fitzpatrick, 2 vols. (New York: Longmans, Green and Co., 1888), vol. ɪɪ, p. 430.

13 O'Connell, *Speeches*, vol. ɪ, p. 331.

14 W.H. Curran's sketch, quoted in P. Geoghegan, *King Dan: the rise of Daniel O'Connell, 1775–1829* (Dublin: Gill & Macmillan, 2008), p. 64.

murder, gained him support, even though he was personally against the agitation. It was a difficult balancing act to sustain but it positioned O'Connell as the peaceful agitator with the potential to call on the violent forces he alone could control. The threat of latent force was one of O'Connell's most potent weapons. James Donnelly has shown how O'Connell was able to benefit from balancing the legal with the political, and tap into millenarian prophecies about the destruction of the Irish Protestants to benefit his cause.[15]

The Campaign for Emancipation, 1815–1829

The year 1815 is an appropriate starting point for any assessment of O'Connell's impact on politics, because it was the year when O'Connell emerged as the champion of Irish Catholics. Provoked into fighting a duel by John Norcot D'Esterre, a member of Dublin Corporation, who saw in O'Connell's 'perforated corpse' a chance of financial redemption and political advancement, O'Connell's success on the duelling ground in February 1815 answered those doubters who questioned his capacity to lead the movement for full civil rights for Catholics.[16] There had been some doubts about O'Connell's courage since 1813 when he accepted a compromise rather than pursue an affair of honour to its logical conclusion. Even his brother-in-law warned him that an 'unfavourable impression' had been created by withdrawing from the field before any shots had been fired.[17] By facing down D'Esterre, a former royal marine who had a reputation as a crack shot, O'Connell established himself as someone as adept on the field of battle as he was in the courtroom or in a public debate.

This proved important in the struggle for the leadership of Catholic opinion, which was split over whether to accept conditional emancipation (the securities demanded by the British government, and specifically a 'veto' on the appointment of bishops). O'Connell's position on the issue was unambiguous and consistent until the point when he was prepared to compromise on his terms. He opposed the 'veto' throughout this period, sacrificing the unity of the movement in 1813 because he was not prepared to compromise. He also abandoned his childhood hero, Henry Grattan, for taking a different

---

15 See J.S. Donnelly, *Captain Rock: the Irish agrarian rebellion of 1821–1824* (Cork: Collins Press, 2009), chapter 4.

16 *Irish Magazine and Monthly Asylum for Neglected Biography*, 8 (March 1815), p. 101.

17 Rickard O'Connell to Daniel O'Connell, 4 Feb. 1815, in *The correspondence of Daniel O'Connell*, ed. M.R. O'Connell, vol. ii, p. 7; J. Kelly, *'That Damn'd Thing called Honour': duelling in Ireland, 1570–1860* (Cork: Cork University Press, 1996).

position on the issue, accusing him of a 'style of superiority better suited, perhaps, to periods when the Catholics were more depressed, the Protestants more elevated'.[18] The movement split, and the seceders formed their own movement and prepared their own petitions for parliament. The irony is that O'Connell was prepared to accept conditions in 1825, when a deal was on the table, and it appeared that Catholic emancipation was finally within his grasp. The difference then was that it was a deal on his terms. As his friend and colleague Charles Phillips noted, 'implicit obedience was the homage he demanded'. O'Connell's most obvious weakness was that he was incapable of tolerating alternative voices to his own in the movement. O'Connell himself would compromise, and adjust, and turn depending on the circumstances and the opportunities; but he was furious whenever someone else tried to do the same. As Phillips concluded: 'contradiction incensed him, equality affronted him; and while invoking "liberty", he waved an iron sceptre'.[19]

On 23 February 1815, fresh from his duel with D'Esterre, O'Connell established his ascendancy over his opponents in the Catholic movement. He took the opportunity to undermine the leadership pretensions of Arthur, 8th Earl of Fingall, who he dismissed in withering terms, and to denounce those who were prepared to compromise with the government. Preaching unanimity but practising division he declared that 'we are for independence, the seceders are for ... dependence'.[20] He encouraged a siege mentality amongst his supporters, insisting that their 'friends' had abandoned them, their 'enemies' had oppressed them, and the 'seceders' had betrayed them.[21] The movement that resulted was a smaller one, but it was forged in O'Connell's image, and was prepared to follow his agenda for as long as it thought he might succeed. O'Connell only became vulnerable when it looked as if other strategies from other sources might bear greater results, and these proved to be his greatest threats in the 1820s.

His biggest challenge was to mobilise people who were used to disappointment, year after year, and who had become convinced that emancipation would never come. The established strategy of putting their faith in sympathetic politicians in London was explicitly rejected by O'Connell. But the alternative of persuading people to campaign was slow to gather momentum. In 1817, the newly renamed Catholic Board suffered from increasing apathy, and was then wound up because of financial issues. In 1818 a decision was

---

18 O'Connell, *Speeches*, vol. I, p. 424.
19 C. Phillips, *Curran and his contemporaries* (Edinburgh: Blackwood, 1850), p. 259.
20 O'Connell, *Speeches*, vol. II, p. 12. The speech is incorrectly dated as 1814.
21 Ibid., p. 15.

taken not to petition parliament, O'Connell's advice to the contrary notwithstanding, and although he published an open letter to the Catholics of Ireland on 1 January 1819 listing various grievances, the *Dublin Journal* dismissed his letter as a 'strange jumble of egotism and misrepresentation'.[22] It seemed for a time that O'Connell had reached too far, and that the movement would soon burn itself out.

The impetus for change was stronger elsewhere, and it seemed at the time that more moderate forces in Britain would be able to deliver what O'Connell was unable. In 1821 it looked as though a Catholic Relief Act would pass the British parliament when William Plunket brought forward legislation which included a provision increasing the level of securities offered to the state. O'Connell opposed it furiously, accusing Plunket of 'out-Heroding' Herod by offering to extend the veto, but he failed to get enough signatures to call an aggregate meeting of the Catholics in Dublin to attack the bill.[23] Plunket's bill passed in the House of Commons on 2 April, but its defeat on 17 April in the House of Lords by 159 votes to 120 saved O'Connell's leadership.[24]

The real achievement of O'Connell in the 1820s was in the way he succeeded in mobilising the demoralised and defeated Catholics. He did so by demanding that Catholics take responsibility for winning their own freedom, rather than wait for others to give it to them. His philosophy and approach was best summed up by the two lines of poetry he quoted most often, regularly beginning his political addresses with them. From Lord Byron's *Childe Harold's pilgrimage*, they were his inspiration as well as his rallying cry: 'Hereditary bondsmen! Know ye not/Who would be free, themselves must strike the blow.' The great O'Connell scholar Oliver MacDonagh later entitled the first volume of his biographical study *The hereditary bondsman*. But O'Connell never saw himself as that bondsman: his self-image was that of the hereditary chieftain who would lead his slaves to freedom. Yet MacDonagh was correct to focus on the words. They encapsulated O'Connell's political strategy in the 1820s. If Catholics wished to be free, they must prove to the world that they deserved to be free; they must strike the blow themselves to secure freedom.

This explains the tactics employed in the 1820s. O'Connell no longer wanted a movement that was financed by a middle-class elite in Ireland, patronised by a Catholic aristocracy, and reliant on friendly supporters in the British parliament. He aspired to a movement from the bottom up. It was to

22 *O'Connell correspondence*, ed. O'Connell, vol. II, p. 187.
23 O'Connell, *Speeches*, vol. II, p. 127.
24 *O'Connell correspondence*, ed. O'Connell, vol. II, p. 312.

be a transformative proposition for modern Irish politics, as it combined a grass-roots organisation, a method of raising funds using a form of crowd-sourcing (church-gate collections), and a way of politicising the general public and aligning them behind a cause. It was to be a mass, democratic political movement, dependent on moral suasion rather than physical force, and it was to have a profound impact on the campaign for emancipation. In the early days of the new organisation, which was named the Catholic Association, there was no evidence that this new approach would succeed. O'Connell's son, John, who was present at one of the early meetings in the autumn of 1823, was disappointed to find that the two-room floor in Capel Street was only half-full, that there were 'scanty returns of money, few communications from the country, and informal haste' in the manage-ment of business. With only 'captious, uncertain, half-timid' members in attendance, it seemed as if, like its predecessors, the movement was destined to fail.[25]

It was the proposal for a great national subscription – the Catholic rent – that changed everything. O'Connell floated the idea in February 1824, hav-ing tried and failed for some weeks to introduce it for want of a quorum. The inability to achieve a quorum – a simple ten members – shows just how apathetic Catholic politics had become. The idea was not completely new. Viscount Kenmare had suggested some kind of national subscription back in the 1780s, and O'Connell himself had attempted a temporary subscription in 1812. But this was a more ambitious long-term project. Each subscriber was to pay not less than a penny a month and not more than two shillings, and O'Connell boasted that 'The Catholic rent will surely emancipate us.'[26] Because the sums individuals undertook to pay were relatively small, the hope was that it would encourage mass participation, and that everyone who agreed to contribute would feel they had a share as well as a stake in the movement. As Oliver MacDonagh observed: 'O'Connell saw the rent as the transformer of sentimental support into real commitment.'[27] From the beginning, O'Connell insisted the rent could raise £50,000.[28] And while some mocked the very idea – John O'Connell, then at school at Clongowes College,

25 O'Connell, *Speeches*, vol. II, p. 231.
26 O'Connell to John Primrose, 18 Dec. 1824 in *O'Connell correspondence*, ed. O'Connell, vol. III, p. 89.
27 O. MacDonagh, *The Hereditary bondsman: Daniel O'Connell 1775–1829* (London: Weidenfeld & Nicolson, 1988), p. 210.
28 O'Connell to Mary O'Connell, 14 Feb. 1824 in *O'Connell correspondence*, ed. O'Connell, vol. III, p. 32.

was teased about his father's 'penny-a-month plan for liberating Ireland' – the idea soon gathered momentum, raising vital funds as well as interest.[29] When O'Connell addressed an aggregate meeting of Irish Catholics on 27 February 1824 he was unable to speak for several minutes 'amidst the most enthusiastic cheering' and 'deafening shouts', and he pointedly began his speech by quoting his favourite lines – his 'old and favourite motto' of 'hereditary bondsmen'.[30] By the end of the year the subscription amounted on average to £1,000 a week.[31] As Bill Kissane has identified, O'Connell was able thereby 'to construct a political movement that was expansive, rather than restrictive in its attitude towards membership, [and] geared towards politicising the people rather than excluding them'.[32]

Connected to this was O'Connell's positive conception of democracy, and democracy in an Irish context. He believed that a 'spirit of democracy' would lead to prosperity; without it, 'governors are tyrants, and the people are slaves'.[33] He feared extreme forms of radical activity, as represented by the mob violence of the French Revolution, and the way the 1798 rebellion descended into sectarian atrocities and official reprisals against civilians. This was what he termed a kind of 'fierce democracy'. It was, O'Connell believed, the product of having no limits on democratic activity, and because it would destroy society it was to be avoided at all costs.

The Catholic Association was suppressed in February 1825 when the chief secretary for Ireland declared in the British House of Commons that it had links with the traitors of old, Wolfe Tone, Thomas Russell and Robert Emmet.[34] O'Connell was not too concerned, convinced that 1825 would be the year of destiny predicted in the Pastorini prophecies, and that a deal would be done with the British government to secure emancipation. A Catholic petition was presented in the House of Commons, and its acceptance, by thirteen votes, prepared the way for a new emancipation bill. Anticipating victory, O'Connell was prepared to compromise precisely because it seemed success was now achievable. Having railed against securities for years, he was now prepared to accept the disenfranchisement of the forty shilling freeholders and a state provision

29 O'Connell, *Speeches*, vol. II, p. 286.
30 Ibid., p. 295.
31 Ibid., p. 438. By the end of 1824 approximately £8,000 from the rent had been invested in government securities: Catholic Association papers, 60/2, Dublin Diocesan Archives.
32 B. Kissane, *Explaining Irish democracy* (Dublin: UCD Press, 2002), p. 85.
33 Speech from 1841, quoted in L. Colantonio, 'Democracy and the Irish people' in J. Innes and M. Philp (eds.), *Re-imagining democracy in the age of revolutions: America, France, Britain* (Oxford: Oxford University Press, 2013), p. 164.
34 *Parliamentary Debates*, 12 (1825), col. 172.

for the clergy (what became known as the 'wings'). O'Connell had little faith in the forty shilling freeholders, believing they were too easily controlled by their landlords; he was willing to sacrifice them for the sake of a deal, although he recognised it was 'a very hard card to play'.[35] The bill passed through the House of Commons in April, but was rejected in the Lords on the night of 17 May.

O'Connell's reputation was damaged by the defeat, and he struggled to restore his authority. As Thomas Wyse recounted in his account of the Catholic Association, published a few years later, there had been a 'host of errors and sins'.[36] A New Catholic Association was founded, and there was a return to agitation. Because O'Connell stood to gain personally from the deal – with a patent of precedence to be granted to advance his legal career – he was accused of acting from 'corrupt and personal motives' and there was a backlash, which O'Connell survived, but at some cost.[37] The lesson that O'Connell took was that *temperateness, moderation* and *conciliation*' were 'suited only to perpetuate our degradation' and that the only solution was to 'rouse in Ireland a spirit of *action*'.[38]

The 1826 general election in County Waterford convinced O'Connell that the forty shilling freeholders could be a force for change. The key move, however, was made in 1828, when O'Connell agreed to stand in a by-election in County Clare, even though he would not be able to take his seat if elected. Believing that 'moral force' would trump 'physical force', he called on the people of Clare to avoid violence, drinking or illegality.[39] The 'union of physical force with moral sentiment' would, he pronounced, leave the British government with no option but to concede emancipation. O'Connell's appeal was explicitly to 'Old Ireland' and he hoped that his mass movement would triumph. The election of O'Connell – 2,057 votes to Vesey Fitzgerald's 982 – was a transformative moment in Irish politics. Robert Peel, the home secretary, recognised that British power in Ireland had been 'shivered to atoms', not only because the people had voted for O'Connell, but also because they had followed his instructions to avoid drinking and violence and to give no

35 O'Connell to Mary O'Connell, 22 April 1825 in *O'Connell correspondence*, ed. O'Connell, vol. III, p. 153.
36 T. Wyse, *Historical sketch of the late Catholic Association of Ireland*, 2 vols. (London, 1829), vol. I, p. 220.
37 *O'Connell correspondence*, ed. O'Connell, vol. III, p. 198; *Dublin Evening Post*, 20 Oct. 1825.
38 P. Geoghegan, *King Dan: the rise of Daniel O'Connell 1775–1829* (Dublin: Gill & Macmillan, 2008), chapter 12.
39 Speech of 16 Jan. 1827: Catholic Association papers, 59/1/I f. 32, Dublin Diocesan Archive; O'Connell to Knight of Kerry, 31 Dec. 1826 in Fitzpatrick (ed.), *Correspondence*, vol. I, p. 135.

excuse to the soldiers who had been sent to maintain order.[40] Realising that the government could be won over, O'Connell sacrificed the forty shilling freeholders for the sake of a deal.

The loss of the forty shilling franchise represented a significant diminution of democratic power in Ireland, reducing the electorate from about 300,000 to close to 37,000. Donal McCartney and others have described this as 'a necessary sacrifice to achieve equal rights across confessions', but Laurent Colantonio has posed the question as to whether this was 'a democratic retreat'.[41] Although Colantonio provides a necessary corrective to some of the more over-stated claims about O'Connell's leadership, the fact remains that to sacrifice emancipation to protect the forty shilling franchise would have been a short-term act of political self-sabotage, given the stakes involved, and the way the franchise issue was to be addressed within the next few years. The deal agreed, emancipation passed in 1829, after George IV failed in his attempts to change the ministry, and the prime minister, Wellington, convinced him that there was no alternative.

Years later, when trying to rally people to support repeal of the Union, O'Connell reminded them that emancipation had seemed a hopeless cause at one time. He was clear about how it had been achieved: 'the united force of a people'. It was 'the force of opinion, the force of reason, the force of justice' which had triumphed, he pointed out; 'physical force' was not necessary.[42] As he asserted at his trial in 1844, he was proud 'that Catholic emancipation, and every achievement of my political life, was obtained without violence and bloodshed'.[43] O'Connell's central role in the winning of emancipation was recognised by contemporaries. In 1839, O'Connell was profiled in a major study of the leading figures of British politics. The author was certain that when future generations asked the question of how the civil disabilities of the Catholics were removed there could only be one answer: 'Daniel O'Connell removed them ... Alone he did it.'[44] Similarly, William Ewart Gladstone was insistent that O'Connell's 'was the genius and the tact, the energy and the fire, that won the bloodless battle of emancipation'.[45] Donal McCartney has

---

40 Lord Mahon (ed.), *Memoirs of the Right Honourable Sir Robert Peel*, 2 vols. (London: John Murray, 1857), vol. 1, p. 116.

41 Colantonio, 'Democracy', p. 167.

42 P.M. Geoghegan, *Liberator: the life and death of Daniel O'Connell* (Dublin: Gill & Macmillan, 2010), chapter 3.

43 Ibid., chapter 10.

44 Mask [James Grant?], *St. Stephen's: Or, Pencillings of politicians* (London: Hugh Cunningham, 1839), p. 160.

45 Geoghegan, *Liberator*, chapter 4.

correctly identified O'Connell's movement as the first modern political structure in Europe: 'an unprecedented organisation of democratic power'.[46]

The winning of Catholic emancipation was O'Connell's greatest victory, even
though he insisted that it was only a first step. His key objective was to restore
the Irish parliament, and at the start of the campaign for emancipation he admitted that he would not be satisfied until he had repealed the Union. Moreover,
the winning of emancipation was a remarkable achievement in itself. It had
been secured after almost three decades of agitation, and numerous false steps,
mis-steps and mistakes by O'Connell. The key thing was not that it had been
achieved, but how it had been achieved. With the assistance of O'Connell's leadership, it had been secured by the Irish Catholics themselves, by their activities
and exertions, not as a gift from the British state but as something that had been
extracted from it.

Emancipation in itself did not change Ireland dramatically. In the short term it
only affected a small number if measured in terms of the numbers of Catholics
elected to parliament, or financial or professional advancement, or the opportunities opened up to middle-class Catholics. Yet it was meaningful for all the Irish
Catholics who cheered O'Connell's electoral victory in 1828 and telegraphed the
news across the country by lighting bonfires on every hill. It was meaningful
because emancipation was seen as a great civil rights issue, as a way of recognising in law that Catholics were equal to Protestants, and an acknowledgement
that the majority population on the island need no longer feel inferior. The Penal
Laws had largely been deconstructed by the end of the eighteenth century, but
a sense of inferiority remained. Theobald Wolfe Tone had asserted in 1791 that
Catholics lived in a state of 'absolute slavery', in his *Argument on behalf of the
Catholics of Ireland*, and for many in the 1820s it was still a slavish existence, even
if not so 'absolute'. O'Connell articulated that sense of shame, and also articulated a solution. To a modern ear the comparisons with slavery may seem overstated, but they resonated with a people who felt inferior and ashamed in their
own country. The victory of 1828–9 was understood and remembered in Ireland
as an act of 'Catholic emancipation'.

To O'Connell's European contemporaries, the real impact of the movement was that it served as a source of inspiration, and a model for mass
democratisation Not just liberal Catholics were influenced by O'Connell;
republicans and radicals also identified possibilities in what was called 'the
Irish democracy'.[47] Even though the Irish example had a specific Catholic

---

46 Donal McCartney, *The dawning of democracy* (Dublin: Helicon, 1987), p. 113.
47 See Colantonio, 'Democracy', p. 162.

aspect, they recognised a 'universal' dimension, namely the way people could become involved in politics, and it had a particular resonance in France where it was forbidden to assemble. *Le National* hailed O'Connell as 'the orator of democracy' and, as Laurent Colantonio has noted, he was championed as 'the advocate of peoples oppressed by tyrants and kings, the natural representative of the masses excluded from the vote – a status to which republicans themselves aspired'.[48] O'Connell, in the words of one French radical, was 'this gigantic revolutionary', who, with 'his vigorous arm, is pushing the old world into the depths, and proclaiming the advent of a new right – the right of peoples – and the reign of equality and liberty'. When there were two failed rebellions in France in 1834 the arrested leaders sought unsuccessfully to have O'Connell defend them at their trials. Touring Ireland in the 1830s, Gustave de Beaumont viewed O'Connell as 'the prototype of the modern politician', someone who could position himself 'between submission and revolt'.[49] O'Connell's greatest political skill was his ability to straddle the two, raising fears and expectations of rebellion to convince both his own side and his opponents that he was serious in order to secure reforms that made violent protest unnecessary.

Sean O'Faoláin was not certain about what exactly O'Connell's legacy was, summarising it as 'much good, much bad', but he was clear about one thing that was 'priceless': it was 'the principle of life as a democracy'. His role was everything: 'He thought a democracy and it rose. He defined himself, and the people became him.'[50] Colantonio has queried O'Connell's democratic convictions, recognising his authoritarian tendencies, and his fears of extreme forms of political activity.[51] But this only reflects the contradictions that made up the man. O'Connell was the champion of freedom who swaggered around like a bully, and the defender of equal rights who assumed an automatic right of superiority in any movement with which he was associated. While never a supporter of revolutionary change, and rooted in an essentially conservative world-view of property and society, he fostered a new kind of involvement in politics.

Irish Protestantism also underwent serious change in this period, in part a response to the rise of O'Connell. Daragh Curran has pointed out that 'Protestant society was under strain at a number of levels in the years

---

48 Ibid., p. 163.
49 Ibid.
50 S. O'Faoláin, *King of the beggars: a life of Daniel O'Connell* (Dublin: Poolbeg Press, 1986), pp. 329–30.
51 Colantonio, 'Democracy', p. 167.

immediately prior to the Famine.'[52] The ultra-Protestant identity, which had developed into a coherent ideology following the passing of the Act of Union, was slow to recognise and then to respond to the challenge posed by the Catholic Association and its model of participatory politics. As James Kelly has noted in his study of Richard Musgrave, the figure who epitomised this identity more than anyone else, it viewed the strategies of O'Connell 'with a combination of incomprehension and intransigent resistance'.[53] Fragmented, it took time to mobilise, concerned about the danger of political violence, and largely ignored what was happening away from Ulster. Curran has suggested that, 'had someone of the charisma of O'Connell emerged on the Protestant side ... a more unified response' could have delayed the government from legislating for emancipation.[54] Instead the mobilisation of Protestant interests only began properly in 1828, and assumed a coherent form in the 1830s and 1840s in opposition to O'Connell's advocacy of repeal.

The Impact of O'Connell on British Politics, 1830–1839

The British parliament was not prepared for the force of O'Connell's personality. Aggressive, abusive and unwilling to follow the normal rules of conduct, he appeared to many to be an unscrupulous figure who was impossible to work with. The raising of an annual subscription to allow O'Connell to dedicate his time completely to politics in an age when MPs were not paid was also viewed with great suspicion. The O'Connell Tribute raised approximately £14,000 a year until 1834, when it went into decline, and led to charges that O'Connell was 'The Great Beggarman', and 'The King of the Beggars', living off the hard work of the people.[55] The diarist Charles Greville, by contrast, defended the arrangement, describing it as 'an income nobly given and nobly earned'.[56]

Some of the abuse O'Connell directed at his opponents shocked. In 1830, Sir Henry Hardinge, the chief secretary for Ireland, was brutally dismissed as a 'paltry, contemptible little English soldier' and 'a chance child of fortune

---

52 D. Curran, *The Protestant community in Ulster, 1825–45: a society in transition* (Dublin: Four Courts Press, 2014), p. 157.

53 J. Kelly, *Sir Richard Musgrave, 1746–1818: ultra-Protestant ideologue* (Dublin: Four Courts Press, 2009), p. 227.

54 Curran, *Protestant community*, pp. 69, 73.

55 M. MacDonagh, *The life of Daniel O'Connell* (London: Cassell, 1903), p. 217.

56 *The Greville Memoirs: a journal of the reigns of King George IV and King William IV*, 8 vols. (London: Longmans, Green and Co., 1874–87), vol. VI, p. 86.

and war'.[57] When Hardinge sought to uphold his injured honour by challenging O'Connell to a duel he was rebuffed, with O'Connell stating that he thought 'fighting a duel would be a bad way to prove that Sir Henry was right and Mr. O'Connell wrong'. Being so quick to abuse, and then to refuse to withdraw the words, or to fight a duel when challenged, was identified as a serious breach of the 'code of social law' that existed at this time.[58] O'Connell did not care – he felt he already had blood on his hands from the D'Esterre killing and he was increasingly concerned by this as he grew older and more religious – but it marked him out as someone who existed outside of society's norms. Even his supporters warned him about his behaviour. The *Northampton Mercury* in 1832 praised O'Connell for refusing to duel, but at the same time advised him to refrain from making verbal assaults because of his refusal to honour the code which existed.[59] Charles Greville was prepared to justify O'Connell's aggression, saying that, 'Had he never been violent, he would not be the man he is, and Ireland would not have been emancipated.'[60] But it led to much criticism in print, allowing *The Times* to ask: 'Safe from challenge – safe from law / What can curb thy callous jaw?'[61] (Illustration 3)

During his first years in the British House of Commons O'Connell became 'a noisy bore' by speaking too often, and by bringing repeal of the Union into too many debates.[62] As he admitted himself, he 'shipwrecked his parliamentary fame' by trying to do too much.[63] Nonetheless, he marked himself out as a leading radical by identifying openly with a 'small and sacred band of radical reformers'.[64] Supporting a number of parliamentary causes, including rights for Jews and other minorities, tithe reform, anti-slavery legislation, a reformed and elected House of Lords, a secret ballot and the abolition of the death penalty, O'Connell was a warm advocate of the Great Reform Act of 1832. However, he believed the prime minister, Lord Grey, had a 'foolish and envenomed prejudice against everything Irish' and, as a result, never showed him any gratitude for ensuring Irish support in 1832.[65] In the event, O'Connell was directly responsible for bringing down Grey's administration in 1834, by

---

57 *Annual Register* (1831), p. 176.
58 *Greville Memoirs*, vol. II, p. 328.
59 *O'Connell correspondence*, ed. O'Connell, vol. VIII, p. 234.
60 *Greville Memoirs*, vol. I, p. 228.
61 *The Times*, 26 Nov. 1835.
62 Mask, *St. Stephen's*, p. 160.
63 O'Connell to Jeremy Bentham, 22 Feb. 1831 in *O'Connell correspondence*, ed. O'Connell, vol. VIII, p. 229.
64 Speech of 12 March 1830, quoted in Colantonio, 'Democracy', p. 166.
65 O'Connell to Richard Barrett, [*c.* 11 July 1834] in *O'Connell correspondence*, ed. O'Connell, vol. V, p. 152.

3. Little Red-Riding Hood's (John Russell, 1st Earl Russell) meeting with the Wolf (Daniel O'Connell), 1835. Though a characteristically gentle satire by 'HB', this image offers a vista onto the uneasiness O'Connell's influence and impact generated at Westminster in the 1830s. Lithograph by 'HB' (John Doyle), published by Thomas McLean, 3 April 1835.

revealing publicly assurances he had been given in private, in an off-the-record briefing by the chief secretary for Ireland. Those closest to the event considered it 'a black act of perfidy', but O'Connell was unrepentant and insisted on doing things his own way.[66]

In terms of his parliamentary reputation, it was his point-by-point opposition to the 1833 coercion bill that established him as a parliamentary gladiator of serious note. One political opponent described him as 'indisputably the greatest orator in the House – nervous, passionate, without art or ornament; concise, intrepid, terrible, far more in the style of old Demosthenic directness and vehemence than anything I have heard in this modern world'.[67] But others were quick to dismiss O'Connell's speeches as failures, even when they went well, and it took time to overcome the prejudice against him. O'Connell's contribution to a debate on the repeal of the Union on 22 April 1834 largely silenced his critics. It was the moment when he was seen to have 'established his reputation' in the form of a superb five-hour oration on the necessity of an Irish parliament.[68]

The huge majority at Westminster against repeal convinced O'Connell that a change of direction was necessary. Following the 1835 general election, O'Connell faced a series of political and personal challenges. He was unseated following a petition against his return after a long and expensive investigation, and he found himself pursuing a number of risky strategies to try and stay afloat. Discovering that he and his Repeal MPs held the balance of power, he availed himself of the opportunity to negotiate a loose alliance with the Whigs. Not quite the formal 'compact' it was described as being, it enabled O'Connell to pursue 'Justice for Ireland'. The repeal campaign was suspended temporarily, not because O'Connell was not serious about it, but because it was in a weak state, and this enabled him to look as if he was acting from a position of strength. In any case he was tormented on a number of fronts. There was a parliamentary investigation into the claims that he attempted to sell a seat in Carlow to an English banker, and then reneged on the deal; he was only saved because the Whigs, reluctantly, came in behind him for the sake of his parliamentary support. His wife Mary (1778–1836) died amidst allegations of serial adultery, and their son, John, was arrested for assaulting a man who claimed to be a half-brother. Some allies turned

---

66 Edward Littleton to Lord Wellesley, 4 July 1834 in H. Reeve (ed.), *Memoir and correspondence relating to political occurrences in June and July 1834 by the Right Hon. Edward John Littleton, first Lord Hatherton* (London: Longmans, Green and Co., 1872), p. 52.
67 MacDonagh, *Life*, p. 228.
68 Geoghegan, *Liberator*, p. 51.

to enemies. Feargus O'Connor, the political agitator and MP, fell out with O'Connell in 1836 and denounced him in print as a 'Dictator', and a 'licensed defamer', who only succeeded because 'timid individuals submit to his slander'.[69] And the relentless abuse in the media, especially *The Times*, eroded his reputation, for example the infamous, 'Scum condensed of Irish bog!/ Ruffian – coward – demagogue!'[70]

In 1840 O'Connell launched a new campaign for repeal, but it suffered from the same apathy that had previously held back the emancipation movement for years. The return of a Tory ministry in 1841 reinforced his conclusion that further gains must be secured outside of parliament, rather than in it. He was aided in this by a brilliant group of people around him, who later became known as Young Ireland, and who were able to channel their energies into organising and promoting the new movement, employing their newspaper, *The Nation*, as a way of using the past to motivate and inspire in the present. Declaring publicly that 1843 would be 'The Year of Repeal', O'Connell prevailed in a debate on the subject at Dublin Corporation, and embarked on a series of weekly public addresses in venues across the country, in what soon became known as 'monster meetings'.

These meetings, an opportunity to explain the reasons for repeal to a domestic audience, and to provide evidence of popular support for the movement to external watchers, were a bold exercise in mass democratic politics. Between March and October 1843 O'Connell criss-crossed the country, travelling approximately 5,000 miles, to address increasing numbers of people in an atmosphere that was part festival, part political theatre. It was essentially the Clare strategy from 1828 made national and it energised the movement. The impact of the monster meetings can be seen in the level of international attention they were afforded. Newspapers daily followed his activities, and travellers came to Ireland specifically to see O'Connell in action.

While claiming to speak on behalf of '9 million' people – 8 million in Ireland and 1 million in Britain – O'Connell appealed to moral force to induce the government to respond positively to the demand for repeal of the Union, with the implicit threat of physical force in the background if things went wrong. O'Connell always insisted that violence would not be necessary, but he hinted that force would be met with force, and that if the government provoked a confrontation the Repeal Association would not

69 Ibid.
70 'The Whig missionary of 1835', *The Times*, 26 Nov. 1835.

back down. O'Connell also clung, naively, to a belief that Queen Victoria would support his cause, and would be an ally in favour of compromise. The key problem was that he did not possess a realistic alternative strategy if the government did not back down. As O'Connell was unwilling to countenance the use of force it had no value except as a threat. He insisted that he 'always preferred one living patriot to ten dead ones', and dismissed any talk about dying being an alternative to freedom as only 'an oratorical phrase'.[71] So even if the Clontarf meeting had not been proscribed in October 1843 the campaign would have lost momentum naturally in the face of determined government opposition.

In the event the government acted first. Clontarf was proscribed, O'Connell cancelled the meeting, the leaders were arrested, and the repeal movement went into decline. O'Connell's guiding principle in his later years, or, as he stated at his trial, 'the principle of my political career', was that political changes were 'purchased at too dear a price if they could only be obtained at the expense of one drop of human blood'.[72] Sentenced to a year in prison, O'Connell became an object of international interest, and prayers for his deliverance were said across continental Europe. Upon his release after a few months, when his conviction was overturned, O'Connell repeated his belief that 'no human revolution is worth the effusion of one single drop of human blood. Human blood is no cement for the temple of human liberty.'[73] His unrivalled standing in the country was shown by the celebrations marking his release. The public reaction was described in the newspapers as the 'unexampled spectacle of a whole people, in a delirium of triumph, maintaining moderation and courtesy'.[74] Another insisted that O'Connell had 'first been made a martyr, and then a conqueror'. O'Connell's influence over the public – his hold over the Irish nation that he had recast in his own image – was shown by the failure of an attempt by the British government to enlist the Vatican against him in 1845. The government succeeded in getting an instruction requiring priests to abstain from political activity, but it was largely ignored. The Duke of Wellington admitted that O'Connell and his 'democracy' were 'too strong for the Roman Catholic nobility, gentry, and hierarchy, with or without the pope'.[75]

71 Geoghegan, *Liberator*, p. 145.
72 Ibid., p. 134.
73 Ibid., p. 195.
74 Charles Gavan Duffy quoted in ibid.
75 Ibid., p. 214.

The Break with Young Ireland

Though they had worked together in promoting the cause of repeal, the relationship of Young Ireland and O'Connell's Repeal Association was not tension free, and the break occurred for many reasons. There was fundamental disagreement between the two interests about the use of physical force, or even the possibility of using physical force to forward their objectives. Second, Young Ireland were disquieted by O'Connell's denunciations of the slave-owners in the United States, and the feeling that he was interfering in another country's internal affairs and losing support and critical finance. Some, like John Mitchel, were supporters of slavery. Others, like Charles Gavan Duffy, believed that tenants in counties Mayo and Kerry were more badly treated than the slaves in Alabama and South Carolina.[76] Third, there was a generational conflict with underlying ideological differences. O'Connell, the heir to the Enlightenment and constitutional patriotism, epitomised the values of 'Old Ireland', whereas the Young Irelanders were a product of the Romantic era and adherents of the values of modern nationalism. Fourth, there was a sublimated succession battle, with a fear that one of O'Connell's sons would seek to emulate his ascendancy and assume the leadership and direction of the movement. Fifth, there was religion. There were elements of suspicion and sectarianism on both sides. Thomas Davis notably attacked O'Connell for being dominated by 'superstition' in a leader in *The Nation*.[77] O'Connell, for his part, bristled easily at any hint of religious condescension/superiority, or any aspersion of Catholicism. The eventual split in 1845 dealt the repeal movement a fatal blow, but in many ways it was unavoidable. The tensions, which were present from the beginning, could be controlled as long as the campaign was active and had momentum; by 1845 the movement had nowhere to go except in on itself. The 1848 rebellion, in the middle of the catastrophic Famine, was a last desperate attempt by the Young Ireland movement to shape events, and it is a measure of their limitations as revolutionaries that it was so easily quenched. By avoiding any executions, and transporting the leading figures for treason-sedition, the government avoided adding to the Irish martyrology, and cheated the movement out of any chance of winning a victory in defeat.

---

76 C. Gavan Duffy, *Four years of Irish history* (Dublin, London and New York: Cassell, Petter, Galpin, 1887), p. 34.
77 R. Davis, *The Young Ireland movement* (Dublin: Gill & Macmillan, 1987), p. 171.

The Great Famine dominated O'Connell's final years. He studied weather conditions and joined scientific committees in an attempt to address what was happening, and used his own money to pay for relief efforts. His final speech in the House of Commons, on 8 February 1847, was a last, dramatic appeal on behalf of a starving population. As Oliver MacDonagh notes: 'He attempted no argument, attributed no blame, [but] threw his country upon the mercy of his foes.'[78]

> Ireland is in your hands, in your power; if you do not save her she cannot save herself. I solemnly call on you to recollect that I predict, with the sincerest conviction, that one-fourth of her population will perish unless you come to her relief.

His one request was for 'a great national act of charity' to save the country. But it went unheard and unheeded, and O'Connell died on 15 May 1847 en route to Rome, believing he had failed his people. The Famine confirmed and reinforced the division of Ireland along sectarian lines, and ensured that land as much as the distribution of political power would become the locus for future agitation.

Critiquing O'Connell

Central to the negative image of O'Connell is the perception that he equated Irish nationalism with Catholicism, and permitted the priests too much influence in politics. Bringing the clergy into the emancipation campaign in the 1820s was probably necessary, as O'Connell employed the existing parish structures to collect funds, and relied on the bishops and priests to provide support. But he sought to avoid equating Irish nationalism with Catholicism, even though it was the religion of the majority. During the campaign for repeal in the 1830s and the 1840s he attempted to forge as broad a coalition as possible, in an attempt to make the movement a genuinely national one. He was only partly successful; the Repeal Association was ever marked by the fact that those links did exist, and that O'Connell was seen both by his supporters as well as by his opponents as the Catholic champion. Publicly as well as privately, O'Connell spoke in favour of the separation of church and state. At a banquet in honour of Polish independence in 1831 O'Connell insisted that church and state should always be kept apart, and described whenever

---

78 O. MacDonagh, *The emancipist: Daniel O'Connell, 1830–1847* (London: Weidenfeld and Nicolson, 1989), p. 313.

they were joined as 'an adulterous connection'.[79] He told the British Jewish leader Isaac Goldsmid that it was 'an eternal and universal truth that we are responsible to God alone for our religious belief and that human laws are impious when they attempt to control the exercise of those acts'. Similarly, W.E. Gladstone never forgot hearing O'Connell demand a complete separation of church and state during a particularly heated debate in parliament. It was clear that O'Connell's vision for Ireland was not the church-dominated ideal his later detractors imagined, or came to believe was created after independence.[80]

The diaries of Thomas Goff, a Protestant clergyman and landlord, provide a good insight into how O'Connell was viewed by more traditional voices in Ireland. Over a twenty-five-year period he attacked O'Connell for his 'vulgar and impertinent oratory', his 'mad and extravagant schemes', his 'most perverse despotism' and his 'usual style of gross deception, fraud, and lying'.[81] O'Connell was blamed for mobilising a 'base rabble', and raising up 'his infatuated and priest-ridden countrymen' for 'his own aggrandisement' and to put 'cash in his pocket'. In stark terms he was 'the Arch Enemy of all Peace and Order', the 'Arch Fiend' and the 'Arch Anarchist'.[82] O'Connell was feared because he was not understood. He was unlike any political activist who had been seen before: demotic, aggressive, egotistical and unreliable. Worse, he was unmistakeably Irish, Catholic and Gaelic, everything that the Ascendancy feared and had tried for so long to suppress. O'Connell was the realisation of their worst fears about Catholic politicians.

O'Connell is often blamed for the decline of the Irish language. One critic has called him 'the greatest enemy of the language', a supporter of 'English-speaking imperialism'.[83] Another has suggested that O'Connell, like the Catholic Church, 'did much' to further its abandonment.[84] Most such commentaries fail to locate O'Connell's comments in the context of the ongoing decline of the language in his lifetime.[85] He did not contribute to it; but he did not express much regret at it happening. At a St Patrick's Day dinner in London in 1833 he admitted that he was 'sufficiently utilitarian not to

---

79 M. Robinson, 'Daniel O'Connell: a tribute', *History Ireland*, 5:4 (1997), 26–31.
80 See, for example, P. Buckland, *Daniel O'Connell: an appraisal* (Ireland in Schools, www.iisresource.org/Documents/0A5_04_Daniel_OConnell.pdf).
81 D. Doyle, *The Reverend Thomas Goff, 1772–1844: Property, Propinquity and Protestantism* (Dublin: Four Courts Press, 2015), p. 36.
82 Ibid.
83 P. Beresford Ellis, *A history of the Irish working class* (London: Pluto Press, 1985), p. 100.
84 R. Welch, *Irish writers and religion* (Gerrard's Cross: Colin Smythe, 1992), p. 101.
85 See Aidan Doyle, Chapter 14 below, pp. 362–8.

regret its gradual abandonment'.[86] Drawing a link with the Tower of Babel, he admitted that although the Irish language was a real source of national pride, the English language was 'the medium of all modern communication', and that he could 'witness without a sigh the gradual disuse of the Irish'. Yet O'Connell's love of the Irish language was unambiguous. It was his native tongue, and he was able to conduct business and legal cases in Irish; sometimes he even spoke in Irish at political events to confuse government reporters. After emancipation he regretted not changing the spelling of his surname to 'O'Conal' (insisting the other form was an English imposition).[87]

Reflecting on O'Connell's reputation in 1844, Thomas Babington Macaulay claimed that O'Connell had attained a position in 'the estimation of his countrymen such as no popular leader in our history, I might perhaps say in the history of the world, has ever attained'.[88] In the same year, James Grant noted that O'Connell has 'for the last thirty years filled so large a space in England's and Ireland's eye, and in the eye of the world'.[89] It is unsurprising therefore that the abolitionist James Cannings Fuller believed that 'there is a charm in the name Daniel O'Connell all over the universe'.[90] Even Charles Gavan Duffy, when attacking O'Connell, described him as 'the greatest tribune of modern times'.[91]

O'Connell's international reputation was enhanced by his campaign against slavery. Of all the causes that O'Connell espoused it was his opposition to slavery, in all forms, that had the greatest impact. His speeches against slavery, most notably in the 1830s and 1840s, reached an international audience and were often republished. Introducing one such edition in 1842, William Lloyd Garrison claimed they 'scathe like lightning and smite like thunderbolts', and credited O'Connell with having done more than anyone else to denounce 'the soul-drivers of this land'.[92] At a Boston anti-slavery rally in the same year, Wendall Phillips insisted that 'the voice of O'Connell, which now shakes the three kingdoms, has poured across the waters as a thunderpeal for the cause of liberty in our own land'.[93] The great black abolitionist

---

86 Geoghegan, *Liberator*, p. 9.
87 Ibid.
88 *Works of Lord Macaulay*, ed. Lady Trevelyan, 8 vols. (London: Longmans, Green and Co., 1866), vol. VIII, p. 261.
89 Geoghegan, *Liberator*, p. 188.
90 Quoted in C. Kinealy, 'The Liberator: Daniel O'Connell and anti-slavery', *History Today*, 57:12 (2007), 51–7.
91 C. Gavan Duffy, *Young Ireland* (Dublin, London and New York: Cassell, Petter, Galpin, 1880), p. 657.
92 Ibid., p. 205.
93 D. O'Connell, *Daniel O'Connell upon American slavery, with other Irish testimonies* (New York: American Anti-Slavery Society, 1860), p. 40.

Charles Lenox Remond claimed that he learnt what true abolitionism was from listening to O'Connell; he praised his 'soul-stirring eloquence and burning sarcasm'.[94] Frederick Douglass too was inspired by stories of O'Connell from childhood; he came to Ireland specially to hear him in action, and took pride in being anointed 'the black O'Connell' of the United States.

Some of that reputation was lost during the squabbles of 1844–7 with the Young Irelanders. On his death, the *Spectator* compared him to Moses, Mohammed and Napoleon, but complained that he had squandered his power after winning emancipation, and by always aiming for some future achievement that never came.[95] Charles Greville concurred; he described O'Connell as 'one of the most remarkable men who ever existed', a man who, like Napoleon, had risen 'from the humblest situation to the height of empire', but regretted that his reputation was tarnished by infighting, as a result of which he had become 'morally and politically defunct'.[96] In France the Comte de Montalembert was more positive; he hailed O'Connell as the man who had 'reigned without ever having spilled one drop of blood and without encouraging one drop of blood or violent act'.[97]

As many of these assessments suggest, O'Connell was divisive in life and he remained so after death. John Henry Newman claimed his 'unspeakable aversion to the policy and acts of Mr. O'Connell' turned him off becoming a Roman Catholic. The revolutionary generation of 1916 detested O'Connell because he retreated from confrontation at Clontarf in 1843 and for shirking the biggest tests.[98] But Éamon de Valera came to recognise that his greatness was justified because of the way he had raised a people who were degraded and defeated, and gave them confidence in themselves. He suggested that O'Connell convinced his followers that 'those who pretended they were superior were not superior in any way except that they had superior forces'. While O'Connell's legacy in Ireland continues to be debated, outside of Ireland he is remembered as the champion of liberty, and for leading a new kind of political movement. When Barack Obama, the forty-fourth president of the United States, visited Ireland in May 2011, he singled out O'Connell uniquely for

94 Charles Lenox Remond to Charles B. Ray, 30 June 1840 in C. Peter Ripley (ed.), *The Black Abolitionist papers*, vol. I: *The British Isles, 1830–1865* (Chapel Hill: University of North Carolina Press, 1985), p. 73.
95 P. Bew, *Ireland: the politics of enmity, 1789–2006* (Oxford: Oxford University Press, 2007), p. 215.
96 Geoghegan, *Liberator*, p. 235.
97 Quoted in G.F. Grogan, *The noblest agitator: Daniel O'Connell and the German Catholic movement 1830–50* (Dublin: Veritas, 1991), p. 14.
98 *The Irish Times*, 21 Aug. 1967.

special mention. Within Ireland, O'Connell's name is still invoked by causes relating to civil rights. During the marriage equality referendum campaign in 2015, O'Connell was quoted by a leading minister (and future Taoiseach) in a major Dáil speech, and suggested as a reference point.[99]

O'Connell remains as elusive in death as he was in life: enigmatic, divisive, overpowering, individualistic, energetic and aggressive. By making himself the hero in his own narrative about Irish political progress, and ruthlessly dismissing and destroying any critics, he became impossible to assess objectively. He was a transformative political figure who wrecked as much as he created, but who forged, fostered and left behind an ideal of a democratic way of pursuing political progress that endures because it did not involve violence. Thus, for some, his reputation has become stronger not despite but rather because of other methods being used to achieve independence.

99 Daniel McDonnell, 'Health Minister Varadkar cites Daniel O'Connell in powerful speech on same sex marriage referendum', *The Irish Independent*, online edition, 10 March 2015.

5

Popular Politics, 1815–1845

MAURA CRONIN

Introduction

Did you know who you were going to vote for?
Yes, I was going to vote for Lord Bantry's friend.
That was all you knew about the matter?
It was indeed.
You did not know whether [he] was a Conservative or a Liberal?
I heard he was a Conservative.
[What] did you admire him for?
For [being one of] Lord Bantry's friends.[1]

This evidence was given before a select committee by Dennis Sullivan of
Berehaven, a supporter of the conservative candidates in the Cork County
election of 1841. Travelling with other voters to the poll in Cork city, he was
waylaid at Upton near Bandon, badly beaten, and prevented by his injuries
from completing the journey to cast his vote. Sullivan's noncommittal testimony before the bemused select committee raises several questions about
the nature of popular politics in the age of O'Connell – questions about the
level of popular politicisation, the concerns and loyalties of voters, and the
intersection between the elite and common people.

The term 'the people' was elastic. In the cities it described those below
the merchant and manufacturer – retailers of different degrees of prosperity,
skilled artisans and unskilled labourers. Paralleling this hierarchy in smaller
towns and in the countryside were the clergy, who were considered (to a
greater or lesser degree depending on denomination) the 'natural' leaders of
society; they were followed by graziers and strong farmers, and beneath these
were those referred to as the *cosmhuintir* – smallholders, cottiers and labourers,

---

1 *Petition ... and evidence taken before the Select Committee on the Cork County Election*, H.C.
1842 (271), p. 63.

and the nameless poor.[2] Popular politics in the pre-Famine decades, therefore, must be taken as meaning different things in different places and different groups. At its most visible, it refers to involvement by the Catholic majority (along with a minority of Protestants and Dissenters) in successive and some-times overlapping campaigns to weaken Protestant Ascendancy – campaigns for parliamentary, municipal and other reforms. But 'popular politics' must not be associated exclusively with the Catholic-inspired agitation: it also involved the Protestant minority in *counter*-campaigns to preserve the status quo, move-ments that (though denominationally exclusive) were as socially representative as those seeking change. And there were other complications: the social vari-ety of those involved on both sides of the pro- and anti-reform divide meant that denominational distinctions were sometimes blurred by urban–rural ten-sions. Within loyalism, the political outlook of the loyal Protestant farmer was quite different from that of his artisan counterpart in the city, while on the reform side disgruntled city retailers, side-lined in the race for office following municipal reform in 1840, directed their ire at liberal merchants and manufac-turers who made it onto the corporation.[3] Finally there is the matter of how to label the opposing sides in this struggle for political dominance: those who supported change are here referred to collectively as O'Connellites (though this masks the tensions within their ranks), while those opposing reform are described interchangeably as Tories, conservatives or loyalists (again decep-tively cohesive terms, but at least echoing contemporary terminology).

As Dennis Sullivan's experience at Upton shows, mass political involve-ment brought its own problems, and the attempted political neutralising of plebeian trouble-makers by disenfranchising rural forty shilling freeholders in 1829 proved ineffective for several reasons. First, it was impossible to estab-lish a uniformly 'respectable' vote, especially in boroughs where a multiplic-ity of voting qualifications still prevailed and a wide range of lane dwellers and impecunious traders continued to vote side-by-side with the wealthy and upwardly mobile – their wildly different attitudes making for a volatile political atmosphere.[4] Secondly, political engagement was not dependent on

---

2 Though the term *cosmhuintir* (literally 'people at the bottom' or inferiors) is generally used in relation to the lower levels of O'Connellite society, the present chapter will apply it to both sides of the political divide.

3 I. D'Alton, *Cork Protestant society and politics in Cork 1812–1844* (Cork: Cork University Press, 1980), pp. 202–5; M. Murphy, 'Municipal reform and the repeal movement in Cork, 1833–1844', *Journal of the Cork Historical and Archaeological Society*, 81 (1976), 11–12.

4 B. Walker (ed.), *Parliamentary election results in Ireland, 1801–1922* (Dublin: Royal Irish Academy, 1978), pp. xii–xiii; *First report from the Select Committee on Fictitious Votes, Ireland*, H.C. 1837 (308), pp. 195–6, evidence of William Smith. Forty shilling freeholders, though

enfranchisement: disruptive spectator participation in the growing number of contested parliamentary elections continued up to and well beyond the Great Famine, suggesting that politics was an all-consuming passion among 'the people'.[5] There is no doubt that distinct senses of popular political identity had solidified by the 1820s, bolstered by political speeches, imagery and the verses on broadsides and in cheap songbooks.[6] Within loyalism, the amalgam of Protestantism, Irishness and Britishness that shaped its outlook from the late eighteenth century spread through all classes, accelerated by the fear of Catholic emancipation. On the O'Connellite side there were several forms of popular political identity, predating but sharpened by the expectation of emancipation. The rural *cosmhuintir*'s ethnic-religious world-view was that of *Gael* versus *Gall*; the Ribbon societies (combining agrarianism, sectarianism, racketeering and proto-nationalism) undertook to be 'true to Ireland'; while, in the cities, there emerged a distinctly anti-English economic nationalism which blamed post-war economic depression on the Union: 'No people have ever been so cruelly treated as we have been … British tyranny [demands] taxes without trade.'[7]

Popular Political Commitment

But how acute was political awareness in reality among non-voters and the enfranchised? The commitment required to vote with the minority, be it O'Connellite or loyalist, suggests a firm attachment to political principles among country voters who were obliged to travel long distances to polling

disenfranchised in the rural areas following the 1829 Emancipation Act, still remained as voters in the boroughs.

5 In the sixty-six parliamentary constituencies on the island, the number of contested elections increased from fourteen in 1818 to twenty-seven in 1847, with the greatest number of contests (forty-five and forty respectively) in 1832 and 1837: Walker, *Parliamentary election results*, pp. 26–86.

6 G.D. Zimmermann, *Songs of Irish rebellion: political street ballads and rebel songs 1780–1900* (Dublin: Allan Figgis, 1967), pp. 23–4.

7 A. Blackstock, *Loyalism in Ireland, 1789–1829* (Woodbridge: The Boydell Press, 2007), pp. 120–1; F. Lane, *In search of Thomas Sheehan: radical politics in Cork 1824–1836* (Dublin: Irish Academic Press, 2001), pp. 50–1; M. Cronin, *Country, class or craft: the politicisation of the skilled artisan in nineteenth-century Cork* (Cork: Cork University Press, 1994), pp. 38–9; N. Ó Ciosáin, *Print and popular culture in Ireland, 1750–1850* (Basingstoke: Macmillan, 1997), pp. 104–6, 194–7; *Cork Mercantile Chronicle*, 13 June 1832; T. Garvin, 'Defenders, Ribbonmen and others: underground political networks in pre-Famine Ireland', *Past and Present*, 96 (1982), 146, 153; M.R. Beames, 'The Ribbon societies: lower-class nationalism in pre-Famine Ireland', *Past and Present*, 97 (1982), 138–40; J. Kelly, 'An outward looking community? Ribbonism and popular mobilisation in Co. Leitrim 1836–46', PhD thesis, Mary Immaculate College, University of Limerick, 2005, p. 41.

booths in county towns.[8] Conservatives from the northernmost parts of County Tipperary risked being ambushed by O'Connellite crowds on their 150 mile trek to the polling booths at Clonmel, while, as Dennis Sullivan's experience shows, the 90 mile combined sea and land journey to the Cork polls from the west of the county could be equally hazardous.[9] The greatest danger was at a journey's end: the attack on Sullivan occurred just 10 miles from Cork, while Graigue, where Queen's County conservatives voting in the 1835 Carlow county election ran a gauntlet of 'individuals of the lowest class', was less than fifteen minutes from the polling booths.[10] It is not surprising therefore that the less politically committed dodged registration or fled the polls to avoid the pressure of competing authority figures, neighbours and majority opinion.[11]

Yet, as Sullivan's exchange with the parliamentary select committee suggests, political commitment on the part of voters and non-voters on both sides of the political divide was determined by more than reverence for the Protestant constitution or a consuming desire for the repeal of the Union. Sullivan seems to have shrugged off party politics as irrelevant, and this well over a decade after the emergence of mass democracy under O'Connell. Or perhaps his decision to vote Tory – made at the request of his landlord's agent – was a reluctant submission to superior strength, much like the County Carlow farmers who voted O'Connellite in 1835 in response to the crowd and priestly pressure.[12] Or was he simply guided by a healthy sense of economic self-interest? Or were his loyalties determined by pre-existing patronage networks – he first registered as a voter in 1817 – rather than by any new-fangled views of democracy?

Leaders and Followers

The description in 1848 of Irish popular political feeling as innately 'ultra-democratic' was hardly an accurate description of the leader–follower patterns

---

8 Cronin, *Country, class or craft*, p. 147.
9 *Select Committee on the Cork County Election 1841*, pp. 61–3; T.G. McGrath, 'Interdenominational relations in pre-Famine Tipperary' in W. Nolan and T.G. McGrath (eds.), *Tipperary: history and society* (Dublin: Geography Publications, 1985), pp. 278–9.
10 Chief Secretary's Office Registered Papers, Private Index, 1836/203/1/9, 13: Correspondence between Dublin Castle and various officials in Carlow, 6 July 1835, National Archives of Ireland (henceforth NAI).
11 F. O'Ferrall, *Catholic emancipation: Daniel O'Connell and the birth of Irish democracy 1820–30* (Dublin: Gill and Macmillan, 1985), pp. 119, 128–9.
12 Outrage Reports, Carlow, 1835, 7/135, 7 Jan. 1835, 13/107, 6 Feb. 1835; *Carlow Sentinel*, 4 July 1835; Rent due by tenants who voted for O'Connell, Bruen papers, MS 29,778 (6), National Library of Ireland (henceforth NLI).

that were manifest during the preceding three decades.[13] All popular political movements from the 1820s onwards were, to a greater or lesser extent, leader-centred – rooted in established structures of deference, landed, commercial or clerical.[14] In loyal Ireland, the cultivation of top-down leader–follower relationships built on the patriarchal rural hierarchies that the estate system sustained: 'magnates of large fortune' like Lords Roden and Abercorn figured prominently in the Ulster anti-repeal campaigns of the 1830s, while in Munster magistrates and petty gentry in County Tipperary gave the lead in rallying local Protestants.[15] Moreover, popular acceptance of such leadership crossed denominational and political divides, as evident in the acceptance in 1841 by the Berehaven voters (Catholic and Protestant) of the political guidance of Lord Bantry, while aristocrats like Edmund Burke Roche in County Cork and Lord Ffrench in County Galway were popular O'Connellite leaders.[16] Similar patron–client relationships underlay the interaction between the populace and middle-class leaders. In the larger urban centres, for instance, the collection of the O'Connell Tribute and Repeal Rent was coordinated by pro-O'Connell employers, large and small, while house landlords (sometimes of relatively humble social status) were most effective in galvanising their enfranchised tenants at election time. On both sides, retailers and newspaper men, emerging figures of influence in towns throughout the country, figured within leadership circles: in loyal Ulster they were particularly active in the network of Brunswick Clubs in the late 1820s, and in Munster in the 1830s they took a prominent part in the anti-tithe campaign.[17] The pattern of clerical political leadership was more varied. Catholic priests, unimpeded by dependence on the landed classes, treated the voters 'at their disposal' with as proprietorial an attitude as any landlord.[18] Protestant clergymen's involvement in popular politics showed

13 M.J. Barry to W. Smith O'Brien 22 Feb. 1848, MS 442, letter 2374, Smith O'Brien papers, NLI.

14 K. Whelan, 'An underground gentry? Catholic middlemen in eighteenth century Ireland' in K. Whelan, *The Tree of Liberty: radicalism, Catholicism and the construction of Irish identity, 1760–1830* (Cork: Cork University Press, 1996), pp. 8–9; D.P. Reid, 'The Tithe War in Ireland, 1830–1838', PhD thesis, Trinity College Dublin, 2012, p. 296.

15 D. Curran, *The Protestant community in Ulster, 1825–45: a society in transition* (Dublin: Four Courts Press, 2014), p. 72; J. Bardon, *History of Ulster* (Belfast: Blackstaff Press, 1992), pp. 254, 257; McGrath, 'Interdenominational relations', p. 265.

16 *Southern Reporter*, 6 June 1841; M. Cronin, ' "Of one mind": O'Connellite crowds in the 1830s and 1840s' in P. Jupp and E. Magennis (eds.), *Crowds in Ireland c. 1720–1920* (Basingstoke: Macmillan, 2000), p. 151.

17 Curran, *Protestant community*, p. 149; Blackstock, *Loyalism in Ireland*, pp. 236–8; Cronin, *Country, class or craft*, p. 145; Reid, 'Tithe War', p. 298.

18 McGrath, 'Interdenominational relations', p. 262; S.J. Connolly, *Priests and people in pre-Famine Ireland 1780–1845* (Dublin: Gill and Macmillan, 1982), pp. 229–36, 256–60;

sharp regional variations: the Church of Ireland clergy, especially in the cities, took something of a back seat, but evangelical clerics like the Revd Henry Cooke in Ulster and Revd Tresham Gregg in Dublin yielded nothing to their Catholic equivalents in their capacity to rally their humbler followers at a time when political Protestantism was challenged by demands for liberal reforms.[19]

Despite their leader-centric nature, popular movements of all political hues were accepting of manipulation from above, since the pervading 'ideology of status' was predicated not only on the followers' deference, but also on the leaders' capacity to fulfil public expectations.[20] Leaders that failed to meet expectations risked losing control over the popular forces that they or others expected to harness. Even the priests, despite their undoubted success as a 'sacred gendarmerie', were unable to curb either faction fighting or agrarian violence, and their authority in the political sphere lasted only as long as they led where 'the people' wished to follow. The Catholic priest – and there were several – who opposed the anti-tithe agitation in the 1830s risked, as one observer put it, 'forfeiting [his people's] confidence and being stripped of his influence'.[21] Loyalist leaders experienced similar challenges, the swaggering sectarianism of plebeian Orangemen proving as difficult to control as the inter- and intra-denominational divisions within loyal society.[22] Even the Order's Grand Master, the Duke of Cumberland, was unable to prevent Ulster Orangemen from defying the ban on parades in the tense summer of 1832, while the Dublin Protestant Operative Society's stand against any sign of liberalism within Protestant leadership caused serious headaches for local conservative leaders in the 1840s.[23]

Authority, affability, lineage (real or imagined) and familiarity with the concerns of the followers all were vital antidotes to the leader's loss of control. The loyalist Lord Roden's populist approach on his O'Connell-like progress

Freeholder, 12 Feb. 1831; *Cork Mercantile Chronicle*, 14 Dec. 1832; *Cork Constitution*, 14 Nov. 1840; *Southern Reporter*, 18 Oct. 1836; *Cork Examiner*, 25 June 1847.

19 Curran, *Protestant community*, pp. 71, 131, 140; C. Hirst, 'Politics, sectarianism and the working class in nineteenth-century Belfast' in F. Lane and D. Ó Drisceoil (eds.), *Politics and the Irish working class, 1830–1945* (Basingstoke: Palgrave Macmillan, 2005), p. 67; F. Wright, *Two lands on one soil: Ulster politics before Home Rule* (Dublin: Gill and Macmillan, 1996), p. 48; K.T. Hoppen, *Elections, politics and society in Ireland 1832–1885* (Oxford: Clarendon Press, 1984), pp. 311–12.

20 Ó Cíosáin, *Print and popular culture*, pp. 170–4.

21 Connolly, *Priests and people*, pp. 229–36, 256–60; Outrage Reports, Cork, 1834: 6/376, NAI.

22 Curran, *Protestant community*, pp. 60–1, 90; McGrath, 'Interdenominational relations', p. 261; D.W. Miller, *Queen's rebels: Ulster loyalism in historical perspective* (Dublin: UCD Press, 2007), pp. 47, 60.

23 Curran, *Protestant community*, p. 77; Hoppen, *Elections, politics and society*, pp. 312–13.

through Ireland in the later 1830s was particularly effective in this regard.[24] But O'Connell was the master: he could bully his followers unmercifully (expelling a whole village in east County Galway from the Repeal Association in 1843 when it flouted his rules against violence) while at the same time wooing mass audiences in Tipperary (or Tralee, or Waterford, or Drogheda) as the bravest men (with 'physical force, muscular strength and bravery') and the most beautiful and virtuous women in Ireland.[25] He did nothing to discourage popular belief in his descent from pre-plantation nobility – 'an planda fíor den' Ghael-fhuil' (the true plant of Irish blood) – and his speeches always touched on the issues most relevant to his hearers.[26] Other popular leaders showed an equal awareness of the reciprocal nature of popular leadership, exploiting the popular penchant for a gentleman on the one hand while, on the other, exercising a 'common touch' to play the crowd more effectively. Feargus O'Connor, described by the ballad singers as being 'descended from nobles', used (one unkind but astute observer noted) his 'brazen audacity, fine sonorous voice, and copious supply of words ... to put himself on a level with all the cobblers and tinkers in the crowd'.[27] His contemporary, the substantial landed proprietor Dominick Ronayne, became the darling of the east Cork peasantry through his prominent part in the campaign against market tolls and his imprisonment for involvement in the anti-tithe campaign.[28]

For those leaders lower down the social ladder – from the 'classes above the masses' – it was even more important to reflect the concerns of their followers. Sam Grey, publican and local Orange District Master in County Monaghan, was established firmly in the pantheon of popular loyalist heroes when he mobilised the Orangemen and yeomen of Ballybay to repulse violently John Lawless' promotion of the Catholic Association in Ulster. The admittedly less flamboyant Master of the Clonmel Orange Lodge, an ironmonger's clerk, played just as vital a role in rallying local conservative opinion as did the small shopkeepers who led the Orange Lodges in the towns of County Cork.[29] It was a similar awareness of the concerns of the humble that gave Catholic priests their clout as political leaders in rural areas, though less so in the cities, where professionals, merchants and retailers held the reins. Older priests

---

24 Hoppen, *Elections, politics and society*, p. 309.
25 *Tipperary Constitution*, 25, 30 May 1843; Cronin, ' "Of one mind" ', pp. 153–4, 163.
26 Ó Cíosáin, *Print and popular culture*, p. 179.
27 D.O. Madden, *Ireland and its rulers*, 3 vols. (London: Newby, 1843–4), vol. I, pp. 179–81.
28 'A new song in praise of Mr Dominic P. Ronayne, or the Downfall of the Tories of Youghal', Outrage Reports, 1835, 6/95, NAI.
29 Blackstock, *Loyalism in Ireland*, p. 233; Hoppen, *Elections, politics and society*, p. 322; D'Alton, *Protestant society*, p. 206.

like Martin Doyle of Graigue and Matt Horgan of Blarney were, like the Anglican clergy and middle-rank gentry in loyalist Ulster, among the most influential 'intermediaries' between the local community and the state.[30] Less hot-headed than some of the younger priests, they balanced pastoral concern and social control, restraining election crowds, curbing factions, providing (or withholding) character references in court, and – vitally important for their position as 'people's priests' – speaking out on behalf of the poor, even to the extent of challenging O'Connell on his opposition to a poor law.[31]

Conservatives and O'Connellites each portrayed their rivals – 'tory deceivers', 'peasant priests', 'big beggarman', 'demagogues' – as manipulating gullible people for political ends.[32] Such accusations were not without foundation. Remote political issues like the franchise or the repeal or maintenance of the Union were artificially made to appear universally relevant. The modest membership subscriptions instituted by the Catholic and Repeal Associations and the Brunswick Clubs encouraged even the humblest to feel part of a great movement; the attractive rituals of the Orange Order allowed high and low to mix (even briefly) on equal terms; and a reassuring though totally illusory sense of one-ness was fostered by mass meetings – the ultimate social control mechanism in tense times.[33] Aptly described by Owens in the O'Connellite context as 'dramatic performances', such meetings' historic pageantry, music, fairground atmosphere and carefully honed speeches heightened political excitement but did so in a manner that sublimated disruptive popular tendencies and encouraged the emotional genie back into the bottle once the business of the day was over.[34] The ruse worked. Within loyalism, the network of Brunswick Clubs active in the late 1820s and early 1830s fostered controlled political enthusiasm in the ranks beneath the elite by attracting a multiplicity of Protestant political and social opinions and in the long run, helping to 'shift loyalism ... towards modern political activism'.[35] On the other side, the Catholic Association's message, spread through mass

30 *Pilot*, 26 April 1837; Blackstock, *Loyalism in Ireland*, pp. 269–70.
31 Outrage Reports, Carlow, 1835, 9/107, 8 Feb. 1835, NAI; *Cork Mercantile Chronicle*, 5 Dec. 1842; *Borris Chapels: Copies of Correspondence between the Roman Catholic Priests of Borris, Robert Doyne, Esq and the Lord Lieutenant of Ireland, on the alleged attendance of the Military at the Roman Catholic Chapels*: H.C. 1835 (198), xlv, 493, pp. 3–6; O'Ferrall, *Catholic emancipation*, p. 128; *Pilot*, 16 Sept. 1836.
32 *Freeman's Journal*, 8 Sept. 1840, 17 April 1841; *Cork Constitution*, 14 Oct. 1843; *The Repealer Repulsed: a correct Narrative of the Rise and Progress of the Repeal Invasion of Ulster* (Belfast: McComb, 1841), pp. 38, 152.
33 Curran, *Protestant community*, pp. 54, 133; Blackstock, *Loyalism in Ireland*, p. 235.
34 Owens, 'Nationalism without words', p. 243.
35 Curran, *Protestant community*, pp. 71–2, 77; Blackstock, *Loyalism in Ireland*, pp. 242–3.

meetings in 1828, achieved the unachievable – the (temporary) suspension of faction fighting in Munster, and the fusion of the tamed factions into the mainstream political campaign.[36] In the following decade, the anti-tithe movement channelled popular violence into parliamentary petitions and replaced the potentially disruptive anti-tithe 'hurling meetings' organised 'from below' with stage-managed gatherings where the country crowd could be induced to cheer as lustily for the unquestionably irrelevant cause of corporate reform as for the abolition of tithe or repeal of the Union.[37]

Past and Place

When the anti-O'Connellite Daniel Owen Madden wryly described rural repealers as 'an impulsive, hearty, romantic race, who rejoiced in dreaming of the glories of Old Ireland', he identified an essential element shaping popular political identity – the remembered (or misremembered) past.[38] For all, from O'Connell to agrarian redressers operating well outside the law, the backward glance shaped political perspectives. Displaced smallholders looked to the 'restoration' of land lost to newcomers, whether consolidating farmers in the present or the recent past, or the beneficiaries of seventeenth-century plantation:

> The wind a long time has blown contrary
> Which made poor Erin's sons so sad,
> To see their property in the hands of strangers
> And no releasement to be had.[39]

In the party political sphere, O'Connellite and loyalist popular attitudes were driven alike by competing pasts that were recalled or re-invented to keep the fires of animosity burning: Protestants, high and low, recalled the massacres of 1641, the triumph of William of Orange over James II in 1690 and the atrocities perpetrated against Wexford Protestants in 1798.[40] Catholics shared the 1798 memories – but from the vantage point of the defeated. To these they added vague but powerful stories of dispossession such as those motivating

---

36 McGrath, 'Interdenominational relations', pp. 261–4.
37 J.S. Donnelly, *Captain Rock: the Irish agrarian rebellion of 1821–1824* (Cork: Collins Press, 2009), pp. 70–3; Reid, 'Tithe War', pp. 31–40; Outrage Reports, 1836, 6/37, 87, NAI.
38 Madden, *Ireland and its rulers*, vol. I, p. 194.
39 'Sleeve na Mon', ballad sung in Bray, County Wicklow, 16 Aug. 1842: Chief Secretary's Office Private Index, 1832, A/1581, NAI.
40 Blackstock, *Loyalism in Ireland*, p. 266; Zimmermann, *Songs of Irish rebellion*, pp. 300–5.

the Molly Maguire agrarian movement in pre-Famine County Leitrim or the mutterings of Catholic hill farmers in Ulster recorded in semi-fictional form by William Carlton:

> Look at them, Jimmy *agrá* – only look at the black thieves! How warm an' wealthy they sit there in our ould possessions, an' here we must toil till our fingers are worn to the stumps.[41]

Equally powerful was the recall of minor triumphs in the more recent past, especially local incidents appertaining to anti-tithe agitation – the battle of Keimaneigh in west Cork where locals routed the local Yeomanry in 1822, and still sing of the event two centuries later, or the 1831 confrontation at Carrickshock in south County Kilkenny, where a crowd stoned to death a process server and thirteen police.[42]

Annual commemorations, especially those of Williamite triumphs at the Boyne and Aughrim, ensured the regular reinforcement of loyalist memories. In the later eighteenth century such commemorations were forsaken by the state as too divisive, but by the 1820s, and more particularly following emancipation, they became an essential feature of the popular loyalism which strutted defiantly in the annual Orange parades of 1 and 12 July – even (or perhaps especially) following the prohibition of such parades by the Party Processions Act of 1832.[43] Lower-order Catholics did not possess an equivalent commemorative calendar – largely because there was little to celebrate from a litany of defeats and dispossession – but the feast of Mary's assumption on 15 August (a religious rather than a political occasion) provided the opportunity to exhibit identity through provocative behaviour. Each group thumbed its nose at the other by marching on contested routes, disturbing the other's divine services with party tunes, and engaging in brawls that escalated on occasion into inter-community battles such as took place at Garvagh in 1813 or Dolly's Brae in 1849.[44] Nor was an anniversary required in order to rouse hostilities: the relevance of past to present was stressed in partisan (and not necessarily inaccurate) histories and memoirs published in pamphlet and book

---

41 Wright, *Two lands*, p. 84, quoting from William Carleton's 'The Black Pig's Dyke'.
42 J. Kelly, 'Local memory and manipulation of the past in Leitrim' in T. Dooley (ed.), *Ireland's polemical past: views of Irish history in honour of R.V. Comerford* (Dublin: UCD Press, 2010), pp. 40–1; Zimmermann, *Songs of Irish rebellion*, pp. 62–4; B. Brennan, *Máire Bhuí Ní Laoire: a poet of her people* (Cork: Collins Press, 2000), pp. 2–8; G. Owens, 'The Carrickshock incident: social memory and an Irish cause célèbre', *Social and Cultural History*, 1:1 (2004), 36–64.
43 Curran, *Protestant community*, p. 51.
44 Bardon, *History of Ulster*, pp. 242–3, 302–4.

form from the late eighteenth century onwards. Reprints of both Crouch's Protestant *History of Ireland* and Reilly's Catholic *Impartial history* perpetuated into the pre-Famine decades a seventeenth-century world-view of the elemental struggle between Protestantism and Popery, while Richard Musgrave's *Memoirs of the different rebellions in Ireland*, presenting the 1798 rebellion as religiously motivated, informed a whole series of ultra-Protestant writings.[45] Nor was the perpetuation of memories dependent on the printed word. The past was evoked in a particularly powerful way through oft-told tales, musical airs, even place names. Henry Cooke's 1840 evocation of Scullabogue (the site of a rebel atrocity during the Wexford rebellion in 1798) reminded his listeners at Belfast in 1841 (as it had Musgrave's readers four decades earlier) of the perfidy of Catholics; the place names Carrickshock or Gortroe (the east Cork village where a 'tithe massacre' occurred in 1834) similarly served as a rallying cry against the police and local Protestants well into the 1840s.[46] Just as 'to sing is to pray twice', the transmission of contested memories through song was doubly provocative. The antiquarian Thomas Crofton Croker concluded in the 1820s that the 'verses current among the Irish [are the means] by which their feelings of revenge or love are kept up for generations'.[47] Such a musical recall of events long past played a major part in reflecting, if not in shaping, both O'Connellite and loyalist popular attitudes, and it was sufficient to whistle a party tune (the 'Protestant Boys' by the Orange party, the 'Shan Van Vocht' by the O'Connellites) to rouse the other to anger. Where place name, memory and evocative air came together the potential for provocation of the enemy was even greater. Just as the name Slievenamon (*Sliabh na mBan*), a hill in south Tipperary and the scene of a rebel defeat in 1798, was invoked in popular O'Connellite songs in the 1830s both as a reminder of past disasters and a promise of future revenge, songs like the 'Sprigs of Kilrea', 'Battle of Garvagh', 'Aughalee Heroes', 'Lurgan Town' and 'Dolly's Brae' reminded rebels and papists that croppies would be compelled to 'lie down'.[48]

This essentially local emphasis also coloured leader–follower relations. At the election of 1841, Dennis Sullivan's main loyalty (if we can deconstruct his rather guarded evidence) was to his land agent and the local lord of the soil,

45 Ó Cíosáin, *Print and popular culture*, pp. 103–7; J. Kelly, *Sir Richard Musgrave, 1746–1818* (Dublin: Four Courts Press, 2009), pp. 91–105, 227–32.
46 Wright, *Two lands*, p. 50; *Cork Constitution*, 29 Jan. 1835; *Waterford Mail*, 6 July 1833; *Southern Reporter*, 5, 29 June 1841.
47 T. Crofton Croker Correspondence. Add. MS 20,096, f. 41, BL.
48 M. Cronin, '"By memory inspired": the past in popular song, 1798–1900' in Dooley (ed.), *Ireland's polemical past*, pp. 40–1; Zimmermann, *Songs of Irish rebellion*, pp. 315–18.

Lord Bantry, and the group of Tory voters with whom he travelled to Cork seem to have belonged to one or more local kin-groups – Sullivans, Kellys and Murphys.[49] Moreover, local leaders who were part of the 'supporting cast to O'Connell' or Roden could displace great men in the popular pantheon.[50] In the early 1830s among the *cosmhuintir* of south Leinster and north Munster, the renowned 'JKL' (James Doyle, bishop of Kildare and Leighlin) often out-shone O'Connell; the 'great Dan' was rivalled in County Cork by the colour-ful Feargus O'Connor; while less prominent figures involved (depending on region and context) in the anti-tithe or anti-emancipation movements exer-cised considerable sway at local level; popular admiration increased accord-ing as they either defied the law like Sam Grey, or fell foul of it like Dominic Ronayne.[51]

Such localism simultaneously reflected broader issues – truly a matter of 'the republic in the village'.[52] Just as the larger constitutional conflict was waged between the upholders and opponents of Protestant Ascendancy, popular politics was at heart concerned with enforcing the claim of both in-groups and out-groups (religious, ethnic and political) to control the local area. This place-centredness was particularly powerful in cementing popular loyalist unity in Ulster, where Orangemen encountering Catholics in sectar-ian brawls saw themselves as defending not only crown, religion and constitu-tion but also the honour of their townland or village – 'you can stop counting beads, and quit midnight parades, and put on Orange shoes when you come to Kilrea'.[53] Ordered events displayed the same localism and machismo. The contingents of Orange 'boys' or O'Connellites marching to meeting grounds, bands playing, banners aloft, and headed by the local gentry (or priest) whose presence solidified that sense of political, denominational and local identity that characterised popular politics, were identifying clearly with their village or parish.[54] Newspaper reports made clear the combined sense of

49 *Select Committee on the Cork County Election 1842*, evidence of Patrick Sullivan, pp. 20–1.
50 G. Ó Tuathaigh, 'Gaelic Ireland, popular politics and Daniel O'Connell', *Journal of the Galway Archaeological and Historical Society*, 34 (1974), 24.
51 Reid, 'Tithe War', p. 294; D. Read and E. Glasgow, *Feargus O'Connor, Irishman and Chartist* (London: Edward Arnold, 1961), pp. 20–9.
52 M. Agulhon, *The republic in the village* (Cambridge: Cambridge University Press, 1982); K. Whelan, 'The republic in the village' in Whelan, *The Tree of Liberty*, pp. 59–98.
53 J.H. McIlfatrick, *Sprigs around the Pump Town: Orangeism in the Kilrea district* (Derry: McIlfatrick, 1995).
54 D. Curran, 'The great Protestant meeting of Dungannon, 1834' in W. Sheehan and M. Cronin (eds.), *Riotous assemblies: rebels, riots and revolts in Ireland* (Cork: Mercier Press, 2011), pp. 102–3; Wright, *Two lands*, p. 55; A. Blackstock, 'Tommy Downshire's Boys: popular protest, social change and political manipulation in mid-Ulster 1829–1847', *Past and Present*, 196 (2007), 136–7; *Tralee Mercury*, 3 Aug. 1832.

masculinity, religious affiliation and local pride that went with such occasions: a 'great anti-tithe meeting at the foot of Mount Gabriel', county Cork, in July 1832 saw the convergence of 'the men of Muintervara ... the tithe-payers of Ballydehob ... the men of Crookhaven' – all headed by their priests – with the mounted strong farmers of the area ('a fine bold yeomanry') as a vanguard.[55] This sense of local pride was equally evident in the urban context, where the Irish manufacture campaigns of the 1830s and 1840s were inherently local, defending Cork (or Waterford, or Dublin, or Galway) from the 'importation' of goods from other towns.[56] Such hard-nosed localism was politically adaptable: Henry Cooke's rousing speech *against* repeal in Belfast in 1841 was equally and unashamedly localist – and well received for that very reason:

> Look at the town of Belfast ... the masted grove within our harbour (cheers) – our mighty warehouses teaming with the wealth of every climate (cheers) – our giant manufactories lifting themselves on every side (cheers).[57]

The Sectarian Divide

For Cooke's audience, local pride was inseparable from religious superiority, and religious sectarianism provided them – and O'Connellites – with a terminology useful in defining their own identity and in increasing awareness of the otherness of the 'enemy'.[58] Loyalist speeches, newspaper squibs, polemical pamphlets, songs and evangelical sermons all harped on the inbuilt capacity of Catholics' for political treachery – summed up in 1831 by one Cork city Tory's outrage at the decision of the local Catholic conservative MP to jump ship to become a repealer: 'I trusted in a Papist and was deceived, and I was only served as every Protestant ought to be who puts his trust in Popery.'[59] Among the O'Connellite *cosmhuintir*, broadside ballads churned out by jobbing printers, like the Irish-language poetry transmitted orally in the rural areas, focused popular animosity on 'Luther's cruel reformation' and the modern representatives of 'sliocht Calvin' (Calvin's breed).[60] By 1843 such compositions were proving a headache for law-abiding citizens, law enforcers

---

55 *Cork Mercantile Chronicle*, 18 July 1832; Owens, 'Nationalism without words', p. 243.
56 Cronin, '"Of one mind"', p. 147.
57 *The Repealer Repulsed*, p. 110.
58 Whelan, *The Tree of Liberty*, p. 140.
59 *Cork Constitution*, 5 May 1831.
60 'A new song composed by Kate na Greeny', Madden Ballads, v, 307, Cambridge University Library; Ó Tuathaigh, 'Gaelic Ireland', p. 33; Zimmermann, *Songs of Irish rebellion*, pp. 44–5.

and Dublin Castle: as an outraged Tory newspaper in County Louth saw it, 'in proportion to the degree of rancour exhibited in them is their value enhanced and their reception secured'. Ballad singers sometimes made more money in one day from the sale of such songs than a farm labourer could earn in a week.[61]

What made these sectarian songs so popular? Attributing their appeal to theology seems simplistic given the widespread laxity in religious observance among all creeds, especially in rural areas.[62] Yet, the basic theological differences between religions were well known to the lower classes in pre-Famine Ireland. Northern Protestants and Presbyterians acquainted with the preaching of Henry Cooke and other evangelicals were certainly *au fait* with theological matters at some basic level, and Munster's Catholic *cosmhuintir* was also aware of the religious tenets separating them from the denominational and political 'other'. Devout works like Tadhg Gaelach Ó Suilleabháin's *Pious miscellany* were widely disseminated, while broadside ballads listing the beliefs 'betrayed' by converts from Catholicism to Protestantism – belief in the Eucharist, veneration of Mary and of the saints – were bought with avidity.[63] Receptivity to the sentiments of these songs was increased by the 'Second Reformation' of the late 1820s onwards.[64] It was a short step from the theological to the political: Protestants, particularly those whose charitable work among the local poor was now being set at naught, painted the Catholic masses as dangerous fools obedient to 'the nod of a priest'; Catholics, discounting many Protestant clergymen's objections to evangelicals, tarred all Protestants as economic exploiters: 'Táimíd féin agus ár máithreacha romhainn le trí chéad bliain nach beag faoi chrúba na ministrí. Is le hallas ár mailí do shaothraíomar an deachú doibh chun iad a choimead i ngradam.'[65]

Religion and status were closely interlinked: sectarian tensions at popular level simply reflected in microcosm what was happening higher up – the

---

61 *Drogheda Conservative*, 28 Oct. 1843; M. Murphy, 'The ballad singer and the role of the seditious ballad in nineteenth-century Ireland: Dublin Castle's view', *Ulster Folklife*, 25 (1979), 90.

62 Connolly, *Priests and people*, pp. 83–97; Bardon, *History of Ulster*, pp. 251–2.

63 'David O'Brien's advice to Denis O'Sullivan', Outrage Papers, 1836, Cork, 6/240, NAI; Ó Cíosáin, *Print and popular culture*, pp. 118–31.

64 D. Bowen, *Souperism: myth or reality: a study in Souperism* (Cork: Mercier Press, 1970), pp. 126–50.

65 Outrage Reports, 1844, 6/15769, NAI; *Cork Constitution*, 18 Dec. 1832; Ó Tuathaigh, 'Gaelic Ireland', p. 32. 'We and our mothers before us have, for almost three hundred years, been oppressed by the ministers. With the sweat of our brows we have toiled to give them the tithe to keep them in luxury.'

displacement of Protestant Ascendancy by assertive political Catholicism.[66] Fears of what 'the other' might do – fears increased by the power of rumour and memories of past atrocities – underlay popular political attitudes on all sides. In 1832, a panic spread among Protestant smallholders and weavers that they were about to be massacred by Catholics. While neither side feared locals of 'the other' creed, all were convinced that an outside force (papist or Orange, depending on the area) could compel locals to join in the conspiracy and murder their neighbours in their beds.[67] The equalising reforms beginning with emancipation in 1829 widened the sectarian gap and increased popular fears on both sides. This was because they touched on the vital matter of status – the status of individuals and, more importantly, of communities in a local context. Though most of these reforms had as little immediate impact on lower-class loyalists as they had on their O'Connellite equivalents, the reform of the police and the magistracy in the mid-1830s, precisely because the impact was local, made lower-class Protestants intensely conscious of their position as a plebeian elite.[68] As paid magistrates appointed by government gradually supplanted the local justices of the peace (usually, though not always, Protestant), as cocky liberal attorneys took up the case of Catholic petty offenders, and as it became more difficult to summon exclusively Protestant juries in party-political cases, loyal Protestants felt vulnerable and betrayed.[69] Their resentment was sharpened by daily encounters with O'Connellite street singers (outside loyal Ulster where the Orange singers were equally belligerent) who bawled out 'horrible compositions' repeating the Pastorini prophecies that Protestantism was to be extirpated and Protestants humiliated by being reduced to the condition of 'ag treabhadh is a' fuirseadh is a' briseadh na tíre' (ploughing, harrowing and breaking up the sod).[70] For the humbler classes of loyalists, the threat of lowered status was most seriously felt in those areas where there was an even demographic balance between creeds, as in the Ulster counties of Tyrone, Armagh, Londonderry/Derry and Fermanagh, or where their minority share of the

66 J. Hill, 'The meaning of "Protestant Ascendancy", 1787–1840' in *Ireland after the Union: proceedings of the second joint meeting of the Royal Irish Academy and the British Academy, London 1986* (Oxford: Oxford University Press, 1989), pp. 1–22.

67 Wright, *Two lands*, p. 97.

68 V. Crossman, *Local government in nineteenth-century Ireland* (Belfast: Institute of Irish Studies, 1994), pp. 2–4.

69 *Kilkenny Journal*, 30 June 1843; *Western Argus and Galway Commercial Chronicle*, 14 March 1832; *Waterford Weekly Chronicle*, 26 Aug. 1832; Curran, *Protestant community*, pp. 88–9.

70 Outrage Reports, 1836, 6/240, NAI; 'Eastig a Deena, a new song composed by Kate na Greeny', Madden Ballads, Cambridge University Library, v, 307; *Cork Constitution*, 14 Feb. 1833.

population was, as in Carlow, Wexford or Queen's County, large enough to generate assertiveness but too small to profit thereby.[71] Relative harmony, maintained while the minority group kept a low profile, could be shattered once heads were raised above the parapet as a result of a fracas at a fair, in the excitement of an election, or on the Orange Twelfth.[72] When Monaghan Orangemen, returning from the Newbliss parade in July 1835, aggravated two local Catholics by singing 'Croppies lie down', the response of one of those taunted – 'there wasn't an Orange puppy on the road that he wouldn't kick' – led to a not unfamiliar party riot.[73]

But sectarian animosity was neither universal nor continuous. Generally speaking, the further up the social scale on either side, the less intense the sectarian rancour. In the cities, sectarian divisions were frequently bridged by common civic patriotism, philanthropy and cultural activity.[74] In the countryside, established church clergy or intensely loyal Protestant landlords could be on friendly terms with local Catholic priests even during the tense twenties and thirties, while some Brunswick Clubs, established to protect the Protestant constitution, admitted respectable Catholics to membership.[75] Further down in society, inflammatory O'Connellite ballads took care to distinguish between the 'liberal Protestant' and the 'Orange tory', and to bless or curse them accordingly.[76] In the daily round, neighbours of different religions from Ulster to west Cork co-existed in a relative if uneasy harmony, the evidence suggesting that even explosions of party violence were fuelled as much by over-consumption of alcohol as by sectarian hatreds. The exchange of insults at Newbliss in July 1835 led to a major disturbance largely because the parties involved were, one witness explained euphemistically, 'highly elated, and in great spirits'.[77] Shared economic grievance, moreover, could transcend religious difference, as when in the 1830s Protestant and Catholic artisans in

71 Curran, *Protestant community*, p. 109.

72 The population of Queen's County in the 1830s was estimated at four Catholics to one Protestant: S.R. Gibbons, 'Captain Rock in the Queen's County' in P. Lane and W. Nolan (eds.), *Laois: history and society* (Dublin: Geography Publications, 1999), p. 491.

73 Curran, *Protestant community*, pp. 114, 116; D'Alton, *Protestant society*, pp. 104–5; *Cork Mercantile Chronicle*, 30 Oct. 1835.

74 *First report of the commissioners appointed to enquire into the municipal corporations in Ireland*, H.C. 1835, xvii, p. 57; *Cork Mercantile Chronicle*, 9, 18 July 1832; *Cork Constitution*, 25 April, 2 May 1839; D'Alton, *Protestant society*, p. 35.

75 Wright, *Two lands*, p. 88; Blackstock, *Loyalism in Ireland*, p. 236; D'Alton, *Protestant society*, pp. 73, 138.

76 'A Speedy Repeal', Outrage Reports, 1843, County Clare, 5/13187; County Cork, 6/17767; 27/12177, 13337; County Waterford, 29/13599, NAI.

77 Curran, *Protestant community*, pp. 114, 116; D'Alton, *Protestant society*, pp. 104–5; *Cork Mercantile Chronicle*, 30 Oct. 1835.

Cork city came together in the (ultimately unsuccessful) Irish manufacture campaign, or Tommy Downshire's Boys along the Down–Armagh border, equally burdened by tithe and rent, 'burnt the symbols of their respective parties, and raised a common and tri-coloured flag'.[78]

Economic Issues

Once the veneer of denominational identity was removed, popular politics was revealed as essentially economic in its motivation. Most local leaders, irrespective of political complexion, were driven, as one sardonic observer put it, by the quest for 'the fruits of public employ [*sic*] ... offices for public prosecution, clerkships of the peace and of the Crown'.[79] Economics (but in this case survival rather than advancement) were equally important for those at the bottom of the social ladder, as is clear from the County Carlow Whitefoot leader's complaint in 1833 that 'Emancipation has done nothing for us. Mr O'Connell and the rich Catholics go to parliament. We are starving to death just the same.'[80] In the cities too, popular politics focused on shillings and pence. On the loyalist side, Henry Cooke's rallying of Belfast in 1841 linked the Union with 'the genius of Industry ... shower[ing] down his blessings on the fair and smiling lands of [Ulster]'.[81] On the opposite side, trade unions in Dublin, Cork and Waterford in the 1830s became stalwart supporters of repeal as the means to alleviate the economic hardship caused by post-war contraction in local manufacture.[82] Even in the 'repeal year' of 1843, political questions were frequently side-lined by economic issues: south Mayo was far less agitated by repeal than by opposition to priests' dues, while along the Munster coast from Waterford to the Shannon estuary the capacity of new 'scotch weirs' to destroy the earning power of local salmon fishermen

---

78 Lane, *In search of Thomas Sheehan*, pp. 50–3; Blackstock, 'Tommy Downshire's Boys', pp. 142–3.

79 Joseph Hayes to O'Connell, 14 Aug. 1840, O'Connell Correspondence, vi, letter 2755, NLI; Cronin, '"Of one mind"', pp. 150–3; M. Hanrahan, 'The Tithe War in County Kilkenny 1830–1834' in W. Nolan and K. Whelan (eds.), *Kilkenny: history and society* (Dublin: Geography Publications, 1990), p. 490; Reid, 'Tithe War', pp. 297–9.

80 Whelan, *The Tree of Liberty*, p. 54.

81 *The Repealer Repulsed*, p. 110.

82 Cronin, *Country, class or craft*, pp. 129–31; R. O'Higgins, 'Irish trade unions and politics, 1830–50', *Historical Journal*, 4 (1961), 212; J. Boyle, *The Irish labour movement in the nineteenth century* (Washington, DC: Catholic University of America Press, 1988), pp. 40–2; F. D'Arcy, 'The artisans of Dublin and Daniel O'Connell 1830–1847: an unquiet liaison', *Irish Historical Studies*, 17 (1970), 222–5; *Southern Reporter*, 2 Dec. 1830; *Cork Mercantile Chronicle*, 19 March 1832.

was a major source of popular grievance.[83] A similar prioritisation of the economic over the political is identifiable in 1848 in the unlikely location of the Orange village of Garvagh in County Londonderry/Derry where, in response to the burden of rent arrears, poor rates and county cess, the local Twelfth celebrations featured a banner proclaiming (and the sequence is significant) 'Tenant Right and No Surrender'. The experience of shared economic grievance could, as the Tommy Downshire protests show, briefly bridge the party divide; a witness before a select committee in 1835 explained that 'the lower class of Orangemen [were] as much opposed to tithe as' were the Quakers.[84]

Tithe, more than any other issue, epitomised the economic focus of popular politics and, at the same time, the hazards involved in building the political on economic foundations. In 1836 a Clonmel witness before the Select Committee on Fictitious Votes summed up the concerns of the 'popular side' as 'cheap government and the abolition of tithes' – an objective fundamentally similar to that driving the violent agrarian Rockite movement in counties Cork and Limerick in the early 1820s.[85] By the mid-thirties the now largely constitutional anti-tithe campaign derived its energy from its continuing 'appeal to [the peasantry's] purses', enforced by the economic concerns of graziers and large farmers who had been caught in the net when pasture land, previously exempt, was made liable to tithe in 1823.[86] This fusion of the economic interests of leaders and followers, which gave the anti-tithe agitation cohesion, was epitomised by the combined presence at meetings of priests along with Protestant and Catholic gentlemen, acting as platform speakers and as marshals of contingents marching in from the surrounding areas.[87] In the case of other issues of popular concern, however, the social gap separating leaders and followers within both O'Connellism and loyalism meant that the highlighting of economic grievance had the capacity to be divisive, which it was essential to avoid in movements that aimed to 'think as one man and see as one man'.[88] O'Connell was personally wary of the tithe issue, considering it a diversion from the issue of repeal, but he added it to his political agenda, on the advice of local leaders like that Cork priest who advised that

---

83 Outrage Reports, 1843: Mayo, 21/665, 1735, 1787, 5997; Waterford, 29/9661, NAI.
84 Wright, *Two lands*, p. 128; Curran, *Protestant community*, p. 110; Blackstock, 'Tommy Downshire's Boys', pp. 142–3.
85 *Select Committee on Fictitious Votes, Ireland,* H.C. 1837 (308), p. 334; Donnelly, *Captain Rock*, pp. 122–7, 172–4.
86 *Cork Constitution,* 6 Dec. 1834; Reid, 'Tithe War', pp. 25–8.
87 *Cork Mercantile Chronicle,* 18 July 1832.
88 *Tipperary Constitution,* 30 May 1843.

'on the question of tithes, [the peasantry] would go with him against their landlord, but he was afraid he could not drag them out on Repeal so readily'.[89] Other economic issues relevant to the non-elite were side-lined by the movers and shakers of popular politics, precisely because of their divisive potential. O'Connell actively combatted the spread of Chartist ideas in Cork and Dublin, and came down heavily on trade union activity in the same places, condemning not just violent attacks by the trades on persons and property, but any manifestation of 'ingratitude' to employers.[90] Similarly, the Orange Order in Ulster quickly stamped on the not inconsiderable anti-tithe feeling among its members lest such an agitation would serve as an entrée to repeal of the Union.[91]

The reluctance to link politics with potentially disruptive economic issues was especially obvious in relation to agrarian issues. Since the mid-eighteenth century access to land had become the most pressing matter for the *cosmhuintir* whose livelihood was threatened by a fast-rising population pressure and the accelerated commercialisation of agriculture.[92] In one sense, land-related issues hardly intersected at all with politics: the reaction against change (whether the mass disturbances that finally tailed off in the early 1820s or the ongoing clandestine but violent activities of small local gangs) was *apolitical* in its thrust. It bypassed the law and the machinery of state to seek redress for grievances through direct action at local level – by targeting the persons and property of those who initiated or benefited from economic change at the expense of the broader *cosmhuintir*.[93] Even within the sphere of constitutional and electoral activity, what was interpreted as political was largely economic in motivation. When Tory landlords were (sometimes accurately) accused of evicting tenants who had voted O'Connellite, the election simply provided the opportunity to replace improvident or stroppy tenants with more substantial Protestant farmers willing to promote agricultural improvement. Similarly, popular attacks on farmers (Catholic or Protestant) who voted Tory were motivated less by political animosity than by the understandable resentment of the weak, landless and voteless of the enfranchised and successful.[94]

---

89 *Cork Constitution*, 11 Dec. 1832.
90 *Cork Constitution*, 18 Nov. 1834, 6 June 1837; F.A. D'Arcy, 'The trade unions of Dublin and the attempted revival of the guilds: an episode in mid-nineteenth century Irish labour history', *Journal of the Royal Society of Antiquaries of Ireland*, 101 (1971), 114–15; Boyle, *Irish labour movement*, pp. 41–3; O'Higgins, 'Irish trade unions and politics', p. 212.
91 Curran, *Protestant community*, p. 110.
92 S. Clark, *Social origins of the Irish Land War* (Princeton: Princeton University Press, 1979), pp. 362–3.
93 M. Cronin, *Agrarian protest in Ireland 1750–1960* (Dundalk: Irish Economic and Social History Society, 2012), pp. 12–18.
94 Outrage Reports, Carlow, 1835, 7/135, 7 Jan. 1835, NAI; Wright, *Two lands*, p. 95.

Yet, at another level, land-related grievance was eminently political. Agrarian protest was rooted in socio-political attitudes that were frequently couched in the language of 'moral economy'. The inherent right of all to the means of survival (in this case land) was emphasised and – even more pointedly – the obligation of those *with* to help those *without*. Still greater challenges to social and political structures were presented by the widespread popular contention that political change (either revolutionary or constitutional) would automatically remove the burdens pressing on the rural poor: 'Tá an téarma ag teacht gan mhoill go mbeidh Éire arís ag Gaeil gan cíos.'[95] It is unclear if these proto-political sentiments reflected deeply held beliefs or were simply a rhetorical device that was usefully deployed in threatening notices and broadside ballads. Contemporaries took them seriously, however, particularly in the context of violent agrarian protest, whether mass or small-scale. From the early nineteenth century onwards the state was forced to engage directly in the containment of Irish agrarian unrest, combining strong-arm and reformist tactics. In the half-century before the Famine, thirty-five pieces of coercive legislation were enacted to deal with Irish land-related unrest, while from the early 1820s onwards the building of road networks accelerated to facilitate military access to disturbed areas. Parallel with this, a series of parliamentary commissions of inquiry into the nature of Irish landholding and agrarian unrest culminated in the Devon Commission which in 1845 exhorted the landlord 'to advance the improvement of the district in which he lives, and the increasing comfort of the people around him'.[96] Other challenges to agrarian relationships were posed by individual administrators, most especially the under-secretary, Thomas Drummond, whose reminder to Tipperary magistrates that property had 'its duties as well as its rights' ran counter to the received view among the social and economic hierarchy.[97]

But land was a political hot potato. Just as Drummond made himself as many enemies as friends through his pronouncement, leaders of popular political movements found themselves walking a knife edge when agrarian questions cut across political issues like repeal of the Union and parliamentary reform. At the height of the Great Famine, a small and unrepresentative

---

95 'The time is fast approaching when the Irish will have rent-free land.' 'An Irish elegy by James O'Brien', Madden Ballads, v, 392, Cambridge University Library.

96 P. and G. Ford, *Select list of British Parliamentary Papers 1833–1899* (Shannon: Irish University Press, 1969), pp. 120–7; *Report from Her Majesty's Commissioners of Inquiry into the state of the law and practise in respect to the occupation of land in Ireland*, H.C. 1845 [605], p. 44.

97 L. O'Dea, 'Thomas Drummond', *Dublin Historical Record*, 24:4 (1971), 120–1.

number of politically active middle-class individuals linked agrarian and political change: Irish Confederates James Fintan Lalor and John Mitchel, who had
broken from O'Connell's Repeal Association in the mid-1840s, urged the transfer of land from landlord to tenant by whatever means were available.[98] If such
beliefs were far too 'levelling and ultra-democratic' for most Confederates,
constitutional political leaders were even more cautious, dependent simultaneously as they were on the support of the *cosmhuintir* and of 'natural' leaders
of their own class in the locality. While O'Connellite leaders' speeches, electoral and otherwise, occasionally targeted evicting landlords (but only those
of the opposing party), the reality was that most of those on the platforms
at public meetings were themselves landholders – priests, clergymen, professionals and strong farmers – and almost all representative of the social groups
increasingly targeted by agrarian protestors from the late 1820s onwards.[99]
No platform orations from such leaders could convince the land-hungry in
their audience to refrain from violence against those who displaced them. No
exhortations to obey the law (the keystone of O'Connell's campaigns) could
shake the 'alternative law' of agrarian gangs – the 'law which is paramount
to [the law of the land], it is the law of nature, which the very worm when
trodden upon acknowledges' – and agrarian protest movements proliferated
as a result.[100] It was not surprising that in pre-Famine political movements
held together by 'identity defined against an enemy', the divisive land question (though it was never so termed until later in the century) received little
attention.[101]

Conclusion

Popular politics in the pre-Famine decades possessed some of the qualities
of a hologram, its essence changing according to when and where it manifested itself. It centred, as did Irish politics at an elite level, on the future of
Protestant Ascendancy, and whether the political structures should preserve
or shake off the shape imposed on them in the late seventeenth century.
But, involving as it did the harnessing of a mass following (or, rather, two

---

98 S.R. Knowlton, 'The quarrel between Gavan Duffy and John Mitchel: implications for
    Ireland', *Albion*, 21:4 (1989), 588–90; M.J. Barry (Cork) to W. Smith O'Brien, 22 Feb.
    1848, Smith O'Brien Papers, MS 442, letter 2374, NLI.
99 M. Beames, *Peasants and power: the Whiteboy movements and their control in pre-Famine
    Ireland* (Brighton: Harvester Press, 1983), pp. 220–5.
100 Whelan, 'The republic in the village', p. 93.
101 Blackstock, *Loyalism in Ireland*, p. 264.

mass followings), popular politics was both complicated and unpredictable. As a consequence, astute leaders on both sides of the political divide had to convince their incompletely politicised followers that remote constitutional issues were of relevance – by playing the sectarian card, by fostering an illusory sense of one-ness between elite and 'people', and by implying that the economic or social position of the humble was dependent on political alignment with the great. But political manipulation was not as easy as it appeared: it required an admixture of authority and empathy on the part of those who led, which was a difficult balance to strike when dealing with a volatile and internally divided mass following. Nor were 'the people' as malleable as their leaders desired. Their politics was coloured by their selective views of the past, by the adulation of individual leaders, and by a narrowly local focus. This notwithstanding, politics 'from below' could be as clear-sighted as from the top, for though the *cosmhuintir* on each side of the political divide was frequently obsessed with status, sectarian animosity, pride of place and (less frequently) a vague and unrealistic proto-nationalism, popular politics was at heart based on pragmatic economic considerations.

PART II

*

ECONOMY AND DEMOGRAPHY

6

Society and Economy in the Long Eighteenth Century

DAVID DICKSON

Peace and Poverty

Northern Europe experienced its coldest winter in half a millennium in the first weeks of 1740. The cold was most intense far from the ocean, but its social impact was greatest on the Atlantic periphery. The so-called Little Ice Age had brought several harsh seasons to Ireland in the previous hundred years, notably in the icy winter of 1683/4. But the havoc wreaked by the frost was unparalleled, principally because it ushered in a whole series of extreme weather events – drought, floods, snows, storms – running from New Year 1740 to late summer 1741. The initial collapse in air temperatures caused immediate shock and hardship, but the huge population losses in town and countryside and the massive livestock mortality came months later and in several waves, the perverse domino effect working its unpredictable course. The 'Great Frost Famine' was in many respects the defining event in the social history of eighteenth-century Ireland.[1]

The vulnerability of Ireland to disaster on this scale had not been foretold, although there had been an intense public debate over the previous twenty years on all that appeared wrong in the Irish economy – the shortage of coin, the imbalance of foreign trade, the recurrence of food shortages, an irresponsible landowning class that directed its spending onto imported luxuries or, worse still, lived it up outside the country, spending nothing at home. Jonathan Swift's tirades in the 1720s were literary masterpieces that had immediate public impact, but they were not typical of the hundred-plus tracts and essays that calmly debated the ills of Irish society. The most reflective writings were those

---

1 M. Drake, 'The Irish demographic crisis of 1740–41' in T.W. Moody (ed.), *Historical Studies VI* (London: Routledge and Kegan Paul, 1968), pp. 101–24; J.D. Post, *Food shortage, climatic variability and epidemic disease in preindustrial Europe: the mortality peak of the early 1740s* (Ithaca, NY: Cornell University Press, 1985); D. Dickson, *Arctic Ireland: the extraordinary story of the great frost and forgotten famine of 1740–41* (Belfast: White Row Press, 1997).

by Lord Molesworth (1723), David Bindon (1729), Thomas Prior (1729), Arthur Dobbs (1729–31), George Berkeley (1735–7) and Samuel Madden (1738), all of which were grounded on empirical observation and in most cases on personal knowledge of the world outside Ireland.[2] These writers were genuinely concerned with the self-evident poverty of the kingdom, whether measured against the more promising state of things in the Restoration era or the far more resilient economy across the Irish Sea. They were nearly all Protestant gentry or clergy, yet were critical of their own governing caste. Molesworth, the earliest writer in the genre, warned of the links between recurring food shortages and woefully short-sighted estate management, and he suggested that it was imperative for the Irish parliament to intervene and regulate agriculture as it was already doing in the linen industry. A particularly severe run of grain harvest failures in 1727–9 served to reinforce the call for new policies, and the most substantial outcome was Arthur Dobb's two-volume treatise *An essay on the trade of Ireland* (1729–31), which blended a profusion of statistical data with pleas for the establishment of a public association dedicated to the material improvement of the kingdom. Out of such ideas emerged the Dublin Society in 1731, its mission to transform Irish farming and eliminate food and other raw-material imports that could be produced at home, with the collateral benefits of outlawing begging and improving the money supply. It took some decades before it became 'the principal agent of economic development in the country', but the Society's identity was shaped in the 1730s and reflected the exclusively Protestant but relatively apolitical environment of those years.[3]

Most writers shared a fervent belief in the possibility of Irish economic 'improvement' (i.e. development) and regarded enlightened governance and public policy as critical. This belief had old roots. It can be found in the reflections of Nicolas Plunkett, an exiled Jacobite writing in the 1690s,[4] and in the most original if oblique commentator of the 1730s, George Berkeley, whose *Querist* (initially appearing anonymously) challenged conventional assumptions as to the primacy of foreign trade as generator of wealth and

---

2 R. Molesworth, *Some Considerations for the promoting of Agriculture and employing the Poor* (Dublin, 1723); D. Bindon, *A Scheme for supplying Industrious Men with money . . .* (Dublin, 1729); T. Prior, *A List of the Absentees of Ireland . . .* (Dublin, 1729); A. Dobbs, *An Essay on the Trade and Improvement of Ireland*, 2 vols. (Dublin, 1729–31); [G. Berkeley], *The Querist . . .* (Dublin, 1735–7); S. Madden, *Reflections and Resolutions proper for the gentlemen of Ireland* (Dublin, 1738).

3 J. Livesey, 'The Dublin Society in eighteenth-century Irish political thought', *Historical Journal*, 47:3 (2004), 631–2, 639–40.

4 P. Kelly, 'The improvement of Ireland', *Analecta Hibernica*, 35 (1992), 45–84.

public welfare. He posited a fundamental alternative for Ireland: an economy protected by high import tariffs and reconstructed on paper credit, with the money supply controlled by a national bank; the poor would be enticed into the market economy through an abundance of paper money, which would create in them an appetite (i.e. a demand) for non-subsistence goods, while tariffs would deter the rich from their propensity to consume imported fashions and luxuries. But he did not elaborate on his radical if patrician prescription for the moral reordering of the economy.[5]

Shortly afterwards, Berkeley became a prime witness at his east Cork home of the unfolding of the 'Great Frost' Famine. He distinguished himself as one of the most active donors and organisers of private charity and, in its final months, predicted that the human losses would not be repaired in fifty years. Such a judgment was grounded on the modest rate of population growth since the 1690s and on the prevailing pessimism as to the country's economic prospects. But just how feeble had the economy been in the previous fifty years? If viewed through the pamphlet literature, the picture seems dark indeed: in Molesworth's words, 'we have always either a glut or a dearth, very often there are not ten days distance between the extremity of the one and the other'; in Madden's words, 'so many of the best families and hands in the nation live abroad, and are gone or going off to *America*, that in a little time, betwixt madness and despair, we shall be left desolate'.[6]

Customs and inland excise receipts, which exist from the 1680s, point to a pattern of short-term oscillation rather than any clear long-term trend. Sharp economic fluctuations were of course a feature of all pre-industrial economies involved in international exchange; severe weather at home or abroad, external market changes, the outbreak of international war, or a specifically financial crisis could precipitate a sharp reversal in economic activity and fill the debtors' prisons. Ireland was repeatedly buffeted by all of these in the late seventeenth and early eighteenth centuries, although it was not until the collapse of Burton's Bank in Dublin in 1733 that a local financial crisis precipitated recession.[7] But Irish customs returns indicate some strong growth spurts in foreign trade and, by implication, in economic activity, notably at the turn of

---

5 P. Kelly, 'The politics of political economy in mid-eighteenth-century Ireland' in S.J. Connolly (ed.), *Political ideas in eighteenth-century Ireland* (Dublin: Four Courts Press, 2000), pp. 105–29.

6 Dobbs, *Essay on trade*, p. 2; Madden, *Reflections*, p. 4.

7 L.M. Cullen, 'Problems and sources for the study of Irish economic fluctuations', *Irish Economic and Social History*, 41 (2014), 1–13; P. Walsh, *The South Sea Bubble and Ireland: money, banking and investment, 1690–1721* (Woodbridge: The Boydell Press, 2014).

the century and in the years after the peace of Utrecht (1713). And although the momentum was on each occasion soon lost, each expansionary phase left a legacy. The stuttering character of the economy in the 1720s and 1730s, as suggested by customs and revenue data, masks considerable structural changes occurring under the surface. For instance, there was strong population growth in Dublin and Cork cities, where the number of households may have risen by as much as a third between 1720 and 1740 in each case; local coal imports, perhaps a more sensitive barometer of urban activity, rose by even more; the first brick terrace appeared in Dublin in the 1720s (with Henrietta Street's great mansions), and the marshes to the east and west of the old walled city of Cork were vigorously colonised in these decades.[8] It was also the time when the first Palladian mansions were built in the Irish countryside, many by the German architect Richard Castle (ranging from Castle Hume in County Fermanagh and Hazelwood in County Sligo to Summerhill and Belvedere in County Meath and Powerscourt in County Wicklow), and others by native architects (notably John Rothery, who was responsible for Doneraile Court in County Cork and Mount Ievers in County Clare). These great unfortified buildings with their superb interiors and ambitious landscaping plans reflected increasing rent-rolls and an abundance of cheap labour for construction work. The greatest of them all, Castletown House, was Speaker William Conolly's vast palace west of Dublin: it was a quite deliberate statement in stone, commissioned by the elderly and childless parliamentarian who had grown immensely rich, first as a dealer in lands, later as an office-holder. The statement was directed at his peers – to imitate and build – and perhaps at his betters too.[9]

Conolly's estates were principally in counties Derry and Donegal, on the edge of the new 'linen economy'. He had been one of the most consistent champions of linen, and during his lifetime the manufacture had grown from a small exotic activity in the Lagan valley to become the staple of the north, helped on its way by duty-free access to the English market and by Irish parliamentary oversight and subvention. Its momentum continued even through the depressed 1730s, and in the 1740s cloth exports averaged around 7.5 million yards per annum, roughly three times the volume in the 1710s; linen yarn exports nearly doubled over the same period.[10] The story in

---

8 Compare John Carty's Cork city map of 1726 and Charles Smith's in 1750: www.corkpastandpresent.ie/mapsimages/corkinoldmaps.

9 P. Walsh, *The making of the Irish Protestant Ascendancy: the life of William Conolly, 1662–1729* (Woodbridge: The Boydell Press, 2010); Chapter 16, pp. 401–12.

10 The National Archives (henceforward TNA), CUST/15; C. Gill, *The rise of the Irish Linen industry* (Cambridge: Cambridge University Press, 1925), pp. 339–42.

the south was, by contrast, the ascendancy of livestock farming, supplying continental and Atlantic markets. Wool's seventeenth-century pre-eminence was now declining, and it was beef and butter, salted and barrelled for distant markets, that became the great export earners, expanding from small beginnings in the Restoration era. The beef trade, which included the valuable by-products of hides and tallow, was generally the more valuable sector, and in the 1720s and 1730s it enjoyed rapid growth and strong prices, helped by robust French colonial demand (see Table 1). Cork was the processing and financial centre for both beef and butter, but it never held a monopoly. Wholesale commercial activity in general was now being concentrated on the large port cities at the expense of secondary centres, a trend first evident in the Restoration years. In 1699 Dublin and Cork between them handled 65.1 per cent of the recorded tonnage of shipping entering Irish ports from overseas and they generated 65.5 per cent of national customs revenue that year. These shares strengthened in the decades that followed, averaging over 70 per cent and in some years over 75 per cent of national revenue, with the smaller port towns along the east, south and south-west coasts being the most severely eclipsed.[11]

Revenue statistics also give some clue as to population change, although it is always hazardous to construct population estimates based on the fragmentary

Table 1. *Irish beef and butter exports, 1683–1780 p.a.*

	Beef	Beef index	Butter	Butter index
	(barrels)	(1701–119/20 = 100)	(cwt)	(1701–19/20 = 100)
1683–6	74,187.5	79.2	132,495	88.9
1701–20	93,657.8	100	149,071.7	100
1720–40	142,665.7	152.3	157,052.7	105.4
1740–60	150,584.7	160.8	201,375	135.1
1760–80	192,872.9	205.9	263,174.6	176.5
1781–1800	138,671.6	148.1	288,927.5	193.8

Note: 1683–6 are calendar years; 1700–7 data are for years ending 25 December, and thereafter for years ending 25 March (British Library, Add. MS 4759; TNA/CUST 15; Thomas Newenham, *A view of natural, political and commercial circumstances of Ireland* (London, 1809), appendix 9).

11 TNA, cust/15; D. Dickson, 'The place of Dublin in the eighteenth-century Irish economy' in T.M. Devine and D. Dickson (eds.), *Ireland and Scotland 1600–1850: parallels and contrasts in economic and social development* (Edinburgh: John Donald, 1983), pp. 178–82; www.duanaire.ie/trade.

hearth tax evidence: thus the apparently dramatic 76 per cent rise in hearth tax between 1693 and 1702 may principally reflect post-war rural resettlement and administrative normalisation. However a modest growth of hearth tax in the first quarter of the new century probably reflected the reality of limited population growth at national level, and the subsequent dip the likelihood of negligible change or decline between the mid-1720s and mid-1740s. But a more interesting story lies beneath national aggregates: hearth tax data at county level hint at contrasting local fortunes: growth in the first quarter of the century in south Leinster and the coastal counties of Munster and its absence from the richer inland counties (Tipperary, Limerick, Roscommon) and the north-west. Higher-growth counties were areas where cereal production and mixed farming survived, whereas in the inland counties of low or negative growth big tenant-graziers expanded their herds of store cattle or sheep and outbid small tenant-farmers, consequently thinning the rural population on the good limestone soils. It was precisely this phenomenon that sparked the only social protest of the era, a campaign to 'hough' (i.e. to maim) the sheep and cattle of 'strangers': it began west of the town of Galway in 1711 and for a brief period swept across seven western counties from Clare to Fermanagh. What is perhaps remarkable is the absence of any other signs of resistance in districts affected by the spread of ranching. Perhaps it was because the graziers involved were rarely strangers.[12]

Another new element in these unsettled times was emigration. The effects of short-distance movement to the burgeoning ports is implied in the sluggish growth of hearth tax in counties around Dublin, but what was new was a substantial overseas migration, notably the departure of up to 10,000 migrants from Ulster to the American colonies during the 1720s. These were predominantly Presbyterian, male and of rural background. The migration continued at fluctuating levels throughout the century (although it was always restricted in wartime), and the numbers of women and non-Ulster migrants gradually rose.[13] The precise mix of religious, economic and family

12 D. Dickson, C. Ó Gráda and S. Daultrey, 'Hearth tax, household size and Irish population change 1672–1821', *Proceedings of the Royal Irish Academy*, 82c (1982), 157–60, 180–1; S.J. Connolly, 'The Houghers: agrarian protest in early eighteenth-century Connacht' in C.H.E. Philpin (ed.), *Nationalism and popular protest in Ireland* (Cambridge: Cambridge University Press, 1987), pp. 139–62.

13 K.A. Miller, A. Schrier, B.D. Boling and D.N. Doyle (eds.), *Irish immigrants in the Land of Canaan: letters and memoirs from colonial and revolutionary America, 1675–1815* (Oxford: Oxford University Press, 2003). For a conservative estimate of the scale of this migration: A. Fogelman, 'Migrations to the thirteen British North American colonies, 1700–1775: new estimates', *Journal of Interdisciplinary History*, 22:4 (1992), 705–6.

pressures that triggered the first exodus is still debated. At first sight it is surprising that Ulster, diversifying economically and developing by far the strongest rural industry in the country, should have been the main source of indentured labourers seeking a better life far away. But it is less surprising when seen at the sub-regional level: it was not the heartland of the fine linen industry in east Ulster but rather the less favoured districts in counties Derry, Tyrone and east Donegal that contributed most to the first waves of migrants (areas of heavy Scottish immigration a generation or two previously). And a key ingredient that kept passage costs low and ventures profitable was the growth of a return trade in flaxseed from the Middle Colonies: there was comparative advantage for the vast number of petty flax producers in Ulster to harvest the flax plant for the spinning wheel before it went to seed, and to purchase American-grown seed for the next planting. Thus the flourishing trades in servants and flaxseed were entirely complementary.[14] However, few left the new weaving districts in east Ulster, areas that began to show signs of rapid population growth by the 1740s.

But the first half of the 1740s was a bitter time for town and countryside across the island. The impact of the 'Great Frost' Famine was, it is true, primarily in the southern half of the country, with the boundary line between high and low population losses running roughly from Clew Bay to Waterford Harbour. Current estimates are that the famine led to excess deaths of between 250,000 and 400,000, which means that in *relative* terms it was a greater human catastrophe than the Great Famine of the 1840s. Then, in 1744, appalling summer weather devastated the cereal harvest, particularly in the centre and north of the country, and the hay crop everywhere; the effects on food supply, public health and the rural economy in some north Connacht and west Ulster districts were indeed quite as severe as the earlier crisis across the south. Between them they constituted the worst years for the common people in a century.

Tide Rising

There was a palpable link between the Palladian mansions now peppering the landscape and the anguished patrician discourse about pervasive poverty. The link lay in the fact that economic development in the early eighteenth century, such as it was, was highly regressive socially. There were several strands

---

14 T.M. Truxes, 'Connecticut in the Irish-American flaxseed trade, 1750–1775', *Éire-Ireland*, 12:2 (1977), 34–62.

to this. Old agricultural leases negotiated in the insecure aftermath of the Jacobite War turned out to be good bargains for thousands of tenants as internal peace held and agricultural prices rose, a time when

farmers liv'd like gentlemen
E're lands were raised from five to ten,
Again from ten to three times five,
Then very few cou'd hope to thrive.[15]

As post-war contracts expired in the 1710s and 1720s, landlords insisted that new farm leases reflected higher land values. The net effect was a pronounced redistribution of agricultural income back towards the owners of land. This was also a time when beef exports were particularly strong and large-scale fatstock farming expanded; the behaviour of opportunistic graziers as they displaced smaller mixed-farming tenants became notorious, particularly in those districts in west Leinster, north Munster and east Connacht where good-quality lowland soils could be kept permanently under grass. What were in effect bullock or sheep ranches were created as grazier tenants built up portfolios of townland leases, often renting from different landlords, their attraction as tenants being that they were easier to manage than small mixed-farmers and more secure as rent-payers. Mixed farming of course survived across the country, not least near the coast and on thinner or poorly drained soils, but smallholders everywhere were affected by the abrasive effects of increased market exposure and by the oscillations of seemingly capricious prices.

What of those further down the ladder? Francis Brewster, a merchant turned land speculator, claimed in 1702 that

before the wars, the Irish had cows, even the very beggars from door to door have their cows, and potato gardens, and whilst they can have milk and potatoes, they will do little work. Now the Irish had [sic] generally lost their cattle, and that forced them to spin to get them bread.[16]

Whatever the stereotype of the lazy cottager and his potato patch, Brewster's contention that war and local upheaval had created a new rural proletariat was an over-simplification. Even before the Jacobite War, the distribution of cattle ownership had already been skewed. Sir William Petty (like Brewster, familiar mainly with Munster) suggested in the 1670s that as much

---

15 L. Whyte, 'The parting cup ...', in A. Carpenter, *Eighteenth-century Irish verse in English* (Cork: Cork University Press, 1999), p. 291.
16 F. Brewster, *New Essays on trade ...* (London, 1702), p. 96.

as 40 to 45 per cent of the population had no land to speak of and possessed little more than two or three head of cattle; he may have overstated their relative importance, but the rootless poor were already very much part of the landscape that he knew in County Kerry. Up to the 1740s all commentators assumed the existence of a vast substratum of leaseless, if not landless, poor who dwelt in single-room mud cabins, lacked all material amenities, and were usually referred to as cottiers or 'cottars'.

Such labels mislead, because they embraced a fluid amalgam of (a) small partnership or 'village' tenants, operating in groups of up to eight families, each of whom farmed from 5 to 20 hectares (excluding upland common-age), usually held a lease from a landlord or a chief tenant spanning 11 to 31 years, and paid rent in money, labour services, produce or a combination of all three; and (b) tied labourers, whose 'garden' and cow's grazing, amounting to, at most, a single hectare, was the extent of their farming, and whose tenancy was a one-year unwritten agreement with employers large and small that they paid off in labour.

The balance between these two social groups changed over time and between regions of the country. Between the 1690s and the 1740s the former were in the majority in most areas, but the latter were growing in relative importance. Distinctions were muddied by the fact that most cottier-labourers still owned a few head of cattle, while many cottier-farmers did not necessarily own all of theirs. And there was an important intermediate type, the dairyman. Since the first expansion of commercial butter-making for overseas markets in the seventeenth century, only very substantial tenants possessed the resources to respond to market opportunity and expand herd numbers, but the management of their cows was generally devolved to 'dairymen' on one-year agreements: such families undertook to mind and milk herds of up to thirty cows and to produce all the marketable butter, drawing little profit beyond the sale of a few calves, the use of up to a hectare of ground, and an ample supply of butter milk. The herd-owners or 'dairy masters' oversaw the sale of the butter and had to live with high levels of livestock mortality, made worse by their skimping on winter fodder. When extreme weather prematurely halted grass growth or decimated the supply of fodder, as happened in the savage winter of 1744/5, countless dairymen as well as independent cottier-farmers (particularly the upland smallholders rearing young stock) were literally beggared by the loss of cattle. There is a hint of this devastation in the 267,780 calfskins exported from Ireland during the following year, which was more than double the normal total.

From the mid-1740s to the 1770s a more benign scenario unfolded. The most telling evidence as to how much the Irish countryside was changing is provided by the raw travel-notes made by that champion of English agricultural enlightenment Arthur Young, most of whose Irish observations were made in 1776. Young's primary concern was to report on the agricultural practices on the hobby-farms of resident landlords and hand-picked chief tenants, but he also sought information on the state of 'the poor' and 'the cottars', specifically on whether their circumstances had changed in recent decades, what material resources they had at hand, and what they ate. Visiting almost every county, Young found that about two-thirds of his informants believed that conditions for the poor had improved since mid-century, with the most consistently positive reports coming from Ulster, the least positive from the Munster interior, and that the wages of unskilled labourers had risen nearly everywhere (although the variations reported to Young point to a decidedly imperfect labour market). An improvement in clothing was consistently mentioned, and some claimed that housing was now better and the diet more secure, 'the poor ... being freed from those scarcities which were felt before the laws for the increase of tillage'.[17]

A shift back towards mixed farming and the expansion of commercial tillage was indeed one of the big changes between the 1740s and the 1770s, although this was driven more by a long-term shift in relative prices between grain and cattle products on international markets than by the generous parliamentary subsidy on the carriage of wheat and flour to Dublin introduced in 1758, important as that was regionally. Young was surprised to find that, in contrast to his native East Anglia, tillage in an Irish context nearly always meant small-scale operations, part subsistence and part commercial. Yet, requiring little capital, cereal farming offered small tenants a ladder for social advancement as well as providing steadier employment on and off the land.

In most years Irish agriculture managed to supply most of the bread and meal consumed by humans and horses across the country, but between the 1720s and 1770s there was rarely a surplus available to export, and in the bad years there were large-volume imports of wheat and flour from England, the southern Baltic and the American colonies (notably in the late 1720s and in 1745/6). Matters changed in the 1770s when Ireland became a net grain exporter once again. Coastal districts in the south and south-east, strongholds of tillage farming, were now joined by numerous districts across the south

17 A. Young, *A Tour in Ireland: with general observations on the present state of that Kingdom*, 2 vols. (Dublin, 1780), vol. I, p. 412; vol. II, appendix, pp. 38–9.

midlands where lighter soils had heretofore favoured intense sheep produc-tion. In such districts, tenant-farmers above the cottier-farmer category now became more visible, managing farms from 20 to 100 hectares that combined both pastoral and tillage operations. The fact that many of these were the under-tenants of established leaseholders who were no longer bona fide farm-ers infuriated Young, and in his recurring critique of Irish estate practices he introduced the term 'middlemen' to shame them. He failed to recognise that it was the changing rural economy, not bad management, that was responsi-ble for turning graziers and cattlemen into petty landlords.[18]

The primary reason for the positive tone among Young's informants in the 1770s was not the tillage revival, important though that was in many dis-tricts, but the great expansion of opportunities for poorer country people to earn cash, whether in the spinning of wool (notably in the south midlands and most Munster counties), in the cultivation of flax and spinning of linen yarn (in the north midlands and the north-west), in the geographical expan-sion of the areas involved in domestic linen manufacture (now spreading far outside its east and central Ulster heartlands), and in the rearing of poultry and pigs, which was almost universal in the Irish countryside by the 1770s (and reflected in the remarkable fourfold growth of pork exports since 1750). These supplementary 'Z-goods' products were not unknown in the 1740s, but their importance was transformed over the following thirty to fifty years. None of them required access to farmland but some necessitated hard-learnt skills, and all involved the family, or at least the women and older children. The intensification of such activities brought the near-landless (or at least the menfolk) into more regular contact with the cash economy. Demand for the end product was to a great extent generated within England, and without the powerful and enduring demand coming from the other island for Irish woollen, worsted and linen yarn (for its burgeoning textile industries), linen cloth (for its domestic and colonial consumers) and pork (for ship provision), it would have been a very different story for rural Ireland.

Young left his readers in no doubt that the potato was central to the sub-sistence of 'the labouring poor', and he characterised it as a standard element in agricultural rotations and an efficient pioneer crop bringing marginal soils into productive use, an activity he associated with labourers and cottier-farm-ers, not big tenants or graziers. Occasionally he noted how much the overall cultivation of the potato had increased in recent years, not least because it

18 D. Dickson, 'Middlemen', in T. Bartlett and D.W. Hayton (eds.), *Penal era and golden age: essays in Irish history, 1690–1800* (Belfast: Ulster Historical Foundation, 1979), pp. 162–85.

had become the chief diet for the ubiquitous pig.[19] Young's characterisation of the role of the potato in the 1770s is now broadly accepted, but precisely how that ascendancy came about remains opaque. Its adoption as a garden crop had been evident generations earlier in Munster, where it was well established by the late seventeenth century as the winter food of 'the poor', but even there potatoes only became a field crop in the 1720s. The ferocity of the 'Great Frost' Famine in Munster a decade later reflected the particular importance of the potato in that province: it was the wholesale destruction of potatoes in the ground in the first days of 1740 that was the catalyst for all the horrors that followed. New practices that protected the potato against harsh frost were subsequently adopted, but it was not until the 1760s that varieties of potato that could safely be kept in the ground throughout the year became widely known; this helped to diminish the importance of oatmeal and other foodstuffs in springtime and summer diets. The ascendancy of the potato occurred more slowly in Connacht and Leinster, and later still in Ulster, where it never completely displaced oatmeal in lower-class diets. However, its agricultural value in extending cultivation into the hills and onto poorly drained lowland was an enormous boon everywhere. It was a land-intensive crop peculiarly well suited to a natural environment of temperate winters, and to a social environment where labour was cheap and marginal land abundant. Cultivated as a garden crop, the potato required only short bursts of activity in a few weeks of the working year, releasing cottier-labourers to work for around 200 days a year for the farmers who rented them land, or to go off elsewhere in search of harvest work. But as a field crop the potato was still the most demanding element in the crop rotation, and the necessary soil preparation and transport of natural fertilisers like sea-sand and seaweed added greatly to the effort involved. Cottier-farmers who persisted in this kind of potato-centred land improvement (and were fortunate in their timing) could save, expand their little herds of cattle, and rise up in the world.

The consolidation of the independent cattle-owning small farmer, owning his own ploughs, draught animals and tackle, a cart and agricultural implements, was perhaps the most important – yet almost invisible – change that took place in the second half of the century. Such families, who had some cash to spend on Sunday clothes, on dowries for the daughters and on funerals for the adult members of the household, were more than a cut above their cottier neighbours. In those parts of the country where commercial butter production was central – inland south and west Munster, the Barrow valley – the

19 Young, *Tour*, vol. I, p. 56; vol. II, p. 235, appendix, pp. 32–5.

old dairy system allowed dairymen to better themselves, initially by rearing up their calves and mingling personal stock with the rented herd and by paying for the hire of cows in cash, not butter. At the time of Young's tour, most dairying districts were still operating the old system (he noted independent herds in only two districts), but it was already in decline, and by the end of the century dairy farmers large and small – except in the remoter parts of west Munster – owned their own cattle.[20] Occasionally loans from landowners and butter dealers may have helped in the process, but for the most part small tenant-farmers raised themselves up by their own boot-straps.

Yet during this era the cottier-labourers were coming under pressure: the labour required to pay for a fixed acreage of potato-ground was rising, certainly in the last quarter of the eighteenth century, meaning that the freedom to have a head or two of cattle, a horse and some sheep, which was still common in Young's day, became progressively rarer. It is true that money wages for those in employment rose sharply in the following generation: Thomas Newenham, drawing on evidence from nineteen counties in 1809, reckoned that monetary wages had risen by two-thirds since Young's time (from 6.5 to 10.5 pennies *per diem*). However, his claim that this reflected the revival of tillage, which had 'greatly improved the conditions of the labourers', was misplaced, since in the long run the increase in cottier-labourers' rents and in their cost of living more than cancelled out these gains.[21] The weakening in *real* wages was first evident in Munster (where as it happened most of Young's pessimists as to the state of the poor were based); it was soon to be the common pattern across three provinces.

An Economy Opening

Young travelled Ireland in the first year of the American War of Independence. The essential optimism of his account is all the more striking given what was happening around him. The early 1770s were very difficult economically; land values fell after a generation of growth and the linen industry experienced an unprecedented recession; emigration to North America (now including quite large numbers of young men from Leinster and Munster) reached record levels. Then in February 1776, with a transatlantic war looming, the government placed a blanket embargo on the export of Irish salted provisions – other than

20 Ibid., vol. I, p. 79; vol. II, p. 142.
21 T. Newenham, *A view of the natural, political and commercial circumstances of Ireland* (London: Cadell and Davies, 1809), p. 231.

to Britain and the loyal colonies. This unprecedented degree of government control over foreign trade remained in place for more than three years. But how crucial was this, or indeed any, war in reshaping the economy?

Two periods of extended maritime war between 1689 and 1713 had been disastrous commercially, what with several key overseas markets closed and French privateers active around Irish coasts; some decades later, eight years of warfare in the 1740s coincided with internal harvest disasters with similar results; nevertheless naval contracting swelled the pockets of Munster traders. The economic impact of war was more clear-cut during the Seven Years War (1756–63): it was broadly positive for graziers, landowners and provisions traders, but bad for consumers. High food prices, bank failures (in 1759/60), and speculative demand for land triggered novel episodes of social protest: in the early months of the war in the town of Belfast 'the mob' took control of the markets for several weeks and sought to cap the price of meal. A still more formidable challenge to public order emerged in central Munster in 1761–2. The initial issue there was contested access to common grazing land, but the agenda of grievances widened in the first few months. The agitation, the first 'Whiteboy' movement, transmuted into a wider social protest involving cottier-farmers and cottier-labourers from at least four Munster counties, and it escalated into something akin to a classic peasants' revolt. And although the first outbreak was successfully repressed by local gentry with large-scale military support, it was the first in a series of spasmodic agrarian protests in many of the southern farming districts, in which the near-landless usually (but not always) featured prominently, and where the social issues were generally closer to the concerns of labourers than to those of independent farmers.[22]

The American War was also a time of mixed economic fortunes. The direct effects of government restriction on trade were not as severe as the vocal opponents of the embargo on exports claimed, but a toxic mix of external market dislocation, a financial crisis in London and harvest failure at home produced one of the sharpest downturns in half a century in 1778/9. The following year, when the Irish parliament was debating a general 'combination' act to outlaw the unofficial craft associations that had developed strongly in several port cities, there was the first large-scale protest by journeymen craft-workers in Dublin, a non-violent affair involving thousands of protestors,

---

22 G. Benn, *A history of the town of Belfast* …, 2nd edn (London: Marcus Ward, 1877), pp. 593–6; D. Dickson, 'Novel spectacle: the birth of the Whiteboys 1761–2' in D.W. Hayton and A. Holmes (eds.), *Ourselves alone? Religion, society and politics in eighteenth- and nineteenth-century Ireland* (Dublin: Four Courts Press, 2016), pp. 61–83.

which demonstrated for the first time the existence of a new social constituency. Urban unemployment was eased, however, by unprecedented recruitment into both the Royal Navy and army regiments.

Despite further severe economic difficulties at the end of the war which were exacerbated by harvest failure, the economy bounced back quickly and entered a fifteen-year 'goldilocks' period between 1784 and 1797, a time of highly visible and apparently benign structural change in manufacturing, infrastructure and urban development. Later commentators, accepting the importance of these years, emphasised the political context – the enlarged powers of the Irish parliament after 1782, the repeal in 1778 and 1782 of the Penal Laws that had affected Catholics' freedom to buy, sell and mortgage land – but modern interpretations, while not discounting either the impact of parliamentary support for industrial innovation and cereal exports, or the role of Catholic relief in altering the investment climate, have tended to emphasise the exceptional importance of contemporary British developments and the synergistic effects of early-stage industrialisation on Ireland.

The interconnectedness of Irish and British developments in manufacturing was striking. Nowhere was this truer than with 'flour factories', the sophisticated water-powered mills that produced fine flour for urban consumption. The first such mills appeared close to Dublin, Cork and Waterford in the 1730s and 1740s, but they were modest by comparison with new-style 'bolting' mills first seen in the south of England; the vast London market was the catalyst there, but mills on the English south coast found an additional outlet in supplying Irish cities. The 1758 Irish parliamentary subsidy offsetting the cost of transporting local wheat, and more than offsetting the cost of bringing Irish flour to Dublin, was in part a response to this inflow of English flour. Within a decade the scheme resulted in a wave of investment in flour-milling across the wheat-growing districts of Leinster and Munster, spreading to parts of Connacht two decades later. The most famous of these enterprises was the elegant five-storey Slane Mill, sited beside the Boyne. It was built by a partnership involving two gentry investors and David Jebb, son of a Drogheda merchant, who had managed a technically advanced tide-mill near Chichester before gaining additional experience as overseer in the construction of the Boyne Navigation. The Slane Mill, with its sophisticated water management and complex system of power transmission, was Jebb's creation and something of a wonder to behold: it began operations in 1766, drawing its wheat from a 10 mile radius and producing some 15 tons of flour per day for despatch both to the northern linen districts and (principally) to Dublin city. The plant and ancillary works cost nearly £20,000, but through prudent management the debt was cleared by the end of the century. Slane Mill remained the largest industrial building in Ireland for many years.

In all, over 240 flour-mills were constructed between the 1750s and 1790, most of them quite modest and very few approaching the scale of Slane. Many of the larger enterprises were financed or part-financed by local gentry, with city-based flour factors also heavily involved. But all flour-millers were active traders, providing a price point for the tillage farmer and often a vital credit line. Yet to the embattled consumer at times of high bread prices, the mills became objects of hostility: four west Cork flour-mills were torched by gangs of artisans from neighbouring towns in the hungry autumn of 1792.[23]

One of the biggest flour-mills in the Dublin suburbs, the Hibernian Mills at Kilmainham, was built *c*.1790 by a successful and articulate brewer-made-good, Arthur Guinness. Beer production was one of the many processing trades present in every Irish town, dependent entirely on local sales. Quality was unpredictable and superior ales and porter imported from England commanded an increasing market share in the ports. Capitalised brewers were slow to emerge; Guinness was one of the first to expand, albeit tentatively. It was only in the 1790s that there was heavy investment in brewing, most notably in Cork. This drew on new English technologies but was dependent on surging local consumption, aided by military demand from official contractors. Excise and regulatory changes were critical in the timing of this take-off, but Guinness's early diversification into flour-milling suggests the limitations of the market for beer. At almost the same time and for similar reasons, industrial-scale distilling began in the larger urban centres, encouraged by a sharp decline in rum and brandy consumption following tariff changes. But unlike the pattern with flour-milling, the first generation of large-scale alcohol producers were port-based, reflecting the heavy use of coal in the production process. Their precursors in the heavy use of coal had been the sugar-refiners, who throughout the century operated smoky but highly lucrative enterprises in the heart of Dublin and Cork.

Steam engines were introduced at the end of the century to supplement waterpower at a few locations (Lisburn, Dublin and Cork) in large cotton- and flour-mills and in several distilleries, a sign of the need to escape the seasonal uncertainties of rainfall. English and Welsh coal was much cheaper in the ports than inland, so coal-consuming industrial processes (apart from

---

23 L.M. Cullen. 'Eighteenth-century flour milling in Ireland' in A. Bielenberg (ed.), *Irish flour milling: a history, A.D. 600–2000* (Dublin: Lilliput Press, 2003), pp. 37–56; C. Rynne, *Industrial Ireland 1750–1930: an archaeology* (Cork: Collins Press, 2006), pp. 257–60.

malting) were almost entirely restricted to the coastal cities. True, the first stationary steam engine in Ireland had been erected in 1740 on the Kilkenny coalfield to assist in pumping water from the pits, and much later others were built at the Tyrone and Leitrim coalmines, but none of these coalfields lived up to early hopes or generated spin-off industrial activity.[24]

Steam power was therefore little more than a footnote in Ireland until the nineteenth century. The greatest concentration of industrial enterprises was up to then to be found beside harnessable water – within or close to the port cities and along nearby rivers – the Dodder in south Dublin and the Camac to the west, the Glanmire near Cork, and the Lagan and its tributaries beside Belfast. But the processing of grain was a small part of the story here. Since early in the eighteenth century textile processes had predominated along these rivers – bleach greens and printing works for linens, dye yards and tenter fields for woollens – and the numbers employed at these sites were much greater than in the mills, the breweries or the distilleries. But even this workforce constituted a very small percentage of the vast numbers employed elsewhere in textile manufacturing, whether in the home or in small workshops, as independent artisans or as wage-earners. And larger workshops were by no means unknown, as where intricate foot-powered looms were installed (as in damask making) or where there were economies of scale in bringing handicraft production under a single roof (as in sail-cloth manufacture). But all this began to change rapidly in the 1780s, reflecting developments in England and the mechanisation of cotton production: cotton spinning machines using horse- or waterpower quickly crossed the Irish Sea. The first mills were rural, with the biggest enterprises at Blarney (County Cork), Balbriggan (County Dublin), and the new town of Prosperous (County Kildare). These were vertically integrated, badly planned, and usually dependent on imported management. And as with the early linen industry and, more recently, with flour-milling, landlord sponsorship was important in the initial stages, but their dispersed rural location reflected strong parliamentary encouragement for new enterprises that would draw Dublin's turbulent weaving population to quieter environs. Some of these firms survived and thrived for a generation or more, whether as spinning mills or printing yards, but the profitable ones were those closest to Dublin, Belfast and Cork, and some of them endured.[25]

The bitter irony of these headline developments was that overall employment in the textile industries was negatively affected by the early industrial

24 Rynne, *Industrial Ireland*, pp. 53–60.
25 Ibid., pp. 211–14.

revolution. Linen manufacture, it is true, continued to spread geographically in the late eighteenth century, most notably into north Connacht and parts of the south-west. By the early 1790s annual exports of whitened cloth passed 40 million yards, the industry employing according to one (perhaps conservative) estimate 300,000 weavers and spinners. And cotton weaving may briefly have employed another 60,000 in the port hinterlands of Dublin, Cork and Belfast.[26] But in the east Ulster heartlands, earnings in the finer branches of linen were depressed by the cotton revolution, and after the early 1790s there was no long-term growth in Irish linen exports until the 1820s when the technology to spin finer counts of flax was finally perfected. The vast and dispersed woollen and silk weaving trades were a different story. Production of medium and fine fabrics – for bourgeois and upper-class consumption – had for generations been carried on within the country, and the finer the fabric the more likely it was to be a big-city product. Towns like Kilkenny, Clonmel, Carrick-on-Suir and Bandon had long specialised in the production of mid-priced worsted and heavier cloths for sale at fairs and markets across the country, but fashion goods with finer finishes were associated with Blackpool in Cork city, Limerick and the Liberties of Dublin.[27] In the 1760s the finer branches, where craft organisations were well developed and wages high, came under pressure from English, mainly Yorkshire, manufacturers, and this became even more serious in the 1780s and 1790s. And although the coarser branches of Irish woollen manufacture survived far into the nineteenth century, the declining status of weavers (and their employers) in the finer branches of wool and silk had a profound effect on the Dublin economy, where the numbers employed in woollen and silk manufacturing declined from over 12,000 in the 1760s to perhaps half that number by 1800. The falling living standards of those who remained were highlighted at moments of commercial depression, as in 1778/9 and 1792/3, but the relentless de-skilling of the handicraft textile sector and the increased prominence of women and children at the loom was a fifty-year process of craft emasculation. Not surprisingly, in the 1780s and 1790s old textile districts like the Dublin Liberties were highly responsive to political radicalism, but also to military recruitment into the forces of the crown.

26 Newenham, *View*, p. 231.
27 L.A. Clarkson, 'The Carrick-on-Suir woollen industry in the eighteenth century', *Irish Economic and Social History*, 16 (1989), 23–41.

Infrastructure

In the final decades of the century the country's physical and commercial infrastructure underwent dramatic improvement or, rather, long-planned developments finally bore fruit: the canals began to have economic impact; the principal trunk roads were sufficiently robust to accommodate high-speed mail-coaches between the main cities; and a national bank of sorts was established.

Investment in river improvement and 'artificial navigation' was publicly debated from the 1690s when the idea of linking Lough Neagh with the Irish Sea was first investigated. That was a generation before coal was discovered west of the great lake, and the illusory prospect of making Ireland self-sufficient in coal sustained a great variety of canal-building projects north and south, not least the two vastly expensive schemes to link Dublin with the south midlands and Castlecomer coal (the Grand Canal), and with the north midlands and Arigna (the Royal). Substantial public and private money was lost over the decades before cargo and passenger services on an eastern section of the Grand commenced in 1779, and it was another quarter of a century before direct services between Dublin and the River Shannon began. That milestone was far less important than the opening up of sections further east which generated heavy canal traffic in cereals, building materials and fuel; by the 1790s about a third of the wheat and flour entering Dublin came by canal, a third by road and a third by coastal shipping. Other canal and river-deepening schemes benefited Drogheda, Newry, Belfast, Limerick, Clonmel and New Ross. But these were dwarfed by the two Dublin canals, both in terms of the capital consumed in their construction and in their eventual commercial impact.

Road improvement was incremental, but the spread to Ireland of turnpiking led to major changes in the 1730s. The sometimes controversial privatisation of most trunk roads by parliamentary statute led to substantial investment in highway maintenance and to some improvement in gradient and alignment, notably on the Dublin to Cork road, facilitating heavier coaches and carts and reducing the impact of heavy rainfall on wheeled traffic. Scheduled coaching services first operated out of Dublin in the 1710s, and the routes served increased slowly. By the 1780s there were more than a dozen destinations, but the step-change came with the introduction in 1788 of mail-coaches on four routes from the capital. The undertakers involved took control of several turnpike trusts, strengthened the roads and perfected the logistics of managing large numbers of horses and coaches under the discipline of the clock. Travellers could now get from Cork to Dublin within twenty-four hours, and while mail-coaches were only for wealthier patrons, the provision of a faster and more reliable postal service had much broader commercial and social impact. Meanwhile county grand juries were given progressively greater powers to raise local taxation for road improvement: in the case of County Cork, a modest budget for infrastructural spending of £1,050 in 1731 had risen to £18,903 by 1790 and to £66,849 by 1810, and roads were the main item of expenditure throughout. Central government loans only became available for road improvement in 1805.[28]

No data survive to document the inexorable growth of inland trade that accompanied such improvements: Young admired Irish roads but noted the absence of heavy wheeled vehicles and the modest volume of traffic, but his comparison was with England and a more advanced economy, and perhaps he neglected to notice the hundreds of smaller carts carrying linen and flour amongst much else. Of course a major part of the traffic was cattle on the hoof. The international success of the Irish provisions trade was built on a series of inland exchanges of cattle between different types of farming district; these were mediated through fairs, some located in market towns, some in far more modest locations. In the 1680s there were around 500 privately sponsored fairs in the country, by the 1770s nearly 3,000. Some fairs were held once in a year (for up to five days), others on a single day and up to six times in the year. In the early days of Cork's beef export trade, fattened bullocks were driven to a great three-day fair on the city's edge in mid-September, but as trade grew there were thrice-weekly markets through the autumn, then daily cattle markets. And a few of the country fairs became almost national events, notably the great wool and livestock fairs at Clonmel, County Tipperary, and Ballinasloe, County Galway (which got off the ground in the 1750s).[29]

Trade at such venues had formerly been transacted by means of coin, large and small, foreign and British, sound and debased. But promissory notes, inland bills of exchange, and private and eventually public bank notes assumed a dominant role in wholesale (but not retail) transactions around the country during the eighteenth century. Only the linen trade in Ulster remained solidly based on coin. The growth of monetary substitutes and the rise of paper was an inexorable process, punctuated by short-term collapses

---

28 D. Broderick, *The first toll roads: Ireland's turnpike roads 1729–1858* (Dublin: Irish Academic Press, 2002); D. Dickson, *Old World colony: Cork and South Munster 1630–1830* (Cork: Cork University Press, 2005), pp. 429–31.
29 P. O'Flanagan, 'Markets and fairs in Ireland 1600–1800', *Journal of Historical Geography*, 11:4 (1985), 364–78.

in public confidence when private banks failed, most painfully so in 1759/60 when no less than three Dublin banks closed their doors. And the supply of coin, a matter of extreme concern in the 1720s, probably increased threefold or more by the 1770s, and continued to expand rapidly up to 1797.

The statutory creation of the Bank of Ireland in 1782, for all the institution's early limitations, was more than symbolically important: its emergence gave a new solidity to the private banking system, and although Munster was convulsed by an old-style failure in Cork in 1784, the banking sector as a whole proved robust enough in 1797 to adapt to the wartime suspension of the convertibility of national bank paper to gold. Backed now by a state-backed lender of last resort, a proliferating array of private banking establishments helped lubricate the Napoleonic economic boom through the sometimes profligate issue of their own bank notes. The Bank of Ireland also helped create a structured bond market: a regular trade in government debt, canal stock and a small number of other public issues was already growing when the Irish Stock Exchange was formally established in Dublin in 1799.

The Stock Exchange was housed in a new privately financed complex, the Commercial Buildings, close to the Parliament House. Dublin's street system running west from parliament and north-east across the river had at enormous cost and much controversy been widened and remodelled on a scale unusual by any European standard. The 'metropolitan improvements' involved much else, but the startling reconstruction of the city centre in the 1780s and 1790s, partly on public account, was the most striking instance of Irish urban renewal, coming at a time when public buildings, assembly rooms, market houses, monumental private terraces, open spaces and a novel concern for civic appearance were evident in many towns. Outside the capital, Belfast and Limerick provided the strongest examples of new streetscapes, but even in Cork, despite the constriction of its island site, the reclamation of the waterways changed the whole feel of the city, and in Derry and Waterford the construction of great wooden bridges transformed access into the two cities. This growth in urban investment late in the century suggests two factors at work: first, the growth and growing complexity of the urban middle classes, both as an aggregate entity and in terms of their disposable income, that could also be seen in the range and size of fixed retail establishments and in the growth of specialist shops and retail warehouses that imported consumer goods and fabrics from Manchester, Leeds, Birmingham and beyond; secondly, the strengthening attraction of the larger towns for the middling orders of the countryside, as the incomes of free-standing tenants improved and a taste for urban standards spread, thanks to the growing volume of print in circulation. One small but telltale marker of the process was the rise of coffee consumption, the international staple of the urban public sphere: between 1753 and 1782 Irish imports averaged a modest 401 cwt p.a.; between 1783 and 1802 the annual figure rose to 693 cwt, and demand accelerated in the following decade.[30]

Entrepreneurship

The eighteenth-century transformation in the scale and complexity of sea-borne trade in Irish and Atlantic waters was achieved through the actions of thousands of independent trading houses, small and large, sole traders and robust partnerships. But most of the shipping dropping anchor in Irish ports, whether in 1700 or 1800, was English, Dutch or Scottish, although locally owned vessels controlled coastal traffic and dominated some long-distance trades (notably in exchanges with Bordeaux, Lisbon and southern Spain). For most of the century the bulk of Irish foreign trade was conducted on commission, with orders coming from merchant houses outside the country. Independent Irish venturing overseas was therefore quite modest. How far this reflected the regulatory environment and Ireland's restricted access to English colonial trades in the century before 'free trade' came in 1780 remains contentious. The remarkable rise of Glasgow as a premier Atlantic port in the wake of Anglo-Scottish union in 1707 is certainly suggestive of what might have been – if Irish ports could have competed in transatlantic trading on more equal terms with those in Britain. Yet the supposed inferiority of 'passive' commission trading against active ship-owning and venturing at sea can be misleading: Irish ports that did build up a stock of ocean-going vessels – Belfast, Derry and Limerick – were less favourably positioned to service English ships entering Atlantic waters than were Dublin, Waterford or Cork. In fact there were great merchant dynasties in all these ports, exclusively Protestant in the northern ports, predominantly so in the south (although less so by the 1780s). The particular mode of trading of the big houses reflected local opportunity, and they were not self-evidently more risk-averse than their correspondents in Bristol or Boston. The history of private banking is further proof of this, and no merchant could thrive without a long list of debtors. Outside of Dublin, merchant capital played a critical role in urban property development throughout the century. Water-powered industrial

---

30 L.A. Clarkson and E.M. Crawford, *Feast and famine: a history of food and nutrition in Ireland 1500–1920* (Oxford: Oxford University Press, 2001), p. 51.

development, both in the ports and across their hinterlands, was driven by merchant investment, albeit in partnership with local landowners in the case of flour-milling and out-of-town linen drapers in the case of bleach greens.

That said, the capital of all religious colours accumulated in trade continued to flow relentlessly into rural land acquisition (although Quaker trading families seem to have been the least attracted by gentrification and its delights). Thus, as a consequence of the recurring preference for property investment, there were very few multi-generational business dynasties, making families like the La Touches (centred on banking) and the Guinnesses (on grain and brewing) unusual. Overseas, it is true, there were instances of extraordinary wealth built up in one or two generations by Irish families like the Fitzgeralds, the great London-based tobacco factors, or the Walshs of Nantes, slavers, sugar producers and plantation owners in the Caribbean. No eighteenth-century Irish-based firm scaled such heights, although a few may have aspired so to do. Edward Byrne, regarded by his contemporaries as the richest trader in Dublin, left property worth in the order of £40,000 plus stated legacies of £91,523 on his death in 1804, but that would not have placed him in the top tier of Irish landowners.

The End of a Cycle

Three decades after Arthur Young published his Irish travels, another English writer, Edward Wakefield, published a vast survey (*An account of Ireland: statistical and political*) in 1812. Like Young, Wakefield grew up in East Anglia and came to Ireland with a mission, making an extended stay and gathering a vast corpus of agricultural and commercial information on which he struggled to impose some order. Like Young, he was critical of the way power was monopolised in the country, and he supported the completion of Catholic emancipation. Wakefield documented an economy that had been demonstrably changed by twenty years of warfare, not least by the high land prices that benefited established leaseholders and all those engaged in agricultural production and processing (although modern scholarship emphasises that the division of the benefits of inflation varied greatly from farm to farm and estate to estate, depending on the timing of lease renegotiation and the management policies on each estate).[31] Beef exports were now overshadowed by pork, and grain-based products were

---

31 A large-scale analysis of land values in County Armagh has revealed that 'rents at new settings grew steadily from the early 1740s until the early 1770s, increasing by about 170 per cent' and well ahead of food prices, but then there was little upward movement for

being despatched from some thirty Irish ports large and small, destined almost entirely for England. There were signs that farmers in many parts of the country were generating sufficient savings to copy their social superiors and build more elaborate homesteads – two-storey buildings with parlours and private spaces within, stables and granaries outside. Perhaps some had the ambition to set up younger sons as seminarians or apprentices in small-town professions and businesses, thereby protecting the farm as an integral unit to be handed down to a single heir.[32] Such ambition was probably the exception for now: partible inheritance and the apparently unstoppable sub-division of tenancies was still the norm across the country, and was seen by outsiders as the evil consequence of population growth.

Until the final years of the eighteenth century the rise of population evident across the island had been seen as entirely positive and a key marker of economic improvement. But as Thomas Malthus' warnings began to be popularised, some saw negative implications.[33] No one disputed that growth was occurring, but both cause and consequence were obscure. The causes are still unclear, given the absence of robust statistical evidence, but four aspects of the phenomenon now seem incontrovertible: (a) Irish population growth occurred at a time of almost universal European growth, but at rates of growth towards the higher end of the spectrum; (b) the upward trend that commenced, or recommenced, in the late 1740s showed no signs of deceleration before 1815; (c) while growth was universal across Ireland, the highest rates shifted markedly between regions over the course of the period; and (d) no one factor can account for the phenomenon, as the precise triggers of rapid growth in one region are unlikely to have been identical to those in other regions.[34]

Prior to the first national census in 1821, the hearth tax remains our principal if treacherous source: a reworking of post-1750 data (see Table 2) suggests that Ulster and Munster counties may have witnessed the highest rate of

---

two decades, followed by a wartime rise of about 80 per cent; but given the distinctively industrial character of the county, the sharpness of the mid-eighteenth-century rise and the less emphatic wartime movement of rents, it remains to be seen whether these results will be replicated elsewhere: P.M. Solar and L. Hens, 'Land under pressure: the value of Irish land in a period of rapid population growth, 1730–1844', *Agricultural History Review*, 61:1 (2013), 40–62.

32 L.M. Cullen, *Economy, trade and Irish merchants at home and abroad 1600–1988* (Dublin: Four Courts Press, 2012), pp. 78–80.

33 For example, W. Stokes, *Projects for re-establishing the internal peace and tranquility of Ireland* (Dublin: James Moore, 1799), pp. 5–12.

34 See Gurrin, Chapter 8, pp. 213–17.

Table 2. *Provincial population growth-rate estimates, 1753–1821.*

	Growth rate band (p.a.)	Growth rate (p.a.)
Leinster	1.0–1.4	1.3
Munster	1.5–1.9	1.6
Ulster	1.8–2.2	1.1
Connacht	1.5–2.1	2.0
Ireland	1.4–1.5	1.4

Source: D. Dickson, C. Ó Gráda and S.Daultrey, 'Hearth tax, household size and Irish population change 1672–1821', *Proceedings of the Royal Irish Academy*, 82c (1982), 170.

population growth between mid-century and the 1790s, with Connacht and the less well-endowed western counties then assuming a lead position during the French wars, and with Ulster decelerating sharply. Modern interpretations have championed the importance of both external factors and local agency, but explanations as to why Irish growth was atypically high have focused on crop innovation (the potato), on the elastic stock of reclaimable land, on the permissive land system and on proto-industrialisation. Future research may help pin down whether rapid growth was triggered primarily by a rise in fertility (lower marriage age and increased nuptiality) or in fecundity (improved female health and changes in weaning practices), or by a fall in mortality (whether because of higher infant and/or child survival rates, or through the absence of general mortality crises arising from famine or pandemic). Fertility changes were critical in accelerating population growth in eighteenth-century Britain, but there are strong grounds for suspecting that Ireland was different, that marriage age had always been lower in Ireland, and that improved survival rates and life expectancy after the 1740s may explain much of the spring tide. But that of course leaves other questions of causality unanswered.

Wakefield was less curious than Young as to the state of the poor, but his evidence confirms that of many others: the lot of the wage-earner in town and countryside by 1812 was now more precarious, and a great many were severely under-employed in the good years and vulnerable to disease and distress at times of scarcity, as in the near-famine of 1800/1. Nevertheless, given the unremitting speed of Irish population growth, perhaps the remarkable thing is that the cost of living did not rise sooner or more sharply than it did.[35] The cottier-labourer was indeed no longer a

35 L. Kennedy, 'The cost of living in Ireland, 1698–1998' in D. Dickson and C. Ó Gráda (eds.), *Refiguring Ireland: essays in honour of L.M. Cullen* (Dublin: Lilliput Press, 2003), pp. 257–8.

distinct social category, for a chasm had emerged between the *tied* labouring family, still hiring potato ground (but in many parts of the country no longer able to earn enough to rent grazing for a cow or even enough money to buy milk), and the *untied* labouring family, renting even less, the menfolk searching for work locally or through temporary migration eastwards or across the Irish Sea, the women forced to tend a diminished potato garden, or simply to take to the roads and beg. As long as abundant handicraft work was available and wartime demand kept pig prices high, the former could cope, rear a family and possibly come up in the world; for the latter their exposure to risk was ever present, as the 'perfect storm' of 1816–18 painfully revealed.

Global weather aberrations beginning in 1814 overlapped with the post-Napoleonic fall in commodity prices and with the return of the vast numbers who had served in army and navy. However, despite the fact that hundreds of thousands succumbed to fevers in 1816–17, excess mortality was far lower than in 1740–1, possibly around 50,000.[36] Public health practices (if not the underlying science) were now superior to those of the 1740s, and the greater wealth held by the middle and upper classes in the wake of a long and profitable war seems to have been translated into a broad-based philanthropic response. But a deflationary peace and intensified British industrialisation soon transformed the economic climate and cruelly exposed the weaknesses and vulnerabilities of Irish society after seventy years of growth.[37]

36 D. Dickson, 'The gap in famines: a useful myth?' in E.M. Crawford (ed.), *Famine: the Irish experience, 900–1900* (Edinburgh: John Donald, 1989), pp. 107–8.

37 For contrasting views on trends in wages and living standards over the following decades, see J. Mokyr and C. Ó Gráda, 'Poor and getting poorer? Living standards in Ireland before the Famine', *Economic History Review*, 41:2 (1988), 209–35; F. Geary and T. Stark, 'Trends in real wages during the Industrial Revolution: a view from across the Irish Sea', *Economic History Review*, 57:2 (2004), 362–95.

7

The Irish Economy, 1815–1880: Agricultural Transition, the Communications Revolution and the Limits of Industrialisation

ANDY BIELENBERG

Introduction

In 1817, the Irish Treasury was amalgamated with the British Treasury in London; the Irish currency was subsequently assimilated with sterling in 1826. By then all duties between the two islands had been removed so that Great Britain and Ireland thereafter constituted a unified monetary and trading zone. George O'Brien's *Ireland from the Union to the Famine*[1] (published in 1921 just at the point when what is now the Republic of Ireland was leaving the Union) conveyed the negative nationalist interpretation of these developments, an appraisal that prevailed until the publication in 1972 of Louis Cullen's *An economic history of Ireland since 1660*.[2] Cullen highlighted the more dynamic features of Irish economic development, and divested the topic of its political overtones (which in simple terms revolved around the benefits of the relationship with Britain for unionists and its malign impact for nationalists). Yet even before Cullen's new departure, various revisions to the received wisdom had been advanced. In 1966, Raymond Crotty argued that the end of the Napoleonic wars in 1815 rather than the Great Famine was the key watershed in nineteenth-century Irish economic history on the grounds that the latter event merely accelerated the transition from arable to pasture farming that was already well underway.[3] This influential assessment has since been challenged on several fronts. In 1983, Joel Mokyr's *Why Ireland starved*[4] brought the Great Famine back into focus. This widely read monograph marked the beginning of a more quantitative turn in Irish economic history. Since then,

---

1 G. O'Brien, *Ireland from the Union to the Famine* (London: Longmans, Green and Co., 1921).
2 L.M. Cullen, *An economic history of Ireland since 1660* (London: Batsford, 1972).
3 R. Crotty, *Irish agricultural production: its volume and structure* (Cork: Cork University Press, 1966).
4 J. Mokyr, *Why Ireland starved: a quantitative and analytical history of the Irish economy 1800–1850* (London: Allen and Unwin, 1983).

work on agricultural prices and trade (cited later in the article) have conclusively disproved Crotty's revisionist contention. The most recent synthesis of this new turn (the so-called 'new economic history') published in 1994 by Cormac Ó Gráda, *Ireland: a new economic history 1780–1939*,[5] offered a number of new approaches and interpretations utilising quantitative methods. This has since been complemented by new trade evidence carefully built up by Peter Solar, who has also worked with Liam Kennedy to produce a far more refined picture of agricultural prices. Frank Geary and Tom Stark's work (cited below) on Irish GDP and wages constituted another significant quantitative advance. This group have collectively enhanced our understanding of Irish agriculture, trade, demography and living standards. This chapter provides an outline of developments between 1815 and 1881 across the three major sectors of the economy (agriculture, industry and services), while the final section focuses on discernible changes in living conditions and the distribution of wealth.

Agriculture

British industrialisation and urbanisation played a profound and increasingly influential role in accelerating the commercialisation of Irish agriculture, which remained the mainstay of the Irish economy between 1815 and 1881 in terms of employment. In the early 1840s agriculture accounted for 53 per cent of the Irish labour force, or roughly 1.8 million persons (including 1.3 million farm servants or labourers). The following decades witnessed a substantial decline in the agricultural workforce; by 1881 the dominance of livestock in the production mix had been firmly established. Yet up to the Great Famine, crops actually accounted for a higher share of output (see Table 3), underpinned, first, by the Corn Laws which afforded protection to United Kingdom grain growers up to 1846, and, second, by the extensive share of Irish land given over to growing potatoes on which many smallholders depended. By 1845, according to the estimates of Clarkson and Crawford, about two-fifths of the population of 8.5 million depended chiefly on potatoes for survival. Although agricultural exports rose at an impressive rate between 1815 and 1845, the lion's share of Irish agricultural output on the eve of the Famine (about three-quarters according to Ó Gráda) was consumed in Ireland.[6]

---

5 C. Ó Gráda, *Ireland: a new economic history 1780–1939* (Oxford: Oxford University Press, 1994).
6 F. Geary and T. Stark, 'Trends in real wages during the Industrial Revolution: a view from across the Irish Sea', *Economic History Review*, 57 (2004), 375; L.A. Clarkson and

In the pre-Famine period, potato cultivation was central to this labour-intensive system of crop rotation that boosted tillage yields. Although labour inputs increased dramatically between 1815 and 1845, the relatively low animal population meant that manures and fertilisers were at a premium as farmers and cottiers sought to increase fertility and offset soil depletion. This was achieved in various ways; the higher rents for land near the coast demonstrated the significance of the availability of sea-sand, seaweed or estuarine mud in improving soil fertility; mud scrapings from ditches and bogs or turf mould were also utilised. Lime in particular but also ashes and human waste were also applied. Animal dung was a most precious commodity and it was predominantly preserved for the potato crop. Potato yields of between 5 and 6 tons per acre were maintained in the decades after 1815, which compared favourably with Great Britain, and these yields were not surpassed in Ireland in the century following the early 1850s. On the eve of the Great Famine the area used for growing potatoes peaked at about 2 million acres, or approximately a third of all tilled land, with the potato harvest approaching 15 million tons.[7] Multiple other strategies were adopted to intensify land use between 1815 and 1845, reducing fallow in rotations, and reclaiming waste land to increase corn and potato production to feed a population expanding fast by European standards. Agricultural output had to rise to facilitate this population growth as well as the increase in agricultural exports. With increased commercialisation, farmers are likely to have benefited more than labourers or landlords, more notably after the 1820s when rent increases were limited.[8] Most tillage land was still prepared by hand (using a spade or loy) rather than by plough, which became more commonplace in the second half of the nineteenth century as the labouring population contracted and the cost of farm labour rose.

M. Crawford, *Feast and famine: food and nutrition in Ireland 1500–1920* (Oxford: Oxford University Press, 2001); P. Solar, 'Irish trade in the nineteenth century' in D. Dickson and C. Ó Gráda (eds.), *Refiguring Ireland* (Dublin: Lilliput Press, 2003); C. Ó Gráda, *Ireland before and after the Famine: explorations in economic history, 1800–1925*, 2nd edn (Manchester: Manchester University Press, 1993), p. 61.

7 C. Ó Gráda, 'Poverty, population and agriculture 1801–45' in W.E. Vaughan (ed.), *A new history of Ireland*, vol. v: *Ireland under the Union, I, 1801–70* (Oxford: Oxford University Press, 1989), pp. 108–33; M. Cooper and J. Davis, *The Irish fertiliser industry: a history* (Dublin: Irish Academic Press, 2004), pp. 12–38. On human waste see A. Bourke, '*The visitation of God'? The potato and the Great Irish Famine* (Dublin: Lilliput Press, 1993), p. 63.

8 K.H. Connell, 'The colonization of wasteland in Ireland 1780–1845', *Economic History Review*, 50 (1950), 44–71; on rents and output see Cullen, *An economic history of Ireland since 1660*, p. 113. His conclusions on rent are broadly supported by P. Solar and L. Hens, 'Land pressure: the value of Irish land in a period of rapid population growth, 1730–1844', *Agricultural History Review*, 61 (2013), 40–62.

The Inquiry into the Condition of the Poorer Classes in the mid-1830s reveals the extent to which women and older children in labouring households contributed to rural income generation through the maintenance and sale of poultry and eggs and pigs, by engaging in fieldwork, and by spinning textile yarn for the market. However, whereas farmers paid rents in cash, the co-existence and persistence of semi-subsistence strategies among labourers and cottiers is evident from Mokyr's tabulations from the same inquiry which reveal that about 53 per cent of wage payments from farmers to cottiers and labourers in Ireland were made with cash, with the remainder covered by provisions or with land. There were significant regional variations; in Connacht and Munster under 44 per cent of transactions were in cash, whereas in Ulster it stood at 64 per cent and in Leinster 55.[9] The growth in population in the century before the Great Famine (accompanied by exceptional levels of potato cultivation and consumption) appears also to have been fastest in those areas where wages were lower and land quality was poor, notably in the west; population growth was slowest in more prosperous farmlands near Dublin and the south-east, while the northern linen manufacturing districts and the south-west witnessed growth rates between these extremes.[10]

If the rise in demand for food arising from population growth was the primary driver of output growth, the benefits were highly unevenly divided across the rural population. Rents to landlords by the early 1840s accounted for something in the order of 25–30 per cent of agricultural output. At the bottom of the social spectrum, a vast army of hard-pressed cottiers and labourers and their families precariously lived off less than 13 per cent of all available land. By the eve of the Famine, a narrower group of about 400,000 farmers and their families farmed some 70 per cent or so of the available land and produced the bulk of agricultural output. This starkly reveals the highly uneven income distribution of the pre-Famine economy, which left much of the bottom third of the population highly vulnerable to harvest fluctuations and limited recourse to the market. Yet at this stage about two-thirds of agricultural output was sold for cash.[11]

9 M. Cullen, 'Bread winners and providers: women in the household economy of labouring families 1835–6' in M. Luddy and C. Murphy (eds.), *Women surviving: studies in Irish women's history in the nineteenth and twentieth centuries* (Dublin: Poolbeg Press, 1989), pp. 85–116; Mokyr, *Why Ireland starved*, p. 23.
10 M. Kelly and C. Ó Gráda, 'Why Ireland starved after three decades: the Great Famine in cross-section reconsidered', *Irish Economic and Social History*, 42 (2015), 61; P. Solar, 'Why Ireland starved and the big issues in pre-Famine Irish economic history', *Irish Economic and Social History*, 42 (2015), 62–75.
11 Solar and Hens, 'Land pressure', 58–9; Ó Gráda, 'Poverty, population and agriculture 1801–45', pp. 108–33.

The disastrous failure of the potato over a series of years from 1845 to 1848 left a gaping hole in the food supply, in a society where the potato-dependent portion of the population was far higher than in other parts of Europe. Poor harvests across Europe led to a rise in cereal prices in 1846, making it more difficult to find potato substitutes, even for those with cash.[12] In terms of the wider Irish cash economy, the decline in bank note circulation between September 1846 and September 1849 by almost half (or double the decline in Britain) reveals the vulnerability of the economy at large to fluctuations in agriculture. This was still apparent in less severe agricultural downturns recorded during the recessions of the early 1860s and late 1870s.[13]

The closing years of the Great Famine witnessed some important legislative reforms with significant implications for Irish agriculture. Under the Encumbered Estates Acts of 1848–9, about a quarter of the land acreage passed to 7,489 new owners (predominantly Irish), resulting in the departure of many insolvent landlords. Another significant outcome of the Famine was that many smallholdings were consolidated, following the death of the original tenants, or their departure through evictions (which rose dramatically), or voluntary surrender. Smallholders were increasingly displaced by the expanding grazier class which focused on rearing and fattening cattle and sheep. This more highly commercialised activity was favoured by landlords, as it simplified estate management, regularised rental payments and reduced poor rate liabilities. The graziers included townspeople with accumulated surplus capital, and existing graziers extending their ranching activities, exploiting the new opportunities created by the Famine.[14] As a result exports of live cattle and sheep increased dramatically in the third quarter of the nineteenth century, with some improvement in carcass weights. A more specialised cattle rearing zone was clearly discernible by the 1880s, with young cattle raised in north Munster and east Connacht transferred to north Leinster for the final stages of fattening prior to export or slaughter. The expanding class of

12 P. Solar, 'The Great Famine was no ordinary subsistence crisis' in E.M. Crawford (ed.), *Famine: the Irish experience 900–1900* (Edinburgh: John Donald, 1989), pp. 112–33.
13 J. Lee, 'The dual economy in Ireland 1800–50' in T.D. Williams (ed.), *Historical studies VIII, papers read before the Irish Conference of Historians* (Dublin: Gill and Macmillan, 1971), p. 194; K. O'Rourke, 'Monetary data and proxy GDP estimates: Ireland 1840–1921', *Irish Economic and Social History*, 25 (1998), 22–51.
14 T.P. O'Neill, 'Famine evictions' in C. King (ed.), *Famine, land and culture* (Dublin: UCD Press, 2000), pp. 29–70; D.S. Jones, 'The transfer of land and the emergence of the graziers during the Famine period' in A. Gribben (ed.), *The Great Famine and the Irish diaspora in America* (Amherst: University of Massachusetts Press, 1999), pp. 85–103.

graziers, strong farmers and cattle dealers associated with this trade assumed increasing importance within the Irish economy and within rural society.[15]

Wheat production declined during the Famine, and wheat was increasingly imported thereafter, underpinning the food supply as bread consumption increased. The third quarter of the nineteenth century witnessed a major transition in the production mix in Irish agriculture away from cereals and potatoes to a far greater focus on dairy, livestock and meat. Between the 1840s and the 1870s prices changed more dramatically in favour of livestock and livestock products, while the price of corn remained relatively stagnant. Solar and Kennedy have also revealed that relative price trends favoured pasture both before and after 1815, which has finally laid to rest Crotty's argument that the key shift in the balance of prices favouring pastoral over tillage products in Irish agriculture occurred in 1815.[16] Moreover, it would be hard to square Ó Gráda's estimates of agricultural output on the eve of the Great Famine (see Table 3) with any marked shift away from arable in the interim, since it still accounted for a very significant share of output. The transition was more likely to have occurred from the 1840s onwards, as reflected in the Irish agricultural statistics returned annually from 1847.

Post-Famine adjustment and land use changes are apparent from the rapid rise in livestock numbers, which attest to the rise in investment in stock. Total cattle numbers in Ireland rose from 1,863,000 in 1841 to 3,816,000 in 1861, while sheep rose during the same years from 2,106,000 to 3,556,000. Irish farmers became increasingly more specialised and commercialised in the third quarter of the nineteenth century, focusing to a greater extent on livestock in which both prices and the terms of trade were improving. The post-Famine decades down to the early 1870s witnessed a major growth in agricultural exports to Britain, as farmers proved highly responsive to the greater opportunities opening up in that market.[17]

Crop acreages and yields fell in the immediate aftermath of the Famine, as the fertility built up in the soil was depleted and the labour intensive strategies adopted in the pre-Famine period were no longer feasible. By the 1860s and

---

15 J. O'Donovan, *The economic history of livestock in Ireland* (Cork: Cork University Press, 1940), pp. 214–15; J. Gilligan, *Graziers and grasslands: portrait of a rural Meath community 1854–1914* (Dublin: Irish Academic Press, 1998), p. 26.

16 L. Brunt and E. Cannon, 'The Irish grain trade from the Famine to the First World War', *Economic History Review*, 57 (2004), 33–79. L. Kennedy and P. Solar, *Irish agriculture: a price history* (Dublin: Royal Irish Academy, 2007), pp. 96–105.

17 B.R. Mitchell, *British historical statistics* (Cambridge: Cambridge University Press, 1988), p. 205; M. Turner, *After the Famine: Irish agriculture 1850–1914* (Cambridge: Cambridge University Press, 1996), pp. 69–88; P. Solar, 'Irish trade in the nineteenth century' in Dickson and Ó Gráda (eds.), *Refiguring Ireland*, pp. 277–89.

Table 3. *Irish agricultural output at current prices, 1840–76.*

	1840–5		1854		1876	
Crops						
Wheat	4.2		4.1		0.9	
Oats	7.4		5.7		2.6	
Barley	1.7		1.6		1.2	
Flax	1.1		2.3		1.7	
Potatoes	8.8		6.7		3.2	
Hay	0.3		0.4		0.8	
Other	1.2		1.1		0.6	
Subtotal	**24.7**	**59.2%**	**21.9**	**46.2%**	**11.0**	**23.5%**
Stock						
Cattle	4.4		7.9		11.3	
Butter	5.8		8.4		10.6	
Pigs	3.5		3.9		5.5	
Sheep	1.0		2.0		3.6	
Wool	0.4		0.9		0.9	
Eggs	0.9		1.1		2.1	
Other	0.8		1.3		1.9	
Subtotal	**16.8**	**40.8%**	**25.5**	**53.8%**	**35.9**	**76.5%**
Total	**41.7**	**100**	**47.4**	**100**	**46.7**	**100**

Source: C. Ó Gráda, *Ireland before and after the Famine: explorations in economic history,*
1800–1925, 2nd edn (Manchester: Manchester University Press, 1993), pp. 57, 68, 154.

1870s, yields were recovering as land less suitable for tillage was switched to pasture more quickly, the dung supply increased, and farmers increasingly resorted to guano and artificial fertilisers.[18] Falling population in rural Ireland and increased productivity in Irish agriculture improved the position of the farming community in the third quarter of the nineteenth century. However, consecutive bad harvests between 1877 and 1879 marked the beginning of a more difficult period. This economic downturn drew into sharp relief the conflicting interests between the landowners, living on relatively consistent annual rents, and the tenants who bore the brunt of output and market fluctuations. When the Irish National Land League was formed in 1879, this effectively marked the beginning of the end for the privileged position of landlords with respect to what still remained the premier economic resource

18 Cooper and Davis, *The Irish fertiliser industry*, pp. 102–9.

in Irish society, land. The conflict arising out of this recession ultimately created the conditions (starting with the 1881 Land Act) which led to the major redistribution in Irish landownership in the decades that followed.

Fishing, Forestry and Turf

The years between 1815 and the Great Famine witnessed a general expansion of both commercial and semi-subsistence based fishing. A Fishery Board was established in 1819 and funding was provided to build piers, harbours, boats and curing stations to encourage the herring fishery in particular. As a result, the numbers employed in fishing climbed to almost 65,000 by 1830, which increased the supply and quality of fish landed.[19] Despite the termination of government supports by 1830, and the subsequent contraction in numbers to just over 54,000 fishermen in 1836, there appears to have been significant expansion in the following decade, which peaked in 1846 when 113,073 fishermen were engaged. This reflected both the pressure on the food supply and the abundance of fish in that particular year. Coastal counties during and after the Great Famine experienced lower mortality, implying that access to fishing, coastal resources and sea transport may have been more helpful than is generally supposed. Clarkson and Crawford's survey of the Poor Law Inquiry reveals the significance of herring in particular as a cheap source of protein in the diet of the poor in the 1830s. Herrings were consumed in every county in the mid-1830s and in over a quarter of all parishes throughout the country; other types of fish were less commonly consumed.[20]

Although the fishing industry lacked vital infrastructure, which inhibited the landing and marketing of fish in many locations, commercial fisheries emerged in places close to major market outlets in towns like Arklow, which was one among only six ports across the country where fishermen were engaged full time. The scale of the industry in employment terms declined during and after the Famine; the herring and mackerel fisheries were highly seasonal, and Irish demand was relatively limited. The English

19 J. De Courcy Ireland, *Ireland's sea fisheries: a history* (Dublin: Glendale Press, 1981); C. O'Mahony, 'Fishing in nineteenth-century Kinsale', *Journal of the Cork Historical and Archaeological Society*, 98 (1993), 113.

20 *Commission of inquiry into the resources and industries of Ireland: report on the sea fisheries* (Dublin: Stationary Office, 1921); B. Walsh, 'Urbanization and the regional distribution of population in post-Famine Ireland', *Journal of European Economic History*, 29 (2000), 121; C. Ó Gráda, *Black 47 and beyond: the Great Irish Famine in history, economy and memory* (Princeton: Princeton University Press, 1999), p. 33; Clarkson and Crawford, *Feast and famine*, p. 76.

market accounted for about three-quarters of the Irish fresh herring catch in 1875.[21]

Various British innovations were adapted. For example, the trawl net carried on a wide beam was brought to Ringsend by Devonshire trawlermen who settled there from 1819 onwards, serving the Dublin market for sole and turbot. In 1855, Scottish fishermen introduced the cotton net, which improved catches.[22] By 1870, mackerel and herring accounted for two-thirds of the value of all fish taken on the Irish coastline. A boom in the herring fishery took place from the early 1860s to about the early 1880s. Access to the British market provided a major advantage to fishing centres on the east coast. They also had ready access to the Dublin market, with the result that fishing communities based in Howth, Skerries, Balbriggan and Arklow experienced growth from the 1860s. From the 1870s, Ardglass and Kilkeel in County Down also participated in the east coast herring fishery, largely serving the British market.[23]

Compared to other European maritime economies, sea fisheries made a relatively modest contribution to the Irish economy between 1815 and 1880. From the Great Famine to 1881 there was a contraction in employment in this sector in excess of the general decline in population; the combination of fishing and potato cultivation common before the Famine was deemed a particularly high-risk survival strategy in its aftermath. By contrast, the salmon fisheries steadily increased in value on about 120 salmon rivers, where weirs had long been utilised to trap fish.[24] Salmon constituted by far the most valuable branch of the inland fisheries, though most were caught in tidal waters and exported to Britain.

The Irish forestry sector was also of relatively minor consequence in economic terms, with most land cleared of trees for agriculture. Wakefield noted in 1812 that 'the whole island is remarkably bare of trees and exhibits a naked appearance'.[25] Indigenous timber supplies were so limited that the recovery

---

21 De Courcy Ireland, *Ireland's sea fisheries*, passim; J. Rees, *The fishery of Arklow 1800–1950* (Dublin: Four Courts Press, 2008), p. 15; V. Pollock, 'The herring industry in County Down 1840–1940' in L. Proudfoot and W. Nolan (eds.), *Down: history and society* (Dublin: Geography Publications, 1997), p. 417.

22 E. Symes, 'The Torbay fishermen in Ringsend', *Dublin Historical Record*, 53 (2000), 139–49; W. Andrews, 'On the herring fisheries of Ireland', *Journal of the Royal Dublin Society*, 35 (1866), 12–23.

23 O'Mahony, 'Fishing in nineteenth-century Kinsale', 113; De Courcy Ireland, *Ireland's sea fisheries*; M. McCaughan, 'Dandys, luggers, herring and mackerel' in M. McCaughan and J. Appleby (eds.), *The Irish Sea: aspects of maritime history* (Belfast: Institute of Irish Studies, 1989), pp. 121–6.

24 *Thom's Directory* (Dublin: Alex. Thom & Co., 1859), p. 580; A. Went, 'The pursuit of salmon', *Proceedings of the Royal Irish Academy*, 63c (1964), 191–244.

25 E. Wakefield, *An account of Ireland, statistical and political*, 2 vols. (London: Longman, Hurst, Rees, Orme, and Brown, 1812), vol. I, p. 9.

Table 4. *Forestry acreage in Ireland, 1841–91.*

1841	374,482
1845	345,000
1851	304,906
1861	316,597
1871	324,990
1881	328,703
1891	311,554

Source: E. Neeson, *A history of Irish forestry* (Dublin: Lilliput Press, 1991), pp. 97–100; A. Bourke, 'The agricultural statistics of the 1841 census of Ireland: a critical review', *Economic History Review*, 2nd ser., 18 (1965), 376–91; *Agricultural statistics, Ireland 1913*, [*Forestry operations*].

of bog wood was a profitable activity. Nonetheless, tree planting gathered momentum during the first third of the nineteenth century, followed by a lull in the 1840s,[26] with very modest increases thereafter down to 1881 (see Table 4).

Most forestry was located on landed estates where economic returns were secondary to its aesthetic and recreational value. Efforts to utilise waste land for forestry were relatively limited, with only 1.5 per cent of the total area of Ireland under forestry by the end of the nineteenth century, compared to 5.2 per cent in England and 4.5 per cent in Scotland.[27] Following the second Land Act of 1881, landlords and new owners began to cut down trees and sell the timber, with the result that acreages gradually declined. Added value in the forestry sector appears to have been fairly limited by European standards.

The exploitation of bogs for cutting turf was significantly more important to the Irish economy in these years than fishing and forestry combined. Ó Gráda estimates that turf may easily have contributed £2 million to pre-Famine rural incomes, when about £2 per family is allowed for about one million families for domestic heat and cooking purposes, with most of the

26 A.T. Lucas, 'Bog-wood, a study in rural economy', *Bealoideas*, 23 (1954), 71–121; E. Neeson, *A history of Irish forestry* (Dublin: Lilliput Press, 1991), p. 92; W.J. Smyth, 'The greening of Ireland – tenant tree planting in the eighteenth and nineteenth centuries', *Irish Forestry*, 54 (1997), 55–72; R. Tomlinson, 'Trees and woodlands of County Down' in Proudfoot and Nolan (eds.), *Down*, pp. 239–65; D. McCracken and E. McCracken, 'A register of trees, Co. Cork, 1790–1860', *Journal of the Cork Historical and Archaeological Society*, 81 (1976), 39–60.
27 W. Coyne (ed.), *Ireland industrial and agricultural* (Dublin: Browne and Nolan, 1902), pp. 323–4.

turf harvest not marketed.[28] Using household consumption data from the Coolatin estate (of 8 tons per turf-using household), Liam Kennedy has estimated that Irish turf output and consumption rose from somewhat over 5 million tons in 1801 to a peak of over 8 million in 1845, before falling back to over 6 million by 1851; his pre-Famine estimate fits with that of Ó Gráda.[29] But these estimates are probably too conservative; while £2 might suffice for the turf consumption of poorer households, Wakefield's estimates in 1810 allowed much higher consumption among better-off households.[30] It was also utilised for a host of other industrial and agricultural purposes, including distilling, lime burning, linen bleaching, brick making, by blacksmiths, etc. Proudfoot notes that the core linen manufacturing districts in Ulster in the mid-nineteenth century created a huge demand for agricultural products, notably cattle, potatoes, oats and turf.[31] Allowance must also be made for sales to a variety of institutions, businesses and better-off households, from offices to military barracks, police stations, hotels, hospitals, schools, convents, pubs and so forth, which collectively would have increased consumption levels above those estimated by Kennedy and Ó Gráda. Production was heavily affected by weather conditions, notably excessive rainfall, which resulted in major fuel famines in, for example, 1816–17 and 1861–2 in the west and northwest.[32] Turf remained a valuable source of fuel and income for turf cutters and was probably as important to the Irish economy at large, or more so, than the proceeds of forestry, fishing, mining and quarrying combined.

Services, Urban Development and the Communications Revolution

One of the most notable structural changes in the Irish economy in the nineteenth century was the decline in the share of the population engaged in agriculture and industry, and the corresponding rise in the proportion engaged

---

28 Ó Gráda, *Ireland: a new economic history*, p. 116.
29 L. Kennedy, 'The peoples fuel: turf in Ireland in the nineteenth and twentieth centuries' in R.W. Unger (ed.), *Energy transitions in history: global cases of continuity and change*, RCC *Perspectives* 2013, no. 2, pp. 25–30.
30 Wakefield, *Ireland statistical and political*, vol. 1, pp. 624–5.
31 L. Proudfoot, 'Markets, fairs and towns in Ireland, *c*.1600–1853' in P. Borsay and L. Proudfoot (eds.), *Provincial towns in early modern England and Ireland* (Oxford: Oxford University Press, 2002), p. 86.
32 J.S. Donnelly, 'The Irish agricultural depression of 1859–64', *Irish Economic and Social History*, 3 (1976), 47.

in services from less than 20 per cent of the occupied population in 1841 to almost 40 per cent in 1881 (see Table 5).

While market towns provided financial, legal and commercial services, periodic fair and market days provided intensive interfaces between rural and urban populations. Village and small-town Ireland, notably in the south, was therefore usually strongly connected with the service requirements of the agricultural population. The impact of extensive nineteenth-century chapel construction at intersections frequently gave rise to other localised services such as a school, shop, public house, forge, post office, etc.[33]

A few larger ports provided a more specialised range of services and infrastructure that facilitated trade. In Cork city, for example, between 1841 and 1881 there was a general contraction in manufacturing employment, and a rise in employment in transport, dealing, public and professional services, and domestic service.[34] London excepted, Dublin's position as a provider of legal, medical and educational services was unequalled in the United Kingdom. Its decline in the rankings from the second city in the early nineteenth century to seventh by 1881 reminds us of the relatively slower pace of urbanisation in Ireland compared to the rest of the UK, if we leave aside the exceptional growth of Belfast. Yet extensive suburban development in Dublin between 1815 and 1881 could not have been sustained in the absence of expanding employment opportunities, which were availed of by the middle classes in services in particular, as the city emerged as the chief centre of the wholesale and retail trade in Ireland.[35] The construction of the Irish rail network

Table 5. *Employment shares in the Irish economy, 1841–81.*

% share in occupied workforce	1841	1851	1861	1871	1881
Agriculture and fishing	51.1	48.8	43.2	41.1	41.6
Industry and construction	29.5	25.2	23.5	22.0	18.8
Services	19.4	26.0	33.3	36.9	39.6

Source: Derived from S.A. Royle, 'Industrialization, urbanization and urban society in post-Famine Ireland c. 1850–1921' in B.J. Graham and L.J. Proudfoot (eds.), *An historical geography of Ireland* (London: Academic Press, 1993), p. 264.

33 K. Whelan, 'The Catholic parish, the Catholic chapel, and village development in Ireland', *Irish Geography*, 16 (1983), 1–15.
34 S. Royle, 'Industrialization, urbanization and urban society in post-Famine Ireland, c. 1850–1921' in B.J. Graham and L. Proudfoot (eds.), *An historical geography of Ireland* (London: Academic Press, 1993), pp. 258–92.
35 D. Dickson, *Dublin: the making of a capital city* (London: Profile, 2014), pp. 279–368.

bolstered the city's commercial significance. The shipping tonnage handled by the port of Dublin trebled between 1841 and 1878. The continuing importance of road transport is apparent from the fact that half of the 7,500 jobs in transport in the city by 1871 were connected with this sector, a further third were engaged in canals, maritime or port employment, while the balance worked in railways, which had five major termini in the city. The improving road system increased mobility between inland districts and the ports, expanding inter-regional and cross-channel trade.

Solar's work on shipping records the acceleration in the tonnage entering Irish ports between the mid-1820s and the late 1870s. This period witnessed the transition from sail to more dependable and predictable steamships. Belfast's share of steamship tonnage cleared in Ireland rose from 22 per cent in 1841 to 29 per cent in 1881, by which time it had become Ireland's premier port, just eclipsing Dublin, which declined from 34 to 28 per cent during these years. The growth of steamship usage facilitated the expansion of certain types of trade, notably the export of live animals, eggs and poultry destined for the expanding British market, while greater regularity enabled Irish retailers to bypass import merchants through direct orders.[36]

The coasting trade was important for ports and harbours. There was a canal network serving inland locations, but it was relatively small compared to that in Britain; with only 600 miles of inland navigation in operation by 1845, its impact was restricted. For passenger traffic the canals were slow, but they were well suited for carrying bulky heavy goods, like coal, building materials, turf, flour, grain and beer. When the first railway line opened on the suburban route between Dublin and Kingstown in 1834, Ireland tentatively entered the railway age and it was this mode of transport that ultimately brought the communications revolution into the heart of the Irish countryside; by 1874 Ireland had nineteen different railway companies operating 2,049 miles of track. Of the investment in Irish railways between 1831 and 1852, which predominantly came from private investors, Ireland contributed about £4.4 million and England £4.3 million.[37]

Building railways was extremely labour-intensive; in 1846–8 about 40,000 men were employed on average on various railway construction projects. Much of the unskilled labour was hired locally, supplemented by a more

---

36 P.M. Solar, 'Shipping and economic development in nineteenth-century Ireland', *Economic History Review*, 59 (2006), 717–42.

37 M. Gould, 'The effects of government policy on railway building in Ireland', *The Newcomen Society*, 62 (1990–1), 84; W.A. Thomas, *The stock exchanges of Ireland* (London: Francis Cairns, 1987), p. 109.

transient group of navvies and skilled craftsmen. After lines had been built, labour was then required to run the railways, amounting to over 9,000 persons already by 1860. Construction costs were cheaper in Ireland than in Britain due to lower labour and land costs, and to the reduced requirement for bridges, viaducts and tunnels.[38]

The knock-on effects of railway development in Ireland were not as great as in other European economies. The iron and coal industries benefited enormously in Europe and Britain from their growth and the railways in turn derived much income from transporting iron and coal. Ireland had limited coal and iron resources, however, so much of the construction benefit passed to English industry. The major effect of the railways was the enormous improvement in Ireland's communications infrastructure. This was probably the single most important impact of the British industrial revolution in Ireland. The average cost of road haulage in the mid-1830s was 5d per ton-mile. Average freight rates on the railways worked out at less than half of this. The rail network was also safer and less susceptible to seasonal weather conditions. It widened markets, stimulated competition and reinforced tendencies towards regional specialisation, by providing regions with opportunities to export products in which they had comparative advantage. Ireland, as a result, increasingly exported more agricultural produce to Britain and in turn imported more goods from British industrial districts. Rail was critical in the major extension of retailing, by facilitating the entry of a flood of factory-produced goods which were sold in hardware stores and draperies in provincial towns, and in larger department stores displacing local artisan production in the cities.[39]

Tourism and the hotel business also expanded in Ireland as a consequence of railway investment. Many hotels built in the second half of the nineteenth century were located close to rail stations. Killarney is perhaps the best example of a town which developed significantly as a tourist centre, as a consequence of the investment in a hotel by the Great Southern and Western Railway. Rail companies published guides for tourists, to encourage them to visit specific locations on their routes. Railways also opened up new

---

38 J.C. Conroy, *A history of railways in Ireland* (London: Longman, 1928), p. 320; J. Lee, 'The construction costs of Irish railways 1830–1853', *Business History Review*, 9 (1967), 95–109.

39 J. Lee, 'The railways in the Irish economy' in L.M. Cullen (ed.), *The formation of the Irish economy* (Cork: Mercier Press, 1968), pp. 77–87; L. Kennedy, 'Regional specialization, railway development, and Irish agriculture in the nineteenth century' in M. Goldstrom and L.A. Clarkson (eds.), *Irish population, economy and society* (Oxford: Oxford University Press, 1981), pp. 173–93; Ó Gráda, *Ireland: a new economic history*.

opportunities for visitors; Thomas Cook began organising low-cost excursions to Ireland from Britain in 1849 and his son opened the first Cook office in Dublin in 1874, bringing many British tourists to Ireland subsequently.[40]

Railways also created new possibilities for extending recreational facilities such as seaside resorts. Proximity to major urban centres opened up sea bathing in emerging resorts such as Bray, Bangor, Tramore, Youghal and Salthill, accommodating those eager to take the air, swim and escape the confines and pollution of the cities for a day at least. Bray, for example, had long been a destination and tour base for travellers and day trippers; in 1815 it had a hotel, in addition to a growing number of lodging houses for the upper classes. The arrival of the railway in 1854 opened up the seafront to day trippers from Dublin and marked the beginning of an impressive new phase of development, which resulted in new hotels, the esplanade, pleasure grounds and a Turkish bath.[41]

The core rail routes, complemented by the road network, provided for an improved and more integrated transport infrastructure throughout Ireland, which dramatically transformed and compressed time–space relationships across the island. Rail infrastructure also accommodated much of the newly developed telegraph services and the mail services. The circulation and distribution of newspapers gradually widened in the post-Famine decades as literacy rose and costs came down. The number of provincial newspapers expanded from 65 in 1850 to 125 by 1880, extending the public sphere.[42]

Other developments in the services sector included the radical improvement in banking provision from the mid-1820s. Ireland's banking infrastructure was exceedingly limited in 1815, with the Bank of Ireland operating in Dublin alone, and various private banks operating in the larger commercial centres. During the banking crisis of 1820, sixteen of the thirty-one private banks on the island went bankrupt, leaving only six centres in the entire country with banking facilities. Prior to 1824, the Bank of Ireland refused to develop branches outside Dublin, but in 1825 it opened branches in Cork,

40 Lee, 'The railways in the Irish economy', pp. 77, 80; I. Furlong, *Irish tourism 1880–1980* (Dublin: Irish Academic Press, 2009), pp. 17–18.

41 K.M. Davies, 'For health and pleasure in the British fashion: Bray, Co. Wicklow as a tourist resort, 1750–1914' in B. O'Connor and M. Cronin (eds.), *Tourism in Ireland: a critical analysis* (Cork: Cork University Press, 1993); for seaside resorts see R. Foley, *Healing waters: therapeutic landscapes in historic and contemporary Ireland* (Farnham: Ashgate, 2010), pp. 111–42.

42 A. Horner, 'Ireland's time-space revolution; improvements in pre-Famine travel', *History-Ireland*, 15:5 (2007), 22–7; T. Wall, 'Railways and telecommunications', *Journal of the Irish Railway Record Society*, 20143 (2001), 479–85; M.-L. Legg, *Newspapers and nationalism: the Irish provincial press 1850–1892* (Dublin: Four Courts Press, 1999), pp. 30, 125.

Waterford, Clonmel, Newry, Belfast, Londonderry and Westport, and over the next decade the Provincial Bank also developed a branch network. The various bank failures in the preceding decade led to new legislation (the Banking Co-partnerships Regulation Act in 1825), which facilitated the subsequent formation of banking partnerships, the first being the Northern Bank in Belfast in 1824. A series of joint stock banks were established thereafter, creating more competition. Yet, it was not until the collapse of the City of Glasgow Bank in 1878 that Irish banks adopted limited liability status. There were eight unlimited liability joint stock banks operating in Ireland by the mid-1830s; the fact that seven of these were still operating by the mid-1870s reveals the greater stability in Irish banking after the 1820s.[43]

By 1875 there were 326 bank branches in Ireland, helping to transfer funds saved in deposits generated in rural areas to loans in the towns and cities where borrowing was more commonplace. A substantial remainder was invested in London. Philip Ollerenshaw has challenged the traditional view that conservative Irish bankers starved the Irish economy of much needed capital in this period, demonstrating that generally banks provided credit to those seeking short-term working capital. However, he found that credit lines to farmers could be severely curtailed during major recessions such as those in 1859–64 and 1877–9. His work reveals the highly seasonal nature of the demand for credit both in agriculture and in industry. Irish bank deposits rose marginally from 5.8 per cent of UK deposits in 1871 to 5.9 by 1881, demonstrating a somewhat lower level of savings pro rata to the population compared to the rest of the UK.[44] Nevertheless, Irish banking had made huge advances since 1815.

The development of company law within the United Kingdom between 1844 and 1856 opened the way to extend the operation of joint stock companies. Revisions to company law brought about by the Limited Liability Act in 1855 and the Joint Stock Companies Act in the following year helped to increase the availability of investment capital for Irish companies in the following decades, when there was a significant increase in the demand for financial assets, and commercialisation accelerated in the economy at large. Within the services sector this

---

43 P. Ollerenshaw, 'Business and finance, 1780–1945' in L. Kennedy and P. Ollerenshaw (eds.), *An economic history of Ulster* (Oxford: Oxford University Press, 2013), pp. 177–94; F.G. Hall, *The Bank of Ireland* (Dublin: Hodges Figgis, 1949); C. Hickson, J. Turner and C. McCann, 'Much ado about nothing: the limitation of liability and the market for 19th century Irish bank stock', *Explorations in Economic History*, 42 (2005), 459–76.
44 Ó Gráda, *Ireland: a new economic history*, pp. 140–6, 358–65; Hall, *The Bank of Ireland*, p. 261; P. Ollerenshaw, 'Aspects of bank lending in post-Famine Ireland' in R. Mitchison and P. Roebuck (eds.), *Economy and society in Scotland and Ireland 1500–1939* (Edinburgh: John Donald, 1988), pp. 222–32.

was apparent among new hotels and gas and insurance companies registered as joint stock companies in the late 1850s and 1860s. In the 1870s transport, warehousing, distribution and retailing featured strongly, in addition to restaurants, clubs, coffee houses and even roller skating rinks, which attest to the increasing significance of distribution, retailing, consumption and recreation.[45]

The general expansion of the service economy is also evident in the growth of professional services in education, health and law, in transport and dealing and in the range of institutional services. The national school system (founded in 1831) employed many teachers, extended primary education and dramatically improved literacy and numeracy levels thereafter. The establishment of a host of institutions and organisations – hospitals, workhouses, reformatories and asylums, orphanages, convents and seminaries – and the presence of various other state-funded bodies, including the armed forces, the police, customs and excise, the prison system and government administration, all provided expanding employment opportunities. Domestic service accounted for a significant share of female employment, almost doubling its share of total employment to 18 per cent by 1881.[46] By 1881 the Irish service sector provided more than twice as many jobs in the Irish economy as the industrial sector, and it was fast approaching the percentage level of employment provided by the agricultural sector. This structural shift was symptomatic of an economy which was becoming increasingly more diversified.

Industry and Mining

While Britain's industrial revolution was in full spate in the early nineteenth century, industrial development in Ireland was altogether more limited. It followed a pattern with parallels in such continental European economies as Spain, Austria and the Scandinavian countries.

In 1815, the most marked feature of Ireland's premier industry, linen, was its concentration in the province of Ulster. At this proto-industrial stage, it was still largely a domestic industry, apart from the bleaching process, which was more mechanised and centralised. Critically the industry had long been geared to international markets, with about two-thirds of output sold outside

---

45 C. Hickson and J. Turner, 'Pre and post Famine indices of Irish equity prices', *European Review of Economic History*, 12:1 (2008), 3–38; Thomas, *The stock exchanges of Ireland*, pp. 144–50.

46 C. Clear, *Social change and everyday life in Ireland 1850–1922* (Manchester: Manchester University Press, 2007), pp. 30–54, 90–123; H.D. Gribbon, 'Economic and social history 1850–1920' in W.E. Vaughan (ed.), *A new history of Ireland*, vol. vi: *Ireland under the Union, II, 1870–1921* (Oxford: Oxford University Press, 1996), p. 333.

Ireland.[47] It was extremely labour intensive and the slowest textile to become mechanised, so cheaper Irish labour costs and a tradition of flax cultivation were important comparative advantages over linen manufacturing in Britain. The spinning sector only began to become mechanised from the late 1820s, with an increasingly heavy concentration around Belfast in the following decades, and yarn increasingly put out to weavers. There was a marked spatial realignment of the handloom weaving workforce also, as it became more concentrated in counties Antrim, Down and Armagh and the greater Belfast area in proximity to the major spinning mills in the 1840s and 1850s. Weaving was slower to mechanise, with power looms introduced only from the 1850s onwards; handloom weavers continued in the manufacture of fine cambrics and damask, and it was claimed in 1880 that there was still £5 million invested in the handloom trade and 100,000 weavers were employed.[48]

While industrialisation was concentrated in the greater Belfast region, it was also identifiable in towns and villages across Ulster, notably but not exclusively in the east. The majority of the province's industrial villages had their genesis between 1830 and 1870 when linen production became mechanised; their number includes Annsborough and Dunbarton, County Down, Sion Mills in County Tyrone, and Bessbrook in County Armagh. Earlier industrial villages, like that at Hilden near Lisburn, were extended. Impressive developments in the Irish cotton industry in the first third of the nineteenth century were not sustained as British competition proved increasingly more intense, reducing profitability relative to linen where Irish textile investment was increasingly focused thereafter. But it is revealing that, as late as the mid-1830s, cotton was still the most important source of employment in mechanised spinning mills, accounting for almost 44 per cent of employment in such concerns compared to under 39 per cent in flax spinning.[49]

---

47 L.A. Clarkson, 'Ireland 1841; pre-industrial or proto-industrial; industrializing or de-industrializing' in S. Ogilvie and M. Cerman (eds.), *European proto-industrialization* (Cambridge: Cambridge University Press, 1996), pp. 67–84.

48 P. Solar, 'The birth and death of European flax, hemp jute spinning firms: the Irish and Belgian cases' in B. Collins and P. Ollerenshaw (eds.), *The European linen industry in historical perspective* (Oxford: Oxford University Press, 2003), pp. 245–58; K. James, *Handloom weavers in Ulster's linen industry 1815–1914* (Dublin: Four Courts Press, 2007).

49 P. Solar, 'The linen industry in the nineteenth century' in D. Jenkins (ed.), *The Cambridge history of western textiles*, 2 vols. (Cambridge: Cambridge University Press, 2003), vol. II, pp. 809–23; D.S. MacNeice, 'Industrial villages of Ulster, 1800–1900' in P. Roebuck (ed.), *Plantation to Partition: essays in honour of J.L. McCracken* (Belfast: Blackstaff Press, 1981), pp. 172–90; P. Ollerenshaw, 'Industry 1820–1914' in Kennedy and Ollerenshaw (eds.), *An economic history of Ulster*, pp. 62–108; R. Harrison, *The Richardsons of Bessbrook; Ulster Quakers and the linen industry, 1845–1921* (Dublin: Original Writing, 2009); D. Greer and J. Nicholson, *The Factory Acts in Ireland 1802–1914* (Dublin: Four Courts Press, 2003), p. 19.

The impact of industrialisation on Ireland was geographically limited and relatively late by British standards. A substantial number of cottage producers engaged in textile production were displaced between the 1820s and the 1880s, the majority as a consequence of the industrialisation of linen production in Ireland. While total employment in Irish textiles and clothing recorded by the census fell from over 898,000 persons in 1841 to 290,860 in 1881, the scale of this decline is misleading since it was largely comprised of part-time domestic producers. Employment in Irish mechanised textile mills actually rose from merely 2.7 per cent of UK employment in such concerns in 1835 to 6.6 by 1885, revealing advances in Irish mechanised production. Moreover, when textiles are removed from the census data, taken collectively there was no marked decline in other forms of industrial employment in these years, and significant growth was recorded in the 1870s.[50]

East Ulster in general was strongly connected to the great industrial network of northern Britain, drawing upon its coal and iron resources and human capital to complement the considerable indigenous skills and entrepreneurial talent that had been cumulatively built up in the linen industry, assisted by privileged access in the eighteenth century to the rapidly growing British market and that of her colonies, notably in North America. As linen became more concentrated in east Ulster between the 1820s and 1880s, it became progressively more difficult for other regions in Britain and Europe to compete. Mechanised linen manufacture also gave rise to the dynamic growth of a number of textile engineering firms, which exported linen manufacturing machinery to Britain and Europe from the mid-nineteenth century. From the 1840s, the shirt making and clothing industry increased around Derry.

Dublin became the major centre of southern Irish industry, notably in the food and drink sectors, but also in railway engineering. Cork became the main centre of mechanised woollen manufacture in Ireland during the second half of the nineteenth century. Developments in Dublin and Cork were fairly limited when compared to the critical mass built up in Ulster. The second wave of development in east Ulster in textiles and clothing took place from the 1860s, notably during the American Civil War when cotton was in short supply. Ulster became one of the leading linen manufacturing centres

---

50 A. Bielenberg, *Ireland and the Industrial Revolution: the impact of the Industrial Revolution on Irish industry 1801–1922* (London: Routledge, 2009), pp. 180, 199.

in the world at this point, specialising in the production of fine linens for the British and American markets in particular.[51]

Iron shipbuilding emerged as the fastest-growing industry in the country from the 1860s, again centred increasingly in Belfast. Harland and Wolff (established in 1858) depended largely on British demand, since Britain dominated the dramatic expansion of world trade in these years. Unlike linen, the iron shipbuilding and engineering sectors in Belfast owed much to British entrepreneurs, while part of its skilled labour was also hired from Britain at premium rates of pay, but the shipyards and engineering works could simultaneously take advantage of the lower cost of unskilled and semi-skilled labour in Ireland. Belfast's industrialisation and rapid urbanisation were exceptional by Irish standards; its population grew spectacularly from a little under 28,000 in 1811 to over 208,000 by 1881.[52]

Industrial development in the remainder of Ireland was far more limited. The food processing and drink sector was relatively more significant, even developing exports to the expanding British market, most notably in bacon curing, biscuit making, distilling and brewing. By 1880, there was a greater concentration of such industries in Dublin than elsewhere, but Belfast was also a major centre of food processing, distilling and tobacco production.[53] Outside the north-east, Guinness was the major success story. The firm already dominated the Dublin market for beer by 1815, and with the growth of the railway network in both Britain and Ireland it extended its trade dramatically in Britain, before cornering most of the growing Irish market. Yet food processing and drink did not benefit the southern Irish economy as textiles or shipbuilding did in Ulster, since food and drink were far less labour intensive. Moreover, many of the smaller craft industries which had been important in Dublin and Cork gave way to mass-produced factory goods increasingly imported from Britain.

Belfast was Ireland's only major nineteenth-century industrial city. Outside east Ulster, no counties and only a few of the larger urban centres had over 43 per cent of the labour force engaged in industry; these were Dublin city with 55.1 per cent, Cork city with 48.3, Limerick city with 43.9 and Waterford city with 50.8 in 1881. In that year, by comparison, 68.2 per cent of the workforce was engaged in industry in Belfast. In a wider UK context, total industrial

---

51 Ibid; P. Solar 'The Irish linen trade 1852–1914', *Textile History*, 36 (2005), 46–68.
52 R. Gillespie and S. Royle, *Belfast, part 1*, Irish Historic Towns Atlas 12 (Dublin: Royal Irish Academy, 2003) p. 10; S. Royle, *Belfast, part 2*, Irish Historic Towns Atlas 17 (Dublin: Royal Irish Academy, 2007), p. 7.
53 C. Rynne, *Industrial Ireland 1750–1930* (Cork: Collins Press, 2006), pp. 235–66; M. Daly, *Dublin the deposed capital: a social and economic history 1860–1914* (Cork: Cork University Press, 1985).

employment in Ireland declined during the post-Famine decades in contrast to the experience in England, Scotland and Wales.[54]

One of the factors that limited Ireland's capacity to industrialise was a lack of raw materials, iron and coal in particular, which prevented it from pursuing the development path that England, Scotland and Wales all successfully followed. Ireland accounted for less than 0.25 per cent of UK coal output between 1854 and 1881, with the result that the cost of fuel was greater than on the major industrial coalfields of Britain around which energy intensive industries congregated. This greatly influenced the evolution, profile and character of its industrial sector relative to that of Great Britain both during and after the industrial revolution.[55]

Living Conditions and Wealth Distribution

Between 1815 and 1881 Ireland experienced exceptional levels of emigration by European standards.[56] Consequently, the US and British labour markets began to exert an influence on developments in Ireland. Kevin O'Rourke has revealed the far greater influence of higher wages and labour demand in these economies in pulling people out of rural Ireland than any endogenous factors between 1856 and 1876. O'Rourke and others have also tracked the growth in post-Famine wages and the extent of wage convergence with the British and American economies between 1850 and 1914, highlighting the significant contribution of emigration.[57] Geary and Stark's assessment of movements of wages and GDP within the regions of the UK between 1861 and 1911 has also found evidence of Ireland catching up with Great Britain, but concludes that improvements in the Irish position arose more from growth in capital accumulation and total factor productivity than from emigration.[58]

---

54 Royle, 'Industrialization, urbanization and urban society', 263; F. Geary and T. Stark 'Examining Ireland's post-Famine economic growth performance', *Economic Journal*, 112 (2002), 919–35.

55 A. Bielenberg, 'What happened to Irish industry after the Industrial Revolution? Some evidence from the first UK Census of Production in 1907', *Economic History Review*, 61 (2008), 820–41.

56 See Gurrin, Chapter 8, pp. 226–7 below; Kenny, Chapter 25, pp. 666–87 below.

57 K. O'Rourke, 'Rural depopulation in a small open economy: Ireland 1856–1876', *Explorations in Economic History*, 28 (1991), 409–32; G. Boyer, T. Hatton and K. O'Rourke, 'The impact of emigration on real wages in Ireland 1850–1914' in T. Hatton and J. Williamson (eds.), *Migration and the international labor market, 1850–1939* (London: Routledge, 1994), pp. 221–39; J. Williamson, 'Economic convergence: placing post-Famine Ireland in comparative perspective', *Irish Economic and Social History*, 21 (1994), 5–27.

58 F. Geary and T. Stark, 'Regional GDP in the UK, 1861–1911: new estimates', *Economic History Review*, 68 (2015), 123–44.

Yet the distribution of Irish wealth remained highly uneven. In the mid-1830s, the Poor Inquiry estimated that roughly 2.4 million people were annually in a state of extreme privation and in need of assistance during the 'meal months' between the point when the supply of the previous year's potato crop had run out and the harvesting of the new crop began. Food shortages attributable to the failure of the potato crop occurred in 1817, 1822, 1831, 1835–7, 1839 and 1842, with far worse to come between 1845 and 1849, when famine raged for several years with devastating consequences.[59] This reality must be incorporated into any discussion of living standards in this period. Trends in the standard of living in pre-Famine Ireland (after 1815) remain an issue of dispute.[60] If there was a rise in average living standards derived from wages, salaries, rents, etc. between 1815 and 1845, this was among the majority of the population which lived above the abject living conditions observed by the Poor Inquiry. Following the Great Famine, the general rise in living standards is more clear-cut, with some limited convergence with the rest of the UK.[61]

Within agriculture, W.E. Vaughan has argued that between the mid-nineteenth century and the mid-1870s, rents moved upwards more slowly than the rise in agricultural prices, so tenants benefited more than landlords. Michael Turner disagrees. He argues that while both groups benefited, any advantage to tenants was exceedingly marginal and, more critically, that advances were wiped out between the early 1870s and the early 1880s when output fell and the net incomes of tenants took a nose dive.[62]

Yet across society at large, general improvements in Irish living conditions are apparent in the improved quality of housing from the mid-nineteenth century. In 1841 under a quarter of the housing stock was defined as better-quality first- and second-class houses; by 1881 this had risen to over half of all houses. Fourth-class housing, by contrast, which accounted for almost 37 per cent of the housing stock in 1841, fell to less than 5 per cent by 1881, but much of this shrinkage was a consequence of the grim fallout from the Great

---

59 L.M. Geary, ' "The whole country was in motion"; mendicancy and vagrancy in pre-Famine Ireland' in J. Hill and C. Lennon (eds.), *Luxury and austerity: Historical Studies XXI* (Dublin: UCD Press, 1999), pp. 121–37; T.P. O'Neill, 'Poverty in Ireland 1815–45', *Folklife*, 11 (1973), 22; see Gray, Chapter 24 below, pp. 639–65.

60 See J. Mokyr and C. Ó Gráda, 'Poor and getting poorer? Living standards in Ireland before the Famine', *Economic History Review*, 46 (1988), 209–35 for a pessimistic view, and Geary and Stark, 'Trends in real wages during the Industrial Revolution: a view from across the Irish sea', *Economic History Review*, 57 (2004), 363–95 for an optimistic view.

61 Geary and Stark, 'Regional GDP in the UK, 1861–1911', pp. 123–44.

62 Turner, *After the Famine*, 206.

Famine, which raised average living standards by default, as it removed much of the poorest strata of Irish society (see Table 6).

Another indicator of rising living standards is provided by increased per capita consumption of commodities such as tobacco, beer, flour and tea between 1815 and 1881. By the early twentieth century, there are some indications that this rise in purchasing power was enjoyed to a greater degree in Ulster, as a result of the relatively higher household incomes available there consequent on the wider employment opportunities arising from industrialisation.[63]

While Irish living standards had clearly risen since the pre-Famine era, the benefits of these general improvements in the performance of the Irish economy were highly unevenly distributed. In the countryside, the tabulation in the mid-1870s of landownership starkly reveals the concentration of wealth within the Irish gentry. Although official returns revealed that there were about 6,500 landlords (with upwards of 500 acres), about 48 per cent of the country was comprised of estates of 5,000 acres or more in the possession of an elite group of 700 landlords, whose large country houses and conspicuous consumption graphically displayed their status at the economic and political apex of Irish society.[64] Turner's work on Irish wealth concentration in the six counties of Ulster, based on an analysis of the estates of deceased persons probated, indicates that the expanding middle classes (merchants, industrialists, professionals and retailers) increased their share of all estates probated from under 23 per cent in the late 1850s to over 35 by 1881, thereby eclipsing the gentry, whose share declined from over 51 per cent to under 31 during

Table 6. *The number of houses (in thousands) returned in different classes in the census years 1841–81.*

	1st class	2nd class	3rd class	4th class	Total	1st + 2nd %
1841	40	264	533	491	1328	22.90
1851	50	319	542	136	1047	35.20
1861	55	361	490	89	995	41.80
1871	60	381	363	157	961	45.90
1881	67	422	384	41	914	53.50

Source: 1841–81 censuses.

63 A. Bielenberg and J. O'Hagan, 'Consumption and living conditions 1750–2016' in M. Daly and E. Biagini (eds.), *Cambridge social history of Ireland* (Cambridge: Cambridge University Press, 2017), pp. 195–211.
64 W.E. Vaughan, *Landlords and tenants in mid Victorian Ireland* (Oxford: Oxford University Press, 1994), p. 6.

the same period. This provides additional evidence of the growing relative economic significance of the middle classes during the period in question. Although farmers also made some advance from about 10 per cent of estates probated to almost 15 in these years, the gentry were still well ahead of them in terms of wealth concentration in the countryside. At the economic apex (e.g. those bequeathing more than £30,000) across all Ireland, the gentry still accounted for the majority of estate shares probated in the 1880s.[65]

Urbanisation in Ireland proceeded at a limited pace during these years, with less than 8 per cent of the Irish population in towns of over 10,000 persons at the beginning of the nineteenth century, rising to 18 per cent by 1891; this was an exceedingly low level of urbanisation when compared to 62 per cent in England and Wales or 50 in Scotland in the latter year, or even the 29 to 35 per cent range witnessed in Belgium, the Netherlands, France, Denmark or Spain. Yet in a wider European context, Ireland was still more urbanised than Norway, Switzerland, Austria, Hungry, Sweden or Portugal by 1891.[66] It is when Ireland's position is considered within the United Kingdom that it stands out as anomalous, and in keeping with its far more limited level of industrialisation.

Conclusion

Those born in Ireland during the early nineteenth century who lived to witness the 1880s would have noticed a number of notable economic changes in the interim. An improvement in living standards and housing conditions was perhaps the most obvious. The decline in the rural population, with many abandoned dwellings, and a general rise in livestock numbers in farming and the dramatic reduction in tillage acreages would have been notable features in a changing rural landscape since the Great Famine. The aged would have noted a marked reduction in domestic cottage industry in the countryside, as Irish industrial production became increasingly more concentrated in workshops and factories, notably in Ulster. Yet the impact of industrialisation was far more limited than in Britain, despite major improvements in productivity

---

65 J. Turner 'Wealth concentration in the European periphery: Ireland 1858–2001', *Oxford Economic Papers*, 62 (2010), 625–49. For some insights into elements of the middle class see F. Campbell, *The Irish establishment 1879–1914* (Oxford: Oxford University Press, 2009); A. Bielenberg, 'The industrial elite in Ireland from the Industrial Revolution to the First World War' in F. Lane (ed.), *Politics, society and the middle class in modern Ireland* (London: Palgrave Macmillan, 2010).
66 Royle, 'Industrialization, urbanization and urban society', p. 266.

and the emergence within the Irish economy of several exceedingly large industrial firms.

This chapter has revealed that the most far-reaching advances in the economy in these years were made in the services sector. The communications revolution and the resulting increase in mobility centred on the railway network were probably the most dramatic changes witnessed and experienced across Irish society at large. The transformation of retailing was also remarkable, while trade assumed greater significance in Irish GDP. Service sector employment doubled its share of total employment in the economy between the 1840s and the 1880s, by which time its employment share almost rivalled that of agriculture while its GDP share is likely to have surpassed it. The emergence of a diverse range of service employments in these years is itself a testimony to the growing sophistication of the economy and the increase in purchasing power to sustain such services. Yet, agriculture remained centrally important to the Irish economy, and Ireland benefited in this period from improvements in the terms of trade as the price of livestock and livestock products rose, while the price of major industrial imports from Britain, like textiles and clothing, fell. Much of the Irish industrial sector processed raw materials derived from agriculture. Moreover, much of the service sector was geared to servicing the needs of the agricultural population. Fluctuations in the agricultural economy therefore still made a far deeper impact on Irish society than in Great Britain. It is hardly surprising, therefore, that events like the Great Famine and the severe agricultural recession of the late 1870s, which gave rise to the Land War, had the capacity to transform Irish politics, as they brought into sharp focus the highly unequal distribution of the benefits of economic production, more particularly in the Irish countryside.

8

Population and Emigration, 1730–1845

BRIAN GURRIN

The population of Ireland more than tripled, from some 2.5 million people to more than 8 million, between 1730 and 1845. This growth was uneven in both regional and temporal terms. At the national level the population grew rapidly in the second half of the eighteenth and the opening two decades of the nineteenth century, but growth slowed thereafter. In regional terms, the population increase was most rapid in Ulster and Connacht, and more muted in the south and the east. Ulster, with the third largest provincial population in 1730, was in 1821 the most populous province, though it was subsequently surpassed by Munster, which had the largest population by 1841. Connacht possessed the smallest population of all four provinces across the period 1730–1845.

Irish Population Studies

Although Ireland's population trends elicited the interest of notable early political economists such as William Petty, Richard Price, James Laffan and Arthur Young, their propositions, typically founded on house-count numbers emanating from the Revenue Commissioners, relied heavily on speculation and unsubstantiated supposition. It was not until 1821, when a national census was successfully completed, that some statistical clarity was brought to bear. The first notable modern-day inquiry into Irish population history – K.H. Connell's *The population of Ireland, 1750–1845,* published in 1950 – drew on surviving hearth-tax house-count data to propose revised national population figures for the period between 1687 and 1791.[1] Its age notwithstanding, Connell's work is still useful, not least because he provided a readable commentary on Ireland's population estimation between 1672 and 1821. But the identification of errors and invalid or questionable assumptions in his treatment and

---

1 K.H. Connell, *The population of Ireland, 1750–1845* (Oxford: Clarendon Press, 1950), p. 25.

interpretation of sources make his conclusions insecure. For example, his speculation that the collection of the hearth-tax became more efficient 'as the country became more thickly populated' is incorrect, and his assertion that it was 'quite impossible to give any precise opinion' on the degree of deficiency in the hearth-tax house-counts before the 1780s is followed by the assumption that an adjustment of 50 per cent is 'perhaps' appropriate. Then, using his adjusted house-count figures he presented fifteen national population estimates for the period 1687–1791. According to Connell, the population of Ireland rose from in excess of 3 million in the mid-1720s, to 4 million by the early 1780s and to over 4.75 million by 1791.[2]

His 'rudimentary' approach notwithstanding, Connell's was the 'standard work' on pre-Famine Irish population for three decades, in large part because it was felt that there was little more that could be done with the patchy and imprecise data available.[3] In the early 1980s, however, serious reservations were entered against his population-growth thesis, first by Leslie Clarkson and then by David Dickson, Cormac Ó Gráda and Stuart Daultrey. Both proposed 'a new chronology of population growth for the eighteenth century' on the grounds that Connell's adjustment of the hearth-tax figures caused him to exaggerate the national population in the first decades of the eighteenth century.[4] The publication in 1982 of Dickson et al.'s 'Hearth tax, household size and Irish population change, 1672–1821' was particularly important because of the manner in which it tested the reliability of the surviving house-count figures published by the Revenue Office. They comprehensively disproved Connell's key assumption that the hearth-tax house-counts became more efficient over time, showing the contrary to have been the case. Drawing on a wider array of sources, including five additional national house-counts, and applying a more sophisticated analytical approach than Connell or Clarkson, they rejected Connell's 50 per cent upward adjustment of the official house-counts between 1712 and 1785 in favour of smaller upward adjustments of between 14 and 34 per cent. Clarkson's proposed upward adjustment was

---

2 Ibid., pp. 4–5, 13, 25, 255–60.

3 J. Lee, 'Introduction' in *The population of Ireland before the nineteenth century* (Farnborough: Gregg International, 1973), fn. 3; D. Dickson, C. Ó Gráda and S. Daultrey, 'Hearth tax, household size and Irish population change, 1672–1821', *Proceedings of the Royal Irish Academy*, 82c (1982), 128, 129.

4 L.A. Clarkson, 'Irish population revisited, 1687–1821' in J.M. Goldstrom and L.A. Clarkson (eds.), *Irish population, economy, and society: essays in honour of the late K.H. Connell* (Oxford: Clarendon Press, 1981), pp. 13–35; Dickson et al., 'Hearth tax', *passim*; W. Macafee, 'The pre-Famine population of Ireland, a reconsideration' in B. Collins, P. Ollerenshaw and T. Parkhill (eds.), *Industry, trade and people in Ireland* (Belfast: Ulster Historical Foundation, 2005), p. 76.

15 per cent; but this was, by his own admission, no more than a 'hypothetical addition' on his part.[5]

Connell, Clarkson and Dickson et al. converted their adjusted house-counts to population estimates by employing household-size multipliers. Connell's multiplier ranged from 5.2 to 5.65, based on the number of hearths in a house, though this was offered 'with no certainty'. Clarkson averred that a mean household size of 5 was 'more appropriate', but employed a range of multipliers (5.0, 5.25 and 5.5) for 1791 on the reasonable grounds that 'regional rather than national multipliers ought to be established'; but, he pronounced, 'we are a long way yet from possessing such data'. Dickson et al., however, did precisely this; they used an array of demographic sources to construct a series of hypothetical provincial household multipliers, which they deployed to generate provincial population estimates. Significantly, their provincial multipliers were well below Connell's national multiplier.[6]

The more advanced analytical approach of Dickson et al. permitted them to propose eight new national population estimates for the period 1687 to 1753, and a further estimate for 1791.[7] These are shown, along with Connell's figures, in Table 7. The differences are of great consequence, as they suggest a pattern of population growth very different from that implied by Connell, particularly for the seven decades between 1753 and 1821. Employing Joseph Lee's proposed national population figure for 1821 of 7.2 million Connell's yearly rate of increase of 1.2 per cent between 1753 and 1821 is significantly in arrears of Dickson et al.'s figures of between 1.5 and 1.8 per cent.

The Population of Ireland in 1732

Dickson et al.'s reworked figures suggest an island-wide population in 1732 of between 2.16 and 2.53 million, well below Connell's estimate of 3 million. Their figure also highlights a decline, albeit of a modest order, on their estimate for 1725. This decline can be attributed to the sequence of poor harvests in the late 1720s, famously satirised in Jonathan Swift's *Modest proposal*, which plunged parts of the country into famine, as a result of which 'hundreds perished', and 'we have hundreds of families (all Protestants) removing out of the north to America'. It is impossible to offer a secure estimate of the numbers that succumbed and emigrated, but the population estimates indicate

---

5 Dickson et al., 'Hearth tax', pp. 129, incl. fn 21, 149–50; Clarkson, 'Irish population revisited', p. 17.
6 Connell, *The population of Ireland*, pp. 17–25; Clarkson, 'Irish population revisited', pp. 24–5; Dickson et al., 'Hearth tax', pp. 150–3.
7 Dickson et al., 'Hearth tax', p. 156.

Table 7. *Reworked national population estimates, 1687–1753 and 1791 (in millions).*

Year	Connell's estimate	Dickson et al.'s lower estimate	Dickson et al.'s upper estimate	Difference
1687	2.17	1.97	1.97	10.2%
1712	2.79	1.98	2.32	20.3–40.9%
1725	3.04	2.18	2.56	18.8–39.4%
1732	3.02	2.16	2.53	19.4–39.8%
1744		1.91	2.23	
1749		1.95	2.28	
1753	3.19	2.20	2.57	24.1–45%
1791	4.75	4.42	4.42	7.5%

Source: Dickson et al., 'Hearth tax', p. 156.

that it interrupted the upwards growth in population that was a feature of the early eighteenth century. It also inaugurated a pattern of regional emigration. Donald MacRaild notes that in the five decades after 1720 the number of migrants from Ulster to North America was not far short of the numbers moving there from England.[8]

In addition to their national population estimate, Dickson et al. also employed their suggested provincial household multipliers, ranging from 5.2 for Munster and 5.0 for Leinster, to 4.6 for Ulster and 4.7 for Connacht, to generate provincial population figures for 1732 (Table 8). According to their calculations, the two most populous provinces were Munster, with between 700,000 and 800,000 inhabitants, and Leinster, with a population ranging from 660,000 to 770,000. Ulster, with at least half a million people, was well ahead of Connacht, which had the smallest population of the four provinces.[9]

These 1732 population estimates are based on the county hearth-tax household-count figures issued by the Revenue Commissioners. A year earlier, an 'Inquiry into the State of Popery' provided detailed statistics on the human and capital infrastructure of the Irish Catholic Church, and revenue officials used the fiscal mechanisms available to them in 1732 to gather further

8 J. Kelly, 'Harvests and hardship: famine and scarcity in Ireland in the late 1720s', *Studia Hibernica*, 26 (1992), 65, 83; Boulter to Duke of Newcastle, 7 March 1727/8, Boulter to Newcastle, 16 July 1728, Boulter to Newcastle, 13 March 1728/9 in *Letters written by his excellency Hugh Boulter, D.D.*, 2 vols. (Dublin: George Faulkner, 1770), vol. I, pp. 181, 202, 231; D. MacRaild and M. Smith, 'Migration and emigration, 1600–1945' in L. Kennedy and P. Ollerenshaw (eds.), *Ulster since 1600: politics, economy, and society* (Oxford: Oxford University Press, 2013), p. 144.

9 Dickson et al., 'Hearth tax', pp. 153, 155.

Table 8. *Provincial population estimates, 1732.*

Province	Population (in millions)		Provincial proportion of national population
	Lower estimate	Upper estimate	
Munster	0.70	0.80	28.8–35.4%
Leinster	0.66	0.77	27.3–33.9%
Ulster	0.52	0.61	21.3–27.1%
Connacht	0.28	0.35	11.4–15.7%
Ireland	2.16	2.53	

Source: Dickson et al., 'Hearth tax', p. 155.

information on Irish 'popery' by ordering the hearth-tax collectors to 'inquire if the princip[a]l p[er]son of each family be Protestant or Papist'. Thus, the 1732 hearth-tax returns can be viewed as the first attempt to conduct a religious census of households in Ireland. Religious household-breakdowns are available at county level for all of Ireland, but data have also survived for most baronies, and parish breakdowns exist for County Louth.[10] The provincial data that resulted from this religious 'census' are shown on Table 9, though it is virtually certain that they overestimate the Protestant proportion of the population in all regions.

It is not proposed here to offer alternative population estimates to those postulated by Dickson et al., although some general comment is necessary, given the importance of the hearth tax for pre-census Irish population estimation. Evidence suggests that the tax was collected more vigorously in areas that were familiar to collectors and readily accessible.[11] Furthermore, tax-based house-counts are compromised by a number of factors, including, most critically, tax avoidance by the populace and corruption on the part of the collectors. The adjustments to the 1732 house-count figures provided by Dickson et al. allow for discrepancies in the figures; but these adjustments were only applied at the national level. Additional provincial adjustments are made too, but only to the extent of applying different household multipliers

10 'Report on the state of Popery, Ireland, 1731', *Archivium Hibernicum,* 1 (1912), 10–27; 2 (1913), 108–56; 3 (1914), 124–59; 4 (1915), 131–77; Minute book of the Revenue Commissioners, 23–4 Jan. 1732, CUST 1/24, p. 47, The National Archives; [D. Bindon], *An Abstract of the Number of Protestant and Popish families* (Dublin, 1736), pp. 3–6; An abstract of the number of Protestant and Popish families as returned to the Hearth money office Anno 1732 (Lambeth Palace Library, MS 1742, ff. 43–8); 'Ardee Corporation reports', *Journal of the County Louth Archaeological Society*, 5:1 (1921), 70–1.

11 B. Gurrin, K. Miller and L. Kennedy (eds.), *Catholics and Protestants in eighteenth-century Ireland* (Dublin: Irish Manuscripts Commission, forthcoming), table 4.

Table 9. *Number of religious households by province, 1732.*

Province	Protestant families	Popish families	Total	Protestant proportion
Connacht	4,299	44,101	48,400	8.9%
Leinster	25,241	92,434	117,675	21.4%
Munster	13,337	106,407	119,744	11.1%
Ulster	62,624	38,459	101,083	62.0%
Ireland	105,501	281,401	386,902	27.3%

Source: An abstract of the number of Protestant and Popish families (Dublin, 1736), pp. 5–6.

to provincial house-counts.[12] The problem is that there is a wealth of evidence to indicate that the collection regime was highly defective along the west coast and in rural areas. The authors cite Charles Smith's observation for County Kerry that

> the number of Roman Catholics are here under rated, for the hearth-money collectors, in the wild uncultivated mountains, are obliged to compound for this tax, and take a certain sum for many cabins, otherwise they could collect nothing; besides many poor families, who are Roman Catholics, are excused on account of their poverty, by certificates from the magistrates; and are not numbered.

Similar testimony is available for other locations and time periods and it was commonly reported that houses could be abandoned or demolished when the tax collector arrived.[13]

If, as this suggests, hearth-tax inspired population estimates for remote areas understated the population to the greatest degree, it may be that the population of Connacht in 1732 was closer to the 350,000 upper-bound figure proposed by Dickson et al. than to their lower-bound estimate of 280,000, and that allowances may have also to be made for west Munster and west Ulster. The figures for religious adherents returned by the hearth-tax collectors that year support this contention. It is doubtful, for example, that Protestants ever outnumbered Catholics in County Donegal; yet the presentation of its data report 4,144 Catholic and 5,543 Protestant households in the county; the numbers for Inishowen barony are even starker, with Protestant households outnumbering Catholics by almost two to one, which is improbable.[14]

12 Dickson et al., 'Hearth tax', p. 155.
13 Ibid., p. 135; J. McVeagh (ed.), *Richard Pococke's Irish tours* (Dublin: Irish Academic Press, 1995), p. 60; Harrowby papers, T/3228/2/1, Public Record Office of Northern Ireland; *Freeman's Journal*, 24 Dec. 1763, p. 2, col. a.
14 Abstract of the number of Protestant and Popish families, 1732, f. 43v.

Famine and Economic Challenge, the 1740s

Extrapolating from the hearth-tax data for 1744, Dickson et al. estimate the population of Ireland in the mid-1740s at between 1.91 and 2.23 million people. This implies a population decline since 1732 of as much as 620,000. Since benign economic conditions prevailed for most of the 1730s it is likely that the national population at the close of the decade had advanced from its 1732 level. Thus, any decline between 1732 and 1744 must have occurred in the early 1740s, when Ireland was plunged into crisis as a result of a series of unprecedented weather events across Europe.

John Post's study of the impact of the weather on mortality in Europe in 1740–1 concludes that starvation was more acute in Ireland, Norway and Finland than elsewhere in the continent, but that 'the deaths from hunger and hypothermia combined proved less demographically significant than the mortality that resulted from the elevated incidence of epidemic diseases'. Echoing this, Dickson has concluded that the crisis was proportionately more devastating than the Great Famine of the 1840s, and proposes that between 13 and 20 per cent of the population or 'between 310,000 and 480,000 people may have perished'. The crisis did not impact the country evenly; excess mortality was particularly acute in the south and west, with Munster contributing perhaps 50 per cent of the total, whereas Ulster emerged 'earlier and less badly scarred than elsewhere'.[15] The devastation was so severe that figures such as Bishop Berkeley and Richard Cox predicted that the country might not recover from the blow for a half century or more, although public relief schemes and private philanthropy saved countless lives, and 'there was not a poor distressed person in the great city of Dublin who applied, that was not daily relieved to the full'. So great was the suffering that 1741 became ingrained in folk memory as *bliain an áir* – the year of the slaughter – and even in the succeeding century some still remembered the 'memorable year of the Great Frost'.[16]

Although national house-counts are available for only a handful of years during the eighteenth century the revenue accruing from the hearth tax is

---

15 J.D. Post, *Food shortage, climatic variability, and epidemic disease in preindustrial Europe: the mortality peak in the early 1740s* (Ithaca, NY: Cornell University Press, 1985), pp. 37, 226; D. Dickson, *Arctic Ireland* (Belfast: The White Row Press, 1997), pp. 58, 69, 72.

16 Dickson, *Arctic Ireland*, pp. 62–3, 68, 70–2; *Boulter's letters*, vol. I, p. 224, note; J. Kelly 'Coping with crisis; the response to the famine of 1740–41', *Eighteenth-Century Ireland*, 27 (2012), 99–122; W. Shaw Mason, *A statistical account or parochial survey of Ireland*, 3 vols. (London: Longman, Hurst, Rees, Orme, and Brown, 1814–19), vol. II, p. 509.

available for all years after 1720, and these data permit a slightly more nuanced story of the 1740–1 crisis (see Fig. 1).[17] In the 1727–8 fiscal year net revenue from the hearth tax amounted to £42,937, which was the highest to date. Net revenue in each of the three subsequent years reflects the demographic challenges of the late 1720s. By 1732, however, net revenue had rebounded and an upward trajectory was maintained, albeit with a slight dip in the mid-1730s, until 1739–40, when the tax exceeded £45,000 for the first time. The 1739–40 net revenue figure was £2,108 above the sum reported for 1727–8, the equivalent of well above 20,000 hearths, or more than 100,000 people.

Then 'the worst human disaster [in Ireland] since 1650–1, possibly since the Elizabethan conquest' occurred, and it was vividly reflected across the economy. Grain prices on the Dublin market reached an all-time high in 1741 for the period 1700–60, and fiscal returns plummeted. The hearth-tax revenue declined by £350 in 1740–1, but retreated by a staggering sum of almost £3,000 the following year. By 1742–3 the net revenue from the tax was only £41,166, which was almost £4,000, or 8.6 per cent, down on the total collected in 1739–40.[18]

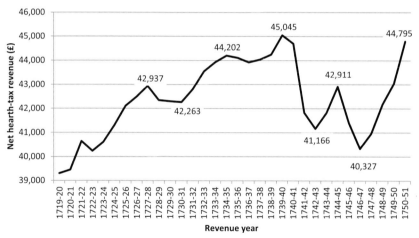

FIGURE 1. Net revenue from hearth tax, 1719–20 to 1750–1.

Source: Dickson et al., 'Hearth tax', pp. 180–1.

17 Various revenue series are available in Dickson et al., 'Hearth tax', pp. 180–1.
18 D. Dickson, 'The gap in famines: a useful myth?' in E.M. Crawford (ed.), *Famine: the Irish experience, 900–1900* (Edinburgh: John Donald, 1989), pp. 97, 98, chart; Dickson et al., 'Hearth tax', p. 181.

Although the decline in tax income confirms that famine conditions impacted the population severely, it also poses some questions. First, the 1742–3 net revenue for the hearth tax is roughly the same as that for 1724–5, yet there is only a marginal overlap between Dickson et al.'s national population range for 1725 (2.18–2.56 million) and their estimate of 1.91 to 2.23 million for 1744. More troublingly, once the crisis was over, net revenue rebounded vigorously, increasing by more than £1,700 over the following two years (Fig. 1). It seems counter-intuitive that revenues recovered so quickly if the national population declined by as much as one fifth. Rather, it seems more likely that the rapid recovery in revenues resulted from households being re-incorporated into the hearth-tax system, having being exempted on poverty grounds during the crisis, than that the population suffered to the extent suggested.

Mean household size is the only means by which the competing evidence of rapidly recovering hearth-tax revenues and substantial demographic collapse can be reconciled, and Dickson et al. propose that household size may have declined in the early 1740s, although the evidence for this is regional, and patchy. They recognise that if population loss in the early 1740s was caused primarily by starvation mean household size would have declined, while the number of households would have held firm. However, if contagious diseases were the principal cause of excess mortality, household numbers would have collapsed, but mean household size would have been impacted less.[19] Both Post and Dickson argue that the death toll in the early 1740s was primarily accounted for by contagious diseases, which is not readily compatible with the prompt recovery that occurred in the net returns.

It was a short-lived recovery, however, as conditions disimproved once more in 1744. Known colloquially as the 'Rot Year', Ulster bore the brunt on this occasion as 'much grain was spoiled in the fields; all over the north of Ireland ... provisions were scarce and dear the following spring, and a considerable mortality arose among the cattle from the bad quality of their food'.[20] It has been suggested that mortality in north Connacht and Ulster in 1744–5 was 'as great or greater than in 1740–1', although large-scale grain imports provided some respite. Net revenue from the hearth tax plunged again, retreating to £40,960 in 1747–8, which was barely above the figure collected a quarter of a century previously. However, tax receipts rebounded rapidly once the impact of the 'Rot Year' subsided, and the £44,795 net sum accruing in 1750–1

19 Dickson et al., 'Hearth tax', pp. 152, 165.
20 S. McSkimin, *The history and antiquities of the county of the town of Carrickfergus*, new edn (Belfast: Mullan and Son, 1909), pp. 79–80.

was fractionally below the £45,045 collected in 1739–40, before the challenges of *bliain an áir*. The fears expressed by Berkeley and Cox a decade previously had not been realised, although the population estimate of between 1.95 and 2.28 million in 1749 proposed by Dickson et al. is some way below their estimate for 1725. What is certain is that the impact of the double dip of the 1740s exceeded the scale and impact of the difficulties experienced in the second half of the 1720s, although the fact that the population decline during the previous quarter century had been made good by 1753 is in keeping with the interpretation suggested here that its impact may have been less severe than many commentators have concluded (Table 7).[21]

Irish Population Change, 1751–1813

Though the country experienced further subsistence crises in the second half of the eighteenth century – in 1756–57, when Dublin grain prices rose to little below 1741 levels, 1766, 1783–84 and 1800–1 – these were not accompanied by significant excess mortality, with the result that, from mid-century, Irish population growth embarked on a new and sustained upwards trajectory. The population soared during the second half of the eighteenth century, perhaps reaching about 4.5 million by 1791, and it continued to grow rapidly in the opening decades of the nineteenth century. Connell proposed two reasons for 'the extraordinarily rapid rate of natural increase' that he believed 'to have begun by the 1780s'.[22] First, he argued that Irish marital fertility increased after 1780 as a result of a falling age at marriage, meaning that 'women spent more of their childbearing years in the state of marriage, and therefore, in the absence of contraception, bore more children'. Second, on the basis that crises were usually 'well documented', he invoked the 'rarity of comment' as evidence that there was a 'gap in the famines', which facilitated an unprecedented population increase.[23]

Both propositions have been overturned. Shortly after the publication of *The population of Ireland*, Geary demonstrated that marital fertility was 'lower in Ireland than in England and Wales in 1841', leading Connell to acknowledge

---

21 Dickson, 'Gap in famines', pp. 98, 101; Dickson et al., 'Hearth tax', pp. 156, 180–1.

22 C. Ó Gráda, *The Great Irish Famine* (London: Macmillan, 1989), p. 20; Dickson, 'Gap in famines', p. 98, chart; K.H. Connell, 'Land and population in Ireland, 1780–1845' in D.V. Glass and D.E. Eversley (eds.), *Population in history: essays in historical demography* (London: Edward Arnold, 1965), p. 424.

23 Connell, *The population of Ireland*, p. 144; K.H. Connell, 'Land and population in Ireland, 1780–1845', *Economic History Review*, n.s., 2:3 (1950), 280–1; Connell, 'Land and population in Ireland, 1780–1845', p. 425.

that his contrary hypothesis was invalid. Michael Drake also showed that there was 'no difference in fertility' within English and Irish marriages in spite of Irish female marriage age being lower in the 1830s.[24] The 'gap in famines' hypothesis proved harder to dislodge, since it ostensibly accounted for the demographic growth that had occurred in the half century or more before 1820, but it is now viewed as a 'useful myth'. Using various economic indicators, including grain prices in the Dublin market and grain imports, Dickson has shown that the death rate increased during subsistence crises. He has identified peaks in Protestant burials in Dublin in 1756–7 and 1782–4, and observed regional Catholic peaks in 1774, 1783, 1794 and 1800, although in each case the excess mortality was on a smaller scale than that evidenced during the 1740s, or later experienced in the 1840s.[25]

In spite of these intermittent demographic challenges it is clear that the population grew between the early 1750s and the early 1790s at the unprecedented level of between 1.5 and 2 per cent per year. This contrasts sharply with Connell's figures, which suggested a more modest annual rate of increase of about 1 per cent during these four decades. Significantly, the hearth-tax returns are of little assistance in explaining this. Dickson et al. argue that 'a decline in the quality of hearth-tax administration and, consequently, of the relevant returns and receipts' from about the middle of the eighteenth century render the available house-counts unsuitable for determining population levels; they offer no national population figures between 1753 and 1791.[26]

Ironically, though the quality of the hearth-tax returns disimproved, the second half of the eighteenth century witnessed a growing interest among contemporaries in Irish population levels. The 'Population Controversy', a drawn-out debate on English population trends, had commenced in England in 1755, and some of the participants, notably the Dissenting minister and political radical Revd Richard Price, the agriculturist Arthur Young and Revd John Howlett, looked to Ireland in search of evidence to support their positions. Their estimates varied widely. Price argued that the Irish population had yet to reach 2 million in 1767; Young put it at 3 million in 1778, while Howlett settled on a figure of

24 R.C. Geary, 'The population of Ireland, 1750–1845 – review', *Studies: An Irish Quarterly Review*, 39156 (1950), 473; K.H. Connell, 'Some unsettled problems in English and Irish population history, 1750–1845', *Irish Historical Studies*, 7 (1951–2), 228–9, note; M. Drake, 'Marriage and population growth in Ireland, 1750–1845', *Economic History Review*, 2nd series, 16 (1963–4), 307.
25 Dickson, 'Gap in famines', pp. 101–2.
26 Dickson et al., 'Hearth tax', pp. 136, 155, 156; Connell, *The population of Ireland*, p. 25.

Table 10. *Contemporary national population estimates, 1767–88.*

Year	Author	Estimate of national population	Proposed mean household size
1767	Price	1,908,207	4.5
1777	Laffan	2,475,000	5.5
1778	Young	3,000,000	
1781	Howlett	2,500,000–2,750,000	5.5
1788	Bushe	'above 4,040,000'	6.25

Source: Connell, *Population of Ireland*, p. 4.

2.5 to 2.75 million in 1781 (Table 10).[27] Meanwhile, two attempts were made in the 1760s to determine Ireland's religious demography; the first was a failed scheme in 1764–5 to do so using hearth-tax officials; the second, in 1766, involved the clergy of the established church returning lists of their parishioners to the House of Lords. This ecclesiastical-based census is important for two reasons. First, it is the only eighteenth-century population survey that is not based on house-counts derived from the hearth tax. This is significant as the 1731 Inquiry into the State of Popery had concluded that the returns from clergymen were more reliable than the contributions from secular officials. Second, although doubts persist as to its completeness, it was more comprehensive than the hearth-tax returns for 1764–5, which reported 424,046 houses; this was less than the religious census, which returned at least 435,943 and perhaps as high as 465,000 'families'.[28]

Arthur Young appealed in the 1770s for an Irish census to be held.[29] The merits of this suggestion, which fell on deaf ears, were made clear in the late 1780s when, following his appointment in 1784 to the Revenue Commission, Gervaise Parker Bushe introduced sweeping reforms of the collection process resulting in a dramatic increase in the number of houses enumerated by the hearth-tax collectors. In 1785, 'the year before the new [reform] plan was formed', the Revenue Office reported 474,237 houses, but within six years their count had jumped by almost 50 per cent as some of the endemic corruption

27 J. Howlett, *An essay on the population of Ireland* (London, 1786); R. Price, *Observations on reversionary payments*, 4th edn, 2 vols. (London: Cadell, 1783), vol. I, pp. 253–4, note; Connell, *The population of Ireland*, p. 4.

28 Dickson et al., 'Hearth tax', p. 178; E. Wakefield, *An account of Ireland, statistical and political*, 2 vols. (London: Longman, Hurst, Rees, Orme, and Brown, 1812), vol. II, p. 587.

29 [Arthur Young], *Proposals to the Legislature for numbering the people* (London: W. Nicoll, 1771), p. 9; A. Young, *A Tour in Ireland: with general observations on the present state of that Kingdom, 1776, 1777, and 1778*, 2 vols. (Dublin, 1780), vol. II, p. 88.

was expunged.[30] Armed with more reliable house-count figures, and with new information on mean household size Bushe proposed a national population of 'above 4,040,000' for 1788. This was more than a third greater than any previous estimate (Table 10).

Bushe arrived at his figure using a mean household size of 'nearly 6¼', derived from a sample of more than 14,000 households in sixteen counties. This multiplier was significantly higher than those employed by Price (4.5), Howlett and Laffan (5.5), and it is now generally accepted that his mean household size figure was too high.[31] By comparison, for 1791 Connell employed a multiplier of 5.65 and Clarkson one of 5 to 5.5, whereas Dickson et al. had recourse to provincial multipliers ranging from 5.3 for Connacht to 5.9 for Leinster and Ulster. The latter also proposed provincial population levels (Table 11) consistent with the substantial demographic changes that had occurred in Ireland since 1753. Growth had stabilised in Leinster, but surged elsewhere. Ulster and Munster now exceeded Leinster, with Ulster accounting for almost one third of the national population in 1791. Connacht remained the least populated province, with about 600,000 inhabitants.[32]

There is widespread agreement, as William Macafee has observed, that Ireland's population embarked on a period of sustained growth at some point before the 1780s; probably in the 1750s. Various factors contributed to this. They include the increased dominance of the potato in the diet of the cottier and small-farmer classes; a move from pastoral agriculture towards arable farming that facilitated changed tenancy arrangements; an increase in the number of smallholdings; the emergence of an industrial sector, which provided cash incomes, thus aiding the emergence of a market economy; and a fall in mortality rates.[33] The impact of these factors varied according to region. The northern part of the country was the engine of proto-industrial growth, particularly in textiles, and 'local markets flourished in consequence'. The number of holdings of between 1 and 5 acres increased in every region, but it was most marked in Connacht, where in 1841 64 per cent of all holdings were less than 5 acres compared with 45 per cent nationally. There was,

30 G.P. Bushe, 'An essay towards ascertaining the population of Ireland', *Transactions of the Royal Irish Academy*, 3 (1789), insert; Connell, *The population of Ireland*, p. 5.

31 Bushe, 'Population of Ireland', pp. 147, 154 and insert; Price, *Observations on reversionary payments*, vol. 1, p. 254, note; Howlett, *Population of Ireland*, p. 16, note; J. Laffan, *Political arithmetic of the population, commerce and manufactures of Ireland* (Dublin, 1785), p. 2.

32 Connell, *The population of Ireland*, p. 24; Clarkson, 'Irish population revisited, 1687–1821', p. 26; Dickson et al., 'Hearth tax', pp. 153, 155.

33 Macafee, 'The pre-Famine population of Ireland', p. 76; L.M. Cullen, *An economic history of Ireland since 1600*, 2nd edn (London: Batsford, 1987), pp. 77–83.

Table 11. *Provincial population levels, 1753 and 1791.*

Province	Population (millions)		Proportionate size, 1791	Yearly growth rate
	1753	1791		
Ulster	0.62–0.72	1.43	32%	1.8–2.2%
Munster	0.59–0.68	1.20	27%	1.5–1.9%
Leinster	0.71–0.82	1.18	27%	1.0–1.4%
Connacht	0.28–0.35	0.61	14%	1.5–2.1%
Ireland	2.20–2.57	4.42		

Source: Dickson et al., 'Hearth tax', p. 155.

as Louis Cullen has pointed out, a strong correlation between the growth of tiny holdings and population advance, with numbers increasing most rapidly along the western seaboard.[34]

These fundamental structural and social changes placed Ireland's cottier and small-farmer classes in the perilous position of being dependent on a subsistence foodstuff – the potato – which was prone to periodic failures when weather conditions were unfavourable. Crises were inevitable, and so too was increased excess mortality. Though Thomas Newenham seemed relieved that 'the two years of scarcity' that gripped the country in 1800–1 'did not … occasion a greater loss of people than 40,000', 'the last great subsistence crisis in the western world', in 1816–17, may have resulted in 65,000 deaths.[35] Both of these crises coincided with difficult years across western Europe, but specifically Irish crisis years were still more commonplace as, for example, in 1812, 'a season of uncommon scarcity', 1822, 1830–1 and 1840–1.[36]

The rapid growth in Ireland's population after 1750 is still more impressive when the impact of emigration is factored in. Although pre-Famine emigration figures are unreliable, William Forbes Adams has calculated that a remarkable 1.14 million departed Ireland for the United States and Canada in the sixty-five years after 1780, with an additional 600,000 migrating to Britain.[37]

---

34 Connell, 'Land and population in Ireland, 1780–1845', p. 284; Cullen, *Economic history of Ireland*, p. 117.

35 T. Newenham, *A statistical and historical inquiry into the progress and magnitude of the population of Ireland* (London: Cadell and Davies, 1805), pp. 131–2; J.D. Post, *The last great subsistence crisis in the Western World* (Baltimore: Johns Hopkins University Press, 1977).

36 Ó Gráda, *The Great Irish Famine*, p. 20; Shaw Mason, *Parochial survey*, vol. I, p. 582; vol. II, p. 338; vol. III, pp. 201–2.

37 W. Forbes Adams, *Ireland and Irish emigration to the New World from 1815 to the Famine* (New Haven: Yale University Press, 1932), p. 69; Connell, *The population of Ireland*, p. 27.

This is well in excess of previous patterns, which may have seen 100,000 Presbyterians – 70 per cent of all emigrants from Ulster ports – departing for the American colonies between 1717 and 1776. Miller et al. suggest that as many as 200,000 migrants in total may have travelled to America between the late 1690s and the mid-1770s.[38] The different figures are not easily reconciled, but they point in only one direction; increased emigration could not have occurred in the absence of a rapidly rising population.[39]

The First Irish Statutory Censuses, 1813–15 and 1821

The English 'Population Controversy' was brought to an end by the 1801 census which, though deficient, and known to be so at the time, confirmed that a significant increase in the country's population had occurred during the eighteenth century.[40] After 1801 censuses were held decennially in Great Britain, but no equivalent provision existed for Ireland until July 1812, when parliament approved *An Act for taking an account of the population of Ireland, and of the increase or diminution thereof.*[41] Overseen by William Shaw Mason, the census commenced on 1 May 1813, but it was terminated almost two years after it was begun, with some parts of the country not enumerated and other parts inadequately surveyed.[42] Be that as it may, the fact that the 1813–15 census enumerated some 4.635 million people permitted a more accurate calculation of the population than previously possible. Allowing for omissions and deficiencies, an 'ingenious friend' of Shaw Mason calculated, with impressive precision, that Ireland's population in 1813 was 5,937,856.[43]

The organisational issues that frustrated enumeration in 1813–15 were remedied before a second census was attempted in 1821. The process was assisted by the decision to scale back the administrative unit from the barony to the parish, as well as by the attention that was devoted to allaying the 'determined hostility [that] ... shewed itself openly in some districts', and it paid

---

38 Connell, *The population of Ireland*, p. 27; MacRaild, 'Migration and emigration', p. 144; K. Miller, A. Schrier, B. Boling and D. Doyle (eds.), *Irish immigrants in the Land of Canaan: letters and memoirs from colonial and revolutionary America, 1675–1815* (Oxford: Oxford University Press, 2003), p. 7.

39 See Chapters 6 (Dickson), pp. 158–9 and 22 (Griffin), pp. 596–7.

40 D.V. Glass, *Numbering the people: the eighteenth-century population controversy* (Farnborough: Saxon House, 1973), pp. 11–46; D.V. Glass, *The population controversy* (Farnborough: Gregg International, 1973).

41 *Hansard I*, XXI (1812), cols. 399–401 (29 Jan. 1812).

42 52 Geo. III, c. 133, sect. 3; P.M. Froggatt, 'The census of Ireland in 1813–15', *Irish Historical Studies*, 14 (1964–5), p. 229.

43 Shaw Mason, *Parochial survey*, vol. III, p. xxi.

dividends as a population of 6,801,827 was reported for the entire country.[44] It was far from problem free, however, and, guided by the conclusion of the 1841 census commissioners that it 'was rather below than above the truth', Joseph Lee concludes that the true population in 1821 was 'comfortably in excess of 7 million', and proposes 7.2 million as 'more plausible than the official return'.[45]

The 1821 census confirmed that Ulster was still the most populous province, followed closely by Munster and Leinster, with Connacht some way in arrears (Table 12). The availability of the census figures meant that mean household size, which eighteenth-century 'statistical writers' assumed to be about 5 or 5.5, could now be determined with tolerable accuracy. The national figure of 5.95 persons per house exceeded most eighteenth-century estimates, but was well short of Bushe's 1791 figure.[46] It also masked significant provincial variations; Ulster and Connacht, with the smallest household sizes (5.55 and 5.62 respectively), were far behind Leinster (6.31) and Munster (6.30).

On the assumption that a cluster of 100 houses qualifies as an urban centre, 16.6 per cent of Ireland's 6.8 million inhabitants were urban dwellers in 1821. It will come as no surprise that the provinces with the largest mean household size also had the largest proportion of their population living in urban settings. In Leinster, almost one in four of the population were urban dwellers by comparison with fewer than one in ten in Connacht (Table 13). The largest urban settlements were located in Leinster and Munster. Only Dublin and Cork had populations exceeding 100,000 people and only one other city – Limerick – exceeded 50,000. These were followed by Belfast's 37,000, which made it the largest urban centre in Ulster, and by Waterford, Galway and Kilkenny, which were the three remaining urban centres with populations above 20,000. Drogheda was next with 18,000 people, followed by Clonmel and Bandon, which were larger than Newry and Londonderry, Ulster's second and third most populous urban centres respectively.[47]

Dublin was Ireland's largest city, with a population of 178,603 within the city's boundaries, and an additional 48,732 living beyond its administrative limits, but within the two canals and the two circular roads that defined it

44 *Abstract of answers and returns, pursuant to act 55 Geo. 3, for taking an account of the population of Ireland in 1821*, H.C. 1824 (577), xxii, p. xi (hereinafter *Cen. Ire., 1821*).
45 *Report of the commissioners appointed to take the census of Ireland for the year 1841* [504], H.C. 1843, xxiv, 1, p. viii; J. Lee, 'On the accuracy of the pre-Famine Irish censuses' in Goldstrom and Clarkson (eds.), *Irish population, economy, and society*, pp. 44–6.
46 Lee, 'On the accuracy of the pre-Famine Irish censuses', p. 53.
47 *Cen. Ire., 1821*, pp. xxii, 10, 54, 162, 172, 198, 204, 222, 228, 238, 250, 282, 298, 338.

Table 12. *Provincial populations, 1821.*

Province	Houses	Males	Females	Total population	Proportionate size	Mean household size
Connacht	197,408	553,948	556,281	1,110,229	16%	5.62
Leinster	278,398	859,798	897,694	1,757,492	26%	6.31
Munster	306,999	960,119	975,493	1,935,612	28%	6.30
Ulster	359,801	968,061	1,030,433	1,998,494	29%	5.55
Ireland	**1,142,606**	**3,341,926**	**3,459,901**	**6,801,827**		**5.95**

Source: Census of Ireland, 1821, p. 378.

Table 13. *Urban and rural populations, 1821, by province.*

Province	Urban population	Rural population	Total	Urban proportion
Connacht	100,241	1,009,988	1,110,229	9.0%
Leinster	412,021	1,345,471	1,757,492	23.4%
Munster	411,912	1,523,700	1,935,612	21.3%
Ulster	202,867	1,795,627	1,998,494	10.2%
Ireland	**1,127,041**	**5,674,786**	**6,801,827**	**16.6%**

Source: Census of Ireland, 1821.

Note: Clusters of 100 or more houses are categorised as urban.

geographically. Mean household size within the city's boundaries was 12.7, but household size was highest in the historic southern core of the city, in the vicinity of the two cathedrals and Dublin Castle, and north of the river Liffey, in St Michan's parish. St John's parish, which was proximate to Christchurch Cathedral, was the only Dublin parish where mean household size exceeded sixteen, but in seven other parishes the mean size of a household was larger than fourteen. By contrast, the suburban parishes to the east and north – St George's, St Peter's and St Thomas' – all had mean household sizes of ten, or lower.[48] Cork had the second largest mean household size among the principal urban settlements (9.0), followed by Limerick (8.2) and Waterford (7.8). In Ulster, Londonderry boasted the largest mean household size (7.4), ahead of Belfast (6.8), Newry (6.8) and Carrickfergus (5.9), the country's smallest county borough; it also exceeded Galway (7.0).

Rural population density varied greatly, but was highest in the northern half of the country, and lowest in Leinster, particularly in the eastern counties proximate to Dublin (Map. 2). Densities were especially high in a band stretching from Strangford Lough to Donegal Bay encompassing counties Down, Longford, Monaghan, Sligo and Armagh, which was the most densely populated county. Rural industry was prevalent in many of these areas, particularly in the 'linen triangle' in east Ulster, and this provided economic opportunities and cash wages in non-urban settings. It is unsurprising, therefore, to observe a strong positive correlation between rural population density and large numbers of people engaged in employments other than agriculture. Only six Irish counties had fewer than 30 per cent of those in work employed in agriculture – the five north-eastern counties and Dublin.

48 Ibid., p. xxii.

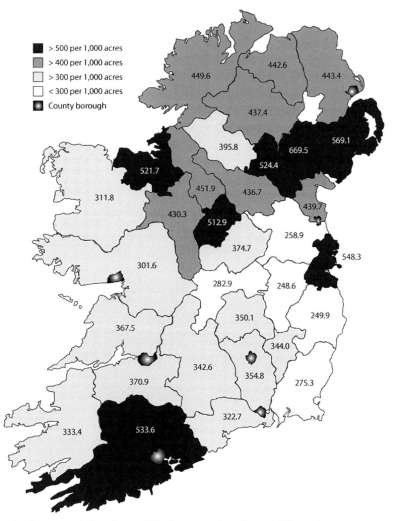

> 500 per 1,000 acres
> 400 per 1,000 acres
> 300 per 1,000 acres
< 300 per 1,000 acres
County borough

MAP 2. Rural population density, 1821, by county (people per 1,000 acres).
Source: Census of Ireland, 1821.

County Armagh, with the highest rural population density, was also the
county with the lowest proportion of its population employed in agriculture
(26.1 per cent).[49] In the five north-eastern counties, slightly above one in four
were 'chiefly employed' in agriculture, compared with almost half in the rest

49 The other five counties were Antrim, Down, Londonderry, Tyrone and Dublin.

of the country (Table 14). By comparison, rural population density was particularly low in the counties proximate to the capital, and particularly high in
County Dublin. In this instance the summer timing of the census may be relevant. Seasonal migrants were attracted towards Dublin and Britain, thereby
depressing population densities in the counties supplying this labour.

Population Growth, 1821–1841

According to official census figures, Ireland's population increased by 14.2
per cent, from 6.8 million to 7.767 million, between 1821 and 1831, but in the
subsequent decade the growth was a more modest 5.2 per cent, or 408,000
(Table 15).[50] These figures were contested at the time, and they have continued to be challenged since. As a result, many are disposed to favour those proposed by Joe Lee, who 'tentatively suggests' alternative population estimates

Table 14. *Principal employments, 1821.*

Counties (grouped by rural population densities)	Chiefly employed in:		
	Agriculture	Trade, manufacture, handicraft	Other
Armagh, Cork, Down, Dublin, Longford, Monaghan, Sligo	278,773 (36.6%)	329,338 (44.4%)	133,215 (18.0%)
Antrim, Cavan, Donegal, Leitrim, Londonderry, Louth, Roscommon, Tyrone	285,105 (34.9%)	424,303 (52.0%)	106,532 (13.1%)
Carlow, Clare, Fermanagh, Galway, Kerry, Kilkenny, Limerick, Mayo, Queen's, Tipperary, Waterford, Westmeath	438,188 (50.4%)	267,666 (30.8%)	163,375 (18.8%)
Kildare, King's, Meath, Wexford, Wicklow	112,718 (48.6%)	61,592 (26.6%)	57,524 (24.8%)
Counties (5 north-eastern counties)			
Antrim, Armagh, Down, Londonderry, Tyrone	180,448 (27.6%)	379,669 (58.0%)	94,064 (14.4%)
Twenty-seven other counties	934,336 (46.6%)	703,230 (35.1%)	366,582 (18.3%)

Source: Census of Ireland, 1821.

50 W.E. Vaughan and A.J. Fitzpatrick (eds.), *Irish historical statistics: population, 1821–1971*
(Dublin: Royal Irish Academy, 1978), p. 3.

Table 15. *Provincial populations, 1821–41.*

Year	Connacht	Leinster	Munster	Ulster	Ireland
1821	1,110,229	1,757,492	1,935,612	1,998,494	6,801,827
	(16.3%)	(25.8%)	(28.5%)	(29.4%)	
1831	1,343,914	1,909,713	2,227,152	2,286,622	7,767,401
	(17.3%)	(24.6%)	(28.7%)	(29.4%)	
1841	1,418,859	1,973,731	2,396,161	2,386,373	8,175,124
	(17.4%)	(24.1%)	(29.3%)	(29.2%)	

Source: Vaughan and Fitzpatrick, *Irish historical statistics: population*, pp. 15–16.

for Ireland's three census years, 1821, 1831 and 1841; these are shown in Table 16. Whatever the precise figures, it should be borne in mind that the 1831 results were seriously questioned in the wake of the publication of the 1841 census returns, because many people disbelieved that the rate of population growth had slowed down to the extent that the censal figures suggested. In point of fact, as Lee has argued, the 1831 census was probably the most accurate of the four pre-Famine censuses. He speculated that it underestimated the national population by only 1.7 per cent, or about half the deficiency in the 1841 survey.[51]

The religious information extracted from the 1831 census returns provided the first island-wide perspective on Ireland's religious demography since the religious censuses of the 1760s. The Public Instruction Commissioners, which oversaw its preparation, published the parish returns, organised by diocese, then parish.[52] As some parish boundaries crossed provincial boundaries it is not possible to compile precise provincial estimates, but the discrepancies are negligible. The provincial and national religious breakdowns that emerged from this comprehensive denominational survey are shown in Table 17. It is apparent from this that Catholics were the majority denomination in all four provinces on the eve of the Great Famine, accounting for between 52.6 per cent of the total population in Ulster, and 95.3 per cent in Connacht. Within the Protestant denominations Presbyterianism predominated in Ulster (57 per cent of the Protestant population), but as the remaining three provinces contained barely 5,000 Presbyterians, compared with 386,224 members of the Church of Ireland, the latter was strongest throughout Ireland.

51 Lee, 'On the accuracy of the pre-Famine Irish censuses', p. 54, table.
52 *First report of the Commissioners of Public Instruction, Ireland* [45] [46] [47] H.C. 1834, xxxiii.1, 829, xxxiv.1.

Table 16. *National population estimates, 1821–51, and 1791.*

Year	Census figures (millions)	Reworked figures (millions)	Deficiency (millions, proportion deficient)	Yearly growth rate (period)
1791		4.42		
1821	6.802	7.2	0.4 (5.9%)	1791–1821: 1.6%
1831	7.767	7.9	0.133 (1.7%)	1821–31: 0.9%
1841	8.175	8.4	0.225 (2.8%)	1831–41: 0.6%
1845		8.525		1841–5: 0.4%
1851	6.552			1845–51: -4.3%

Sources: For 1791, Dickson et al., 'Hearth tax', p. 156; for 1821–41, Lee, 'On the accuracy of the pre-Famine Irish censuses', p. 54, table (1821–41); for 1845, Boyle and Ó Gráda, 'Famine trends, excess mortality and the Great Irish Famine', p. 556 (1845); for 1851, Vaughan and Fitzpatrick, *Irish historical statistics: population*, p. 3.

Table 17. *Religious adherents by province, 1831.*

Province	Church of Ireland	Catholic	Presbyterian	Other Protestant denominations	Others & omitted
Connacht	60,424	1,262,657	564	364	549
	(4.6%)	(95.3%)	(0.0%)	(0.0%)	(0.0%)
Leinster	221,578	1,638,488	3,886	3,470	11,338
	(11.8%)	(87.2%)	(0.2%)	(0.2%)	(0.6%)
Munster	104,222	2,108,664	729	2,180	3,651
	(4.7%)	(95.0%)	(0.0%)	(0.1%)	(0.2%)
Ulster	447,752	1,201,513	615,278	15,019	3,579
	(19.6%)	(52.6%)	(26.9%)	(0.7%)	(0.2%)
Ireland	**833,976**	**6,211,322**	**620,457**	**21,033**	**19,117**
	(10.8%)	**(80.6%)**	**(8.1%)**	**(0.3%)**	**(0.2%)**

Note: The total number of people recorded in the Public Instruction report is 7,705,905, which is 61,496 below the official population figure. In addition, 64,717 people were recorded in parishes which crossed provincial boundaries; these have been assigned to the province in which the majority of each parish's population lived.

Less than 5 per cent of the 3.5 million people enumerated in Connacht and Munster in 1831 embraced reformed faiths.[53]

The 8,175,124 people reported in the 1841 census was the largest population ever recorded in an Irish national census (Table 15). Ten years later, after

53 The religious figures given in this paragraph and in Table 17 are based on research

the country had been ravaged by potato failure, infectious diseases and star-vation, the population had declined to 6,552,385. The 'fearful visitation' of '"cholera" in potatoes in Ireland' was first identified in September 1845, but since both excess mortality and emigration remained muted during the second half of 1845, 'the population total for the end of 1845 [was] the highest ever achieved in Ireland'. Phelim Boyle and Cormac Ó Gráda suggest a population of 8,525,000 on the eve of the Great Famine (Table 16).[54]

It is apparent from this that the population of Ireland continued to increase until the onset of widespread famine in 1846, although the rate of advance slowed as the nineteenth century progressed. The reworked figures presented in Table 16 suggest a yearly increase of 1.6 per cent in the three decades to 1821, falling to 0.9 per cent in the decade after 1821, and declining still further to 0.6 per cent during the decade 1831 to 1841. Emigration was a key factor in the decline in population growth. Forbes Adams has identified the 1816–19 economic crisis as the commencement of 'the true emigrant trade' from Ireland to North America; the figure of 6,000 emigrants from Ireland to North America in 1816 was 'extraordinary', 'the 20,000 who followed in 1818 inaugurated a new era'.[55] The scale of Irish migration was remarkable. Forbes Adams' figures show 130,000 leaving for North America in 1831 and 1832, while Sir Thomas Larcom, commenting on the 1841 census, argued that above 500,000 departed between the 1831 and 1841 censuses, with 428,000 settling in North America and 105,000 in Britain. For the preceding decade he presumed only 70,000 emigrants. It must be borne in mind that Larcom was not an unbiased commentator – the discrepancy between the official rates of population increase in the 1820s and 1830s required explanation, and low emigration in the period 1821–31 followed by high migration between 1831 and 1841 fitted his narrative. Modern calculations greatly exceed Larcom's estimate for the decade after 1821.[56]

The 1841 census, the first British census to include birthplace details, also reported almost 420,000 Irish-born living in Britain (Table 18). Crucially, the census was taken in early June; had it been held a few weeks later thousands of seasonal Irish agricultural migrants would have assumed temporary residence. As it was, the Irish migrants were concentrated in the great industrial cities

undertaken with Professors Liam Kennedy and Kerby Miller.

54 *Freeman's Journal*, 11 Sept. 1845, p. 2; P. Boyle and C. Ó Gráda, 'Famine trends, excess mortality and the Great Irish Famine', *Demography*, 23:4 (1986), 556.

55 Forbes Adams, *Ireland and Irish emigration*, p. 70.

56 Captain Larcom, 'Observations on the census of the population of Ireland in 1841', *Journal of the Statistical Society of London*, 6:4 (1843), 329; Forbes Adams, *Ireland and Irish emigration*, pp. 413–14; Vaughan and Fitzpatrick (eds.), *Irish historical statistics: population*, p. 259.

Table 18. *Irish-born in Britain, 1841.*

Country	Irish-born	Total population	Irish proportion of population
England	284,128	14,995,138	1.9%
Scotland	126,321	2,620,184	4.8%
Wales	5,276	911,603	0.6%
Britain	415,725	18,526,925	2.2%

Sources: Enumeration abstract, pt 1, *England and Wales* H.C. 1843 (496) pp. 398–9 (England), 458 (Wales); *Enumeration abstract*, pt 2, *Scotland* H.C. 1843 (498), pp. 77–8.

Note: The total Irish population in Great Britain is given as 419,256: *Abstract of answers and returns made pursuant to acts 3 & 4 Vic. c. 99, and 4 Vic. 7; enumeration extract*, part 1, *England and Wales*, H.C. 1843 (496), p. 464.

along the west coast of Britain. In Scotland, 44 per cent of all Irish-born were located in industrial Lanarkshire, and seven out of ten Irish in the country lived in the adjoining counties of Ayr, Lanarkshire and Renfrewshire (Table 19).[57]

A similar pattern was evident in England (Table 19). More than one in three of all Irish-born enumerated in the English census were recorded in industrial Lancashire, with the neighbouring counties of Cheshire and Yorkshire West Riding accounting for above 4 per cent of the Irish-born total. England had a second centre for Irish-born, however – one in four of all Irish-born were situated in and proximate to London. In Wales 61 per cent of all the Irish-born in that country were resident in Glamorgan, where the cities of Swansea and Cardiff were located.[58]

The Irish community in Scotland was also proportionately strongest in the western part of the country; the five adjacent counties of Ayrshire, Dumbartonshire, Lanarkshire, Renfrewshire and Wigtownshire were the counties where the Irish-born population was proportionately greatest. Wigtownshire, across the North Channel from east Ulster, had the largest proportionate Irish-born population of all British counties. In England, Lancashire had the largest Irish community (Table 19), but it also had the strongest Irish community; 6 per cent of the 1.67 million population of the county were Irish-born, which was well in excess of Middlesex, where 3.7 per cent of its population were Irish-born (Table 20).[59]

57 *Abstract of answers and returns made pursuant to acts 3 & 4 Vic. c. 99, and 4 Vic. 7; enumeration extract*, part 2, *Scotland* H.C. 1843 (498), p. 78.
58 *Enumeration extract*, part 1, *England and Wales*, pp. 399, 458.
59 Ibid., pp. 398–9; *Enumeration extract*, part 2, *Scotland*, pp. 77–8.

Table 19. *Distribution of Irish communities in England and Scotland, 1841.*

County/city	Irish-born	Proportion of total Irish community
Scotland		
Lanarkshire	55,915	44.3%
Renfrewshire	20,417	16.2%
Ayrshire	12,035	9.5%
Edinburgh (Lothian)	7,100	5.6%
Forfar (Angus)	6,474	5.1%
Rest of Scotland	24,380	19.3%
England		
Lancashire	105,916	37.3%
Middlesex	58,068	20.4%
Yorkshire, West Riding	15,177	5.3%
Surrey	13,822	4.9%
Cheshire	11,577	4.1%
Rest of England	79,568	28.0%

Note: For Scotland the percentages show the proportion of the entire Scottish-based Irish-born by county/city; similarly, the English percentages show the proportion of the entire English-based Irish-born community by county.

Table 20. *Relative strength of Irish populations in England and Scotland, 1841.*

County	Irish-born	Population	Irish-born as proportion of county's population
Scotland			
Wigtownshire	5,772	39,195	14.7%
Renfrewshire	20,417	155,072	13.2%
Lanarkshire	55,915	426,972	13.1%
Dumbartonshire	4,891	44,296	11.0%
Ayrshire	12,035	164,356	7.3%
Rest of Scotland	27,291	1,790,293	1.5%
England			
Lancashire	105,916	166,7054	6.4%
Middlesex	58,068	157,6636	3.7%
Cheshire	11,577	39,5660	2.9%
Cumberland	4,881	17,8038	2.7%
Surrey	13,822	58,2678	2.4%
Rest of England	89,864	10,595,072	0.8%

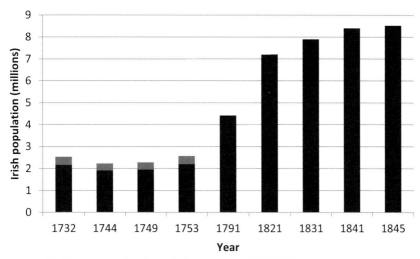

FIGURE 2. Reworked national population estimates, 1732–1845.

Sources: Dickson et al., 'Hearth tax', p. 156; Lee, 'On the accuracy of the pre-Famine Irish Censuses', p. 54; Boyle and Ó Gráda, 'Famine trends, excess mortality and the Great Irish Famine', p. 556.

Note: For 1732, 1744, 1749 and 1753 dark shading indicates Dickson et al. lower-bound estimates and lighter shading indicates upper-bound estimates.

Conclusion

It is now generally accepted that K.H. Connell overestimated the population of Ireland in the first half of the eighteenth century, and that the rapid and sustained increase in the Irish population commenced in the 1750s, three decades earlier than he proposed. According to the population estimates of Dickson et al., Lee, and Boyle and Ó Gráda the population of Ireland rose from no more than 2.5 million people in the early 1730s and the early 1750s to above 8.5 million on the eve of the Great Famine (Fig. 2). This suggests a rapid increase in population in the seven decades before 1821, in the order of 2.1 per cent per year between 1753 and 1791, and 1.6 per cent from 1791 to 1821 (Tables 11 and 16). Thereafter, the population continued to increase, although at a rate slowed primarily because of the rise of mass emigration from Ireland to Britain and to British North America. The figures available suggest a yearly increase of 0.9 per cent between 1821 and 1831, 0.6 per cent in the subsequent decade, and merely 0.4 per cent between 1841 and 1845.

The final word on Ireland's population history in the century before the Great Famine has not been written, but it will not be possible, because of the limited availability of parish records, to emulate Wrigley and Schofield's *The population history of England, 1541–1871* for Ireland.[60] This notwithstanding, some valuable parish-register-based studies have been completed for a handful of regions, primarily in Ulster, and local censuses and surveys have been successfully deployed on occasion to examine social ordering at the parish or town level.[61] Although it is unlikely that the thesis of rapid population growth between the 1750s and the 1820s, followed by a gradual tempering of the rate of increase over the next twenty-five years, will be overturned, considerable scope still remains for the study of the growth and ordering of populations at local, regional and provincial levels.

60 E.A. Wrigley and R.S. Schofield, *The population history of England, 1541–1871: a reconstruction* (Cambridge: Cambridge University Press, 1989).
61 See, for example, W. Macafee, 'Pre-Famine population in Ulster: evidence from the parish register of Killyman' in P. O'Flanagan et al. (eds.), *Rural Ireland: modernisation and change, 1600–1900* (Cork: Cork University Press, 1987), pp. 142–61; V. Morgan, 'A case study of population change over two centuries: Blaris, Lisburn 1661–1848', *Irish Economic and Social History*, 3 (1976), 5–16; C. Thomas, 'The city of Londonderry: demographic trends and socio-economic characteristics, 1650–1900' in G. O'Brien (ed.), *Derry and Londonderry: history and society* (Dublin: Geography Publications, 1999), pp. 359–78.

9

Women, Men and the Family, *c.*1730–*c.*1880

SARAH-ANNE BUCKLEY

Introduction

The numerous publications on Irish demography in the eighteenth and nineteenth centuries have been amplified in recent years by investigations of the family, childhood, the place of women and sexuality. These studies have highlighted the importance of the arranged marriage ('the match'), social class, geographical location, religion, migration, fertility, mortality and inheritance in generating a history of the family, and, for women, of the crucial importance of reputation, respectability and sexuality. This historiography can be said to have commenced with the publication in 1978 of *Women in Irish society: the historical dimension*, edited by Margaret MacCurtain and Donnchadh Ó Corráin, which prepared the way, after an interval, for the publication of various inquiries into the impact of gender and patriarchy on family life.[1] In respect of the era that is the focus of this chapter, the publication in 2006 of an enlarged edition of A.P.W. Malcomson's pioneering study of aristocratic marriage, *The pursuit of the heiress*, can be identified as a key moment.[2] Since then, Deborah Wilson's *Women, marriage and property in wealthy landed families in Ireland, 1750–1850* has provided a nuanced account of the interrelationship of women, property and marriage, while Rachel Wilson's *Elite women in Ascendancy Ireland, 1690–1745*

---

1 See M. MacCurtain and D. Ó Corráin (eds.), *Women in Irish society: the historical dimension* (Dublin: Arlen House, 1978); M. O'Dowd and S. Wichert (eds.), *Chattell, servant or citizen: women's status in church, state and society* (Belfast: Institute of Irish Studies, 1995); B. Whelan (ed.), *Women and paid work in Ireland, 1500–1930* (Dublin: Four Courts Press, 2000); M. Valiulis (ed.), *Gender and power in Irish history* (Dublin: Irish Academic Press, 2008); M. MacCurtain, M. O'Dowd and M. Luddy, 'An agenda for women's history in Ireland, 1550–1900', *Irish Historical Studies*, 28 (1992–3), 1–37; D. McLoughlin, 'Women and sexuality in nineteenth century Ireland', *Irish Journal of Psychology*, 15 (1994), 266–75; M. O'Dowd, 'Family, sex, and marriage, 1600–1800' and D. Urquhart, 'Gender, family, and sexuality, 1800–2000' in L. Kennedy and P. Ollerenshaw (eds.), *Ulster since 1600: politics, economy and society* (Oxford: Oxford University Press, 2012).
2 A.P.W. Malcomson, *The pursuit of the heiress: aristocratic marriage in Ireland, 1740–1840* (Belfast: Ulster Historical Foundation, 2006).

has produced a broader engagement with the role, place and contribution of aristocratic women during the early eighteenth century.[3] In the case of the family more generally, Mary O'Dowd's ambitious *History of women in Ireland, 1500–1800* has highlighted many gaps in the literature relating to women and the family while addressing the experience of women in regard to education, religion, class and background.[4] Currently, Mary O'Dowd and Maria Luddy are embarked on a history of marriage and the family in Ireland from 1660 to 1925, which promises to provide a more socially inclusive account, while work in print by James Kelly and Tom Power on the harsher aspects of gender relations has highlighted the vulnerability of women to abduction and sexual assault, and the pressures that prompted those who experienced unwanted pregnancies to have recourse to infanticide.[5]

In the context of an exploration of the history of women, the family and the economy, this chapter will engage with marriage, gender, mortality, infanticide, abduction, domestic violence, divorce, celibacy, and households and families (including children). Acceptable and unacceptable family structures are also addressed in the context of an engagement with the treatment of unmarried mothers, foster parents and extended family structures. Central to this is an analysis of the removal of children from the family, to charter schools and the foundling hospital in the eighteenth century, and industrial schools and reformatories in the nineteenth century, and the assumption by Catholic religious orders of the initiative in this area.

There is much to be gleaned about the experience of men and women across the class structure by looking at family 'types'. With regard to women specifically, the eighteenth century was a time of significant change in the lives of middle- and upper-class women as a consequence of increased literacy and the inauguration of a consumer society. As a result of the Enlightenment

---

3 D. Wilson, *Women, marriage and property in wealthy landed families in Ireland, 1750–1850* (Manchester: Manchester University Press, 2009); R. Wilson, *Elite women in Ascendancy Ireland, 1690–1745: imitation and innovation* (Woodbridge: The Boydell Press, 2015).

4 M. O'Dowd, *A history of women in Ireland, 1500–1800* (Harlow: Pearson Longman, 2005).

5 M. Luddy and M. O'Dowd, 'Marriage in Ireland, 1600–1925', AHRC funded project; J. Kelly, ' "A most inhuman and barbarous piece of villainy": an exploration of the crime of rape in eighteenth-century Ireland', *Eighteenth-Century Ireland*, 10 (1995), 78–107; J. Kelly, 'The abduction of women of fortune in eighteenth-century Ireland', *Eighteenth-Century Ireland*, 9 (1994), 7–43; 'Responding to infanticide in Ireland, 1680–1820' in Elaine Farrell (ed.), *'She said she was in the family way': pregnancy and infancy in modern Ireland* (London: Institute of Historical Research, 2012), 189–204; J. Kelly, 'Infanticide in eighteenth-century Ireland', *Irish Economic and Social History*, 19 (1992), 5–26; T. Power, *Forcibly without her consent: abductions in Ireland, 1700–1850* (New York: iUniverse, 2010).

and improved access to education, women's public role expanded.[6] While the impact of these trends on societal attitudes to women is barely visible before the final decades of the nineteenth century because of the strength of patriarchal attitudes, it is important to acknowledge the beginnings of this shift. The chapter commences with an exploration of women and the family; this is followed by an examination of childhood and 'unacceptable' family structures, and familial and gendered violence. The chapter concludes with a brief assessment of the impact of the Great Famine on the family.

Women, the Family and the Economy

Marriage

The legal framework defining women's place within the family was laid down in the seventeenth century. Though the legal age of marriage was 14 for a male and 12 for a girl, the 1634 act targeted at preventing abduction stipulated that a girl under 16 could not marry without parental consent. This set the tone for the eighteenth century, and for the provision, ratified by the Irish parliament in 1735 and affirmed ten years later, that minors could not marry without parental consent if they or their parent were possessed of property worth more than £100.[7] The priority of the legislature was to prevent 'clandestine' marriages between Protestant heiresses who were abducted by Catholic men, but the act inevitably had a wider impact.[8] Under English common law and the prevailing concept of female coverture, unmarried daughters were legally subordinate to their fathers, and their male heirs. While married women were comparably subordinate to their husbands, this and other interventions of legislators had the effect of increasing patriarchal authority within the family.

Below the level of the elite, the mechanics of marriage arrangements are more difficult to detect before the second half of the eighteenth century. By the 1750s, in common with the elite, arranged marriage was established practice, as was the need for a dowry, as inheritance practices developed among landed families in the seventeenth century 'had filtered downwards to other social groups by the mid-eighteenth century'.[9] One of the reasons offered for the strength of patriarchal authority in the home was the prevalence of

---

6 G. Meaney, M. O'Dowd and B. Whelan, *Reading the Irish woman: studies in cultural encounter and exchange, 1714–1960* (Liverpool: Liverpool University Press, 2013), 13–86.

7 Wilson, *Elite women in Ascendancy Ireland*, p. 17.

8 O'Dowd, *A history of women in Ireland*, p. 225; Kelly, 'The abduction of women of fortune', pp. 11, 23–4.

9 O'Dowd, *A history of women in Ireland*, p. 105.

arranged marriages, particularly within the farming or substantial tenant class, but this was not unique to rural families.[10] Patriarchy increased among all social groups. In her study of landed families, Deborah Wilson has shown that the replacement of the common law dower arrangement with the jointure disadvantaged women. Women did, as Wilson shows, inherit property of their own, but, she concludes, 'the affective family model and the interests of women within marriage were subordinated to the transfer intact of property'.[11]

There has been a vigorous debate on marriage and fertility in demographic and anthropological studies. These exchanges have focused on (among other issues) the age of marriage, numbers marrying, marital fertility, and the impact of migration, urbanisation and inheritance. While marriage rates were high in Ireland at the start of the eighteenth century and at the end, the most contested issue is the age at first marriage. According to Connell's classic study, the peasantry married young, and from the 1780s teenage marriage was commonplace: 'In Dublin, for example, the age at marriage among poor females was 21.5 in 1810 and 23 on the eve of the [Great] Famine.'[12] The age rose thereafter, as did the proportion of the population that never married. By 1871, the proportion of married women aged 15–45 years in Ireland had fallen to 43 per cent, and it fell further to 36 per cent in 1911. The average marriage age for women in 1841 was 24–25 years; in 1911 it was 28 years.[13] In view of these trends, S.J. Connolly maintains that any consideration of marriage in pre-Famine Ireland 'must begin and revolve around discussions of the social structure', as the majority of the Irish lower classes married young, 'partly because economic conditions permitted them to do so, and partly because there was no realistic prospect of improving their condition by prudence or self-denial'.[14] In County Clare, the Poor Inquiry was informed in 1835 that 'a farmer's son will wait till he gets a fortune, or till he settles his sisters; but with the labourer an acquaintance begun the night before at a wake or a dance is sometimes consolidated the next morning into matrimony'.[15] Clearly, parental

10 Ibid., p. 256.
11 Wilson, *Women, marriage and property*, p. 8; J. Kelly, review of Deborah Wilson's *Women, marriage and property in wealthy landed families in Ireland, 1750–1850*, *Irish Economic and Social History*, 38 (2011), 167–9.
12 O'Dowd, *A history of women in Ireland*, p. 163.
13 M.E. Daly, *A social and economic history of Ireland since 1800* (Dublin: Educational Company of Ireland, 1981), p. 92.
14 S.J. Connolly, 'Marriage in pre-Famine Ireland' in A. Cosgrove (ed.), *Marriage in Ireland* (Dublin: College Press, 1985), p. 79.
15 Ibid., p. 80.

power was less crucial in the case of the labourer than a tenant farmer or the elite because there was no property at stake.

In post-Famine Ireland, 'marriage was a minority experience for the Irish people', David Fitzpatrick argues, due to emigration and the rising marriage age.[16] The spread of celibacy reflected the increasing restrictiveness of the marriage institution, and the closeness of the link between the acquisition of a spouse and property. Yet in regard to parental control, he maintains that Connell's study 'underestimated parental control of marriage before the Famine and overstated it afterwards'.[17] Caitríona Clear echoes this conclusion, as, she maintains, the 'reasons for marrying or not marrying are complex and idiosyncratic'.[18] In particular, Clear queries the assumption that the post-Famine marriage was loveless, pointing to the fact that not all marriages were late; not all marriages involved a business or farm; and not all reasons for marrying can be gleaned from the existing records. Clear provides a rationale for marriage patterns that combines emotion with reason for the period after 1850 – 'perhaps', she argues, 'caution had its origins in emotion rather than economics'.[19] While she acknowledges the arguments of Joseph Lee and others as to the significance of changing inheritance patterns among farmers on marriage patterns in the post-Famine period, she questions the assumption that the Catholic Church and its clergy were key factors when the greatest single proportion of single women in 1881 were Protestants.[20]

Changing Role of Women

Patriarchy notwithstanding, the eighteenth century was a time of appreciating economic involvement by women. Urban growth increased the participation of women in paid work. Employment in the home as well as in family businesses provided girls with skills, while there were increased opportunities for wives to set up businesses separate from but auxiliary to those of their husbands.[21] Women, especially widows, were well represented in the running of inns or taverns, as a study of trade directories in Belfast has documented. Furthermore, more widows were appointed executors and administrators of their husbands' estates in the eighteenth century than was the case previously,

---

16 D. Fitzpatrick, 'Marriage in post-Famine Ireland' in Cosgrove (ed.), *Marriage in Ireland*, p. 116.
17 Ibid., p. 121.
18 C. Clear, *Social change in everyday life in Ireland, 1850–1922* (Manchester: Manchester University Press, 2009), p. 75.
19 Clear, *Social change in Ireland*, p. 86.
20 Ibid.
21 O'Dowd, *A history of women in Ireland*, p. 116.

and some were notably effective in that capacity; though it should be noted that O'Dowd has found that the majority of widows chose not to remain in business.[22] A comparable study of Dublin trade directories from 1766 to 1800 indicates that the majority of women listed were engaged in the food or cloth business. Women were also active as tallow chandlers, as proprietors of book, printing and paper businesses, and, as consumption patterns evolved, as sellers of consumer goods, particularly those used by women such as china, delph and glass. By the end of the century, they were also actively engaged as owners of schools for girls in small towns.[23]

In urban settings, the textile industry was the primary means of women making a living, with many working as spinners, milliners and mantua makers. Apprenticeships allowed girls of modest means to access work, and they were coveted by families seeking to emerge from poverty or to raise their standard of living. How women spent their money and advertised their services was also socially determined. By comparison with middle-class women who were provided for by their husbands, and for whom working for remuneration was viewed disapprovingly, 'the urban-based women who were compelled to earn a living by working outside the home' had direct access to money, though their employments and lifestyle are elusive since they 'could not afford to advertise their services or register their name in trade directories'.[24] Some supplied dairy products, fruit and other foodstuffs to better-off households; others were street sellers or employed as servants, charwomen or washerwomen. Urbanisation offered opportunities for work previously unavailable, yet not all this work was respectable, still less beneficial. There was, for example, an increasing involvement in prostitution and sex work. This led, among other things, to the opening, at the behest of a number of philanthropically minded women from the elite and middling sort, headed by the widowed Lady Arabella Denny (1707–92), of the Magdalen Asylum in Dublin in 1766.[25] Domestic service, which had begun to expand from 1650, and was integral to the maintenance of the aristocratic order, also had its hierarchy. Women who took employment in the lower grades of domestic staff as house, kitchen or dairy maids generally came from poor, rural backgrounds, and they had limited opportunity to advance. With regard to remuneration in a rural environment, hiring fairs and work for women on farms, for example

---

22 Ibid., p. 119.
23 Ibid., p. 122.
24 Ibid., p. 130.
25 Ibid., p. 133; D.F. Fleming, 'Public attitudes to prostitution in eighteenth-century Ireland', *Irish Economic and Social History*, 32 (2005), 1–19.

flax growing, became more common, although much of the paid agricultural work available was seasonal and occasional. Linen spinning, which was largely undertaken by women, became a vital part of the family economy over much of the northern half of the country in the eighteenth century, while in the early nineteenth women made a significant contribution to family budgets selling eggs and making butter.

Women and the Family Economy

As O'Dowd has observed, 'the factional basis of eighteenth-century Irish political life meant that family networks could also be political networks'.[26] This facilitated the presence of women from the social elite at notable events in court life in Dublin Castle, and permitted some to exercise political as well as social influence. O'Dowd has pointed to the influence some women had over their husbands and male relatives in electoral and political matters, and, once Catholics assumed a more visible public profile from the 1780s, the increasing part elite Catholic women played in philanthropy. Improved conditions for women were not class determined, but progression was neither linear nor irreversible. The eighteenth century witnessed an expansion in their social life, increased spending, and the acquisition of new skills in cooking, housework and domestic (including medical) care. However, economic opportunities remained 'highly volatile' and dependent on the state of the Irish economy.[27] Setbacks ensued at different points as a result of the decline of the textile industry, subsistence crises and migration, which prompted an increase in the number of unemployed women in Dublin, and an expanding demand for charitable institutions. There was also the impact of the growth in population, which has been attributed to a reduction in the marriage age and a decline in infant mortality in the eighteenth century.[28] As a result, for the poor and marginal at least, 'the main economic contribution of women to the family economy was earned not through spinning but through begging'.[29] This would remain a feature of poor women's lives in the nineteenth century, despite the attempts of the legislature to deter women and children from vagrancy and begging.

For those unmarried, the terms 'spinster' and 'old maid' achieved currency at the beginning of the eighteenth century, coinciding with an increase in

---

26 O'Dowd, *A history of women in Ireland*, p. 43.
27 Ibid., p. 143.
28 See Gurrin, Chapter 8 above, pp. 204–30.
29 O'Dowd, *A history of women in Ireland*, p. 143.

the pressure to marry.[30] With these terms came the distinctive genteel titles of 'Miss' and 'Mrs' about half a century later.[31] Both Malcomson and Wilson have illuminated the world of elite women who were spinsters or became widows. While they were recognised as 'legal individuals', society showed far less respect for unmarried, mature women than for those who were married. Spinsters were, however, afforded more legal status in Britain and Ireland than elsewhere in Europe, where it was legally mandatory that a woman, regardless of marital situation, was represented by a male.[32] In his study of the gentry of County Galway in the nineteenth century, Patrick Melvin has shown that unmarried sisters remained in the family home after the estate was passed on to a new male heir.[33] For those that did not marry, there was little hope of waged employment. Daughters of Anglo-Irish gentry, and lesser gentry, were usually educated at home, often sharing governesses or tutors with their brothers before the boys were of an age to be sent to boarding school.[34] Governesses outnumbered tutors by ten to one in 1861, and played a significant role in the lives of these girls and young women.[35]

Unlike spinsters, widows were expected to head their own households, as on the death of her husband a woman's legal identity was automatically restored.[36] Widows were more visible, because they were statistically numerous, and more respected than spinsters.[37] A subservient wife, widowed with children at a young age and well provided for financially, might evolve into a controlling matriarch.[38] Historians agree that the financial burden on an estate of sustaining the widow's jointure was a topic of grievance in England and Ireland.[39] There is less evidence that the same antipathy was manifest in respect of the payment of portions, though there is evidence of delayed payment. Upon remarriage, widows forfeited their legal independence and,

30 A.L. Erickson, 'Property and widowhood in England 1660–1840' in S. Cavallo and L. Warner (eds.), *Widowhood in medieval and early modern Europe* (Harlow: Pearson, 1999), p. 162.

31 A.L. Erickson, *Women and property in early modern England* (London: Routledge, 1993), p. 100.

32 A.L. Erickson, 'Coverture and capitalism', *History Workshop Journal*, 59 (Spring 2005), 8.

33 P. Melvin, *Estates and landed society in Galway* (Dublin: Edmund Burke, 2012), p. 166.

34 D. Raftery, J. Harford and S.M. Parkes, 'Mapping the terrain of female education in Ireland, 1830–1910', *Gender Education*, 22:5 (2010), 566.

35 J. Logan, 'Governesses, tutors and parents: domestic education in Ireland, 1700–1880', *Irish Educational Studies*, 7:2 (1988), 3.

36 A. Vickery, *The gentleman's daughter: women's lives in Georgian England* (New Haven: Yale University Press, 1988), p. 208.

37 Erickson, *Women and property in early modern England*, p. 154.

38 Vickery, *Behind closed doors*, p. 218.

39 Ibid., p. 219; D. Large, 'The wealth of the greater Irish landowners, 1750–1815', *Irish Historical Studies*, 15 (1966–7), 27.

unless carefully managed, their rights to property. Guardianship of children was a key issue. As a result, it was customary for widows to submit to an appropriate mourning period, to ensure there was no confusion about the paternity of a subsequent child.[40] Unlike other parts of Europe, a mother in Ireland and England was not the natural legal guardian to her children; and while widows may have had the benefit of financial independence, their rights to their children were not guaranteed, especially if they chose to remarry. With regard to widowers, many were encouraged to remarry in order to have a woman available to manage a household and children.[41] This sometimes resulted in second and more families.

Among the middle and upper classes, running a household and maintaining authority over children and servants was a highly gendered activity.[42] Fathers provided the material necessities for the family; mothers managed the household. With regard to the house itself, the gendered character of domestic spaces during the Georgian era influenced the manner in which rooms were presented and decorated. The dining room, for example, was a 'symbol of the family's pedigree and a repository of values transcending fashion'. It was regarded as a 'masculine' space. For that reason, it was less frequently redecorated than the 'feminine' drawing room – to which women 'withdrew from male company' after dining.[43] Within the home, mothers were expected to provide care and emotional support, though this responsibility might be delegated to nursemaids and servants in aristocratic households. Historians differ in their interpretation of the extent to which parents manifested affection for their children and each other, with some suggesting that prior to the eighteenth century it was lacking. Others argue that affection was not absent but that its expression was limited.[44] Both mothers and fathers within the lesser gentry appear to have maintained a close involvement in the lives of their offspring and many decisions regarding financial matters were made jointly. Medical care was predominantly a domestic function, and as

---

40 Cavallo and Warner (eds.), *Widowhood in medieval and early modern Europe*, p. 11.

41 L. Davidoff and C. Hall, *Family fortunes: men and women of the English middle class, 1780–1850* (London; Routledge, 1987), p. 325.

42 Vickery, *The gentleman's daughter*, p. 72.

43 C. Lucey, 'Redecorating the domestic interior in late eighteenth-century Dublin' in E. FitzPatrick and J. Kelly (eds.), *Domestic life in Ireland* (Dublin: Royal Irish Academy, 2012), p. 175.

44 S.J. Connolly, 'Family, love and marriage: some evidence from the early eighteenth century' in M. MacCurtain and M. O'Dowd (eds.), *Women in early modern Ireland* (Edinburgh: Edinburgh University Press, 1991), p. 277.

such primarily administered by women.[45] The dangers associated with child-birth and infant mortality was a concern for all. For women who were fertile, the early years of marriage were frequently punctuated by confinement and birth.[46] Literature regarding birth control was not produced in Ireland prior to 1868, though information may have been accessible to those who travelled to England, and certain proprietary medications may have been employed to induce a miscarriage.[47] Mortality rates among children were high, such was the prevalence of epidemic diseases such as smallpox, and it was accepted up to the middle of the eighteenth century that up to a third of children might not survive to their fifteenth birthday. The practice of making a mother's guardianship conditional on not remarrying was guided by the desire to provide appropriately for young children.[48]

Children, Childhood and Institutions

Scholars agree that the history of childhood is a product of Philippe Ariès' 1960 study, translated into English as *Centuries of childhood*. Ariès instigated the development of a new field of scholarship, utilising age, gender, class, religion and ethnicity as tools for research. Following Ariès, Lloyd de Mause, Edward Shorter and Laurence Stone all argued that there had, over time, been major changes to the attitude and treatment of children. In 1983, Linda Pollock provided a major critique of existing theories, arguing that Ariès' contention 'that in medieval society the idea of childhood did not exist' was incorrect.[49] She also pointed out that British historians did not concur with Stone's char-acterisation of the parent–child relationship in the seventeenth century. With this intervention, Pollock established a new paradigm that was less reliant on an over-arching theory and more firmly grounded on the actuality of par-ent–child relationships. In the Irish context, emerging work suggests that the eighteenth century was a significant moment, as a concept of childhood as a distinct life phase achieved greater recognition among elite families. Gabrielle

45 J. Kelly, 'Domestic medication and medical care in late early modern Ireland' in J. Kelly and F. Clark (eds.), *Ireland and medicine in the seventeenth and eighteenth centuries* (Farnham: Ashgate, 2010), pp. 109–36,

46 Vickery, *The gentleman's daughter*, p. 97.

47 M. Luddy, *Women in Ireland, 1800–1918: a documentary history* (Cork: Cork University Press, 1995), p. 32; J. Kelly, 'Health for sale: mountebanks, doctors, printers and the sup-ply of medication in eighteenth-century Ireland', *Proceedings of the Royal Irish Academy*, 108c (2008), 95.

48 Wilson, *Women, marriage and property*, p. 94.

49 L. Pollock, *Forgotten children: parent–child relations from 1500 to 1900* (Cambridge: Cambridge University Press, 1983).

Ashford has concluded that the eighteenth-century elite experienced the 'discovery' of their children in the sense that they came to share their company as well as to care and provide for their health and education. She has also suggested that they were more comfortable with family intimacy than their English peers.[50] Yet invoking the work of Joseph Robins on the Foundling Hospital and extending his framework to embrace childhood illness, Ashford accepts that the prevailing model of childhood in eighteenth-century Ireland was broadly comparable to that in eighteenth-century England. It was not always so. Mary O'Dowd has demonstrated that the relationship between the state and the child in Ireland during the Tudor and Stuart periods was almost the reverse of that between the state and the English or Welsh child. While the sons of elite Gaelic families were identified as a suitable agent of English language and customs as well as security for the loyalty of their fathers, there was little provision for the welfare of poor or abandoned children.[51]

By the early eighteenth century, the abandonment of children, particularly illegitimate children, was a matter of tangible public concern, and from 1703 the newly established House of Industry was charged with receiving foundling children aged between 5 and 16 years in order to educate them in the Protestant faith and to apprentice them to Protestant masters. In 1725 the workhouse was reorganised as the Dublin Foundling Hospital and Workhouse, and in 1730 it began admitting children of all ages, with infants usually handed over to the care of wet-nurses in the community. As a system it lent itself to abuse. The Foundling Hospital had an appalling infant mortality rate, with suggestions that 75 per cent of infants admitted in the mid and late eighteenth century died.[52] Conditions improved somewhat thereafter but, like the smaller Cork and Galway institutions, the Dublin Foundling Hospital was characterised by corrupt administration, poor diet, disease, infestation and cruelty until its closure in the 1820s. It set a precedent for the institutional care of orphaned, abandoned and otherwise problematic children that was to endure. The rate of institutional infant mortality would remain high throughout the nineteenth century – and feature prominently in the concerns expressed about the Poor Law system.

---

50 G.M. Ashford, 'Childhood: studies in the history of children in eighteenth-century Ireland' (unpublished PhD thesis, St Patrick's College, Dublin City University, 2012), p. 56.

51 M. O'Dowd, 'Early modern Ireland and the history of the child' in M. Luddy and J.M. Smith (eds.), *Children, childhood and Irish society: 1500 to the present* (Dublin: Four Courts Press, 2014), p. 42.

52 J. Robins, *The lost children: a study of charity children in Ireland, 1700–1900* (Dublin: IPA, 1980), p. 17.

The Poor Law

From the beginning of the nineteenth century, orphanages, ragged schools, industrial schools and reformatories were founded to cater for orphaned and deserted children, and, later, for neglected children. In keeping with the religious polarisation of society, most of these institutions were denominational in character. This was essentially true also of the poor law unions that were authorised to receive poor families and their children when the Poor Law was approved by parliament in 1838, and, as a result, they were quickly enmeshed in the concern with proselytism that preoccupied the Catholic Church. It was manifest, for example, in such areas as the debates on the setting up of reformatories for young offenders in 1858, during which the Catholic hierarchy demanded that all boys and girls be sent to schools of their own denomination. It was not an exclusively Catholic preoccupation, moreover; during the debates on the formation of industrial schools, Ulster Protestants expressed equivalent fears that working-class Protestant children might be ill treated or stigmatised if they were placed in Catholic industrial schools.

A majority of the children in the care of the Poor Law were kept in workhouses. As the system was designed to 'reform as well as relieve', the intention was to mould children into valuable citizens. Not only were children not boarded out, most were put to work as early as possible. Furthermore, parents and children in the workhouse were separated at the age of 2 years, and, since most parents did not apply for formal visitation, workhouse children grew up with little parental contact. Given this context, it is not difficult to establish why philanthropists prioritised the need to develop other options for destitute children. As a result, the children were caught in an attitudinal and ideological crossfire. As Virginia Crossman has demonstrated, it was inevitable that the authorities would focus on the family in a period of rapid change, as it represented a unit that could be influenced and moulded. And they were not alone in so doing; as Anna Clark points out, Irish nationalists, the Catholic Church and philanthropic women also 'used the issue of poor infant children as leverage in their confrontation with the British state'.[53]

In the first quarter of 1844, the 22,585 children in workhouses amounted to about half the total workhouse population. By 1850 the number had surged to an estimated 120,000.[54] Although an improvement on the conditions in which

---

53 A. Clark, 'Orphans and the Poor Law: rage against the machine' in V. Crossman and P. Gray (eds.), *Poverty and welfare in Ireland, 1838–1948* (Dublin: Irish Academic Press, 2011).

54 V. Crossman, 'Cribbed, contained and confined? The care of children under the Irish Poor Law, 1850–1920' in Luddy and Smith (eds.), *Children, childhood and Irish society*, p. 82.

they were kept in the Foundling Hospital, the care afforded children within the workhouse left much to be desired. Children were usually allowed three meals a day – of milk and oatmeal, potatoes or bread – which was one more than the two permitted to adults. Yet mortality rates were high, especially in the larger urban unions. Children were supposed to attend school for a minimum of three hours per day but this generally amounted to little more than mass supervision in cold and dirty surroundings. Like adults, and their predecessors in the charter schools, children were expected to engage in manual labour. In some workhouses they were trained in trades or in agricultural or domestic work, or hired out as farm labourers. In many instances, children spent their days without any occupation. Unruly or violent behaviour, and instances of absconding, were frequent as a result. Improvements in dress, diet and educational and training standards occurred as numbers declined in the 1850s, and as a result of the amalgamation of poor law unions for educational purposes, which was permitted from 1855.

The boarding out system (later known as fostering), which allowed poor law guardians to board out children, who would otherwise be placed in the workhouse, with local families was introduced under the Irish Poor Law Amendment Act (1862). This act gave boards of guardians the power to place orphan and deserted children up to the age of 5 years 'out to nurse', with the proviso that guardians could extend this to children aged up to 8 years if they deemed it advantageous to the child's health.[55] Despite clear guidance from the Poor Law Commission, the response was far from uniform. In contrast to the situation in Scotland, a majority of poor law children in Ireland (and in England) remained in some form of institutional care throughout the nineteenth century, as poor law unions availed themselves of the discretion allowed to boards of guardians to act as they deemed appropriate.[56] Catholic critics denounced the workhouse as an unsuitable environment for pauper, orphaned, deserted or illegitimate children, but they were less than objective when it came to their own institutional provision, which was also not without serious failings.

The guardians' reluctance to authorise boarding out was partly guided by the fear that an interventionist approach to poverty alleviation would

---

55 See S.A. Buckley, ' "Found in a dying condition": nurse children in Ireland, 1872–1952' in Farrell (ed.), *'She said she was in the family way'*, pp. 145–62.

56 Crossman states that 'the slow take-up of boarding out was a consequence of the misgivings of local guardians, not the poor law commissioners': ' "Cribbed, contained and confined?" ', p. 50; H.J. MacDonald, 'Boarding-out and the Scottish Poor Law, 1845–1914', *Scottish Historical Review*, 75 (1996), 197–220.

encourage parental irresponsibility and the abandonment of children. With regard to conflicting views on the upper age limit to which children should be cared for, disagreement reflected the debate over the merits of industrial over domestic care.[57] The pressure brought to bear by philanthropists and the awareness of the limitations of the workhouse convinced government that they must intervene and introduce improvements to the system. These were slow in coming, but in 1898 they increased the age to which children had to be cared for to 15 years and extended the powers available to boards of guardians to implement boarding out arrangements. Two issues were critical to the success of boarding out – the choice of foster parent and the quality/frequency of inspections. An examination of both issues reveals the problems with the system. Most foster parents were identified by members of boarding out committees, philanthropists and other interested persons. Occasionally, advertisements were placed in the local press seeking suitable adoptive parents. In 1877, the Local Government Board for Ireland issued a list of conditions that prospective foster parents had to satisfy in an attempt to ensure the well-being of children. The stipulated criteria embraced moral character, religion, health, housing and economic status. In respect of the latter, it was provided that 'no child shall be permitted to continue with any foster-parent who ... shall keep any pig, cow, donkey or other such animal in the dwelling house'.[58] Most unions also sought references or testimonials signed by a local clergyman, magistrate or medical officer attesting to the good conduct and respectability of applicant foster parents. With regard to inspections, inspectors or relieving officers were required to oversee and monitor the supervision and well-being of children in foster homes, provide regular reports to the Local Government Board on the workings of the system and make recommendations in particular cases. Despite these good intentions, both the selection of foster parents and inspections varied in quality from union to union. When carried out regularly, the inspections indicated that many foster parents lived up to their responsibilities. In 1873, the inspector for the Galway region noted: 'children are in good hands and well cared for. I inspected them on Saturday last, and found them well housed, comfortably clothed and presenting a clean and healthy appearance'; he also observed positively 'some degree of kinship' between the children and the family.[59] But it was not always so. Dr Roughan

---

57 See C. Skehill, 'The origins of child welfare under the Poor Law and the emergence of the institutional versus family care debate' in Crossman and Gray (eds.), *Poverty and welfare in Ireland*, pp. 115–29.

58 *Annual Report of the Local Government Board for Ireland*, 1877 [c1761], p. 44.

59 *Annual Report of the Local Government Board for Ireland*, 1873 [c794], 61–2.

of the Sligo district described a house he visited in the Collooney region in the same year as 'a damp hovel, with filthy surroundings. It consisted of one apartment, containing 2 beds, each occupied by four persons. A cow, a calf and a pig occupy or share a portion of it.'[60]

How many children were actually boarded? In their 1870 report on the administration of poor relief in Ireland, the Commissioners calculated that 1,207 children were in fosterage. This was an increase of 57 per cent on the 689 children in that position the previous year, and it is attributable to 'the extension of the age to which this class of children may be relieved out of the workhouse' and 'to the further adoption of the system by Boards of Guardians'.[61] Nevertheless, when set beside the 15,000 children residing in workhouses at the time, it is striking just how deep rooted was the institutional approach to pauper relief. At an average of £6 per child per year, boarding out was half the cost of residential care, but local authorities preferred the institutional approach; what they lost in financial terms they recouped in human resources and energy, as it was easier to send children to workhouses (and later to industrial schools) than to engage in the task of seeking and vetting applications and pursuing inspections. The problem was that it was not in the best interests of the child, but, Marie Dickie pointed out, 'philanthropy [was] not so widespread as to provide an open door for one orphan after another from the local workhouse'.[62]

Industrial Schools and Reformatories

Debates about childhood and criminality also shaped attitudes, and the decision to authorise the foundation of reformatories and industrial schools. Legislation to establish reformatories for young offenders aged between 12 and 16 was passed in 1858 and to establish industrial schools a decade later. In keeping with developments on continental Europe, both were built and managed through voluntary effort, with the state certifying and inspecting the institutions and, together with local authorities, providing capitation grants. Both were segregated according to religion and gender, and both were required to provide moral and literary education as well as occupational training. The extent to which these aims were pursued, as well as the extent to which inspections were carried out thoroughly, is debatable. Under the

---

60 Ibid., p. 80.
61 *Annual Report of the Commissioners for Administering the Laws for the Relief of the Poor in Ireland*, 1870 [c156], p. 13.
62 *Annual Report of the Local Government Board for Ireland*, 1910 (c5319), p. 24.

Industrial Schools (Ireland) Act of 1868, children under 14 could be committed to an industrial school if they were encountered begging, if they were without a home or proper guardianship, if they were destitute, or if they 'frequent the company of reputed thieves'.[63] Children under 12 convicted of a misdemeanour could also be sentenced to detention in an industrial school. The great majority of children were committed for begging and from the outset industrial schools were associated with poor, destitute or abandoned rather than 'criminal' children. As a result, they gradually replaced the workhouse in this role. The abuses, which this system permitted in the twentieth century, cannot be identified for the nineteenth century – as the testimony of the children committed to care does not exist. However, the records of the religious orders (which are not currently accessible) may in time shed light on a system which, for a variety of reasons, resulted in the splitting up of thousands of families.

Marital, Familial and Gender Violence

The prevalence of infanticide, abduction, domestic violence, sexual violence, divorce, bigamy and desertion all attest to the abusive practices that marriage and family arrangements permitted in the eighteenth and nineteenth centuries. Work by James Kelly, Maria Luddy, Timothy Guinnane, Marilyn Silverman, Liam Kennedy, Liz Steiner-Scott, Diane Urquhart, Carolyn Conley and Elaine Farrell have identified, and in certain cases illuminated, some of these issues. This section will address them while also focusing on the importance of gender, geography and class to the experiences of men and, particularly, women.

From the 1750s, it was not uncommon in Dublin and other urban areas for couples who wished to marry to do so with the assistance of a priest without any public declaration or investigation into their marital status or suitability. This was contrary to law if not religious practice and, as the century drew to a close, officials, lay and clerical, sought to tighten the regulatory apparatus in an attempt to curtail the prevalence of abduction, marriage by 'couple begging' clergy, rape, infanticide, bigamy and elopement.[64] Consistent with the prevailing patriarchal order, women were more harshly affected than men by abusive practices within marriage. The limits of medical knowledge and

---

63 Ibid., p. 42.
64 J. Kelly, 'Some harsh realities of love and marriage in eighteenth-century Ireland' (unpublished paper).

access to medical services made childbirth and pregnancy extremely hazardous, and even when legislation was introduced in 1853 to combat wife-beating, it was underutilised for economic and other reasons. Sexual assault within marriage was not an offence; the law declined to sanction males who physically assaulted their wives, and separation / desertion was commonplace. Moreover, this occurred against a backdrop of an idealised image of female virtue that brought particular pressure to bear on women, as the following commentary from the 1760s attests:

> A women ought not only to be virtuous ... all the earth should think of her so; a female might as well be in reality a prostitute as imagined so. What a shocking creature a women is who has lost her virgin innocence? She is a poor wretch ... a woman cuts a despicable figure depriv'd of her honour ... a woman's honour is centr'd on her virtue.[65]

Illegitimacy and Infanticide

One abuse where a woman's reputation and sexual history were particularly pertinent was infanticide. Historians have investigated the history and occurrence of this phenomenon, demonstrating not only its enduring prevalence, but also, by implication, a willingness to engage in premarital and extramarital sex on which other sources are silent. Addressing the years 1680 to 1820, James Kelly contends that the pattern of infanticide in Ireland has much in common with that identified in England and Scotland during the same period; the fact that it was primarily a women's offence is indicative of the preoccupation with 'female reputation', and the patriarchal character of the prevailing code of sexual morality. The seriousness of the consequences certainly encouraged some single (and some married) women not only to conceal their pregnancy but also in the immediate aftermath of childbirth to dispose of the child in order to maintain their reputation. The existing narrative is one involving women in domestic service, girls and young women engaged in prostitution, and a disposition to legal severity that resulted in the eighteenth century in the capital conviction and execution (by burning and by hanging) of a small proportion of those who were brought to trial, which represented a still smaller proportion of those who committed infanticide.[66] Capital sentences were rarely handed down from the early nineteenth century, but the change

---

65 *Freeman's Journal*, 7 Feb. 1764.
66 J. Kelly, 'Responding to infanticide in Ireland, 1680–1820', *passim*; J. Kelly, 'Infanticide in eighteenth-century Ireland', 5–26.

to the law then, which militated against the application of capital sentences even in cases where infanticide was proven, had little impact on the predisposition to commit the offence. Indeed, infanticide became more commonplace. Elaine Farrell has identified 4,645 cases of suspected infant murder, attempted infanticide and concealment of birth between 1850 and 1900.[67] While Farrell reveals that only twenty-nine women were found guilty of child murder during this time, the larger number of suspected cases shows that infanticide was an option single women with unwanted pregnancies felt compelled to employ. It also suggests that premarital and extramarital sexual relationships were not unusual. Similarly, in her examination of breach of promise cases in the late nineteenth century, Maria Luddy has shown that premarital sex was not uncommon, suggesting 'a greater tolerance of such activity within society' than the moral structures of opinion formers in church and state imply.[68]

Female and Child Abductions

There were fewer instances of the abduction and forcible marriage of women by comparison with the number of cases of infanticide. But the sample of some 200 instances assembled by Kelly, Power and Luddy permit the identification of its main features during the eighteenth and early nineteenth centuries, when necessitous men, many of whom were of some social standing, perceived the abduction of women of fortune as a solution to their financial problems.[69] In the eighteenth century, the 'typical' rural abductors and their targets were from the lower gentry and 'yeoman' or strong farmer classes. In Dublin, abductors were often journeymen, while the target was usually a sole heir of a merchant or shopkeeper, and the motivation there, as in the countryside, was essentially financial.[70] This was sufficient to sustain the practice until the late eighteenth century, when the combination of the increased daring of abductors and the decision of the authorities to respond with exemplary sanctions in a number of high-profile cases served to discourage the hitherto prevalent practice of abducting young Protestant heiresses. It did not bring about the end of the practice, however. It continued to be pursued

67 E. Farrell, 'A most diabolical deed': infanticide and Irish society, 1850–1900 (Manchester: Manchester University Press, 2013), p. 247.
68 M. Luddy, Matters of deceit: breach of marriage cases in nineteenth- and twentieth-century Limerick (Dublin: Four Courts Press, 2011), p. 10.
69 Kelly, 'The abduction of women of fortune in eighteenth-century Ireland', pp. 7–43; Power, Forcibly without her consent; M. Luddy, 'Abductions in nineteenth-century Ireland', New Hibernia Review, 17:2 (2013), 17–44. Kelly's sample embraces 180 abductions, 1701–1800; Power's 138 instances, 1700–1802, and Luddy's 192 cases, 1700–1802.
70 Kelly, 'Some harsh realities of love and marriage'.

in the countryside in the early nineteenth century, when a majority of practitioners were from the peasantry, and (when it was not collusive) the manner in which it was pursued mirrored the tactics employed by those engaged in agrarian protest. One may instance the case of Honora Goold – a young girl who was mistakenly identified as the eldest daughter of Richard Goold, the son of a prosperous farmer. On 4 March 1822, twelve armed men entered the house in which she lived and removed Honora. Over the following weeks, she was repeatedly sexually assaulted and advised that her ordeal would conclude with her release if she married her abuser, whose name was William Brown. Goold's refusal to cooperate frustrated her abductors, who were left with no alternative but to agree to release her if she signed a document in which she stated she was present of her own free will. This was not sufficient to protect her assailants, however. Following Goold's release, a number of prosecutions to conviction ensued.[71] This notwithstanding, the practice persisted, albeit within an increasingly narrow social circle and geographical space, until at least the Great Famine.

By comparison, the abduction of children, which also took place on occasion in the eighteenth century, was seldom practised in the early nineteenth, though children continued to be targeted, then and later, and taken to an isolated location to be stripped of their clothing and jewellery. In a recent account, it has been demonstrated that the practice was pursued under the umbrella of the emigrant trade – especially to the crown's American colonies – in the second half of the eighteenth century. The primary target was children aged between 5 and 10 years. Its scale is difficult to pin down, but its occurrence, and the weakness of the legislative and police response, is revealing both of the willingness of an element within the population to exploit children and, when set beside 'the shocking levels of mortality revealed by the inquiries in 1791 into the operation of Dublin's Foundling Hospital', of the tardiness of the authorities in developing an appropriate response.[72]

Domestic Violence and Divorce

Wife-beating was a regular occurrence in nineteenth-century Ireland and one that featured frequently in the courts and in the press, as Liz Steiner-Scott has shown. An examination of domestic violence and desertion draws together a number of themes: the economic dependence of wives; the societal roles

---

71 Luddy, 'Abductions in nineteenth-century Ireland'.
72 J. Kelly, ' "This iniquitous traffic": the kidnapping of children for the American Colonies in eighteenth-century Ireland', *Journal of the History of Childhood and Youth*, 9:2 (2016), 244.

assigned to mothers, wives, husbands and fathers; class differences; and the continuing subordination of women to men. By the mid to late nineteenth century, as with incest and cruelty to children, wife-beating was portrayed by middle-class temperance advocates and social reformers as a working-class problem committed by 'barbaric' men, whose 'pathetic' wives needed protection by the state. In 1853 the Aggravated Assaults on Women and Children Act was introduced to address the issue. Unsurprisingly, very few women prosecuted their husbands because of 'their economic dependency, fear of reprisals, and distrust of the law'.[73] The following case is typical of those that came to court that were not prosecuted to conviction:

> A man named —, a labourer living at 134 Great Britain Street was charged in the Northern Divisional Police Court, Dublin before Mr O'Donal with having assaulted his wife. When the case was called, the complainant, a respectably-dressed woman, refused to prosecute … The Complainant said that if her husband was sent to jail she and her children would starve. Mr. O'Donal said they could go to the poorhouse, and the woman still declining to prosecute, his worship discharged the prisoner.[74]

In the context of a discussion of the family, the woman's recognition of the economic distress that both she and her children would experience if her husband was imprisoned is revealing. Had she been childless she might have been in a position to leave her husband and live a separate life (although this was very rarely the case), but her economic dependence reduced her room to manoeuvre. Offered the choice of the workhouse or a violent husband, she concluded logically that staying with the latter would disrupt her and her children's lives the least.

The 1853 act legislated against wife-beating, but it did nothing to engage with the structural inequalities that enabled husbands to beat their wives without fear of the consequences. Even in the cases that were prosecuted, the economic dependence of wives and economic independence of men ensured that women were and remained at a disadvantage, as men were in a position to pay the fines imposed by judges in the courts. In those cases which made it to court that women refused to prosecute, most women informed the judge they were prepared to forgive their husband in the hope that a warning would effect change. Saliently, as Steiner-Scott has noted, though

73 L. Steiner-Scott, '"To bounce a boot off her now and then …": domestic violence in post-Famine Ireland' in M. Valiulis and M. O'Dowd (eds.), *Women and Irish history* (Dublin: Attic Press, 1997), 125–43; Buckley, *The cruelty man*, 189–96; D. Urquhart, 'Irish divorce and domestic violence, 1857–1922', *Women's History Review*, 22:5 (2013), 820–37.
74 Buckley, *The cruelty man*, p. 189.

cases were reported in the press and dealt with in the courts, there was no sustained movement against wife-beating in Ireland. In contrast to Britain and the United States, where feminists campaigned against wife-beating, battered wives elicited little attention and had little recourse. They were in no position, certainly, to seek a divorce.

In her study of divorce following the introduction of the 1857 Divorce and Matrimonial Causes Act (from which Ireland was excluded), Diane Urquhart argues that 'parliamentary divorce provided an uneasy, if permanent, solution to marital problems, but access was dictated by class, gender, and post-1857, by geography'.[75] Urquhart demonstrates the gendered nature and grounds for granting a divorce in Westminster – to the extent that, prior to 1857, only four women were granted divorces by comparison with 300 men. The situation was still more inequitable in Ireland in the eighteenth century, when a private act was required, as a result of which a mere eleven divorces were authorised by law between 1730 and 1800.[76] The 'sexual double standard' was integral to this unequal state of affairs. By the terms of the 1857 Act, adultery on the part of the wife or the bogus transmittal of property provided adequate evidence for a husband to secure a divorce. Wives, by contrast, had to prove aggravated adultery on the part of the husband: incestuous adultery and adultery coupled with bigamy or cruelty, rape or sodomy were grounds. The publicity given to cases was also more difficult for women since it meant that their married, sexual and family lives would be placed in the public arena. Bad as this was, the failure to extend the provisions of the 1857 Act to Ireland excluded the many people 'who could ill afford financially, morally, or socially to pursue a parliamentary divorce'. Divorce 'Irish style', which in popular parlance referred to desertion or agreed separation by means of migration, provided a solution of sorts for many more unhappy marriages than legal divorce.[77]

The Great Famine and the Family

In the debate on the demography of the Irish family, the Great Famine features large. As discussed earlier in this chapter, Irish society in the post-Famine period was characterised by a late age of first marriage and a high

75 D. Urquhart, 'Ireland and the Divorce and Matrimonial Causes Act of 1857', *Journal of Family History*, 38:3 (2013), 301–20.

76 J. Bergin, 'Irish private divorce bills and acts of the eighteenth century' in J. Kelly, J. McCafferty and C.I. McGrath (eds.), *People, Power and Politics: essays on Irish history, 1660–1850* (Dublin: UCD Press, 2009), pp. 94–121.

77 Ibid.

rate of permanent celibacy. Although Kennedy and Clarkson contend that the Famine had 'only a limited impact on patterns of marriage and family formation', a comparison of the pre- and post-Famine periods demonstrates that it accelerated existing trends in marriage age and celibacy rates, among farmers particularly. Before the Great Famine, nine out of ten adults married, but by 1871, 17 per cent of Irish men and 16 per cent of Irish women did not.[78] This percentage continued to increase in the late nineteenth century. Was this a consequence of the 'psychic trauma' of the Famine or other material/economic factors? Kennedy et al. argue, from the fact that the changes were limited between 1841 and 1851, that the drift away from marriage was primarily a post-Famine phenomenon.[79] Additionally, as emigration resulted in a growing awareness of the living standards in Britain and the United States, this was a factor in people's calculations of the likely benefits of marriage and of their future. In 1850, the level of permanent celibacy in Ireland was still much the same as in England and Scotland. By 1911, the celibacy levels for women had doubled, while they had more than doubled among men.[80] Inevitably, marriage rates impacted the birth rate. After the Famine, 'the crude birth rate fell from an estimated 38–40 births per thousand of the population in 1841 to 23 in 1911'.[81] In conjunction with these shifts, there were changes to the formation, type and make-up of households, as fewer marriages resulted in more diverse households.

With respect to where families resided, the declining population of the post-Famine period prompted an improvement in the quality of the country's housing stock. In 1861, Henry Coulter noted the gradual disappearance of 'wretched-looking hovels with fermented manure heaps outside' in Scariff, County Clare.[82] The improvement in housing was due to a number of issues – legislation, town planning and cultural change. Furthermore, by the 1880s changes had begun to be introduced with respect to hygiene, child welfare and diet.[83] The impact of this was uneven; in counties Kerry and Mayo, fourth-class houses still represented 60 per cent of all housing; in Galway,

---

78 L. Kennedy and L.A. Clarkson, *Mapping the Great Irish Famine* (Dublin: Four Courts Press, 1999).
79 Ibid., p. 43.
80 Ibid., p. 164.
81 Ibid., p. 169.
82 Cited in Clear, *Social change*, p. 142.
83 See for example D. Birdwell-Pheasant, 'Family systems and the foundations of class in Ireland and England', *History of the Family*, 3:1 (1988), 17–34; D. Birdwell-Pheasant, 'Irish households in the twentieth century: culture, class and historical contingency', *Journal of Family History*, 18 (1993), 19–38.

50 per cent. As Barry O'Reilly has observed: 'until the mid-nineteenth century the vast majority of the people of Ireland lived in houses that they built themselves with the help of family and neighbours'.[84]

Geographical location also impacted gender balance. In the post-Famine period, there was a growing imbalance in gender ratios, as the excess of females in more urbanised and industrialised regions in the east was mirrored by a surplus of males in the rural west. Gender changes were influenced by employment opportunities and emigration, and they are important for what they reveal of family life, inward and outward migration, the availability of marriage partners, the sexual division of labour, and the celibacy rate. Comparing 1841 and 1851, the Famine had the greatest impact on the far west of the island, as Connemara moved from a male surplus to a female surplus. This may reflect survival rates, which, Robert Durks suggests, are a product of the greater biological capacity of women to negotiate famine.[85] Others argue that women suffered disproportionately. What recent studies have demonstrated is that change was slow, falling from ninety-seven males for every hundred females in 1841 to ninety-five males for every hundred females in 1871. Moreover, many parts of the country were little affected. After the Famine, we see more women than men in the north-east and south-east, and in Dublin and Limerick. Of the male surplus areas, County Kildare was the worst affected, but other factors contributed to this. Women migrated for work and in order to enhance their marriage opportunities.

How did these changes affect the make-up of family homes? Birdwell-Pheasant describes the now dominant stem family by the end of the nineteenth century as 'one in which there was cross-generational continuity of households, as with the patriarchal family, but in which most children were dispersed, as in the nuclear family'.[86] While scholars continue to debate the speed at which change occurred and the extent to which the Famine was responsible, there is little question but that the Irish family experienced identifiable change after 1870.

---

84 B. O'Reilly, 'Hearth and home: the vernacular house in Ireland from c.1800', in E. Fitzpatrick and J. Kelly (eds.), *Domestic life in Ireland* (Dublin: Royal Irish Academy, 2012), pp. 193–215.

85 R. Dirks, 'Social responses during severe food shortages and famine', *Current Anthropology*, 21:1 (1980), 21–44.

86 D. Birdwell-Pheasant, 'The early twentieth century Irish stem family: a case study from Co. Kerry' in M. Silverman and P. Gulliver (eds.), *Approaching the past: historical anthropology through Irish case studies* (New York: Columbia University Press, 1992), p. 207.

Conclusion

In the introduction to their 2001 collection *Family life in the long nineteenth-century, 1789–1913*, David Kertzer and Marzio Barbagli observe that 'the picture we present here should encourage [scholars] to avoid simple mono-causal theories and to dive instead into the messy, but fascinating, whirlwind of forces that together shaped and continue to shape family life'.[87] The Irish family changed substantially between 1730 and 1880. There are a number of reasons for this, most notably the changing role of women; the emergence of an improved understanding of childhood; the cautious willingness of the judiciary and the legislature to address abuses and gender violence; changes to inheritance and land allocation patterns; and the devastating effects of the Great Famine. With the increasing role of the state and religion in the lives of the working class and the rural poor, and the emergence of an educated, literate population, the twentieth century would see a very different 'type' of Irish family. Yet, as Kertzer and Barbagli highlight, the reasons for these changes are complex – ranging from (to name a few) the impact of urbanisation, to the emergence of the women's movement and changing mortality rates. What this chapter has shown is that the experience of family life could as easily involve pain and endurance as love and commitment, and that those on the margins experienced the negative effects most acutely. It is also clear that the patterns, practices and pursuits then adopted and engaged in laid the foundations for problems that would become major issues in the twentieth century. Much of this can be ascribed to the longer-term effects of the model of patriarchy and controlled sexuality that was pursued. But the negative consequences of institutionalisation were hardly less consequential for the lives of women and children. For historians of the family, there remain many unanswered questions, but this is to be expected of a subject that continues to take shape.

---

87 D. Kertzer and M. Barbagli (eds.), *Family life in the long nineteenth century, 1789–1913* (New Haven: Yale University Press, 2001), p. xxxviii.

PART III

*

RELIGION

10

The Catholic Church and Catholics in an Era of Sanctions and Restraints, 1690–1790

THOMAS O'CONNOR

Introduction

For generations, the narrative of late seventeenth- and eighteenth-century Irish Catholicism was dominated by the body of anti-Catholic legislation commonly known as the Penal Laws. According to traditional accounts, their passage through the Dublin parliament in the 1690s and early 1700s inaugurated a period of ethnically tinted religious oppression against Irish Catholics that endured for the best part of a century.[1] Because of its enormous popularity and the consecrated place it came to occupy in the Catholic nationalist and colonialist narratives of Irish history, this view of the early modern Irish Catholic experience was largely unquestioned until the middle of the last century. The beginnings of a change are associated with the work of Maureen Wall.[2] The Catholic Ireland that emerged from her research was not the oppressed monolith of tradition but a congeries of communities and interests whose Penal Law experiences varied over time and space.[3]

After Wall, more sophisticated Catholic narratives took root. They tended to relativise the oppressive aspects of the Penal Laws, presenting Catholics as a not especially disadvantaged order within a classic old regime estate structure.[4] In contrast to traditional accounts, these narratives located the Penal Laws in a longer historical time-frame that started in the 1650s and stretched into the nineteenth century. Although the more generous time-span was broadly accepted, at least on the seventeenth century end, the so called *ancien*

---

1 For a survey of traditional interpretations see J. Kelly, 'The historiography of the Penal Laws' in J. Bergin et al. (eds.), *New perspectives on the Penal Laws* (Dublin: Eighteenth-Century Ireland Society, 2011), pp. 27–52.

2 M. Wall, *Catholic Ireland in the eighteenth century: collected essays of Maureen Wall*, ed. G. O'Brien (Dublin: Geography Publications, 1989).

3 H. Fenning, 'Some problems on the Irish mission, 1733–1774', *Collectanea Hibernica*, 8 (1965), 58–109; J. Brady (ed.), *Catholics in the eighteenth-century press* (Maynooth: Catholic Record Society, 1966).

4 S.J. Connolly, *Divided kingdom: Ireland 1630–1830* (Oxford: Oxford University Press, 2006).

régime interpretation has its critics.[5] Inter alia, they note its tendency to neglect the variety within Catholicism and to overlook the significance of its international dimension. Furthermore, revisionist accounts, by emphasising strategies of connivance and collusion between Protestants and Catholics, are taxed with underestimating the role of religious sectarianism, not only in the bloody final decades of the eighteenth century but throughout the entire period.[6]

Interpretations of all hues have tended to underestimate the importance of economic factors, particularly as they pertain to Protestant–Catholic interdependency. Whether viewed as a colonial elite or an *ancien régime* order, Protestant landowners, except in parts of Ulster, relied on Catholic tenants and labour. Given the overwhelming demographic superiority of the Catholics this was inevitable and not necessarily problematic. The general purpose of *anciens régimes*, after all, was to maintain third-estate majorities, like Irish Catholic or French peasants, in deferential obedience to ruling noble minorities. What did compromise the security of Irish Protestantism, turning its economic dependency into a potential political vulnerability, was the lack of effective means of assimilating into the Irish political nation those Catholics who were entitled to a place there. In the prevailing early modern confessional context, this could never have been done on the basis of religious tolerance. That was always a bridge too far. Nonetheless, a stable settlement required more sophisticated forms of Catholic political and social association than those hewn from the victories of 1649 and 1690 and enshrined in penal legislation.

That is not to say that the denominational door was completely closed. Conversion to Anglicanism did allow limited movement across the Protestant–Catholic divide. Catholic converts were relatively few in number, however, for reasons that were as much structural as attitudinal.[7] Mass conversion to the established church risked an uncontrolled influx into the Protestant political nation, with negative political, economic and social consequences for the establishment. For this reason, few Protestants, whether lay or ecclesiastical, pursued serious missionary work among their papist neighbours. But this is only half the story. On the other side, Catholic elites knew they were entitled by law to the free exercise of their religion. They were also conscious of their

---

5 I. MacBride, *Eighteenth century Ireland* (Dublin: Gill and Macmillan, 2009), pp. 194–5.

6 V. Morley, 'The continuity of disaffection in eighteenth-century Ireland', *Eighteenth-Century Ireland*, 22 (2007), 189–205.

7 E. O'Byrne and A. Chamney (eds.), *The Convert Rolls 1703–1838* (Dublin: Irish Manuscripts Commission, 2005).

indispensable role in mediating relations between the Protestant landowners and Catholic tenants. Furthermore they could exploit foreign pressure on the London government on their behalf. Given these circumstances, Catholics continued to hold out for political and social inclusion on their own terms. Their aspiring after what amounted to a cross-confessional polity had contradictory results. On one level, it maintained *esprit de corps* among lay and clerical elites. It was insufficiently inclusive, however, to attract pan-Catholic support. In-house disagreements, stretching across the Jacobite–Hanoverian spectrum, splintered the Catholic interest, generally to the benefit of the Protestant status quo.[8]

With the mid-century eclipse of the Jacobite cause, inherited Catholic divisions softened, exposing the inadequacies of the Williamite settlement and its penal appendages. From the 1750s, as many of them became more prosperous, Catholics grew less tolerant of their political exclusion and less accepting of social and economic disadvantage. By the 1780s the officially proscribed seventeenth-century Catholic Church and its civilly marginalised adherents were emerging as a resented but un-ignorable player on the British political stage. Although the 1780s did not bring an end to anti-Catholic sanctions, they did see stronger Catholic organisation and more successful lobbying. By then Catholics had a renewed sense of their political weight, and of their enhanced capacity, however indirect, to exercise political agency. They could permit themselves to expect more. For the Protestant Ascendancy this was a dangerously destabilising situation. Their tragedy was that in 1782 they were no more capable of dealing with Catholic entitlement than they had been in the 1690s.

The Making of the Irish Catholic Order

The defeats of the 1690s left James II's Irish Catholic supporters, especially the Old English interest, at the mercy of the restored Protestant establishment. Thanks to their demographic superiority, their indispensability to the economy, their international links and their sense of political entitlement, they remained an important if subjugated constituency.[9] To maintain them in a state of restraint, the Protestant establishment turned to the law. The

---

8 P. Fagan, *Divided loyalties: the question of an oath for Irish Catholics in the eighteenth century* (Dublin: Four Courts Press, 1997); G. O'Brien, 'The beginning of the veto controversy in Ireland', *Journal of Ecclesiastical History*, 38:1 (1987), 80–94.

9 P. Corish, *The Irish Catholic experience: a historical survey* (Dublin: Gill & Macmillan, 1984), p. 108.

restored administration's ambitions for legal restraint of Catholicism were hindered by the Treaty of Limerick. Under its terms, William III, anxious to conclude the war, had guaranteed the property rights of certain Catholics and promised all Catholics religious concessions in line with Irish law and privileges extant under Charles II. For Irish Protestants, the Catholic aspiration to undo the Cromwellian settlement, so brazenly displayed by the 1689 parliament, needed much stronger medicine.[10] So too did their persistent presumption to a political role in the kingdom and their disturbing success in wheedling concessions, usually in cahoots with overseas Catholic powers, from the monarchy. Furthermore, by virtue of their putative political subjection to a foreign potentate and their enduring thralldom to the exiled Stuarts, all Catholics were an *ipso facto* risk to the safety of Protestant life and property. The persistent threat of French incursions, even after formal hostilities concluded in 1697, gave substance to Protestant fears, a fact that coloured the legislative mood of Irish parliaments in the 1690s and 1700s. Members accepted that it was both impractical and uneconomical to suppress Catholicism completely but they were concerned to put Catholics back in their box and to keep them there.[11] By means of sixty acts, the most important of which had been passed by 1710, parliament erected a legal bulwark against domestic and foreign Catholic sedition.[12] By means of the popery or Penal Laws, all of which were on the statute books by 1750, parliament ensured the security of the Protestant interest, limited Catholics' access to land and circumscribed the activities of their clergy.

Security was parliament's first priority and here Irish Protestants had form. In the early 1690s, they had helped scotch William III's proposal to absorb Jacobite combatants into the army. Concurrently, through a series of government proclamations, they hounded disbanded Jacobites at home. In the same vein, the 1695 parliament passed laws disarming Catholics, denying them access to war-worthy horses and prohibiting their offspring travelling abroad for educational purposes.[13] The elaboration and passage of these laws were the result of complex bargaining, involving the Irish Privy Council, the Irish House of Commons and, thanks to Poynings' Law, the English Privy

---

10 See J. Morrill in 'The causes of the popery laws: paradoxes and inevitabilities' in J. Bergin et al. (eds.), *New perspectives on the Penal Laws*, p. 73.

11 Ibid., p. 252.

12 J. Kelly, 'Sustaining a confessional state: the Irish parliament and Catholicism' in D.W. Hayton, J. Kelly and J. Bergin (eds.), *The eighteenth-century composite state: representative institutions in Ireland and Europe 1689–1800* (Basingstoke: Palgrave, 2010), pp. 44–77.

13 C.I. McGrath, 'Securing the Protestant interest: origins and purpose of the Penal Laws of 1695', *Irish Historical Studies*, 30 (1996–7), 25–46.

Council. Given the real security risk in the immediate post-war period, all parties agreed on the need to restrain Irish Catholics. Subsequently, however, unanimity could not be assured, in particular when the English (later British) Privy Council was subject to mitigating Catholic petitions and the persuasions of continental diplomats.

Because the Irish Protestant interest was based on the possession of confiscated landed wealth, safeguarding the Cromwellian and Williamite land settlements was another key legislative priority. An early token of parliamentary intent came in 1697, with an act passed to prevent Catholic access to land by way of mixed marriages. Much more comprehensive was the 1704 act to prevent the further growth of popery. In the main, this complex piece of legislation extended to Ireland measures to restrict Catholic access to land already in force in England. Catholics were prevented from inheriting land from Protestants, barred from acquiring it by purchase and confined to leases of thirty-one years or less.[14] The inclusion of measures to reduce Catholic patrimonies, however, was without precedent in English statute law and revealed the distinctiveness of the Irish Protestant settlement. In a remarkable departure from English legal tradition, the act provided that Catholic properties were to descend by partible inheritance (gavelkind) rather than primogeniture. The 1704 measures were strengthened by a 1709 act which made provision for filing bills of discovery against breaches of the 1704 provisions, granting rights of inheritance to the discoverer.[15]

The implications of this legislation were grave for surviving Catholic landowners, who were mostly of Old English ancestry. For some, retaining property required conversion to the state religion and, at least technically, to the Protestant interest. Over the following century there was a steady Catholic trickle into Anglican pews.[16] The same legal provisions pushed some Catholic leaseholders across the confessional divide. This was particularly the case during periods of economic prosperity, when Catholics who wished to protect investments converted in order to conceal illegal leases. Election years also triggered conversions among Catholics who wanted to vote or harboured political ambitions. Of course, circumventing the legislation did not always necessitate a change of religion. Catholic landowners threatened by discovery

---

14 11 Anne c. 6 (1703).

15 T.P. O'Neill, 'Discoverers and discoveries', *Dublin Historical Record*, 37 (1983), 2–13.

16 Over 5,000 Catholic converts are accounted for but information on their social background and geographical distribution is uneven and incomplete: see T.P. Power, 'Converts' in T.P. Power and K. Whelan (eds.), *Endurance and emergence: Catholics in Ireland in the eighteenth century* (Dublin: Irish Academic Press, 1990), pp. 101–27.

could convince well-disposed Protestants, perhaps recent converts and/or relatives, to file collusive discoveries and thereby frustrate genuine discoverers. Although it is difficult to measure the real effects of these naturally clandestine arrangements, it is a fact that between 1708 and 1778 over 90 per cent of the 2,000 discovery cases filed against Catholic property dealings were collusive. Convert lawyers, sympathetic to Catholic interests, played a pivotal role in this sort of avoidance. In response to their activities, parliament approved measures against them in 1727 and 1733.

This parliamentary concern was justified. Because the bulk of these conversions were strategic, the converts retained strong links with their Catholic families and networks. In some parts of the country, notably Connacht and Munster, they constituted a separate, intermediate political and social interest that was largely pro-Catholic and could act as a sort of Catholic lobby. It is difficult to quantify the political importance of this group. It does seem that, along with convert lawyers and other pro-Catholic professionals, certain converts petitioned successfully against proposed anti-Catholic legislation in London, using the opportunities provided by the operation of Poynings' Law to appeal to the English and later to the British Privy Council.[17] They also made representations to protect both surviving and emerging Catholic interests, particularly in the commercial sphere. These activities were networked overseas, through the Catholic embassies, to the Catholic courts, not always, it must be said, with the wholehearted approval of the Holy See.[18] This was a weak Catholic voice but not entirely unheard, and during the eighteenth century it tended to become stronger and more sophisticated.

None of this was a comfort to Irish Protestants. The memory of 1641, the experience of 1689 and the ongoing occurrence of collusive discovery, strategic conversion and clandestine lobbying made them chary about conversion, whatever the evangelistic platitudes issued from the pulpit or figuring in the penal legislation. Although the continued existence of the Catholic religion was taken for granted, parliament baulked at the exercise of papal jurisdiction in Ireland and legislated in 1697 to banish bishops and regular clergy. Later, in 1703, another act prohibited the entry of priests to the kingdom. The 1704 and 1705 acts to register remaining Catholic clergy, measures that constituted *de facto* government recognition of Catholicism, indicate that Irish

---

17 J. Bergin, 'Irish Catholics and their networks in eighteenth century London', *Eighteenth-Century Life*, 39:1 (2015), 75–85.
18 For evidence of the complex Roman reaction to Irish Catholic attempts to organise representation at the Treaty of Soissons, see St St F4c (1728), Archivio della sacra congregazione della Dottrina della Fede, Rome.

Protestants were content enough to leave Catholics to their superstitious religious practices, provided they behaved. This apparent failure in religious zeal troubled some more sensitive Protestant consciences, including the odd bishop, but they consoled themselves by blaming the laity. According to Edmund Synge of Tuam, 'it is a melancholy reflection that the true Christian way of reducing popery is not much regarded. Nor can I but fear that there are too many amongst us who had rather keep the Papists as they are, in an almost slavish subjection than have them made Protestants and thereby entitled to the same liberties and privileges with the rest of their fellow-subjects.'[19] There was probably some truth to this. Fundamentally, the law of the land had the protection of the Cromwellian and Williamite settlements at heart and, viewed from College Green, the conversion of Catholics, rather like proposals later in the century to give them the vote, was unwelcome. Protestant lawgivers preferred less ambitious legislative goals than mass conversion and were generally content if the law merely kept papists in awe.[20] In this more modest mission, they were effective. Domestic Catholic sympathy for the Jacobite cause never stiffened into armed support, even during the heady days of the '45.

Keeping the papists in awe, however, was only one side of the coin. It was also necessary to maintain taut and tended Protestant fears of a Stuart invasion and dread of a papist uprising. This was no great challenge, given the intensity of the Protestant memory of 1641 and 1689 and the frequently fraught relations between Britain and its Catholic neighbours. The combination of the dynastic, religious and economic threats justified continuing tight control of Irish Catholics.[21] These factors helped to sustain Protestant emotional investment in the settlement and its associated legislation, which reason alone could not always easily justify. For the first half of the eighteenth century, Irish Protestant fears also resonated with general British sentiment and interests. But this convenient coincidence had its Achilles heel. As the Williamite wars had testified, Irish Protestant security depended on the connection with England. Up to 1705, partners on both sides of the Irish Sea sang from the same hymn sheet. However, as the century progressed, this partnership of convenience came under strain. If after 1750 no new anti-Catholic legislation was passed, this was not because Irish Protestant attitudes had softened but because the British Privy Council was increasingly loath to

---

19 Synge to Wake, Dublin, 19 Nov. 1719, Add MS 6117, f. 143, BL.
20 Kelly, 'Historiography of the Penal Laws', p. 60.
21 J. Kelly, ' "Disappointing the boundless ambition of France": Irish Protestants and the fear of invasion, 1661–1815', *Studia Hibernica*, 37 (2011), 27–105.

approve them.[22] By the 1770s, when free trade and parliamentary independence were on the College Green agenda, Whitehall's attitude towards the Irish Protestant interest grew still more ambivalent. For Catholic lobbyists this opened up opportunities not only to plead for the mitigation of proposed legislation but also to petition for relief from laws already on the statute book.

Catholic Life under Restraint

Away from College Green, life went on. The Penal Laws made provision for little more than the bare bones of a Catholic ecclesiastical structure, served by registered parish clergy and bereft of hierarchy, religious orders, income and educational/charitable infrastructure.[23] However, even as the legal apparatus of restraint was being put together between 1695 and 1709, the complex and inevitably compromising business of cohabitation, necessary over the greater part of the kingdom, had already commenced. The Cromwellian land confiscations had displaced Catholic landowners, leaving most Catholics tenants *in situ*, a situation unaltered by its Williamite successors. This gave the surviving eighteenth-century Catholic landed leadership its distinctive geographical distribution. Connacht, specifically counties Galway and Mayo, had received the bulk of transported Catholic landowners from Leinster and Munster in the seventeenth century. Thanks to its dense Catholic networks and its overwhelmingly Catholic population, the western province was the most amenable zone for Catholics under restraint. It sustained an active Catholic culture, and was well represented among the senior clergy and foreign regiments, and later, as Catholicism politicised, in the Catholic Committee, founded in 1756, and in the Catholic Convention of 1792.[24] In Munster and south Leinster, where the bulk of Catholic proprietors had disappeared, many subsequently assumed senior tenancies on their former estates, with a small number diversifying into other activities, including trade.[25] This created a second Catholic heartland where, overall, Catholic life was more or less tolerable. In the traditional Old English heartlands, which included counties Meath and Westmeath, Kildare, Louth and Dublin, Catholic families, including the lords of the Pale, survived surprisingly well, often as senior tenants. They provided

---

22 Kelly, 'Sustaining a Protestant state', p. 68.
23 E. O'Flaherty, 'An urban community and the Penal Laws: Limerick 1690–1830' in Bergin et al. (eds.), *New perspectives on the Penal Laws*, p. 209.
24 C. Woods, 'The personnel of the Catholic Convention, 1792–3', *Archivium Hibernicum*, 57 (2003), 26–76.
25 L. Cullen, 'Catholics under the Penal Laws', *Eighteenth-Century Ireland*, 1 (1986), 31–2.

leadership for a resilient Catholic presence on the very doorstep of Protestant Dublin. Ulster was the exception. There significant Protestant immigration reduced Catholics to a large minority and, more significantly, no Catholic landowners survived the seventeenth century to emerge later as large tenants exercising social function, on the model of Munster and Leinster. Lacking landed leadership, Ulster Catholics occupied a more marginalised position than their co-religionists in the remaining provinces. For them, religious harassment was more common and they were comparatively under-represented in the Irish foreign regiments, colleges and international business networks. They were conspicuously absent from the Catholic Committee. By the 1780s, harsh conditions and the lack of alternative forms of political activism had created the environment for the growth of Catholic militancy in the form of Defenderism.

The economic and social structure of penal Catholicism was overwhelmingly rural.[26] Outside parts of Ulster, Protestant landowners depended on Catholic tenants, cottiers and labour to operate their properties. A crucial role in organizing and maintaining these Protestant–Catholic economic relations was played by the 'middlemen' or leaseholding 'middle tenants'. They were often former proprietors and *de facto* 'intervening landlords'. In general, they accumulated multiple leases, working some and subletting others to Catholic and Protestant subtenants. This indirect form of patronage allowed them to display status and exercise influence not only over Catholic but also over Protestant tenants, including some who had the vote.[27] It also gave them influence over their clergy, who depended on them financially. Although conversion, sales of land and bad luck eroded the proportion of land in Catholic ownership during the eighteenth century, it is true that, from the 1750s, Catholic leasehold wealth actually increased. This was prompted in great part by the contemporary boom in cattle rearing for the provisions trade, and in the dairying sector. In overall wealth terms, this growth in Catholic leasehold wealth compensated for the shrinkage in Catholic ownership and helps to account for the relative vibrancy of rural life in the Catholic heartlands from mid-century onwards. As certain Catholics accumulated the profits of the mid-century economic recovery, the clamour for their return to the political nation gathered pace.

---

26 For an extended local study see T.P. Power, *Land, politics and society in eighteenth-century Tipperary* (Oxford: Oxford University Press, 1993).

27 D. Dickson, 'Middlemen' in T. Bartlett and D.W. Hayton (eds.), *Penal era and golden age: essays in Irish history 1690–1800* (Belfast: Ulster Historical Foundation, 1979), pp. 162–85.

Many middlemen were wealthy enough to bear the burden of maintaining the social status and style of life of quasi-gentry. For smaller leaseholding middle tenants, however, the need to squirrel away capital for foreign education or a marriage dowry, or to purchase a career for a son, imposed a frugal, even bleak lifestyle. It certainly did not leave much disposable income, a fact that helps explain the modesty and plainness of penal churches and the straitened financial circumstances of the Catholic clergy. Beneath the smaller leaseholder level were much more numerous small tenants and cottiers, who were sensitive to changing economic conditions. The agricultural boom after the mid-1750s, accompanied by the enclosure of common land and the expansion of dairying, disadvantaged many of them, particularly in Munster and south Leinster. Additionally, they paid tithes to the Church of Ireland, a charge now exacerbated by the growing financial demands of their own clergy. In response to the resulting economic stress, some of the discontented formed defensive groups like the Whiteboys and the Rightboys. These associations often enjoyed broad community support and, given the complexity of issues involved, were as likely to target Catholic as Protestant proprietors, middlemen and clergy. In the sectarian environment of the time, however, many local Protestants chose to see these disturbances as harbingers of popish insurrection.[28] The notorious 1766 trial of the Catholic priest Nicholas Sheehy for alleged complicity in Whiteboyism and foreign conspiracy was a salutary reminder of the depth and persistence of sectarian passions. Whatever their strength elsewhere in Ireland, the mid-century winds of Enlightenment blew feebly among the Protestant gentry of Munster.

The vibrancy of Catholic rural society, especially after the 1750s, profited from the greater integration of rural hinterlands into urban economies, linked, in turn, into increasingly commercialised and internationalised markets. It was in urban centres like Dublin, Cork and Limerick that Catholic mercantile groups first began to enjoy prosperity. Protestant observers, like Archbishop William King, complained as early as 1717 'that the Papists being made incapable to purchase lands, have turned themselves to trade and already engrossed almost all the trade of the kingdom'.[29] In truth, his worries were unfounded. Although Catholics in Ireland were reputed to have prospered

---

28 J.S. Donnelly, 'The Whiteboy movement 1761–85', *Irish Historical Studies*, 21 (1978–9), 20–55; J. Kelly, 'The genesis of Protestant Ascendancy: the Rightboy disturbances of the 1780s and their impact upon Protestant opinion' in G. O'Brien (ed.), *Parliament, politics and people: essays in eighteenth-century Irish history* (Dublin: Irish Academic Press, 1989), 93–127.

29 King to Wake, Dublin, 6 Feb. 1717, Add. MS 6117, f. 57, BL.

in trade, one of the few avenues of wealth-making to which they retained access, it is easy to exaggerate the importance of their business and entrepreneurial roles. Certainly, they made their mark in printing and publishing, for instance,[30] and also in the declining ports of Galway and Limerick, but, revealingly, only a quarter of booming Dublin's wholesale merchants were Catholic.[31] They were scarce too in prosperous Cork, where Protestant opposition to Catholics in the trades and in trade was especially strong. Indeed, it was perhaps only overseas that Catholic commercial performance was plainly visible, mainly in the Irish mercantile colonies flourishing in French, Portuguese and Spanish ports.[32] The domestic picture did change later in the century, however, when Dublin Catholic merchants, stealing a march on their provincial co-religionists, emerged as influential political activists, first in the Catholic Committee founded in 1756 and later in the Catholic Convention of 1792. They also spearheaded a gradual but steady transformation of Catholic religious culture and social solidarity, especially in primary education, orphan support and relief of the poor, which set the trend for other urban centres.[33]

Across the countryside, surviving Catholic landowners and the much more numerous leaseholders were crucial for the maintenance of both the Catholic interest and its social infrastructure. To provide education and opportunity for family members whose domestic employment prospects were bleak, Catholic landowners and middle tenants were networked into an interlocking set of overseas institutions.[34] In sheer numerical terms, the most important of these were the military networks in foreign Catholic armies, particularly those of Spain, France and Austria. To integrate Irish men into their respective fighting machines, the Catholic monarchies established specific Irish units, especially in the 1690s and 1700s, when the largest single outflows of Catholics of military background and fighting age took place. The Williamite

---

30 For example, see H. Fenning, 'Dublin imprints of Catholic interest, 1701–1739', *Collectanea Hibernica*, 39/40 (1997–8), 106–54.

31 L.M. Cullen, 'The Dublin merchant community in the eighteenth century' in P. Butel and L.M. Cullen (eds.) *Cities and merchants: French and Irish perspectives on urban development 1500–1900* (Dublin: Department of Modern History, University of Dublin, 1986), p. 201; D. Dickson, 'Catholics and trade in eighteenth-century Ireland: an old debate revisited' in Power and Whelan (eds.), *Endurance and emergence*, pp. 85–100.

32 See the detailed local study by Agustín Guimerá Ravina, *Burgesia extranjera y comercio Atlantico: la Empresa commercial Irlandesa en Canarias 1703–1771* (Tenerife: Consejeria de Cultura y Deportes Gobierno de Canarias, 1986); Chambers, Chapter 21, pp. 581–5.

33 C. Begadon, 'The renewal of Catholic culture in eighteenth century Dublin' in Bergin et al. (eds.), *New perspective on the Penal Laws*, pp. 227–47.

34 L.M. Cullen, 'The Irish diaspora of the seventeenth and eighteenth centuries' in N. Canny (ed.), *Europeans on the move: studies on European migration 1500–1800* (Oxford: Oxford University Press, 1994), pp. 113–49.

settlement alone facilitated the transport of about 20,000 soldiers to France, but thereafter, until the middle of the century, perhaps about a thousand men a year on average travelled to Europe to pursue military careers. These men enlisted in all ranks but it was the 500 or so European commissions, reserved to Irish Catholics, that most interested the surplus sons of middling to upper-level Catholic families, particularly from Munster.[35] The commissions were obtained through family and geographical networks and provided acceptably dignified if not enormously remunerative employment. Irish Catholic families maintained a firm hold on these until the revolutionary wars at the end of the century.

From mid-century, Irish Catholics began to enter British military service, despite the religious ban. It is impossible to arrive at precise numbers, but it is clear that Catholic marines were recruited from 1757 and there was more general but still unofficial recruitment of Catholics into the army from the 1770s. With the immiseration of the Leinster Catholic poor due to rapid population growth after mid-century, and the emergence of the poorer west as a military recruitment territory in the 1770s, traditionally non-military Catholic populations began to enter the army, with some signing up for the East India Company. The lifting of the ban on Catholics bearing arms in 1793 permitted large-scale official recruitment of Irish Catholics into the British forces, especially the Royal Navy, just in time for the carnage of the revolutionary wars.[36]

As might be expected, these international military extensions of Catholic Ireland fed Irish Protestant phobias of foreign invasion and papist rebellion.[37] Blind to the crucial social function of the Catholic regiments in absorbing surplus Catholic sons, the College Green parliament legislated in 1721 to prevent unlicensed enlisting in Ireland for foreign service. Subsequent bans on Irish officers serving abroad came in 1746 and 1756. These measures struck terror into the hearts of solid Catholic families, who depended on commissions to absorb younger sons denied entry to the army and the professions at home. However, even if the Irish parliament remained alive to the presumed security threat of Catholic Ireland's foreign legions, the government's mood gradually changed. In the later stages of the Seven Years War, for instance, it considered a scheme from the Catholic leadership to raise six regiments

35 Cullen, 'Irish diaspora', p. 138; Morley, Chapter 1 above, pp. 27–8; Chambers, Chapter 21 below, pp. 570–1.
36 H. Murtagh, 'Irish soldiers abroad, 1600–1800' in T. Bartlett and K. Jeffery (eds.), *A military history of Ireland* (Cambridge: Cambridge University Press, 1996), pp. 294–314; Bartlett, Chapter 3 above, pp. 74–7.
37 Kelly, ' "Disappointing the boundless ambition of France" ', *passim*.

of Catholics to serve England's ally, Portugal. Faithful to its old phobias, the Dublin parliament shot down the plan, but the proposal and the government's reaction were straws in the wind.[38] Later in the century the political manoeuvring necessary to give British army recruiters free access to Catholic populations sufficiently thawed official attitudes, at least in London, to consider Catholic relief measures.

The regiments were not the only foreign employment networks available to Irish Catholics to disperse their sons. A colleges network was also at their disposal, consisting of seminaries, hostels and schools located in the main in Portugal, Spain, France, Italy and the Spanish Netherlands. Originally founded either by Old English clergy of the ports and Pale or by scions of Gaelic learned families, by the early eighteenth century these institutions were increasingly reserved to the siblings of those serving in the Irish regiments. At their height, in the third quarter of the eighteenth century, the so-called 'Irish colleges' provided about 500 places for male students. These were complex entities, performing a broad range of functions that included the provision of clergy for some of the thousand or so Catholic parishes spread over the four ecclesiastical provinces of the kingdom. Young men accessed the colleges through a network of informal secondary schools at home, run by clergy and laity and operating under the penal radar. Some of these had already been set up before the Williamite wars and survived the relatively severe persecution in the early eighteenth century to expand thereafter. In 1731, for instance, it was reported that there were forty-five Catholic schools in Dublin alone, catering for both urban and rural students.[39] In the following decade, the institution of the Protestant charter schools roused Catholics to establish more comprehensive educational networks. These schools provided students with a grounding in the classics, especially Latin, facilitating admission to philosophy, canon law and theology programmes on the continent.

In a departure from normal church discipline, Irish students intended for the priesthood were sometimes ordained at home, without any seminary formation. They later travelled abroad for a stint in one of the continental colleges. Roman tolerance of antecedent ordination was initially justified by the precarious status of Catholicism in Ireland and the hardships endured by the episcopate. It was also argued that pre-ordained mature students were more

---

38 T. Bartlett, *The fall and rise of the Irish nation: the Catholic question 1690–1830* (Dublin: Gill and Macmillan, 1992), pp. 57–8.

39 J.J. McCracken, 'The ecclesiastical structure, 1714–1760' in T.W. Moody and W.E. Vaughan (eds.), *A new history of Ireland*, vol. IV: *Eighteenth-century Ireland* (Oxford: Oxford University Press, 1986), p. 95.

likely to return home following a stint abroad than lay youngsters. The practice brought its own difficulties, however, as it was not unknown for ordained men to refuse to travel abroad, episcopal entreaties notwithstanding.[40] Later in the century, as domestic conditions for Catholics improved, a proportion of priests, perhaps over half in remoter dioceses, still lacked training in an overseas seminary. Even for those who did travel, the practice of antecedent ordination continued, due in part to episcopal fears concerning student attrition. To some extent the figures appear to confirm the bishops' fears. In Paris, at the end of the eighteenth century, the return rate to the home mission of antecedently ordained clergy seems to have been about 80 per cent. Among the non-ordained sent out, the return rate was much lower but this was in part because about half of these were never intended for religious ministry in the first place. Of those who were, probably 50 per cent returned to ministry in Ireland.

The college network was densest in Spain and the Netherlands, but the greatest numbers of students were accommodated in France, principally in Paris and Nantes, which between them provided nearly half the total number of student places.[41] Incoming students, depending on their prior level of academic formation, took programmes in humanities and philosophy before studying theology.[42] Courses were generally taken outside the colleges proper, in Spain invariably with the local Jesuits, though this was not the case in Paris or Nantes. Course content was standard fare, generally Aristotelian philosophy and scholastic theology. There is evidence of more varied and adventurous intellectual influences but theological high flyers were few. In general the peripatetic Irish gave theological controversy a wide berth and, when pushed, were careful to side with state and church authorities in academic and ecclesiastical disputes.[43] They were particularly allergic to Jansenism, which they took pains to shun. It was common, however, for warring clerical factions to

40 See C. Mac Murchaidh, ' "My repeated troubles": Dr James Gallagher (bishop of Raphoe 1725–37) and the impact of the Penal Laws' in Bergin et al. (eds.), New perspectives on the Penal Laws, p. 158; P. Fagan, Ireland in the Stuart papers, 2 vols. (Dublin: Four Courts Press, 1995), vol. I, p. 217.

41 L. Chambers, 'Rivalry and reform in the Irish College, Paris, 1676–1775' in T. O'Connor and Mary Ann Lyons (eds.), Irish communities in early modern Europe (Dublin: Four Courts Press, 2006), pp. 103–29; Chambers, Chapter 21, pp. 575–80.

42 L.W.B. Brockliss, 'The Irish colleges on the continent and the creation of an educated clergy' in T. O'Connor and M.A. Lyons (eds.), The Ulster Earls in Baroque Europe (Dublin: Four Courts Press, 2010), pp. 142–65.

43 P. O'Connor, 'Irish students in Paris faculty of theology: aspects of doctrinal controversy in the ancien regime, 1730–60', Archivium Hibernicum, 53 (1998), 85–97; T. O'Connor, 'The role of Irish clerics in Paris University politics, 1730–40', History of Universities, 15 (1997–8), 193–225.

use accusations of Jansenism as a cover for the settlement of old scores, to the great confusion of later historians.

For those returning to Ireland on completion of their studies, like those who remained at home, parochial appointments depended as much on family connections as on episcopal approval. Given the relative weakness of the bishops' authority, it was not unknown for priests, aided and abetted by lay supporters, to intrude themselves on parishes. In Limerick city, for instance, local clergy profited from episcopal absences to build up their own networks of influence and to ingratiate themselves with the laity.[44] Intrusion through lay interference could also occur through the operation of hereditary rights of presentations to clerical livings, a practice with roots in Reformation times. Such collusive networking functioned particularly well within Old English families.[45] In this as in so many other ways, the laity called the tune and there is evidence that parish priests, who acted as quasi-domestic chaplains, devoted relatively little time to strictly parish ministry. That seems to have been left to their assisting clergy, underlings who were in the parish priest's pay and at his beck and call.

Despite their financial dependency on the laity, the clergy were not completely supine. Clerical reluctance to dispense with forbidden degrees of kindred in marriage, for instance, was a common cause of lay–clerical tensions. Among the clergy themselves, disputes were not infrequent, often the result of disciplinary squabbles and competition for scarce resources.[46] These could lead to civil court cases, and, when Catholic bishops were involved, Protestant magistrates exploited the occasion to ferret out proscribed prelates. In 1733, for instance, the parish priest of Doneraile swore information against several Munster bishops for complicity in an alleged Jacobite plot. In general, the operation of the penal legislation tended to favour the unruly priest against the 'skulking hedge pretender-bishop'.[47]

Despite the banishment act of 1697 and various other measures to prevent priests entering the country, clerical numbers recovered quickly in the early eighteenth century. In fact, from the 1720s until mid-century there was a surplus of priests in parts of the kingdom.[48] The college clerical surplus, following the example of their regimental brothers, made their careers abroad,

---

44 O'Flaherty, 'An urban community and the Penal Laws', p. 212.
45 E. Derr, 'The Irish Catholic episcopal corps 1657–1829: a prosopographical analysis', PhD thesis, 2 vols., National University of Ireland, Maynooth, 2013, p. 182.
46 E. O'Flaherty, 'Clerical indiscipline and ecclesiastical authority in Ireland, 1690–1750', *Studia Hibernica*, 26 (1992), 7–29.
47 King to Wake, Dublin, 2 April 1723, Add. MS 6117, f. 81, BL.
48 J. Kelly, 'The impact of the Penal Laws' in J. Kelly and D. Keogh (eds.), *History of the Catholic Diocese of Dublin* (Dublin: Four Courts Press, 2000), pp. 153–61.

many of them preferring the risk of possible hardship abroad to the certainty of poverty at home.[49] Unsurprisingly, about half the Irishmen who took out French letters of naturalisation were priests.[50] Conditions abroad, however, were by no means easy. In 1714, James Merrick, superior of the Irish College, Paris, complained that there were over 300 Irish priests in the city, most of them living in misery.[51] For the more motivated and better connected, there was the possibility of integrating local patronage networks. Some of these took up parochial ministries and canonries, but competition from continental colleagues pushed many into less attractive posts, like hospital and military chaplaincies. For the college students who did not persevere to holy orders or who were never intended for the church, the regiments, medicine, trade and other avenues provided career options after college.

For young clerics who could not aspire either to a parish in Ireland or a foreign living, there was the option of joining a religious order. In 1697 all regular clergy were officially banned from the kingdom but in the early eighteenth century their numbers recovered. In 1723, for instance, no fewer than seventeen returning friars were arrested in Dublin, provoking a minor Protestant panic. Later, in 1731, the reports to the House of Lords' committees inquiring into the State of Popery painted a rather alarmist picture of a priest- and friar-infested countryside.[52] Their concern was shared by some Catholics, as the growth in domestic clerical numbers, particularly relative to the laity's means to support them, became an internal church issue. Propaganda Fide intervened in 1742 to limit the number of secular ordinations. It was much tougher on regular clergy. In 1751, they were forbidden to accept any novices in Ireland. These harsh measures worked only too well, reducing overall clerical numbers by nearly a quarter, mostly from among the regulars. Because this fall in clerical numbers coincided with a rapid rise in population, about 45 per cent between 1750 and 1770, there was a dramatic deterioration in the ratio of priests to people. This resulted in a crisis of pastoral provision that overwhelmed the institutional church, despite a modest recovery in clerical numbers later in the century.[53] The

49 B. Hoban, *A melancholy truth: the travels and travails of Fr. Charles Bourke c. 1765–1820* (Dublin: Banley House, 2008).

50 L.M. Cullen, 'Catholic social classes under the Penal Laws' in Power and Whelan (eds.), *Endurance and emergence*, p. 76.

51 H. Fenning, *The undoing of the friars of Ireland: a study of the novitiate question in the mid eighteenth century* (Louvain: Publications Universitaires de Louvain, 1972), p. 92.

52 'Report on the state of popery, Ireland, 1731', *Archivium Hibernicum*, 1 (1912), 10–27; 'Report on the state of popery in Ireland, 1731: diocese of Dublin', *Archivium Hibernicum*, 4 (1915), 131–77.

53 E. Larkin, *The pastoral role of the Roman Catholic clergy in pre-Famine Ireland, 1750–1850* (Dublin: Four Courts Press, 2006), pp. 9–41.

relative dearth of clergy was exacerbated by the continuing haemorrhage of college students to overseas careers and by the calculated reluctance of better-off parents to encourage religious vocations as improved economic opportunities opened up elsewhere.[54]

For most of the period, the Catholic episcopate was a cowed body. Officially they had been banished by an act of parliament in 1697. In 1703 only three prelates remained in the country and thereafter their numerical recovery was slow. Rome, linked administratively to Ireland through the nunciature which was based at Brussels, began to appoint bishops in 1707 but it was not until 1750 that all Irish sees were again occupied. By then episcopal absenteeism, long excused on account of official persecution, had become a cause for complaint and sanction.[55] Strengthening numbers did not necessarily betoken increasing influence. Returning bishops faced a clergy and laity grown used to autonomy in church affairs. Even where bishops managed to function pastorally, their financial dependency on the laity obliged them to act more as adjuncts to rich Catholic families than as leaders of an independent institution. Further compromising their situation, at least in the eyes of the government, was their nomination by the exiled Stuarts, a right originally claimed by James II in the 1680s and successfully reasserted by his son. Inevitably this skewed appointments towards Jacobite supporters, often regulars of Old English extraction. On the plus side, the Stuart nomination helped maintain the episcopal appointment process and papal interest in Ireland during the difficult early decades of the eighteenth century. However, it also fostered ecclesiastical cliques, like the Munster Butlers. Jacobite favouritism alienated political 'outsiders', including some Dublin senior clergy and certain Ulster-based prelates. By the 1740s the latter had sufficiently shaken off the dust of Jacobite loyalty to voice dissent with royal nomination, reflecting a broader disillusionment with Jacobitism. Michael O'Reilly, bishop of Derry and later of Armagh (d.1758), complained that the royal preference for regulars increased episcopal frictions.[56] After 1766, the papacy's decision to ignore the Stuart right of nomination helped broaden the geographical spread of episcopal appointments across all the Catholic heartlands. It also ensured that sitting bishops were freer to influence their succession, leading to a rise in the number of coadjutors with rights of succession. This apparent strengthening of episcopal clout was checked by continuing lay influence and by the

---

54 Fenning, *Undoing of the friars*, pp. 41–3.
55 H. Fenning, 'John Kent's report on the state of the Irish mission, 1742', *Archivium Hibernicum*, 28 (1966), 59–103; Derr, 'Prosopography', p. 84.
56 Fenning, *Undoing of the friars*, pp. 154–210.

increasingly active middle clergy, who were progressively better organised into cathedral chapters.

Lay influence conspired to curb episcopal pretensions. So too did poverty. Bishops had sporadic access to emergency income from Propaganda Fide, but this was modest and short term. More substantial sustenance came from the French *Assemblée du clergé*, which supported about 10 per cent of the Stuart episcopal cohort. Some Irish clergy had foreign benefices, generally acquired during continental sojourns and retained, if at all possible, on return to Ireland.[57] Bishops also drew on domestic sources, notably the annual levy on their clergy and revenues drawn on so-called mensal parishes, which were reserved to the bishop. Like all clergy, bishops charged stole fees for the administration of the sacraments. Because of financial pressures, it appears that some bishops were tempted to treat ordination, a sacrament reserved to them, as a source of revenue. It was observed in 1733, for instance, that 'Mr [Dominic O']Daly, a Dominican friar bishop of Achonry alone, if not stopped, will ordain enough for the whole kingdom.'[58]

In spite of poverty, state prohibition and lay influence, by the end of the century bishops and priests were timidly reassertive.[59] The recovery was from a very low base. There was synodal activity at diocesan level from 1712 and provincial activity from 1752.[60] At deanery level, clergy met at monthly conferences, although there was great variation between dioceses, with the more remote western dioceses sustaining the thinnest ecclesiastical organisation. By the 1780s, at least in wealthier dioceses, a bishop could expect his priests to attend diocesan conferences, to confess regularly and lead lives broadly in line with the Christian gospel.[61] Preaching was not always up to scratch and catechesis could be patchy, but around parochial clergy a pastoral infrastructure of teachers and midwives was falling into place. In more and more places bishops and clergy felt confident enough to take on the *bêtes noires* of reformed Catholicism: adultery, cohabitation, debauchery, drunkenness,

---

57 Derr, 'Prosopography', p. 192.

58 Fenning (ed.), 'Some problems of the Irish mission, 1733–1774', *Collectanea Hibernica*, 8 (1965), 63.

59 E. Derr, 'Episcopal visitations of the diocese of Cloyne and Ross, 1785–1828', *Archivium Hibernicum*, 66 (2013), 261–393.

60 For the situation in Munster see R.F. Cummins and H. Fenning, 'The constitutions of the diocese of Cashel: the New Psalter of Cashel (1737) and three pastoral letters of Archbishop Christopher Bulter', *Archivium Hibernicum*, 56 (2002), 132–88.

61 M.J. Curran, 'Instructions, admonitions etc of Archbishop Carpenter, 1770–86', *Reportorium Novum*, 2:1 (1957–8), 150–2.

swearing and the allurements of folk religion.[62] As agents of social control, the Catholic clergy were less effective than their established church contemporaries assumed. With superb condescension, the Anglican Bishop George Berkeley of Cloyne exhorted Catholic prelates and clergy to induce their flock to cooperate with 'the public spirit of the legislature and men in power'.[63] He was overly sanguine. Clerical attempts to resolve feuds and faction fights, for instance, were often futile and could come with a hefty human price tag. In 1732, John Hoey, the 90-year-old parish priest of Ballyboggan in County Meath, was killed by a stray missile when he interposed himself to quell a local disturbance.[64] Nonetheless, there were some successes, especially in urban areas, but these were largely lay-led. From mid-century, wealthier Catholics in Dublin began to organise themselves to improve church infrastructure, extend educational provision and poor relief, deepen piety and support general moral improvement.[65] This set an influential pattern that strengthened across the country in the following decades.

In general, the institutional church's public self-confidence and moral authority remained slight throughout the era. Bishops were officially proscribed and, along with their clergy, played second fiddle to Catholic laity who retained the decisive directive role in the Catholic community. Before bishops and clergy could attain the poise of an independent ecclesiastical caste, they had to cut their financial and social moorings with the powerful family interests which up to then had both sustained and crippled them.[66] This would not happen in the eighteenth century.[67]

Catholic politicisation

The problem of divided Catholic loyalties, inherited from the Reformation past, remained alive throughout the eighteenth century, dominating the claustrophobic political world of Irish Catholicism.[68] The Penal Laws may

---

62 S.J. Connolly, *Priests and people in pre-Famine Ireland 1780–1845* (Dublin: Gill and Macmillan, 1982), pp. 74–218.

63 G. Berkeley, *A word to the wise: or the Bishop of Cloyne's exhortation to the Roman Catholic clergy of Ireland* (Dublin: George Faulkner, 1749), p. 13.

64 A. Cogan, *Diocese of Meath: ancient and modern*, 3 vols. (Dublin: Joseph Dollard, 1867), vol. II, p. 397.

65 C. Begadon, 'Laity and clergy in the Catholic renewal of Dublin c.1750–1830', PhD thesis, National University of Ireland, Maynooth, 2009.

66 Cullen, 'Catholic social classes', p. 82.

67 E. Larkin and C. Hargett, 'Clerical income and its sources in the parish of Moycullen in the wardenship of Galway, 1786–1823', *Archivium Hibernicum*, 62 (2009), 221–35.

68 Fagan, *Divided loyalties*, pp. 9–21.

have placed all Irish Catholics in one legal category but this did not encourage political *esprit de corps*. Efforts to square participation in the Protestant state with loyalty to pope and pretender were reactivated with every new legal restriction imposed on Catholics, triggering afresh the search for the holy grail of an acceptable oath of allegiance. In 1704, for instance, an oath of abjuration of the Stuarts was required of Catholic voters. This was extended to all solicitors in 1707, and two years later to all registered priests. In the 1720s failed proposals to pay Catholic clergy a state stipend and educate them in Trinity College included a new oath of loyalty, which again set the loyalist cat among the Jacobite pigeons.

Attempts to find a single Catholic voice on the issue failed. Lord Delvin's 1727 address of loyalty to George II roused Bishop Sylvester Lloyd to denounce compromising laity and clergy.[69] The issue erupted again in the 1750s when the Anglican bishop of Elphin, Edward Synge, floated proposals that included the appointment of Catholic clergy by a troika of principal Catholic laity, grand juries and the lord lieutenant. Even well-disposed Catholics baulked at this suggestion but their efforts to produce acceptable alternatives met with little success, foundering on the state requirement that Catholic clergy pray publicly for the king's health. Although acceptable to the Pale gentry, this demand was too much for Munster Jacobites. Horrified Anglican bishops put their oar in too, refusing to accept what they saw as state recognition of popery and an encroachment on their ecclesiastical privileges.

But the problem of divided loyalties only became more acute as increasingly prosperous Catholic laity considered trading their loyalty for legal relief, social status and political participation. Some of the clergy opposed all compromise, in part because they feared Rome's displeasure, in part because they believed they could strike a more favourable deal. In either case, their dithering fed lay impatience at perceived clerical heel-dragging. According to Charles O'Conor, writing in 1756, clerical reluctance to cooperate was down to self-interest, ambition and the desire to curry favour with Rome.[70] He probably overstated his case, as a great number of clergy, including the bishops, were by and large open to the idea of an oath, if only a suitable form of words could be agreed.[71] From 1760, the lay-dominated Catholic Committee,

---

69 I. McBride, 'Catholic politics in the penal era: Father Sylvester Lloyd and the Delvin addresses of 1727' in Bergin et al. (eds.), *New perspectives on the Penal Laws*, pp. 114–47.

70 M. Wall, 'Catholics in mid-eighteenth century Ireland' in *Catholic Ireland in the eighteenth century*, ed. G. O'Brien, p. 95.

71 C.D.A. Leighton, *Catholicism in a Protestant kingdom: a study of the Irish ancien régime* (Dublin: Gill and Macmillan, 1994), pp. 145–56.

originally set up to lobby for commercial privileges, broadened its base and its agenda, diffidently entering the political fray with petitions of loyalty. Over the following years the Committee served to educate Catholics in the realities of power and to place the question of Catholic relief on the political agenda. They enjoyed some success in the 1760s and 1770s, notably in lobbying on behalf of Catholic tradesmen and merchants in the ongoing quarterage dispute.

In the meantime, the congeries of interests that constituted Protestant Ireland remained resolutely attached to its constitutionally privileged position and to the land settlements that underpinned it. There was some establishment willingness, however, to reward good Catholic behaviour with measured relief from disabilities. The milder attitude was practical in nature, supported by the general culture of improvement and economic rationalisation. It enjoyed the backing of economic eminences like Arthur Young, whose liberal programme for the modernisation of Ireland included harnessing the personal wealth of Catholics for the general good.[72] In 1771, as a modest token of economic intent, Catholics were allowed to rent bog-land for sixty-one years, in the interests of encouraging drainage. Other softening forces may have been at work too in more liberal corners of the Irish Protestant mind. The news from Enlightenment Europe, for instance, was encouraging, with the suppression of the Jesuits suggesting that, even in the benighted Catholic monarchies, old-style persecuting Catholicism was on the wane. This reassured some Irish Protestants as they considered the wisdom of indulging their Catholic neighbours. However, political sympathy based on the anticipated death of Catholicism proved a flimsy foundation for broadening the Irish political nation. Apart from the fact that the *infâme* proved doughtier than hoped, such thinking risked confusing the apparent plight of international Catholicism with the real state of Irish Catholic grievance, concealing rather than defusing the gathering threat it posed for the Irish Protestant establishment.

In any case these rather cosmetic changes in Irish Protestant attitudes to Catholics proved relatively unimportant. More significant were the higher-level shifts in relations between Dublin and London, already discernible in the 1750s. At that stage there was a cooling in London's attitudes to Dublin, in time developing into a rift between the Irish executive and the legislature. This was in part the legacy of the Money Bill dispute of the 1750s, which

---

72 M.A. Mullett, *Catholics in Britain and Ireland 1558–1829* (Basingstoke: Macmillan, 1998), p. 182.

had nothing to do with Catholics, but tried London's patience with College Green, introducing an element of conditionality into its relationship with Dublin.[73] This trend continued in the late 1760s during the lord lieutenancy of George, 4th Viscount Townshend. He came from London with instructions to increase Ireland's contribution towards imperial defence, primarily by the augmentation of the permanent Irish military establishment. To overcome local opposition he found it useful to sideline the local power brokers or undertakers, who had traditionally managed parliament for the government. Instead he determined to manage parliament from Dublin Castle, through state patronage. In time this change enhanced the roles of both the lord lieutenant and the chief secretary and opened up new lobbying opportunities for Catholics.

The London and Dublin governments had no intention of weakening their commitment to the maintenance of Protestant interests in Ireland. They were increasingly aware, however, of the benefits of associating Irish Catholics more closely with the state, not only for economic reasons but also in the interests of international security. This created an opportunity for the friends of Catholic relief, but early efforts in parliament, despite their modesty, were rebuffed. In 1772, for instance, Lord Charlemont's proposal to allow Catholics to hold ninety-nine years leases was resoundingly defeated. Shortly afterwards, however, the London parliament approved the Quebec Act, granting civil guarantees to Canadian Catholics. In the same year, 1774, the Dublin parliament approved a new act of allegiance, with a form of words designed to win broad Catholic endorsement. This provided loyal Catholics with an acceptable alternative to conversion, promising them limited political recognition. Meanwhile, English Catholics were granted a measure of relief. Consequently, only six years after the defeat of Charlemont's modest proposal, the Dublin parliament, pressed by the government, approved the more far-reaching bill presented by Luke Gardiner, permitting Catholics who swore the 1774 oath to take out 999 year leases. The act also ended the compulsory gavelling of Catholic estates. As the bill survived fresh amendments in August 1778, 'the shoal of papists in the gallery were so elated with their success that they clapped and shouted, as in a play house'.[74] Two more relief acts passed in 1782 allowed Catholics to purchase land, except in parliamentary boroughs, and removed most of the restrictions affecting their clergy and education.

73 T. Bartlett, 'The origins and progress of the Catholic question in Ireland' in Power and Whelan (eds.), *Endurance and emergence*, pp. 6–7; see Kelly, Chapter 2 above, pp. 54–60.
74 M. Wall, 'The quest for Catholic equality 1745–1778' in *Catholic Ireland in the eighteenth century*, ed. G. O'Brien, p. 132.

With these concessions, certain Irish Catholic clergy were now prepared to embrace the Hanoverians.[75]

These concessions were the result of multi-interest hardball rather than doe-eyed mutual trust, and the peculiar facilitating conjunction of circumstances and personalities did not endure. Parliamentary approval of these measures in 1782 was inextricably tied up with Patriot strategies to outflank the government on the issue of legislative independence. For College Green there was absolutely no question of broadening the political nation, as the bar on Catholics acquiring land in boroughs reaffirmed.[76] These were not extreme Protestant positions. Even the wayward Protestant liberal William Drennan believed that Catholics were, at least for the moment, 'absolutely incapable of making a good use of political liberty'.[77] If liberal Protestants had such doubts about Catholics, it is no surprise that their hard-line co-religionists continued to deal in the certainties of old-style prejudice. The government, fretting over the political and social risks posed by Catholic relief, gradually retreated back to inherited bias. The opportunistic and inconsistent politics of the Catholic interest, particularly its flirtations with political radicalism, were contributory factors. There were older and nastier animosities too. Sectarian violence had erupted in Armagh, intensifying over the following years, while in Munster agrarian unrest justified sectarian repression. Irish Protestantism was closing ranks, drawing the apparently more polite phase of Catholic relief to a close. But as Protestant and government apprehension grew, so too did the political self-awareness of Catholics and the extravagance of their demands. The talk of concessions was now marbled with the vocabulary of rights, transforming the question of relief for Catholics into the Catholic question in the 1790s. Although a long, frustrated future stretched ahead, it was now an unavoidable item on the British political agenda.

---

75 J. Kelly, '"A wild Capuchin of Cork": Arthur O'Leary (1729–1802)' in G. Moran (ed.), *Radical Irish priests* (Dublin: Four Courts Press, 1998), pp. 39–61.

76 J. Kelly, 'The parliamentary reform movement of the 1780s and the Catholic question', *Archivium Hibernicum*, 44 (1988), 95–117.

77 Cited in Connolly, *Divided island*, p. 436.

11

The Re-energising of Catholicism, 1790–1880

COLIN BARR

Introduction

The lord lieutenant was not amused. In late 1849, Pope Pius IX played a 'shameful trick', and chose as the new archbishop of Armagh and primate of Ireland 'the most malignant enemy of the English & the English government in Ireland'.[1] In Paul Cullen, the 4th Earl of Clarendon raged, 'we have a new and powerful enemy coming into the field'.[2] Cullen came, Clarendon quickly noticed, with 'unusually extensive' powers. For the lord lieutenant, and for the British state, the appointment represented a retrograde step in their relations with the Holy See and consequently in their ability to manage the island's Catholic majority. They preferred the emollient and clubbable Archbishop Daniel Murray of Dublin, who was prepared to sit on government boards and talk to government men. The thoroughly Romanised Cullen was neither emollient nor clubbable, and when he arrived in Ireland he flatly refused to meet the lord lieutenant, despite Murray's entreaties. He joined no board, despite Clarendon saving his place on several. He was, it seemed, 'quite as black as he was painted'.[3] A few months later, Clarendon informed the prime minister that the first national synod of the Irish Catholic Church (held at Thurles, County Tipperary) had produced a set of decrees 'which for intolerant Bigotry is worthy of the middle ages – of Louis Blanc for its Socialist doctrines and of the Devil for its misquotation of Scripture'.[4] The whole 'medieval farce' was presided over by Cullen, who 'comported himself

---

1 Clarendon to Lord John Russell, 5 Jan. 1850, Clarendon dep. Irish vol. 5, Bodleian Library, Oxford University (henceforth Bodl.).
2 Clarendon to Russell, 30 Apr. 1850, Clarendon dep. Irish vol. 5, Bodl.
3 Clarendon to Russell, 12 May 1850, Clarendon dep. Irish vol. 5, Bodl.
4 Clarendon to Russell, 22 Sept. 1850, Clarendon dep. Irish vol. 6, Bodl.

in the most arrogant and tyrannical manner' and used his Roman authority to silence all opposition.[5]

Clarendon never changed his opinion of Cullen (still a 'viper' in 1869),[6] and his portrait of a crypto-socialist Anglophobe has never been widely accepted. But both contemporaries and subsequent commentators recognised in Archbishop Cullen the most important and influential Irishman in the generation between the death of Daniel O'Connell and the rise of Charles Stewart Parnell. As *The Times* remarked on his death in 1878, 'No man in the kingdom has exercised a greater personal influence, or wielded more absolute power.'[7] Clarendon's view of Cullen as a fundamentally new force in Irish Catholicism, however, has been widely accepted, most strikingly by the American historian Emmet Larkin. In his seminal 1972 article, 'The devotional revolution in Ireland', Larkin claimed that it was only through the efforts of Paul Cullen that 'the great mass of the Irish people became practicing Catholics'.[8] Before Cullen's arrival, Larkin wrote, it was an open question whether Ireland's majority 'were Catholics at all'.[9]

Pre-Famine Catholicism, 1790–1815

Larkin grounded this claim in the condition of the institutional church in the years before the Famine. In 1800, he calculated, there were some 1,860 priests in Ireland, or 1 per 2,260 people. By 1840, the number of priests had climbed to 2,400, but the population had grown even faster with the result that the ratio of priests to people was now 1:2,750. Even this was not uniform across the island, but ranged from 1:2,150 in the prosperous ecclesiastical province of Dublin to 1:3,080 in the impoverished province of Tuam. In Catholic Austria, by contrast, the ratio was 1:750; in Protestant Prussia, 1:900. The French bishops believed the ideal was 1:650.[10] If clerical numbers as a whole were growing too slowly to match the surging population, some categories were actually

---

5 Clarendon to Russell, 31 Aug. 1850; Clarendon to Lord Grey, 20 Sept. 1850, Clarendon dep. Irish vol. 6, Bodl.

6 Clarendon to Odo Russell, 25 Jan. 1869, quoted in N. Blakiston (ed.), *The Roman question: extracts of the despatches of Odo Russell from Rome, 1858–1870* (Wilmington, DE: Michael Glazier, 1980 [1932]), p. 358.

7 *The Times*, 25 Oct. 1878.

8 E. Larkin, *The historical dimensions of Irish Catholicism* (Washington, DC: The Catholic University of America Press, 1997 [1984]), p. 58; E. Larkin, 'The devotional revolution in Ireland, 1850–75', *American Historical Review*, 77 (1972), pp. 625–52.

9 Larkin, *The historical dimensions of Irish Catholicism*, p. 84.

10 E. Larkin, *The pastoral role of the Roman Catholic Church in pre-Famine Ireland, 1750–1850* (Dublin: Four Courts Press, 2006), pp. 9–10.

declining. In 1800, for example, there were some 120 Franciscan friars, but there were only 65 in 1850.[11] In the years leading up to the Great Famine, the Irish church largely did not have the personnel to provide more than a rudimentary service to its flock. In some areas it had trouble even with that.

The problem of an insufficient clergy was amplified by an inadequate ecclesiastical infrastructure. To a degree this had been addressed before 1800, with a notable surge of building beginning around 1790. By 1834, there were some 2,109 chapels serving the island's 1,029 parishes. This apparent success – an average of two chapels per parish – masked some important realities, most obviously stark regional variations. The ecclesiastical province of Dublin, for example, managed 416 chapels for its 163 parishes across the four wealthy eastern and south-eastern dioceses. Further west and north-west, the situation was very different. In the worst-provided dioceses the number of people per chapel could rise to 1:4,038 (Raphoe, in the ecclesiastical province of Armagh) or even 1:4,546 (Killala, in Tuam). The populous archdiocese of Dublin managed 1:3,231, the highest in a province that could also boast 1:1,899 in Ferns (centred on County Wexford) and 1:2,232 in Ossory (centred on Kilkenny).[12] The raw numbers also conceal the varied state of the provision, which ranged from large, well built and in accord with the latest liturgical and architectural trends, to small and ramshackle. As Paul Cullen remarked in Rome after a visit home in 1835, he could not help remembering the 'poor miserable buildings destined to the purposes of Catholic worship in Ireland' and 'could not avoid drawing a contrast between them and the sumptuous churches which adorn almost every town on this side of the Alps'.[13]

An inevitable consequence of this lack of spiritual and spatial provision was an idiosyncratic Catholicism that was uniquely Irish. But the enduring and wholly heterodox belief in the world of the fairies and the efficacy of magic more generally was not the result of the survival of an earlier, somehow more authentic, Gaelic or Celtic faith, but a byproduct of an inefficient and thinly spread orthodoxy. Nor were such practices the peculiar possession of Catholic Ireland. As R.V. Comerford has pointed out, 'belief in magic, curses, cures, and the malevolent attentions of an underworld not known to

---

11 P. Conlan, 'Reforming and seeking an identity 1829–1918' in E. Bhreathnach, J. MacMahon and J. McCafferty (eds.), *The Irish Franciscans 1534–1990* (Dublin: Four Courts Press, 2009), p. 104.

12 Larkin, *Pastoral role*, pp. 149–50.

13 Cullen to Murray, 13 April 1835, Murray papers [MP], 34/9, Dublin Diocesan Archives (henceforth DDA).

the Christian churches was part of a customary common culture'.[14] These survivals could have benign consequences, some still visible in rural topography, and more malign ones, as the unfortunate Bridget Cleary, who was perceived to be a changling and was murdered by her family, discovered in 1895. Magical practices inevitably overlapped with and were overlaid by more conventionally Catholic ones. Croagh Patrick, for example, was sacred to pagans long before it became so to Christians. So were numerous holy wells. S.J. Connolly has enumerated the survival into the immediate pre-Famine era of a number of quasi-Catholic rituals and objects, including the delightful lie-detecting crozier of County Mayo, one of several such.[15] What *was* uniquely Catholic was the custom of 'Stations'. This was the practice of the sacraments being offered and dues collected in private homes on a rotating basis. A natural adaptation to the lack of suitable places of worship and the scarcity of parochial clergy, Stations were manifestations neither of an older Irish faith nor of resistance to Roman, episcopal or parochial authority.[16]

On the eve of the Great Famine, the Irish Catholic Church was in many ways still that of penal times. It could not provide enough priests or religious, and was falling further behind with each passing year. It could not build enough chapels or churches, although it was doing its best. Magic, fairies, and syncretic objects and practices remained widespread, especially in rural areas and in the west and north. Mass attendance – a rough measure of piety, but the best available – was relatively low, especially among the poor, particularly when measured against what came later. David Miller's estimate that by the mid-1830s attendance in rural areas was probably on average no more than 40 per cent still seems the most plausible number available, even if it should be treated as indicative and not definitive.[17] As always, there were regional variations: attendance was more assiduous in the east than further west or north-west; English-speaking areas seem to have been more conventionally devout than Irish-speaking ones.

---

14 R.V. Comerford, 'Deference, accommodation, and conflict in Irish confessional relations' in C. Barr and H.M. Carey (eds.), *Religion and Greater Ireland: Christianity and Irish global networks, 1750–1950* (Montreal and Kingston: McGill-Queen's University Press, 2015), p. 50.

15 S.J. Connolly, *Priests and people in pre-Famine Ireland, 1780–1845* (Dublin: Four Courts Press, 2001 [1982]), p. 116.

16 Larkin, *Pastoral role*, chapter 4.

17 See D.W. Miller, 'Mass attendance in Ireland in 1834' in S. Brown and D. Miller (eds.), *Piety and power in Ireland, 1760–1960: essays in honor of Emmet Larkin* (Notre Dame, IN: University of Notre Dame Press, 2000).

Larkin's thesis has been challenged, not least by Thomas McGrath, who argues that he overestimated Cullen's impact. The Synod of Thurles, McGrath suggests, was important, but not itself transformative or novel. Other bishops had pursued similar reforms for many years, and Cullen is best seen as consolidating the work of others rather than sparking a revolution.[18] McGrath points in particular to the reforms implemented in the 1820s in the eastern diocese of Kildare and Leighlin by Bishop James Doyle, better known as the politically prominent 'JKL'. Treating the Council of Trent as a 'source-book of ecclesiastical government', Doyle radically improved the quality and social standing of his priests, imposed episcopal authority, built churches, and insisted upon an 'exact attention to the rubric of the liturgy'.[19] Although he resisted Roman orders to abolish Stations, Doyle was otherwise an enthusiastically Tridentine reformer whom McGrath convincingly situates within a wider European 'Catholic recovery' after 1815.[20]

The same was true of Dublin, where Daniel Murray was coadjutor to Archbishop John Troy from 1809 and archbishop in his own right from 1823. Like Doyle, Murray was a reformer and a builder. Although poorly served by scholarship, Murray's importance is undeniable. He erected some ninety churches, doubled the number of clergy, and oversaw the creation of the Irish Vincentians and the foundation of All Hallows Missionary College. Murray was particularly encouraging of women religious, helping to establish the Sisters of Charity, the Irish branch of the Loreto Sisters, and the most numerous and globally important of all the Irish religious orders, the Sisters of Mercy. A willingness to protect and promote female religious leaders such as Mary Aikenhead, Teresa Ball and Catherine McAuley was Murray's greatest and most enduring achievement. It was also easier in the urban setting of the capital to oversee the clergy and eliminate the lusher manifestations of popular piety or practice. Although Murray, who had been educated in pre-revolutionary Spain, was not a champion of the Roman devotions later favoured by Cullen, he was hardly an opponent either. He encouraged devotion to the Sacred Heart and the Virgin Mary, and was an assiduous reformer of the internal structures and practices of his diocese. At the Synod of Thurles, his opposition was limited to the decrees dealing with education, not to those dealing with clerical discipline or ecclesiastical organisation.

---

18 T. McGrath, 'The Tridentine evolution of modern Irish Catholicism, 1563–1962: a re-examination of the "devotional revolution" thesis', *Recusant History*, 20 (1991), 512–23.

19 T. McGrath, *Religious renewal and reform in the pastoral ministry of Bishop James Doyle of Kildare and Leighlin, 1786–1834* (Dublin: Four Courts Press, 1999), pp. 210–11.

20 Ibid., p. xi.

Yet these manifestations of pre-Cullen reform should not be pushed too far. As Emmet Larkin pointed out in his detailed analysis of the pre-Famine church, Kildare and Leighlin was the 'upper limit in what could be achieved in terms of providing priests', and even with Doyle's 'heroic efforts' the ratio of priests to people there was slightly worse in 1835, a year after Doyle's death, than it had been in 1800. And by 1840, the number of priests had actually declined, from 131 to 120, and the ratio of priests to people had worsened by some 12 per cent.[21] Doyle's influence was real but transient, and Kildare an outlier that even in his pomp lacked adequate clerical provision.

In Dublin, Murray's reforms were more enduring, partly because he had greater resources, partly because he lived longer, until 1852, and partly because his immediate successor was Paul Cullen. But in the vast majority of Ireland's twenty-seven dioceses, there were too few priests, too many of whom were unsatisfactory, overseeing a too numerous people who continued, in many cases, to prefer the ad hoc arrangements and idiosyncratic devotions of earlier times. The social and coercive power of the clergy was attenuated because it was so diluted. It is true that almost everywhere things were improving, but those improvements were everywhere outpaced by the rapid growth of the pre-Famine population. The situation with women religious demonstrates this real but inadequate progress: in 1800, there were only 122 nuns in Ireland; by 1850, there were around 1,000.[22] A great improvement, but not nearly enough, largely dependent on the initiative of a single bishop, and nothing like the explosion that was to come.

Ecclesiastical structures were not the only concern of Irish Catholics in the early nineteenth century. In fact, one of the most important pre-Famine manifestations of Catholic revival owed its origins to an elderly Quaker, William Martin. It was Martin who convinced the charismatic Capuchin friar Theobald Mathew to assume the leadership of the Cork Total Abstinence Society. It was obvious to the society's Protestant founders that Catholic clerical leadership was necessary if temperance was to have any chance of success in the face of the some 12.2 million proof-gallons of alcohol consumed by the Irish in 1838. From April of that year to November 1839, some 50,000 people, mostly in County Cork, took the pledge. By December, Mathew's itinerant preaching secured perhaps another 100,000, mostly in counties Limerick and Waterford. By 1840 it was a national phenomenon, excluding only the north-east. As Catherine McAuley, the foundress of the Sisters of

---

21 Larkin, *Pastoral role*, p. 21.
22 Larkin, *Historical dimensions*, pp. 58–9.

Mercy, noted delightedly in November 1840, 'the Publicans of Dublin are in terror at Father Mathew's approach'. 'You can scarcely form an idea', she continued, 'of the moral improvement throughout the country.'[23] By 1843, largely through the charisma of Mathew's preaching, about half the adult population had taken the pledge. Despite its lay (and Protestant) origins, the Cork Total Abstinence Society and its pledge soon became distinctively Irish, Catholic and clerical. This was true not only in Ireland but also globally. In 1844 in Madras, for example, some 3,000 Irish soldiers and civilians took the pledge at the urging of their Irish bishop.[24] The temperance campaigns were, as Paul Townend notes, 'the single most extraordinary social movement that occurred in pre-Famine Ireland'.[25]

Politics too saw an increasingly active episcopate and clergy. The proximate cause was the attempt in the wake of the Act of Union to secure a government veto over episcopal appointments as a surety against eventual political emancipation. Most Catholic states and some Protestant ones enjoyed such privileges, and its appeal to the government was obvious. Rome was minded to comply, and by no means all Irish Catholics were opposed, including Archbishop Troy of Dublin. The long-running campaign against the veto consequently took on some of the characteristics of a civil war. Bishops like Daniel Murray warned 'misguided Catholics' against betraying the church and thus emulating the 'treacherous disciple', Judas.[26] Rising young priests such as John England of Cork, later an influential American bishop, rallied public opposition to both the government and those inclined to concede to it. In their struggle against the veto, they made common cause with a new generation of Catholic laity.

Among them, Daniel O'Connell quickly emerged as the leading intransigent voice demanding Catholic emancipation without conditions. He was also active in trying to establish a representative Catholic body in the face of determined ultra-Protestant opposition. After several attempts, he finally succeeded in 1823 with the creation of the Catholic Association. It successfully created a common Catholic political identity that transcended diocesan,

23 McAuley to Frances Ward, 13 Nov. 1840 in M.C. Sullivan (ed.), *The correspondence of Catherine McAuley* (Dublin: Four Courts Press, 2004), pp. 319–20.
24 *Madras Catholic Expositor*, 4:1 (March 1844), p. 22.
25 P.A. Townend, *Father Mathew: temperance and Irish identity* (Dublin: Irish Academic Press, 2002), p. 1.
26 Quoted in W. Meagher, *Notices of the life and character of . . . Rev. Daniel Murray, late Archbishop of Dublin, as contained in the Commemorative Oration pronounced in the Church of the Conception, Dublin, on the occasion of his grace's Month's Mind, with historical and biographical notes* (Dublin: Gerard Bellew, 1853), pp. 72–3. He was speaking in 1816.

regional, social and even linguistic divisions, and O'Connell himself became a talisman for Irish Catholics at home and abroad. This sense of a shared communal identity was amplified by resentment directed at a renewed and aggressive campaign of Protestant proselytisation from the mid-1820s.

By using the Catholic parish structure to raise the so-called 'Catholic rent' and deliver votes to pro-emancipation candidates and then himself, O'Connell effectively invited the church into Irish political life for the first time since the mid-seventeenth century. As long as his aims were civil, social and economic equality for Catholics, he enjoyed overwhelming ecclesiastical support. James Doyle of Kildare and Leighlin, for example, insisted on emancipation as a matter of justice to a loyal population, explicitly denying that the pope had any power whatsoever 'to interfere directly or indirectly with the rights of our sovereign'.[27] These assurances (the importance of which should not be underestimated), and O'Connell's growing political power, were ultimately enough to secure emancipation in 1829. It was only when O'Connell challenged Ireland's constitutional position that he lost some clerical support.

Bishops like Murray, Doyle and William Crolly (bishop of Down and Connor from 1825, archbishop of Armagh from 1835) were satisfied with the achievement of emancipation, reconciled to the Union, and pleased by the steadily improving place of Catholics in political and economic life. They opposed the government when necessary, and defended what they saw as Catholic rights, but always with a view to compromise. This was less true of a new generation of prelates, trained not in the Irish colleges of pre-revolutionary Europe but in Ireland. Most prominent among them was John MacHale, the first bishop since the Reformation to have been educated entirely on the island. MacHale made his name as a polemically aggressive professor at Maynooth, and as a dynamic bishop of Killala from 1825. In 1834, he was translated to the archiepiscopal see of Tuam over the strenuous opposition of the British government, who knew him to be an implacable and noisy opponent. To MacHale and those who thought like him, the British state and Irish Protestants were equally and unambiguously the enemy.

Despite differences in background and temperament, the Irish bishops largely maintained their outward unity until the late 1830s. In particular, they successfully navigated the introduction of the national system of education, accepting it as an imperfect but real improvement on the state-funded but Protestant-run schools of the Kildare Place Society. Murray and then Crolly

---

27 J. Doyle, *An essay on the Catholic claims, addressed to the right honourable the Earl of Liverpool, K.G., &c. &c.* (Dublin: Richard Coyne, 1826), p. 11.

joined the system's governing board. But episcopal unity was shattered in 1838, when John MacHale published a letter addressed to Lord John Russell, then home secretary in Lord Melbourne's Whig government. It was a blistering condemnation of the national system, which MacHale thought was usurping oversight of religious education. To Russell, MacHale announced that 'to no power on earth, save the Pope, shall I submit the books from which the children of my diocese are to derive their religious instruction.'[28] To Daniel O'Connell, he explained that the national system was intended 'to place the religious education of Catholics in the hands of the Crown'.[29] The majority of the bishops thought this was delusional: the idea that MacHale could secure state-funded denominational education was, Daniel Murray explained, 'so utterly visionary that no rational person could entertain it for a moment'.[30] They were right: it was politically impossible for any British government to grant what MacHale demanded, and his refusal to countenance the national system in Tuam achieved nothing beyond denying an education to the poor in Ireland's most deprived region.

Although Rome accepted the majority's view that the national system was a legitimate compromise with reality, the fissures opened by MacHale only widened. The cause was the determination of the administration of Sir Robert Peel to drain support for O'Connell's revivified campaign for repeal of the Union. A former Irish chief secretary, Peel knew that without the backing of the clergy O'Connell would fail. As he put it to the newly appointed lord lieutenant in July 1844, it was absolutely necessary to disunite 'by the fair legitimate means of a just, kind and conciliatory policy, the Roman Catholic body and thus [break] up a sullen and formidable *confederacy* against the British connexion'.[31] Peel ultimately identified three primary areas of legitimate Catholic grievance and set out to prove the Union could work by legislating for each. Two of these, reform of the laws governing charitable bequests and the provision of higher education in Ireland, badly divided Irish Catholics. The third, providing the seminary at Maynooth with an adequate and permanent income, split his own party.

---

28 MacHale to Russell, 12 Feb. 1838 in B. O'Reilly, *John MacHale, Archbishop of Tuam: his life, times, and correspondence*, 2 vols. (New York: Fr. Pustet, 1890), vol. I, p. 417.

29 MacHale to O'Connell, 27 Feb. 1838, in ibid., vol. I, p. 419.

30 Murray to Cullen, 28 April 1838, Cullen papers [CP], 423, Pontifical Irish College, Rome, Archives [PICRA].

31 Peel to Heytesbury, 8 Aug. 1844, quoted in D.A. Kerr, *Peel, priests and politics: Sir Robert Peel's administration and the Roman Catholic Church in Ireland, 1841–1846* (Oxford: Oxford University Press, 1982), p. 120.

In 1844, Peel introduced legislation on bequests that he hoped would satisfy Catholics without proving too unpalatable to his backbenches. The reform allowed property to be willed to the Catholic Church as such, although not to religious orders. Protestant fear of the power of confessors over dying penitents was to be ameliorated by various restrictions, and by the creation of a government board to oversee all bequests. Murray and Crolly saw progress, and joined the board. MacHale and his allies smelled tyranny, and opposed it heatedly. John Cantwell of Meath thought that those bishops who had joined 'will very soon be pronounced insane, should they persist in their unprincipled, unwise, and mad career'.[32] Another bishop noted that the 'education question was the first wedge to [inflict] our body, and the enemy has now put another at its back'. It would be necessary, he continued, for the 'orthodox' bishops to resist.[33] Both sides appealed to Rome.

The divisions over charitable bequests were nothing compared to those that soon arose over higher education. Since 1592, the only university in Ireland was the University of Dublin and its sole college, Trinity. Although open to Catholics, Trinity was avowedly Protestant in its ethos. With a few exceptions, Oxford, Cambridge and the ancient Scottish universities were also closed or uncongenial to Catholics, and Peel accepted that Irish Catholics had a legitimate claim to indigenous university education. As political realities made a state-endowed Catholic university impossible, he offered three secular 'Queen's Colleges' at Cork, Galway and Belfast. Murray and Crolly negotiated hard, secured some concessions, and then welcomed the colleges as a boon to Catholic Ireland. A strong minority of bishops agreed with them. But a majority backed MacHale, including the previously quiescent fourth Irish archbishop, Michael Slattery of Cashel. He thought the proposed colleges 'dangerous in the highest degree to the morality & to the religious principles of the Catholic Youth who might resort to them'.[34] Again, both sides appealed to Rome.

In 1846, the newly elected Pius IX condemned the colleges. Murray and his allies formally submitted, but never abandoned their view that they were the best that could be obtained under Irish circumstances. Rome's proposed alternative, a locally funded Catholic University, was dismissed as impracticable in good times and wholly impossible in the context of the Famine. It was now apparent that the Irish Catholic Church was hopelessly divided. Two of the

32 Cantwell to MacHale, 29 Jan. 1845 in O'Reilly, *MacHale*, vol. I, p. 566.
33 William Higgins to Cullen, 2 Oct. 1844, CP/956, PICRA.
34 Slattery to Cullen, 6 Feb. 1846, Slattery papers, Cashel Diocesan Archives.

four archbishops thought the other two imprudent fools, and were considered in turn borderline heretics and traitors. Cullen was not alone in describing Archbishop Crolly as 'a decided government man', nor in wishing the primate would receive 'a lecture from higher quarters'.[35] An aging O'Connell had no choice but to condemn both the bequests act and the colleges, which delighted MacHale and Slattery and infuriated Murray and Crolly. His tenure as the political avatar of a united hierarchy was over. This all occurred against the backdrop of famine, in which Murray took the lead in soliciting and distributing government funds and private charity. Yet even in 1847 serial denunciations and explanations regularly appeared in the press and arrived in Rome.

Cullen's Church, 1849–1878

It was the demonstrable inability of the Irish church to manage its own affairs that caused Rome to intervene so decisively in late 1849. The final straw was the failure of the bishops to agree a successor following the death of William Crolly earlier that year. Each faction had a preferred candidate, and each denounced that of the other. As the intemperate Bishop William Higgins of Ardagh wrote, 'All those who deserve the name of Catholics in Ireland' supported MacHale's candidate, 'whilst the Heretics and place-hunting lukewarm Catholics will do anything to malign and misrepresent him'.[36] With the bishops so deeply divided, Archbishop Slattery and then MacHale privately suggested Paul Cullen. A frustrated and distracted Rome agreed, leaving a genuinely horrified Cullen no option but to accede.

By 1850, Cullen was by his own admission more an Italian than an Irishman. Born in Prospect, County Kildare in 1803, he had arrived in Rome in 1820 to study at the college of the Propaganda Fide, the Roman congregation with responsibility for mission territories such as the British Isles, the British Empire and the United States. His time in the college was crucial. He mastered Italian, learned to love the devotions, discipline, architecture and theology of papal Rome, and built important and enduring relationships. Living for more than ten years in the Propaganda also taught him how its power was exercised. He became the protégé of Mauro Cappellari, the cardinal prefect of Propaganda from 1826, and a crucial indirect influence on the development

---

35 Cullen to Tobias Kirby, 20 Sept., 25 Jul. 1845, New Kirby Papers [NKP], 1/1/34, 1/1/32, PICRA.
36 Higgins to Cullen, 7 July 1849, CP/1757, PICRA.

of Irish Catholicism both in Ireland and globally. It was Cappellari's theological preferences and convinced papalism that shaped Cullen and were in turn inculcated in the Irish College and other seminaries, although crucially not in Maynooth. It was Cappellari who kept Cullen in Rome after his ordination, much against the wishes of Bishop Doyle of Kildare, who wanted him at home. He invented various jobs for Cullen, including the production of a polyglot Bible and teaching oriental languages. In early 1831 Cappellari was elected pope as Gregory XVI, and later that year suggested the Irish bishops appoint Cullen rector of the recently revivified Irish College in the city. He became their agent to the Holy See, where he used his access to represent their needs, explain their mistakes and carry out their commissions. By 1833, he was unofficially performing the same function for the growing Irish faction among the American bishops. He was recommended for various dioceses, including New York City, and for the presidency of Maynooth. Doyle wanted him as his successor in Kildare. In 1834, he was briefly appointed coadjutor bishop of Charleston, South Carolina. Cullen preferred to remain in Rome, the favourite of the reigning pope and the Holy See's expert on Irish affairs. (Illustration 4)

His power was accentuated by chance: very few of the senior officials who governed the church and almost none of the *minutanti* who staffed its bureaucracy spoke or read English. This was particularly true of the Propaganda, which came to rely on Cullen to explain English-language disputes and recommend solutions. In the 1830s, he used this opportunity to secure the appointment of Irishmen as bishops of dioceses in the United States, British North America, the Cape of Good Hope and India. In 1839, the Propaganda asked him to investigate the national system of education in Ireland. His pragmatic advice was that it was flawed, but better than any realistic alternative. In 1844, he allied with MacHale and opposed the Charitable Bequests Act. Archbishop Murray was furious, and a chastened Cullen repented of his involvement with 'the keenest mental agony' and promised to 'never take any public step again'.[37] The Queen's Colleges caused him to abandon that resolution. Although he retained his nominal role as agent for the entire hierarchy, Cullen worked successfully with MacHale and Slattery to secure multiple Roman condemnations of the colleges. The government believed that the archbishop of Tuam had 'a regular agency through Dr Cullen of the Irish College for the propagation of falsehood', and its envoy warned the pope

---

37 Cullen to William Walsh, 10 Feb. 1845, cp/66/16, DDA.

4. Paul, Cardinal Cullen (1803–78), archbishop of Dublin, 1852–78, and Ireland's first cardinal (1866), exerted a formative influence on the Catholic Church in Ireland. Portrait (copy), Irish School, nineteenth century. Oil on canvas.

directly that Cullen was lying to him.[38] Although Pius IX listened politely, he did nothing to curtail Cullen's influence. It was no wonder that MacHale and his allies were delighted by his appointment, or that Murray and Clarendon were appalled.

Cullen arrived in Ireland in early May 1850. It was only his fourth visit home since 1821, and what he found in his new diocese shocked him. The seminary and bishop's house belonged to Crolly's under-age nephew – in a nicely ironic twist, the archbishop had failed under the terms of the Charitable Bequests Act to sign his will soon enough before his death. His executors were planning to sell the furniture. The cathedral was 17 feet, a roof and £20,000 short of completion. There were no records of any kind, and he knew nothing about his priests. Nor were there enough in the first place. 'Every thing', he complained, 'is primitive.' Liturgical practice was nothing like he knew in Rome, especially in rural areas. 'There is scarcely a cap or a surplice', he complained, and there was a scandalous paucity of liturgical candles. He might as well have been beginning his episcopate in Oregon or California.[39] But Cullen was determined: within weeks he raised £1,000 to give to the pope, approached several orders about establishing a convent and poor school in Armagh town, and ordered greater liturgical solemnity throughout the archdiocese. The change Cullen's arrival represented can be illustrated in the seemingly simple choice of an archbishop's processional cross. Archbishop Murray, he noted disapprovingly, carried a plain wooden one 'without an image of our saviour'. Cullen ordered his cross directly from Rome, giving instructions that 'I would wish to be like the Pope.'[40]

Cullen's desire to be like the pope was central to his episcopate. His goal was nothing less than the wholesale importation of *Roman* Catholicism into Ireland; that is, the devotional, architectural, liturgical and theological norms current in post-Napoleonic Rome. Cullen would have an early opportunity to implement this agenda, as he had been sent to Ireland with the power of an apostolic delegate and instructions to convene the first national synod of the Irish Catholic Church. Prior to 1850, there had been no mechanism for an archbishop, bishop or majority of bishops to impose their will on a recalcitrant colleague. Rome could intervene, but only after some delay and multiple appeals. But the decrees of a synod ratified by Rome were at least notionally

---

38 Lord Minto to Lord John Russell, 14 April 1848 in F. Curato (ed.), *Gran Bretagna e Italia nei documenti della Missioni Minto*, 2 vols. (Rome: Istituto storico italiano per l'età moderna e comtemporanea, 1970), vol. II, p. 195.
39 Cullen to Kirby, 28 May 1850, NKP/I/II/21, PICRA.
40 Cullen to Kirby, 1 July 1850, NKP/I/II/29, PICRA.

binding on all, and Cullen was determined that his would be the mechanism by which the Irish church was not only unified, but also Romanised.

For a template he looked to America, where the institution of regular synods had been the first goal of the Hiberno-Roman bishops whom Cullen had aided from the early 1830s. In particular, he looked to Francis Patrick Kenrick of Philadelphia, from whom he eagerly sought 'hints regarding our Synod'. 'You see so many of our poor people in America', he wrote, 'that you must know what their wants are, better than we do.'[41] Also an Irish-born product of the Propaganda college, the slightly older Kenrick had long pursued policies similar to those Cullen would introduce in Ireland. His emphasis on episcopal control, clerical education and discipline, uniform devotions and Roman theology shaped the American church for decades. Like Cullen, Kenrick took the practices and preferences of post-revolutionary Rome to be identical with orthodoxy and best practice. He even went so far as to write lengthy works of dogmatic and moral theology specifically for the United States to prove this. Cullen supplied the books he worked from, advised on content, helped in the editing, and presented the finished products to a delighted Gregory XVI. All three men were influenced by the work of Alphonsus Liguori, an eighteenth-century Italian theologian whose teachings rejected the rigours of Jansenism without quite embracing the flexibility of the Jesuits. This could have surprising results, not least given Irish Catholicism's later reputation for sexual puritanism. As Peter Gardella put it, Kenrick was the 'first American writer to prescribe orgasm' and to insist on a woman's right to sexual pleasure and a man's duty to provide it.[42] Although Liguorian theology fell out of fashion in the Rome of Pius IX, it was in the ascendant in the time of Pius VII and Gregory XVI, who canonised Liguori in 1839. In one of the most significant failures of his tenure, Cullen never succeeded in embedding Liguorian moral theology in Ireland, particularly at Maynooth; his protégés were more successful abroad.

Kenrick's 1832 diocesan synod in Philadelphia served as a model for many that followed in America, and much of what it introduced remained normative into the twentieth century. In addition to concerns peculiar to the United States, Kenrick insisted that no new church could be built, or orphanage or school opened by a religious order, without the relevant bishop's written permission, and that all church property was to be vested in the bishop's name.

---

41 Cullen to Kenrick, 5 July 1850, Kenrick papers, 28 T2, Associated Archives St. Mary's Seminary and University, Baltimore.
42 P. Gardella, *Innocent ecstasy: how Christianity gave America an ethic of sexual pleasure* (Oxford: Oxford University Press, 1985), p. 9.

Other decrees involved the placement of baptismal fonts and other liturgical furniture, and the correct keeping of the records, especially of marriage, that were necessary for effective social control. The intent was to centre worship and devotional life in the parish under the watchful eye of the parish priest, who was in turn under the watchful eye of the bishop. Thurles would imitate Philadelphia, and in turn be copied by Kenrick when, in his new role as archbishop of Baltimore, he convened the first plenary synod of the American church in 1852. Both then shaped the first national synod of Australasia, convened in 1885 by the archbishop of Sydney (and Cullen's nephew), Patrick Francis Moran.

On 21 August 1850, some 10,000 people gathered to watch the bishops of Ireland process through the streets of Thurles. They were there to celebrate the formal opening of the national synod the next day. It was an unabashedly Roman display, carefully planned by Cullen and a small group of Irish College graduates. As one reported, the opening mass was celebrated by Cullen himself, the church was modelled 'as far as possible on the plan of the Papal Chapels', and the form of the service 'the old Irish College Mass in four parts quite in the Palestrina style'.[43] As a statement of intent it could not have been clearer.

The synod was dominated by the politically charged debate over the Queen's Colleges, with Archbishop Murray resurrecting memories of the 'veto controversy' to argue that Rome could err and the colleges should not be condemned. Although the line of argument and its level of support appalled Cullen, there was little doubt of the ultimate outcome: had Murray won, as he very nearly did, Rome would have repeated its condemnation and perhaps removed him from his see. The synod simply confirmed that the bishops remained irreparably divided. Indeed, Murray and twelve others unsuccessfully urged Pius IX not to ratify the decrees on the colleges, an act that apparently 'enraged' the pope.[44] But this was politics, undeniably important at the time but of limited long-term consequence. What were ultimately much more important were the specifically ecclesiastical decrees written by Cullen and his Roman-trained assistants. These dealt with clerical discipline, record keeping, liturgical practice and episcopal authority, and were all drawn from American precedents. Unlike the propositions regarding education,

---

43 Laurence Forde to Kirby, 22 Aug. 1850, quoted in E. Larkin, *The making of the Roman Catholic Church in Ireland, 1850–1860* (Chapel Hill: University of North Carolina Press, 1980), p. 27.

44 Diary of Patrick Francis Moran, '1851', T1208, Archives of the Archdiocese of Sydney (henceforth AAS).

they passed with little dissent, and cumulatively represented the introduction of Tridentine norms of discipline and organisation to the entire Irish church. This was Thurles' enduring legacy.

Before the synod Cullen had hoped for unity; after, he concluded that he would have to neutralise his opponents in the hierarchy and replace them with men willing to do his bidding. Murray's supporters were the obvious first target, but Cullen soon realised that MacHale and his allies also posed a threat to his vision of a fully Romanised Irish Catholicism. Although MacHale supported Cullen's appointment, and backed him at Thurles, he soon proved recalcitrant, not least over the establishment of Cullen's beloved Catholic University. Although the archbishop genuinely objected to what he saw as Cullen's centralising tendencies and willingness to deal with Englishmen, his opposition was ultimately temperamental: John MacHale was incapable of working with others. Nor was he at all attracted to Cullen's Roman devotions or ultramontane theology. Indeed, MacHale was one of only two Irish bishops to oppose papal infallibility at the First Vatican Council in 1870, while Cullen was not just a leading infallibilist, he actually wrote the definition.

As the unofficial agent of the Irish bishops abroad, Cullen had learned how to manipulate the Propaganda to alter the balance of a national church. His strategy in Ireland was simple: impugn uncongenial bishops as defiant, aged, ill, indolent, incompetent or some combination. Cullen wrote regularly to the Propaganda describing (in Italian) their inadequacies, in some cases urging the appointment of a coadjutor bishop with the right of succession, in others separating historically joined sees and appointing new bishops. Often he simply laid the groundwork for the succession at an incumbent's death or incapacitation. These reports collectively rendered a picture of institutional and individual failure across the country and at every level. They made for grim reading in Rome, and were meant to. Although strict accuracy was not Cullen's first concern, the level of detail and specificity of example convinces, and his letters to the Propaganda remain the best available picture of Irish Catholicism at the cusp of the devotional revolution.

The Propaganda listened because Cullen's successor and close ally, Tobias Kirby, continued to ensure that the *minutanti* had a correct understanding of Irish affairs. And those bureaucrats were in turn overseen by Cullen's most important surviving patron, Alessandro Barnabò, who was elevated from secretary to cardinal prefect in 1856. Over time Cullen was thus able to fill almost every Irish diocese with an appointee either of his choosing or with his acquiescence. This was in spite of the Irish convention that the parish priests of a vacant see voted for three names to forward to the bishops of the relevant province, who in turn ratified or amended the list before sending it to Rome with a recommendation. When they produced an appropriate choice, Cullen simply endorsed it; when they did not, he intervened with one of his own, if possible also from the priests' *terna*. By 1860, he had succeeded in creating a new and unified hierarchy: MacHale was isolated in the west with a handful of remaining allies while Murray's faction was no more. Relatively few of these new bishops were Roman-trained, as Cullen tended to reserve his former students (and relatives) for overseas appointments. In Ireland, his concern was to secure efficient and compliant candidates whose appointment was congenial to the diocese. As a result, while the bishops uniformly understood where power lay in the Irish Church, and what was necessary to placate it, they did not necessarily all share Cullen's ideological and personal *Romanità*, although of course some did. His posthumous influence was consequently greater abroad than in Ireland.

Cullen's dominance was confirmed by his appointment to succeed Daniel Murray as archbishop of Dublin in late 1852. When rumours of Rome's intentions reached London and Dublin, the government panicked. Unofficial envoys dropped heavy hints about the consequences of defiance ('God grant', one piously told the pope, 'we do not see an English fleet at Ancona'), and as in 1848 attempts were made to have jurisdiction for Ireland transferred from the Propaganda to the more pliable secretariat of state. Pius nearly yielded, and the appointment was saved only when Barnabò threatened to resign during a heated interview with him.[45] News of British pressure and the pope's resistance confirmed Cullen's singular position within the Irish church. His 1866 appointment as Ireland's first ever cardinal merely ratified it.

Cullen's power was amplified by demographic catastrophe. Before the Great Famine the church was unable to meet the needs or even to keep pace with Ireland's population. Had starvation and emigration not intervened, no change in its administrative composition or theological posture could have produced enough clergy or infrastructure to effect the social, devotional, organisational or political changes that Cullen desired. The Famine changed matters at a stroke. What had once been a wholly inadequate number of priests suddenly became otherwise, and the unequal distribution of mortality and flight meant that effectual clerical surveillance and oversight became possible in precisely those areas (western and north-western, rural and Irish-speaking) where idiosyncratic practices were most embedded and challenges to clerical authority most prevalent.

45 Moran diaries, 7 Sept. 1852, T1208, AAS.

Although remaking the hierarchy was a necessary precondition, it was not sufficient. It took time for new and more active bishops to transmit their requirements to the clergy and to ensure their compliance. In many places resources remained severely stretched, even allowing for depopulation. The most effective solution was a nation-wide campaign of parish missions. Primarily associated with the Irish Vincentians, which had been founded in Dublin in the mid-1830s, the missions rapidly expanded after 1850, soon reaching every parish on the island at least once. A sort of flying squad of Roman orthodoxy, the missioners descended on a parish for several days or a week. During the day they gave lectures on scripture and doctrine, heard confessions, and celebrated mass with as much liturgical solemnity as possible; extravagant altar decorations and the liberal use of candles contributed to the effect. In the evening there were hymns, short moral or dogmatic lessons, the rosary, climaxing with the benediction of the blessed sacrament. The mission culminated in the renewal of baptismal vows, communion (often first communion) and more singing, all staged as impressively as possible. Finally, participants were enrolled in a confraternity or sodality designed to maintain regular and orthodox practice and devotion after the missioners had left. This was the antithesis of Stations, and the cumulative effect was to centre devotional life in the parish, and to orient the devotions themselves to the wider norms of the church of the mid-nineteenth century.

Just as the Great Famine radically altered the ability of the church to reach and oversee its members, it also profoundly changed Irish politics. Under Daniel O'Connell, the bishops and clergy had taken an active (sometimes very active) part in political life, but they were almost invariably in a supporting role. O'Connell's death in 1847 and the failure of the Young Ireland revolt the next year left Catholic and nationalist Ireland leaderless, and the easing of the Famine and the expansion of the franchise in 1850 meant that such a vacuum could not long endure. There were already signs of a new political movement coalescing around the rights of tenant farmers. The question was whether Cullen would passively await a return to the status quo, or push the church towards an entirely new political posture.

The need for a Catholic political vehicle became undeniable when the clumsy re-establishment of the English hierarchy in 1850 triggered an atavistic spasm of British anti-Catholicism. Although the offence had been given in England, the United Kingdom's Catholics were overwhelmingly located in Ireland, and it was there that the political response to the so-called 'Papal Aggression' was most keenly felt. The defence of the church against external attack was a cause in which all strands of Irish Catholic opinion could join, and Cullen sanctioned not only the creation of a Catholic Defence Association, but also its subsequent alliance with the Irish Tenant League. The bishops endorsed their collective political demands and tests for supporting prospective parliamentary candidates, and gave their clergy great latitude in lending support. The 1852 general election was consequently an outstanding success, with nearly fifty candidates returned pledged to land reform, religious freedom and independent opposition. It appeared that O'Connell's alliance of priests and people might be restored even in the absence of a charismatic leader.

But Paul Cullen had no intention of permitting an oppositional nationalist party to exist except under exigent circumstances. When Lord Aberdeen's ramshackle coalition emerged, that need no longer existed. Aberdeen had opposed the anti-Catholic Ecclesiastical Titles Act in the House of Lords, earning a private letter from Cullen praising his 'powerful and generous advocacy of the principles of religious freedom'.[46] As prime minister, he invited Irish Catholics to join the government, and looked to their votes in the House of Commons. For Cullen this was enough, and he countenanced if he did not actually encourage John Sadleir and William Keogh to break their pledge of independent opposition and accept office. From his perspective this made sense: the interests of the church were best served by a cautiously transactional relationship with the state, not by mindless or malevolent opposition. Although Daniel O'Connell remained Cullen's *beau ideal* of political Catholicism, his genuine loathing of the English and of the Union was exceeded by his fear of Irish nationalism and its likely consequences.

The politics of mid-Victorian Ireland were consequently distorted by Cullen's unshakeable belief that the leaders of the new Independent Irish Party (IIP) were alike in kind and intent to Italian nationalists in general and Giuseppe Mazzini in particular. His animus was directed particularly at Charles Gavan Duffy, the editor of *The Nation*, formerly a leading Young Irelander, now an MP and leading figure in the IIP. To Cullen, the party was merely Young Ireland with a new name, and the 'young Irelanders desire to destroy all the power of the priests – they seem to act just as the Mazzinians did in Italy – Evviva Pio Nono just as they are going to crucify him'.[47] Duffy was an Irish Mazzini. Cullen was not, but it did not matter: he saw Italy, and acted accordingly. First in Armagh and then in Dublin, he promulgated and enforced regulations prohibiting the clergy from taking an active role in

---

46 Cullen to Aberdeen, 22 May 1851, Aberdeen papers, Add. MS 43246, f. 190, BL.
47 Cullen to Bernard Smith, 18 Dec. 1843, Smith papers, Irlanda file, San Paolo fuori le muri.

politics. In 1854, he secured a similar ban from a synodical meeting of the Irish bishops. Without clerical support, the party could not function as the political voice of Catholic Ireland. This was an existential threat, and Archbishop MacHale and Duffy's ally Frederick Lucas (the English convert editor of *The Tablet*) set off to Rome. Like the British before them, they sought to convince the authorities that Cullen was deceiving them as to the true situation in Ireland, and they enjoyed exactly the same success. Soon Lucas was dead, Duffy in Australia, MacHale isolated in Tuam, and the Independent Irish Party spent. As Lucas put it, Cullen had laboured 'diligently, in season and out of season, by all practicable methods, to accomplish this disastrous result'.[48]

Cullen's destruction of the Independent Irish Party and subsequent hostility to the Fenians and wariness of the movement for home rule should not be confused with hostility to Irish national aspirations as such. Rather, Cullen did not believe that the Irish nationalists of his era offered a realistic or safe alternative. This was particularly true of the Fenians, who offered only a 'libertà alla Mazziniana' in which the church would be persecuted.[49] At times he wondered if the British were fomenting a revolt in order to justify the sort of violent repression they had visited on India or Jamaica. Irish nationalists could not win, would get many killed, and if by chance they did succeed they would prove no better than the anti-clerical Mazzini.

Under Cullen the Irish Catholic Church was manifestly not apolitical. The bishops were prepared to advocate (and allow their clergy to advocate) for what they understood to be Catholic rights, particularly the provision of chaplains in official settings, the relief of the poor, and education at all levels. As these were matters of natural justice and religious freedom, Cullen saw no contradiction in maintaining the ban on clerical political activism. Archbishop MacHale and a handful of others went beyond these limits, and almost all prelates worked to ensure satisfactory outcomes in local elections, but most were content to leave national politics to the archbishop of Dublin. Few priests publicly dissented, and those such as Patrick Lavelle that did usually enjoyed the protection of MacHale. Cullen almost wholly controlled the church's political posture and activity in the 1860s: as the Fenian supporting newspaper *The Irish People* complained in 1865, 'Dr Cullen *is the hierarchy*.'

Cullen preferred to exercise his influence indirectly through Catholic or sympathetic Protestant politicians such as William Monsell, Myles O'Reilly,

---

48 See E. Lucas, *The life of Frederick Lucas, M.P.*, 2 vols. (London: Burns & Oates, 1886), vol. II, p. 145.

49 Cullen to Kirby, 3 Dec. 1863, CP63/316, PICRA.

Sir John Gray and John Blake Dillon. Although important and in some cases influential figures in their own right, Cullen was clearly the dominant partner, even with the former Young Irelander Dillon. Although he preferred indirect influence and quiet negotiation, Cullen was also prepared to take advantage of passing opportunities. In 1857, for example, he privately threatened at the height of the Indian mutiny to compromise British military recruiting in Ireland unless long-standing grievances about chaplaincy provision were addressed, which they promptly were. On issues that he thought within his competence, and above all education, Cullen was willing to engage the government and to punish Catholics who compromised too far. As he told Dillon in 1866, 'we have a right to use spiritual arms in order to preserve the faith'.[50]

In the mid-1860s, Cullen even reluctantly countenanced the creation of a quasi-political party, the National Association, in order to provide a safe outlet for the patriotic feelings stimulated by the Fenians. Too much the archbishop's creature, it was not a popular success, and Cullen returned to his preferred informal alliance with the Liberals. This approach was soon vindicated by what Cullen considered his greatest political triumph: the disestablishment of the Church of Ireland and the dispersal of its endowments. Cullen finally fell out with the Liberals in 1873 over university education, and subsequently worked productively with Disraeli's Conservatives, who consulted him on their Intermediate Education Act of 1878. Under Cullen, the Irish Catholic Church was unprecedentedly powerful and politically active, but only on a narrow ground of its own choosing. The price of this was the absence for nearly twenty years of a substantive constitutional nationalist party, or popular lay political leader. It was only when the Home Government Association emerged (significantly, under Protestant leadership) that a political party enjoyed enough popular support to force Cullen to grant it a wary toleration.

During this long interregnum, love of the papacy and fear for its fate became the outstanding public cause of Catholic Ireland. This manifested itself most strikingly in the surprise Irish victory of the Conservatives in the 1859 general election, despite the bitter anti-Catholic and anti-nationalist character of the party's Irish leaders. As Jennifer O'Brien has pointed out, Irish Catholics voted against their own domestic interests in support of a party thought to be more favourable to the maintenance of the papal states.[51] In London, Irish migrants confronted a pro-Garibaldi crowd with a chorus

---

50 Cullen to Dillon, 6 May 1866, Cullen Letter Book 4/263–5, DDA.
51 J. O'Brien, 'Irish public opinion and the Risorgimento through the eyes of the press, 1859–60' in C. Barr, M. Finelli and A. O'Connor (eds.), *Nation/Nazione: Irish nationalism and the Italian Risorgimento* (Dublin: UCD Press, 2014), pp. 110–30.

of 'God and Rome'. In Galway and Tralee, as Anne O'Connor has noted, visits by the Italian nationalist and anti-Catholic lecturer Alessandro Gavazzi were met by riots.[52] Pro-papal ballads such as Patrick Murray's enduring 'A song for the Pope' became popular, neatly fusing ultramontane devotion and Irish patriotism. In County Kerry, a priest addressing an Irish-speaking crowd asked what they would do if given arms: stick them 'Into the guts of the enemies of the Holy Father' was the reply.[53] Many thousands volunteered to fight for the papal armies, and some thousand actually served. Across the island, the Peter's Pence collection raised nearly £80,000 for the papacy in 1860–1, with even impoverished dioceses raising substantial sums. This was the largest amount ever raised in Ireland, exceeding both O'Connell's 'Catholic rent' and the spectacular first collection for the Catholic University. John Pollard has calculated that by the end of the century Ireland had sent nearly £500,000 to Rome, which was more than the United States, Brazil or Canada.[54]

At home the Cullenite church pursued a more aggressive, a more sectarian and a more socially segregated agenda. The goal was to ensure that Catholics did not mix with Protestants in hospital, in schools, at university, in the workhouse or prison, in bed or in the grave. A Catholic could work with or for a Protestant, and even vote for one, but that was the extent of it. Cullen himself rarely met Protestants except on business and there is a probably apocryphal story that he never dined with one. Mixed marriages were particularly frowned upon and the rules governing them ruthlessly enforced. Proselytism was violently opposed, and Miriam Moffitt has pointed out the extent to which Protestant evangelism drove the church's relief activities, particularly in Dublin where the Society for Irish Church Mission to the Roman Catholics was especially active.

Margaret Aylward's Ladies' Association of Charity of Saint Vincent de Paul (LAC), for example, was founded in 1851 largely to monitor the lives and behaviour of poor urban Catholics in an effort to repel proselytisers, retrieve backsliders and buttress the faith of the weak. As Moffitt has put it: 'they were

52 A. O'Connor, 'An Italian inferno in Ireland: Alessandro Gavazzi and religious debate in the nineteenth century' in N. Carter (ed.), *Britain, Ireland and the Italian Risorgimento* (Basingstoke: Palgrave Macmillan, 2015), pp. 127–50.

53 David Moriarty to Kirby, 14 Dec. 1859, quoted in E. Larkin, *The consolidation of the Roman Catholic Church in Ireland, 1860–1870* (Chapel Hill: University of North Carolina Press, 1987), p. 8.

54 J.F. Pollard, *Money and the rise of the modern Papacy: financing the Vatican, 1850–1950* (Cambridge: Cambridge University Press, 2005), p. 33.

ever watchful at death-beds, providing beads and crucifixes ensuring that the dying would receive the last rites and, above all, would die as Catholics'.[55] Aylward established St Brigid's Orphanage in 1856 largely to prevent Catholic orphans falling into Protestant hands, and was later imprisoned for refusing to return a Catholic child to its mother for fear of its spiritual fate. Aylward enjoyed the enthusiastic support of Cullen, who agreed with her that sinfulness was the result of poverty, not poverty the result of sinfulness. He funded the LAC's provision of food and clothing to the poor, allowed it a place on the annual charity sermon, and twice addressed its annual meeting. He and other bishops were equally generous to similar groups, and Cullen himself was a regular and powerful public voice for the proper treatment of the poor.

Like Daniel Murray, Cullen understood the importance of religious women, and the number of nuns in Ireland surged from around 1,000 in 1850 to more than 3,700 at his death in 1878.[56] Convents were established in almost every town, many with associated schools, refuges or medical facilities. Orders such as the Dominican, Presentation and Loreto sisters also exported members in large numbers to Ireland's spiritual empire, as did the Sisters of Mercy. Although firmly under the overall control of the male hierarchy, these women enjoyed a latitude and scope of operation unprecedented in Ireland and unavailable to all but the most elite or determined laywomen. They managed their own affairs, enjoyed high social status, and built large and complex organisations that stretched across Ireland and beyond. It is little wonder that membership proved attractive to so many Irishwomen.

Conclusion

The explosion in the number of religious women was matched across every facet of the Irish church. In the first twenty years of Cullen's rule, for example, the number of priests increased by some seven hundred while the ratio of priests to people improved from 1:3,300 in 1850 to 1:1,100 in 1870. As with religious women, this was achieved against the backdrop of a substantial export market for Irish clergy. As Emmet Larkin put it, 'cathedrals, churches, chapels, convents, monasteries, seminaries, parochial houses, episcopal palaces, schools, colleges, orphanages, hospitals and asylums all mushroomed in every part of Ireland' in a boom that lasted from Cullen's arrival to the late 1870s.[57]

55 M. Moffit, *The Society for Irish Church Missions to the Roman Catholics, 1849–1950* (Manchester: Manchester University Press, 2010).
56 Larkin, *Historical dimensions*, p. 77.
57 Ibid., p. 27.

Although local variations endured (especially in the west), the Irish church became and remained more uniform, more Roman, more centred on the parish and more responsive to episcopal authority. It also came to enjoy a vastly greater capacity and appetite for imposing social controls on its flock. Politically, it remained powerful but constrained within its self-imposed boundaries until Cullen could no longer contain popular enthusiasm for constitutional nationalism. Under Cullen, the Irish church also pursued a surprisingly moderate course. As Joe Lee has put it: 'the most piously popular religion in northern Europe eschewed the spirit of the Syllabus of Errors and remained politically pragmatic'. This was largely, Lee concluded, the work of 'Paul the Prudent'.[58] In re-engergising his church, Cullen created modern Irish Catholicism out of the wreckage of famine and internal division. Paul Cullen did not make the great mass of the Irish people into practising Catholics, but he went a long way towards making them Roman Catholics.

58 J. Lee, *The modernisation of Irish Society, 1848–1918* (Dublin: Gill & Macmillan, 1989 [1973]), p. 49.

12

Protestant Dissenters, *c.*1690–1800

IAN MCBRIDE

Introduction

No constituent of eighteenth-century Irish society was more dynamic than its Presbyterian population. The century after the battles of the Boyne and Aughrim is traditionally portrayed as the era of Protestant Ascendancy and, increasingly, an age of 'endurance and emergence' for Catholics. But it was also a period of spectacular advances for Presbyterians, whether measured in terms of demographic strength, economic and social power, political ambition or intellectual vitality. Ulster Presbyterians made seminal contributions to three major eighteenth-century inventions with an enduring and controversial legacy: the philosophical ferment of the Enlightenment, the United States of America and Irish republicanism. They shared the same experiences as their Anglican and Catholic contemporaries – famine and economic growth, transatlantic migration, warfare, revolution and counter-revolution. They also attracted an extraordinary amount of hostility and suspicion from the authorities at the beginning of the century and again at its close: to their critics, 'Dissenter' was synonymous with 'republican', and many of their local communities would be shattered by the brutal repression that followed the 1798 rebellion.

What made Presbyterians different – and what made them distrusted – was their refusal to conform to the established church. There were other Protestant nonconformists, originating in the great upheavals of the English Civil Wars (Quakers, Independents) or refugees from Catholic aggression on the continent (French Huguenots, German Palatines). But these microgroups rarely troubled the government or interested the political economists who anatomised Ireland's demography, agriculture and commerce. The Presbyterians formed a large and cohesive bloc. Their numerical strength meant that the terms 'Presbyterian' and 'Dissenter' were used interchangeably. Since they were subject to legal disabilities as well as social disadvantages, the Presbyterians formed a distinct political unit – the 'Dissenting interest' – as well as a confessional community. As in England, their religious traditions and their experience of political exclusion made them natural Whigs in politics, and they became enthusiastic supporters of parliamentary reform, the movement for American independence and the French Revolution.

The Presbyterian Revolution

The 1690s to the 1720s was an age of revolutionary change. Political controversy raged for three decades over the meaning of the upheavals of 1688–9, when James II was overthrown and his crown seized by William of Orange. This 'Glorious Revolution' had apparently delivered England, Scotland and Ireland from the conjoined evils of popery and slavery; henceforth the three kingdoms were constituents of a limited monarchy in which power was shared between king, lords and commons. Just as unsettling was the altered relationship between church and state, with Toleration Acts in England (1689) and Ireland (1719) guaranteeing legal protection for Protestant Dissenters; in Scotland, meanwhile, Presbyterianism was re-established in 1690 and underwritten by the Anglo-Scottish Union of 1707. European wars, waged with unprecedented intensity, saw the Protestant succession defended against the might of Louis XIV's France, at the price of massive strains at home. Finally, this domestic and international turmoil coincided with the intellectual upheavals that Paul Hazard once called 'the crisis of the European mind', as the defenders of confessional orthodoxy struggled to reconcile traditional Christian doctrine with the innovations of Locke and Newton.

Alongside these dramatic developments there took place what might be called the Presbyterian revolution in the north of Ireland, as the infrastructure of Presbyterian discipline was established, with congregational sessions, presbyteries and synods meeting openly for the first time.[1] In the fierce pamphlet warfare of Queen Anne's reign (1702–14), the strategy pursued by Presbyterian apologists was to portray these two revolutions – the overthrow of Stuart absolutism and the confident self-assertion of Ulster Presbyterianism – as mutually dependent. In a sermon published to mark the accession of George I, James Kirkpatrick of Belfast boasted that the Scots colony in the north was 'the *Great Bulwark* of the Protestant Interest in the

---

1 R. Gillespie, 'The Presbyterian revolution in Ulster, 1660–1690' in W.J. Sheils and D. Wood (eds.), *The churches, Ireland and the Irish*, Studies in Church History 25 (Oxford: Blackwell, 1989), pp. 159–70.

Nation'.[2] In part, the argument was a pragmatic one. The celebrated Siege of Derry had demonstrated the central value of the Ulster Scots as a counterweight to Jacobite ambition. Subsequently, the invasion threats and militia arrays of 1708, 1715 and 1719 presented Dissenters with regular opportunities to vaunt their loyalty and assert their territorial predominance. In February 1716, indeed, Presbyterian militiamen not only flaunted their right to bear arms, but also organised a series of house searches, seizing the weapons of Anglican clergymen whose loyalties they considered suspect.[3]

It was not only their numbers that recommended the Presbyterians to government, but also their political orientation. Dissenting clergymen depicted the events of 1688 as an act of popular resistance against a tyrannical monarch. They exhibited none of the inhibitions and equivocations of their Anglican counterparts. When Kirkpatrick and others denounced 'the slavish Doctrines of the *Unlimited, irresistible* power of Princes, [and] their *Hereditary, Divine, indefeasible* Right', they were not merely advertising their political reliability; they sought also to embarrass their Tory neighbours.[4] Scots Presbyterians had a long history of resisting and coercing their monarchs. The legal harassment of Dissenters in Ireland ebbed and flowed with the electoral strength of Tories at Westminster, peaking in 1702–4 and 1710–14. Consequently there were strong incentives for Presbyterians in all three kingdoms to emphasise their ideological affinities with the constitutionalism of the English Whigs, whose dominance at Westminster owed more to the support of the new Hanoverian dynasty than to electoral majorities. The flipside of this bid for metropolitan respectability was a willingness to repudiate the militant, sectarian vestiges of the seventeenth-century Scots Covenanting tradition, represented in extreme form by the Solemn League and Covenant of 1643, which had attempted to impose a Presbyterian settlement on Charles I and all three of his kingdoms.

Perhaps the most striking thing about Irish Presbyterians during the three decades after the Williamite war was the suspicion, resentment and contempt with which they were regarded by the ruling elite. This is a remarkable fact. In London, and particularly under the Whig ministries favoured by the Hanoverians, the received wisdom was that the Dublin parliament should 'put

---

2 J. Kirkpatrick, *God's dominion over kings and other magistrates* (Belfast: James Blow, 1714), pp. 23–4.
3 *The insolence of the Dissenters against the Established Church* (London: J. Baker and T. Warner, 1716), esp. pp. 3–10.
4 Kirkpatrick, *God's dominion over kings*, pp. 19–20.

an end to all other Distinctions in *Ireland*, but that of *Protestant* and *Papist*'.[5] Given the religious demography of Ireland, where Catholics outnumbered Protestants by four to one, calls for solidarity might seem like common sense. 'Popery', moreover, was not merely a corruption of true religion. Its defining feature was violence. A crowded calendar of royal and military anniversaries observed in cities and towns reminded Protestant congregations of the sufferings their brethren had endured under Catholic domination, both at home and abroad, and of the characteristic method by which Rome propagated its slavish doctrines: the massacre. Each year, Irish Protestants commemorated the rebellion of 1641, when settlers in Ulster had been stripped naked and exposed to death by cold and hunger, or herded into barns and houses and burned alive, or driven off bridges and drowned. The resilience of Catholic ecclesiastical structures, the existence of a Stuart court-in-exile on the continent, sheltered by Britain's Catholic enemies, the periodic threat of invasion by France or Spain all fuelled fears of another 1641. The size of Ireland's Catholic majority, as the Earl of Wharton observed in May 1709, demanded not only the reinforcement of the penal code, but also measures to consolidate 'a good Understanding amongst all the *Protestants* of this Kingdom'.[6] The inevitable price of conciliation was the admission of Dissenters to the small share of civil and military offices appropriate to their social and economic position. But every concession along these lines was bitterly opposed by members of the established Church of Ireland.

Presbyterians were not subject to 'penal laws' but neither were they part of the system of privilege now known as Protestant Ascendancy. The House of Commons, the pinnacle of Ascendancy power, was never legally closed to Protestant Dissenters, although in practice there was only ever a handful of MPs from Dissenting backgrounds. Unlike Catholics, they were not excluded from the franchise, or denied that equally important mark of citizenship, the right to bear arms. Direct interference with their capacity to acquire and inherit property was unthinkable. Provided they were willing to take the oath of allegiance, their right to worship freely was guaranteed by the 1719 Toleration Act. They even received a modest state subsidy – the *regium donum* – to assist them in doing so. Following the Hanoverian succession, Whigs monopolised political power in London and therefore in Dublin, with the result that legislative attempts to restrict Presbyterian worship or education

---

5 *His Grace Charles Duke of Grafton, and His Excellency Henry Earl of Gallway, Lords Justices General and General Governors of Ireland: their speech to both Houses of Parliament* (Dublin: Andrew Crooke, 1715).

6 *Journals of the House of Lords*, 8 vols. (Dublin: William Sleater, 1779–1800), vol. II, p. 244.

ceased. But attempts to ameliorate the legal position of Presbyterians were consistently defeated in the Irish parliament, and the Toleration Act was whittled down to the bare minimum. The remaining restrictions – such as the authorities' refusal to recognise Dissenting marriages as valid – were now all the more galling.

Official hostility to Dissent was fuelled partly by the migration of tens of thousands of Scots to Ulster in the 1690s. In the 1730s the Revd John Abernethy claimed confidently that there were some 216,000 Dissenters in the northern province, which represented just over a third of the Ulster total, and around a tenth of the Irish population.[7] Ulster maintained a higher growth rate than the other provinces between the 1740s and 1790s of around 2 per cent per annum, closely linked to the expansion of the domestic linen industry. In the 1780s the Revd William Campbell calculated that there were 72,000 Presbyterian families in the north, amounting to somewhere between 360,000 and 432,000 souls, depending on whether the average family size was five or six; to this figure he added 82,000 members of the breakaway Secession congregations.[8] From the 1790s, however, Ulster's position as the most demographically vibrant province was superseded as growth rates fell to 1.1 per annum. Local studies suggest that the Presbyterian numbers grew particularly slowly from this point, and in some areas suffered absolute as well as relative decline.[9]

The territorial concentration of 'Scotch' Presbyterians in Ulster encouraged their assertiveness and fuelled the sense of confidence and frustrated entitlement that characterised their behaviour. Their dynamism as a social force was combined with the efficient pyramid structure of church courts or 'sessions', presbyteries and synods, which, some Anglicans felt, amounted to a subversive state within the state. Session books show how congregations attempted to maintain sexual discipline in their localities at a time when the new market economy based on linen manufacture promoted greater mobility. Kirk sessions heard complaints of women remaining at fairs at 'unseasonable hours' or staying out all night 'drinking with idle persons'. Too many, it was feared, were consorting with wool combers, 'strollers' and 'yearn merchants'.

---

7 J. Abernethy, *Scarce and valuable tracts and sermons* (London: R. Griffiths, 1751), p. 61.

8 W. Campbell, 'Journal' (Dec. 1783), pp. 3–4, Presbyterian History Society of Ireland, Belfast.

9 L. Kennedy, K.A. Miller and B. Gurrin, 'People and population change, 1600–1914' in L. Kennedy and P. Ollerenshaw (eds.), *Ulster since 1600: politics, economy, and society* (Oxford: Oxford University Press, 2013), pp. 70–1; D. Dickson, C. Ó. Gráda and S. Daultrey, 'Hearth tax, household size and Irish population change 1672–1821', *Proceedings of the Royal Irish Academy*, 82c (1982), 155.

In 1704, a woman was called before the session of Connor for marrying a soldier 'upon Shane castle fare day [at] the back of a hedge with a priest'. Patrick Griffin, who has used these session books to best effect, has pointed out that congregants often sought to cheat congregational discipline by appealing to the civil magistrate or the bishop's court. In 1713, for example, Richard Berry defied the kirk session of Burt, County Donegal, by bringing a colourful accusation of slander before the local justice of the peace. According to one of his fellow congregants, Berry was supposed to have said that he had no need of a mistress 'for he had milked himself over the bed-stock by taking his yeard in his hand or between his fingers and thumb'. Berry was so enraged that he pursued a legal remedy rather than 'stand to the determination of the session'. A few years earlier another man compared the proceedings of the Burt session to the 'heathens and pagans and the conclave of Rome'.[10] The same messy reality is evident in session books from other Ulster congregations, but these internal commotions were invisible to Anglicans; they saw only the rapid increase of Presbyterian congregations, punishing their fornicators, Sabbath-breakers and other backsliders, while the episcopal courts, which had taken for granted the full backing of the state, were experiencing the sudden shock of powerlessness.

The Presbyterian Enlightenment

The decades between the 1720s and the 1770s witnessed the intellectual and cultural transformations we now think of as the Enlightenment. That term had not yet been invented, admittedly, but contemporaries were certainly aware that they lived in an 'enlightened age'. They took pride in the scientific achievements of Newton, which apparently proved the existence of a harmonious universe presided over by a benevolent God. Many hoped that the application of scientific methods might also disclose the laws governing human behaviour, and the various forms of our political and social organisation. The most brilliant and subversive philosopher of the Scottish Enlightenment, David Hume, demonstrated how moral systems, and even religion itself, could be understood as merely human constructs. But most enlighteners, like Hume's most celebrated precursor, the celebrated Francis Hutcheson, took it for granted that the truths of Christianity, once purged of

---

10 P. Griffin, *The people with no name: Ireland's Ulster Scots, America's Scots Irish, and the creation of a British Atlantic World, 1689–1764* (Princeton: Princeton University Press, 2001), pp. 40–3.

superstitions and false notions, would clarify and reinforce the basis for moral and religious belief.

Hutcheson's importance as a foundational figure of the Scottish Enlightenment is now generally recognised. He was not, however, a Scot, but signed himself as 'Scoto-Hibernus' in the matriculation album at Glasgow, where he studied between 1710 and 1718, and where he became a hugely popular professor of moral philosophy between 1730 and 1746. The culture of the Scottish universities is as vital to the history of Ulster Presbyterians in the eighteenth century as the continental seminaries were to Catholic Ireland. Excluded from Trinity College Dublin until 1793, Irish Presbyterians sent their sons to Glasgow and, to a lesser extent, to Edinburgh for their training in the arts, medicine and, of course, divinity. These *Scoto-Hiberni* dominated the intellectual life of Presbyterian Ulster, and as Scots-Irish emigrants to North America they became exporters of enlightenment to the colonies.[11] The common sense philosopher Thomas Reid estimated that 'near a third' of the four or five hundred students who went to Glasgow University came from Ireland. He dismissed them as 'stupid Irish teagues' who attended classes for two or three years to qualify as school teachers.[12] This was unfair. Irish Presbyterians accounted for almost a sixth of those who signed the matriculation register between 1690 and 1820 but a much higher proportion of those who went on to graduate: from 24 per cent in the 1750s, the Irish proportion of graduates rose to 46 per cent in the sixties; it peaked at 47 per cent in the seventies and thercafter gradually declined.[13]

The most basic feature of Hutcheson's thought was his unusually positive depiction of human existence. Look inside yourself, Hutcheson told his readers, examine the world around, and you will discover that happiness outweighs suffering, that benevolence and compassion come naturally, while real malice is rare; that we act to help others, not because of any perceived advantage to ourselves, but because we *feel* it is right to do so. We derive spontaneous pleasure and fulfilment from following the impulses of our 'moral sense' – a concept that Hutcheson spent his most creative period elaborating and defending against his critics. Human beings are designed in such a way that they desire to promote the common good, and work instinctively

---

11 D. Sloan, *The Scottish Enlightenment and the American college ideal* (New York: Teachers College Press, 1971), chapter 2.
12 Reid to Andrew Skene, 14 Nov. 1764, *The works of Thomas Reid, D.D.*, ed. William Hamilton, 2nd edn (Edinburgh: McLachlan, Stewart, 1849), pp. 40–3.
13 I.M. Bishop, 'The education of Ulster students at Glasgow University during the eighteenth century', MA thesis, Queen's University Belfast, 1987.

towards 'the greatest happiness for the greatest numbers'. It is our very concern for the well-being of others that creates the gravest problems for Hutchesonian man, since we cannot help but get depressed when we see our fellow men suffer. The fact that humans are subject to error, together with the stubborn persistence of pain and loss in this world, means that the spontaneous responses of the moral sense are not always, on their own, sufficient to guarantee a life of virtue and happiness. They must be reinforced by our broader understanding of God's creation and our belief in the rewards and punishments of the next world: 'belief of a Deity, a Providence, and a future state, are the only sure supports to a good mind'.[14]

It was Hutcheson's determination to prove that the process of moral judgment is really based on sentiment, rather than reason, that so impressed David Hume and his own pupil Adam Smith. But his cult status at Glasgow depended less on the technicalities of moral-sense theory than his contributions to a new language of morality, drawn primarily from the classical world and especially the Stoics, and fused with the new 'science of man'. Hutcheson was an early exponent of the experimental method: as a close friend explained, his ambition was to examine 'the various natural principles or natural dispositions of mankind, in the same way that we enquire into the structure of an animal body, of a plant or of the solar system'.[15] If this sounds dry, it should be remembered that Hutcheson wanted to turn philosophy away from scholastic disputes and towards the 'ordinary human affairs' of an increasingly commercial society. We can find 'more virtuous action in the life of one diligent good-natured trader', he remarked, 'than in a whole sect of such speculative pretenders to wisdom'.[16] The point of philosophy, as the ancients had known, was to make us feel better about ourselves, but contemporary moralists, Hutcheson complained, were 'sour and morose'.[17] It was time to lighten up.

Two other emphases in Hutcheson's teaching both reflected and powerfully reinforced tendencies in Irish Dissent. One was his eloquent and expansive treatment of the right of resistance. A crucial chapter in his *System of moral philosophy* (1755) acknowledged that there was often a 'popular outcry'

---

14 J.A. Harris, 'Religion in Hutcheson's moral philosophy', *Journal of the History of Philosophy*, 46:2 (2008), 214–15.

15 W. Leechman, 'Preface' in F. Hutcheson, *A system of moral philosophy*, 2 vols. (Glasgow: R. and A. Foulis, 1755), vol. I, p. xiv.

16 T. Mautner (ed.), *Francis Hutcheson on human nature* (Cambridge: Cambridge University Press, 1993), p. 105.

17 Ibid., p. 97.

against theories of resistance, which were held responsible for civil disturbances. In fact, he countered, it was the proponents of absolutism who had
produced unrest by encouraging rulers to exceed the limits of legitimate
power. Even where rebellion was perfectly justified, human beings were so
risk-averse, and so attached to traditional structures, that it was difficult to
rally a sufficient number to attempt the violent overthrow of an established
ruler. 'Mankind have generally been a great deal too tame and tractable', he
concluded, 'hence so many wretched forms of power have always enslaved
nine-tenths of the nations of the world, where they have the fullest rights
to make all efforts for a change.'[18] Both Hutcheson's distinctive moral-sense
theory and his views of resistance were recycled in the political sermons of
his Irish disciples.[19]

Another key section of the *System* explored the right of private judgment.
'Every rational creature' has the right, and indeed has a duty, to interpret
the Bible for themselves. Since men cannot make themselves agree to a proposition that conflicts with the evidence as they find it, 'this right is plainly
unalienable'.[20] The *System* echoed the psychological argument put forward
in Locke's *Letter concerning toleration* (1689). The magistrate had no right to
inflict penalties on those who refused to conform to the established religion,
because sincere belief could only be formed by reasoning and persuasion.
These mental processes were beyond the reach of state coercion, which
merely multiplied the number of hypocrites. Penal Laws were thus 'mon-
strous usurpations on the most sacred rights of all rational beings'.[21] Like all
political theorists, Hutcheson acknowledged that the magistrate had a right
to restrain opinions which undermined the political and social order. But in
a revealing footnote, he stipulated that magistrates had no business intervening in the interminable controversies between Calvinists and Arminians.
Nor should they concern themselves with squabbles over the doctrine of the
Trinity. In all these factions Hutcheson recognised the core Christian doctrines, 'the same motives to all social virtues from a belief of a moral providence, the same acknowledgements that the goodness of God is the source
of all the good we enjoy'. None of their principles incited disorder, he concluded, 'except that horrid tenet too common to most of them, the right of
persecuting'.[22]

18 Hutcheson, *System of moral philosophy*, vol. II, p. 280.
19 For a good example, see A. Maclaine, *A sermon preached at Antrim, Dec. 18, 1745, being the National Fast* (Dublin: A. Reilly, 1746), pp. 23, 11.
20 Hutcheson, *System of moral philosophy*, vol. II, p. 311.
21 Ibid., vol. II, p. 311.
22 Ibid., vol. II, p. 316 note.

Hutcheson's mission in Scotland was to promote 'more moderate and charitable sentiments in religious matters'.[23] As one of his Scottish pupils recalled, he also brought to Scotland an 'aversion to subscription' – opposition, that is, to the requirement that all candidates for the Presbyterian ministry subscribe to the Westminster Confession of Faith.[24] The crucial period for Hutcheson's theological commitments, and for his philosophical writings, was the 1720s, when he was master of a Dissenting academy in Dublin. The Irish capital contained half a dozen substantial Presbyterian congregations, accounting for a significant section of the city's tradesmen, shopkeepers and artisans. They were supplied largely by 'Scots' ministers from Ulster. In 1719, however, their peace was shattered by an incendiary sermon entitled *Religious obedience founded on personal persuasion* by John Abernethy of Antrim, and the furious reaction it provoked. Interestingly, Abernethy's sermon was published in London as well as Belfast, an indication of the cosmopolitan orientation of its author; and it was English rather than Scottish intellectual influences that shaped the latitudinarian strain of theology which became known as 'New Light' and the series of dramatic clashes over the practice of subscription to the Westminster Confession of Faith.

Abernethy's quarrel was not so much with the Calvinist doctrines contained in the Confession as with the right of ecclesiastical authorities to compel professions of belief. For Presbyterians the church was a spiritual kingdom, a corporate body comprised of its own assemblies and courts, administered in the name of a divine king, entirely separate and distinct from the temporal kingdom of the civil magistrate. Not only was Christ the king and lawgiver of the church, but he was its *only* king and lawgiver, and the interference of human authorities in the government of his kingdom was regarded as a usurpation of his power. The old term for such usurpers, derived from biblical prophecy, was antichrist. In common with most Protestants, Presbyterians believed that the Church of Rome was an antichristian force because it had replaced scripture with human tradition. That the papacy was antichrist, Abernethy thought, was 'beyond all rational contradiction'. But it was also possible to think of antichrist in more abstract terms as the use of persecution to enforce uniformity; Abernethy emphasised that the Protestant churches retained within them much of 'the spirit of popery'.[25]

---

23 See Francis Hutcheson to Thomas Steward, 12 Feb. 1740, MS 64, f. 279, Magee College, Derry.
24 Alexander Carlyle quoted in C. Kidd, 'Subscription, the Scottish Enlightenment and the moderate interpretation of history', *Journal of Ecclesiastical History*, 55:3 (2004), 517.
25 J. Abernethy, *A sermon recommending the study of scripture-prophecie* (Belfast: James Blow, 1716), pp. 12, 17.

Abernethy and his New Light brethren were taking the key principles of reformed religion – the sufficiency of scripture, the right of private judgment, and 'the sole dominion of Christ in his own kingdom' – and turning them against the Synod of Ulster itself.[26] There was some justice in the horrified reaction of conservatives, who regarded the non-subscribers as 'a sett of men . . . pretend[ing] to give new light to the world, by putting *personal perswasion* in the room of Church government and discipline'.[27] But the argument that the imposition of any human creed or confession infringed upon the individual's right of self-determination was directed not just at the Presbyterian clergy but at the Anglican confessional state. For the civil magistrate to enforce religious uniformity by earthly rewards and penalties jeopardises 'the *sincerity* of obedience, and consequently is a real prejudice to true religion'.[28] It is hardly a coincidence that objections to subscription took shape during the protracted struggle for the repeal of the test which ended in failure in 1719. It is also possible that the dispute over ministerial subscription to creeds was catalysed by the behind-the-scenes negotiations over the terms of the Toleration Act. An early version of the toleration bill, discussed in July 1719, granted legal security to Dissenters on condition that they subscribed all but three of the Thirty-Nine Articles, and the Nicene and Apostolic Creeds, and were prepared 'to own yᵉ Trinity and Divinity of yᵉ Saviour'.[29]

Periodically, New Light ministers were accused of being closet Arians, an ancient label for those who believed that Christ was a lesser divinity than God the Father. The implications of such theological deviance were grave. Denial of the Trinity was blasphemy and liable to punishment by the civil authorities, as the Revd Thomas Emlyn of Wood Street, Dublin, discovered when his *Humble inquiry into the scripture account of Jesus Christ* (1702) resulted in a fine of £1,000 and two years in prison. He was ostracised by his Presbyterian brethren. The clergy detested Arianism because it was not obviously reconcilable with the radical contrast between human depravity and divine omnipotence that was so basic to the Protestant Reformation. Orthodox Presbyterians maintained that an unbridgeable chasm separated man from God. The sole means of salvation was the imputation of Christ's righteousness to the sinner,

26 J. Duchal, *A sermon on occasion of the much lamented death of the Late Reverend Mr John Abernethy* (Belfast: James Blow, 1741), pp. 48–62.

27 J. Malcome, *Personal perswasion no foundation for religious obedience* (Belfast: Robert Gardner, 1720), p. [4].

28 J. Abernethy, *Religious obedience founded on personal persuasion* (Belfast: James Blow, 1720), p. 23.

29 [Bishop Evans] to [Wake], 9 July 1719, Wake MS, Christ Church, Oxford.

a unilateral act in which fallen man was essentially passive. The election of the saved and the damnation of the rest was the apparently arbitrary decision of an unfathomable God. But without the full divinity of Christ it was not clear that he could give full satisfaction for human sin. By 1718 rumours were circulating in Dublin that Samuel Clarke's *The scripture-doctrine of the Trinity* (1712), a carefully reasoned, comprehensive work of scholarship, setting out the discrepancies between the orthodox doctrine and the actual contents of the New Testament, had 'made several unfixed in their old opinions'.[30]

Perhaps some of the New Light ministers really concluded that Christ was a sort of super-angelic being, as Isaac Newton believed, occupying a unique rung on an elaborate ladder of celestial beings.[31] The notion that the Father, Son and Holy Ghost formed a single divine being was impenetrable at the best of times, and its complex entanglements with scholastic philosophy had not made it more digestible. The various passages of Scripture relating to Christ's human and divine characteristics are not easily reduced to a coherent viewpoint. No doubt some determined readers came honestly to the Arian conclusion that Christ was *pre*-existent (created before the world) but not *self*-existent (as only God the Creator could be). Arianism was sometimes the first step on a slippery slope towards Socinianism, which held that Christ was straightforwardly human; these views appeared to fit with the general assault on metaphysical reasoning characteristic of the Enlightenment. If they speculated along these lines there is little sign of it in their public or private reflections. But the tendency of New Light preaching was to present Jesus not as a mediator between corrupt man and his creator, but as a moral exemplar, rather like one of the conscientious but companionable professors of moral philosophy in enlightened Glasgow and Edinburgh who inspired in their students just and lively sentiments of human virtues and of the perfections of God.

We have already seen that happiness was one of the buzzwords favoured by Hutcheson. It has been claimed, indeed, that the famous phrase 'life, liberty and the pursuit of happiness' in the Declaration of Independence reflects the influence of his former students and readers in the American colonies.[32]

---

30 William Wright to Robert Wodrow, 27 Sept. 1718, Wodrow Letters, Qu. xx, f. 228, National Library of Scotland (henceforth NLS).
31 M. Wiles, *Archetypal heresy: Arianism through the centuries* (Oxford: Oxford University Press, 1996), chapter 4.
32 G. Wills finds echoes of Hutcheson in the Declaration of Independence in *Inventing America: Jefferson's Declaration of Independence* (New York: Doubleday, 1978), esp. pp. 192–205, 228–39, 250–5.

But what did it really mean, for Hutcheson and his followers, to be happy? A considerable amount of scattered correspondence still survives from the Glasgow professor and the 'numerous set of old comerads and kinsmen' he visited in Ireland.[33] They included Thomas Drennan, his assistant at the Dissenting Academy in Dublin, and subsequently minister of First Belfast; his cousin William Bruce, printer, bookseller and the political spokesman for the Dissenting interest up to the 1750s; the essayist James Arbuckle, whose 'Letters of Hibernicus' aspired to bring literary taste and polite culture to Dublin; and the prolific clerics Abernethy and Duchal, who established the 'New Light' theology that characterised the eighteenth-century Presbyterian pulpit. Collectively, they come across as an attractive bunch: they were warm and affectionate with each other, gregarious, good-humoured and worldly. Like Hutcheson, they seem to have celebrated 'the delights of humanity, good nature, kindness, mutual love, friendships, [and] societies of virtuous persons'.[34] But they exhibit none of the emotional or psychological drama associated with 'vital' religion. One thing noticeably missing from their writings is any sense that an encounter with Jesus Christ could be a transformative experience.

The Limits of the New Light

In Ireland enlightenment and evangelicalism were oil and water. Confidence in the efficacy of Christ's saving grace required certainty about his full divinity. Evangelicals emphasised 'spiritual conflict, the active agency of the Devil, individual sinfulness in all its intensity and virulence, the possibility of redemption through and only through faith in Jesus Christ, and the certainty of future Judgement'.[35] This vital religion takes us a long way from Hutcheson's minimalist characterisation of Christianity as 'a religion which gives us the truest idea of virtue, and recommends the love of God, and of mankind'.[36] The God of the Enlightenment didn't go about intervening in history or communicating with earthlings. He had already equipped humans with the means of grasping the basic moral structure of the universe, if only they could free themselves from superstition and priestcraft. It makes sense to think of Hutcheson as a *practical* Arian or Socinian, if not a theoretical one.

---

33 Hutcheson to Lord Minto, 4 July 1744, Minto Papers, MS 11004, f. 57, NLS.
34 Mautner (ed.), *Francis Hutcheson on human nature*, p. 105.
35 B. Hilton, *A mad, bad, and dangerous people? England 1783–1846* (Oxford: Oxford University Press, 2006), p. 176.
36 Harris, 'Religion in Hutcheson's moral philosophy', p. 221, n.45.

His teaching stressed the indispensability of a providential scheme and hopes of an afterlife to a virtuous life, but he never recommended the core Calvinist doctrines of grace, atonement or election. One notably sophisticated and original study of his writings finds it difficult 'to see why it would matter to the virtuous agent as described by Hutcheson whether or not Christ is to be regarded as consubstantial with God the Father, or indeed as divine in any sense at all'.[37]

The urbanity of the New Light men and their defence of religious freedom have made them attractive to modern readers. In contrast their Old Light rivals have received less attention, both because they published less, and because what they did publish was less readable. But did the theological liberals really have a monopoly on enlightenment? It has been pointed out recently that some evangelicals of the early nineteenth century subscribed to notions of progress and improvement; they were intellectually serious and self-consciously rational. So far, however, the evidence produced to suggest that orthodox Presbyterians combined evangelical doctrines with enlightenment language has been thin; more obviously, it involves a very hazy idea of what the Enlightenment actually meant.[38] Enlightenment defined itself by way of a contrast with the darkness from which it had emerged. To the extent that it was not just a mood but a movement of ideas, it was given direction by its hostility to intolerance and persecution.[39] 'Popery' was of course the paradigm case. But a major theme of the Protestant Enlightenment in the Dutch Republic, Geneva, England and North America was the series of interrelated campaigns fought for the right of private judgment against the man-made creeds imposed by earlier generations of reformers. In Scotland the dominant 'Moderate' party in the Kirk avoided open confrontation with the guardians of subscription. With their usual self-satisfaction, the professors of Edinburgh and Glasgow suggested instead that allowances must be made for the fact that the Westminster Confession was framed in an era of narrow fanaticism

---

37 Ibid., p. 221.
38 A. Holmes, 'Tradition and Enlightenment: conversion and assurance of salvation in Ulster Presbyterianism, 1700–1859' in M. Brown et al. (eds.), *Converts and conversion in Ireland, 1650–1850* (Dublin: Four Courts Press, 2005), pp. 129–56. Holmes does not engage with the very extensive historiography on the Enlightenment in the British world (e.g. the standard works by Pocock, Porter, Robertson) with its strong emphasis on the importance of Protestant heterodoxy.
39 For an influential statement of this case see J.G.A. Pocock, 'Clergy and commerce: the conservative Enlightenment in England' in R. Ajello (ed.), *L'Età dei Lumi: studi storici sul settecento Europeo in onore di Franco Venturi*, 2 vols. (Naples: Jovene, 1985), vol. I, pp. 523–62; J.G.A. Pocock, 'Enthusiasm: the antiself of Enlightenment', *Huntington Library Quarterly*, 60:1–2 (1997), 7–28.

and imperfect knowledge. It was a fundamental assumption of the Scottish Enlightenment that theology, 'like other sciences, marched in step with the recent progress of the European mind'.[40] Christianity was a work in progress.

The limitations of the New Light persuasion become apparent when it is considered as a social phenomenon as well as a theological trend. A visitor to Belfast in the 1750s found that 'the richer people' were all New Light and most of the others were Old Light or Catholics.[41] On closer inspection, the division was never quite so clear-cut. Belfast's Third Congregation, formed in the 1720s by opponents of the New Light tendency, was built by the leading merchant Samuel Smith, who raised money in Glasgow and Edinburgh, as well as locally, for the erection of a meeting-house. But social tensions often revealed themselves in the fierce polemics between New Light and Old. Thus Hutcheson rather spoiled his eloquent defence of the right of private judgment by remarking that 'scarce one in an hundred' actually bothered to exercise it, either because they were too lazy or because of the inescapable drudgery that characterised the lives of the masses. This elitism was wholly in keeping with New Light assumptions. There is little evidence to suggest that the non-subscribers viewed the enlightenment of the common people as possible, or even desirable. At the other end of the Dissenter spectrum, we find Francis Pringle warning his fellow Seceder ministers to keep things plain and simple in the pulpit, and to avoid 'the embellishments of polite style'. After all, he explained, 'the souls of the poor and unlearned are of equal value with the souls of the learned and the rich'.[42] Financial hardship was the inevitable price the Seceders paid for ministering to the lower sorts. In 1791, for example, it was reported that the congregation of Lylehill (Antrim) was £74 in arrears and paid a stipend of only £30 annually, that Roseyards (Antrim) owed £150 and Markethill (Armagh) £67, and that Gilnahirk (Down) was three years in arrears.[43]

If the Enlightenment requires careful definition, the same is true of evangelicalism. In both Ulster and Scotland, 'evangelical' is a retrospective term that can only be applied to conservatives within the Synod and their Secession rivals with some difficulty. The two outstanding scholars in the field are at

---

40 Kidd, 'Subscription', 511.

41 R.W.M. Strain, *Belfast and its Charitable Society* (Oxford: Oxford University Press, 1961), p. 11.

42 F. Pringle, *The Gospel Ministry, an ordinance of Christ; and the duty of ministers and people* (n.p., 1796), pp. 18–20.

43 D. Stewart, *The Seceders in Ireland with annals of their congregations* (Belfast: Presbyterian Historical Society, 1950), p. 97.

odds on precisely this issue. Andrew Holmes has produced an impressive body of work asserting the theological and pastoral continuities between the Old Light party and the Seceders, who between them commanded the loyalties of a large majority of Presbyterians, and the evangelicals who came to dominate the Synod in the 1820s. The alternative, what we might call the discontinuity thesis, is that of David W. Miller, who insists that the Old Light were 'confessionalist' rather than conversionist. Miller has suggested that subscription, and other means of policing the orthodoxy of clergymen, constituted rituals of 'lay harassment' that gave agency to ordinary hearers; confessional rectitude thus provided an Ulster-Scots equivalent of the rituals of revivalism that were to be found in the American colonies, complete with their trances, physical convulsions and altered states of consciousness.[44] Miller tends to explain changes in religious systems in terms of the social functions they serve, while Holmes prefers to reconstruct the beliefs and experiences of Presbyterians with sympathy and sensitivity, provided they are not liberals. The trouble is that no serious investigation of the eighteenth-century Old Light has ever been attempted, and so neither view has been backed up by detailed empirical research. Closer inspection is almost certain to reveal that the Old Light was less moribund than historians have assumed. On the other hand, two of the accepted characteristics of evangelical religion – the emphasis on personal conversion and religious and social activism – seem present in eighteenth-century Ulster only in very weak form.

It should be stressed that the theological disputes discussed above were not confined to the clerical intelligentsia. That much is clear from the unusually high turnout of elders at the annual synods of the 1720s and from the number of congregations that split over the issue of subscription. Yet we know hardly anything about how doctrinal issues were interpreted by the ordinary country folk who made up the vast majority of the Presbyterian population. A rare insight comes from the recollections of the United Irishman John Caldwell (1769–1850), who grew up in the market town of Ballymoney, and moved to Belfast in 1784. The Ballymoney congregation was composed mostly of Calvinists, he recalled, but there were also 'an enlightened few, who had the temerity to presume to think for themselves'.[45] As he grew up Caldwell joined

---

44 D.W. Miller, 'Religious commotions in the Scottish diaspora: a transatlantic perspective on "evangelicalism" in a mainline denomination' in D.A. Wilson and M.G. Spencer (eds.), *Ulster Presbyterians in the Atlantic World: religion, politics and identity* (Dublin: Four Courts Press, 2006), pp. 22–38.

45 J. Caldwell, 'Particulars of a north county Irish family', p. 80, Caldwell papers, T3541/5/3, Public Record Office of Northern Ireland.

his father, a prosperous farmer and linen manufacturer, in private conversations with the local minister, in which some of the doctrines contained in the Westminster Confession were called into question. As he read the Bible for himself, Caldwell became convinced that 'many of the opinions and dogmas imposed on us as divine truths were merely the offspring of priestcraft, kingcraft and moneycraft'.[46] By the 1780s, however, Calvinists and theological liberals co-existed within the Synod in relative peace. Caldwell explained that at the large communion festivals held annually in May and October, Presbyterians of different opinions would gather together in crowds of up to 700 and, by a tacit arrangement, received communion from the minister of their choice.[47]

Sadly, we can only speculate about how Caldwell's thinking few were regarded by the ordinary citizens of Ballymoney. But what we know of the Presbyterian communion season suggests some of the means by which orthodoxy retained its vitality. The open-air preaching of the Seceders attracted large crowds. Their communion festivals were raucous affairs, branded by one critic as 'a noisy, drunken, idolatrous feast'.[48] Indeed it was a general expectation everywhere that many of those leaving the meeting-house headed straight for the public house. Preparations for communion included fast days, and the examination by the clergy of those who intended to approach the Lord's Table.[49] In theory, at least, communion tokens were distributed only to those who could demonstrate knowledge of the Reformed faith and were of sound moral character. Added refinements could be found on the ultra-orthodox fringe. In the middle decades of the century the Seceders made the renewal of the Scottish National Covenant (1638) and Solemn League and Covenant (1643) a condition of communion, reminding their congregations that the British monarchy would not be fully legitimate until Presbyterianism was established in all three kingdoms. The Covenanters remained frozen in the radical reformation of mid-seventeenth-century Scotland, summoning before the kirk session those who took the oath of allegiance, served on juries or voted in elections – all unacceptable compromises with an erastian regime in which the monarch, as head of the church, had usurped the position of Christ.

---

46 Ibid., p. 80.
47 Ibid., pp. 80–1.
48 T.L. Birch, *Physicians languishing under disease: an address to the Seceding, or Associate Synod of Ireland* (Belfast: s.n., 1796), p. 36.
49 A.R. Holmes, *The shaping of Ulster Presbyterian belief and practice, 1770–1840* (Oxford: Oxford University Press, 2006), chapter 6.

Since the 'ignorant or scandalous' were excluded from communion, male and female members of all the Presbyterian bodies were required to submit themselves to the discipline of the kirk session for lapses in sexual conduct and other misdemeanours. Almost twenty session books survive from the eighteenth century, which is enough to reveal that levels of discipline varied widely. In the four decades between 1740 and 1780 the kirk session of Ballycarry, a non-subscribing congregation, tried just fifty-nine cases, all but three of them concerning fornication or adultery. The wealthiest New Light congregations, First and Second Belfast, do not seem to have enforced session discipline at all. Over a comparable period (1767–1805), the Old Light congregation of Carnmoney tried 171 sexual offences. Predictably, the Seceders outdid the Synod. In just six years between 1752 and 1758 the Burgher session at Cahans, County Monaghan, tried twenty-three cases of fornication, twenty of irregular marriage, three of adultery and twenty-three other offences. Future research is likely to show in more detail that the everyday experience of worship reflected differences between the various liberal and conservative strands of Dissent.

The Kingdoms of this World: America, France and Ireland

Presbyterianism was prone to fragmentation. Throughout the eighteenth century the Synod of Ulster contained the great majority of northern congregations but was periodically assaulted by various offshoots who found its adherence to the Westminster Confession either too rigid or too lax. Relations with the liberal non-subscribers of the autonomous Presbytery of Antrim were generally polite. So were dealings with the Southern Association, the umbrella organisation that included the wealthy and influential congregations in Dublin. In contrast, the Synod and its more energetic rival, the Secession, regarded each other with hostility. Finally, there were the militant Covenanters or 'mountain men', who denounced all other Presbyterians as apostates. Their tiny band of preachers resembled wild prophets, gathering their hearers in barns and fields to renounce all the pragmatic compromises of the eighteenth century. What unified these rival organisations and tendencies was a powerful sense of inherited disadvantage. Memories of past wrongs, notably the legislation of Queen Anne's reign, were kept alive by the continuing exclusion of Dissenters from political and social power at local as well as national levels.

Presbyterians evidently relished disputation. But the theological battles that absorbed so much clerical energy tended to revolve around the relationship between the civil and ecclesiastical spheres. The connection between the kingdom of Christ and the kingdoms of this world was a perennial problem. The Seceders established almost fifty new congregations between the 1740s and the 1790s, offering a combination of rigid Calvinism and fervid preaching to country folk alienated by the rarefied Hutcheson-speak of the New Light men. But their origins lay in a long-running quarrel within the Church of Scotland over the rights of landowners to impose ministers on congregations. When the Secession itself split into two rival factions in 1747, it was once again over a political issue, the Scottish burgher oath. These divisions were replicated across the Irish Sea despite their irrelevance to the Irish situation. Resistance to subscription, as we have seen, was entangled with the campaign to repeal the test in 1719, and was re-energised by the English campaigns against the Test and Corporation Acts of 1787–90.

For the vast majority of ordinary Presbyterians the most bitterly resented aspect of Anglican superiority was the exaction of tithes and parochial dues. Poor harvests and slumps in the linen trade made the payment of tithes particularly onerous for the mass of tenant farmers, artisans and labourers. The oppressions of the tithe system featured prominently among Presbyterian explanations of the exodus to America; in the colonies it was believed that there would be 'no tythe (or task masters, as they call them) to vex or oppress them'.[50] Two waves of agrarian protest, the Hearts of Oak (1763) and the Hearts of Steel (1770–2), targeted the collection of excessive tithes by middlemen; Oakboys particularly resented 'small dues', the fees charged by the Anglican church for christenings, marriages, churchings and funerals, which were collected from Protestant, Catholic and Dissenter alike. In the 1790s the United Irishmen highlighted the tangible benefits that would follow from parliamentary reform, with the abolition of tithes and church rates high on the agenda. The established church was a major target of radical propaganda, including the popular satire 'Billy Bluff and Squire Firebrand', which was serialised in the *Northern Star* in 1796. The author was the Revd James Porter of Greyabbey, who was hanged near his meeting-house on 2 July 1798. When the dialogues were reissued in 1797 they were accompanied by a 'POLITICAL CREED', denouncing hereditary monarchy, aristocracy and, of course, the established church:

---

50 E.R.R. Green, 'The "strange humours" that drove the Scotch-Irish to America, 1729', *William and Mary Quarterly*, 3rd ser., 12 (1955), 118.

> *Religion* I believe to be an affair between the conscience of man and his Creator, and that it ought to be as free as the air in which we breathe. That all national churches are national defects, and that the state which compels me to contribute to any teacher, particularly to a teacher whose doctrines I cannot approve, is guilty of robbery.[51]

This was the language of Tom Paine's *Rights of man* (1790), famously described by Wolfe Tone as the 'Koran' of Belfast. As we have already seen, however, the ideas and commitments of the revolutionary decade were superimposed upon pre-existing notions about the relationship between church and state that had long and complex histories of their own.

The causes of the great revolutionary upheavals of the late eighteenth century were only indirectly related to religion. The issues raised by the American Revolution were centred on taxation and representation, and stemmed from the attempts of the Westminster parliament to make the colonists pay for their own defence. American opponents of the legislative claims of the Westminster parliament, like Molyneux and Swift before them, countered that liberty only existed under a constitutional system in which the people gave consent to the laws binding them, and that those who did not live in such a 'free state' or commonwealth were reduced to the condition of slaves. The origins of the French Revolution lay in the bankruptcy of the Bourbon monarchy resulting from France's participation in the American War, which brought the royal government to the point of collapse in 1788. The intensification of interstate warfare was a common factor, as in Irish politics, in encouraging central governments to consolidate its administrative powers over peripheral regions, and to mobilise the material and human resources of their populations on a greater scale than ever before.

Perhaps the single greatest cause of politicisation in the north was the rise of the Irish Volunteers in 1778, in response to the withdrawal of regular soldiers during the American war and the apprehension of a French invasion.[52] This movement assisted the transformation of the Patriot cause from a small group of parliamentarians, never representative of more than a minority of the ruling elite, into a massive citizen militia capable of pressurising the London government into a series of humiliating concessions. The excitement and the sense of empowerment created by volunteering caused a shift in the balance of power, not simply between Britain and Ireland, but within Protestant society. As the Belfast-born doctor William Drennan explained,

---

51 *Billy Bluff and Squire Firebrand or, a sample of the times* (Belfast: s.n., 1797), p. 27.
52 See Kelly, Chapter 2 above pp. 65–9.

the use of arms, the frequent meetings and political debates and the elections of delegates all made volunteering a social equaliser. It disseminated
'an independence and republicanism of spirit' through the lower ranks that
eroded their 'servile awe of estated tyrants' and promoted demands for parliamentary reform.[53] More than anything else, it was the experience of volunteering that enabled people in northern towns and farmlands to imagine
themselves as engaged in a single national discussion. The achievement of
legislative independence, by a combination of parliamentary agitation and
Volunteer mobilisation, was depicted as the act of a sovereign people, organised outside the conventional structures of Irish politics and, in a sense, in
opposition to them.

As so often, then, militarisation was a primary driver of radicalisation.
But the revolutionary upheavals that transformed America in the 1770s and
France in the 1790s had ecclesiastical as well as civil meanings. Both wars saw
the Anglican clerical establishment mobilised on behalf of the state, underlin-
ing the fact that the established church was still an essential part of the structure of power and privilege. The American Revolution was widely construed
as a civil war, moreover, and this was true above all in Ulster. Family ties, economic relationships and cultural connections were all reinforced by the recent
resurgence of emigration: around 40,000 left the province between 1769 and
1774.[54] A continuing identification with their colonial brethren bolstered the
ideological attachment of Irish Dissenters to the British Empire, widely conceived as uniquely based on Protestantism, liberty and commerce. It is not
surprising, then, that Ulster Presbyterians identified with the American cause,
regardless of their theological differences. The Revd Benjamin McDowell of
Ballykelly rallied Presbyterian voters in County Derry in 1775 by reminding
them that 'our friends and fellow subjects' across the Atlantic were 'bleed-
ing in defence of their rights'.[55] McDowell himself was an evangelical who
had been born in New Jersey and educated at Princeton. At the other end of
the spectrum we find the Revd Samuel Barber advising his Ulster brethren at
the annual synod in 1791 to turn their eyes westward to the new, expanding
American empire, where there was no ecclesiastical establishment, and every
man worshipped God as his conscience dictated.[56]

---

53 [W. Drennan], *A letter to Edmund Burke . . . containing some reflections on patriotism, party-
spirit, and the union of free nations* (Dublin: William Hallhead, 1780), 15–16.
54 See Griffin, Chapter 22 below, pp. 599–600, 604–5.
55 [McDowell,] 'To the free electors of the County of Londonderry', *London-Derry Journal*,
9 Sept. 1775.
56 S. Barber, Manuscript sermon on Revelation 18:20, June 1791, pp. 18–19, Presbyterian
Historical Society of Ireland Library and Archive.

The entire discourse of the French Revolution radiated a quasi-religious enthusiasm. Thus Samuel Neilson, rhapsodising in the Belfast *Northern Star*: 'like the dew of heaven, [the French Revolution] inspires all Europe, and will extend the blessing of liberty to all mankind as citizens of the world, the creatures of one Supreme Being'.[57] The collapse of the *ancien régime* had apparently swept away centuries of restrictions and prejudices, promising an end to despotism and superstition everywhere. The rights of man were regarded as a fundamental feature of God's creation and therefore sacred. But admiration for the utopian experiment of the new republic was bound up with a fascination with the dismantling of the French confessional state. The French Revolution, which saw the nationalisation of the French church and the appropriation of its lands by the National Assembly, could be read as an assault on Roman Catholicism and on all civil establishments of religion.

When the *Northern Star* was launched at the beginning of 1792, its first editorial boasted of the 'increasing commerce, population and wealth of the province of Ulster, which are daily producing new establishments in every art and manufacture'.[58] Economic and technological transformations facilitated an explosion of public and private discussion of political matters. This ferment was most obvious in Belfast. New wealth transformed this Presbyterian redoubt – wealth derived partly from the growing demand across the Irish Sea for Ulster livestock, partly from the retailing of manufactured products from Britain, and above all from the expanding linen industry in the triangle formed by Dungannon, Lisburn and Newry. The success of the town's white linenhall (1784) allowed northern linen drapers to operate independently of Dublin, and confirmed that Belfast, rather than its rival Newry, was the economic hub of the north. Belfast was also the capital of volunteering. The very first Ulster company of Volunteers was founded there on St Patrick's Day, 1778. Dozens of companies made their way from all over the province for the annual reviews held on the Fall meadows. During the American war Belfast became a byword for republicanism and subversion.

The economic growth and technological innovations that transformed Ulster politics were embodied in Samuel Neilson, a poorly documented figure who was at least as important as Theobald Wolfe Tone and Thomas Russell in shaping the United Irish movement. Neilson was the son of a Presbyterian minister of Ballyroney (County Down), who settled in Belfast in 1777 as an apprentice to his brother, a woollen merchant. By the age of 30 he had

---

57 *Northern Star*, 7 Nov. 1792.
58 'To the people', *Northern Star*, 4 Jan. 1792.

established his own business, the Belfast Woollen Warehouse, and was said to be worth £8,000. Although he associated with local gentry in the Northern Whig Club, founded by the Earl of Charlemont in 1789, he also helped form a secret committee within the First Belfast Volunteer company (whose uniform Wolfe Tone was so proud to wear) from which the Belfast Society of United Irishmen emerged in October 1791. The man nicknamed 'the Jacobin' now embarked on a new career as a professional revolutionary. It was Neilson who authorised the Defender link, having established connections with the underground Catholic fraternity in south Down in 1792. Overloaded with intelligence, often totally unreliable, Dublin Castle failed to follow up a tip-off from the Belfast stamp office in June 1795 that 'a Counsellor Tone' was being despatched for France with a subscription of £1,500 raised by Neilson and his Belfast associates. In May 1796 a government informant explained: 'Sam Neilson . . . is the medium thro' which the North and South correspond', adding that 'their plans are laid . . . and advised by him'.[59] By now the secret committees of the United Irishmen were linked to disturbances throughout the north, where they already claimed 50,000 members.

Neilson was the principal shareholder and editor of the remarkable *Northern Star* newspaper, and the driving force behind the massively successful propaganda war fought by the radicals. 'Being Presbyterians ourselves', the editors celebrated 'the characteristick of our persuasion, a manly opposition to religious domination, as well as political injustice'.[60] The *Star* embodied the radicalism of the northern Dissenters for five years, before Neilson's presses were destroyed by the Monaghan Militia in 1797. Although it spoke with a recognisably northern accent it represented an Irish nation in which the confessional divisions between Protestant, Catholic and Dissenter had been dissolved. The printing presses at the *Star* office were responsible for many of the key radical works of the decade, ranging from the revolutionary songbook *Paddy's Resource* and the Irish dictionary *Bolg an Tsolair*, to a cluster of millenarian tracts predicting that the world was about to be transformed by the Second Coming of Christ and the establishment of the kingdom of God on earth. The 1790s witnessed a reawakening of millenarian expectancy, as the fall of the European monarchies, the captivity of the pope and the rise of Napolean Bonaparte were all interpreted as fulfilling scriptural prophecies. France's military victories in Italy, for example, were portrayed in the

---

59 John Cleland to Viscount Castlereagh, 16 May 1796, Rebellion papers, 620/30/87, National Archives of Ireland.
60 *Northern Star*, 31 Dec. 1795, editorial.

Northern Star as the overthrow of the papacy. 'It is a long period of time since the Gallican Catholic Church threw off the Roman Yoke', the editors commented in June 1796, 'and why should the Irish Catholic Church wish to hug her chains in this enlightened period?'[61]

Presbyterian clergymen reacted to the cataclysmic events on the continent by conjuring with the well-known symbols and numbers found in Daniel and Revelation – what John Abernethy called 'Apocalyptical Synchronisms'.[62] This science was a scholarly and sophisticated pursuit, but it also provided one of the most important and interesting ways in which radical thought connected with the fears and aspirations of ordinary people. At the annual meeting of the Synod of Ulster in 1791, Samuel Barber opened the proceedings with a sermon on Revelation 18:20, rejoicing that French Catholics had thrown off the shackles of civil and religious tyranny, and urging his hearers to prepare for the collapse of all religious establishments and the imminent 'fall of the great city Babylon'.[63] Two years later it was the turn of Thomas Ledlie Birch, a member of the staunchly orthodox Presbytery of Belfast and the founder of a United Irish society in Saintfield, to inform the Synod that the admission of French Protestants to full citizenship was one of the decisive victories foretold in the struggle against antichrist.[64] It was at this synod that the Presbyterian clergy passed a resolution congratulating their Roman Catholic countrymen on having the franchise restored to them. In later years Birch would be troubled by the evidence of growing infidelity in the new republic, but he persisted in his view that the French had adopted a more rational form of worship, while in Ireland the Catholics had become 'as enlightened as others'.[65]

Predictably it was the Covenanters, on the ultra-orthodox fringe of Ulster Presbyterianism, who were most explicit in their claim that the war was part of the struggle against antichrist. At the Reformation, they believed, the usurped power of the papacy had merely been transferred to the crown, whose assertion of supremacy over the church was an affront to the sovereignty of Christ. In an eschatological work entitled *War proclaimed and victory ensured* (1795), the leader of their Reformed Presbytery, William Stavely,

---

61 *Northern Star*, 20 June 1796.
62 Abernethy, *Study of scripture-prophecie*, p. 23.
63 Barber, Sermon on Revelation 18:20, p. 21, Presbyterian Historical Society of Ireland Library and Archive.
64 T.L. Birch, *The obligations upon Christians and especially ministers to be exemplary in their lives* (Belfast: Hugh Dowell, 1794), esp. 26–32.
65 T.L. Birch, *A letter from an Irish emigrant to his friend in the United States* (Philadelphia: s.n., 1799), pp. 24, 26–7.

identified the European monarchies which had risen from the Roman Empire as the ten crowned horns of the beast whose fall was predicted in the coded chronologies of Daniel and Revelation. By taking upon themselves such titles as 'eldest son of the church' and 'defender of the faith', the rulers of Europe had implicated themselves in the usurped and tyrannical claims of the Roman Catholic Church.[66] For Stavely the struggle with France was in the most literal sense a war of religion in which England had elected to join a coalition of antichristian powers in propping up papal tyranny. The implication, that the French had been chosen as God's instrument for toppling the corrupt and tyrannical priests and princes of Europe, was spelt out by other Covenanters who itinerated through Antrim and Down at this time, preaching to large crowds and predicting 'the immediate destruction of the British monarchy'.[67]

By no means all Ulster's Presbyterians were sympathetic to radical mobilisation, still less to the insurrections of 1798. Proposals for parliamentary reform had attracted widespread support since the 1780s. Some measure of Catholic emancipation was now recognised as a desirable or at least inevitable component of reform, although there were divisions over the extent and timing of change. A significant party of moderates in Belfast shared the anxieties of the Revd William Bruce, who warned against granting political power to a people 'ignorant, illiberal, intolerant, superstitious and justly exasperated against their future subjects' without a lengthy decontamination period.[68] During the mid-1790s, debates over the reform programme of the United Irishmen were short-circuited by the rapid militarisation of Irish society brought about by war with revolutionary France. The alternative world of politics created by volunteering was now suppressed. Where the United Irishmen predominated, they effectively paralysed the structures of local government, infiltrating militia units and intimidating magistrates and loyalists with nocturnal raids. It was the very strength of the United Irish 'system' in the north that led to the brutal disarming of the population and the arrest of so many leaders in 1797.

Throughout the 1790s the United Irishmen had demonstrated a remarkable confidence that they would remain in control of the process of democratisation they had initiated. Part of the explanation lay in their conviction that

---

66 W. Stavely, *War proclaimed, and victory ensured; or, The Lamb's conquests illustrated* (Belfast: Thomas Storey, 1795), pp. 55–6.
67 S. McSkimmin, *Annals of Ulster: or Ireland fifty years ago* (Belfast: John Henderson, 1849), p. 54.
68 I.R. McBride, *Scripture politics: Ulster Presbyterians and Irish radicalism in the late eighteenth century* (Oxford: Oxford University Press, 1998), p. 172.

a genuine community of interests united Protestant, Catholic and Dissenter. One of the most dramatic developments of the 1790s was the new social radicalism that called upon the mercantile and professional classes, urban artisans, and the tenant farmers and the weavers of the countryside to unite against a parasitic landed elite. Another factor was the triumphant feeling that 'popery' – that is, superstition and priestcraft – had entered irreversible decline both at home and on the continent. Perhaps many Ulster radicals also shared the sense of social superiority evident in Wolfe Tone's suggestion that although the Defenders were an 'undisciplined rabble' the Catholic population, 'with proper rulers', might become of 'very great service to the cause'.[69] This self-assurance was shaken by accounts of events in Wexford in 1798, when the Catholics apparently displayed 'all the bigotry and intolerance of the middle ages'.[70]

It would be unwise, however, to allow the bloody upheavals of 1798 to obscure longer-term continuities in Presbyterian politics and the broader determinants of religious developments. The continuing political liberalism among Presbyterians through the nineteenth century is now recognised by all serious scholars. It reflected the same social circumstances emphasised above – their numerical strength and regional concentration in the north-east, their dominance in the trading, manufacturing and professional classes, their resentment at the constitutional alliance of church and state and at the social and political advantages unjustly enjoyed by their Anglican neighbours. The rise of a new evangelical style within the Synod and the Secession has been linked to the sectarian friction rekindled in the Ulster borderlands, and especially in County Armagh, during the 1780s; but vital religion triumphed over enlightenment in England and Scotland as well as Ireland. As for the revolution, the gospel of liberty, equality and fraternity had been tarnished by the ruthless exploitation of its occupied territories by France. 'Plundering by French soldiers', Tim Blanning comments, became 'the most obtrusive, ubiquitous, constant – and hated – feature of revolutionary warfare'.[71] The reasons for the decline of Presbyterian radicalism, like its origins, are to be found in Britain and Europe, as much as in Ireland itself.

69 T. Bartlett (ed.), *The life of Theobald Wolfe Tone* (Dublin: Lilliput Press, 1998), p. 120.

70 H. Joy (ed.), *Historical collections relative to the town of Belfast* (Belfast: John Berwick, 1817), p. x.

71 T.C.W. Blanning, 'Liberation or occupation? Theory and practice in the French Revolutionaries' treatment of civilians outside France' in M. Grimsley and C.J. Rogers (eds.), *Civilians in the path of war* (Lincoln: University of Nebraska Press, 2002), p. 118.

13

Protestantism in the Nineteenth Century: Revival and Crisis

ANDREW R. HOLMES

Protestantism in nineteenth-century Ireland was energised by the experience of religious revival that transformed the ability of the churches to meet the needs of their own members and of society in general. At the same time, Protestants faced a series of internal and external crises, particularly the growing challenge to their privileged minority position. This pattern of revival and crisis was not unique, yet historians have become reticent at interpreting religious revival in Europe or North America as a simple product of political and cultural crisis. They find it more helpful to point to complex interrelationships and to acknowledge the sincerity of religious belief as a motive for human action. In that regard, much of the impetus towards a common Protestant experience of revival was provided by evangelicalism – a movement of revitalisation amongst Protestants that in the eighteenth century was associated with the growth of Methodism and religious awakenings that affected Calvinist Protestants throughout the North Atlantic world. Evangelicalism united Protestants irrespective of denominational, social or geographical background on the basis of a shared experience of individual conversion and a desire to spread their version of Christianity across the world. This fervent form of Protestantism stimulated reform within the Church of Ireland and the Presbyterian churches, led to the revitalisation of smaller Protestant groups, awakened the potential of the Protestant laity through voluntary missionary and philanthropic effort at home and overseas, shaped Victorian notions of respectability and gender roles, and gave renewed impetus to the long-desired goal of effecting the conversion of Ireland. It led to a remarkable outbreak of religious revival in Ulster in 1859 and helped the Church of Ireland to deal in part with the trauma of disestablishment. Yet it is necessary from the outset to note the limits of a common Protestant experience. The separate structures and vested interests of the various denominations militated against institutional convergence. Evangelicalism had both its limits and its opponents within the churches, especially the High Church party within the Church of Ireland and a handful of theologically liberal Presbyterians. Moreover, resentment and grievance against the Church of Ireland persisted amongst northern Presbyterians, some of whom had been in the radical vanguard in the 1790s and many more of whom remained in the nineteenth century politically liberal and opposed to the social and political ascendancy of Episcopalians. By the 1880s, intra-Protestant difference had been eased by the influence of evangelicalism, but perhaps more significant was the concern about the minority Protestant interest in Ireland and the threat posed by Catholic democracy and the spectre of 'Rome Rule'.

Religious Revival and Reform, 1790–1830

The crisis of the late eighteenth century prompted an extraordinary outbreak of religious revival amongst Protestants across the North Atlantic world. In the vanguard was Methodism. Between 1785 and 1790 alone, the number of Methodists in the United States jumped from 18,000 to 57,631 – an increase of 220 per cent – and it continued to grow at a rapid pace; by 1830 there were 476,153. This pattern was replicated in Britain, where the number rose tenfold from 30,760 in 1775 to 302,048 in 1830. Methodism in Ireland likewise experienced significant expansion and there were 36,903 Methodists by 1830.[1] This growth in Ireland occurred mainly in south Ulster and was unpredictable and often transient. Sectarian tensions, rising prices and food shortages stimulated the longing for religious meaning, and this was supplied by a striking collection of eager itinerant preachers, both male and female, who were inspired by a desire to convert souls and whose often modest social origins gave them better access to the bulk of the population in comparison to college-educated clergymen.

The desire to spread the gospel affected Presbyterians as well. The fastest-growing sector of Presbyterianism after 1750 was Seceder Presbyterians whose preachers first came to Ireland from Scotland in the 1740s. The origins of the movement can be traced to those who seceded from the established Presbyterian Church of Scotland in 1733 in protest at lay patronage and a perceived relaxation of doctrinal rigour. Their opportunism, lively preaching, strict moral code and orthodox theology appealed to many ordinary Presbyterians in the north who were increasingly dissatisfied with the Synod of Ulster, the largest and most representative Presbyterian organisation in

---

1 Figures from D. Hempton, *Methodism: empire of the spirit* (New Haven: Yale University Press, 2005), p. 216.

Ireland. Seceder congregations grew especially in south Ulster, and it is unsurprising that Seceder ministers in County Armagh were instrumental in the formation of the Evangelical Society of Ulster in October 1798. The object of the society was to promote itinerant preaching and the inaugural meeting was attended by thirteen ministers from four different Presbyterian denominations as well as Episcopalians and Independents. Though the Evangelical Society of Ulster was short-lived, the turmoil of the 1790s encouraged individual evangelicals throughout Ireland to join together in voluntary societies in order to promote both home and foreign mission during the first two decades of the nineteenth century. They desired individual conversions, but the instability of the time focused attention on the capacity of evangelicalism's 'moral creed and its anti-Catholicism to act as compelling antidotes to civil and political unrest'. It also stimulated reform within the various Protestant churches in the early nineteenth century, though the 'delicate task of church leaders in these years was to encourage religious zeal without stirring up religious controversy, and to harness evangelical enthusiasm to the broader interests of the church'.[2]

This injection of religious intensity benefited the state churches in Britain and Ireland. The United Kingdom by the end of the Napoleonic wars had two established churches – the Presbyterian Church of Scotland and the United Church of England and Ireland, which had been created by clause five of the Act of Union, though in practice the two churches remained distinct organisations. As S.J. Brown has noted, all state churches, irrespective of their differences, struggled to come to terms with the impact of political revolution, industrialisation and urbanisation, and the growing challenge of alternative forms of Christianity. At the same time, these exceptional threats to social order prompted policy makers to seek a response through revitalised state churches. At the instigation of William Pitt, parliament voted monies, and the scale of direct financial aid to all three churches rose substantially under Tory governments between 1809 and 1824. It also led to a proper audit of the effectiveness of the churches. On paper, the Church of Ireland had four archbishops, eighteen bishops and around 1,200 parish livings funded largely through tithe paid by Catholics. This basic structure hid fundamental problems, not least the fact that its minority position attracted increasing criticism arising from the nineteenth-century emphasis on utilitarian appraisal and efficiency. A survey commissioned by the archbishop of Armagh in 1807 found

---

2 D. Hempton and M. Hill, *Evangelical Protestantism in Ulster society, 1740–1890* (London: Routledge, 1992), pp. 23, 67.

that of the 1,133 clergy in Ireland, 561 were regularly non-resident and that 274 held more than one parish (pluralism); only 582 church buildings were in good repair and 155 glebes were habitable.[3] In an attempt to assist the church to ease these difficulties, the state provided building grants averaging £10,000 per annum for the first decade of the century and £60,000 per annum in the years from 1810 to 1816. In 1808 legislation was passed to help bishops deal with non-resident clergy, and grants reaching £9,000 per year by 1823 were made to the voluntary Association for Discountenancing Vice, whose main task was to publish and distribute religious materials acceptable to the doctrines of the Church of Ireland.[4]

Similar reforms were pursued by other Protestant churches. Methodist attempts to consolidate the gains made during the revivals of the 1790s and to clarify their relationship with the Church of Ireland led in 1816 to a split in the denomination over the administration of the sacraments. Presbyterians underwent an extensive process of internal reform. It has been suggested that the evangelical emphasis on personal conversion was not part of the traditional Presbyterian world-view, but this ignores the spiritual and doctrinal continuity with the Old Light party in the Synod of Ulster and the Seceders. The type of evangelicalism that came to dominate Ulster Presbyterianism during this period was conservative in its adherence to Calvinist theology and to the Presbyterian organisation of the church. A commitment to structural efficiency was exemplified in the Synod of Ulster's *The constitution and discipline of the Presbyterian Church* (1825), which codified procedure and provided a framework for reform. Though prepared by a theologically mixed committee, evangelicalism energised reform, and the driving force in its publication was the prominent evangelical Henry Cooke (1788–1868). In a sermon preached at the Synod in 1825, Cooke called for the thorough reform of Presbyterian church life and structures in order to promote 'vital religion'. Cooke's desire to make the Synod clearly evangelical inspired his campaign against a handful of Arian ministers who denied the divinity of Christ. He began by opposing the influence of Arian professors on ministerial students in the Belfast Academical Institution, but by the late 1820s his target had widened to include Arians within the Synod. The Arian Controversy aroused considerable public interest as Cooke and his principal opponent, Henry Montgomery (1788–1865), engaged in vigorous debate about the doctrine of the Trinity and the

---

3 S.J. Brown, *Providence and Empire: religion, politics and society in the United Kingdom, 1815–1914* (Harlow: Pearson Longman, 2008), p. 18.
4 Brown, *Providence and Empire*, p. 46.

right of churches to impose statements of faith upon their clergy. Eventually thirteen ministers led by Montgomery left the Synod in 1829 to form the Remonstrant Synod of Ulster. The expulsion of the Arians and their sympathisers laid the basis for the formation in 1840 of the General Assembly of the Presbyterian Church in Ireland, a product of the union between the Synod of Ulster and the Secession Synod. (Illustration 5)

Within the Church of Ireland, reforms were implemented by a revived episcopate comprising High Churchmen as well as evangelicals. It was these conscientious churchmen from different theological traditions that began the campaign to achieve what the Reformation of the sixteenth century had failed to do – the conversion of Catholic Ireland to Protestantism. The origin of the so-called Second Reformation has usually been traced to an address delivered in October 1822 by William Magee, the High Church archbishop of Dublin, who claimed that the state church was 'hemmed in by two opposite descriptions of professing Christians' – Catholics, 'possessing a Church, without what we can properly call a Religion', and Presbyterians, 'possessing a Religion, without what we can properly call a Church'.[5] Though Magee's High Church principles made evangelicals wary, Alan Acheson notes that he was successful in integrating them into the life of his archdiocese. Evangelicalism led to the formation of various voluntary societies to promote conversion, and this associational culture provided Church of Ireland evangelicals with the opportunity to encourage each other and to promote church reform, especially as they congregated in Dublin at the annual meetings of these societies in April. They also received support from other church leaders. Though initially unsympathetic to conversionist religion, Power Le Poer Trench, the archbishop of Tuam, publicly supported evangelicalism from 1819. In that year he issued an address to his clergy, in which he declared he would reward their support 'by exerting myself in the cause of true religion upon the earth, and by upholding, by my influence, by my patronage, and by my personal countenance, every institution in aid thereof'.[6] Magee's challenge to extend the Church of Ireland across the island was taken up for religious and social reasons by evangelical landlords such as the Farnhams of County Cavan, the Lortons of north Roscommon, and the Rodens of Tollymore in County Down. According to Irene Whelan, there also emerged an 'Irish Clapham Sect' whose membership included the banker James Digges

---

5 W. Magee, *A charge delivered at his primary visitation: in St. Patrick's Cathedral, Dublin, on Thursday the 24th of October 1822* (Dublin: Richard Coyne, 1822), pp. 25–6.
6 'Clergy address to the archbishop of Tuam', *Christian Observer*, 18 (Dec. 1819), 814.

Engraved by W. Holl, from a Photograph.

REV? HENRY COOKE, D.D. L.L.D.

WILLIAM MACKENZIE, GLASGOW, EDINBURGH & LONDON.

5. Henry Cooke (1788–1868), Presbyterian leader, spearheaded the reform and evangelical revitalisation of Presbyterianism in Ulster. Line engraving by William Holl Jr, after unknown artist, mid-nineteenth century.

La Touche, the educator John Synge, the physician Charles Edward Orpen and the moral reformer Thomas Langlois Lefroy. Despite significant expenditure of resources and extensive newspaper coverage, the Second Reformation did not convert Catholic Ireland and provoked opposition from groups without and within the churches, including politically liberal members of the established church such as John Jebb, the High Church bishop of Limerick.[7]

Political Challenges and Options, 1829–1850

Many Protestants went on the political defensive in the late 1820s as it seemed to them that the Protestant character of the state was being undermined by the demand to admit Catholics to parliament. The passage of Catholic emancipation in 1829 meant that the United Kingdom was no longer a semi-confessional Protestant state. Some Protestants perceived this development as national apostasy while many others were bewildered. Protestant opinion in Ulster ranged from angry Orange populism to politically liberal yet theologically orthodox members of the Synod of Ulster who made little or no comment. In hindsight, 1829 marked the beginning of the end of the Church of Ireland as an established church. The dark mood of Protestants was exacerbated by popular resentment amongst the Catholic population at having to pay tithe to a church they clearly did not support. The 'Tithe War' that began in autumn 1830 produced violent confrontations and fatalities, and by the end of 1832 less than half of tithe was being collected. The strength of popular opposition to the tithe drew attention to the anomalous position of the Irish state church and it was clear that the Whig governments of the 1830s were committed to making the institution as acceptable as possible to popular opinion. In 1831 the state withdrew grants from voluntary Protestant schools under the superintendence of such avowedly confessional organisations as the Kildare Place Society and embarked on an attempt to create a non-denominational system under a National Board of Education. In response, the Church of Ireland set up its own Church Educational Society in 1839 and so lost out on a significant injection of state funds. Matters were to get worse; by passing the Church Temporalities Act of 1833, 'parliament acknowledged that the Protestant Church of Ireland would never become the church of the whole Irish people'.[8] Under this legislation, the structures

---

7 J. Ridden, 'The forgotten history of the Protestant crusade: religious liberalism in Ireland', *Journal of Religious History*, 31 (2007), 78–102.
8 Brown, *Providence and Empire*, p. 82.

of the church were streamlined by reducing the archbishoprics of Tuam and Cashel to bishoprics, uniting small parishes and abolishing the payment of cess. An Ecclesiastical Commission was also established to control and distribute funds from church resources, which amounted to almost £3 million by 1861. Combined with the Tithe Rentcharge Act (1838), which put the onus on landlords to pay tithe, these were significant reforms that clearly demonstrated the subservience of church to state. It was, as Acheson had observed, 'the acceptable face of erastianism'.[9]

As a consequence, reform of the Irish church alarmed supporters of state churches in Britain while encouraging those who advocated the voluntary principle and called for disestablishment. The reaction of many within the Church of Ireland was to redouble their efforts to improve the religious life of the church. The Revd Henry Irwin argued in 1831:

> The church can no longer trust to her prescriptive grandeur, opulence, and authority. The power of the civil arm is now a very precarious resource. Her fidelity to herself is, under God, her all in all. It was always so, but never more than now, that she must depend on the personal character of her ministry.[10]

A handful of radicals abandoned the church altogether. Influenced by the conferences on biblical prophecy held on the Powerscourt estate in the 1820s, John Nelson Darby's rejection of the erastianism of the Irish church led to his secession and his connection with what came to be known as the Plymouth Brethren. Darby and his fellow millenarians believed that the significance of the threats to the Protestant constitution meant that the Second Coming of Christ was imminent and that believers ought to keep their spiritual purity until the tribulation had occurred. This deeply pessimistic reading of the 'End Times' would eventually become a marked feature of conservative evangelicalism throughout the Anglo-American world in the twentieth century.

Other members of the established church sought to make common cause with their fellow Protestants in other churches, especially Presbyterians. The tensions between the two main sections of Irish Protestantism should not be underestimated. They had fought each other during the seventeenth century and penal legislation had been imposed on Presbyterians at the behest of the Church of Ireland establishment during the early eighteenth century. It was these experiences of conflict and coercion that caused many Presbyterians to

---

9 A. Acheson, *A history of the Church of Ireland 1691–2001*, 2nd edn (Dublin: The Columba Press/SPCK, 2002), p. 146.
10 'Substance of the address of the Rev. Henry Irwin', *Christian Examiner*, 11 (April 1831), 321–2.

join with Catholics in rebellion against the Irish confessional state in 1798. Yet the sectarian character of the rebellion had a profoundly chastening effect on Presbyterian rebels, and even former United Irishmen began to see the benefits of an Act of Union that offered the framework for significant political reform. By the 1830s, Protestant unity within the context of union seemed an obvious option given the order of the threats posed by Whig reforms and Catholic democracy. Henry Cooke was instrumental in promoting Protestant political unity in defence of the Protestant character of the British state. Cooke was deeply influenced by the piety and outlook of evangelicals within the Church of Ireland and was later a correspondent and confidant of Robert Peel. At a meeting convened in October 1834 by the third Marquis of Downshire to protest at Whig reforms, Cooke in a personal capacity called on Episcopalians and Presbyterians to forget past persecution and make common cause, pronouncing 'banns of marriage' between the two forms of Protestantism. The *Dublin University Magazine* was delighted by Cooke's attitude. It claimed that he 'spoke almost the unanimous sentiments of the Presbyterians of the North'. 'These are times when all minor differences are merged in the common epithet of Protestant', it continued, before noting Presbyterian support for bible education, the need to protect 'Protestant property and life', and their resentment at the actions of government. As a consequence, a Presbyterian

> makes common cause with his brethren of the established church; and, in indignation at the treatment that Protestants have received, he never stops to inquire whether those who are in the same danger with himself worship their God in the same posture, or adopt the same orders of church government, or the same regulations of public worship, that he does.[11]

Generally speaking, Presbyterians objected not to the principle of established churches but to the particular form of church that was established in Ireland. They were beneficiaries of a state subsidy known as the *regium donum* and increasingly saw themselves as one with the Presbyterian Church of Scotland. Cooke emerged as a champion of established churches and received in 1837 an honorary degree from Trinity College, Dublin, in recognition of his efforts, yet it was his defence of the Union against Daniel O'Connell in January 1841 that sealed his popularity as a Protestant and unionist hero. In his various public campaigns Cooke 'fused together in his own person a particular combination of conversionist theology, social conservatism, and anti-Catholicism that would eventually come to dominate popular politics in the

11 'The Downshire Meeting', *Dublin University Magazine*, 4 (1834), 693–5.

north of Ireland'.[12] It is certainly the case that his response to the events in the 1820s and 1830s was almost indistinguishable from that of Episcopalian evangelicals such as Roden and Farnham and 'was informed by a powerful mixture of religious, social and political convictions'. These convictions made such figures fearful of the resurgence of the 'Man of Sin', and, though the effort to convert Catholic Ireland was a failure, 'Protestantism became both more vigorous and more defensive as it became clear neither British governments nor British public opinion could be relied upon to resist Irish Catholicism with sufficient fortitude.'[13]

Cooke's evangelicalism and unionist politics were shared by virtually all orthodox Presbyterians, but his desire to unite with the Church of Ireland was rejected by most of his ministerial colleagues and obscures the considerable support amongst Presbyterian tenant farmers – the social backbone of Presbyterianism – for liberal politics in mid-Victorian Ulster. Generally speaking, Presbyterians were well disposed to favour political reform, and their frustration with the status quo was heightened from the late 1830s as their rights and privileges were denied by some episcopal Protestants and Peel's Conservative government. The legality of their marriages was called into question in the early 1840s because of the High Church claim that Presbyterian ministers were not properly clergymen as they had not been ordained by bishops, and in 1843 the Presbyterian Church of Scotland was torn apart by the failure of Peel's government to recognise the Presbyterian principle of the spiritual independence of the church. It is quite clear that grass-roots Presbyterians, especially in counties Antrim, Down and Londonderry, rejected episcopacy as a church in error and because it was the church of their landlords. At election times, many of them supported liberal candidates as they stood for the legalisation of the Ulster Custom or tenant right. Along with fair rents and fixity of tenure, this freedom of sale of one's interest in improved land was one of the 'three Fs' that became the platform for land reformers before the Land Act of 1881. Yet prior to the extension of the franchise and the introduction of the secret ballot in 1872, Presbyterian electors and candidates found it very difficult to gain electoral success as landlord influence on parliamentary and local government representation in Ulster remained strong.

Problems with the electoral system did not stop Presbyterians from criticising Conservative governments, landlordism or the Church of Ireland. In the

---

12 I.R. McBride, *Scripture politics: Ulster Presbyterians and Irish radicalism in the late eighteenth century* (Oxford: Clarendon Press, 1998), p. 216.
13 Hempton and Hill, *Evangelical Protestantism*, p. 102.

aftermath of the Disruption of the Church of Scotland and during the high-point of the marriage controversy, the General Assembly of the Presbyterian Church in Ireland passed a resolution in June 1843 which recognised the 'powerful influences' marshalled against Presbyterianism 'to wrest from her the rights and privileges of her ministers and people' and recommended to their members 'such a united and faithful discharge of their duty, as Christian electors, as shall most effectually secure a full and adequate representation of the principles and interests of Presbyterianism in the British Legislature'.[14] Cooke was angered by this challenge to his policy of working with Peel and the Conservatives and withdrew from the Assembly for four years until it was repealed. When he returned, he found his defence of landlord interests out of sympathy with the overwhelming majority of the General Assembly who in July 1850 passed a resolution in favour of the legalisation of tenant right. Presbyterian evangelical ministers at mid-century appeared on platforms supporting land reform and opposed the Orange Order owing to its disreputable behaviour and defence of the privileges of the Church of Ireland. It was only from the 1870s onwards that Presbyterians began to join the Order in sizeable numbers. A graphic example of a Presbyterian evangelical who shared Cooke's unionist politics but rejected his political conservatism was the Revd Richard Smyth, the son of a tenant farmer in north Antrim, a fervent evangelical, professor at Magee College, Derry, and Liberal MP for County Londonderry between 1874 and 1878. In his review of a biography of Henry Cooke published in 1872, Smyth claimed that Cooke's 'real life's work began and ended' when he expelled the Arians from the Synod of Ulster in 1829. 'But for this great achievement it would scarcely have been worthwhile to write his life at all.' Smyth disparaged Cooke's opposition to national education and tenant right, and his support for established churches, the Tory party and Protestant political unity. Smyth concluded that

> it remains undeniable on the face of history, that, since the day he fought so nobly and so successfully for truth and purity in the Synod of Ulster . . . almost every wall which was buttressed by his eloquence has been thrown down, and the principal movements to which he gave the impulse have fallen upon check and disaster. Provincial annals hardly furnish any more striking instance of the total collapse of public policies than in the cases we have mentioned.[15]

14 Cited in A.R. Holmes, 'Covenanter politics: evangelicalism, political liberalism and Ulster Presbyterians, 1798–1914', *English Historical Review*, 125 (2010), 351.
15 Cited in Holmes, 'Covenanter politics', p. 362.

Famine Relief and Revival in Ulster, 1845–1860

One of the reasons why Presbyterians in the 1840s took up the issue of land reform was the onset of the Great Famine. Interpretations of the actions of the Protestant and Dissenting churches during the Famine tend to focus on either the humanitarian ecumenism of the Quakers or the activities of ultra-Protestant proselytisers in the west of Ireland. Quaker soup kitchens were open from November 1846 and their graphic accounts of the catastrophe in the British press were instrumental in stimulating voluntary relief efforts. Protestants such as the Church of England clergyman Alexander Dallas saw the Famine as an opportunity to convert Catholics. With substantial support from evangelicals in England, Dallas formed in 1849 the Society of Irish Church Missions to Roman Catholics. Though it had notable success, the claims that is was dispensing relief as an incentive to conversion (souperism) caused a significant Catholic reaction and its work had faltered by the late 1860s. Yet to focus disproportionately on proselytism during the Great Famine obscures the Christian and humanitarian decency that characterised those Protestants who did not have limelight or opprobrium directed upon them. As Brown reminds us,

> hundreds of Protestant clergymen of the Church of Ireland and other churches remained in their neighbourhoods, serving on local relief committees, distributing food at soup kitchens, writing letters to the newspapers or to wealthy relatives begging for financial aid, visiting the sick and dying, conducting funerals, consoling the bereaved – and often succumbing to famine fever.[16]

The Great Famine did not produce a devotional revolution within Irish Protestantism, but it did extend the influence of evangelicalism within the Protestant churches. The period between 1845 and 1895 was one of 'Evangelical ascendancy' within the Church of Ireland, and the Presbyterian Church was even more solidly evangelical in its outlook and ethos.[17] Evangelicalism did inform the conservative reaction of Irish Protestants to higher biblical criticism and materialist science, but those responses were thoughtful, scholarly and accommodating where possible.[18] The dominance of evangelicalism was most clearly demonstrated by the remarkable religious revival that swept

---

16 Brown, *Providence and Empire*, p. 155; see Gray, Chapter 24 below.
17 Acheson, *History*, p. 182.
18 G. Jones, 'Darwinism in Ireland' in D. Attis (ed.), *Science and Irish culture*, vol. 1 (Dublin: Royal Dublin Society, 2004), pp. 115–37; D.N. Livingstone, *Dealing with Darwin: place, politics, and rhetoric in religious engagements with evolution* (Baltimore, MD: Johns Hopkins

Protestant Ulster between March and October 1859.[19] The revival was part of a transatlantic evangelical awakening that began in the eastern United States in 1857 and spread to the Celtic fringe of the United Kingdom and primarily affected Protestants outside the state churches. In Ulster it saw the conversion of unbelievers in large numbers and the spiritual quickening of believers within the churches. It affected Protestants from all denominations, but whereas the Presbyterian Church was supportive, the leadership of the Church of Ireland was less enthusiastic. It had its origins in mid County Antrim when unobtrusive conversions occurred during the winter of 1858/9, though the revival publicly announced itself at Ahoghill on 14 March 1859 when converts were 'struck down' at the thought of their sinful condition. Such physical manifestations helped to stimulate interest, and the revival quickly spread throughout the north-east and attracted significant international interest and spiritual tourism to the affected areas. Thousands attended a prayer meeting in Botanic Gardens in Belfast on 29 June and the UK-wide Evangelical Alliance had its annual meeting in the town in September.

This outbreak of religious fervour has puzzled historians. An older tradition of scholarship sought to link the revival to dislocation caused by the onset of factory production in the linen industry that produced two especially receptive social groups – financially ruined male handloom weavers and female mill workers who faced the prospect of delayed marriage or spinsterhood. However, similar economic conditions had not produced revival in the 1830s and the revival began in mid Antrim where domestic linen production remained strong. Religious competition certainly played its part and the revival is interpreted as a response to the rise of a distinctively Roman form of Irish Catholicism under the leadership of Paul Cullen. Recent scholarship has sought to emphasise the importance of the earlier religious reforms within the Protestant churches outlined above and that revivals tend to occur within communities that prepare the ground and expect them to happen. The Presbyterian Church assumed leadership in 1859 because it had been praying for revival since the Arian Controversy and had organised church life in such a way as to promote spiritual renewal. The revival they wanted was respectable and controlled, but the Ulster awakening soon got out of control.

The revival caused significant bewilderment and controversy at the time. The clergy were uncomfortable that the leadership of the revival was

University Press, 2015), pp. 58–88; A.R. Holmes, 'Biblical authority and the impact of Higher Criticism in Irish Presbyterianism, *c.* 1850–1930', *Church History*, 75 (2006), 343–73.

19 A.R. Holmes, 'The Ulster revival of 1859: causes, controversies and consequences', *Journal of Ecclesiastical History*, 63 (2012), 488–515.

dominated by the laity and were concerned at the bizarre physical symptoms that accompanied some conversions. Addresses by the converts were very popular and lay-led prayer meetings provided an opportunity for unregulated freedom of religious expression. For critics, the physical manifestations defined the revival, as these had not been a feature of Presbyterian spirituality in Ireland since the 1630s or of the recent American revival. They affected a small proportion of converts and declined in prominence as the revival continued, but they disproportionately affected women and children, and for sections of the laity they defined true conversion. The chaos was especially liberating for working-class women who assumed leadership roles arising out of the authority thus gained from a personal encounter with God expressed through a bodily experience. The trances, visions, stigmata and other physical manifestations were invoked by working-class females to define a public role for themselves and to challenge male authority. The following account from Belfast is typical:

> A girl of about twenty years of age was leading some persons in most boisterous hymn singing round a girl, who had fainted at a meeting which had just closed, and who was evidently suffering under a hysterical affection; but this young person resisted even the authority of the doctor, who wished to have the girl removed to near the air, and her dress loosened a little, saying she had been a 'case', and understood it much better, and nothing was so good as hymn singing.[20]

The revival proved a short-lived stimulus to female empowerment, and other supposed effects were often just as temporary. Of the estimated 100,000 converts, most were reintegrated into the evangelical subculture of which they had previously been part rather than experiencing conversion for the first time. It was reported that 307 Presbyterian congregations received 10,661 new members and that Methodist membership increased by 53.7 per cent between 1859 and 1860. Yet in the latter case there was a dramatic fall in subsequent years and Presbyterianism lost numbers to smaller denominations who demanded a more obvious commitment from their members, including Baptists, Congregationalists and the Plymouth Brethren. Much of the evidence used by supporters to demonstrate the reality of the revival also proved transient as incidents of prostitution, drunkenness and petty crime soon returned to pre-revival levels. The same was true of sectarian tension.

20 G. Salmon, *The evidences of the work of the Holy Spirit: a sermon preached in St Stephen's Church, Dublin, on Sunday, July 3, 1859 . . . with an appendix on the Revival Movement in the north of Ireland*, 3rd edn (Dublin, 1859), pp. 36–7n.

Supporters made much of the lack of trouble on 12 July 1859, but the revival did not spell the end of populist Orangeism. Ultimately, the revival was a Protestant revival for Protestants that played an important role in shaping Protestant identity and self-confidence in mid-Victorian Ireland. It also demonstrated the importance of evangelical religion and the growing respectability of Ulster Protestantism.

Missionary Activity at Home and Overseas in Mid-Victorian Ireland

The 1859 revival stimulated missionary activism and provoked a shift in how evangelicals understood revivals, which thereafter tended to be planned rather than interpreted as sudden outbreaks of religious zeal. The new form of organised revivalism was led by professional revivalists, the most famous of whom was the American Dwight L. Moody, and appealed to middle-class churchgoers who were increasingly concerned about the threats posed to organised religion by intellectual developments and social and economic change. Moody first visited Ireland in 1874, and again in 1883 and 1892, and his respectable revivalism greatly appealed to Protestants throughout Ireland. For evangelicals in Dublin, Moody's non-denominational approach offered an opportunity to attract Catholics to evangelical Christianity. According to one contemporary observer:

> no one would question now the magnitude and importance of the spiritual work which has gathered round our American brethren in Dublin. No similar movement has ever produced a like impression. At any previous time of revival, the interest was confined within a narrow circle, but at present it penetrates the entire city; and the country – and not the serious people in the country only – is as much moved as the city.[21]

Once more, this impression proved wildly optimistic, but it did reflect the confidence that religiously minded Protestants had in their religious calling. The remarkable network of voluntary societies that had emerged earlier in the century was extended to meet the spiritual and practical needs of the Irish population – Sunday schools, temperance societies, Bible and tract distribution, clothing and poor relief. Voluntary societies offered both spiritual regeneration and 'moral elevation', which was more than social control; it was also a means of self-improvement. The working-class use of these services was

21 J. Hall and G.H. Stuart, *The American Evangelists, D.L. Moody and Ira D. Sankey, in Great Britain and Ireland* (New York: Dodd and Mead, 1875), pp. 276–7.

judicious as they availed themselves of the opportunity to acquire basic skills and relief in tough times as well as the psychological comfort and social validation provided by communal life. Moreover, associational culture would have been significantly less efficient and effective if women were not involved to the active degree they were. Many middle-class women saw their involvement as an extension of their domestic roles, though others developed an awareness of broader social issues and their own subservience, which they challenged on the basis of religious principle as well as notions of gender equality.

Much has been made of the spiritual empire of Irish Catholicism during the nineteenth century, but little attention has been given to Protestant foreign missions. This is remarkable, as the main impetus for Christian mission from the 1790s was evangelical Protestantism, which quickly eclipsed Catholic missionary orders in its global reach.[22] From 1814 to 1878, the Church of Ireland provided eighty-seven missionaries to the Church Missionary Society, the majority of whom were clergy and served in India and Africa. A South American Missionary Society was formed in 1844 and a Colonial and Continental Mission in 1851. In 1878 a Mission to the Lepers was instituted, and Dublin University missions to China and India were established in 1886 and 1891 respectively. The Hibernian Church Missionary Society supported 165 female missionaries overseas, while a female mission, the Zenana Bible and Medical Mission, was formed in 1880. Several Church of Ireland clergy became colonial bishops, including George Pilkington who was martyred in Uganda in 1897.

The first official act of the inaugural meeting of the General Assembly of the Presbyterian Church in Ireland in June 1840 was to appoint the Revd James Glasgow and the Revd Alexander Kerr as missionaries to India. In the early years, the Foreign Mission of the church concentrated on India, but in the late 1860s the focus moved to China, where the mission had remarkable success. Other Presbyterian agencies were established. These included a Jewish Mission (1841) that operated in Damascus and Hamburg, a Colonial Mission (1846) that supplied over sixty ministers to the colonies within the first twenty years, and a Continental Mission (1855) that worked with the French Reformed Church and the Waldensians in Italy. The most successful was the Female Association in Connection with the Foreign Missions of the Presbyterian

---

22 B. Stanley, 'Christian missions, antislavery and the claims of humanity, c. 1813–1873' in S. Gilley and B. Stanley (eds.), *World Christianities, c.1815–c.1914: The Cambridge history of Christianity*, vol. VIII (Cambridge: Cambridge University Press, 2006), pp. 443–57.

Church in Ireland (1873), otherwise known as the Zenana Mission, which was designed to recruit and support teachers and medical workers amongst females in the East. By 1914 there were 101 Irish Presbyterian women, just over 40 per cent of the total number of Presbyterian missionaries, at work in India or China. Once again, missionary activity provided the chance for well-educated, adventurous and idealistic young women to gain status and abilities that would have been significantly curtailed at home. Outside of these denominational societies, a new breed of non-denominational 'faith missions' emerged, such as the Qua Iboe Mission (1887), which harnessed the zeal of the evangelical laity and which would become a dominant strand of Protestant missions in the twentieth century.

Disestablishment and Opposition to 'Rome Rule'

Post-Famine religious renewal deeply affected the Church of Ireland, yet by the 1860s it found itself in a paradox: 'Assured in her integrity and vitality as a religious communion, the Church of Ireland was insecure as "the Church established".' Pluralism and non-residence were no longer significant, the activities of the church were streamlined and cost-effective, and the scale of voluntary contributions by its members was remarkable. In 1868, £188,000 was given to the Church Missionary Society and the Society for the Propagation of the Gospel, £126,593 to the Church Mission to Jews, and over £400,000 to Protestant Orphan Societies.[23] At the same time, the 1860s witnessed a renewed challenge to established churches, provoked, in part, by the extension of the franchise in 1867 and 1868. According to the 1861 census, 77.6 per cent of the Irish population were Catholic, 11.9 per cent Church of Ireland and 9 per cent Presbyterian. For W.E. Gladstone, the prime minister, 1868–74, and the National Association of Ireland, the religious renewal of the church was irrelevant as it was indefensible for the state to support a minority church that contained the wealthiest in Irish society. As the law and order situation in Ireland deteriorated, Gladstone decided to act and in March 1868 brought resolutions before the House of Commons calling for disestablishment. He was opposed by the Tories and members of his own party who saw his plans as a threat to the Union and the rights of property in general. Yet the disestablishment legislation received royal assent in July 1869 and came into effect in January 1871. The state in Ireland was now religiously neutral and religious equality was established by law. For the Church of Ireland, the

23 Acheson, *History*, pp. 168, 172.

act was one of 'severance' from the state, 'spoliation' of its endowments, and 'self-government' in its internal arrangements.[24] The church adjusted remarkably well to its new voluntary status, forming a General Synod to provide representation and the Representative Church Body properly to manage its resources. Yet the sense of betrayal, perhaps even worse the sense of English indifference, was palpable and it prompted Isaac Butt to form the Home Government Association in 1870.

Disestablishment also affected Presbyterians who lost the *regium donum,* and who were enraged that the episcopal church retained the title 'The Church of Ireland'. Yet the act removed one of the principal grievances between Presbyterians and Episcopalians and it thereby helped prepare the way for united opposition to 'Rome Rule' in the 1880s. As Alvin Jackson has reminded us: 'Late Victorian and Edwardian Unionism was a formidable if unlikely combination of landed and commercial capital, of the southern gentry and Belfast industrialists, of small-town Orange brokers as well as metropolitan Tories and imperialists.'[25] In that context, a shared sense of Protestantism was an integral part of this unionist coalition. The process of reform and revival united Protestants together in a shared religious ethos, opposition to Catholicism, and missionary activity. All Protestant churches were against Home Rule and only a very small minority of individual Protestants were in favour. It is important to remember that unionist opposition to the first Home Rule bill in 1885–6 was all-Ireland in its focus and was indebted to the numerical and social power provided by southern Protestants. This was channelled through the Irish Conservative Party and episcopal landowners who defended the remaining privileges of the Church of Ireland (especially Trinity College), property rights and the British connection. They provided leadership, money, and social and familial contacts with the upper echelons of political society in Britain. Working-class Episcopalians were especially represented within the Orange Order – the only populist organisation that could be used to mobilise anti-Home Rule sentiment. The Order united Protestants from different classes, though it was not egalitarian and deference towards social superiors was deeply engrained. The Presbyterian Church in Ireland was geographically much more cohesive within its numerical heartland in the north-east. Presbyterians brought to the coalition financially well-off tenant farmers and the urban middle class, precisely the social groups from which

---

24 Ibid., pp. 200–1.
25 A. Jackson, *Ireland 1798–1998: war, peace and beyond* (Malden: Wiley-Blackwell, 2010), p. 221.

Gladstone derived his support in Britain, and their Liberal Unionism provided a respectable alternative to Orange populism.

For Irish Protestants, the prospect of 'Rome Rule' challenged their religious principles as well as their social position and economic prosperity. A special meeting of the General Synod was held in Dublin on 23 March 1886. It passed four resolutions in response to Gladstone's Home Rule policy that summed up Protestant opposition. The first three declared their attachment to the legislative union as Irishmen who desired the best for their native land, their horror at the violence and intimidation of the previous years that was a harbinger of what Ireland under Home Rule would be, and their devotion to the British Empire. The final resolution reiterated their belief that Home Rule 'would be injurious to the best interests – social, moral, and religious – of our country', before stating that they would resist such a policy 'as tending to impoverish, if not to extirpate, many of those on whose support the maintenance of our Church, under God, depends, and thereby disable her in the efforts which she is making to supply the spiritual needs of her people'.[26]

Conclusion

By 1880, the Protestant churches of Ireland operated with unprecedented efficiency and zeal. The challenges of the nineteenth century had stimulated religious revival that had in turn forged resilient church structures, mobilised the laity, contributed to the spectacular growth of missionary outreach, and shaped the language of respectability and gender roles. Religious revival had not, however, led to the conversion of Catholic Ireland; rather, as Colin Barr has shown in Chapter 11 above, the Irish Catholic Church had itself undergone a significant period of renewal and reorganisation.[27] As a consequence, religious reform in general contributed to a renewed bout of religious and political polarisation. The prospect of a Catholic-dominated Irish parliament exposed the extent to which the assumptions and rhetoric of religious revitalisation had permeated Protestant society in general. As a consequence, 'Rome Rule' threatened not only the gains of religious reform, but also the worldly position and political future of the Protestant minority.

---

26 *Irish Times*, 27 March 1886.
27 See Barr, Chapter 11, pp. 280–304.

PART IV

*

SHAPING SOCIETY

14

Language and Literacy in the Eighteenth and Nineteenth Centuries

AIDAN DOYLE

Introduction

During the century and a half spanning the period 1730–1880 the Irish language was marginalised as a medium of everyday communication. This language shift is a much-contested topic. Generations of scholars across a range of disciplines have failed to arrive at an agreed explanation either of the chronology or of the causes of that shift, and, as the practice of describing the process in negative terms as a decline or loss indicates, have traditionally approached the subject from a fixed position or engaged with the issue in ideological terms. This is consistent with the strong reactions the subject generates among historians and members of the public to this day. This chapter attempts a reappraisal of the facts in the light of recent research in history and in sociolinguistics.

The common view of the history of the language is that until *c.*1800 Irish was widely spoken all over the country, with the exception of Dublin and its hinterland, and other cities and large towns. In the period 1800–50, according to this account, it was replaced by English as the main language for a majority of the population. Thus, in a standard history of Irish literature we read: 'There were four million speakers of Irish out of a population of five million at the beginning of the nineteenth century in Ireland. That is, Ireland was for the most part Irish in language and custom as late as that.'[1] This implies that 80 per cent of the population then spoke Irish. If this version of events were true, we would have to assume the replacement of Irish by English over the course of little more than two generations, since, according to the census returns of 1851, only 23 per cent of the people are reported as being able to speak Irish. In other words, there would have been a decline of

---

1 J.E. Caerwen Williams and P.K. Ford, *The Irish literary tradition* (Cardiff: University of Wales Press, 1992), p. 255.

almost 60 per cent in half a century, which is dramatic. I will argue that this seemingly cataclysmic change never occurred.

One of the problems facing the historian of the Irish language is that we have no reliable figures for either the number or the proportion of the population that were speakers before 1851. Many commentators in the eighteenth and nineteenth centuries offered general estimates, but these vary considerably. However, modern scholars have subjected the available statistical evidence to rigorous examination. Their work enables us to form a more nuanced picture of the linguistic reality in the 120 years before 1850 than was previously possible.

Another important aspect of my reappraisal will be the application of the sociolinguistic notion of diglossia. This appertains to the contemporaneous use of two linguistic codes within a community in different domains. A typical example would be a high register for writing and official purposes, and a low register for informal contacts. Bilingual diglossia arises when two different languages are used within a community in this way. Further on in the chapter I shall explore how, in the period considered here, Ireland exhibited different patterns and degrees of this sociolinguistic phenomenon.

In diglossic situations literacy is a key factor, in that one language tends to be used in written communication. In Ireland in the eighteenth and nineteenth centuries, levels of literacy increased substantially, but it was literacy in English, not in Irish. Given that the ability to read was of the same significance then as the capacity to use a computer today, this had far-reaching consequences for the decline of Irish. Accordingly, the question of education and literacy will also be considered in some detail.

When dealing with language, histories of Ireland have habitually emphasised the negative, namely, the loss of Irish. However, this loss was balanced by a gain – the acquisition of English. This had many positive consequences, for the simple reason that English offered access to a world of print and books previously denied to Irish speakers. The Gaelic written tradition was elitist and exclusive. Literacy in English was a major democratising influence in the nineteenth century, which contributed to social, cultural and economic change.

The branch of language study known as historical sociolinguistics seeks to identify the patterns of language use in the past. Prior to the commencement of sound recording in the twentieth century, we are reliant on written sources. Very often, the records that survive emanate from within the elite, and are of limited value in identifying wider patterns of language use. In recent years, historical linguists, like historians in general, have broadened the scope of their inquiry to embrace diaries, merchants' account books, even graffiti, in order to arrive at a more complete picture of how language was spoken across society. One notion that has emerged from this is that some forms of language are more visible than others. For example, in nineteenth-century Schleswig, which was located on the border between Germany and Denmark, the standardised codes of High German and Danish possessed a high visibility, while local spoken varieties, Low German and South Jutish, were at first sight far less present.[2]

Likewise, in Ireland English enjoyed a high profile in the eighteenth and nineteenth centuries, whereas Irish was nearly invisible. Thus, official sources such as census reports, travellers' narratives, business and personal letters etc. are written in English by people who did not speak Irish. The texts in Irish that have survived are not official documents; they comprise literature for the most part, and very often this literature is non-naturalistic. As a consequence, it has to be treated with caution when it is used as a source. This notwithstanding, we will have occasion to refer to it in what follows, as it offers a view from the inside, and an alternative to the official version of events.

The Spoken Language *c.*1730–*c.*1800

In 1730, Dublin and most urban spaces in Ireland were mainly English-speaking. In the countryside, the people associated with the 'big house' – landlords, agents, Church of Ireland clergy, dealers of all types and the wealthier Catholic tenants – were Anglophone. In the south and west, most of the peasants were Irish speakers. In the eastern counties of Leinster, and in much of Ulster, English predominated, even among small farmers and agricultural labourers.

Estimates of numbers of speakers vary significantly. In the last thirty years or so, two approaches have been employed in an attempt to arrive at more reliable figures. One is to take the results of the 1851 census for the oldest decennial cohort, those born in the 1770s. This is the method employed by Garret Fitzgerald.[3] The other approach, used by William Smyth, is to look at levels of literacy in English, on the premise that those who could read English could also speak it.[4] On the basis of the work of Fitzgerald and Smyth, it can

---

2 For more on visible and invisible languages see A. Havinga and N. Langer (eds.), *Invisible languages in the nineteenth century* (Berne: Peter Lang, 2015).

3 G. Fitzgerald, 'Estimates for baronies of minimum level of Irish-speaking amongst successive decennial cohorts: 1771–1781 to 1861–1871', *Proceedings of the Royal Irish Academy*, 84c (1984), pp. 117–55.

4 W. Smyth, *Map-making, landscapes and memory* (Cork: Cork University Press, 2006).

be argued that *c*.1750 roughly half the population spoke mainly Irish, and half spoke English.

What we do not know is how many people were bilingual. We are pretty sure that those at the top of the social ladder spoke only English. At the opposite end of the spectrum, landless labourers from the west and south spoke only Irish. But in between these two extremes there existed a whole range of abilities in the two languages. Landlords' agents, tradesmen, professional men, publicans, soldiers, administrators and schoolmasters who engaged with members of both linguistic communities would have had an active competence in both languages, although, depending on the time and place, one language would have been dominant. In Ulster, Leinster and the midlands, most people would have had contact with the other language on a daily basis. In a mixed language setting like that of eighteenth-century Ireland, what is termed receptive bilingualism, where one can understand a language but not speak it, seems to have been common. Evidence for this kind of communication is provided by macaronic poetry. Not infrequently such compositions take the form of a dialogue between the male poet-narrator and a girl he is trying to seduce:

> Do dhruideas ina coinne is gan dabht tháinig fonn orm,
> Is é dúirt sí liomsa: 'No more of your tricks!'
> 'A ainnir ná diúltaigh – do sheinnfinn suas tiún duit.'[5]

In bilingual poems such as these, the male tends to speak Irish, and the girl to answer in English. Yet they have no trouble understanding each other. This is not just a literary device – one observes the same practice between speakers of different languages in the present. In other words, macaronic poems are reflections of the linguistic behaviour of the communities that produced them.

From modern studies of bilingual practice,[6] we know that those fluent in two languages move effortlessly from one language to another in a process known as code-switching. This behaviour is widespread when a society is in transition from one language to another. Indeed, monolingual observers

---

5 'I drew near to her and I really took a fancy to her / what she said to me was: 'No more of your tricks!' / 'O maid don't refuse – I would play a tune for you': D. Ó Muirithe, *An t-amhrán Macarónach* (Baile Atha Cliath: An Clóchomhar, 1980), p. 41.

6 For a good introduction and survey of research see T.K. Batia and W.C. Ritchie (eds.), *The handbook of bilingualism* (Oxford: Blackwell, 2004).

can have trouble determining what language a given individual is speaking. Macaronic poetry provides copious examples of code-switching:[7]

> Yesterday morning, ar maidin inné,
> I spied a young damsel is thug mé di spéis,
> D'fhiosraigh mé den bhruinneall but she went away,
> Is d'fhág sí faoi bhrón mé, I'm sorry to say.[8]

There are, in addition, numerous accounts dating from the later eighteenth century which attest to the ability to speak both languages. William Tighe's description of the situation in County Kilkenny *c.*1800 is illustrative:

> English being taught at all schools, it is understood by most of the younger part of the lower classes; but there are many persons, and particularly women, in the hilly districts who cannot speak a word of English: in the hills of Idagh, Irish is said to be tolerably well spoken. The common people seldom speak any other language among themselves; but Irish is more prevalent about Kilkenny and near Munster, than near the county of Carlow. The priests often preach alternately in Irish and English; but always in Irish if they are desirous to be well understood.[9]

In keeping with its location in south-west Leinster, Kilkenny was part of the transition zone between the mainly English-speaking and mainly Irish-speaking regions of the country. Reports like the above were written mainly by monoglot English speakers, most of whom were outsiders. The fact that locals spoke Irish in their presence is not to be wondered at, since Irish was the language of the dispossessed, a code used not so much to communicate as to conceal.

Nicholas Wolf interprets Tighe's commentary as indicative of stable bilingualism, meaning that two languages exist side by side without any change in their relative status.[10] This seems to have been the case until the middle of the

---

7 For more on linguistic aspects of the macaronic poems, see L. Mac Mathúna, *Béarla sa Ghaeilge – cabhair choigríche: an códmheascadh Gaeilge/Béarla i litríocht na Gaeilge 1600–1900* (Baile Atha Cliath: An Clóchomhar, 2007), pp. 183–221; L. Mac Mathúna, 'Verisimilitude or subversion? Probing the interaction of English and Irish in selected warrants and macaronic verse in the eighteenth century' in J. Kelly and C. Mac Murchaidh (eds.), *Irish and English: essays on the Irish and English cultural frontier, 1600–1900* (Dublin: Four Courts Press, 2012), pp. 116–40.

8 'Yesterday morning, yesterday morning / I spied a young damsel and took a fancy to her / I asked her but she went away / And left me pining, I'm sorry to say': Ó Muirithe, *An t-amhrán Macarónach*, p. 64.

9 W. Tighe, *Statistical observations relative to the County of Kilkenny, made in the years 1800–1801* (Dublin: Graisberry and Campbell, 1802), p. 515. For a discussion, and other examples, see N.M. Wolf, *An Irish-speaking island: state, religion, community, and the linguistic landscape in Ireland, 1770–1870* (Madison: University of Wisconsin Press, 2014).

10 Wolf, *An Irish-speaking island*, p. 57.

eighteenth century. However, when we examine the quotation more closely, we can see that something has changed. First, the writer refers to the fact that younger people are learning English and understand it. Second, preaching in the Catholic Church is in both languages, which means that the full congregation could not understand Irish, even if the majority did. As early as 1800, one of the most influential institutions of the day was using English as well as Irish.

In an age when religion played a central role in people's lives, and when the churches oversaw many activities now dealt with by the state, the relationship that existed between language and religion was crucial. This relationship was not straightforward or stable in eighteenth-century Ireland. While it is true that nearly all Protestants, whether Anglican or Presbyterian, spoke English, not all Catholics spoke Irish. Furthermore, because of the Penal Laws, priests were educated in continental seminaries. This meant that when it came to church affairs, and preaching in particular, many of them were more at ease in English and in French, Spanish or Italian than in Irish. Moreover, the Catholic Church did not possess a coherent language strategy. Bishops and priests were keenly aware of the need for Irish-speaking priests in the west of Ireland in particular. From time to time the authorities in the Irish College in Paris introduced Irish classes for seminarians, but with limited success.[11] Cases have also been cited of priests being obliged to learn Irish in order to perform their pastoral duties.[12] But these were isolated interventions by individual priests or bishops to remedy what they perceived as an unsatisfactory situation. As Ciarán Mac Murchaidh remarks, 'no successful initiative was undertaken to provide systematic support for priests who were struggling with the language'.[13] The same author describes the attitude of the Catholic Church towards the Irish language in the eighteenth century as 'at best neutral'.[14]

Previous accounts of language change have highlighted the large numbers speaking Irish at the beginning of the nineteenth century. There seems to be a consensus that about half of the population spoke Irish in 1800, which would equate with a figure of roughly 2.5 million. This is a sizeable number, but it fails to take into account two factors. One is the question of bilingualism. Many of these 2.5 million speakers used English as well as Irish on a daily basis, and many of them did not pass Irish onto their children. By contrast,

11 See C. Mac Murchaidh, 'The Catholic Church and the Irish language' in Kelly and Mac Murchaidh, *Irish and English*, pp. 162–88.
12 Ibid., pp. 172–9.
13 Ibid., p. 178.
14 Ibid., p. 187.

very few of the 2.5 million or so English speakers were able to speak or understand Irish. In other words, despite the large Irish-speaking population, the balance had already tipped in favour of English. The other factor is literacy, which is of such importance it will be addressed in the next section

Literacy and Education *c.*1730–*c.*1800

In his pioneering exploration of popular reading material from the mid-eighteenth to the mid-nineteenth century, Niall Ó Ciosáin notes three developments which drove the demand for literacy in this period: economic growth, increased participation in civic affairs and in litigation, and religion.[15] For the first two, literacy in English was essential; for religious activity, English was also necessary, while Irish was at best desirable. This demand for literacy in turn prompted a rise in the number of educational institutions: 'the state, its major institutions, and the public identified education as an improving force, and … the eighteenth and early nineteenth centuries witnessed a dramatic expansion in the number of schools in the kingdom'.[16]

Schools were run by both the Church of Ireland and the Catholic Church. There was also an informal network of fee-paying private schools ('hedge schools'). In the Protestant schools, which enjoyed state support, the language of instruction was English: 'state policy involved a consistent push to create new educational institutions in which the vernacular used was English in the explicit hope of seeing it displace all others'.[17] Given that Catholics were reluctant to send their children to schools which actively tried to proselytise them, it might be thought that English-medium education would have been limited. What is striking is that in the Catholic parish schools established after 1730 there was the same emphasis on English: 'Such evidence as exists would suggest that one of their primary functions was to provide children with the basics of the English language, the Catholic faith, and knowledge of the classics.'[18]

This was true also of the hedge schools. Folklore about the poet Eoghan Rua Ó Súilleabháin has it that he worked for a while as a schoolteacher. In the following composition he advertises his accomplishments:

15 N. Ó Ciosáin, *Print and popular culture in Ireland 1757–1850* (Dublin: Lilliput Press, 1997).
16 J. Kelly, 'Print and the emergence of mass education in Ireland, *c.*1650–*c.*1830' in J. Kelly and S. Hegarty (eds.), *New perspectives on the history of education in Ireland and Europe, 1700–1900* (Dublin: Four Courts Press, 2017), p. 35.
17 Wolf, *An Irish-speaking island*, p. 125.
18 Mac Murchaidh, 'The Catholic Church and the Irish language', p. 166.

The Catechism I will explain
To each young nymph and noble swain,
With all young ladies I'll engage
To forward them with speed and care,
With book-keeping and mensuration,
Euclid's Elements and Navigation,
With Trigonometry and sound gauging,
And English grammar with rhyme and reason.[19]

Note that there is no mention of Irish grammar. The poet was anxious to display his knowledge of English to the parents of prospective pupils, which he did both by mentioning English as a school subject and by composing the notice in English.

It so happened that one person sometimes combined the positions of community poet, scribe and hedge schoolmaster. Apart from the priest, the poet-scribe might be the only person in an Irish-speaking community who was literate in Irish. The attitude of the Gaelic literati towards English was ambiguous. On the one hand, until the end of the Jacobite era, when there was still a slender chance of the Stuarts being restored, English was the language of the intruders, a language that was the conduit of an alien culture and religion. At the same time, it was the language of literacy, the language that gave the poet-scribes access to the world of print. Recent work has shown that there was considerable interaction between print and manuscript cultures in the second half of the eighteenth century.[20] Furthermore, even in the scribal bastion of the Gaelic world, English becomes more evident from the middle of the century onwards: 'The amount of English in the manuscripts, first added by the owners and increasingly by the scribes themselves, increased massively in the manuscripts from the 1750s and 1760s.'[21]

Much has been made of the fact that schooling, and hence literacy, was only available through English. Past commentators have ascribed this to the fact that the administration of Ireland was overseen by a small elite who were hostile to the use of Irish.[22] This is undoubtedly true, but it does not explain

19 P. Ua Duinnín (ed.), *Amhráin Eoghain Ruaidh Uí Shúilleabháin* (Baile Atha Cliath: Connradh na Gaedhilge, 1901), p. xxii.
20 M. Ní Urdail, *The scribe in eighteenth- and nineteenth-century Ireland: motivations and milieu* (Munster: Nodus Publikationen, 2000); L. Ní Mhunghaile, 'Bilingualism, print culture in Irish and the public sphere', in Kelly and Mac Murchaidh, *Irish and English*, pp. 218–42.
21 L. Cullen, 'Patrons, teachers and literacy in Irish: 1700–1850' in M. Daly and D. Dickson (eds.), *The origins of popular literacy in Ireland: changes and educational development 1700–1920* (Dublin: Department of Modern History, 1990), pp. 15–44.
22 J. Kelly, 'Irish Protestants and the Irish language in the eighteenth century' in Kelly and Mac Murchaidh (eds.), *Irish and English*, pp. 189–217.

the scale of the demand for English. After 1730, private pay schools operated freely all over the country, often being taught by the poet-scribes mentioned in the previous paragraph. They were entirely free to teach through whatever medium they chose. The printing industry was mainly based in Dublin, but if there was nothing to prevent printers producing Catholic devotional material despite the Penal Laws, there was even less pressure on them to refrain from producing material in Irish.[23] A similar situation obtained in Wales regarding the Welsh language, and yet there was much more printing in Welsh in the eighteenth century: 'Altogether, there were perhaps three thousand works printed in Welsh before 1820, compared to less than two hundred in Irish.'[24]

The problem in Ireland is that the choice was not a straightforward one between reading in Irish and reading in English. The main form of literacy available in Gaelic Ireland, both before and after the seventeenth-century conquest and colonisation of the country, was manuscript literacy, and this was restricted to a small elite. There was never any question in Gaelic Ireland of mass education or mass literacy. The trade of scribe tended to pass down from father to son. One of the best-known examples of this in the eighteenth and nineteenth centuries was the Ó Longáin family of County Cork, three generations of whom were employed as copiers of texts.[25] Reading and writing were arcane skills that were jealously guarded, and there seem to have been no attempts to make them accessible to the community as a whole. The one body that might have been able to provide the kind of institutional support for education, literacy and print culture in Irish was the Catholic Church. By the time this institution was able to operate freely, it was too late – the mould was already set, and English was the only language through which the church as a whole could function.[26]

Those who have grown up in monolingual nation-states can have difficulty understanding how somebody can use one language for speaking and another for written communication. And yet this practice was widespread in the past and is still to be found in many parts of the world outside Europe. For about a thousand years in western Europe, reading and writing meant reading and writing in Latin, while people spoke their local vernacular. In

23 J. Kelly and C. Mac Murchaidh, 'Introduction: establishing the context' in Kelly and Mac Murchaidh (eds.), *Irish and English*, pp. 15–42.
24 Ó Ciosáin, *Print and popular culture*, p. 188; N. Ó Ciosáin, 'The print culture of the Celtic languages, 1700–1900', *Cultural and Social History*, 10:3 (2013), 347–67.
25 See Ní Urdail, *The scribe* for an in-depth study of this family.
26 N. Ó Ciosáin, 'Print and Irish, 1570–1900: an exception among the Celtic languages', *Radharc*, 5–7 (2004–6), 73–106.

post-colonial Africa and Asia, it is not uncommon for people to speak a local or national language and to receive their education through the medium of English or French. Thus, in the circumstances of eighteenth-century Ireland, the fact that many people spoke Irish and read English is not at all remarkable, particularly since the Gaelic manuscript culture was unavailable to all save a chosen few, and could never provide the same range of written material that English did.

This is not to minimise the significance of certain scribal families and their patrons who served as mediators between English and Irish via translation. Meidhbhín Ní Urdail shows how two religious texts were translated into Irish in the eighteenth century, and circulated in manuscript form; one of them even found its way into print,[27] and was copied later by the Ó Longáins.[28] Ní Urdail contrasts this earlier activity with the translations produced by Mícheál Óg Ó Longain in the early nineteenth century: 'It is the case, however, that although this material was adapted into Gaelic scribal culture from its counterpart in print, the contact itself cannot be said to have been extensive as the texts were not transmitted in manuscripts by other scribes in Cork city and its environs.'[29] It is clear that the sporadic efforts of mid-eighteenth-century scribes to disseminate new texts in Irish were petering out by 1800.

Before concluding this section, it is worth mentioning one other form of bilingual diglossia, illustrated by the case of Riocard Bairéad, the folk-poet from County Mayo. According to the editor of his works, Bairéad could read and write English but wrote Irish using English orthography; presumably, he was unable to read the manuscripts that were still being produced elsewhere in the Gaelic script.[30] This pattern was to become increasingly common after 1800, as literacy in English increased and the manuscript tradition declined.

The Spoken Language 1800–1880

Because the use of the Irish language, as evidenced by the number of speakers, contracted sharply between 1800 and 1880, this period has attracted much

---

27 *Eagna fhírinneach – true wisdom (English and Irish): with short instructions for reading Irish* (Cork, 1736).

28 Ní Urdail, *The scribe*, pp. 219–20.

29 Ibid., p. 218.

30 N. Williams, *Riocard Bairéad – Amhráin* (Baile Atha Cliath: An Clóchomhar, 1978) pp. 39–40; see also N. Williams, 'Gaelic texts and English script' in M. Caball and A. Carpenter (eds.), *Oral and print cultures in Ireland 1600–1900* (Dublin: Four Courts Press, 2010), pp. 85–101.

attention from both historians and philologists.[31] I will commence with a brief outline of what might be described as the traditional view of events, before examining some recent reappraisals and reworkings of this account. As with the eighteenth century, I will deal with education and literacy separately.

Political events in nineteenth-century Ireland had a formative impact on the relative status of the Irish and English languages. In the first half of the century, public life was dominated by Daniel O'Connell. As the commanding influence of his generation, O'Connell has been assigned a major role in the language shift, mainly because he has been portrayed as somebody who could have saved Irish, and instead used his influence to urge his devoted followers to abandon it. I have shown elsewhere that this is too simplistic, and that O'Connell is better conceived of as a bilingual who spoke Irish in certain circumstances, but who operated through English in public life and when reading and writing. He did not possess an ideological agenda with respect to Irish, but based his linguistic choices on what was expedient.[32]

Romantic nationalists took a different view, of course, but romantic nationalism, with its focus on national languages, was a late arrival on the Irish political scene. The Young Irelanders of the 1840s, and Thomas Davis in particular, claimed that there was an indissoluble link between the Irish nation and the Irish language, but this philosophy did not gain widespread support until after 1880. In fact, while Davis was urging his countrymen to speak Irish, he and other ideologues of nationalism created a body of writing in prose and verse in *English* that was to prove a powerful inspiration for their own and future generations. The Fenian movement of the 1850s and 1860s maintained this tradition. Irish was seen as a goal to be pursued, but the linguistic means they employed were English. Not surprisingly, the means subverted the end.

Nicholas Wolf has recently challenged the version of events which denies Irish any role in public life in the nineteenth century.[33] His claim is that, contrary to what the received wisdom would have us believe, Irish played a prominent role in community affairs. He points out that provision was frequently made in the courtroom for those who could not speak English, and that at election time it was permitted to administer oaths in Irish. There are also

---

31 See G. Ó Tuathaigh, *Ireland before the Famine 1798–1848* (Dublin: Gill & Macmillan, 1972); B. Ó Cuív, 'Irish language and literature, 1691–1845' in T.W. Moody and W.E. Vaughan (eds.), *A new history of Ireland*, vol. III (Oxford: Oxford University Press, 1986), pp. 509–45; C. Ó Huallacháin, *The Irish and Irish* (Dublin: Assisi Press, 1994); A. Doyle, *A history of the Irish language* (Oxford: Oxford University Press, 2015), pp. 107–60.

32 A. Doyle, 'A sociolinguistic analysis of a national language: Irish in the nineteenth century' in Havinga and Langer, *Invisible languages*, pp. 117–34.

33 Wolf, *An Irish-speaking island*, pp. 149–80.

reports of speakers addressing crowds in Irish during election campaigns. This is all true, and it is important that we be reminded of it. However, it hardly undermines the thesis that English was the dominant language. Irish was tolerated, if and when there were intermediaries available to accommodate those who had no English.[34]

One cannot deal with matters linguistic in nineteenth-century Ireland without engaging with the attitudes of and language policies of institutional religion. As part of the so-called Second Reformation, various Bible societies sought to convert Irish speakers by teaching them to read in Irish, in the hope that they would be encouraged to read the Bible and evangelical religious tracts in translation. A network of schools was established, and local Catholic schoolmaster-scribes were employed to do the teaching. After some initial success, the campaign provoked a fierce response from the Catholic clergy. Bishops and priests denounced the so-called *Bíobloírí* 'proselytisers', as a result of which many were ostracised by their communities. The net effect was a lasting and deep-rooted suspicion among the ordinary people of those who were literate in Irish, and of the Irish language in general.[35]

Meanwhile, the Catholic Church was embarked on its own missionary activity. The traditional version is that this activity was conducted mainly through English, but Nicholas Wolf argues that the opposite was the case: 'the church … exhibited a keen awareness of the need to administer to their flocks in Irish if devotional revolution was to make any headway'.[36] To some extent, one's interpretation of church activity is a matter of perspective, and whether one views the glass as half-empty or as half-full. Wolf invokes every identifiable instance of Irish being used, and recommendation that it be spoken. In so doing, he rightly corrects those who denied the clergy any credit in attempting to preach or conduct services in Irish. Individuals frequently translated sermons into Irish for use in Sunday services. The archbishop of Tuam, John McHale, encouraged his priests to preach in Irish, and to prepare children for confirmation in this language. There was, as Wolf reminds us, a large cohort of Irish-speaking students in Maynooth between 1800 and 1870.

Yet Wolf's claim that 'centuries of received understanding about conquest and dispossession had marked English as a threat to Catholicism' is

---

34 See A. Doyle, 'The "decline" of the Irish language in the eighteenth and nineteenth centuries: a new interpretation', *Studia Hibernica*, 41 (2015), 165–76.

35 For an account of the Bible Societies see P. de Brún, *Scriptural instruction in the vernacular: the Irish Society and its teachers, 1818–27* (Dublin: Dublin Institute for Advanced Studies, 2009).

36 Wolf, *An Irish-speaking island*, p. 267.

contestable if not simply misleading.[37] This may have still been the case in 1730, in that there were parts of Ireland (e.g. Ulster) where there was a direct connection between ethnicity, language and religion.[38] By 1800 language no longer played a major part in Irish identity:

> in the vast majority of eighteenth-century *aislingí* [Jacobite poems] the role-reversal forecast by the poet as a consequence of Ireland's deliverance is described with reference to religious and linguistic labels ... By the early nineteenth century, however, the linguistic label is found less often in the poems, and the religious distinction becomes the primary test in discussing the past and future.[39]

We can map this change by tracing the changing meaning of a single Irish word, *Sasanach*. In the seventeenth century, the main meaning of this word was 'Englishman'. From about the middle of the eighteenth century, it begins to acquire a second meaning, that of 'Protestant'. By the time we get to the nineteenth century, the religious meaning is dominant, and that of 'Englishman' is confined to literary texts. Writing in 1824, when the Bible societies were at their most active, one of their teachers complains that his neighbours are accusing him of being a Protestant: 'Tá go leor insan áit so dhá rá gur Sagsanach mé' [Many in this place are saying that I'm a Protestant].[40] Given that the author, Labhrás Ó Séaghdha, was writing in Irish, and had a Gaelic surname, it is clear that religion was more divisive in Ireland in the nineteenth century than language or even ancestry.

It would be wrong, however, to conclude that the Catholic Church was more aggressively anti-Irish than other sections of the Irish population. Most bishops and priests were pragmatic. Because the written word played a vital role in their work and because the Catholic Church was active in so many aspects of public life – education and health most notably – it was inevitable that the church would function mainly through the medium of English. The same pragmatic impulse led individuals to conduct pastoral work through the medium of Irish when this was appropriate. But they did so in the absence of a uniform language policy among the clergy as a whole. It would have required a bishop like John McHale in every diocese, supported by a carefully

37 Ibid., p. 274.
38 For an exploration of religious-linguistic antagonism, see C. Dillon, 'English, Irish and the south Ulster poets and scribes' in Kelly and Mac Murchaidh, *Irish and English*, pp. 141–61.
39 G. Ó Tuathaigh, 'Gaelic Ireland, popular politics and Daniel O'Connell', *Journal of the Galway Archaeological and Historical Society*, 34 (1974), 29.
40 P. de Brún (ed.), 'Bíoblóir á chosaint féin', *Éigse* 23 (1988), 82.

planned system of bilingual education in Maynooth, for Irish to become the language of worship and instruction. In other countries, the clergy acted as a bulwark for the local language.[41] In Ireland, the use of Irish in preaching was not ideologically driven; it was an immediate and provisional response to circumstances, in the same way that interpreters were employed by the courts when and if the need arose.

Whenever the language question in the nineteenth century arises, the Great Famine and its consequences are invariably adduced as important factors in the decline of Irish. The assumption is that since the poorer members of society in the south and west of the country were hardest hit by the Famine, and that these were Irish speakers, then Irish must have experienced a larger drop in numbers than English.[42] The secondary, and more lasting, effect was emigration; as emigration to Britain and the USA became a permanent feature of Irish life after 1850, and emigration post-Famine was higher in the south and west than elsewhere, it increased demand for English.

One of the more contentious issues surrounding emigration is the fate of Irish overseas, particularly in the New World. The traditional view was that Irish speakers concealed their knowledge of Irish on arrival. Before the 1880s, there is very little evidence of Irish being spoken in the immigrant communities, but this is not surprising – spoken languages leave few traces.[43] A number of features distinguished the Irish from other newcomers. The first was that, given the level at which bilingualism stood in pre-Famine Ireland, there was no Irish person who would not have been previously exposed to English, even if it was only on the emigrant ship. Second, since it is not such a big step for bilinguals to increase their use of one language and reduce that of another, emigrants faced with this choice would not have had to engage in a major adjustment in linguistic behaviour. Thirdly, Irish immigrants were linguistically mixed, but insofar as they had a language in common, it was English, not Irish. In the difficult conditions of the New World, being Irish was far more important than being Gaelic. Fourth, since Irish identity was defined in religious terms, there was a pre-existing institution with which the newcomers could comfortably identify – the Catholic Church. And the churches of the

---

41 Ó Ciosáin, *Print and popular culture*, pp. 187–91; H. Wolbersen, 'The decline of the South Jutish in Angeln: a historical case of transformation into the modern age around 1800' in Havinga and Langer, *Invisible languages*, pp. 149–72.

42 As far as I know, no attempt has been made to quantify the effect of the Famine in linguistic terms.

43 For more on the fate of Irish in the USA see J. Callahan, 'The Irish language in Pennsylvania' in T.W. Ihde (ed.), *The Irish language in the United States: a historical, sociolinguistic and applied linguistic survey* (Westport, CT: Bergin and Garvey, 1994), pp. 18–26.

Irish community were solidly Anglophone: 'Unlike the role of Hebrew in Judaism, Arabic in Islam, Greek, Armenian and Serbian in Eastern Orthodox churches, the role of Irish in Catholicism was not one of religious necessity.'[44]

This negative view of the presence of Irish in the USA has been challenged by Deirdre Ní Chonghaile. Focusing on a community of Irish speakers in Philadelphia in the 1880s and 1890s, she has shown that it was common for members of this community to come together to sing and play music in each other's houses.[45] The Irish-Americans of Philadelphia that she writes about were certainly proud of their heritage, both linguistic and musical. However, Ní Chonghaile is writing about the period after 1880, when societies like the Philo-Celtic Society provided support for enthusiasts and collectors of manuscripts, folklore and music. It seems that attitudes towards Irish changed after 1880, just as they did in Ireland around the same time. Before this, there is little evidence that Irish was visible (as distinct from audible) at events in the Irish-American community. The attitude of Irish-Americans to the Irish language was complex. On the one hand, many emigrants took with them Irish-language manuscripts as mementos.[46] But they rarely added to them, or wrote new ones. Regarding a scribe who emigrated to the USA and took a manuscript with him, we read: 'Go bhfios dúinn, níor bhreac sé focal eile Gaeilge tar eis dó an tír a fhágaint sa mbliain 1827' [As far as we know, he didn't write another word of Irish after he left the country in 1827].[47] And when the same scribe wrote to his brother, he wrote in English. A parallel may be drawn with balladry; while many Irish-language songs were collected in the USA, nearly all the nineteenth-century ballads of emigration were composed in English. There seemed to be some insurmountable barrier to transporting Irish across the sea.

In conclusion, there is the question of quantifying the order of the language shift. The 1851 census included a question about language. Allowing for the usual inaccuracies, and for the fact that some respondents denied that they knew Irish, we can conclude that approximately a quarter of the population (23 per cent) spoke Irish, and of these less than a third spoke Irish only. Working backwards from this figure, it is possible to form a rough estimate

44 J. Kallen, 'Irish as an American ethnic language' in Ihde (ed.), *The Irish language in the United States*, p. 35.

45 D. Ní Chonghaile, ' "Sagart gan iomrádh": an tAthair Domhnall Ó Morchadha (1858–1935) agus amhráin Pennsylvania' in R. Nic Congáil et al. (eds.), *Litríocht na Gaeilge ar fud an domhain* I (Baile Atha Cliath: *Leabhair* Comhar, 2015), pp. 191–214.

46 P. Ó Macháin, 'Imirce agus filleadh lámhscríbhinní na nGael' in Nic Congáil et al. (eds.), *Litríocht na Gaeilge ar fud an domhain* I, p. 133.

47 Ó Macháin, 'Imirce', p. 114.

of the numbers who were brought up speaking Irish in the decade 1771–81. On the basis of such a study, Garret Fitzgerald concluded that 45 per cent of the children born in this decade were brought up speaking Irish.[48] This in turn enables us tentatively to suggest a figure of about half the population who could speak Irish in 1800. This would then mean that the proportion of Irish speakers halved in the period 1800–50.

Some commentators have interpreted the post-Famine number of Irish speakers as a sign of vigour, not of decline: 'More than one million men and women still spoke Irish in 1861', Nicholas Wolf has pointed out.[49] The problem with such statements is that they ignore the fact that the communities in question were bilingual. Some of the census respondents undoubtedly had spoken Irish in their youth, and perhaps still did so with their co-evals, but by the 1860s in most of the country they would have had no choice but to speak English to the next generation. Furthermore, literacy and education had become available to all, and since this was through English it meant that English continued to advance and expand as a language of conversation as well as commerce.

Literacy and Education 1800–1870

One of the main causes traditionally invoked in explaining the 'decline' of Irish in the nineteenth century is the introduction of a system of free primary education for all in 1831: 'Today nearly every school child in Ireland will tell you that Daniel O'Connell, the Catholic clergy and the National schools together killed the Irish language.'[50] The spread of education following the Education Act of 1831 certainly accelerated the language shift, but the trend had been established long before that. As early as 1824, roughly 40 per cent of children were attending some kind of school. As discussed earlier, both the state schools and the private pay-schools of the late eighteenth century operated almost exclusively through English. When the national schools were set up, they simply continued this practice. The exclusion of Irish was partly a legacy of the Bible societies, which had created a link in the 1820s between the reading and writing of Irish and proselytisation. Another point worth considering is put forward by Nicholas Wolf, namely, that the national schools were slow to catch on in Connacht and Munster, partly because John McHale

---

48 Fitzgerald, 'Estimates for baronies of minimum level of Irish-speaking', pp. 117–55.
49 Wolf, *An Irish-speaking island*, p. 268.
50 M. Wall, 'The decline of the Irish language' in B. Ó Cuív (ed.), *A view of the Irish language* (Dublin: The Stationery Office, 1969), pp. 81–90.

opposed them.[51] This meant that many Irish-speaking children did not attend them until the 1860s. And yet Irish continued to decline in both these provinces between 1830 and 1860.

Regardless of how they acquired it, the ability to read English was extremely high among the Irish prior to the Great Famine: 'In 1841 . . . 47 per cent of the population over five years of age were able to read.'[52] While connected with formal education, literacy could be acquired independently of it, in that one could also learn to read in a Sunday school or at home. There is evidence also that women in Ulster were more literate than in other parts of the country, and that this may have been connected with the higher number of Protestants in this province.[53] Bible-reading at home would have been normal for Protestant women, unlike their Catholic counterparts.

With respect to formal schooling, we can form a picture of the way that reading and writing were taught. For the English-speaking areas in the east and north of the country, and the main cities and towns elsewhere, there was a wide range of primers and grammars available for purchase.[54] While the price could be forbidding for poorer parents, bodies like the Kildare Place Society supplied texts in large numbers at more affordable prices. As well as the elementary textbooks, works of fiction were made available in cheap editions. Titles ranged from classics like *Robinson Crusoe* and *Aesop's Fables,*[55] to more local works like *Irish highwaymen.*[56] It may be that these were read by more advanced students. But, one way or another, judging by the amount of cheap print available in Ireland in this era, the demand for instruction in reading and writing was high.

The situation was different in the mainly Irish-speaking areas. The long-term goal of the Bible societies was to teach people to read in English, but it was recognised that it would be helpful to teach them to read Irish first; the same approach was applied in Scotland in the Gaelic-speaking areas of the Highlands. Thanks to the work of Padraig de Brún, we know quite a lot about the books used to teach people how to read Irish.[57] The most common primer was called *An Irish and English spelling-book: being a few easy steps to a right understanding of the English language, through the medium of Irish. For the*

51 Wolf, *An Irish-speaking island*, pp. 141–2.
52 Ó Ciosáin, *Print and popular culture*, p. 39.
53 Ibid., p. 42.
54 For more on this, see Kelly 'Print and emergence of mass education', *passim*.
55 Ibid., pp. 68–9.
56 Ó Ciosáin, *Print and popular culture*, pp. 94–111.
57 de Brún, *Scriptural instruction*, pp. 104–16.

use of schools, and persons in the Irish parts of the country. This was popularly known as the 'Catbrack', from the phrase *cat breac* 'speckled cat' in Lesson Two. If one reads through the list of titles printed for the Irish Society, the most active of the Bible societies, a few features stand out.[58] One is the obviously 'missionary' nature of the content. Thus on p. 6 of the Catbrack primer, we find the phrase *fear geal* ['white man'], which would hardly have been an essential item of vocabulary in nineteenth-century Ireland. Secondly, texts for reading are taken from the Bible, comprising extracts from the Gospels or the Book of Proverbs. The other common feature of these books is that they are in both Irish and English. In other words, their purpose was as much to teach English as to teach the reading of Irish. In fact, in 1825 the Irish Society gave explicit instructions to its officials not to distribute any books besides the Bible, for fear that people would not progress to the reading of English.[59]

It is extremely difficult to ascertain how many people did actually learn to read Irish, either in the schools of the Bible societies or elsewhere. Contemporary reports are conflicting in the extreme. On the one hand, one finds references to the teaching of Irish in non-Protestant schools: 'there are very many schools in the darkest parts of Ireland, in which the Irish language is taught for the mere love of that language alone; these are scarcely supplied with printed books, making use of MSS grammars, transcripts from old books, or fragments of print'.[60] On the other hand, the fact that all commentators, regardless of their religion or background, mention the fact that Irish was taught by specific individuals supports the conclusion that it was unusual. Moreover, many of the missionaries did not know Irish, and seemed happy to believe that the Bible societies were more successful than they really were. Education and books were prized commodities, and the fact that people enrolled for classes and took free copies of bibles does not mean that they ever made use of them. Finally, as we saw earlier, the ability of a schoolmaster to read and write manuscripts in the Gaelic script is not to be equated with a modern literacy programme. The third generation of Ó Longáins continued to copy manuscripts for bodies like the Royal Irish Academy until the 1880s, but this was a niche activity aimed at wealthy patrons.

The Catholic Church, while it never undertook the kind of concerted campaign that other Christian churches did, supported the printing of catechisms and other works of popular devotion. Niall Ó Ciosáin has argued that 'there

---

58 Ibid., pp. 115–17.
59 Ibid., p. 105.
60 Irish Society's 5th report (1823), pp. 4–5; quoted in de Brún, *Scriptural instruction*, p. 64.

was a minor explosion in Irish-language printing between 1800 and 1850'.[61] The *Pious miscellany* of Tadhg Gaelach Ó Súilleabháin, a collection of religious verse, was printed twenty times in this period.[62] Reprints of catechisms enjoyed a comparable popularity.[63] However, such works were nearly always stopgaps, produced in response to local conditions. By and large, their titles and introductions are in English, and they contain guidelines for readers literate in English as to how the Irish characters are to be pronounced. Not infrequently, the texts are written using English orthography. Another point to be borne in mind is that reading aloud was a common form of textual transmission in this era. It sufficed for one person in a district, either the priest or the schoolmaster, to be able to read a catechism out loud, while the rest of the community learnt its precepts off by heart, without seeing them in written form. Such measures cannot be compared with an organised literacy programme, supported by qualified teachers and a range of suitable textbooks.

Lest it be thought that Ireland was exceptional with respect to language, it is worth briefly considering the case of southern Denmark around the same time. There, German enjoyed high status, while the local dialect of South Jutish was a low-register language. Even when Danish ministers tried to introduce (standard) Danish into services, the congregation did not always welcome such changes: 'The language used for worship had been Latin and H[high] G[erman]. This meant that for the common people who spoke the Danish vernacular German was seen as some kind of holy language.'[64] Before 1800, High German was the language of writing: 'Nearly all printed media was written in H[high] G[erman], so the practice of reading and writing ... trained the locals increasingly in mastering a former foreign language.'[65] In the end, standard Danish triumphed over High German, but only because the Lutheran church conducted a vigorous campaign aimed at making Danish the official language for services and writing. Left to their own devices, the local people would have continued to use High German as the status language.

In situations of diglossia, once a pattern of language use becomes established, it is very difficult, sometimes impossible, to persuade people to behave otherwise. To this day, it is not unusual for Gaeltacht people to speak Irish to

---

61 Ó Ciosáin, *Print and popular culture*, p. 179.
62 R. Sharpe, 'Tadhg Gaelach Ó Súilleabháin's *Pious miscellany*: editions of the Munster bestseller in the early nineteenth century', *Proceedings of the Royal Irish Academy*, 114C (2014), 235–93.
63 Wolf, *An Irish-speaking island*, p. 188.
64 Wolbersen, 'The decline of the South Jutish', p. 164.
65 Ibid., p. 167.

each other, but to write in English. In the period 1800–80, it is not that books were not printed in Irish, or that nobody was able to read them. Archbishop McHale produced his own catechism and translation of the New Testament to counter the work of the Bible societies. The reports of those same societies make it clear that it was possible to teach people to read Irish.[66] English orthography is far more inconsistent and opaque for a learner than Irish spelling, and yet the Irish mastered it relatively painlessly. In the end, the barrier to literacy in Irish was psychological rather than technical. One of the *Bíoblóirí* who converted to Protestantism and continued to proselytise all his life, Thomas Stack, describes the reaction of a group of country people to the reading of a letter in Irish in 1850:

> on last Sunday I went my cousin's house. I asked him to come with me to this [other] house … In a short time after going in, my cousin asked me to read the last Irish letter that I got from America for them. So I did; and whilst reading it, there was not another word in the house. When I was done, they were all surprized at having a letter written in Irish in America, and also at the great information in it concerning the country and the state of the people in it.[67]

Had the letter been in English, it would have caused no surprise, but the fact of its being in Irish made it an event which was unlikely to be repeated.

Given the wealth and variety of material published in English in the nineteenth century, there was no way that the Irish would have been content only to read the Bible and other religious material, as was the hope of the Bible societies. In Gaelic Scotland, where there was no opposition from the Catholic Church, various literacy missions were far more successful than in Ireland. But as in Ireland, the students wanted more:

> In late eighteenth- and early nineteenth-century Scotland, when evangelical societies established schools to teach the reading of scripture in Gaelic, pupils were disappointed if they did not proceed to reading and writing in English later on … Literacy in regional languages was possible and desirable, but not as desirable as literacy in an official, high-prestige language.[68]

In the twentieth century, even with the full support of the state and publishing subsidies, the variety and range of material published in Irish was limited. Two hundred years ago, there was virtually nothing to publish besides

---

66 de Brún, *Scriptural instruction*, pp. 59–83.
67 Ibid., p. 461.
68 Ó Ciosáin, *Print and popular culture*, p. 179.

religious matter and poetry. This did not satisfy the demand for reading material that accompanied the various educational and social changes of the era. Only English-language print provided what the people were looking for.

The English Language in Ireland 1730–1880

In histories of Ireland since 1900, language change is invariably presented from the perspective of Irish. By this I mean that authors write of the *decline* of Irish, rather than of the *rise* of English. The implication is that the language change was bad for the Irish people. Obviously, though, one could view the same occurrence in a positive light, or at least in a neutral fashion. There was loss, but there was gain as well. This section explores the rise of Irish English[69] and its consequences.

Although English was spoken in Ireland before 1600, it was during the period 1600–1700 that it took root over large parts of the country, assisted by the various plantations of that century. Outside of Ulster, the new settlers came mainly from the north and west of England, bringing with them their local dialects. In Ulster, the settlers spoke Scots. This resulted in the development of two main varieties of English in Ireland by 1750: Ulster Scots, and what one might call southern Irish English. These two varieties, and a metropolitan supra-regional dialect in Dublin, were to become the speech of most Irish people in the period 1750–1850. Before 1800, written sources for Irish English are meagre. Furthermore, as they are the work of educated people, they rarely differ from the kind of material we find in England at the same time. Thus, in the case of Jonathan Swift, the only text which we can identify as unmistakeably Irish English is his satirical representation of the speech of country landowners.[70] In the nineteenth century, we find evidence of all kinds for Irish English from regional writers like William Carleton to letters written by emigrants to the New World and Australia.[71]

As mentioned above, the change from Irish to English was preceded by a period of prolonged language contact and bilingualism. In such situations, it is usual for speakers to carry some features from one language into the other.

---

69 Irish English seems to have replaced Hiberno-English and Anglo-Irish as the name of the dialect of English spoken in Ireland.

70 J. Swift, 'A dialogue in Hibernian style between A and B' in H. Davis and L. Landa (eds.), *Prose writings*, vol. IV (Oxford: Blackwell, 1973).

71 For letters see M. Filppula, *The grammar of Irish English: language in Hibernian style* (London: Routledge, 1999), pp. 42–7, 296–8.

Not surprisingly, this also happened in Ireland.[72] If a lexical item is borrowed, then it is easy enough to identify Irish as the source, as in this quotation from John O'Donovan, one of the main figures employed on the Ordnance Survey of Ireland in the 1830s: 'a man may be very learned, and at the same time a very great *amadawn*'.[73] The epithet *amadawn* is clearly a borrowing of Irish *amadán* ['fool']. However, with other features of Irish English, it is harder to pinpoint their source. One phenomenon which has become particularly associated with Irish English is the use of reflexive pronouns (*myself, yourself* etc.) as subjects of sentences: *Himself was having a drink* (Standard English: *He was having a drink*). This usage corresponds to an identical one in Irish, so it has been argued in one article that the pattern was borrowed from one language into the other.[74] However, it has been pointed out elsewhere that there are sporadic instances of the same construction in Shakespeare and other Early Modern English texts, which leads the authors to conclude: 'This leaves open the possibility of converging adstratal influences between the Celtic languages, earlier "mainstream" English, and the dialects of English which have evolved in Scotland and Ireland.'[75]

Some authors argue that Irish English is simply Irish with English words:

> The term 'Hiberno-English' comprises two strands, the Irish language and the English language. It is a macaronic form of English which derives its power and uniqueness from the competition between two grammars and two lexicons which is experienced by every user of Hiberno-English who has to exercise choice all the time ... There is a continual interplay between Irish and English, which involves questions of correctness, class, ethnicity, religion, culture, superstition, and many other concerns.[76]

The above could be said of any non-standard variety of English: Scottish, Welsh, Yorkshire, etc. Speakers of these dialects usually write, and at times speak, standard English, and revert to the local dialect in informal settings. But the existence of two codes in Ireland proves nothing about the origins of Irish English. Nobody would deny that it is a contact variety, but there

---

72 For more on this, see J. Kallen, 'Irish English: context and contacts' in J. Kallen (ed.), *Focus on Ireland* (Amsterdam: John Benjamins, 1997), pp. 1–33; Filppula, *The grammar of Irish English*, pp. 22–9.

73 M. Herity (ed.), *Ordnance Survey letters: Meath* (Dublin: Four Masters Press, 2001), p. 31.

74 T. Odlin, 'Bilingualism and substrate influence: a look at clefts and reflexives' in Kallen, *Focus on Ireland*, pp. 35–50.

75 M. Filppula et al., *English and Celtic in contact* (London: Routledge, 2008), p. 176.

76 T. Dolan, 'Translating Irelands: the English language in the Irish context' in M. Cronin and C. Ó Cuilleanáin (eds.), *The languages of Ireland* (Dublin: Four Courts Press, 2003), pp. 78–92.

is no direct one-to-one correspondence between the grammar, vocabulary and phonetics of Irish and of Irish English. In other words, Irish English is an *English* dialect, accessible to any speaker of English. One can establish certain parallels and mutual influences with Irish, but they are separate languages.

Whatever its origins, there is no doubt that by 1850 Irish English had established itself as a distinct dialect of English. The wider English-speaking world became aware of this dialect as more and more Irish people emigrated to Britain, its colonies and North America. In Britain, the Irish accent and turn of phrase was the subject of parody, embodied in the character of the stage Irishman. In America, the emigrant ballads of the post-Famine era helped to disseminate what was rightly or wrongly regarded as a distinctly Irish way of talking. Irish writers, in their turn, were not slow to utilise the emerging dialect in their work. Novelists like William Carleton, Maria Edgeworth and Charles Kickham wrote dialogues which purport to represent the speech of peasants, many of whom were bilingual. Another genre which can yield linguistic evidence for nineteenth-century Irish English is folklore as recorded by people like Crofton Croker and William Wilde. We also know much about the speech of ordinary people thanks to letters, diaries, newspapers and court records, which frequently contain examples of speech or mistakes that reveal something about the Irish English dialect.

It must constantly be borne in mind, however, that most of the writing that survives of Irish people in the nineteenth century was produced by members of the upper or middle classes, and that it differs little from English writing of the time. Using standard English in the public arena – in the courtroom, in the Westminster parliament, in newspapers and political tracts, in trade and commerce, in ecclesiastical affairs – enabled the educated classes to participate fully in the life of their country and to influence its development.

Conclusion

The period 1730–1880 witnessed a profound change in language use in Ireland. At the beginning of this century and a half, roughly 50 per cent of the population spoke Irish on a daily basis. By 1880 it survived marginally in some counties on the western and southern seaboards. This language shift has been the object of numerous studies. The present contribution has sought, by combing history and sociolinguistics, to provide some new perspectives.

One factor the previous commentators have failed to acknowledge is the nature and implications of bilingual diglossia, which was much higher in the eighteenth century than previously recognised. This in turn meant that by

1800 the number of people using Irish on a daily basis, and passing it on to the next generation, was much lower than mere statistics would suggest. The decline of Irish was not a cataclysmic event therefore. It happened over a period of 150 years. Brian Ó Cuív described it thus:

> I consider that the acquiring of English as a second language by one genera-
> tion was the first step in the transition in the succeeding generations, firstly
> to the position where Irish was a secondary language, and ultimately to that
> where Irish was unknown, the stages being expressed thus: Irish only: Irish
> and English: English and Irish: English only.[77]

The above scheme represents a slow, gradual process, imperceptible to the very communities in which it took place. The depiction of the language change as a traumatic blow to the Irish psyche derives from the Gaelic Revival of the post-1880 era, and it is a product of the conflation of nationalist think-ing with genuine linguistic anxiety.

In keeping with its identification as perhaps the 'most profound social change to take place on the island between the early sixteenth and the mid-nineteenth centuries', the language shift that took place in Ireland cannot be accounted for simply.[78] It was a product of multiple forces, some of which were particular to a specific time, others of longer duration. One may instance the general desire to advance and progress economically and socially, which in turn led to an awareness of the advantages of literacy in English. This force, which was initially felt among the better-off Catholics of the late eighteenth century, was to gather momentum as the nineteenth century progressed, and it is difficult to see how in the circumstances it could have been resisted. We can certainly point to more specific institutional issues such as the impact of the national schools system, or economic crises such as the Great Famine – there is no denying their contribution to the language change. But these are not the real issue. Alan Titley makes the interesting point that even if the United Irishmen had been successful, or Daniel O'Connell had managed to have the Act of Union repealed, attitudes to Irish among the new ruling class would not have been favourable.[79] I would add to this that the attitude of the general populace would not have changed either, even without the effect of the Famine and emigration.

77 B. Ó Cuív, *Irish dialects and Irish-speaking districts* (Dublin: Dublin Institute for Advanced Studies, 1951), pp. 26–7.
78 Kelly and Mac Murchaidh, *Irish and English*, p. 11.
79 A. Titley 'An náisiúnacht Ghaelach agus náisiúnachas na hÉireann' in M. Ó Cearúil (ed.), *Aimsir Óg* II (Baile Atha Cliath: Coiscéim, 2000), p. 47.

I have not dwelt equally on all of the pertinent factors, particularly with respect to the decline of Irish in the nineteenth century, as these have been thoroughly examined in other accounts.[80] I have prioritised the results of more recent research on three issues in particular. One is the role of religion in general, and particularly that of the Catholic Church. As argued above, the attitude of the church towards Irish was one not so much of hostility as of neglect. This in turn was in keeping with the emerging nationalist identity, which was based on religion rather than language.

Another aspect of the decline that I have dwelt on is emigration, and attitudes towards Irish in North America in particular. The traditional view that emigrants abandoned Irish as soon as they boarded ship has been challenged recently, and we now have more information about the use of Irish by individuals and communities in the New World. Nevertheless, the overall impression is that here, just as in Ireland, it was Catholicism rather than language which bound Irish-American communities together. Language became an emblem, something to be displayed on banners on St Patrick's Day and occasions of this sort.

I have devoted much attention to education and literacy, partly because a lot of work has been done in these areas recently, and also because they are closely connected to bilingualism and diglossia. It has been argued that because literacy in Irish was not available to the masses, while access to literacy in English was, there was a huge demand for education in English. This was met by a variety of institutions, some of them run by the Protestant and Catholic churches, some by the state. In itself, this is not a new discovery. However, recent work has provided us with a deeper and more nuanced understanding of how the skill of reading was mastered, and what kind of material was used to aid learners. As we saw, printing and writing were not exclusively in English, but the use of printing in Irish was limited in the way

---

80 See Ó Cuív, *Irish dialects*, pp. 20–7; S. de Fréine, *The great silence* (Baile Átha Cliath: Foilseacháin Náisiúnta Teoranta, 1965); Wall, 'The decline of the Irish language'; Ó Cuív, 'Irish language and literature, 1691–1845'; M. Nic Craith, *Malartú teanga: an Ghaeilge i gCorcaigh sa naoú haois déag* (Baile Átha Cliath: Cumann Eorpach Léann na hÉireann, 1993); Ó Huallacháin, *The Irish and Irish*, pp. 24–33; M. Ó Murchú, 'Language and society in nineteenth-century Ireland' in G. Jenkins (ed.), *Language and community in the nineteenth century* (Cardiff: University of Wales Press, 1998), pp. 341–68; G. Denvir, 'Literature in Irish, 1800–1890: from the Act of Union to the Gaelic League' in M. O'Kelleher and P. O'Leary (eds.), *The Cambridge history of Irish literature*, 2 vols. (Cambridge: Cambridge University Press, 2006), vol. I, pp. 544–98; Mac Mathúna, *Béarla sa Ghaeilge*, pp. 219–68; M. Nic Craith, 'Legacy and loss: the Great Silence and its aftermath' in J. Crowley et al. (eds.), *Atlas of the Great Irish Famine* (Cork: Cork University Press, 2012), pp. 580–8.

6. Image of Irish 'Bard' as presented by Joseph Cooper Walker. Line engraving by C. Maguire, published by J. Christie. From J.C. Walker, *Historical memoirs of the Irish bards* (Dublin, 1818), pp. 20–1.

that the production of manuscripts had been: ultimately, written texts were for an elite, whether this consisted of scribes and antiquarians or of members of the clergy. In such a situation, the masses had no choice but to turn to English.

Finally, I outlined briefly the emergence of a distinct form of Irish English, the dialect which was destined to become the main language on the island after 1880. The seeds for the flowering of English literature in Ireland in the twentieth century were planted in the period 1730–1880.

In the introduction, I mentioned the notion of languages being visible or invisible. Applying this to Ireland in the period under survey, we can say that in 1730 Irish enjoyed a low degree of visibility, but was audible to a high degree. By 1880 it was largely invisible and inaudible. While eighteenth-century commentators all noted the presence of Irish in the areas outside Dublin, Irish figured less and less as the nineteenth century progressed, and by the 1870s it seemed that it had disappeared from view totally. Surprisingly, it was to emerge into the public space quite spectacularly soon afterwards, being accorded a degree of visibility that it had never possessed before. But that is another chapter in the history of this language.

15

Futures Past: Enlightenment and Antiquarianism in the Eighteenth Century

MICHAEL BROWN AND LESA NÍ MHUNGHAILE

Introduction

The eighteenth century in Ireland was scarred by the outcome of the War of the Two Kings (1688–91), which dashed the hopes of a Catholic kingship in the Stuart line and secured a Protestant succession across the British and Irish archipelago. As a consequence, cultural life in Ireland was shaped by the intersection of religious and political division. Catholics predominantly espoused a Jacobite politics that sought the return of King James II or subsequently his son James III and grandson Charles Edward; Protestants by contrast upheld the legitimacy of the 'Glorious Revolution' and, in 1714, they supported the accession of the Hanoverians to the crowns of Scotland, England and Ireland. Although there were some Protestant Jacobites, and Catholic Hanoverians, the authorisation of an extensive penal code which reduced non-Anglicans to second-class legal status underlined the bifurcated nature of the Irish state system. Yet, despite these realities, Ireland permitted significant cultural and intellectual innovation. In what follows, we outline how Irish philosophers and antiquarians contributed to the broader European intellectual milieu, writing significant works in the domains of theology, aesthetics, political economy and antiquity. In so doing we will argue that Irish commentators in the eighteenth century produced a sustained reflection on Ireland's condition, forming grand narratives of the possible pasts and futures the country might inhabit.

Enlightenment

To begin, three pieces of evidence speak against the validity of this topic; evidence which suggests that the Irish Enlightenment is a misnomer, and that the broad European experiment in living in a secular domain was stillborn on Irish soil. In September 1697, following a vote of the parliament sitting in

College Green, the public hangman burnt a copy of John Toland's freethinking tract, *Christianity not mysterious* (1696). He fled before the attack became more personal.[1] In 1758 the Anglican bishop of Clogher, Robert Clayton, was threatened with legal proceedings for publishing a denunciation of the Nicene and Athanasian creeds as fundamental tests of religious orthodoxy because of their espousal of the doctrine of consubstantiality of Christ and God. He died before judgment could be announced.[2] In 1779 Charles O'Conor, the Catholic advocate and doyen of antiquarians, was entangled in a dispute over his family's estate caused by the conversion of his younger brother to the established church; penal legislation trumped primogeniture when this occurred. Though subjected to house arrest, he stood and fought, eventually retaining his control of the property once the statute of limitations lapsed.[3] In all three cases, Ireland is configured as a country under tight confessional control and experiencing stultifying intellectual stagnation. And at the heart of this conception lies the anti-Catholic legislative cluster known as the Penal Laws. Edmund Burke, in a public letter to Hercules Langrishe penned in 1792, acerbically, and influentially, described them as 'a machine of wise and elaborate contrivance, as well fitted for the oppression, impoverishment and degradation of a people, and the debasement in them of human nature itself, as ever proceeded from the perverted ingenuity of man'.[4]

Yet, far from establishing a context in which intellectual discussion was precluded, the penal system can be understood to have set the terms for the Irish Enlightenment. What is striking about these incidents of censorship, persecution and legal pursuit is not that they occurred in the context of a confessional state but that the precipitating factor was intellectual daring and social prominence. Despite the obstacles, legal and political, Ireland was in fact a venue for extensive debate about the implications of Enlightenment methods, making major contributions in the fields of theology, aesthetics, political economy and the nascent theory of civil society. Moreover, this last prompted a profound reconsideration of the Irish condition, one that enabled an extensive

---

1 M. Brown, *A political biography of John Toland* (London: Pickering and Chatto, 2012), p. 26.

2 C.D.A. Leighton, 'The enlightened religion of Robert Clayton', *Studia Hibernica*, 29 (1995–7), 157–84.

3 C. O'Halloran, '"A Revolution in our moral and civil affairs": Charles O'Conor and the creation of a community of scholars in late eighteenth-century Ireland' in L. Gibbons and K. O'Conor (eds.), *Charles O'Conor of Ballinagare: life and works* (Dublin: Four Courts Press, 2015), pp. 81–2.

4 E. Burke, 'Letter to Sir Hercules Langrishe' in *The writings and speeches of Edmund Burke*, vol. IX: I: *The Revolutionary War, 1794–1797*; II, *Ireland*, (Oxford: Oxford University Press, 1991), p. 637.

reimagining of the relationship between the confessions by focusing on the critical study of primary sources and the theory of social development, both found in the intersectional world of antiquarian writing.

One can begin to rehearse this history by looking afresh at John Toland, who has been described by David Berman as 'the father of Irish philosophy', although a 'hated father'.[5] The hatred emanated from his derision of the clergy. Indeed *Christianity not mysterious* can be read as an early volley in the conflict between a freethinking Enlightenment and the religious establishment across the British Isles, and the resulting legal imbroglio as the first engagement in what has been termed 'the deist controversy'.[6]

Christianity not mysterious provided a rationalist treatment of faith, arguing that the individual should not be under compulsion to believe something that was not understood. Faith was, in the terms of the contemporary debate, not above but compatible with reason. As a consequence, the Bible did not promulgate mysteries; rather it explained them with reference to God's active revelation. 'Thus God is pleased to reveal to us in Scripture several wonderful matters of fact', Toland wrote:

> Whoever reveals anything, that is, whoever tells us something we did not know before, his words must be intelligible and the matter possible. This rule holds good, let God or man be the revealer. If we count that person a fool who requires our assent to what is manifestly incredible, how dare we blasphemously attribute to the most perfect being what is an acknowledged defect in one of ourselves?

This apparently innocuous notion exploded the pretensions of those clerics who claimed to have privileged access to divine truths: something Toland was quick to underline and emphasise. He denounced priests for being

> fond enough of their own ridiculous systems to count the things of God foolishness, because they did not agree with their precarious and sensual notions; because every sentence was not wrapped up in mystery, and garnished with a figure: not considering that only false or trivial matters need the assistance of alluring harangues to perplex or amuse.[7]

5 D. Berman, 'The Irish freethinker' in P. McGuinness et al. (eds.), *John Toland's* Christianity not mysterious: *text, associated works and critical essays* (Dublin: Lilliput Press, 1997), p. 224.

6 R.E. Sullivan, *John Toland and the Deist Controversy: a study in adaptations* (Cambridge, MA: Harvard University Press, 1982); J. Champion, *The pillars of priestcraft shaken: the Church of England and its enemies, 1660–1730* (Cambridge: Cambridge University Press, 1992).

7 J. Toland, *Christianity not mysterious* in McGuinness et al. (eds.), *John Toland's* Christianity not mysterious, pp. 40, 41 (first quote); p. 46 (second quote).

His conceit, that scripture was accessible to all reasonable men, stripped Christianity of its supernatural character, and secularised its content. As he later adjudged in *Hodegus* (1720), such accounts as that of the pillar of cloud and fire in Exodus 13:21–2 was no more than 'a pillar of smoke, and not a real cloud, that led the Israelites in the wilderness; and that there was not two (as by most believed) but one and the same pillar, directing their march with the cloud of its smoke by day, and with the light of its fire by night'.[8] In his determination to rationalise religion he turned the miraculous mundane.

In this clarion call to anti-clericalism Toland anticipated Voltaire's campaign to crush infamy by decades. Indeed, the Frenchman came to recognise Toland as a fellow warrior against religious authority. In 1755 he recalled how 'persecution exasperated him, and he wrote against Christianity, at once out of hatred and of revenge'.[9] However, two other aspects of the text, and of Toland's subsequent career, also mark him out as an enlightener of European significance. First, his antagonism towards clerical authors was expressed through a critical engagement with the biblical and other textual sources that underpinned church tradition. Second, he was an able narrator of an imagined counter-history, utilising the past as a moral lesson in the consequences of spiritual hubris. Toland's subsequent literary career built on both these themes, challenging the validity of the Bible by providing source material around apocrypha (the Gospel of Barnabus for example) and positing the existence of a pre-Christian Irish civilisation corrupted by the intrusion of Druids similarly to how he speculated that the Culdees – imagined as a community of primitive Christians – were corrupted by Roman orthodoxy.

Toland was in many ways a religious seeker, ultimately foregrounding a kind of pantheism that was indebted heavily to the freethinking of Spinoza.[10] Yet although he can be set aside as maverick – 'the Donegal heretic', to use J.G. Simms' belittling title – the challenge he set the Irish confessional state system was profound, and it prompted a number of his contemporaries to think through the foundations of the polity's religious coloration and the legitimacy of its claim to secular supremacy. While David Berman has accorded this cluster of clerical writers the title of the 'Irish Counter Enlightenment', it is perhaps more accurate to see them as endeavouring to apply Enlightenment methodologies of empirical analysis and rational deduction to the problematic of justifying and legitimating the outcome of the War of the Two Kings

---

8 J. Toland, *Hodegus* in J. Toland, *Tetradymus* (London: J. Brotherstow, 1720), p. 6.
9 Cited in Brown, *A political biography of John Toland*, p. 24.
10 It is in this capacity that Toland appears in J. Israel, *Radical Enlightenment: philosophy and the making of modernity, 1650–1750* (Oxford: Oxford University Press, 2001), pp. 609–14.

(1688–91), in which an Anglican church was left to rule a population which was predominantly Catholic in affiliation.

While Peter Browne (1665–1735) was the most vocal antagonist of Toland's speculative heterodoxy, writing *A letter in answer to a book entitled Christianity not mysterious* (1697), and Narcissus Marsh (1638–1713), the archbishop of Dublin, led the charge to indict Toland in the Irish parliament for the promulgation of heresy, William King (1650–1729) was a more emblematic figure of the grouping. Bishop of Derry during the contestation of the late 1680s, he was to write an extended defence of the actions of the Anglicans in forsaking the Stuart claimant in favour of the intruding William III. In *The state of the Protestants of Ireland*, King deployed a heavily freighted empirical register to compile a legal case against James II for mistreating his Protestant subjects. Presenting a litany of abuse under nine separate headings, he contended 'I do not see how they [Irish Roman Catholics] can condemn us for what we have done; or what else they could have expected from us; except they would have had us held up our throats till they cut them; which no man had reason to expect from a whole body of a people, and they least of all, who designed to be actors in it.'[11] In rehearsing this history of trial and redemption, King saw in the recent history of the Anglican community a confirmation of the view that they enjoyed divine favour.[12] This view was informed by King's development of what David Berman has called theological representationalism, whereby comprehension of God is reached by developing analogies to man's positive attributes.[13] This position was fully elucidated in his masterwork of philosophical reflection, *De origine mali* (1704; translated by Edmund Law in 1731 as *Essay on the origin of evil*). In this theodicy, which was praised by Leibniz for its elegance of argumentation, man was deemed capable of approximating the divine nature of God, whom King depicted as singular, infinite in nature and power, conscious, intelligent, purposeful and good.[14] This likeness was only limited by humanity's mediocre understanding and feeble competency, while God's benevolence and generosity were underscored by his grant of free will

---

11 W. King, *The state of the Protestants of Ireland under the late King James' Government* (London: Samuel Roycroft, 1691), p. 5.

12 This contention informs W. King, *Europe's deliverance from France and slavery* (Dublin: Tim Goodwin, 1691).

13 D. Berman, 'The Irish Counter-Enlightenment' in R. Kearney (ed.), *The Irish mind: exploring intellectual traditions* (Dublin: Wolfhound Press, 1985), pp. 119–40; D. Berman, 'The Irish pragmatist' in C. Fauske (ed.), *Archbishop William King and the Anglican Irish context, 1688–1729* (Dublin: Four Courts Press, 2004), pp. 123–34.

14 W. King, *Essay on the origin of evil*, trans. Edmund Law (London: R. Knaplock, 1731), pp. 45–51. For Leibniz's response see C. Fauske, *A political biography of William King* (London: Pickering and Chatto, 2011), p. 175.

to such humble creations. God was wholly independent of influence. Hence, King concluded: 'He is ... wholly indifferent to all external things, and can neither receive benefit nor harm from any of them ... He determines himself, and creates to himself a kind of appetite by choosing.'[15] That God is free to choose and that he had chosen to create the world implied, for King, an immediate and active involvement in its affairs.

King's commitment to the Church of Ireland may have had something of the enthusiasm of a convert. He was born in County Antrim to Presbyterian parents and adopted Anglicanism during his time as a student in Trinity College Dublin. However, his was not the only cosmology to emerge from that institution in the half century following the Battle of the Boyne. George Berkeley (1685–1753) was a fellow of the college before his translation to the church and his rise to the position of bishop of Cloyne, and he too offered an analysis of the relationship between the microcosm and the macrocosm, the earthly and the supernatural, that was predicated on an analogy between the human and the divine.

At the centre of Berkeley's conception of understanding was the faculty of sight. To see was literally to believe in its existence, for the idea of a thing was generated by the witness to it, and, in a nice logical turn, things that were not witnessed did not exist. He admitted in the *Principles of human knowledge* that:

> It will be objected that from the foregoing principles it follows, things are every moment annihilated and created anew. The objects of sense only exist when being perceived: the trees therefore are in the garden, or the chairs in the parlour, no longer than while there is somebody by to perceive them. Upon shutting my eyes all the furniture in the room is reduced to nothing, and barely upon opening them it is again created ... For my part after the nicest inquiry I could make, I am not able to discover that anything else is meant.[16]

This power of perception was, for Berkeley, identical with the possession of a spirit and this he defined as 'one simple, undivided active being: as it perceives ideas, it is called the *understanding*, and as it produces or otherwise operates about them, it is called the *will*'.[17] The existence of other spirits was then evidenced by the unwilled nature of much of an individual's perception. At the apex of this system of active spirits lay the presence of God, an all-perceiving

15 King, *Origin of evil*, p. 185.
16 G. Berkeley, *Principles of human knowledge* in *Philosophical works*, ed. M. Ayers (London: Everyman, 1993), p. 105.
17 Ibid., p. 99.

eye who was the guarantor of the continued and persistent existence of the external world. A radical form of occasionalism which had some roots in Malebranche, Berkeley was polemically drawing out the consequences of Enlightenment ideas about the reduction of knowledge into personal experience to defend the presumption of the existence of God.

Argument through analogy was also a defining characteristic of the work of the Ulster Presbyterian Francis Hutcheson (1694–1746). He is commonly associated with the Scottish Enlightenment through his work as the professor of moral philosophy at the University of Glasgow from 1730 until his early death. During that time he taught Adam Smith, corresponded with David Hume over issues raised in the latter's *Treatise of human nature* (1739/40), and helped to embed a socially tolerant 'New Light' variant of Presbyterianism. Yet his most creative writing was actually completed in Dublin in the 1720s.[18] And his *Inquiry into the original of our ideas of beauty and virtue* (1725) was structured to parallel aesthetic and moral experience. Rejecting the idea of innate ideas (espoused by John Locke), Hutcheson presumed the existence of a series of internal senses that operated to generate pre-rational judgments concerning the quality and temper of the world. Just as an individual might respond to a beautiful object positively or recoil from something repulsive without discerning the immediate cause of their response until later reflecting on the event, so Hutcheson argued that a moral sense operated in a similar fashion to this internal sense of beauty. Moral judgments were therefore inherent in human nature, even if moral qualities were not inherent in external objects. This immediate, pre-rational, judgment might be tempered or reversed in the light of subsequent contextual information coming to light, but Hutcheson insisted that neither calculations of self-interest nor extenuating circumstances could overthrow the fundamental assertion of the moral calibre of an action. In this he overtly rejected the egoism of Thomas Hobbes and instead co-opted, Christianised and crucially democratised the connoisseurship model proposed by the 3rd Earl of Shaftesbury. Whereas Shaftesbury was thought to be a freethinker, Hutcheson remained determinedly a communicant of the Presbyterian church – rejecting rumours of a proposed conversion to the Church of Ireland in the 1720s; and while Shaftesbury's moral philosophy was inherently Platonic and elitist, Hutcheson suggested that the moral sense was a universal faculty and that even 'The poor creatures we

---

18 M. Brown, *Francis Hutcheson in Dublin, 1719–1730: the crucible of his thought* (Dublin: Four Courts Press, 2002).

meet in the streets seem to know the avenues to the humane breast better than our philosophers.'[19]

If Hutcheson's moral arguments were taken up by his Scottish contemporaries, there is some allusive evidence to suggest that his aesthetic concerns informed the writing of Edmund Burke's *Philosophical enquiry into the origin of our ideas of the sublime and beautiful* (1757) – the very title seems to be a gesture towards Hutcheson's influence. Burke (1730–97) had yet to turn to politics when the book – an entrée piece to London's literary circles – was published. Differentiating between a mode of aesthetic experience that originated in fear and one that emerged from attraction, Burke deployed a highly gendered register to describe the contrasting emotions evoked by darkness, grandeur and threat on the one hand, and illumination, delicacy and fragility on the other. The first response was grounded in the desire for self-preservation; the second in the desire to procreate. Navigating between the two responses was the faculty of sympathy, being the capacity to envision imaginatively oneself in the place of another. As he argued, sympathy ensured that 'we enter into the concerns of others; that we are moved as they are moved, and are never suffered to be indifferent spectators of almost anything which men can do or suffer'.[20]

If the argument from analogy can be extended into Burke's later career, this emphasis on sympathy can be related to his subsequent concern for the right ordering of government, in particular in Britain's imperial domains. Burke's own family heritage may also play a role in grounding this identification with the colonised communities of Ireland and India. His mother was a Catholic, and his father may have been a convert to the Church of Ireland prior to pursuing his legal career. Burke retained extensive Catholic connections in the Blackwater area of County Cork, and was frequently dismissed as an Irish adventurer by his English political rivals. Certainly Burke was overtly willing to argue for the repeal of the Penal Laws, and this empathy for the residual native cultures may also have prompted his laboured campaign against the perceived maladministration of India personified in Burke's mind by Warren Hastings. The impeachment trial that Burke led before the House of Lords provided the moment for Burke to argue at once (and counter-intuitively)

---

19 F. Hutcheson, 'Reflections on the common systems of morality' in T. Mautner (ed.), *Francis Hutcheson: two texts on human nature* (Cambridge: Cambridge University Press, 1993), p. 103.

20 E. Burke, *Philosophical enquiry into the origin of our ideas of the sublime and beautiful*, ed. A. Phillips (Oxford: Oxford University Press, 1990), p. 41.

against 'geographical morality' and for the moral value of local customary practice.[21]

Burke's sophisticated allegiance to the native community reached its limit in the American colonies, where he sided expressly with the colonial community in their conflict with Britain. (In contrast, Burke was derisive when describing the Irish ascendancy caste.[22]) In a series of speeches, notably 'On American taxation' (1774) and 'On conciliation with America', Burke asserted that the miscreant cause of the conflict was the centralising administration in London and not the patriotic colonials whose assertions of liberty were a direct consequence of the active and ill-considered intervention of the British government in their affairs. However, he was less sanguine about the extent of Native American virtue. He did not subscribe to the common conceit of the noble savage, arguing instead that it should be the priority of both the British government and the colonists to bring

> gradually that unhappy part of mankind into civility, order, piety and virtuous discipline, than to conform their evil habits, and increased their natural ferocity, by fleshing them in the slaughter of you, whom our wiser and better ancestors had sent into the wilderness with the express view of introducing, along with our holy religion, its humane and charitable manners.[23]

With the publication of his *Reflections on the Revolution in France* (1790), Burke began to understand how apparently virtuous claims to liberty might destabilise and ultimately overturn a government. Appalled by the misuse of the concept of liberty, Burke crusaded against the sophistries of the French revolutionaries by recapturing their vocabulary for the use of the establishment. Popular politics was depicted as the intrusion of a 'swinish multitude'; prejudice was inscribed as virtuous habits (a deployment he co-opted from Hume); and history was reconfigured as regressive in that 'the age of chivalry is gone; the age of sophisters, economists and calculators has succeeded, and the glory of Europe is extinguished forever'.[24]

---

21 E. Burke, *Writings and speeches*, vol. VI: *India: the launching of the Warren Hastings impeachment, 1786–1788* (Oxford: Clarendon Press, 1991), p. 346.

22 F.P. Lock, *Edmund Burke*, vol. II: *1784–1797* (Oxford: Oxford University Press, 2006), pp. 567–9. For a nuanced examination of this issue see E. O'Flaherty, 'Burke and the Irish constitution' in S.P. Donlan (ed.), *Edmund Burke's Irish identities* (Dublin: Irish Academic Press, 2006), pp. 102–17.

23 E. Burke, 'Address to the Colonists' (1777) in E. Burke, *Writings and speeches*, vol. III: *Party, parliament and the American war, 1774–1780* (Oxford: Clarendon Press, 1996), p. 282.

24 E. Burke, *Reflections on the Revolution in France*, ed. J.C.D. Clark (Stanford: Stanford University Press, 2001), pp. 242, 238.

What is frequently overshadowed in critical comment on these works by concentrating on the aesthetic effects generated by his writing is Burke's deployment of arguments drawn from perceived utility. Both 'On conciliation with America' and *Reflections* are informed by his understanding of political economy. In his defence of the American Revolution he concentrated his fire on the repercussions for American trade of the introduction of the controversial navigation acts. These, he professed, were 'strangling' the commerce of the country 'with regulations which in a manner put a stop to the coasting intercourse of the colonies'.[25] In his denunciation of the French Revolution, he mocked the introduction of paper currency – the *assignat* – backed by church confiscations, as a republican recourse to miracles:

> With these philosophic financiers, this universal medicine made of church money is to cure all the evils of state. These gentlemen do not perhaps believe a great deal in the miracles of piety; but it cannot be questioned that they have an undoubting faith in the prodigies of sacrilege. Is there a debt which presses them – issue *assignats* – are compensations to be made, or a maintenance decreed to those who they have robbed of their freehold in their office, or expelled from their profession – issue *assignats* ... They are all professors of *assignats*.[26]

In these cases, as oftentimes elsewhere, Burke's political polemic can be perceived as a late flowering of an Irish school of political economy dating back to the 1720s, which was expressly concerned with matters of trade and money. In *An essay on the trade and improvement of Ireland* (1729), Arthur Dobbs (1689–1765) argued that the economic interests of Great Britain and Ireland were 'inseparable', and that British trade laws that hindered Irish commerce risked making the country 'a perpetual charge to England ... or so turbulent as to be apt to join in with any prince who should invade us'.[27] David Bindon (d.1760), in contrast, saw the conundrum of Irish economic woes as revolving around the circulation of specie, and the lack of small coinage in the country. He proposed the establishment of a national mint to overcome the difficulties that arose from the presence of foreign coinage in the Irish market.

---

25 E. Burke, 'Speech on American taxation' in E. Burke, *Writings and speeches*, vol. ii: *Party, parliament and the American crisis, 1766–1774* (Oxford: Clarendon Press, 1981), p. 433.
26 Burke, *Reflections on the Revolution in France*, p. 403. See also J.G.A. Pocock, 'The political economy of Burke's analysis of the French Revolution' in J.G.A. Pocock, *Virtue, commerce and history: essays on political thought and history, chiefly in the eighteenth century* (Cambridge: Cambridge University Press, 1985), pp. 193–212.
27 A. Dobbs, *An essay on the trade and improvement of Ireland* (Dublin: J. Smith, 1729), pp. 3, 69.

Jonathan Swift (1667–1745) personified both concerns. With regard to money, he was to gain renown as the author of the *Drapier's letters* (1724–5), which mocked a government proposal to create small coins for the Irish economy. The privilege had been granted by the British prime minister Robert Walpole to a Wolverhampton ironmonger William Wood, and Swift made his personality a central feature of his rebuttal of the scheme. He profoundly distrusted the quality of the coin being issued, and used the occasion to defend the status of Ireland as an independent – and not a dependent – kingdom. Although attention has rightly focused on the constitutional aspects of Swift's campaigning, his stance on the value of the money was of a piece with his dismissal of paper money and his support for a land bank for the country when the idea of a national bank was mooted in the early 1720s.

This concern for Irish self-sufficiency informed Swift's broader economic writings also. During the 1720s, Swift moved from a position of advocating domestic responsibility to mockery of its pretensions to humane paternalism. In *A proposal for the universal use of Irish manufacture* (1720), Swift rejected the idea of Anglo-Irish reciprocity in economic matters, recalling how 'I heard the late Archbishop of Tuam mention a pleasant observation of somebody "That Ireland would never be happy till a law were made for burning everything that came from England except their people and their coals." '[28] This dismissal of the mutual benefits to be derived from trade pushed Swift back onto the indigenous resources of the island. Subsequent to the Wood's Halfpence affair, the dean of St Patrick's was less sanguine about such improvisational and piecemeal proposals. His macabre *Modest proposal* (1729) dismissed many of the ideas he had proposed earlier in the decade. In their place, he projected a trade in the bodies of children, killed to serve up on the plates of the landlords, 'who as they have already devoured most of the parents, seem to have the best title to the children'.[29] Among the advantages he foresaw was that of political security, for the scheme 'would greatly lessen the number of Papists, with whom we are yearly over-run, being the principal breeders of the nation, as well as our most dangerous enemies, and who stay at home on purpose with a design to deliver the kingdom to the Pretender'.[30]

This cannibalistic and highly confessional rendition of Irish economic activity can be read as a counsel of despair; yet others were less pessimistic

28 J. Swift, *A proposal for the universal use of Irish manufacture* in J. Swift, *Major works*, ed. A. Ross and D. Wooley (Oxford: Oxford University Press, 2003), p. 40.
29 J. Swift, *A modest proposal* in *Major works*, p. 494.
30 Ibid., p. 496.

about the possibility of taking economic improvement into their own hands.[31] Indeed, in the wake of the famine conditions of the early 1740s, the Dublin Society – founded in 1731 precisely to ameliorate the condition of domestic agriculture – was resuscitated by the actions of Samuel Madden (1686–1765). He galvanised the Society by introducing a system of competitive premiums, awarded for innovative practice in the growing of crops and the use of technology. Madden also articulated a vision of associational life that came close to a form of nascent Irish civil society.[32] Writing of the actions of the Linen Board, he saw in that body's labours

> indisputable evidence for the use and efficacy of such societies. And as the whole attention and care of our trustees is taken up in the linen manufacture; and as I shall show hereafter, that there are a number of very difficult, though most useful improvements, which want as much to be nursed up and encouraged in Ireland, it will, when that is proved, be as demonstrable, that is in the highest manner incumbent on us, as our duty, as our interest, to set up such societies; and when set up, to support, by larger contributions (adequate to such great and generous designs) every attempt they shall make, of new improvements among us.[33]

Perhaps the most enlightened of these voluntary associations was the Freemason lodge. If not an improving society itself, its ethos of cross-confessional sociability embodied a particular brand of Enlightenment idealism. Catholic membership in Dublin may have risen as high as 40 per cent in the 1760s, and Ulster was home to a number of lodges in which fraternisation across the religious divide was openly institutionalised.[34] Whether the inherent secrecy of meetings within the Lodge enabled this sociability or deterred the establishment from joining in the first place is rather less clear, but masonic parades – on St John's Day – publicised their fraternal values to the wider community as well as highlighting the esoteric nature of their symbolic regalia.[35]

---

31 For a more moderate, constructive reading of the text see J. Kelly, 'Jonathan Swift and the Irish economy in the 1720s', *Eighteenth-Century Ireland*, 6 (1991), 7–36.

32 On this see J. Livesey, *Civil society and empire: Ireland and Scotland in the eighteenth-century Atlantic world* (New Haven: Yale University Press, 2009), pp. 85–8.

33 S. Madden, *A letter to the Dublin Society on improving their fund* (Dublin: R. Reilly, 1739), p. 13.

34 P. Fagan, *Catholics in a Protestant country: the papist constituency in eighteenth-century Dublin* (Dublin: Four Courts Press, 1988), p. 131; Petri Mirala, *Freemasonry in Ulster, 1733–1813* (Dublin: Four Courts Press, 2007).

35 Petri Mirala, '"A large mob calling themselves Freemasons": masonic parades in Ulster' in E. Magennis and P. Jupp (eds.), *Crowds in Ireland, c.1720–1920* (London: Palgrave Macmillan, 2000), pp. 117–38.

If the Freemasons were to split in the 1790s over the issue of Catholic participation in politics, the Catholic committee was first convened in 1756 to petition for just such a breach in the confessional character of the Irish *ancien régime* state. Seeking to agree an oath to the Hanoverian state to which Catholics would subscribe, the Committee deployed the accumulated social capital of Dublin's Catholic merchant community to an overtly political end. In that, though an acceptable oath was not introduced until 1774, the Committee was symbolic of the emerging challenge the Enlightenment set the confessional construction of the Irish polity. Its inauguration foreshadowed the pamphlet petition of Arthur O'Leary, a Capuchin priest, who in 1780 published an *Essay on toleration, or plea for liberty of conscience* which contended that 'error in faith is not a crime'.[36]

The Catholic Committee also echoed Enlightenment concerns in other ways. It is perhaps significant that the Committee was led by two antiquarians of substance: John Curry and Charles O'Conor. Both were to engage in polemical pamphleteering over the causes and consequences of the 1641 rebellion in Ulster, challenging David Hume's account in his multi-volume *History of England* (1754–61).[37] In the case of O'Conor, the pre-Christian history of Ireland, which concerned Toland at the beginning of the century, was again a focus of interest in his *Dissertations*.[38] And in projecting there a commercial, tolerant and civilised society, O'Conor was again to beg questions about the nature of knowledge formation if a confessional foundation were not to be assumed, and about Ireland's religious conflicted past and the possibility of a tolerant futurity. These issues were to be the central currents of debate within the community of scholarly antiquarians that reflected on the Irish condition in the period.

Antiquarianism

The intellectual worlds of the native Gaelic and Anglo-Irish communities in Ireland intersected in two key areas pertinent to Enlightenment thinking during the eighteenth century, namely in the critical study of primary sources and in the employment of theories relating to human social development.

---

36 A. O'Leary, *An essay on toleration, or Mr O'Leary's plea for liberty of conscience* (1780) in A. O'Leary, *Miscellaneous tracts*, 2nd edn (Dublin: Thomas McDonnel, 1781), p. 366; J. Kelly, '"A wild capuchin of Cork": Arthur O'Leary (1729–1802)' in G. Moran (ed.), *Radical Irish priests, 1660–1970* (Dublin: Four Courts Press, 1998), pp. 39–61.

37 D. Berman, 'David Hume on the 1641 Rebellion in Ireland', *Studies*, 258 (1976), 101–12.

38 C. O'Conor, *Dissertations on the ancient history of Ireland* (Dublin: James Hoey, 1753).

Both of these concerns were brought together in the fields of antiquarianism and historiography as each community examined and re-examined the Irish past. In doing so they sought to validate the rights of their respective religious communities and, in the case of Protestant descendants of sixteenth- and seventeenth-century English settlers, to root themselves in the country's past as they began to develop an Irish identity. This involved a complex process whereby they appropriated the Gaelic past as their own, which development was facilitated by an abatement of the antagonism shown towards both Irish history and the Irish language by Protestant writers such as Richard Cox, author of *Hibernia Anglicana* (1689), in the previous century.[39] Competing views of the pre-Conquest Gaelic past were advanced by scholars in their attempts either to vindicate or to denigrate Gaelic culture and civilisation. Owing to these conflicting political concerns, however, historical narratives on both sides during this period were often characterised by 'confusion and inconsistency'.[40]

The various antiquarian and historiographical debates were informed by discussions appertaining to the treatment of documentary sources. The Enlightenment emphasis on analysis, rationalism and experimentation advocated a critical approach to such material. Gradually, Irish-language manuscripts came to be regarded as valuable sources for Irish history by a number of Anglo-Irish scholars, which in turn, sparked an interest in the collecting and interpretation of those documents. The activities of learned bodies such as the Dublin Philosophical Society (1683–1708), the Physico-Historical Society (1744–52), the Select Committee on Antiquities of the Dublin Society (1772–4), the Hibernian Antiquarian Society (1779–83) and the Royal Irish Academy (1785–) gave added impetus to the study of historiography and antiquarianism. Although these were predominantly Protestant bodies, they offered a fruitful opportunity for cooperation between native and non-native scholars, as the majority of the latter were unable to read Irish-language manuscripts and were therefore dependent on the assistance of native scholars. Through

---

39 D. Hayton, 'Anglo-Irish attitudes: changing perceptions of national identity among the Protestant Ascendancy in Ireland, ca. 1690–1750', *Studies in Eighteenth-Century Culture*, 17 (1987), 145–57; J. Leerssen, *Mere Irish and Fíor-Ghael: studies in the idea of Irish nationality* (Cork: Cork University Press, 1996), pp. 294–376; C. O'Halloran, *Golden ages and barbarous nations* (Cork: Cork University Press, 2004); J. Kelly, 'Irish Protestants and the Irish language in the eighteenth century' in J. Kelly and C. Mac Murchaidh (eds.), *Irish and English: essays on the Irish linguistic and cultural frontier, 1600–1900* (Dublin: Four Courts Press, 2012), pp. 189–217.

40 C. O'Halloran, ' "The island of saints and scholars": views of the early church and sectarian politics in late-eighteenth-century Ireland', *Eighteenth-Century Ireland*, 5 (1990), 7.

their patronage of such scholars, Anglo-Irish antiquarians began to take the place of traditional patrons. Gaelic scholars and scribes were concerned with sourcing and transcribing ancient codices containing annals, genealogies and lists of regnal succession in an effort to preserve them for posterity. They also sought to demonstrate the nobility, piety, learning and civility of their race. They understood that this desire dovetailed with the antiquarian interests of some Protestant scholars and that they could serve such an interest through the transcription and translation into English of ancient Irish-language manuscripts.[41]

Linked to discussions on written sources were debates on the validity of oral sources. Prior to the eighteenth century, scholars did not accept that a substantial body of material could be transmitted orally, fully intact, through the ages. Only written sources were believed to possess true authority. Thus, for example, Samuel Johnson argued that the Erse or Scottish Gaelic language 'never was a written language' and therefore 'merely floated in the breath of the people'.[42] Only written sources were reliable in his estimation:

> Books are faithful repositories, which may be a while neglected or forgotten; but when they are opened again, will again impart their instruction: memory once interrupted, is not to be recalled, written learning is a fixed luminary, which, after the cloud that had hidden it has past away, is again bright in its proper station. Tradition is but a meteor, which, if once it falls, cannot be rekindled.[43]

In direct opposition to this theory was the new ethnographic idea of 'oral tradition'. Scholars who idealised primitive cultures, the most prominent of whom was the Scotsman James Macpherson, argued that it was possible for non-literate cultures to possess a substantial body of well-developed poetry, customs and laws that could be passed down orally through the centuries.[44] Thus, he claimed that the poetry of the third-century AD bard Ossian was preserved intact in the Scottish Highland. Scholars in Ireland took opposing sides in the debate depending on whether they wished to vindicate or denigrate Gaelic culture, although the concept proved challenging for those

---

41 A. Harrison, *The Dean's friend: Anthony Raymond 1675–1726, Jonathan Swift and the Irish language* (Dublin: de Burca Publishers, 1999), p. 62.

42 S. Johnson, *A journey to the Western Isles of Scotland* (London: W. Strahan, 1775), p. 268.

43 Ibid., pp. 257–8.

44 N. Hudson, '"Oral tradition": the evolution of an eighteenth-century concept' in A. Ribeiro and J. Basker (eds.), *Tradition in transition: women writers, marginal texts, and the eighteenth-century canon* (Oxford: Clarendon Press, 1996), pp. 161–76.

Gaelic scholars who wished to argue for a sophisticated literate pre-Christian past, as the Gaelic literary tradition existed in both written and oral forms.[45]

Emerging methods of social analysis that were developed during the second half of the eighteenth century by Scottish Enlightenment thinkers such as Adam Ferguson (1723–1816) and William Robertson (1721–93) proved useful to a number of Anglo-Irish scholars in formulating their arguments.[46] One such method of social analysis, stadialism, viewed the progress of mankind as passing through three consecutive stages of development, beginning with savagery, moving on to barbarism and ending with civilisation. As far back as the sixteenth century the concept of the noble savage and the ignoble barbarian had been employed in discussions on primitive societies outside Europe, but by the early decades of the eighteenth century the noble savage had come to be identified with peasants living in remote areas of Europe such as parts of Ireland and Wales, the Scottish Highlands and the Shetlands.[47] The inhabitants of such regions were regarded as still existing in a state of primitive savagery. According to this model, civilisation was identifiable in those eighteenth-century European societies that adhered to advanced ethical and social norms.

Stadialism informed the writings of Protestant Irish scholars such as the historian Thomas Leland (1722–85), the Church of Ireland clergymen Thomas Campbell (1733–95) and Edward Ledwich (1737?–1823), who subscribed to the negative view of the Gaelic Irish presented in Edmund Spenser's 'A view of the present state of Ireland' (1596) and Sir John Davies' *Discovery of the true causes why Ireland was never entirely subdued* (1612). These works established a link between ethnic identity and the issue of civility, which justified the English conquest of Ireland by denigrating Gaelic culture and that of the Old English community, who, it was believed, had degenerated by adopting the customs and dress of the native Irish. Eighteenth-century Protestant scholars who upheld the ascendancy of the Protestant interest argued that since ancient Gaelic civilisation was barbarous the contemporary Catholic nation was unfit for self-government. Coupled with Gothicism, a current of thought that centred on the heritage of the historic Germanic barbarian tribes, the stadialist model can be located in the respective works of Leland, Campbell and

---

45 F. Stafford, *The sublime savage: James Macpherson and the poems of Ossian* (Edinburgh: Edinburgh University Press, 1988).

46 A. Ferguson, *An essay on the history of civil society* (Edinburgh: Kincaid and Bell, 1767); W. Robertson, *History of America* (Edinburgh: J. Balfour, 1777).

47 M. Rubel, *Savage and barbarian: historical attitudes in the criticism of Homer and Ossian in Britain, 1760–1800* (Amsterdam: North-Holland, 1978), p. 18.

Ledwich: *The history of Ireland from the invasion of Henry II with a preliminary discourse on the ancient state of that kingdom* (1773), *Strictures on the ecclesiastical and literary history of Ireland from the most ancient times* (1789) and *The antiquities of Ireland* (1790).

Linked to the stadialist approach was the use of origin myths in narratives of the ancient Gaelic past. This tendency mirrored that of a number of other countries throughout Europe where national ancestry myths were utilised for the purpose of political debate.[48] In support of their arguments, scholars on each side adapted, developed or contested the Gaelic Milesian origin myth found in the medieval manuscript *An Leabhar Gabhála* (The book of invasions), which posited a Scythian origin for the Irish race. Edward Ledwich, by contrast, promoted a Scandian theory of Irish origins which argued for a Scandinavian route of colonisation and emphasised the Gothic racial origins of the entire British nation. In doing so, it negated any ethnic differences between the Irish and English and undermined the Gaelic claim to a culturally superior civilisation prior to the Norman invasion.[49] Furthermore, this argument assisted efforts by Protestant scholars to demonstrate that the early Irish church was independent of Rome and, in so doing, facilitated the efforts of the Anglican Church in Ireland to justify its position as the state church.[50]

As the campaign for an amelioration of the Penal Laws intensified from the middle of the eighteenth century, the Scottish model of the history of man unfolding in progressive stages was rejected by Irish scholars, Catholic and Protestant, who sought parliamentary reform and religious toleration. As a counter-argument, they advanced a model of progress that was cyclical in nature, one of a golden age in which ancient Gaelic civilisation was civilised and literate and on a par with the classical civilisations of Greece and Rome. According to this model, Ireland was an 'Island of Saints and Scholars' while the rest of Europe was in a state of barbarism and the eventual decline of that great civilisation came about as a result of the Danish and Anglo-Norman invasions. Drawing on Geoffrey Keating's (Seathrún Céitinn) (*c.*1580–1644) *Foras Feasa ar Éirinn* (A basis of knowledge about Ireland) (*c.*1634), the earliest Catholic attempt to vindicate Gaelic civility, they adapted and developed the Milesian origin myth which Keating in turn had adapted from *An Leabhar*

---

48 J. Leerssen, *Remembrance and imagination: patterns in the historical and literary representation of Ireland in the nineteenth century* (Cork: Cork University Press, 1996), pp. 27–8.
49 O'Halloran, *Golden ages*, pp. 61–2.
50 O' Halloran, ' "Island of saints and scholars" ', pp. 7–20.

Gabhála.[51] A landmark work, *Foras Feasa* offered a synthesis of Irish history down to the twelfth century. Together with 'Tuireamh na hÉireann', a long poem composed *c*.1657 by Seán Ó Conaill, it shaped Gaelic understanding of Irish history and gave expression to the new political ideology that had emerged among the Catholic community during the early decades of the seventeenth century that promoted a Catholic nation encompassing the Old Irish and Old English under the common title of *Éireannach*.[52] Other Gaelic historians such as Peter Walsh (*c*.1616–88) and Ruaidhrí Ó Flaithbheartaigh (Roderick O'Flaherty) (1629–1718) based their work on *Foras Feasa*, while Protestant scholars such as Sir Richard Cox (1650–1733) dismissed it in *Hibernia Anglicana* (1689) as nothing 'more than *an ill-digested Heap of very silly Fictions*'.[53]

Keating's defence of Gaelic Ireland remained an influential treatise until well into the eighteenth century, serving as both a source and a foundational text for both native and non-native scholars alike.[54] It should be noted, however, that it remained in manuscript until the Limerick scribe Dermot O'Connor (Diarmaid Ó Conchubhair) (*c*.1690–*c*.1730) published the first printed English translation in 1723 under the title *The general history of Ireland*.[55] This translation immediately came under fire from a number of quarters and O'Connor was accused of having taken liberties with the text. The Catholic Gaelic scholar Charles O'Conor (1710–91) called it 'the grossest imposition that has been ever yet obtruded on a learned age'.[56] Nonetheless, it was the version of Keating most accessible to Protestant antiquarians in the eighteenth century who were unable to read Irish or did not have access to other translations. Ironically, these were readers 'who could no longer be expected

---

51 For a detailed consideration of this text, see B. Cunningham, *The world of Geoffrey Keating: history, myth and religion in seventeenth-century Ireland* (Dublin: Four Courts Press, 2000).

52 M. Mac Craith, 'Literature in Irish, *c*.1550–1690: from the Elizabethan settlement to the Battle of the Boyne' in M. Kelleher and P. O'Leary (eds.), *The Cambridge history of Irish literature*, 2 vols. (Cambridge: Cambridge University Press, 2006), vol. I, pp. 191–231; V. Morley, *Ó Chéitinn go Raifteараí* (Dublin: Coiscéim, 2011), pp. 33–138.

53 P. Walsh, *A prospect of the state of Ireland* (London: Johanna Broom, 1682); R. O'Flaherty, *Ogygia* (London: R. Everingham, 1685); R. Cox, *Hibernia Anglicana, or, the history of Ireland, from the Conquest thereof by the English, to this present time with an introductory discourse touching the ancient state of that kingdom*, 2 vols. (London, 1689), vol. I, 'To the reader'.

54 Cunningham, *World of Geoffrey Keating*, pp. 201–25.

55 D. O'Connor, *The general history of Ireland . . . collected by the learned Geoffrey Keating, D.D., faithfully translated from the original Irish language* (London: B. Creake, and Dublin: James Carson, 1723); D. Ó Catháin, 'Dermot O'Connor, translator of Keating', *Eighteenth-Century Ireland*, 2 (1987), 67–87.

56 O'Conor, *Dissertations on the ancient history of Ireland*, p. x, quoted in Ó Catháin, 'Dermot O'Connor', pp. 84–5.

to understand the nuances of the political, social and moral issues that had been central to the world of Geoffrey Keating'.[57]

One such non-native scholar was the Church of Ireland vicar of Trim, Anthony Raymond (1675–1726). His efforts to publish a refined English version of *Foras Feasa*, and his connection with Dermot O'Connor and the wider Ó Neachtain circle of scholars and scribes in Dublin during the period 1718–26, serve as an example of how the interests of the Protestant/Anglo-Irish and Catholic/Gaelic intellectual worlds intersected during the early decades of the century. Raymond's intention was to supplement Keating's text with material from other manuscripts and from the works of later seventeenth-century Catholic apologists. It is noteworthy that he felt obliged to vindicate the character of the ancient Gael by undertaking his history of Ireland:

> I was induced to acquaint myself with their history delivered by their own approved writers and foreign authors of undoubted credit and finding they have been most injuriously misrepresented out of ignorant malice or private views, I thought myself obliged in justice to vindicate the character of an injured people.[58]

Raymond initially employed O'Connor to assist him in his research for the planned edition of Keating's history, and probably for other projects that included a dictionary and genealogies, but the latter left his patron's employment some time in 1720 and published his own translation, thereby thwarting Raymond's plan. Raymond had some competence in the Irish language. He claimed to have learned to speak it in order to communicate with his parishioners in Meath and it appears that he could both read and write the language as he corresponded with the scribes through Irish.[59] There are also a number of examples of his transcriptions from Irish-language manuscripts in his personal papers.[60] His main interest in the language, however, derived from his interest in the ancient history of Ireland and, as the primary sources for that history were Irish-language manuscripts written in middle and classical Irish, it is likely that the language of these older manuscripts would have been beyond his ability. He needed the assistance of those skilled in reading them, and turned to members of the Ó Neachtain circle for assistance. This coterie of twenty-six scholars and scribes based in Dublin and County Meath during the early decades of the eighteenth century compiled a substantial corpus of

---

57 Cunningham, *World of Geoffrey Keating*, p. 225.
58 Harrison, *Dean's friend*, p. 100.
59 Ibid., p. 74.
60 RIA 24G 11–24 G 14.

manuscripts, of which approximately one hundred are still extant.[61] An inner circle that included Tadhg Ó Neachtain (1671–*c*.1752), Risteard Tiobar (Richard Tipper), Seon Mac Solaidh (John Mac Solly), Stiabhna Rís (Stephen Rice) and Aodh Buí Mac Cruitín had a particular interest in historical texts and they had access to a number of different exemplars of *Foras Feasa*. Their contact with Raymond proved to be mutually beneficial: 'knowledge, manuscripts, transcribing and interpretation ability and the Irish language itself being the gain for Raymond, and money, status and recognition for their beleaguered culture for the scholars'.[62]

The Ó Neachtain scribes and scholars realised the importance of salvaging their literary heritage from extinction and regarded Raymond as an ally in their attempts to do so. Tadhg Ó Neachtain, for example, in a poem praising Raymond, compared the scholar's work on the ancient history of Ireland to that of the bee extracting honey from the thorny briars:

> An mhil chéadna chum bhur gcneasadh
> Bhur gcríche is a coimhneasa,
> Chugaibh í gan chlaonta bréige
> Ón ollamh caomh ollmhór' Éire.

(This same honey the mighty gentle scholar has given to you O Ireland to heal you, your neighbours and your territories without any false deflection.)[63]

Ó Neachtain regarded Raymond's elucidation of Gaelic sources as possessing a healing property and presumably regarded it has having the potential for reconciliation or at least explicating Gaelic culture to other members of Raymond's class in Ireland and in Britain.

The foundation of the Select Committee of Antiquities of the Dublin Society in 1772 in order 'to rescue the antient reputation' of Ireland and to demonstrate that the Irish were not 'a barbarous or a contemptible people' serves as a further important example of the willingness of certain Protestant and Catholic antiquarians to create a community of Irish antiquarians of all creeds working together with the common goal of elucidating the ancient

---

61 For the Ó Neachtain circle, see A. Harrison, *Ag Cruinniú Meala* (Dublin: An Clóchomhar, 1988); L. Mac Mathúna, 'Getting to grips with innovation and genre diversification in the work of the Ó Neachtain circle in early eighteenth-century Dublin', *Eighteenth-Century Ireland*, 27 (2012), 53–83; L. Ní Mhunghaile, '"An Solamh sochmadh": Seon Mac Solaidh agus ciorcal Neachtain' in L. Mac Mathúna and R. Uí Chollatáin (eds.), *Saothrú na Gaeilge scríofa i suímh uirbeacha na hÉireann, 1700–1850* (Dublin: Four Courts Press, 2016), p. xx.

62 Harrison, *Dean's friend*, p. 104.

63 Ibid., p. 71.

Irish past.[64] It also marked a new phase in Protestant associational life, as the Committee admitted some Catholic antiquarians. Charles O'Conor was elected to honorary membership, while his friend the Catholic archbishop of Dublin, John Carpenter, was made a corresponding member. The committee's brief existence also attests to the difficulties associated with such an undertaking because of enduring political tensions. Nevertheless, the belief that the study of Irish antiquity could ameliorate relations between the main ethnic groupings in Ireland began to be clearly articulated during the latter half of the eighteenth century by the Catholic scholars Charles O'Conor and Sylvester O'Halloran (1728–1807).[65] In his first publication on the history of Ireland, *An introduction to the study of the history and antiquities of Ireland* (1772), O'Halloran argued that close blood ties existed between the native Irish and the Old English:

> For, though unhappily for this antient kingdom, unnatural distinctions have but too long been kept up by artful and designing enemies, to the almost entire ruin of the whole; yet are we in fact, but one people, and as unmixt a race as any in Europe. There is not at this day a Milesian, or descendant of Strongbow, whose bloods are not so intimately blended, that it would be impossible to determine which should preponderate.[66]

He continued this conciliatory tone and expressed his motives for undertaking the work as follows:

> I do affirm them to have been of the purest kind; a love of my country, and ALL her sons; a desire to place them and their ancestors, in that point of view which their courage, their hospitality, and other *manly* virtues, justly intitle [*sic*] them to: a wish that a spark of public spirit might catch every breast and banish for ever from amongst us all ruinous distinctions.[67]

O'Conor, who has been described as 'one of the most important cultural mediators between native and ascendancy Ireland', and O'Halloran

---

64 Sir Lucius O'Brien to O'Conor, 26 May 1772, cited in C. O'Halloran, 'Charles of Conor and the creation of a community of scholars' in Gibbons and O'Conor (eds.), *Charles O'Conor*, p. 86.

65 O'Conor, *Dissertations on the ancient history of Ireland* (1753); C. O'Conor, *Dissertations on the history of Ireland*, 2nd edn (Dublin: George Faulkner, 1766); S. O'Halloran, *An introduction to the study of the history and antiquities of Ireland* (Dublin: Thomas Ewing, 1772); S. O'Halloran, *A general history of Ireland*, 2 vols. (London: A. Hamilton, 1778). It should also be noted that the refutation of James Macpherson's Ossian and his account of Irish history also played an important role in their works.

66 O'Halloran, *Introduction to the study*, p. i.

67 Ibid., p. xvii.

were conscious of the Enlightenment's emphasis on improvement in their respective occupations as gentleman farmer and surgeon. In their historical works they portrayed a civilised and literate pre-Christian Gaelic civilisation.[68] O'Conor was particularly concerned with proving the compatibility between Catholics and civil society and argued that 'the ancient Milesians had been governed by a regular constitutional mechanism' akin to the English parliamentary tradition.[69] Unlike Keating who had stressed the religious piety of the early Irish, O'Conor's emphasis was more secular.[70] Specifically, he highlighted the existence of literacy among the ancient Irish:

> Descended from the most humane and knowing Nation of all the old Celts, they imported, very early, the Elements of Letters and Arts into Ireland: Here they improved those Elements into Systems of Government and Philosophy, which their undisturbed State from foreign ambition left them at full Liberty to cultivate, thorough [*sic*] a long Succession of Ages.[71]

O'Halloran, by contrast, emphasised the militaristic aspects of Gaelic society, arguing that Ireland had been a maritime power and that it 'was very early an extensive commercial country'.[72]

O'Halloran and O'Conor were joined in their cause by the Protestant scholars Charles Vallancey (1725?–1812), Joseph Cooper Walker (1760–1810) and Charlotte Brooke (*c*.1750–93), who all had patriotic leanings and regarded the study of Irish antiquities as rendering a service to their country.[73] They found common ground in the areas of music and poetry, arguably topics that were free from sectarianism.[74] O'Conor and O'Halloran were encouraged by their interest and enthusiastically offered advice and provided copies of texts and translations. The following comment by the Chevalier Thomas O'Gorman (1732–1809) in a letter to O'Conor is revealing of their motivation: 'It must indeed be very pleasing to us old Irish to see such a Spirit at present diffused

---

68 Gibbons and O'Conor (eds.), *Charles O'Conor of Ballinagare*; C. Lyons, 'Sylvester O'Halloran's *General history* (1778): Irish historiography and the late eighteenth-century British Empire', PhD thesis, National University of Ireland, Galway, 2011.

69 C. Kidd, *British identities before nationalism: ethnicity and nationhood in the Atlantic world 1600–1800* (Cambridge: Cambridge University Press, 1999), p. 160.

70 O'Halloran, *Golden ages*, p. 24.

71 O'Conor, *Dissertations* (1753), p. v.

72 O'Halloran, *General history*, vol. II, p. 145.

73 For a consideration of patriotism in the eighteenth century, see Leerssen, *Remembrance and imagination*, pp. 14–20.

74 L. Ní Mhunghaile, *Ré Órga na nGaeil: Joseph Cooper Walker 1760–1810* (Indreabhán: Cló Iar-Chonnacht, 2013); L. Ní Mhunghaile, *Charlotte Brooke's Reliques of Irish poetry* (Dublin: Irish Manuscripts Commission, 2009).

among our late oppressors and it is incumbent on us to give them every Aid in our Power towards forwarding and keeping up such Zeal in them.'[75]

The main focus of Walker's *Historical memoirs of the Irish bards* was a history of Irish poetry and poets from the earliest times to the eighteenth century, and he cited liberally therein from the works of Keating, O'Flaherty, O'Halloran, O'Conor and others. It also included a discussion of Irish musical instruments and a biography of the harper Turlough O'Carolan. Because Walker lacked competence in the Irish language he relied heavily on O'Conor and the Gaelic scholar Theophilus O'Flanagan for translations. He claimed to have 'marked out a path which may facilitate the pursuit of those who shall hereafter follow me'.[76] His portrayal of ancient Gaelic society was similar to that of O'Conor and O'Halloran as he sought to demonstrate that the ancient Irish were not barbaric: 'Can that nation be deemed barbarous, in which learning shared the honours next to royalty? Warlike as the Irish were in those days, even arms were less respected among them than letters. – Read this, ye polished nations of the earth, and blush!'[77] (Illustration 6). Similarly, in *Reliques of Irish poetry* (1789) Charlotte Brooke aspired to counter the arguments of those writers she termed 'anti-Hibernian', who represent 'our early ancestors' as '*barbarians, descended from barbarians, and ever continuing the same*'.[78] She believed that the study of Irish poetry could foster reconciliation between the various communities in Ireland, as well as a more sympathetic view of the Irish by English commentators, and she downplayed any distinction between the Anglo-Irish and the native Irish: 'Let them tell her, that the portion of her blood which flows in our veins is rather ennobled than disgraced by the mingling tides that descend from our heroic ancestors.'[79] As proof of the glorious Gaelic past she wished to portray, she offered examples of Irish poetry composed between the fifteenth and eighteenth centuries:

> The productions of our Irish Bards exhibit a glow of cultivated genius, – a spirit of elevated heroism, – sentiments of pure honour, – instances of disinterested patriotism, – and manners of a degree of refinement, totally astonishing, at a period when the rest of Europe was nearly sunk in barbarism: And is not this very honourable to our countrymen? Will they not be benefited, – will they not be gratified, at the lustre reflected on them by ancestors so very different from what modern prejudice has been studious to represent them?[80]

---

75 Thomas O'Gorman to O'Conor, 19 July 1781 cited in O'Halloran, *Golden ages*, p. 112.
76 J. Walker, *Historical memoirs of the Irish bards* (London, 1789), p. v.
77 Ibid., p. 5.
78 *Brooke's Reliques*, p. 27n.
79 Ibid., p. viii.
80 Ibid., p. vii.

Brooke's use here of the first person pronoun echoes that of Walker and it provides a clear indication that they regarded the Gaelic literary heritage as their own.

Another key area in which Gaelic and Anglo-Irish scholars could assert Gaelic civility was in debates surrounding the antiquity of the Irish language. In the early decades of the eighteenth century Anthony Raymond and the Ó Neachtain scribes sought to present the language as one worthy of study. It was crucial for them to prove its antiquity in order to validate the value and authenticity of works written in it.[81] They adapted Ruaidhrí Ó Flaithbheartaigh's speculations in *Ogygia* that Irish was related to the Phoenician language, which in turn was related to Hebrew. The implication of this argument was that Irish could not be a barbarous language if it were related to the language of the Bible.[82] Charles Vallancey enthusiastically adopted this theory and claimed that the Irish language was the oldest and most unadulterated of all languages and was closest to the language spoken before Babel. He argued that it had 'the strongest affinity' with 'the Celtic, Punic, Phoenician and Hebrew languages' and asserted that it was a 'Punic-Celtic Compound'. As a result, he believed it to be 'a language of the utmost importance, and most desirable to be acquired by all antiquarians and etymologists'.[83] This was an important argument as it supported the origin myth that the Irish had descended from the Phoenicians from whom they had acquired writing. This then strengthened the argument for a literate early Irish civilisation. Charlotte Brooke termed Irish 'a neglected language' and hinted at its superiority over English:

> In the pathetic, it breathes the most beautiful and affecting simplicity; and in the bolder species of composition, it is distinguished by a force of expression, a sublime dignity, and a rapid energy; as it sometimes fills the mind with ideas altogether new, and which, perhaps, no modern language is entirely prepared to express. One compound epithet must often be translated by two lines of English verse, and, on such occasions, much of the beauty is necessarily lost.[84]

These scholars were challenged by Edward Ledwich, who rejected attempts to use the antiquity of the language as evidence of the eastern origin of the early Irish. In a lengthy discussion on the origin of the language, he claimed

---

81 Harrison, *Dean's friend*, p. 85.
82 Ibid., p. 87.
83 C. Vallancey, *An essay on the antiquity of the Irish language: being a collation of the Irish with the Punic language* (Dublin: S. Powell, 1772), p. 1.
84 *Brooke's Reliques*, p. vi.

that 'no genuine specimen of old Celtic has been produced' and argued that there were no Irish-language manuscripts extant from earlier than the eleventh century. He concluded that 'the pretensions of the Irish to an eastern origin is a vain and groundless notion, generated in ignorance and mistaken patriotism, disgraceful to the good sense of the nation, and not to be supported by reason, history, or learning'.[85]

Two distinct strands can be identified in the interactions that occurred between the intellectual worlds of Catholics and Protestants throughout the eighteenth century, namely the vindication of Gaelic civility and reconciliation between the various ethnic groupings in Ireland. Works such as Walker's *Historical memoirs* and Brooke's *Reliques* demonstrate optimism that these dual aims would succeed. The political events of the 1790s had a profoundly negative register, however, as Anglo-Irish antiquarians such as Walker distanced themselves from their earlier endeavours and turned their attention to less politically sensitive topics of inquiry. Nevertheless, the collaboration that occurred between the Gaelic and Anglo-Irish worlds in the field of antiquarianism during the eighteenth century laid the foundation for a process of 'cultural hybridisation', one that would 'become the very cornerstone of cultural and (later) political nationalism in the nineteenth century'.[86]

Conclusion

If ultimately the desire to create a confessionally tolerant system of government was thwarted by the tensions of the 1790s, it was not because either side was inherently antipathetic to identifying a *modus vivendi*. While the government was willing to pass a series of acts repealing the articles constitutive of the penal code, the United Irishmen speculated about the possibilities of a republican futurity open to all creeds. Both parties to the conflict were later to rehearse versions of Irish history that accorded with their political sentiments; as a result, the 1798 rebellion was itself to be a historically contested event. However, the bloody denouement of the century also posed a significant new question for Irish thinkers and writers: namely, what did it mean to be Irish? The Act of Union of 1800 repositioned Irish politics within the confines of British institutional life. Westminster not Dublin became the central venue for discussion of how to ameliorate the lives of fellow citizens. This posed the stark question: was the population of Ireland distinct from

85 E. Ledwich, *Antiquities of Ireland* (Dublin: Arthur Grueber, 1790), pp. 83–5.
86 Leerssen, *Mere Irish*, p. 383.

the English, Scots and Welsh that equally found a home in the British state system? And if they were distinct, what made them so? Was it their religion, their ethnicity or their language? In other words, the closure of the Dublin parliament and its integration into the parliament of Great Britain and Ireland shifted the question from one of civility to one of ethnicity. In the nineteenth century, a variety of solutions to the puzzle of Anglo-Irish affairs were to be articulated: the Age of Enlightenment and Antiquarianism had closed and the Age of Empire and Nationalism had opened.

16

Art and Architecture in the Long
Eighteenth Century

CHRISTINE CASEY

Introduction

In a censure of 'pretenders to art at home' and 'intruding mercenaries from abroad' the author of a pamphlet published in 1729 identified a central issue in artistic production and consumption in Ireland in the long eighteenth century: the premium placed on foreign expertise and its negative impact on the careers of native artists.[1] It was a concern echoed by others throughout the century. Writing in 1759, Henry Brooke observed: 'In the case of building, and in truth, in many others, we are apt to set too high a value on foreigners, of whom some have appeared to be nothing more than forward prating, superficial pretenders.' John Aheron (d.1761), an eccentric architect from County Clare, thought likewise; he accused Trinity College in 1754 of the conviction 'that no native of this kingdom can equal a foreigner in point of taste and judgment'.[2] While Ireland was not without native artistic genius in the eighteenth century, local fine art production was, with notable exceptions, slow to achieve the highest international standards. To some extent the history of art and architecture of Ireland in the long eighteenth century might be read as a game of two halves: the first dominated by resident foreign architects and craftsmen, by the commissioning and procurement of art works from abroad, and by the process of design and patronage by correspondence; the second characterised by a growing sophistication and originality in native production, by the increased migration of Irish artists to London and Rome, and by the foundation of Irish art institutions. Throughout the entire period, ambitions

---

1 *Considerations on the act for encouraging in-land navigation in Ireland* (Dublin: William Smith, 1729) cited in C. Casey, 'Books and builders: a bibliographical approach to Irish eighteenth-century architecture', PhD thesis, University of Dublin, 1991, pp. 205–6.
2 [H. Brooke], *An essay on the antient and modern state of Ireland* (Dublin: P. Lord, 1759), p. 77; Casey, 'Books and builders', p. 126.

were high. In architecture, high standards in scale and quality of materials and craftsmanship set the bar for the entire period, while Grand Tour sculpture and painting and imported furnishings and silver spurred local emulation. In the wider British context, provincial ambition resulted in precocity across a range of media.[3] In terms of self-conscious patronage and production, there are distinct parallels in the relationship of Dublin with London and of Vienna, Dresden and Munich with the fringes of the Holy Roman Empire where the desire for status within the *Reich* was paramount.[4] Mrs Delany's colourful pen-picture of Robert Clayton, successively bishop of Killala, Cork and Clogher (1729–58), if inspired by tributes to the grandiose patronage of the 1st Duke of Chandos, vividly evokes the conscientious cosmopolitanism of Irish patrons of the period: 'he eats, drinks and sleeps in taste. He has pictures by ... Morat, music by Corelli, castles in the air by Vitruvius'.[5]

The Art of Self-representation: Architecture, Sculpture, Portraiture and Plate

The 'intruding mercenaries from abroad' referred to by the pamphleteer Patriophilus in 1729 were most probably the recently appointed architect of the Irish parliament house, Edward Lovett Pearce, and his assistant Richard Castle. Indeed 'Patriophilus' may have been Pearce's thwarted rival for the commission, the native-born surveyor-general, Thomas Burgh, who was summarily side-lined by the building committee.[6] The pamphlet was published in the year in which the foundation stone of the parliament house was laid, accompanied by effusive tributes to 'the great architect ... Captain *Pierce*'. Though not an independent legislature, the Irish parliament gained increasing significance in the opening decades of the eighteenth century largely due to its ability to raise money with increasing legislative artistry. The 'Pile Majestick' raised to house the Irish legislature surprised even its incumbents, and though reflationary motives may well have informed the project, magnificence and its effects were undoubtedly its principal aim.[7] Universally

---

3 E. McParland, 'Eclecticism: the provincial's advantage', *Irish Arts Review Yearbook 1991–1992*, 210–13.

4 J. Whaley, *Germany and the Holy Roman Empire*, vol. II: *From the Peace of Westphalia to the Dissolution of the Reich 1648–1806* (Oxford: Oxford University Press, 2012), pp. 133–5, 220–30.

5 E. McParland, *Public architecture in Ireland, 1680–1760* (New Haven: Yale University Press, 2001), p. 188.

6 E. McParland, 'Edward Lovett Pearce and the parliament house in Dublin', *Burlington Magazine*, 131:1031 (1989), 91–100.

7 Ibid., p. 177.

acclaimed, it is the most accomplished classical building in Ireland, a work of international significance in terms of typology, and the most significant public building in the new Palladian manner in Britain (Illustration 7). The chief pictorial ornaments of the building commissioned for the House of Lords are telling: 'two pieces of Fine Irish Tapestry ... one representing the Glorious Victory obtained at the Boyne, by our Valiant Defender, King William of Immortal memory and the other the Valiant Defence of Londonderry'.[8] Parliament met for the first time in its newly completed chambers in October 1731 and Pearce was knighted there on 10 March 1732. It may well have provided the impetus for a new parliament house at Westminster, for at precisely the same moment designs were mooted in the London press and Nicholas Hawksmoor wrote to the Earl of Carlisle of 'much' talk about the proposed building. A parliamentary report on the topic was submitted in May 1732, and in March 1733 the *Gentleman's Magazine* noted the Earl of Burlington's plan for the new building.[9] An extensive series of designs was prepared by Burlington's associate, William Kent, between 1733 and 1740, but none came to fruition. Unsurprisingly, visitors to Dublin in the eighteenth century were struck by the splendour of the parliament house by comparison with the shambolic accommodation of the parent legislature in Westminster.[10] At almost three times the size of the Dublin building, the Westminster project posed significant problems in terms of embanking the site, incorporating existing buildings and adequately framing parliamentary ceremony. Pearce was unfettered by parliamentary tradition, and the most problematic aspect of the site was its restricted street frontage, as it was hemmed in by neighbouring buildings on three sides. While in formal terms there is much common ground between the designs of Pearce, Burlington and Kent, drawing as they do on Palladio and the Antique, the Dublin parliament house is strikingly unconventional. At Westminster, tradition dictated a symmetrical arrangement of Lords' and Commons' chambers at either end of a transverse circulatory sequence that optimised the Black Rod ritual during the state opening of parliament. In Dublin, symmetry (and equal status of the chambers) was dispensed with; the domed Commons' chamber formed the core of the plan, with the House of Lords set off to the right of the dominant axis (Illustration 8).

8 *Dublin Evening Post*, 11–15 Sept. 1733.
9 F. Salmon, 'Public commissions' in S. Weber (ed.), *William Kent: designing Georgian Britain* (New Haven: Yale University Press, 2013), p. 329.
10 A. Gilchrist, 'The greatest traveller in eighteenth-century Ireland', *Bulletin of the Irish Georgian Society*, 3 (1960), 7–8.

7. Elevation of the parliament house, Dublin, by Roland Omer.

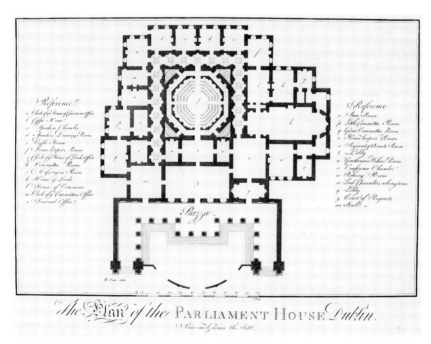

8. Plan of the parliament house, Dublin, by Roland Omer.

409

The elevation and interiors of the parliament house bear witness to the complex architectural personality of its author. Pearce imbibed the monumentality and grandeur of buildings by his cousin, Sir John Vanbrugh, and the rigorous proportional relationships and antique reconstructions of Andrea Palladio. The superb colonnaded portico with its relatively plain entablature and starkly solid parapet elicits conflicting similes which capture the very pure character of its architecture. They are redolent of Pearce's decidedly and precociously 'Grecian' sensibility, a taste that he shared with a sophisticated group of patrons and practitioners self-styled as the 'new Junta for Architecture'.[11] The group included several members of the prominent Molesworth family, Thomas Hewett, surveyor of the King's Works in London (1719–26) and the Italian architect Alessandro Galilei. The latter, who was brought to Ireland in 1717 by Robert Molesworth, provided designs for Ireland's first great house of the period, Castletown in County Kildare, which was built from 1722 by William Conolly, then Speaker of the Irish House of Commons. Since Galilei did not remain in Ireland, the extent to which his designs were followed at Castletown remains unclear. In 1722 George Berkeley noted that construction had begun before the façade had been settled upon and mentioned designs 'by several hands'. The candidates include Conolly's County Kildare neighbour Thomas Burgh, and Edward Lovett Pearce who arrived back from the Grand Tour in 1725. Conolly too was ascribed a role, and the synthesis of dynastic Roman palazzo and Palladian villa design was surely the outcome of mediation between patron and practitioner (Illustration 9). The monumental central block with its alternating pediments to the piano nobile windows was always considered plain and, though softened by the Ionic colonnaded quadrants, the wings too are sober constructions and the overall effect is of imposing and restrained grandeur (Illustration 10). Compared to Robert Walpole's grandiose house at Houghton in Norfolk (also begun in 1722) with its cupolas, portico and pedimented wings, Castletown is forthright in its sobriety. As at Houghton, the hall is a monumental double-height space, but in contrast to the rich Roman sculptural adornment of Walpole's stone hall, the Castletown hall relies for its impact on architecture, here of the same pure eloquence as that seen at the parliament house and unquestionably the work of Edward Lovett Pearce, who appears to have been executant architect by the mid-1720s. A drawing by Pearce for the cornice of the central block

11 E. McParland, 'Sir Thomas Hewett and the new Junta for Architecture' in Giles Worsley (ed.), *The role of the amateur architect* (London: Georgian Group, 1994), pp. 21–6.

9. Entrance front of Castletown House, County Kildare, begun *c.*1722.

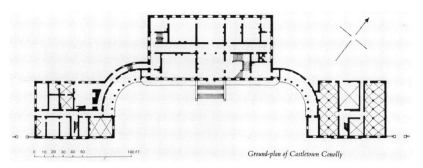

10. Plan of Castletown House, County Kildare, by John Stewart.

has been shown to derive from the Antique as mediated through Palladio's *Quattro libri*: Conolly, who eschewed a portico, was content to complete his house with a monumental moulding from the entrance to the Pantheon in Rome.[12] Though Castletown was absolutely exceptional in an Irish context, and remained until the 1770s 'the only house in Ireland to which the term

---

12 M. McKenna, 'Castletown: the British context', BA thesis, Department of History of Art and Architecture, Trinity College Dublin, 2014, p. 26.

411

palace may be applied', it had counterparts in Britain, and Giles Worsley concluded that it 'would not look out of place in the volumes of *Vitruvius Britannicus*'.[13] Though Conolly might fairly be seen as Walpole's equivalent in Ireland, his wealth and influence did not compare to that of Britain's first minister. Castletown bears greater resemblance to astylar buildings such as Cliveden or Colen Campbell's Rolls House in Chancery Lane, the official residence of the Master of the Rolls, which was begun in 1718 just as Conolly was contemplating building.[14] Conolly died in 1729, before the completion of his great representative mansion. He and his wife Katherine were childless and the vast interior remained unfinished until the 1770s. However, as with the parliament house, the building set a standard in scale and quality, and the double-pile plan with a columnar hall screen and spinal corridor exerted direct influence on Irish country house design.[15] Built as a statement of social and political status, a place for astute entertaining and retreat within easy reach of the capital, it was soon emulated but never wholly outdone.

More overt evidence of Conolly's self-fashioning is found in portraiture, the most prolific genre of eighteenth-century painting in Ireland. Conolly sat to Charles Jervas (*c*.1675–1739), the most successful Irish painter of the early eighteenth century, who was appointed principal painter to George I in 1723. Of gentry stock from King's County, Jervas trained in London with Sir Godfrey Kneller, who commented acerbically on the meteoric rise of his erstwhile pupil.[16] Jervas spent a decade in Italy from 1698 where he became an avid copyist of Raphael. Grand Tourist connections aided his rise in London and Robert Walpole was among his most significant early patrons. Swift and Pope were friends and the latter joked that Jervas 'peopled Ireland with a world of beautiful shadows'.[17] Jervas was a regular visitor to Ireland, and Conolly's portrait was probably painted during the artist's sustained sojourn from 1717 to 1721. It depicts the Speaker in parliamentary robes with the scroll and mace of office and was reproduced as a line engraving and a mezzotint, giving the Speaker's full honours as revenue commissioner, privy councillor

13 G. Worsley, 'Castletown, County Kildare', *Country Life*, 188:11 (17 March 1994), 52–7.
14 McKenna, 'Castletown', p. 3.
15 M. Craig, *The architecture of Ireland* (London and Dublin: Batsford and Eason & Son, 1982), pp. 177–99.
16 W.G. Strickland, *A dictionary of Irish artists*, 2 vols. (Dublin and London, 1912; reprint, Shannon: Irish University Press, 1968), vol. I, p. 547; C. Pegum, 'Charles Jervas' in N. Figgis (ed.), *Art and architecture of Ireland* (hereafter AAI), vol. II: *Painting 1600–1900* (New Haven: Yale University Press, 2014), pp. 323–5.
17 A. Crookshank and the Knight of Glin, *Ireland's painters 1600–1940* (New Haven: Yale University Press, 2002), p. 30.

and 'ten times' lord justice (Illustration 11).[18] It was more than likely Jervas who recommended the author of Conolly's funerary monument, Thomas Carter, a London sculptor promoted by the portraitist who developed one of the largest workshops in the capital, employing in 1746 no less than forty craftsmen.[19] The monument arrived in Ireland in 1736 and was installed in a Doric aedicule in the now ruinous Conolly mausoleum (Illustration 12).

The choice of London-based painters and sculptors for portraits and monuments was symptomatic of the metropolitan pretensions of Irish grandees. Thomas Carter's executor and fellow sculptor, Henry Cheere, was chosen by the Countess of Kildare for the ambitious funerary monument at Christ Church Cathedral to her husband Robert, the 19th Earl of Kildare, who died in 1744. If Conolly was Ireland's principal commoner, the Earl of Kildare assumed the role of its foremost peer following the attainder of James Butler, 2nd Duke of Ormonde in 1715. Cheere's design is unusual in that Lord Kildare is posed as a recumbent robed figure, as if lying in state, attended by his wife and children. In this period the deceased was almost invariably represented standing or reclining (Illustration 13). The Countess lays her hand on her husband's waist while his grieving son and daughter mourn him at either end of the catalfalque. The absence of religious elements and the resemblance of the pose to an entombment add to the monument's individuality.[20] Of Cheere's vast output of fashionable funerary statuary, Rupert Gunnis concluded: 'I doubt if he ever produced a finer, more human and touching memorial than the group of Lord Kildare's family.'[21] In these theatrical marble set-pieces Georgian Ireland achieved its closest brush with the European baroque tradition.

The principal resident portrait painter in Ireland during the 1730s and 1740s was James Latham, who was 'by a long way, the most distinguished painter of the first half of the eighteenth century and the only Irish portrait painter who transcends the parochial picture of Irish art at this time'.[22] A late eighteenth-century commentator considered Latham's portraits superior to those of Jervas. He was chosen for the full-length portrait of Charles Tottenham painted to commemorate a celebrated patriotic occasion in 1731 when the

18 P. Walsh, *The making of the Irish Protestant Ascendancy: the life of William Conolly, 1662–1729* (Woodbridge: The Boydell Press, 2010).

19 I. Roscoe, E. Hardy and M.G. Sullivan, *A biographical dictionary of sculptors in Britain 1660–1751* (New Haven: Yale University Press, 2009), pp. 212–15.

20 P. Ward-Jackson, 'Church monuments' in P. Murphy (ed.), AAI, III, pp. 398–9.

21 R. Gunnis, *Dictionary of British sculptors 1660–1851*, 2nd edn (London: Abbey Library, 1968), pp. 97–8.

22 Crookshank and Glin, *Ireland's painters*, p. 36.

11. 'The Right Honble William Conolly Esqr', engraving by Paul Foudrinier after Charles Jervas.

12. Monument to William and Katherine Conolly by Thomas Carter.

13. Sir Henry Cheere, monument to the 19th Earl of Kildare (d.1744), Christ Church Cathedral.

MP for New Ross, County Wexford, rode 60 miles to reach the House of Commons in time to provide the casting vote against giving a surplus of £60,000 to the London parliament.[23] Posed with boots, spurs and riding crop against a giant column evocative of the parliament house, the picture demonstrates Latham's distinctive ability to combine virtuoso naturalism with the conventional swagger portrait (Illustration 14). The superb handling of leather, silk, velvet and silver embroidery is clear and precise, in contrast to the later double-portrait of Pole Cosby and his daughter of 1741 in which a freer French manner is evident. Cosby's spectacular embroidered waistcoat reveals the taste for sumptuous personal attire expressed in his manuscript autobiography and was most likely acquired from Paris.[24] The Conolly mezzotint inscription, Tottenham's boots and Cosby's waistcoat are testament to the wider signifying role of portraiture in eighteenth-century Ireland: like building and collecting, portraiture was a cultural practice, a communicative act by which the individual and the collective addressed society.[25]

That portraits signified independently of their sitters is forcibly demonstrated by the wide currency of mezzotint engravings after painted portraits and by the population of interiors with busts of great men. 'Illustrious Heads' ennobled halls, state rooms and libraries – the most spectacular example being the fourteen ancient and modern heads by Scheemakers and Roubiliac commissioned for the Long Room of Trinity College Library, where Irishmen Robert Boyle and James Ussher feature alongside Homer, Cicero and Shakespeare (Illustration 15). Political portraits commissioned or presented to Dublin Corporation reflected the fluctuating loyalties of the city fathers.[26] James McArdell, 'a native of Ireland and the most eminent in this Art in his time', dominated the mezzotint portrait business in London until his early death in 1765 aged 37.[27] Among his many portraits of politicians, peers and beauties was a pair of mezzotints, after Joshua Reynolds, of the 20th Earl and Countess of Kildare (Illustration 16).

23 E.M. Johnston-Liik, *History of the Irish parliament 1692–1800: commons, constituencies and statutes*, 6 vols. (Belfast: Ulster Historical Foundation, 2002) vol. VI, p. 416; F. Cullen, *The Irish face: redefining the Irish portrait* (London: National Portrait Gallery, 2004), p. 30.

24 'Manuscript autobiography of Pole Cosby', *Journal of the Kildare Archaeological Society*, 5 (1906–8), 79–99, 165–84, 253–73, 311–24, 423–36.

25 M. Pointon, *Hanging the head: portraiture and social formation in eighteenth-century England* (New Haven: Paul Mellon Centre for Studies in British Art, 1998), p. 4.

26 M. Clark, *The Dublin Civic Portraiture Collection: patronage, politics and patriotism, 1603–2013* (Dublin: Four Courts Press, 2016), *passim*.

27 Strickland, *Dictionary*, vol. II, p. 46.

14. James Latham, *Charles Tottenham*. Oil on canvas, *c*.1731.

15. The Long Room, Trinity College Dublin, by Thomas Burgh with busts by Scheemakers and Roubiliac.

The Kildares did not hesitate to underline their position at the apex of the Irish peerage. The acquisition in 1738 of former ancestral lands at Carton in County Kildare bounding the Conolly's Castletown estate facilitated the creation of a new dynastic seat that 'sounded a fanfare for the Kildare's re-entry into politics and high society'.[28] In the year after his father's death in 1744, James, 20th Earl of Kildare and future Duke of Leinster, commenced construction of a grandiose town house on the south-eastern periphery of Dublin City (Illustration 17). Its foundation stone bore his name, the date and the inscription: 'Hence learn, when in some unhappy time you chance on the ruins of so magnificent a house, how great was he who erected it.'[29] In the absence of Edward Lovett Pearce, who had died in 1733, the Kildares employed Richard Castle to design their new buildings. Castle remained in their employment until his death in 1750 which occurred at Carton. Like Charles Jervas, Richard Castle was of landed background: his father was a court Jew of English ancestry

---

28 T. Barnard, *Making the grand figure: lives and possessions in Ireland, 1641–1770* (New Haven: Yale University Press, 2004), p. 69.
29 D. Griffin and C. Pegum, *Leinster House* (Dublin: OPW, 2000), p. 2.

16. James FitzGerald, 20th Earl of Kildare. Mezzotint by James McArdell after Sir Joshua Reynolds, 1754.

17. Richard Castle, elevation of Kildare (Leinster) House begun 1745.

employed as a trade envoy by the Saxon monarchy at Dresden.[30] Though
Castle's training remains a mystery, his drawing skills were superb. He
evidently worked for Edward Lovett Pearce in London before travelling to
Ireland in 1728 with his patron and business associate Sir Gustavus Hume
of Castle Hume, County Fermanagh, a courtier of George I who had travelled in Germany.[31] Castle's architecture is less sophisticated than that of
Pearce, with a lesser command of proportion and the classical orders. His
buildings are, however, immensely impressive as material objects, lovingly
crafted and with a robust handling of mass and detail that finds resonance
in modest Georgian buildings of the Irish countryside (Illustration 18).
His architecture is closest in temper to that of the Scottish architect James
Gibbs, and it may not be merely a coincidence that Gibbs' draughtsman,
Johann Borlach, was also a Dresden Jew of English ancestry. Borlach was
much involved in the production of Gibbs' richly illustrated folio treatise
A book of architecture whose publication in 1728 coincided with Castle's

---

30 L. Calderón and K. Dechant, 'New light on Hugh Montgomerie, Richard Castle and
Number 85 Saint Stephen's Green' in C. Casey (ed.), *The eighteenth-century Dublin town
house: form, function and finance* (Dublin: Four Courts Press, 2010), pp. 174–96.
31 M. Hayes, 'Anglo-Irish architectural exchange in the early eighteenth century: patrons,
practitioners and pieds-à-terre', PhD thesis, Trinity College Dublin, 2015, pp. 30–1, 51–3.

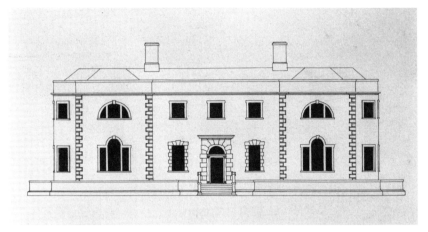

18. Richard Castle, Belvedere House, County Westmeath, *c*.1740. Elevation by David Griffin.

arrival in Ireland. Like Gibbs and unlike Pearce, Castle had a taste for richly ornamental interior effects and his buildings were decorated with sumptuous plasterwork decoration and inlaid wooden floors. At Carton he employed Swiss-Italian *stuccatori* for the crafting of the Kildare's great room, the eating parlour, now saloon, which has aptly been described as 'one of the most extravagant displays of baroque plasterwork in the British Isles' (Illustration 19).[32] Again the Kildares looked to London: Paolo Lafranchini had recently decorated the picture gallery of Bedford House, the largest and most impressive in the city. His spectacular debut at Carton in 1738, assisted by his brother Filippo, secured their command of interior decoration in Ireland until the 1760s.

In the mid-1740s a third prodigy residence was built within a short distance of the capital. Though significantly smaller than its peers, Russborough, County Wicklow, punches considerably above its weight in terms of opulence and grandeur and retains many of its sumptuous fittings and contents (Illustration 20). Its builder, Joseph Leeson, 1st Earl of Milltown, was zealously arriviste and much parodied for his pretensions and for his father's history as brewer and property developer. Like Kildare, he not only began building immediately after his father's death (1741) but also engaged Richard Castle, who built a compact villa-like block of two principal storeys over a

---

32 J. Cornforth, *Early Georgian interiors* (New Haven: Yale University Press, 2004), p. 47.

19. Carton, County Kildare, eating parlour, Paolo and Filippo Lafranchini, 1738.

basement joined by advanced colonnaded quadrants to kitchen and stable blocks. While Conolly and Kildare chose limestone for their seats, Leeson used local Wicklow granite whose gritty texture, glistening quartz and attendant lichens create an architectural palette of distinction and permitted Castle's elegant reductionism in the detailing of the subsidiary elements: for example, in the pavilions the full entablature of the stylar centrepiece with its

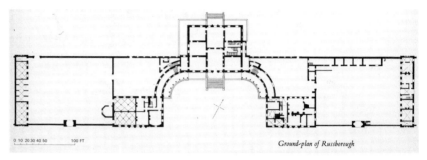

Ground-plan of Russborough

20. Russborough, County Wicklow, plan by John Stewart.

pulvinated frieze is truncated in the outer bays and side elevations to a deep flat band and cornice, amusingly 'carried' on brackets flanking the first-floor windows. Work began on the demesne in the spring of 1742; in 1748 a visitor noted 'artificers from most parts of Europe ... employed in this great new work'. By 1759 Lady Kildare noted 'furniture magnificent'.[33]

Leeson made two Grand Tours of Italy in 1744–5 and 1750–1 in search of art and furnishing for the house, employing as his secretary the antiquarian and author Robert Wood who, though of Scottish ancestry, was born and raised in County Meath. Leeson sought out paintings, statuary and furniture to fill the seven rooms of parade on his piano nobile and to populate twelve niches cut into the back of his forecourt arcades. As was the norm in Britain, the pictures were mostly copies of Seicento originals, several from the Palazzo Colonna in Rome. Domenichino, Guercino and Rubens were among those copied. His distinct taste for Roman Catholic iconography mirrors that of Sir Robert Walpole at Houghton, while his penchant for fleshy nudes has been seen to reflect Leeson's amorous appetites. The colonnade statues were copies after the Antique while small-scale interior statuary derived from artists such as Giambologna. The finest antiquity in the collection was a Venus Genetrix now at the J. Paul Getty Museum.[34] For his drawing room Leeson procured in Rome four atmospheric landscapes symbolising the times of the day by Claude-Joseph Vernet: ovals whose size was determined by robust plasterwork frames on the walls of the room. They are set too high for the viewpoint in the pictures and are thus reflective of patronage by correspondence.

33 W. Laffan and K. Mulligan, *Russborough: a great Irish house, its families and collections* (Russborough: Alfred Beit Foundation, 2014), p. 51.
34 W. Laffan and C. Monkhouse (eds.), *Ireland: Crossroads of art and design, 1690–1840* (Chicago: The Art Institute of Chicago, 2015), pp. 24, 264.

21. Russborough, saloon with inlaid floors and plasterwork by the Lafranchini brothers.

Leeson commissioned scagliola pier tables in Florence and gilt frames in Rome, and retained a French upholsterer in Ireland.[35] The copies after Guercino and Rubens are set in spectacular carved frames whose authorship has eluded identification. Italian polychrome table tops were combined with locally made furniture, including grandiose dining room side tables with the vigorous foliate and zoomorphic ornaments that were grist to the mill of Irish carvers. Even the floors at Russborough are objects of beauty; crafted in polychrome parquetry, they bear comparison to Castle's lost interiors at Powerscourt House in County Wicklow, which he remodelled ostentatiously in the 1730s for the Wingfield family (Illustration 21). The walls and ceilings of the piano nobile interiors at Russborough were enriched with decorative plasterwork of such diversity in design and handling that a staggered execution period has been mooted: this is 'possible', if unlikely, given the hive of activity described in 1748 and Leeson's acquisitive determination.[36] The opulence of these rooms and the curiously disjointed character of the decoration certainly

35 Ibid., pp. 92–3, 122–5.
36 Ibid., p. 69.

suggests a lack of unified architectural control in the final stages of the project such as is frequently encountered in Britain and Ireland in the period, and which points up the burgeoning role of craftsmen in the design, execution and decoration of buildings in city and countryside. The preservation of the Milltown collection provides a rare glimpse of the Georgian aristocratic interior and the extent to which the art in the eighteenth-century country house, both in Britain and Ireland, was not of native origin.

Through the ample sash windows of these houses the occupants viewed designed landscapes initially inspired by the classical manner of Claude and Poussin but increasingly inclined towards the picturesque. The refashioning of the Irish landscape in the eighteenth century and the painting which amplifies it has been read as an integral part of Britain's colonial project in Ireland.[37] Contemporaries were less analytical. Thomas Campbell claimed in 1778 that 'the Irish, by taste and opportunity are landscape lovers', and his view was echoed by Thomas Brownwell, a County Meath wood ranger in 1759: outraged by the removal of modest white-thorn trees from the Stackallan estate, Brownwell spoke lyrically of his response to the landscape: they were 'very beautiful trees in their kind', gave 'ornamental shelter in winter' and 'shade in summer' and 'by cutting the said trees the places where thay stood look very blake [sic] and naked and the beauty of the place much lessened by the loss of the said trees'.[38]

Though most Georgian demesnes have been altered over time, much eighteenth-century planting survives and it is an element of the first importance in the Irish rural landscape. Richard Castle, who had experience of hydraulic engineering, designed arresting structures for his clients' demesnes, most notably the vast Conolly folly built by Katherine Conolly as a relief work during the famine year of 1741; the idea of an obelisk set above a staggered set of arches may well have been inspired by the Roman fountains of the Pamphili family on the Janiculum Hill and Piazza Navona (Illustration 22). Beyond the lawns, ditches and tastefully planted tree clumps at Russborough and Powerscourt were natural features that attracted burgeoning numbers of visitors for their emotional effects – an aesthetic response articulated in Edmund Burke's precocious undergraduate essay, *An enquiry into the origin of our ideas on the sublime and the beautiful* (1757).

Surprisingly perhaps, Joseph Leeson played an active role in the encouragement of a native school of landscape painting by making his collection available to young artists and by having an Irish painter make copies of his continental

---

37 W. Laffan, 'Landscape painting in Ireland' in Figgis (ed.), AAI, II, pp. 71–7.
38 National Archives of Ireland, 1148/5/3.

22. The Conolly folly, Castletown, County Kildare, attributed to Richard Castle, 1741.

capricci. His commissioning, *c*.1750, of Roman landscapes from the young George Barret for plaster aedicules in his dining room was an important step in the artist's career. Barret progressed from copies and variants of classical landscapes to a picturesque manner comparable to that of Richard Wilson

427

in England and related to the aesthetic ideas of Edmund Burke who would eventually champion his work in London, where he exhibited views of Wales and the Lake District, together with the celebrated Powerscourt and Dargle canvases. These helped steer the direction of taste towards the Wicklow landscape (Illustration 23). Barret's removal to London in 1763 favoured a young landscape painter from Waterford, Thomas Roberts (1748–77), the son of the architect of the same name who was an accomplished provincial exponent of Palladianism much influenced by the work of Richard Castle.[39] In 1769, Roberts exhibited two canvases in Dublin whose realism, delicacy and lyricism derived from his study of Vernet, Dutch landscape painting and attentive observation of the Irish countryside including ruinous thatched cabins. The inclusion of ruins and natives in Roberts' paintings has been interpreted as an ideological framing device akin to the role of later publications in shaping a voyeuristic view of the Irish landscape and in dictating those sites worthy to be painted and engraved and ultimately to be visited.[40] Like Barret, Roberts' market was primarily in the painting of demesne views and the relatively tame landscape of the Carton estate provided the subject for a late series of paintings considered his masterpiece in which diminutive figures of the Duke and Duchess and their assiduous estate workers are set in river landscapes of intense idealism and serenity (Illustration 24). For all their idealism, romantic convention and political dimension, the landscapes of Barret and Roberts are deeply evocative of Ireland's lush and verdant countryside, and were singled out for their quality and originality by Anne Crookshank and the Knight of Glin in their pioneering study of Irish painting.[41]

No less than architecture, sculpture and painting, silver played a significant role in social and political representation and the plate amassed by the 19th and 20th Earls of Kildare 'signified to those within and beyond their circle the family's pre-eminent position in Irish society'.[42] As with other artistic media, patrons sought expertise at home and abroad, and local goldsmiths

39 Irish Architectural Archive, Dictionary of Irish Architects, 'Thomas Roberts'; W. Laffan, 'Thomas Roberts' in AAI, ii, pp. 435–8.

40 F. O'Kane, *Ireland and the picturesque: design, landscape painting and tourism 1700–1840* (New Haven: Yale University Press, 2013) pp. 26–31, 185–9.

41 A. Crookshank and the Knight of Glin, *The painters of Ireland 1660–1920* (London: Barrie and Jenkins, 1979), p. 200.

42 D. Bennett, *Irish Georgian silver* (London: Cassell, 1972); A. FitzGerald, 'The production and consumption of goldsmiths' work in eighteenth-century Dublin', PhD thesis, Royal College of Art, London, 2005; A. FitzGerald, 'A sterling trade: making and selling silver in Ireland' in Laffan and Monkhouse (eds.), *Ireland: crossroads of art and design*, p. 175.

23. George Barret, *Powerscourt waterfall*. Oil on canvas, c.1760.

emulated and vied with the London trade.[43] The production of silver in Ireland increased from 25,000 ounces in 1696–7 to 84,000 ounces in the 1780s, with silversmiths in Dublin, Cork, Kinsale, Limerick and Galway.[44] The remarkable silver gilt toilet service commissioned by the 19th Earl of Kildare for his wife following the birth of their first son in 1720 was made in London by the French goldsmith David Willaume while a splendid Kildare wine cistern of 1727 by Robert Sutton and a wall fountain by Robert Calderwood of 1753 demonstrate the consummate skills of Dublin goldsmiths (Illustrations 25, 26).[45] The cistern with tasselled bowl and mask handles is engraved with the Kildare coat of arms while the sheer bulbous body surface of the fountain is a foil for a raised armorial crest, a FitzGerald monkey tap, and a coronet lid complete

43 A. FitzGerald, 'Cosmopolitan commerce: the Dublin goldsmith Robert Calderwood', *Apollo*, 162:523 (Sept. 2005), 46–50.
44 Barnard, *Making the grand figure*, p. 140.
45 E. Taylor, 'Silver for a countess's levee: the Kildare toilet service', *Irish Arts Review*, 14 (1998), 115–25. For the wall fountain, see Laffan and Monkhouse (eds.), *Ireland: crossroads of art and design*, pp. 174–5.

24. Thomas Roberts, *A sheet of water at Carton, with the Duke and Duchess of Leinster about to board a rowing boat.* Oil on canvas, 1775–6.

with illusionistic velvet. In 1746, the year before his marriage to Lady Emily Lennox, daughter of Charles Lennox, 2nd Duke of Richmond and grandson of Charles II, the 20th Earl commissioned an astonishing rococo dinner service from George Wickes of London on which the arms of FitzGerald are impaled with those of Charles II. Those who enjoyed the hospitality of the Kildares' eating parlour did so in the presence of thousands of pounds worth of ornately chased silver, far more than might be found in a contemporary goldsmith's shop. A silver dinner service was also procured at great expense from London for Russborough in 1742–4 – its centrepiece an epergne and stand whose masks, scallop shells and vegetal ornament find echo in the modelled walls and ceilings of the dining room.[46] These objects were viewed by their owners as family heirlooms to be passed down together with the house and estate. The dowager Countess of Kildare gave the Willaume toilet service to her daughter-in-law, Emily, and expected that she in turn would present it

46 Laffan and Monkhouse (eds.), *Ireland: crossroads of art and design*, pp. 23–4.

25. Kildare Toilet service, David Willaume, c.1720.

26. Kildare wine cistern, Thomas Sutton, 1727.

to her son's wife. Evidently the dowager duchess needed some persuasion. In 1776 her sister Sarah Bunbury wrote:

> I also forgot to tell you that Lady Kildare mentioned both to Louisa and me, at separate times, that you had said you would give the little Duchess all that Lady Kildare had given to you. And so she enquired much for a set of gold dressing boxes, which I told her I had not heard anything of, but ... then I supposed you would give them if you had said so ... Now, perhaps, my dear sister, these boxes have slipped your memory, though to be sure, it is time enough to give them. But I thought it right to mention it to you.[47]

Buildings, monuments, portraits and personal objects together and singly operated as vehicles for the display of wealth and aspiration and for the progressive consolidation of dynastic identity.

Art and Architecture in the Public Realm

Country houses and their collections tell one story about artistic production in eighteenth-century Ireland but they are by no means the full picture. A wealth of modest buildings both public and private, with occasional surviving contents, document ordinary lives. Market houses, estate cottages and vernacular dwellings ranged from ambitious emulative structures, such as the singular market house, *c.*1740, at Dunlavin, County Wicklow, to modest limewashed thatched buildings, such as the Church of Saint James of 1762 on the Cooley peninsula, which is one of the oldest surviving pre-emancipation chapels in the country (Illustration 27). Vernacular dwellings range from one-storey, single-room cabins to substantial farmhouses of several rooms on two storeys with attendant outbuildings, with distinct regional variations in plan, elevation and materials. Many cabins were windowless and without a chimneystack though John Wesley noted that the Ulster cabins commonly had windows, doors and a chimney.[48] A conspicuous feature of traditional dwellings is the placement of the gable end to the road, an attractive and distinctive aspect of Ireland's rural built environment. The legacy of estate planning is felt in the broad main streets of towns and villages, such as Strokestown, County Roscommon, and in designed towns such as Westport in County

47 B. FitzGerald (ed.), *Correspondence of Emily, Duchess of Leinster (1731–1814)*, 3 vols. (Dublin: Stationery Office, 1949–57), vol. II, p. 163.
48 N. Roche, 'Vernacular architecture', R. Loeber, 'Vernacular farmhouses' and R. McLoughlin 'Vernacular farmsteads' in AAI, IV, pp. 330–7.

27. St James, Grange, Cooley peninsula, 1762.

Mayo.[49] More ambitious architecture was undertaken in the principal ports and survives in towns such as Drogheda, Wexford, Waterford, Cork and Limerick. John's Square in Limerick built in the 1750s has been likened to 'a corner of Dublin or London ... shipped west and deposited in one corner of the city'.[50] Waterford is unique in having two cathedrals of the late eighteenth century, both denominations served by the architect Thomas Roberts, whose intriguing work merits further exploration, as do the European origins of Davis Ducart, who, besides Castletown Cox in County Kilkenny, designed the former mayoralty house at Cork (1765–73) and the Custom House at Limerick (1765–9).[51]

Though lighting was a feature of fundamental importance in the eight-eenth-century interior, few original chandeliers or sconces survive to tell

49 L. Hurley and K. Whelan, 'Planning of towns and villages from the seventeenth to the nineteenth century' in AAI, IV, pp. 393–7.
50 J. Hill, *The building of Limerick* (Cork: Mercier Press, 1991), p. 70.
51 J. Logan, '"Dropped into this kingdom from the clouds": the Irish career of Davis Dukart, architect and engineer, 1761–1781', *Irish Architectural and Decorative Studies*, 10 (2007), 34–89.

the tale and nineteenth-century glass now predominates. A twelve-branch Galway chandelier, now in the Winterthur Museum, is one of two surviving silver chandeliers made in Ireland in the first half of the eighteenth century for Roman Catholic chapels. The Galway example was made c.1742 for the Dominican chapel in Kirwan's Lane in Galway. It splendidly evokes the unexpected visual culture of eighteenth-century chapels in a period of penal legislation against Catholicism, itinerant clergy and back-street worship.[52] Other important survivals include a copy of *The Descent from the Cross* by Rubens in a superlative Irish Chinoiserie frame, formerly the altarpiece of the Townsend Street chapel and now in St Andrew's, Westland Row (Illustration 28). Likewise in Navan parish church in County Meath there is a monumental, polychrome, limewood crucifix carved in 1790 by the sculptor Edward Smyth, whose father was a native of County Meath.[53] A similar back-street chapel of the late eighteenth century houses the most celebrated devotional monument of late Georgian Ireland: *The dead Christ* by John Hogan, sculpted in Rome, exhibited in Dublin in the year of Catholic emancipation (1829) and acquired by the Revd Fr L'Estrange for the Carmelite Church on Clarendon Street in Dublin (Illustration 29).[54]

Smyth and Hogan return us to sculpture, a medium dominated by English and continental artists for much of the eighteenth century. Royal equestrian statues by Grinling Gibbons (William III, College Green, 1701), John Van Nost II (George I, Essex Bridge, 1717) and John Van Nost III (George II, Saint Stephen's Green) were the capital's most conspicuous public monuments of the period and an inextricable part of popular political culture, the focus of Hanoverian celebration and patriotic protest, alternately garlanded with lilies and assailed by motley missiles.[55] Of the three sculptors, John Van Nost III is of most significance for Ireland, having moved to Dublin following his father's death and the collapse of the family business. From Van Nost the Elder and Peter Scheemakers he inherited a Flemish propensity to naturalism which he brought to late baroque conventions of funerary and portrait sculpture. Like Richard Castle, he was in the right place at the right time: his

52 J. McDonnell, *Ecclesiastical art of the penal era* (Maynooth: St Patrick's College, 1995), pp. 32–3.
53 P. Murphy, 'Edward Smyth' in AAI, III, pp. 321–3.
54 J. Turpin, *John Hogan: Irish Neoclassical sculptor in Rome 1800–1858* (Blackrock: Irish Academic Press, 1982), pp. 164–7.
55 P. McEvansoneya, 'Royal monuments and civic ritual in eighteenth-century Dublin' in C. Chastel-Rousseau (ed.), *Reading the royal monument in eighteenth-century Europe* (Farnham: Ashgate, 2011), pp. 173–94.

28. Mid-eighteenth-century Chinoiserie altarpiece frame, St Andrew's, Westland Row, Dublin.

29. John Hogan, *The dead Christ*, Church of St Theresa, Clarendon Street, Dublin, 1829.

subjects included Dr Samuel Madden and Thomas Prior, founding members of the Dublin Society, and a figure of George III for the Royal Exchange (NGI) commissioned by the lord lieutenant (Illustration 30). He worked in stone and lead at a sculpture yard near St Stephen's Green and supplied statuary for the pleasure gardens at the Lying-in Hospital and for the Upper Castle Yard, where his lead figures of Justice and Fortitude (1753) are painted to appear as stone. Van Nost's significance for Irish eighteenth-century sculpture extends beyond his own output to that of his pupils.

Though undocumented, Van Nost's workshop is the likeliest contender for the apprenticeship of Christopher Hewetson, 'unquestionably the finest Irish-born sculptor of the eighteenth century'.[56] Hewetson came from landed stock in County Kilkenny and rose to international fame in the heated antiquarian atmosphere of late eighteenth-century Rome where he is first recorded in 1765. Though of the reformed faith and described by one Roman cleric as 'one of those unfortunate hardened unbelievers', Hewetson nevertheless succeeded in 1771 in securing the commission for a celebrated bust of Pope Clement XIV. Connections helped: Hewetson was much in demand among the British, Roman and Spanish nobility and his clients included the antiquaries Charles Towneley, Sir Watkin Williams-Wynn and Frederick Hervey, the 'earl-bishop' of Derry. Though his final years coincided with the emergence of the young Antonio Canova, Hewetson remained at the top of his profession, in 1783 sculpting a marble bust of Anton Raphael Mengs for the Pantheon and in 1797 travelling to Naples to make busts of Sir William and Lady Hamilton. His monument to Dr Richard Baldwin in the Public Theatre at Trinity College Dublin is considered 'the outstanding performance of its time in Ireland' and a 'seminal work in the evolution of Neo-Classical sculpture' (Illustration 31).[57] Baldwin, who was provost from 1718 to 1760 and who bequeathed £80,000 to the University, is represented in a reserved manner, markedly removed from the more dramatic Roman funerary ensembles of the period.

Lesser known in Rome though of considerable significance for Ireland was the Anglo-Flemish sculptor Simon Vierpyl, who spent seven years in the capital (1748–56) at a crucial moment in the emergence of Franco-Roman Neoclassicism. Chiefly a copyist of antique sculpture, Vierpyl operated in the circle of William Chambers and James Caulfeild, 1st Earl of Charlemont. An

---

56 H. Potterton, *Irish church monuments 1570–1880* (Belfast: Ulster Architectural Heritage Society, 1975), p. 48.
57 M.G. Sullivan, 'Christopher Hewetson' in AAI, III, pp. 163–7.

30. John Van Nost, bust of Samuel Madden.

incredible four-year commission from Charlemont's tutor, Edward Murphy, produced a series of twenty-two statues and seventy-eight terracotta busts of the Roman emperors and their families housed in the Capitoline Museum (Illustration 32). Vierpyl's taxing vigil, winter and summer, showed his mettle and prepared the way for a career in Dublin, primarily as a carver of architectural ornament. Though William Chambers criticised his carved chimney-piece output in London, he was satisfied with the work for Charlemont on

31. Christopher Hewetson, monument to Provost Richard Baldwin, 1771–83, Public Theatre, Trinity College Dublin.

the Casino at Marino, 'built by Mr Verpyle with great neatness and taste'.[58] Also master mason at the Royal Exchange in Dublin and a speculative builder in his own right, Vierpyl's superb craftsmanship in stone was immensely important in the realisation of Neoclassical designs by resident and non-resident architects.[59] His pupil Edward Smyth was spotted by James Gandon and,

58 M.G. Sullivan, 'Simon Vierpyl' in AAI, III, pp. 346–8.
59 H. Byrne, 'The speculative building activities of Simon Vierpyl', *Bulletin of the Irish Georgian Society*, 37 (1995), 31–5.

32. Simon Vierpyl, terracotta portrait busts after originals in the Capitoline Museum, begun 1751.

though his work is jauntier and more robust than that of Vierpyl, his remarkable carving skills were marshalled to excellent effect by Gandon and, later, by Francis Johnston. Though Gandon's likening of Smyth to Michelangelo speaks of a modest local industry, and the work is derivative of Chambersian London models, the brooding riverine heads of the Dublin Custom House are architectural carving of the first quality (Illustration 33).

Hewetson's fame was long eclipsed by that of Canova and Thorvaldsen by the time the young John Hogan arrived in Rome from his native Cork in 1824. Like Smyth, he had received strong encouragement as a carver of architectural ornament and, in his own words, claimed that the architect Thomas Deane had 'placed the chisel in my hands'.[60] Supported by private patrons and art institutions in Cork and Dublin, Hogan expressed his esteem 'for the truly patriotic and noble spirit in combating so successfully the existing prejudices which fettered so often the efforts of many an Irish artist'.[61] While the bulk

60 Turpin, *Hogan*, p. 23.
61 Ibid., p. 34.

33. Edward Smyth, riverine head, Custom House, Dublin.

of his output was achieved after 1830, his sophisticated Neoclassical oeuvre, like that of Hewetson before him, is a measure of the impact that munificent patronage, high-quality exemplars and a competitive professional environment could have in developing the skills of gifted provincial artists.

The proximity of Carton, Castletown and Russborough to the capital speaks of Dublin's pre-eminence as the 'chief planet' of the country throughout the eighteenth century.[62] Seat of the vice-regal court, parliament, government departments, the law courts and the university, it also offered a range of professional services unavailable in provincial centres.[63] The iconography, nomenclature and public architecture of the city reflect its position as a Protestant capital.[64] While the country house and its contents remained the dynastic seat secured by primogeniture, town houses were more transitory dwellings, and were more often than not bought complete from a building developer. Speculative domestic building activity was already well advanced in the city by the early eighteenth century, with impressive standards in scale and planning employed by the Corporation at St Stephen's Green, and on the adjacent Aungier estate. Generous plot sizes with broad frontages bounding wide thoroughfares were adopted by the city's most influential eighteenth-century developer, Luke Gardiner, and his associates, in seminal developments at Henrietta Street (from the late 1720s) and Sackville Street and the Mall (from *c.*1740). The latter was a particularly novel design, with two roadways of 50 feet flanking a central mall or promenade, gravelled and bounded by low walls surmounted by lantern-bearing obelisks (Illustration 34). Plan types ranged from the economical model of two rooms alongside a hall and stairhall to a showy arrangement predicated on a grand double-height entrance-cum-stairhall that devoted one quarter of the plan to circulation. The most curious aspect of these streets of palatial houses was the consistent absence of external elaboration, such as the stringcourses, quoins, cornices and other dressings usual in British town houses of the period (Illustration 35). While streets of plain houses were built in other British cities, it is the consistent choice of plain red brick in both modest and large houses that is so distinctive in Dublin: this was clearly an arrangement acceptable to clients of varying social status and the solution of choice for Dublin builders. Economical and anonymous, these cliff-like terraces contained interiors of surprising richness, cheaply fashioned in lime plaster by exponents of

---

62 McParland, *Public architecture*, p. 1.
63 Barnard, *Making the grand figure*, p. 282.
64 R. Usher, *Protestant Dublin, 1660–1760: architecture and iconography* (Basingstoke: Palgrave Macmillan, 2012).

34. Joseph Tudor, *Sackville Street and Gardiner's Mall*, c.1750.

a burgeoning craft industry that was much indebted to the virtuoso continental productions of the Lafranchini et al. at Carton, Russborough and
Kildare House, and to the innovations of a Flemish stuccodore, Bartholomew
Cramillion, who arrived in Dublin *c*.1754.[65] An idiosyncratic style that replaced
figuration with acanthus arabesques, birds and C scrolls has attracted the designation the Dublin 'School' of plasterwork (Illustration 36).[66] A proliferation
of decorative plasterwork distinguishes Dublin from other British cities of
the period; comparisons clearly show the greater elaboration of speculatively
built interiors and a higher number of master plasterers in the Irish capital.[67]
These grand brick boxes with granite window sills, limestone doorcases and
sumptuously decorative interiors were most likely the result of economic,
industrial and social pragmatism: they were seasonal dwellings economically
produced by 'knots' of craftsmen who supervised the building from rough

65 J. McDonnell, 'The art of the sculptor-*stuccatore*: Bartholomew Cramillion in Dublin
and Brussels 1755–72', *Apollo*, 156:487 (Sept. 2002), 41–9.
66 J. McDonnell, *Irish eighteenth-century stuccowork and its European sources* (Dublin:
National Gallery of Ireland, 1991), p. 13.
67 C. Lucey, 'The scale of plasterwork production in the metropolitan centres of Britain
and Ireland' in C. Casey and C. Lucey (eds.), *Decorative plasterwork in Ireland and Europe*
(Dublin: Four Courts Press, 2012), pp. 194–218.

35. Henrietta Street, Dublin.

foundation to refined plaster ornaments. Ludwig Wittgenstein's pronouncement on Dublin's Georgian streetscape during his sojourn there in 1948–9
captures the spirit of uncomplicated consumption evoked by contemporary
correspondence: 'the people who built these houses had the good taste to

36. Stairhall, no. 20 Lower Dominick Street, Dublin.

know that they had nothing very important to say: and therefore they didn't attempt to express anything'.[68]

The pragmatic character of Dublin's speculatively built streets and squares renders all the more remarkable the achievement of the Wide Street Commissioners, a parliamentary body established in 1757 for making a wide street from the newly rebuilt Essex Bridge to Dublin Castle. Compulsory purchase powers enabled a tortuous process of acquisition and demolition, and the resulting Parliament Street set the standard for later and more extensive projects at Dame Street, Sackville Street, Great Brunswick Street and elsewhere. The most dramatic intervention was the opening of two radiating avenues on the south side of the new Carlisle Bridge, a *coup de théâtre* which created a dynamic baroque termination to the monumental Sackville Street artery established by Gardiner and extended southward to the river by the Wide Street Commissioners (Illustration 37). No such concerted government

68 M. O'Connor Drury, 'Conversations with Wittgenstein' in R. Rhees (ed.), *Recollections of Wittgenstein* (Oxford: Oxford University Press, 1984), p. 137.

37. Carlisle Bridge with D'Olier and Westmoreland Streets, *c*.1880.

intervention in urban fabric is encountered elsewhere in Britain in the eighteenth century, and the achievement of the Commissioners mirrors the particular political condition of late eighteenth-century Ireland and the fact that
the management of a growing and increasingly vociferous local political
interest, exacerbated by international revolution, required the appeasement
of government supporters.[69] Patriotism as a stated impetus to the production
of art and architecture was not new to Ireland: in 1722 Lord Perceval wrote
to George Berkeley describing Castletown as a potential cabinet of native
materials and craftsmanship, an 'epitome of the kingdom and all the natural
rarities she affords'. The eleventh-hour, surplus-retaining vote of Tottenham-
in-his-boots reflected a consistent tension in Anglo-Irish politics that came to
a head in the Money Bill dispute of 1753: in December 1753 the 'Patriot' party
led by Henry Boyle and the Earl of Kildare succeeded in rejecting the bill on
grounds that it prevented the Irish parliament from spending surplus revenue
without royal consent. The public rejoicing that ensued provided the context

---

69 R. Rodger, 'Recording the fabric of great cities', Survey of London, English Heritage,
London, 10 May 2010.

for the McArdell mezzotints of the Kildares, a subscription for which was opened in March 1754.[70]

Architecture profited from the controversy as major grants were made to Trinity College, which constructed the appropriately named 'Parliament' Square and the vast adjoining west front of the university which represented an appropriately monumental foil to Pearce's colonnade (Illustration 38). This too was designed and executed by English architects: Theodore Jacobsen, an amateur, drew the design that was executed by John Sanderson and Henry Keene, who were brought to Dublin by the 4th Duke of Bedford, viceroy from 1757 to 1761. Bedford was instrumental in the appointment of Francis Andrews as provost in 1758 and John Smyth who drew plans of the new Provost's House may well have been John Sanderson's long-standing assistant. On the face of it, the west front and the Provost's House appear to emulate early eighteenth-century Palladianism; it is possible, however, that the well-travelled Andrews was aware of a precocious historicising architecture at the court of Frederick the Great that employed Palladian exemplars in a novel associational manner prophetic of nineteenth-century historicism, and it is also possible that the model adopted for the Provost's House, the town house of the Irish, Hanoverian general George Wade had political connotations (Illustration 39).[71] The sophisticated Ardbraccan stone façade emulates the aristocratic residences of Lords Kildare and Tyrone and the few other Dublin houses which emulated public architecture in being stone fronted, and points up the chasm between the monumental set pieces of the city and the sea of brick terraces between. A tension between the architectural ambition of the aristocrats and ambitious office holders who constituted the Wide Street Commissioners and the developers who built the city is revealed in a row over cut stone embellishments proposed for the façades of the newly widened Dame Street (Illustration 40). Proprietors clubbed together, engaged a senior counsel and ensured that no such dressings would be applied without compensation 'for the difference of the expense between fronting such houses in [the] manner aforesaid and erecting plain fronts of brick with stone window stools and doorcases'.[72] The cost proved preclusive and pragmatism won the day.

---

70 Strickland, *Dictionary*, vol. ii, p. 48.
71 C. Casey, 'A Palladian palazzo in Ireland's capital', *Country Life*, 204: 50 (8 Dec. 2010), 44–50; E. McParland, 'An academic palazzo in Ireland – the Provost's House, Trinity College, Dublin – ii', *Country Life*, 160:4138 (21 Oct. 1976), 1106–9.
72 Wide Street Commissioners minutes (hereafter WSC), 22 Dec. 1786, 2 March 1787, DCLA/WSC/Mins, f.221, Dublin City Archives.

38. Samuel Byron, 'A bird's-eye perspective plan of Trinity College park and gardens', 1780.

39. Trinity College Dublin, Provost's House, 1760.

Taste and the Antique: The Impact of Neoclassicism

While the west front of Trinity College was rising, a new interpretation of classicism was being advanced in avant-garde architectural, antiquarian and artistic circles. Johann Joachim Winckelmann's lyrical championing of Greek over Roman art, Abbé Laugier's argument for a correct, structural and antique use of the classical orders, the experiments of artists and architects of the French Academy in Rome, and the archaeological expeditions of British and European antiquarians converged to produce a taste for monumental classical architecture which eschewed the applied orders and elaborations of post-Renaissance design and advocated a return to noble simplicity and quiet grandeur. The fortuitous encounter of Lord Charlemont, William Chambers and Simon Vierpyl in Rome in the mid-1750s was the catalyst to Ireland's whole-hearted adoption of the new sensibility.[73] This was also the moment when the young Edmund

---

73 M. Craig, *The Volunteer Earl: being the life and times of James Caulfeild, the first Earl of Charlemont* (London: Cresset Press, 1948); J. Harris, *Sir William Chambers, Knight of the Polar Star* (London: Zwemmer, 1970); W.B. Stanford and E. Finopoulos (eds.), *The travels of Lord Charlemont in Greece & Turkey, 1749* (London: Trigraph for the A.G. Leventis Foundation, 1984); C. O'Connor, *The pleasing hours: James Caulfeild, first Earl of Charlemont 1728–1799: traveller, connoisseur and patron of the arts* (Cork: Collins Press, 1999); M. McCarthy, *Lord Charlemont and his circle: essays in honour of Michael Wynne* (Dublin: Four Courts Press, 2001).

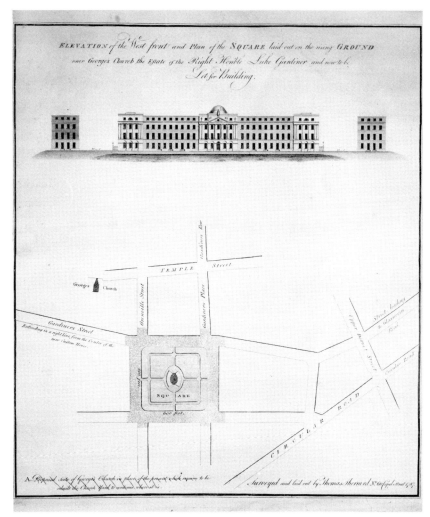

40. Unexecuted design by Thomas Sherrard for Mountjoy Square, Dublin, 1787, with ambitious stone enrichments.

Burke was writing his revolutionary essay on 'the sublime and the beautiful', and the aesthetic dynamism of the mid-eighteenth century was as much about cultural relativism as it was about the Antique. Indeed, a precocious illustrated account of Irish architectural antiquities, Thomas Wright's *Louthiana* of 1748, was penned for an Irish peer by an English astronomer, architect and garden designer, whose work was significant in the emerging taste for Gothic

449

Revival.[74] However, in the 1750s the taste for Gothic was in its infancy, and in the second half of the eighteenth century painting, sculpture and architecture in Ireland were dominated by Neoclassicism.

The void created by Richard Castle's death in 1750 was filled by local and foreign architects of varying ability. The most notable was Davis Ducart, an engineer of Piedmont origin who designed elegant buildings in counties Cork, Kilkenny and Limerick. His most significant achievement was the mansion of Archbishop Michael Cox in County Kilkenny, which was modelled on Buckingham House in London, an early eighteenth-century house then recently acquired by George II and the nucleus of the future Buckingham Palace; this was a clear case of 'backward-movement' in design with strong emulative purpose (Illustration 41). The quality of craftsmanship in sandstone and Kilkenny limestone is echoed in contemporary work by Thomas Roberts at Waterford and points to the high level of skill in quarrying and stone-cutting in Kilkenny and beyond (especially counties Down and Meath) that was such a significant feature in the delivery of Neoclassical refinement in Irish architecture. This mastery of materials is nowhere better seen than at the Casino at Marino, County Dublin, which was begun in 1759. An exquisite and early realisation of the new taste, it is an entertaining pavilion on a grand scale whose monumental single-storey appearance conceals a basement, piano nobile and attic, and a roof terrace with expansive views of Dublin Bay (Illustration 42). Executed entirely in gleaming white Portland stone, its cruciform volume is encircled in a peristyle of free-standing Doric columns that proclaim the tectonic principle of the antique order. Vierpyl's vase-like chimney-pots, Capitoline lions and delicate pedestal bas-reliefs are amplified by classical mouldings of immense elegance and precision. Inside, doors are curved to follow the bowed inner wall of the hall, and floors are luxuriously inlaid. This refinement of detail, ultimately inspired by the ornaments of antique buildings, was the life-blood of Neoclassical architecture in Ireland and was largely achieved by craftsmen and master builders whose lack of Grand Tour experience was compensated for by the proliferation of books and engravings illustrative of 'antique and modern' interiors. Indeed, the agency of craftsmen was vital during the 1760s and 1770s when design by correspondence was the norm, as is vividly revealed by the epistolary exchange between Charlemont and Chambers. In response to Charlemont's complaints of his Dublin workmen, Chambers urged his patron to be phlegmatic.

---

74 E. Harris, 'Thomas Wright and Viscount Limerick at Tollymore Park', *Irish Architectural and Decorative Studies*, 16 (2013), 50.

41. Davis Ducart, Castletown Cox, County Kilkenny, *c.*1767.

Neither Chambers, Adam, James Stuart nor Wyatt visited Ireland and their works there were largely dependent upon executant architects, overseers and local craftsmen.[75] Adam did little in Ireland; his sole surviving work is the recently conserved interior of Headfort House in County Meath. James

75 C. Lucey, ' "Made in the new taste": domestic neoclassicism and the Dublin building industry, 1765–1801', PhD thesis, University College Dublin, 2009, *passim*.

42. Sir William Chambers, the Casino at Marino, begun 1759.

'Athenian' Stuart's Irish oeuvre likewise consists of decorative remodelling, with superb surviving interiors at Rathfarnham Castle in Dublin.[76] Wyatt's legacy was more profound; he undertook a series of impressive remodellings and the single most important country house of the late Georgian period in Ireland. Castle Coole in County Tyrone (Illustration 43) was built for Armar Lowry-Corry, 1st Earl of Belmore (1740–1802), as a grand statement of social and political aspiration, and this austerely beautiful building arguably represents the zenith of European Neoclassicism in Ireland.[77] Built and decorated by English craftsmen, its pristine ashlar elevations, volumetric interior and spare ornament were exemplars for many smaller houses. Its spirit is keenly felt in the work of Armagh-born architect Francis Johnston, who became Ireland's foremost architect of the Regency period. Johnston's Townley Hall, completed c.1798, and a group of smaller houses in Leinster

76 E. McParland, 'Rathfarnham Castle, Co. Dublin', *Country Life*, 172:4438 (9 Sept. 1982), 734–7; G. Madden, 'Rathfarnham Castle', *Irish Arts Review*, 4:1 (1987), 22–6.
77 P. Marson, *Belmore: the Lowry Corrys of Castle Coole 1646–1913* (Belfast: Ulster Historical Foundation, 2007); J.M. Robinson, *James Wyatt (1746–1813): architect of George III* (New Haven: Yale University Press, 2012), pp. 96, 103–4, 118–24, 314, 347.

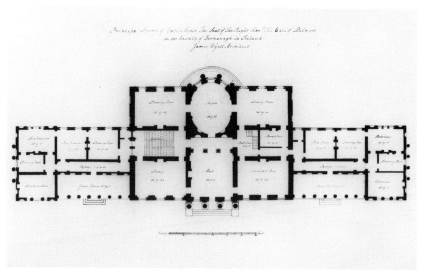

43. James Wyatt, Castle Coole, County Fermanagh, 1789–96.

exhibit a conscientious reticence and material precision much indebted to Wyatt (Illustration 44).[78]

The impact of Franco-Roman Neoclassicism was first seen in public architecture in the competition for the Royal Exchange in Dublin in 1769. The precocious public exhibition of the submitted designs prompted widespread comment in the press and bears witness to the level of sophistication among Irish patrons and aficionados that is the subtext to the activities of the Wide Street Commissioners.[79] Only two of the designs survive: Thomas Cooley's winning entry, and that of another English Neoclassical architect, William Newton, who is best known for the first English translation of Vitruvius.[80] Cooley's ambulatory-enveloped rotunda looks to Chambers and Robert Mylne in its richly rusticated envelope and imposing Corinthian order

78 E. McParland, 'Francis Johnston, architect, 1760–1829', Irish Georgian Society Bulletin, 12:3–4 (1969), 61–139. C. Casey and A. Rowan, The buildings of Ireland, vol. II: North-Leinster (Harmondsworth: Penguin, 1993), pp. 51–5, 58–60, 453–4, 466–7, 478–82, 503–8.
79 E. McParland, 'James Gandon and the Royal Exchange competition 1768–69', Journal of the Royal Society of Antiquaries of Ireland, 102 (1972), 58–72; R. Thorpe, 'Thomas Cooley before the Dublin Royal Exchange', Irish Architectural and Decorative Studies, 8 (2005), 71–85; K.V. Mulligan The buildings of Ireland, vol. IV: South Ulster (New Haven: Yale University Press, 2013), pp. 31–2; Casey, 'Books and builders', p. 253.
80 Casey, 'Books and builders', pp. 152–5.

44. Francis Johnston, Townley Hall, County Louth, completed *c*.1798.

(Illustration 45). Extravagantly dressed in Portland stone inside and out, carved by Vierpyl and his team, this is an Augustan edifice whose ambition far outweighs its commercial function and was the velvet glove that delivered the final strategic blow to the ancient city of Dublin. The site at the foot of the Castle precinct, intended for a grand piazza, was granted by the Wide Street Commissioners, several of whom promoted the eastern expansion which threatened the old city's mercantile interest. By the time the building was finished, plans were well advanced for the removal of the Custom House downstream and the construction of the bridge that would link the new north-eastern and south-eastern residential suburbs and sound the death-knell for the Castle quarter. James Gandon, who received the second premium in the Exchange competition, was brought to Dublin to build the new Custom House, a vast riverside classical building (Illustration 46). It cost roughly one quarter of the administration's revenue for 1786, an expenditure matched in magnificence of form and material, and echoed in Gandon's later Four Courts further upstream. The largest public building of the Georgian period in Ireland, its arcades, portico and pantheon-like columnar screens are

45. Thomas Cooley, Royal Exchange, Dublin, from 1769.

magnificently crafted in Portland stone, the grey Ardbraccan stone dome, reconstructed in the 1920s, a talisman of post-Revolution protectionism.

Athenian Stuart's London drawing office was the unlikely starting point for the career of Ireland's most ambitious painter of the entire eighteenth century, the Cork-born artist James Barry (1741–1806), whose meteoric rise and fall at the Royal Academy in London has all the melodrama of Barry's remarkable history paintings.[81] Trained in drawing at the newly established

81 W.L. Pressly, *The life and art of James Barry* (New Haven: Yale University Press, 1981), *pas-sim*; T. Dunne (ed.), *James Barry 1741–1806: 'The Great Historical Painter'* (Cork: Crawford Art Gallery and Gandon Editions, 2005); S. Bennet, *Cultivating the human faculties: James Barry (1741–1806) and the Society of Arts* (Bethlehem, PA: Lehigh University Press,

46. James Gandon, The Custom House, Dublin, begun 1781.

Dublin Society School of Drawing, Barry spent some five years in Europe, principally in Rome, before taking up residence in 1771 in London where in 1782 he was appointed professor of painting at the Royal Academy. His heroic commitment to history painting in a period dominated by portraiture and landscape resulted in a series of frescoes entitled *The progress of human culture*, executed gratis, in the Great Room of the Adelphi, the headquarters of the Society of Arts (Illustration 47). Complex in iconography and redolent of Barry's fervent Catholicism and republicanism, the cycle ranges from brilliance to dullness and is an impressive achievement irrespective of quality or pictorial convention. 'The breadth and profundity of his vision' and 'the heroic vocabulary' used to express it have been likened to the art of William Blake, who likewise 'desperately wanted to create monumental works in public spaces'.[82] There were few such opportunities for grand-scale history painting in Ireland and the vice-regal commission for St Patrick's Hall at Dublin Castle (1787–1802), the inauguration chamber for the newly established order of Knights of Saint Patrick, went to the viceroy's tried and trusted Italian

2009); T. Dunne and W.L. Pressly (eds.), *James Barry, 1741–1806: history painter* (Farnham: Ashgate, 2010).

82 W.L. Pressly, *James Barry's murals at the Royal Society of Arts: envisioning a new public art* (Cork: Cork University Press, 2014), *passim*.

47. James Barry, 'Crowning the victors at Olympia' (*detail*) from *The progress of human culture*, Great Room, Royal Society of Arts, London, 1777–83.

painter, Vincenzo Waldré. His urbane scenes of the life of St Patrick, flanking George III with justice and liberty, lack the conviction and complexity of Barry's history painting.[83] However, for all the singularity and heroism of his Adelphi *chef d'œuvre*, it is arguable that James Barry's smaller and focused paintings are more accomplished works of art, in particular his *Self-portrait as Timanthes* in the National Gallery of Ireland which was begun in 1783 and completed in 1803 (Illustration 48). In a remarkably compressed composition Barry works grand mythological themes and complex personal associations into a portrait which speaks boldly of the artist's passion and ambition.

Smaller again are the masterpieces of Barry's contemporary and a prior student of the Dublin Society Drawing Schools, Hugh Douglas Hamilton (1740–1808), who likewise spent time in London and in Rome. Hamilton

83 For Waldré see N. Figgis, 'Vincent Waldré' in AAI, II, pp. 85–486; U. Waldré and C. Lynch, 'Vincenzo Waldré (Faenza 1740–Dublino 1814): un artista versatile in Inghilterra ed Irlanda', *Torricellianan, bolletino della Società de Scienze e Lettere, Faenza*, 60 (Oct. 2010), 79–216. For a political reading of the scheme see F. Cullen, *Visual politics: the representation of Ireland 1750–1930* (Cork: Cork University Press, 1997), p. 80.

48. James Barry, *Self-portrait as Timanthes*, 1783–1802.

excelled in drawing and pastel, and among his best works are miniatures of the Conolly-FitzGerald families of Castletown and Carton. His draughtsmanship and skilful observation are seen to optimum effect in an early sketchbook which records the street criers of Dublin.[84] Like Barry, Hamilton was initially

84 W. Laffan (ed.), *The cries of Dublin* (Tralee: Churchill House Press, 2003), *passim.*

successful in London though in the very different commercial genre of speedy pastel portraiture, his fame fuelled by portraits of George III, Queen Charlotte and their children. Eclipsed by the mid-1770s, he lived in Rome in the 1780s and returned to Ireland in 1791 due to the revolutionary wars. Oil painting followed and two canvases at the National Gallery of Ireland exhibit the range of his talent from 'soft' Neoclassicism to fashionable melancholia. The affecting figure of Richard Mansergh St George mourning at his wife's tomb (*c.*1795) has been seen to represent 'a cry for the continuation of a class', the *fin-de-siècle* Anglo-Irish ascendancy (Illustration 49).[85] Hamilton's English contemporary, Francis Wheatley, produced an alternative form of portraiture likened to historical reportage and to the new realism of the American history painter Benjamin West, as seen in his two famous canvases *Henry Grattan addressing the Irish House of Commons* (1780) and *A view of College Green with a meeting of the Volunteers on 4th November 1779, to commemorate the birthday of King William* (1780).[86]

The Early Nineteenth Century

The Act of Union, which came into effect on 1 January 1801, had long-term implications for artistic activity in Ireland and by the 1830s the craftsmen of Dublin publicly lamented the loss of earnings resulting from the abolition of the Irish parliament and the exodus of peers and politicians to London.[87] However, the impact was not as sudden or as dramatic as the remarks of these craftsmen suggested and a wealthy landed class, together with a burgeoning Roman Catholic middle class, sustained building activity and related crafts throughout the early decades of the new century.[88] Indeed some of the finest furniture produced in Ireland dates to the Regency period.[89] In Dublin and provincial towns much building activity dates to the late Georgian and Regency periods. In the decades after the Union the activities of the Wide Street Commissioners were even more in evidence and grants from the Board of First Fruits made possible the erection of small parish churches – modest

---

85 Cullen, *Visual politics*, p. 114.
86 J. Kelly, 'Francis Wheatley: his Irish paintings' in A.M. Dalsimer (ed.), *Visualizing Ireland: national identity and the pictorial tradition* (London: Faber and Faber, 1993), pp. 145–63; Cullen, *Visual politics*, pp. 50–9.
87 Royal Irish Academy, Haliday MS 4B.
88 A. Cowhey, 'Dublin cabinetmakers and their clientele 1800–1841', PhD thesis, University College Dublin, 2007.
89 Ibid.; Knight of Glin and J. Peill, *Irish furniture* (New Haven: Yale University Press, 2007), pp. 180–90.

49. Hugh Douglas Hamilton, *Richard Mansergh St George, c.1795*.

50. Louth County Courthouse, Dundalk, 1813–19.

Gothick buildings whose towers are a characteristic feature of the Irish rural landscape.[90] Likewise, county grand juries invested in high-quality classical architecture for courthouses and prisons that were as much a reflection of local economic and political ambition as instruments of the judicial and penal system (Illustration 50).[91] In the capital a spate of post-Union public building included the splendid Neoclassical General Post Office, a monumental column to Admiral Nelson, a vast obelisk for the Duke of Wellington, a Neoclassical parish church on Hardwicke Place of St Martin-in-the-Fields ambition, and a new, extravagantly decorative vice-regal chapel at Dublin Castle, which assumed the title Chapel Royal and looked to the Tudor chapels of Windsor and Westminster Abbey.[92]

90 The National Inventory of Architectural Heritage provides the most comprehensive survey of Ireland's provincial architecture (www.buildingsofireland.ie).

91 R. Butler, 'Westminster, the Irish Grand Juries and the political context for Assize Court building, 1800–1850', History of Art Postgraduate Research Seminar, Trinity College Dublin, 12 March 2014; C. Casey, 'Court houses, market houses and townhalls of Leinster', MA thesis, University College Dublin, 1982; C. Brett, *Court houses and market houses of the province of Ulster* (Belfast: Ulster Architectural Heritage Society, 1973).

92 Casey, *Dublin*, pp. 147–9, 212–14, 308, 320–2, 358–60.

The architect of the Church, Chapel and Post Office was Francis Johnston, whose life and work encapsulates the state of art and architecture in Ireland at the end of the Georgian era.[93] Born in Armagh of Scottish ancestry, Johnston was sent to Dublin by Archbishop Richard Robinson to train with Thomas Cooley whom he succeeded as Robinson's architect. His most conspicuous project in Dublin was the remodelling of the parliament house for the Bank of Ireland. Pearce's building had been extended in the 1780s; the new accommodation for Lords (east) and Commons (west) was concealed by curved screen walls of very different appearance – Gandon's reticent niche-patterned wall answered by Edward Parke's Pearcian colonnade. Johnston sensitively amalgamated the variegated extensions and added a monumental top-lit cash office whose grandeur impressed George IV on his visit to Dublin in 1821. Johnston was an avid collector who assembled a vast collection of painting and sculpture in his residence at Eccles Street which had a *Tribuna*-like octagon and a Gothic garden belfry for the architect's passionate pastime, campanology. In 1821, Johnston was one of fourteen founder members of the Royal Hibernian Academy, whose palazzo-like premises on Abbey Street he designed and built at his own expense. The Academy was the outcome of a lengthy process. Its ancestry lay in the Dublin Society drawing schools, in the Society of Artists in Ireland which held its first exhibition in a purpose-built octagonal gallery in 1765, and in the exhibition activity of the Royal Irish Institution founded in 1810.[94] Johnston's friend, the artist Thomas Mulvany, elicited the support of royal academicians, including Sir Thomas Lawrence, and secured a royal charter for the RHA in 1823. Mulvany was a painter primarily of landscape and genre and Johnston owned several of his works. More significant for the history of Irish art and architecture was Mulvany's literary activity: a series of 'memoirs' of Irish artists published in the *Citizen* and a biography of James Gandon which were important steps in the historiography of 'Irish' art and architecture. Johnston received honourable mention in Thomas Bell's *An essay on the origin and progress of Gothic architecture* (Dublin, 1829) which praised the Castle Chapel and Johnston's wider oeuvre, and expressed the 'gratitude and admiration' of Ireland to 'such an artist – such a patriot – such a man'.[95] Johnston died in 1829 and his letter of

---

93 McParland, 'Johnston'. A comprehensive study of the life and work of Francis Johnston is much needed.

94 J. Turpin, 'Dublin art institutions' in AAI, II, pp. 28–31.

95 T. Bell, *An essay on the origin and progress of Gothic architecture with reference to the ancient history and present state of such architecture in Ireland, to which was awarded the prize proposed by the Royal Irish Academy for the best essay on that subject* (Dublin and London: W.F. Wakeman and Baldwin and Cradock, 1829), p. 256.

support for Bell's project was appended posthumously to the published text. Addressing Mulvany, Johnston referred to the 'attention Mr Bell has paid to my name … I thank him kindly, but indeed he has over-rated it'.[96] Precisely a century after the lament of 'Patriophilus', the perception of native 'genius' had come full circle.

Conclusion

In terms of taste and formal conventions the art and architecture of Ireland of the long eighteenth century conform broadly to those of Britain but differ in terms of achievement and character: landscape painting, architecture and silver being its most distinctive features. Though Dublin was a cosmopolitan capital of considerable pretension, it did not attract European or British painters and sculptors of the first rank and produced few native artists of international reputation. The premium placed upon European and English art and the consequent paucity of local patronage was a major factor in the slow development of native 'genius', together with the absence of major collections and the competitive artistic environments of cities such as London, Paris and Rome. The same is true of other provincial cities in Britain, for while Dublin was for a period the second city of the realm, little justice is done by habitual comparison with the artistic achievement of London, a city of infinitely greater wealth. Given its lesser social, economic and political status, the achievement of eighteenth-century Dublin in terms of architecture and urbanism is distinctive. The arts that thrived in eighteenth-century Ireland were those which related to necessity: in sheer volume, architecture, furniture, silver and glass trumped the higher arts of painting and sculpture by virtue of their utility, thereby enabling the nurture of local skills through widespread patronage. Ireland's Protestant Ascendancy, eager to make its mark, required houses, churches and public buildings and the expertise to build, furnish and ornament them. Pictures and statuary were costly and movable and as such were best obtained from the highest quarter in Britain and Europe. Gradually, Irish artists achieved renown, aided by increasing patronage, travel in Europe and the support of institutions such as the Dublin Society, the Royal Irish Academy and the Royal Hibernian Academy. The marginalisation of native artists lamented throughout the century is at one level the provincial's plight, whether in Dublin, Bamberg or Linz. At another it is a political issue, and art historians opposed to the conservatism

96 Ibid., p. 270.

of connoisseurial scholarship have discovered ideological motives in the art and architecture of the period. Indeed it has been argued that 'it is the political dimension, above all, which justifies a specific focus on "Irish" art, since in most other respects the work can be analysed in terms of European norms, and particularly, as part of the British response to European developments'.[97] While much penetrating work has been done in identifying the ideological under-currents of eighteenth-century artistic production, national perspectives, born of the nineteenth-century nation-state, are inclined to exceptionalism, and on occasion anachronism, while the conceptual turn of the late twentieth century has tended to privilege idea over object, resulting in a reductionism of vastly different media to bearers of meaning. The 'material turn' of recent years returns the focus to the specific object, its making, maker and achievement, while the evidence-based study of material culture and consumption seeks to situate artistic production within contemporary society. The connoisseurial art history of the nineteenth and twentieth centuries, criticised as 'a legacy of the Anglo-Irish tradition', has a new resonance in a global context where craftsmanship, quality and relationship to international visual culture are once again key concerns.[98] Indeed strong opposition to conservatism is increasingly seen as 'a rigid position' and the 'ageing' 'new' art history as the new academy.[99] Happily, the swings and roundabouts of historiography do not change the buildings, paintings, sculpture and objects which adorned eighteenth- and early nineteenth-century Ireland, merely our perception of them.

97 T. Dunne, 'Politics in Irish painting 1700–1900' in AAI, II, p. 112.
98 N. O'Sullivan, 'History of art: the academic discipline' in AAI, V, pp. 207–12.
99 K. Jôekalda, 'What has become of the New Art History?', *Journal of Art Historiography*, 9 (2013), 1–7.

17

Civil Society, *c.*1700–*c.*1850

MARTYN J. POWELL

Introduction

In 1848 the radical Catholic priest Thaddeus O'Malley, commenting on his support for repeal clubs, noted: 'If . . . the idea of a "club" necessarily implied something mischievous . . . I would not press that question.'[1] Ireland's clubs of 1848 were mischievous, and more. So too were many others both before and afterwards. One could write a history of modern Irish politics through the prism of its club culture: Volunteers, United Irishmen, Orange Order, Catholic Association, Brunswick Clubs, repeal clubs, the Fenians, IRB, UVF and IRA. The history of civil society in Ireland has frequently had a paramilitary aspect, and, the Fenians apart, by highlighting this dimension of activity has not accorded sufficient attention to the sociability that was the common thread that bound together these groups, and many others besides.

Thanks to Alexis De Tocqueville and, more recently, Robert Puttnam, civil society and its near relation associational culture have been portrayed as an unalloyed good; they are conceived of as part of a teleological process whereby populations located spaces to interact with each other outside of the state, improving the quality of their lives and the democratic potential of their homelands in the process. They would have concurred with the *Cork Examiner*'s take on club-life in the 1840s: 'Individuals are weak, segregated, inactive. Clubs are strong, compact, full of energy.'[2] Yet, Puttnam also put an end to the tendency to see the efflorescence of club and society culture in the nineteenth and twentieth centuries as the culmination of a process, or a permanent state; in his exemplar, American society descends back into the selfish and, more importantly, powerless individualism of 'bowling alone'.[3] The

---

1 *Freeman's Journal*, 10 July 1848.
2 Quoted in *Nation*, 10 June 1848.
3 A. de Tocqueville, *Democracy in America*, trans. G. Lawrence (New York: Anchor, 1969); R. Puttnam, *Bowling alone: the collapse and revival of American community* (New York: Simon and Schuster, 2001).

notion that associationalism is possessed of innate virtue is problematic, of course, and there has been revealing work qualifying the image of 'clubs' as 'agents of democracy'. In the German and Italian instances it has been argued that the proliferation of societies – even those that were apolitical – bolstered the nationalist cause.[4] In Ireland one can identify a close relationship between the growth of civil society and sectarianism. Networks of associations can, in the right environment, accentuate political polarisation. This point about the 'right environment' is important as one can argue that Ireland's polity encouraged a kind of associationalism different from that seen in Great Britain. Bermeo has observed that a chasm between government and civil society can exacerbate the kinds of sectarian tensions evident in Ireland. It is a point made in relation to Irish nationalism in the twentieth century.[5] But this disjuncture began earlier – with the mass politicisation of Catholics in the late eighteenth century fostered by groups like the United Irishmen and the Defenders.

Moreover, networks formed through associational culture were resorted to frequently to advance the interests of a religious or ethnic group, which in Ireland served to reinforce sectarian divisions. There were others, of course, that aspired to overcome the more divisive elements of identity politics. Commenting on the repeal clubs of the 1840s, Fr O'Malley wrote approvingly that each club was 'a miniature association, a league, a local focus for the concentration of opinion in its district, a *ganglion* serving for the more equal distribution of the nervous action of the brain of the political body'.[6] O'Malley's definition of club-life was progressive; democratic even. Certain reformers in the 1840s saw the possibility of new linkages being forged based on class rather than religion. And while it cannot be said that 'class' was a dominant feature of civil society organisations in eighteenth- and early nineteenth-century Ireland, it is one of the complicating factors that requires that any study of Irish associationalism must take notice of other features of Irish life in this period – political cleavages, the differences between rural and urban environments, and the role played by groups committed to the maintenance of the connection to the British state.

---

4 N. Bermeo and P. Nord (eds.), *Civil society before democracy: lessons from nineteenth-century Europe* (Lanham, MD: Rowman and Littlefield, 2000); S. Berman, 'Civil society and the collapse of the Weimar Republic', *World Politics*, 49:3 (1997), 401–29; N. Bermeo, *Ordinary people in extraordinary times* (Princeton: Princeton University Press, 2003).

5 N. Bermeo, 'Civil society after democracy: some conclusions' in Bermeo and Nord (eds.), *Civil society before democracy*, pp. 237–60; J. Cormier and P. Couton, 'Civil society, mobilization and communal violence: Quebec and Ireland, 1890–1920', *Sociological Quarterly*, 45:3 (2004), 490.

6 *Freeman's Journal*, 10 July 1848.

It is arguable, moreover, that the eighteenth century sustained an 'open' civil society model, before a hardening occurred that resulted in more defined class stratification and intensified sectarianism in the nineteenth century. Freemasonry, for example, was open to Catholics in this earlier period, but the likelihood of their participating was effectively closed off by papal edict in 1814. Other associational opportunities open to Catholics in the eighteenth century included commercial bodies, annuity societies and book clubs. Some groups embraced a middling and artisan membership. Guilds and journeymen organisations morphed into both civic patriot groups like the Free Citizens of Dublin and workers 'combinations'. The amiable Friendly Brothers of St Patrick possessed a sizeable membership from the middling sort. So too did the charitable organisations that provided relief during times of crisis, and, in a more targeted fashion, to specific social groups – as was the case, for example, of the Sick and Indigent Roomkeepers Society founded in Dublin in 1790. The relatively modest achievements of charitable groups in the eighteenth century were due at least in part to the limitations of the early conduits between state and civil society – in this period they rarely represented Catholics. Indeed, more than just lacking in links, Catholic and oppositional civil society was inherently unstable, as indicated by the regularity with which certain groups – even those legal in the public sphere – found themselves at odds with the authorities. From the United Irishmen Oliver Bond and Simon Butler to repeal leader William Smith O'Brien, leadership of respectable reform bodies rendered one vulnerable to prosecution by a state that was prone to spasms of insecurity.[7]

In the Irish context then, there are obstacles in the way of the open, clubbable world, dominated by coffee houses and taverns that, by way of Jürgen Habermas, is presented in Peter Clark's *British clubs and societies, 1580–1800* and Roy Porter's *Enlightenment Britain*.[8] Clark's model sees the nineteenth century usher in a more exclusive, private associational culture. In Ireland there is plenty of evidence to support his thesis. Daly's Club, the Kildare Street Club and the Friendly Brothers moved into private premises, as notions of politeness and respectability drew the middle classes away from more rambunctious urban environments. But even if associational groups met in bespoke

---

7 For sociability and club-life in the eighteenth-century context see J. Kelly and M. Powell (eds.), *Clubs and societies in eighteenth-century Ireland* (Dublin: Four Courts Press, 2010).

8 J. Habermas, *The structural transformation of the public sphere*, trans. Thomas Burger (Cambridge, MA: MIT Press, 1989); P. Clark, *British clubs and societies, 1580–1800: the origins of an associational world* (Oxford: Oxford University Press, 2000); R. Porter, *Enlightenment: Britain and the creation of the modern world* (London: Allen Lane, 2000).

premises, was that necessarily an indication of a shift in associational practice? After all, the whole point of club-life was its exclusivity. Nevertheless, although we might find stasis at the top end of associational culture, it is clear that it accommodated variety, and there was greater variation amongst the forms of association that the lower orders signed up to – these could be religious, political, social or based on violent collective action. And then there is the question of definition. Were the attendees of the O'Connellite Monster Meetings technically club-men? The repealers who met on Dublin's Donnybrook Green in 1848 certainly were. At various points in the nineteenth century huge numbers of Irish people participated in club-life – in radical or reform societies, Orange Order lodges, the Freemasons, and social and charitable groups. Clubs proliferated and faded away. Individuals joined multiple associational groups, while others morphed into new bodies: Steelboys to Volunteers to United Irishmen, and Catholic Association to Repeal Association to Tenant League. It can be suggested that more than the power of ideas was required to bring individuals together in these cases; the true binding force was sociability. This chapter will seek to explore these issues during an era when a once predominantly Protestant public sphere became increasingly Catholic – by looking at Irish civil society in the eighteenth and nineteenth centuries from a number of vantage points. These are its intellectual and improving origins; conviviality; ritual and practice; religion and sectarianism; and the tensions between public and private.

Emergence: Philosophy and Improvement

Club-life may have commenced slowly in Ireland as a consequence of the demographic, social and economic instability that was a feature of the seventeenth century, and the slow spread of such key facilitators as taverns and coffee houses. But groups like the Freemasons made up for lost time in the more stable environment of the eighteenth century. There were, for example, more masonic lodges in Ireland than in Great Britain by 1790, and while they were predominantly urban based, it would be a mistake to assume that civil society was exclusively urban. The importance of the horse to its development cannot be gainsaid, and though groups involved in hunting and racing had urban meeting places – the Sportsmen's Club met in Dublin's Eagle Tavern and Rose and Bottle, and the Kildare Hunt met in Morrison's Hotel in Dawson Street – their focus was rural pursuits. Taverns were popular places of congregation, and a day's hunting or racing concluded invariably with eating and drinking. Ritualistic behaviour might also play a part – toasting, for example. Yet politeness encouraged some regulation of the amount of alcohol consumed and decorum in personal conduct.

Improvement was a leitmotif of Irish club culture in the eighteenth century, and although this catch-all term is perhaps a little careworn through overuse, there was a strong relationship between Irish clubs and improvement. The Society of County Down Horse Breeders is a case in point, and some of the earliest intellectual clubs such as the Dublin Philosophical Society, formed in 1683, and the (later Royal) Dublin Society (RDS), founded in 1731, were at their core improving organisations, the latter with a very practical edge. Although the RDS is a notable survivor in a landscape that was not characterised by longevity, it experienced periods of languor and internecine squabbling. The Act of Union delivered a different kind of Ireland, and the RDS's new premises in Kildare Street offered succour to similar minded bodies, such as the Sanitary Association, the Society for the Promotion of Irish Manufacture and Industry, and mechanics' institutes, which hosted public presentations by RDS sponsored lecturers. Its urban headquarters notwithstanding, the RDS was much occupied with rural Ireland, and it contrived, along with a host of regional bodies, to prioritise improving approaches to agriculture.

Moreover, the communication of information and expertise was not one way – from metropole to provinces. The Royal Agricultural Improving Society acted as the parent body for dozens of local farming societies. And the 'patronising' – in both senses of the word perhaps – of regional associations, whose members possessed more modest incomes and fewer club privileges, by elite societies based in Dublin was a feature of Irish associationalism in this period. One may instance the Mechanics' Institute, which, beginning in 1824, was to be found in thirty-one towns in the first half of the nineteenth century.[9] This was impressive, though the top-down nature of some of these bodies make, it difficult to see them as symptomatic of a thirst for an improving club culture amongst the artisan class.

The Royal Agricultural Improving Society typified the sober, respectable improving body with a Dublin base. In its early years it discussed publishing a journal of its transactions and the formation of a farmers' club with a library.[10] This was in obvious contrast to the self-indulgence that characterised some dining clubs, and yet, improving associations should not be taken out of the sociable milieu of Irish club-life. The lengthy toast lists of the Free

---

9 E. Neswald, 'Science, sociability and the improvement of Ireland: the Galway Mechanics' Institute, 1826–51', *British Journal for the History of Science*, 29:4 (2006), 504.
10 *Freeman's Journal*, 17 May 1852.

Citizens of Dublin and the Aldermen of Skinners Alley in the eighteenth century spoke to an improving agenda. The Free Citizens drank to the Dublin
Society and the Farmers' Clubs, as well as a host of commercial causes. The
Aldermen in 1784 launched a non-consumption campaign to protect the
interests of the Irish brewing trade. Though their toasting lists were generally
shorter, O'Connellite clubs had similar concerns. William Smith O'Brien's '82
Club, formed in 1845, toasted to 'the Industrial Resources of Ireland, and their
speedy development'. The Clonmel Liberal Club toasted to 'prosperity of
agriculture' and 'the trade and commerce of Clonmel'. The Royal Yacht Club
toasted 'the fisheries of Ireland' and 'the health of the Directors of the Dublin
and Kingstown Railway'. The familiar sociable rituals of associational culture
could also, it seems, be put to an improving purpose. The Portlaw Farming
Society issued 'challenges' to members between toasts. In October 1839 the
scientific gardener of Curraghmore invited its members to produce 'an essay
to be read at the next meeting on the cause of the failure in the potato crop,
and the means of its prevention'.[11]

A century earlier, the Physico-Historical Society in the 1740s offered a distinctly political – and anti-Catholic – take on improvement, and the nature of
Irish associational life, which attests to the fact that, then as later, associationalism echoed wider political allegiances. It was certainly the case with some
hunt clubs: the Bishopscourt Hunt was connected with prominent Whiggish
politicians, including the Ponsonbys and John Philpot Curran; both the
Kildare Hunt and the Leinster Harriers wore Foxite blue and buff. Nenagh's
Gentlemen's Sporting Club organised celebrations in honour of the acquittal
of the Whig Admiral, Lord Keppel, after his court martial in 1779.[12] In the
1840s Goldenbridge's Agricultural Club was reconstituted as a confederate
repeal club, and, more generally, the confederate repeal societies' lectures and
libraries offered improvement with a political edge. In the 1870s the Limerick
and Clare Farmers' Club differed over whether it was a Farmers' Club or a
Home Rule Club.[13]

The dressing of club members in clothing of Irish manufacture was an
enduring feature of Irish club-life; it was advocated by a range of societies
including the Dublin Society, the Aldermen of Skinner's Alley, the Volunteers
and the Repeal Association. William Smith O'Brien urged the Sarsfield Club
to wear only clothes of Irish manufacture in 1848. Sometimes this assumed

11 *Freeman's Journal*, 7 Oct. 1839, 18 Feb. 1846, 3 Jan., 13 Aug. 1849.
12 *Limerick Chronicle*, 1 March 1779.
13 *Nation*, 24 June 1848, 9 Aug. 1873.

a local aspect – for example the Kilkenny Citizens Club favoured dressing in clothes of Kilkenny manufacture, and a member of Cork's Desmond Confederate Club made a similar point.[14] The relevance of earlier non-consumption campaigns was made explicit on this occasion by the recitation of Swift's famous exhortation to burn 'everything that came from England except the coals'.[15] The consumerist responsibility of elite women also elicited attention, though predictably the membership of the societies that did so was often exclusively male.

Eating, Drinking and Conviviality

The activities of the Patriot clubs of the 1750s, Dublin's Bar Club in the 1780s and the United Irishmen in the 1790s suggest that at least one of the attractions of club culture in the eighteenth century was its bacchanalian character. The *Universal Advertiser* published special toast supplements in the 1750s, while Wolfe Tone's diaries reveal that radical politicking would have been a much greyer affair in the 1790s without sociability. Although it is tempting to identify the birth of a new sober, middle-class Ireland – and especially Dublin – post Union, there is little evidence to suggest that there was a dramatic change in sociable behaviour in the nineteenth century. The charitable Catholic Club, meeting in 1821, enjoyed 'a reasonable circulation of the juice of the grape'. The variegated clubs backing Daniel O'Connell appeared to enjoy toasts and bumpers as much as their eighteenth-century predecessors.[16]

Toasts and songs possessed a long history, and they were a sufficiently popular repository of anti-establishment feeling both to concern government and to encourage the composition of alternatives by opponents. Toasts could be threatening enough to result in beatings, arrests, defenestration or, as Charles James Fox found to his cost, expulsion from the Privy Council. Such was the power of this ritual of club-life that fictional toasts (and fictional clubs for that matter) were an effective form of satire. This was the height of drinking as performance. The toasts raised, whether by patriots in the 1750s, citizens' debating societies in the 1770s or United Irishmen in the 1790s, were crafted, negotiated and ranked, and designed for publication.[17] Moreover, there is no sense that this changed after the Union. In fact if we look at the clubs that supported Catholic emancipation in the 1820s and repeal

---

14 *Freeman's Journal*, 17 Jan. 1848, 28 Sept. 1840; *Nation*, 22 Jan. 1848.
15 *Freeman's Journal*, 28 Sept. 1840.
16 *Freeman's Journal*, 10 Sept. 1821, 11 Jan. 1830.
17 M.J. Powell, 'Political toasting in eighteenth-century Ireland', *History*, 91 (2006), 510.

in the 1840s there are clear signs that performance, ritual, even public speaking achieved new levels. Many clubs of the O'Connell period combined toasts with music, whereby every health offered was accompanied by 'a delightful and appropriate air'. When the Drogheda Independent Club drank to 'the people – the true source of legitimate power' in the 1830s in the presence of Daniel O'Connell, it was accompanied by 'Hearts of Oak'; 'The speedy repeal of the Union' was accompanied by 'Should auld acquaintance be forgot'; and the 'Marquis of Anglesey' by 'St Patrick's Day'.[18] Protestant Brunswick clubs did likewise – though Irish airs were replaced with loyal tunes such as 'Rule Britannia' and 'Britons strike home'.[19] Another addition to toasting ritual that was entrenched by the early nineteenth century was the waving of handkerchiefs at popular toasts. In some clubs this allowed females an opportunity to participate; it was a development popular with O'Connellite clubs like the Duleek Independents, the Drogheda Independents and the Monaghan Independents.

Gourmandising, more generally, was an attraction of many clubs; the Beefsteak and Hellfire clubs – and Ireland had a few of the latter – are obvious examples.[20] However, it could also lay clubs open to ridicule. In the 1790s, the Irish Whig Club was denigrated by its opponents because of its commitment to dining.[21] There is no question but that some clubs, and some occasions, encouraged excess, and the sanctions that were applied suggest it was not always regarded with disapproval. Indicatively, the Duhallow Hunt and the Bar Club fined individuals for misdemeanours in bottles of wine.[22] At a banquet at the Rotunda in 1845 the '82 Club did not go out of its way to present itself as a sober body that encouraged restraint. During the dinner the 'rarest viands' were 'in the utmost plenty; the dessert was excellent and in profusion'. It may have reflected on these excesses, as it was reported after the next meeting that 'Economy is to rule their proceedings; and, except the preliminary expense of uniforms, it will not be found that the club will press at all heavily on its members.' In the wake of the Great Famine, clubs were acutely aware of the indelicacy of boasting about plentiful repasts.

---

18 *Freeman's Journal*, 1 Feb. 1820, 11 Jan., 6 Dec. 1830.
19 S.T. Kingon, 'Ulster opposition to Catholic emancipation, 1828–9', *Irish Historical Studies*, 34 (2004–5), 148.
20 D. Ryan, *Blasphemers and blackguards: the Irish Hellfire Clubs* (Dublin: Irish Academic Press, 2012).
21 J. Kelly, 'Elite political clubs, 1770–1800' in Kelly and Powell (eds.), *Clubs and societies in eighteenth-century Ireland*, p. 284.
22 J. Kelly, 'The Bar Club, 1787–93: a dining club case study' in Kelly and Powell (eds.), *Clubs and societies in eighteenth-century Ireland*, p. 385.

The Clonmel Liberal Club, for example, in 1849, 'remembered the poor, and heightened their own enjoyment by providing an excellent dinner for a large number to be distributed under the judicious management of the Sisters of Charity'.[23]

Clubs sought to pre-empt criticism by imposing codes of politeness. These could include non-smoking (Citizens' Confederate Club), non-swearing (Jason Lottery Club)[24] and, most commonly, a more moderate approach to drinking. A number of bodies, from charitable societies to hunting clubs, introduced either bottle limits or spending limits as a way of regulating expenditure and behaviour. This was most evident in the early nineteenth century as the virtues of temperance achieved greater public acceptance. The rules and orders of the Cork Harbour Water Club stated that, 'unless the company exceed the number of fifteen, no man shall be allowed more than one bottle to his share'.[25] Some clubs even sought to impose alcohol limits on auxiliary societies with a less well-heeled membership. For Brunswick Club taggers-on no more than 2d. was to be spent on liquor at any meeting,[26] which may explain why it failed to excite lower-order Protestant participation beyond its start-up phase. In this way some clubs and societies – ostensible advocates of the interests of the artisan class – were also about social control; the Irish Mechanics' Institutes, for example, were much concerned with addressing issues around drink and other forms of intemperate behaviour. The second mechanics' institute formed in Galway was titled the 'Galway Trades Mechanics' Institute, Total Abstinence, and Morality Association', though its initial pledge-based entrance criteria were later watered down to an encouragement to moderation.[27]

The temperance movement had an impact upon Irish club-life beyond the proliferation of temperance societies. Temperance halls became useful venues for clubs. The Anti-Early Burial Committee met in the Temperance Hall in Cuffe Lane, Dublin. The Inns-Quay Ward Registration Club met at the Temperance Hall in Halston Street in the same city. The O'Meara and Fulton Club met at the Temperance Hall in Nenagh and, when it came to organising festivities on St Patrick's Day, the Davis Confederate Club opted for a

---

23 *Freeman's Journal*, 17, 25 April 1845, 3 Jan. 1849.
24 *Nation*, 27 May 1848; R. Dudley, *The Irish lottery, 1780–1801* (Dublin: Four Courts Press, 2005), p. 123.
25 RCYC, 'The Cork Harbour Water Club', *Dublin Penny Journal*, 1:49 (1833), 387.
26 Kingon, 'Ulster opposition', p. 145.
27 Neswald, 'Science, sociability and the improvement of Ireland', p. 522.

tea party. Temperance groups even spawned their own literary and scientific societies.[28]

Some societies which incorporated a sociable dimension to their activities in the eighteenth century adopted a more businesslike form in the nineteenth. Mutual insurance companies at one point embraced a dining culture. Newry's Amicable Annuity Society met in McClatchey's tavern and Dublin's Hibernian Annuity Company met at Fay's in Essex Street. But such clubs were increasingly disposed to meet in commercial premises – the Belfast Annuity Company in the Market House; and Dublin's Patriotic Assurance Company held its annual meeting at the company's office in Dame Street. Also relatively abstemious were the charitable societies that proliferated in the eighteenth and nineteenth centuries. The charitably minded Bull's Head Musical Society was among Ireland's first clubs. Charitable focus did not, of course, imply an entirely benevolent attitude towards others. Bishop Richard Woodward (1726–94) found his involvement in a range of charities – including the Society for the Recovery of Persons Drowned and Apparently Dead – entirely compatible with his support for unlimited Protestant Ascendancy. There was a contretemps in the County Galway Bible Society in 1830 over the founding of a Tuam branch, when it emerged that Catholics attended the foundation meeting.[29] As with other clubs, charitable societies had a close relationship with the press, and donors and recipients might advertise in newspapers. There are numerous examples of individuals and groups making public donations to help imprisoned debtors. Daniel O'Connell ensured that his name was connected with the Teresian Orphan Society by giving his name and address for donations to that body.[30]

Significantly, Irish charitable societies, emphatically Protestant in the eighteenth century, became noticeably more Catholic in the nineteenth – the Catholic Institution for the Deaf and Dumb, founded in the 1840s, is just one example of the way in which civil society changed. Catholic confraternities and sodalities were a crucial element of the sociability enjoyed by many communities in the nineteenth century, as well as a means of organising charity.[31] The Olivemount Association was charitable in focus, and consisted for the most part of Catholic tradesmen, but most of its activities – from

---

28 E. Malcolm, *Ireland sober, Ireland free: drink and temperance in nineteenth-century Ireland* (Syracuse, NY: Syracuse University Press, 1986).

29 *Freeman's Journal*, 22 Jan. 1830.

30 *Freeman's Journal*, 1 Feb. 1845.

31 Colm Lennon (ed.), *Confraternities and sodalities in Ireland: charity, church and sociability* (Blackrock: Columba Press, 2012).

charitable sermons, to more general Sunday services – were religious in content, and sociability seemed incidental. A similar point could be made about the Christian Brothers, though the latter did follow some tried and tested associational tactics – advertising the names and amounts of donations in the press. During the Great Famine there was an upsurge in the scale of charitable involvement in the public sphere. Dublin's Central Relief Society had close O'Connellite connections, and the standing of the Royal Dublin Society was acknowledged by a visit from the newly arrived viceroy, the Earl of Clarendon, in July 1847.[32]

Club Personalities and Practices

A student of the clubs and societies that shaped Ireland's social life in the eighteenth and early nineteenth centuries will soon recognise that the involvement of individuals with civil society were rarely monogamous. The Irish were inveterate clubbers. At the wealthy end of the spectrum in the eighteenth century one might have a commitment to a hunting pack in the country and, at key moments of historical drama, a rank in a Volunteer regiment or a senior position in a radical club or lodge of the Orange Order. In towns there were political, charitable and cultural societies to join. Commitment to societies during this period was frequently influenced by political developments, and changed over time. Volunteering had radical phases in 1783–4 and in the early 1790s, and many graduated to become members of the United Irishmen. Meanwhile, the Aldermen of Skinner's Alley splintered into radical and loyalist factions in 1793; prior to this, the society had a sizeable membership of United Irishmen. In the 1780s, Ralph Mulhern was rumoured to have been a member of the shadowy (and possibly fictional) radical Block and Axe Club, whereas in the early nineteenth century he was a member of the loyalist Aldermen of Skinner's Alley.[33]

The names of clubs also speak of reinvention and indebtedness – note Dundalk's Northern Rangers, which might have been a Volunteer regiment; and County Roscommon's Mirth and Good Humour Club, which sounds like a dining or glee club; in each case the name disguised a commitment to hunting. Other clubs chose to highlight their Protestant lineage: thus Volunteer corps manifested a predilection for titles such as the True Blues, the Boyne and

---

32 *Freeman's Journal*, 13 Aug., 31 Dec. 1849, 10 July 1847.
33 M. Powell, 'The Aldermen of Skinner's Alley: ultra-Protestantism before the Orange Order' in Kelly and Powell (eds.), *Clubs and societies in eighteenth-century Ireland*, p. 222.

the Aughrim. The rank and file of the Orange Order did likewise; it included lodges named after King William ('the Williamite Lodge'), the Boyne Water, Aughrim, Cumberland and Schomberg. There were also Nelson clubs; Belfast had one and a Trafalgar Club in addition. The new generation of repeal clubs formed in Dublin and elsewhere in 1848 followed the same pattern. The names offer a window onto a complex and varied radical heritage that embraced Catholic rebels and military leaders – the Roger O'Moore Club and the St Ruth Club; Patriots of various hues – the Molyneaux Club, the Swift Club, the Curran Club and the Grattan Club; and United Irishmen – the Oliver Bond Club, the Arthur O'Connor Club, the Emmet Club and the Fitzgerald Club.[34] On both sides of the political and religious divide, club formation was pursued with an acute awareness of historical tradition.

In order for civil society to develop, certain features were required – a degree of urbanisation and a print culture were perhaps the most critical preconditions. There was an intimate link between print and club-life in Ireland from the early eighteenth century. Even rural groupings, hunt clubs for example, were dependent upon print to advertise their meetings and to circulate information about their activities. It is not surprising, therefore, that printers were active participants in the associational world. The attempt by John Giffard, the controversial printer of *Faulkner's Dublin Journal*, to join the Aldermen of Skinner's Alley contributed to its fracturing; he was also in the Orange Order. John Exshaw of the eponymous journal was in the Skinner's Alley club.[35] When Matthew Carey of the *Volunteers Journal* was arrested in 1784, various Volunteer regiments and clubs used the press to offer messages of support. In 1790 the Whig Club complained that the imprisonment of John Magee, the printer of the *Dublin Evening Post*, placed the liberty of the subject in 'imminent danger'.[36] The sanctioned destruction, a few years later, of the printing presses of the United Irishmen newspaper, the *Northern Star*, made the limits of this freedom very clear, a point eloquently made by Richard Brinsley Sheridan in the British Commons in 1810. By the early nineteenth century, 'The liberty of the Press' was one of the most popular toasts at O'Connellite and Repeal gatherings. The Monaghan Independents toasted to 'the Press, the Palladium of Liberty' in 1832, and when the leading

---

34 *Nation*, 1 July 1848; *Irish Examiner*, 19 July 1848; see G.M. Owens, 'Popular mobilisation and the rising of 1848: the clubs of the Irish Confederation', in L.M. Geary (ed.), *Rebellion and remembrance in modern Ireland* (Dublin: Four Courts Press, 2001), pp. 51–63.
35 Powell, 'The Aldermen of Skinner's Alley', pp. 217–18; Royal Irish Academy, 23H51, Alphabetical index of the Aldermen of Skinner's Alley, 1813–63.
36 *Belfast News-Letter*, 26 Feb. 1790.

repealer Stephen Curtis gave the toast to the 'Liberty of the Press' in the '82 Club in 1846, he reflected that 'it is only since these words became understood amongst mankind, that civil liberty has been rightly cherished by them, or liberty of any kind possessed'. A confederate repealer agreed that 'the press was now the only refuge of the people'.[37]

It was claimed erroneously by a member of a repeal club in the 1840s that 'Conservative clubs did not allow their proceedings to go to the public.'[38] In fact loyalist clubs sustained a similarly close relationship with printers and the press. Londonderry's True Blue Society deposited its articles of subscription with a bookseller.[39] The Aldermen of Skinner's Alley published its proceedings in a range of newspapers; *Faulkner's Dublin Journal* was the mouthpiece of the ultra-Protestant faction in the 1790s, and later of Orange and Brunswick clubs. The Portadown Brunswick Club agreed that its proceedings should be inserted in the *Dublin Evening Mail*, the *Belfast Guardian* and the *Newry Telegraph*, and other Brunswick clubs did likewise.[40] The value of the publicity the press provided for clubs was revealed by one wing of the Post-Office Ward Club; a meeting of five or six was rendered by an advertisement placed by the secretary as 'a numerous and highly respectable one'. In 1832, the Clonmel Independent Club discussed circulation, local versus national status, and commitment to the issue of reform, when considering in which papers to advertise.[41] Newspapers were not just a crucial vehicle for club news and propaganda. The increasing tendency of clubs to establish permanent club houses or club rooms meant that clubs displaced coffee houses as locations where members could conveniently consult a wide range of newspapers. Galway's Amicable Literary Society, founded in 1791, offered newspapers and library facilities to its well-heeled clientele – and in a sense became a more exclusive version of the Mercantile Coffee Room.

Membership of a club was determined by ballot (Aldermen of Skinner's Alley) or blackball (the '82 Club); and should it be necessary to deprive an individual of membership, by expulsion. Clubbability was reinforced by recourse to the press – a member of the Limerick Annuity Company had his expulsion for non-payment of subscription publicised in the *Limerick Chronicle* in 1779, and a member of the Meath Independent Club experienced a similar fate in 1830.[42] The Turf Club moved in the late 1830s to eject a Mr Ferguson

---

37 *Freeman's Journal*, 1 Sept. 1832, 18 Feb. 1846; *Nation*, 22 April 1848.
38 *Freeman's Journal*, 23 April 1844.
39 *Londonderry Journal*, 2 July 1776.
40 Kingon, 'Ulster opposition', p. 143.
41 *Freeman's Journal*, 25 Feb. 1840, 10 Feb. 1832.
42 *Limerick Chronicle*, 3 May 1779; *Freeman's Journal*, 21 Oct. 1830.

because he went to the London press with details of a dispute with Lord Milltown arising out of an alleged plot to prevent his horse Harkaway from maximising the number of races that it could win – a cause célèbre that made its way across the Atlantic.[43] Clubbability depended on one's capacity to pay one's way, and this applied as much to the accoutrements of club-life as to membership fees. A host of eighteenth- and nineteenth-century clubs, including the Volunteer regiments of the 1770s and 1780s, the Monks of the Order of St Patrick, the Knights of Tara and the Orange Order, required members to wear uniforms. At an '82 Club banquet on 16 April 1845, no member not in the uniform of 'a Green Body Coat with Velvet Collar, White Skirt Linings and Gilt Buttons inscribed "1782" in a wreath of Shamrocks' was allowed to dine.[44]

The cost of participating in club-life provides a direct link between credit and sociability. Club or society members had to possess a certain amount of credit in order to be accepted by the formal grouping. Economic and political credit was bound together in the associational world. The United Irishmen may have sought to boycott Bellingham beer and to use lottery clubs as a mode of recruitment, but the number of United Irishmen whose involvement in radical politics resulted in their bankruptcy is still more significant. This was true also in the O'Connellite period. When anti-tithe protestors were jailed in the 1830s, clubs raised funds to provide them with financial support. The Mayo Independent Club subsequently paid the rents of tenants whose occupancy was endangered by voting against the landlord interest. Personal credit could also intermingle with financial credit on a significant scale as clubs became wealthier. There was a minor controversy in the press over the bank used by O'Connell for Precursor Society funds. Nevertheless, thanks to O'Connell and his organisations, there was a change to the manner in which popular clubs were financed. The practice of taking relatively small amounts from a mass membership – as in the case of the Catholic Association's one penny minimum monthly subscription – permitted a less hand-to-mouth existence. Indeed the proceedings of the Repeal Association, as reported in the press, were in some ways a demonstration of the economic vitality of the club; they listed – at some length – the groups and individuals that paid their remittances.[45]

---

43 *American Turf Register and Sporting Magazine*, Jan./Feb. 1839, pp. 6–8.
44 *Freeman's Journal*, 18 Jan., 17 April 1845.
45 *Freeman's Journal*, 4 Oct. 1833, 19 Jan. 1839, 3 June 1845.

Religion and Sectarianism

The Orange Order, formed in 1795, poses two issues for progressive civil society models. First, its pursuit of a sectarian agenda is problematic, as it demonstrated by its activities in the 1790s that associationalism could be violent. Second, if we seek to locate the emergence of Irish civil society outside of the state, then this body was compromised in a number of ways. Yet Orangeism emerged out of a milieu that was as much about civic patriotism as religious contestation. The progenitor of Orangeism in Dublin was the Aldermen of Skinner's Alley. It contained a sprinkling of civic worthies in its ranks throughout its eighteenth-century phase, and there was always a core of members for whom the society was a vehicle for the expression of a Dublin city identity.[46] In the Dublin lodges of the Orange Order there are signs of the presence also of a group that prioritised civic life – identifiable, for example, in the willingness of the Dublin lodge to oppose the Anglo-Irish Union.[47] If the cabinet-makers, carpenters and tailors of Dublin were 'Orange' in the nineteenth century, one might argue also that this was a natural historical extension of the guild system, which was hostile to Catholic membership. In Dublin in the 1840s, the Saddlers Guild marshalled its members to support Conservative candidates at election time. The issue of tenant right is another interesting case, as the Gavan Duffy-led movement not only was non-sectarian in its early phases, but also possessed of a distinctly urban dimension, and an appeal that embraced a host of urban clubs. The Dublin District Tenant Society sought the affiliation of the Carpenters' Society as well as the Bricklayers'. In addition there was some discussion of affiliating Friendly and Building Societies.[48]

Following the Act of Union, the Dublin Orange Order incurred the displeasure of George IV for its supporters' free and easy attitude towards the statue of William III on College Green – though the Dublin Lodge sought to curb this behaviour. The Grand Orange Lodge of Ireland was dissolved in 1825 as a consequence of the Unlawful Associations Act, and the viceroy, Lord Anglesey, subsequently banned the annual twelfth of July festivities. As a result, parades became an increasingly divisive issue within Irish Protestantism; even within the Order itself. In 1829, the Grand Lodge urged members not to process on the twelfth, fearing – correctly – sectarian violence

---

46 Powell, 'The Aldermen of Skinner's Alley', pp. 220–3.
47 In an oblique acknowledgement of this, a Newry confederate repeal club chose the name 'Foster', after the anti-union champion, Speaker John Foster, though it was later renamed the 'John Mitchel Club': *Nation*, 22 April, 17 June 1848.
48 *Freeman's Journal*, 30 June 1841, 5 Aug. 1851.

in the wake of Catholic emancipation. In 1838, a Grand Master cast doubt on the usefulness of parading, suggesting that it was revealing of the body's weakness. He maintained that it was part of a Catholic tradition, echoing a point made previously about Freemason processions.[49]

The usefulness of parading was also debated by confederate repealers. On 12 July 1849, in an incident redolent of the ongoing clashes between sectarian bodies and local populaces over access to streets and public spaces, the Orange Order and the military clashed with Catholics during a march through Dolly's Brae, in County Down, as a result of which the latter incurred heavy casualties. In some ways it may be better to understand the Orange Order – and indeed loyalist civil society more generally – as two distinct, but overlapping, strains of club-life – one civic and urban, and the other paramilitary and semi-rural. This is not, of course, to say that they did not possess shared aims.

Attracted by the common convivial currency of so much associational activity – drinking, dining, ritual – Catholics slotted comfortably into what was once a near exclusively Protestant public sphere. From the late eighteenth century, Catholics participated publicly for the first time (though, as we will see below, they were already covert joiners). In the 1780s, Catholics became Volunteers in significant numbers – to the chagrin of those Protestants who were uneasy about any manifestation of Catholic assertiveness. The Dublin branch of the United Irishmen admitted more Catholics to membership than its Belfast counterpart, and recent work has uncovered high levels of United Irish membership in some of Ireland's most Catholic counties. Following the ratification of the Act of Union, and the rise of Catholic emancipation, repeal and tenant right movements, there was a further gear change. The number of Catholic priests in leadership roles during the 1798 rebellion may have been exaggerated, but they made their influence felt across a range of associations in the nineteenth century. Protestant clergymen were leading lights in associational culture in the eighteenth century – hunting, gourmandising, politicking; in the nineteenth century they were prominent in the Brunswick clubs. The new breed of priestly civil society leaders was a departure. This meant not only a presence in clubs, but also the appearance of named Catholic members (Catholic priests included) in newspapers.

When the County Clare Liberal Club was formed in September 1847 it was noted that 'the Catholic clergy have rendered ... valuable aid in its

---

49 J. Hill, 'National festivals, the state and Protestant Ascendancy', *Irish Historical Studies*, 24 (1984–5), 30–51; Petri Mirala, 'Masonic sociability and its limitations: the case of Ireland' in Kelly and Powell (eds.), *Clubs and societies in eighteenth-century Ireland*, p. 319.

construction'. The Repeal organisation minus the Young Irelanders – the 'Old Irelanders' – was branded by William Smith O'Brien as 'the organ of Mr John O'Connell and the Catholic clergy ... in point of fact very much a Catholic association', although a club cleaving to the Smith O'Brien line (the Brian Borhoimhe Club in Glanworth) was chaired by a Catholic priest.[50] Later variants of mechanics' societies maintained close connections with the Catholic Church, and indeed with the political fortunes of O'Connell and the Repeal Association. Thaddeus O'Malley thought priestly involvement in club-life was essential. In this sense he was tempering worldly concerns, and international socialist concerns, with native moral codes:

> For my part I should wish (if it be permitted me) that there was not one single club in Ireland that had not a clergyman as a member, were it only as a honorary member, for that would be enough to enable him to look in amongst them occasionally as a moral overseer, and use his opportunity seasonably in strengthening every good and restraining every mischievous tendency.[51]

In its founding resolutions the Cavan Liberal Club made it clear that this was a club to further Catholic interests.[52] The Clonmel Liberal Club did likewise; it toasted the health of Pius IX, 'the great reformer of the age – the high priest of liberty – the Sovereign Pontiff'. There was also a toast to 'the Hierarchy and Clergy of Ireland'.[53] In some ways what is most interesting about the increasingly Catholic nature of club culture in the nineteenth century was how little changed in terms of ritual and procedure. The toasts may have been different, but much else was retained by those now dominant in certain areas of civil society.

The Limits of Civil Society: Public versus Private

Catholics participated in organised popular protest during the eighteenth century as members of the Houghers, Whiteboys, Rightboys and other organised manifestations of agrarian discontent. Their resort to violence may seem to rule such groups out of a progressive vision of civil society. But that would also necessitate excluding the Defenders, who, Jim Smyth has shown, had close structural links to Freemasonry.[54] Such an approach might also require the

---

50 *Freeman's Journal*, 11 Sept. 1847, 17 Jan., 8 July 1848.
51 *Freeman's Journal*, 10 July 1848.
52 *Anglo-Celt*, 18 July 1868.
53 *Freeman's Journal*, 3 Jan. 1849.
54 J. Smyth, *The men of no property: Irish radicals and popular politics in the late eighteenth century* (Basingstoke: Macmillan, 1992).

exclusion of the Orange Order and the United Irishmen, their obvious associational qualities notwithstanding. Some of the key features of associational
culture were embraced by popular protest groupings, in other words; these
include the use of ritualised behaviour (the costumes of the Whiteboys); or the
commitment to fraternal loyalty, which can be perceived in their preparedness
to stage daring rescues of arrested comrades. One might even suggest that Irish
history has extended a place within civil society to respectable clubs and parties, but that any group smacking of paramilitarism (unless state-sponsored)
has been ostracised. And yet given the manner in which they were organised –
whether we are talking about Defenders or Fenians – it is clear that the same
rituals of sociability were important. Moreover, some of these groups had a
very intimate relationship with the community; compensation was paid by
rural houghers to a farmer whose cattle were attacked in error, for example.[55]
Given that so many leading clubs and societies possessed a paramilitary aspect,
why not add Whiteboys, Defenders and Ribbonmen to the mix? It would fit
broader trends in the study of civil society, which focus on social movements
and their adoption of disruptive tactics in order to secure their goals.[56]

Tensions between types of associational culture can be identified from the
late eighteenth century. The early Orange Order was too robust for an elite
that could clearly see the value of its numbers and muscle. Some United Irish
leaders – William Drennan for example – baulked at the Defender alliance.
In the 1770s and 1780s, Volunteers were active in policing rural protest movements (and urban combinations). Daniel O'Connell urged his supporters to
do likewise and 'put an end to the Whitefeet crimes'. Although the language
of the O'Connellites appeared to speak to the democratisation of the public
sphere, the reality was that not only individuals were subjected to a suitability
test, but also clubs themselves. Daniel O'Connell denounced in public the club
culture of 'secret societies' and 'illegal oaths' – he singled out Whiteboyism
and Ribbonism, and would later add the Molly Maguires – as harmful to the
Repeal cause. Some of those who expressed strong opposition to protest
groups also focussed on their target's club-like features. When a member of
the Licensed Retail Grocers' and Vintners' Trade Protection Society noted
that he 'firmly refused' a request from a Ribbon club for the use of a room,
his experience was echoed by another member of the society.[57] It was clearly

---

55 M. Powell, 'Ireland's urban houghers: moral economy and popular protest in the late
   eighteenth century' in M. Brown and S. Donlan (eds.), *The laws and other legalities of
   Ireland, 1689–1850* (Farnham: Ashgate, 2011), pp. 231–54.
56 M. Giugni, D. McAdam and C. Tilly, *How social movements matter* (Minneapolis: University
   of Minnesota Press, 1999).
57 *Freeman's Journal*, 21 Oct. 1830, 25 Feb. 1833, 3 June 1845, 8 May 1852.

a problem for popular urban clubs. The breakaway Davis Confederate Club complained that 'persons who had rooms to let' were influenced by 'the emissaries' of the Repeal Association to refuse them.[58] Club-life at a popular level was as shape-shifting and multifarious as its elite equivalent.[59]

Some ascendancy-oriented clubs enjoyed a complex relationship with the Protestant lower orders. Most were only interested in representing them in a virtual sense. The Metropolitan Conservative Society felt that it offered the best way of protecting the rights and privileges of the poor.[60] And yet the transference of club votes to potential members of parliament was a means of moving beyond the 'virtual' in the political system. Ireland could arguably be said to have been in the vanguard of a democratising club culture in this sense, as attempts to get MPs to commit to particular political principles originated in the 1750s with the Free Citizens of Dublin. There were a number of ways in which this could work. Clubs initially sought promises in the press, and then later facilitated voter registration; some became election clubs. Beyond that, it was possible in certain instances for clubs to promise a block of votes. The Louth Club proposed to deliver all of its votes to a single candidate if three-quarters of the club were in favour. In the Brunswick clubs it seems that the Cork club had a similar electoral focus, but that this was not typical of the movement as a whole.[61]

The class divide in club-life was rigidly enforced, and applied by Catholic as well as Protestant associations. Just as there was an exclusivity to the Catholic Association's Liberal clubs, so the county versions of the Brunswick clubs were dominated by the gentry – inevitably given the one guinea membership and strict nomination rules. Local Brunswick clubs were more permissive. Membership and subscription fees were one way of ensuring exclusivity. Such a tack did not always work. The Royal Agricultural Improvement Society of Ireland permitted tenant farmers to join at a reduced rate, but offered such limited benefits that not a single tenant joined up. One supporter of 'tenant farmer admission … attributed the sinking condition of the society heretofore to its exclusiveness'.[62] Similar tensions were in evidence among

---

58 *Nation*, 14 Aug. 1847.
59 Oakboys and Steelboys could be Volunteers and then United Irishmen, and in the nineteenth century peasants drifted in and out of Ribbonism and successive O'Connellite reform movements: Hereward Senior, 'The place of Fenianism in the Irish Republican tradition', *Irish University Review*, 4:3 (1967), 253.
60 *Freeman's Journal*, 30 June 1841.
61 *Freeman's Journal*, 1 Dec. 1832; Kingon, 'Ulster opposition to Catholic emancipation', p. 143.
62 *Freeman's Journal*, 17 May 1852.

the Galway Mechanics, with one artisan bemoaning the fact that Catholic artisan members were treated disrespectfully if they attempted to bring forward motions.[63] The Repeal Association – though it opened its doors to women and the poor – continued to offer privileges, such as the best seats in the Corn Exchange, to wealthy attendees. There was a complex system of entrances and seating for those attending meetings, depending upon gender and whether they were paid-up members. There were separate seats for women attending free, and those who were members, though men who paid £1 could also introduce a lady to the reserved seats. The Dublin Mechanics' Institution likewise gave members the power to introduce a lady.[64]

Women were part of club culture throughout the eighteenth century, and were welcomed by debating clubs, music groups and charitable societies, as well as the more nebulous salon culture. They did not participate on equal terms with male members, however. This was obviously true of those who were proprietors, serving staff or entertainment.[65] But even where women were part of the club proper, they were frequently rendered passive observers by society rules or membership conditions. At the Hibernian Temperance Society women were confined to the audience; only men were allowed to speak from the platform. In 1807, the Cork Harbour Water Club passed a resolution, 'that the wives and daughters of the members of the club, be also considered members of the club, and entitled to wear their uniform'; breeches were another matter.[66] Be that as it may, there is no doubt that women clubbed in increased numbers in the nineteenth century – and not just in Dublin. The Carrickfergus Coterie, which was open to men and women, met at the town's Court House. In the political arena, the formation of the Precursor Society – which saw O'Connell actively encourage female membership – was an important development. The body lasted only a year, but a precedent had been set, and women were also admitted subsequently to the Repeal Association. The lists published in the press would indicate their number to be around 15–20 per cent.[67] Some organisations surpassed this level; at a meeting of the new Orangeist Clarendon Club in Dublin in 1848,

63 Neswald, 'Science, sociability and the improvement of Ireland', p. 515.
64 M. O'Dowd, 'O'Connell and the lady patriots: women and O'Connellite politics, 1824–1845' in A. Blackstock and E. Magennis (eds.), *Politics and political culture in Britain and Ireland, 1750–1850* (Belfast: Ulster Historical Foundation, 2007), p. 292; *Freeman's Journal*, 18 Jan. 1845, 31 Dec. 1849.
65 In Belfast's Nelson Club, for example, a Mrs Hirst had overall responsibility for entertainment and catering: *Belfast News-Letter*, 5 March 1824.
66 RCYC, 'The Cork Harbour Water Club', p. 387.
67 O'Dowd, 'O'Connell and the lady patriots', p. 291.

'the ladies present seemed somewhat to exceed in number the male portion of the company'.[68]

As already observed, an influential strand of thinking on British civil society perceives a shift from a public to a private associational culture – from public coffee houses and taverns to private club rooms and houses – at the close of the eighteenth century. In Ireland coffee houses were the engines of club culture in the eighteenth century. They were assisted by their close connection to the world of print, as in the case of Dick's Coffee House, which was established by Richard Pue of *Pue's Occurrences*. Some clubs even shared names with coffee houses: Anthing's Club met at Anthing's Coffee House in Granby Row. Coffee houses like Dublin's Exchange Coffee House provided an important connection with modern chambers of commerce. But they declined in importance as club venues in the nineteenth century. The Turf Club's coffee house continued, however, and its walls remained the repository of the names of the members. The relationship with taverns was more enduring. One of the great venues for eighteenth-century Irish club-life, the Donegall Arms in Belfast – host to the Northern Whig Club and the Belfast Hunt – was still used as a club venue in the early nineteenth century, by, for example, the Monthly Club and the Card Club; indeed the waiter of the Donegall Arms collected subscriptions for the latter.[69] The early nineteenth-century Catholic Club met at the Union Tavern in Dublin. Dublin's Licensed Retail Grocers' and Vintners' Trade Protection Society met at O'Hara's Royal College Tavern. One might even argue that Irish popular associationalism in the first half of the nineteenth century became ever more 'public'. In the 1750s and 1760s the Mallow Loyal Association eschewed pubs in favour of dinner at private houses. There was nothing private about the monster meetings of the Repeal movement. And if we include rural Gaelic-speaking groups – poetry circles and the like – they might also congregate outdoors, although they were more likely to meet in taverns.

Between 1830 and 1832 the Repeal-supporting Meath Independent Club switched venues from an inn at Dunshaughlin to a hotel. This shift from public houses to hotels appears to have been commonplace – at least among clubs with middling- and upper-class memberships. The Beefsteak Club assembled in the Morrison Hotel in Dawson Street, and the Liberal Club of St Anne's Parish met in the Shelbourne Hotel on St Stephen's Green, both in Dublin. The same trend is identifiable in the provinces. The Louth Club met

68 *Freeman's Journal*, 13 July 1848.
69 *Belfast News-Letter*, 24 Feb., 23 Oct. 1807, 19 April 1811.

at Mouritz's Hotel in Dundalk, and the County Limerick Club at Quinlivan's Hotel in Limerick. In some towns hotels hosted a number of clubs, much as taverns had once done. Both the County Cavan Club and the Farmers' Club met at the Globe.

The number of clubs boasting their own club rooms increased in the nineteenth century. Dublin's Royal Horticultural Society had rooms on Grafton Street while the Citizens' Club of Kilkenny had 'Rooms' on High Street in that city. There was a tangible difference between rented rooms and purpose-built premises. Dublin's Post-Office Ward Club met in its 'Committee' or 'Club' Room in Henry Street, and later at their rooms in Elephant Lane. A splinter faction met at Hart's Great Rooms, which has an 'assembly room' ring to it, while the United Repealers of Kilkenny also met in assembly rooms. A hostile description by the Ward Club of their rivals makes it clear that some clubs continued to function in a manner redolent of the eighteenth century – in public houses: 'they had been obliged a few evenings since to put Hart, the owner of the public house where they met, in the chair'. Allegedly 'the only persons present were ... brawlers who threw ... dirt on the respectable members of that club', whose number included Coyne, 'the Ciceronian hatter'. In the 1780s, lower-order Volunteers were mockingly depicted as members of a fictional Fishmongers corps. In 1848 a club that eventually morphed into the John Mitchel Club met at the fishery in Lower Glanmire Road, in Cork.[70] Things did not, as this suggests, remain the same; although writers in the Augustan period invoked fictional clubs of beggars to satirise club-life, in the nineteenth century Thaddeus O'Malley set up a club for the poor in Dublin.[71]

At the other end of the social spectrum, the Kingstown Royal Irish Yacht Club lived it up in its purposely designed club house. Opened in 1849, it had a number of 'noble rooms' overlooking the harbour.[72] The increasingly middle-class identity of the Galway Mechanics' Institute was manifested in an expensive new hall, which left the society heavily indebted. The Cork Club, by 1861, also had a club house. Meanwhile, in towns and smaller cities, clubs might possess rooms or apartments in a shared club house. The Clonmel Liberal Club 'had their anniversary dinner in their splendid apartments in the Club-House, Main-street' in 1849.[73] The increasingly Catholic nature of club-life

70 *Freeman's Journal*, 25 Feb. 1840, 8 July 1848.
71 *Hibernian Journal*, 1–3, 12–15 Jan. 1776; F. D'Arcy, 'Labour, nationality and religion in nineteenth-century Ireland: the case of Thaddeus O'Malley', *Old Limerick Journal*, 31 (1994), 11.
72 *Freeman's Journal*, 2 Aug. 1849.
73 *Freeman's Journal*, 3 Jan. 1849.

is indicated by the fact that some clubs met in religious buildings. Although not quite making club culture 'public', the increasing preference of clubs to favour large venues helped make club-life a less exclusive activity. The Corn Exchange in Dublin was used by a variety of clubs connected with O'Connell, until it was replaced by the purpose-built Conciliation Hall, headquarters of the Repeal Association. When the Ulster Constitutional Association met in the Music Hall in Belfast in 1840 around 700 people attended, including women, who occupied the gallery. The confederate repealers used the Music Hall in Dublin – again with ladies in the gallery – as did the Protestant Repeal Association.

Conclusion

Ireland's civil society for most of the eighteenth century was Protestant, urban, elite or middling-sort, and male. And although there were exceptions – rural hunt clubs, the Freemasons, charitable societies with female members, radical societies with an artisanal base that admitted Catholics to membership – the nineteenth century witnessed a major shift in Ireland's public culture. By 1850, Catholics had become an integral part of civil society. This, it might be suggested, brought with it an opportunity for a public sphere to emerge that was independent of the state. Some commentators even opined that civil society was one of the few remaining possibilities for optimism in Irish political and social life: 'Fox-hunting and Freemasonry are mainstays of society wherever they are cherished, and there are yet in Ireland many choice spirits of different creeds and various political opinions who meet at lodge and covert-side with the cordial feelings of brethren of the ancient craft and of the joyous chase.'[74] But the moments then and earlier when this prospect seemed real – whether in the Aldermen of Skinner's Alley, the United Irishmen or the confederate Repeal movement – failed to come to pass. Perhaps this was a result of the fact that when Catholics entered this public world they did so in a manner that pushed them into their own particular silos. Many Catholic societies had close relationships with the Catholic Church; furthermore, Protestant clubs were antipathetic to Catholic incursions into the public arena. Catholic emancipation stimulated opposing Protestant groups, and the Great Famine made it clear that the right to sit in parliament was no solution to an economic system that kept millions of Catholics at a dangerous level of subsistence.

74 *Sporting Magazine*, Sept. 1844, p. 157.

If we accept that the nature of civil society changed as a result of the altered sectarian dynamic, can we say that the very nature of Irish associational life also shifted as we move through the eighteenth and early nineteenth into the second half of the nineteenth century? For example, did the privatisation and the Catholicisation of the public sphere lead to a diminution in the level of riotous sociability? The intersection of the temperance movement and repeal is symptomatic of changes in the patterns of sociability, but there is little to indicate that the sociable dimension of club culture was fundamentally changed in the long term. Temperance in Ireland enjoyed a short-lived peak – a confederate repeal body supplanted a Father Mathew temperance group in a set of Galway club rooms – and much of the evidence for the Catholic associational culture that sprang up around O'Connell suggests business as usual.[75] For some Catholics and Protestants, new commitments – political, religious, moral – may have filled a void, but for many others the pleasures of sociability, eating, drinking and enjoying exclusive ritualised behaviour were persisted in. The point perhaps was where such diversions featured in the club's priorities. As one radical critic of the '82 Club put it in 1845, a club now had to have 'meaning': 'Not to gossip gentlemanly, or bow gracefully surely; but to take counsel how best the bold thought of liberty might be pushed through the assuming crowd.'[76]

75 *Nation*, 10 June 1848.
76 *Nation*, 22 Nov. 1845.

18

Sport and Recreation in the Eighteenth and Nineteenth Centuries

JAMES KELLY

The recreational and sporting proclivities of the population of Ireland in the eighteenth and nineteenth centuries echoed the social hierarchy that defined that society. Thus the aristocratic elite, whose authority was at its most secure in the eighteenth century, embraced horse racing, hunting, the theatre, classical music, sociability and association, reading and other activities that possessed the cachet of respectability. The aristocracy did not possess, or seek to assert, an exclusive entitlement to these pursuits, still less a monopoly on sport and recreation. The recreational culture of the elite existed alongside a demotic recreational culture (with distinct urban and rural features) whose defining pursuits included bull baiting, throwing at cocks, a number of ball games, tests of physical and athletic strength, and a rich diet of social interaction at fairs, patterns and domestic gatherings at which folk music, dancing, drinking, storytelling and games were normative. The involvement of elements of the elite in promoting hurling in the second half of the eighteenth century, the cross-sectoral appeal of cockfighting, and the enthusiasm of the populace for horse racing demonstrate that these recreational cultures intersected at a number of points. Moreover, the space separating elite and popular recreations narrowed, as the expanding ranks of the respectable contrived in the late eighteenth century to exclude certain popular recreational activities (the pursuit of blood sports and low-purse race meetings particularly) from the public arena. This object was not easily achieved. The respectable had powerful allies, however, and they contrived with the assistance of municipal and state authorities, first, to prohibit contested activities such as bull running and throwing at cocks and to consign cockfighting to the margins, and, second, to compel other 'recreations' such as pugilism and, eventually, traditional field sports to modify in order to survive, and traditional fairs and patterns to cease or to change. The evolution of pugilism into boxing and the abolition of the notorious Donnybrook fair occurred in the nineteenth century when the attitudinal convergence of the elite and the middling sort, the growth of the state, and the increasing moral sway of evangelical religion and the Catholic Church ensured that the sports and recreations that were pursued and the manner in which people sought recreation answered increasingly to what respectable opinion judged acceptable. This did not produce a dramatic narrowing of the range of recreational activity. As well as the pursuits that grew and flourished because they were inherently diverse and possessed of wide social acceptance (hunting, for example), the recreational milieu expanded and diversified. In addition to the emergence of new pursuits (many of them enduring minority interests, others short lived), and the increased reliance on the club as the fulcrum of organised sport, there was a palpable intensification of what, in another context, John Rule has denominated 'recreational polarisation' both within and across the social orders.[1] One highly visible manifestation of this was the emergence of temperance halls as a counter-attraction to the public house, which consolidated its position as the primary venue of popular male sociability in the nineteenth century. Another arose out of the increased withdrawal of the elite behind the demesnes walls. Yet, there was still plenty of space for individuals, groups and interests to pursue particular pursuits, as the combination of opportunity (fuelled by greater disposable income and leisure time most notably), social identification and political outlook sustained patterns of activity that mirrored the expanding range of options. And as exemplified by the history of the music hall and team sports, these were manifestations of forms of recreation that reflected the increasing influence of the middling sort and the attraction of mass participation.

Patterns of Elite Recreation in the Eighteenth Century

In keeping with their position at the top of the prevailing hierarchal order, the recreational pursuits of the landed elite were more developed than those of other social interests in the eighteenth century. They are, as a result, more amenable to reconstruction. Moreover, they had by that point largely shaken off the medieval inheritance that had, for example, prompted major landowners in the seventeenth century to create expansive deer-parks as bespoke play areas. Deer continued to be hunted throughout the eighteenth and early nineteenth centuries; but whereas seventeenth-century magnates such as the Duke of Ormonde and the Earl of Orrery equated hunting with the pursuit

---

1 J. Rule, *The labouring classes in early industrial England, 1750–1850* (Harlow: Longman, 1986), p. 220.

of the stag, this was no longer the case in the eighteenth century. Hunting flourished as a socially defining activity, and deer continued to attract pursuers, but the most popular quarry was the fox because it facilitated more regular and more affordable chases. This notwithstanding, cost was still a factor in sustaining organised hunting as an elite pursuit. The maintenance of a pack of dogs and a hunting horse and the remuneration of the stable hands, kennel men, beaters, earthstoppers, etc. necessitated a considerable outlay. This was one of the reasons why the hunt club emerged in the course of the eighteenth century as the defining feature of the sport. As well as assisting the development and maintenance of a hunting infrastructure, it was a means by which the costs associated with hunting were shared. Committed individuals continued to maintain packs of hunting dogs and to organise hunts into the nineteenth century, but the impetus lay with the club, and before the eighteenth century was over, the better circumstanced – the Kilkenny Fox Hunting Club (1797), for example – were fixed features on the local landscape with club houses and a defined social calendar.[2] There was, in short, a financial and organisational logic to the proliferation of hunt clubs, but the story of their emergence and consolidation is also indivisible from that of the burgeoning associational culture that was also a feature of the era. Their near ubiquity further reflected the close links hunting maintained with horse racing, which was the kingdom's most notable organised sport.

The surge in interest in horse racing in Ireland and Britain that can be traced to the Restoration era had taken sufficiently firm root by the early eighteenth century to sustain an identifiable pattern of organised race meetings. The number of identifiable courses was still small at that point, and they were located preponderantly in Leinster and east Ulster. But the structured manner in which the notice of impending meetings was circulated, and in which the 'articles' that governed individual meetings (determining who was eligible to enter, the length and number of heats, the prize money and who functioned as stewards) were readied, was indicative of an activity that was sufficiently firmly rooted by 1731 to justify the contemporary observation that 'horse racing is become a great diversion'.[3] It had certainly arrived at a point where it could embark on a phase of rapid expansion.

Based upon reports which permit the conclusion that the number of racing venues may have grown fivefold, from less than twenty in the years 1701–30 to

---

2 J. Kelly, *Sport in Ireland, 1600–1840* (Dublin: Four Courts Press, 2014), pp. 124–56; M.J. Powell, 'Hunting clubs and societies' in J. Kelly and M.J. Powell (eds.), *Clubs and societies in eighteenth-century Ireland* (Dublin: Four Courts Press, 2010), pp. 392–408.
3 *Dublin Intelligence*, 5 Aug. 1731.

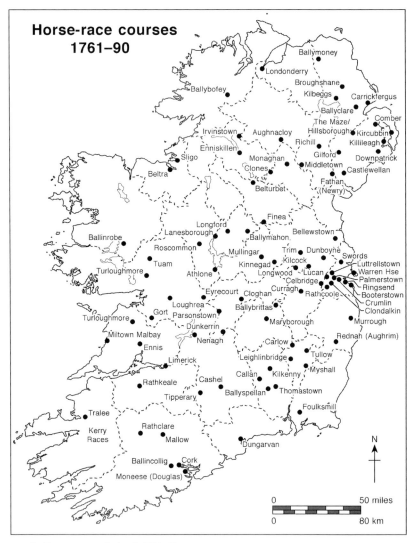

MAP 3. Racecourses, Ireland, 1731–60.

nearly a hundred in the thirty years 1731–60, horse racing was transformed from a regional to a national activity in the mid eighteenth century. Still strongest in Leinster and Munster, but with an identifiable footprint in east Ulster and south Connacht, it failed only to register a definite presence in mid and western Ulster, northern Connacht and the extreme south west (Map. 3).[4] The growth in horse racing was facilitated by a parallel expansion in the circulation of print

4 Kelly, *Sport in Ireland*, pp. 35–43.

(specifically the newspaper) as this was the medium through which race organisers circulated information as to eligibility, prize money, and other matters to prospective entrants and audiences and, once race meetings (which generally extended over four or five days) were underway, communicated results.

The centrality of horse racing to the increasingly structured recreational world of the elite in the eighteenth century is demonstrable from an examination of newspaper notices, datable from the early 1730s onwards, which advised putative spectators that, as well as enjoying racing, they could partake of fox, doe, rabbit, hare or otter hunting and cockfighting during the racing week. The provision of these diversions was a feature of the expanded recreational programmes that race organisers developed to attract an audience that went beyond owners and the discrete bands of aficionados that provided their core audience. With this in mind, it became commonplace to alert prospective attendees to the availability of 'good accommodation' and places to dine. It was, in truth, the minimum required to attract an audience from beyond the immediate locality, and it had the additional merit of involving innkeepers, ostlers and tavern owners, who were the usual providers of these facilities, in the organisation of race days, and by extension of deepening the social pool of likely participants. It was insufficient to attract women and to animate locals for whom racing possessed little appeal, however. They required particular provision, and the staging from the early 1730s of 'plays and assemblies for the diversion of the ladies every night' or, still more commonly, of 'a ball and other diversions' indicates that, by reaching out beyond the men who were the primary audience, the organisers of race meetings contrived to make these events a highlight of the social calendar in many communities.[5] The recreational options available on course possessed less broad appeal to be sure, but once it was recognised that there was money to be made selling alcohol, it became commonplace for race organisers to stipulate, as at Comber, County Down, in 1756, that 'no tent or booth will be allowed on … course without paying' a fee, which varied according to whether the tent or booth specialised in the sale of spirits, wine, beer, ale or cider.[6]

Though there are no specific accounts of the size or social composition of the crowds that attended horse races in the eighteenth century, both the variety of courses and the range of prizes on offer are consistent with the conclusion that participation was not exclusive to the upper classes and their retainers. They may have provided the runners, and have predominated among those present at the courses, both regional and national, that attracted the best horses by providing the highest prizes, but there were so many opportunities

5 *Pue's Occurrences*, 6, 24 June 1732, 17 July, 23 Aug. 1734.
6 *Belfast Newsletter*, 29 July 1756; *Limerick Chronicle*, 15 Aug. 1771.

open to inferior horses to race for small or non-cash prizes that few had good reason to feel excluded from the sport as it grew in the course of the eighteenth century. As a result, it is reasonable to conclude that (other than the exclusive king's plate meetings at the Curragh and the small purse meeting targeted at the populace) most race meetings attracted an audience that spanned the social order. Yet, contrary to legend, the rich, middling sort and poor did not mingle freely on the racecourse, for while the absence of other than the most basic viewing platforms (stands), enclosures and reserved areas outside of the better courses – the Curragh specifically – may have necessitated some social intermixing, the request by the organisers of Limerick races in 1771 'that gentlemen will not entertain during the races' and the provision of a stand 'to accommodate ladies and gentlemen' at Derry in 1773 (for which the price of admission was 1s. 1d.) indicates that social exclusivity persisted.[7]

Its cross-sectoral appeal notwithstanding, the capacity of horse racing to sustain its position as the country's premier sport in the eighteenth century was dependent on its retention of the goodwill of the elite. Signally, this resulted over time in a contraction in the number of locations at which race meetings were held, as landowners reprioritised, and others were obliged by debt to exit the sport.[8] Since there were always owners on the side-lines willing to take their place, a sufficiency of well-wishers forthcoming with money and trophies, punters prepared to bet, and (increasingly) newspapers willing to report on events on (and off) course, the sport remained strong. As well as the factors already mentioned, its success can be ascribed, at least in part, to the fact that it was more organisationally advanced than other recreational activities. It may be that sport was in arrears of the charitable and popular political sectors (both loyalist and patriot), which set the standard in this respect, but the establishment in the late 1740s of the Sportsman's Club, and its evolution over time into the Sportsman's Society culminating in the 1780s in the Turf Club, gave racing an organisational advantage, since attempts by other sports (hunting and cockfighting, for example) to establish comparable organisations were stillborn. It served, certainly, to place horse racing in the vanguard of those sporting pursuits (hunting was next) which were beneficiaries of the social and cultural shift that the emergence of a vigorous associational world fostered.[9] It is not merely coincidental, in other words, that the Sportsman's Club habitually concluded its gatherings with a convivial dinner, or that the Coffee House it constructed in the proximity of

---

7 *Limerick Chronicle*, 15 Aug. 1771; T. Deeney, *History of Ballyarnett Racecourse and the Derry/ Londonderry races* (Ballyarnett: Ballyarnett Books, 2012), p. 29.
8 Kelly, *Sport in Ireland*, pp. 73–100.
9 Kelly and Powell (eds.), *Clubs and societies in eighteenth-century Ireland, passim*.

the Curragh was as much a place of assembly as a place of business. It is easy to ascribe more significance to this, and to the Turf Club (which had modest powers), than it merits, but it was an emblematic recreational feature of the era.

The variety of clubs and societies – commemorative, political, social and, to a lesser extent, recreational – that combined communal dining and business, and the regularity with which elite households entertained, are indicative of the centrality of recreational dining to the life and lifestyle of the elite and, increasingly, the emerging middling sort in the eighteenth century. Taking the domestic arena first, the manner in which Katherine Conolly, the widow of William Conolly (1662–1729), the powerful Speaker of the House of Commons, entertained at Castletown, their grand country residence, provides a retrievable illustration of how this operated in practice; she contrived thereby not only to develop and to maintain bonds with a wide circle of family and friends but also to attempt to perpetuate her authority within her extended circle once her husband was no more.[10] Katherine was happy to host large parties of family and friends, which she did frequently and for extended periods, in keeping with the contemporary practice which meant it was commonplace 'to spende the hollydays' with friends or relations and for visits to last for weeks or even months.[11] While this was important in enabling families and friends to sustain personal relationships, it also dovetailed with the expectation of those invited to participate in a day's hunting, or other social activity; invitations were offered and accepted on the assumption that participants would assemble at four or five o'clock for dinner, and remain at table, eating and drinking for a number of hours, or until they rejoined the women who had left the table earlier. Such occasions lent themselves to over-indulgence, of course, for which the Irish elite acquired a reputation. The observation of George Edward Pakenham after a 'delightful' season hunting in County Westmeath in the 1730s that 'the fox hunters live much after the same manner as in England and drink as hard' cautions against stereotyping the Irish gentry as especially bibulous, but it does not contradict the more numerous reports that the heavy consumption of alcohol was a feature of recreational sociability, and of male recreational sociability particularly.[12] French wine was favoured by the elite, and it can be assumed, based on the volume imported and the available accounts of its consumption, that it was imbibed in amounts that permitted regular inebriation. However, the

---

10 M. Jennings and G.M. Ashford (eds.), *The letters of Katherine Conolly, 1707–47* (Dublin: Irish Manuscripts Commission, forthcoming).

11 Ibid.; Matthew to Fitzwilliam, 26 Dec. 1749; Pembroke Estate papers, 97/46/1/2/5/73, NAI.

12 'Survey of documents in private keeping: Longford papers', *Analecta Hibernica*, 15 (1944), 120; J. Kelly, 'The consumption and sociable use of alcohol in eighteenth-century Ireland', *Proceedings of the Royal Irish Academy*, 115c (2015), 244–9.

infrequency with which reference is made to drunkenness in the home, and the practice whereby 'everyone serves himself as much as he wants', observed in 1783, suggests that it was less commonplace than the highly quotable accounts of excess and the rhetoric of temperance advocates imply.[13]

Moreover, sociability in the home was not dependent on alcohol. The publication from the 1740s of multiple Dublin editions of titles by Edmond Hoyle on backgammon, quadrille, piquet, brag and whist indicates that card playing was a popular option.[14] There was, to be sure, no shortage of moralists ready to condemn card play in the home as a particularly 'detestable vice' in keeping with the prevailing patriarchal assumption that 'odious as it is in a man, [gambling] is still worse in a woman'.[15] Yet the publication in 1790 of an Irish edition of Jacques Ozanam's (1640–1717) *Recreations for gentlemen and ladies*, in which he outlined various 'tricks on cards and dice ... to promote diversion in company', demonstrates that there was another point of view, and that the condemnations rained down on those who enjoyed cards and allied games did not always hit the mark.[16] Dancing, by comparison, was viewed more positively. The existence of 'dancing schools', the inclusion of dancing on the curriculum of some of 'the chief schools' in the country, and the fact that 'dancing masters' in the 1770s and 1780s advertised their availability to wait upon 'gentlemen and ladies ... at their houses in town or country', is illustrative of the social importance afforded this recreational skill and of the effort that went into its acquisition.[17] And this was not all; published guides to 'the most fashionable country dances', minuets and cotillions, selections of 'English, Scotch and Irish songs, catches, duets, medleys, ballads and cantatas', 'solos for the German flute or violin', scores for the harpsichord, and other music tailored for use in the home, point to the importance of music and dancing among the recreations of the elite and, increasingly, the middling sort.[18]

The domestic environment was also the location where reading was pursued; in the words of Eliza Heywood, 'one of the most improving as well

13 Observation of Karl Gottlib Kütter, 1783, in E. Bourke (ed.), *Poor green Erin: German travel writers' narratives on Ireland from before the 1798 Rising to after the Great Famine*, 2nd edn (Frankfurt: Lang, 2013), p. 19.

14 E. Hoyle, *The polite gamester: containing short treatises on the games of whist, quadrille, backgammon, piquet and chess ...* (Dublin: Ewing, 1745).

15 *Hibernian Chronicle* (Cork), 28 April 1785, 8 June 1786.

16 J. Ozanam, *Recreations for gentlemen and ladies: being ingenious sports and pastimes . . .*, 4th edn (Dublin, 1790).

17 *Dublin Evening Journal*, 18 April 1778; *Hibernian Chronicle* (Cork), 8 March 1779, 7 Feb. 1780, 8 Jan. 1781, 31 Jan. 1785.

18 *Limerick Chronicle*, 21 Jan., 4 July 1771, 24 Aug. 1772; *Hibernian Chronicle* (Cork), 23 Nov. 1778, 28 Aug. 1783.

Table 21. *Known English-language titles published in Ireland (main locations), 1750–1800, as a percentage of total number of titles to 1800.*

Location	Total to 1800	Total 1751–1800	Percentage published 1751–1800
Dublin	26,294	15,097	61.5
Belfast	803	583	72.6
Cork	727	603	83
Limerick	118	98	83
Newry	108	197	99
Waterford	80	49	61
Kilkenny	57	18	31.6
Drogheda	33	33	100
Armagh	28	21	75
Derry/Londonderry	27	27	100

Source: English Short Title Catalogue.

as agreeable amusements'.[19] The increased availability of English-language print, demonstrated by the number of surviving titles (Table 21), extended the opportunities for recreational reading, and the eagerness with which these were grasped is clearly signalled by the number of Irish editions of English novels.[20] These largely pirated editions were not all printed for the Irish market, but the advertisement in 1772 by William Whitestone, the proprietor of 'the paper, accompt-book and stationery warehouse' located on Skinner's Row, Dublin, that as well as 'country chapmen's books of every denomination', he stocked 'new entertaining novels, as soon as published', points to a robust local demand.[21] Moreover, it was not only Dublin booksellers who sought to capitalise. The 'catalogue of books' issued by the Limerick printer John Ferrar for circulation in counties Clare, Tipperary and Limerick in the same year included novels by Daniel Defoe, Tobias Smollett, Samuel Richardson, Henry Fielding, Sarah Fielding and other lesser-known authors, volumes of poetry by John Gay, John Dryden, Thomas Parnell, Oliver Goldsmith and Matthew

19 T. Barnard, 'Reading in eighteenth-century Ireland: public and private pleasures' and M. Kennedy, 'Women and reading in eighteenth-century Ireland' in B. Cunningham and M. Kennedy (eds.), *The experience of reading: Irish historical perspectives* (Dublin: Economic and Social History Society, 1999), pp. 60–77, 78–98; G. Meaney, Mary O'Dowd and B. Whelan, *Reading the Irish woman: studies in cultural encounter and exchange, 1714–1960* (Liverpool: Liverpool University Press, 2013), pp. 13–53.
20 R.C. Cole, *Irish booksellers and English writers, 1740–1800* (London: Mansell, 1986).
21 *Limerick Chronicle*, 22 Oct. 1772.

Prior, and a host of adventures, travel books, histories, popular classics and collections of essays aimed at the recreational rather than the serious reader.[22] Interestingly, Ferrar did not include magazines in his catalogue. Possibly he did not stock them, but if so he overlooked an expanding market, as these illustrated compendia of 'entertaining knowledge' were tailored to suit the recreational reader, and the heavy advertisement they were afforded in the press suggests they enjoyed a wide circulation.[23] The key to their success was their thematic range and the variety of subjects addressed therein. Thus readers interested in international affairs were more likely to seek out the *Annual Register* than *Walker's Hibernian Magazine*, which combined politics, gossip and extracts from current publications in a manner Irish readers found appealing, and male readers to look to *Exshaw's Gentleman's and London Magazine* rather than to 'the collections of science, *belles lettres* and history' which was the confection that *Anthologia Hibernica* offered readers over twenty-four issues in the 1790s. What is clear is that the combination of foreign and domestic news, parliamentary reports, memoirs, stories, chronicles, travel accounts, romance, scandal, book extracts, designs, obituaries and marriage notices that was the standard stock in fare, albeit in different proportions, was seldom so rarefied it did not offer something for the perusal of every adult family member.[24] Furthermore, recent investigations of the reading practices of Mary Leadbeater, a Quaker resident at Ballitore, County Kildare, and Eliza McCracken, a Presbyterian residing in Belfast, indicate that women were enthusiastic readers, and that while they did so with the object of self-improvement, they did not confine themselves to 'solid improving books'.[25]

Though the centrality of the domestic environment as a recreational space cannot be gainsaid, much recreational activity required a larger company and a public space. The various parks, residential squares, gardens, pleasure grounds, parades, malls and 'walks' that the eighteenth-century building boom sustained provided endless opportunities for the *beau monde* and the leisured to pursue the fashionable pursuit of promenading. It was a less

---

22 *Ferrar's catalogue of books prints etc* (Limerick, 1772) is printed in *Limerick Chronicle*, 22 Oct., 2 Nov. 1772.

23 See *Freeman's Journal*, 2, 23 Jan. 1773; *Hibernian Chronicle (Cork)*, 13 March 1780, 8 Jan. 1781; *Hibernian Morning Post*, 23 Feb. 1775; *Cork General Advertiser*, 24 April 1777.

24 *Hibernian Magazine*, Feb. 1771; *Walker's Hibernian Magazine*, 1778, 1780; *Exshaw's Gentleman's and London Magazine*, Jan. 1773; *Annual Register*, 1781; *Anthologia Hibernica*, advertised in *Hibernian Journal*, 4 June 1794.

25 M. O'Dowd, 'Mary Leadbeater: modern woman and Irish Quaker' and J.J. Wright, 'Love, loss and learning in late Georgian Belfast: the case of Eliza McCracken' in D.W. Hayton and A.R. Holmes (eds.), *Ourselves alone: religion, society and politics in the eighteenth and nineteenth centuries* (Dublin: Four Courts Press, 2016), pp. 147, 187–9.

genderised and more family-friendly activity than frequenting the coffee houses that were to be encountered in expanding numbers in urban centres across the country. Moreover, 'promenading' better reflected the expansive pattern of sociability that was a feature of the surge in the number of clubs and societies – specifically of dining clubs – that the appreciating appeal of association promoted. It could be countered, based on the example of the Bar Club, a dining club of mainly junior barristers that met in Dublin during legal term between the 1770s and 1790s, that these bodies simply supplied bibulous males with the opportunity to get drunk in congenial company, but the fact that loyalist, patriot and radical political clubs were no less likely than hunt clubs, the Freemasons, friendly societies and others to integrate dining into their proceedings, and that many sought actively to discourage excessive consumption, demonstrates that the recreational and the purposeful aspects of associational life were not disconnected activities.[26] Not all clubs and societies combined work and play of course, but many did, and the fact that bodies as diverse as the Patriot clubs, the Free Citizens of Dublin, the Volunteers, the Order of the Monks of St Patrick, and the Whig Club sustained this *modus operandi* over four decades points to the conclusion that this was recreation with a purpose.[27] These gatherings served to bind individuals into groups and, as is exemplified by the practice of drinking toasts, provided the membership (and the wider public when they were published) with a tableau of easily remembered slogans around which they could unite.[28] The best-known bodies of this kind functioned in the political realm, and often in the vanguard of those demanding change, but the importance of regular communal dining in solidifying the ranks of the ultra-loyalist 'True Blue County of Tipperary Club', which was committed to upholding Protestant values and encouraging conversion to the Church of Ireland in the 1760s and 1770s, illustrates that recreational dining was not reserved to those who advocated reform.[29] Conservatives gathered for the same purpose, and with the same result.

This was equally true of the political elite whose lives rotated around Dublin Castle and Parliament House. The centrality of dining to the political

26 See J. Kelly, 'The Bar Club, 1787–93: a dining club case study' and M.J. Powell, ' "Beef, claret and communication": convivial clubs in the public sphere, 1750–1800', both in Kelly and Powell (eds.), *Clubs and societies in eighteenth-century Ireland*, pp. 353–92.

27 B. Harris, 'The Patriot clubs of the 1750s', M.J. Powell, 'The Society of Free Citizens and other popular political clubs', and James Kelly, 'Elite political clubs, 1770–1800' in Kelly and Powell (eds.), *Clubs and Societies in eighteenth-century Ireland*, pp. 224–89; above p. 472.

28 Kelly, 'The consumption and sociable use of alcohol', pp. 251–4; M.J. Powell, 'Political toasting in eighteenth-century Ireland', *History*, 91 (2006), 508–29.

29 *Limerick Chronicle*, 14, 17, 21 Jan., 25 Feb., 25 March, 25 April, 23 May 1771.

life of Ireland was famously highlighted by the remark of Edward Cooke, the powerful under-secretary, in October 1798 that the plan to bind the kingdoms of Great Britain and Ireland in a legislative union would have to be 'drunk up' as well as 'written up, spoken up, intrigued up ... and bribed up' if it was to be implemented.[30] Cooke's remark was informed by years of observing chief secretaries and lords lieutenant, and the usefulness of sociable dining in enabling them to forge a working majority in the House of Commons, but he might also have noted that it served a broader purpose. The public was disposed to look favourably upon a lord lieutenant who recognised the value of entertaining as well as public spectacle, and while none of the hoi polloi ever attended a 'vice-regal banquet', a 'grand dinner' followed by dancing, a fancy dress 'gala', or a 'concert and supper' at Dublin Castle, these events generated an impression that extended well beyond the ranks of those who were present.[31] They also underlined the enduring importance of the court as a sponsor of recreation in the capital and, to a lesser extent, in other cities and garrison towns, since royal birthdays and military and naval victories were occasions of cheer and celebration across the island during the eighteenth century.[32]

Next to the Curragh racecourse, the theatre was the primary recreational beneficiary of the patronage of the vice-regal court, for though it was a site of contention on occasion, the preparedness of lords lieutenant in the 1730s and 1740s to command as many as fifty performances, and for their successors to attend on red letter days such as the anniversary of William of Orange's birthday, assured the theatre a public profile that no other recreational site possessed. It did not mean, by comparison with musical venues or, later, places of assembly, that Dublin and the other main urban centres in the kingdom were well supplied with bespoke theatrical venues, or that the recreational fare that was presented to the audience was invariably good. But the Dublin winter theatre season was a high point in the recreational year, and John Greene's exhaustive calendars of performances in the capital between 1720 and 1780 indicate that the Anglophone public had plenty to choose from.[33] Greene's arresting calculation that between 1,700 and 2,000 'patrons would have had

---

30 Cooke to Auckland, 27 Oct. 1798, Sneyd papers, T3229/2/37, Public Record Office of Northern Ireland.
31 *Hibernian Chronicle (Cork)*, 22 March 1784; *Freeman's Journal*, 27 Jan. 1791.
32 S.J. Connolly, 'Ag deanamh *commanding*: elite responses to popular culture, 1660–1850' in J.S. Donnelly and K.A. Miller (eds.), *Irish popular culture, 1650–1850* (Dublin: Irish Academic Press, 1998), pp. 17–18; *Hibernian Chronicle (Cork)*, 30 May 1782, 27 May 1784.
33 J.C. Greene and G.L.H. Clark, *The Dublin stage, 1720–1745: a calendar of plays, entertainments and afterpieces* (Bethlehem, PA: Lehigh University Press, 1993); J.C. Greene, *Theatre in Dublin, 1745–1820: a calendar of performances*, 6 vols. (Bethlehem, PA: Lehigh University Press, 2011).

to attend each night ... for the theatres to survive financially' also indicates that the theatre-going audience extended well beyond the elite, and the provision of separate low-cost seating for tradesmen and servants was one of the practical consequences.[34] Reports of full houses in the 1780s and early 1790s also indicate that audience interest in drama may not have fluctuated as dramatically as it did in music, where Italian grand opera and English ballad and comic opera competed for favour. There were also 'grand concerts', and music to dance to, which reinforces the conclusion that there was plenty of variety.[35] Moreover, though the choice was richest in the metropolis, the development in the 1730s and 1740s of a summer touring circuit provided the populations of Cork, Limerick, Waterford, Kilkenny, Drogheda, Newry and Belfast with access to theatrical performance prior to the emergence of provincial venues. Cork was the first; Limerick followed some time afterwards; both were heavily reliant on the charitable benefit to attract an audience.

Though resort to the benefit performance can be traced back at least to the 1730s in Dublin, the enduring appeal of this theatrical form was more visible in the provinces later in the century, when it dovetailed with the philanthropic impulse that had surged in the interval. Benefits on behalf of named individuals in the theatrical world continued to be staged, but in Cork, for example, they encountered increased competition in the 1780s from charitable bodies such as the House of Industry and the Cork Society for the Relief and Discharge of Persons Confined for Small Debts.[36] More pertinently, the emergence of assembly rooms in provincial centres provided a more flexible space with greater audience appeal. It is notable, for example, that the North and South Charitable Infirmaries, which were among the most active charities in Cork in the 1780s, held their annual fancy dress ball in the Great Assembly Room in the city, while the North Infirmary benefited from a drum (or social gathering) held at the same location every Thursday.[37]

Provincial assembly rooms served a multiplicity of functions. They provided those who did not have the resources or reason to take a townhouse in Dublin with an accessible recreational facility, equivalent to the Ranelagh Gardens and the Public Rooms on Rutland Square in Dublin,

34 J.C. Greene, *Theatre in Dublin, 1745–1820: a history*, 2 vols. (Bethlehem, PA: Lehigh University Press, 2011), vol. I, p. 508; C. Morash, *A History of Irish theatre, 1601–2000* (Cambridge: Cambridge University Press, 2002), p. 35.
35 *Hibernian Chronicle (Cork)*, 14 April 1785, 2 Oct. 1786; *Dublin Morning Post*, 5 July 1791.
36 *Hibernian Chronicle (Cork)*, 22 Oct., 3 Nov. 1778, 20 Sept. 1781, 23 Sept. 1782.
37 *Hibernian Chronicle (Cork)*, 4 Nov. 1779, 6 Oct., 14 Dec. 1780, 4 April 1782, 30 Jan., 3 March, 1 Dec. 1783.

and a programme of drums (ordinary and subscription), assemblies, concerts, balls and other occasions during which they could socialise with their peers. Moreover, because the cost was within the compass of the 'middling sort', and admission was permitted to anyone who paid the required fee and behaved properly, assembly rooms served both to assist the upwardly mobile to follow in the path of their betters, and to foster the attitudinal convergence of the elite and the middling sort that gathered pace in the late eighteenth century. They were assisted in this, moreover, by the willingness of successive lords lieutenant to endorse such gatherings when they had a charitable purpose and, in the case of the Public Rooms in Dublin, by making it known in advance when they would grace the venue with their presence.[38] Comparable promises from local eminences carried less weight. Yet the centrality of assembly rooms to the recreational world of Kilkenny, Youghal, Mallow, Armagh and Ennis, as well as Cork, Limerick and Dublin, and the use elsewhere of halls and court houses, contributed to the changing nature of recreational patterns as the eighteenth century drew to a close. By then much of what was once exclusive to the elite was now shared. It is this which makes the assemblies and drums at which people paid to dance, dine, play cards and pursue other recreations, and to intermix and be seen, more than ordinarily socially significant. The impact of the commitment to respectability that facilitated this was to leave a still deeper impression in the nineteenth century, as the assault on popular recreational habits that was already underway intensified.

Popular Recreations under Pressure

By comparison with the habits of the elite, the recreational activity of the populace in the eighteenth century is more resistant to reconstruction. It was not as diverse or as extensive as that which has been identified for England by R.W. Malcolmson, and the fact that the sports played possessed distinctively regional distributions cautions against assuming that those pursuits that have been located, and described, were embraced equally across the island. It was certainly the case that the recreational worlds of the elite, 'middling sort' and populace functioned largely independently each of the other, though there were, as already mentioned, a number of shared activities, and others that

---

38 Both the Earl of Westmorland and Earl Fitzwilliam attended 'assemblies' in the 'Public Rooms, Rutland Square' in support of the Lying-In Hospital: *Dublin Morning Post*, 9 March 1790; *Freeman's Journal*, 3 Feb. 1795.

were pursued after a parallel fashion by elements of the elite, middling sort and populace.

Recreational consumption is a case in point. There is little evidence to suggest, major rites of passage apart, that the populace engaged in communal dining in a manner comparable to the elite and middling sort in the eighteenth century, but they did engage extensively in the communal consumption of alcohol. There were certainly plenty of venues in which to do so. John Rutty's familiar computation that there were 300 taverns, 2,000 alehouses and 1,200 brandy shops in Dublin in 1749 does seem inflated (it would correspond to a ratio of one outlet to some thirty-five people), but comparable assertions that there were '240 dram shops' in Limerick in 1790, and '500 alehouses and taverns in Cork' in 1806, and that 'almost every house' on the Belturbet–Enniskillen road sold 'aquavitae or whiskey' in the 1740s are consistent with the conclusion that there was no shortage of drinking venues.[39] Moreover, the prevalence of reports of illicit distillation and of alcohol smuggling strongly suggests that alcohol was also actively consumed in the home. Certainly the bottle was reached for as a matter of course when important domestic events were being marked, and though the connection is not explicitly drawn, it is difficult to imagine that it was not integral also to the enjoyment of the ordinary gatherings that were commonplace throughout the country at which music (played by 'a piper or blind fiddler') and dancing were central. Indeed, it may be suggested, based on the observations of Arthur Young and others, that dancing was so 'very general among the poor people' that it was the most common recreational pursuit pursued by the populace.[40] Dancing was certainly as integral as drinking to the merriment that drew people in droves to celebrate the anniversaries associated with local saints (the pattern), to major fairs such as that held annually at Donnybrook on the outskirts of Dublin city, and to the monthly fairs and markets where, as well as buying and selling, people availed themselves of the recreational opportunity on offer.[41] And this was not all. The observation of Shrove Tuesday and Mayday, and days particular to municipalities, such as Cork which long provided for 'two public days of entertainment ... on election and swearing-in days', was strong in many parts of the country. These days were a welcome addition to

---

39 Kelly, 'The consumption and sociable use of alcohol', pp. 243–4.
40 A. Young, *Tour in Ireland*, 2 vols. (London: G. Bell and Sons, 1892), vol. I, p. 446.
41 S.J. Connolly, *Priests and people in pre-Famine Ireland, 1780–1845* (Dublin: Gill and Macmillan, 1982), pp. 135–48; S. Ó Maitiu, *The Humours of Donnybrook: Dublin's famous fair and its suppression* (Dublin: Irish Academic Press, 1995).

Sundays, which, as the only day of the week that 'the peasantry . . . are exempt from labour', was the primary opportunity they had 'to amuse themselves'.[42]

The 'spirit of gaiety', which was what the early nineteenth century travel writer John Carr maintained prevailed in Ireland 'after the hours of devotion' on Sundays, encouraged a variety of recreational activities that the respectable were increasingly prone to characterise as 'a scandal to all religion'.[43] Previously, during the eighteenth century the attitudinal chasm that separated the respectable from the populace was not unbridgeable. Many landlords then possessed a keen sense of the value of fostering good communal recreations, and while few went to the same lengths as the Kingsboroughs, who in the 1780s hosted 'a dinner and dance' annually on Mitchelstown Castle lawn for 'all the women' employed in the local cotton manufacture, the communal celebration of red letter days and rites of passage (the birth of an heir or marriage of the eldest son of the estate owner) is an index of the efforts that were made to ease the legacy of suspicion that divided the ruling elite from the populace.[44] This was a mutable relationship, however, as the history of the engagement of the elite and the populace in sports such as hurling attests.

As one of the country's traditional sports, hurling was long viewed with suspicion by Ireland's ruling elite, and it remained securely anchored in that unpromising space until the 1740s when it was taken up by elements within the gentry and aristocracy. The reasons for this are elusive, but a combination of admiration of the skill of the game that was most marked among the descendants of once major Catholic families, a diminution of the sectarian suspicion that was a legacy of the seventeenth century, the flowing associational tide, and the prospect of financial gain combined to elevate what till then was a local recreational pastime into a regionally vibrant activity. Anchored in a compact core area that encompassed south Leinster, much of Munster and parts of east Connacht, its footprint embraced the counties of Tipperary, Kilkenny, Limerick, Cork, Waterford, east Clare, east Galway, King's County, Queen's County, Kildare, Carlow and Wexford. In addition, the sport was played in the environs of Dublin city, but this was a consequence, first, of the mobility of the rural population that played the game (matches also took place occasionally in London, Paris and New York[45]), and, second,

---

42 *Hibernian Chronicle (Cork)*, 31 Aug. 1786; *Ramsey's Waterford Chronicle*, 16 Oct. 1787.
43 J. Carr, *The stranger in Ireland* (London: R. Phillips, 1806), p. 254.
44 Connolly, 'Ag deanamh *commanding*', p. 18; C.J. Woods (ed.), 'Charles Abbot's tour of Ireland, 1792' (unpublished manuscript).
45 J. Bergin and E. Kinsella, 'Hurling in London (1733–1818) and New York (1781–2)', *Archivium Hibernicum*, 68 (2015), 139–67.

of its attraction as a spectator sport. Indeed, in the wake of the successful hosting of a sequence of four 'grand hurling matches' between teams representing the provinces of Munster and Leinster on Crumlin Common (on the outskirts of Dublin) in 1748 and 1749, and a number of 'exhibitions', including one attended by the lord lieutenant and members of the nobility in 1755, hurling was riding high. The orchestration of an irregular sequence of competitive games involving county teams between the 1750s and 1780s may have encouraged some to conclude that hurling might emulate cricket in England, and successfully make that transition from a local pastime into a structured sport with written rules and a regulatory body, but the failure of a number of initiatives in the 1770s to pay their way, the identification of the sport with violence, and the congenital fear with which the ruling elite regarded any public congregation from the 1790s, proved insuperable obstacles, with the result that the gentry and nobility who had supported it withdrew their patronage and participation. Hurling survived as a popular recreational activity in its traditional heartland, but only as a rural, local peasant sport.[46]

Other popular recreations were pursued in this manner during the eighteenth and early nineteenth centuries. They included commons, an allied ball and stick game played mainly in Ulster; and football, which has left its deepest evidential imprint in north Leinster, and which was a standard pastime of urban artisans who gathered on Sundays on open areas such as Oxmantown Green, the Phoenix Park and other green spaces dotted about the city of Dublin.[47] The fortunes of these sports depended to a considerable extent on the disposition of the elite, and also, as it became an increasingly influential force, on the respectable middling sort. This can be illustrated by the experience of cockfighting, which grew in the space of a few decades in the mideighteenth century from a low-key activity into an organised sport with a near island-wide footprint. Once pursued by individuals with a handful of fighting cocks, it acquired a more visible profile when it was taken up by members of the elite who, following on the practice in England, bred enough birds to warrant the employment of 'feeders' and others expert in their preparation for the cockpit. The object was to present enough birds to sustain a main (for which twenty-one cocks was usual), which (like a race meeting) might last a week. The opening of a 'cock pit royal' on Cork Hill, Dublin in the late 1730s provided the first clear signal of the sport's appeal, for though the personal rivalries that fuelled competition in the middle decades of the

46 Kelly, *Sport in Ireland*, pp. 238–67.
47 Ibid., pp. 274–5, 276, 277.

century ensured the mains involving the country's leading owners were reported in the press, the sport had few champions at that point. This was no longer the case when, following the precedent established in England, teams replaced individuals as the sport's standard bearers. Competitions between 'county' teams emerged first in Leinster, where, as well as the availability of cockpits in Dublin and other locations, the sport profited from its association with horse racing. It was less expensive to pursue than horse racing, moreover, which assisted it to take root in Ulster, and, over a number of decades, to establish an infrastructure that embraced a network of cockpits and competitions at county, barony, town and community level. In common with horse racing, it was reliant on the press – in this instance the *Belfast News Letter* – to communicate news of impending mains, and the diversions that were available to distract audiences during the long intervals that were part and parcel of the manner in which mains were conducted. It also served to generate trust in the rules, which was as essential in this sport as it was in horse racing because of their shared reliance on gambling.[48]

Cockfighting was at its height in Ireland during the middle decades of the eighteenth century, when it was pursued by the elite, by elements of the rural middling sort in Ulster particularly, and by those among the ordinary folk who kept a cock or two which they presented at 'shake bag' competitions in taverns, inns and other places of popular assembly and recreation. This was an inherently unstable complex of interests, however, for though the sport flourished as long as each element was well disposed, it was not destined to last. The fragility of the public's enthusiasm for cockfighting was first manifest in Dublin when, as a consequence of urban development, the cockpit royal was relocated at some remove from the symbolic heart of the city in 1763. This anticipated a contraction in the number of inter-county mains in Leinster, but the disengagement of the respectable in Ulster beginning in the 1780s was of greater consequence. First identifiable in the reduced number of notices of cockfights carried in the *Belfast News Letter*, it achieved greater visibility as the public disquiet mounted at the intimacy of the link between cockfighting and other ostensibly immoral practices – gambling and alcohol consumption most notably.[49] This change in attitude had less visible impact on those who kept a few birds than it had on the network of cockpits and competitions that defined the sport when it was at its peak. They continued to pursue cockfighting in the traditional way into the nineteenth century, but

---

48 Ibid., pp. 157–88.
49 Ibid., pp. 200–3.

the flight from what was for several decades the most vibrant sport in Ulster was a harbinger of the more general retreat of aristocratic mores in the face of the rising tide of respectability that was a defining feature of the shift in the late eighteenth and early nineteenth centuries from an aristocratic to an identifiably bourgeois sensibility.

Moreover, cockfighting was not the only popular recreation to encounter problems of this kind. Bull baiting, bull running and throwing at cocks were venerable urban popular recreations that were subject to intense criticism in the second half of the eighteenth century. It would be misleading to imply, the increasing volume of print objecting to the abuse of animals notwithstanding, that public disquiet at the inherent abusiveness of throwing sticks at cockerels, setting trained dogs on bulls that were tied to a bull ring, and chasing bulls with dogs through the streets of Dublin was what fuelled this criticism. The respectable were increasingly discommoded by accounts of animal abuse, but their criticism of these activities was impelled first and foremost by their unwillingness any longer to accommodate the populace by ceding control of the streets and thoroughfares of the mainly urban locations where they took place. They advanced this line of argument for some time before they were able, with the assistance of municipal officials – mayors, magistrates, sheriffs and justices of the peace – first to force these activities onto the margins, and then, incrementally, to prosecute them out of existence. Throwing at cocks was the first to be eclipsed; bull running followed thereafter, and by the beginning of the nineteenth century bull baiting was in rapid contraction in its surviving urban strongholds.[50]

Abolition was the most dramatic outcome. Other recreations underwent significant but less profound change. The ratification by the Irish parliament in 1790 of legislation proscribing low-value horse races within 9 miles of Dublin Castle, on the grounds that it was wasteful when those concerned could be engaged in productive work, and morally and behaviourally dubious because it encouraged drinking, fighting and other disagreeable behaviour, dealt a blow to popular horse racing. The heightened attendances that were reported at meetings in the capital's hinterland in the immediate aftermath of its proscription demonstrated that the sport did not simply cave in in the face of this onslaught.[51] Yet, the unrelenting verbal assault on 'idlers and vagabonds ... playing and gambling on the [Sabbath] holyday',[52] the ferocious criticism

50 Ibid., pp. 208–33.
51 31 George III, chap 43; Kelly, *Sport in Ireland*, pp. 99–101, 103.
52 *Limerick Chronicle*, 11 May 1772.

directed at dram houses and at whiskey drinking (the 'liquid poison' to which the populace had ready access), the intensified policing of traditional fairs, and holidays such as Mayday and Shrove Tuesday, and the reduced opportunities available for traditional recreational pursuits, demonstrated that the tide was well and truly with the respectable. Indicatively, when the incoming mayor of Cork, Samuel Rowland, proposed in 1786 to 'abolish ... the two public days of entertainment' that traditionally marked the election and swearing in of a new mayor and to assign the money saved to charitable purposes, he was publicly applauded at a meeting of freemen.[53]

Recreational Patterns in the Nineteenth Century: The Triumph of Respectability, Organisation and Mass Participation

The assault on popular recreational practices initiated in the eighteenth century was maintained in the nineteenth. The net effect of this was a further contraction in the range of traditional sports and popular recreations as the forces arrayed against them grew in strength and influence. The increased pervasiveness of reformed religion – both evangelical Protestant and Roman Catholic – was particularly consequential in this respect, as it strengthened the attempt that was underway to eradicate patterns and to regulate festive wakes and allied popular recreations that encouraged alcohol consumption and 'games' that the respectable found repellent.[54] The withdrawal of the Catholic clergy from patterns, the purging of wakes and the embrace of a code of behaviour that esteemed decorum were important milestones for this reason. It was echoed, and energised, by the emergence in the 1830s of an organised temperance movement, spearheaded by Fr Theobald Matthew (1790–1856), which dovetailed with the expanding willingness of the state, through its agents – with the newly established Royal Irish Constabulary to the fore – to police contested recreational practices.

Following the demise of throwing at cocks and bull baiting, the highest-profile sporting casualty was cockfighting, for though the occurrence of 'shake bag' battles in public houses in the early decades of the nineteenth century indicates that it survived the withdrawal of the elite and middling

---

53 R. Loeber and M. Stouthamer-Loeber (eds.), 'Dublin and its vicinity in 1797', *Irish Geography*, 35:2 (2002), 247; *Hibernian Chronicle*, 31 Aug. 1786.
54 Connolly, *Priests and people in pre-Famine Ireland*, pp. 152–6; D. Ó Giollain, 'The pattern' and G. Ó Crualaoich, 'The merry wake' in Donnelly and Miller (eds.), *Irish popular culture*, pp. 201–21, 173–200.

sort, it was subsequently forced underground by the decision of parliament to make the sport illegal in 1835.[55] Road bowls was another casualty of the assumption by the authorities of the responsibility of policing public spaces. This led inevitably to the curtailing of the practice, long accommodated, of playing sports and games on the streets and in open areas. Moreover, as the commitment to regulation acquired increased traction, there was greater willingness to intervene to regulate fairs and allied gatherings, culminating in the symbolically significant closure in 1855 of Donnybrook fair.[56] Other popular recreations also endured testing times. The loss of elite patronage encouraged critics who were repelled by the violence associated with hurling, which persisted as a popular regional recreation, prompting calls in the 1850s and 1860s for its suppression.[57] Pugilism also experienced problems. The image of this popular gladiatorial pursuit, which was largely conducted in public spaces in the last quarter of the eighteenth century, was boosted in the early nineteenth century by the deeds of the Irish 'champions' Dan Donnelly and John Langan, and an attempt was made to develop it into a more structured activity. This undertaking was partly successful, but it was not sustained, and the reversion in the 1830s to the brutal street contests that were commonplace in the 1780s reflected a sport that had regressed.[58] As a result, pugilism, like hurling, remained vulnerable to its critics until the elaboration in the 1860s of the Queensbury rules provided it with a lifeline.[59]

The early nineteenth century was, as a transitional era, a challenging time for various recreations. Even horse racing, which was the most successful and organised sport, experienced problems, as an ill-conceived attempt to establish a number of Irish 'classics' on the English model in the late 1810s, along with internal disputes that racked the Turf Club, prompted a haemorrhage of members.[60] There was a contraction also in the number of courses, though this did not cause permanent damage as the sport sustained an appeal that crossed social class. 'The city of tents' that Johann Kohl encountered at Kilkenny races in 1844 'where every earthly desire an Irishman could form might be gratified' even suggests that racing may have profited from

---

55 Kelly, *Sport in Ireland*, pp. 205–6; *Leinster Independent*, 9 July 1836.
56 Kelly, *Sport in Ireland*, pp. 340–3; Ó Maitiu, *Humours of Donnybrook, passim*.
57 P. Rouse, *Sport and Ireland: a history* (Oxford: Oxford University Press, 2015), pp. 91–8.
58 See the observation of Frederick von Raumer in 1835 in Bourke (ed.), *German travel writers' narratives*, pp. 247–8.
59 Kelly, *Sport in Ireland*, pp. 288–308.
60 F.A. D'Arcy, *Horses, lords and racing men: the Turf Club, 1790–1990* (The Curragh: Turf Club, [1991]), pp. 64ff.

the increased surveillance of fairs and patterns.[61] It certainly contributed to attendances in the tens of thousands at meetings across the country in the 1820s and 1830s, and to the preparedness of those who knew little of 'the fame of the horses' that ran at the Curragh, Kilkenny or other established courses to pay a shilling in 1837 for admission to the 'stand house' to watch ponies race in Dublin's Cobourg Gardens, and to attend local meetings when, as at Lucan, also in 1837, horses entered in 'hack races' competed for a 'bridle and saddle'.[62] Yet, success was not assured. The ability of an Anti-Race Committee in Derry/Londonderry, driven by the evangelical belief that horse racing was contrary to 'the general interests of good order and morality' and an induce-ment to the 'ungodliness that is fruitful in vice of all kinds', to put an end to racing at Ballyarnett racecourse in the late 1830s, helped to explain its con-traction over much of Ulster.[63] Yet, if this was a manifestation of 'the prevail-ing indifference to public amusements' identified in County Londonderry by the author of the Ordnance Survey memoir, it was not uncontested, and the resumption of horse racing at Ballyarnett in 1860 attested to the enduring appeal of the country's premier sport. As a result, horse racing contrived, when it overcame its internal organisational difficulties after the Great Famine, to attract even larger attendances to its network of established and better-appointed new courses. It came at the price of increased social segrega-tion on the racecourse, and at the 'race balls' and suppers that were now an integral feature of race weeks up and down the country.[64]

The social separation that was a feature of racing was still more in evidence in the hunt club, though in other respects hunting was illustrative of a trend which saw the club consolidate its position as the foundation unit of sporting organisation. With a grand total of sixty-six mounted hunt packs in 1875, and one at least in every county, fox and deer hunting was sufficiently popular to justify the publication by the *Freeman's Journal* of a detailed schedule of hunts, with the date and location of when and where they were due to take place.[65] In addition, though hunting embraced a wide variety of less structured activity – shooting, trapping and netting – which also increased in the course of the

61 Johann Georg Kohl, *Ireland: Dublin, the Shannon, Limerick, Cork and the Kilkenny races …* (London: Chapman and Hall, 1844), pp. 114–15.

62 *Freeman's Journal*, 5, 9 May 1837.

63 Deeney, *History of Ballyarnett Racecourse*, pp. 165–6.

64 D'Arcy, *Horses, lords and racing men*, pp. 188–205; Deeney, *History of Ballyarnett Racecourse*, pp. 98, 162–3, 181.

65 K. Theodore Hoppen, *The mid-Victorian generation, 1846–86* (Oxford: Oxford University Press, 1998), p. 358.

nineteenth century, organised fox chases such as that engaged in by the lord lieutenant, Earl Spencer, and the Kilkenny Hunt in December 1870 reinforced the reputation for exclusivity that membership of a hunt club brought with it and that the hunt ball extended into the recreational sphere. Though accepted by many as a manifestation of the natural order of things, the elitism of equine sport was not without consequence, as the emergence of a distinctly anti-hunt movement during the Land War in the 1880s highlighted the negative outcome for the sport of the chasm that had emerged between hunt clubs and the population at large.[66]

Hunting apart, the club played an increasingly important role in the structured development of organised sport. The nineteenth century witnessed a dramatic growth in the number of bespoke clubs, which facilitated a variety of activities to make the transition from inchoate or disaggregated practices into definably modern sports. Athletics is a case in point, as the foundation of athletics clubs, beginning in the 1860s, provided a structure whereby races for wagers and tests of strength and endurance gave way to structured competitions. Rowing, yachting, fencing, gymnastics, coursing and, in the final decades of the century, cycling, lawn tennis and golf were also organised on club lines.[67] The appeal of fishing, which attracted a host of literary champions during the nineteenth century, and billiards, which sustained a network of public billiard rooms across the century, demonstrated that a structure such as the club provided was not a prerequisite for a sport to take root. This remained the case with individual pursuits; the situation was otherwise with respect to collective or team recreations.

The earliest illustration of the suitability of the club to the development of team sport was provided by cricket. Building upon shallow foundations put in place in the 1820s and 1830s, and capitalising upon a sense of Britishness that then possessed broad appeal, cricket expanded rapidly beyond its original class and ethnic boundaries during the middle decades of the nineteenth century. Partisan claims were advanced in the 1880s suggesting that the success of cricket was due to the fact that it transcended 'social distinction [and] politics and religious differences', but this is to exaggerate.[68] The eclipse of various 'low' sports, and the stagnation or decline of others, hurling and

---

66 *Leinster Express*, 3 Dec. 1870; L.P. Curtis, 'Stopping the hunt, 1881–1882: an aspect of the Irish Land War' in C.H.E. Philpin (ed.), *Nationalism and popular protest in Ireland* (Cambridge: Cambridge University Press, 1987), pp. 349–402.

67 Rouse, *Sport and Ireland*, pp. 135–41; Kelly, *Sport in Ireland*, pp. 330–3.

68 The words are those of Arthur Samuels, Irish cricket's first historian: quoted in Rouse, *Sport and Ireland*, p. 119.

cockfighting notably, combined with the transmission of the game by students educated at English public schools and military men to create a space that cricket and hand ball could occupy. Indeed, the brief *floruit* of the ball alley and ball court during the middle decades of the century suggests that cricket may have expanded from the elite circles it initially occupied to fill the vacuum handball left during the 1860s and 1870s when cricket was at its most vibrant. It is hardly coincidental that it was at this point also that the Irish Football Union (1874), which became the representative body for rugby, and the Irish Football Association (1880), which assumed responsibility for soccer, were established.[69] The era of modern team sports was taking shape.

The fact that the amateur ethic that team sports embraced sat easily with the culture of respectability associated with the 'middling sort' is consistent with the increasingly bourgeois character of sport and recreation in the second half of the nineteenth century. It was by no means all embracing, however. The landed elite was still sufficiently firmly entrenched to sustain its own discrete recreational realm (witness the network of residential and social clubs in Dublin and regional towns, and the elitist character of the Dublin season). The populace too sustained a recreational world anchored in music, dance, story and the traditional calendar in the countryside, and the public house, and its antithesis the temperance hall which provided a venue for brass bands, in urban areas.[70] But the norms were increasingly set by the middle ranks and they assumed an increasingly prominent presence in the landscape. These included masonic halls, citizens clubs and social clubs of various kinds, temperance and total abstinence clubs, 'young men's' society venues, literary clubs, reading rooms (repeal and others), learned societies, the premises of intellectual societies devoted to the promotion of science, the arts, history and archaeology, and myriad voluntary bodies, which hosted meetings, lectures and performances committed to improvement, advancement and edifying recreation. These are all important, and insufficiently well known, but the extent to which recreational life answered to the mood of the middling sort can be demonstrated still more clearly by the manner in which in the second half of the nineteenth century the growth of the music hall embraced the upwardly mobile working class within the realm of respectability.

The emergence in the nineteenth century of what Christopher Morash has identified as a 'national theatre' represented a shift in direction away from

---

69 Rouse, *Sport and Ireland*, pp. 129–33.
70 Bourke (ed.), *German travel writers' narratives*, pp. 93–4, 142; J. Borgonovo, 'Politics as leisure: brass bands in Cork, 1845–1918' in L. Lane and W. Murphy (eds.), *Leisure and the Irish in the nineteenth century* (Liverpool: Liverpool University Press, 2016), pp. 23–40.

the anglicised theatrical world that flourished in Dublin in the eighteenth century.[71] A majority of the plays and performances presented on the Irish stage continued to originate in England, notwithstanding, and traditional 'high culture' was not forsaken. The Theatre Royal included 'Italian opera' on its programme in the 1860s, while the Philharmonic Society (1826–79), which maintained concert rooms in Brunswick Street, presented a season of 'grand concerts' for many years.[72] However, these offerings were not what drew the majority of the concert-going audience, and the development of musical theatre and its evolution into music hall offers a clearer perspective on the increasingly bourgeois nature of musical entertainment and of the audience to which it appealed.

Following a number of false starts, the opening of the 'New Music Hall' on Lower Abbey Street, Dublin in February 1841 was received as a major addition to the city, which was then without a dedicated large 'concert room'. With a reputed capacity of 'about 4,000', the venue was certainly commodious, and the positive public response to the mix of concerts, 'vocal and instrumental', and 'entertainments illustrative of the national music of Ireland' that Robert J. Mackintosh, the hall's 'enterprising manager', presented suggests that there was a healthy cross-section of society able to pay 3 shillings for admission to the 'dress circle' and £1 11s. 6d. for a private box (which held fifteen guests).[73] There were signs, however, even before the testing economic environment of the late 1840s took its toll, that the 'Music Hall' was experiencing difficulties. Mackintosh responded by adapting the programme; he booked 'Ioway [*sic*] Indians' (whose performance embraced 'war dances, war songs … and … feats of archery') in 1845, and a troupe of 'danseuses Viennoises' in 1846; he staged a 'monster' concert featuring 'upwards of two hundred military wind instruments' in 1847 and, when it was apparent that they appealed as much to white Irish audiences as they did to their British and American peers, groups of 'negro minstrels'.[74] Though the inherent racism of the presentation of minstrels as 'Ethiopian serenaders' is still more revealing of the nature of the Music Hall's audience than its fascination with all things American, the inability of the venue to attract full houses during the 1850s meant it failed to 'resume its former position amongst the fashionable places of resort'.[75]

71 Morash, *A history of Irish theatre*, pp. 67–93.
72 *Freeman's Journal*, 1 June 1847, 5 Dec. 1861, 11 Dec. 1865.
73 *Freeman's Journal*, 3 Feb. 1841, 5 Jan., 16 Feb. 1842, 23 Feb. 1844; *Kerry Examiner*, 14 Feb. 1843.
74 *Freeman's Journal*, 13 March 1845, 9 Sept. 1846, 25 Dec. 1847.
75 *Freeman's Journal*, 26 Oct. 1846, 16, 24 March 1847, 16 March 1855, 3 Dec. 1857; *Belfast News Letter*, 20, 23 April 1847.

In an attempt to compete with the various crowd-pleasing entertainments – dioramas, panoramas, exhibitions, lectures, dramatic readings, flower shows, magic and illusion, equestrian performances, waxworks, circuses, acrobatic displays, comedy, concerts and plays – that the regular theatre, the Rotundo and other venues offered in Dublin, Belfast and elsewhere, the Hall presented a series of 'peoples' concerts' in 1857, but this proved no more successful. Unable 'to secure first-class artistes', this experiment in 'cheap concerts' cut little ice with the predominantly bourgeois theatre-going city audience.[76] As a result, when in December 1861 the *Freeman's Journal* presented the public with a menu of 'Christmas amusements', the Music Hall did not feature among the list of venues whose programmes embraced pantomime (at the Theatre Royal and Queen's Royal Theatre), 'a most interesting performance in natural magic' (at the Rotundo), and a lecture on 'electro biology' that combined 'instruction with amusement'.[77]

Having failed to pay its way as a respectable venue, the Music Hall served as a 'mechanics music hall' for a time until it was rebranded as 'the people's music hall' in the late 1860s, in which capacity it ostensibly targeted a largely 'working-class' audience.[78] But if its combination of competitive pricing and its menu of 'singing, dancing and juggling' was directed at those of modest incomes, it marketed itself as a bastion of bourgeois values. Hence, the assertion by its 'sole proprietor', G. Steele, in 1867 that he aspired 'to supply a want long felt by a large and respectable portion of the community – viz, to enjoy a pleasant evening at a small charge without being obliged to pay for intoxicating liquor' – echoed that of St Patrick's Music Hall (subsequently the 'city music hall of varieties') three years later. Then it was claimed that the Maryland Minstrels could be enjoyed by all: 'there is not a trace or shade of vulgarity mixed up with their mirthful and versatile entertainment, whilst nothing is offered in word, look, or action that can in the least degree offend the most fastidious taste'.[79] It was not a claim that every music hall, and they were to be found in Cork and Belfast as well as Dublin by the 1860s, chose to make, but it illustrated the extent to which respectability had penetrated mass consciousness. There were, to be sure, some who maintained that 'the music hall tribe ... were ... entirely destitute of any claim to musical talent', but the observation printed in the *Cork Examiner* in 1869 that 'the music hall has now

---

76 *Freeman's Journal*, 31 July 1857, 3 Sept. 1866.
77 *Freeman's Journal*, 24 Dec. 1861.
78 *Freeman's Journal*, 13 Feb. 1865, 5 Oct. 1867.
79 *Freeman's Journal*, 5 Oct., 30 Nov., 3 Dec. 1867, 5 Feb. 1870. St Patrick's Music Hall was located on Capel Street.

become a distinct and firmly-established class of entertainment' was more accurate and more perceptive.[80] The era of the variety show was underway. The public had to wait another decade before its most famous Irish exponent, Dan Lowrey, established his first music hall in Dublin in 1879. At first, 'nice people' chose to stay away, but their reserve was not sustained, and the success of Lowrey's initiative demonstrated that, in the world of recreation as well as in sport, the nineteenth century closed with bourgeois values in the ascendant.[81]

Conclusion

The argument advanced by J.H. Plumb that late eighteenth- and early nineteenth-century England witnessed the 'emergence of a commercial leisure industry responding to a bourgeois desire to emulate the existing minority culture of the elite' cannot be transferred easily to Ireland.[82] Yet Ireland, like England, did evolve from a position in the eighteenth century when the aristocratic elite determined what sports and recreations were esteemed, and shaped the manner in which they were pursued. Though it was seldom referred to at the time, and it has not featured high on the historical agenda since, the weakening social ascendancy of the aristocracy as a consequence of the emergence of a more broadly based emphasis on respectability had a formative effect on recreational and sporting pursuits, even if its impact on aristocratic behaviour was mixed. Some pastimes and pursuits – horse racing, assemblies and social dining most notably – that were already firm fixtures on the sporting and recreational landscape continued hardly altered. Others such as real tennis disappeared, or, like the sport of lawn bowls, which was played on public greens in most towns and cities for more than a hundred years spanning the seventeenth and eighteenth centuries, survived behind the barrier of the demesne wall. The pattern of popular recreation was not altogether different, as games and recreations that were once commonplace either disappeared or, like hurling, endured and were to flourish in a modernised form in the era of the club and mass attendance that was still in its infancy as the nineteenth century drew to a close. In the main, the sports and recreations

---

80 *Tuam Herald*, 27 June 1868; *Cork Examiner*, 20 Sept. 1869.

81 E.R. Watters, *Infinite variety: Dan Lowrey's Music Hall, 1879–1897* (Dublin: Gill and Macmillan, 1975).

82 J.H. Plumb, 'The commercialization of leisure' in N. McKendrick, J. Brewer and J.H. Plumb, *The birth of a consumer society: the commercialization of eighteenth-century England* (London: Hutchinson, 1983), pp. 265–85; Rule, 'Popular recreation', p. 219.

favoured by the respectable fared better because, in Ireland as in England, they reflected the values of the combination of the elite, the middling sort and the improving artisans that constituted the respectable in the nineteenth century, and which, as the example of the music hall demonstrates, continued to grow in size and influence. The process whereby what is known as bourgeois values achieved ascendancy in Ireland was thus more prolonged than that identified by Plumb for England; it was also more complex because it possessed a religious dimension that has been insufficiently addressed here. Yet when all is said and done, because it answered to larger, international, trends and tendencies, the outcome bears comparison to what happened in England in the round if not in every particular.

19

Bourgeois Ireland, or, on the Benefits of Keeping One's Hands Clean

CIARAN O'NEILL

Introduction

Who and what was the Irish bourgeoisie? When did it emerge, when were its peak years, and what are its main features? The 'expanding middle class' is a phrase that has been invoked by historians of Europe in the sixteenth, seventeenth and eighteenth centuries and it is as elusive a concept as this broad chronological range would suggest. Indeed, there are some who dispute its very existence.[1] It sometimes seems as if the middle classes are at all times expanding or 'emerging', and this presents a problem for historians in general, not only those concerned with Ireland.[2]

It is odd that we should separate the Irish bourgeoisie from its European counterparts, or indeed treat it as somehow separate from the complex 'social imaginary' of British society. And yet it is equally unacceptable that we should ignore what is distinctive about the Irish manifestation of this elusive and ill-defined social stratum. Much ink has been spilled on the differences and similarities between what the English term the 'middle classes', what the French call the *bourgeoisie* and what is known in Germany as the *bürgertum* or *bürgerlich*, never mind how these social categories translate into a global context.[3] Recently scholars of the subject have sought to distance themselves from

---

1 T. Munck, *Seventeenth-century Europe: state, conflict and social order in Europe 1598–1700*, 2nd edn (Basingstoke: Palgrave Macmillan, 2005), chapter 5; S.C. Maza, *The myth of the French bourgeoisie: an essay on the social imaginary, 1750–1850* (Cambridge, MA: Harvard University Press, 2003).

2 I follow W.H. Crawford and others in using 'middle classes' rather than the more limiting 'middle class', or 'middling sort'; see J. Wright, *The natural leaders and their world: politics, culture and society in Belfast, c.1801–1832* (Liverpool: Liverpool University Press, 2012), pp. 8–12.

3 J. Kocka and A. Mitchell (eds.), *Bourgeois society in nineteenth-century Europe* (Oxford: Berg, 1993); J. Kocka, *Industrial culture and bourgeois society: business, labor, and bureaucracy in modern Germany* (New York: Bergahn, 1999); J. Siegel, *Modernity and bourgeois life: society, politics, and culture in England, France and Germany since 1750* (Cambridge: Cambridge University Press, 2012).

the dominant interpretative tradition that sees the middle classes expanding from a western European base via the Anglo world, driving modernity in the process, and franchising a Eurocentric 'progress' that was embraced and replicated by the 'developing' world.[4] The middle classes of any society did not grow at a steady or predictable pace, and they do not replicate according to a set model. Nonetheless, it seems clear enough that we can identify the nineteenth century as the bourgeois century *par excellence* and that this is also true of Ireland, and the Irish bourgeoisie. It was the moment when the educated and polished middle classes reigned supreme, having finally wrested control of the poor from the rich through control of philanthropy, charity and education, and in the process usurped the asset-rich and landed as the natural governors of society. The structural and societal change that resulted owed much to the rise of capitalist economics, a way of seeing the world that popularised ideas of the potentially positive outcomes of competition for resources as well as meritocratic principles. Though important, these economic ideologies will only be alluded to in this chapter, which concentrates on the social consequences of structural and demographic change. Before engaging with these matters it is imperative first that we address a more basic question: who in its Irish context are the people we term the bourgeoisie, and can we define the constituent elements of a bourgeois identity?

Becoming Bourgeois

Most scholars of bourgeois society in the nineteenth century have argued that bourgeois identity can only be understood as a culture or way of being with which an individual might want to identify. In other words, it is considered either a lived or aspirational category for most of the people we might include in it. In this chapter we will locate the Irish bourgeoisie very much in the classic way, in the European and imperial context in which it expands, and according to occupational category and social interactions.

In a recent work Franco Moretti has isolated distinctive features of the bourgeois value system as it emerged in western cultures from the eighteenth century, and provided a formulation that can usefully be placed alongside G.M. Young's classic articulation of Victorian bourgeois identity in his essay *Portrait of an age* (1936). Together, they can take us closer to defining what we mean by bourgeois Ireland. Young's interpretation is a useful point of

---

4 A. Ricardo López and B. Weinstein (eds.), *The making of the middle class: toward a transnational History* (Durham, NC: Duke University Press, 2012), pp. 5–8.

departure, as it highlights some of the reasons why a predominantly Catholic, socially underdeveloped and altogether lesser partner in the 'Union' of Great Britain and Ireland produced a similar but different bourgeois code from that of its neighbours. On the basis of the English experience that was his focus, Young maintained that an evangelical discipline underpinned the Victorian code of 'respectability' that defined the middle classes. The rigid stability of early modern society, reductively personified by 'a nobleman, a gentleman, a yeoman', was disrupted in the nineteenth century by the expansion of the middle classes of men. Society was, he argued, 'splitting into a hundred aristocracies, a hundred democracies, button makers and gentleman button-makers'. All of this expansion was accomplished in a rarefied public sphere of civility and modern manners. The evangelical bourgeois class 'imposed on society . . . a code of Sabbath observance, responsibility and philanthropy; of discipline in the home; regularity of affairs'.[5] Religious observance was important, but work, and work ethic, was still more central.[6] After all, who could respect an idle man?

The centrality of *work* to bourgeois identity is present also in Moretti's definition of bourgeois value systems, though he locates its core features further back in the eighteenth century and sees the Enlightenment as merely an accelerator of the process. In analysing Defoe's famous novel *Robinson Crusoe* (1719), Moretti asks a simple question: why did Crusoe feel the need to work so hard on his island? After all, nobody was looking. Crusoe had no superior to impress, no inspector, no need to account for his idle hours. To what extent had he internalised the need to work and why was it so important to him to do so? To answer, Moretti isolates distinctive goals or ideals as ways to understand the world-view of the western bourgeois. First, there is an emphasis on the 'working master', or wealth accumulation by non-manual labour.[7] In fact, clean hands – clean of filthy lucre and clean of physical work – might be presented as a short-hand definition of bourgeois identity. The politics of payment are also fundamental. The visible accumulation of money over a counter-top meant ostracism from the bourgeois classes, just as completely as calloused hands debarred entry. Nevertheless, adherence to a work ethic

5 G.M. Young, *Portrait of an age*, 2nd edn (London: Phoenix Press, 2002), pp. 4–7. This connects to the thesis expounded by Norbert Elias, *The civilizing process* (New York: Urizen Books, 1978, original 1939).

6 L. Davidoff and C. Hall maintain religious observance was a 'central plinth' of middle-class culture: *Family fortunes: men and women of the English middle classes 1780–1850* (London: Routledge, 2002), p. 73.

7 F. Moretti, *The bourgeois: between history and literature* (London: Verso, 2013), pp. 6–11, 25–8, 67–73.

defined and separated them from those who lived fat and idle on the sweat and toil of others. The bourgeois working master worked similar hours to those who worked for him, albeit for much greater recompense, but in a non-manual way. In modern societies it was the idea of hard work and 'seriousness' that was central to the legitimation of the acquisition by the middle classes of social power. This works well enough for the Anglo- and Francophile middle classes, but how might the Irish – infamous in the nineteenth century for their alleged slovenly incivility – be embraced within this bourgeois code?

Our search for the Irish bourgeois equivalent to Defoe's Crusoe can begin in Oliver Goldsmith's hamlet of Auburn – the siting of his most famous work, *The deserted village* (1770). Auburn is a most useful location, since it is set somewhere in the confused haze of Ireland, England and the New World. Moreover, Goldsmith's critique of wealth accumulation still resonates, as it was evoked to devastating effect by Tony Judt in his posthumous book on the failures of capitalism, *Ill fares the land* (2010), which takes its title from a line in Goldsmith's poem. What Goldsmith laments is not – as Judt and others have argued – the power wielded by a privileged elite, *or* the loss of a self-sufficient but poor peasantry whose rood might have maintained them. Instead, Goldsmith's land was 'ill-fared' because it lacked a responsible middle layer, a bourgeoisie, to whom Goldsmith (and maybe Judt) could relate and conceived of as morally reliable. When he reached for the village preacher, Goldsmith sought the respectable exemplar, that earnest and useful man of the middling sort, without whom society might collapse.

> Unpractised he to fawn, or seek for power
> By doctrines fashioned to the varying hour
> Far other aims his heart had learned to prize
> More skilled to raise the wretched than to rise.

Throughout *The deserted village* Goldsmith's exemplars conform perfectly to the Moretti definition of bourgeois identity. His preacher is 'serious' and 'pious'. His village master is 'severe' and 'stern'.[8] There is a responsible middle layer of society, a backbone. Like every great piece of art, Goldsmith's pastoral is many different things at once. It is an indictment of colonial government as well as a lament for pre-industrial society. It is a covert endorsement of the benevolent benefits of responsible monarchy, and a lament about rural depopulation. But most of all, it is a celebration of the virtues of industry and commitment. We

---

8 O. Goldsmith, *The deserted village* (London: W. Griffin, 1770), pp. 144–7, 180, 187, 196; M. Griffin, *Enlightenment in Ruins: The Geographies of Oliver Goldsmith* (Lewisburg, PA: Bucknell University Press, 2013).

might even argue that what Goldsmith deemed most admirable was a governing class of hard-working bourgeois ascetics like Robinson Crusoe.

Goldsmith is still more explicit as to the importance of this middle layer in *The Vicar of Wakefield* (1766), where he extols a 'middle order' between the 'rabble' and the very rich:

> In this middle order of mankind are generally to be found all the arts, wisdom, and virtues of society. This order alone is known to be the true preserver of freedom, and may be called the People ... For he divides the power of the rich, and calls off the great from falling with tenfold weight on the middle order placed beneath them. The middle order may be compared to a town of which the opulent are forming the siege, and which the governor from without is hastening the relief.

Goldsmith's contemporary, Adam Smith, had much to say in *The wealth of nations* about this responsible middle layer. In fact, one of Smith's arguments in favour of the legislative union of Ireland and Britain (which would come about, of course, in 1801) was that it would 'elevate the middling and inferior ranks' of Ireland at the expense of the aristocracy in the manner that it had already done in Scotland.[9] He too saw the bourgeois as a necessary buffer between rich and poor, not rich enough to be corrupt, not poor enough to be obliged to concentrate solely on survival.

Moretti and Young provide us with a 'type' to begin with, an identity as a higher category of worker, who depended for his livelihood on his mind. A conformist from below, the bourgeois was serious and earnest, and disposed to work hard to provide for those he worked for and those who worked for him. He was also religiously conscientious; in the Irish context a greater degree of respectability was accorded to the non-Catholic bourgeoisie, but Protestantism was not necessarily a defining feature. Instead, devotion, religious observance and, more particularly, a willingness to invest in one's religion of choice were as important as brand loyalty.

So who was in and who was out of the responsible middle layer? This changed significantly over time, but let us take Kocka's typology of the German *Burgertum* as a guide:

> Not counted among the *Burgertum* are the nobility, peasants, workers, and the lower strata altogether. Always counted among the *Burgertum* are merchants, manufacturers and bankers, owners of capital, and entrepreneurs and their

---

9 A. Smith, *The wealth of nations*, 2 vols. (London: John Dent & Sons, 1901, original 1776), vol. II, p. 427.

top management – in other words the *Wirtschaftsburgertum*, the economic middle class … We also include among the *Burgertum*, as a rule, physicians, lawyers, and other independent professionals, secondary school teachers and professors, judges and higher civil servants, as well as natural scientists, engineering graduates and other qualified experts.[10]

Knowledge is thus the final piece in the puzzle. Access to controlled and applied knowledge was the means through which Kocka's professional classes could access and hold power as the nineteenth century unfolded, and their ranks swelled as a result. By the 1870s and 1880s there was a general recognition that these groups had amassed enough cultural coherence and social control to constitute a new social stratum.[11] Their increasing importance came at the expense of the noble classes across Europe who, although they retained in some cases vast wealth and assets, found their political leverage and social importance on the wane.

Though no scheme will ever be fully adequate, it is appropriate that we proceed by locating the bourgeois in relation to the 'work' that is central to their identity and position in society. There are three main spheres in which much of the literature on the European bourgeoisie clusters. Broadly speaking the first of these spheres can be labelled the bureaucratic realm: the world of clerks, teachers and knowledge workers of various sorts. These occupations are state-sustained and, increasingly, credentialist in character. The significant growth of the state post-1760 was dependent on an expanding number of bureaucrats, all of whom were white-collar *workers*. Secondly: the world of money and merchants was also very obviously bourgeois. Populated by new and old money, there were of course merchants and traders who were emphatically not bourgeois, but they were in the minority. The third traditional category is one of the most difficult to isolate, the *professions*. There is some overlap between this category and the first, of course, as there is between all three. Quite what professions from the 'old' and the 'new' are included is a matter of surprisingly vigorous debate, but all studies of the bourgeois note their centrality. Beyond these three traditional and male-dominated categories is a less well-researched territory. In what follows, we will concentrate on these three categories, but seek also to complicate them with sections on bourgeois women, bourgeois childhoods, and new directions that might emerge from environmental, material and transnational ways of looking at the Irish bourgeois.

---

10 Kocka, *Industrial culture and bourgeois society*, pp. 192–3.
11 C. Charle, *Les élites de la République 1880–1900* (Paris: Fayard, 1987).

Bourgeois Bureaucrats

The state was integral to bourgeois expansion. The striking infrastructural growth of the state in the early nineteenth century is well known, but the state had already grown in bursts through the seventeenth and mid-eighteenth centuries, and was a considerable enterprise by the time the Act of Union dramatically changed the relationship between policy formulation, democratic representation and the actual administration of Ireland. This resulted in what James H. Murphy has termed a sort of 'bi-furcated' government structure where the roles of lord lieutenant, chief secretary and under-secretary were to some extent all dependent on the chemistry that existed between the three post-holders. Below them lay a quintessentially bourgeois layer of clerks, office-holders and tax collectors all of whom fit well with our definition of the 'working masters' of Ireland. This unsatisfactory situation lent itself to conspiracies and suspicions about accountability. The situation is beautifully captured in an excerpt from *The Evening Packet* in December 1840, which is to be found among the news-cuttings in Thomas Larcom's (under-secretary of Ireland, 1853–68) papers:

> *Irish Government*! There is something slippery – something of an *ignis fatuus* idea is conveyed in the very name. Were the Irish ever governed? Can they be ever governed? Will they be ever governed? Was it ever intended they could, would, should, or might be governed? What is the Government? Where is it? Who constitute it? Was it in Conciliation Hall? Is it in Downing-street? Will it ever be at the Castle? ... Irish Government, kind readers, is a fluctuating commodity, now in the possession of this individual, and then of that.[12]

We can conceive of Ireland under the Union as subject to a gradually accelerating project of 'civilisation', epitomised by the laying down of the Wicklow military road post-Union and culminating at the century's end in an impressively networked society overseen by what Michael Moran has described as the modern 'regulatory state'. In general European terms, the state expanded exponentially only after 1850.[13] In this respect state expansion in Britain and Ireland was prescient, as others have noted. Building on foundations put in place in the eighteenth century, the state began to expand

---

12 'Irish Government', *Evening Packet*, 30 Dec. 1840 in Larcom Papers, MS 7511, NLI. Conciliation Hall, Burgh Quay in Dublin, was the headquarters for Daniel O'Connell's Repeal Association in the 1840s. The Castle alluded to is Dublin Castle, the administrative centre of government in Ireland.
13 C. Bayly, *The birth of the modern world 1780–1914: global connections and comparisons* (Oxford: Blackwell, 2004), pp. 261–6.

visibly in the first half of the nineteenth century. Every aspect of Ireland was increasingly documented, processed and logged as the century wore on. This process had many phases, and many meanings. Regional radical agitation in Sheffield, Manchester and elsewhere in the industrial north from the 1780s demonstrated that the public sphere was no longer simply centred on London and on national politics, but was possessed also of a regional, yet distinctively urban, character that was most visibly manifest in extra-parliamentary politics.[14] This developing feature of popular politics, which had Irish manifestations in the Volunteers in the 1770s and 1780s and the United Irishmen in the 1790s, meant that a change in the style of government was discernible by the early union period. London could no longer consider itself legitimate alone. Britain and Ireland would need to be governed in a more totalising, all pervasive, but more decentralised manner. It needed meaningful municipal representation, and rural reform. It needed, in short, several new layers that the bourgeois would fill. It would become a state of agents, of networks, of man-made rules enforced by 'experts' made by, and for, government.

The initial phase of infrastructural development in the 1810s and 1820s may have been animated primarily by security concerns – thus the military road built in Wicklow served to protect from a Napoleonic invasion from the south-east, while the latent domestic threat led to changes in policing and army deployment under the energetic chief secretaryship of Sir Robert Peel, 1812–18. From the 1820s to the Great Famine a more totalising impulse was witnessed, with the development of a surveillance state that sustained an extensive infrastructure. This expanding state mirrored the growth of the professional and mercantile classes discussed in the following section, and was to a great degree composed of people drawn from the same economic bracket – the middle classes. In the new government of Ireland, policy was to be devised, debated and enacted in London, but implemented in Ireland by a mixture of British and Irish civil servants and clerks.

The first four decades or so of the nineteenth century witnessed an extraordinary proliferation of large-scale government-sponsored projects that would define the character of Irish interaction with the state over the subsequent forty years. Put summarily, these embraced a communications revolution exemplified by the development of Howth (1807–13) and Kingstown (1817–21) harbours, the railways and the post-office network. Power over the population

14 D. Read, *The English provinces c.1760–1960: a study in influence* (London: Edward Arnold, 1964); P. Corfield, *The impact of English towns 1700–1800* (Oxford: Oxford University Press, 1982); K. Theodore Hoppen, *Governing Hibernia: British Politicians and Ireland 1800–1921.* (Oxford: Oxford University Press, 2016).

was ensured first by mapping (Ordnance Survey of Ireland), then by instruction (the national education system) and by containing social disruption (workhouses, asylums, prisons). Much work has been done on this galloping, enumerating, state of bureaucrats in this period, with particularly impressive coverage of the Poor Law and mapping. Ireland moved from a very light-touch libertarian state with alarming rapidity. By the 1840s it had a totalising, pervasive, state infrastructure with arguably as extensive an information network as any other contemporary society. This period of intense activity has generally been referred to as the 'revolution in government' in British historiography, and mapped out, contested and debated vigorously since the late 1950s.[15] And yet the position and importance of the state in Ireland is contested in Irish historiography, where it has often been described as consistently precarious, or weak. Claims of its illegitimacy certainly dogged the developing state in its first twenty-nine years, as the issue of Catholic emancipation proved a troubling public embarrassment to successive governments.

Scholars have traced and theorised this pattern in other societies. Oliver MacDonagh was happy to declare a revolution in government in his history of bureaucratic change in England, but his tone in assessing Ireland was softer and more cognisant of issues of legitimacy.[16] The same state was built on both islands in much the same way, but the treatment of the systems by historians has been different. Jo Guldi has recently argued that this early 'infrastructure state' was usurped by 'localists' who succeeded in de-nationalising the transport and communications networks built and part funded by the centralising state, weakening the 'big state' approach and returning Britain to its more consistent small-state style of governance.[17] This is a compelling argument that holds true in Ireland, where the post-Famine era was notable for the privatisation of public services and the insecure control wielded by Dublin Castle.

What is just as significant as the state of things – that is to say the expansion of the material and networked power of the state in the nineteenth century – is the state of the people.[18] A quick glance at the directories of clerks and junior clerks all the way up to the under-secretary of Ireland (the unofficial

15 J. Hart, 'Nineteenth-century social reform: a Tory interpretation of history', *Past and Present*, 31 (1965), 39–61.
16 O. MacDonagh, 'The nineteenth century revolution in government: a reappraisal', *Historical Journal*, 1 (1958), 52–67; O. MacDonagh, *The Inspector General: Sir Jeremiah Fitzpatrick and the politics of social reform, 1783–1802* (London: Croom Helm, 1981).
17 J. Guldi, *Roads to power: Britain invents the infrastructure state* (Cambridge, MA: Harvard University Press, 2012), pp. 4–5, 22–3, 201.
18 P. Joyce, *The state of freedom: a social history of the British state since 1800* (Cambridge: Cambridge University Press, 2013), pp. 216–28.

and unelected head of practical government in Ireland) indicates that these were a mixture of well-educated Scottish, English and Irish men with an extended school education and/or a university career. Take, for example, two men from the very top of the rapidly expanding cohort of bourgeois bureaucrats: Thomas Drummond (1797–1840) and Thomas Larcom (1801–79). Both were British; both worked their way up through the Irish system, cutting their teeth on the great cartography project of the age, the Ordnance Survey of Ireland. Both rose to the height of under-secretary for Ireland, a position that only became permanent under Larcom, but was effectively the most important position in the Irish Civil Service from the 1830s. Both were classic bourgeois workaholics. Their writings are humourless, statistic heavy and scientifically minded. In fact, Larcom's aide memoire on the life of Drummond (occasioned by his death in 1840) is almost a paean to the bourgeois qualities discussed above. Published, somewhat fittingly and to no fanfare, in the fourth volume of *Papers on subjects connected with the duties of the Corps of Royal Engineers*, Larcom singled out his predecessor's dispassionate work rate as his single greatest quality, and characterised his energetic professional career as that of a 'scientific soldier'.[19]

Recent work by Fergus Campbell has amplified understanding of the social and cultural composition of the Castle and the Irish administration more broadly, but more remains to be done, particularly on the administration prior to the 1880–1920 period.[20] Little is known of the everyday governance of Ireland for fifty years either side of the Act of Union, outside of what correspondence between politicians can tell us, and next to nothing has been done on the clerks and white-collar workers who governed Ireland from one file and memo to the next.

Merchants and Money

Money was at the very centre of the bourgeois world. Yet, one's 'competence' or income was never spoken about overtly or freely. We are provided with vivid insight into how central the matter of annual income was to bourgeois and elite society in the fictional world of Jane Austen, where suitors of both sexes were ranked according to their income levels first, and other

19 T. Larcom, 'Memoir of the professional life of the late Captain Drummond', in *Papers on subjects connected with the duties of the Corps of Royal Engineers*, 4 (1840), pp. ix–xxiv.
20 F. Campbell, *The Irish establishment 1879–1914* (Oxford: Oxford University Press, 2009), pp. 53–98; R.B. McDowell, *The Irish administration, 1801–1914* (London: Routledge and Kegan Paul, 1964).

attractions second. The bourgeois relationship with money was a complex one, and nobody was better acquainted with the vagaries of financial acquisition than the merchant classes, in some respects the most open of all the bourgeois categories. Acquiring money through trade or manufacture reaped more instant rewards and losses than the steadier and rival options of a state job, or a life in one of the respected professions. But it also brought with it the possibility of disgrace in a way that the latter options did not. It also made entry into the upper reaches of the aristocracy or even gentry classes more problematic. The most successful Irish industrial family of the nineteenth century, the Guinnesses, had to endure the condescension of the ascendancy classes even as they dwarfed their collective wealth. This was the price of being a household name in every public house in the land. Only those with vast fortunes could overcome that sort of wealth origin, and then never fully.

The Guinness family sat at the very pinnacle of Britain's rich list for several generations before they were finally admitted to the peerage in 1891 and to its upper ranks with an earldom in 1919. The road to that earldom speaks volumes for the social barriers placed before 'new' money. Never had a family to demonstrate more philanthropic goodwill to receive such grudging political and social endorsement. It cost Benjamin Guinness the (considerable) sum of £150,000 assigned to the restoration of St Patrick's Cathedral in order to secure a baronetcy for the family in 1867, the most junior of all titles. The eventual acquisition of the titles of Lord Iveagh and Lord Ardilaun was greatly assisted by the Guinness family's infrastructural and social investment in the Liberties area adjoining their factory, not to mention the gift of St Stephen's Green to the city *c.*1880 and the careful endorsement given to Gladstone and the Liberals and later Salisbury and the Conservatives in return for honours.[21] For all of this, industrial peers of this type, the Guinnesses or the Bass family of Derby, were lumped together in the popular imagination as the 'beerage', derided by people either side of them on the social scale for the manner in which they were perceived to have 'bought' social status. Fortunes were likewise made in whiskey, a source of money that also ranked low in Irish and British society in terms of social status.[22]

If the Guinness family eventually climbed out of the industrial class, what of the countless that remained there, at various income levels? Much of Ireland's

21 A. Bielenberg, 'Late Victorian elite formation and philanthropy: the making of Edward Guinness', *Studia Hibernica*, 32 (2002), 133–54.
22 F. Shovlin, '"Endless stories about the Distillery": Joyce, death and whiskey', *Joyce Studies Annual* (2007), 134–58.

financial market was dispersed among the various banks of Dublin, and of Belfast, which became a centre for medium-scale finance in the second half of the nineteenth century.[23] Indeed, an argument can be made that Belfast, and not Dublin, is the archetypal bourgeois city of Ireland, since it grew on the basis of industry and commerce, and in conjunction with the early nineteenth-century expansion of the middle classes. This, as Jonathan Wright and Alice Johnson have pointed out, facilitated the rise of a relatively homogenous 'civic' elite, almost entirely bourgeois in character, which occupied most prominent social and financial roles in the city. Similar work has been done on the composition of the chambers of commerce and trade guilds of the other cities and major towns of Ireland, pointing to the importance of understanding the roles of mayor, alderman and freemason in the topography of local commercial exchange. It is also important to point out that religious divisions encouraged the channelling of money and business in ways that were revealing of practical segregation. Certain banks were Protestant, Catholic or Dissenter, just as certain chambers of commerce discriminated against one sect or the other.[24] This financial market was controlled – to some extent – by the stock exchanges of Belfast, Cork and Dublin, but most major Irish companies traded in London. Of the three Irish exchanges the former two were nineteenth century in origin.[25]

In business circles one singularly important divider between those who qualified as bourgeois and those who did not stands out: the question of whether one traded on one's name or not. Wholesale business, manufacture and subsidiary industry were all socially acceptable, but trading across a counter, and against one's own name, was altogether more problematical. Great fortunes could be made as a merchant, but social condescension would only allow so much social mobility. Susan Galavan has shown how the Meade family of builders rose from carpenters and builders to lord mayors of Dublin in just two generations, but also the limitations of that rise. The family made its fortune from building suburban mansions for the rich while renting their

---

23 N.E. Gamble, 'The business community and trade of Belfast 1767–1800', PhD thesis, University of Dublin, 1978; W.H. Crawford, 'The Belfast middle classes in the late eighteenth century' in D. Dickson et al. (eds.), *The United Irishmen: republicanism, radicalism and rebellion* (Dublin: Lilliput Press, 1993), pp. 62–73.

24 A.M. Johnson, 'The civic elite of mid-nineteenth century Belfast', *Irish Economic and Social History*, 37 (2010), 131–3; J.B. O'Brien, *The Catholic middle classes in pre-Famine Cork.* The O'Donnell Lecture, 1979 (Dublin: National University of Ireland, 1980).

25 C.R. Hickson and J.D. Turner, 'The rise and decline of the Irish stock market, 1865–1913', *European Review of Economic History*, 9 (2005), 3–33.

former townhouses as tenement slums.[26] Such class-exploitation in both directions was rare, but it spoke well to the role that finance could play in the hands of the successful bourgeois business family.

The Professionals

It is clear that professionals were at the heart of bourgeois identity. They were socially respectable workers, with clean hands (although not always morally clean, of course) and upstanding social status. But the professional class possessed a very different character across different societies. In France, for example, the established professions were an extension of state corporatism. Entry was state-controlled, and regulated by means of a tightly administered educational elitism. In Britain and Ireland, the picture was very different. Here, the professions were largely deregulated or left unregulated in the eighteenth and nineteenth centuries, and the distinction which occurred at the higher branches of law or medicine, for example, was socially filtered. With significant expenses associated with training, professionals in the nineteenth century most often derived from the various branches of gentry families, or from merchant houses. Thus, access was economically and socially controlled, and the outcome was not all that dissimilar to elsewhere.

Surprisingly little has been written on the Irish professions that made up the backbone of the white-collared bourgeoisie. I propose dividing up this layer of society between the old professions – medicine, divinity, military and law –and the newer credentialled professions such as engineering, dentistry, pharmacy and veterinary science. My reason for doing so is the social barrier between them. Civil servant and physician might both consider themselves bourgeois but not equal. We can see a formula for this, one noted by Moran and others but not often stated unequivocally. The classic professions were less regulated by the state than the newer professions. Broadly speaking, the less regulated an industry is the higher its social status. Medicine, divinity and law remain to some extent self-regulated to the present day, as does the army. The reasons for this derive from the nineteenth century, when impressive levels of state regulation failed to penetrate these professions, just as they failed to penetrate the financial markets of London. Why? Moran argues it is because the state was sold the fiction that because the professions were stocked with the offspring of elite families they could be trusted to behave

---

26 S. Galavan, 'Building Victorian Dublin: Meade & Son and the expansion of the city' in C. O'Neill (ed.), *Irish elites in the nineteenth century* (Dublin: Four Courts Press, 2013), pp. 51–67.

honourably as gentlemen. To this we might add that the state officials seeking to regulate lacked the leverage or social clout to win the argument with their social superiors. Newer or lower professions did not have the luxury of antiquity or social capital on their side, and so they were highly regulated as they began to incorporate at a time when the regulatory power of the state was already much higher than it could ever be with professions that predated it.

Broadly speaking, the classic professions (army, medicine, law and divinity) only began to expand as career options for a diverse segment of the population in the second half of the eighteenth century, when the middle classes constituted about 3 per cent of the population in Britain and Ireland.[27] This figure would increase gradually to about 10 per cent by the twentieth century. It is clear from this that the character of Irish society changed in the interim in terms of occupational structure. What difference that made to Irish society is quite another matter, however, and much more difficult to capture.

What the focus on individuals has brought into sharp relief, is that to focus exclusively on the island of Ireland is to neglect a major enabling space for social mobility, or several. Recent studies tracking the Irish in the military or Irish in the Empire have revealed a large number of individuals who utilised career and trade routes advantageously. Likewise, the literature on the Irish abroad has of late switched emphasis from Irish paupery to Irish prosperity, with new studies emerging on eighteenth- and nineteenth-century groups flourishing in the New World.[28]

We have increasingly rich resources on the professions in the eighteenth century.[29] Coverage in the nineteenth century is more hit and miss, perhaps owing to the emergence of so many new professions in the period, as well as to the entrance of women into certain professions towards the end of the century.[30] We do not yet possess an equivalent to the sophisticated literature that exists on the urban middle class in Britain, America

---

27 The numbers are disputed: see M. Ackroyd et al., *Advancing with the army: medicine, the professions, and social mobility in the British Isles 1790–1850* (Oxford: Oxford University Press, 2006), p. 10.

28 C. Bailey, *Irish London: middle-class migration in the global eighteenth century* (Liverpool: Liverpool University Press, 2013); W.A. Jenkins, *Between raid and rebellion: the Irish in Buffalo and Toronto, 1867–1916* (Montreal: McGill-Queen's University Press, 2013); D.H. Akenson, *Ireland, Sweden and the great European migration, 1814–1914* (Montreal: McGill-Queen's University Press, 2011).

29 T. Barnard, *A new anatomy of Ireland: the Irish Protestants 1649–1770* (New Haven: Yale University Press, 2003).

30 F. Lane (ed.), *Politics, society and the middle class in modern Ireland* (Basingstoke: Palgrave, 2010).

and elsewhere,[31] though recent work on Dublin, Belfast and Cork is beginning to redress this absence in Irish urban history.[32] To understand fully the
picture of class diversity in Ireland we will need sophisticated analyses of
the social hierarchy of large towns – such as Clonmel, Nenagh or Tuam –
as well as cities in the nineteenth century.[33]

The separation of paying customer from service provider distinguished
the law, medical or religious professional from his social inferiors. Bills were
settled on the presumption of honour, and money was never discussed directly
with a barrister or doctor. The bill was simply issued and it was expected
that it would be paid in due course. Officers in the army were reasonably
well remunerated also, and certainly on a par socially with the others, while
the more socially advantaged of the religious professionals in Ireland were
those of the Anglican persuasion. Catholics were located at the lower end of
the spectrum socially – and often excluded. Until the relief acts of the 1790s,
Catholics enjoyed limited access to the law as a career. Medicine was more
open, but medical practitioners at the lower end could expect to earn much
less than any of the other established professions – just £90–£200, which was
a quarter of what a typical barrister might make.[34] Likewise, only careers
that reached the episcopal bench in the Anglican Church delivered significant
earning power and social mobility to those in holy orders. Furthermore, all
three professions required significant family investment in order for the requisite qualifications to be obtained – even a lowly Anglican curate required
in the region of £400 to be sunk into their education in the late eighteenth
century to deliver at best a living of about £200 a year.[35]

31 R.J. Morris, *Class, sect and party: the making of the British middle class, Leeds 1820–
50* (Manchester: Manchester University Press, 1990); S. Gunn, *The public culture of
the Victorian middle class: ritual and authority in the English industrial city 1840–1914*
(Manchester: Manchester University Press, 2007).

32 O. Purdue, *Belfast: the emerging city 1850–1914* (Dublin: Irish Academic Press, 2013); S.J.
Connolly (ed.), *Belfast 400: people, place and history* (Liverpool: Liverpool University
Press, 2012); D. Dickson, *Old World colony: Cork and South Munster 1630–1830* (Cork: Cork
University Press, 2005), *passim*; D. Dickson, *Dublin: the making of a capital city* (London:
Profile, 2014); P. Fagan, *Catholics in a Protestant country: the papist constituency in eight-
eenth century Dublin* (Dublin: Four Courts Press, 1998).

33 For some good examples see M. Byrne, *Tullamore: a portrait* (Tullamore: Esker Press,
2010); P. Grace, *The middle class of Callan, Co. Kilkenny, 1825–45* (Dublin: Four Courts
Press, 2015).

34 Barnard, *A new anatomy of Ireland*, pp. 115–42; C. Kenny, 'The exclusion of Catholics
from the legal profession in Ireland, 1537–1829', *Irish Historical Studies*, 25 (1987), 337–
57; F.O.C. Meenan, 'The Catholic University School of Medicine 1860–1880', *Studies*,
66:262–3 (1977), 135–44; T. Farmar, *Privileged lives: a social history of middle-class Ireland
1882–1989* (Dublin: A. & A. Farmar, 2012), pp. 75–82.

35 Barnard, *A new anatomy of Ireland*, pp. 84, 87.

Of the three 'learned' professions, law was potentially the most transform-ative in terms of lifestyle and income. Great fortunes could be made from one's own wit and reputation, as the career of Daniel O'Connell attests.[36] Yet most law professionals cut their teeth at the more competitive end of the profession, as lower-ranking solicitors. Gauging the impact of the professions beyond the prosaic matter of income and into the world of the political is difficult, but it served a minority well. It is clear that the courts served as a very adequate training for those interested in a parliamentary career, as fewer entered that world from the medical or religious sphere. Military men were, by comparison, more likely to re-enter society at the level of county elite, whether by serving as a resident magistrate or a poor law guardian. Few enough entered politics unless they were members of a landed family with an established profile. Likewise, a rich historiography on those bourgeois figures of priest, vicar and nun is available to us, with the 'devotional revolution' and the second great awakening driving huge recruitment into that profession from the late eighteenth century until relatively recent times.[37] As with the lower ranks of law and medicine, there was a spectrum of bourgeois identity. A Loreto nun in Dalkey was not on the same social plane as a Sister of Mercy down the road, any more than a barrister was the same as a solicitor, or a surgeon on a level with a GP. But there is no doubting the fact that these pro-fessions were at the heart of bourgeois culture. By about the 1850s and 1860s their pre-eminence was obvious, not only in the bourgeois citadel of Belfast, the social circles of post-parliament Dublin and the suburbs of Cork, but also across the north of England as well. In 1857 William Thackeray, chronicler of the pan-British bourgeois class, announced in an after-dinner speech that he 'belonged to the class ... of lawyers, merchants, and scholars, of men who are striving on in the world, of men of the middle classes of this country'.[38]

Locating the rising status of new professionals is more difficult. Old pro-fessional boundaries loosened to include broader catchments. So solicitors became a broad church that embraced unsuccessful practitioners as well as recognisably bourgeois legal professionals. Apothecaries made some pro-gress towards inclusion within the medical profession, as did nurses, albeit both at inferior rank. The new professions were nonetheless something quite

36 P.M. Geoghegan, *King Dan: the rise of Daniel O'Connell, 1775–1829* (Dublin: Gill and Macmillan, 2008).

37 J.H. Murphy (ed.), *Evangelicals and Catholics in nineteenth-century Ireland* (Dublin: Four Courts Press, 2004), pp. 15–60; M.P. Magray, *The transforming power of the nuns: women, religion, and cultural change in Ireland, 1750–1900* (Oxford: Oxford University Press, 1998).

38 Quoted in D. Newsome, *The Victorian world picture* (London: Fontana, 1998), p. 64.

different: a creature of scientific and technological advancement and inno-vation, sometimes resented by the more prestigious professionals. Stephen Walker has described how barristers and solicitors came together to lambast the new, liminal and industry-aimed, professional group of accountants in mid-Victorian England. As late as 1867 the *Law Times* referred to accountants as 'men of small standing', or 'half professionals' who lacked etiquette, social grace and formal qualification.[39]

Other new professions were regarded with similar condescension, but as the need for diversified services expanded as the state apparatus grew and general wealth rose, the new professions found respectability easier to come by. Veterinary science provides a useful example. In 1800 the Royal Dublin Society poached Thomas Peall, a prominent veterinary surgeon from Bristol. The syllabus for his 1802 series of lectures to the Society show a man much exercised by the horse's foot, with five of his eighteen lectures given over to that subject. Peall's post was allowed to lapse on his death in 1825. At that point there were only four veterinarians working in Dublin, suggesting that the profession was not taken for granted in the way it was later in the century. Another abortive attempt to appoint a self-sustaining lead veterinarian for Ireland occurred in 1832, providing coverage until 1858, but no national over-sight for the profession (there were 221 vets on the 1891 register) was provided until 1900.[40]

In what we might call the technical professions – mining, engineering, sur-veying – only France had an elaborate state infrastructure in place for their training by the late eighteenth century. In Britain and Ireland these profes-sions developed in response to industrialisation, but without any direct tie to university education. Academic recognition for the engineer would not come about until the mid to late nineteenth century, when chairs were estab-lished in London, Glasgow and Edinburgh; further such initiatives were taken across the industrial north of England from the 1870s. In Ireland engineering and 'applied' sciences had also been routed outside of the academy and the state through the Royal Dublin Society. The first major step in recognising the applied sciences came with the founding of Newman's Catholic University in Dublin; this institution opened its doors with six professors in 1854, one of whom was a civil engineer – the most prestigious and lucrative of the various

---

39 S.P. Walker, ' "Men of small standing"? Locating accountants in English society during the mid-nineteenth century', *European Accounting Review*, 11:2 (2002), 378.

40 K. Bright, *The Royal Dublin Society 1815–45* (Dublin: Four Courts Press, 2004), pp. 30–1, 80.

branches. Elsewhere it fell to the Museum of Industry in Dublin to employ an engineer as a lecturer; Christopher Lane was employed in this role in 1853.[41]

Bourgeois Badges

The idea that the various categories outlined above were easily distinguishable is of course a fiction. Many individuals held several professional positions in the nineteenth century. Likewise, many professions were characterised by layers of social gradation that were replete with social consequence. What is more interesting, perhaps, is to identify the social signifiers that alerted the wider public that bourgeois status had been attained or retained, and how that changed over the course of the nineteenth century. With a much smaller and more socially exclusive state in operation in the late eighteenth century, how were 'bourgeois badges' distributed across society, and in what ways did they divide or unite the various factions?

Some of these badges were in the gift of the state. These included the socially important shrievalty posts – a relic of the medieval state. High sheriffs, deputy lieutenant and justice of the peace were locally important roles overseen by the lord lieutenant of each of the thirty-two counties, an expensive and cumbersome role that was shared among the leading gentry families resident in a county.[42] These were all crown appointments made on the recommendation of Dublin Castle and the lord lieutenant of Ireland, who screened for loyalty to the state first, and competence second. The efficacy of the system was called into question by the reforms of 1836, which saw resident magistrates appointed to help with the (predominantly legal) functions carried out by those who comprised bourgeois government at county level. Later in the century this was complicated by the imposition of an alternative local government cohort as a result of the poor law system (1838) and the municipal reforms of the 1840s, which created another layer of bourgeois control, this time even more socially diverse.[43] The effect in the long term

41 J. Adelman, 'Communities of science: the Queen's Colleges and scientific culture in provincial Ireland, 1845–1875', PhD thesis, NUI Galway, 2006, pp. 107–9; C. Cullen, 'The Museum of Irish Industry, Robert Kane and education for all in the Dublin of the 1850s and 1860s', *History of Education*, 38:1 (2009), 99–113.

42 The lord lieutenant of the county was always a senior nobleman of the district. Until the 1830s this role was known as county governor, similar to the county lieutenants in England: V. Crossman, *Local government in nineteenth-century Ireland* (Belfast: Institute of Irish Studies, 1994), pp. 11–23.

43 P. Gray, *The making of the Irish Poor Law, 1815–43* (Manchester: Manchester University Press, 2009), *passim*; M. Potter, *The municipal revolution in Ireland: a handbook of Urban government in Ireland since 1800* (Dublin: Irish Academic Press, 2010).

was the embourgeoisement (or *déclassement*, some contemporaries might have argued) of local government in Ireland long before the local government reforms of the 1870s and 1898, which completed the job.[44] The long-term effect of this was to transfer power away from the gentry, who found themselves progressively channelled away from ground-level government in a way that would have been unimaginable in the eighteenth century.

In many respects the resident magistrate (RM) was the quintessential bourgeois badge holder. A paid post-holder, though on a relatively low salary of about £400, the typical RM was an ex-military officer or policeman, and slightly more likely to be Protestant than Catholic. He was acceptable socially to the gentry with whom he would cooperate on day-to-day matters, but also loyal to his employer – the Castle – to whom he was expected to provide local intelligence on crop yields, unrest or 'outrage', and anything else of relevance.[45]

Membership of clubs, sporting organisations, yacht clubs and beneficial groups such as the Freemasons was also central to bourgeois life.[46] One other feature of this world deserving of notice is the credentialist revolution that facilitated the professional expansion of the era. With only Trinity College Dublin supplying university degrees in the eighteenth century, the expanding bourgeoisie demanded, and acquired, religiously neutral alternatives, not only through the Queen's Colleges established in 1845, but also through the Catholic (later Royal) University in 1854. In addition, the ambitious and the able could avail themselves of the much-exploited backdoor route of the decentralised University of London external examination system, and, to a lesser extent, of continental universities, and courses at Edinburgh, Glasgow and elsewhere in Britain.[47] With Trevelyan's redesign of the Indian Civil Service entrance exam in 1855 matched by a later democratisation of the home Civil Service in 1870, it was clear that the government had to bow to the merit principle – which was advantageous to the Irish middle classes. The secondary schools that catered for the various religious divisions within Ireland and Britain aimed specifically at this market, and even trespassed on

44 W.L. Feingold, 'The tenants' movement to capture the Irish Poor Law Boards, 1877–1886', *Albion*, 7:3 (1975), 216–31.

45 P. Bonsall, *The Irish RMs: the resident magistrates in the British administration of Ireland* (Dublin: Four Courts Press, 1997), pp. 11–15.

46 See J. Kelly, *Sport in Ireland 1600–1840* (Dublin: Four Courts Press, 2014); P. Rouse, *Sport and Ireland: a history* (Oxford: Oxford University Press, 2015), pp. 84–148.

47 C. Shepard, 'Cramming, instrumentality and the education of Irish imperial elites' in D. Dickson, J. Pyz and C. Shepard (eds.), *Irish classrooms and British Empire: imperial contexts in the origins of modern education* (Dublin: Four Courts Press, 2012), pp. 172–83.

it. By the 1880s Blackrock College in Dublin, for example, was offering Civil Service training on site.[48] The usage of these routes to bourgeois membership can tell us much about the Irish middle classes.

Bourgeois Women

Studies of bourgeois women tend to focus on their consumption practices, charitable work or gradual professionalisation and education.[49] This particular aspect of *fin-de-siècle* Irish bourgeois women has also generated a small body of work, which has been amplified more recently by work on the cultural and interior world of women of the revolutionary period.[50]

Bourgeois professional categories were firmly resistant to female infiltration, even from women who were born into that class. This was less marked in ostensibly 'caring' professions, such as medicine, but even medicine channelled women into badly remunerated and menial sub-categories of the profession for as long as was feasible. By the late nineteenth century this was being challenged more broadly, with the 'new woman' movement promoting greater professional equity as one of its main causes.[51] Progress was slow and socially coded, and, as Gillian Sutherland has recently cautioned, less was achieved, and more slowly, than is sometimes claimed. Many entered the professions at the lowest levels; most worked as clerks or teachers, and in other low-status white-collar jobs, while many more worked as members of the religious or as shopkeepers, small business proprietors and other occupations on the margins of bourgeois identity. The definition of the bourgeois woman was, arguably, one that did not visibly work, and it is perhaps possible to argue that the bourgeois layer of society was the most restrictive and disempowering of all until the second half of the twentieth century. This leaves the Irish historian with a conundrum few have even attempted to resolve: how do we

---

48 C. O'Neill, *Catholics of consequence: transnational education, social mobility and the Irish Catholic elite* (Oxford: Oxford University Press, 2014), chapter 1; J. Pyz, 'St Columba's College: an Irish School in the age of Empire' in Dickson et al. (eds.), *Irish classrooms and British Empire*, pp. 124–33.

49 See L. Tiersten, *Marianne in the market: envisioning consumer society in fin-de-siècle France* (Los Angeles: University of California Press, 2001); for bourgeois consumption see R. Rich, *Bourgeois consumption: food, space and identity in London and Paris, 1850–1914* (Manchester: Manchester University Press, 2011).

50 R.F. Foster, *Vivid faces: the revolutionary generation in Ireland 1890–1923* (London: Penguin, 2014); S. Rains, *Commodity culture and social class in Dublin, 1850–1916* (Dublin: Irish Academic Press, 2010); L. Kelly, *Irish women in medicine, c.1880s–1920s: origins, education and careers* (Manchester: Manchester University Press, 2012).

51 G.M. Sutherland, *In search of the new woman: middle-class women and work in Britain 1870–1914* (Cambridge: Cambridge University Press, 2015).

integrate or unite an analysis of bourgeois domestic life? What defines middle-class female existence post-enlightenment?[52] One rich seam will be the relationship between female heads of household and domestic servants, children and other visitors, which can be explored through the lens of the home life of the bourgeois family. A recent book by Alison Light exploring that relationship between the writer Virginia Woolf and her servants suggests a line of research that would add to Mona Hearn's singular study of domestic service in Ireland.[53] But what of women who did manage to infiltrate that public bourgeois world?

The case of Oonagh Keogh (1903–89) provides an impression of the barriers preventing women of the same class and background who sought to break into male-only ranks. Oonagh was the daughter of a prominent stockbroker, John Keogh, himself a classic bourgeois success story. Keogh worked his way up to membership of the Dublin Stock Exchange (DSE) via management of a Hibernian Bank branch in Swinford, County Mayo, and marriage to Annie Doyne of Mullingar. By the 1920s he was running a prominent stockbroking company and his success was reflected in his choices of address. Moving first to a large house in County Wicklow, he later took up residence at 'Rossbegh' on Shrewsbury Road, Dublin, where the family employed five domestic servants. Reflecting the family's new financial muscle, Oonagh was sent to Princethorpe convent in Warwickshire for two years, before completing her education in Alexandra College and 'finishing' with a Grand Tour, in the course of which she visited Dalmatia and North Africa in addition to Bayonne in the south of France in her late teens. By 1925 she was back in Dublin, where, because of her father's ill-health, she was tasked with taking over the family business temporarily.[54] Oonagh's decision to apply for membership of the DSE in 1925 caused a sensation. Moreover, the DSE had no legal grounds to stop her, since she had traded with her father for several years and had acquired the sort of social and cultural capital through her education that made debarring her on class status difficult to justify.[55] In the end,

52 G. Meaney, M. O'Dowd and B. Whelan (eds.), *Reading the Irish woman: studies in cultural encounter and exchange, 1714–1960* (Liverpool: Liverpool University Press, 2013).

53 M. Hearn, *Below stairs: domestic service remembered in Dublin and beyond 1880–1922* (Dublin: Lilliput Press, 1993); A. Light, *Mrs Woolf and the servants: the hidden heart of domestic service* (London: Fig Tree, 2007).

54 She traded as full partner between 1926 and 1933: see B. Nolan, *Oonagh Keogh: a celebration* (Dublin: Irish Stock Exchange, 2014); 'Woman on 'change', *Irish Press*, 21 Sept. 1956; 'First woman stockbroker', *Irish Times*, 6 June 1925.

55 She was not the first female applicant; a Mrs Bolger, widow of the stockbroker D.S. Bolger, had applied *c.*1905, but was rejected: see 'Dublin Stock Exchange: lady's application for membership', *Irish Times*, 25 May 1925.

the Stock Exchange admitted her, which was an unprecedented event as the New York and London Exchanges only admitted their first female stockbrokers in 1967 and 1973 respectively.

Oonagh Keogh represented a rare victory, however, as in reality the expression of bourgeois values for most women, whether aspirant or actual bourgeois, was revealed in a non-work sphere. This extended beyond the obvious outreach areas of philanthropy and charity, to the domestic sphere, and the locality that the bourgeois life was lived in.[56] Political mobilisation has attracted a lively literature in the Irish case, with recent publications on the revolutionary generation of political activists and suffragists revealing a bourgeois urban sphere of sororal circles.[57]

Bourgeois Children and Bourgeois Pets

Without drawing an immediate comparison or parallel between children and pets, a survey of what aspects of the identities adults project or imbue on both may well prove instructive in the search for the Irish bourgeoisie. We more or less accept that the strategies of child-rearing, schooling and upbringing more generally that parents deploy reflect their expectations or wishes about their children's imagined future. In education this involves choices about the type of school they will attend, and the type of academic or physical environment they will be exposed to, as well as the social milieu in which they will be educated. Several studies illuminate the gendering and politicising of Irish 'youth' culture in the late nineteenth and early twentieth centuries, but a real gap is evident in our understanding of bourgeois childhood outside of school contexts before this point.[58] Everything from the construction of childhood to the language, leisure time and physical education surrounding children and young adults can tell us more about the Irish family – itself an understudied unit in a culture much exercised by family values.

Little has emerged since Steve Baker and Kathleen Kete's seminal work on the relationship between the keeping of pets and middle-class or bourgeois

---

56 See C. Harrison, *The bourgeois citizen in nineteenth-century France: gender, sociability, and the uses of emulation* (Oxford: Clarendon Press, 1999).
57 S. Pašeta, *Nationalist women in Ireland, 1900–1918* (Cambridge: Cambridge University Press, 2013); W. Murphy, *Political imprisonment and the Irish, 1912–1921* (Oxford: Oxford University Press, 2014), pp. 11–34.
58 See M. Hatfield, 'Games for boys: masculinity, boyhood, and play in Ireland, 1890–1939' in R. Barr, S. Brady and J. McGaughey (eds.), *Ireland and masculinities in history: from the sixteenth century to the present* (Basingstoke: Palgrave, 2016).

identity in the nineteenth century.[59] Juliana Adelman's work aside, even less has yet emerged on the class dimensions to animal ownership in Ireland.[60] Work on British 'exotic' pets is suggestive of the potential, and some scattered essays inspired by environmental history and eco-criticism promise to open up new avenues of enquiry.[61] The keeping of a prize herd, a rare breed of dog, a well-maintained horse and pair, were all marks of what Bourdieu would call distinction – a way to signal wealth and taste to the wider world. On his ramble through Ireland in the 1830s, William Gibson met with the pet-crazed surgeon Sir Philip Crampton, whose obsession with dogs and horses was vividly described in Gibson's memoir of his visit.[62] And after all, what could be more bourgeois than a lapdog or a poodle?

New Directions

So far we have established that there is an advanced literature on the state, education and bourgeois professions, and that rather less work has been done on the financial capital of the bourgeois classes, or on the bourgeois female, excepting some studies of her post-1890s political mobilisation. There are, however, other sites towards which we might look. Some recent studies have begun to highlight the gradual but usually successful middle-class penetration of the Irish diaspora – too often associated with tales of rags or riches, and to the exclusion of any discussion of the many in between.[63] A history of the globalised Irish middle classes would be a most useful addition to the literature. In the same vein – trying to locate the Irish bourgeoisie spatially – more work might be done on the possibility of a *rural* bourgeoisie. Studies of the middle classes have an inherently urban bias for good reason. Doctors, lawyers and merchants all cluster in large towns and cities. But what of the

---

59 K. Kete, *The beast in the boudoir: petkeeping in nineteenth-century Paris* (Berkeley: University of California Press, 1994); S. Baker, *Picturing the beast: animals, identity, and representation* (Chicago: University of Illinois Press, 1993).

60 J. Adelman, 'Animal knowledge: zoology and classification in nineteenth-century Dublin', *Field Day Review*, 5 (2009), 109–21.

61 H. Cowie, *Exhibiting animals in nineteenth-century Britain: empathy, education and entertainment* (Basingstoke: Palgrave, 2014). In the Irish case see K. Kirkpatrick and B. Farago (eds.), *Animals in Irish literature and culture* (Basingstoke: Palgrave, 2014).

62 W. Gibson, *Rambles in Europe in 1839: with sketches of prominent surgeons, physicians, medical schools, hospitals, literary personages, scenery, etc.* (Philadelphia: Lea and Blanchard, 1841), pp. 226–31. My thanks to Juliana Adelman for this reference.

63 J. Herson, *Divergent paths: family histories of Irish emigrants in Britain 1820–1920* (Manchester: Manchester University Press, 2015); W. Jenkins, *Between raid and rebellion: the Irish in Buffalo and Toronto, 1867–1916*; M. Moulton, *Ireland and the Irish in interwar England* (Cambridge: Cambridge University Press, 2014).

social status accorded the so-called parish gentry, strong farmers and land agents, in the Irish countryside? Might these not be incorporated into our vision of the bourgeoisie, along with the proto-typical itinerant knowledge-worker, the hedge schoolmaster?

Focused studies of sport, leisure and vacation patterns will tell us much about how the Irish middle classes reinforced their emerging identity. Likewise, an expanded consumption history will reveal how bourgeois identity was sold, bought, gendered and embodied in the eighteenth and nineteenth centuries. Print consumption, circulation and reception history will illuminate in a similar vein. Some work on advertising, for example, is beginning to emerge, but much more is required.[64] Studies that focus on taste, distinction and different forms of capital will also help us to understand social gradation within elite and bourgeois groups in a way that currently eludes us, and it stands to reason that these ought to be studied in much the same way as they were experienced – transregionally and transnationally. The ideas that flowed through bourgeois trends in food, music and fashion itself are inherently fluid and contingent. The gradual Americanisation of the Anglo world will be just as important as a more nuanced understanding of how Irish involvement in Empire informed domestic culture, material culture and everyday consumption practices. There is, in this sense, arguably no such thing as an Irish bourgeois 'taste', whatever about the argument we can advance for an Irish bourgeoisie in general terms. Instead, fads and fashions at the core in London, Paris and, increasingly, New York, were transmitted and altered on their journey to the peripheries. Even the inherently bourgeois values of the Irish revival were a reworking of similar literary and cultural projects across Europe.

Conclusion

The purpose of this chapter has been to outline the main features of the Irish bourgeoisie between the late eighteenth century and the end of the nineteenth. By that I mean that amorphous category of people in between those in want and those who never knew want. That constantly shifting morass of people between the elite and the landless labourer has proven difficult to quantify, and probably always will. The bourgeois class is more elastic than any other, and was resistant to active female participation well into the

---

64 S. Rains, '"Do you ring? Or are you rung for?": mass media, class, and social aspiration in Edwardian Ireland', *New Hibernia Review*, 14:3 (2014), 17–35.

twentieth century. One could be above it as a noble fallen on hard times, but contained or constrained within it as a merchant prince with enormous financial resources. A junior clerk in Dublin Castle in the 1870s could fairly be considered within the same broad bourgeois class as the doctor who treats his illness, and the barrister who defends the malpractice case if he came to harm during treatment. Despite existing under the same umbrella, it was clear to all three who was the more refined, and who was the better paid. What they all shared was a preoccupation with keeping their hands clean. A bourgeois could not make money by the sweat of his brow, but then he could not possess a hereditary title either. How much money one had in one's pocket was largely irrelevant, in other words; being bourgeois was about a set of values. Ambition was everything, and the only real fear was that of *déclassement*. Bourgeois membership depended on taste and distinction; as Mauss once wrote, 'the domain of social life is essentially a domain of differences'.[65]

---

65 M. Mauss, 'La civilisation' (1913) quoted in M. Lamont and M. Fournier, *Cultivating differences: symbolic boundaries and the making of inequality* (Chicago: University of Chicago Press, 1992), p. 1.

20

The Growth of the State in the
Nineteenth Century

VIRGINIA CROSSMAN

Introduction

If there is one thing on which historians of nineteenth-century Ireland tend to agree, it is that the early decades of the century saw a significant expansion of the state. 'In the fields of education, economic development, police, prisons, and public health', Oliver MacDonagh observed, 'the state intervened to a degree and in a fashion scarcely conceivable in contemporary Britain'; a point echoed by Vincent Comerford, who describes the state in Ireland as 'interventionist and centralising to a precocious degree'.[1] Unlike England, where the organisation and regulation of society remained for the most part the responsibility of local government, voluntary associations or the individual, in Ireland responsibility was increasingly vested in the state and delegated to local officials. By the middle of the nineteenth century Ireland possessed a range of institutions and services that had no parallel in other parts of the United Kingdom; these included a national system of elementary education, a national police force and, according to MacDonagh, a health system. The impact of these innovative initiatives was not just administrative moreover. Institutional buildings such as police stations, workhouses and lunatic asylums changed the appearance of the countryside while the salaried officers who occupied them added a new dimension to Irish society.

Seeking explanations for these developments has led some historians to see Ireland as a site of experimentation, or a 'social laboratory'. Ireland, Stanley Palmer observes, was 'a natural place to experiment: the country was wretchedly

---

1 O. MacDonagh, 'Ideas and institutions, 1830–45' in W.E. Vaughan (ed.), *A new history of Ireland*, vol. v: *Ireland under the Union, I, 1801–70* (Oxford: Oxford University Press, 1989), p. 206; V. Comerford, *Inventing the nation: Ireland* (London: Arnold, 2003), p. 37; P. Carroll, 'Science, power, bodies: the mobilization of nature as state formation', *Journal of Historical Sociology*, 9 (1996), 139–67.

542

poor, local government was weak because Protestants were scarce and the bulk of the population hostile, and the need to court public opinion was felt to be slight'.[2] While recent studies have tended to dismiss the social laboratory thesis, the concept of the centralising interventionist state remains highly influential. To focus on the centralising tendency of administrative reforms is, however, to ignore the importance of local factors in shaping the genesis, evolution and operation of the systems created. Far from being uniform and regularised, administration of the poor law system, for example, was highly localised, and characterised by diversity and irregularity. The following account offers a fresh perspective on the expansion of the state locating its origins in the eighteenth century, highlighting its political context, and exploring the unintended consequences of some of the key reforms introduced in the early nineteenth century.

The Eighteenth-Century Legacy

It is generally assumed in a nineteenth-century context that 'the state' can only mean the British state, since Ireland did not possess a parliament, an army or control over foreign policy. Even in the eighteenth century, when Ireland possessed a parliament and an army establishment, sovereign power and thus ultimate control lay in London. Yet, as Tom Bartlett has argued, it is possible to detect a nascent Irish state in the eighteenth century, one moreover that grew stronger over time, and that demonstrated an ability to attract the loyalty of its citizens. Indeed, it was the growing strength of the Irish state, he argues, and the threat it 'appeared to pose to imperial unity, that prompted British ministers to urge its absorption into the greater British state'.[3] Over the course of the eighteenth century, the Irish parliament engaged with a variety of economic and social issues and approved acts to promote industry, to regulate prison management, to address poverty and to improve public health. These legislative initiatives were a reflection of the underdeveloped state of local government and the lack of active local elites; they were also evidence of the utility of an Irish parliament that provided the propertied class with a public forum as well as access to funds.[4] Awareness

---

2 S.H. Palmer, 'The Irish police experiment: the beginnings of modern police in the British Isles 1785–95', *Social Science Quarterly*, 56:3 (1975), 411.

3 T. Bartlett, 'From Irish state to British Empire: reflections on state-building in Ireland, 1690–1830', *Études Irlandaises*, 20:1 (1995), 23–37.

4 J. Innes, 'What would a "Four Nations" approach to study of eighteenth-century British social policy entail?' in S.J. Connolly (ed.), *Kingdoms united? Great Britain and Ireland since 1500: integration and diversity* (Dublin: Four Courts Press, 1998), pp. 197–8.

of the eighteenth-century background is crucial for understanding developments in the nineteenth century. Centralised administrative systems were built on frameworks that were already established. Moreover, many of the features assumed to be nineteenth-century innovations were first introduced in the eighteenth century; these include the creation of uniform administrative structures that extended across the whole country, and the central regulation of local administration.

Much of the impetus for reform came from the weak and fragmented nature of local administration in Ireland. The main organs of local government, municipal corporations in major urban areas and county grand juries, were exclusive, inefficient and often partisan. Irish local government initially developed along lines similar to that in Britain. The earliest representatives of central authority in the Irish localities, the county sheriff and local magistrates, were part of the legal system imported to Ireland from England. Division of the country into counties and boroughs also followed English practice. The main divergence was the survival in Ireland of the grand jury, which remained a central element of county administration until the end of the nineteenth century. In England the administrative functions of the grand jury had largely devolved by the nineteenth century to parish vestries and magistrates sitting at quarter sessions. Having been granted the power to levy a local tax to pay for the upkeep of roads and bridges in the early seventeenth century, grand juries acquired a range of further powers and responsibilities over the course of the eighteenth century; these included the building and repair of jails and courthouses (1708), and the establishment of county infirmaries (1765) and houses of industry (1772).

Measures to address poverty and the social evils associated with it were actively discussed in Ireland during the seventeenth and eighteenth centuries with many commentators looking to England for inspiration. Arguing from the premise that it was the responsibility of the ruling classes to provide employment for the poor and thus to develop the economy, George Berkeley, bishop of Cloyne, suggested in the 1730s that parishes in Ireland should be obliged to find work for their resident poor, as was the case in England under the Elizabethan poor law. Similar ideas were advanced by Richard Woodward. When dean of Clogher, he proposed that workhouses should be constructed in each county in order to accommodate the sick and aged as well as able-bodied beggars who would be put to work, to be funded by local taxation and under the control of grand juries.[5] This provided the basis for the act

---

5 P. Gray, *The making of the Irish Poor Law 1815–43* (Manchester: Manchester University

of 1772 that made provision for houses of industry funded by a combination of subscriptions and grants. This act was typical of much of the reforming legislation of the eighteenth century in being permissive in character; a county subscription had to be raised in order for a house of industry to be established. As a result, houses of industry were erected in only a minority of counties; most opted to ignore the act's provisions.[6] Where action was deemed essential to public order or public health, an element of compulsion was sometimes introduced. Legislation approved in 1765 providing for county infirmaries, for example, required infirmaries to be built at the direction of the lord lieutenant and funded by a mixture of local taxation, government grants, voluntary subscriptions and donations. The 1765 act, Andrew Sneddon notes, 'conceived a unified, national system, set up and run in specified locations, according to detailed rules of finance, governance and patient intake, by provincial elites who, largely, regarded it as a statutory obligation'. This represented a significant shift in the approach of central government since it meant that 'the state took at least some responsibility for the country's sick poor', and it can, therefore, be regarded as a 'forerunner to the regulatory institutions of the succeeding century'.[7] But while the act ensured that infirmaries were erected, it did nothing to ensure the buildings were fit for purpose or to regulate the services provided in them. As a result county infirmaries varied enormously. Some were well designed and appropriately equipped but many were small, poorly maintained and inadequately funded.[8] The state also made some direct financial provision for poor relief and health care. The Dublin house of industry, for example, was almost entirely state-funded by the end of the eighteenth century.[9] Hospitals were also beneficiaries; indeed MacDonagh described voluntary hospitals in this period as 'semi-state institutions'. Seven of the major voluntary hospitals received annual grants from

Press, 2009), pp. 20–2; J. Kelly, 'Defending the established order: Richard Woodward Bishop of Cloyne (1726–94)' in J. Kelly and I. McGrath (eds.), *Parliament and politics in seventeenth and eighteenth-century Ireland* (Dublin: UCD Press, 2009), pp. 148–54.

6 The counties taking action were Cork, Waterford, Limerick, Clare, Queen's County, Wexford and Dublin. Existing initiatives in Belfast, Coleraine and Lisburn came under the terms of the act: D. Dickson, 'In search of the Old Irish Poor Law' in R. Mitchison and P. Roebuck (eds.), *Economy and society in Scotland and Ireland 1500–1939* (Edinburgh: John Donald, 1988) p. 155; M. Cousins, 'The Irish parliament and relief of the poor: the 1772 legislation establishing houses of industry', *Eighteenth-Century Ireland*, 28 (2013), 95–115.

7 A. Sneddon, 'State intervention and provincial health care: the county infirmary system in late eighteenth-century Ulster', *Irish Historical Studies*, 38 (2012), 20.

8 L.M. Geary, *Medicine and charity in Ireland 1718–1851* (Dublin: UCD Press, 2004), p. 51.

9 Dickson, 'In search of the Old Irish Poor Law', p. 156.

Westminster in the wake of the ratification of the Act of Union, despite the fact that no other hospitals either in Britain or throughout the Empire were state supported.[10]

One of the areas where the Irish parliament was most active was prison reform. The combination of humanitarian concerns over the treatment of prisoners, growing interest in ideas of moral reform, and alarm over the threat posed to public health by the spread of jail fever provided opposition MPs with an issue they could use to embarrass the government by exposing local maladministration.[11] A parliamentary inquiry into debtors' prisons in 1729–30 led to the Gaol Regulation Act of 1763, which introduced salaries for local gaolers together with basic classification of prisoners, and encouraged Protestant clergy to visit gaols in their localities and to provide food and medicine at public expense to prisoners. This legislation, which predated similar legislation in England, had little practical effect but it did prompt reformers to look for ways of prodding grand juries into action. One result was the Prison Inspection Act 1786 which established a system of prison inspection. Local inspectors appointed by grand juries were required to report to a government-salaried inspector general in Dublin who collated their reports for parliament and gathered statistical data on crimes committed and sentences imposed. Initially a temporary appointment, the position of inspector general was made permanent in 1787: a development presented by MacDonagh as prefiguring the general increase in government power in the nineteenth century.[12] Reviewing progress in 1793, the first inspector general, Sir Jeremiah Fitzpatrick, reported improvements in prison administration and conditions, as well as the erection of new gaols. However, when he resigned shortly afterwards in order to pursue other interests, the post was not filled until 1796 and then by a much less active incumbent (Illustration 51).

Imposing financial responsibilities on local authorities without allowing them control over how the money was spent proved very unpopular. Legislation enacted by the Irish parliament in 1787 empowered the lord lieutenant to appoint a chief constable to command a force of locally appointed Protestant constables in disturbed districts, provided that the cost was met partly by government and partly by grand jury presentment. The original plan was for all appointments to be made centrally but the bill was amended

---

10 MacDonagh, 'Ideas and institutions', p. 210.

11 Innes, 'What would a "Four Nations" approach to study of eighteenth-century British social policy entail?', p. 191.

12 O. MacDonagh, *The Inspector General: Sir Jeremiah Fitzpatrick and social reform, 1783–1802* (London: Croom Helm, 1981), p. 316.

51. Sir Jeremiah Fitzpatrick (*c*.1740–1810) was a physician, inspector of prisons and pioneering social reformer, who paved the way for social reform in the nineteenth century. Mezzotint by William Barnard, after Samuel Drummond, 1801.

during its passage through parliament to allow for the appointment of constables (but not chief constables) to be made locally by grand juries. Despite the change, the act was fiercely criticised as an assault on Irish liberties, and in 1792 control of the force was transferred to local magistrates and all appointments vested in grand juries. Furthermore thirteen northern and eastern counties were exempted from the provisions of the act until 1796, when it was extended to the country as a whole.[13] Known as baronial constables, the men appointed were widely represented as ill disciplined and inefficient.[14]

The Age of Reform

The early decades of the nineteenth century were a period of relative optimism encouraged by the widespread belief that improvement in Ireland was possible. With the restoration of political stability following the Act of Union, politicians of all shades of opinion looked to the Westminster parliament to effect reforms that would address Irish grievances and provide solutions to long-standing problems. Popular politicians such as Daniel O'Connell sought justice for the Catholic population together with practical improvements such as reform of the legal system and measures to extend education and reduce the extent of poverty. Liberal Protestants such as Sir John Newport, Sir Henry Parnell and Thomas Spring Rice campaigned for similar measures, hoping to promote social cohesion and thus secure their position as the natural leaders of Irish society. Notwithstanding the gloomy predictions of some commentators suggesting that Irish problems were insoluble, many British politicians shared the general sense of optimism. The attention focused on Ireland in public discourse and in parliament is evidence of the interest in and commitment to bringing about beneficial change.[15]

Anxious to integrate the country more closely into the United Kingdom and to reduce the chasm that separated England and Ireland in the arenas of economic development and political and social stability, successive governments were disposed to respond to pressing problems by establishing administrative structures and introducing institutions that had no equivalent in Britain. There was less contradiction here than might appear, since the aim of exceptional measures was to speed up development in Ireland in order to bring it more

---

13 S.H. Palmer, *Police and protest in England and Ireland, 1780–1850* (Cambridge: Cambridge University Press, 1988).

14 See for example, W.R. Wilde, *Irish popular superstitions* (Dublin: J. McGlashen, 1852), p. 53.

15 N. Ó Ciosáin, *Ireland in official print culture 1800–1850* (Oxford: Oxford University Press, 2014).

closely into line with Britain. Ireland appeared more disordered, more discontented, more divided, poorer and more vulnerable to contagious diseases than other parts of the United Kingdom. If the country was to achieve the stability and prosperity of England, these problems needed to be addressed. How best to do this was the subject of much debate. Some argued for stronger government. The French writer Gustave de Beaumont expressed a common view when he noted that while the English landowner acted as a 'patron of the soil and its inhabitants', the Irish proprietor was merely 'desirous of deriving ... the greatest profit possible'. What Ireland needed, he maintained, was 'a strong administration ... beneath whose shadow the middle classes might grow up, develop themselves, and acquire instruction, whilst the aristocracy would crumble away'.[16] But while some in Britain were inclined to agree – Ireland, the lord lieutenant, Lord Anglesey, declared in 1831, 'wants a Bonaparte'[17] – many others distrusted intervention and centralisation as foreign to British traditions and practices. As Robert Peel had warned the Irish chief secretary in 1828, 'to take [local administration] into the hands of Government is to widen the distinction between England and Ireland and postpone the period at which Irish local affairs can be satisfactorily managed by local authorities'.[18]

Ministers remained anxious to strengthen and stimulate local authorities without superseding them. Central inspection was extended, but as a way of prompting local authorities into action. Thus prison inspection underwent further reform in the 1820s, with the introduction of a second inspector general. The two inspectors were required to divide the country between them and visit each prison at least every other year. Their reports were to be sent to grand juries at assizes, and a joint national report presented to parliament. In 1823 central government was empowered to close unsatisfactory bridewells and amalgamate others. The result was the closure of numerous smaller bridewells and the erection or alteration (with government funding) of others. Three years later prison administration was consolidated and a code of regulations introduced. Grand juries remained responsible for county prisons but their management was devolved to boards of management of which half were to be local magistrates. Speaking in the Commons in 1831, Spring Rice credited inspection with improving prison discipline and establishing it 'in the good state in which it now was'.[19] The trend towards greater centralisation

---

16 G. A. de la Bonniere de Beaumont, *Ireland, social, political and religious*, ed. W.C. Taylor, 2 vols. (London: R. Bentley, 1839), vol. i, p. 288; vol. ii, pp. 213–14.

17 Anglesey to Holland, 3 Sept. 1831, Anglesey papers, D619/27B, f. 36, PRONI.

18 Peel to Gower, 26 Dec. 1828, Peel papers, Add. MS 40336, f. 187, BL.

19 *Hansard*, 3rd series, 6, 944.

continued in subsequent decades with the opening of the first state prison, Mountjoy, in 1850 and the establishment of a centralised system of prison management in 1877.[20]

Concern about the state of the country in the early nineteenth century led to further attempts to encourage local authorities to take a proactive approach to poverty and public health. The most important manifestation of this was legislation to provide for the establishment of voluntary dispensaries (1805) and fever hospitals (1818). These acts were permissive but the 1817 act establishing district lunatic asylums was compulsory. The act enabled the lord lieutenant to order the establishment of district asylums for the lunatic poor, the involvement of grand juries being restricted to raising the necessary funds. Looking back on the legislation from the 1850s, Thomas Larcom admitted that the act was 'in advance of public opinion', but explained that it had been necessary to take the initiative since, 'if the grand juries had been left to erect them … few if any would have been erected'. The act followed years of campaigning by Irish MPs such as Sir John Newport, who had introduced an unsuccessful bill to establish four asylums throughout Ireland in 1805. Catherine Cox has described the act as part of 'the trend towards the centralisation of powers away from local government and landlords and to Dublin Castle'. Subsequent legislation established a central board of control and in 1845 a separate lunacy inspectorate. It is important to note, however, that the management of district asylums was left in local hands, being entrusted to boards of governors composed of local landowners, magistrates, merchants, clergy and, after 1838, poor law guardians.[21] From 1875 central government contributed a portion of the establishment costs, providing 4 shillings per patient per week, amounting to around two-fifths of the average yearly cost of a patient's upkeep.[22]

By the middle of the nineteenth century, Ireland possessed what MacDonagh described as 'one of the most advanced health services in Europe in the first half of the nineteenth century. It was to a large degree state-supported, uniform and centralised.'[23] The British government, it has been observed, was 'far more interventionist' with regard to public health

20 S. Kilcommins, I. O'Donnell, E. O'Sullivan and B. Vaughan, *Crime, punishment and the search for order in Ireland* (Dublin: IPA, 2004), pp. 16–18.

21 C. Cox, *Negotiating insanity in the southeast of Ireland 1820–1900* (Manchester: Manchester University Press, 2012), pp. 5, 11.

22 V. Crossman, *Local government in nineteenth-century Ireland* (Belfast: Institute of Irish Studies, 1994), p. 39.

23 MacDonagh, 'Ideas and institutions', p. 210.

in Ireland than elsewhere in the United Kingdom, and took an active role in shaping and directing medical provision.[24] By the mid-1830s there were around 500 dispensaries, forty-one county and city infirmaries and seventy fever hospitals.[25] But with much still depending on local initiative and local funding, the distribution of these institutions across the country was uneven, and the quality of the service provided extremely variable. County infirmaries and fever hospitals tended to be small and accessible only to those living in the immediate vicinity.[26] Neither the income nor the number of beds available in county institutions bore any relation to medical need, or the size of the local population.[27] As David Dickson observes, county facilities 'were ultimately dependent on the willingness of the wealthier classes to become involved and make substantial recurring contributions', and with increasing interference from the centre and the growing challenge of poverty and disorder, by the 1830s 'the vulnerability of voluntarism was exposed'.[28]

Education

If the root causes of Ireland's problems, poverty, ignorance and disorder were generally agreed on, so were the remedies: economic development, education and the establishment of the rule of law, all of which were seen to be closely linked. Education had been on the reform agenda for many years. All agreed that the education of the lower orders would help to bring about improvements in Ireland. The problem was how to achieve this, and how to ensure that it was the right kind of education. In the eighteenth century, plans to introduce a general system of education had come to grief over the issue of moral and religious instruction. In the early nineteenth century, British ministers remained committed to education in principle but were wary of the political controversy that any extensive scheme was likely to provoke. It was thus left to Irish MPs to take the initiative on the issue. Education was a particular interest of moderate reformers such as Spring Rice and Richard Bourke. The

---

24 E. Malcolm and G. Jones, 'Introduction: an anatomy of Irish medical history' in E. Malcolm and G. Jones (eds.), *Medicine, disease and the state in Ireland, 1650–1940* (Cork: Cork University Press, 1999), p. 6.

25 *Poor Inquiry (Ireland): Second Report of the Commissioners for Inquiring into the Condition of the Poorer Classes in Ireland*, Parl. Papers, 1837 (68), Appendix 5, p. 15.

26 *Second Annual Report of the Commissioners for Administering the Laws for Relief of the Poor in Ireland, under the Medical Charities Act*, Parl. Papers, 1854 [1759], p. 12.

27 Geary, *Medicine and charity in Ireland*, pp. 52–3.

28 Dickson, 'In search of the Old Irish Poor Law', p. 157.

latter, Jennifer Ridden notes, had 'established non-denominational schools on his [Limerick] estate from as early as 1820'.[29]

Making the most of his influence within Whig circles, Spring Rice was appointed chair of the Select Committee on Irish Education in 1828. This enabled him to have a major role both in the conduct of the committee and in the drafting of the final report, which recommended a system of mixed education that did not interfere with religious beliefs.[30] When the Whigs took office in 1830 a plan based on the committee's report was promptly submitted to the new chief secretary, Edward Stanley. Stanley was sympathetic to the principle of mixed education. He had also been in correspondence with the Catholic cleric James Doyle, bishop of Kildare and Leighlin, and he incorporated a number of Doyle's recommendations into the bill he presented to parliament in September 1831.[31] The resulting act established a board of national education with powers to supervise the curriculum and to provide funding to cover school buildings, equipment, salaries and other running expenses. There was to be an inspectorate to report on schools and to set and maintain standards, and model schools to act as teaching training colleges.

Credited with making Ireland 'a country of literates', the national school system, which predated the establishment of a similar system in England by almost forty years, reflected the desire for education amongst the Catholic population as much as the desire of government to foster an educated and orderly populace.[32] While more than half the population aged 5 years and over was recorded as illiterate in 1841, this proportion had dropped to one third by 1871. By 1881, 59 per cent of the population were able to read and write, compared to 33 per cent in 1851.[33] While it was a national system in that it extended across the country and was funded in part by an annual parliamentary grant, it was not under direct government control and was, as Comerford explains, designed to operate at arm's length from the state. The controlling body was a board of commissioners over whose actions the government had no direct control, although the lord lieutenant was required

29 J. Ridden, 'Irish reform between the 1798 Rebellion and the Great Famine' in R.A. Burns and J. Innes (eds.), *Rethinking the age of reform* (Cambridge: Cambridge University Press, 2003), p. 286.

30 Ridden, 'Irish reform between the 1798 Rebellion and the Great Famine', pp. 286–7.

31 I. Murphy, 'Primary education' in P.J. Corish (ed.), *History of Irish Catholicism: the church since emancipation* (Dublin: Gill and Macmillan, 1971), pp. 5–6.

32 D.H. Akenson, 'Pre-university education 1782–1870' in Vaughan (ed.), *A new history of Ireland*, vol. v: *Ireland under the Union, I, 1801–70*, p. 536.

33 C. Hutton, 'Publishing the Irish cultural revival 1891–1922' in C. Hutton and P. Walsh (eds.), *The Oxford history of the Irish book*, vol. v (Oxford: Oxford University Press, 2011), p. 19.

to approve any changes of rules governing national schools, and could dismiss the commissioners. Individual schools had considerable autonomy. The board monitored activities and provided funding but did not operate or own the schools. Having created a system designed to minimise direct state involvement, ministers could do little to prevent it becoming almost entirely denominational. Moreover, because of the local autonomy built into the system, national schools were able to develop an ethos that was antipathetic to the British state. Many responded to the rise of cultural nationalism in the early twentieth century by embracing the teaching of Irish. Whereas only 105 national schools presented pupils for examination in Irish in 1899, more than 2,500 (comprising over 30 per cent of the total) did so in 1912.[34] If this was a state system, therefore, it was a very peculiar one.

Social and Economic Development

The board of national education was just one of a number of initiatives undertaken in the 1830s that signalled a more radical approach to reform in Ireland and a greater willingness to challenge the power of local elites in an attempt to accelerate the pace of change. Having long supported Catholic emancipation, Whig ministers wanted to put emancipation into practice and to demonstrate that Union government could benefit all the people of Ireland. In addition to education provision, the Whig administration headed by Lord Grey established the Board of Works in 1831, and introduced a modest measure of grand jury reform. Headed by three salaried commissioners, the Board of Works was empowered to make loans not exceeding £500,000 in total for works initiated either by local authorities or by private individuals. A further £50,000 was made available for distribution as grants to facilitate the construction of roads and bridges in poorer areas.[35] In an attempt to provide for the more satisfactory scrutiny of grand jury expenditure, an act of 1833 allowed a small number of cess-payers (chosen by the grand jury) to examine presentments prior to their consideration by the grand jury. It also required all approved presentments to be executed by contracts made on sealed tenders, and overseen by qualified surveyors appointed by the government. This was a far more modest measure than critics of the grand jury system sought;

---

34 R.V. Comerford, 'The British state and the education of Irish Catholics 1850–1921' in J. Tomiak et al. (eds.), *Schooling, educational policy and ethnic identity* (London: Institute of Education, 1991), pp. 15–16, 25.

35 R.B. McDowell, 'Administration and the public services, 1800–70' in Vaughan (ed.), *A new history of Ireland*, vol. v: *Ireland under the Union, I, 1801–70*, p. 550.

O'Connell had called for an end to county administration by grand juries and the introduction of a new system of democratically elected county boards. The reform process continued with a further act of 1836 extending cess-payer involvement.[36] More importantly perhaps, the grand jury was increasingly eclipsed as an organ of local administration by the poor law board.

If the Board of Works was an attempt to reduce poverty and disorder through indirect means, the poor law was an attempt to alleviate poverty directly. The Irish Poor Relief Act of 1838, which was modelled on the English New Poor Law of 1834, was a compromise measure that was greeted with little enthusiasm in Ireland. Most Irish reformers were opposed to the idea of a poor law. Newport and Spring Rice for example argued that a poor law based on a parochial rate would manufacture poverty, not relieve it.[37] But if ministers opted for a workhouse system partly as a way of avoiding the kind of large-scale public expenditure recommended by the Whateley Commission 'on the poorer classes' in 1833, they also embraced the measure as a positive way of helping and improving Ireland. One great advantage of the measure in Whig-Liberal eyes was that it would make Irish property pay for Irish poverty. The prime minister, Lord John Russell, was convinced that progress in Ireland depended on the emergence of responsible, resident gentry in place of irresponsible rack-renting absentees. A poor law would force Irish landlords to take responsibility for the Irish poor. As he explained on the introduction of the bill in December 1837, no one should expect a poor law to eradicate poverty; rather it should be seen as 'one of many improvements by which the security of property may be increased – by which order may be maintained – by which poverty may be relieved – and by which the various classes in Ireland may be better united'.[38]

Advocates of the poor law hoped that the experience of working together on poor law boards would bring the various classes in Ireland together, and create a bond of union between them that would help to reduce sectarian and partisan feeling. In their annual report for 1841 the poor law commissioners revealed that they had always considered that the creation of poor law unions and

> a local machinery for their government, would afford important facilities for the introduction of other local improvements in Ireland. Hitherto, there has been a want of means for the origination and carrying out of such objects,

36 Crossman, *Local government in nineteenth-century Ireland*, pp. 36–9.
37 Gray, *The making of the Irish Poor Law*, p. 65.
38 *Hansard*, 3rd series, 39 (1 Dec. 1837), 492.

but the union authorities now afford the means and possess the requisite degree of influence and consideration, for setting on foot and supporting undertakings calculated to benefit its inhabitants.[39]

This hope was not to be realised. Nonetheless, the boards did prove a convenient alternative to grand juries, which were increasingly seen as unrepresentative and ineffectual.

Administered partly by guardians elected by ratepayers and partly by local magistrates sitting *ex officio*, boards of guardians were more representative of ratepayers' interests, while still providing a major role for local landowners. In the post-Famine period poor law boards were given a wide range of responsibilities in addition to the management of the workhouse; their remit was extended to embrace the administration of health and safety legislation such as the Sanitary Act of 1866, and the Public Health Acts of 1874 and 1878, while grand juries were gradually side-lined. This process was reflected in local expenditure levels. Whilst the county cess, which had risen dramatically from £0.4m in 1803 to £1.3m in 1840 in the first half of the nineteenth century, remained fairly static in the second half of the century, poor law expenditure rose from £0.75m in the mid 1850s to £1.4m in 1886.[40]

Prior to the Great Famine, poor relief was only available within the workhouse. Under the pressure of mass starvation and with many workhouses full to overflowing, the system was extended in 1847 to allow poor law boards to grant outdoor relief to the sick and disabled, and to widows with two or more legitimate children. Outdoor relief could only be granted to the able-bodied if the workhouse was full, or a site of infection. Furthermore, anyone occupying more than one quarter of an acre of land was excluded from receiving relief. Initially a relatively minor element of the poor law system, medical provision became increasingly central to poor law administration. As part of the expansion of the poor law system in 1847, boards of guardians were empowered to establish separate hospitals 'for the reception and treatment of "poor persons" affected by dangerous contagious disease'. As a result many of the fever hospitals that had been established by grand juries under previous legislation closed. In 1847 there were 104 grand jury fever hospitals, together with 63 under the control of boards of guardians. In 1852 there were just 40 grand jury hospitals remaining, and 147 poor law fever hospitals.[41] The

39 *Sixth Annual Report of the Poor Law Commissioners*, Parl. Papers, 1840 (245), p. 24.
40 Crossman, *Local government in nineteenth-century Ireland*, pp. 40, 52.
41 *Second Annual Report of the Commissioners for Administering the Laws for Relief of the Poor in Ireland, under the Medical Charities Act*, Parl. Papers, 1854 [1759], p. 12.

expansion of poor law medical services continued in the decades after the Famine. In 1851 dispensary provision was reorganised and reconstituted as part of the poor law system, and in 1862 workhouse hospitals were opened to the non-destitute poor.

The poor law established new administrative units in Ireland (poor law unions) and new administrative bodies (poor law boards) to which central government could delegate local responsibilities. The system was far from uniform, however, and there were limits to the control which the central authorities could exercise. In contrast to grand juries that operated relatively free from central interference, poor law boards conducted their business under the watchful eye of the poor law commissioners, who were empowered to dissolve any board that failed to administer the poor law according to statutory regulations. But while the central poor law authorities were responsible for maintaining the integrity of the system as a whole, local poor law boards were responsible for the actual administration of relief. Poor law guardians were responsible for deciding on individual applications for relief and their decisions could not be over turned unless they contravened statutory regulations. The extent of local autonomy became clear in the later decades of the nineteenth century. However much the central authorities preached the virtues of economy and urged boards of guardians to enforce the workhouse test for all able-bodied applicants, many boards increasingly chose to relieve people outside rather than inside the workhouse. What was in theory a uniform system thus permitted considerable local variation both between regions and within them. This is evident in terms of the relief provided, and levels of expenditure. Unions on the eastern seaboard, together with those in the central south-eastern portion of the country, provided significantly higher levels of relief proportionate to the population, and spent more on relief and related administration, than those in the north, west and south-west.[42]

Much like the education system, the poor law system evolved in ways that its architects neither envisioned nor intended. The period of the Land War saw many boards come under the control of elected local tenant guardians. Prior to this, the landed elite dominated poor law administration. The transfer in power across much of the south and west of the country from *ex officio* to elected guardians was to produce a far more politicised and polarised system.[43] It was also to enable people who previously had no access to political

---

42 V. Crossman, *Poverty and the Poor Law in Ireland 1850–1914* (Liverpool: Liverpool University Press, 2013), pp. 52–62.

43 This process is explored in V. Crossman, *Politics, pauperism and power in late nineteenth-century Ireland* (Manchester: Manchester University Press, 2006).

power to gain executive experience. Feingold argued that one reason why Ireland managed to establish stable democratic government after independence was that the people had active experience of local democracy through local bodies such as poor law boards.[44] However, the highly politicised character of poor law administration and of local government generally had a polarising effect; it increased community divisions and prioritised national questions over local issues.

Law and Order

Perhaps the most pressing problem besetting post-Union Ireland was the lawless nature of the country. As the commentator George Cornewall Lewis noted in 1836, 'in a large part of Ireland there is still less security of person and property than in any other part of Europe'.[45] In an age when the role of central government was strictly limited, maintenance of the law and the preservation of life and property were regarded as primary responsibilities. The perceived extent of crime and disorder thus acquired a critical political significance, being taken as an indicator of government effectiveness. And since disorder in Ireland took the form primarily of agrarian disturbances the issue inevitably was linked with the whole question of land and land tenure. A government that was unable to maintain order not only failed to protect life and property, but also failed to get to grips with the land question. Under these circumstances it is not surprising that the state played an increasingly active role in overseeing the local administration of justice.

In England, magistrates who presided over petty and quarter sessions were believed to operate with the confidence of the local population. In Ireland there was little public confidence in the local magistracy because the majority of magistrates were drawn from the Protestant landed gentry. Magistrates who were not inactive or incompetent were generally believed to be corrupt. Magisterial lists were revised on a number of occasions in the early decades of the nineteenth century in order to weed out unsuitable people, and a determined effort was made, particularly by Whig administrations, to appoint more Catholic magistrates. At the same time steps were taken to regularise the conduct of magisterial proceedings by encouraging magistrates to act jointly in petty sessions rather than singly at their own residences, and by

---

44 W.L. Feingold, *The revolt of the tenantry: the transformation of local government in Ireland 1872–1886* (Boston, MA: Northeastern University Press, 1984), pp. 234–5.

45 G.C. Lewis, *On local disturbances in Ireland, and on the Irish church question* (London: B. Fellowes, 1836), p. 1.

requiring a registry to be kept of all acts and proceedings to be signed by all the magistrates present.[46]

Ministers also attempted to enhance the image and authority of the law by strengthening the professional element over the amateur through the creation of salaried legal officers such as assistant barristers and crown solicitors. Once again, the idea was to improve the efficiency and efficacy of the legal process and to lessen the degree to which the law was seen to be the instrument of Protestant landlords. Assistant barristers were originally appointed to act as 'a constant assistant to the justices' at quarter sessions. As a result of the Rightboy disturbances in the south of Ireland, the lord lieutenant was empowered in 1787 to appoint a barrister of at least six years' standing to assist justices at quarter sessions in disturbed districts. In 1796 this provision was extended to all Irish counties and the assistant barrister empowered to hear civil bills as sole and exclusive judge. Jurisdiction was initially limited to suits involving less than £20, but this was extended in 1814 to cover actions for damages for assault where the amount claimed was less than 5 guineas, and in 1816 to the recovery of small landholdings.[47] Meanwhile, more serious cases were increasingly prosecuted by crown solicitors rather than left to private prosecutions. Appearing before a commons select committee in 1829, Matthew Barrington, the crown solicitor for Munster, stated that virtually all serious felonies were then prosecuted as crown cases, commenting that this had helped to preserve the peace by increasing the certainty of prosecution and confidence in the law.[48]

In addition to assistant barristers appointed to support local justices at sessions, government had recourse to the services of stipendiary magistrates. One of the first appointments was that of Edward Wilson in 1799. Having initially acted as a police magistrate in Dublin, Wilson was sent to Kerry in 1808 to coordinate the authorities' efforts to contain disturbances in that county. Ministers were wary of deploying stipendiaries more widely, fearing that this would discourage the ordinary magistracy as well as provoke complaints. As the chief secretary, Sir Arthur Wellesley (later Duke of Wellington), observed in 1808, it was not that this would not 'be a very efficient mode of keeping the peace, but it would be very unconstitutional and

46 McDowell, 'Administration and the public services', p. 545.
47 R.B. McDowell, *The Irish administration 1801–1914* (London: Routledge and Kegan Paul, 1964), pp. 113–14.
48 *Report of the Select Committee on Irish Miscellaneous Estimates*, Parl. Papers 1829 (342), p. 148.

would be objected to in parliament'.[49] Stipendiary magistrates were thought to be efficient but problematic in the long term since they provided ordinary magistrates with an excuse for inactivity. Henry Hardinge (chief secretary 1830) remarked that the problem with relying on stipendiaries was that 'a temporary measure of relief becomes a confirmed habit rendering the resident gentry more inert than they were before'.[50] Increasingly, however, the advantages were seen to outweigh the disadvantages. Resident magistrates were active and, in theory at least, they were impartial, being assumed to be more detached than ordinary magistrates and less influenced by local feeling. Moreover, if they proved unsatisfactory, they could simply be removed or dismissed. It is important to emphasise that stipendiary magistrates never replaced ordinary magistrates. Court records from across the country demonstrate that ordinary magistrates continued to form an essential part of the legal process, acting both in petty sessions and alone.[51]

The highest degree of central regulation and control was evident in law enforcement. During the course of the nineteenth century, the administration and enforcement of emergency powers were increasingly taken out of the hands of local magistrates and entrusted to government officials.[52] Furthermore, in contrast to police forces in Britain that operated under the control of local authorities, from 1836 the Irish constabulary was directed and controlled from the centre. Organised along military lines and accommodated in barracks, this was a force serving not the locality, but the state. Whereas in Britain the emphasis by the later part of the nineteenth century was on the detection of crime and policing by consent, in Ireland the priority remained the suppression of disorder, so that the police were frequently obliged to operate by force. Personifying stability and order, the constabulary force, Elizabeth Malcolm concludes, 'was more about power than about crime. It was a ubiquitous, all-purpose arm of government, rigidly disciplined and strictly controlled, and intended to observe and regulate most major aspects of Irish political, economic and social life.'[53]

---

49 Wellesley to Littlehales, 9 Dec. 1808, 2nd Duke of Wellington (ed.), *Civil Correspondence and Memoranda (Ireland)* (London, 1860), p. 85, cited in Crossman, *Politics, law and order*, p. 18.
50 Hardinge to Peel, 23 Sept. 1830, Peel papers, Add. MS 40313, f. 34, BL.
51 See for example Balbriggan Petty Sessions Order Book, CSPS, 1/350, National Archives of Ireland.
52 Crossman, *Politics, law and order*, passim.
53 E. Malcolm, *The Irish policeman 1822–1922: a life* (Dublin: Four Courts Press, 2006), p. 128.

Policing

The evolution of a national police force has often been presented as a gradual but irreversible transfer of power from the localities to the centre, a prime example of the 'centralized authoritarianism and national uniformity' believed to have characterised Irish government at all levels.[54] What is often overlooked in such accounts is that progress was both uneven and contested. As we have seen, early initiatives were hampered by an inherent contradiction in attempting to strengthen the hand of central government in responding to disorder without undermining the authority of local magistrates and grand juries. The idea of deploying specially appointed temporary police forces to restore order to disturbed districts was animated in the early nineteenth century by Robert Peel (chief secretary 1812–18). Introducing the Peace Preservation Act in 1814, Peel was careful to present it as an exceptional measure.[55] The bill provided for a special force consisting of a chief magistrate, a chief constable and fifty sub-constables to be deployed in any district proclaimed to be in a state of disturbance, the cost to be met from grand jury presentments. Peel was well aware of the sensitive nature of such a proposal, since MPs were notoriously resistant to anything resembling a 'gendarmerie' because of its associations with state tyranny. He was careful to stress that the chief magistrates would not be invested with extraordinary powers and would only be called upon to perform those tasks, such as accompanying search parties at night, which it was unreasonable to expect ordinary magistrates to undertake. The Peace Preservation Act was thus intended to act as both a spur and a support to local magistrates.[56]

Peel's initiative has often been presented as a prime example of centralisation. Palmer describes Peel's approach to the government of Ireland as 'based on innovation and centralization ... His ideas on the police were a Castle-orientated version of enlightened despotism.'[57] But this is to misrepresent Peel's underlying philosophy and his attachment to the principle of local autonomy. Far from embracing centralisation, he resorted to it reluctantly and resisted it where possible. Replying to a motion for a select committee to consider the office of constable in Ireland in 1818, Peel rejected the suggestion

---

54 This phrase occurred a number of times in MacDonagh's work: see, for example, *Early Victorian government 1830–1870* (London: Holmes and Meier, 1977), p. 181; *The Inspector General*, p. 316.
55 *Hansard*, 1st series, 28 (23 June 1814), 163–72.
56 Crossman, *Politics, law and order*, p. 20.
57 Palmer, *Police and protest*, p. 531.

balance.[65] It was this situation that the Whig-Liberal 'justice to Ireland' policy was intended to redress.

Police reform was a central feature of the reform programme of the Whig-Liberal administration that took office in 1835. Lords Mulgrave and Morpeth, who became lord lieutenant and chief secretary, and the under-secretary, Thomas Drummond, were united in believing that radical action was needed to restore people's confidence in government. The law had to be seen to be administered fairly and measures promoted that would improve the material condition of the mass of the population. Drummond was convinced that the existing organisation of the constabulary, which was divided into four distinct provincial forces each under a separate head, was inconvenient and inefficient. Moreover, leaving appointments in the hands of local magistrates had, he concluded, allowed a 'bad description' of men to enter the constabulary. As a result, 'the people regard the police as a partisan force'.[66] Drummond's proposed solution, the creation of a unified force with appointments vested in the lord lieutenant, was to return to the model first proposed in the 1780s. If the model was familiar, so was the opposition it faced from Irish landowners who resented the potential threat to their influence and authority. Following complaints that the new force would be both expensive and filled with Catholics, the bill was amended, significantly reducing the number of constabulary inspectors to be invested with magisterial powers, thus removing the prospect of an inspector-magistrate in every county, which was particularly objectionable to the resident gentry. The lord lieutenant retained his power to appoint stipendiary magistrates at will, but these individuals would not be members of the force and would have no direct control over it. The Irish Constabulary Act of 1822 nevertheless represented a major reform, establishing a national police force with a military ethos. Members were instructed 'to avoid, in every respect, the most remote appearance of partisanship, or the expression of sectarian or political opinions'. They were not to serve in their native county, or in any county where they had connexions 'by marriage or otherwise'.[67] Reform did go some way to improve the public image of the constabulary, amongst the Catholic community at least. One of the most powerful means available to the government to maintain tranquillity in Ireland, Mulgrave was to claim in 1838, was the confidence felt by the great

---

65 Littleton to Blackburne, 3 Dec. 1833, cited in Crossman, *Politics, law and order*, p. 66.

66 Drummond to Morpeth, 6 Aug. 1835, cited in Crossman, *Politics, law and order*, p. 70.

67 *Standing Rules and Regulations for the Government and Guidance of the Constabulary Force in Ireland; as approved by his excellency the Earl of Mulgrave, Lord Lieutenant General and General Governor of Ireland* (Dublin: G. and J. Grierson, 1837), p. 6.

body of the people 'that the constabulary was no longer a party force'.[68] The impetus for police reform came from the desire to create an impartial force that could operate effectively throughout the country and not be drawn into local conflicts or political divisions. The military character of the police was, and remained, a focus of criticism but it was strongly defended by members of the constabulary as essential to its operations. As the inspector general, Colonel Duncan McGregor, commented in 1847, it would be impossible to organise a large armed force without some military spirit. It would also, one suspects, have been impossible to maintain discipline amongst men drawn from different parts of Ireland as well as different religions. It was, McGregor observed, a matter of 'great wonder' to him that the men were so free of political and religious bias in the execution of their duties and lived together in harmony with one another.[69]

With a presence in even the remotest districts, and an established identity within the community, the police were well placed to take on duties that required regular contact with local people. By the early 1850s their duties included distributing and collecting voting papers for the election of poor law guardians, compiling statistical returns, assisting the board of health, and inspecting weights and measures. In 1857 the constabulary took over the task of suppressing illicit distillation, previously performed by a separate force of revenue police. Charged with enforcing an increasing volume of legislation designed to regulate and to control a whole range of activities, from keeping a dog to begging, the force found itself at the forefront of efforts to impose new standards of public behaviour. The imposition of such duties, Elizabeth Malcolm and William Lowe have argued, helped 'substantially to transform and domesticate the force's character', so that by the early years of the twentieth century, external appearances notwithstanding, it constituted 'a thoroughly domesticated, civil police force'.[70]

The process of domestication, like that of centralisation, was partial and patchy. What determined the character of the constabulary were the duties they performed and the manner in which they were deployed. Even during the widespread disturbances of the early 1830s when the Tithe War was at its height, many parts of Ireland remained peaceful. In these districts the police were largely confined to attending quarter sessions and assizes and

---

68 Mulgrave to Russell, 28 March 1838, cited in Crossman, *Politics, law and order*, p. 72.
69 Observations of Col. MacGregor on the Constabulary Force, 10 Dec. 1847, Official Papers (MA), 145/8, NAI.
70 W.J. Lowe and E. Malcolm, 'The domestication of the Royal Irish Constabulary', *Irish Economic and Social History*, 19 (1992), 32.

appearing at fairs and markets. In districts where the police were regularly required to enforce the payment of tithes, however, they acted more as a coercive force, with consequences for the men deployed and the reputation of the force. Recalling his experiences in County Longford in the 1840s, head constable Robert Dunlop contrasted the demanding nature of police work in the northern part of the county, where the prevalence of agrarian outrages necessitated nightly outings by joint police and army patrols, with the much lighter duties of a posting to Lisryan near the border with County Westmeath, where the main task was to be present at Granard market every alternate Monday.[71]

Centralisation was initially introduced as a means of giving the force popular legitimacy. That legitimacy was bound up with the legitimacy of central government. As central government came more into conflict with the mass of the population, so the police came to be aligned once again with the forces of reaction and repression. Thus while police duties throughout much of Ireland increasingly acquired a domestic character, in disturbed districts where the constabulary were required to carry out evictions and arrest those suspected of political disaffection, the police performed a role that brought them into direct conflict with the local populace. The most immediate point of contact with authority for most ordinary people, the constabulary personified law and order and were duty-bound to neutralise potential threats to the fabric of society whether in the form of immoral behaviour or political disaffection. It is hardly surprising therefore that loyalty was highly valued. While the majority of Irish policemen were drawn from the Catholic community, their officers remained predominantly Protestant. Moreover, the proportion of Catholics among senior officers, which had increased up to the 1880s, declined in the decades thereafter. Viewed as potentially disloyal, Catholic recruits, Fergus Campbell argues, experienced a glass ceiling.[72] Whereas Protestant officers were assumed to be loyal, Catholics had to prove their loyalty, making it more difficult to advance within the force. Such obstacles, Campbell suggests, may have contributed to the sense of frustration and resentment within the Catholic middle class that was to stimulate recruitment to the separatist cause in the early twentieth century.[73]

---

71 Memoirs of head constable Robert Dunlop, T/2815/1, PRONI.
72 F. Campbell, *The Irish establishment 1879–1914* (Oxford: Oxford University Press, 2009), pp. 132–4.
73 F. Campbell, 'The social composition of the senior officers of the Royal Irish Constabulary, 1881–1911', *Irish Historical Studies*, 36 (2009), 540–1.

Conclusion

The nineteenth century saw the emergence of new kinds of government and administration throughout the United Kingdom, and a new kind of state, one that intervened more directly in the lives of its citizens. In Britain this process was driven largely by the demands of industrialisation. This was not the case in Ireland, where government focused more on addressing the consequences of centuries of political upheaval and the fractured nature of Irish society. In understanding the reform process it is important to look beyond the particular problem being addressed to consider the individuals addressing it and the political context. Administrative reform was the product not simply of the pressure of events, or bureaucratic pragmatism, although these were important, but of individual and collective action. It reflected a belief in the power of government, central and local, to improve the fabric of society and the lives of the people. Generally presented in negative terms as providing evidence of the oppressive nature of British rule, and reinforcing the colonial relationship in which Britain and Ireland were bound, the growth of the state in the nineteenth century was a more complex process than is often suggested, and its consequences more varied and unpredictable. While there was an undoubted power differential between the two jurisdictions, and while British always trumped Irish interests in ministerial decision making, the developments described here contributed to the development of an educated, well-ordered, democratic society, whose members had access to a range of local services that were to some extent need-dependent. The reform process moreover helped to propel Ireland towards modernity and independence. That was not the intention but it was ultimately the effect.

PART V

*

THE IRISH ABROAD

21

The Irish in Europe in the Eighteenth Century, 1691–1815

LIAM CHAMBERS

Introduction

Tens of thousands of Irish migrants settled in continental Europe in the 'long' eighteenth century, extending well-established patterns of mobility with roots in sixteenth-century state building, confessionalisation and trade patterns. France, Spain, Portugal and the southern Netherlands continued to attract the largest proportion of migrants, with more moderate numbers drawn to the Italian states and Austria, and a smaller proportion again making their way to destinations in northern Europe. Modern scholarship on the 'Irish in Europe' emerged in the late nineteenth century, when the pioneers of the subject focused on the valour of Irish soldiers and the piety of Irish clergy abroad.[1] The professionalisation of Irish history in the twentieth century brought new standards to bear on migration studies, while greater access to European repositories after the conclusion of the Second World War opened fresh lines of inquiry, notably on merchants and women.[2] Since the 1980s, Irish and continental European historians have produced a stream of new research, attuned to developments in social, economic and gender histories. Detailed quantitative investigation, particularly on military and student migration, has produced more accurate figures and challenged long-standing assumptions. The result has been a more realistic reconstruction of the 'Irish in Europe' which pays due attention to the full range of migrants, encompassing those who succeeded and integrated effectively into their host

---

1 T. Bartlett, ' "Ormuzd abroad ... Ahriman at home": some early historians of the "Wild Geese" in French service, 1840–1950' in J. Conroy (ed.), *Franco-Irish connections: essays, memoirs and poems* (Dublin: Four Courts Press, 2009), pp. 15–30; L. Chambers, 'Patrick Boyle, the Irish colleges and the historiography of Irish Catholicism', *Studies in Church History*, 49 (2013), 317–29.

2 For an overview written in the 1970s, published in 1986, see J.G. Simms, 'The Irish on the continent, 1691–1800' in T.W. Moody and W.E. Vaughan (eds.), *A new history of Ireland*, vol. IV: *Eighteenth-century Ireland* (Oxford: Oxford University Press, 1986), pp. 629–56.

societies, as well as those for whom the migration experience was a 'harsh inelegant business'.[3] Historians have also been more concerned to place Irish migration within wider patterns of European mobility: the recruitment of foreign soldiers into European armies, the movement of students seeking appropriate higher education, the creation of foreign merchant colonies in the port cities of the Atlantic seaboard and the migration of those in search of better opportunities abroad.

The Nature and Scale of Irish Migration, 1691–1815

While their movement to the continent must be understood within the broader parameters of eighteenth-century mobility, Irish Catholics, like French Protestants or Sephardic Jews, migrated in particularly large numbers for specific political and religious reasons. Ultimately, early modern Irish emigration was driven by conflict. The Nine Years War (1594–1603) and the Cromwellian conquest (1649–52) resulted in the mass migration of defeated Irish Catholic soldiers and their dependants to the continent. The Glorious Revolution and subsequent 'War of the Two Kings' precipitated a comparable movement. In 1690, 5,300 soldiers transferred from the army of James II to the service of his ally Louis XIV and were subsumed into the French army in three Irish regiments.[4] The Treaty of Limerick permitted defeated soldiers and their dependants to depart *en masse*. Historians have cited varying figures for the number of soldiers who left, but the best-informed estimate suggests that 15,000 soldiers and up to 4,000 women and children departed for northern France in the winter of 1691.[5] From 1692 to the 1730s a less dramatic, but steady, flow of military and civilian emigration of Catholics from Ireland to the continent (notably to France and Spain) ensued. Ascertaining the level of annual migration to Europe is challenging, but Cullen has suggested a figure of 1,000 for the early eighteenth century. Some patterns of migration are, however, relatively clear: France was the single most important destination,

3 N. Canny, 'Ireland and continental Europe, *c.*1600–*c.*1750' in A. Jackson (ed.), *The Oxford handbook of modern Irish history* (Oxford: Oxford University Press, 2014), p. 342; L.M. Cullen, 'The Irish diaspora of the seventeenth and eighteenth centuries' in N. Canny (ed.), *Europeans on the move: studies on European migration, 1500–1800* (Oxford: Oxford University Press, 1994), pp. 113–49; T. O'Connor and M.A. Lyons, *Strangers to citizens: the Irish in Europe, 1600–1800* (Dublin: Wordwell Books, 2008).

4 N. Genet-Rouffiac, *Le grand exil: les Jacobites en France, 1688–1715* (Mercuès: Service Historique de la Défense, 2007), pp. 145–60.

5 G. Rowlands, *An army in exile: Louis XIV and the Irish forces of James II in France, 1691–1698* (London: Royal Stuart Society, 2001), p. 5.

followed by Spain, with smaller numbers dispersed around Catholic territories in western and central Europe. Military migrants predominated in the early century, followed by students, but this pattern had changed significantly by mid-century as large-scale recruitment into the French and Spanish armies tailed off while student mobility continued apace. Indeed, while migration continued until the 1780s and even into the 1790s, it is now clear that the rate of migration had slowed considerably by the 1740s, with significant consequences for the Irish communities on the continent.[6]

Historians have accounted for the relatively high level of migration between the 1690s and 1730s in a number of ways. First, Irish Catholic soldiers and civilians continued to hope for a Jacobite restoration throughout the 1690s and well into the eighteenth century. Many Irish Jacobites were drawn to the court established at Saint-Germain-en-Laye just outside Paris, though, as the detailed work of Genet-Rouffiac and Corp has shown, the Irish contingent lacked the political influence of the numerically smaller English and Scottish courtiers.[7] Undeterred, Irish migrants on the continent were involved in a series of Jacobite plots, as well as the major risings of 1715 and 1745. More generally, Jacobite ideology and imagery remained important for recruitment to the Irish regiments in the French and Spanish armies.[8] A second factor driving migration was the enactment of penal legislation against Catholics from 1695. The prohibition on bearing arms and the inability of Catholics to partake in higher education encouraged them to move to other European states. Meanwhile, the banishment of bishops and regular clergy, enforced in 1698, precipitated the arrival of hundreds of destitute priests in French towns and cities.[9] Third, while the political and religious dimensions of migration were important, so were more mundane economic realities. Unsurprisingly, the period of heaviest emigration from Ireland to the continent, between the 1690s and 1730s, coincided with a period of sustained economic stagnation. Ultimately, it is impossible to disentangle the complex impulses driving Irish

6 Cullen, 'The Irish diaspora', p. 140.
7 Genet-Rouffiac, *Le grand exil*, p. 308; E. Corp, *A court in exile: the Stuarts in France, 1689–1718* (Cambridge: Cambridge University Press, 2004).
8 É. Ó Ciardha, *Ireland and the Jacobite cause, 1685–1766* (Dublin: Four Courts Press, 2002), pp. 105–8, 137–51, 219–23, 251–69, 295–9, 349–58; H. McDonnell, 'Some documents relating to the involvement of the Irish Brigade in the Rebellion of 1745', *Irish Sword*, 16 (1984–6), 3–21; B. Ó Buachalla, *Aisling Ghéar: Na Stíobhartaigh agus an tAos Léinn, 1603–1788* (Baile Átha Cliath: An Clóchomhar, 1996).
9 H. Fenning, *The Irish Dominican Province, 1698–1797* (Dublin: Dominican Publications, 1990), pp. 19–23; J. McMahon, 'The silent century, 1698–1829' in E. Bhreathnach, J. McMahon and J. McCafferty (eds.), *The Irish Franciscans, 1534–1990* (Dublin: Four Courts Press, 2009), pp. 77–8.

Catholics to the continent, but the sharp decline in migration as the economy improved appreciably from the 1740s is surely telling.[10]

The recruitment of foreigners remained an important feature of European armies in the eighteenth century and, consequently, soldiers were among the most visible Irish migrants on the continent.[11] During Louis XIV's reign the French recruited substantial numbers of Swiss, Italians, Germans and others from outside France, constituting 21 per cent of the army according to a 1693 estimate.[12] Rowlands has emphasised the complex military and political impulses driving this foreign recruitment, including the need 'to stop them swelling the ranks of Louis's enemies'.[13] Irish military migration to France had, of course, deep roots, but the arrival of substantial numbers of Irish soldiers in 1690–1 laid the basis for Irish regiments which survived until the French Revolution.[14] Unlike the Irish soldiers who arrived in France in 1690, those who poured into Brest in the final months of 1691 formed a separate army of James II from 1692 to 1698. Supported by Louis XIV, these regiments of Irish soldiers provided an essential military force for the Jacobite court-in-exile, but they were under-funded and poorly administered. Even if it had been better managed, James' army could not have survived the Treaty of Ryswick, which provided for French recognition of William's English title. As a consequence, the Jacobite army was disbanded, with six Irish regiments integrated directly into the French army.[15] Thereafter the number of *regiments irlandais* fluctuated, being reduced, for example, following the War of the Spanish Succession.

The reduction of the French army after the Treaty of Ryswick encouraged the movement of demobilised Irish soldiers into other forces in Europe and the outbreak of the War of the Spanish Succession naturally drew Irish soldiers across the Pyrenees. Irish military service in Spain had an even longer pedigree than in France, but it had declined considerably in the later

10 D. Dickson, 'Famine and economic change in eighteenth-century Ireland' in A. Jackson (ed.), *The Oxford handbook of Irish history* (Oxford: Oxford University Press, 2014), pp. 422–38.

11 P.H. Wilson, 'The German "soldier trade" of the seventeenth and eighteenth centuries: a reassessment', *International History Review*, 19 (1996), 757–92; P.H. Wilson, 'The politics of military recruitment in eighteenth-century Germany', *English Historical Review*, 117 (2002), 536–68.

12 G. Rowlands, 'Foreign service in the age of absolute monarchy: Louis XIV and his *forces étrangères*', *War in History*, 17:2 (2010), 145–6.

13 Rowlands, 'Foreign service', 149.

14 É. Ó Ciosáin, 'Irish soldiers and regiments in the French service before 1690' in N. Genet-Rouffiac and D. Murphy (eds.), *Franco-Irish military connections, 1590–1945* (Dublin: Four Courts Press, 2009), pp. 15–31.

15 Rowlands, *An army in exile*, p. 18.

seventeenth century. The weakness of the Spanish Bourbon military, the acquiescence of Louis XIV and the availability of Irish soldiers after Ryswick explain the establishment of Irish regiments in Spain from 1709 onwards, three of which endured until 1818. Though the regiments recruited successfully in Ireland, the numbers were never substantial and had declined significantly by the middle of the eighteenth century.[16] France and Spain were not the only destinations for Irish soldiers, who could be found in substantial numbers in smaller European armies, including those of Parma, Naples, Lorraine and Bavaria.[17] Persistent attempts to constitute an Irish regiment in the Austrian army between 1692 and 1710 did not succeed. Nevertheless, Austrian military service drew a small but significant number of Irishmen, mainly to its officer ranks, throughout the eighteenth century.[18]

Historians of Irish military migration have traditionally focused on Irish participation in campaigns and battles, stretching from the Nine Years War to the American War of Independence, with Fontenoy during the War of the Austrian Succession serving as the apogee of Irish engagement on the European battlefield (helpfully, against the British).[19] More recent work has emphasised the importance of military service as a means of social integration by elite Irish migrants., For example, Charles O'Brien, Viscount Clare, who fought at Fontenoy, reached the rank of *maréchal de France*.[20] The officer positions of the Irish regiments provided important means of career development and social mobility for Irish Catholic families at home and abroad, and some rose rapidly through the ranks. For example, Charles Edward Rothe

---

16 D.M. Downey, 'Beneath the harp and the Burgundian cross: Irish regiments in the Spanish Bourbon army, 1700–1818' in H. O'Donnell (ed.), *Presencia irlandesa en la milicia española* (Revista Internacional de Historia Militar 92) (Madrid: Ministerio de Defensa, 2014), pp. 83–105; Ó. Recio Morales, *Ireland and the Spanish Empire, 1600–1825* (Dublin: Four Courts Press, 2010), pp. 167–234.

17 É. Ó hAnnracháin, 'The Duke of Parma's company of Irish Guards, 1702–1733', *Irish Sword*, 29 (2014), 362–85; F. Richard-Maupillier, 'The Irish in the regiments of Duke Leopold of Lorraine, 1698–1729', *Archivium Hibernicum*, 67 (2014), 285–312; J. Garland, 'Irish officers in the Bavarian service during the War of the Spanish Succession', *Irish Sword*, 14 (1981), 240–55; J. Garland, 'Irish officers in the Neapolitan service' in *Irish Genealogist*, 5 (1979), 728–9. See also: H. Murtagh, 'Irish soldiers abroad, 1600–1800' in T. Bartlett and K. Jeffery (ed.), *A military history of Ireland* (Cambridge: Cambridge University Press, 1996), pp. 294–314.

18 D.M. Downey, 'Wild geese and the double headed eagle: Irish integration in Austria, *c*.1630–*c*.1918' in P. Leifer and E. Sagarra (eds.), *Austro-Irish links through the centuries* (Diplomatic Academy of Vienna, 2002), pp. 41–57.

19 J.C. O'Callaghan, *History of the Irish Brigades in the service of France* (Glasgow: Cameron and Ferguson, 1870).

20 P. Clarke de Dromantin, *Les réfugiés Jacobites dans la France du XVIIIe siècle* (Presses Universitaires de Bordeaux, 2005), pp. 190–1.

was a lieutenant general by the age of 33.[21] Families like the Dillons used their position in the French army to establish dynastic legacies which endured throughout the eighteenth century. In reality, however, a military career in France offered fewer opportunities than one in Spain. Their close associations with France ensured that Irish officers integrated well into Bourbon Spain, and the ensuing militarisation of Spanish politics and society meant that Irish migrants with successful army careers enjoyed social integration via the military orders. As Óscar Recio Morales puts it: 'Although it may seem paradoxical, the army in a sense turned out to be a dynamic institution, capable of bringing about social advancement in a highly rigid society structured on the basis of separate estates.'[22]

Access to officer positions in the French, Spanish and Austrian armies remained important throughout the century, though by the 1780s the number of Irish regiments in France and Spain had been reduced to six. The recruitment of rank-and-file soldiers followed a very different pattern. Until recently, determining the number of Irish soldiers in the French army was problematic, not least in the light of grossly inflated claims made by contemporaries like MacGeoghegan.[23] Drawing on the new system of troop inspections introduced in 1716, Ó Conaill has estimated that 19,994 soldiers fought in the Irish regiments between 1716 and 1791, though only 6,534 were actually Irish. Using O'Callaghan's calculations for the period to 1698, Ó Conaill offered an estimate of 24,725 Irish soldiers in France between the Treaty of Limerick and the French Revolution.[24] The evidence suggests that solders were drawn from across the island of Ireland, with the largest proportions from the counties of Munster and southern Leinster.[25] Recruitment was strongest from the 1690s to the 1730s. Using *contrôles de troupe* figures, Ó Conaill has estimated that of the 3,742 soldiers serving in Irish regiments in 1729, 2,652 were Irish (71 per cent). The overall number had fallen to 2,697 by 1737, while the Irish contingent remained proportionately similar at 1,810 (67 per cent). The collapse in Irish recruitment occurred in the following decade. By the late 1740s

---

21 Ibid., p. 197.
22 Recio Morales, *Ireland and the Spanish Empire*, p. 223.
23 J. MacGeoghegan, *Histoire de l'Irlande ancienne et moderne*, 3 vols. (Paris: Antoine Boudet, 1758–62; Amsterdam: n.p., 1763), vol. III, p. 754.
24 C. Ó Conaill, 'The Irish regiments in France: an overview of the presence of Irish soldiers in the French service, 1716–1791' in E. Maher and G. Neville (eds.), *France–Ireland: anatomy of a relationship* (Frankfurt: Peter Lang, 2004), pp. 331–7; C. Ó Conaill, ' "Ruddy cheeks and strapping thighs": an analysis of the ordinary soldiers in the ranks of the Irish regiments of eighteenth century France', *Irish Sword*, 34:98 (2005), 411–25.
25 Ó Conaill, ' "Ruddy cheeks" ', 421; E. Ó hAnnracháin, 'Irish veterans at the Hôtel Royal des Invalides (1692–1769)', *Irish Sword*, 31:83 (1999), 5–39.

only 30 per cent of the soldiers serving in the Irish regiments were actually Irish and their proportion continued to fall, to 14 per cent at the start of the Seven Years War and to just 5 per cent by the mid-1770s. Years of impressive recruitment still occurred in the early 1750s and in 1763, but the pattern from mid-century was very low.[26] Recruitment to the rank and file of the Irish regiments in Spain declined even more markedly. As early as 1715, the regulations of the Bourke regiment provided for alternative arrangements if Irish recruitment proved tardy. Instead, the Irish regiments were filled with Spaniards, Portuguese, Italians, Germans and Swiss, all commanded by an almost entirely Irish officer elite.[27] The Spanish and French remained acutely conscious of the impact of Irish legislation against recruitment for foreign service until at least the 1750s, but by this stage large-scale military migration from Ireland to the continent had already ended.[28] Though patterns of rank-and-file recruitment are now clearer, the social history of ordinary soldiers in the armies of France and Spain remains to be written.[29] Familiar problems of military life, including drunkenness, desertion and duelling, occupied the lives of the Irish too. Of course, thousands died in the major conflicts of the eighteenth century, while the wounded and elderly survivors struggled to survive outside their regiments. In France, their lives may be glimpsed in the registers of institutions such as the Hôtel Royal des Invalides.[30]

The Irish Colleges and the Irish in Eighteenth-Century Europe

Student mobility was another recurring feature of early modern society. As Hilde de Ridder-Symoens has noted, confessionalisation 'shattered and re-moulded' patterns of student mobility, pushing Catholics and Protestants excluded from lecture halls at home to universities and colleges abroad.[31] Catholic minorities from England, Scotland, the Dutch Republic, Germany and Scandinavia quickly established colleges abroad, frequently attached

---

26 Ó Conaill, 'The Irish Regiments', pp. 334–5.
27 Recio Morales, *Ireland and the Spanish Empire*, pp. 194.
28 Archives du Ministère des Affaires Étrangères, Affaires Diverses Politiques, 10, dossier 233, ff. 5–9.
29 P.-L. Coudray, ' "Irlandois de nation": Irish soldiers in Angers as an illustration of Franco-Irish relationships in the seventeenth and eighteenth centuries' in Genet-Rouffiac and Murphy (eds.), *Franco-Irish military connections*, pp. 94–108.
30 Ó hAnnracháin, 'Irish veterans', 5–39.
31 H. de Ridder-Symoens, 'Mobility' in H. de Ridder-Symoens (ed.), *A history of the university in Europe*, vol. II: *Universities in early modern Europe, 1500–1800* (Cambridge: Cambridge University Press, 1996), p. 419.

to universities closely identified with the Counter-Reformation (Paris, Salamanca, Douai and Rome were all prominent), to facilitate the education of students. Irish Catholics followed a similar model so that by the 1690s more than forty colleges already existed across the continent, stretching from Lisbon to Leuven and from Prague to Paris. The Irish regular clergy, notably the Franciscans and Dominicans, had impressive college networks. Their houses in Leuven, Rome, Prague and Lisbon provided vital support when the regular clergy were banished from Ireland following legislation passed by the Irish parliament in 1697. Indeed, the Franciscans established a new college at Boulay in 1700, with the support of the Duke of Lorraine, in part to cater for the increased pressure brought about by newly exiled brethren. Colleges for the formation of secular clergy and lay students operated in Spain, the southern Netherlands and Rome, but most were small, and the larger French colleges, especially those in Paris, Nantes and to a lesser extent Bordeaux, attracted the greatest proportion of students in the eighteenth century.[32]

The colleges varied greatly as they adapted to local circumstances and fulfilled a range of functions as student hostels, university colleges, lay schools, friaries and seminaries. The Jesuits exercised an important influence on most of the colleges in Spain, as well as the Irish secular college in Rome, but Irish priests, usually under local ecclesiastical and university superintendence, managed the colleges in France and much of the southern Netherlands.[33] The regular colleges provided instruction internally, but many were not teaching institutions. Instead, students attended classes at local colleges and universities where they rubbed shoulders with cosmopolitan student populations, especially in the larger urban centres. The significance of the colleges lay instead in the 'controlled environment' they provided, which anticipated that Irish students were monitored through a detailed daily timetable. The variation in the colleges was matched by the complexity of the Irish student populations. Financial pressures ensured that Irish bishops continued to ordain students in their mid-twenties before they travelled to the continent for a higher education, an unorthodox system which had the benefit of allowing students to earn an income from clerical duties and therefore to fund their studies. Alongside these older students, most colleges also took in much

32 L. Chambers and T. O'Connor (eds.), *College communities abroad: education, migration and Catholicism in early modern Europe* (Manchester: Manchester University Press, 2017).
33 L.W.B. Brockliss, 'The Irish colleges on the continent and the creation of an educated clergy' in T. O'Connor and M.A. Lyons (eds.), *The Ulster Earls and Baroque Europe: refashioning Irish identities, 1600–1800* (Dublin: Four Courts Press, 2010), pp. 142–65.

younger students destined, at least in theory, for the priesthood. These were funded either from family resources or by means of bursaries, which were increasingly important in Paris and Leuven.[34] Of course, Irish Catholic students could be found outside the Irish colleges too. Lack of places, especially in the first half of the eighteenth century, was one reason. Elite Irish Catholic families, like the Plunketts of Fingal, employed alternative educational strategies on the continent, using the network of English colleges in Flanders to strengthen relationships with contacts across the Irish Sea.[35]

Large-scale prosopographical studies of Irish students in Paris, Leuven, Toulouse and Rome have underlined the level of Irish student migration to the continent throughout the eighteenth century.[36] For Paris, Brockliss has identified 827 Irish students for the period 1690–1789. Nilis has identified 598 students at the University of Leuven between 1690 and 1794. In fact, studies of student registration and matriculation underestimate the scale of Irish student migration, for many did not formally register or take degrees, presumably for reasons of expense. This was certainly the case in Paris. For example, of the 197 Irish priests who signed petitions drawn up during a dispute at the Irish Collège des Lombards in Paris in the 1730s, only twenty-three appear in the university records.[37] Geographical trends have also been sharpened by recent investigations. Studies of students in Paris and Leuven, as well as Rome, illustrate that these major centres of Catholic education attracted students from across Ireland. Ferté's work on Toulouse and other similar studies indicate that the smaller colleges catered to students with specific provincial or even county backgrounds.[38] The most significant finding to emerge from the prosopographies, specifically from the work of Brockliss on Paris and Ferté on Toulouse, is that a large proportion (possibly even a majority) of students did not return to Ireland on completion of their studies. This finding undermines the traditional

---

34 L. Chambers, 'Irish *fondations* and *boursiers* in early modern Paris, 1682–1793', *Irish Economic and Social History*, 35 (2008), 1–22.

35 See P.R. Harris (ed.), *Douai College documents, 1639–1794* (St Albans: Catholic Record Society, 1972), pp. 125, 263, 265, 269, 272, 356, 366.

36 L.W.B. Brockliss and P. Ferté, 'Irish clerics in France in the seventeenth and eighteenth centuries: a statistical study', *Proceedings of the Royal Irish Academy*, 87C (1987), 527–72; L.W.B. Brockliss and P. Ferté, 'A prosopography of Irish clerics in the universities of Paris and Toulouse', *Archivium Hibernicum*, 58 (2004), 7–166; J. Nilis, 'Irish students at Leuven University, 1548–1797', *Archivium Hibernicum*, 60 (2006–7), 1–304; M. Binasco and V. Orschel, 'Prosopography of Irish students admitted to the Irish College, Rome, 1628–1798', *Archivium Hibernicum*, 66 (2013), 16–62.

37 Brockliss and Ferté, 'Irish clerics in France', pp. 536–7; Four student petitions, Irish Collège des Lombards, Paris, 1734–7 (Archives of San Clemente, Rome, Codex II, volume 2, ff. 412r–v, 464–5, 466–7, 497–8v).

38 Brockliss and Ferté, 'Irish clerics in France', pp. 559–61.

argument that the colleges were important primarily for the formation of clergy for the Irish mission. Instead, it suggests that the college networks operated as part of the migration process, facilitating the permanent movement of Irish Catholics, particularly younger sons, to the continent and into careers in the church, medicine and the law among others.[39] Indeed, while the bursaries established for Irish students at Paris and Leuven, largely by Irish migrants, provided funding for students to pursue theology, many also facilitated legal and medical studies.[40] The University of Reims awarded medical degrees to 598 Irish students in the early modern period, the vast majority from the 1680s onwards, with a high point in the 1730s. A substantial proportion of these students had studied previously at Paris, Montpellier or Leuven, before opting to graduate from the relatively inexpensive faculty at Reims.[41] While some medical graduates, like the Catholic writer and activist John Curry, returned to Ireland, others settled permanently on the continent. In Paris, Irish doctors and medical students even formed themselves into a masonic lodge, *l'Irlandaise du soleil levant*, in the 1770s.[42] In Spain, a series of prominent Irish medical practitioners utilised their skills to advance themselves socially and to make pioneering contributions to medical knowledge. Timoteo O'Scanlan was a prominent case. Educated in Paris, he moved to Spain through Irish military and administrative circles and was at the forefront of smallpox inoculation.[43]

The Irish college networks were important for other reasons too. They were not isolated exile outposts, but were closely connected to the wider Irish migrant communities on the continent. Family connections linked administrators and students at the colleges with soldiers in Irish regiments (especially in France). In Paris, the college provided a range of services to the Irish migrant communities around them: students and priests assisted the

39 Brockliss and Ferté, 'Irish clerics in France', p. 548; P. Ferté, 'Étudiants et professeurs irlandais dans les universités de Toulouse et de Cahors (xviie–xviiie siècles): les limites de la mission irlandaise' in T. O'Connor and M.A. Lyons (eds.), *Irish communities in Early Modern Europe* (Dublin: Four Courts Press, 2006), pp. 69–84.

40 Nilis, 'Irish students at Leuven University', p. 11; Chambers, 'Irish *fondations* and *boursiers*', p. 15.

41 L.W.B. Brockliss, 'Étudiants de médecine des Îles Britanniques inscrits en France sous l'ancien régime' in P. Ferté et C. Barrera (eds.), *Étudiants de l'exil: migrations internationals et universités refuges (XVIe–XXe s.)* (Toulouse: Presses Universitaires du Mirail, 2009), pp. 81–104; L.W.B. Brockliss, 'Medicine, religion and social mobility in eighteenth- and early nineteenth-century Ireland' in J. Kelly and F. Clark (eds.), *Ireland and medicine in the seventeenth and eighteenth centuries* (Farnham: Ashgate, 2010), pp. 73–108.

42 P.-Y. Beaurepaire, *L'autre et le frère: l'étranger et la Franc-maçonnerie en France au XVIIIe siècle* (Paris: H. Champion, 1998), pp. 226–32 and, more generally, pp. 215–57.

43 M. White, 'The role of Irish doctors in eighteenth-century Spanish medicine' in D.M. Downey and J. Crespo MacLennan (eds.), *Spanish–Irish relations through the ages* (Dublin: Four Courts Press, 2008), pp. 149–74.

destitute, managed finances, provided legal advice and services, translated documents and prepared the attestations of identity which were so crucial in *ancien régime* society.[44] Of course, the relationship was not unidirectional: Irish patrons and benefactors among the migrants donated money to the college networks.[45] The Paris physician Bartholomew Murry was a major benefactor of the Irish College in the French capital.[46] While host communities also continued to provide assistance to students and colleges, in the course of the eighteenth century the colleges came to rely more heavily on the patronage of Irish Catholics abroad and at home. The rise of a Catholic 'middle class' encouraged college administrators to launch funding appeals in Ireland in the later eighteenth century.[47]

The colleges facilitated migration, but it is clear that they were also important for the reconstruction of the Irish church. Most eighteenth-century Irish bishops passed through the continental colleges before returning to Ireland, bringing with them their experience of late baroque Catholicism.[48] The colleges also had less obvious impact as the church rebuilt, especially from the 1730s. In the absence of a strong Irish episcopacy in the early eighteenth century, the colleges controlled by Irish secular clergy operated with surprising autonomy. Indeed, they provided career opportunities for ambitious priests, creating a unique group of administrators with the potential to influence the direction of the Irish church. In 1730s Paris, prominent Irish college administrators argued that the practice of bishops ordaining men before they proceeded to the continent should be terminated in favour of a more orthodox system of educating younger students. This position dovetailed with new thinking emanating from sections of the Irish church (especially in Armagh and Dublin) which aimed to reconstruct the relationships between the bishops, the clergy and the Irish colleges as the impact of the Penal Laws slackened. The suggestions created a storm of protest from Irish bishops who feared that, with penal legislation still on the statute books, a flexible ordination system was necessary to guarantee pastoral structures. Ultimately, the bishops prevailed, but, as Hugh Fenning has shown, the closure of the novitiates of

---

44 P. O'Connor, 'Irish clerics and Jacobites in early eighteenth-century Paris, 1700–30' in T. O'Connor (ed.), *The Irish in Europe, 1580–1815* (Dublin: Four Courts Press, 2001), pp. 175–90.

45 Recio Morales, *Ireland and the Spanish Empire*, p. 264.

46 Papers relating to the Fondation Murry (Archives du Collège des Irlandais, Paris, MS B2.g.1).

47 C. Begadon, 'Laity and clergy in the Catholic renewal of Dublin, c.1750–1830', PhD thesis, National University of Ireland, Maynooth, 2009, pp. 196–7.

48 Brockliss and Ferté, 'Irish clerics in France', pp. 567–72.

the regular clergy in Ireland by Rome in 1751 was an indirect result with far-reaching consequences.[49]

Historians have long recognised that student mobility and the college networks also afforded opportunities for cultural and intellectual innovation. Irish scholars across Europe produced philosophy and theology from scholastic perspectives until well into the eighteenth century.[50] The Irish College in Paris emerged as an important centre for Irish-language publication from the 1730s, with the appearance of Begley and MacCurtain's *An Focloir Bearla Gaoidheilge* (1732), followed by Andrew Donlevy's *An Teagasg Críosduidhe* (1742) and John O'Brien's *An Focalóir Gaoidhilge-Sax-Bhéarla* (1768).[51] In the late 1750s and early 1760s, James MacGeoghegan produced an ambitious *Histoire d'Irlande* for French consumption, but one especially attuned to the sensitivities of the increasingly well-integrated Irish migrant communities. At the same time another Paris-based Irish priest, the influential David Henegan, penned his own Irish history for inclusion in the latest edition of the *Dictionnaire de Moréri*. This marked a shift away from the Jacobite allegiances evident in MacGeoghegan towards a more accommodationist line in respect of the Hanoverian regime reminiscent of Catholic activists like Charles O'Conor and John Curry.[52] Henegan's work points to the innovative and even Enlightenment scholarship produced by Irish migrants. The fact that thousands of Irish students attended classes in the lecture halls of European universities ensured that they experienced the dramatic intellectual changes which occurred over the course of the eighteenth century, even if the colleges and universities themselves were slow to respond. Outside their walls, innovative thinking was evident in the work of the linguist and lexicographer Pedro Sinnot, the naturalist Guillermo Bowles, the theologian Luke Joseph Hooke, the mathematician Patrick D'Arcy and the economists Richard Cantillon and Bernardo Ward.[53]

---

49 L. Chambers, 'Rivalry and reform in the Irish College, Paris, 1676–1775' in O'Connor and Lyons (eds.), *Irish communities in early modern Europe*, pp. 103–29; H. Fenning, *The undoing of the friars of Ireland: a study of the novitiate question in the eighteenth century* (Louvain: Publications Universitaires de Louvain, 1972), pp. 92–236.

50 L. Chambers, 'Irish Catholics and Aristotelian scholastic philosophy in early modern France, c.1600–c.1750' in J. McEvoy and M. Dunne (eds.), *The Irish contribution to European scholastic thought* (Dublin: Four Courts Press, 2009), pp. 212–30.

51 P. MacCana, *Collège des Irlandais, Paris and Irish studies* (Dublin: Dublin Institute for Advanced Studies, 2001), pp. 81–8, 98–121.

52 *Le grand dictionnaire historique, ou le mélange curieux de l'histoire sacrée et profane*, 10 vols. (Paris: Les Libraires Associés, 1759), vol. VI, pp. 405–33.

53 A.E. Murphy, *Richard Cantillon: entrepreneur and economist*, 2nd edn (Oxford: Oxford University Press, 1989); T. O'Connor, *An Irish theologian in Enlightenment France: Luke*

Merchants, Professionals and Others
among the 'Irish in Europe'

Richard Cantillon's *Essai sur la nature du commerce en général*, published post-humously in 1755, was one of the most important economic tracts of the eighteenth century and underlines the point that, alongside the soldiers and students, the merchants and professionals (doctors, lawyers, bankers and others) formed another core group among the 'Irish in Europe'. The expansion of trade from the great Atlantic ports like Bordeaux and Cadiz resulted in the emergence of colonies of foreign merchants, among them significant populations of Germans, Dutch, Italians, English and Scots. Irish merchants began to establish permanent bases on the western European Atlantic seaboard from the middle of the seventeenth century, but their number expanded in the ports of the southern Netherlands, France and Spain in the eighteenth century.[54] In the Irish case, the scale and nature of migration to Europe only strengthened economic opportunities on the continent. Their success, Cullen has noted, 'is a striking example of the ability of expatriate minorities to exploit a widespread network of family relationships by virtue of their dispersal'.[55] In the southern Netherlands, the Irish presence was concentrated in Ostend, Bruges and Dunkirk.[56] The Ostend connection was especially significant. It emerged in the mid-seventeenth century but was reinforced by the arrival of a new wave of Irish merchants after 1691. Most important among these was Thomas Ray, whose activities in both privateering (during the War of the Spanish Succession) and global trade networks stretching to the Caribbean and to East India ensured that Irish merchants 'dominated the international maritime trading world of Ostend in the years 1715–1735'. In part, this success

Joseph Hooke, 1714–96 (Dublin: Four Courts Press, 1995); Recio Morales, *Ireland and the Spanish Empire*, pp. 254–5.

54 A. Crespo Solana (ed.), *Communidades transnacionales: colonias de mercaderes extranjeros en el mundo Atlántico, 1500–1830* (Madrid: Doce Calles, 2010); D. Dickson, J. Parmentier and J. Ohlmeyer (eds.), *Irish and Scottish mercantile networks in Europe and overseas in the seventeenth and eighteenth centuries* (Ghent: Academia Press, 2007).

55 L.M. Cullen, 'The Irish merchant communities of Bordeaux, La Rochelle and Cognac in the eighteenth century' in P. Butel and L.M. Cullen (eds.), *Négoce et industrie en France et en Irlande aux XVIII et XIX siècles* (Paris: Éditions du Centre National de la Recherche Scientifique, 1980), p. 53.

56 J. Parmentier, 'The Irish connection: the Irish merchant community in Ostend and Bruges during the late seventeenth and eighteenth centuries', *Eighteenth-Century Ireland*, 20 (2005), 31–54; C. Pfister, 'Dunkerque et l'Irlande, 1690–1790' in Dickson et al. (eds.), *Irish and Scottish mercantile networks*, pp. 93–114.

was built on rapid assimilation, which in Ray's case was reflected in the fact that he was mayor of Ostend between 1728 and 1738.[57]

In France, mid-seventeenth-century migration patterns focused on St Malo and La Rochelle were already giving way, in the 1690s, to a stronger concentration on Nantes. Some families, like the Lees, were well established before the 1690s and along with new arrivals they created a network of Irish merchants who developed the Nantes economy as it expanded into the Atlantic. The case of Thomas and Daniel Macnemara is very striking; by the 1720s the brothers were reputed to be among the richest merchants in Nantes.[58] Unsurprisingly, Irish merchants were heavily involved in Nantes' flourishing slave trade. As Clarke de Dromantin has pointed out, Irish (along with English and Scots) merchants accounted for around 3 per cent of the merchant population, but acted as *armateurs* to around 8 per cent of slave voyages. In part, this is explained by the very significant involvement of Antoine Vincent Walsh. A committed Jacobite who played a central role in the Jacobite rising of 1745, Walsh was responsible for forty-six slave voyages between 1734 and 1759, more than four times the number of the O'Sheills (his relatives by marriage) or Roches, who were the next largest of the Irish slave traders in the port and for whom the slave trade formed but a part of their large and lucrative transatlantic activities.[59]

By the time Walsh had established himself as a dominant force in Nantes, it had declined in significance with the rise of France's great Atlantic port of the eighteenth century: Bordeaux. From a low base at the start of the eighteenth century, the number of Irish merchants settled in Bordeaux rose rapidly as the port expanded. The wine trade was the initial stimulus, but developments in the mid-century beef trade and, especially in the 1760s, the brandy trade were also significant. By the second half of the eighteenth century Bordeaux was undoubtedly the most important centre for Irish commercial activity in France. Unlike other centres of Irish trade that were dominated by Irish merchants from particular localities, the Bordeaux Irish were remarkably broadly based, with strong representation from Dublin, Cork, Limerick, Clare and Galway. Ulster Protestants also arrived in the 1720s, 1730s and 1740s, a reminder that Irish migration to France was not exclusively Catholic. Cullen has argued

---

57 J. Parmentier, 'The Ray dynasty: Irish mercantile empire builders in Ostend, 1690–1790' in O'Connor and Lyons (eds.), *Irish communities* pp. 367–82.
58 G. Saupin, 'Les réseaux commerciaux des Irlandais de Nantes sous le règne de Louis XIV' in Dickson et al. (eds.), *Irish and Scottish mercantile networks*, pp. 132–6; Clarke de Dromantin, *Les réfugiés Jacobites*, pp. 413–18.
59 Clarke de Dromantin, *Les réfugiés Jacobites*, pp. 450–6.

that the Bordeaux Irish actively saw themselves as a colony, a separate group from the merchant and wider communities around them. This was reflected not only in patterns of intermarriage but also in social relationships, with Irish group cohesion manifested in events such as the balls held at the Hôtel d'Angleterre. This stood in sharp contrast to the Irish in Nantes, who presented themselves as *Irlandais réfugiés*, integrated much more readily, and gradually moved from trade to the life of country gentlemen on estates outside the city. The Bordeaux Irish also maintained strong links with Ireland and with the Irish migrant communities elsewhere in Europe.[60]

The other great centre of Irish merchant activity in Europe in the eighteenth century was Cadiz, Bordeaux's Spanish equivalent, which enjoyed a virtual monopoly of Spanish American trade between 1717 and 1778. Among the range of nationalities attracted to Cadiz was a substantial proportion of Irish and their families. A 1714 census enumerated just ten Irish (and eight English) families out of a total of 520 foreign heads of household. The scale of change in the course of the eighteenth century is illustrated by the remarkable 1773 census, when 127 Irish households were recorded, though this represented only 3.3 per cent of the foreign presence (which stood at 3,839 households). This figure masks the incredible reach of the Irish merchant community in Cadiz, given that in the same year 227 of the 949 ships that put in to the port of Cadiz were Irish, more than the Spanish or French. Cullen has noted that the emergence of such a strong Irish presence in Cadiz was the result of the departure of English (Protestant) merchants, while Mario del Carmen Lario has pointed to the significance of family and national ties among the Irish community, noting in particular the strength of Waterford families.[61] Though Cadiz attracted most Irish merchants in the eighteenth century, Seville, Huelva, Malaga, the Canary Islands and, indeed, Madrid all had significant Irish merchant presences.[62] As Recio Morales has argued, their success was predicated on the fact that 'Irish merchants in Spanish ports were part of a small elite cosmopolitan class, that of foreign merchants of the Atlantic

---

60 Cullen, 'The Irish merchant communities', pp. 51–63; L.M. Cullen, *The Irish brandy houses of eighteenth-century France* (Dublin: Irish Academic Press, 2000); L.M. Cullen, J. Shovlin and T. Truxes (eds.), *The Bordeaux–Dublin letters, 1757: correspondence of an Irish community abroad* (Oxford: Oxford University Press, 2013), pp. 31–59.
61 M. del Carmen Lario, 'The Irish traders of eighteenth-century Cadiz' in Dickson et al. (eds.), *Irish and Scottish mercantile networks*, pp. 207–26.
62 M. Begoña Villar Garcia, 'Irish migration and exiles in Spain: refugees, soldiers, traders and statesmen' in O'Connor and Lyons (eds.), *Irish communities in early modern Europe*, pp. 172–99; various essays in M. Begoña Villar Garcia (ed.), *La emigración Irlandesa en el siglo XVIII* (Malaga: Universidad de Málaga, 2000).

world, and they managed to situate themselves at the very heart of the economic, political and cultural life of the cities.'[63]

Irish merchant networks in Ostend, Bordeaux and Cadiz all reflected
the general pattern of colonies of foreign merchants which congregated in
Atlantic ports to take advantage of their trading potential. At the same time,
Cullen and Recio Morales are correct to highlight the benefits afforded by the
specific contours of Irish Catholic migration, which facilitated international
financial transactions. Indeed, London was also important for Irish Catholic
merchant activity. The careers of the Arthur banking family provide remarkable examples. Daniel Arthur, originally from Limerick, moved from London
to France in 1679 and was ideally placed to act as banker for English, Scots and
Irish Jacobites after 1688. In the early eighteenth century the family consolidated a European network, with sons in Paris, Madrid and London.[64] Cullen
has shown that the two George Fitzgeralds of London (uncle and nephew),
active from the late 1710s to the 1750s, transacted business with 'peripatetic
members of the Irish brigade and wandering gentry on the continent'.[65] The
Fitzgeralds were not unusual for, as Bergin has demonstrated, a complex
world of Irish Catholic lawyers, doctors, merchants and bankers operated in
the English capital, many with connections to family members settled in continental Europe. He has pointed out that when the Limerick merchant Martin
Harrold died in the English capital in 1725, he left legacies to individuals in
Antwerp, Bayonne, Bordeaux, Madrid, Nantes and Paris.[66]

While much recent research has expanded knowledge of Irish Catholic
trade networks and activities, migrants also prospered in other ways. Clarke
de Dromantin has pointed to the involvement of a whole range of Irish
'Jacobites' in mining, glassware and earthenware manufacturing, textiles, and
the metal and chemical industries.[67] Research has also shown that success
was sometimes built on questionable foundations including smuggling, privateering and the slave trade. The denominational range of Irish migrants is
also becoming clearer. Irish Protestant merchants settled in Catholic Europe,
notably in Bordeaux where religion was less problematic than elsewhere. The
Blacks of Belfast, established in Bordeaux from the 1690s, followed strikingly

63 Recio Morales, *Ireland and the Spanish Empire*, p. 263.
64 Genet-Rouffiac, *Le grand exil*, pp. 373–400.
65 L.M. Cullen, 'The two George Fitzgeralds of London, 1718–1759' in Dickson et al.
   (eds.), *Irish and Scottish mercantile networks*, p. 252.
66 J. Bergin, 'Irish Catholics and their networks in eighteenth-century London', *Eighteenth-
   Century Life*, 39:1 (2015), 79.
67 Clarke de Dromantin, *Les réfugiés Jacobites*, pp. 285–399.

similar patterns of dispersal to their Catholic counterparts.[68] Indeed, recent work has also extended our understanding of the 'Irish in Europe' to incorporate the smaller groups and individuals who travelled north. Murdoch, for example, has underlined the mixed confessional and dynastic allegiances of the Irish who migrated to Sweden in the early eighteenth century.[69] Irish Protestants attended European centres of education, notably the faculty of medicine at Leiden.[70] They also travelled with growing ease to predominantly Catholic states on the continent as the eighteenth century progressed. Dozens of Irish artists based themselves in Rome in the later eighteenth century, while the Grand Tour emerged as a staple undertaking of the Irish aristocracy in the same period.[71] Indeed, the worlds of Irish Protestant travellers and Irish Catholic migrants increasingly came into contact as the century wore on.[72]

Women, the Poor and Irish Emigrant Communities

If the mobility of Irish Protestants or the significance of the northern continent for the 'Irish in Europe' constitutes something of a hidden migration, the more glaring historiographical omissions until recently involved women and the poor. The overwhelming attention paid to male soldiers, students, priests and merchants has meant that the migration of Irish women to Europe has largely gone unnoticed. Among the most studied were the least visible of all, the Irish Benedictine community which settled at Ypres. Drawn from among elite Irish Catholics, they maintained unsurprisingly strong Jacobite associations. The only other enduring Irish female community was the Dominican convent in Lisbon. As a result of this lack of opportunity to participate in female religious life, Irish women turned to the far more numerous English foundations concentrated in the

---

68 J. Livesey, *Civil society and empire: Ireland and Scotland in the eighteenth-century Atlantic world* (New Haven: Yale University Press, 2009), pp. 131–3.

69 S. Murdoch, 'Irish entrepreneurs and Sweden in the first half of the eighteenth century' in O'Connor and Lyons (eds.), *Irish communities in early modern Europe*, pp. 348–66; A. Byrne, 'Irish soldiers in Russia, 1690–1812: a re-assessment', *Irish Sword*, 28 (2011), 43–58.

70 E. Mijers, 'Irish students in the Netherlands, 1650–1750', *Archivium Hibernicum*, 59 (2005), 66–78.

71 T. Barnard, *Making the grand figure: lives and possessions in Ireland, 1641–1770* (New Haven: Yale University Press, 2004), pp. 310–44; N. Figgis, 'Irish artists in Rome in the eighteenth century' in W. Laffan (ed.), *The sublime and the beautiful: Irish art, 1700–1830* (London: Pyms Gallery, 2001), pp. 18–27.

72 J. St John, *Letters from France to a gentleman in the south of Ireland*, 2 vols. (Dublin: P. Byrne, 1788), vol. ii, pp. 51–86.

southern Netherlands and France, though Irish identities did not always fit comfortably into English convents.[73] Outside the convents, thousands of Irish women settled on the continent though few have been the subjects of serious study.[74] Among those leaving Ireland in the final months of 1691, perhaps 4,000 women and children arrived in France. For many arrivals, life must have been difficult, particularly as husbands, fathers and brothers died on European battlefields. Those gathered near the Jacobite court-in-exile at Saint-Germain-en-Laye or in the French capital turned to a number of charitable sources: the network of James II's queen, Mary of Modena, before her death in 1718, as well as the French state and church, and Irish groups in the capital.[75] Despite the problems that some women encountered, their significance for the development of the migrant community in Paris is evident from the files of notaries like Jean Fromont who took care of much of the Irish business in the French capital in the early eighteenth century.[76] Like their male counterparts, women continued to migrate throughout the eighteenth century, with economic opportunity a factor.[77] Men also experienced destitution. The demobilisation of thousands of Irish soldiers in the army of James II created an epidemic of poverty and criminality in the late 1690s.[78] Among the students and clergy some found it difficult to secure a foothold in European society and, presumably, many eked out a living as a *prêtre habitué*. *Inventaires après décès* sometimes provide poignant reminders of the poverty of their lives, like that of one Richard Moore who died in Paris in 1723 and left behind an old trunk with worn-out clothes and a handful of books.[79] Among the thousands who found life difficult were not just destitute soldiers and poor students and priests, but those of limited means

---

73 P. Nolan, *The Irish dames of Ypres* (Dublin: Browne and Nolan, 1908); Marie-Louis Coolahan, 'Archipelagic identities in Europe: Irish nuns in English convents' in C. Bowden and J.E. Kelly (eds.), *The English convents in exile, 1600–1800: communities, culture and identity* (Farnham: Ashgate, 2013), pp. 211–28.

74 See, for example, Clarke de Dromantin's discussion of marriage strategies of elite Irish migrants in France: *Les réfugiés Jacobites*, pp. 113–33. The best-known woman among the Irish migrant families in France is probably Henriette Lucie Dillon, on account of her autobiography which first appeared as *Journal d'une femme de cinquante ans, 1778–1815*, 4 vols. (Paris: R. Chapelot, 1907–11).

75 M.A. Lyons, ' "Digne de compassion": female dependants of Irish Jacobite soldiers in France, c.1692–c.1730', *Eighteenth-Century Ireland*, 23 (2008), 55–75.

76 L. Swords, 'Irish material in the files of Jean Fromont, notary at Paris', *Collectanea Hibernica*, 34–5 (1992–3), 77–115; 36–7 (1994–5), 85–139.

77 Cullen, Shovlin and Truxes (eds.), *The Bordeaux–Dublin letters, 1757*, pp. 63–4.

78 D. Bracken, 'Piracy and poverty: aspects of the Irish Jacobite experience in France, 1691–1720' in O'Connor (ed.), *The Irish in Europe*, pp. 127–42.

79 Swords, 'Irish material in the files of Jean Fromont, notary at Paris', *Collectanea Hibernica*, 36–7 (1994–5), 108–9.

who migrated to the continent, particularly in the difficult economic circumstances in Ireland in the first half of the eighteenth century. In short, alongside the personal successes of mobility were the demobilised and destitute who have left little or no trace of their existence.

From the 1690s, Irish communities in Europe were strengthened and expanded with the arrival of new migrants. Though frequently assigned to distinct categories by historians, the various soldiers, students, merchants, professionals and others formed communities where they congregated in sufficient numbers. In the largest centres of eighteenth-century migration, like Paris, it is clear that Irish communities were close knit.[80] This was also true of more modest destinations, like Lisbon, where the Irish merchant community buried their dead inside the church of the Irish Dominicans at Corpo Santo.[81] Irish migrant networks also stretched beyond the European continent into the expanding French, Spanish, Danish and, indeed, British empires. Irish mercantile interests in France quickly acquired property across the Atlantic. The O'Sheills of Nantes, for instance, built up an extensive interest in Saint-Domingue.[82] Irish families also operated within French networks in India, China and Cochinchina, particularly in the second half of the eighteenth century, and some like François de Rothe constructed lucrative careers with the Compagnie française des Indes.[83] Spanish America attracted Irish merchants like Ambrosio O'Higgins, who started his career in the Irish merchant houses of Cadiz and took full advantage of mid-century Irish influence at the Spanish court to build a spectacularly successful career as administrator in Chile and Peru.[84] Irish traders also operated outside their main French and Spanish networks. Nicholas Tuite grasped the advantages of St Croix in the Danish West Indies to extend his Caribbean trade in the 1750s.[85]

---

80 O'Connor, 'Irish clerics and Jacobites', pp. 175–90.
81 P. O'Neill Teixeira, 'The Lisbon Irish in the 18th century' in I. Pérez Tostado and E. García Hernan (eds.), *Irlanda y el Atlántico Ibérico: molividad, participación e intercambio cultural (1580–1823)* (Valencia: Albatros Ediciones, 2010), p. 259.
82 Clarke de Dromantin, *Les réfugiés Jacobites*, pp. 436–9.
83 Ibid., pp. 440–50.
84 Recio Morales, *Ireland and the Spanish Empire*, pp. 284–95; idem, 'Los estudios Irlandeses y el Atlántico Ibérico (siglos xvi–xviii): una selección bibliográfica' in Tostado and García Hernan (eds.), *Irlanda y el Atlántico Ibérico*, pp. 323–35.
85 O. Power, 'The 18th century sugar and slave trade at St Croix, Danish West Indies' in Tostado and García Hernan (eds.), *Irlanda y el Atlántico Ibérico*, pp. 51–7.

In Decline, 1750–1815

By mid-century, the high point of Irish migration to Europe was over but, arguably, the apogee of Irish migrant influence occurred at this juncture. After 1691, the Stuart court-in-exile provided a focal point for recent arrivals, even if Irish influence was limited. By the middle of the eighteenth century the Jacobite court was located in Rome, and while it remained an important nexus for the Irish in Europe generally, migrants reached positions of prominence elsewhere around alternative figures. In France, Cullen has identified a group which coalesced around the dominant French statesman of the period, Étienne François, duc de Choiseul, in the 1760s.[86] Simultaneously, Irish influence in Spain reached its zenith under Ricardo Wall, who like many other prominent Irish migrants in eighteenth-century Spain arrived via France. As Secretary of State and Secretary of the Indies, between 1754 and 1763, he provided a centre point of Irish patronage in Spain and its empire.[87] In Austria, where migration was largely an elite phenomenon, Franz-Moritz de Lacy was president of the Imperial War Council between 1766 and 1778.[88] This Irish migrant elite integrated smoothly into *ancien régime* society. It was well represented among visitors to elite Europe's most significant health resort, at Spa, where dozens of Irish officers in European armies, aristocrats, merchants and even the superiors of Irish colleges figured in the published lists of visitors which appeared between 1763 and 1787[89] (see Illustration 52).

If some Irish migrants reached positions of unprecedented prominence in the 1760s and 1770s, this masked the deeper reality that the mass migration on which their success rested had long ended.[90] Though the Irish population expanded dramatically in the eighteenth century, economic growth from the 1740s offered new opportunities and reduced the necessity for mass migration. The tacit relaxation of penal legislation, surreptitious recruitment into the

---

86 L.M. Cullen, 'Choiseul's Irish circle and the Irish community: the end of the *ancien régime*', *Eighteenth-Century Ireland*, 24 (2009), 62–83.

87 D. Téllez Alarcia, 'Política y familia en el grupo irlandés de XVIII: ¿un partido irlandés en la Corte?' in E. García Hernán and Ó. Recio Morales (eds.), *Extranjeros en el ejército: militares Irlandeses en la sociedad Española, 1580–1818* (Madrid: Ministerio de Defensa, 2007), pp. 263–7; Recio Morales, *Ireland and the Spanish Empire*, pp. 238–57.

88 Downey, 'Wild geese and the double headed eagle', p. 53.

89 L. Chambers, 'Les confessions au carrefour. Catholiques et Protestants irlandais à Spa au XVIIIe siècle' in D. Droixhe (ed.), *Spa, carrefour de l'Europe des Lumières: les hôtes de la cité thermale au XVIIIe siècle* (Paris: Hermann, 2013), pp. 59–63.

90 L.M. Cullen, 'Apotheosis and crisis: the Irish diaspora in the age of Choiseul' in O'Connor and Lyons (eds.), *Irish communities in early modern Europe*, pp. 6–31.

52. Michel van Loo, *Ricardo Wall (1694–1777), Spanish ambassador to Great Britain, 1746, and chief minister to King Ferdinand VI (1746– 59) and Charles III (1759– 88)*. Oil on canvas, 1746 (National Gallery of Ireland).

British army, and the emergence of alternative migration options across the Atlantic and within the British Empire, further reduced the imperatives propelling Catholics to the continent. As we have already seen, the Irish regiments in France (of which only three remained) and Spain were almost completely devoid of rank-and-file Irish recruits by the 1780s. The Irish college networks began to shrink from the 1760s, under pressure from reforming forces within European states rather than because of a lowering demand for places. The suppression of the Jesuits in 1773 resulted in the closure of the colleges the society operated in Lisbon, Seville, Santiago de Compostella and Poitiers. Woeful administration caused the suppression of the college in Alcalá de Henares, while the reforms of Joseph II accounted for the Irish Franciscan college in Prague and exerted pressure on the Franciscans and Dominicans at Leuven. The effective collapse of the Irish college network in Spain only reinforced the significance of the Irish college network in France. The construction of a new college in a fashionable quarter of Paris in the 1770s, funded largely by Irish benefactors at home and abroad, might suggest confidence, but the two Paris colleges were in serious financial difficulties in the 1780s, something equally true of the colleges in Bordeaux and Nantes.[91] Of course, without an alternative, the Irish student migration to the continent continued apace. Economic pressures also explain the decline of the Irish merchant strongholds in Bordeaux and Cadiz in the 1780s. As Cullen has noted: 'business houses were fewer, and there was no replacement for those who disappeared.'[92]

It is now abundantly clear that Irish migration to Europe was in decline well before the French Revolution and, consequently, that the events of the 1790s accelerated an on-going process. Initially unaffected, the Irish colleges in France gradually came under sustained pressure as the Revolution radicalised and war with Britain broke out. In 1793, the revolutionary authorities shut down colleges and in some cases imprisoned the priests and students who remained. As the French exported revolution, so most of the Irish colleges across Europe closed.[93] The Irish identity of the Walsh, Dillon and Berwick

---

91 L. Chambers, 'Revolutionary and refractory? The Irish colleges in Paris and the French Revolution', *Journal of Irish and Scottish Studies*, 2:1 (2008), 31–5; Fenning, *Undoing of the friars*, pp. 354–74; Lettres patentes portant suppression de titre de la chapelle Jean Martin, 1766 (AICP, MS c1.d13); Dossier sur l'union du prieuré de Saint-Crespin à la maison du séminaire des prêtres irlandais de Nantes, 1772–6 (AICP, MS c3.a3).

92 Cullen, 'Apotheosis and crisis', p. 27.

93 Chambers, 'Revolutionary and refractory?', pp. 36–47.

regiments was abolished in 1791, while emigration, desertion, wartime loss (especially in the Caribbean), purges and executions (most notably that of Arthur Dillon in 1794) destroyed a century of military tradition.[94] For Irish merchants the early French Revolution posed few problems, but war and the disruption of imperial trade impacted heavily on business.[95] In Ireland, important shifts in government policy ensured that neither military nor student migration would easily resume: from 1793 Catholics could legally join the army, while Maynooth College provided a government-subsidised education for Irish Catholics. Instead, France became a magnet for a new kind of radical Irish migrant. United Irish agents and refugees now joined more established Irish migrants, including priests, students, doctors and soldiers who had embraced the Revolution. The failed rebellion of 1798 brought a major wave of refugees to France. Surprisingly, this facilitated the re-creation of Irish migrant infrastructure which would have been familiar to those who had been in France before 1789. In 1803 Napoleon established an Irish Legion which lasted until 1815 (three years before the final suppression of the Irish regiments in Spain). He also united what remained of the Irish (and Scots and English) colleges in France into a single 'British' establishment, which re-opened the Irish college in Paris as a school for the children of Irish refugees and the French elite. After 1815, transformed into a seminary for Irish students, it was one of only a handful of Irish colleges on the continent to emerge successfully from the upheaval of the 1790s.[96]

Conclusion

Our understanding of eighteenth-century Irish migration to Europe has been transformed since the 1980s. The shape of that migration is now clearer: the unique circumstances of military defeat prompted a mass migration in 1691 and large-scale mobility continued until at least the 1730s, before giving way to a much smaller movement which endured into the 1790s. If attention to specific Irish political, religious and economic circumstances is essential to understanding mobility, it is now evident too that Irish migration history

---

94 S. Scott, 'The French Revolution and the Irish regiments in France' in H. Gough and D. Dickson (eds.), *Ireland and the French Revolution* (Dublin: Irish Academic Press, 1990), pp. 14–27.
95 Cullen, *Irish brandy houses*, pp. 161–75.
96 M. Rapport, *Nationality and citizenship in Revolutionary France: the treatment of foreigners, 1789–1799* (Oxford: Oxford University Press, 2000); L. Swords, *The green cockade: the Irish in the French Revolution, 1789–1815* (Dublin: Glendale, 1989).

has striking parallels not only with the most obvious diasporic comparisons in terms of scale, the Huguenots or Jews, but also with the intra-European and imperial migration of soldiers, students, merchants and those in search of a better life. Protestants as well as Catholics migrated to and travelled in Europe in the eighteenth century, but the development of Irish communities in Europe, with their colleges, regiments and merchant houses, was especially important in providing outlets for Irish Catholics, particularly in the first half of the eighteenth century. The recurring eighteenth-century complaints about the failure of students to return to the Irish mission missed the point: the colleges and universities, as much as the regiments and merchant houses, were facilitators of permanent migration. The availability of opportunities on the continent underlay the resilience of Catholic Ireland and the revival evident in politics, trade and ecclesiastical structures in the course of the eighteenth century, even if this is still improperly understood.[97] Indeed, Catholic revival at home was one reason why migration was already in decline by the 1780s, long before the French Revolution destroyed the traditional patterns of *ancien régime* Irish migration.

97 Cullen, 'The Irish diaspora', p. 143.

22

'Irish' Migration to America in the Eighteenth Century? Or the Strange Case for the 'Scots/Irish'

PATRICK GRIFFIN

Introduction

The very idea of eighteenth-century migration from Ireland to America presents an interpretative challenge. For a start, by and large the phrase 'Irish migration' for this period is a bit of a misnomer. There is no doubting that men and women sailed from Ireland for the British colonies in America and to the new republic after the American Revolution. In fact, those leaving represented the largest non-African movement of men and women across the Atlantic to British North America, surpassing English, Scottish and German numbers. And this movement is anything but forgotten or overlooked. Scholars and antiquarians have written scores of books on the subject, and the numbers and passion of some testify to the enduring interest, scholarly and popular, in the subject of migration from Ireland to America.

But though tens of thousands ventured from Ireland, not many Irish left. Or so we have learned. The eighteenth-century movement to colonial America is one defined by the 'Scotch Irish', who do not fit comfortably into the conventional Irish-American story. The reason why the Irish have gone missing stems from ethnic boosterism and the indifference of American colonial historians to such chauvinism. From the early nineteenth century, the descendants of those who left Ireland for America called themselves 'Scotch Irish'. The use of the term was innocent enough. It was employed to dissociate a group of what were regarded as largely Protestant migrants to America, many of whom were descended from settlers who had ventured from Scotland to Ulster in the seventeenth century, from the new migrants, largely Catholic, streaming into American ports from Ireland during the Great Famine.[1] By the 1840s, no one could doubt that 'Irish' migration had begun. Subsequent Scotch Irish hagiographers insisted on the use of the

---

1 On this, see K. Miller, *Emigrants and exiles: Ireland and the Irish exodus to North America* (Oxford: Oxford University Press, 1985); K. Miller, ' "Scotch Irish," "Black Irish" and "Real Irish": emigrants and identities in the Old South' in A. Bielenberg (ed.), *The Irish diaspora*

formulation, and some scholars have stuck with this tried and true term to this day. People at the time, some argue, knew themselves by the name Scotch Irish. Or so the argument goes.[2]

American colonial historians, with no proverbial dog in this fight, have followed suit. A glance at any American history textbook or monograph – none really written by those with Scotch Irish sympathies – will confirm that the Scotch Irish migration is the one that linked Ireland to the colonies in the eighteenth century.[3] The Irish story picks up with the Famine. The upshot is that, as Kerby Miller has shown, migration from Ireland was comprehended within what he calls the 'two traditions' model, and more lately what he has referred to as a 'partitionist' perspective on the past.[4] Catholics had the nineteenth century, and Protestants had the eighteenth. The Scotch Irish left Ireland but they were not 'Irish'.

Lately, scholars have begun to try to address the question of nomenclature. Warren Hofstra's willingness in an edited collection to wrestle with the thorny issues of identity that go hand-in-hand with names, as well as the criticism he has encountered, is a case-in-point. Tellingly, the scholars in his collection arrive at no firm conclusion on what to call these people, and they revert to older, tried-and-true definitions that speak to their distinctive perspectives.[5] This is understandable. The two traditions idea leaves all parties somewhat content. And the rest do not care one way or the other. But it comes at a cost. It makes it impossible to incorporate in any meaningful way those who do not fit the model of the typical 'Scotch Irish' migrant before the Revolution,

(New York: Longman, 2000), pp. 139–57; K. Miller, ' "Scotch-Irish Myths" and "Irish" identities in eighteenth- and nineteenth-century America' in C. Fanning (ed.), *New perspectives on the Irish diaspora* (Carbondale, IL: Southern Illinois University Press, 2000), pp. 75–92; K. Miller, 'Ulster Presbyterians and the "two traditions" in Ireland and America' in T. Brotherstone, A. Clark and K. Whelan (eds.), *These fissured isles: Ireland, Scotland and the making of modern Britain 1798–1848* (Edinburgh: John Donald, 2005), pp. 260–77.

2 Of the latest work, see M. Montgomery, 'Searching for security: backcountry Carolina, 1760s–1780s' in W. Hofstra (ed.), *Ulster to America: the Scots-Irish migration experience, 1680–1830* (Knoxville: University of Tennessee Press, 2012), pp. 147–64.

3 See, for instance, B. Bailyn, *The peopling of British North America: an introduction* (New York: Knopf, 1986); B. Bailyn, *Voyagers to the West: a passage in the peopling of America on the eve of the Revolution* (New York: Knopf, 1986); M. Jones, 'The Scotch-Irish in British America', in B. Bailyn and P. Morgan (eds.), *Strangers within the realm: cultural margins of the first British Empire* (Chapel Hill: University of North Carolina Press, 1991), pp. 284–313.

4 Miller, 'Ulster Presbyterians and the "two traditions" '; for 'partitionist' see his review of Richard MacMaster's *Scotch-Irish merchants in colonial America*, *Journal of Social History* 44:4 (2011), 1293–5.

5 Hofstra (ed.), *Ulster to America*; reviews by Celeste Ray in *Journal of American Ethnic History* 33:2 (2014), 98–100, and, more positively, by Howard Keeley in *Pennsylvania Magazine of History and Biography* 136:3 (2012), 295–7.

and there were plenty of such people. Moreover, it makes it difficult to integrate the migration of people from Ireland to the new republic in the years after the Revolution but before the Famine. Though larger in scale than the colonial-era movement, this period does not fit into the 'two traditions' formula. As such, it inhabits a grey space between those migrations that have defined the ways subsequent generations of Americans deploy the ideas of Irishness and Scotch-Irishness to make sense of who they were and who we are. In the tug-of-war over identity, the later part of the eighteenth century lies in a no-man's land.[6]

This chapter seeks, in the first instance, to insert the word 'Irish' into eighteenth-century migration from Ireland to America as a way of capturing what has gone missing. It does not do so to overturn older and enduring myths. Such myths, of course, arise for all sorts of reasons, most not germane to this topic. Rather, it seeks to situate the movement from Ireland to America within the *longue durée* of movement between the places. What we find is that the eighteenth-century migration fits comfortably in the larger story, once we establish its proper parameters. If there is one common feature of migration from Ireland to America since the seventeenth century it is this: migrants left from those places most dynamically immersed into a broader Atlantic world of commerce mediated by British culture, commerce and the state. They left those regions in Ireland most enmeshed in the Atlantic for those most integrated in the Atlantic in America. Ongoing movement, then, corresponded to the ongoing consolidation of the Atlantic world into a system.[7]

The chapter will also venture to explore how these migrants considered themselves not only in chronologically expansive ways but also in more geographically ambitious ways. In a word, a great many, the lion's share really, did regard themselves as 'Irish', however much that definition deviates from our own. They did not have an uncomplicated sense of what this meant, nor did they embrace nineteenth-century understandings of the term. To be Irish was to be from and of Ireland. That said, as we shall see, such self-definition

---

6 On this, see P. Griffin, 'Irish migration to the colonial south: a plea for a forgotten topic' in B. Giemza (ed.), *Rethinking the Irish in the American South: beyond rounders and reelers* (Jackson: University Press of Mississippi, 2013), pp. 51–74; P. Griffin, 'The two migrations myth, the Scotch Irish, and Irish American experience' in A. H. Wyndham (ed.), *Re-imagining Ireland: how a storied island is transforming its politics, economy, religious life, and culture for the 21st century* (Charlottesville: University of Virginia Press, 2006).

7 N. Canny and P. Morgan (eds.), *The Oxford handbook of the Atlantic world, c.1450–c.1850* (Oxford: Oxford University Press, 2011), especially Joyce Chaplin's contribution, 'The British Atlantic', chapter 13.

was complicated by the fact that a number who left places like Derry/
Londonderry for New Castle came from families that spent no more than
one generation in Ireland. They were not necessarily consciously Scots, but
their movement was a feature of a complex series of interactions between
the two kingdoms and a multi-staged process that tied areas of the Atlantic
archipelago to each other and to America.

Even though migrants, as best we can establish, by and large called themselves and were known as 'Irish', their distinctive experiences reflected the ways
that Ireland and Scotland were yoked together into a broader Atlantic world of
motion and the ways each was affected by the growth and expansion of the
British state. It is, in fact, difficult to disentangle the two places. Nineteenth-century anachronisms cannot do justice to these people, their sense of self-conception, or the proper way to make sense of their movement. This chapter offers
a different, and hopefully richer, way of considering them. It also offers a new
name for the eighteenth-century movement.

The Nature and Dimension of Emigration
to Eighteenth-Century America

Perhaps we should start with what we know, or what we think we know. Over
the course of the eighteenth century, or the 'short' American eighteenth century
that runs until the beginning of the War of Independence, somewhere between
50,000 and 250,000 men and women set sail from Irish ports for British North
America. The American Revolution represents a logical endpoint because large-
scale migration would stop until the signing of the Treaty of Paris marked the
end of what had become a disruptive world war. Migration to the new republic soon recommenced, and numbers picked up until the Napoleonic wars. We
reckon 60,000 left between 1783 and 1799. If we expand that end date to 1815,
perhaps as many as 150,000 left Ireland for America in these years.[8]

The massive range we have for the pre-revolutionary numbers should give
us pause, but we can safely dispense with the low and high figures. The low
one uses the official sources that have survived to arrive at this figure. But we
know just from shipping records and notices in newspapers of ships coming

---

8 M.J. Bric, *Ireland, Philadelphia and the re-invention of America, 1760–1800* (Dublin: Four
   Courts Press, 2008); and K. Miller, 'Introduction' in K. Miller, A. Schrier, B. Boling and
   D. Doyle, *Irish immigrants in the land of Canaan: letters and memoirs from colonial and
   revolutionary America, 1675–1815* (Oxford: Oxford University Press, 2003). J. Kelly, 'The
   Resumption of Emigration from Ireland after the American War of Independence,
   1783–1787', *Studia Hibernica*, 24 (1984–8), 61–89.

and going that the number is far too small.[9] The other extreme, frankly, must be fanciful. Migration would have had to be on a consistently sustained scale throughout the century for it to have any value. The most reliable numbers are R.J. Dickson's. He puts the numbers at somewhere near 150,000.[10] The numbers for the later period through to the signing of the Treaty of Ghent (1814) appear more reliable.

Where emigrants left from and where they went is easier to pin down, and most scholars agree on the particulars. The same goes for status or condition. Though migrants came from nearly all regions, most left Ulster. They tended to sail from port towns like Derry/Londonderry and Coleraine directly for the colonies. Two areas of Ulster predominated: the east in and around the Lagan valley, especially the 'linen triangle'; and the area in and around the River Foyle further to the west. Counties Antrim, Down, Coleraine or Derry/Londonderry, Armagh, Tyrone and Donegal would have sent the greatest numbers, though those aspiring to go were concentrated in these strips of territory in the east and west of the province.

Most went where the ships took them. In most cases throughout the century, this meant the Middle Colonies, including New York, or the upper Chesapeake colony of Maryland. But Pennsylvania, serviced by Philadelphia and New Castle in Delaware, became the place of choice for a plurality of migrants. Many stayed where they landed, and large communities of men and women from Ireland settled in the city of Philadelphia; a larger number continued to move. The patterns for those landing in the Delaware River ports and, after the Seven Years War, in Baltimore are unmistakeable. They went in search of land they could work, purchase or settle on with an eye towards improving and acquiring, what we might call squatting, in a sequence of regions as the century progressed. Earliest migrants headed to south-east Pennsylvania in what would be Lancaster County. Later arrivals leapfrogged these to establish themselves over the Susquehanna River, beginning in the late 1730s. The next wave landed in the same ports but headed further south on what was quickly becoming a wagon road in the Shenandoah

---

9 L.M. Cullen, 'The Irish diaspora' in N. Canny (ed.), *Europeans on the move: studies on European migration* (Oxford: Oxford University Press, 1994), pp. 113–49; M. Wokeck, *Trade in strangers: the beginnings of mass migration to North America* (University Park: Pennsylvania State University Press, 1999).

10 R.J. Dickson, *Ulster emigration to colonial America* (London: Routledge, 1966); G. Kirkham, 'New introduction' to R.J. Dickson, *Ulster emigration to colonial America* (Belfast: Ulster Historical Foundation, 1988); G. Kirkham, 'Ulster emigration to North America, 1680–1720' in H.T. Blethen and C.W. Wood (eds.), *Ulster and North America: trans-Atlantic perspectives on the Scotch-Irish* (Tuscaloosa: University of Alabama Press, 1997), pp. 76–117.

valley of Virginia. Others travelled still further south along the edge of the Appalachians to the backcountry of North and South Carolina.[11]

Those who left in the earliest waves tended to travel as free passengers before what one scholar calls the 'trade in strangers' began to take shape. Indentured servitude may have defined the seventeenth-century movement to the Chesapeake. It did not do so for early crossings from Ulster to America. The famine of 1741 changed this dynamic, and what we find is that the numbers of those travelling as indentured servants far surpassed those leaving as free passengers. It would remain unbalanced this way until the American Revolution, and after that period the earlier pattern of free passage would predominate.[12]

There were outliers of course. Early in the movement, some groups set sail for Massachusetts Bay expecting a warm welcome. They were disappointed. Some also established settlements in New Hampshire and in Maine. Some too sailed directly for ports in the South such as Charleston, but like their fellow travellers to New England, their numbers were dwarfed by those disembarking in the Middle Colonies. The same goes for places migrants left from. Colonial newspapers record Irish from all over the kingdom, but a relatively smaller number came from the west or south-west of the island. If Ulster was over-represented, with a smattering from the midlands, Munster and Connacht were under-represented in the movement.

The exceptions speak to a seeming rule about the people migrating. Most were Presbyterian, and many left with a sense of grievance. We know that a group of migrants left in 1718 complaining of the disabilities they suffered because of their dissent from the established church. The Revd James McGregor from the Bann valley led a group to Boston, and he focused on their experiences as Dissenters to explain the decision to leave.[13] Like Catholics, they were subject to paying tithes to a church they did not adhere to. They could not own land. They did not have the political privileges of the established church. And for a time, marriages performed by their ministers were not considered valid. Yet it is beyond debate that many of these disabilities were lifted as the century wore on.

11 The latest work to explore this movement can be found in the relevant essays in Hofstra (ed.), *From Ulster to America*.

12 Wokeck, *Trade in strangers*; A. Fogleman, 'From slaves, convicts, and servants to free passengers: the transformation of immigration in the era of the American Revolution', *Journal of American History*, 85:1 (1998), 43–76.

13 P. Griffin, *The people with no name: Ireland's Ulster Scots, America's Scots Irish, and the creation of a British Atlantic World, 1689–1764* (Princeton: Princeton University Press, 2001), p. 90.

Clearly more than religion was at issue. To be sure, Quakers also travelled in these years. Yet, so did members of the Church of Ireland. More to the point, Catholics did as well, but their percentage paled in comparison to the weight of their numbers at home. Though discriminated against in a more thoroughgoing way than Dissenters, they did not as a rule opt to escape to America.[14]

Therefore, we have to look beyond religious persecution. Migrants certainly left because of economic shocks. And we find that the spikes in mass migration (1717–19, late 1720s, early 1740s, early 1750s, 1763–75 and 1783–84) coincided with subsistence crises, economic crashes of key industries in Ulster, and rising rents.[15] For a majority of people who saw the world through a religious world-view, the shocks and calamities were interpreted through providential lenses, but keeping body and soul together or bettering oneself for the benefit of the next generation drove most. Put another way, though the press to leave stemmed from more prosaic reasons, such as subsistence or betterment, those departing made sense of these decisions, and often rationalised them, in ways culturally attuned to who they were. Coming from a kingdom in which religious confession determined access to power, religion served this function. Since most of the migrants were leaving as dissenters, they were fleeing Ireland with a sense of grievance; they also departed with hope that their disabilities would be relieved in the New World. The choice of Pennsylvania as destination, or as it was once called in the eighteenth century 'the best poor man's country' where the founding Quakers had established religious toleration, spoke both to their economic plight and their religious justifications.[16]

More importantly, focusing on the religious aspect of experience occludes the broader patterns rooted in region. These were an Ulster people. That is what matters, not in the sense that they embraced an 'Ulster' identity. No such thing existed. Rather, decisions to leave were premised on what was happening in that place in the years prior to migration.[17] And the place had been changing dynamically since the time of the Glorious Revolution. Of

---

14 For an explanation of this dynamic, rooted in deep cultural patterns, see Miller, *Emigrants and exiles.*

15 Dickson, *Ulster emigration* is especially strong on these waves; also Kelly, 'The resumption of emigration', 64–80.

16 These dynamics are captured in Griffin, *People with no name, passim*; and J. Lemon, *The best poor man's country: a geographical study of early southeastern Pennsylvania* (New York: W.W. Norton, 1976).

17 For a thoughtful usage of the term 'Ulster', see B. Bankhurst, *Ulster Presbyterians and the Scots Irish diaspora, 1750–1764* (Basingstoke: Palgrave Macmillan, 2013).

course, war transformed Ulster, and contemporaries testified to the destruction and upheaval it wrought. The reach and power of the central state expanded as well. More prosaically – but more importantly – areas of Ulster were being remade by the production of linen. One of the few industries relatively untouched by British mercantilist policy, the manufacture in linen was encouraged by the Irish parliament and by improving landlords. Tenants took up the spinning of linen in places like the Foyle river valley and the weaving of it in the eastern part of the province as a way of supplementing income. Such a mundane set of tasks set this place apart from the rest of Ireland, immersing men and women living in such regions into a broader British economy. The flaxseed they sowed came from Middle Colony ports. The linen they produced travelled back in the same ships to the New World and in others to Britain and the continent. Linen made this Atlantic world go round, literally.[18]

To put it another way, migrants ventured from the region most thoroughly integrated into a consolidating Atlantic system. In the seventeenth century, the Atlantic was bound together by the sporadic movement of Puritans and indentured servants from places like England to the New World and by intermittent spikes in economic activity. This changed in the following century. The eighteenth century witnessed a steady flow of peoples, goods and ideas, yoking the littoral regions of the Atlantic together as never before. It became an integrated system, by and large through the movement of migrant groups, the demand they created for consumer goods, and what they produced. The areas that migrants from Ireland predominantly settled typified this process. Scattered along the eastern edges of the Appalachians, those who left Ireland, and soon their descendants, did not live in backward regions. Far from it. These now became integral parts of the system, as what was produced on their farms – and lands in places like south-east Pennsylvania and the Shenandoah were some of the best for growing in the world – made their way up what was a 'great wagon road' to the entrepôt of Lancaster, created in 1729, en route to the burgeoning port city of Philadelphia for places throughout the broader Atlantic.

These people left dynamic regions for progressive areas. And they left where the ships with linen would take them. Even though the trade in persons to the New World arose as an ancillary to the transportation of linen, and migrants often left with what they had produced, soon enough it became as important as the trade of any good. The movements of peoples and of

18 Griffin, *People with no name*, pp. 27–32.

goods, therefore, emerged side-by-side, both further deepening connections between America and Ireland, transforming certain Irish regions and serving to develop and enmesh those areas in America to which they and their goods sailed. Migrants did not leave Ulster because it was backward. They left the area of Ireland, for lack of a better term, most modernised and most fully invested in a burgeoning Atlantic system. They travelled to those parts of America not furthest removed from port towns but those most fully integrated into a world of new possibilities. The 'frontier' regions where many settled, therefore, represented those places where opportunity most clearly beckoned.

What they did once they reached the New World reflected these patterns. Though the movement was diverse and composed of peoples from different confessional groups, a broad pattern can be seen reflecting the changing nature of Atlantic integration in the eighteenth century. So, for instance, migrants from Ireland included traders who created merchant houses in Philadelphia, and whose work tied Ireland to the colonies ever closer through the flow of goods.[19] From Ireland came colonial proprietors, such as Arthur Dobbs, the wealthy member of the Church of Ireland who became governor of North Carolina and who invited others from Ireland to settle in the colony, encouraging the movement of bodies across the ocean.[20] James Logan, a Quaker from Ireland, played a similar role in Pennsylvania. He also sought out the 'Irish', as he called them, to establish footholds on the very edges of settled areas, all with an eye to creating a 'hedge' against Indians further to the west. Those who had 'bravely defended Derry and Enniskillen' during the Glorious Revolution, he wrote, were well suited to doing the same against Indians.[21]

It also included a number of prominent frontier traders and diplomats, such as George Croghan and Sir William Johnson. The former, most likely a converted Catholic from the Strabane area, became 'the king of the traders', was adopted by the Shawnee as their own, and even helped the historiographer royal of Scotland, William Robertson, in his ethnographic work on Native Americans.[22] Johnson came from a Jacobite Catholic family in County

---

19 See R. MacMaster, *Scotch-Irish merchants in colonial America* (Belfast: Ulster Historical Foundation, 2009).
20 See, for instance, D. Gleason (ed.), *The Irish in the Atlantic world* (Columbia: University of South Carolina Press, 2013) on variety and others like Dobbs.
21 Griffin, *People with no name*, p. 104.
22 For Croghan, see P. Griffin, *American Leviathan: empire, nation, and revolutionary frontier* (New York: Hill and Wang, 2007).

Meath, journeyed to America to look after the New York estates of his uncle Sir Peter Warren, and eventually became the crown's superintendent of Indian affairs and a chief of the Mohawks. Croghan and Johnson epitomised a certain stock type of the migrant from Ireland, the hustling trader who lived on the edges of settlements and who travelled to areas far afield to encompass Indians in the burgeoning 'empire of goods' and also to pave the way for white settlement of Indian lands. For all of their abilities as cultural brokers, both Croghan and Johnson were not above defrauding Indians of their lands.[23]

These prominent individuals were joined by thousands of faceless men and women who also contributed to the transformation of a land-rich, labour-hungry America into a vital cog of the Atlantic system. Through trade, encouraging settlement and migration, and pressing the bounds of British North America to the west, those from Ireland were on the cutting edge of a movement that enmeshed America into the world they had left behind. Unsurprisingly, the migrants from Ireland played outsized roles both in tying the Atlantic together through shipping and in pressing the frontier ever westward. They also played larger than life roles in some of the sordid aspects of this dynamic. Those from Ireland did indeed treat Indians with ferocity from time to time, and they perhaps displaced some of their anxieties and feelings of liminality on those seen as savage. Those who had been persecuted in Ireland, to pick up on the old line, became the persecutors in America.[24] The instances do not need recounting here, but the most infamous massacre of Indians, the Paxton Boys episode in 1763–4, took place at the hands of migrants from Ireland and their descendants.[25]

They were not alone in making the Atlantic system, of course. German migrants did much of the same, though in different ways. But it is the timing that matters. Coming when they did ensured that they would contribute to the transformation of the Atlantic from a world into a system. They included those who were settling in cities, as well as those moving further west over the Appalachians. In short, though not as central as those streaming in from Africa to toil as slaves on plantations, these people became parts of the engine of a vast system increasingly mediated by London, drawing in

---

23 F. O'Toole, *White savage: William Johnson and the invention of America* (New York: Farrar, Straus, and Giroux 2005); J. Merrell, *Into the American woods: negotiators on the Pennsylvania frontier* (New York: Norton, 2000).

24 J. Merritt, *At the crossroads: Indians and empires on a mid-Atlantic frontier, 1700–1763* (Chapel Hill: University of North Carolina Press, 2003).

25 K. Kenny, *Peaceable kingdom lost: the Paxton Boys and the destruction of William Penn's holy experiment* (Oxford: Oxford University Press, 2009).

the near peripheries like Ireland, and yoking in places further afield on the Atlantic littoral, such as West Africa and the Rhine river valley.

For post-revolutionary movement, it is perhaps the figure of the canal worker that captures this moment best.[26] At the very end of the eighteenth century, these men tied the newly settled hinterlands into the Atlantic economy. They sustained – and connected in a concrete way – the Jeffersonian and Madisonian vision of westward expansion with the Hamiltonian ideal of trade and development out east. They helped develop an American political economy, one that could thrive in a post-revolutionary Atlantic and one premised on the idea of free trade.[27] The revolutionary generation of migrants, if we can call them that, also reflected what was happening in the broader Atlantic, how America changed after the Revolution, and how Ireland was transformed by the British state. When the strains, tensions and contradictions of integration exploded into Atlantic revolution, those from Ireland were also part of the flotsam and jetsam of a system disintegrating. This included the political radicals, of course.[28] It also included the faceless of this generation, coming from areas imperfectly tied into a capitalist world transitioning from one defined by empires to one dominated by republics.

These were, moreover, a people ideally and cruelly suited to the sort of difficult work they did. Wrenched from places like north Leinster by the commercialisation of agriculture there, they were a pre-modern people who built the modern world, a people prepared for the backbreaking and thankless work of making America. Avowedly Catholic – though not catechised in the conventional sense – these appeared as Irish bogeys, almost perfectly anti-American, in a republican America now firmly and consciously Protestant. There was no mistaking that these were Irish.[29]

Contextualising Irish Emigration

Once we appreciate this slice of time this way, we can then place the eighteenth-century movement in its proper context. Though this movement

26 P. Way, *Common labour workers and the digging of North American canals, 1780–1860* (Cambridge: Cambridge University Press, 1993).

27 D. McCoy, *The elusive republic: political economy in Jeffersonian America* (Chapel Hill: University of North Carolina Press, 1996); J. Appleby, *The relentless revolution: a history of capitalism* (New York: Norton, 2011).

28 D. Wilson, *United Irishmen, United States: immigrant radicals in the early Republic* (Ithaca, NY: Cornell University Press, 1998).

29 Bric, *Ireland, Philadelphia and the re-invention of America*; Miller et al., *Irish immigrants in the land of Canaan.*

may seem *sui generis*, it was not. Stepping back, we see the same dynamics at work a century earlier. In the seventeenth century, the predominant movement from Ireland to America revolved around Munster and the Caribbean. The forced migration of thousands by Cromwell's conquest leaps to mind. This happened. But it was part of a pattern for the period. Munster ports like Kinsale tied Irish sites of production to plantations in places such as Barbados and Montserrat, particularly before the rise of chattel slavery there. A number also left via Galway because of connections between merchant families and the Caribbean. Key points for provisioning, Kinsale and Cork and their hinterlands were drawn into the production of provisions to the Caribbean, the Shenandoah valley of its day. Here opportunity beckoned, and now men imaginatively part of the broader system through what they produced made the decision to try their luck in what was the dynamic region of its time. Needless to say, it was not Presbyterians who went. Largely Catholics did. Religion, though, proved incidental.[30] Many also sailed from Ireland for the Chesapeake, though these numbers paled in comparison to the movement to the Caribbean. Both movements came to a sudden halt with the transition to slave labour. Though Munster ports still served the provisioning trade, the demand for labour from Ireland plummeted.[31]

Before the migration ended, however, those in places most fully immersed in the Atlantic left for those places they were most closely tied to by trade, and again the extension of the English state played a prominent role in catalysing movement. If the scale differed, it did so because the level of integration in the seventeenth century was more rudimentary and the hinterlands affected were smaller, hence the draw of migration did not pull others from areas further afield. The Atlantic was more a world than the system it would become a century later, and the reach of the Atlantic into Irish and American hinterlands reflected this reality.[32]

In the eighteenth century, the ties would deepen and draw from and to areas more deeply in the interiors of each place, reflecting the heightened level of systemic integration. And as before, the state – now British – played the catalytic role, in this case through the disruption caused by the War of the Two Kings in Ireland. The pattern continued throughout the century. So, for instance, the movement in the period between the end of the Seven Years

30 D. Akenson, *If the Irish ran the world: Montserrat, 1630–1730* (Montreal: McGill-Queen's University Press, 1997).
31 D.B. Quinn, *Ireland and America: their early associations 1500–1640* (Liverpool: Liverpool University Press, 1991); Griffin, 'Irish migration to the colonial south'.
32 Canny and Morgan (eds.), *Oxford handbook*, passim.

War and the beginning of the War of Independence enveloped those people living in linen-producing regions on the Earl of Donegall's estates. They were responding to a severe shock to the linen market that imperilled their ability to pay rents. And so they followed their linen to the New World, at the very moment that the state – now starved for manpower and looking towards Ireland – was reaching more deeply into their lives.

That such a decision by this time seemed so commonsensical testifies to a few things. First, migration between Ulster and the Middle Colonies was so well established by this time that economic setbacks occasioned subsequent movement, proverbial chain migration. Second, the America these men and women left for was already a part of their imaginative world. The leap did not seem so great because the Atlantic was less a barrier than a highway, and migrants in fact likely left on ships carrying the material that they produced with their own hands. These were by this time, because of the transformation of their region of Ireland, a British Atlantic people.

Others from other areas of Ireland did not migrate *en masse* for the simple reason that they had not made the imaginative leap of those like the tenants on Lord Donegall's estates. They were not enmeshed in a broader world that included America. Yet, that is. So, by and large, Catholics did not flee Ireland in the eighteenth century. It would be a mistake, however, to suggest none or very few went. And to focus on the idea of 'Scotch Irishness' misses this diversity. Estimates by modern scholars put the percentage of Catholics going over at anywhere between a quarter and a third. This may be too high, but it points to the fact that Catholics did not represent an anomaly.[33] But the key here is that most who went, regardless of faith, left from the north. The north, mainly Ulster but also adjacent regions drawn into the linen economy, became the site where a land-rich but labour-poor America met a land-poor but labour-rich part of Ireland. The process was mediated by a more intrusive state now growing through war-making capacity. This equation never changed for Ireland, though the regions and people negotiating it did with time.

The eighteenth-century movement, more importantly for our purposes, only makes sense when we situate it within the story of subsequent migration as well. For after the American Revolution, when shipping resumed once more, more parts of Ireland were drawn into an Atlantic system, still mediated by Britain, with people still setting sail for the most dynamic regions

---

33 D. Doyle, *Ireland, Irishmen, and Revolutionary America, 1760–1820* (Cork: Mercier Press, 1981); Miller et al., *Irish immigrants in the land of Canaan*; Kelly, 'The resumption of emigration', 75–6.

of the New World. After the Revolution, the pace of migration picked up, again reflecting changing circumstances in Ireland. Of course, we know that a group of radical émigrés set sail for America as the United Irish movement was repressed by the state in Ireland. These saw America as a safe-haven for radicalism, or so they thought. And they would play prominent roles in American politics, helping, ironically, to push politics not to the revolutionary fringes but to the conservative middle.[34] But a quieter story was also taking place, one far larger in terms of numbers and more dramatic still in terms of impact. Ordinary men and women left Ireland in these years. In this case, they departed newly commercialising areas, such as south Ulster and north Leinster.

These people were, of course, not the well-to-do, but the people most exposed to the pressures of a commercialising economy and rendered economically precarious by population growth and the end of the Napoleonic war economic boom. Many became migrant workers, leaving Ireland for Britain to dig canals. They were ideally suited for the world of movement they were about to enter, and in their case, again taking a page from the Ulster movement a generation before, they were attracted to the most progressive areas in the New World. In this case, thousands sailed to work on internal improvement projects in the new United States. Their hands created America. After 1815, the floodgates opened, and some have estimated that as many as a million would leave Ireland for America between this year and the start of the Great Famine.[35]

Later migrants continued to conform to this pattern, even through the Great Famine. The Atlantic, far from being closed off by the severing of America's ties with Britain, became even further integrated, and Irish movement reflected that level of consolidation. By now, as migration became an almost natural aspect of this system, American cities and work sites could regard parts of Ireland as their natural hinterlands. With the Famine, it was those areas that had already been drawn into the system that sent massive numbers to America when the blight struck. Tragically, those places, like much of Munster and almost all of Connacht, that had not been pulled into the system in a thoroughgoing way saw the highest levels of mortality. The Great Famine integrated these areas, and we could regard it as the most brutalising aspect of modernity to strike Ireland. And following the pattern

---

34 On political culture, see S. Cotlar, *Tom Paine's America: the rise and fall of transatlantic radicalism in the early Republic* (Charlottesville: University of Virginia Press, 2011).

35 K. Kenny, *The American Irish: a history* (New York: Longman, 2000); Miller, *Emigrants and exiles*.

established over *la longue durée*, from this point forward all of Ireland had been atlanticised and all regions now sent their people to America.[36]

From this perspective stretching from the seventeenth to the mid-nineteenth century, the eighteenth century does not appear that distinctive. The people, of course, by and large, appear as outliers in terms of their faith and how they conceived of themselves. These markers, however, are almost incidental. The migration from Ulster to the colonies fitted into the broader pattern perfectly. This was, then, unambiguously an Irish migration.

Being Scots Irish

Or was it? Maybe these people are best described the way some ethnic champions described them at the end of the nineteenth century. Maybe they were truly Scotch-Irish. Maude Glasgow, perhaps the most colorful of this group, argued that by calling them 'Scotch Irish' we recognise their essential Scottish traits. These traits were not attenuated in Ireland at all. In fact, they were heightened, and the contests with the 'Irish' in their midst prepared them for their providential mission in the New World, to push the bounds of a Protestant republic ever westward. They were, as another explains, 'God's frontiersmen'.[37] We could take all of this with a grain of salt, but this interpretation held sway for a while among members of the Scotch-Irish Society, which concerned itself with the triumphs in America of the 'race'.[38] The term also reflects the ethnic pride some of the descendants of the group in America embrace even to this day. Though far less visible than those considering themselves 'Irish' in the United States, there is a vibrant sense of Scotch-Irishness in some places in the South. Senator James Webb's *Born fighting*, which resurrects the earlier hagiographic stories, serves as a great example.[39]

There is, however, one way a different though similar term – 'Scots Irish' – works well, and this complicates the Irish story of migration, though I hasten to add it is not the reason this term is advocated by historians. Kerby Miller employs it conventionally to suggest that, however much the 'two traditions' thesis is myth, many of these people still differed in some fundamental ways from the

---

36 J.S. Donnelly Jr, *The Great Irish Potato Famine* (Stroud: Alan Sutton, 2001).

37 M. Glasgow, *The Scotch Irish in Northern Ireland and the American Colonies* (New York: G.P. Putnam's Sons, 1936); R. Fitzpatrick and K. McNally, *God's frontiersmen: the Scots-Irish epic* (Chatswood, New South Wales: Peribo, 1989).

38 See Griffin, 'Irish migration to the colonial south', p. 55. More recently, see Miller's collected essays in *Ireland and Irish America: culture, class, and transatlantic migration* (Dublin: Field Day Publications, 2008), in which he further develops the 'two traditions' theme, as well as the Scotch Irish myth.

39 J. Webb, *Born fighting: how the Scots-Irish shaped America* (New York: Broadway Books, 2004).

masses that would leave Ireland in the nineteenth century. Scottish historians offer a different story. The Scottish historian Tom Devine and the Americanist Ned Landsman both suggest that much of the movement from Ireland in the eighteenth century is better considered a variant of Scottish migration, and any movement of 'Ulster Scots' proves difficult to disentangle from it. We know, for instance, that many who left in the early waves in the eighteenth century, especially from areas adjacent to Derry, were first-generation immigrants themselves. With perhaps as many as 60,000–90,000 men and women sailing from Scotland in the wake of the Glorious Revolution for western Ulster, the region had a distinctively Scottish complexion. Many of those streaming over signed leases as tenants that expired in the late 1710s or 1720s. The early movement coincided with the expiration of those early lease terms and the ratcheting up of new terms.

Ulster Scot proved an offshoot of Scot, a regional variation on a broader theme. So, for instance, maybe we should, as Landsman does, consider Gilbert Tennant, a revival preacher at the time of the Great Awakening, a Scot in terms of his theological leanings, along with Francis Allison, who would train a number who would go on to sign the Declaration of Independence at the Academy of Philadelphia. Both were descended from Scots. And the Presbyterianism they embraced, however much their variants differed from each other, originated in Scotland. Devine clearly spells out that this is how it worked. To be in Ireland for only a generation or two did not make a person Irish at all, or even Scots Irish, but really Scottish. To be sure, neither Devine nor Landsman can be counted 'Scotch Irish' supporters. They do not consider those who emigrated from Ulster to be part of a narrowly construed ethnic group that coheres to mythic conceptions. They are not 'in search of Ulster Scots land', as one recent author is, nor are they trying to revive the long-dead Celtic mist thesis that places all of these peoples and their folkways into an essentialist interpretation of southern American culture.[40] They write on Scottish themes, but the patterns from Ireland they see fitting into broader patterns that also included Scotland.[41]

---

40 B. Vann, *In search of Ulster-Scots land: the birth and geotheological imagings of a transatlantic people, 1603–1703* (Columbia: University of South Carolina Press, 2008); G. McWhiney, *Cracker culture: Celtic ways in the Old South* (Tuscaloosa: University of Alabama Press, 1988); D.H. Fischer, *Albion's seed: four British folkways in America* (Oxford: Oxford University Press, 1989).

41 See Landsman's contribution to T.C. Smout, N.C. Landsman and T.M. Devine, 'Scottish emigration in the seventeenth and eighteenth centuries' in Canny (ed.), *Europeans on the move*. For Devine on the 'Ulster Scots' see Devine, *Scotland's empire and the shaping of the Americas* (Washington, DC: Smithsonian Books, 2004) as well as T. Devine, *To the ends of the earth: Scotland's global diaspora 1750–2010* (Washington, DC: Smithsonian Books, 2011). Also see L.E. Schmidt, *Holy fairs: Scottish communions and American revivals in the early modern period* (Princeton: Princeton University Press, 1989).

These people still left, therefore, because of Irish dynamics and because of the nature of Ireland's immersion in the Atlantic. But Scotland too was a critical element in this sub-system of movement. Maybe we should consider Ireland and Scotland – both dynamically changing in these years because of similar processes – as a single unit, politically disconnected to be sure but culturally and economically linked. If this is the case, the earliest migrants to the colonies are best considered the flotsam and jetsam of marchland integration into the Atlantic, mediated by the British state. And that combination was manifest in both the Glorious Revolution and the economic shocks and economic development that followed in its wake. Today we see Scotland and Ireland as distinct places. This was not the case in the eighteenth century. Granted the two jurisdictions were not linked as closely as they had been in the early modern period when, together, regions of Scotland and Ireland formed an integrated cultural area. And they had different constitutional relationships with the English centre. Nonetheless, as margins within an English-centred archipelago, each kingdom was affected by common systemic dynamics in similar ways, occasioning movement from each and between each.

We would, therefore, be mistaken to follow Devine's lead and consider this earliest movement simply 'Scottish migration', and do away with the Irish label; but we would be just as foolish to jettison 'Scots' altogether. Devine's formulation can be applied with some justice to the few who stayed for one generation in Ulster. But it does not account for the many. It does not apply so clearly to those men and women who left in the 1740s or thereafter. They lived in Ulster for generations, and the migration ties between Ireland and Scotland had dried up by then. With the 1750s, as we know, a growing number of migrants from Scotland proper, in the wake of the '45 and the subsequent reformation of the Highlands, sailed directly for America. The movements from Ireland and Scotland paralleled each other, but stemmed ultimately from the same Old World pressures, New World promises, and the ties between both.

Maybe we should, therefore, consider if the term 'Irish migration' fits at all. In other words, even if the migrants were from Ireland, does it follow they were of Ireland? The thickets become thicker with this question. And here we run into Maude Glasgow's nemesis, the ethnic hagiographer and her mirror image, Michael O'Brien. The head of the Irish American Historical Society at the turn of the twentieth century, O'Brien argued that Scotch-Irishness was a myth created to dissociate the group from Catholics streaming into America, especially with the Famine. All were unambiguously Irish. Maybe we could ditch all qualifiers and use Kevin Kenny's simple but apt formulation of 'America's Irish'.[42]

But what did migrants in the eighteenth century call themselves? The answer is a bit confused. For a start, we know that, aside from the early modern examples James Leyburn has uncovered, the term Scotch-Irish was virtually unknown in Ireland, and when it was used it referred to the linkages between Catholics in Ulster and Highland brethren in Scotland. Highlighting the use of national monikers in a way that spoke to the earlier unity of a cultural Gaeldom that encompassed Ireland and the Highlands, the term reflected new English understandings of both places. And James I would famously look to divide this cultural reality through the wedge of plantation policy along the Scotch-Irish hyphen.[43]

Newspapers offer the best clues to how natives and how those from Ireland conceived of themselves in America. The *Pennsylvania Gazette*, which captured much of the comings and goings of the chief port of entry and settlement for migrants from Ireland, produces some fascinating results.[44] The term 'Scotch Irish', just for a start, when pertaining to people and not 'Scotch, Irish trade', for instance, produces a tiny number of hits for the period between the 1720s and 1780s. Adding the term 'Scots Irish', which was virtually unknown, the grand total grows by one. These come from the years 1756, 1763, 1766, 1775, 1785 and 1787 for 'Scotch Irish'. The results pertain to seven persons, as advertisements for a few runaways were carried twice.[45]

Here are the specifics for the use of the term 'Scotch Irish'. In 1763, Isaac Morgan stole a horse. He had 'the Scotch-Irish tone'.[46] In 1766, a servant named Samuel Evans ran away from his master, and the notice said that he spoke 'on the Scotch-Irish order'.[47] In 1775, the Kerr brothers were described as 'Scotch Irish servant men'.[48] Twelve years later, James McCib was similarly characterised.[49] Finally, and most interestingly,

---

42 Kenny, *The American Irish*, p. 3.
43 J. Leyburn, *The Scotch Irish: a social history* (Chapel Hill: University of North Carolina Press, 1962).
44 www.accessible.com.proxy.library.nd.edu / accessible / preLog?Search=The%20 Pennsylvania%20Gazette. I was inspired to examine newspapers closely by a talk by Michael Montgomery at the Ulster-American Symposium in 2012 at Omagh. There he used newspapers to try to reconstruct the usage of the term 'Scotch Irish'. He, too, found that the term could be used to denote accent. I, however, employ other terms in my analysis for comparative purposes.
45 *Pennsylvania Gazette* (henceforth *PG*), 19 July 1759. On accents see following footnotes.
46 *PG*, 30 June 1763.
47 *PG*, 14 Aug. 1766. This advertisement was reprinted in the same paper, on 18 Sept. 1766.
48 *PG*, 15 March 1775.
49 As a 'Scotch-Irish SERVANT MAN': *PG*, 25 April 1787.

in 1785 Bill and George Mullon ran away. The paper described them as twins descended from a half-Indian slave, 'not to be distinguished from white persons'. The Mullons were both talkative and drunks, 'talk on the Scotch-Irish dialect, [and] may pass for Irishmen'. George, it concluded, is fond of the fiddle.[50]

In general, the obscure term refers to their accents to help readers recognise them and to lead to their apprehension. The more description, the better. The better refinement of their dialect, the better. In our parlance today, this small handful of runaways was being profiled, and advertisements carried anything by which they could be distinguished and apprehended. The accent was akin to a scar. Outside of runaways – with one exception – the term 'Scotch Irish' is not used in the *Pennsylvania Gazette*.

Other searches yielded other results that can help us in labelling. In the same newspaper, 'Irish' yielded 4,327 hits. Considering the goods and ships arriving on a regular basis, this does not surprise. Digging a bit deeper, 'Irish servant' accounted for 1,774 hits. Compare this to 'Scotch Irish servant', which produced three hits, the aforementioned Robert and John Kerr (1775), James McCib (1787) and the Kerr brothers again (1775). Searching for Scotch Irish servant (without quotes) nets forty-five results, but this includes '2 Irish servant men with … [one having] a Scotch accent' and a number of comparable uses.[51] In fact 'Irish servant' with a Scotch accent outnumbers the term 'Scotch Irish'. Ireland servant (without quotes) accounts for 463 hits, and Scotch servant yields 197, though these terms can relate to things other than people. Most of these, it should be noted, are Scottish, and only an Irish servant is described as speaking 'with a Scotch tone'. The term 'brogue' (380 results) is used far more often than referents to Scots/Scotch Irish accent or tone (about three). For instance, in 1770, one runaway from 'north of Ireland' could be identified by his 'brogue'.[52]

The trend holds for other newspapers in the colonies.[53] In fact, it is rarer still. I could not find one that referred to 'Scotch Irish servants' or 'Scotch Irish' tone or accent. A search for 'Scotch Irish' yielded fifty-nine hits for that time period. Many of these, again, refer to 'Scotch, Irish, Dutch' varieties of linens or other goods. And those coming from the *Pennsylvania Gazette* we may discount. A similar search for 'Scots Irish' yields ten results, one of

---

50 *PG*, 31 Aug. 1785.
51 *PG*, 9 May 1751.
52 *PG*, 21 June 1770.
53 'America's Historical Newspapers' database.

which reprints in the *Boston Newsletter* the same reference to 'Scots Irish set-tlers' mentioned in the *Pennsylvania Gazette* above from 1759.[54] I did encounter two other uses of the term. The *Virginia Gazette* in 1776 referred to Scotch highlanders and 'Scotch Irish *regulators*' in the Battle of Moore's Creek.[55] And the *Boston Newsletter* ran an extract from a letter from Philadelphia to London decrying 'Scotch Irish Pr—ns' and their 'diabolical conduct' in the Paxton Boys raid.[56]

Three more are worth mentioning. The first, from *The New-York Journal; or, the General Advertiser* for 5 September 1771, involves a letter from a gentleman in Virginia addressing the controversy over a potential bishopric in America. In it, he argues that nearly all of the assemblymen for Virginia would support the measure; only Dissenters opposed on principle. 'And these being only the members for some back counties', he reports, 'which were chiefly settled by the Scots Irish Presbyterians, I suppose would not amount to a tenth part of the Assembly.' The second is from the *Freeman's Journal; or The North-American Intelligencer*, published in Philadelphia, for 18 February 1784. The paper ran an advertisement for a runaway indentured servant named Sarah Campbell, who was, the paper noted, 'born in the North of Ireland … very artful tho' ignorant, gives Scotch Irish blarney plentifully, to make up for her laziness, says she is a good spinner'. The third, from *Greenleaf's New York Journal and Patriotic Register*, 27 September 1794, is a news item describing the Governor of Virginia's efforts to recruit militia to take on the whiskey rebels. 'What is strange, but true', the writer finds, is that 'the Irish lately imported joined these unhappy people', and he also notes that 'Governor Lee will have to con-tend with Governor Simcoe – Scotch Irish Pennsylvanians, rank Irish, Virginia negroes, and British deserters – These poltroons must soon fly before our gal-lant buckskins.'

The first and the third complicate our picture. Sandwiching the descrip-tor used to apprehend a servant, these point to some sort of 'identity'. The first, however, may in fact refer to Scots *and* Irish. The third, our latest example, points most strongly in the direction of self-conception. By dis-sociating the 'Scotch Irish' from the 'rank Irish', it suggests that some sort of splintering is occurring. This would comport with the work of Kerby Miller, who argues that it was just about this time – really the first stirrings – that we can discern the creation of Scotch-Irishness in America. The idea of

54 *Boston Newsletter*, 23 Aug. 1759.
55 *Virginia Gazette*, 4 May 1776.
56 *Massachusetts Gazette, and Boston News-Letter*, 2 Aug. 1764.

Scotch-Irishness, conventional wisdom now holds, is an early nineteenth-century phenomenon, and it had as much to do with class concerns as it did with ethnic or religious preoccupations. The middle-class descendants of migrants sought to carve out a respectable and politically conservative profile after the tumult of Atlantic Revolution and the associations of Irishness with radicalism. Many considered the so-called Whiskey Rebellion as a continuation, and an unwelcome one at that, of revolutionary radicalism that many wanted consigned to oblivion. To be Scotch Irish, Miller argues, was to reject such radicalism. To be Irish was to continue to embrace it. Although the term 'Irish' enjoyed a radical chic appeal at the time of the Revolution, by 1800 it did not.

That makes for a total of five identifiable 'Scotch Irish' mentions in papers other than the *Pennsylvania Gazette* for the years 1700–1800. Keeping track overall, including seven from the *Pennsylvania Gazette*, that makes twelve cases of Scotch Irish mentions, not counting reprinted advertisements for servants and only counting the 1759 reference to settlers once. Five of them refer to an accent, tone or 'blarney'; the others use it as a label for people themselves. When all is said and done, it is hard to escape the fact that 'Scotch Irish' was exceptional and that it was used in these newspapers in two contexts with one meaning. When it was used, it was employed as a term of derision or as a way, in some circumstances, to denote an accent, to finger these people when they were being sought by a master. Undoubtedly, the accent mattered. But much, much more common was to call these people 'Irish'. Perhaps, after all, they were not a 'people with no name'. But they had few, and 'Irish' is closer to the mark.

In fact, if we look at the mentions in newspapers, their identities appear fluid. This should not surprise us, and perhaps the term 'identity' was an anachronism during the eighteenth century. In fact, mixing and fluidity, found again in the *Pennsylvania Gazette*, captures who these people were much more effectively than either Irish or Scotch Irish. Here is a small taste. The paper listed two Scotch servants (in separate advertisements) who speak Irish, as well as an Irish servant man with Irish and Scotch.[57] We encounter Irish servants who speak with a Scotch tone. We also come across a native Irish man named Laughlin O'Dennysey, who 'speaks good English, nothing on the brogue, but rather on the Scotch tongue,

---

57 Scotch servants who speak Irish: *PG*, 10 Nov. 1773; *PG*, 28 Aug. 1776 (an advertisement for Andrew Urquhart, a 'Scotch servant lad' who 'has something of the Scotch dialect, and can speak Erse tongue'; the reference to 'Erse' may be to Scottish Gaelic). Irish servant man: *PG*, 14 Oct. 1772.

by reason of his living in the north of Ireland'.[58] He was not alone. The *Pennsylvania Gazette*, again in runaway notices, lists 'an Irish servant' lad 'who speaks a little on the Scotch dialect', a fellow calling himself Patrick Hamilton, alias McConnell, who is described as an Irishman who 'speaks much on the Scotch dialect', an Irish servant girl 'slow in speech, and has something of the Scots accent', and another Irish servant girl who 'speaks very improper, between Scotch and English'.[59] The paper also lists an 'Irish' couple six weeks out from Ireland. The man, it finds, is 'a little inclined to the Scotch accent', while she 'speaks broad Scotch'. Similarly, we come across 'a fellow born in the north of Ireland, and talks something of the Scotch'.[60]

These examples are fascinating, and they suggest that our conventional understanding of these people does not do justice to how they thought of themselves and how both sending and receiving societies made sense of them. They were a people perfectly suited to the world of motion they inhabited and came to define. They shifted both place and shape. Most embraced Presbyterianism, but as we know in the New World, many would come to redefine who they were in light of the Great Awakening. Catholics also came, though in smaller numbers, and as far as natives in America were concerned, there was little to distinguish them from their Presbyterian neighbours. They crossed what we would later consider to be rigid confessional boundaries with ease.

Conclusion

To a great extent, we have seen the migration from Ireland in the eighteenth century through the prism of what happened thereafter. In America, after a revolutionary era when Irishness was justifiably associated with radicalism, those coming over from Ireland now seemed to be troubling holdovers from a radical age most Americans wanted to consign to pious memory. As Americans neutered their revolutionary past for a post-revolutionary present, the Irish reverted to what they had been in the English/American imagination: bogeys. Unsurprisingly, the term Scotch Irish grew in prominence from

58 *PG*, 24 March 1747.
59 'Speaks a little': *PG*, 8 Nov. 1770; Hamilton: *PG*, 9 July 1772; 'Slow in speech': *PG*, 2 Nov. 1758; 'Very improper': *PG*, 6 Sept. 1753.
60 Couple: *PG*, 30 Oct. 1766; 'a fellow': *PG*, 4 Aug. 1748.

this period. Moreover, changes in Ireland created the conditions for the two-traditions ideal to take shape. As confessional lines hardened and as they mapped onto political programmes, summed up as nationalist and unionist, the earlier heady period faded from view. The sundering of the Atlantic politically by revolution did not stem the flow – both places were still enmeshed in a system – but it did change the way the Irish saw themselves and the world saw them. Our conundrum of Irishness and migration dates from this period.

But in the eighteenth century, in this grey space between the early modern and the modern, these people inhabited a murky middle between the processes that in the seventeenth century sent the Irish to the Caribbean and that created unambiguous Scotch-Irish identity in the nineteenth. Before the modern construction of nation, theirs was a world that included for a long time Scotland, and this was a good reason to call some of them Scots Irish or Scots-Irish, because the eighteenth-century migration did and did not fit into the broader Irish story.[61]

But perhaps we should use the term in a slightly different way. Adding a slash between Scots and Irish, a 'Scots/Irish migration', captures the ways in which movement to America from Scotland and Ireland, between Scotland and Ireland, and sequentially from one to the other defined the eighteenth-century marchland experience within the Atlantic archipelago. The term Scots/Irish also reminds us, helpfully, that many of our modern conceptions of nation and ethnicity, which gave rise to the very concepts of Irish and Scotch Irish migration, and which create exclusivities based on subsequent history and myth, cannot help us understand how people at the time understood themselves. Migration, simply, incorporated both kingdoms in the eighteenth century as both were immersed in a British-mediated world of trade and of coercion. It incorporated all sorts of people from both places: Catholic, Dissenter and churchman from Ireland; lowlander and highlander from Scotland. For a few people the term speaks to the fluid and open world of limitations and possibilities migrants encountered in both the Old and the New World, and captures how those on the margins of a British-mediated world made sense of changes in the system by moving through it. Ultimately, as the advertisements suggest, their world was one of staged movement, collisions, collusion and hybridity. Those from Ireland, no doubt, outnumbered those leaving from Scotland, but they both left from and settled

---

61 See Miller, *Irish immigrants in the land of Canaan.*

in places newly enmeshed in the system, they both had similar settlement patterns, and they both had the same mixed relations with Indians.[62] The trouble picking a name, and perhaps settling for the Scots/Irish hybrid, also speaks to how these people helped create a world and had to become a people with no name for it.

---

62 See, for instance, D.A. Wilson and G. Morton (eds.), *Irish and Scottish encounters with indigenous peoples: Canada, the United States, New Zealand, and Australia* (Montreal: McGill-Queen's University Press, 2013).

23

Ireland and the Empire in the Nineteenth Century

BARRY CROSBIE

In December 1882, following a controversial twenty-year career that spanned the geographical breadth of the British Empire, the Irish-born, British colonial administrator Sir John Pope-Hennessy secured what would be his last official appointment, as governor of the former French colony of Mauritius. Ever a thorn in the side of the Colonial Office, Hennessy's previous governorships in Labuan, Sierra Leone, the Bahamas, the Windward Islands and Hong Kong had been shaped by what contemporaries referred to as his unfailing 'pro-native sympathies' and his refusal to accede to the demands of white settler interests.[1] During his time in Mauritius, Hennessy openly championed the cause of the Francophone Creoles – who demanded 'Mauritius for the Mauritians' – and the marginalised Indian migrant community. While publicly condemning British colonial rule on that island, he became embroiled in a series of high-profile disputes with British officials, most notably Charles Dalton Clifford Lloyd, the lieutenant-governor. Hennessy's detractors alleged that much of the conflict in which he became embroiled was attributable to his Irish Catholic nationalist background and the particular political views he held.[2] According to Sir Charles Bruce, a guest of the governor in Mauritius in 1884, Hennessy 'seemed never tired of expounding to all and sundry his opinions on the question of Home Rule for Ireland', and was seen constantly to draw covert analogies between Home Rule there and in Mauritius. Observing the many books and pamphlets on Irish Home Rule

---

1 P. Howell and D. Lambert, 'Sir John Pope Hennessy and colonial government: humanitarianism and the translation of slavery in the imperial network' in D. Lambert and A. Lester (eds.), *Colonial lives across the British Empire: imperial careering in the long nineteenth century* (Cambridge: Cambridge University Press, 2006), pp. 228–57.

2 K. Lowe and E. McLaughlin, 'Sir John Pope-Hennessy and the "native race craze": colonial government in Hong Kong, 1877–1882', *Journal of Imperial and Commonwealth History*, 20 (1992), 223–47.

that littered the tables and reading rooms of Le Réduit, the governor's official residence, Bruce was convinced that Hennessy and his cabal of advisers were 'working in perfect harmony ... to produce in the European community of Mauritius ... a little Ireland'.[3] Indeed, Hennessy's attitude and increasingly volatile behaviour prompted the Colonial Office to take the unprecedented step of issuing a royal commission to Sir Hercules Robinson, governor of Cape Colony, high commissioner in South Africa, and fellow Irishman, to inquire into Hennessy's administration. Of particular interest to the authorities was the issue of Hennessy's poor relations with Lloyd, his apparent pro-Creole partisanship, his alleged 'persecution' of English Protestant officials, and his ambitious programme of penal reform. Suspended by Robinson in December 1886, Hennessy was eventually ordered back to London by the colonial secretary, Lord Knutsford, where a long inquiry ensued. However, in July of the same year, Knutsford concluded that although Hennessy had been found guilty of 'want of temper and judgment', 'vexatious and unjustifiable interference' and undue partisanship, no further action against him would be taken on the grounds that there was insufficient evidence to support his removal. Accordingly, Hennessy returned to Mauritius where he served out his time as colonial governor, retiring on full pension and returning to Ireland in December 1889.

Personal histories of Irish involvement in British imperialism overseas, such as that of Sir John Pope-Hennessy, litter the history of the nineteenth century. Indeed, the experiences of Hennessy in many respects mirror the complex nature of nineteenth-century Ireland's relationship with the British Empire. During this period, Ireland was bound legislatively to the United Kingdom through the Act of Union (1801–1922). But rather than serving as a model of nineteenth-century British political and social engineering (as it was hoped), Ireland evolved its own peculiar dynamic with the Union-state, proving at times an important link in the imperial chain but also a critical fault-line at the Empire's core.[4] For much of the century (and, indeed, long before) the Empire functioned as a source of opportunity and outlet for almost all sections of Irish society, from the aristocratic landed gentry and professional middle classes, to rural peasant labourers and the urban poor.[5] Up to the end

3 J. Pope-Hennessy, *Verandah: some episodes in the Crown Colonies, 1867–1889* (London: George Allen and Unwin, 1964), pp. 257–8.
4 A. Jackson, *The two Unions: Ireland, Scotland and the survival of the United Kingdom, 1707–2007* (Oxford: Oxford University Press, 2015).
5 K. Jeffery (ed.), *An Irish empire? Aspects of Ireland and the British Empire* (Manchester: Manchester University Press, 1996).

of the Union in 1922 and beyond, the best Irish university graduates were absorbed into the Empire's vast bureaucratic, educational, scientific, legal, military and medical machinery.[6]

But if the Empire provided Irish people with employment and opportunity, and was an important source of social advancement, Irish people also played a significant role in undermining and subverting the imperial agenda.[7] Recent research on the role of the Irish has made it clear that, for the most part, Irish people of various religious denominations in the service of the Empire viewed themselves as being both part of and separate from the British imperial system.[8] For the poorer classes, 'taking the Queen's shilling' and serving in the Imperial Armed Forces was essentially an economic imperative bound up with the fortunes of the Irish agricultural sector that was more often appealed to in the years after the Great Famine.[9] For the middle and upper classes, careers in the Empire provided a direct route to upward social mobility and betterment.[10] Although many were ambivalent about or even ignorant of the ideological underpinnings of Britain's imperial mission, the vast majority seemed to identify with and to support British colonial rule and policies.

A lack of awareness of the imperial ideal or mission was, of course, partly attributable to Ireland's cultural and geographical distance from the metropolitan core; though a formal part of the United Kingdom during the nineteenth century, Ireland (unlike Scotland and Wales) was fundamentally removed from 'mainland' Britain and was never fully absorbed into the Union-state. Similarly, the extent to which the Empire pervaded the consciousness and psyche of people in mainland Britain (and influenced British culture and identity) was not replicated in Ireland.[11] The vast majority of Irish men and women did not perceive themselves as a 'ruling' people in the English imperial tradition. The subaltern classes, lacking the luxury of an education and a stable income, rarely reflected on the nature of the jobs they were engaged in, while

---

6 B. Crosbie, *Irish imperial networks: migration, social communication and exchange in nineteenth-century India* (Cambridge: Cambridge University Press, 2012).

7 K. O'Malley, *Ireland, India and Empire: Indo-Irish radical connections, 1919–1964* (Manchester: Manchester University Press, 2008).

8 K. Kenny, 'The Irish in the Empire' in K. Kenny (ed.), *Ireland and the British Empire*: Oxford History of the British Empire companion series (Oxford: Oxford University Press, 2004), pp. 90–123.

9 T. Bartlett and K. Jeffery (eds.), *A military history of Ireland* (Cambridge: Cambridge University Press, 1997).

10 C. O'Neill, *Catholics of consequence: transnational education, social mobility and the Irish Catholic elite, 1850–1900* (Oxford: Oxford University Press, 2014).

11 A. Thompson, *Britain's experience of Empire in the twentieth century*: Oxford History of the British Empire companion series (Oxford: Oxford University Press, 2011).

the educated classes tended to view the Empire pragmatically, through a distant and neutrally observant lens.[12] While most appreciated the freedom of movement and privilege that the Empire bestowed, some Irish people looked upon the Empire as 'foreign' and 'alien', and saw it as an oppressive economic and political system based on the subordination and domination of others.[13] Indeed, by the end of the nineteenth century, in spite of its long-established role in supplementing and aiding the spread of British imperialism overseas, Ireland and Irish people were more synonymous with attempts to reform or dismantle the Empire than to sustain or enlarge it.

This chapter sets out to make sense of some of the inherent contradictions and complexities that lie at the heart of the relationship between Ireland and the British Empire in the nineteenth century. In doing so, it seeks to identify the defining features of that relationship in an attempt to unravel the enigma that is Ireland's imperial past. It is divided into two sections. The first explores the broad impact that the Empire had on nineteenth-century Ireland, particularly in relation to its political culture, economic performance and cultural transformation. The second section discusses the role of Ireland and Irish people in the Empire, and assesses the impact that the movement of Irish people, ideas and practices had upon nineteenth-century Britain and its overseas territories. Both sections incorporate discussions of new methodological approaches to the study of Ireland and the British Empire in the nineteenth century and areas of current research.

The Political, Cultural and Economic Impact of the Empire on Nineteenth-Century Ireland

Although never officially a 'colony' of the British Empire, the historical reliance of the crown and its ministers on the Protestant Ascendancy in Ireland sustained an attitude to government and a pattern of administration that survived the abolition in 1800 of the Irish parliament by the Act of Union.[14] Just as the Ascendancy dominated the Irish parliament in the absence of Catholics and nonconformists (who were prohibited from sitting in parliament) in the eighteenth century, Irish representation in the United Kingdom

---

12 T. McDonough, *Was Ireland a colony? Economics, politics and culture in nineteenth-century Ireland* (Dublin: Irish Academic Press, 2005).

13 M. Silvestri, *Ireland and India: nationalism, empire and memory* (Basingstoke: Palgrave Macmillan, 2009).

14 See Volume II, Chapters 2, 5 and 6, by Edwards, McGrath and Hayton, and in this volume, Chapters 2 and 3, by Kelly and Bartlett.

House of Commons remained firmly in the hands of Irish Protestants during the early part of the nineteenth century. It was anticipated that the Union would transform Ireland into a dynamic and prosperous region of the United Kingdom, but the Irish administration that emerged after 1801 bore many of the classic hallmarks of a colonial regime that was subordinate to the central government in London. Moreover, though the admission of Catholics to the Westminster legislature in 1829 can be perceived as the beginnings of a shift that followed a trend identifiable throughout the Empire, whereby successive Liberal governments sought to displace established 'settler' allies by affecting collaborative relationships among English-speaking colonial elites, the government of nineteenth-century Ireland remained resolutely Protestant in character for most of the nineteenth century. Alongside the physical distance that separated the vast majority of Irish people from parliament and an executive headed by a colonial-style viceroy (or 'lord lieutenant'), Ireland developed its own unique political administration within the Empire; neither fully colonised nor absorbed within the metropolitan core, it had its own distinct legal system, Civil Service (with branches in both Dublin Castle and Whitehall) and separate paramilitary-style police force.[15] As depicted by Alvin Jackson, Ireland stood as a 'half-way house' without clear political definition in the nineteenth-century Empire – a failure of the Westminster government that resulted in Ireland being 'ruled partly in colonial and partly in metropolitan terms, and … partly assimilated within a British cultural context'.[16]

Economically, the situation was not altogether better, though it was legally clearer. The removal in 1824 of the protective tariffs that had served to nurture small-scale manufacturing and handicraft industries in parts of Ireland had a stifling effect on the once vibrant and profitable Irish cotton and linen industries. In saying that, however, recent research has demonstrated that the application of an overarching model of economic exploitation will not suffice. While the catastrophe of the Great Famine exposed the fault-line at the heart of the political Union between both islands, there were positive benefits to Ireland's economic ties with the Empire. The inauguration of free trade between both countries in the 1820s, for example, provided Irish merchants with greater access to British imperial markets and was an important stimulus for Irish agricultural development and the promotion of industrial growth

---

15 D. Fitzpatrick, 'Ireland and Empire' in A. Porter, *The Oxford history of the British Empire*, vol. III: *The nineteenth century* (Oxford: Oxford University Press, 1999), pp. 494–521.
16 A. Jackson, 'Ireland, the Union and the Empire, 1800–1960' in K. Kenny (ed.), *Ireland and the British Empire*: The Oxford History of the British Empire companion series (Oxford: Oxford University Press, 2004), p. 124.

and expansion in eastern Ulster. Central to both stimuli was the position of Ireland as one of Britain's major trading partners throughout the period of the Union, a trade whose value at times exceeded that between the United Kingdom and Australia, and at various stages was second only to that of Britain and India. Increased trade between the two jurisidictions during the first half of the nineteenth century encouraged significant capital investment, particularly in the form of gilt-edged bonds and stocks from London-based investors keen to establish insurance firms and brokerages on Irish soil. While the direction of the flow of capital was almost always from Britain to Ireland, increased capital investment and monetisation contributed to the establishment of several major Irish banks, railway companies and canal works.

Complementing formal mechanisms of government, law, trade and economic arrangements were a whole series of informal colonial structures and practices aimed at anglicising and integrating Ireland within the broader framework of the United Kingdom. Official reluctance to incorporate Ireland fully, either politically or economically, within the Union-state (and the wider imperial system) had important ramifications for the array of cultural and social policies that Britain imposed on nineteenth-century Ireland. Ireland was not alone in this regard. Metropolitan hesitancy in extending rights of British citizenship to colonial subjects or fully incorporating possessions within formal structures of colonial power was a characteristic feature of the nineteenth-century Empire. As Oliver MacDonagh has argued:

> the need to treat Ireland as a subordinate collided constantly with the policy of converting her into a component of an integrated society in the British Isles. It also vitiated the policy of converting Irishmen to outer Britons. These cross-purposes, strikingly manifested in Anglo-Irish relations, also characterised, more or less, Britain's relations with all her other dependencies at the time.[17]

Here the British policy of cultural assimilation and the advancement of an 'Anglo-civilising' project aimed at the intellectual and moral regeneration of supposedly 'backward' and 'barbarous' colonised peoples also produced mixed results.

The first serious attempt to 'civilise' and 'modernise' Ireland began in 1824 with the establishment of the Ordnance Survey of Ireland under the direction of Colonel Thomas Colby of the Royal Engineers.[18] The cartographic

---

17 O. MacDonagh, *Ireland* (Englewood Cliffs, NJ: Prentice Hall, 1968), p. 22.
18 J.H. Andrews, *A paper landscape: the Ordnance Survey in nineteenth-century Ireland* (Oxford: Oxford University Press, 1975).

achievements of the Irish Survey represented a seminal moment in the history of British engineering, and in colonial science in general, as the resulting six-inch scale maps compiled by the new scientific method of triangulation portrayed a level of detail and accuracy in cartographic images never before witnessed in the Empire.[19] From this perspective, the Irish Survey, which was completed in 1846, proved to be a resounding success. Yet, as Matthew Edney has pointed out, producing maps that allowed a colonising power to access raw materials, and transport people and goods, as well as to inform military planning was one thing; using them to get to *know* the people, culture and society over whom they ruled was something entirely different. In failing to experience the many different aspects of India's societies and cultures beyond areas under direct colonial control as detailed in their maps, the British 'deluded themselves that their science enabled them to know the "real" India', an oversight devastatingly exposed during the Indian Mutiny of 1857–8.[20] This was also true of the Irish Survey's initiative to produce encyclopaedic accounts of local Irish history, archaeology, society and culture parallel with its cartographic enterprise.[21] Here, the primary goal was to produce a richly detailed archive of Irish antiquarian and historical knowledge (known as the 'Memoirs') that would allow the government to describe and to order the physical environment of Ireland and its people. Despite the widespread acclaim with which the publication in 1837 of the Irish Survey's first *Memoir* (Templemore, County Derry) was greeted, the government suspended work on the *Memoirs* less than three years later, citing reasons of economy. The reality was that the Peel administration was anxious about the political implications of the published *Memoirs*. In particular, critics pointed to the sensitive material revealed by the genealogical research and the histories of dispossession recorded by the Irish Survey's officers and translators.[22] As a result, no further volumes of the *Memoirs* were published and the British government remained largely ignorant of many important aspects of Irish culture, history and society, a failure that would ultimately play a part in undermining the Union in a later period.

---

19 S. Ó Cadhla and É. Ó Cuív, *Civilising Ireland: Ordnance Survey, 1824–1842: ethnography, cartography, translation* (Dublin: Irish Academic Press, 2007).

20 M.H. Edney, *Mapping an Empire: the geographical construction of British India, 1765–1843* (Chicago: University of Chicago Press, 1999), pp. 2–3.

21 G.M. Doherty, *The Irish Ordnance Survey: history, culture and memory* (Dublin: Four Courts Press, 2004).

22 Ibid., p. 26.

In terms of its physical environment, Ireland also remained distinctly 'different' from mainland Britain during the nineteenth century. Aside from a substantial army presence (numbering over 25,000 in the 1880s), with its associated military accoutrements and displays within the numerous garrison towns, visual elements of Britishness and of formal colonisation were scattered thinly on the ground. Outside some of the larger Irish cities where British architectural styles and symbolism of the colonial administration were visible in the form of post offices, law courts, hospitals, banks, theatres, libraries and museums, few buildings were erected. Of those that were, by far the most common were the fabled 'Big Houses' or country estates of the Anglo-Irish elite. Dating back to the seventeenth century, these houses represented the symbolic focal point of the landed estate and Ascendancy dominance throughout large parts of Ireland. Yet, despite the central role the landed estate had in determining the social structures and hierarchies of the communities in which they existed, many landowners had little engagement with the community beyond the collection of rents. Concealed behind high walls or natural barriers of dense woodland, the Big Houses epitomised not only the growing social and economic disparity between landed and tenanted families, but also the reality of the physical divide that separated the two communities under British rule. This material symbol of Ascendancy dominance in the eighteenth and early nineteenth centuries experienced a gradual decline in the second half of the nineteenth century as Catholic emancipation, closely followed by the Great Famine, heralded the beginning of a sustained period of social and political unrest focused on land reform and the economic and political disempowerment of the landed elite in the face of the rising might of Irish nationalism.[23]

British imperial influence in Ireland in the nineteenth century was sustained by a spectrum of cultural influences ranging from sport and newspapers to popular literature, theatre and cinema. Sport, in particular, was an effective agent of informal British imperialism in Ireland, where it worked to communicate and spread Victorian values and ideas throughout the country. As was the case in many of Britain's colonies, sport played a key role in incorporating Ireland into a wider 'cultural British world', thereby reinforcing the institutional, political and economic bonds of empire.[24] Several studies on

23 T. Dooley, *The decline of the big house in Ireland* (Dublin: Wolfhound Press, 2001), p. 102.
24 B. Crosbie and M. Hampton (eds.), *The cultural construction of the British world* (Manchester: Manchester University Press, 2015), pp. 1–23.

the history of sport and leisure in nineteenth-century Ireland have stressed just how central Ireland was in the unfolding of a British imperial sporting culture.[25] Far from eschewing 'foreign' sports such as cricket, football, tennis and rugby, Irish people enthusiastically embraced them and flocked in large numbers to join the sporting clubs and societies that emerged in Ireland in the post-Union period. Indeed, according to Paul Rouse, 'nowhere were the games of Empire more rapidly and fully adopted' than in Ireland.[26] Moreover, this was a collective Irish pursuit that crossed class and religious divides. Tom Hunt's analysis of the emergence of cricket as a popular sport played in County Westmeath in the second half of the nineteenth century, for example, debunks the common nationalist interpretation of these sports as elitist and exclusionary. Cricket was a game that was played across the classes and in many villages and towns throughout Ireland in that period.[27] Central to the spread of British games throughout the Empire, of course, was the belief that sport (much like the spread of technology, the English language or the Protestant faith) would have a transformative effect upon host societies; sport in this sense was an integral component of the anglicising mission, a drive to communicate to colonised peoples Victorian (and imperial) ideas of masculinity, fairness and devotion to a cause through fair-play, team-spirit and a clearly defined set of rules.[28] Yet here too, the long-term impact and sustainability of the imperial sporting agenda in Ireland proved relatively short-lived. Irish cultural nationalists identified sport as an important tool in their campaign to promote national liberation, which led to the establishment in 1884 of a distinctly Irish sporting institution in the form of the Gaelic Athletic Association (GAA), committed to the promotion of 'native Irish games [Gaelic football, hurling, handball and camogie] … bathed … in ideas of Irishness', and in a rhetorical language designed 'to make Irish people choose between "Irish laws" and "English laws", between "native" and "foreign" [sporting codes]'.[29] Typical of the inherent anomalies at the core of Ireland's imperial relationship with Britain was the fact that many Irish nationalists actively partook in the sports of Empire and for the most part did not see their Irishness compromised by their sporting affiliations.

25 A. Bairner, 'Ireland, sport and empire' in Jeffery (ed.), *An Irish empire?*, pp. 57–77; T. Hunt, *Sport and society in Victorian Ireland: the case of Westmeath* (Cork: Cork University Press, 2007); P. Rouse, *Sport and Ireland: a history* (Oxford: Oxford University Press, 2015).
26 Rouse, *Sport and Ireland*, p. 2.
27 Hunt, *Sport and society in Victorian Ireland*, p. 3.
28 P. McDevitt, *May the best man win: sport, masculinity and nationalism in Great Britain and the Empire, 1880–1935* (Basingstoke: Palgrave Macmillan, 2004).
29 Rouse, *Sport and Ireland*, p. 2.

Education too was perceived to possess an integrative value. The development of the national education system in Ireland after 1831 initially proceeded on the basis that newly established state-run schools would be multi-denominational and would promote a curriculum that would instil 'the great principles of morality and religion, which are suggested by the law of nature, and are admitted by all Christians of every denomination in Ireland'.[30] By promoting a secular, holistic and far-reaching educational curriculum – one that went beyond the narrow confines of a perceived parochial Ireland – the education commissioners envisaged a school system that would create a body of metropolitan citizens and future colonists.[31] Certainly, throughout the second half of the nineteenth century, the development of a modern Irish education system was closely linked to the British imperial state. Both mass schooling and elite colleges, established for the growing Catholic middle classes, were particularly concerned with preparing children for future careers in the professions.[32] The British Empire, with its increasing emphasis on mobility of labour and opportunities for those with talent (imperial Civil Service entry examinations replaced the old system of patronage in 1855), proved an important outlet for Irish families who believed that education was the key to social and economic advancement.[33] In this respect, at least, the nineteenth-century British Empire was also very much an *Irish* Empire. From the mid-1850s through to the outbreak of the First World War (when numbers began to wane), thousands of Irish-trained doctors, teachers, civil servants, engineers, scholars and missionaries travelled to almost every part of the Empire, where many enjoyed long, lucrative careers. Securing an imperial post was a serious business, and one that invested the collective interests of individuals, families, institutions, and state and church authorities alike. Established in 1845 for the purpose of providing further educational opportunities for Irish Catholics, Queen's College Cork was one of several Irish universities that specifically tailored the curricula of its courses to the needs of the imperial system. Writing in the annual report for 1863, one Civil Service commissioner was keen to direct 'the attention of parents and guardians ... to the new arrangements for the East India Company Service, according to which are open to competition at

---

30 *Royal Commission of Inquiry into Primary Education (Ireland)*, vol. 1, pt 1: Report of the Commissioners, p. 123 [c 6], H.C., 1870, xxviii, pt 1.
31 D.H. Akenson, *The Irish education experiment: the national system of education in the nineteenth century* (London: Routledge, 2012).
32 O'Neill, *Catholics of consequence*.
33 D. Dickson, J. Pyz and C. Shepard (eds.), *Irish classrooms and British Empire: imperial contexts in the origins of modern education* (Dublin: Four Courts Press, 2012).

Examinations prescribed by the Board of Control'. 'The courses of lectures at the Queen's College, Cork', he noted, 'are well adapted to prepare candidates for their Examination.'[34] For a sustained period of time, Irish educational institutions were shaped by policies (some of which were openly supported by the Catholic Church) attuned to the opportunities afforded by the Empire.

Ireland and Irish people in the Empire

The extent to which Irish educational institutions and people went beyond recognising the Empire as a valuable labour-market and embraced the 'imperial mission' varied greatly. For many Irish, the work of Empire was undertaken not 'through a sense of imperial duty … or even a common sense of adventure' but out of a sense of 'professional frustration that, having acquired their education and qualifications, they were unlikely to be able to apply them at home'.[35] Irish involvement in Empire was not simply a nineteenth-century phenomenon, of course. From the beginnings of the British Empire in the sixteenth century, Irishmen played a prominent role in helping to conquer and to govern both Ireland and the various parts of the globe to which British power and influence extended. For the most part, this was done willingly and, depending on the particular socio-economic or religious group concerned, enthusiastically.[36] The Irish, much like their Scottish, Welsh and English counterparts, were to be found in every part of the Empire, occupying positions at all levels of imperial institutions and settler societies, including the military, the administration, the professions and the church. Substantial Irish migration and settlement in Canada, Australia, New Zealand and South Africa was supplemented by smaller movements of Irish people to areas of informal empire, such as Argentina.[37] The Empire also provided opportunities for those in the professions – engineers, lawyers, doctors and teachers. Both Catholics and Protestants served as colonial governors and magistrates, and staffed the Indian civil and medical services, and there was an extensive Irish Catholic presence in the rank and file of both the East India Company and the regular British Army throughout the nineteenth century. Irrespective of the degree to

---

34 'Annual Reports of Her Majesty's Civil Service Commissioners', *Parliamentary Papers*: 1863, XVII (pt 2), 7, pp. 13–14.

35 Dickson et al. (eds.), *Irish classrooms and British Empire*, p. 156.

36 See R.B. McDowell, 'Ireland in the eighteenth-century British Empire' in J.G. Barry (ed.), *Historical Studies IX* (Belfast: Blackstaff Press, 1974), pp. 57–63.

37 A. McCarthy, *Scottishness and Irishness in New Zealand since 1840* (Manchester: Manchester University Press, 2005); L. Proudfoot and D. Hall, *Imperial spaces: placing the Irish and Scots in Colonial Australia* (Manchester: Manchester University Press, 2011).

which jingoistic fervour or a sense of an 'imperial mission' was a motivating factor for the different classes and religious groups of Irish people involved in the Empire, all played some role in the dispossession and subjugation of indigenous peoples and helped to consolidate racially segregated, white-dominated colonial societies through migration and settlement. Thus, although the motivating factors for Irish participation in the Empire varied considerably – ranging from deprivation and economic necessity to social mobility and career progression – most Irish people identified with the Empire to some degree. Significant also was the fact that imperial participation for many Irish people did not necessarily mean compromising their sense of identity or cultural belonging. Although technically classified as 'Britons' as a result of the Act of Union, Irish people (including Catholics and other marginalised non-Anglican Protestant groups such as Presbyterians and Methodists) were never wholly comfortable with a 'British' designation, and did not necessarily see themselves as such. This is perhaps not surprising given that nineteenth-century Ireland was never a homogeneous economic, political or religious entity whose historic relationship with Britain was straightforward or uniform. Instead, Ireland comprised a multiplicity of communities, each with its own distinctive identity, traditions and cultural values, and each with its own particular relationship with the Empire. For William Hoey, a Belfast-born Irish Presbyterian magistrate based in Lucknow in the 1880s, there was a clear distinction between Irish and English people in India that could not be easily reconciled. According to Hoey, 'the Irish Protestant stood outside that English Mutual Admiration Society which he calls the Union or the Empire. The Irish Protestant simply seized on English power; used it for his own purposes … with freedom from the scruples of world politics. The business was Irish business, not English; and he was Irish.'[38] According to Richardson Evans, a Cork-born Wesleyan Methodist, stationed as an assistant magistrate and collector in Mirzapur in the 1860s, an Irish Protestant identity was more compatible with contemporary understandings of Britishness. Once recalling how he had been mistaken for a British 'Chubutra-Wallah with an unusual accent' rather than a 'proud Irishman from Cork', he was filled 'half with pride at being one and half with pride that [he had] been mistaken for an Englishman'.[39] For Patrick Heffernan, a County Tipperary-born Catholic employed in the Indian Medical Service in the 1890s, imperial service did not necessarily confirm the

---

38 W. Hoey, *A Monograph on trade and manufactures in Northern India* (Lucknow: American Methodist Mission Press, 1880), pp. 47, 200.
39 R. Evans Papers, MS. E 404, Box 1, f. 354, Oriental and India Office Collections, British Library.

nationalist view of Irish Catholics in the Empire as typical 'Shawneens' or 'West-Britons'. In his memoir he recalled how he and his colleagues deeply 'believed in the British Empire' and how, as 'Irish Europeans, cosmopolitans and citizens of the world', the Empire enabled them to 'live satisfying lives ... perhaps contributing a share, great or small, to human progress and human civilisation'.[40] According to Heffernan, he and his colleagues' long association with Britain and the Empire did not diminish their sense of Irishness; careers in India, and more broadly within the British imperial administration itself, did not mean 'that we did not consider ourselves good Irishmen, we did'.[41]

Clearly Irish people of various religious denominations in the service of Empire viewed themselves as being both part of, yet separate from, the British imperial system. Within the context of the nineteenth-century Empire, multiple and hybrid Irish identities often co-existed. In this sense, the Irish in the Empire were no more a unified or uniform body of people than they were at home. Just as the Irish in Ireland were divided by politics, religion and class during the nineteenth century, so too were the Irish in the Empire. This is evidenced by the degree of discomfort and defensiveness in the articulation of identities by individuals such as William Hoey, Richardson Evans and Patrick Heffernan. Indeed, the Empire itself was a source of tension between Irish families and individuals throughout the nineteenth century, as those who campaigned for Home Rule and an end to the Union were often the same people who publicly supported the Empire and envisaged an independent Ireland operating fully within a broader imperial framework. For many Irish (particularly middle-class Catholics) the necessity of pursuing a career and upward social mobility meant that patriotism and an ingrained distrust of Britain, or dislike of its colonial mechanisations, often had to be compromised or overlooked. For this reason, it was commonplace too for Irish Home Rulers, even separatists, to occupy positions in the colonial administration during the nineteenth century. Often vociferous opponents of imperial institutions and critics of imperial policy, many of these individuals remained fiercely proud of their work in the Empire and of the children, siblings or family friends whom they supported and secured posts for in colonial service.

Although there was little difference in the extent to which the Irish, as opposed to the Scots or Welsh, embraced the opportunities that the Empire afforded them, recent research has made clear that there were subtle

---

40 Major P. Heffernan, *An Irish Doctor'smemories* (Dublin: Clonmore & Reynolds, 1958), p. 28.
41 Heffernan, *An Irish Doctor's memories*, pp. 1–3.

differences in how different groups of Irish people viewed the Empire, the degree to which they embraced the imperial ideal, and the extent to which the Empire was influenced by specific Irish residua. This is important because understanding what was particularly unique about Irish involvement in the British Empire has replaced an older historiographical concern centred on an examination of the nature of Ireland's constitutional and political ties to Britain under colonial rule.[42] This new historiographical focus in Irish Empire studies is part of a wider trend in British imperial history where an increasing number of scholars, most notably John M. MacKenzie, engage more fully with the distinct experiences of Irish, English, Scottish and Welsh relationships with the British Empire.[43] MacKenzie's 'four nations' approach to the history of the British Empire, in particular, has done much to draw attention to the ways in which the separate ethnic, religious, social and political characters of nineteenth-century Britons impacted upon the Empire both at home and abroad. As an integral component of the larger British world in the nineteenth century, Ireland played a central role in the economic, political and cultural construction of that system; this new research has made clear that during this time Irish people thought of themselves in distinct ethnic and racial terms and saw their contributions to British imperialism and culture as wholly separate from their English, Scottish and Welsh counterparts'. Although the idea of the Irish as agents of Empire is not new, the extent to which Irish personal, commercial, professional and religious associations spun linkages and ethnically based networks of their own, foregrounding 'British' imperialism and culture, is only beginning to be uncovered. Building on the pioneering work of scholars such as Clive Dewey, Howard Brasted and S.B. Cook, scholarship on the role of the Irish in the Empire has moved beyond simply recalling the achievements or deeds of Irish men and women who rose to prominence in the Empire to examine instead the implications that Irish backgrounds, forms of education and understandings of the world had for imperial affairs in different parts of the Empire. Moreover, there is an emerging body of work interested in examining how cultures of religious, scientific and political thought drew from Irish institutions, methods and personnel, and how an awareness of these processes can be used to inform an understanding of the extent to which

42 See, for example, S. Howe, *Ireland and Empire: colonial legacies in Irish history and culture* (Oxford: Oxford University Press, 2002).
43 See J.M. MacKenzie, 'Irish, Scottish, Welsh and English worlds? A four-nation approach to the history of the British Empire', *History Compass*, 6:5 (2008), 1244–63.

'Britishness' was influenced by 'Irishness', and how British imperial culture was suffused with distinctly 'Irish' elements.[44]

Much recent work on Ireland's historical relationship with the British Empire has centred on an examination of the multi-layered nature of Ireland's imperial experience and especially on the networks and connections that underpinned it. Much of this new scholarship focuses on the cultural as well as economic and political ties of the Empire, highlighting how the Empire was not simply an administrative or commercial structure, but also a power-ful cultural entity that facilitated the movement of different peoples, ideas and culture around the globe.[45] Increasingly, the history of Ireland and the British Empire in the nineteenth century is being written within the context of the 'new' imperial history, with its focus on discourses of race, gender and class, and a more expansive global view. Early work by Keith Jeffery examin-ing how aspects of Irish culture – including sport, film and entrepreneurship, 'the sinews of Empire' – served at various times to reinforce British impe-rial authority in both Ireland and the Empire during the nineteenth century represented a significant departure in both Irish and British imperial history. Until then, both had largely ignored Ireland's long and complex relationship with the Empire.[46] Highlighting the diverse nature and geographical scope of Ireland's imperial connections during this period, Jeffery's work was built upon by Christopher Bayly, who in a hugely influential lecture (later pub-lished in the *Transactions of the Royal Historical Society*) discussed a series of important connections and exchanges between nineteenth-century Ireland and India, ranging from mutually reinforcing calls for economic justice and national self-determination, to shared intellectual practices and debate over the role of emerging religious and political ideology in both countries.[47] Bayly's work was particularly significant in its identification of specific groups or 'Indo-Irish' networks of people and institutions, and the impact they had on each other, and on British rule throughout the Empire more generally. In recent years, scholars have attempted to delineate more fully the experi-ence and influence of individual Irish personnel networks and institutions on imperial matters directly. Tony Ballantyne's study of the role of Irish

---

44 See, for example, J.M. MacKenzie, *The Scots in South Africa: ethnicity, identity, gender and race, 1772–1914* (Manchester: Manchester University Press, 2012); T.M. Devine, *Scotland's Empire: The origins of the global diaspora* (London: Penguin, 2012).

45 G.B. Magee and A.S. Thompson, *Empire and Globalisation: networks of people, goods and capital in the British world, c.1850–1914* (Cambridge: Cambridge University Press, 2010).

46 Jeffery (ed.), *'An Irish Empire'?: Aspects of Ireland and the British Empire*.

47 C.A. Bayly, 'Ireland, India and the Empire: c.1780–1914', *Transactions of the Royal Historical Society*, 6th series, 10 (2000), 377–97.

administrators (many of whom were amateur antiquarians, folklorists and linguists) in the production of colonial knowledge, for example, demonstrated the centrality of nineteenth-century Irish 'knowledge communities' in the construction of British hegemony in colonial South Asia.[48] Indeed, a number of recent studies have focused almost exclusively on specific groups of Irish-born and -trained professionals in an attempt to define more clearly the 'Irish' imperial dimension to Britain's Empire. Work by Patrick O'Leary on Irish public servants, engineers and medical personnel, for example, has established that the Irish were at the forefront of British 'engineering imperialism' in Punjab and the North-Western Frontier in the late nineteenth century, where they brought their first-hand experience of working on similar land-related projects in Ireland to bear on the construction of 'canal colonies' and irrigation works in India, the Straits Settlements, Malaya and Ceylon.[49] The role of Irish medical personnel in the nineteenth-century Empire has also received attention. Work by Christopher Shepard, Greta Jones and S. Karly Kehoe has variously uncovered the degree to which Irish doctors, at the forefront of imperial medicine, contributed to the spread of western scientific medical practice and shaped debates concerning the extent to which religiosity, national identity and loyalty were incorporated and understood within the context of imperial defence and public health reform.[50] Michael Silvestri and Alexander Bubb have similarly focused on the role of Irish officers and soldiers in the imperial armed forces to demonstrate how the inter-related processes of historical memory, commemoration and representation were crucial in the construction and articulation of British and Irish identities both during the nineteenth century and in modern times.[51] Other notable work on the role of Irish officers, proconsuls and colonial governors that goes beyond the simple biographical approach pursued by earlier studies of Ireland and Empire includes studies by Jennifer Ridden and Zoe Laidlaw on the influence

48 T. Ballantyne, 'The sinews of empire: Ireland, India and the construction of British colonial knowledge' in McDonough (ed.), *Was Ireland a Colony?*, pp. 145–61.

49 P. O'Leary, *Servants of Empire: The Irish in Punjab, 1881–1921* (Manchester: Manchester University Press, 2011).

50 C. Shepard, ' "I have a notion to go off to India": Colonel Alexander Porter and Irish recruitment to the Indian Medical Service', *Irish Economic and Social History*, 41 (2014), 36–52; G. Jones, ' "Strike out boldly for the prizes that are available to you": medical emigration from Ireland, 1860–1905', *Medical History* 54 (2010), 55–74; S. Karly Kehoe, 'Accessing Empire: Irish surgeons and the Royal Navy, 1840–1880', *Social History of Medicine*, 26:2 (2012), 204–24.

51 M. Silvestri, *Ireland and India: nationalism, empire and memory* (Basingstoke: Palgrave Macmillan, 2009); A. Bubb, 'The life of the Irish Soldier in India: representations and self-representations', *Modern Asian Studies*, 46:4 (2012), 769–813.

of Irishness on imperial governance in the nineteenth century. Their work on Richard Bourke, the one-time colonial governor of New South Wales and the Cape Colony, in particular, has argued that Irish liberalism profoundly shaped Bourke's behaviour as colonial governor of Melbourne, and that this had enduring consequences for Australia as a whole.[52] Similar studies have also been developed for regions of the Empire less well documented in imperial historiography. Jonathan Wright's work on the Belfast-born writer, parliamentarian and colonial administrator James Emerson Tennent is significant in that it highlights the extent of Ulster's imperial connections and influence on governance in Ceylon in the pre-Home Rule era.[53]

There have been a number of innovative attempts to frame the substantial Irish missionary presence in the nineteenth-century Empire in a broader, more nuanced manner. Hilary Carey and Colin Barr, in particular, have done much to advance a global understanding of the impact of the Irish and their religious connections in the nineteenth century. Carey's recent study of the relationship between religion and colonialism in the nineteenth-century British world, for example, demonstrates that Irish religious orders and missionary societies (of various denominations) were central to Britain's transformation from Protestant nation to free Christian empire during the nineteenth century.[54] Barr's work goes further, arguing that the influence of Paul Cullen as rector of the Irish College in Rome, and later as archbishop of Dublin, facilitated the appointment of a close network of Irish Roman Catholic prelates throughout the Empire. Within these different geographical locations, Irish missionaries and priests sought to supplant the work of their predecessors, giving rise to a distinctly 'Hiberno-Roman' devotional and disciplinary model of Catholicism that became the standard in many places.[55] Going beyond the traditional historical focus on the experience of individual religious orders and their impact on Irish diasporic communities and settler societies, Carey and Barr have developed the idea of a 'Greater Ireland' as an appropriate framework for analysing the global impact of nineteenth-century Ireland's 'Spiritual Empire'. For

---

52 J. Ridden, 'Making good citizens: national identity, religion and liberalism among the Irish elite, c.1800–1850', PhD thesis, 1998, King's College London; Z. Laidlaw, 'Richard Bourke: Irish liberalism tempered by Empire' in D. Lambert and A. Lester (eds.), *Colonial Lives across the British Empire: Imperial careering in the long nineteenth century* (Cambridge: Cambridge University Press, 2006), pp.113–44.

53 J. Wright, '"The Belfast Chameleon": Ulster, Ceylon and the imperial career of Sir James Emerson Tennent', *Britain and the World*, 6:2 (2013), 192–219.

54 H.M. Carey, *God's Empire: religion and colonialism in the British world, c.1800–1908* (Cambridge: Cambridge University Press, 2011).

55 C. Barr, '"Imperium in Imperio": Irish episcopal imperialism in the nineteenth Century', *English Historical Review*, 123 (2008), 611–50.

them, 'Greater Ireland' (that is, the collective regions of the world that the Irish populated) was 'a shared cultural space in which a sense of home and shared identity jostled with the varying challenges of the host societies and the inherited divisions of the Irish themselves'. Within this world, Irish clerics and laypeople took advantage of the religious free market of the British Empire and used their faith not only to compete, exploit and thrive in the vast world opened up to them, but also to reshape the very structures of those societies.[56]

Of course, not all Irish people worked to sustain British imperialism during the nineteenth century. Within the more national-focused tradition of twentieth-century Irish historical scholarship, much early work on the relationship between Ireland and Empire centred on the role of Irish nationalists (as either settlers, soldiers in the British Army or employees in the imperial bureaucracy) in undermining both colonial regimes and the imperial system at large. As such, a relatively extensive historiography dealing with Ireland's anticolonial role in the Empire already exists, albeit one that focuses disproportionately on developments occurring within Ireland or Britain itself, or connections between Ireland and one other British colony at most. In recent years, the history of Irish subversive activity and involvement in the end of Empire has been considered in much broader, comparative perspectives. Niall Whelehan's work on nineteenth-century Irish nationalism and political violence in transnational contexts, for example, reveals connections and parallels between Irish radicals and revolutionary groups across Europe and the United States, suggesting that Irish anti-colonial interest in Africa, Asia and the Middle East at this time was part of a broader global trend.[57] Indeed, Whelehan's work on Irish nationalist activity and the imperial endgame is being mirrored by a growing interest among historians in examining Ireland's active role in shaping the post-colonial world. Recent works by Kate O'Malley, Kevin O'Sullivan, Helen O'Shea and Georgina Sinclair have indicated how, despite the forces of nationalism, Irish participation and interest in the British Empire remained strong well into the twentieth century.[58]

---

56 C. Barr and H.M. Carey (eds.), *Religion and greater Ireland: Christianity and Irish global Networks, 1750–1950* (Montreal and Kingston: McGill-Queen's University Press, 2015), p. 21.

57 N. Whelehan, *The Dynamiters: Irish nationalism and political violence in the wider world, 1867–1900* (Cambridge: Cambridge University Press, 2012).

58 O'Malley, *Ireland, India and Empire: Indo-Irish radical connections, 1919–1964*; K. O'Sullivan, *Ireland, Africa and the end of Empire: small state identity in the Cold War, 1955–1975* (Manchester: Manchester University Press, 2014); H. O'Shea, *Ireland and the end of the British Empire: the Republic and its role in the Cyprus Emergency* (New York: I.B. Taurus, 2015); G. Sinclair, *At the end of the line: colonial policing and the imperial endgame, 1945–1980* (Manchester: Manchester University Press, 2006).

Conclusion

Ireland's relationship with the British Empire in the nineteenth century was complex, fraught with multiple contradictions and with no clear narrative upon which to base definitive judgments. The relationship was complex precisely because there were so many factors and variables complicating its multiple layers and facets at any given point in time. To be sure, the nineteenth century was a period of tremendous social, economic, religious and cultural change in a deeply divided Ireland; this transformation took place within the broader context of an organic, ever protean British Empire that was constantly changing in both form and structure at the same time. Within this shifting paradigm, any analysis of the impact of the Empire on Ireland, and conversely of the impact of Ireland on the Empire, cannot be simple or straightforward. What is clear, however, is that the failure of the British government to integrate Ireland fully into the Union-state after 1800 meant that Ireland was never properly defined, in either metropolitan or colonial terms. Official reticence about whether to colonise the country as a whole and render it wholly subordinate to the crown, or to embrace it as a key component of the United Kingdom, conferring the status of equal partner in the imperial process, set Ireland apart from all other components of Britain's Empire. Again, there is no simple explanation. Certainly, the debates leading up to the passing of the Union at the beginning of the nineteenth century offer some clues about British ambivalence on the issue of Ireland's formal integration into the United Kingdom. As Joe Cleary has observed: 'The country was perhaps geographically too close to England to be exotic in the manner of India, the Americas, or Egypt, and culturally too stubbornly Catholic, too frequently rebellious, too commonly a byword for misery and failed policy to be regarded as a showcase either for the benefits of the Union or for those of imperial progress.'[59] In the end, British unwillingness to accommodate Ireland and Irish people fully in the Union was a principal factor in precipitating Irish independence in 1921, as disillusioned Irish nationalists sought to free themselves from British rule, and in the process served as a model for others who would later champion the demise of the Empire itself. Lacking any formal political definition or categorisation within the nineteenth-century British Empire, Ireland and Irish people were ultimately left to construct their own identities and to forge their own individual roles and relationships within

---

59 J. Cleary, 'Amongst Empires: A Short History of Ireland and Empire Studies in International Context', *Eire-Ireland* 42:1 and 2 (2007), 21.

the wider imperial system, some of which worked to Ireland's benefit and Britain's detriment and vice versa. The hybrid identities and multiple roles that Ireland and Irish people adopted facilitated an extraordinary degree of interaction, communication and exchange within the context of the British Empire, most of which is only beginning to be explored. In examining the diversity and breadth of Irish imperial connections during the nineteenth century it is important to remember C.A. Bayly's caution that any attempt to decentre the Empire must not be made at the expense of downplaying the Empire's dominant economic and political machinery in the metropole. It is important for this reason that those interested in examining the many facets of Ireland's historical relationship with the nineteenth-century Empire do not over-emphasise the diffusion and impact of what were evidently less dominant forms of imperial culture emanating from subordinate centres throughout the British world.[60] Clearly, though, as recent scholarship has made clear, the Irish were at the forefront of aiding the spread of British imperialism overseas, and Irish institutions had the ability to supply the Empire with many of its fundamental needs and requirements. Looking at Irish involvement in the nineteenth-century Empire in this manner at once complicates and destabilises how Ireland can be viewed within the imperial system and its relationship with other Britons and centres of metropolitan power. At the same time tracing such connections obliges us to re-evaluate the active circuits of imperialism within both the Union-state and the wider British world while challenging us to rethink some of the traditional orthodoxies within British, Irish and imperial historiography.

---

[60] C.A. Bayly, 'The British and indigenous peoples, 1760–1860: power, perception and identity' in M. Daunton and R. Halpern (eds.), *Empire and others: British encounters with indigenous peoples, 1600–1850* (Philadelphia: University of Pennsylvania Press, 1999), p. 21.

PART VI

*

THE GREAT FAMINE AND
ITS AFTERMATH

24

The Great Famine, 1845–1850

PETER GRAY

Introduction

In the century after the horrendous famine of 1740–1, mass starvation was largely absent from the island. When the spectre of famine returned in the 1840s, it fell on a society transformed both demographically and politically. The population had more than tripled since 1750 with little per capita economic growth, rendering millions vulnerable to crop failure. At the same time, political change and state expansion had raised both the capacities and the expectations of the state to respond effectively to any such crisis. Moreover, the constitutional structure in which the Great Famine occurred had been transformed by the Act of Union in 1800, which ostensibly created the unitary state of the United Kingdom of Great Britain and Ireland, abolishing the kingdom of Ireland as a quasi-autonomous political entity. Given this specific context, there may be some merit in regarding the crisis that struck Ireland and the Highlands of Scotland, and which subjected many parts of England and lowland Scotland to the effects of crisis emigration, as the 'Great British Famine of the 1840s'.[1]

There are several reasons why this label never acquired popularity at the time or subsequently. For Irish nationalists the failure of the UK state to prevent the mass mortality of the later 1840s was proof of the moral bankruptcy of that Union and hence the necessity of Irish autonomy or independence. Famine, they believed, had been thrust specifically on Ireland by the deliberate malevolence, or at the very least the culpable indifference, of the British government.[2] Furthermore, English and Scottish public

---

1 P. Gray, '"The Great British Famine of 1845–50"? Ireland, the UK and peripherality in famine relief and philanthropy', in D. Curran, L. Luciuk and A. Newby (eds.), *Famines in European economic history: the last great European famines reconsidered* (London: Routledge, 2015), pp. 83–96.

2 J. S. Donnelly, 'The construction of the memory of the Famine in Ireland and the Irish diaspora, 1850–1900', *Eire-Ireland*, 31 (1996), 26–61.

opinion, while displaying some temporary sympathy for Irish suffering in 1847, tended to treat the Famine as fundamentally an Irish affair, with specifically Irish causes and characteristics rooted in that island's social backwardness, and, for some, its Catholicism. British reluctance or inability to mobilise the full resources of the industrialising UK economy to relieve famine in Ireland, and the decision in the latter years of the crisis to place virtually all relief costs on Irish resources, led one conservative Irish Protestant observer to conclude that under such circumstances 'the Union [was] a nullity'.[3]

The intensity of polarisation over who or what was responsible for the disaster in Ireland gives rise to a further question – to what extent was the Famine the consequence not just of policy failure and lack of public empathy at the time, but of deeper structural relationships between the islands, long predating the Union of 1800? While nationalists frequently located the Famine within an extended narrative of English / British oppression stretching back to the Anglo-Norman invasion, modern historians have generally been reluctant to do so. However, the historical geographers William Smyth and David Nally, writing in the *Atlas of the Great Irish Famine*, have sought to restore the colonial relationship to the heart of an understanding of the Famine. For these authors, the outcomes were largely determined by the structures of colonial subordination and economic exploitation established over centuries. In Smyth's view, the full political subjection of Ireland to British rule from the sixteenth century was paralleled by the creation of an exploitative extractive economy serving the needs of the colonial elites and the metropolitan centre. This remained as much in place in the 1840s as it had prior to 1800. Nally regards the state's 'biopolitical' response to the Famine as driven by imperial prejudice and the imperative of maintaining British economic interests in Ireland.[4] While some economic historians reject the imposition of any such colonial model on the Irish past,[5] the significance of structural inequalities grounded in the long-standing colonial British–Irish relationship is difficult to dismiss. However, reliance on potentially reductionist and determinist colonial interpretations poses certain problems, not least in diminishing the role

---

3 I. Butt, *The rate in aid: a letter to the rt. hon. the Earl of Roden* (Dublin: J. McGlashan, 1849), p. 27.

4 W. J. Smyth, 'The longue durée – Imperial Britain and colonial Ireland', and D. Nally, 'The colonial dimensions of the Great Irish Famine' in J. Crowley et al. (eds.), *Atlas of the Great Irish Famine, 1845–52* (Cork: Cork University Press, 2012), pp. 46–74.

5 See for example L. Kennedy, *Unhappy the land: the most oppressed people ever, the Irish?* (Sallins: Merrion Press, 2015), pp. 81–126.

that contingency and agency played in both the causation of and the response to the Great Famine.

A Society Vulnerable to Disaster

The ecological trigger for the Famine, the fungus *Phytophthora infestans*, unquestionably fell on an acutely vulnerable society in 1845. The social pressures associated with rapid demographic expansion were exacerbated in the decades after 1815 by the sharp contraction of cottage employment in proto-industrial textile districts and changes in the agricultural economy that saw the living conditions of the lowest social classes – the cottier labourers and rundale peasant farmers – decline yet further. Dependency on potato subsistence increased for the poorer half of the island's population even as commercial grain production for the export trade to Britain continued to expand. While the rate of population growth eased from the 1820s, and rising emigration, especially from south Ulster and north Leinster, offered some relief, Ireland was marked by acute levels of rural impoverishment. The population plateau of the early 1840s, with an average density of around 700 people per square mile placing it second in Europe only to Belgium, rendered the Irish, and especially the economically marginal poor of the western regions, highly vulnerable to any shock to the staple crop of its poorer classes.[6]

Did this – as some commentators later claimed – render famine inevitable? The theory that population growth would always outrun any increase in food production, unless checked by natural disaster, human vice or some form of moral restraint, was developed by the political economist T.R. Malthus from 1798. Malthus' pessimistic theory was not universally accepted by contemporaries, but many British and elite Irish observers would come to see the famine crisis as being brought by the poor upon themselves through improvident patterns of high nuptuality, large families and the rampant subdivision of land. In the words of the conservative *Dublin University Magazine* in 1845, Ireland could not be improved until the people understood the 'Law of God that men cannot multiply like brutes without foregoing [*sic*] the benefits and blessings of social progress'.[7]

6 C. Ó Gráda, 'Poverty, population and agriculture, 1801–45' in W.E. Vaughan (ed.), *A new history of Ireland*, vol. v: *Ireland under the Union, I, 1801–70* (Oxford: Oxford University Press, 1989), pp. 118–22.
7 [S. O'Sullivan], 'Land Commission in Ireland', *Dublin University Magazine*, 25 (May 1845), p. 623.

Thus, although in the early 1840s the country was still able both to feed itself and to generate an export surplus, this was at the cost of unsustainable overdependence on a single staple crop – the potato. Regional potato failures provoked partial famines in western counties in 1800, 1817, 1822 and 1831, and even in 'good' years the limited preservation qualities of the potato produced annual 'hungry months' each summer, during which many thousands, mainly women and children, were driven on to the roads to beg alms from their slightly less worse off neighbours. Yet even during these single-season crises, the availability of certain modes of risk-limitation in the peasant economy (especially the sale of the ubiquitous potato-fattened pig or poultry) and a relatively effective short-term state relief response meant that, while there was some excess mortality connected to typhus fever outbreaks in these years, there was little mass starvation. In the view of modern economic historians such as Cormac Ó Gráda, Joel Mokyr and Peter Solar, social vulnerability did not render famine on the scale of the later 1840s inevitable, not least as it existed alongside more positive economic indicators and a rising tide of emigration. Rather it took an 'exogenous shock' of an extreme and unforeseen character to turn vulnerability into catastrophe.[8] Indeed Ó Gráda concludes that Ireland was more the victim of 'bad luck' in the arrival of potato blight in 1845 and the following seasons than of any pre-ordained Malthusian outcome.[9]

Not all in Ireland were poor; the wealth of its landed, commercial and political elites was evident in architecture and conspicuous consumption that continued after 1815. There was a growing middle class in the more commercially dynamic areas of the east and north, and there is also evidence before 1845 that many 'strong' and 'middling' farming families consumed more luxury goods. Thus despite the country's evident agricultural difficulties after 1815 it is clear that some in Ireland were still making profits out of export-oriented agriculture and textile production.[10]

Yet there is also clear evidence that the living conditions of the labouring and smallholding peasant majority were deteriorating to crisis levels in some places, rendering Ireland an increasingly divided society. Average per capita

8 P. Solar, 'The Great Famine was no ordinary subsistence crisis' in E.M. Crawford (ed.), *Famine: the Irish experience 900–1900* (Edinburgh: John Donald, 1989), pp. 112–29; C. Ó Gráda, *Ireland: a new economic history, 1780–1939* (Oxford: Oxford University Press, 1994), pp. 162–8; J. Mokyr, *Why Ireland starved* (London: Unwin, 1983), pp. 6–10, 15.

9 C. Ó Gráda, *The Great Irish Famine* (Cambridge: Cambridge University Press, 1995), p. 1.

10 J. Mokyr and C. Ó Gráda, 'Poor and getting poorer? Living standards in Ireland before the Famine', *Economic History Review*, 2nd ser., 61 (1988), 209–35.

income was around 40 per cent of that of Britain (which was the highest in Europe) in the early 1840s, but this percentage masked great internal discrepancies.[11] Data for landholding from the Poor Law records in the early 1840s, which included the labourers' micro-plots for 'conacre' (manured potato plots let to labourers) and cottiers' gardens, gave a total of 916,000 landholdings – 15 per cent of which were under one acre, many in Leinster where conacre was more common than in the west.

This increasing social polarisation had evident consequences in terms of class and sectarian antagonisms, and it fuelled the agrarian unrest that came to dominate external perceptions of the country. Violent confrontations between landlords and peasants (small tenants and labourers) over much of the country on economic, religious and political grounds were in many places stimulated by fears that landowners now sought to clear estates of tillage labourers to make way for the restoration of pasture.[12] Violence and the fear of it sharpened economic conflict and arguably scared off investment, leading to some capital flight from Ireland. British government in Ireland and the nationalist challenge to it were soon preoccupied with the dangers posed by agrarian violence and the need to find an answer to it, whether coercive or conciliatory.

The Capabilities of the State

Any assessment of the reaction of the state to the Great Famine needs to start with the basic question: what could government have done? To answer this we need to consider the capacity and ability of the state by the mid-nineteenth century. A contrast might be drawn with the last great Irish famine, in 1740–1. At that time, the state did little more than maintain its military capacity and secure internal 'law and order'; local elites or corporate bodies took some limited responsibility for welfare or infrastructural improvements (although evident in Dublin and its environs and parts of the north, this was minimal elsewhere). In practice the population was abandoned to its fate.[13]

After the Union, the state's capacity to act increased significantly, and this was evident by the time of the regional famine crisis of 1816–17. What made

---

11 Mokyr, *Why Ireland starved*, p. 11.
12 M. Beames, 'Rural conflict in pre-Famine Ireland: peasant assassinations in Tipperary 1837–47', *Past and Present*, 81 (1978), pp. 75–91; Mokyr, *Why Ireland starved*, p. 145.
13 D. Dickson, 'The 1740–41 famine' in J. Crowley et al. (eds.), *Atlas of the Great Irish Famine*, pp. 23–7; J. Kelly, 'Coping with crisis; the response to the famine of 1740–41', *Eighteenth-Century Ireland*, 27 (2012), pp. 99–122.

state intervention possible was the development of executive agencies which gave it both the eyes and the tools to act in different ways. The Commissariat was created during the Peninsula War in 1809 to support the feeding and supply of British armies overseas. Retained in peacetime, it became potentially the supply agency for any humanitarian intervention, as a body uniquely capable of organising the transfer, storage and distribution of large quantities of food on state account.

Several agencies began to provide the state with more accurate statistical information after 1800. From 1821 Ireland acquired an ever more elaborate decennial census, with that of 1841 offering a complex set of social statistics, albeit still liable to some potential undercount of the population. The country was mapped in detail by the Ordnance Survey from 1824; and from 1836 the reformed Irish Constabulary started to provide reports on economic conditions as well as crime to Dublin Castle, and to collect official agricultural statistics from 1847. From 1831 the state took direct responsibility both for the education of the Irish people through the National Education Board and for improving the country's infrastructure through the Irish Board of Works.[14]

State-funded medical relief to the poor was gradually extended from the 1790s through dispensaries, county infirmaries, fever hospitals and asylums, and by the 1830s these institutions reached most parts of Ireland, although they were still scattered and underfunded in the west. Perhaps most importantly, and after long debate, in 1838 Ireland was finally given a poor law, making the state responsible for providing a baseline of welfare relief (albeit minimal) to all those deemed destitute, offered through 'indoor relief' in the new network of 130 union workhouses. Theoretically, after 1838, no one need starve in Ireland, though in practice that would depend on sufficient resources being available and flexibility being manifested to make the system work when circumstances were difficult.[15]

As the state grew in early nineteenth-century Ireland, its agencies were increasingly subject to control from London. The Irish exchequer was abolished in 1816 and new agencies reported not only to the Irish executive at Dublin Castle, but also to the Treasury at Whitehall as the source of their funding. The Poor Law was a partial exception, being funded by local rates on

14 R.B. McDowell, 'Administration and the public services 1800–70' in Vaughan (ed.), *A new history of Ireland*, vol. v, pp. 538–61; Crossman, Chapter 20 above, pp. 548–53.
15 E.M. Crawford, *Counting the people: a survey of the Irish censuses, 1813–1911* (Dublin: Four Courts Press, 2003); P. Gray, *The making of the Irish Poor Law, 1815–43* (Manchester: Manchester University Press, 2009); L.M. Geary, *Medicine and charity in Ireland, 1718–1851* (Dublin: UCD press, 2004).

landed property that fell on both tenant farmers and landowners, but the 1838 system was never intended to cope with a full-scale famine. Whether the state would make effective use of these agencies would depend to a significant degree on political decisions taken in the face of social catastrophe.

Two British governments were confronted with the responsibility of responding to Famine in Ireland. The first, a Conservative government headed by Sir Robert Peel, had been in power since 1841 and had adopted a confrontational attitude towards Daniel O'Connell's Repeal campaign before opting for a more conciliatory strategy aimed at suborning 'moderate' Irish Catholics in 1844–5. Peel's administration was credited retrospectively with adopting a relatively generous policy towards the victims of famine, although its reputation benefited from the fact that its tenure of office terminated in June 1846, shortly before the second and much more extensive potato failure plunged Ireland into a crisis of much greater intensity than that which had resulted from the partial failure in 1845.

The succeeding Whig administration, headed by Lord John Russell, attracted vituperative denunciation of its policies from contemporaries and – despite some apologetic efforts by revisionist historians to minimise its responsibility – remains the object of substantial historical criticism for its manifest failures.[16] Paradoxically, the Whigs had as recently as 1841 been popular in much of Ireland for their pro-Catholic reforms. In that year, over 160,000 people had signed a testimonial, supported by O'Connell and the Catholic clergy, to the outgoing Whig chief secretary Lord Morpeth, and even at the height of the Famine in May 1847 the public funeral in Dublin of the popular lord lieutenant Lord Bessborough (himself an Irish landowner) was respectfully observed.[17] What the Famine revealed was not any latent genocidal intent on the part of a party that had previously sought to conciliate through giving 'justice to Ireland', but rather the severe limitations of the reformist Whig position on Ireland when faced by an extreme socio-economic crisis. Countervailing ideological and political imperatives in the party and the British body politic – a providentialist theodicy and a moralist obsession with self-help, liberal political economy, and the ascendancy of British middle-class pressures for budgetary restraint and transferring the

---

16 See R. Haines, *Charles Trevelyan and the Great Irish Famine* (Dublin: Four Courts Press, 2004).

17 C. Ridgway (ed.), *The Morpeth Roll: Ireland identified in 1841* (Dublin: Four Courts Press, 2013); P. Gray, 'A "People's Viceroyalty"? Popularity, theatre and executive politics 1835–47' in P. Gray and O. Purdue (eds.), *The Irish Lord Lieutenancy c.1541–1922* (Dublin: UCD Press, 2012), p. 171.

fiscal and moral responsibility for the Famine back to the Irish countryside – were to prove too strong for Russell's good intentions.

Peel's Response, 1845–1846

In the wake of the first appearance of potato blight in September 1845, Peel's cabinet mustered sufficient Irish experience to know that an extensive potato failure must lead to significant distress and potentially mass mortality. The prime minister was also all too aware, however, of the acute political sensitivities associated with food policy. An Irish subsistence crisis would inevitably draw hostile British attention to the protectionist restrictions on the import of foodstuffs under the 1815 Corn Law and provoke demands for reciprocity from British taxpayers for relief expenditure in Ireland. The British Anti-Corn Law League had attracted middle-class support since the later 1830s and its leader Richard Cobden was quick to claim that 'Providence had stepped in, and by famine ... set at naught all the contrivances and delays and moderations of statesmen.'[18]

Peel was also under pressure to be seen to be acting promptly in the face of noisy calls for action from the Irish press and the Dublin Mansion House Committee, behind which Daniel O'Connell had thrown his still substantial political weight.[19] Mixed in with these calculations was a genuine perception, shared by Peel and his evangelical home secretary Sir James Graham, that the blight was a manifestation of divine providence, a 'visitation' issued by God for the beneficent purpose of exposing 'unnatural' and hence unsustainable elements in the economic and social constitutions of both Britain and Ireland. These were taken to embrace both the Corn Laws as an unwarranted interference with free trade, and the cottier-based social economy of Ireland.[20]

This combination of political and ideological considerations helps explain the Peel government's response to the crisis in 1845–6 – a reaction that arguably helped stave off significant starvation in the first year of the Famine, at the expense of splitting the ruling Conservative Party and curtailing Peel's political career. As soon as he was persuaded of the extent of the blight, the prime minister committed himself to tying relief to the repeal of the Corn Laws,

---

18 *The Times*, 17 Dec. 1845.
19 O. MacDonagh, *The Emancipist: Daniel O'Connell, 1830–47* (London: Weidenfeld and Nicolson, 1989), p. 276.
20 P. Gray, *Famine, land and politics: British government and Irish society, 1843–50* (Dublin: Irish Academic Press, 1999), pp. 97–8; B. Hilton, 'Peel: a reappraisal', *Historical Journal*, 22 (1979), pp. 585–614.

and hence drew on himself the ire of the landed interest, including many of his own backbenchers. While facilitating the temporary import of maize and rice as cheap substitutes for the potato might have been accomplished without repeal, Peel combined an element of free-trade opportunism with a serious concern for what he hoped would be a long-term replacement of peasant potato subsistence with the consumption of imported grain (purchased in the marketplace by proletarianised wage-labourers), and a belief that the providential warning of the blight could not safely be ignored by the UK.[21] At the same time free-trade doctrine led him to ignore appeals from O'Connell and others for a ban on distillation and a temporary suspension of grain exports from Ireland, a policy his successors would also adhere to assiduously.

Peel's relief policy featured a Relief Commission chaired by Sir Randolph Routh, the head of the Commissariat, which would coordinate the establishment and operation of voluntary local relief committees and grant-aid their charitable subscriptions. Legislation was passed to finance public relief works, principally on roads and drainage schemes, which would be implemented by the Irish Board of Works in collaboration with local landowners acting through the county grand juries, and employ those persons deemed by the relief committees to be deserving of relief. These were features of a well-established response to Irish food crises, used in 1816–17 and 1822 and during the 1830s, now deployed on a larger scale in keeping with the national rather than regional nature of the 1845 crop failure. Although anxious to ensure that Irish landowners were made to bear their responsibilities, and that relief complied with Treasury rules, the home secretary concluded that 'in the last extremity of want, especially when it arises from a dispensation of Providence, these rules must frequently be relaxed'.[22]

The government's other major relief measure was more innovative, but intended as a strictly temporary expedient to pump-prime the as yet underdeveloped grain import trade. In November 1845 the government secretly purchased £100,000 worth of maize (Indian corn) on the New York market for transshipment to Ireland, where it was parcelled out to depots managed by the Commissariat and the Coast Guard. This and later purchases totalled some 20,000 tons of grain, which was a quantity sufficient (had it been so used) to feed some 490,000 persons for three months, a daily dole of one pound per head. But the purpose was not to feed the Irish poor directly, but

21 Gray, *Famine, land and politics*, pp. 110–17.
22 Sir James Graham to Lord Heytesbury, 26 Nov. 1845, Graham Papers, Bundle 95B, British Library.

to regulate the market price of grain and to accustom the peasantry to this new and cheap staple (the Commissariat distributed numerous handbills to educate the people on the preparation of what was labelled 'Peel's brimstone' by his critics). Unfamiliarity initially led to problems of preparation and consequent illness, but over time imported maize (whenever it was available) became the main substitute food of the poor in the Famine years.[23]

As growing distress in spring 1846 led to food and employment riots, the relief works and depots set up by the government were opened, with some degree of success. Peel's measures are generally regarded as having been effective in curbing famine mortality in the first season of the crisis.[24] However, the policy was transitional and suffered from a number of flaws. Having intervened once in the international food trade, the government was reluctant to do so again, and regarded the significant private import of maize to Ireland in summer 1846 as a vindication of its unwillingness to interfere further in the market.[25] In line with paternalist social thought, Peel's relief policy relied heavily on encouraging voluntary contributions from the local landed elite, and offered relatively generous grants and loan terms to reward this.

However, both Dublin administrators and the assistant secretary (the chief civil servant) at the Treasury in London, Charles Trevelyan, grew increasingly critical of what they regarded as the reluctance of landowners to take what was regarded as their fair share of the relief burden, and their apparent readiness to exploit the relief works to improve their estates at public expense, and abuse the relief tickets issued by relief committees to favour their own dependants and tenants rather than the most needy. As the British press picked up these criticisms, a perception that Peel's system had been too generous took hold, and that, in the words of *The Times*, 'whatever we give to the peasant passes through that hungry sieve right into the pockets of the landlord. Benevolence is wasted on those who neither need nor deserve it.'[26] At the same time, Peel's insistence on pressing a robust coercion bill on Ireland to deal with an upsurge in agrarian unrest provoked opposition from Catholic and nationalist voices in Ireland, and provided the opportunity for his parliamentary opponents to combine to bring down his administration in June 1846 (see Illustration 53).

---

23 J.S. Donnelly, *The Great Irish Potato Famine* (Stroud: Sutton, 2001), pp. 49–53.
24 Donnelly, *Great Irish Potato Famine*, p. 56.
25 Gray, *Famine, land and politics*, pp. 125, 228.
26 *The Times*, 19 March 1846.

53. Charles Edward Trevelyan (1807–86), assistant secretary to the Treasury, 1840–59. Though he is properly blamed for the insensitive and incomplete delivery of famine relief, the tone was primarily set by the chancellor of the exchequer, Charles Wood. Stipple and line engraving by Daniel John Pound, after a photograph by John Watkins, *c*.1860–77.

The Failure of Russell's Government, 1846–1850

Many commentators expected the blight to disappear after one year, and the Irish cottiers (lacking any alternative crop to sow) planted the seed potatoes they had preserved to an extent little diminished from the previous year. The sudden and almost universal return of the blight at the end of July 1846, wiping out upwards of 90 per cent of the crop, was thus a crushing blow. With little left to pawn or sell, and farmers unwilling or unable to pay cash wages for labour, reports of famine-related mortality started to multiply as the autumn progressed. The task of responding to the renewed Irish catastrophe fell to Lord John Russell's incoming Whig administration, a weak minority government dependent on the continuing division of its parliamentary opponents for survival. Daniel O'Connell's initial confidence in the goodwill of this Whig government was soon to appear woefully misplaced, but he at least correctly discerned the true scale of the 1846 ecological disaster (he predicted 2 million might perish if the country was not adequately assisted), and unlike his radical nationalist critics he recognised that only the British parliament could command the food and logistical resources sufficient to diminish its fatal impact. O'Connell aimed to revive the lobbying tactics that had elicited significant concessions from governments in the 1830s, but his health collapsed from late 1846, his party machine fell apart following his death in May 1847, and appeals for sympathetic treatment of Ireland made limited inroads when confronted by political and ideological imperatives generated from within the British body politic as the Famine progressed.[27]

The Russell government quickly came under pressure to terminate the perceived 'abuses' of Peel's policy. Corn merchants lobbied successfully to ensure that there would be no repeat of the state's purchase of grain on the international markets. Depots with remaining stocks were retained in the west, but sales would henceforward be at market price. Peel's Relief Commission was stood down, paving the way for stricter and more direct Treasury control of the relief administration. At the same time, Russell announced on 17 August 1846 that his government would use 'the whole credit of the Treasury and means of the country ... as it is our bounden duty to use them ... to avert famine and to maintain the people of Ireland'.[28] The tension between these imperatives – economy and national responsibility – would soon become evident.

27 MacDonagh, *Emancipist*, pp. 297–318.
28 *Hansard's Parliamentary Debates*, 3rd series, 88, cols. 772–8 (17 Aug. 1846).

Despite doubts expressed by lord lieutenant Bessborough, the administration adhered rigorously to its faith in the power of the laws of supply and demand in the food trade to (it claimed) optimise the supply for Ireland. However, after the summer of 1846 private maize imports to Ireland dried up, and what was available on the international markets was drawn to countries where private and state demand was most robust. Although substantially more of the grain harvest – especially the cheaper variety of oats – was retained in Ireland than in previous years, food prices climbed steeply, peaking in February–March 1847 at more than double the normal average, which was well beyond the reach of the destitute poor.[29] Nationalists asserted that famine could be averted if all Ireland's non-potato food output was kept in the country, and damned the administration for refusing to embargo exports. Their claims that the Famine was wholly artificial were driven more by political rhetoric than evidence in the context of a sharp food availability decline produced by potato blight – but they did give vent to genuine moral outrage at the continuing export of foodstuffs from a starvation-racked country. The export of Irish-produced food undoubtedly worsened the 'hunger winter' of 1846–7, but it exacerbated rather than caused the real food shortage due to the loss of the bulk of the subsistence potato crop. Moreover, retaining higher-cost grains such as wheat and expensive livestock products in Ireland would have done little for the rural labouring poor without some effective distribution mechanism (and indeed there is evidence that some of the grain that was retained was fed to cattle previously given potatoes as winter fodder).[30] At the same time, the coastal fishing trade collapsed as poor fishermen – deprived of local market demand for their luxury catch – pawned their nets and boats to raise money to buy the cheapest available foodstuff – maize.

Russell's government initially adhered to the commitment to provide relief by public works, but revamped it under the August 1846 Labour Rate Act. Designed to take a harder line against perceived opportunism by local elites, this measure centralised administration under the Board of Works (itself answerable directly to the Treasury) and made the total cost ultimately repayable from taxation levied on the localities. Despite attempts by officials at Dublin Castle to soften its impact, the underlying purpose of the new system was to introduce a more penal element to the public works, aimed at landowners and labourers alike. Charles Wood, the Chancellor of the Exchequer, declared that 'the time has come when the Irish proprietor must learn to

---

29 M. Daly, *The Famine in Ireland* (Dundalk: Dublin Historical Society, 1986), pp. 80–1.
30 Donnelly, *Great Irish Potato Famine*, pp. 57–64.

depend on himself', and that the new relief mechanism must enforce this responsibility.[31]

The Treasury sought to veto all useful or 'reproductive' works of the sort permissible under Peel's policy in 1845–6 (hoping thereby to oblige landowners to borrow privately to improve their estates and avoid the ultimate costs of useless state relief works). It also moved to impose a scale of 'piece work' payments on the labourers – a measure intended to stimulate work-discipline and reward individual effort but which in practice pushed those least able to exert themselves, such as the malnourished, ill and elderly, below the threshold of subsistence to the lowest point on the payscale. The situation was worsened by the decision to pay only half this minimum rate when bad weather interrupted the works, and by the shortage of both low-denomination coins for wages and sufficient numbers of honest and capable staff willing to oversee this bloated bureaucracy in the localities.[32]

Notwithstanding its gross limitations as a relief mechanism in the harsh and hungry winter of 1846–7, desperation led thousands of the poor to throw themselves on the public works. The official head-count soared from 114,000 in late October 1846 to a scarcely credible peak of 714,390 by March 1847, with each labourer typically seeking to support a family of four or five on their meagre earnings. As numbers escalated, the Board of Works bureaucracy struggled to keep up. Works were disrupted by strikes or riots against petty tyrannies, delays in wage payments and the imposition of piece rates, while rising food prices outran the wage scale which had been deliberately pegged at a low level to encourage labourers to seek a return to private agricultural employment. The consequence was, as one inspector wrote from County Leitrim, that 'the miserable condition of the half-famished people is greatly increased by the exorbitant … price of meal and provisions, insomuch that the wages gained by them on the works are quite inadequate to purchase a sufficiency to feed many large families'.[33]

Despite the high costs of the relief works system (which would account for some £5 million in 1846–7) the unintended outcome was to augment rather than contain excess mortality. Heavy outdoor labour, especially in the cold and snowy winter conditions of 1846–7, placed extreme stresses on the bodies of the malnourished, who began to die in large numbers on the works in early 1847. Social upheaval and distress created the ideal condition for

31 Charles Wood to Henry Labouchere, 22 Sept. 1846, Hickleton Papers, A4/185/1, Borthwick Institute, York.
32 Gray, *Famine, land and politics*, pp. 240–50.
33 Quoted in Donnelly, *Great Irish Potato Famine*, p. 77.

contagious fevers such as typhus and relapsing fever, which now also reached epidemic proportions, and spread by congregating the malnourished at pestilential work sites.[34]

By early 1847 Irish and British press reports were replete with eyewitness accounts of mass mortality in western Ireland and increasingly also with calls for charitable assistance. The sympathetic impulse of early 1847 combined with several factors to spur a radical turn in relief policy. Russell's government, ostensibly 'friendly' towards Ireland, was shamed by public exposures and lobbied by its own officials in Dublin into abandoning the failed public works system. In addition, the costs of the system were becoming prohibitive and its consequences evidently demoralising as well as largely ineffective. After debating various options, the government decided to follow the example of the Quakers and offer direct food aid to those most in need, through a network of state-sponsored soup kitchens. The prime minister observed that 'the pressing matter at present is to keep the people alive'.[35] But other ministers noted different attractions to such a system: a cooked food test of destitution would prevent importunity (ever an obsession for many in the administration, despite the evident collapse of much of Irish rural society); while transferring the ultimate repayment costs of the new scheme onto the local poor law rates would, it was hoped, act as a more direct stimulus to proprietors to offer employment and pave the way for a permanent extension of the poor law system.[36] A temporary relief act was rapidly passed by parliament in February, but establishing a new relief bureaucracy under the directorship of Sir John Burgoyne took an inordinate length of time. Staged lay-offs from the public works took place from March, but few of the soup kitchens provided under the new act were operational before late May or June, throwing tens of thousands into the overcrowded workhouses, or onto the roads, with nothing but the erratic ministrations of private charities and mutual or landlord assistance to support them.

Only when the soup kitchens came fully into operation, distributing free daily rations of a cheap 'stirabout' porridge of maize, rice and oats in upwards of 2,000 poor law districts, did the appalling mortality rates of early 1847 begin to abate. Although far from flawless in operation, and offering a bare minimum of nutrition, the soup kitchen regime issued as many as 3 million

---

34 L. Geary, 'Famine, fever and the bloody flux' in C. Póirtéir (ed.), *The Great Irish Famine* (Cork: Mercier Press, 1995), pp. 86–103.

35 Lord John Russell to Lord Bessborough, 5 Jan. 1847, Russell Papers, 30/22/6A, ff. 48–9, The National Archives.

36 Gray, *Famine, land and politics*, pp. 262–7.

daily rations by July and fed over 90 per cent of the population in some western unions, thus demonstrating the logistical capacity of the Victorian state to curb, if not to avert, the horrors of famine.[37] The initiative also was significantly cheaper than the public works to run, and this was aided by a rapid fall in the market price of grain within Ireland in late spring and summer 1847. As if in belated vindication of Trevelyan's faith in the free market, massive shipments of maize, principally from the USA but also from southern Europe and the Levant, began to arrive in Irish ports, bringing down the price of that commodity by August to half what it had been in February. Maize and rice imports would continue at a high level for the rest of the Famine period, significantly outweighing in terms of volume the export of the more expensive grains of wheat and oats from Ireland in the years 1847–50.[38] This sudden influx of cheap maize had several unexpected effects, undermining (in some cases bankrupting) many of the Irish merchants who had profited from speculating in the inflated prices of winter 1846–7, but also reducing the winter livestock feeding costs of 'strong' farmers who were in a position to shift (with their landlord's encouragement) into the cattle economy in these years. The availability of cheaper food in the markets from mid-1847 did not end the Famine, however, as it was less aggregate food availability that mattered so much as who had an 'entitlement' to it through the ability to produce or purchase it in accessible marketplaces.[39]

All too quickly, the relatively successful soup kitchen relief scheme was abandoned from late August 1847 and replaced as the principal mode of relief by the Poor Law. Despite strong opposition from Irish landowners and their British Conservative allies, there was a growing conviction in British public opinion that 'Irish property must pay for Irish poverty' and that the UK taxpayer had already contributed too much for Ireland.[40] In June 1847 the Irish Poor Law Extension Act was passed, permitting (for the first time) outdoor relief for certain classes of paupers, and for the 'able-bodied' destitute where the workhouses were full, and requiring the elected Boards of Guardians to

---

37 Donnelly, *Great Irish Potato Famine*, pp. 81–92.

38 A. Bourke, *'The visitation of God'? The potato and the Great Irish Famine* (Dublin: Lilliput Press, 1993), pp. 159–69.

39 C. Ó Gráda, *Ireland before and after the Famine: explorations in economic history, 1800–1925*, 2nd edn (Manchester: Manchester University Press, 1993), pp. 106–10; idem., *Black '47 and beyond: the Great Irish Famine in history, economy and memory* (Princeton: Princeton University Press, 1999), pp. 122–5.

40 J.S. Donnelly, ' "Irish property must pay for Irish poverty": British public opinion and the Great Irish Famine' in C. Morash and R. Hayes (eds.), *Fearful realities: new perspectives on the Famine* (Blackrock: Irish Academic Press, 1996), pp. 60–76.

relieve all those classed as destitute and who applied for aid to them. As a concession to landowners, however, the act also contained an amendment permitting relief only to those holding less than a quarter-acre of land (essentially a 'garden' sized plot inadequate to feed a family without wages) – a provision used by many proprietors to facilitate the permanent clearance of smallholding peasants from their estates.[41]

In essence the extended Poor Law, while welcomed by many Irish Catholic clergymen as a well-merited punishment for the landed class who had created the social conditions triggering famine, transferred the full costs of relief from the Treasury to the Irish localities. Several developments made this expedient for the state. Growing economic difficulties in Britain climaxing in a major banking crash in October 1847 made raising government loans in the money markets much more difficult and stimulated middle-class demands for lower taxation. The UK general election of summer 1847 returned a turbulent group of around eighty laissez-faire radical MPs, led by Richard Cobden, who held the parliamentary balance of power and demanded fiscal retrenchment. Russell observed with concern that 'we have in the opinion of Great Britain done too much for Ireland and have lost elections for doing so'.[42] In addition, the potato did not fail in 1847 (although as few were planted, the crop was meagre). The apparent absence of a renewed 'visitation', along with lower food prices in the markets and a good grain harvest across the UK, provided the illusion that the Famine emergency was now over. Charles Trevelyan assured readers of the apologia he produced on behalf of the government in early 1848 that the food crisis had finished and 'the appointed time of Ireland's regeneration is at last come'.[43] This was echoed by T.C. Foster in *The Times*, who urged that the Irish must now be forced to help themselves: 'let them work as we do, and their poverty will become wealth, and their distress will be changed into abundance'.[44]

On top of this, sympathy for Ireland was reduced by the perception that agrarian unrest (which surged in late 1847 in response to a wave of evictions, before being curbed by new coercive legislation), and the highly publicised

41 A case has been made that this 'Gregory clause' has been exaggerated in its effects, although Irish officials were highly critical of its impact: see B.M. Walker, 'Villain, victim or prophet: William Gregory and the Great Famine', *Irish Historical Studies*, 38 (2012–13), 579–99; Gray, *Famine, land and politics*, pp. 277–9, 295–7.
42 Russell to Clarendon, 2 Aug. 1847, Clarendon Deposit Irish, box 43, Bodleian Library, Oxford.
43 C.E. Trevelyan, *The Irish crisis* (London: Longman, Brown, Green and Longmans, 1848), p. 199.
44 *The Times*, 13 Oct. 1847.

activities of the Young Ireland radicals were manifestations of Irish 'ingratitude' for previous British assistance. The Young Irelanders had broken with O'Connell over his attempt to impose a pledge of non-violence on the Repeal movement in July 1846. Even after O'Connell's death in May 1847, the seceders, now branding themselves the 'Irish Confederation', made little headway in the countryside in the face of clerical hostility and peasant preoccupation with survival. However, the Confederation did have significant urban support and its newspapers, *The Nation*, and later John Mitchel's more radical breakaway *United Irishman*, raised its public profile.

The Young Irelanders agreed that Britain bore full responsibility for the suffering of the Famine, but disagreed over how to respond to it. Reunited temporarily by the example of the French Revolution of February 1848, the movement sought to emulate this in Ireland, and the state responded with arrests and the new Treason Felony Act. The disorganised and chaotic rebellion that followed in July 1848 had little chance of success, but was pursued by its leader, William Smith O'Brien, as an act of defiant protest. The government was careful not to make martyrs of the movement's captured leaders, transporting them to Van Diemen's Land rather than executing them, but British opinion tended to regard the rising as evidence of the inveterate rebelliousness and undeserving nature of the Irish people as a whole.[45] The diarist Charles Greville concluded in the aftermath of the rising that in England 'the sources of charity and benevolence are dried up; the current which flowed last year has been effectually choked by the brutality and ingratitude of the people, and the rancorous fury and hatred with which they have met our exertions to serve them'.[46]

The latter years of the Famine, from 1848 through to 1850, and extending in some western districts into 1851 and 1852, were marked by a further withdrawal of state intervention and expenditure, as the burden of relief was thrown almost exclusively on to the grossly underfunded Poor Law. After a brief visit to Ireland in October 1847, Trevelyan agreed to designate twenty-two western poor law unions as 'distressed', but the only additional aid given these was from the remnants of that spring's charitable collections, not from the Treasury. Outdoor relief was permitted from the winter of 1847–8 (with

---

45 S.J. Connolly, 'The Great Famine and Irish politics' in C. Póirtéir (ed.), *The Great Irish Famine* (Cork: The Mercier Press, 1997), pp. 34–49; also C. Kinealy, *Repeal and revolution: 1848 in Ireland* (Manchester: Manchester University Press, 2009).

46 C.C.F. Greville, *The Greville memoirs (second part): a journal of the reign of Queen Victoria from 1837 to 1852*, 3 vols. (London: Longmans, Green and Co., 1885), vol. III, pp. 207–8 [21 July 1848].

the 'able-bodied' required to break stones in workhouse yards in return for food), and workhouse provision greatly expanded with the acquisition of auxiliary buildings and fever sheds, rising to around 250,000 nominal places by autumn 1849. But with numerous localities unable to bear the costs of escalating destitution, and with fever again rampant, many of these build-ings became, in the words of one newspaper, mere 'slaughter asylums'.[47] Another major potato failure in autumn 1848 presaged what the lord lieuten-ant described as a further 'winter of horrors', especially in the west. Several proposed remedial schemes of public works in land reclamation or railway construction or through assisted emigration to the colonies were discussed but were stymied by opposition within the cabinet and parliament, falling victim to a combination of strict economy and laissez-faire doctrine.[48]

In the latter stages of the Famine crisis, public rhetoric was dominated by the trope of 'natural causes' – the unavoidable suffering that Ireland must now face in the process of reconstruction – and for which Britain was no longer morally responsible. Alarmed at the continuing crisis in Ireland, Russell despairingly pointed out that it was less the 'crude Trevelyanism' of his colleagues in government than feelings lying 'deep in the breasts of the British people' that now made any further substantive intervention politically impracticable. The continuation of localised distress appeared to British mor-alists to be self-inflicted, and at the same time necessary for the 'working of a gigantic remedy' that would lead to a (top-down) 'social revolution' in the Irish countryside.[49] In 1849 Trevelyan continued to reject further central state intervention in the western counties using a medical metaphor: 'what the patient now requires is rest and quiet and time for the remedies which have been given to operate. Continual dosing and dependence upon physicians is not good either for the body politic or corporate.'[50]

The one exception to the rule of non-intervention (except to ensure the rigorous application of the Poor Law through the inspection and surveil-lance regime) was the Rate in Aid scheme, itself revealing of the reduction of Ireland to peripheral status in British thinking. In the spring of 1849, in the teeth of strong hostility in parliament, the government proposed a (rela-tively modest) additional relief loan of £50,000 for the distressed and bank-rupt western unions. The political price was that repayment would fall not on national taxation, but on the recovering Irish unions of the north and east

---

47 *Freeman's Journal*, 2 Feb. 1848.
48 Gray, *Famine, land and politics*, pp. 298–311.
49 Ibid., pp. 304–27.
50 Trevelyan to Wood, 20 Oct. 1849, Hickleton papers, A4/59/2 Borthwick Institute, York.

through a rate in aid – an additional levy on the local property rates in Ireland only. The political significance of this taxation was not lost on Irish observers. Many in the north used similar language to British observers to denounce the moral and social degeneracy of the Catholic and Celtic west. However, for Isaac Butt, who penned a pamphlet denouncing the initiative, it was a further denial of the meaning of the British–Irish union through its explicit treatment of Ireland as 'a separate state'.[51]

The government's last major legislative initiative, the Encumbered Estates Act of 1849, was intended to create a 'free trade in land' by facilitating a summary process of sale of indebted estates. Whig ministers and anti-landlord radicals regarded this measure as a panacea, which would reinvigorate Irish agriculture by encouraging investment by British entrepreneurs. While significant quantities of land were indeed sold under the act, it did next to nothing to alleviate distress, but rather added a further motivation to many property owners to clear the estates of 'surplus' population to make way for more profitable cattle pastures and sheep runs. In sum, as a much later British prime minister observed, the government in London 'failed their people through standing by while a crop failure turned into a massive human tragedy'.[52] While not guilty of intentional genocide (for which there is no evidence in the archive), the reasons for this failure include adherence to misplaced ideological dogmas and political calculations that placed the interests of Great Britain and its taxpaying class before those of the destitute masses in Ireland.

The Limits of Private Charity

The Great Famine saw significant manifestations of private charity and philanthropic action from many individuals and groups in Ireland, Great Britain and overseas. Why did people give – of their time, effort or money – to assist Irish famine relief in the 1840s? There were a range of motivations, often overlapping, varying in importance between individuals and over time. For some, there was a sense of Christian (or ethical) duty to assist those in need. For others, the more secular ideal of landed or middle-class paternalism towards the poor operated to some degree. In the early stages of the Famine a number of Irish landowners or their agents sought to act paternalistically,

---

51 Butt, *The rate in aid*, p. 27.
52 'Blair admits British policy failure turned famine into massive human tragedy', *Irish Times*, 2 June 1997.

at least towards the impoverished on their own estates. This took the form of participation in local relief committees, offering rent rebates, opening estate soup kitchens and similar measures.[53] However, many other landowners, whether due to absenteeism, chronic indebtedness or indifference towards the poor, failed to respond, and as the Famine progressed, even many previously generous individuals retrenched or renounced charity. The Marquess of Sligo, for example, whose family were at the forefront of local charity around Westport, County Mayo in the early years of the crisis, became one of the most notorious 'clearers' of small tenants from his estates from 1848, taking the view that the burden of taxation and collapse of rents now meant he must resort to 'ejecting or being ejected'.[54]

Outside Ireland, the fashionability of charity, often related to a sense of social obligation, was important in stimulating elite philanthropic activity. Royal endorsement for Irish Famine charity from early 1847 led to imitative activity in fashionable British circles, with charity balls and bazaars in London and as far away as the British colonies in Florence and Bengal.[55] This sentiment played an important role in early 1847, but was shallow and short-lived. What is striking is the conditionality of much charitable giving for Ireland – charity was often seen as a form of exchange or contract between giver and recipient, and goodwill could turn into contemptuous antagonism if the imagined terms of this bargain were believed to have been broken by the recipients, or when more 'deserving' objects of sympathy presented themselves. The Famine was also regarded by many as a providential opportunity for bringing change (either spiritual or temporal) to that country. For some, charity was a way of promoting Irish gratitude and solidifying the Union, and of preparing the way for social and political transformations. Again, this motivation was liable to disappointment and alienation over time when confronted with Irish realities.[56]

The religious group with the strongest record for active and sustained charitable engagement in Ireland, despite their small size, was the Religious Society of Friends. The Quakers (as they were popularly known) combined commitments to pacifism, philanthropic social action and opposition to

---

53 The most recent survey of famine philanthropy is C. Kinealy, *Charity and the Great Hunger in Ireland* (London: Bloomsbury, 2013).

54 D.E. Jordan, *Land and popular politics in Ireland: County Mayo from the Plantation to the Land War* (Cambridge: Cambridge University Press, 1994), p. 111.

55 E.g. 'Famine in Ireland and distress in Scotland – Ladies' bazaar of useful and ornamental work', *Daily News*, 20 March 1847.

56 P. Gray, 'National humiliation and the great hunger: fast and famine in 1847', *Irish Historical Studies*, 21 (2000), 193–216.

proselytism, and were quick to respond to the social catastrophe in Ireland. Their work came to prominence with the highly publicised 'tours of inspection' led by leading English Quakers William Foster and James Hack Tuke in the winter of 1846–7; their reports, published as pamphlets and in newspapers, exposed to English audiences the sheer scale and horror of mass famine mortality on the western seaboard of Ireland.

As well as raising consciousness, they took practical action. Quakers used English and American funds to establish local soup kitchens giving free doles to the destitute in distressed western localities. On the back of this success they lobbied government for a much larger state soup kitchen scheme in early 1847. Quakers such as William Bennett also toured the west distributing free green-crop seed to destitute small farmers, and Tuke and Jonathan Pim were later prominent in exposing and denouncing landlord clearances. In all, some £200,000 was raised and spent by the Quakers in Ireland in 1846–9, although diminishing resources and despair at the withdrawal of government activity led them to terminate their efforts in June 1849.[57]

Quaker activists were not the only relief workers in 1840s Ireland. Irish clergy of all denominations frequently put themselves in the front line in organising local relief committees, distributing charity and running soup kitchens, as well as (especially for the Catholics) tending as well as they could to the spiritual needs of the dying. Along with local doctors, serving in the fever hospitals and workhouses, those clergy who stayed at their posts (not all did) suffered high mortality from contagious diseases.

They were joined by volunteer relief workers (with various degrees of institutional backing) from many places. Among the most remarkable of these was the American female evangelist Asenath Nicholson – a tireless traveller and dispenser of relief, and severe critic of what she saw as inappropriate conversionism. Her eyewitness account of the Famine has been published in several editions.[58] Count Paul Strzelecki, an émigré Polish nobleman, acted as agent for the British Relief Association in western Ireland, vigorously organising that charity's expenditure there (although also drawing criticism for turning a blind eye to the consequences of clearances).[59] Many less well known

57 H.E. Hatton, *The largest amount of good: Quaker relief in Ireland 1654–1921* (Kingston and Montreal: McGill-Queen's University Press, 1993).
58 A. Nicholson, *Annals of the Famine in Ireland*, [1850], ed. M. Murphy (Dublin: Lilliput Press, 1998); M.O. Murphy, *Compassionate stranger: Asenath Nicholson and the Great Irish Famine* (Syracuse, NY: Syracuse University Press, 2015).
59 W.S. Crawford, *Depopulation not necessary*, 2nd edn (London: Gilpin, 1850), pp. 36–40.

and less recorded charitable bodies, many of them female-led, raised money and appointed agents to spend it in Ireland.[60]

Charity in the Great Famine extended well beyond the highly committed actions of small groups and individuals such as Nicholson and the Quakers – indeed it became, for a time, a mass movement. The attention of the British public (especially the literate middle classes) was first drawn to what was happening in Ireland through the work of individuals and small groups in late 1846. These themes were taken up more generally by the British press in late 1846 and into early 1847, most graphically through the illustrated reports from Skibbereen by the Irish artist John Mahony carried in the *Illustrated London News* in February 1847.[61]

Although often parsimonious in its own famine relief, the state opted to support and encourage charitable giving for Ireland from late 1846. On 1 January the British Association for the Relief of Ireland and Scotland was established in London, with government endorsement, to raise money and coordinate the many local and municipal collections that had already sprung up. Ministers ostentatiously gave significant amounts, and Queen Victoria was prevailed on to give £2,000 (which it appears she was happier to do on hearing the distressed Highlands of Scotland would also be included – in the end this area received a disproportionate one sixth of all the funds raised).[62] The clergy of the state churches (the Church of England, Church of Ireland and Church of Scotland) were instructed to read a Queen's Letter from their pulpits on successive Sundays in January and February, with collections to be made at the church doors for the Irish relief fund. Finally, a National Day of Fast and Humiliation was proclaimed for 24 March 1847, involving the closing of offices and businesses, special church services, and further collections. In all, £435,000 was raised through these means (including some overseas donations) for use by the British Association. However, the price of state endorsement was that this body was open to political influence (Trevelyan had contacts on its board) and some groups, including the Quakers, the Catholics and some evangelical societies, opted to keep their relief collections separate. Given its quasi-state character, it is perhaps not surprising that a decision was made to use these funds to support the operation of the Irish Poor Law.[63]

---

60 Kinealy, *Charity and the Great Hunger*, pp. 143–66, 173–81.
61 *Illustrated London News*, 20 Feb. 1847.
62 Kinealy, *Charity and the Great Hunger*, pp. 167–93.
63 Gray, 'National humiliation', pp. 193–216.

Aid for Ireland came also in significant amounts from overseas. Some of this was in high-profile donations by other political leaders: the Sultan of Turkey (then seeking a political alliance with the UK) made a £1,000 donation to the British Association. Other overseas aid was much more demotic: local relief funds sprang up in many parts of the USA as news of Irish suffering reached there in early 1847, and were coordinated by the New England Relief Committee, which raised over $500,000. Despite lobbying, the US government opted not to intervene, but did supply two warships to convey the food-aid purchased in the USA to Ireland; although these did not arrive until food prices were already falling due to private import in summer 1847, they were still welcomed in Ireland.[64] The Catholic Church internationally also exerted itself under the leadership of Pope Pius IX (who was closely advised on Irish affairs by the head of the Irish College in Rome, Paul Cullen). Large sums were raised under a papal appeal and transferred to Ireland via Archbishop Murray of Dublin.[65]

The explosion of charitable activity for Ireland in the UK and abroad was not, however, sustained and it dwindled from the second half of 1847. What modern aid agencies term 'famine fatigue' – the growing boredom or frustration of a public when a food crisis stretches over a prolonged period – was undoubtedly a factor in the Irish case, and was reinforced by the (false) impression that the absence of potato blight and good grain harvest of summer 1847 meant the Famine was really over. This was supplemented by more negative attitudes towards the Irish developing for a number of reasons. One, common to both Britain and the USA and Canada, was the mass influx of impoverished and often disease-carrying Irish migrants into their cities from spring 1847. This refugee crisis did stimulate some to transfer their work to the Irish on their doorsteps, but it filled others with disgust and fear. From late spring 1847 Britain slid into economic recession in the wake of a banking crisis, leading to tightening purses, and refocusing charity on the local 'deserving' poor, and those suffering from cholera.[66] This was exacerbated by the inter-related perception that the Irish poor had been ungrateful for British aid, and that landlords must be obliged to meet the cost of the crisis

---

64 T.J. Sarbaugh, 'A moral spectacle: American relief and the Famine 1845–9', *Eire-Ireland*, 15 (1980), 6–14; for a more critical reading of US intervention, see D. Sim, *A Union forever: the Irish question in US foreign relations in the Victorian age* (Ithaca, NY: Cornell University Press, 2013), pp. 39–68.

65 D.A. Kerr, 'A nation of beggars'? Priests, people and politics in Famine Ireland 1846–1852 (Oxford: Clarendon Press, 1994), pp. 30–68.

66 F. Neal, *Black '47: Britain and the Famine Irish* (Basingstoke: Macmillan, 1998), pp. 239–81.

their mismanagement had created.[67] War in North America and revolutions in Europe from early 1848 also disrupted overseas charitable activity.

One other, highly controversial, variety of philanthropic activity was 'souperism'. This phenomenon arose from the widespread extension in the west of Ireland from the 1820s of evangelical Protestant colonies, led by highly driven individuals committed to the objects of the 'Second Reformation', a movement zealously focused on missionary activity among the 'papists' of Ireland. A number of missionary colonies existed along the west coast by 1845, in Connemara, north Mayo, Dingle and – most famously – the Achill Island settlement at Doogort, led by the Revd Edward Nangle.[68] It was during the Famine that these settlements attracted greatest controversy, through the charges made by Catholics that they were inducing conversions through offering food ('soup') to adults or children who entered the settlement.

The evidence for this is mixed. It is unquestionably true that the settlements were generously provided with funds from English supporters and were therefore able to command food resources in some remote districts once all other sources had failed in the later stages of the Famine. It is also true that Nangle and others were genuinely convinced that the Famine was a divine judgment on Irish Catholicism and a call to proselytising vigour. They regarded their activities, however, not as bribery, but as the use of resources to 'protect' their converts against Catholic victimisation and to run orphanages and free schools.

The impact of the 'souper' colonies can be exaggerated. There were never very many of them; many of their converts reverted as the Famine ended, or sought assisted emigration from their patrons. But 'souperism' attracted disproportionate attention due both to the propagandising efforts of the missionaries and to the angry reaction of Catholic clergy and communities to what they regarded as an invasion of their territory and exploitation of hunger for spiritual ends. Returning to Ireland from Rome in 1849 as the newly appointed archbishop of Armagh, Paul Cullen saw his mission as not only confronting such proselytism, but also stamping an orthodox ultramontane uniformity on the Catholic Church in Ireland. The consequence would be a new era of religious polarisation in Ireland, where the many incidents of

---

67 Gray, 'National humiliation', pp. 211–13.
68 I. Whelan, 'Edward Nangle and the Achill Mission, 1834–1852' in R. Gillespie and G. Moran (eds.), *'A various county': essays in Mayo history 1500–1900* (Westport: Foilseacháin Náisiúnta Teoranta, 1987), pp. 113–34.

inter-denominational charitable cooperation in the Famine years would be quickly forgotten.[69]

Impact and Consequences

The demographic impact of the Great Famine, and the causes of the mass mortality, were the subject of contestation between the state and Irish nationalists from its immediate aftermath.[70] While responsibility remains a highly contentious issue, and is likely to remain so,[71] an element of consensus on the scale of famine mortality, measured as 'excess deaths', has been established by demographic historians. Of the estimated population of 8.5 million in 1845, between 1 million and 1.1 million perished between then and 1851 of starvation and (more commonly) hunger-related disease. There were a further 0.4 million 'averted births' due to the collapse of fertility during the crisis years.[72] Another million emigrated, reducing the island's population by over a quarter of an anticipated total of just over 9 million by the census of 1851. Local factors (such as variations in social structure, landlord indebtedness and behaviour, and the availability of alternative employment) accounted for some fluctuations in experience, but the most impoverished western counties were hardest hit, and a number of western parishes lost over 50 per cent of their population.[73]

While the long-term economic consequences of the catastrophe remain disputed, it appears likely that the combination of massive demographic loss, concentrated among the cottier-labourer and smallholding tenant classes, and the stimulus and facility the crisis gave to land clearance and farm consolidation, paved the way for the export-oriented pastoral economy that distinguished Irish agriculture from the 1850s.[74] In terms of absolute numbers

---

69 I. Whelan, 'The stigma of souperism', in Póirtéir (ed.), *The Great Irish Famine*, pp. 135–54.

70 P. Gray, 'Accounting for catastrophe: William Wilde, the 1851 Irish census and the Great Famine' in M. De Nie and S. Farrell (eds.), *Power and popular culture in modern Ireland* (Dublin: Irish Academic Press, 2010), pp. 50–66; J. Quinn, *John Mitchel* (Dublin: UCD Press, 2009).

71 For radically different recent attributions of responsibility, see Kennedy, *Unhappy the land*; Haines, *Charles Trevelyan*; D. Nally, *Human encumbrances: political violence and the Great Irish Famine* (South Bend, IN: University of Notre Dame Press, 2011); T.P. Coogan, *The Famine plot: England's role in Ireland's greatest tragedy* (New York: Palgrave Macmillan, 2012).

72 Ó Grada, *Ireland: a new economic history*, pp. 173–87.

73 C. Ó Gráda, 'Mortality and the Great Famine', and W.J. Smyth, ' "Variations in vulnerability": understanding where and why people died' in Crowley et al., *Atlas of the Great Irish Famine*, pp. 170–97.

74 K. O'Rourke, 'Did the Great Famine matter?', *Journal of Economic History*, 51 (1991), 122; T.P. O'Neill, 'Famine evictions' in C. King (ed.), *Famine, land and culture in Ireland* (Dublin: UCD Press, 2000), pp. 29–70.

of excess deaths, the Great Famine was dwarfed by the demographic catastrophes of India, China and the Soviet Union in the nineteenth and twentieth centuries, but proportionately it ranks amongst the most severe, and as one of the 'last great subsistence crises of the western world'.[75]

---

75 C. Ó Gráda, 'The Great Famine and other famines' in *Ireland's Great Famine: interdisciplinary perspectives* (Dublin: UCD Press, 2006), pp. 196–216.

25

Irish Emigration, *c.*1845–1900

KEVIN KENNY

Introduction

The second half of the nineteenth century was the great age of Irish over-seas emigration. Departures from Ireland were already high before the Great Famine, with almost 1 million people crossing the Atlantic Ocean for North America between 1800 and 1845 and as many as half a million set-tling in Britain. Emigration levels remained high in the twentieth century as well, when 2 million people left Ireland and the outflow was directed mainly towards Britain rather than North America. But the most intense phase of Irish emigration took place between 1841 and 1900. About 4 million people emigrated from Ireland to the United States during this period, about 600,000 to Canada, more than 300,000 to Australia and New Zealand, and 40,000 to South Africa, Argentina and other destinations. In addition, as many as one million Irish went to Great Britain. The total – about 6 million emigrants – exceeded the population of Ireland at the beginning of the nineteenth cen-tury (Table 22). By the end of the century, two out of every five Irish-born people were living overseas (not counting those in Britain).[1]

In the context of contemporary European history, Irish emigration was highly distinctive. Due to the combined effects of famine mortality and emi-gration, Ireland's population was cut in half in little over half a century. The number of people living in Ireland declined from *c.*8.5 million in 1845 to 5.7 million in 1855, a reduction by one-third in ten years, and the downward spiral

---

1 A. Schrier, *Ireland and the American migration, 1850–1900* (Minneapolis: University of Minnesota Press, 1958), p. 159; D. Fitzpatrick, *Irish emigration 1801–1921* (Dundalk: Economic and Social History Society of Ireland, 1984), p. 5; D.H. Akenson, *Ireland, Sweden and the great European migration, 1815–1914* (Liverpool: Liverpool University Press, 2011), pp. 169, 182; K.A. Miller, *Emigrants and exiles: Ireland and the Irish exodus to North America* (Oxford: Oxford University Press, 1985), pp. 346–8. Akenson gives a figure of 5,071,336 for 'overseas out-migration from Ireland' (not counting those who settled in Britain) between 1841 and 1900, a figure that includes the first half of the 1840s. In 1891, 38.8 per cent of Irish-born people were living in the United States, Britain, Canada or Australia.

Table 22. *Emigration from Ireland to overseas destinations (not counting Great Britain), 1841–1900.*

Period	USA	% of total	Canada	% of total	Australasia	% of total	Other countries	% of total	Total
1841–50	908,292	70	362,738	27.9	22,825	1.8	4,539	0.3	1,298,394
1851–60	989,880	81.4	118,118	9.7	101,541	8.3	6,726	0.6	1,216,265
1861–70	690,845	84.4	40,079	4.9	82,917	10.1	4,741	0.6	818,582
1871–80	449,549	82.8	25,783	4.8	61,946	11.4	5,425	1	542,703
1881–90	626,604	85.3	44,505	6.1	55,476	7.5	7,890	1.1	734,475
1891–1900	427,301	92.7	10,548	2.3	11,448	2.5	11,520	2.5	460,917
	4,092,471	82.75	**601,871**	9.25	**336,153**	7	**40,841**	6	**5,071,336**

Source: Adapted from D.H. Akenson, *The Irish diaspora: a primer* (Toronto: P.D. Meany Co., 1996), 56.

continued for the rest of the century due to relentlessly heavy emigration. By 1901 the population had fallen to 4.4 million, roughly half what it had been on the eve of the Great Famine. This drastic decline occurred in a period when the populations of most countries in Europe and the Americas were rapidly expanding. About 5 million Germans emigrated to the United States in the same time period, for example, but the German population was four times greater than the Irish at the beginning of the period and fourteen times greater by the end. The annual emigration rate from Ireland (19 per 1,000 people in the 1850s, 16 per 1,000 in the 1880s, and 10 per 1,000 in the 1890s) was almost double that of any other European country. Norway was the only other European country whose emigration rate exceeded 10 per 1,000 during this era.[2]

Irish emigration in the period 1845–1900 is often considered under two separate headings, the Famine decade of 1845–55 and the post-Famine era of 1855–1900. This approach has the virtue of highlighting the unique characteristics of the Famine emigration. But the two periods were closely connected, with the Famine crisis accelerating existing socio-economic trends that endured for the rest of the century. This chapter will examine the Famine emigration and the post-Famine emigration together, under three headings: origins, composition and passage, and settlement. The analysis begins with the causes of emigration, then considers the social background of the emigrants and their mechanisms of departure, and concludes with some reflections on how the Irish fared in their various settlements abroad.

Origins

The population of Ireland reached its historical peak in the early 1840s. The census of 1841 recorded 8.2 million people. About 1.5 million (the poorest rural dwellers) had no significant sources of food other than the potato and another 3.5 million were largely dependent on that crop. Regionally, the greatest dependence was in the south and west. Yet it was the potato that kept the poor alive before the Famine, facilitating the subdivision of landholdings and thereby acting as a significant check on emigration. And because the

---

2 T. Guinnane, *The vanishing Irish: households, migration, and the rural economy in Ireland, 1850–1914* (Princeton: Princeton University Press, 1997), p. 101; Akenson, *Ireland, Sweden and the great European migration*, p. 8; T.J. Hatton and J.G. Williamson, 'After the Famine: emigration from Ireland, 1850–1913', *Journal of Economic History*, 53 (1993), 575–600; T.J. Hatton and J.G. Williamson, *The age of mass migration: causes and economic impact* (Oxford: Oxford University Press, 1998), pp. 33, 75.

potato is highly nutritious when consumed in sufficient quantity, the rural poor were not generally malnourished. A small crop of new potatoes was harvested in the early summer before the main potato crop arrived in August and September. The poor were certainly vulnerable in the interval, known as the 'hungry months', especially if the previous year's crop had been deficient or if the stored potatoes had deteriorated over the winter. The potato suffered several partial failures between 1820 and 1845 due to bad weather or disease, but these failures were local and short-lived and there was no reason to believe that the entire crop would fail nationally. A total failure, far from being inevitable, was unprecedented.[3]

The blight first hit the Irish potato crop in the autumn of 1845; it struck more heavily in 1846, 1848, 1849 and 1850.[4] The disease abated thereafter, but the harvest remained below half the pre-Famine level until the mid-1850s. The rate of emigration, likewise, did not return to pre-Famine levels until the middle of that decade. Historians of emigration therefore take the 'Famine decade' (1846–55) as their unit of measurement. About 2.1 million Irish people emigrated overseas between 1846 and 1855, 1.5 million of them to the United States. An estimated 315,000 went to British North America (many of whom then trekked overland to the United States), and about the same number to England and Scotland, where the Irish-born population almost doubled between 1841 and 1861. These emigrants represented one-quarter of Ireland's population on the eve of the Great Famine and accounted for the largest European mass migration, in proportional terms, in the nineteenth century.[5]

Levels of emigration rose sharply as the crisis escalated. Although the impact of the blight on emigration was limited in 1845, because it appeared halfway through the emigration season, the 75,000 transatlantic emigrants that year (i.e., those going to the United States and British North America combined) represented the highest annual figure in Irish history up to that point. This first outbreak of the blight (*Phytophthora infestans*) affected less than half the crop but its effects were sufficient to raise the number of

---

3 P. Gray, *The Irish Famine* (New York: Harry N. Abrams, 1995), pp. 31–3.

4 See Gray, Chapter 24 above, pp. 641–3, 650–1.

5 K.A. Miller, 'Emigration to North America in the era of the Great Famine, 1845–55' in J. Crowley et al. (eds.), *Atlas of the Great Irish Famine* (Cork: Cork University Press, 2012), pp. 214–27; C. Ó Gráda, 'Mortality and the Great Famine' in Crowley et al. (eds.), *Atlas of the Great Irish Famine*, p. 179; O. MacDonagh, 'The Irish Famine emigration to the United States', *Perspectives in American History*, 10 (1976), 405–7; Miller, *Emigrants and exiles*, pp. 281–2; D.M. MacRaild, *Irish migrants in modern Britain, 1750–1922* (New York: St. Martin's Press, 1999), p. 43. The Irish-born population of England, Wales and Scotland rose from 415,725 in 1841 to 805,717 in 1861.

transatlantic emigrants to 106,000 in 1846. The harvest was comparatively healthy in 1847, but because only a small crop had been planted amidst the devastation of the previous year transatlantic emigration reached a new high of 214,000 in 1847. The number of emigrants leaving for the United States and British North America fell slightly to 177,000 in 1848 after the healthy but small harvest of the previous year, rose to 208,000 in 1849 and 225,000 in 1850, and reached an all-time peak of 245,000 in 1851.[6]

Crop failure in itself does not necessarily lead to famine or mass emigration. In situations of this kind, people end up starving to death, dying of illness or fleeing their country in massive numbers because no adequate source of food is provided as a substitute. When the potato failed in Ireland, the British government experimented with various temporary measures, selling corn meal at cost price in 1846, providing indoor relief in workhouses and outdoor relief via public works projects, and briefly distributing food free of charge to the neediest via soup kitchens in 1847. The absence of blight in 1847 provided a welcome pretext to abandon these centralised efforts in favour of local responsibility and chargeability, on the supposed principle of laissez-faire. The Poor Law Extension Act of that year placed the burden of famine relief on unions funded by local taxes in a country where the poor could no longer pay their rents and landlords were going bankrupt. Any illusion that the crisis was over was dissipated by the return of the blight in full force in 1848, but the new relief mechanism remained in force and proved grossly inadequate.[7]

The poor relief system could hardly have been better designed to encourage evictions, clearances and mass emigration. A tax was levied on landlords and tenants holding property with an annual rateable value of £4 or more, with rates on properties valued at less than this figure chargeable to the landlords. Smallholders whose farms were just above the taxable limit had an incentive to vacate and emigrate, rather than pay the tax. Landlords and middlemen, unable to extract rents with which to pay their poor law rates, had every reason to evict their tenants. The infamous 'Gregory Clause' of the Poor Law Extension Act of 1847 denied public relief assistance to any head of household renting more than a quarter-acre who refused to relinquish the holding to its proprietor. Unable to survive on the land, the rural poor

---

6 Miller, 'Emigration to North America in the era of the Great Famine', pp. 214–15; MacDonagh, 'Irish Famine emigration', pp. 405–7.
7 P. Gray, *Famine, land, and politics: British Government and Irish society, 1843–1850* (Dublin: Irish Academic Press, 2001); J.S. Donnelly, Jr, *The Great Irish Potato Famine* (Stroud: Sutton, 2001); see Gray, Chapter 24 above, pp. 652–5.

abandoned their holdings and, if they survived and could raise the fare, they had little choice but to leave the country. The rate of evictions rose sharply after 1847, with an estimated 50,000 families (representing at least a quarter of a million people) being turned out of their homes permanently between 1849 and 1854.[8]

Little wonder, then, that many of the American Irish were disposed to agree with John Mitchel's verdict on the Famine. From his exile in the United States, Mitchel wrote, notoriously: '[A] million and a half of men, women and children, were carefully, prudently, and peacefully *slain* by the English government.' Potatoes failed all over Europe, Mitchel pointed out, yet there was famine only in Ireland. 'The British account of the matter, then, is first, a fraud – second, a blasphemy', he concluded. 'The almighty, indeed, sent the potato blight, but the English created the Famine.' No professional historian today would accept this charge of genocide: the British did not systematically slaughter the Irish. Yet many government officials and opinion-makers saw the crisis as a heaven-sent opportunity to stamp out Irish poverty, violence and ignorance. God, it seemed, was intervening in history to solve the Irish question. Charles Trevelyan, the English official in charge of famine relief in Ireland, is the most often quoted: 'Our humble but sincere conviction is, that the appointed time of Ireland's regeneration has come.' The 'root of social evil', Trevelyan continued, 'has been laid bare by a direct stroke of an all-wise and all-merciful Providence'. There was more to Trevelyan's work in Ireland than these much-cited words. But Mitchel's response, despite its hyperbole, became foundational, especially in Irish-American circles.[9]

The Great Famine transformed the rural class structure in Ireland, setting the stage for mass emigration for decades to come. As Peter Gray has put it, the relief policy from 1847 onward 'was not pure *laissez-faire* but the use of a penal mechanism – the poor law – to forcibly transform Irish behavior and to prole-tarianise the cottier'. The decimation of the rural poor through mortality and emigration paved the way for the emergence of the Irish-born commercial farmer as the backbone of the rural economy. Holdings of less than 5 acres accounted for 45 per cent of total landholdings in 1841 but only 15 per cent

---

8 Gray, *Irish Famine*, pp. 65–9; Gray, *Famine, land, and politics*, pp. 227–337; Donnelly, *The Great Irish Potato Famine*, pp. 65–168; Miller, *Emigrants and exiles*, p. 287; Guinnane, *Vanishing Irish*, pp. 61–2.

9 J. Mitchel, *The last conquest of Ireland (perhaps)*, ed. P. Maume (Dublin: UCD Press, 2005), p. 219; C. Trevelyan, *The Irish crisis* (London: Longman, Brown, Green and Longmans, 1848), p. 201; R. Haines, *Charles Treveylan and the Great Irish Famine* (Dublin: Four Courts Press, 2004).

a decade later. The proportion of middle-sized farms (between 15 and 30 acres) more than doubled in the same period, from 11.5 per cent to 25 per cent. The figure for farms of 50 acres and above almost quadrupled, from 7 per cent to 26 per cent. Mass emigration continued inexorably for the remainder of the century. About 1.2 million emigrants left Ireland in the 1840s, 780,000 of them for North America. Another 1.2 million left in the 1850s, more than 900,000 of them for North America. Just over 800,000 left in the 1860s and slightly more than 500,000 in the 1870s, with about 436,000 going to the United States in each decade. Emigration rose to more than 700,000 during the economic downturn of the 1880s, with 655,000 settling in the United States. The number of emigrants fell to about 460,000 in the last decade of the nineteenth century, of whom 390,000 went to the United States. Great Britain was always the second most popular destination after the United States (with 500,000 or more Irish settling there in the post-Famine era), followed by Canada and Australia (more than 200,000 each), New Zealand, South Africa and Argentina.[10]

The second half of the nineteenth century, a period of demographic, urban and industrial expansion in western Europe and North America, was a period of precipitous decline in Ireland. In an era when other countries were growing rapidly, Ireland's population was reduced by half. Textile production, the basis of thriving domestic industry in the late eighteenth and early nineteenth centuries, was increasingly concentrated in the Belfast area, while industry elsewhere stagnated. Irish towns and cities declined in population accordingly. The bulk of the Irish population remained dependent on agriculture in an economy that could not provide an adequate supply of land or work. Without urban or industrial employment, those displaced from the countryside had little choice but to move abroad. Given the restrictions on opportunity, the Irish had the lowest rates of matrimony, the highest ages at marriage and the highest levels of permanent celibacy in Europe by the late nineteenth century (with the highest rates of all in the west of Ireland). Marital fertility, by contrast, remained unusually high, in part because children, as David Fitzpatrick notes, 'were reared as potential emigrants'. Rural depopulation, low rates of marriage, high rates of permanent celibacy and high emigration rates were found in other European countries and regions,

---

10 P. Gray, 'Famine relief policy in comparative perspective: Ireland, Scotland, and Northwest Europe, 1845–1849', *Éire-Ireland*, 32:1 (1997), 105; MacDonagh, 'Irish Famine emigration', p. 361 n. 8; Fitzpatrick, *Irish emigration*, pp. 3–4; Akenson, *Ireland, Sweden and the great European migration*, p. 169; P.J. Blessing, 'Irish' in S. Thernstrom (ed.), *The Harvard encyclopedia of American ethnic groups* (Cambridge, MA: Belknap Press, 1980), p. 528; Miller, *Emigrants and exiles*, p. 346.

but their particular combination in the Irish case was distinctive and the rate of emigration was unique.[11]

Post-Famine Ireland differed markedly from pre-Famine Ireland in its economy, social structure and emigration patterns, with the crisis of the 1840s serving as the catalyst for this transformation. Prior to the Famine, potato cultivation and the subdivision of holdings allowed the poor to stay on the land. The social structure of post-Famine Ireland, by contrast, was top-heavy with middling and strong farmers. Between 1861 and 1911, as a result of evictions, consolidation and emigration, the number of smallholders renting 2 acres or less in return for their labour fell by 60 per cent. In the west, the old joint tenancies and rundale farming practices gave way to individual farmsteads. Throughout the country, farmers continued to move from tillage to pasture, replacing humans with animals. Impartible inheritance of landholdings became the norm, and marriage was an economic calculation based on the availability of land. With one child, typically the eldest son, inheriting the land and delaying marrying until he received his inheritance, prospects for non-inheriting siblings were bleak. One daughter might get married if the family could provide a dowry, but other daughters and non-inheriting sons often had few options but to emigrate.[12]

Some historians have challenged this 'gloom and doom' interpretation of post-Famine Ireland. They emphasise that Ireland had a wide variety of family and inheritance patterns, ranging from solitary occupants, through simple or nuclear households, to stem families with two married couples, to complex extended households. Even under primogeniture, younger siblings in better-off families might receive small parcels of land from their parents or a cash payment, which they could use to finance emigration. This interpretation has much to offer, though its emphasis on the profit-maximising actions of rational individual actors cannot do justice to the complexity of emigration as a collective movement of people. Granted, the emigrants did not leave

---

11 Fitzpatrick, *Irish emigration*, p. 29; Miller, *Emigrants and exiles*, pp. 346, 361–70, 380–402; Guinnane, *Vanishing Irish*, pp. 15, 38–42, 48–51, 73–4, 82–5, 92–6, 133–65, 195, 225–33; K.H. Connell, 'Peasant marriage in Ireland after the Great Famine', *Past and Present*, 12 (1957), 76–91; K.H. Connell, 'Peasant marriage in Ireland: its structure and development since the Famine', *Economic History Review*, 2nd ser., 14 (1962), 502–23; R.E. Kennedy, *The Irish: emigration, marriage, and fertility* (Berkeley: University of California Press, 1973), pp. 1, 29; Akenson, *Ireland, Sweden and the great European migration*, pp. 243–4; B.M. Walsh, 'Marriage rates and population pressure: Ireland, 1871 and 1911', *Economic History Review*, 23 (1970), 148–62.

12 Miller, *Emigrants and exiles*, pp. 380–402; Connell, 'Peasant marriage in Ireland after the Great Famine'; Connell, 'Peasant marriage in Ireland: its structure and development since the Famine'; Kennedy, *Emigration, marriage, and fertility*.

Ireland as part of an involuntary mass exodus. But their decisions were made in the context of the family, rather than on a strictly individual basis, and often involved a complex process of step and chain migration. Young women, in particular, left Ireland in the expectation that they would send money home for the upkeep of the farm or to finance the emigration of their siblings. Migration of this kind is best seen as an extension of family control across the Atlantic, rather than a straightforward story of upward individual mobility.[13]

Composition and Passage

What kinds of people left Ireland during the Famine and post-Famine eras? Once the decision to emigrate had been made, how did the emigrants leave? What forms of assistance and transportation were available to them? The answers to these questions vary by time and region but some overall patterns emerge. The emigrants were poor but most of them were not destitute. About three-quarters of them were classified as labourers and servants. Men predominated over women initially, but sex ratios were roughly equal in the post-Famine era, with women predominating in some decades. The emigrants depended heavily on remittances from Irish people abroad, and they travelled via an increasingly efficient transportation network.[14]

Although Famine emigration contained elements of panic and chaos, the general profile is clear. The great majority of those who left Ireland between 1845 and 1855 were rural dwellers without marketable skills. An estimated 60 per cent or more were aged between 20 and 45, Famine mortalities being highest on either side of this age range. Men had outnumbered women by about two to one in the pre-Famine emigration, but this gap narrowed in the late 1840s. The lowest rates of emigration were from the most heavily Protestant regions, especially Belfast and the Lagan valley, the Dublin area and County Wexford. Protestants made up about 10 per cent of the Famine emigrants, at a time when they accounted for 25 per cent of the Irish population. As during the pre-Famine era, the highest rates of emigration were from north-central Ireland (counties Sligo, Roscommon, Longford, Cavan, Monaghan and Fermanagh) and the south-central plains (Queen's County, Tipperary and Kilkenny). In the impoverished counties on the Atlantic seaboard, there was

---

13 Guinnane, *Vanishing Irish*, pp. 15, 38–42, 48–51, 73–4, 82–5, 92–6, 133–65, 195, 225–33. Step migration involves movement through a series of locations. In chain migration, emigrants establish a foothold and then finance the passage of others, typically family members.

14 Guinnane, *Vanishing Irish*, pp. 104–7; Miller, *Emigrants and exiles*, pp. 350–3.

often an inverse relationship between emigration and mortality; Mayo had high rates of both, Donegal had low rates in each category, and Cork had high mortality in the west and high emigration in the east. By volume, as distinct from rate, the six counties with the highest number of emigrants between 1846 and 1855 were, in order, Cork, Tipperary, Mayo, Galway, Limerick and Cavan.[15]

The Famine emigration was dominated by cottiers, smallholders and middling farmers rather than the conacre tenants and landless labourers who sat at the bottom of the social scale. Emigration was disproportionately high among tenants holding 5–15 acres and substantial among middling farmers (holding 15–30 acres) and strong farmers (holding anywhere from 30 to several hundred acres). Those most heavily dependent on the potato, living along the Atlantic seaboard, were the most likely to die of starvation and disease. Some of the most notorious cases of mass starvation occurred in these regions, but emigration rates from western counties (other than Donegal and Kerry) were much higher than they had been in the pre-Famine era. As Galway, Mayo, Kerry and Clare (along with Waterford, somewhat anomalously) contained the heaviest concentrations of Irish speakers, the proportion of emigrants who spoke that language was higher than the proportion in the general population. Between one-quarter and one-third of American-bound emigrants during the Famine decade are thought to have spoken Irish (compared to about one-quarter of the population as a whole). Emigration therefore contributed to the decline of Irish, while making it more common on the streets of America and Britain than it had been earlier in the century. Yet more than 90 per cent of Irish-speaking emigrants could speak English as well, which was a significant advantage over other immigrants in the United States.[16]

15 W.J. Smyth, 'Exodus from Ireland – patterns of emigration' in Crowley et al. (eds.), *Atlas of the Great Irish Famine*, pp. 494–503; MacDonagh, 'Irish Famine emigration', pp. 418–30; Miller, *Emigrants and exiles*, p. 297; S.H. Cousens, 'Regional death rates in Ireland during the Great Famine, from 1846 to 1851', *Population Studies*, 14 (1960), 55–74; S.H. Cousens, 'The regional pattern of emigration during the Great Irish Famine, 1846–51', *Transactions and Papers (Institute of British Geographers)*, 28 (1960), 119–34; S.H. Cousens, 'Emigration and demographic change in Ireland, 1851–1861', *Economic History Review*, 14 (1961), 275–88. The lower emigration from County Donegal was apparently due to a combination of seasonal migration and charitable efforts by landlords and religious groups. In County Mayo, the high emigration rates may have been correlated with the high eviction rate of smallholders, including some assistance.

16 MacDonagh, 'Irish Famine emigration', pp. 380, 423; Miller, *Emigrants and exiles*, pp. 295–7; Guinnane, *Vanishing Irish*, pp. 104–7; B. Ó Cuív, *Irish dialects and Irish-speaking districts: three lectures* (Dublin: Dublin Institute for Advanced Studies, 1980), pp. 23–7. According to the census of 1851, 1,524,286 people (23 per cent of the population) spoke Irish, of whom 319,602 were monolingual (5 per cent of the population, 21 per cent of

In the post-Famine era, emigrants continued to leave from all parts of Ireland but emigration was especially intense in the west. Munster and Connacht provided slightly more than half the emigrants between 1855 and 1900, even though they contained only about 40 per cent of the country's population. Almost one-third of post-Famine departures came from the densely populated province of Ulster, including hundreds of thousands of Protestants whose favoured destination was Canada. But the rate of emigration was heaviest in Connacht, followed by Munster, Ulster and Leinster. Emigration from the west had been relatively low in the pre-Famine era. Post-Famine emigration reached its peak in the 1880s, when the fragile economies of the western seaboard collapsed. In the 1880s and 1890s, Connacht and Munster each lost 15 per cent of their population to emigration, whereas Ulster lost 5 per cent and Leinster only 4 per cent in the latter decade. Emigration from Ireland as a whole declined by 18 per cent in 1881–1910 when compared to 1856–80, but it declined by only 13 per cent in Munster and increased by fully 53 per cent in Connacht. During the last two decades of the nineteenth century, nearly all the counties with the heaviest emigration were on the western seaboard – Cork, Kerry, Clare, Galway, Mayo and Donegal – though the emigration rate remained high in north-central Ireland (especially Cavan, Longford and Tyrone), as it had since the early nineteenth century.[17]

Emigrants in the post-Famine era were younger and more likely to be single and female than in previous periods. Between 1852 and 1891 the median age of Irish emigrants was 22.5 for males and 21.2 for females. In each of the last four decades of the nineteenth century, emigrants aged 15 to 24 made up between 46 and 60 per cent of the outflow and those between 25 and 34 made up an additional 20 to 25 per cent. Roughly 75 per cent of the post-Famine emigrants were unmarried and the great majority left Ireland as individuals rather than in family groups. Men considerably outnumbered women in the emigration to Australia but the number of Irish women equalled or exceeded the number of Irish men on the Atlantic route. Not only were half of these Irish emigrants women, they also crossed the Atlantic as single individuals.

the Irish speakers). Irish-speaking women, as Ó Cuív notes, were less likely to know English than Irish-speaking men (which means that the census figures on monolingualism, to the extent that they were extrapolated from male heads of household, may be somewhat low; see also Doyle, Chapter 14, pp. 366–8 above.

17 Miller, *Emigrants and exiles*, pp. 349–51, 370–9, 397–402, 469–81, 571; Fitzpatrick, *Irish emigration*, p. 9; S.H. Cousens, 'The regional variations in population changes in Ireland, 1861–1881', *Economic History Review*, 17 (1964), 301–21; B.M. Walsh, 'A perspective on Irish population patterns', *Éire-Ireland*, 4 (1969), 3–21; C. Ó Gráda, 'Seasonal migration and post-Famine adjustment in the west of Ireland', *Studia Hibernica*, 13 (1973), 48–76.

Jewish gender ratios were comparable to those of the Irish but most Jewish women emigrants were married or travelled with their parents. Only about 20 per cent of southern Italian emigrants in the late nineteenth century were female and they did not cross the Atlantic unaccompanied. For young Irish women in the post-Famine era, emigration provided a means of escape from a society in which opportunities were severely restricted, even if they were expected to send remittances back to their families. Women could find temporary work in Ireland as farm servants, usually living in the homes of their employers. Beyond that, given the stagnation of urban and industrial life, employment opportunities were few and marriage was unlikely in the absence of a dowry. Irish women were, however, in considerable demand for domestic work in the United States. Only Swedish gender ratios resembled the Irish, with large numbers of single Swedish women also entering domestic service in America.[18]

Once the decision to leave was reached, the emigrants had to figure out how to fund their passage and by what means to travel. Given the scale of the catastrophe in the 1840s, and the extent of rural poverty, remarkably little assistance was available. Landlords provided monetary assistance to some 50,000 emigrants between 1846 and 1855, but their motives were more self-interested than humanitarian. Eviction accompanied by compulsory assisted emigration was an effective way of clearing the land of destitute tenants. Lord Palmerston's estate in County Sligo sent out 2,000 tenants in this way, Sir Robert Gore Booth cleared 1,340 tenants from his Sligo estates, the Marquess of Lansdowne sent 3,500 from County Kerry, and Denis Mahon sent 1,000 from his estate in County Roscommon. The crown also took the opportunity to clear some of its estates. All the tenants on the crown estate at Ballykilcline, County Roscommon, for example, were evicted in 1847 and

---

18 Akenson, *Ireland, Sweden and the great European migration*, pp. 173, 239; Miller, *Emigrants and exiles*, p. 352; Guinnane, *Vanishing Irish*, pp. 53–5, 94–106, 166–76, 193–240, 266–7; Kennedy, *Emigration, marriage, and fertility*, pp. 76–85; Hatton and Williamson, 'After the Famine: emigration from Ireland, 1850–1913', 587; Hatton and Williamson, *The age of mass migration*, p. 84; P.J. Blessing, 'Irish emigration to the United States, 1800–1920: an overview' in P. J. Drudy (ed.), *Irish in America: emigration, assimilation, and impact* (Cambridge: Cambridge University Press, 1985), p. 19; Guinnane, *Vanishing Irish*, pp. 105–6, 176–86; M. Lynch-Brennan, *The Irish Bridget: Irish immigrant women in domestic service in America, 1840–1930* (Syracuse, NY: Syracuse University Press, 2009); H. Diner, *Erin's daughters in America: Irish immigrant women in the nineteenth century* (Baltimore, MD: Johns Hopkins University Press, 1983), pp. 1–42; J. Nolan, *Ourselves alone: women's emigration from Ireland, 1885–1920* (Lexington: University Press of Kentucky, 1989), pp. 2–6, 26–54; P. Jackson, 'Women in nineteenth-century Irish emigration', *International Migration Review*, 18 (1984), 1006, 1010, 1018.

those willing to emigrate to America were offered free passage as part of the package. A small number of emigrants received assistance under the revised Poor Law of 1847, which allowed local unions to pay one-third of the passage if the landlord paid the remainder. As the landlords could no longer collect rents, however, and the union boards on which they served were in financial disarray, this scheme covered at most 5,000 people. In addition, poorhouses and orphanages despatched some 15,000 inmates directly to America between 1851 and 1855, mostly young women and children. The vast majority of Famine emigrants, then, had to pay their own way. Selling a pig or heifer and using the proceeds to finance emigration rather than to pay the rent was an option for some. But the chief form of assistance came from relatives in America. Official returns indicate that North American immigrants sent more than £34 million in remittances to the United Kingdom between 1848 and 1887, the great bulk of it from the United States to Ireland and about 40 per cent in the form of prepaid passage tickets.[19]

Public assistance was more readily available in the post-Famine era than earlier. The Poor Law boards sent about 80,000 Irish paupers to the United States in the late nineteenth century. Landlords, charitable and friendly societies, and philanthropists also provided assistance, with Vere Foster and James Hack Tuke, for example, financing 30,000 departures from the west of Ireland to the United States in the 1880s alone. A majority of emigrants to Australia and New Zealand received some form of assistance from the state, but they made up a small proportion (well under 10 per cent) of the total outflow in the post-Famine era. For the nineteenth century as a whole, the best estimate of the number of Irish transatlantic emigrants who received aid from all sources (landlords, government, poor law unions and philanthropists) is 300,000. The vast majority of emigrants, in other words, had to fund their own passages.

---

19 G. Moran, *Sending out Ireland's poor: assisted emigration to North America in the nineteenth century* (Dublin: Four Courts Press, 2013); T. Anbinder, 'Lord Palmerston and the Irish Famine migration', *Historical Journal*, 44 (2001), 441–69; T. Anbinder, 'From Famine to Five Points: Lord Lansdowne's Irish tenants encounter North America's most notorious slum', *American Historical Review*, 107 (2002), 351–87; Cousens, 'Regional pattern of emigration during the Great Irish Famine', 121–3; Gray, *Irish Famine*, 101; R.J. Scally, *The end of hidden Ireland: rebellion, famine, and emigration* (Oxford: Oxford University Press, 1995), especially pp. 105–29; Miller, *Emigrants and exiles*, pp. 296, 356–7, 413–24; MacDonagh, 'Irish Famine emigration', 358–9, 362, 395; R. Doan, 'Green gold to the emerald shores: Irish immigration to the United States and transatlantic monetary aid, 1854–1923', PhD thesis, Temple University, 1998; Schrier, *Ireland and the American migration*, pp. 106–13, 151–2, 167; Nolan, *Ourselves alone*, pp. 55–72; Guinnane, *Vanishing Irish*, pp. 108–11; Fitzpatrick, *Irish emigration*, pp. 18–20.

Those who went to the United States, in particular, relied on an increasingly elaborate system of chain migration and emigrant remittances.[20]

North America was the primary destination for Irish emigrants in the nineteenth century and Liverpool was the main point of departure. Already before the Great Famine, two out of every three Irish emigrants who crossed the Atlantic Ocean did so via Liverpool rather than from Irish ports. During the Famine decade, the number of Irish emigrants to North America who left from Liverpool was four to five times greater than the number who left from Irish ports. Steamships were crossing the Irish Sea by the 1840s, but were not introduced on the Atlantic until just after the Famine. Ships carrying emigrants across the Irish Sea, unlike those crossing the Atlantic Ocean, were not subject to regulations on numbers, space, provisions or hygiene. The more fortunate travelled by steamer to Liverpool, the rest in fishing boats and other vessels equipped to carry livestock and other merchandise rather than human cargo. Those who remained in Britain – where the Irish-born population increased from about 415,000 in 1841 to 727,000 in 1851 – spread out through the industrial towns of Lancashire and beyond. But most of the Irish moved on from Liverpool as quickly as they could, continuing their journey across the Atlantic. Transatlantic emigrant boarded sailing ships that took four to six weeks to cross the ocean but they often had to wait for days or even weeks before boarding. They lived meantime in squalid boarding-houses or camped out along the waterfront, where they were preyed upon by the usual parasites of the emigrant trade, often their own countrymen – shipping agents, runners, hucksters and conmen. Herman Melville observed that, 'of all seaports in the world, Liverpool, perhaps, most abounds in all the variety of land-sharks, land-rats and other vermin, which make the hapless mariner their prey'. Descending on the emigrant in 'the shape of landlords, barkeepers, clothiers, crimps and boarding-house loungers, the land-sharks devour him, limb by limb; while the land rats and mice constantly nibble at his purse'.[21]

Although the primary route from Liverpool was to New York City, much of the emigrant trade was temporarily diverted to Canada in 1847. When the United States passed a new Passenger Act that year requiring passengers to be provided with more space, ship captains responded to the resulting reduction

---

20 Schrier, *Ireland and the American migration*, pp. 106–13, 151–2, 167; Doan, 'Green gold to the emerald shores'; Guinnane, *Vanishing Irish*, pp. 108–11; Miller, *Emigrants and exiles*, p. 357. The 300,000 who received assistance over the century as a whole are the subject of Moran's *Sending out Ireland's poor*.

21 Scally, *End of hidden Ireland*, pp. 181–219; H. Melville, *Redburn: his first voyage* (1849; London: J. Cape, 1937), pp. 162–3.

in numbers by raising fares. Also in 1847, the state of New York imposed a head tax on all immigrants to cover the cost of those who might become public charges. Together these policies had the effect of diverting passengers to the cheaper, less-regulated Canadian route. Of the 214,000 Irish emigrants who travelled to North America in 1847, 97,000 went to Canada. The New York–Liverpool trade recovered the following year, in part because the United States Supreme Court declared the New York head tax unconstitutional, but not before scenes of death and devastation on Canadian shores made 'Black '47' the most notorious year of the Famine. Some 30 per cent of Irish emigrants bound for British North America that year, and 9 per cent of those sailing to the United States, perished on board the 'coffin ships', succumbing to starvation or the variety of diseases that went under the name of 'fever'. Overwhelmed by the sudden influx, the Canadian authorities converted an old cholera quarantine centre on Grosse Île, 30 miles downstream from Quebec City on the Lawrence River, for use as a clearing house. The hospital there was equipped to hold only 150 patients but already by the end of May 1847, the beginning of the emigrant season, 12,500 Irish immigrants were waiting in ships off Grosse Île. By June, about 21,000 Irish immigrants were housed on the island. An estimated 12,000 Irish Famine victims are buried there.[22]

The development of steam-powered ships capable of crossing the Atlantic Ocean transformed the experience of emigration after the Famine. Steamships began to replace sailing ships on the transatlantic voyage in the 1850s, and by the 1870s nearly all Irish emigrants travelled to America by steam. The ships introduced by the Cunard company in the 1850s and 1860s – made of wood, propelled by paddles, and capable of 8–12 knots – reduced the transatlantic voyage from six weeks to two to three. By the 1880s, ocean-going steamships were 500 feet long, built mostly of iron and steel, driven by screw propellers, and capable of twice the speed of the ships in the 1860s. By 1900 it took only a week to ten days or less to cross the Atlantic. In the post-Famine era, moreover, Irish emigrants no longer had to travel via Liverpool. The major British ocean liners called at Queenstown in Cork harbour and at Moville, just north of Derry, to pick up Irish passengers before crossing the Atlantic.

---

22 Gray, *Irish Famine*, pp. 103, 106–7; D. MacKay, *Flight from Famine: the coming of the Irish to Canada* (Toronto: McClelland and Stewart, 1990); M. O'Gallagher, *Grosse Île: gateway to Canada, 1832–1937* (St. Foy, Quebec: Carraig Books, 1984); M. Quigley, 'Grosse Île: Canada's Famine memorial', *Éire-Ireland*, 32 (Spring 1997), 7–19; MacDonagh, 'Irish Famine emigration', 410–11; Scally, *End of hidden Ireland*, pp. 39, 219; Miller, *Emigrants and exiles*, pp. 287, 316.

'Emigration', as David Fitzpatrick once put it, 'had become a massive, relentless, and efficiently managed national enterprise.'[23]

What was the impact of mass emigration on Ireland? Given that so many people left Ireland in their prime working years, emigration may have had a dampening effect on enterprise, with reduced competition for resources discouraging innovation in farming techniques. Yet those who remained received tens of millions of dollars in emigrant remittances, less than half of which was used to finance additional emigration. While this steady flow of income may have discouraged innovation by allowing small and medium farmers to stay on the land, emigration clearly benefited individuals and their families. The nationalist farmers who protested emigration as a form of 'extermination' and blamed it on British misrule, Kerby Miller has argued, not only benefited from emigration financially, but were often directly responsible by displacing poorer tenants, converting their holdings from tillage to pasture, and consolidating them into larger, more commercially viable units. Mass emigration also acted as a significant social safety valve, defusing tensions between the landless poor and commercial farmers as well as landlords. As a result, post-Famine Ireland lacked the pervasive tradition of internal class conflict and secret society violence, stretching from the 'Whiteboys' through the 'Ribbonmen' and the 'Molly Maguires', which had pitted Irishmen against Irishmen for almost a century before the Famine. Strong tenant farmers, who would soon own their land outright, reigned triumphant by the end of the nineteenth century. And, by removing 'surplus' population, mass emigration contributed to a general increase in wage levels and living standards for those who remained in Ireland.[24]

Settlement

Irish emigration was a global phenomenon in the period 1845–1900. After the United States, the areas of the world that received significant numbers of Irish immigrants were, in descending order, Britain, Canada, Australia,

23 Miller, *Emigrants and exiles*, pp. 380–402; Guinnane, *Vanishing Irish*, pp. 38–42; D. Fitzpatrick, 'Emigration, 1871–1921' in W.E. Vaughan (ed.), *A new history of Ireland*, vol. VI: *Ireland under the Union, II, 1870–1921* (Oxford: Oxford University Press, 1996), p. 607.
24 Fitzpatrick, *Irish emigration*, pp. 5, 38–40; Fitzpatrick, 'Emigration, 1801–1921', p. 262; Guinnane, *Vanishing Irish*, pp. 4, 22–3; Akenson, *Ireland, Sweden and the great European migration*, p. 243; G.R. Boyer, T.J. Hatton and K. O'Rourke, 'The impact of emigration on real wages in Ireland, 1850–1914' in T.J. Hatton and J.G. Williamson (eds.), *Migration and the international labor market, 1850–1939* (New York: Routledge, 1994), pp. 221–39; Hatton and Williamson, *The age of mass migration*, pp. 186–90.

New Zealand, Latin America and South Africa. Irish men and women were also active as individuals in the non-settler colonies of the British Empire as soldiers, administrators and missionaries. Although the number of Irish immigrants was always much larger in the United States than elsewhere, the Irish-born constituted a greater proportion of the populations of Scotland, Ontario, New Brunswick, New Zealand and the Australian provinces in 1870. Irish overseas settlement has generated a vast scholarly literature, and the focus here will be on providing a broad outline of the Irish impact on the host countries along with a brief analysis of the main historiographical debates.[25]

Regional variations in emigration from Ireland had important consequences for the development of immigrant communities abroad. The impoverished province of Connacht was over-represented in emigration to the United States in the second half of the nineteenth century but under-represented in emigration to Britain and Australia. Ulster sent disproportionate numbers of emigrants, many of them Protestants, to Canada, Scotland and New Zealand. The fertile, commercially developed south midlands of Leinster and Munster provided the majority of Irish Catholic emigrants to Australia. 'Thus Irish emigration may usefully be envisaged', Fitzpatrick has noted, 'as a complex network of distinct streams flowing from particular regions of origin to particular countries of settlement, even though the United States remained everywhere the majority choice'. Census records on immigration in the host countries generally provide only the country, and not the region or county, of origin. But by using other sources, historians have demonstrated how regional and local pre-migration conditions influenced the development of immigrant social history, labour organisation and nationalist movements, typically at the local or microhistorical level.[26]

25 Fitzpatrick, *Irish emigration*, p. 5. Standard works on the Irish abroad include Miller, *Emigrants and exiles*; K. Kenny, *The American Irish: a history* (New York: Longman, 2000); K. Kenny, 'The Irish in the Empire' in K. Kenny (ed.), *Ireland and the British Empire*: The Oxford History of the British Empire companion series (Oxford: Oxford University Press, 2004), pp. 90–122; D.M. MacRaild, *The Irish diaspora in Britain, 1750–1939*, 2nd edn (New York: St. Martin's Press, 2011); G. Davis, *The Irish in Britain, 1815–1914* (Dublin: Gill and Macmillan, 1991); D. Wilson, *The Irish in Canada* (Ottawa: Canadian Historical Association, 1989); M. Campbell, *Ireland's new worlds: immigrants, politics, and society in the United States and Australia, 1815–1922* (Madison: University of Wisconsin Press, 2008); D. Fitzpatrick (ed.), *Oceans of consolation: personal accounts of Irish migration to Australia* (Ithaca, NY: Cornell University Press, 1994); P. O'Farrell, *The Irish in Australia* (Kensington, New South Wales: NSWU Press, 1987); L. Fraser, *To Tara via Holyhead: Irish Catholic immigrants in nineteenth-century Christchurch* (Auckland: Auckland University Press, 1997); A. Bielenberg (ed.), *The Irish diaspora* (Harlow: Longman, 2000); D.H. Akenson, *The Irish diaspora: a primer* (Toronto: P.D. Meany Co., 1993).

26 Fitzpatrick, *Irish Emigration*, pp. 11–13; Fitzpatrick (ed.), *Oceans of consolation*, pp. 3–36; Miller, *Emigrants and exiles*, passim; D.M. Emmons, *The Butte Irish: class and ethnicity*

Irish immigrants had a considerable impact on the countries in which they settled. Although those who went to Australia were a small proportion of the total outflow from Ireland, they were the second largest immigrant group there, after the English. In Canada, people of Irish descent made up one-third of the population of Ontario and New Brunswick in 1871 and a majority of the population in the city of St John's, Newfoundland. The Irish were the single largest immigrant group in the United States in the 1840s, when they accounted for 45 per cent of the inflow, and the second largest (slightly below the Germans) in the 1850s, when they accounted for 35 per cent of the total. The scale of the Irish influx into the United States in the 1840s and 1850s was such that American immigration reached one of its three historical peaks.

To gauge the impact of Irish immigration, some comparison with later periods is instructive. During the 1840s and 1850s an average of 300,000 immigrants a year entered the United States, mainly from Ireland, Germany and England, and to a lesser extent from China. The number of people entering the United States during the next great wave of immigration in American history, at the turn of the twentieth century, approached one million annually at its peak. The number in the opening decade of the twenty-first century, part of the third great wave of immigration, exceeded one million a year (counting the estimated figure of the undocumented). But because the population of the United States rose from 31 million in 1860 to 75 million in 1900 and to 308 million in 2010, immigration must be measured in proportionate terms as well as in gross numbers.

There are two ways of doing so. The first is to calculate the foreign-born share of the population, which reached its highest level (15 per cent) at the turn of the twentieth century. The figures for 1860 and 2010 (roughly 13 per cent in each case) are comparable. The second measure is to calculate the number of arrivals per thousand people in the population in a given year or decade (the immigration rate). Whereas the first measure counts all people born abroad, both naturalised and unnaturalised, regardless of how long they have lived in the United States, the second measure counts only those who entered the country as immigrants during the period in question. For a single decade, the American immigration rate reached its peak in 1901–10 at about

in an American mining town, 1875–1925 (Urbana: University of Illinois Press, 1989); T.M. O'Neil, 'Miners in migration: the case of nineteenth-century Irish and Irish-American copper miners', *Éire-Ireland*, 36 (Spring/Summer 2001), 124–40; V.A. Walsh, ' "A fanatic heart": the cause of Irish-American nationalism in Pittsburgh during the Gilded Age', *Journal of Social History*, 15 (1981), 187–204; Anbinder, 'From Famine to Five Points'; K. Kenny, *Making sense of the Molly Maguires* (Oxford: Oxford University Press, 1998).

11 immigrants per 1,000 people. For a two-decade unit, however, the rate was highest in the 1840s and 1850s.[27]

Although the Irish-born accounted for only a small percentage of the American and British populations in the late nineteenth century, their concentration in urban and industrial areas made them unusually visible. The Irish-born share of the US population reached its historical peak of about 5 per cent in 1870, at which time the Irish were concentrated in four states – Massachusetts, New York, Pennsylvania and Illinois, with California in fifth place (a pattern that has endured among their descendants). German immigrants, by contrast, scattered widely across the country. Three-quarters of the American-Irish lived in urban-industrial counties in 1870, compared to about one-quarter of the American population as a whole. One in every four New Yorkers and Bostonians at mid-century was Irish-born, along with one in every six residents of Philadelphia, and by the end of the century more Irish-born people lived in New York City than in either Dublin or Belfast. Likewise, the Irish-born, which made up about 3 per cent of the British population in the late nineteenth century, were highly concentrated in London, Liverpool, Manchester and Glasgow. The Irish were much more widely dispersed in Ontario and Australia, where more than half the Irish settlers (Catholic as well as Protestant) worked as farmers and agricultural labourers in the late nineteenth century.[28]

When it comes to a general interpretation of the Irish experience abroad, the starting point is Kerby Miller's great interpretive survey, *Emigrants and exiles: Ireland and the Irish exodus to North America*, and the responses it has elicited. Seeking to explain why Irish emigrants came to see their departure as a matter of exile and banishment rather than opportunity and self-improvement, Miller located the origins of the exile motif not in the poverty

---

27 R. Ueda, *Postwar immigrant America: a social history* (New York: Bedford/St. Martin's, 1994), p. 11. The immigration rate in the United States in both 1891–1900 and 1911–20 was between 5.5 and 6, compared to 11 in 1901–10, resulting in an average rate of 8.5 per 1,000 for both 1891–1910 and 1901–20. By comparison, the rate in the 1840s (8.5) and the 1850s (9.5) together give an average immigration rate of 9 per 1,000 over a twenty-year period. The corresponding figure today is less than 4 because the population is so much higher than it was a century ago while the number of immigrants is only slightly larger.

28 D.N. Doyle, 'The remaking of Irish-America, 1845–80' in Vaughan (ed.), *A new history of Ireland*, vol. VI, pp. 732–3, 726, 741; D.N. Doyle, 'The Irish as urban pioneers in the United States, 1850–1870', *Journal of American Ethnic History*, 10 (Fall 1990–Winter 1991), 36–59; Fitzpatrick, 'Emigration, 1801–70' in W.E. Vaughan (ed.), *A new history of Ireland*, vol. V: *Ireland under the Union, I, 1801–70* (Oxford: Oxford University Press, 1989), p. 569; O'Farrell, 'Irish in Australia and New Zealand, 1801–70' and 'Irish in Australia and New Zealand, 1870–1990' in Vaughan (ed.), *New history of Ireland*, vol. V, pp. 661–81 and vol. VI, pp. 703–24.

and alienation of immigrant life but in the pre-migration culture of Ireland itself. The beliefs and practices of rural Catholics, he argued, predisposed them to regard emigration in negative terms. Miller does not equate emigration with exile, observing merely that the Irish poor were predisposed to see it that way. In a related but distinct argument, he has also demonstrated how Irish commercial farmers, who benefited from mass emigration, and often initiated the process by evicting sub-tenants and consolidating their holdings, invoked the exile theme expediently, blaming emigration on British misrule as a way of masking their own self-interested actions. Miller's critics, concentrating their animus on the first argument and ignoring the second, have questioned his characterisation of Irish rural culture as communalist rather than individualist, fatalistic rather than forward-looking, passive rather than active. They have done so largely by investigating whether a pre-migrant Catholic rural culture of any kind hindered the adaptation and progress of the Irish overseas.[29]

Led by Donald Harman Akenson, these historians have pursued a sustained critique of Miller's conception of Irish culture and the putative disabilities bequeathed to the Irish abroad. They have focused their inquiries on the Irish in Canada, South Africa, Australia, New Zealand and the American West. In this global context, they have found that Irish Catholic migrants did just as well on average as Irish Protestants. But their alternative portrait of Irish emigrants as entrepreneurs rather than exiles is more persuasive for Canada, Australia and the American West than for the north-eastern United States or Britain, where the vast majority of Irish immigrants settled. To overturn the Miller thesis, historians would need to analyse the mainly urban and industrial settings in the United States that he examined in such depth. Nonetheless, by demonstrating the upward social mobility of Irish emigrants in other settings, they have called into question Miller's portrait of Irish culture and, implicitly at least, his portrait of Irish America. By studying the Irish globally, they have moved the field beyond the old 'gloom and doom' approach. A new synthesis of Irish-American history along these lines, however, has yet to be written.[30]

29 Miller, *Emigrants and exiles*, especially pp. 345–492; K. Miller with B. Boling and D.N. Doyle, 'Emigrants and exiles: Irish cultures and Irish emigration to North America, 1790–1922', *Irish Historical Studies*, 22 (1980–1), 97–125.

30 D.H. Akenson, 'An agnostic view of the historiography of the Irish-Americans', *Labour/ Le Travail*, 14 (Fall 1984), 123–8, 152–8; Akenson, *Irish diaspora*, pp. 237–42; Doyle, 'Remaking of Irish-America, 1845–80', pp. 732–3; R.A. Burchell, *The San Francisco Irish, 1848–1880* (Manchester: Manchester University Press, 1979); O'Farrell, 'Irish in Australia and New Zealand, 1791–1870', p. 664; O'Farrell, 'Irish in Australia and New Zealand, 1870–1990', pp. 704–5; Campbell, *Ireland's new worlds*, pp. 3–36, 65–103, 132–85.

This new global approach is especially relevant when considering the involvement of the overseas Irish in the political affairs of their homeland. Historians use the term 'ethnic nationalism' to describe activity of this kind. Irish immigrants in Britain, North America and Australia were active in the major varieties of nationalism – constitutional, physical force republican and socially radical. Within each country, support for different types of Irish nationalism varied by class, gender and time of arrival. There was also significant variation by country, with republican and anti-imperial nationalism finding a natural home in the United States, whereas the strong imperial connections of Australia and New Zealand favoured moderate constitutionalism. Leading political figures such as Charles Stewart Parnell and Michael Davitt made extensive tours of the United States. The American Irish orchestrated the escape of Irish political prisoners from Australia to the United States and sent money, arms and munitions to support insurrection in Ireland. Revolutionaries and journalists in New York City, London and Dublin engaged in a sustained transnational dialogue over Ireland's future.[31]

In an apparent paradox, ethnic nationalism of this kind could serve as a powerful force for assimilation. The origins of Irish-American nationalism, as Thomas N. Brown first argued half a century ago, lay not so much in direct concerns with Ireland as in the alienation and poverty of the immigrant experience in the urban United States. Interestingly, his thesis is the opposite of Miller's, who looked for the origins of the exile motif in Ireland's pre-migration culture. Irish-American nationalists fought for Irish freedom, but they also fought, in more direct and concrete terms, for acceptance and respectability in their adopted countries. An independent Ireland, they believed, would raise their status internationally and the act of political organising would demonstrate their fitness for citizenship. Given that physical force extremism was an unlikely path to assimilation, Brown's thesis applied mainly to constitutional nationalists. And Eric Foner provided an important corrective by pointing out that most Irish-Americans were working class, rather than middle-class or lower-middle-class aspirants to bourgeois respectability. The supporters of Patrick Ford and Henry George in the 1880s belonged to an American 'oppositional working-class culture' as well as supporting Irish freedom. Yet Foner's radical nationalism, like Brown's middle-class version,

---

31 J. Belchem, 'Nationalism, republicanism and exile: Irish emigrants and the revolutions of 1848', *Past and Present*, 146 (1995), 103–35; Walsh, ' "A fanatic heart" '; B. Nelson, *Irish nationalists and the making of the Irish race* (Princeton: Princeton University Press, 2012); N. Whelehan, *The dynamiters: Irish nationalism and political violence in the wider world, 1867–1900* (Cambridge: Cambridge University Press, 2012).

was directed mainly towards American ends. David Brundage has recently integrated these and other debates into the first comprehensive history of Irish-American nationalism as a whole.[32]

Conclusion

Despite their continued involvement in Irish affairs, the overseas Irish sustained remarkably low rates of return migration. Distance and cost made return from Australia and New Zealand all but impossible for most, but the rate of return from the United States was also strikingly low. Systematic studies have not yet been conducted, but the American Irish vied with Jewish immigrants in having the lowest return migration at the turn of the twentieth century. By contrast, more than half of all Italian and east European immigrants at this time came to the United States as 'birds of passage', who worked for three to five years before returning to their homelands. Well under 10 per cent of the Irish, by contrast, returned to Ireland. In this respect, the Irish case was highly distinctive, resembling the Jewish case but differing from most other European migrations of this period. Irish emigrants sent millions of dollars to their families in Ireland, but they saw nothing to go back to for themselves. Emigrants who left Ireland for overseas destinations in the second half of the nineteenth century – unlike the twentieth – left the country for good. In this respect, as in the extraordinarily high rate of departure and the extraordinarily high number of female emigrants, Irish emigration in the second half of the nineteenth century was highly distinctive. And the departure of so many people in so short a period of time was a defining feature of modern Irish history.[33]

---

32 T.N. Brown, *Irish-American nationalism, 1870–1890* (Philadelphia: Lippincott, 1966); E. Foner, 'Class, ethnicity, and radicalism in the Gilded Age' in E. Foner, *Politics and ideology in the age of the Civil War* (Oxford: Oxford University Press, 1980), pp. 194–5; D. Brundage, *Irish nationalists in America: the politics of exile, 1798–1998* (Oxford: Oxford University Press, 2016).

33 Akenson, *Ireland, Sweden and the great European migration*, pp. 241–2.

26

Post-Famine Politics, 1850–1879

DOUGLAS KANTER

Introduction

'There seems to me no more hope for the Irish cause than for the corpse on the dissecting table.'[1] Thus the Young Ireland activist turned tenant right advocate Charles Gavan Duffy bid his country a bitter farewell on the pages of the *Nation* in the summer of 1855. Having been disappointed in his attempt to revive Irish popular politics in the aftermath of the Great Famine, Duffy sailed for Australia later the same year, following in the wake of some 2 million men, women and children who had left Ireland in the preceding decade. But his corporeal metaphor continued to resonate long after he had departed, and for generations of nationalists it captured what they perceived to be the moribund state of post-Famine politics in contrast to what obtained elsewhere. On the continent, the third quarter of the nineteenth century was distinguished by the triumph of nationalism, as the Italian *Risorgimento*, German unification and the Austro-Hungarian *Ausgleich* redrew the geopolitical map and transformed international politics. In Ireland, however, the collapse of the agitation for the repeal of the Act of Union in 1848 was followed by a period of relative quiescence, and a sustained nationalist campaign enjoying broad popular support re-emerged only with the advent of the home rule movement in the 1870s. Duffy's successor as proprietor of the *Nation*, A.M. Sullivan, conceded the unfavourable comparison in 1877, admitting in a survey of recent Irish history that, when juxtaposed 'with the development of nations in the long enjoyment of healthy life, the progress of Ireland – material and intellectual, social, industrial, educational and political – may be found sadly slow, and in some respects cruelly retarded'.[2]

---

1 *Nation*, 18 Aug. 1855.
2 A.M. Sullivan, *New Ireland*, 2 vols. (London: Sampson Low, Marston, Searle, and Rivington, 1877), vol. II, p. 406.

Though such remarks reveal the frustrations of mid-century nationalists, they under-rate the resilience of Irish politics after the Great Famine. The dissolution of the repeal movement and the trauma of the Great Famine encouraged moderate nationalists and Irish liberals to seek a redress of grievances within the Union. As post-Famine social and economic change enhanced the status of substantial tenant farmers and the Catholic Church, while further eroding the position of cottiers and landless labourers, popular politicians sought legislation calculated to satisfy the needs and aspirations of these ascending interest groups. During the 1850s and 1860s, consequently, the demand for self-government ceded its earlier primacy to a programme of sectional reform dominated by concerns related to land and religion. When the British response proved to be unsatisfactory, the option of a revivified nationalist campaign became increasingly attractive. But the fragmentation of popular politics resulting from the failure of sectional reform made mobilisation in support of self-government difficult to achieve. Isaac Butt finally succeeded in effecting a *rapprochement* between liberals and nationalists in the 1870s, by wedding interest group politics to the demand for home rule. In so doing, he returned Ireland's constitutional status to the forefront of politics for the first time since the era of O'Connell.

The Structure of Post-Famine Politics

The character of the electorate, the existence of a robust public sphere and the nature of political identity shaped post-Famine political activity. The period opened with a major reform of the franchise, the Parliamentary Voters (Ireland) Act of 1850, which did much to give post-Famine politics its distinctive complexion. The measure addressed the hitherto much-abused registration process and lowered the basic franchise qualification, admitting within the pale of the constitution occupiers of property valued at £8 in boroughs and £12 in counties. It nearly quadrupled the Irish electorate, which increased from some 45,000 to over 163,000 voters.[3] The chief beneficiaries of the act were tenant farmers occupying at least 30 acres of land, who profited at the expense of both their social inferiors and superiors. On the one hand, the £12 county franchise excluded the rural proletariat of smallholders and agricultural labourers, which was already embarked on an irreversible demographic decline. On the other hand, landowners were too few in number to

3 K.T. Hoppen, *Elections, politics, and society in Ireland, 1832–1885* (Oxford: Clarendon Press, 1984), pp. 17–18.

counter-balance the numerical preponderance of the tenant farmers, who comprised over three-quarters of the county electorate by the late 1860s.[4] The Parliamentary Voters Act had less impact on borough constituencies, where the electorate remained heterogeneous and small. The Irish Reform Act of 1868, which lowered the borough occupation franchise to 'over £4' and introduced a borough lodger franchise, only partially remedied these short-comings. In Ulster – where the borough electorate expanded by 131 per cent, and many working men were enfranchised – the changes wrought by the measure were substantial.[5] But its impact was less dramatic in the south and west, where the number of borough voters increased by only 19 per cent.[6]

In the counties, the new electors constituted a potentially cohesive and formidable voting bloc; but they found their freedom of action circumscribed in practice. A sustained period of agricultural prosperity, interrupted only by the depression of 1859–64, enlarged the rent-rolls of Irish landlords and increased their political confidence. The Catholic Church experienced a parallel efflorescence, as the 'devotional revolution' overseen by Paul Cullen, archbishop successively of Armagh (1849–52) and of Dublin (1852–78), made Irish Catholicism not only more Roman, but also more assertive. Though Cullen took a dim view of clerical electioneering, many priests – including the archbishop himself – sought to translate their spiritual authority into political influence. In Ulster, where the Presbyterian Church experienced an analogous revival, ministers held comparable sway. Voters also contended with pressure from below, as the unfranchised had recourse to collective action to convey their political opinions. Local social, economic and political relationships constrained voter choice at every stage of the election process, until the introduction of the secret ballot in 1872 provided some relief.

Despite the pressure and influence that was often brought to bear, Ireland's resilient public sphere ensured that politics continued to possess ideological and partisan dimensions. Voluntary associations played a significant role in popular politics, with nationalists, liberals and conservatives all contriving to mobilise public opinion for their own purposes. Though the reservoirs of support for many post-Famine political organisations were shallow, and their lifespans frequently brief, they provided outlets for political activism and expression throughout the period, collectively serving as vehicles for speech-making, fund-raising, petitioning, parading and banqueting, and for

---

4 Ibid., p. 105.
5 G.R. Hall, *Ulster liberalism, 1778–1876* (Dublin: Four Courts Press, 2011), pp. 211–12.
6 Adapted from B.M. Walker, 'The Irish electorate, 1868–1915', *Irish Historical Studies*, 18 (1973), 372–3.

the orchestration of public meetings. The most prominent political societies conceived of politics in national – and not necessarily in nationalist – terms. Independent clubs, conservative societies and liberal associations, organised on a local basis for electioneering purposes, mediated between provincial preoccupations and national priorities. And many organisations that eschewed formal political commitments, such as mechanics' institutes, trade associations, literary clubs and Catholic young men's societies, also fostered politicisation.

The press was the most vibrant component of the post-Famine public sphere. Increasing rates of literacy, urbanisation and improvements in transportation and communication throughout the period – as well as the repeal of advertising, stamp and paper duties between 1853 and 1861 – fuelled the growth of the newspaper industry. Politics was central to the post-Famine press. Technological innovation made it possible for papers to provide extensive and increasingly timely coverage of parliamentary proceedings, the activities of Irish pressure groups, foreign events and imperial affairs. Newspaper editors embraced partisan affiliations, conveying their views in leaders and, in the case of a minority, organising political campaigns or serving as members of parliament. Newspapers fostered political debate, but they also performed an integrative function. The contemporary editorial practice of excerpting and commenting upon material published in other press outlets connected Ireland's metropolitan and provincial newspapers to each other, as well as to the press in Britain, the empire, America and Europe. Historians of Irish journalism, following Benedict Anderson, have often credited the mid-century press with helping to create an 'imagined political community'.[7] This was certainly the case; but the historiographical inclination to identify this community with nationalism requires qualification, as the diversity of the press ensured that the polity was defined differently depending on the political sympathies of editors and readers. Some newspapers adopted an expansive perspective, extending to the United Kingdom and the British Empire; others embraced a more exclusive outlook, limited primarily to Ireland.

The multiplicity of political views expressed in the press points to the multifarious nature of political identity after the Famine. Ireland's parliamentary representation was assimilated to the British party system for most of this period, as third parties identifying themselves with specifically Irish concerns secured a plurality or majority of seats at only the first and last

---

7 See M.-L. Legg, *Newspapers and nationalism: the Irish provincial press, 1850–1892* (Dublin: Four Courts Press, 1999), p. 73.

of the six general elections held between 1852 and 1874 (Table 23). Political loyalties were rooted in religious affiliation and socio-economic position. The Conservative Party was closely identified with the Church of Ireland and the landed elite, though conservatives also sought to attract Catholic support. The evangelical inflection of the party appealed to some Ulster Presbyterians, which helped to make the north of Ireland a Conservative stronghold. The Liberal Party was more heterogeneous, sheltering under its big tent not only Whiggish Anglican aristocrats, but also landed and middle-class Catholics, Presbyterian ministers, merchants, manufacturers, professionals and farmers. By emphasising tenant right and Catholic religious grievances, the Independent Irish Party briefly became 'the party of the Catholic farmer and small townsman' in the 1850s.[8] Two decades later, the Home Rule Party also captured votes by championing the interests of the Catholic tenant farmers and their church.

Yet while religion and class exerted a powerful influence on political identity, birth and confessional allegiance were not all-defining. On the contrary, boundaries were permeable, and ideologies overlapped. Into the 1870s, moderate nationalists shared with their conservative and liberal counterparts a deferential attitude to two of the main symbols of the Anglo-Irish connection: the monarchy and the viceroyalty.[9] Despite much reflexive nationalist anti-imperialism, support for empire remained compatible with the tenets of moderate nationalism for most of the period.[10] Post-Famine nationalists inherited from O'Connell a set of classical liberal values, including freedom of expression, assembly and the press, liberty of conscience, and equality of opportunity, that were also embraced by Irish liberals. Catholic liberals were in broad agreement with nationalists on the desirability of 'greening' Irish government. Their avidity for patronage, dismissed by contemporary nationalists as a symptom of 'Castle Catholic' venality, can be regarded more reasonably as an attempt to secure Catholic civil and religious rights, and to improve Catholic prospects by exploiting Britain's imperial network.[11] Such intersections made moderate nationalism and Irish liberalism broadly compatible, even if the ultimate aim of nationalists – some form of political

8 S.R. Knowlton, *Popular politics and the Irish Catholic Church: the rise and fall of the Independent Irish Party, 1850–1859* (New York: Garland, 1991), p. 107.

9 J.H. Murphy, *Abject loyalty: nationalism and monarchy in Ireland during the reign of Queen Victoria* (Washington, DC: Catholic University of America Press, 2001), chapters 4–5.

10 P.A. Townend, 'Between two worlds: Irish nationalists and imperial crisis, 1878–1880', *Past and Present*, 194 (2007), 172.

11 R.A. Keogh, ' "Nothing is so bad for the Irish as Ireland alone": William Keogh and Catholic loyalty', *Irish Historical Studies*, 38 (2012–13), 234.

Table 23. *Party affiliation of MPs returned for Irish constituencies, 1852–74.*

Election year	Conservative	Liberal	Independent	Home Rule
1852	41	16	48	–
1857	47	45	13	–
1859	55	43	7	–
1865	47	47	11	–
1868	39	66	–	–
1874	33	10	–	60

Note: Adapted from A. Shields, *The Irish Conservative Party, 1852–1868: land, politics and religion* (Dublin: Irish Academic Press, 2007), p. 15; B.M. Walker (ed.), *Parliamentary election results in Ireland, 1801–1922* (Dublin: Royal Irish Academy, 1978), p. 193.

autonomy – was at odds with that of liberals, who saw greater possibility for the satisfaction of Irish needs and desires within the United Kingdom. Even here, however, the differences were rarely static or unchanging. In the 1850s moderate nationalists shelved the demand for the repeal of the Act of Union, while in the 1870s liberal support for local self-government shaded into milk-and-water varieties of home rule. There were also affinities between conservatism and nationalism. Some Protestant conservatives retained a romantic sense of Irish national identity, and regarded the Union not as a sacrosanct constitutional settlement but as a contract – subject to renegotiation if Britain violated its terms. Some nationalists expressed scepticism of free trade, laissez-faire and non-denominational education, providing other areas of potential agreement. In sum, post-Famine political identities were fluid, relational and contextual, rather than rigid and fixed. The political developments outlined in the remainder of this chapter, consequently, were contingent rather than foreordained, and appeared as such to contemporaries.

Sectional Politics and Independent Opposition, 1850–1859

Between 1850 and 1855, popular politics was dominated by sectional concerns related to land and religion. In an attempt to win concessions on these issues, moderate nationalists declined to pursue repeal, and adopted a policy of independent opposition to any government that was not amenable to reform in the interests of the tenant farmers and the Catholic Church. A number of developments encouraged the eclipse of an explicitly nationalist programme in these years. With O'Connell dead and Young Ireland scattered around the

English-speaking world, the leadership necessary for a revival of agitation did not exist. The abandonment of repeal also reflected a tacit recognition, forced upon nationalists by the vigour with which successive governments had defended the Union in the 1840s, that the British ruling class would not renegotiate its terms. Equally, the decision of popular politicians to set a social and economic agenda stemmed from the trauma of the Famine, which left nationalists with 'unresolvable doubts about the capacity of Ireland to fend for itself', and fostered a sense of 'vulnerability' in 'even the more prosperous farming families'.[12] Under these circumstances, a reordering of political priorities had much to recommend it.

Initial efforts to reorient popular politics centred on the reform of the laws relating to land tenure. In August 1850, a conference in Dublin on tenant right brought together liberals and moderate nationalists from all four provinces, in order to provide a voice for a campaign that had gathered momentum at grass-roots level as the Famine exposed the insecurity of Irish farmers. Its chief organisers included Gavan Duffy, the most distinguished nationalist of the 1840s to remain active in Irish politics, and James McKnight, Presbyterian editor of the liberal *Banner of Ulster*, whose 'object' was 'to have *the soil of Ireland for the Irish*'.[13] The conference established the Irish Tenant League and defined its ends, which came to be known as the three Fs – 'fair rents', set by independent arbitration; 'free sale' of the outgoing tenant's interest in his farm; and 'fixity of tenure'. Recognising that British politicians were unlikely willingly to approve so radical an infringement of property rights, proponents of the League hoped to advance their demands by establishing an Irish party in parliament, composed of MPs pledged to 'withhold all support from any cabinet' that did not endorse its programme.[14]

A denominational agenda soon imposed itself upon this platform. Nearly two weeks after the League was founded, a very different meeting began at Thurles, where Cullen convened the Catholic hierarchy in synod, secured a public condemnation of the state's non-denominational Queen's Colleges, and obtained approval for the foundation of a Catholic University. The synod's decisions provided an unwelcome confirmation to Lord John Russell's Liberal government that the archbishop's appointment signalled the

---

12 R.V. Comerford, 'Churchmen, tenants, and independent opposition, 1850–56' in W.E. Vaughan (ed.), *A new history of Ireland*, vol. v: *Ireland under the Union, I, 1801–70* (Oxford: Oxford University Press, 1989), p. 399; P. Gray, 'Famine and land, 1845–80' in A. Jackson (ed.), *The Oxford handbook of modern Irish history* (Oxford: Oxford University Press, 2014), p. 555.

13 J. McKnight to C.G. Duffy, 13 May 1850, Gavan Duffy papers, MS 7404/4, National Library of Ireland.

14 *Freeman's Journal*, 10 Aug. 1850.

beginnings of an era of ultramontane assertiveness. And more was to come. At the end of September, Rome announced the restoration of the Catholic hierarchy in England. Though primarily a response to the pastoral needs of Irish Catholics who had migrated to England during the Famine, news of the decision sparked an anti-Catholic furore in Britain.

When parliament assembled in 1851, Russell introduced legislation forbidding the assumption of territorial titles by members of the Catholic hierarchy throughout the United Kingdom. The threat to freedom of religion prompted a mass demonstration of Irish Catholic opinion against the measure, and propelled an 'Irish Brigade' of Catholic Liberal MPs into opposition to the government. The leaders of the Brigade, G.H. Moore, William Keogh and John Sadleir, were powerless to prevent the passage of the Ecclesiastical Titles Act, but they were instrumental in launching a Catholic Defence Association, with the support of Cullen and other members of the Catholic hierarchy, at an aggregate meeting in August. Those assembled agreed to pursue the repeal of the odious Titles Act, as well as the achievement of religious equality, by supporting the efforts of 'an independent party' of Catholic MPs.[15] The Tenant League and the Brigade entered into an uneasy alliance before the end of the summer, coalescing around a policy of independent opposition with the aim of securing land reform and Catholic civil rights. It was a set of issues that was well calculated to appeal to those predominantly Catholic tenant farmers that the Parliamentary Voters Act of 1850 had recently enfranchised.

These popular politicians demonstrated the disruptive potential of independent opposition in 1852. Though the Russell administration refrained from pursuing prosecutions under the Ecclesiastical Titles Act, the prime minister was unrepentant when parliament reconvened in February. The Brigade helped to oust the government before the month had ended, with eleven Irish Catholic liberals providing the opposition's margin of victory in the division that sealed the ministry's fate.[16] A caretaker Conservative administration, formed by Lord Derby after the Liberal government's resignation, proved scarcely more acceptable to Irish Catholic opinion by sending mixed signals on land reform and flirting with anti-Catholicism in anticipation of a July general election. Catholic voters in the south and west of Ireland registered their disillusionment with both British parties by returning forty-eight proponents of parliamentary independence when the poll was called. Most

---

15 Quoted in E. Larkin, *The making of the Roman Catholic Church in Ireland, 1850–1860* (Chapel Hill: University of North Carolina Press, 1980), p. 100.

16 *Freeman's Journal*, 23 Feb. 1852.

of these MPs subsequently affiliated to the emerging Independent Irish Party (IIP), pledging to oppose any ministry that did not support tenant right and the repeal of all Catholic disabilities. Led by Duffy, Moore, Keogh, Sadleir and the editor of the *Tablet*, Frederick Lucas, the IIP played a crucial role in overthrowing the Derby administration at the end of the year, dividing against the government's budget in an impressive display of united action after the prime minister reaffirmed his hostility to tenant right.

The defeat of the Derby ministry was a signal but Pyrrhic victory for the independent opposition, as over the next three years the popular coalition that supported the IIP dissolved into its constituent parts. The disintegration of the party was precipitated by a dispute over the acceptance of government patronage, the refusal of which was fundamental to the policy of independent opposition. With Liberal and Conservative administrations having been ousted in quick succession, the Peelite parliamentary faction, led by Lord Aberdeen, formed a coalition government with Liberal support at the end of the year. The most prominent Peelites had distinguished themselves by their hostility to the Ecclesiastical Titles Act, and they were determined to adopt a more eirenic Irish policy. This included the offer of subordinate government offices to prominent Irish Catholics at the ministry's formation; but when Keogh and Sadleir accepted positions in the administration, it precipitated a schism in the IIP. The less tractable proponents of independent opposition, led by Duffy and Lucas, accused them of violating their pledges, condemned them in parliament and the press, and contested their returns in the by-elections necessitated by their acceptance of office. Though the break between nationalists and liberals was not a clean one, the cleavage was symptomatic of unresolved tensions within the party.

The eruption of internecine warfare sapped much of the independent opposition's extra-parliamentary support, alienating both Presbyterian liberals and Cullen. Presbyterian reformers were uncomfortable with the increasingly sectarian drift of Catholic politics. 'Protestants', McKnight warned Duffy in 1851, 'are universally enraged at the style in which their faith is habitually spoken of.'[17] Significantly, none of the independent opposition MPs elected in 1852 were returned by constituencies in Ulster, where success at the polls depended upon cooperation between Presbyterians and Catholics. The row over patronage proved to be the final straw for McKnight, who dissociated himself from the IIP in 1853. Presbyterian liberalism and moderate

17 J. McKnight to C.G. Duffy, 5 Sept. 1851, Gavan Duffy papers, MS 7404/7, NLI.

nationalism were both damaged by the collapse of their alliance. In the view of some frustrated northern reformers, Presbyterian liberals had lapsed into a state of 'hopeless lethargy' and 'voluntary degradation' by the end of the decade.[18] The IIP, in turn, received little support from Ulster's small coterie of Liberal MPs, who 'largely remained aloof' from the independent opposition, preferring closer association with British liberals instead.[19]

The quarrel over patronage also encouraged Cullen's growing reservations with the IIP. The archbishop's priorities were neither nationalist nor liberal; they were Roman. Cullen was sceptical of the Tenant League – 'I never did and never will join them', he assured a close confidant – and unenthusiastic about independent opposition, which he regarded as a *pis aller*.[20] Concerned that the fractiousness of popular politics would undermine the spiritual authority of the clergy, the archbishop secured decrees at the Synod of Dublin in 1854 whose purpose was to restrain clerical politicking. Without the support of the Catholic Church, the IIP was doomed; but Duffy and Lucas hastened the party's decline by mounting a public protest against the synod's decision, and by launching an inevitably unsuccessful appeal to Rome at the end of the year. Their behaviour confirmed Cullen's suspicions of the IIP's incipient 'Mazzinianism', and impelled the archbishop towards the pragmatic support for British liberalism that was to characterise his mature politics.[21] The failed appeal to Rome proved deeply divisive within the party itself, driving many independent oppositionists back into the Liberal fold. By the end of 1855, Lucas had died, a demoralised Duffy had emigrated to Australia, and the IIP was in disarray.

Though the party endured, it never recovered its early momentum. Rising prosperity made the reform of land law less urgent in the later 1850s, and the tenant right agitation that had served as the initial stimulus for independent opposition temporarily lapsed. The Catholic Church demonstrated increased confidence in articulating its grievances as Cullen remade the hierarchy with Roman assistance; but the archbishop held aloof from the IIP,

18 Quoted in A.R. Holmes, 'Covenanter politics: evangelicalism, political liberalism and Ulster Presbyterians, 1798–1914', *English Historical Review*, 125 (2010), 360.

19 J. Bew, *The glory of being Britons: civic unionism in nineteenth-century Belfast* (Dublin: Irish Academic Press, 2009), p. 171.

20 P. Cullen to T. Kirby, 9 Dec. 1853, New Kirby papers, carton i, folder iii, no. 114, Irish College Rome.

21 C. Barr, 'Giuseppe Mazzini and Irish nationalism, 1845–70' in C.A. Bayly and E.F. Biagini (eds.), *Giuseppe Mazzini and the globalisation of democratic nationalism, 1830–1920* (Oxford: Oxford University Press, 2008), p. 139.

which he continued to regard as a 'radical and violent party'.[22] Under Lord Palmerston, prime minister in 1855–8 and 1859–65, British liberals adopted a policy of *quieta non movere* in respect of Ireland. Palmerston's lack of enthusiasm for reform, and Britain's preoccupation with foreign and imperial affairs, pushed Irish policy down the parliamentary agenda during his first premiership. Cumulatively, these developments took a heavy toll on party morale. In 1858, the O'Donoghue of the Glens, upon whom popular hopes for a revival of the IIP rested, privately wrote its epitaph: 'my experience of the House of Commons, convinces me that *there*, there exists no Irish party'.[23] The IIP split in 1859, after which its members ceased to coordinate their activities in any consistent manner. Yet the failure of British politicians to allay Irish sectional concerns ensured that the impotence of independent opposition after 1855 reflected a failure of leadership and organisation, rather than popular satisfaction with British government.

Alternatives to Independent Opposition, 1855–1865

The decline of the IIP provided scope for the emergence of alternatives to independent opposition. This resulted in an exceptionally fragmented political culture, as conservatives, liberals and nationalists all sought to occupy the space vacated by the party. Grievance politics remained ascendant, but demands for self-government resurfaced. In electoral and parliamentary terms, the second half of the 1850s was distinguished by the resurgence of the Irish Conservative Party. Economic and social developments underpinned the party's impressive recovery in these years, as growing landlord confidence in the south and evangelical revival in Ulster strengthened core Conservative constituencies. The Conservative renaissance owed much to superior political organisation – a Central Conservative Society served as the party machine from 1853 – and something to the narrow franchise, which ensured that landowners continued to exercise disproportionate influence.

Conservative efflorescence also resulted from the willingness of the party's elite to support sectional reform. As early as 1851, the leading British Conservative, Benjamin Disraeli, looked forward to 'an Irish alliance of a very comprehensive character', to be achieved by co-opting Irish Catholics

---

22 P. Cullen to Sir J. Acton, 21 Nov. 1857, Acton papers, Add. MS 8119(2), c326, Cambridge University Library.
23 D. O'Donoghue to W.S. O'Brien, 30 April 1858, Smith O'Brien papers, MS 446/3030, NLI.

and by breaking the 'accidental' bond 'between Toryism and Orangeism'.[24] Prominent Irish conservatives were inclined to proceed more cautiously, but they were hardly the atavistic reactionaries that nationalists believed them to be. Lord Naas, who served three terms as Irish chief secretary in the minority Conservative governments of 1852, 1858–9 and 1866–8, proved to be particularly formidable, displaying considerable gifts as 'a shrewd party manager … an efficient administrator', and 'an excellent electoral strategist'.[25] But he was not alone in favouring prudential reform. Joseph Napier introduced legislation during Derby's 1852 ministry providing compensation to outgoing tenants for improvements made to their holdings, while Sir James Emerson Tennent served as a channel for negotiations between Disraeli and Gavan Duffy in 1853, helping to inaugurate more than a decade of intermittent cooperation between the Conservative Party and the independent opposition.

Conservative efforts to cultivate Irish Catholic opinion enjoyed limited success in the early 1850s; but as the IIP disintegrated they bore fruit. After tentative approaches in 1855, the Conservative Party reached out to a section of the independent opposition at the general election of 1857. When Palmerston's resignation the following year led to Derby's return as prime minister, Conservative leaders presented a modest reform programme intended to appeal to Irish Catholic interests. The administration increased the number of Catholic army chaplains, raised their pay and promised to consider granting a royal charter to the Catholic University. Ministers also articulated guarded support for legislation providing compensation for tenant improvements, and sought to foster economic development in western Ireland by offering a subsidy to the Galway Company for steamship services to North America. In foreign affairs, the government's Austrian sympathies were regarded favourably by Irish Catholics, at a moment when the resurgence of Italian nationalism threatened the temporal power of the pope. Such manoeuvres had an obvious electoral intent – the Conservatives were running 'a cheap campaign for the Catholic vote' ahead of the 1859 general election.[26] But they also reflected the 'commitment' of prominent Irish conservatives 'to economic modernisation … coupled with a vision of "social harmony"'.[27]

---

24 J. Vincent (ed.), *Disraeli, Derby and the Conservative Party: journals and memoirs of Edward Henry, Lord Stanley, 1849–1869* (Hassocks: Harvester Press, 1978), p. 40.

25 Shields, *Irish Conservative Party*, p. 19.

26 K.T. Hoppen, 'Tories, Catholics, and the general election of 1859', *Historical Journal*, 13 (1970), 53.

27 Bew, *Glory of being Britons*, p. 198.

Conservative meliorism secured Catholic support at the polls in 1859, and encouraged a section of the IIP to cooperate with the Conservative Party into the mid-1860s. But the dalliance with Catholic opinion also strained relations between party leaders and the conservative grass roots. Irish conservative opinion-makers were unenthusiastic about Derby's position on Italy, and suspicious of Disraeli's flirtation with Catholicism. Over the next six years, the conservative press looked to Palmerston for a defence of property rights and Anglican ascendancy. In Ulster, some members of the Orange Order went further, envisaging the establishment 'of a new "Protestant" party' under Palmerston's leadership.[28] Though senior Irish conservatives had no appetite for such a political realignment, they felt increasingly isolated. One symptom of their insecurity was a renewed emphasis on the Union as 'a treaty and a contract, any aspect of which (if dishonoured) might bring the voiding of the whole'.[29]

The collapse of the IIP also facilitated Liberal electoral success. The reluctance of British Liberals to redress Catholic grievances, however, ensured that Irish liberalism remained fractious. During the second Palmerston administration (1859–65), new disagreements inflamed existing animosities. The government's support for the Italian *Risorgimento*, welcomed by Irish Protestant liberals, placed ministers at odds with the leaders of Catholic opinion, who encouraged financial and military support for the beleaguered papacy in 1859–60. Palmerston's response to ultramontane activism was the appointment of an irascible evangelical, Sir Robert Peel, third baronet, to the post of chief secretary in 1861. Cullen still hoped to secure concessions relating to the church establishment ('a nuisance') and non-denominational education ('a great grievance'), but the government refused to act.[30] The agricultural depression of 1859–64, meanwhile, underscored the insecurity of the tenant farmers, awakening agrarian and fiscal grievances. The administration's response to continued pressure for land reform, the Cardwell-Deasy Land Acts of 1860, failed to allay farmers' anxieties, providing compensation for tenant improvements only when they had the express consent of the landowner, and making 'relations between landlord and tenant a matter of contract'.[31]

---

28 Ibid., p. 213.
29 A. Jackson, *The two Unions: Ireland, Scotland, and the survival of the United Kingdom, 1707–2007* (Oxford: Oxford University Press, 2012), p. 294.
30 P. Cullen to Sir J. Acton, 16 May 1863, 5 June 1863, Acton papers, Add. MS 8119(2), c328, c329, Cambridge University Library.
31 *Hansard*, 3rd ser., CLVIII, 1346 (15 May 1860).

The administration also caused grave offence by refusing to acknowledge the severity of the depression until 1863.

Dissatisfaction with Palmerston and Peel induced many Catholic liberals to adopt an attitude of 'parliamentary independence' from the government.[32] Only nine of the thirty-five Irish Catholics who sat and voted in the parliament of 1859–65 proved reliable supporters of the Liberal Party.[33] Hostility to the administration impelled a few Liberal MPs, including the most prominent Irish Catholic politician of the era, William Monsell, into a position 'virtually indistinguishable' from independent opposition.[34] But Palmerston was unmoved, as the divisions amongst Irish liberals ensured that they lacked the coherence necessary to function as a consistently effective pressure group. In 1864, Cullen and the quondam Young Irelander John Blake Dillon belatedly sought to provide a focus for Irish liberalism by establishing the National Association with the goal of securing compensation for tenant improvements, disestablishing the Church of Ireland and obtaining state support for denominational education.

Cullen's initiative was motivated in large part by the re-emergence of more assertive forms of Irish nationalism, which attracted renewed public interest as demands for sectional reform went unmet. In 1858 Dr Robert Cane, a Young Ireland veteran, garnered favourable coverage in the popular press when he proposed a nationalist campaign along O'Connellite lines, calling for 'home rule' in his journal, *The Celt*.[35] Moderate nationalism was certainly capable of generating substantial grass-roots enthusiasm: a National Petition Committee, organised in 1860 to circulate a petition requesting a plebiscite on the Union, collected over 423,000 signatures within a year. Yet attempts to establish a more permanent nationalist association faltered. When an Irish National League was finally launched in 1864, it struggled to enrol members.

As moderate nationalism stalled, advanced nationalism emerged briefly as the more dynamic force in Irish politics. Such a development could not have been anticipated in the early 1850s, when Irish separatism was in disarray. An Irish Democratic Association, which drew inspiration from the radical wing of Young Ireland associated with the exiled John Mitchel, flourished briefly

---

32 E. Larkin, *The consolidation of the Roman Catholic Church in Ireland, 1860–1870* (Chapel Hill: University of North Carolina Press, 1987), pp. 343–4.

33 D.T. Horgan, 'The Irish Catholic Whigs in parliament, 1847–74', PhD thesis, University of Minnesota, 1975, pp. 67–71, 136–41.

34 M. Potter, *William Monsell of Tervoe, 1812–1894: Catholic unionist, Anglo-Irishman* (Dublin: Irish Academic Press, 2009), p. 111.

35 [R. Cane,] 'Home rule', *The Celt*, 1 (1858), 193.

amongst urban artisans at the beginning of the decade, before being co-opted by tenant right activists. Pockets of revolutionary conspiracy also survived, and in the mid-1850s Britain's unsettled international relations revived separatist hopes. Irish-America proved to be especially fertile ground for advanced nationalism, as expatriate Young Irelanders and refugees from the Famine nurtured a smouldering hatred of British misgovernment, most influentially expressed in Mitchel's *Jail Journal* (1854) and *The last conquest of Ireland (perhaps)* (1861).

Attempts to revitalise Irish separatism culminated in the formation of an oath-bound secret society, established in Dublin at Irish-American instigation, on 17 March 1858. James Stephens, a Kilkenny native of obscure origins who had been 'out' with Young Ireland in 1848, was its organising genius. Formally dedicated to the establishment of an independent Irish republic through the force of arms, Stephens' (initially nameless) society came to be known as the Irish Republican Brotherhood (IRB), and its members were denominated Fenians. Fenianism 'was the decisive proof that a greater Ireland beyond the seas' had emerged as a result of the Famine.[36] Irish-American financial and military support – and, still more, the prospect of Irish-American assistance – proved to be crucial to the IRB's survival and expansion. But Fenianism also flourished because it appealed to the urban working and lower-middle classes in Munster, Leinster and Connacht, where young men of no property found that membership in the IRB met a number of needs. Socially, it provided a sense of belonging and offered recreational opportunities, 'filling the functions of a variety of kinds of association: literary and debating society and sports club'.[37] Politically, Fenianism served as a vehicle for the aspirations of classes that had been poorly served by the Catholic elite after the Famine. Particularly important in this regard was the IRB's newspaper, the *Irish People* (1863–5), which promoted a Mitchelite programme of 'peasant proprietorship, social egalitarianism, working-class self-reliance, [and] independence from ecclesiastical influence in political matters'.[38] The IRB expanded rapidly following the paper's launch, with total membership peaking at perhaps 50,000 in 1865. By this time, the conspiracy seriously alarmed the British government. Acting on intelligence that the Fenians were preparing for rebellion,

---

36 P. Bew, *Ireland: the politics of enmity, 1789–2006* (Oxford: Oxford University Press, 2007), p. 245.
37 R.V. Comerford, 'Fenianism: the scope and limitations of a concept' in F. McGarry and J. McConnell (eds.), *The black hand of republicanism: Fenianism in modern Ireland* (Dublin: Irish Academic Press, 2009), p. 183.
38 M. Ramón, *A provisional dictator: James Stephens and the Fenian movement* (Dublin: UCD Press, 2007), p. 158.

the authorities raided the office of the *Irish People* in September, confiscated its property, and arrested a number of leading conspirators. Though Stephens ultimately escaped to America, the trials of his close associates began in November. In the interim, Palmerston's death raised the prospect of a political realignment.

Gladstone and Ireland: Alliance and Misalliance, 1865–1873

During Palmerston's final years in office, British Liberals began to reassess their party's Irish policy. The Irish agricultural depression, the sour relationship with Irish liberalism, the efflorescence of separatist sentiment, and wider developments in British intellectual life combined to foster a slowly dawning awareness amongst many Liberals that Irish 'difference', rooted in historical experience and cultural distinctiveness, deserved greater recognition.[39] Palmerston had contained these pluralistic impulses while he lived, but his departure from the stage freed liberals to act upon them. In practice, this meant demonstrating a commitment to the redress of those grievances related to land and religion that had underpinned post-Famine popular politics. Early signs of a *rapprochement* between British liberals and their Irish counterparts appeared during the premiership of Palmerston's replacement, the aging Earl (formerly Lord John) Russell. But Russell's administration collapsed after only eight months, to be replaced by a minority Conservative government under Derby (1866–8) and Disraeli (1868). Thus, it was left to Russell's successor as Liberal leader, William Gladstone, to pursue an alliance with Irish liberals and moderate nationalists on the basis of sectional reform.

Gladstone's support for Irish reform was conditioned by a complex amalgam of historicist and relativist tendencies in British thought, his own deeply held religious convictions, and the pressure of political circumstances. Chief amongst the latter was the continued menace of Fenianism. As the most prominent Irish republicans, save Stephens, were convicted and sentenced between December 1865 and February 1866, the separatist movement splintered, impelling rival factions into action. Irish-American Fenians launched abortive invasions of Canada in December and February 1866, while the IRB attempted a rising in Ireland on 5 March 1867. Though the rebellion was

---

39 K.T. Hoppen, 'Gladstone, Salisbury and the end of Irish assimilation' in M.E. Daly and K.T. Hoppen (eds.), *Gladstone: Ireland and beyond* (Dublin: Four Courts Press, 2011), pp. 49–50.

easily suppressed, sporadic Fenian violence continued in its aftermath. Two episodes attracted particular attention. In September 1867, the rescue of two senior Fenians from a police van in Manchester resulted in the death of a police sergeant and the execution, some two months later, of three Fenians involved in the operation – who were soon immortalised by Irish nationalists as the 'Manchester Martyrs'. In December, another rescue attempt, at London's Clerkenwell House of Detention, resulted in mass casualties when an explosion intended to bring down a prison wall levelled adjacent tenement housing. The Russell administration responded to the threat to public order by suspending habeas corpus in 1866, apprehending suspected Fenians, and deploying military reinforcements. Derby and Disraeli followed suit, and by early 1868 some 1,100 Fenians had been arrested.[40]

The spate of Fenian violence did much to determine the timing of Gladstone's engagement with Irish politics. As late as December 1865, he was loath to be seen to move hastily on Irish legislation: 'what I fear is treading prematurely in Irish matters with English public opinion'.[41] By the close of 1867, Irish separatism had sharpened his focus:

> The Irish question which has long been grave is growing *awful*. In my opinion this empire has but one danger. It is the danger expressed by the combination of the three names Ireland, United States and Canada. English policy should set its face two ways like a flint: to support public order, and to make the laws of Ireland such as they should be.[42]

In broad outline, Gladstone borrowed his agenda from Cullen's National Association, which provided him with a bridge to the Catholic hierarchy. Speaking at Southport in December 1867, he emphasised the need to allay Irish concerns related to higher education, land tenure and the church establishment. Gladstone did so in emollient, albeit ambiguous, language, contending that Irish policy 'should be dictated, as a general rule, by that which may appear to be the mature, well-considered, and general sense of the Irish people'.[43] The word was made flesh in March 1868. After Disraeli's government announced an intention to undertake its own Irish reform programme, Gladstone moved resolutions expressing support for the disestablishment of the Church of Ireland. Unable to outbid the leader of the opposition, the

---

40 *Hansard*, 3rd ser., CXC, 1371 (10 March 1868).
41 W. Gladstone to C. Fortescue, [25 Dec.] 1865, Carlingford papers, DD/SH/61/324/1/3, Somerset Record Office.
42 W. Gladstone to C. Fortescue, 11 Dec. 1867, Carlingford papers, DD/SH/61/324/1/10, Somerset Record Office.
43 *The Times*, 20 Dec. 1867.

Conservatives were obliged to defend the Irish church. Gladstone carried his resolutions despite them, rallying the Liberal Party around disestablishment.

Gladstone's endorsement of Irish reform in 1867–8 allied moderate nationalists, Irish liberals and the Catholic hierarchy to British liberalism. In substance, he reconstructed the popular coalition of the early 1850s and united it behind the Liberal Party. The significance of this achievement was evident at the general election of November 1868, which was called by the Disraeli administration after the passage of the Irish Reform Act. In the south and west, advocates of the Liberal alliance swept to victory on a platform of disestablishment and land reform, returning sixty-two Liberal MPs, absorbing the independent opposition and marginalising the Conservatives. In Ulster, Liberal gains were much less substantial, though cooperation between Catholics and Presbyterians helped the party to capture four seats. With the return of sixty-six MPs, Irish liberals registered their largest victory of the post-Famine period. British electors demonstrated similar enthusiasm for Gladstone, who became prime minister at the end of the year.

Liberal electoral success masked the fragility of Gladstone's Irish coalition. Moderate nationalist attitudes to British liberalism remained equivocal; Ulster liberalism was vulnerable to intercommunal tensions, and the support of the Catholic hierarchy was contingent on the provision of assistance to the struggling Catholic University. Had the prime minister's ostensible commitment to govern in conformity with Irish ideas resulted in a redress of those long-standing sectional grievances related to land and religion, his coalition might have survived. But Gladstone expressed himself in characteristically guarded language, and the limitations of his approach soon revealed themselves. The Gladstone ministry's first major legislative initiative – the Irish Church Act of 1869 – was also its greatest success, for on this issue British liberal opinion aligned with Irish popular prepossessions. The measure disestablished and partially disendowed the Church of Ireland, while simultaneously discontinuing the *regium donum* for Presbyterian ministers and the grant to the Catholic seminary at Maynooth. Henceforth, the state was to be secular in Ireland, despite the maintenance of religious establishments in Britain.

The administration's conciliatory policy faltered thereafter, because the liberals proved unable to meet the needs and desires of the tenant farmers and the Catholic hierarchy. In late 1869, a revived Tenant League urged the reform of land law on the basis of 'fixity of tenure at fair rents'.[44] Privately, the prime

44 *Nation*, 2 Oct. 1869.

minister was prepared to go some way to meet this demand, sounding his colleagues on the possibility of legalising Ulster tenant right and extending its practice throughout Ireland. His proposal failed to gain traction in the cabinet. The government's Land Act of 1870 represented an unsatisfactory compromise, which gave customary rights the force of law where they already existed, but offered most tenants only compensation for improvements and 'disturbance' (eviction). The measure also authorised the state to lend money to farmers for land purchase, and while this provision served as an important precedent for future legislation it had only a modest immediate impact.

Following the passage of the Land Act, Gladstone's Irish coalition began to dissolve, as moderate nationalists concluded that cooperation with British liberals had resulted in a misalliance. The government retained the support of Irish liberals and the Catholic Church, because the bishops were determined to sustain the Liberal Party until Gladstone proposed a reform of higher education. On this subject, however, the prime minister's deeply felt dislike of ultramontanism constrained his ability to legislate in a manner satisfactory to the hierarchy: 'it seems to me that in the main we *know* what we ought to give them whether they will take it or not'.[45] Recognising that the bishops might reject what the government was prepared to offer, Gladstone refrained from introducing his university education (Ireland) bill until 1873. In the interim, the eruption of religious controversy strained relations between the Catholic Church and the Liberal Party. The declaration of papal infallibility, sanctioned by the Vatican Council in 1870 with Cullen's crucial support, bolstered British anti-Catholicism and furnished Gladstone with a pretext to delay education reform. Disputes over clerical electioneering in County Galway, as well as Cullen's role in the dismissal of Robert O'Keeffe, a suspended parish priest in Callan, from his positions as a poor law chaplain and a national school manager, were additional sources of friction. The government refrained in these years from pursuing an Irish *Kulturkampf* along continental lines – indeed, ministers repealed the Ecclesiastical Titles Act in 1871 – but the hierarchy's enthusiasm for the Liberal alliance cooled.[46]

When Gladstone finally presented his university education bill in 1873, it was merely the last in a series of disappointments so far as the hierarchy was concerned. The prime minister's plan to affiliate various institutions of higher learning, including the Catholic University, to a remodelled Dublin

---

45 W. Gladstone to C. Fortescue, 19 Aug. 1870, Carlingford papers, DD/SH/61/324/1/125(a), Somerset Record Office.

46 C. Barr, 'An Irish dimension to a British *Kulturkampf* ?', *Journal of Ecclesiastical History*, 36 (2005), 494–5.

University failed to meet Cullen's expectation of state-subsidised, denominational higher education. Cullen condemned the bill prior to the division on its second reading, and 'the ailing Irish Catholic alliance with the liberals finally died'.[47] Gladstone's bill went down to defeat, as thirty-seven Irish liberals voted against the measure, helping to deliver the opposition a narrow majority.[48] Only Ulster liberals clung to the alliance with Gladstone, in the hope that the prime minister might amend the Land Act.

The problem of the Liberal Party's narrowing base in Ireland was compounded by the alienation of that Irish conservative support which it had enjoyed during Palmerston's ascendancy. The threat of disestablishment mobilised Anglican opinion in the late 1860s, with Church of Ireland activists launching a Central Protestant Defence Association in 1867, as well as a Lay and Clerical Association in 1869. By then, some alienated Protestants had begun to demand 'a parliament in Dublin for purely Irish matters'.[49] Most Irish conservatives, however, concluded that there was no real alternative to reunion with the British Conservative Party. In the north, where Fenianism revived Orange activity, continued differences between Orange populists and the Protestant elite were gradually subsumed by a shared hostility to Liberal meliorism, with 'anti-Gladstone rallies' becoming 'a regular feature of Ulster life' from 1868.[50] Partisan polarisation left some Irish liberals uneasy – the leading northern liberal, Lord Dufferin, expressed a desire to 'compose the quarrel between the government and the Orangemen' in 1871 – but the Palmerstonian consensus could not be restored.[51]

The Emergence of Home Rule, 1870–1879

The gradual dissolution of Gladstone's Irish coalition facilitated the emergence of the home rule movement, which served as the primary manifestation of nationalist opinion into the First World War. Nationalism was not entirely subsumed by the Liberal alliance in the later 1860s, however. The

---

47 J.H. Murphy, *Ireland's Czar: Gladstonian government and the lord lieutenancies of the red Earl Spencer, 1868–86* (Dublin: UCD Press, 2014), p. 130.

48 E. Larkin, *The Roman Catholic Church and the Home Rule movement in Ireland, 1870–1874* (Chapel Hill: University of North Carolina Press, 1990), pp. 173–4.

49 Quoted in J.J. Golden, 'The Protestant influence on the origins of Irish home rule, 1861–1871', *English Historical Review*, 128 (2013), 1491.

50 S. Farrell, 'Recapturing the flag: the campaign to repeal the Party Processions Act, 1860–1872', *Éire-Ireland*, 32 (1997), 69.

51 The Earl of Dufferin to the Duke of Argyll, 21 Dec. 1871, Dufferin papers, D1070/H/B/C/95/56, PRONI.

Nation continued to advocate independence from British party politics, and in 1868 1,600 Catholic clergy subscribed to the Limerick Declaration, which called for the 'restoration' of Irish 'nationality'.[52] That same year, nationalists inaugurated a campaign for the amnesty of Fenian convicts, amidst allegations of their mistreatment in prison. Disappointment with the Land Act of 1870 thus served to confirm – rather than to awaken – nationalist reservations about British liberalism. More fundamentally, dissatisfaction with the measure suggested to nationalists that a reconsideration of political priorities was in order. A reassertion of the demand for self-government was the outcome of nationalist frustration with the meagre benefits of sectional reform. Dean O'Brien, author of the celebrated Limerick Declaration, conveyed the nationalist position with great clarity. 'Mr. Gladstone has closed the line of statesmen in whom I had any hope', O'Brien confided to Isaac Butt in early 1870, after perusing Gladstone's land bill. 'Landlords and statesmen have only one remaining chance of saving us from coming confusion, and that is to permit us to make our own laws.'[53]

Butt, a Protestant lawyer and former MP with a chequered personal and political history, was deeply involved in popular politics by this time. The son of an Anglican clergyman, Butt was a staunch defender of Protestant Ascendancy while editor of the *Dublin University Magazine* in the 1830s; but a romantic sense of Irish identity, along with a conviction that British social, economic and fiscal policies served Ireland poorly, encouraged him to regard the Union as a 'conditional' settlement.[54] From the mid-1860s, Butt sought to make common cause with nationalists. To this end, he defended the Fenian leaders at trial, and placed himself at the head of the amnesty and tenant right agitations. By the autumn of 1869, Butt was amongst the minority of Irish Protestants moving towards an explicitly patriotic position, admonishing the Catholic Young Men's Society of Dundalk that 'there can be no hope for Ireland except in giving Irishmen the management of their own affairs'[55] (see Illustration 54).

As nationalist support for Gladstone ebbed, Butt was well positioned to provide an alternative focus for popular politics. He attended the portentous

---

52 *The Times*, 31 Dec. 1867.
53 R.B. O'Brien to I. Butt, 17 Feb. 1870, Butt papers, MS 8692/2, NLI.
54 J. Spence, 'Isaac Butt, Irish nationality and the conditional defence of the Union, 1833–70' in D.G. Boyce and A. O'Day (eds.), *Defenders of the Union: a survey of British and Irish unionism since 1801* (London: Routledge, 2001), pp. 65–89.
55 *Nation*, 20 Nov. 1869.

54. Isaac Butt (1813–79), founder of the Irish Home Rule Party. Pencil and wash by Sir Leslie Ward, [1874].

conference at Bilton's Hotel in Dublin on 19 May 1870, at which forty-nine alienated Protestants and disaffected nationalists agreed to inaugurate a new campaign for self-government. Continued discussion following the meeting led to the establishment in September of the Home Government Association, dedicated to a restructuring of the Anglo-Irish relationship along federal lines. Butt claimed a leading role in the new organisation by issuing a pamphlet entitled *Irish federalism* just as it was formally launched.

Irish federalism provided a thorough exposition of Butt's policy. Its author called not for a repeal of the Union, but for its 're-adjustment or modification', by which 'an Irish parliament' would enjoy 'control over all the domestic affairs of Ireland, while an imperial parliament still preserved the unity and integrity of the United Kingdom as a great power among the nations of the world'. The Union, Butt claimed, had 'failed in giving to Ireland either prosperity or peace'. As a result, he warned, in a delicate allusion to Fenianism, 'Ireland is now the weakness of England.' Butt conceived of home government as an exercise in prudential reform, designed to contain advanced nationalism by removing those grievances, born of misgovernment, on which Irish disaffection thrived. A prompt amendment of the Anglo-Irish constitutional relationship would realise the objects of the Union's architects, who had hoped 'to consolidate the power of the empire'. The proposal, he contended, was consistent with recent developments in British North America, where the Constitution Act of 1867 had federated the Canadian provinces and confirmed Canadian self-government within the British Empire.[56] In sum, Butt's aims were conservative and integrative rather than nationalist and separatist.[57]

As the campaign for self-government gathered momentum, Butt's support for federalism meant he was an isolated figure within the movement that he led. Despite his hopes, Protestant conservatives did not affiliate to the Home Government Association in large numbers. Catholic nationalists were more enthusiastic, but for them 'the idea of self-government . . . exerted more appeal than did a concrete scheme of federalism'.[58] Often, moderate nationalists simply conflated federalism with repeal. It was significant, in this regard, that the specific and limited demand for federalism was never as prevalent as the more ambiguous call for 'home rule' – a phrase that only entered the popular lexicon in 1870. The revolutionary alternative having been discredited, many advanced nationalists also redirected their energies into the movement. The amnesty agitation provided a bridge for their entry into constitutional politics, and the IRB's reorganised governing body, the supreme council, acquiesced in the involvement of rank-and-file Fenians by agreeing in 1873 to give home rule a trial period.

The nationalist complexion of home rule was softened by the flow of Irish liberals into the movement. As the Gladstone administration proved itself

---

56 I. Butt, *Irish federalism! Its meaning, its objects, and its hopes*, 3rd edn (Dublin: John Falconer, 1871), pp. 17, 23, 25–6, 28.

57 C.W. Reid, ' "An experiment in constructive unionism": Isaac Butt, Home Rule and federalist political thought during the 1870s', *English Historical Review*, 129 (2014), 333, 340.

58 A. O'Day, *Irish Home Rule, 1867–1921* (Manchester: Manchester University Press, 1998), p. 29.

unable to deliver on the promise of sectional reform – and as the electoral potential of home rule revealed itself in a series of by-election victories that returned eight home rulers (one of whom was unseated on petition), including Butt, to parliament in 1871–2 – some Irish liberals gravitated towards self-government. The stream became a flood after the defeat of Gladstone's university education bill. When, in November 1873, Butt convened a conference in Dublin to establish the Home Rule League in anticipation of a general election, eighteen Irish Liberal MPs were present. A fundamentally conservative imperialist thus found himself presiding over a coalition of aggrieved nationalists and disappointed liberals.

Butt's achievement was remarkable, but incomplete. The mobilising capacity of home rule was demonstrated when voters went to the polls in February 1874. Without the formal support of the Catholic hierarchy, fifty-nine home rule candidates won sixty parliamentary seats, typically on a platform identifying self-government with denominational education, tenant right and Fenian amnesty. The Liberal Party was routed, and the Conservative Party continued its retreat to the north of Ireland. The election, however, also underscored the limitations of Butt's coalition, as voters in Ulster proved resistant to the allure of self-government. The geography of home rule victories underscored Butt's failure to realise the non-sectarian and bipartisan alliance of Protestant conservatives and Catholic nationalists that he had envisioned. The composition of the party – which included only three former Conservative MPs and thirteen Protestants – told much the same story. Butt's triumph was not merely partial, it was also unfortunately timed, as British voters delivered the Conservative Party a substantial majority in the election. Disraeli returned to Downing Street with little incentive to pursue an active programme of Irish reform, and Gladstone's locum tenens as leader of the Liberal opposition, Lord Hartington, confirmed his hostility to home rule after parliament reconvened.

Given these adverse circumstances, Butt demonstrated considerable resourcefulness in sustaining the home rule movement over the next few years. The Home Rule Party was formally established, with Butt as chairman, in March 1874. Though the antipathy of British politicians ensured that constitutional reform could not be expected from parliament, Butt dutifully introduced home rule motions in 1874 and 1876, both of which were overwhelmingly defeated. He took these rebuffs in his stride, emphasising the educative function of the debates, and reaffirming his commitment to moral suasion as the best means of influencing British opinion. More practically, between 1874 and 1876 members of the party introduced a substantial quantity of legislation related to local government, the franchise, public expenditure, land law and higher education. Though the home rulers succeeded in securing only minor concessions, their activities confirmed the party's role 'as an umbrella for what were essentially Catholic materialist aims'.[59] Butt's willingness to meet the wishes of the Catholic hierarchy where university reform was concerned, moreover, enabled him to outmanoeuvre the aging Cullen and to capture the support of a majority of the bishops, some two-thirds of whom publicly signalled their approval of home rule in 1877 by collecting for a Testimonial Fund intended to repair the chronically indebted party leader's finances. Butt's movement had subsumed, rather than abandoned, sectional politics.

The Home Rule Party's inability to deliver substantive reform exposed its underlying weaknesses. In part, its deficiencies were structural. The parliamentary equation ensured that home rulers could exert little influence on policy, and the heterogeneous composition of the party resulted in cross-voting and internal disagreement. Inevitably, these problems took their toll on morale, and by 1876 nearly half of the Home Rule MPs elected in 1874 had drifted out of the party.[60] In part, the party's shortcomings reflected Butt's inadequacies as a leader. His relaxed attitude towards electoral organisation and party discipline, and his long absences from parliament because of ill health and poor finances, often left the party rudderless. Butt's suddenly cautious attitude to land reform also dampened support for home rule amongst tenant farmers, while the party's inefficacy encouraged restiveness amongst advanced nationalists. After various manifestations of Fenian dissatisfaction in 1875, the IRB's supreme council repudiated home rule in 1876.

Some Home Rule MPs, concerned about the party's declining standing in the country, also harboured reservations about Butt's approach. Joseph Biggar pointed the way forward for disaffected party members in 1874 when he sought to block the renewal of coercive legislation by exploiting the procedural rules of the Commons – a tactic that came to be known as obstruction. Though Butt disapproved, regarding the device as counter-productive, nationalists had no such qualms. In 1875, Biggar again had occasional recourse to obstruction, attracting a small group of followers in the process. This cohort included Charles Stewart Parnell, a Protestant landlord from County Wicklow with a distinguished Patriot pedigree, who had been returned at a by-election for Meath in the spring. By 1877, the charismatic, patrician and

---

59 Ibid., p. 40.
60 D. Thornley, *Isaac Butt and Home Rule* (London: MacGibbon and Kee, 1964), p. 272.

increasingly self-assured Parnell had become the senior figure in the partnership with Biggar. That year, the two men began a campaign of systematic obstruction in the Commons, backed by a minority of the party, which climaxed with marathon sittings on the government's South Africa bill in July. Obstruction served multiple purposes: it penalised parliament and the government for inattention to the Home Rule Party's agenda; it exposed Butt's shortcomings as party leader; and it appealed to advanced nationalists. Butt was certainly alive to the second and third uses of obstruction, condemning the tactic and publicly associating it with Fenianism in 1877.

The ensuing struggle for power between Butt and Parnell played out on the floor of the House of Commons, on the platform, in the press, and at party meetings and League conferences. Their rivalry should not obscure the broad similarities of the two politicians with respect to both ends and means. Parnell, no less than Butt, 'hoped for reconciliation between the Catholic democracy and the southern Irish Protestant ascendancy'.[61] And, like his adversary, 'Parnell was essentially a parliamentarian.'[62] If Parnell's object was fundamentally conservative, his strategy was superficially radical, and as a technique of parliamentary confrontation obstruction rekindled the enthusiasm of advanced nationalists for home rule. Parnell's apparent intransigence played particularly well amongst Irish emigrants in Britain and America. In 1877, he deposed Butt as president of the Home Rule Confederation of Great Britain, an association dominated by Fenian sympathisers. That same year, he was approached by a representative of Clan na Gael, an Irish-American separatist organisation. Following exploratory discussions between Parnell and the Clan in early 1878, its leading figure, John Devoy, proposed an alliance with Parnell, grandiosely termed the 'new departure', in the autumn. A more assertive nationalism – hostile to the British connection, critical of the monarchy, anti-imperial and wedded to essentialist notions of Irish national identity – was thus beginning to marshal itself under Parnell's banner.

Butt fought a skilful rear-guard action against Parnell until his health failed in early 1879. He not only commanded the support of the Catholic clergy, the Home Rule League and the party's moderate majority, but also received assistance from the government, which sought to stifle obstruction, appeal to moderate Catholic opinion and arrest the declining fortunes of the Conservative Party in Ireland in advance of an approaching general election.

---

61 P. Bew, *Enigma: a new life of Charles Stewart Parnell* (Dublin: Gill and Macmillan, 2011), p. 194.
62 A. Jackson, *Home Rule: an Irish history, 1800–2000* (Oxford: Oxford University Press, 2003), p. 39.

The administration began to release the last of the Fenian prisoners in 1877; passed an Intermediate Education Act in 1878, which conceded denominational education and tacitly endowed Catholic schools through a programme of payment by examination results; and established a Royal University in 1879, which was empowered to grant degrees to students at the Catholic University. Conservative concession enabled Butt to pivot towards support for the government. The politics of the late 1870s thus paralleled, in a striking manner, those of the mid-1850s, when an earlier popular coalition had broken into its constituent parts amidst much bitterness and mutual recrimination.

The social upheaval of the late 1870s, however, transformed the situation, rescuing the home rule movement from seemingly inevitable collapse. Between 1877 and 1879, Irish tenant farmers were subjected to a disastrous combination of two harvest failures and a steep decline in the price of agricultural commodities. In 1879, a recently paroled Fenian convict, Michael Davitt, set about directing agrarian discontent into political channels. After meeting with Devoy and Parnell early in the year, Davitt convinced the latter to appear on the platform at a June meeting of tenant farmers in Westport. In his speech, Parnell deftly aligned the cause of the tenants with the demand for home rule: 'if we had the farmers on the soil tomorrow', he pronounced, we would not be long in getting an Irish parliament'.[63] Four months later, Parnell was elected president of the newly established Irish National Land League. With the increasingly desperate tenant farmers in an angry mood, the way was clear for a fresh polarisation of Irish politics.

Conclusion

Post-Famine politics fits uneasily into the teleology of nationalist history. In the absence of charismatic leadership and with few substantive political achievements, the three decades between 1850 and 1879 may appear to be merely a hiatus between the more eventful eras of O'Connell and Parnell. Though the nationalist frame of reference has long since been abandoned by academic historians, its lingering influence is reflected in the modest scholarly interest in Irish politics after the Famine – with the telling exception of Fenianism, which continues to command significant attention and to generate sometimes heated debate. Yet the post-Famine period was, in some respects, a formative one in modern Irish politics. It was marked by an expansion of

63 Quoted in Bew, *Enigma*, p. 55.

the public sphere, with associational activity and print culture deepening the politicisation of the tenant farmers and the urban middle class, and Fenianism extending this politicisation down the social scale. The growth of the political public in Ireland at mid-century paralleled developments in contemporary Britain, continental Europe, and North America. The emergence of the tenant farmers as the dominant electoral bloc and the cautious re-engagement of a re-energised Catholic Church with popular politics were further crucial developments, which imparted a more distinctive character to Irish politics and continued to shape its contours beyond 1879. Nor did the post-Famine emphasis on sectional reform represent a historical blind alley. Though the rise of the home rule movement in the 1870s was a testament to the failure of grievance politics, the Home Rule Party provided a vehicle to pursue sectional ends by nationalist means. And the relative fluidity of post-Famine political affiliation, however difficult to reconcile with essentialist notions of Irish national identity, may appear less alien in twenty-first-century Ireland, where attempts are being made to redefine political communities in more inclusive ways.

27

Afterword

TOBY BARNARD

Omissions from the eighteenth-century volume of the *New history of Ireland* prompted one critic – now the general editor of *The Cambridge history* – to object in *Past and Present*.[1] Themes being developed by scholars were overlooked. Essentially, the texts had been completed by 1973, although published only in 1986. The terminal date was unhelpful, as also reliance on 'colonial nationalism' as an explanation of the tense relationship between Ireland and England. The contributors failed to make use of D.W. Hayton's analyses of the structures and practices of early eighteenth-century Irish politics or indeed the illuminating reformulations for the later eighteenth century presented by Anthony Malcomson. This was the more surprising as it was 'high' politics, played out chiefly through the Dublin parliament and Dublin Castle, which dominated the account, most of it composed by just two scholars.

Now, freer to choose dates, left ragged at the ends, full use is made of Hayton's and Malcomson's publications, as of numerous other scholars, notably the editor of this volume. The powers, procedures, composition and achievements of the Irish parliament, especially before 1782, are better understood. Its dealings with its counterpart in Westminster have been clarified, and searching comparisons made with estates and representative assemblies elsewhere in Europe.[2] Meanwhile, Malcomson has tackled seemingly rebarbative topics, such as the minutiae of administration and government

---

1 T.W. Moody and W.E. Vaughan (eds.), *A new history of Ireland*, vol. IV: *Ireland 1690–1800* (Oxford: Oxford University Press, 1986); Tom Bartlett, 'Review article – *A new history of Ireland*', *Past and Present*, 116 (1987), 206–19.

2 D.W. Hayton, *The Anglo-Irish experience, c.1680–1730: religion, identity and patriotism* (Woodbridge: The Boydell Press, 2012); D.W. Hayton, *Ruling Ireland, 1685–1742: politicians and parties* (Woodbridge: The Boydell Press, 2004); D.W. Hayton (ed.), *The Irish parliament in the eighteenth century: the long apprenticeship* (Edinburgh: Edinburgh University Press, 2001); D.W. Hayton, J. Kelly and J. Bergin (eds.), *The eighteenth-century composite state: representative institutions in Ireland and Europe, 1689–1800* (Basingstoke: Palgrave Macmillan, 2010).

finance as handled by members of the Clements clan, and how an Irish politician and office-holder adjusted to the demands of Union after 1801: an otherwise neglected matter.[3] Equally active in discussing the attitudes and careers of prominent parliamentarians has been James Kelly, with studies of Newenham, Flood, Musgrave and Bishop Woodward, formulator of the notion of Protestant Ascendancy. Alongside these numerous helps has been the publication of a history of the Irish parliament, the core of which is a biographical dictionary of the members, together with sketches of their constituencies.[4] In addition, the most prominent members are included in the nine-volume *Dictionary of Irish biography*.[5] None of this was available, much of it not even projected, in the 1970s.

The happier situation owes much to an astonishing growth in historical research. One objection to the *New history* was its ambitious scale, which hardly looked commensurate with the state of learning. That reservation has disappeared completely. During the 1950s, one series under the imprint of Faber and Faber – 'Studies in Irish History' – brought out monographs, by McDowell, Simms and Beckett, who would write much of the fourth volume of the *New history*. Otherwise, perhaps one or two histories of enduring value appeared each year during the 1950s and 1960s from English or Irish publishers. Matters changed as university departments developed graduate courses and took care that the results were published. Outstanding has been the series linked with the local history master's degree at NUI, Maynooth (now Maynooth University), which has facilitated the publication in pamphlet form since the 1990s of more than a hundred MA theses. Versions of longer dissertations are included in another series devoted to Ireland, published under the auspices of Boydell. Occasionally works focusing on Ireland are included in the Oxford Historical Monographs, the Royal Historical Society 'Studies in History', and Cambridge Studies of early modern British history. As well as a sequence of monographs in the venerable 'Studies in Irish History' series, Cork University Press published a pioneering group of literary studies, both theoretical and empirical, on behalf of Field Day.

---

3 A.P.W. Malcomson, *John Foster (1740–1828): the politics of improvement and prosperity* (Dublin: Four Courts Press, 2011); A.P.W. Malcomson, *Nathaniel Clements: government and the governing elite in Ireland, 1725–75* (Dublin: Four Courts Press, 2005).

4 E.M. Johnston-Liik, *History of the Irish parliament, 1692–1800*, 6 vols. (Belfast: Ulster Historical Foundation, 2002).

5 *Dictionary of Irish biography*, ed. J.I. McGuire and James Quinn, 9 vols. (Cambridge: Cambridge University Press, 2009).

Helpful, too, in underpinning innovation and synthesis are the journals, two of which, *Irish Economic and Social History* (whose first number was published in 1974) and *Eighteenth-Century Ireland* (1986), were unknown when the *New history* was initiated. *Eighteenth-Century Ireland* in particular suggests that the period was proving especially fertile in research. Another sign was the revamping in the 1990s of the long-established *Quarterly Bulletin of the Irish Georgian Society* as a single annual number in order to accommodate substantial pieces of research and reinterpretation.[6] Behind these novelties remained the reassuring presence of the venerable – the Royal Irish Academy and the Royal Society of Antiquaries – and the Irish Manuscripts Commission, which has, over the past decade, sustained a vigorous programme of issuing hitherto unpublished sources in edited volumes and shorter documents in the ancillary *Analecta Hibernica*.

Linked with the enthusiasm for postgraduate inquiry manifested in the university is support for groups. In Ireland, both archaeologists and historical geographers have steered the direction of historical research. When the numbers engaged in such inquiries were few, collaboration may have been both necessary and easy. Moreover, given the history of destruction of written and built records, the terrain itself, together with the unusual amount of mapping and surveying that arose from seizure, forfeiture and dispossession, has left copious evidence. The resulting orientation expresses itself in at least two activities, one institutional, the other voluntary. The Irish Historic Towns Atlas, overseen by the Royal Irish Academy, has overtaken most of the non-Irish models on which it was based, and has issued sets of maps with associated commentary for nearly thirty towns. Rigid, even restrictive, in format, they have further encouraged the appreciation of space, its creation and uses, and of place. A similar zest to explore and understand distinctive sites has brought long life to the Group for the Study of Historic Irish Settlement. To the evanescent pleasures of field trips, alternating between the four provinces, have been added collections of thematic essays: for example, on the manor, parishes and agriculture.[7]

James Kelly, directing a cast of two dozen (instead of the nine who wrote for volume IV of the *New history*), can cover the idiosyncratic as well as the

---

6 *Irish Architectural and Decorative Studies*, from 1996.

7 J. Lyttleton and T. O'Keeffe (eds.), *The manor in medieval and early modern Ireland* (Dublin: Four Courts Press, 2005); E. FitzPatrick and R. Gillespie (eds.), *The parish in medieval and early modern Ireland: community, territory and building* (Dublin: Four Courts Press, 2006); M. Murphy and M. Stout (eds.), *Agriculture and settlement in Ireland* (Dublin: Four Courts Press, 2015).

essential. But the choices also tell of the constant enlargement of what is thought to constitute Irish history. Ireland, it seems, has to comprehend London, where transient and stable populations of Irish are being delineated, and ideally manufacturing towns in Scotland and northern England which attracted numerous Irish.[8] Ports around the Atlantic littoral have long been known as havens for the uprooted Irish; so too in North America and Australasia. To these India must now be added.[9] The hopeful Irish have been tracked to the Danish West Indies, tempted thence by the lucrative sugar trade.[10]

In the Iberian ports, a few of Irish origins flourished and left visible traces of their success, as in Cadiz and Seville.[11] Nor did they always forget the places of their nativity, bequeathing money for funerary monuments or eleemosynary purposes.[12] The scattered participated in and identified with several cultural and social worlds, either simultaneously or *seriatim*. In contemplating the vibrant and variegated communities of Irish expatriates around the world, those which retained functional ties with Ireland, most obviously through the regular or emergency despatch of remittances – as to help famine victims – or offering footholds to later waves of emigrants, need to be distinguished from

---

8 C. Bailey, 'From innovation to emulation: London's Benevolent Society of St. Patrick, 1783–1800', *Eighteenth-Century Ireland*, 27 (2012), 162–84; C. Bailey, *Irish London: middle-class migration in the global eighteenth century* (Liverpool: Liverpool University Press, 2013); J. Bergin, 'The Irish Catholic interest at the London Inns of Court, 1671–1800', *Eighteenth-Century Ireland*, 24 (2009), 36–61; J. Bergin, 'Irish Catholics and their networks in London', *Eighteenth-Century Life*, 39 (2015), 66–102; J. Livesey, *Civil society and empire: Ireland and Scotland in the eighteenth-century Atlantic world* (New Haven: Yale University Press, 2009).

9 B. Crosbie, *Irish imperial networks: migration, social communication and exchange in nineteenth-century India* (Cambridge: Cambridge University Press, 2012).

10 O. Power, 'Friend, foe or family? Catholic creoles, French Huguenots, Scottish dissenters: aspects of the Irish diaspora at St Cruz, Danish West Indies, c.1760' in N. Whelehan (ed.), *Transnational perspectives on modern Irish history* (London: Routledge, 2015), pp. 30–44; O. Power, 'The "quadripartite concern" of St. Croix: an Irish Catholic experiment in the Danish West Indies' in D.T. Gleeson (ed.), *The Irish in the Atlantic World* (Columbia: University of South Carolina Press, 2010), pp. 213–28.

11 M. Lario, 'Irish traders in eighteenth-century Cadiz' in D. Dickson, J. Parmentier and J. Ohlmeyer (eds.), *Irish and Scottish mercantile networks in Europe and overseas in the seventeenth and eighteenth centuries* (Ghent: Academia Press, 2007), pp. 211–30; M. Lario de Oñate, 'Irish integration in the eighteenth century maritime mercantile city of Cadiz' in O. Recio Morales (ed.), *Redes de nación y espacios de poder: la comunidad Irlandesa en España y la América Española, 1600–1825./Power strategies: Spain and Ireland 1600–1825* (Valencia: Albatros Ediciones, 2012), pp. 183–90.

12 R. Ó Floinn (ed.), *Franciscan faith: sacred art in Ireland, AD 1600–1750* (Dublin: Wordwell, 2011); J. McDonnell, 'Art and patronage in the penal era' in Maynooth College, *Ecclesiastical art of the penal era* (Maynooth: St Patrick's College, 1995); cf. K.V. Thomas, *The ends of life: the roads to fulfilment in early modern England* (Oxford: Oxford University Press, 2009), pp. 259–67.

those whose Irishness faded into vague sentimentality. The easy movement between Britain and Ireland, together with its long standing and routines, may make it difficult to analyse in detail. The very familiarity may lead to neglect as novel and alluring destinations beguile researchers.

Emphases alter. Subjects thought beyond the historian's pale in the 1970s have become fair game: gender, age, gesture, humour, emotion. In relation to 'late early modern Ireland', the arrival and reception of ideas are better appreciated as influences over behaviour. Furthermore, the strength of conservative sentiments is being balanced against the radical and revolutionary.[13] In 1987, Bartlett was disappointed by a 'largely trouble-free' narrative. He regretted that the lasting, if fluctuating, influence of John Temple and his 1646 account of the Irish rebellion in keeping alive Protestant fears of their Catholic neighbours was not acknowledged.[14] Subsequently, others have demonstrated the attachment of some Protestants to Temple in the mid-eighteenth century and his influence over the view of 1641 taken by Edmund Burke.[15]

The weight accorded to trouble, weather, war, famine, is decided by individual contributors. Placid and even prosperous passages of time are interspersed with seismic upheavals, especially as the economy is treated. Temple's approach was adopted by an observer and analyst of the 1790s, Sir Richard Musgrave. Bartlett uses Musgrave as testimony to the existence in 1809 of a plot in Munster for 'an universal extermination of Protestants of every description'. However, the extent to which thereafter Musgrave determined how shaken Protestants remembered and understood the events of the 1790s is not discussed.[16] Indeed, in comparison with the eighteenth

13 U. Gillen, 'Monarchy, republic and empire: Irish public opinion and France, *c.*1787–1804', DPhil thesis, Oxford University, 2005; J. Kelly, 'Conservative Protestant thought in later eighteenth-century Ireland' in S.J. Connolly (ed.), *Political ideas in eighteenth-century Ireland* (Dublin: Four Courts Press, 2000), pp. 185–220; J. Kelly, 'Defending the established order: Richard Woodward, bishop of Cloyne (1726–94)' in J. Kelly, J. McCafferty and C.I. McGrath (eds.), *People, politics and power: essays in Irish history 1660–1850* (Dublin: UCD Press, 2009), pp. 143–74; A.P.W. Malcomson, *Archbishop Charles Agar: churchmanship and politics in Ireland, 1760–1810* (Dublin: Four Courts Press, 2002); Malcomson, *John Foster*; V. Morley, *Irish opinion and the American Revolution, 1760–1783* (Cambridge: Cambridge University Press, 2002); S. Small, *Political thought in Ireland: republicanism, patriotism and radicalism* (Oxford: Oxford University Press, 2002).

14 Bartlett, 'A new history of Ireland', pp. 206–19.

15 R. Bourke, *Empire and revolution: the political life of Edmund Burke* (Princeton: Princeton University Press, 2015), pp. 39–40, 64–5, 214–16; T.P. Power, 'Publishing and sectarian tension in South Munster in the 1760s', *Eighteenth-Century Ireland*, 19 (2004), 75–110.

16 M. Brown, *The Irish Enlightenment* (Cambridge, MA: Harvard University Press, 2016), pp. 417–22; D. Dickson, 'Foreword' in R. Musgrave, *Memoirs of the Irish Rebellion of 1798*, 4th edn (Fort Wayne, IN: Round Tower Press, 1995), pp. i–xiii; J. Kelly, *Sir Richard Musgrave 1746–1818: ultra-Protestant ideologue* (Dublin: Four Courts Press, 2009).

century, antiquarian and historical inquiries lacked the earlier hopeful signs of inter-denominational cooperation, although they had not ceased.[17] But what had, or had not, happened in the 1640s now mattered less than the events of 1798 and 1803. In turn, the Famine after 1845 overshadowed all. But decades passed, local groups undertook investigations and Ireland was brought within the remit of the Historical Manuscripts Commission, which was charged with 'editing and publishing' sources. By the 1860s a struggle had developed between prominent and partisan archivists as to whether or not the Commission should undertake an edition of the records relating to 1641.[18]

Moving from the 'Great Frost' of 1740–1 through local subsistence crises and recessions to the climacteric of 1845 to 1850, the sombre and troubled tend to predominate. Yet material improvements, as incomes r0se and population dropped, affected some. Any definitive evaluation of the quality of life for Ireland's inhabitants during more than a century seems to require longer looks at contemporary definitions of poverty, respectability, lawlessness and violence, all of which were thought to stunt lives. Expectations might be low, but started to rise. Bias, intimidation and violence were endemic and were perhaps taken for granted in everyday dealings.[19] Local administration was not notably militarised in the eighteenth century, but the demarcation between civilian and army spheres of action shifted and blurred, and there was greater reliance on the military, and police, intervention in maintaining order in the nineteenth.

Several chapters add to as well as summarising the present state of knowledge, throwing out suggestions for others to ponder. Notable in this respect is Virginia Crossman. In tracing initiatives in local government in the early nineteenth century, she returns to a proposition advanced previously by Oliver MacDonagh: whether as a conscious experiment or through inadvertence, state intervention and spending increased. They were directed onto hospitals, workhouses, lunatic asylums, prisons and schools. Through poor law boards and as salaried resident magistrates, more locals were drawn into and profited from the operations of the government in nineteenth-century Ireland. As Crossman makes clear, activity was increasing already in the eighteenth

---

17 D. Murray, *Romanticism, nationalism and Irish Antiquarian Societies, 1840–80* (Maynooth: Maynooth University, 2000).
18 T. Barnard, 'Sir John Gilbert' in M. Clark, Y. Desmond and N.P. Hardiman (eds.), *Sir John T. Gilbert, 1829–1898: historian, archivist and librarian* (Dublin: Dublin Corporation, 1999), pp. 92–110.
19 N. Garnham, 'How violent was eighteenth-century Ireland?' *Irish Historical Studies*, 30 (1997), 377–92; W.E. Vaughan, *Murder trials in Ireland, 1836–1914* (Dublin: Four Courts Press, 2009).

century. Indeed, the growth of bureaucracy, most conspicuously of the revenue service, has been identified as a source of administrative efficiency, of state-building, and a constructive alliance between a distant government and locals.[20] The most important innovations came from the Dublin parliament, and remained at least loosely under its supervision.[21] With no local parliament after 1800, alternative mechanisms had to be devised. Charitable and educational work, once overseen by voluntary associations such as the Incorporated Society, fell to the state. In addition, through frequent official inquiries, there remained a tradition of assessing specific circumstances, previously arising from cadastral surveys and redistributions.[22] Those involved in running local ventures gained practical experience and status. It was more constructive than idling the day away in the coffee house or club.

A participatory system of this kind, replicating a partnership between locals and central government that had long been the basis of rule throughout England, coming late to Ireland may have divided more than it stabilised.[23] Its potential to prompt new researches can be glimpsed in a second contribution. Ciaran O'Neill pleads for more sustained efforts to locate the bourgeoisie in nineteenth-century Ireland. Members of the professions are the most plausible candidates, together with those serving the state and administering the expanded British Empire. Standing, occupation and revenues helped to define the group, but so too did manner of living and attitudes. Already, as several chapters show, possessions and the physical settings of life can be recreated. In urban Ireland, they were tending towards homogeneity with the prosperous and consciously polite elsewhere. The most helpful terms to classify these

20 C.I. McGrath, *The making of the eighteenth-century Irish constitution: government, parliament and the revenue, 1692–1714* (Dublin: Four Courts Press, 2000); P. McNally, *Parties, patriots and undertakers: parliamentary politics in early Hanoverian Ireland* (Dublin: Four Courts Press, 1997); P. Walsh, 'The Irish fiscal state, 1690–1769', *Historical Journal*, 56 (2013), 629–56; P. Walsh, *The making of the Irish Protestant Ascendancy: the life of William Conolly, 1662–1729* (Woodbridge: The Boydell Press, 2010), pp. 125–52; P. Walsh, 'Enforcing the fiscal state: the army, the revenue and the Irish experience of the fiscal-military state' in A. Graham and P. Walsh (eds.), *The British fiscal-military states, 1660–c.1783* (London: Routledge, 2016), pp. 48–65.

21 D. Broderick, *The first toll roads: Ireland's turnpike roads 1729–1858* (Cork: Collins Press, 2002); H.D. Gribbon, 'The Irish Linen Board, 1711–1828' in L.M. Cullen and T.C. Smout (eds.), *Comparative aspects of Scottish and Irish economic and social history, 1600–1900* (Edinburgh: John Donald [1977]), pp. 77–87; E. Magennis, 'Coal, corn and canals: parliament and the dispersal of public moneys, 1693–1772' in Hayton (ed.), *The Irish parliament in the eighteenth century*, pp. 71–86.

22 N. Ó Ciosáin, *Ireland in official print culture 1800–1850: a new reading of the Poor Inquiry* (Oxford: Oxford University Press, 2014).

23 D. Eastwood, *Governing rural England: tradition and transformation, 1780–1840* (Oxford: Oxford University Press, 1994).

socio-economic orders may not be agreed. For adventurous entrepreneurs of Irish provenance removed to London, 'middle-class' migrants 'in the global eighteenth century' is the preferred description.[24] The middling sorts, even a middle class, of the eighteenth century may have formed the nucleus of O'Neill's nineteenth-century bourgeoisie, or may, through determined acculturation, have evolved into it.

The role of education in this process is recognised. Indeed, the introduction of a system of national schools was the motive behind much of the official interventionism during the 1830s.[25] Divisive and contested, the achievement was visible in the ubiquitous school buildings. How far the formal instruction built on foundations laid at home and in the neighbourhood, is impossible to judge except in the case of a few individuals. Essential skills, notably functional literacy, were inculcated, but the purposes to which they were then applied and the effect on attitudes and indeed on political activism can be gauged safely only for those few who have left autobiographies.[26] Teaching was hardly uniform, so no more than printed propaganda or spoken demagoguery did it result in common outlooks and actions. However, its duration, regularity and content reflected income, status and aspirations. Variations in schooling helped to stratify Irish society and to bring some of its members closer to the outlook of their British and European neighbours.[27]

Schemes for national schools in the 1830s are revealing of long-standing anxieties and particular preoccupations within the executive both in Dublin Castle and in London. The institution of the viceroyalty has attracted intermittent attention, although usually it has been individual lords lieutenant and lords justice who have been characterised, and seldom the larger contingent of the Privy Council or permanent officials.[28] Other branches of government have been delineated much more fully, with the Revenue Commission emerging as the most successful, powerful and (arguably) efficient. In comparison,

24 Bailey, *Irish London.*

25 D.H. Akenson, *The Irish education experiment: the national system of education in the nineteenth century* (London: Routledge, 1970),

26 H. Dorian, *The outer edge of Ulster: a memoir of social life in nineteenth-century Donegal,* ed. B. Mac Suibhne and D. Dickson (Dublin: Lilliput Press, 2000); W. Davis, *The diary of an Offaly schoolboy, 1858–9,* ed. S. Robinson (Tullamore: Esker Press, 2010).

27 T. Barnard, 'Educating eighteenth-century Ulster' in D.W. Hayton and A. Holmes (eds.), *Ourselves alone? Religion, society and politics in eighteenth- and nineteenth-century Ireland* (Dublin: Four Courts Press, 2016), pp. 104–25; C. O'Neill, *Catholics of consequence: transnational education, social mobility and the Catholic elite, 1850–1900* (Oxford: Oxford University Press, 2014).

28 Bailey, *Irish London;* T. Barnard, *A new anatomy of Ireland: the Irish Protestants, 1641–1770* (New Haven: Yale University Press, 2003), pp. 115–279; H.R. French, *The middle sort of people in provincial England, 1600–1750* (Oxford: Oxford University Press, 2007).

the centralised operations of the law, through the Four Courts in Dublin, and indeed during their regular sittings in the localities, have – as yet – seemed less susceptible to a detailed assessment. The loss of the routine records may explain the neglect, although maybe the subject itself does not attract.[29] Gaps of this sort notwithstanding, how eighteenth-century Ireland was governed and taxed can be much better appreciated. Yet any judgment about the intrusiveness, maladroitness or unpopularity of the state and its functionaries, which could include the military, may be premature in the absence of sustained investigations.

In slicing the Irish past into fresh shapes, the general editor Thomas Bartlett satisfies an urge expressed in 1987. The re-arrangements allow illuminating juxtapositions. The era of the Penal Laws gives way to Catholic emancipation, and then to the supposed devotional revolution; Protestant Ascendancy to a 'second' reformation and disestablishment. Schisms and secessionists among the Presbyterians in the eighteenth century cede to coalescence in the nineteenth. The 'Great Frost' of 1740–1 is better understood when set beside the better-known 'Great' Famine of the 1840s. Indeed, these crises and dearths during the 1720s, in 1757 and at other times remind us how vulnerable different localities were. The vulnerability added to anxieties. On the one hand, famines stimulated schemes – collective and individual – to avoid future shortages, as also to mitigate the immediate damage through public relief and works. Another response was for survivors, and others who felt vulnerable, to emigrate. By doing so, they threatened to weaken the working population, perhaps disproportionately in areas of Protestant settlement. Moreover, the recurrence of such events shook the confidence of incumbent proprietors, mostly Protestant. Projects of agrarian and economic improvement disappointed, even failed. Patience was counselled, but it was inevitable that some would question whether or not the divinity favoured the Protestants of Ireland as the people chosen to bring the island to civility, prosperity and authentic Christianity, as had been promised.

Interpretations that have beguiled historians of the eighteenth century – 'composite monarchies', 'multiple kingdoms', centre and periphery, 'colonial nationalism', enlightenment and counter-enlightenment, and an emergent public sphere – generally vanish from view once the nineteenth century is reached. Nationalism and secularisation take over. Historians' interest in organisations and episodes, other than changes in the franchise and ballot which

---

29 M. Brown and S.P. Donlan (eds.), *The laws and other legalities of Ireland 1689–1850* (Farnham: Ashgate, 2011); N. Garnham, *The courts, crime and the criminal law in Ireland, 1692–1760* (Dublin: Irish Academic Press, 1996).

brought those hitherto outside formal politics into it, span the entire period.[30] 'Trouble' – endemic disobedience, violence, protest and outright rebellion – articulates some histories; others emphasise adjustment and accommodation.[31] Underlying continuities are certainly stressed, but so too is change, which was often clearest in the British, European and global contexts in which the Irish were operating.

The local Irish manifestations of both associational and less formal, impromptu socialising have been detailed fully for the eighteenth century. Rituals and purposes, merely sociable and recreational or political and educative, have been identified, and continuities established.[32] Freemasonry flourished. Antiquarian, natural history societies and field clubs proliferated in the nineteenth-century provinces.[33] They attested to local curiosity, the benefits of education, the drive of autodidacts, and the availability of leisure and modest funds. Occasionally groups were manipulated for purposes of self-aggrandisement or collapsed through personal antagonisms. How far they encouraged the meeting of those of differing denominations and social and cultural backgrounds remains to be shown. Overlaps, in membership if not in declared purposes with political and religious organisations, can be detected. Enjoying, investigating and understanding the remains from the past, whether physical or literary, were not necessarily a substitute for agitating for a different and better future, with altered political and legal structures. Accordingly, the periods of ostensible political torpor – for example, after the 1798 rebellion and the Act of Union – may overlook activities that in the longer term subverted conventions. Also, to dwell on the secular may understate the

---

30 T.C. Barnard; 'Considering the inconsiderable: electors, patrons and Irish elections, 1659–1761' in Hayton (ed.), *The Irish parliament in the eighteenth century*, pp. 107–27; J.R. Hill, *From patriots to unionists: Dublin civic politics and Irish Protestant patriotism, 1660–1840* (Oxford: Oxford University Press, 1997); S. Murphy, 'The Dublin anti-union riot of 3 December 1759' in G. O'Brien (ed.), *Parliament, politics and people: essays in eighteenth-century Irish history* (Dublin: Irish Academic Press, 1989), pp. 49–68; J. Kelly, 'The Downfall of Hagan': Sligo Ribbonism in 1842 (Dublin: Four Courts Press, 2008); J. Smyth, *The men of no property: Irish radicals and popular politics in the late eighteenth century* (Dublin: Gill and Macmillan, 1992).

31 S.J. Connolly, *Divided kingdom: Ireland 1630–1800* (Oxford: Oxford University Press, 2008); D. Dickson, *New foundations: Ireland 1660–1800*, 2nd edn (Dublin: Irish Academic Press, 2000); R. Gillespie, *Seventeenth-century Ireland* (Dublin: Gill and Macmillan, 2006); I. McBride, *Eighteenth-century Ireland* (Dublin: Gill and Macmillan, 2009).

32 J. Kelly and M.J. Powell (eds.), *Clubs and societies in eighteenth-century Ireland* (Dublin: Four Courts Press, 2010); R.V. Comerford and J. Kelly (eds.), *Associational culture in Ireland and abroad* (Dublin: Irish Academic Press, 2010).

33 T.C. Barnard, 'Scholars and antiquarians: the clergy and learning, 1600–2000' in T.C. Barnard and W.G. Neely (eds.), *The clergy of the Church of Ireland, 1000–2000: messengers, watchmen and stewards* (Dublin: Four Courts Press, 2006), pp. 231–58.

extent to which reorganised and regenerated churches engaged conscientious laypeople. To daily and annual rituals were added onerous financial and administrative responsibilities.[34]

The interpretations, methods and terminology pioneered in the analysis of societies other than in Ireland are applied to it. Shifting from wrangling as to whether Ireland is better categorised as a kingdom or a colony to its place as a component in a composite monarchy encourages comparisons as well as identifying what may have been distinctive; so too have the sustained efforts to treat Ireland throughout the seventeenth and eighteenth centuries as a variant of the *ancien régime* genus.[35] Further stimulus – and disagreement – can be expected to arise from the historians' quest for an expanding public sphere and for evidence of a more efficiently functioning fiscal-military state.[36] The spread of values that prized politeness, respectability, sociability and refinement has obliged these to be traced sometimes in competition with but often in conjunction with civic activism, industriousness and aggression. These developments sometimes treated as synonymous with modernisation are related to the controversy over the fate of the Irish language, and whether it fell victim because it was in the way of modernising.[37]

---

34 T. Barnard, 'Churchwardens' accounts and the confessional state in Ireland, *c.*1660–1800' in V. Hitchman and A. Foster (eds.), *Views from the parish: churchwardens' accounts c.1500–c.1800* (Cambridge: Scholars Press, 2015), pp. 109–20; T. Barnard, 'The eighteenth-century parish' in FitzPatrick and Gillespie (eds.), *The parish in medieval and early modern Ireland*, pp. 297–324; C. Begadon, 'The renewal of Catholic religious culture in eighteenth-century Dublin' in J. Bergin et al. (eds.), *New perspectives on the Penal Laws* (Dublin: Eighteenth-Century Ireland Society, 2011), pp. 227–47; J. Crawford, *The Church of Ireland in Victorian Dublin* (Dublin: Four Courts Press, 2005); A.R. Holmes, *The shaping of Ulster Presbyterian belief and practice, 1770–1840* (Oxford: Oxford University Press, 2006); C. Lennon (ed.), *Confraternities and sodalities in Ireland: charity, devotion and sociability* (Dublin: Columba Press, 2012).

35 As well as the locus classicus, S.J. Connolly, *Religion, law and power: the making of Protestant Ireland, 1660–1760* (Oxford: Oxford University Press, 1992); P. Fagan, *Catholics in a Protestant country: the papist constituency in eighteenth-century Dublin* (Dublin: Four Courts Press, 1998); C.D.A. Leighton, *Catholicism in a Protestant kingdom: a study of the Irish ançien régime* (Dublin: Gill and Macmillan, 1994).

36 T.C. Barnard, *Brought to book: print in Ireland, 1680–1784* (Dublin: Four Courts Press, 2017); P. Walsh, 'The fiscal military state'.

37 R.A. Breatnach, 'The end of a tradition: a survey of eighteenth-century Gaelic literature', *Studia Hibernica*, 1 (1961), 137; Connolly, *Divided kingdom*, pp. 331–2; A. Doyle, 'The "decline" of the Irish language in the eighteenth and nineteenth centuries: a new interpretation', *Studia Hibernica*, 41 (2015), 117–34; A. Doyle, *A history of the Irish language from the Norman Invasion to Independence* (Oxford: Oxford University Press, 2015); J. Leerssen, *Hidden Ireland, public sphere* (Galway: Arlen Press, 2002); L. Ní Mhungaile, 'Bilingualism, print culture in Irish and the public sphere, 1700–c.1830' in J. Kelly and C. Mac Murchaidh (eds.), *Irish and English: essays on the English linguistic and cultural frontier, 1600–1900* (Dublin: Four Courts Press, 2012), pp. 218–42; N.M. Wolf, *An Irish-speaking island: state, religion, community and the linguistic landscape in Ireland, 1770–1870* (Madison: University of Wisconsin Press, 2014).

After the Union, new nationalisms evolve, originating usually outside Ireland. Lords lieutenant are no longer ranked according to subjective criteria of success or popularity. Instead it is the figures for population, output, exports, imports, wages, prices, urbanisation, which thread through the chapters and shape the arguments and conclusion. In so far as outstanding personalities emerge, they suggest a contrast between the eighteenth and the nineteenth century. Charles O'Conor, scholar, antiquarian and modest landowner based in County Roscommon, and the suave sophisticate Charlemont, living mainly in central Dublin, were steeped in Irish, classical and contemporary culture.[38] Their successors, Daniel O'Connell and Cardinal Paul Cullen (in turn archbishop of Armagh and of Dublin), achieved more. A perhaps necessary coarseness assisted O'Connell to create a national party, in which priests but not the Irish language were prominent. The cardinal gave the Irish Catholic Church a strongly Roman appearance. In the interval since O'Conor and Charlemont, so much had changed – a United Kingdom; nationalist aspirations throughout Europe and beyond; the Irish settling purposefully across the globe.

Historians of recent times are refreshed and likely to have their researches redirected through the emergence of fresh materials. The opening to scholars of the archive of the Bureau of Military History has offered unexpected information and insights about the War of Independence.[39] No supplement on this scale can be expected for earlier centuries. Improved availability and being in formats that are readily searchable means that the documentation relating to the 1640s can be probed exhaustively. Similarly, the English Short-Title Catalogue of books printed before 1800, used in conjunction with electronic texts on Eighteenth-Century Collections On-Line, has made feasible investigations of what was produced and read in eighteenth-century Ireland. Otherwise, although new records come to light, at most they amplify what is already known. Thus, the miscellaneous letters seized on board a ship en route from Bordeaux to Dublin in 1757 add further examples of

---

38 Barnard, *Brought to book*; T. Barnard, 'Delusions of grandeur? "Big" houses in eighteenth-century Ireland', *Eighteenth-Century Ireland*, 30 (2015), 124–49; Doyle, *A history of the Irish language*, pp. 92–5, 102–5; L. Gibbons and K. O'Conor (eds.), *Charles O'Conor of Ballinagare: life and works* (Dublin: Four Courts Press, 2015); M. McCarthy (ed.), *Lord Charlemont and his circle* (Dublin: Four Courts Press, 2001); R. Musielak, *Charlemont's Marino: portrait of a landscape* (Dublin: Office of Public Works, [2014]); C. O'Connor, *The pleasing hours: James Caulfeild, first Earl of Charlemont, 1728–99: traveller, connoisseur and patron of the arts in Ireland* (Cork: Collins Press, 1999).

39 R.F. Foster, *Vivid faces: the revolutionary generation in Ireland, 1890–1923* (London: Penguin, 2014).

transactions, activities and preoccupations that were already familiar.[40] More arresting because sustained over several years are the insights to be gleaned from the letters of a Church of Ireland bishop in County Roscommon, seeking to guide his adolescent daughter in Dublin, or the terse diary of a land agent in County Limerick during the 1740s.[41] Worth returning to are accounts much used in the past. The diary of Humphrey O'Sullivan, a schoolmaster near Callan, is rich enough to be approached from several angles.[42]

Rarely does a rediscovery allow what had previously been imagined to be visualised. Exceptionally, this was the case when an album of drawings of Dublin street traders surfaced in Australia. Composed by Hugh Douglas Hamilton in 1760, the images portray mostly humdrum tasks and occupations, but in one of them condemned priests are carted to their fate.[43] Such an unexpected addition to historical evidence encourages hope that more may survive and be uncovered. Meanwhile, historians work with what they know to be there. By approaching it from novel perspectives, supplying unexpected contexts, and asking new questions, they enliven the placid and uneventful. Imaginative writing – romances, novels and plays – is being annexed by historians.[44] Texts, if written or even set in Ireland, offer insights into behaviour and views, the best of them not laboured but almost accidental. Thorough exploitation of these materials is being assisted, not just with comprehensive listings and guides, but with annotated editions, in which historical and literary contexts are established.[45] They join the landscape, natural and human, as susceptible to historical treatment. They turn attention away from public towards domestic activities.

---

40 L.M. Cullen, J. Shovlin and T.M. Truxes (eds.), *The Bordeaux–Dublin letters, 1757: correspondence of an Irish community abroad* (Oxford: Oxford University Press, 2013).

41 M.L. Legg (ed.), *The diary of Nicholas Peacock 1740–1751* (Dublin: Four Courts Press, 2005); M.L. Legg (ed.), *The Synge letters: Bishop Edward Synge to his daughter, Alicia, Roscommon to London, 1746–1752* (Dublin: Irish Manuscripts Commission, 1996).

42 M. McGrath (ed.), *Cinnlae Amhlaoibh Uí Shúileabháin/The diary of Humphrey O'Sullivan*, 4 vols. (London: Irish Texts Society, 1936–7).

43 H.D. Hamilton, *The cries of Dublin, 1760*, ed. W. Laffan (Tralee: Churchill House Press, 2003), pp. 70–1.

44 J.C. Greene, *Theatre in Dublin, 1745–1820: a history*, 2 vols. (Bethlehem, PA: Lehigh University Press, 2011); R. Loeber and M. Loeber, *A guide to Irish fiction, 1650–1900* (Dublin: Four Courts Press, 2006).

45 Examples include S. Butler, *Irish tales*, ed. I.C. Ross, A. Douglas and A. Markey (Dublin: Four Courts Press, 2010); I. Campbell Ross, ' "One of the principal nations in Europe": the representation of Ireland in Sarah Butler's *Irish tales*', *Eighteenth-Century Fiction*, 7 (1994), 1–16; W. Chaigneau, *The history of Jack Connor*, ed. I.C. Ross (Dublin: Four Courts Press, 2013), pp. 185–6; I.C. Ross, 'Novels, chapbooks, folklore: the several lives of William Chaigneau's Jack Connor, now Conyers: or, John Connor, alias Jack the Bachelor, the famous Irish bucker', *Eighteenth-Century Ireland*, 30 (2015), 60–90.

A family, if amply documented over several generations, offers a prospect of showing responses to changing circumstances.[46] They may remain obstinately the reactions of individuals, wayward and idiosyncratic, but sometimes they are shared and tell of feelings that lead to larger and coordinated movements. Also, they reveal phases of quiescence and withdrawal rather than of public activism. Any whose surviving archive allows detailed reconstruction can be objected to as untypical – members of the Presbyterian and Quaker congregations were more prone than most to autobiographical introspection. Nevertheless, the reflections may show and explain behaviour and beliefs changing over time. Pressures within particular households can be separated from those exerted by education, reading, discussion, travel and age.

---

46 Livesey, *Civil society and empire*; J. Wright, *The 'natural leaders' and their world: politics, culture and society in Belfast, c.1801–1832* (Liverpool: Liverpool University Press, 2012).

Bibliography

Introduction: Interpreting Late Early Modern Ireland

James Kelly

Barnard, T., *A new anatomy of Ireland: the Irish Protestants, 1649–1770* (New Haven: Yale University Press, 2003).

Bartlett, T., *The fall and rise of the Irish nation: the Catholic question 1690–1830* (Dublin: Gill & Macmillan, 1992).

Beresford, W. (ed.), *The correspondence of John Beresford*, 2 vols. (London: Woodfall and Kinder, 1854).

Blackstock, A., *Loyalism in Britain and Ireland, 1793–1839* (Woodbridge: The Boydell Press, 2007).

'The trajectories of loyalty and loyalism in Ireland, 1793–1849' in A. Blackstock and F. O'Gorman (eds.), *Loyalism and the formation of the British World, 1775–1914* (Woodbridge: The Boydell Press, 2014), pp. 103–24.

Bourke, E. (ed.), *'Poor green Erin': German travel writers' narratives on Ireland from before the 1798 Rising to after the Great Famine*, 2nd edn (Frankfurt: Peter Lang, 2013).

Bourke, R., 'Historiography' in R. Bourke and I. McBride (eds.), *The Princeton history of modern Ireland* (Princeton: Princeton University Press, 2016), pp. 271–91.

Brady, C., '"Constructive and instrumental": the dilemma of Ireland's first "new historians"' in C. Brady (ed.), *Interpreting Irish history: the debate on historical revisionism, 1938–1994* (Dublin: Irish Academic Press, 1994), pp. 3–31.

'Arrested development: competing histories and the formation of the Irish historical profession, 1800–1938' in T. Frank and F. Hadler (eds.), *Disputed territories and shared pasts: overlapping national histories in modern Europe* (Basingstoke: Palgrave, 2010), pp. 275–302.

James Anthony Froude: an intellectual biography (Oxford: Oxford University Press, 2014).

Bright, K., *The Royal Dublin Society, 1815–1845* (Dublin: Four Courts Press, 2004).

Connolly, S.J., *Religion, law and power: the making of Protestant Ireland 1660–1760* (Oxford: Oxford University Press, 1992).

Conway, S., *The British Isles and the War of American Independence* (Oxford: Oxford University Press, 2000).

Corkery, D., *The hidden Ireland: a study of Gaelic Munster in the eighteenth century* (Dublin: T.H. Gill, 1924).

Costello, V., *Irish demesne landscapes, 1660–1740* (Dublin: Four Courts Press, 2016).

Curwen, J.C., *Observations on the state of Ireland*, 2 vols. (London: Baldwin, Cradock and Joy, 1818).

Devine, T.M., 'Unrest and stability in rural Ireland and Scotland 1760–1840' in P. Roebuck and R. Mitchison (eds.), *Economy and society in Scotland and Ireland, 1500–1939* (Edinburgh: John Donald, [1988]), pp. 126–39.

Dickson, D., 'The gap in famines: a useful myth' in E. M. Crawford (ed.), *Famine: the Irish experience: subsistence crises and famines in Ireland* (Edinburgh: John Donald, 1989), pp. 96–111.

Donnelly, J.S., 'The Whiteboys, 1761–65', *Irish Historical Studies*, 21 (1978–9), 20–55.

Dunne, T., *The writer as witness: literature as historical evidence* (Cork: Cork University Press, 1987).

Elliott, M., *Partners in revolution: the united Irishmen and France* (New Haven: Yale University Press, 1982).

Robert Emmett: the making of a legend (London: Profile, 2003).

Fagan, P., 'The Dublin Catholic mob, 1700–1750', *Eighteenth-Century Ireland*, 4 (1989), 124–5.

Froude, J.A., *The English in Ireland in the eighteenth century*, 3 vols. (London: Longmans, Green and Co., 1872–4).

Graham, A., and P. Walsh (eds.), *The British fiscal-military states 1660–c.1783* (London: Routledge, 2016).

Graham, B.J., and L.J. Proudfoot (eds.), *Urban improvement in provincial Ireland, 1700–1840* (Dublin: Group for the Study of Irish Historic Settlement, 1994).

Grattan, H., *Memoirs of the life and times of the right hon. Henry Grattan*, 5 vols. (London: Henry Colburn, 1839–46).

Gribbon, H.D., 'The Irish Linen Board, 1711–1828' in L.M. Cullen and T.C. Smout (eds.), *Comparative aspects of Scottish and Irish economic and social history* (Edinburgh: John Donald, 1977), pp. 77–87.

Hall, J., *Tour through Ireland: particularly the Interior and least known parts*, 2 vols. (London: R.P. Moore, 1813).

Hayton, D., J. Kelly and J. Bergin (eds.), *The eighteenth-century composite state: representative institutions in Ireland and Europe, 1689–1800* (Basingstoke: Palgrave, 2010).

Hill, J., 'Loyal societies in Ireland, 1690–1790' in J. Kelly and M.J. Powell (eds.), *Clubs and societies in eighteenth-century Ireland* (Dublin: Four Courts Press, 2010), pp. 181–202.

'Loyalty and the monarchy in Ireland, c.1660-c.1840' in A. Blackstock and F. O'Gorman (eds.), *Loyalism and the formation of the British World, 1775–1914* (Woodbridge: The Boydell Press, 2014), pp. 95–101.

Hoppen, K. Theodore, *Governing Hibernia: British politicians and Ireland, 1800–1921* (Oxford: Oxford University Press, 2016).

Ingram, R.G. (ed.), ' "Popish cut-throats against us": papists, Protestants and the problem of allegiance in eighteenth-century Ireland' in M. Barber et al. (eds.), *From the Reformation to the Permissive Society: a miscellany*, Church of England Record Society 18 (Woodbridge: The Boydell Press, 2010), pp. 151–209.

Ingram, T. Dunbar, *A history of the Legislative Union of Great Britain and Ireland* (London: Macmillan, 1887).

Jackson, A., 'Unionist history' in C. Brady (ed.), *'Interpreting Irish History: the debate on historical revisionism, 1938–1994* (Dublin: Irish Academic Press, 1994), pp. 253–68.

Kanter, D., *The making of British Unionism, 1740–1848: politics, government, and the Anglo-Irish constitutional relationship* (Dublin: Four Courts Press, 2009).

Kelly, J., 'The origins of the Act of Union: an examination of unionist opinion in Britain and Ireland, 1650–1800', *Irish Historical Studies*, 25 (1987), 226–63.

Henry Grattan (Dundalk: Historical Association of Ireland, 1993).

'The Glorious and immortal memory: commemoration and Protestant identity in Ireland 1660–1800', *Proceedings of the Royal Irish Academy*, 94C (1994), 25–52.

'The historiography of the Act of Union' in M. Brown, P. M. Geoghegan and J. Kelly (eds.), *The Irish Act of Union, 1800: bicentennial essays* (Dublin: Irish Academic Press, 2003), pp. 5–36.

(ed.), *Proceedings of the Irish House of Lords, 1771–1800*, 3 vols. (Dublin: Irish Manuscripts Commission, 2008).

'Regulating print: the state and the control of print in eighteenth-century Ireland', *Eighteenth-Century Ireland*, 23 (2008), 141–73.

Sir Richard Musgrave, 1746–1818: ultra-Protestant ideologue (Dublin: Four Courts Press, 2009).

'"Disappointing the boundless ambitions of France": Irish Protestants and the fear of invasion, 1661–1815', *Studia Hibernica*, 37 (2011), 27–105.

'The consumption and sociable use of alcohol in eighteenth-century Ireland', *Proceedings of the Royal Irish Academy*, 115C (2015), 249–54.

Food rioting in Ireland in the eighteenth and nineteenth centuries: the 'moral economy' and the Irish crowd (Dublin: Four Courts Press, 2017).

Kelly, J., and S. Hegarty, 'Writing the history of Irish education' in J. Kelly and S. Hegarty (eds.), *Schools and schooling, 1650–2000* (Dublin: Four Courts Press, 2017), pp. 13–33.

Lecky, W.E.H., *History of Ireland in the eighteenth century*, 5 vols. (London: Longmans, Green and Co., 1896).

Lockhart, J.G., 'Planned villages in Scotland and Ireland 1700–1850' in T.M. Devine and D. Dickson (eds.), *Ireland and Scotland: parallels and contrasts* (Edinburgh: John Donald, 1983), pp. 132–43.

Luckombe, P., *A Tour through Ireland: in several entertaining Letters wherein the Present State of that Kingdom is considered and the most noted Cities, Towns, Seats, Rivers, Buildings etc. are described, interspersed with observations on manners, customs, antiquities, curiosities, and Natural History of that Country* (London: Lowndes, 1780).

MacNeill, J.G. Swift, *How the Union was carried* (London: Kegan Paul, 1887).

Madden, R.R., *The United Irishmen: their lives and times*, 2nd edn, 4 vols. (Dublin: James Duffy, 1858–60).

Malcomson, A.P.W., *John Foster (1740–1828): the politics of improvement and prosperity* (Dublin: Four Courts Press, 2011).

McDowell, R.B., *Irish public opinion 1750–1800* (London: Faber and Faber, 1943).

McGrath, C.I., *Ireland and Empire, 1692–1770* (London: Pickering, 2012).

McGrath, C.I., and C. Fauske (eds.), *Money, power and print: interdisciplinary studies on the financial revolution in the British Isles* (Newark: University of Delaware Press, 2008).

Mitchel, J., *The last conquest of Ireland (perhaps)* (New York: Lynch, Cole and Meehan, 1873).

Mokyr, J., *Why Ireland starved: a quantitative and analytical history of the Irish economy 1800–1850* (London: Allen and Unwin, 1985).

Moody, T.W. and Vaughan, W.E. (eds.), *A new history of Ireland*, vol. IV: *Eighteenth-century Ireland, 1691–1800* (Oxford: Oxford University Press, 1986).

Morley, V., *The popular mind in eighteenth-century Ireland* (Cork: Cork University Press, 2017).

Ó Ciardha, É., *Ireland and the Jacobite cause, 1685–1766: a fatal attachment* (Dublin: Four Courts Press, 2002).

Ó Ciosáin, N., *Ireland in official print culture 1800–1850: a new reading of the Poor Inquiry* (Oxford: Oxford University Press, 2014).

O'Brien, G., *An economic history of Ireland in the eighteenth century* (London: Maunsel, 1918).

O'Brien, G., *Anglo-Irish politics in the age of Grattan and Pitt* (Dublin: Irish Academic Press, 1983).

   Oxford Dictionary of National Biography (Oxford: Oxford University Press, 2004).

Parker, C.S., *Sir Robert Peel: . . . his private correspondence*, 3 vols. (London: John Murray, 1891–3).

Powell, M.J., 'Political toasting in eighteenth-century Ireland', *History*, 91 (2006), 508–29.

Quinn, J., 'The United Irishmen and social reform', *Irish Historical Studies*, 31 (1998), 188–201.

   Young Ireland and the writing of Irish history (Dublin: UCD Press, 2015).

Reid, T., *Travels in Ireland in 1822* (London: Longman, Hurst and Orme, 1823).

Ross, C. (ed.), *Correspondence of Charles, Marquess of Cornwallis*, 3 vols. (London: John Murray, 1859).

Smith, H., *Georgian monarchy: politics and culture 1714–1760* (Cambridge: Cambridge University Press, 2006).

Trotter, J.B., *Walks through Ireland in the years 1812, 1814 and 1817* (London: Richard Phillips, 1819).

Usher, R., *Protestant Dublin, 1660–1760: architecture and iconography* (Basingstoke: Palgrave, 2012).

Vane, H. (ed.), *Memoirs and correspondence of Viscount Castlereagh*, 4 vols. (London: Henry Colburn, 1849).

Vaughan, W.E. (ed.), *A new history of Ireland*, vol. v: *Ireland under the Union, I, 1801–70* (Oxford: Oxford University Press, 1989).

   (ed.), *A new history of Ireland*, vol. vi: *Ireland under the Union, II, 1870–1921* (Oxford: Oxford University Press, 1996).

Whan, R., *The Presbyterians of Ulster, 1680–1730* (Woodbridge: The Boydell Press, 2013).

1 Irish Jacobitism, 1691–1790

Vincent Morley

Manuscript

MS 23 E 12: Royal Irish Academy
State papers SP63: The National Archives
Stuart papers: Royal Archives, Windsor

Printed

Bartlett, T. (ed.), 'Defenders and Defenderism in 1795', *Irish Historical Studies*, 24 (1985), 373–94.

Black, J., *Culloden and the '45* (Stroud: Alan Sutton, 1993).

Brady, J. (ed.), 'Catholics and Catholicism in the eighteenth-century press', *Archivium Hibernicum*, 16 (1951), appendix.

Breatnach, P.A., 'Metamorphosis 1603: dán le hEochaidh Ó hEodhasa', *Éigse*, 17 (1977–8), 169–80.

[Callaghan, John], *Vindiciarum Catholicorum Hiberniae* (Paris: Camusat and Le Petit, 1650).

Campbell, J. Lorne (ed.), *Highland songs of the Forty-five* (Edinburgh: Scottish Gaelic Texts Society, 1984).

Canny, N., *Making Ireland British 1580–1650* (Oxford: Oxford University Press, 2001).

Comer Bruen, M., and D. Ó hÓgáin (eds.), *An Mangaire Súgach* (Dublin: Coiscéim, 1996).

Donnelly, J.S., 'The Whiteboy movement, 1761–5', *Irish Historical Studies*, 21 (1978), 20–54.

Fagan, P., *An Irish bishop in penal times: the chequered career of Sylvester Lloyd OFM, 1680–1747* (Dublin: Four Courts Press, 1993).

(ed.), *Ireland in the Stuart papers*, 2 vols. (Dublin: Four Courts Press, 1995).

Divided loyalties: the question of the oath for Irish Catholics in the eighteenth century (Dublin: Four Courts Press, 1997).

Geoghegan, V., 'A Jacobite history: the Abbé MacGeoghegan's *History of Ireland'*, *Eighteenth-Century Ireland*, 6 (1991), 37–55.

Giblin, C., 'The Stuart nomination of Irish bishops 1687–1765', *Irish Ecclesiastical Record*, 105 (1966), 35–47.

Gilbert, J.T. (ed.), *A Jacobite narrative of the war in Ireland, 1688–1691* (Dublin: Joseph Dollard, 1892).

Hardiman, J. (ed.), *Irish minstrelsy, or bardic remains of Ireland*, 2 vols. (London: J. Robins, 1831).

Keating, G., *Foras feasa ar Éirinn*, ed. D. Comyn, vol. I (London: Irish Texts Society, 1902).

Kelly, J., '"Disappointing the boundless ambition of France": Irish Protestants and the fear of invasion, 1661–1815', *Studia Hibernica*, 37 (2011), 27–105.

Kelly, J. with M.A. Lyons (eds.), *The Proclamations of Ireland 1660–1820*, 5 vols. (Dublin: Irish Manuscripts Commission, 2014).

[Lynch, J.], *Cambrensis eversus*, 3 vols., ed. M. Kelly (Dublin: Celtic Society, 1851).

Mac Cumhghaill, B. (ed.), *Seán de Hóra* (Dublin: Oifig an tSoláthair, 1956).

MacErlean, J.C. (ed.), *Duanaire Dháibhidh Uí Bhruadair*, 3 vols. (London: Irish Texts Society, 1917).

MacGeoghegan, L'Abbé, *Histoire de l'Irlande ancienne et moderne*, 3 vols. (Paris: Antoine Boudet, 1758–63).

McBride, I., 'Catholic politics in the penal era: Father Sylvester Lloyd and the Delvin address of 1727' in J. Bergin, E. Magennis, L. Ní Mhungaile and P. Walsh (eds.), *New perspectives on the Penal Laws* (Dublin: Eighteenth-Century Ireland Society, 2011), pp. 115–47.

McKenna, L. (ed.), *Aithdioghluim dána*, 2 vols. (London: Irish Texts Society, 1939).

Morley, V., 'Hugh MacCurtin: an Irish poet in the French army', *Eighteenth-Century Ireland*, 8 (1993), 49–58.

'Idé-eolaíocht an tSeacaibíteachais in Éirinn agus in Albain', *Oghma*, 9 (1997), 14–24.

'The idea of Britain in eighteenth-century Ireland and Scotland', *Studia Hibernica*, 33 (2004–5), 101–24.

(ed.), *Washington i gceannas a ríochta: Cogadh Mheiriceá i Litríocht na Gaeilge* (Dublin: Coiscéim, 2005).

'The continuity of disaffection in eighteenth-century Ireland', *Eighteenth-Century Ireland*, 22 (2007), 189–205.

'Catholic disaffection and the oath of allegiance of 1774' in J. Kelly, J. McCafferty and C.I. McGrath (eds.), *People, politics and power: essays on Irish history, 1660–1850* (Dublin: UCD Press, 2009), pp. 122–42.

'Peter Walsh' in J. McGuire and J. Quinn (eds.), *Dictionary of Irish biography*, 9 vols. (Cambridge: Cambridge University Press, 2009), vol. IX, pp. 756–60.

(ed.), *Aodh Buí Mac Cruitín* (Dublin: Field Day Publications, 2012).

The popular mind in eighteenth-century Ireland (Cork: Cork University Press, 2017).

Neal, J. and W., *A collection of the most celebrated Irish tunes*, ed. N. Carolan (Dublin: Irish Traditional Music Archive, 2010).

Ní Chinnéide, S. (ed.), 'Dhá leabhar nótaí le Séarlas Ó Conchubhair', *Galvia*, 1 (1954), 32–41.

Nic Éinrí, Ú. (ed.), *An cantaire siúlach: Tadhg Gaelach* (Dingle: An Sagart, 2001).

(ed.), *Canfar an dán: Uilliam English agus a chairde* (Dingle: An Sagart, 2003).

Nic Éinrí, Ú., and M. Spillane (eds.), *Seán Ó Tuama ó Chromadh an tsubhachais* (Dublin: Coiscéim, 2012).

Ó Buachalla, B. (ed.), *Nua-dhuanaire*, vol. I (Dublin: Dublin Institute for Advanced Studies, 1976).

'Briseadh na Bóinne', *Éigse*, 23 (1989), 83–106.

'James our true king: the ideology of Irish royalism in the seventeenth century' in D.G. Boyce, R. Eccleshall and V. Geoghegan (eds.), *Political thought in Ireland since the seventeenth century* (London: Routledge, 1993), pp. 7–35.

Aisling Ghéar: na Stíobhartaigh agus an t-aos léinn 1603–1788 (Dublin: An Clóchomhar, 1996).

The crown of Ireland (Galway: Arlen House, 2006).

(ed.), *Aogán Ó Rathaille* (Dublin: Field Day Publications, 2007).

Ó Ciardha, É., *Ireland and the Jacobite cause, 1685–1766: a fatal attachment* (Dublin: Four Courts Press, 2002).

Ó Conaill, C.J., 'The Irish regiments in France: an overview of the presence of Irish soldiers in French service, 1716–1791' in E. Maher and G. Neville (eds.), *France–Ireland: anatomy of a relationship* (Frankfurt am Main: Peter Lang, 2004), pp. 327–42.

Ó Concheanainn, T. (ed.), *Nua-dhuanaire*, vol. II (Dublin: Dublin Institute for Advanced Studies, 1981).

Ó Cróinín, B. (ed.), *Piaras Mac Gearailt: a shaol agus a shaothar* (Dingle: An Sagart, 2015).

Ó Donnchadha, T. (ed.), *Amhráin Dhiarmada mac Seáin Bhuidhe Mac Cárrthaigh* (Dublin: M. H. Mac Goill agus a Mhac, 1916).

Ó Fiaich, T. (ed.), *Art Mac Cumhaigh: Dánta* (Dublin: An Clóchomhar, 1973).

Ó Foghludha, R. (ed.), *Cois na Cora* (Dublin: Oifig Díolta Foillseacháin Rialtais, 1937).

Eoghan an Mhéirín (Dublin: Oifig Díolta Foillseacháin Rialtais, 1937).

(ed.), *Ar bruach na Coille Muaire* (Dublin: Oifig an tSoláthair, 1939).

(ed.), *Éigse na Máighe* (Dublin: Oifig Díolta Foillseacháin Rialtais, 1952).

Ó Gallchóir, S., 'Filíocht Shéamais Daill Mhic Cuarta', unpublished MA thesis, St. Patrick's College, Maynooth, 1967.

(ed.), *Séamas Dall Mac Cuarta: Dánta* (Dublin: An Clóchomhar, 1971).

Ó hAnluain, E. (ed.), *Seon Ó hUaithnín* (Dublin: An Clóchomhar, 1973).

Ó Muirgheasa, É. (ed.), *Céad de cheoltaibh Uladh* (Dublin: M.H. Mac Giolla agus a Mhac, 1915).

(ed.), *Dhá chéad de cheoltaibh Uladh* (Dublin: Oifig an tSoláthair, 1934).

(ed.), *Dánta diadha Uladh* (Dublin: Oifig Díolta Foillseacháin Rialtais, 1936).

Ó Muirithe, D. (ed.), *An tamhrán macarónach* (Dublin: An Clóchomhar, 1980).

(ed.), *Cois an Ghaorthaidh* (Dublin: An Clóchomhar, 1987).

O'Callaghan, J.C., *History of the Irish brigades in the service of France* (Glasgow: Cameron and Ferguson, 1870).

O'Rahilly, C. (ed.), *Five seventeenth-century political poems* (Dublin: Dublin Institute for Advanced Studies, 1952).

Recio Morales, Ó., *Ireland and the Spanish Empire, 1600–1825* (Dublin: Four Courts Press, 2010).

Rowlands, G., *An army in exile: Louis XIV and the Irish forces of James II in France, 1691–1698* (London: Royal Stuart Society, 2001).

Szechi, S., *The Jacobites: Britain and Europe 1688–1788* (Manchester: Manchester University Press, 1994).

Thomson, D.S. (ed.), *Alasdair Mac Mhaighstir Alasdair: selected poems* (Edinburgh: Scottish Gaelic Texts Society, 1996).

2 The Politics of Protestant Ascendancy, 1730–1790

James Kelly

Manuscript

Additional Sheffield papers, T/3465: Public Record Office of Northern Ireland

Bowood papers, B33: British Library

Chatsworth papers, T/3158: Public Record Office of Northern Ireland

Diary of a journey through England, Wales and Ireland made by Rev. J. Burrowes, 1773, T3551: Public Record Office of Northern Ireland

Hardwicke papers, Add. MS 35615: British Library

Joy papers, MS 11: Linenhall Library

Lansdowne MS 1235: British Library

Newcastle of Clumber papers: Nottingham University Library

Newcastle papers, Add. MS 32874: British Library

Townshend papers, MS 730: National Archives of Ireland

Electronic

Irish Legislation database, 1692–1800, at www.qub.ac.uk/ild/.

Kelly, J., 'The Ponsonby family' in Multi-text project in Irish history: history of early-modern Ireland at http://multitext.ucc.ie/d/The_Ponsonby_Family (accessed December 2015).

Printed

A Collection of the Protests of the Lords of Ireland (Dublin: Milliken, 1772).

Baratariana: a Select Collection of fugitive Political Pieces, published during the Administration of Lord Townshend in Ireland, 3rd edn (Dublin: s.n., 1777).

Bartlett, T., 'The Townshend viceroyalty, 1767–72' in T. Bartlett and D.W. Hayton (eds.), *Penal era and golden age: essays in Irish history, 1690–1800* (Belfast: Ulster Historical Foundation, 1979), pp. 88–112.

'Opposition in late eighteenth-century Ireland: the case of the Townshend viceroyalty', *Irish Historical Studies*, 22 (1981), 66–87.

Burns, R.E., *Irish parliamentary politics in the eighteenth century*, 2 vols. (Washington, DC: Catholic University of America Press, 1989–90).

Conway, S., *The British Isles and the War of American Independence* (Oxford: Oxford University Press, 2000).

Dublin Evening Journal, 1778.

Eighteenth-century Irish official papers in Great Britain, ed. A.P.W. Malcomson, 2 vols. (Belfast: Public Record Office of Northern Ireland, [1973]–1990).

Freeman's Journal, 1763–82.

Garnham, N., *The militia in eighteenth-century Ireland* (Woodbridge: The Boydell Press, 2012).

Grattan, H., *The speeches of Henry Grattan,* 4 vols. (London: Longman, Hurst, Rees, Orme and Brown, 1822).

Higgins, P., *A nation of politicians: gender, patriotism and political culture in late eighteenth-century Ireland* (Madison: University of Wisconsin Press, 2010).

HMC, *10th report appendix 1: C.F. Weston Underwood MSS* (London: Eyre and Spottiswoode, 1885).

    Reports on various collections, vol. VI: Eyre Matcham MSS (London: HMSO, 1909).

Ilchester, Earl of, *Henry Fox, first Lord Holland,* 2 vols. (London: John Murray, 1920).

Kelly, J., 'The origins of the Act of Union: an examination of unionist opinion in Britain and Ireland, 1650–1800', *Irish Historical Studies*, 25 (1987), 236–63.

    'The genesis of Protestant Ascendancy: the Rightboy disturbances of the 1780s and their impact upon Protestant opinion' in G. O'Brien (ed.), *Parliament, politics and people: essays in eighteenth-century Irish history* (Dublin: Irish Academic Press, 1989), pp. 93–127.

    Prelude to Union: Anglo-Irish politics in the 1780s (Cork: Cork University Press, 1992).

    'Parliamentary reform in Irish politics, 1760–90' in D. Dickson et al. (eds.), *The United Irishmen: republicanism, radicalism and rebellion* (Dublin: Lilliput Press, 1993), pp. 74–87.

    Henry Flood: patriots and politics in eighteenth-century Ireland (Notre Dame, IN: University of Notre Dame Press, 1998).

    Sir Edward Newenham, MP, 1734–1814: defender of the Protestant constitution (Dublin: Four Courts Press, 2004).

    'Political publishing, 1700–1800' in R. Gillespie and A. Hadfield (eds.), *The Oxford history of the Irish book, vol. III: 1550–1800* (Oxford: Oxford University Press, 2005), pp. 215–33.

    Poynings' Law and the making of law in Ireland, 1660–1800 (Dublin: Four Courts Press, 2007).

    'Sustaining a confessional state: the Irish parliament and Catholicism' in D.W. Hayton, J. Kelly and J. Bergin (eds.), *The eighteenth-century composite state* (Basingstoke: Palgrave, 2010), pp. 55–63.

    ' "Disappointing the boundless ambitions of France": Irish Protestants and the fear of invasion, 1661–1815', *Studia Hibernica*, 37 (2011), 51–77.

    'Residential and non-residential lords lieutenants: the viceroyalty, 1703–90' in P. Gray and O. Purdue (eds.), *The Irish lord lieutenancy, c. 1541–1922* (Dublin: UCD Press, 2012), pp. 66–96.

    'Mathew Carey's Irish apprenticeship: editing the *Volunteers Journal*, 1783–84', *Eire-Ireland*, 49:3&4 (2014), 201–43.

    'Patriot politics 1750–91' in A. Jackson (ed.), *The Oxford handbook of modern Irish history* (Oxford: Oxford University Press, 2014), pp. 479–96.

Lammey, D., 'The growth of the "Patriot opposition" in Ireland during the 1770s', *Parliamentary History*, 7:2 (1988), 257–81.

    The Letters of Junius, ed. J. Cannon (Oxford: Oxford University Press, 1978).

Letters from an Ulster Land Agent, 1774–1785, ed. W.H. Crawford (Belfast: Public Record Office of Northern Ireland, 1976).

Limerick Chronicle, 1771–2.

Magennis, E. *The Irish political system, 1740–1765: the golden age of the undertakers* (Dublin: Four Courts Press, 2000).

Malcomson, A.P.W., 'Lord Shannon' in Esther Hewitt (ed.), *Lord Shannon's letters to his son* (Belfast: Public Record Office of Northern Ireland, 1982), pp. xxiii–lxxix.

John Foster (1740–1828): the politics of improvement and prosperity (Dublin: Four Courts Press, 2011).

McBride, I., 'The common name of Irishman: Protestantism and patriotism in eighteenth-century Ireland' in T. Claydon and I. McBride (eds.), *Protestantism and national identity: Britain and Ireland, c.1650–c.1850* (Cambridge: Cambridge University Press, 1998), pp. 236–61.

McGrath, C.I., *The making of the eighteenth-century Irish constitution: government, parliament and the revenue, 1692–1714* (Dublin: Four Courts Press, 2000).

Morley, V., *Irish opinion and the American Revolution, 1760–1783* (Cambridge: Cambridge University Press, 2002).

Murphy, S., 'The Lucas affair: a study of municipal and electoral politics in Dublin, 1742–9', MA thesis, UCD, 1981.

O'Connell, M.R., *Irish politics and social conflict in the age of the American Revolution* (Philadelphia: University of Pennsylvania Press, 1965).

O'Donovan, D., 'The Money Bill dispute of 1753' in T. Bartlett and D.W. Hayton (eds.), *Penal era and golden age: essays in Irish history, 1690–1800* (Belfast: Ulster Historical Foundation, 1979), pp. 55–87.

The Orrery letters, ed. Countess of Cork and Orrery, 2 vols. (London: Duckworth, 1903).

Powell, M.J., 'The Society of Free Citizens and other popular political clubs, 1749–89' in J. Kelly and M.J. Powell (eds.), *Clubs and societies in eighteenth-century Ireland* (Dublin: Four Courts Press, 2010), pp. 245–55.

Ramsey's Waterford Chronicle, 1789.

Walsh, P., *The making of the Irish Protestant Ascendancy: the life of William Conolly, 1662–1729* (Woodbridge: The Boydell Press, 2010).

3 Ireland during the Revolutionary and Napoleonic Wars, 1791–1815

Thomas Bartlett

Manuscript

A concise view of the charge of the military establishment of Ireland . . . [1598–1821], MS 999/308/3/18: National Archives of Ireland

Abercorn papers, T/2541: Public Record Office of Northern Ireland

Additional Sheffield papers, T/3725: Public Record Office of Northern Ireland

Camden Transcripts, T/2627/4/: Public Record Office of Northern Ireland

Chatham papers, 30/8/331: The National Archives

Clinton papers, MS 10214: National Library of Ireland

Home Office papers, HO 100/14–188: The National Archives

Military reports, MIC 67/143: Public Record Office of Northern Ireland

Normanton papers, T/3719: Public Record Office of Northern Ireland

Peel papers, Add. MS 40235: British Library

Pitt papers: W.L. Clements Library, Ann Arbor, Michigan

Rebellion papers, 620/: National Archives of Ireland

Richmond papers MS 60: National Library of Ireland

Wellesley transcripts, T/2627/: Public Record Office of Northern Ireland

Printed

Bartlett, T., *The fall and rise of the Irish nation: the Catholic question, 1690–1830* (Dublin: Gill & Macmillan, 1992).

Beresford, W. (ed.), *The correspondence of the Rt. Hon. John Beresford*, 2 vols. (London: Woodfall and Kinder, 1854).

Chart, D.A., 'The Irish levies during the Great French War', *English Historical Review*, 32 (Oct. 1917), 497–516.

Clark, S., and J. Donnelly (eds.), *Irish peasants: violence and political unrest 1780–1914* (Manchester: Manchester University Press, 1984).

Colley, L., *Britons: forging the nation, 1707–1837* (New Haven: Yale University Press, 1992).

Cookson, J.E., *The British armed nation, 1793–1815* (Oxford: Oxford University Press, 1997).

Curtin, N.J., *The United Irishmen: popular politics in Ulster and Dublin, 1791–1798* (Oxford: Oxford University Press, 1994).

Dancy, J. Ross, *The myth of the press gang* (Woodbridge: The Boydell Press, 2015).

Dickson, D., *Old World colony: Cork and South Munster, 1630–1830* (Cork: Cork University Press, 2005).

Donnelly, J.S., 'Pastorini and Captain Rock: millenarianism and sectarianism in the Rockite movement of 1821–4' in S. Clark and J. Donnelly (eds.) *Irish Peasants* (Manchester: Manchester University Press, 1984), pp. 102–39

    Captain Rock: the Irish agrarian rebellion of 1821–4 (Madison, WI: University of Wisconsin Press, 2009).

Doyle, W., 'The Union in a European context', *Transactions of the Royal Historical Society*, sixth series, 10 (2001), pp. 167–80.

Elliott, M., *Partners in Revolution: the United Irishmen and France* (New Haven: Yale University Press, 1982).

    Theobald Wolfe Tone: Prophet of Irish Independence (New Haven: Yale University Press, 1989).

Ferradou, M., 'Histoire d'un "festin patriotique" à l'hôtel White (18 novembre 1792)', *Annales Historique de la Révolution Française* 382 (2015), 123–43.

Grattan, H. (ed.), *Memoirs of the life and times of Henry Grattan*, 5 vols. (Dublin: H. Colburn, 1839–46).

Holmes, R., *Soldiers* (London: Allen Lane, 2012).

Kelly, J., *Sir Richard Musgrave: ultra-Protestant ideologue* (Dublin: Four Courts, 2009).

Knight, R., *Britain against Napoleon: the organization of victory* (London: Allen Lane, 2013).

Linch, K., *Britain and Wellington's army: recruitment, society and tradition, 1807–15* (Basingstoke: Palgrave, 2011).

Madden, Kyla, *Forkhill Protestants, Forkhill Catholics 1787–1858* (Liverpool: Liverpool University Press, 2005).

Miller, D., 'The Armagh Troubles, 1784–95' in S. Clark and J. Donnelly (eds.), *Irish peasants* (Manchester: Manchester University Press, 1984), pp. 155–91.

Musgrave, Sir R., *Memoirs of the different rebellions in Ireland from the arrival of the English . . .* , 2nd edn (Dublin: Milliken, 1801).

Parker, C.S. (ed.), *Sir Robert Peel from his private papers*, 2 vols. (London: John Murray, 1891).

Roberts, P., 'Caravats and Shanavests: Whiteboyism and faction fighting in east Munster, 1802–11' in S. Clark and J. Donnelly (eds.), *Irish peasants* (Manchester: Manchester University Press, 1984), pp. 64–101.

Ross, C. (ed.), *The correspondence of Charles, first Marquis Cornwallis*, 3 vols. (London: John Murray, 1859).

Sack, J.J., *From Jacobite to Conservative: reaction and orthodoxy in Britain, c1760–1832* (Cambridge: Cambridge University Press, 1993).

Smyth, J., *The men of no property: Irish radicals and popular politics in the late eighteenth century* (Basingstoke: Macmillan, 1992).

Whelan, K., *The Tree of Liberty: Radicalism, Catholicism and the construction of Irish identity, 1760–1800* (Cork: Cork University Press, 1997).

4 The Impact of O'Connell, 1815–1850

Patrick M. Geoghegan

Manuscript

Catholic Association papers: Dublin Diocesan Archives

Printed

Aspinwall, B., 'Was O'Connell necessary? Sir Joseph Dillon, Scotland, and the movement for Catholic emancipation' in D.M. Loades (ed.), *The end of strife* (Edinburgh: T. and T. Clark, 1984).

Bartlett, T., *Ireland: a history* (Cambridge: Cambridge University Press, 2010).

Beresford Ellis, P., *A history of the Irish working class* (London: Pluto Press, 1985).

Bew, P. *Ireland: the politics of enmity 1789–2006* (Oxford: Oxford University Press, 2007).

Bew, P., and P. Maume, 'The great advocate', *Dublin Review of Books*, 8 (Winter 2008) (www.drb.ie/essays/the-great-advocate).

Colantonio, L., 'Democracy and the Irish people' in J. Innes and M. Philp (eds.), *Reimagining democracy in the age of revolutions: America, France, Britain* (Oxford: Oxford University Press, 2013), pp. 162–73.

Curran, D., *The Protestant community in Ulster, 1825–45: a society in transition* (Dublin: Four Courts Press, 2014).

Davis, R., *The Young Ireland Movement* (Dublin: Gill & Macmillan, 1987).

Donnelly, J.S., Jr., *Captain Rock: the Irish agrarian rebellion of 1821–1824* (Cork: Collins Press, 2009).

Doyle, D., *The Reverend Thomas Goff, 1772–1844: property, propinquity and Protestantism* (Dublin: Four Courts Press, 2015).

Gavan Duffy, C., *Young Ireland* (Dublin, London and New York: Cassell, Petter, Galpin, 1880).

Four Years of Irish History (Dublin, London and New York: Cassell, Petter, Galpin, 1887).

Geoghegan, P., *King Dan: the rise of Daniel O'Connell, 1775–1829* (Dublin: Gill & Macmillan, 2008).

'Daniel O'Connell and the Irish Act of Union' in J. Kelly, J. McCafferty and C.I. McGrath (eds.), *People, politics and power: essays on Irish history, 1660–1850* (Dublin: UCD Press, 2009), pp. 175–89.

Liberator: the life and death of Daniel O'Connell, 1830–47 (Dublin: Gill & Macmillan, 2010).

[Grant, J.], Mask, *St. Stephen's: or, Pencillings of politicians* (London: Hugh Cunningham, 1839).

Grogan, G.F., *The Noblest Agitator: Daniel O'Connell and the German Catholic Movement 1830–50* (Dublin: Veritas, 1991).

Kelly, J., *'That Damn'd Thing called Honour': duelling in Ireland, 1570–1860* (Cork: Cork University Press, 1996).

Sir Richard Musgrave, 1746–1818: ultra-Protestant ideologue (Dublin: Four Courts Press, 2009).

Kinealy, C., 'The Liberator: Daniel O'Connell and anti-slavery', *History Today*, 57:12 (2007), pp. 51–7.

Daniel O'Connell and the anti-slavery movement (London: Pickering and Chatto, 2011).

Kissane, B., *Explaining Irish democracy* (Dublin: UCD Press, 2002).

Koebner, R., 'The early speeches of Henry Grattan', *Bulletin of the Institute of Historical Research,* 30 (1957), pp. 102–14.

Lecky, W.E.H., *Leaders of public opinion in Ireland,* 2 vols. (London: Longmans, Green and Co., 1903).

MacDonagh, M., *The life of Daniel O'Connell* (London: Cassell, 1903).

MacDonagh, O., *The hereditary bondsman: Daniel O'Connell, 1775–1829* (London: Weidenfeld and Nicolson, 1988).

The emancipist: Daniel O'Connell, 1830–1847 (London: Weidenfeld and Nicolson, 1989).

Mc Cormack, W.J., 'Vision and revision in the study of eighteenth-century Irish parliamentary rhetoric', *Eighteenth-Century Ireland,* 2 (1987), 7–35.

McCartney, D., *The dawning of democracy* (Dublin: Helicon, 1987).

Memoirs of the Right Honourable Sir Robert Peel, ed. Lord Mahon, 2 vols. (London: John Murray, 1857).

O'Brien, G., 'The Grattan mystique', *Eighteenth-Century Ireland,* 1 (1986), 177–94.

O'Connell, D., *The life and speeches of Daniel O'Connell M.P.,* ed. J. O'Connell, 2 vols. (Dublin: J. Duffy, 1846).

Daniel O'Connell upon American slavery, with other Irish testimonies (New York: American Anti-Slavery Society, 1860).

Correspondence of Daniel O'Connell, the Liberator, ed. W.J. Fitzpatrick, 2 vols. (New York: Longmans, Green and Co., 1888).

The correspondence of Daniel O'Connell, ed. M.R. O'Connell, 8 vols. (Shannon and Dublin: Irish University Press (vols. I–III); Stationery Office (vol. IV); Blackwater (vols. V–VIII), 1972–80).

O'Faoláin, S., *King of the beggars: a life of Daniel O'Connell* (Dublin: Poolbeg Press, 1986).

O'Reilly, A., 'Completing the Union: the politics of implementation in Ireland, 1801–1815', PhD thesis, Trinity College Dublin, 2014.

Phillips, C., *Curran and his contemporaries* (Edinburgh: Blackwood, 1850).

Quinn, J., *Young Ireland and the writing of Irish history* (Dublin: UCD Press, 2015).

Reeve, H. (ed.), *Memoir and correspondence relating to political occurrences in June and July 1834 by the Right Hon. Edward John Littleton, first Lord Hatherton* (London: Longmans, Green and Co., 1872).

Robinson, M., 'Daniel O'Connell: a tribute', *History Ireland*, 5:4 (1997), 26–31.

The Black Abolitionist papers, vol. I: The British Isles, 1830–1865, ed. C. Peter Ripley (Chapel Hill: University of North Carolina Press, 1985).

The Greville Memoirs: a journal of the reigns of King George IV and King William IV, 8 vols. (London: Longmans, Green and Co., 1874–87).

Welch, R., *Irish writers and religion* (Gerrard's Cross: Colin Smythe, 1992).

Works of Lord Macaulay, ed. Lady Trevelyan, 8 vols. (London: Longmans, Green and Co., 1866).

Wyse, T., *Historical Sketch of the late Catholic Association of Ireland*, 2 vols. (London, 1829).

5 Popular Politics, 1815–1845

Maura Cronin

Manuscript

Bruen papers, MS 29778: National Library of Ireland

Chief Secretary's Office Private Index: National Archives of Ireland

Crofton Croker papers, Add. MS 20096: British Library

Madden Ballads: Cambridge University Library

O'Connell Correspondence, vi: National Library of Ireland

Outrage papers, 1835, Carlow; 1834–6, 1844, Cork; 1843, Mayo; 1843, Waterford; 1843, Clare: National Archives of Ireland

Smith O'Brien papers, MS 442: National Library of Ireland

Printed

Bardon, J., *History of Ulster* (Belfast: Blackstaff, 1992).

Beames, M.R., 'The Ribbon societies: lower-class nationalism in pre-Famine Ireland', *Past and Present*, 97 (1982), 128–43.

Peasants and power: the Whiteboy movements and their control in pre-Famine Ireland (Brighton: Harvester Press, 1983).

Blackstock, A., *Loyalism in Ireland, 1789–1829* (Woodbridge: The Boydell Press, 2007).

'Tommy Downshire's boys: popular protest, social change and political manipulation in mid-Ulster 1829–1847', *Past and Present*, 196 (2007), 125–72.

Borris Chapels. Copies of Correspondence between the Roman Catholic Priests of Borris, Robert Doyne, Esq and the Lord Lieutenant of Ireland, on the alleged attendance of the military at the Roman Catholic chapels: H.C. 1835 (198), xlv. 493.

Bowen, D., *Souperism: myth or reality: a study in Souperism* (Cork: Mercier Press, 1970).

Boyle, J., *The Irish Labour Movement in the nineteenth century* (Washington, DC: Catholic University of America Press, 1988).

Brennan, B., *Máire Bhuí Ní Laoire: a poet of her people* (Cork: Collins Press, 2000).

Carlow Sentinel, 1835.

Clark, S., *Social origins of the Irish Land War* (Princeton: Princeton University Press, 1979).

Connolly, S.J., *Priests and People in pre-Famine Ireland 1780–1845* (Dublin: Gill & Macmillan, 1982).

Cork Constitution, 1831–43.

Cork Examiner, 1847.

Cork Mercantile Chronicle, 1832–42.

Cronin, M., *Country, class or craft: the politicisation of the skilled artisan in nineteenth-century Cork* (Cork: Cork University Press, 1994).

'"Of one mind": O'Connellite crowds in the 1830s and 1840s' in P. Jupp and E. Magennis (eds.), *Crowds in Ireland c. 1720–1920* (Basingstoke: Macmillan, 2000), pp. 139–72.

'"By memory inspired": the past in popular song, 1798–1900' in T. Dooley (ed.), *Ireland's polemical past: views of Irish history* (Dublin: UCD Press, 2010), pp. 32–50.

Agrarian protest in Ireland 1750–1960 (Dundalk: Irish Economic and Social History Society, 2012).

Crossman, V., *Local government in nineteenth-century Ireland* (Belfast: Institute of Irish Studies, 1994).

Curran, D., 'The great Protestant meeting of Dungannon, 1834' in W. Sheehan and M. Cronin (eds.), *Riotous assemblies: rebels, riots and revolts in Ireland* (Cork: Mercier Press, 2011), pp. 96–109.

The Protestant community in Ulster, 1825–45: a society in transition (Dublin: Four Courts Press, 2014).

D'Alton, I., *Cork Protestant society and politics in Cork 1812–1844* (Cork: Cork University Press, 1980).

D'Arcy, F., 'The artisans of Dublin and Daniel O'Connell 1830–1847: an unquiet liaison', *Irish Historical Studies,* 17 (1970–1), 221–43.

'The trade unions of Dublin and the attempted revival of the guilds: an episode in mid-nineteenth century Irish labour history', *Journal of the Royal Society of Antiquaries of Ireland,* 101 (1971), 113–27.

Donnelly, J.S., *Captain Rock: the Irish agrarian rebellion of 1821–1824* (Cork: Collins Press, 2009).

Dooley, T. (ed.), *Ireland's polemical past: views of Irish history in honour of R. V. Comerford* (Dublin: UCD Press, 2010).

Drogheda Conservative, 1843.

First report from the Select Committee on Fictitious Votes, Ireland, H.C. 1837 (308).

First report of the Commissioners appointed to enquire into the Municipal Corporations in Ireland, H.C. 1835, xvii.

Freeholder, 1831.

Freeman's Journal, 1840–1.

Garvin, T., 'Defenders, Ribbonmen and others: underground political networks in pre-Famine Ireland', *Past and Present*, 96 (1982), 133–55.

Gibbons, S.R., 'Captain Rock in the Queen's County' in P. Lane and W. Nolan (eds.), *Laois: history and society* (Dublin: Geography Publications, 1999), pp. 487–512.

Hanrahan, M., 'The Tithe War in County Kilkenny 1830–1834' in W. Nolan and K. Whelan (eds.), *Kilkenny: history and society* (Dublin: Geography Publications, 1990), pp. 481–506.

Hill, J., 'The meaning of "Protestant Ascendancy", 1787–1840' in *Ireland after the Union: proceedings of the second joint meeting of the Royal Irish Academy and the British Academy, London 1986* (Oxford: Oxford University Press, 1989), pp. 1–22.

Hirst, C., 'Politics, sectarianism and the working class in nineteenth-century Belfast' in F. Lane and D. Ó Drisceoil (eds.), *Politics and the Irish working class, 1830–1945* (Basingstoke: Palgrave Macmillan, 2005), pp. 62–86.

Hoppen, K.T., *Elections, politics and society in Ireland 1832–1885* (Oxford: Clarendon Press, 1984).

Jupp, P., and E. Magennis (eds.), *Crowds in Ireland c. 1720–1920* (Basingstoke: Macmillan, 2000).

Kelly, J., 'An outward looking community? Ribbonism and popular mobilisation in Co. Leitrim 1836–46', PhD thesis, Mary Immaculate College, University of Limerick, 2005.

'Local memory and manipulation of the past in Leitrim' in T. Dooley (ed.), *Ireland's polemical past: view of Irish history* (Dublin: UCD Press, 2010), pp. 51–67.

Kelly, J., *Sir Richard Musgrave, 1746–1818: ultra-Protestant ideologue* (Dublin: Four Courts Press, 2009).

Kilkenny Journal, 1843.

Knowlton, S.R., 'The quarrel between Gavan Duffy and John Mitchel: implications for Ireland', *Albion*, 21:4 (1989), 581–90.

Lane, F., *In search of Thomas Sheehan: radical politics in Cork 1824–1836* (Dublin: Irish Academic Press, 2001).

Madden, D.O., *Ireland and its rulers, 3 vols.* (London: Newby, 1843–4).

McGrath, T.G., 'Interdenominational relations in pre-famine Tipperary' in W. Nolan and T.G. McGrath (eds.), *Tipperary: history and society* (Dublin: Geography Publications, 1985), pp. 256–87.

McIlfatrick, J.H., *Sprigs around the Pump Town: Orangeism in the Kilrea District* (Derry: McIlfatrick, 1995).

Miller, D.W., *Queen's Rebels: Ulster loyalism in historical perspective* (Dublin: UCD Press, 2007).

Murphy, M., 'Municipal reform and the repeal movement in Cork, 1833–1844', *Journal of the Cork Historical and Archaeological Society*, 81 (1976), 1–18.

'The ballad singer and the role of the seditious ballad in nineteenth-century Ireland: Dublin Castle's view', *Ulster Folklife*, 25 (1979), 79–102.

Ó Cíosáin, N., *Print and popular culture in Ireland, 1750–1850* (Basingstoke: Macmillan, 1997).

Ó Tuathaigh, G., 'Gaelic Ireland, popular politics and Daniel O'Connell', *Journal of the Galway Archaeological and Historical Society*, 34 (1974), 21–34.

O'Dea, L., 'Thomas Drummond', *Dublin Historical Record*, 24:4 (1971), 112–23.

O'Ferrall, F., *Catholic emancipation: Daniel O'Connell and the birth of Irish democracy 1820–30* (Dublin: Gill & Macmillan, 1985).

O'Higgins, R., 'Irish trade unions and politics, 1830–50', *Historical Journal*, 4 (1961), 208–17.

Owens, G., 'Nationalism without words: symbolism and ritual behaviour in the repeal "monster" meetings of 1843–5' in J.S. Donnelly Jr and K.A. Miller (eds.), *Irish popular culture, 1650–1850* (Dublin: Irish Academic Press, 1999), pp. 242–69.

'The Carrickshock incident: social memory and an Irish cause célèbre', *Social and Cultural History*, 1:1 (2004), 36–64.

Pilot, 1836, 1837.

Read, D., and E. Glasgow, *Feargus O'Connor, Irishman and Chartist* (London: Edward Arnold, 1961).

Reid, D.P., 'The Tithe War in Ireland, 1830–1838', PhD thesis, Trinity College Dublin, 2012.

Report from Her Majesty's Commissioners of Inquiry into the state of the law and practise in respect to the occupation of land in Ireland, H.C. 1845 [605].

Select Committee on Fictitious Votes, Ireland, H.C. 1837 (308).

Southern Reporter, 1830, 1836, 1841.

The Repealer Repulsed: a correct Narrative of the Rise and Progress of the Repeal invasion of Ulster (Belfast: McComb, 1841).

Tipperary Constitution, 1843.

Tralee Mercury, 1832.

Walker, B. (ed.), *Parliamentary election results in Ireland, 1801–1922* (Dublin: Royal Irish Academy, 1978).

Waterford Mail, 1833.

Waterford Weekly Chronicle, 1832.

Western Argus and Galway Commercial Chronicle, 1832.

Whelan, K., *The Tree of Liberty: Radicalism, Catholicism and the construction of Irish identity, 1760–1830* (Cork: Cork University Press, 1996).

Wright, F., *Two lands on one soil: Ulster politics before Home Rule* (Dublin: Gill & Macmillan, 1996).

Zimmermann, G.D., *Songs of Irish rebellion: political street ballads and rebel songs 1780–1900* (Dublin: Allan Figgis, 1967).

6 Society and Economy in the Long Eighteenth Century

David Dickson

Manuscript

Legers of imports and exports, Ireland, 1698–1829, CUST/15, The National Archives

Printed

Barnard, T.C., *A new anatomy of Ireland: the Irish Protestants, 1649–1770* (New Haven: Yale University Press, 2003).

Making the grand figure: lives and possessions in Ireland, 1641–1770 (New Haven: Yale University Press, 2004).

Improving Ireland? Projectors, prophets and profiteers, 1641–1786 (Dublin: Four Courts Press, 2008).

Benn, G., *A history of the town of Belfast . . .*, 2nd edn (London: Marcus Ward, 1877).

[Berkeley, G.], *The Querist . . .* (Dublin: R. Reilly, 1735–7).

Bindon, D., *A scheme for supplying industrious men with money . . .* (Dublin: Thomas Hume, 1729).

Brewster, F., *New essays on trade . . .* (London: H. Walwyn, 1702).

Broderick, D., *The first Toll Roads: Ireland's turnpike roads 1729–1858* (Dublin: Irish Academic Press, 2002).

Butel, Paul, and L.M. Cullen (eds.), *Cities and merchants: French and Irish perspectives on urban development, 1500–1900* (Dublin: Department of History, Trinity College, 1986).

Clarkson, L.A., 'The Carrick-on-Suir woollen industry in the eighteenth century', *Irish Economic and Social History*, 16 (1989), 23–41.

Clarkson, L.A., and E.M. Crawford, *Feast and famine: food and nutrition in Ireland, 1500–1920* (Oxford: Oxford University Press, 2001).

Cochran, L.E., *Scottish trade with Ireland in the eighteenth century* (Edinburgh: John Donald, 1985).

Collins, Brenda, Philip Ollerenshaw and Trevor Parkhill (eds.), *Industry, trade and people in Ireland, 1650–1950: essays in honour of W.H. Crawford* (Belfast: Ulster Historical Foundation, 2005).

Connolly, S.J., 'The Houghers: agrarian protest in early eighteenth-century Connacht' in C.H.E. Philpin (ed.), *Nationalism and popular protest in Ireland* (Cambridge: Cambridge University Press, 1987), pp. 139–62.

Religion, law and power: the making of Protestant Ireland 1660–1760 (Oxford: Clarendon Press, 1992).

Divided kingdom: Ireland 1630–1800 (Oxford: Oxford University Press, 2008).

Crawford, W.H., *The impact of the domestic linen industry in Ulster* (Belfast: Ulster Historical Foundation, 2005).

Cullen, L.M., *Anglo-Irish trade 1660–1800* (Manchester: Manchester University Press, 1968).

An economic history of Ireland since 1660 (London: Batsford, 1972).

The emergence of modern Ireland 1600–1900 (London: Batsford, 1981).

'Economic development, 1691–1750', and 'Economic development, 1750–1800', in T.W. Moody and W.E. Vaughan (eds.), *A new history of Ireland*, vol. IV: *Eighteenth-century Ireland 1691–1800* (Oxford: Oxford University Press, 1986), pp. 123–95.

'Eighteenth-century flour milling in Ireland' in A. Bielenberg (ed.), *Irish flour milling: a history, A.D. 600–2000* (Dublin: Lilliput Press, 2003), pp. 37–56.

Economy, trade and Irish merchants at home and abroad 1600–1988 (Dublin: Four Courts Press, 2012).

'Problems and sources for the study of Irish economic fluctuations', *Irish Economic and Social History*, 41 (2014), 1–13.

Daultrey, S., D. Dickson and C. Ó Gráda, 'Eighteenth-century Irish population: new perspectives from old sources', *Journal of Economic History*, 41:3 (1981), 601–28.

Delany, R., *The Grand Canal of Ireland*, 2nd edn (Dublin: Lilliput Press, 1995).

Dickson, D., 'Middlemen' in T. Bartlett and D.W. Hayton (eds.), *Penal era and golden age: essays in Irish history, 1690–1800* (Belfast: Ulster Historical Foundation, 1979), pp. 162–85.

'The place of Dublin in the eighteenth-century Irish economy' in T.M. Devine and D. Dickson (eds.), *Ireland and Scotland 1600–1850: parallels and contrasts in economic and social development* (Edinburgh: John Donald, 1983), pp. 177–92.

'The gap in famines: a useful myth?' in E.M. Crawford (ed.), *Famine: the Irish experience, 900–1900* (Edinburgh: John Donald, 1989), pp. 98–111.

Arctic Ireland: [the extraordinary story of the Great Frost and forgotten Famine of 1740–41] (Belfast: White Row Press, 1997).

Old World Colony: Cork and south Munster 1630–1830 (Cork: Cork University Press, 2005).

Dublin: the making of a capital city (London: Profile, 2014).

'Novel spectacle: the birth of the Whiteboys 1761–2' in D.W. Hayton and A. Holmes (eds.), *Ourselves alone? Religion, society and politics in eighteenth- and nineteenth-century Ireland* (Dublin: Four Courts Press, 2016), pp. 61–83.

Dickson, D., and Cormac Ó Gráda (eds.), *Refiguring Ireland: essays in honour of L.M. Cullen* (Dublin: Lilliput Press, 2003).

Dickson, D., C. Ó Gráda and S. Daultrey, 'Hearth tax, household size and Irish population change 1672–1821', *Proceedings of the Royal Irish Academy*, 82C (1982), 125–81.

Dickson, D., J. Parmentier and J. Ohlmeyer (eds.), *Irish and Scottish mercantile networks in Europe and overseas in the seventeenth and eighteenth centuries* (Ghent: Academia Press, 2007).

Dobbs, A., *An essay on the trade and improvement of Ireland*, 2 vols. (Dublin: A. Rhames, 1729–31).

Drake, M., 'The Irish demographic crisis of 1740–41' in T.W. Moody (ed.), *Historical Studies VI* (London: Routledge and Kegan Paul, 1968), pp. 101-24

Geary, F., and T. Stark, 'Trends in real wages during the Industrial Revolution: a view from across the Irish Sea', *Economic History Review*, 57:2 (2004), 362–95.

Gill, C., *The rise of the Irish linen industry* (Cambridge: Cambridge University Press, 1925).

Kelly, J., 'Harvests and hardship: famine and scarcity in Ireland in the late 1720s', *Studia Hibernica*, 26 (1991–2), 65–105.

'Scarcity and poor relief in eighteenth-century Ireland: the subsistence crisis of 1782–84', *Irish Historical Studies*, 28 (1992–3), 38–62.

Kelly, P. (ed.), 'The improvement of Ireland', *Analecta Hibernica*, 35 (1992), 45–84.

'The politics of political economy in mid-eighteenth-century Ireland' in S.J. Connolly (ed.), *Political ideas in eighteenth-century Ireland* (Dublin: Four Courts Press, 2000), pp. 105–29.

Kennedy, L., 'The cost of living in Ireland, 1698–1998' in D. Dickson and C. Ó Gráda (eds.), *Refiguring Ireland* (Dublin: Lilliput Press, 2003), pp. 257–8.

Kennedy, L., and Philip Ollerenshaw (eds.), *Ulster since 1600: politics, economy and society* (Oxford: Oxford University Press, 2013).

Kennedy, L., and P. Solar, *Irish agriculture: a price history from the mid-eighteenth century to the eve of the First World War* (Dublin: Royal Irish Academy, 2007).

Livesey, J., 'The Dublin Society in eighteenth-century Irish political thought', *Historical Journal*, 47:3 (2004), 615–40.

Madden, S., *Reflections and resolutions proper for the gentlemen of Ireland* (Dublin, 1738).

Miller, K.A., A. Schrier, B.D. Boling and D.N. Doyle (eds.), *Irish immigrants in the Land of Canaan: letters and memoirs from colonial and revolutionary America, 1675–1815* (Oxford: Oxford University Press, 2003).

Mokyr, J., and C. Ó Gráda, 'Poor and getting poorer? Living standards in Ireland before the Famine', *Economic History Review*, 41:2 (1988), 209–35.

Molesworth, R., *Some considerations for the promoting of agriculture and employing the poor* (Dublin; Ewing, 1723).

Newenham, T., *A view of the natural, political and commercial circumstances of Ireland* (London: Cadell and Davies, 1809).

O'Flanagan, P., 'Markets and fairs in Ireland 1600–1800', *Journal of Historical Geography*, 11:4 (1985), 364–78.

Post, J.D., *Food shortage, climatic variability and epidemic disease in preindustrial Europe: the mortality peak of the early 1740s* (Ithaca, NY: Cornell University Press, 1985).

Prior, T., *A list of the absentees of Ireland . . .* (Dublin: R. Gunne, 1729).

Rynne, C., *Industrial Ireland 1750–1930: an archaeology* (Cork: Collins Press, 2006).

Solar, P.M., and Luc Hens, 'Land under pressure: the value of Irish land in a period of rapid population growth, 1730–1844', *Agricultural History Review*, 61:1 (2013), 40–62.

Stokes, W., *Projects for re-establishing the internal peace and tranquility of Ireland* (Dublin: James Moore, 1799).

Truxes, T.M., 'Connecticut in the Irish-American flaxseed trade, 1750–1775', *Éire-Ireland*, 12:2 (1977), 34–62.

Irish-American trade, 1660–1783 (Cambridge: Cambridge University Press, 1988).

Walsh, P., *The making of the Irish Protestant Ascendancy: the life of William Conolly, 1662–1729* (Woodbridge: The Boydell Press, 2010).

The South Sea Bubble and Ireland: money, banking and investment, 1691–1721 (Woodbridge: The Boydell Press, 2014).

Young, A., *A tour in Ireland: with general observations on the present state of that kingdom*, 2 vols. (Dublin, 1780).

7   The Irish Economy, 1815–1880: Agricultural Transition, the Communications Revolution and the Limits of Industrialisation

Andy Bielenberg

Andrews, W., 'On the herring fisheries of Ireland', *Journal of the Royal Dublin Society*, 35 (1866), 12–23.

Bielenberg, A., 'What happened to Irish industry after the Industrial Revolution? Some evidence from the first UK Census of Production in 1907', *Economic History Review*, 61 (2008), 820–41.

Ireland and the Industrial Revolution: the impact of the Industrial Revolution on Irish industry 1801–1922 (London: Routledge, 2009).

'The industrial elite in Ireland from the Industrial Revolution to the First World War' in F. Lane (ed.), *Politics, society and the middle class in modern Ireland* (London: Palgrave Macmillan, 2010).

Bielenberg, A., and J. O'Hagan, 'Consumption and living conditions 1750–2016' in M. Daly and E. Biagini (eds.), *Cambridge social history of Ireland* (Cambridge: Cambridge University Press, 2017), pp. 195–211.

Boyer, G., T. Hatton and K. O'Rourke, 'The impact of emigration on real wages in Ireland 1850–1914' in T. Hatton and J. Williamson (eds.), *Migration and the international labor market, 1850–1939* (London: Routledge, 1994), pp. 221–39.

Brunt, L., and E. Cannon, 'The Irish grain trade from the Famine to the First World War', *Economic History Review*, 57 (2004), 33–79.

Clarkson, L.A., 'Ireland 1841; pre-industrial or proto-industrial; industrializing or de-industrializing' in S. Ogilvie and M. Cerman (eds.), *European proto-industrialization* (Cambridge: Cambridge University Press, 1996), pp. 67–84.

Clarkson, L.A., and M. Crawford, *Feast and famine: food and nutrition in Ireland 1500–1920* (Oxford: Oxford University Press, 2001).

Clear, C., *Social change and everyday life in Ireland 1850–1922* (Manchester: Manchester University Press, 2007).

Commission of Inquiry into the resources and industries of Ireland: report on the sea fisheries (Dublin: Stationery Office, 1921).

Connell, K.H., 'The colonization of wasteland in Ireland 1780–1845', *Economic History Review*, 50 (1950), 44–71.

Conroy, J.C., *A history of railways in Ireland* (London: Longman, 1928).

Cooper, M., and J. Davis, *The Irish fertiliser industry: a history* (Dublin: Irish Academic Press, 2004).

Coyne, W. (ed.), *Ireland industrial and agricultural* (Dublin: Browne and Nolan, 1902).

Crotty, R., *Irish agricultural production: its volume and structure* (Cork: Cork University Press, 1966).

Cullen, L.M., *An economic history of Ireland since 1660* (London: Batsford, 1972).

Cullen, M., 'Bread winners and providers: women in the household economy of labouring families 1835–6' in M. Luddy and C. Murphy (eds.), *Women surviving; studies in Irish women's history in the nineteenth and twentieth centuries* (Dublin: Poolbeg Press, 1989), pp. 85–116.

Daly, M., *Dublin the deposed capital: a social and economic history 1860–1914* (Cork: Cork University Press, 1985).

Davies, K.M., 'For health and pleasure in the British fashion: Bray, Co. Wicklow as a tourist resort, 1750–1914' in B. O'Connor and M. Cronin (eds.), *Tourism in Ireland: a critical analysis* (Cork: Cork University Press, 1993).

De Courcy Ireland, J., *Ireland's sea fisheries: a history* (Dublin: Glendale Press, 1981).

Dickson, D., *Dublin: the making of a capital city* (London: Profile, 2014).

Donnelly, J.S., 'The Irish agricultural depression of 1859–64', *Irish Economic and Social History*, 3 (1976), 33–54.

Foley, R., *Healing waters: therapeutic landscapes in historic and contemporary Ireland* (Farnham: Ashgate, 2010).

Furlong, I., *Irish tourism 1880–1980* (Dublin: Irish Academic Press, 2009).

Geary, F. and T. Stark, 'Examining Ireland's post-Famine economic growth performance', *Economic Journal*, 112 (2002), 919–35.

　'Trends in real wages during the Industrial Revolution: a view from across the Irish Sea', *Economic History Review*, 57 (2004), 363–95.

　'Regional GDP in the UK, 1861–1911: new estimates', *Economic History Review*, 68 (2015), 123–44.

Geary, L.M., ' "The whole country was in motion": mendicancy and vagrancy in pre-Famine Ireland' in J. Hill and C. Lennon (eds.), *Luxury and austerity: historical studies 21* (Dublin: UCD Press, 1999), pp. 121–37.

Gilligan, J., *Graziers and grasslands: portrait of a rural Meath community 1854–1914* (Dublin: Irish Academic Press, 1998).

Gould, M., 'The effects of government policy on railway building in Ireland', *The Newcomen Society*, 62 (1990–1), 81–96.

Gribbon, H.D., 'Economic and social history 1850–1920' in W.E. Vaughan (ed.), *A new history of Ireland,* vol. VI: *Ireland under the Union II, 1870–1921* (Oxford: Oxford University Press, 1996), pp. 260–356.

Hall, F.G., *The Bank of Ireland* (Dublin: Hodges Figgis, 1949).

Harrison, R., *The Richardsons of Bessbrook: Ulster Quakers and the linen industry, 1845–1921* (Dublin: Original Writing, 2009).

Hickson, C., and J. Turner, 'Pre and post-Famine indices of Irish equity prices', *European Review of Economic History*, 12:1 (2008), 3–38.

Hickson, C., J. Turner and C. McCann, 'Much ado about nothing; the limitation of liability and the market for 19th century Irish bank stock', *Explorations in Economic History*, 42 (2005), 459–76.

Horner, A., 'Ireland's time–space revolution: improvements in pre-Famine travel', *History Ireland*, 15:5 (2007), 22–7.

James, K., *Handloom weavers in Ulster's linen industry 1815–1914* (Dublin: Four Courts Press, 2007).

Jones, D.S., 'The transfer of land and the emergence of the graziers during the famine period' in A. Gribben (ed.), *The Great Famine and the Irish diaspora in America* (Amherst: University of Massachusetts Press, 1999), 85–103.

Kelly, M., and C. Ó Gráda, '*Why Ireland starved* after three decades: the Great Famine in cross-section reconsidered', *Irish Economic and Social History*, 42 (2015), 53–61.

Kennedy, L., 'Regional specialization, railway development, and Irish agriculture in the nineteenth century' in M. Goldstrom and L.A. Clarkson (eds.), *Irish population, economy and society* (Oxford: Oxford University Press, 1981), pp. 173–93.

'The peoples fuel: turf in Ireland in the nineteenth and twentieth centuries' in R.W. Unger (ed.), *Energy transitions in history: global cases of continuity and change, RCC Perspectives* 2013, no. 2, pp. 25–30.

Kennedy, L., and P. Ollerenshaw (eds.), *An economic history of Ulster* (Oxford: Oxford University Press, 2013).

Kennedy, L., and P. Solar, *Irish agriculture: a price history* (Dublin: Royal Irish Academy, 2007).

Lee, J., 'The construction costs of Irish railways 1830–1853', *Business History Review*, 9 (1967), 95–109.

'The railways in the Irish economy' in L.M. Cullen (ed.), *The formation of the Irish economy* (Cork: Mercier Press, 1968), pp. 77–87.

'The dual economy in Ireland 1800–50' in T.D. Williams (ed.), *Historical Studies VIII, papers read before the Irish Conference of Historians* (Dublin: Gill & Macmillan, 1971), pp. 191–201.

Legg, M.-L., *Newspapers and nationalism: the Irish provincial press 1850–1892* (Dublin: Four Courts Press, 1999).

Lucas, A.T., 'Bog-wood, a study in rural economy', *Bealoideas*, 23 (1954), 71–121.

MacNeice, D.S., 'Industrial villages of Ulster, 1800–1900' in P. Roebuck (ed.), *Plantation to Partition: essays in honour of J.L McCracken* (Belfast: Blackstaff Press, 1981), pp. 172–90.

McCaughan, M., 'Dandys, luggers, herring and mackerel' in M. McCaughan and J. Appleby (eds.), *The Irish Sea: aspects of maritime history* (Belfast: Institute of Irish Studies, 1989), pp. 121–6.

McCracken, D., and E. McCracken, 'A register of trees, Co. Cork, 1790–1860', *Journal of the Cork Historical and Archaeological Society*, 81 (1976), 39–60.

Mitchell, B.R., *British historical statistics* (Cambridge: Cambridge University Press, 1988).

Mokyr, J., *Why Ireland starved: a quantitative and analytical history of the Irish economy 1800–1850* (London: Allen & Unwin, 1983).

Mokyr, J., and C. Ó Gráda, 'Poor and getting poorer? Living standards in Ireland before the Famine', *Economic History Review*, 46 (1988), 209–35.

Neeson, E., *A history of Irish forestry* (Dublin: Lilliput Press, 1991).

Nicholson, J., *The Factory Acts in Ireland 1802–1914* (Dublin: Four Courts Press, 2003).

Ó Gráda, C., 'Poverty, population and agriculture 1801–45' in W.E. Vaughan (ed.), *A new history of Ireland*, vol. v: *Ireland under the Union, 1801–70* (Oxford: Oxford University Press, 1989), pp. 108–33.

Ireland before and after the Famine: explorations in economic history, 1800–1925 (Manchester: Manchester University Press, 1993).

Ireland: a new economic history 1780–1939 (Oxford: Oxford University Press, 1994).

Black 47 and beyond: the Great Irish Famine in history, economy and memory (Princeton: Princeton University Press, 1999).

O'Brien, G., *Ireland from the Union to the Famine* (London: Longmans, Green and Co., 1921).

O'Donovan, J., *The economic history of livestock in Ireland* (Cork: Cork University Press, 1940).

O'Mahony, C., 'Fishing in nineteenth-century Kinsale', *Journal of the Cork Historical and Archaeological Society*, 98 (1993), 113.

O'Neill, T.P., 'Poverty in Ireland 1815–45', *Folklife*, 11 (1973), 22–33.

'Famine evictions' in C. King (ed.), *Famine, land and culture* (Dublin: UCD Press, 2000), pp. 29–70.

O'Rourke, K., 'Rural depopulation in a small open economy: Ireland 1856–1876', *Explorations in Economic History*, 28 (1991), 409–32.

'Monetary data and proxy GDP estimates: Ireland 1840–1921', *Irish Economic and Social History*, 25 (1998), 22–51.

Ollerenshaw, P., 'Industry 1820–1914' in L. Kennedy and P. Ollerenshaw (eds.), *An economic history of Ulster 1820–1939* (Manchester: Manchester University Press, 1985), pp. 62–108.

'Aspects of bank lending in post-Famine Ireland' in R. Mitchison and P. Roebuck (eds.), *Economy and society in Scotland and Ireland 1500–1939* (Edinburgh: John Donald, 1988), pp. 222–32.

'Business and finance 1780–1945' in L. Kennedy and P. Ollerenshaw (eds.), *An economic history of Ulster* (Oxford: Oxford University Press, 2013), pp. 177–94.

Pollock, V., 'The herring industry in County Down 1840–1940' in L. Proudfoot and W. Nolan (eds.), *Down: history and society* (Dublin: Geography Publications, 1997), pp. 405–30.

Proudfoot, L., 'Markets, fairs and towns in Ireland, c. 1600–1853' in P. Borsay and L. Proudfoot (eds.), *Provincial towns in early modern England and Ireland* (Oxford: Oxford University Press, 2002), pp. 69–96.

Rees, J., *The fishery of Arklow 1800–1950* (Dublin: Four Courts Press, 2008).

Royle, S., 'Industrialization, urbanization and urban society in post-famine Ireland, c. 1850–1921' in B.J. Graham and L. Proudfoot (eds.), *An historical geography of Ireland* (London: Academic Press, 1993), pp. 258–92.

Belfast, part 2, Irish Historic Towns Atlas no. 17 (Dublin: Royal Irish Academy, 2007).

Royle, S., and R. Gillespie, *Belfast, part 1,* Irish Historic Towns Atlas no. 12 (Dublin: Royal Irish Academy, 2003).

Rynne, C., *Industrial Ireland 1750–1930* (Cork: Collins Press, 2006).

Smyth, W.J., 'The greening of Ireland – tenant tree planting in the eighteenth and nineteenth centuries', *Irish Forestry*, 54 (1997), 55–72.

Solar, P., 'The Great Famine was no ordinary subsistence crisis' in E.M. Crawford (ed.), *Famine: the Irish experience 900–1900* (Edinburgh: John Donald, 1989), pp. 112–33.

'Irish trade in the nineteenth century' in D. Dickson and C. Ó Gráda (eds.), *Refiguring Ireland: essays in honour of L.M. Cullen* (Dublin: Lilliput Press, 2003), pp. 277–89.

'The birth and death of European flax, hemp and jute spinning firms: the Irish and Belgian cases' in B. Collins and P. Ollerenshaw (eds.), *The European linen industry in historical perspective* (Oxford: Oxford University Press, 2003), pp. 245–58.

'The linen industry in the nineteenth century' in D. Jenkins (ed.), *The Cambridge history of western textiles*, 2 vols. (Cambridge: Cambridge University Press, 2003), vol. II, pp. 809–23.

'The Irish linen trade 1852–1914', *Textile History*, 36 (2005), 46–68.

'Shipping and economic development in nineteenth-century Ireland', *Economic History Review*, 59 (2006), 717–42.

'*Why Ireland Starved* and the big issues in pre-Famine Irish economic history', *Irish Economic and Social History*, 42 (2015), 62–75.

Solar, P., and L. Hens, 'Land pressure: the value of Irish land in a period of rapid population growth, 1730–1844', *Agricultural History Review*, 61 (2013), 40–62.

Symes, E., 'The Torbay fishermen in Ringsend', *Dublin Historical Record*, 53 (2000), 139–49.

Thomas, W.A., *The stock exchanges of Ireland* (London: Francis Cairns, 1987).

Tomlinson, R., 'Trees and woodlands of County Down' in L. Proudfoot and W. Nolan (eds.), *Down: history and society* (Dublin: Geography Publications, 1997), pp. 239–65.

Turner, J., 'Wealth concentration in the European periphery: Ireland 1858–2001', *Oxford Economic Papers*, 62 (2010), 625–49.

Turner, M., *After the Famine: Irish agriculture 1850–1914* (Cambridge: Cambridge University Press, 1996).

Vaughan, W.E., *Landlords and tenants in mid Victorian Ireland* (Oxford: Oxford University Press, 1994).

Wakefield, E., *An account of Ireland: statistical and political*, 2 vols. (London: Longman, Hurst, Rees, Orme, and Brown, 1812).

Wall, T., 'Railways and telecommunications', *Journal of the Irish Railway Record Society* 20:143 (2001), 479–85.

Walsh, B., 'Urbanization and the regional distribution of population in post-famine Ireland', *Journal of European Economic History*, 29:1 (2000), 109–30.

Went, A., 'The pursuit of salmon', *Proceedings of the Royal Irish Academy*, 63C (1964), 191–244.

Whelan, K., 'The Catholic parish, the Catholic chapel, and village development in Ireland', *Irish Geography*, 16 (1983), 1–15.

Williamson, J., 'Economic convergence: placing post-Famine Ireland in comparative perspective', *Irish Economic and Social History*, 21 (1994), 5–27.

8 Population and Emigration, 1730–1845

Brian Gurrin

Manuscript

An abstract of the number of Protestant and Popish families as returned to the Hearth money office Anno 1732 pursuant to the order of the commissioner of revenue, MS 1742: Lambeth Palace Library

Minute books of the Revenue Commissioners, CUST 1: The National Archives

Harrowby papers, T/3228: Public Record Office of Northern Ireland

Printed

Abstract of answers and returns made pursuant to acts 3 & 4 Vic. c. 99, and 4 Vic. 7; enumeration extract, part 1, *England and Wales* H.C. 1843 (496), XXIII.

Abstract of answers and returns made pursuant to acts 3 & 4 Vic. c. 99, and 4 Vic. 7; enumeration extract, part 2, *Scotland* H.C. 1843 (498), XXII.

Abstract of answers and returns, pursuant to act 55 Geo. 3, for taking an account of the population of Ireland in 1821, H.C. 1824 (577), XXII.

Abstract of the population returns, 1831, H.C. 1833 (634), XXXIX.

An abstract of the number of Protestant and Popish families in the several counties and provinces of Ireland (Dublin, 1736).

'Ardee Corporation reports', *Journal of the County Louth Archaeological Society*, 5:1 (1921), 70–1.

Boyce, D.G., *Nineteenth-century Ireland: the search for stability* (Dublin: Gill & Macmillan, 1990).

Boyle, P., and C. Ó Gráda, 'Fertility trends, excess mortality, and the Great Irish Famine', *Demography*, 23:4 (1986), 543–62.

Bushe, G.P., 'An essay towards ascertaining the population of Ireland', *Transactions of the Royal Irish Academy*, 3 (1789), 145–55.

Clarkson, L.A., 'Household and family structure in Armagh city', *Local Population Studies*, 20 (1978), 14–31.

'Irish population revisited, 1687–1821' in J.M. Goldstrom and L.A. Clarkson (eds.), *Irish population, economy, and society: essays in honour of the late K.H. Connell* (Oxford: Clarendon Press, 1981), pp. 13–35.

Connell, K.H., 'Land and population in Ireland, 1780–1845', *Economic History Review*, 2:3 (1950), 278–89.

The population of Ireland, 1750–1845 (Oxford: Clarendon Press, 1950).

'Some unsettled problems in English and Irish population history, 1750–1845', *Irish Historical Studies*, 7 (1950–51), 225–34.

'Land and population in Ireland, 1780–1845' in D.V. Glass and D.E. Eversley (eds.), *Population in history: essays in historical demography* (London: Edward Arnold, 1965), pp. 423–33.

Crawford, E.M., *Counting the people: a survey of the Irish Censuses, 1813–1911* (Dublin: Four Courts Press, 2003).

Cullen, L.M., *An economic history of Ireland since 1660*, 2nd edn (London: Batsford, 1987).

Daultrey, S., D. Dickson and C. Ó Gráda, 'Eighteenth-century Irish population: new perspectives from old sources', *Journal of Economic History*, 41 (1981), 601–28.

Dickson, D., 'The gap in famines: a useful myth?' in E.M. Crawford (ed.), *Famine: the Irish experience, 900–1900* (Edinburgh: John Donald, 1989), pp. 96–111.

Arctic Ireland (Belfast: The White Row Press, 1997).

Dickson, D., C. Ó Gráda and S. Daultrey, 'Hearth tax, household size and Irish population change, 1672–1821', *Proceedings of the Royal Irish Academy*, 82C (1982), 125–81.

Drake, M., 'Marriage and population growth in Ireland, 1750–1845', *Economic History Review*, 2nd series, 16:2 (1963), 301–13.

First report of the Commissioners of Public Instruction, Ireland [45] [46] [47] H.C. 1834, XXXIII.1, 829, XXXIV.1

Forbes Adams, W., *Ireland and Irish emigration to the New World from 1815 to the Famine* (New Haven: Yale University Press, 1932).

Froggatt, P., 'The census of Ireland of 1813–15', *Irish Historical Studies*, 14 (1964–5), 227–35.

Geary, R.C., '*The population of Ireland, 1750–1845* by K. H. Connell, review', *Studies: An Irish Quarterly Review*, 39 (1950), 472–4.

Glass, D.V., *Numbering the people* (Farnborough: Saxon House, 1973).

The Population Controversy (Farnborough: Gregg International, 1973).

Gurrin, B.F., *Pre-Census sources for Irish demography* (Dublin: Four Courts Press, 2002).

Gurrin, B., K. Miller and L. Kennedy, *Catholics and Protestants in eighteenth-century Ireland* (Dublin: Irish Manuscripts Commission, forthcoming).

Howlett, J., *An essay on the population of Ireland* (London, 1786).

Kelly, J., 'Harvests and hardship: famine and scarcity in Ireland in the late 1720s', *Studia Hibernica*, 26 (1992), 65–103.

'Coping with crisis; the response to the famine of 1740–41', *Eighteenth-Century Ireland*, 27 (2012), 99–122.

Laffan, J., *Political arithmetic of the population, commerce and manufactures of Ireland* (Dublin: P. Byrne, 1785).

Larcom, Captain, 'Observations on the census of the population of Ireland in 1841', *Journal of the Statistical Society of London*, 6:4 (1843), 323–51.

Lee, J., 'On the accuracy of the pre-Famine Irish censuses' in J.M. Goldstrom and L.A. Clarkson (eds.), *Irish population, economy, and society: essays in honour of the late K.H. Connell* (Oxford: Clarendon Press, 1981), pp. 37–56.

Letters written by His Excellency Hugh Boulter, D.D., 2 vols. (Dublin: George Faulkner, 1770).

Macafee, W., 'Pre-Famine population in Ulster: evidence from the parish register of Killyman' in P. O'Flanagan, P. Ferguson and K. Whelan (eds.), *Rural Ireland: modernisation and change, 1600–1900* (Cork: Cork University Press, 1987), pp. 142–61.

'The pre-Famine population of Ireland, a reconsideration' in B. Collins, P. Ollerenshaw and T. Parkhill (eds.), *Industry, trade and people in Ireland* (Belfast: Ulster Historical Foundation, 2005), pp. 69–86.

MacRaild, D., and M. Smith, 'Migration and emigration, 1600–1945' in L. Kennedy and P. Ollerenshaw (eds.), *Ulster since 1600: politics, economy and society* (Oxford: Oxford University Press, 2013), pp. 140–59.

McSkimin, S. *The history and antiquities of the county of the town of Carrickfergus*, new edn (Belfast: Mullan and Son, 1909).

McVeagh, J. (ed.), *Richard Pococke's Irish tours* (Dublin: Irish Academic Press, 1995).

Miller, K., A. Schrier, B.D. Boling and D.N. Doyle, *Irish immigrants in the Land of Canaan: letters and memoirs from colonial and revolutionary America, 1675–1815* (Oxford: Oxford University Press, 2003).

Morgan, V., 'A case study of population change over two centuries: Blaris, Lisburn 1661–1848', *Irish Economic and Social History*, 3 (1976), 5–16.

Morgan, V., and W. Macafee, 'Population in Ulster, 1600–1760' in P. Roebuck (ed.), *Plantation to Partition: essays in honour of J.L. McCracken* (Belfast: Blackstaff Press, [1981]), pp. 46–63.

'Irish population in the pre-Famine period: evidence from County Antrim', *Economic History Review*, 2nd series, 37 (1984), 182–9.

Newenham, T., *A statistical and historical inquiry into the progress and magnitude of the population of Ireland* (London: Cadell and Davies, 1805).

Ó Gráda, Cormac, *The Great Irish Famine* (London: Macmillan, 1989).

Ó Tuathaigh, G., *Ireland before the Famine, 1798–1848*, new edn (Dublin: Gill & Macmillan, 1991).

Post, J.D., *The last great subsistence crisis in the Western World* (Baltimore: Johns Hopkins University Press, 1977).

Food shortage, climatic variability, and epidemic disease in preindustrial Europe: the mortality peak in the early 1740s (Ithaca, NY: Cornell University Press, 1985).

Price, R., *Observations on reversionary payments*, 4th edn, 2 vols. (London: Cadell, 1783).

Report of the commissioners appointed to take the census of Ireland for the year 1841 [504], H.C. 1843, XXIV, 1.

'Report on the state of Popery, Ireland, 1731 [Armagh]', *Archivium Hibernicum*, 1 (1912), 10–27.

'Report on the state of Popery in Ireland, 1731 [Cashel]', *Archivium Hibernicum*, 2 (1913), 108–56.

'Report on the state of Popery in Ireland, 1731 [Tuam]', *Archivium Hibernicum*, 3 (1914), 124–59.

'Report on the state of Popery in Ireland, 1731 [Dublin]', *Archivium Hibernicum*, 4 (1915), 131–77.

Shaw Mason, W., *A statistical account or parochial survey of Ireland*, 3 vols. (London: Longman, Hurst, Rees, Orme, and Brown, 1814–19).

   The population of Ireland before the nineteenth century (Farnborough: Gregg International, 1973).

Thomas, C., 'The city of Londonderry: demographic trends and socio-economic characteristics, 1650–1900' in G. O'Brien (ed.), *Derry and Londonderry: history and society* (Dublin: Geography Publications, 1999), pp. 359–78.

Vaughan, W.E., and A.J. Fitzpatrick, *Irish historical statistics: population, 1821–1971* (Dublin: Royal Irish Academy, 1978).

Wakefield, E., *An account of Ireland, statistical and political*, 2 vols. (London: Longman, Hurst, Rees, Orme, and Brown, 1812).

Wrigley, E.A., and Schofield, R.S., *The population history of England, 1541–1871: a reconstruction* (1997 repr., Cambridge: Cambridge University Press, 1989).

[Young, A.], *Proposals to the legislature for numbering the people, containing some observations on the population of Great Britain* (London: Nicoll, 1771).

Young, A., *A tour in Ireland: with general observations on the present state of that kingdom made in the years 1776, 1777, and 1778*, 2 vols. (Dublin: Whitestone et al., 1780).

9 Women, Men and the Family, *c*.1730–*c*.1880

Sarah-Anne Buckley

Ashford, G.M., 'Childhood: studies in the history of children in eighteenth-century Ireland', PhD thesis, St Patrick's College, Dublin City University, 2012.

Barnes, J., *Irish industrial schools, 1868–1908* (Dublin: Irish Academic Press, 1989).

Bergin, J., 'Irish private divorce bills and acts of the eighteenth century' in J. Kelly, J. McCafferty and C.I. McGrath (eds.), *People, power and politics: essays on Irish history, 1660–1850* (Dublin: UCD Press, 2009), pp. 94–121.

Birdwell-Pheasant, D., 'Family systems and the foundations of class in Ireland and England', *History of the Family*, 3:1 (1988), 17–34.

   'The early twentieth-century Irish stem family: a case study from Co. Kerry' in M. Silverman and P. Gulliver (eds.), *Approaching the past: historical anthropology through Irish case studies* (New York: Columbia University Press, 1992), pp. 205–47.

   'Irish households in the twentieth century: culture, class and historical contingency', *Journal of Family History*, 18 (1993), 19–38.

Bradley, A., and M. Valiulis, *Gender and sexuality in modern Ireland* (Amherst: University of Massachusetts Press, 1997).

Buckley, S.A., ' "Found in a dying condition": nurse children in Ireland, 1872–1952' in E. Farrell (ed.), *'She said she was in the family way': pregnancy and infancy in modern Ireland* (London: Institute of Historical Research, 2012), pp. 145–62.

The cruelty man: child welfare, the NSPCC and the state in Ireland, 1889–1956 (Manchester: Manchester University Press, 2013).

Cavallo, S., and L. Warner (eds.), *Widowhood in medieval and early modern Europe* (Harlow: Pearson, 1999).

Clark, A., 'Orphans and the Poor Law: rage against the machine' in V. Crossman and P. Gray (eds.), *Poverty and Welfare in Ireland, 1838–1948* (Dublin: Irish Academic Press, 2011).

Clear, C., *Social change in everyday life in Ireland, 1850–1922* (Manchester: Manchester University Press, 2009).

Conley, C.A., *Melancholy accidents: the meaning of violence in post-Famine Ireland* (Lanham, MD: Lexington Books, 1999).

Connell, K.H., *Irish peasant society: four historical essays* (Oxford: Oxford University Press, 1968).

Connolly, S.J., 'Marriage in pre-Famine Ireland' in A. Cosgrove (ed.), *Marriage in Ireland* (Dublin: College Press, 1985), pp. 78–93.

'Family, love and marriage: some evidence from the early eighteenth century' in M. MacCurtain and M. O'Dowd (eds.), *Women in early modern Ireland* (Edinburgh: Edinburgh University Press, 1991), pp. 276–90.

Cosgrove, A. (ed.), *Marriage in Ireland* (Dublin: College Press, 1985).

Crossman, V., 'Cribbed, contained and confined? The care of children under the Irish Poor Law, 1850–1920' in M. Luddy and J.E. Smith (eds.), *Children, childhood and Irish society: 1500 to the present* (Dublin: Four Courts Press, 2014), pp. 82–99.

Daly, M.E., *A social and economic history of Ireland since 1800* (Dublin: Dublin Educational Co., 1981).

Dirks, R., 'Social responses during severe food shortages and famine', *Current Anthropology*, 21:1 (1980), 21–44.

'Common law versus common practice: the use of marriage settlements in early modern England', *Economic History Review*, n.s., 43:1 (1990), 21–39.

Erickson, A.L., *Women and property in early modern England* (London: Routledge, 1993).

'Property and widowhood in England 1660–1840' in S. Cavallo and L. Warner (eds.), *Widowhood in medieval and early modern Europe* (Harlow: Pearson, 1999), pp. 145–63.

'Coverture and capitalism', *History Workshop Journal*, 59 (Spring 2005), 1–16.

Fitzpatrick, D., 'Marriage in post-Famine Ireland' in A. Cosgrove (ed.), *Marriage in Ireland* (Dublin: College Press, 1985), pp. 116–31.

'The modernisation of the Irish female' in P. O'Flanagan et al. (eds.), *Rural Ireland 1600–1800* (Cork: Cork University Press, 1987), pp. 62–80.

Fleming, D.F., 'Public attitudes to prostitution in eighteenth-century Ireland', *Irish Economic and Social History*, 32 (2005), 1–19.

Guinnane, T., *The vanishing Irish: households, migration and the rural economy in Ireland, 1850–1914* (Princeton: Princeton University Press, 1997).

Kelly, J., 'Infanticide in eighteenth-century Ireland', *Irish Economic and Social History*, 19 (1992), 5–26.

'The abduction of women of fortune in eighteenth-century Ireland', *Eighteenth-Century Ireland*, 9 (1994), 7–43.

'"A most inhuman and barbarous piece of villainy": an exploration of the crime of rape in eighteenth-century Ireland', *Eighteenth-Century Ireland*, 10 (1995), 78–107.

'Health for sale: mountebanks, doctors, printers and the supply of medication in eighteenth-century Ireland', *Proceedings of the Royal Irish Academy*, 108c (2008), 75–114.

'Domestic medication and medical care in late early modern Ireland' in J. Kelly and F. Clark (eds.), *Ireland and medicine in the seventeenth and eighteenth centuries* (Farnham: Ashgate, 2010), pp. 109–36.

'Responding to infanticide in Ireland, 1680–1820' in E. Farrell (ed.), *'She said she was in the family way': pregnancy and infancy in modern Ireland* (London: Institute of Historical Research, 2012), pp. 189–204.

'"This iniquitous traffic": the kidnapping of children for the American Colonies in eighteenth-century Ireland', *Journal of the History of Childhood and Youth*, 9:2 (2016), 233–46.

Kennedy, L., 'Farm succession in modern Ireland: elements of a theory of inheritance', *Economic History Review*, 44:3 (1991), 477–99.

Kennedy, L., and L.A. Clarkson, *Mapping the Great Irish Famine* (Dublin: Four Courts Press, 1999).

Kertzer, D., and M. Barbagli (eds.), *Family life in the long nineteenth century, 1789–1913* (New Haven: Yale University Press, 2001).

Large, D., 'The wealth of the greater Irish landowners, 1750–1815', *Irish Historical Studies*, 15 (1966–7), 21–45.

Lee, J.J., *The modernisation of Irish society, 1848–1918* (Cambridge: Cambridge University Press, 1989).

Logan, J., 'Governesses, tutors and parents: domestic education in Ireland, 1700–1880', *Irish Educational Studies*, 7:2 (1988), 1–18.

Lucey, C., 'Redecorating the domestic interior in late eighteenth-century Dublin' in E. FitzPatrick and J. Kelly (eds.), *Domestic life in Ireland* (Dublin: Royal Irish Academy, 2012), 169–92.

Luddy, M., *Women and philanthropy in nineteenth-century Ireland* (Cambridge: Cambridge University Press, 1995).

Women in Ireland, 1800–1918: a documentary history (Cork: Cork University Press, 1995).

Matters of deceit: breach of marriage cases in nineteenth- and twentieth-century Limerick (Dublin: Four Courts Press, 2011).

'Abductions in nineteenth-century Ireland', *New Hibernia Review*, 17:2 (2013), 17–44.

MacDonald, H.J., 'Boarding-out and the Scottish Poor Law, 1845–1914', *Scottish Historical Review*, 75 (1996), 197–220.

Malcomson, A.P.W., *The pursuit of the heiress: aristocratic marriage in Ireland, 1740–1840* (Belfast: Ulster Historical Foundation, 2006).

Melvin, P., *Estates and landed society in Galway* (Dublin: de Búrca, 2012).

O'Dowd, M., *A history of women in Ireland, 1500–1800* (Harlow: Pearson Longman, 2005).

'Family, sex, and marriage, 1600–1800' in L. Kennedy and P. Ollerenshaw (eds.), *Ulster since 1600: politics, economy and society* (Oxford: Oxford University Press, 2012), pp. 43–57.

'Early modern Ireland and the history of the child' in M. Luddy and J.M. Smith (eds.), *Children, childhood and Irish Society: 1500 to the present* (Dublin: Four Courts Press, 2014), pp. 29–45.

O'Reilly, B., 'Hearth and home: the vernacular house in Ireland from c.1800' in J. Kelly and E. FitzPatrick (eds.), *Domestic life in Ireland* (Dublin: Royal Irish Academy, 2012), pp. 193–215.

Pollock, L., *Forgotten children: parent–child relations from 1500 to 1900* (Cambridge: Cambridge University Press, 1983).

Raftery, D., J. Harford and S.M. Parkes, 'Mapping the terrain of female education in Ireland, 1830–1910', *Gender Education*, 22:5 (2010), 565–78.

Robins, J., *The lost children: a study of charity children in Ireland, 1700–1900* (Dublin: IPA, 1980).

Silverman, M. and P.H. Gulliver (eds.), *Approaching the past: historical anthropology through Irish case studies* (New York: Columbia University Press, 1992).

Skehill, C., 'The origins of child welfare under the Poor Law and the emergence of the institutional versus family care debate' in V. Crossman and P. Gray (eds.), *Poverty and welfare in Ireland, 1838–1948* (Dublin: Irish Academic Press, 2011), pp. 115–29.

Steiner-Scott, L., ' "To bounce a boot off her now and then . . .": domestic violence in post-Famine Ireland' in M. Valiulis and M. O'Dowd (eds.), *Women and Irish history* (Dublin: Attic Press, 1997), pp. 125–43.

Urquhart, D., 'Gender, family, and sexuality, 1800–2000' in L. Kennedy and P. Ollerenshaw (eds.), *Ulster since 1600: politics, economy and society* (Oxford: Oxford University Press, 2012), pp. 245–59.

'Ireland and the Divorce and Matrimonial Causes Act of 1857', *Journal of Family History*, 38:3 (2013), 301–20.

'Irish divorce and domestic violence, 1857–1922', *Women's History Review*, 22:5 (2013), 820–37.

Vickery, A., *The gentleman's daughter: women's lives in Georgian England* (New Haven: Yale University Press, 1988).

Wilson, D., *Women, marriage and property in wealthy landed families in Ireland, 1750–1850* (Manchester: Manchester University Press, 2009).

Wilson, R., *Elite women in Ascendancy Ireland, 1690–1745: imitation and innovation* (Woodbridge: The Boydell Press, 2015).

10 The Catholic Church and Catholics in an Era of Sanctions and Restraints, 1690–1790

Thomas O'Connor

Manuscript

St St F4c (1728), Archivio della sacra congregazione della Dottrina della Fede, Rome
Wake papers, Add MS 6117: British Library

Printed

Bartlett, T., 'The origins and progress of the Catholic question in Ireland' in T.P. Power and K. Whelan (eds.), *Endurance and emergence: Catholics in Ireland in the eighteenth century* (Dublin: Irish Academic Press, 1990), pp. 1–20.

The fall and rise of the Irish nation: the Catholic question 1690–1830 (Dublin: Gill & Macmillan, 1992).

Begadon, C., 'Laity and clergy in the Catholic renewal of Dublin c.1750–1830', PhD thesis, National University of Ireland, Maynooth, 2009.

'The renewal of Catholic culture in eighteenth-century Dublin' in J. Bergin et al. (eds.), *New perspective on the Penal Laws* (Dublin: Eighteenth-Century Ireland Society, 2011), pp. 227–47.

Bergin, J., 'Irish Catholics and their networks in eighteenth-century London', *Eighteenth-Century Life*, 39:1 (2015), 66–102.

Bergin, J. et al. (eds.), *New perspectives on the Penal Laws* (Dublin: Eighteenth-Century Ireland Society, 2011).

Berkeley, G., *A word to the wise: or the Bishop of Cloyne's exhortation to the Roman Catholic clergy of Ireland* (Dublin: George Faulkner, 1749).

Brady, J. (ed.), *Catholics in the eighteenth-century press* (Maynooth: Catholic Record Society, 1966).

Brockliss, L.W.B., 'The Irish colleges on the continent and the creation of an educated clergy' in T. O'Connor and M.A. Lyons (eds.), *The Ulster Earls in Baroque Europe* (Dublin: Four Courts Press, 2010), pp. 142–65.

Brown, M. et al. (eds.), *Converts and conversion in Ireland, 1650–1850* (Dublin: Four Courts Press, 2005).

Chambers, L., 'Rivalry and reform in the Irish College, Paris, 1676–1775' in T. O'Connor and M.A. Lyons (eds.), *Irish communities in early modern Europe* (Dublin: Four Courts Press, 2006), pp. 103–29.

Cogan, A., *Diocese of Meath: ancient and modern*, 3 vols. (Dublin: Joseph Dollard, 1867).

Connolly, S.J., *Priests and people in pre-Famine Ireland* (Dublin: Gill & Macmillan, 1982).

Divided kingdom: Ireland 1630–1800 (Oxford: Oxford University Press, 2008).

Corish, P., *The Irish Catholic experience: a historical survey* (Dublin: Gill & Macmillan, 1984).

Cullen, L., 'Catholics under the Penal Laws', *Eighteenth-Century Ireland*, 1 (1986), 23–36.

'The Dublin merchant community in the eighteenth century' in P. Butel and L.M. Cullen (eds.), *Cities and merchants: French and Irish perspectives on urban development 1500–1900* (Dublin: Department of Modern History, University of Dublin, 1986), pp. 195–210.

'Catholic social classes under the Penal Laws' in T.P. Power and K. Whelan (eds.), *Endurance and emergence: Catholics in Ireland in the eighteenth century* (Dublin: Irish Academic Press, 1990), pp. 57–84.

'The Irish diaspora of the seventeenth and eighteenth centuries' in N. Canny (ed.), *Europeans on the move: studies on European migration 1500–1800* (Oxford: Oxford University Press, 1994), pp. 113–49.

Cummins, R.F., and H. Fenning, 'The constitutions of the diocese of Cashel: the New Psalter of Cashel (1737) and three pastoral letters of Archbishop Christopher Bulter', *Archivium Hibernicum*, 56 (2002), 132–88.

Curran, M.J., 'Instructions, admonitions etc of Archbishop Carpenter, 1770–86', *Reportorium Novum* 2:1 (1957–8), 148–71.

Derr, E., 'Episcopal visitations of the diocese of Cloyne and Ross, 1785–1828', *Archivium Hibernicum*, 66 (2013), 261–393.

'The Irish Catholic episcopal corps 1657–1829: a prosopographical analysis', PhD thesis, 2 vols., National University of Ireland, Maynooth, 2013.

Dickson, D., 'Middlemen' in T. Bartlett and D.W. Hayton (eds.), *Penal era and golden age: essays in Irish history, 1690–1800* (Belfast: Ulster Historical Foundation, 1979), pp. 162–85.

'Catholics and trade in eighteenth-century Ireland: an old debate revisited' in T.P. Power and K. Whelan (eds.), *Endurance and emergence: Catholics in Ireland in the eighteenth century* (Dublin: Irish Academic Press, 1990), pp. 85–100.

Donnelly, J.S., 'The Whiteboy movement 1761–85', *Irish Historical Studies* 21 (1978–9), 20–55.

Fagan, P. (ed.), *Ireland in the Stuart papers*, 2 vols. (Dublin: Four Courts Press, 1995).

Divided loyalties: the question of an oath for Irish Catholics in the eighteenth century (Dublin: Four Courts Press, 1997).

Fenning, H., 'Some problems on the Irish mission, 1733–1774', *Collectanea Hibernica*, 8 (1965), 58–109.

'John Kent's report on the state of the Irish mission, 1742', *Archivium Hibernicum*, 28 (1966), 59–103.

The undoing of the friars of Ireland: a study of the novitiate question in the mid eighteenth century (Louvain: Publications Universitaires de Louvain, 1972).

'Dublin imprints of Catholic interest, 1701–1739', *Collectanea Hibernica*, 39/40 (1997–8), 106–54.

Hoban, B., *A melancholy truth: the travels and travails of Fr. Charles Bourke c. 1765–1820* (Dublin: Banley House, 2008).

Kelly, J., 'The parliamentary reform movement of the 1780s and the Catholic question', *Archivium Hibernicum*, 44 (1988), 95–117.

'The genesis of Protestant Ascendancy: the Rightboy disturbances of the 1780s and their impact upon Protestant opinion' in G. O'Brien (ed.), *Parliament, politics and people: essays in eighteenth-century Irish history* (Dublin: Irish Academic Press, 1989), pp. 93–127.

'"A wild Capuchin of Cork": Arthur O'Leary (1729–1802)' in G. Moran (ed.), *Radical Irish priests* (Dublin: Four Courts Press, 1998), pp. 39–61.

'The impact of the Penal Laws' in J. Kelly and D. Keogh (eds.), *History of the Catholic Diocese of Dublin* (Dublin: Four Courts Press, 2000), pp. 153–61.

'Sustaining a confessional state: the Irish parliament and Catholicism' in D.W. Hayton, J. Kelly and J. Bergin (eds.), *The eighteenth-century composite state: representative institutions in Ireland and Europe 1689–1800* (London: Palgrave, 2010), pp. 44–77.

'"Disappointing the boundless ambition of France": Irish Protestants and the fear of invasion, 1661–1815', *Studia Hibernica*, 37 (2011), 27–105.

'The historiography of the Penal Laws' in J. Bergin et al. (eds.), *New perspectives on the Penal Laws* (Dublin: Eighteenth-Century Ireland Society, 2011), pp. 27–52.

Larkin, E., 'The devotional revolution in Ireland, 1850–75', *American Historical Review*, 77 (1972), pp. 625-52.

The pastoral role of the Roman Catholic clergy in pre-Famine Ireland, 1750–1850 (Dublin: Four Courts Press, 2006).

Larkin, E., and C. Hargett, 'Clerical income and its sources in the parish of Moycullen, in the wardenship of Galway, 1786–1823', *Archivium Hibernicum*, 62 (2009), 221–35.

Leighton, C.D.A., *Catholicism in a Protestant kingdom: a study of the Irish ancien régime* (Dublin, Gill & Macmillan, 1994).

Mac Murchaidh, C., '"My repeated troubles": Dr James Gallagher (bishop of Raphoe 1725–37) and the impact of the Penal Laws' in J. Bergin et al. (eds.), *New perspectives on the Penal Laws* (Dublin: Eighteenth-Century Ireland Society, 2011), pp. 149–72.

McBride, I., *Eighteenth century Ireland: the Isle of Slaves* (London: Gill & Macmillan, 2009).

'Catholic politics in the penal era: Father Sylvester Lloyd and the Delvin addresses of 1727' in J. Bergin et al. (eds.), *New perspectives on the Penal Laws* (Dublin: Eighteenth-Century Ireland Society, 2011), pp. 114–47.

McCracken, J.J., 'The ecclesiastical structure, 1714–1760' in T.W. Moody and W.E. Vaughan (eds.) *A new history of Ireland*, vol. IV: *Eighteenth-century Ireland* (Oxford: Oxford University Press, 1986), pp. 84–104.

McGrath, C.I., 'Securing the Protestant interest: origins and purpose of the Penal Laws of 1695', *Irish Historical Studies*, 30 (1996–7), 25–46.

Morrill, J., 'The causes of the Penal Laws: paradoxes and inevitabilities' in J. Bergin et al. (eds.), *New perspectives on the Penal Laws* (Dublin: Eighteenth-Century Ireland Society, 2011), pp. 55–74.

Morley, V., 'The continuity of disaffection in eighteenth-century Ireland', *Eighteenth-Century Ireland*, 22 (2007), 189–205.

Mullett, M.A., *Catholics in Britain and Ireland 1558–1829* (Basingstoke: Macmillan, 1998).

Murtagh, H., 'Irish soldiers abroad, 1600–1800' in T. Bartlett and K. Jeffery (eds.), *A military history of Ireland* (Cambridge: Cambridge University Press, 1996), pp. 294–314.

O'Brien, G., 'The beginning of the veto controversy in Ireland', *Journal of Ecclesiastical History*, 38:1 (1987), 80–94.

O'Byrne, E., and A. Chamney (eds.), *The Convert Rolls 1703–1838* (Dublin: Irish Manuscripts Commission, 2005).

O'Connor, P., 'Irish students in Paris faculty of theology: aspects of doctrinal controversy in the ancient regime, 1730–60', *Archivium Hibernicum*, 53 (1998), 85–97.

O'Connor, T., 'The role of Irish clerics in Paris university politics, 1730–40', *History of Universities*, 15 (1997–8), 193–225.

O'Flaherty, E., 'Clerical indiscipline and ecclesiastical authority in Ireland, 1690–1750', *Studia Hibernica*, 26 (1992), 7–29.

'An urban community and the Penal Laws: Limerick 1690–1830' in J. Bergin et al. (eds.), *New perspectives on the Penal Laws* (Dublin: Eighteenth-Century Ireland Society, 2011), pp. 197–226.

O'Neill, T.P., 'Discoverers and discoveries', *Dublin Historical Record*, 37 (1983), 2–13.

Power, T.P., 'Converts' in T.P. Power and K. Whelan (eds.), *Endurance and emergence: Catholics in Ireland in the eighteenth century* (Dublin: Irish Academic Press, 1990), pp. 101–27.

Ravina, Agustín Guimerá, *Burgesia extranjera y comercio Atlantico: la empresa commercial Irlandesa en Canarias 1703–1771* (Tenerife: Consejeria de Cultura y Deportes Gobierno de Canarias, 1986).

'Report on the state of Popery, Ireland, 1731', *Archivium Hibernicum*, 1 (1912), 10–27.

'Report on the state of Popery in Ireland, 1731: diocese of Dublin', *Archivium Hibernicum*, 4 (1915), 131–77.

Wall, M., *Catholic Ireland in the eighteenth century: collected essays of Maureen Wall*, ed. G. O'Brien (Dublin: Geography Publications, 1989).

Woods, C., 'The personnel of the Catholic Convention, 1792–3', *Archivium Hibernicum*, 57 (2003), 26–76.

11 The Re-energising of Catholicism, 1790–1880

Colin Barr

Manuscript

Aberdeen papers, Add. MS 43246: British Library
Clarendon dep. Irish vols. 5, 6: Bodleian Library, Oxford University
Cullen papers: Dublin Diocesan Archives
Cullen papers: Pontifical Irish College, Rome, Archives
Kenrick papers: Associated Archives St. Mary's Seminary and University, Baltimore
Moran diaries: Archives of the Archdiocese of Sydney
Murray papers: Dublin Diocesan Archives
New Kirby papers, Pontifical Irish College, Rome, Archives
Slattery papers: Cashel Diocesan Archives
Smith papers: San Paolo fuori le muri, Irlanda file

Printed

Blakiston, N. (ed.), *The Roman question: extracts of the despatches of Odo Russell from Rome, 1858–1870* (Wilmington, DE: Michael Glazier, 1980 [1932]).

Comerford, R.V., 'Deference, accommodation, and conflict in Irish confessional relations' in C. Barr and H.M. Carey (eds.), *Religion and Greater Ireland: Christianity and Irish global networks, 1750–1950* (Montreal and Kingston: McGill-Queen's University Press, 2015), pp. 33–51.

Conlan, P., 'Reforming and seeking an identity 1829–1918' in E. Bhreathnach, J. MacMahon and J. McCafferty (eds.), *The Irish Franciscans 1534–1990* (Dublin: Four Courts Press, 2009), pp. 102–31.

Connolly, S.J., *Priests and people in pre-Famine Ireland, 1780–1845* (Dublin: Gill & Macmillan, 1982).

Curato, F. (ed.), *Gran Bretagna e Italia nei documenti della Missioni Minto*, 2 vols. (Rome: Istituto storico italiano per l'età moderna e comtemporanea, 1970).

Doyle, J., *An essay on the Catholic Claims, addressed to . . . the Earl of Liverpool, K.G., &c.* (Dublin: Richard Coyne, 1826).

Gardella, P., *Innocent ecstasy: how Christianity gave America an ethic of sexual pleasure* (Oxford: Oxford University Press, 1985).

Kerr, D.A., *Peel, priests and politics: Sir Robert Peel's Administration and the Roman Catholic Church in Ireland, 1841–1846* (Oxford: Oxford University Press, 1982).

'A nation of beggars'? priests, people, and politics in Famine Ireland, 1846–52* (Oxford: Oxford University Press, 1998).

Larkin, E., *The making of the Roman Catholic Church in Ireland, 1850–1860* (Chapel Hill: University of North Carolina Press, 1980).

The historical dimensions of Irish Catholicism (Washington, DC: The Catholic University of America Press, 1984).

The consolidation of the Roman Catholic Church in Ireland, 1860–1870 (Chapel Hill: University of North Carolina Press, 1987).

The Roman Catholic Church and the movement for Home Rule in Ireland, 1870–1874 (Chapel Hill: University of North Carolina Press, 1990).

The pastoral role of the Roman Catholic Church in pre-Famine Ireland, 1750–1850 (Dublin: Four Courts Press, 2006).

Lee, J., *The modernisation of Irish Society, 1848–1918* (Dublin: Gill & Macmillan, 1989 [1973]).

Lucas, Edward, *The life of Frederick Lucas, M.P.*, 2 vols. (London: Burns and Oates, 1886).

Madras Catholic Expositor, 1844.

McGrath, T., 'The Tridentine evolution of modern Irish Catholicism, 1563–1962: a re-examination of the "devotional revolution" thesis', *Recusant History*, 20 (1991), 512–23.

Religious renewal and reform in the pastoral ministry of Bishop James Doyle of Kildare and Leighlin, 1786–1834 (Dublin: Four Courts Press, 1999).

Meagher, W., *Notices of the life and character of his grace . . . Daniel Murray, late Archbishop of Dublin, as contained in the Commemorative Oration pronounced in the Church of the Conception, Dublin, on the occasion of his grace's Month's Mind, with historical and bio-graphical notes* (Dublin: Gerard Bellew, 1853).

Miller, D.W., 'Mass attendance in Ireland in 1834' in S. Brown and D. Miller (eds.), *Piety and power in Ireland, 1760–1960: essays in honor of Emmet Larkin* (Notre Dame, IN: University of Notre Dame Press, 2000), pp. 158–79.

Moffit, M., *The Society for Irish Church Missions to the Roman Catholics, 1849–1950* (Manchester: Manchester University Press, 2010).

O'Brien, J., 'Irish public opinion and the Risorgimento through the eyes of the press, 1859–60' in C. Barr, M. Finelli and A. O'Connor (eds.), *Nation/Nazione: Irish nationalism and the Italian Risorgimento* (Dublin: UCD Press, 2014), pp. 110–30.

O'Connor, A., 'An Italian inferno in Ireland: Alessandro Gavazzi and religious debate in the nineteenth century' in N. Carter (ed.), *Britain, Ireland and the Italian Risorgimento* (Basingstoke: Palgrave Macmillan, 2015), pp. 127–50.

O'Reilly, B., *John MacHale, Archbishop of Tuam: his life, times, and correspondence*, 2 vols. (New York: Fr. Pustet, 1890).

Pollard, J.F., *Money and the rise of the modern Papacy: financing the Vatican, 1850–1950* (Cambridge: Cambridge University Press, 2005).

Sullivan, M.C. (ed.), *The correspondence of Catherine McAuley* (Dublin: Four Courts Press, 2004).

The Times, 1878.

Townend, P.A., *Father Mathew: temperance and Irish identity* (Dublin: Irish Academic Press, 2002).

12 Protestant Dissenters, *c.*1690–1800

Ian McBride

Manuscript

Barber, Samuel, Manuscript sermon on Revelation 18:20, June 1791: Presbyterian Historical Society of Ireland Library and Archives

Caldwell papers, T/3541: Public Record Office of Northern Ireland

'Journal of W. Campbell': Presbyterian Historical Society of Ireland Library and Archives, Belfast

Hutcheson letter, MS 64: Magee College, Derry

Minto papers, MS 11004: National Library of Scotland

Rebellion papers, 620/: National Archives of Ireland

Wake MSS: Christ Church, Oxford

Wodrow letters: National Library of Scotland

Printed

Abernethy, J., *A sermon recommending the study of scripture-prophecie* (Belfast: James Blow, 1716).
   Religious obedience founded on personal persuasion (Belfast: James Blow, 1720).
   Scarce and valuable tracts and sermons (London: R. Griffiths, 1751).

Bankhurst, B., *Ulster Presbyterians and the Scots Irish diaspora 1750–1764* (Basingstoke: Palgrave, 2013).
   Billy Bluff and Squire Firebrand or, a sample of the times (Belfast: s.n., 1797).

Birch, T.L., *The obligations upon Christians and especially ministers to be exemplary in their lives* (Belfast: H. Dowell, 1794).
   Physicians languishing under disease: an address to the Seceding, or Associate Synod of Ireland (Belfast: s.n., 1796).
   A letter from an Irish emigrant to his friend in the United States (Philadelphia: s.n., 1799).

Bishop, I.M., 'The education of Ulster students at Glasgow University during the eighteenth century', MA thesis, Queen's University Belfast, 1987.

Blanning, T.C.W., 'Liberation or occupation? Theory and practice in the French Revolutionaries' treatment of civilians outside France' in M. Grimsley and C.J. Rogers (eds.), *Civilians in the path of war* (Lincoln: University of Nebraska Press, 2002).

Connolly, S.J., *Religion, law and power: the making of Protestant Ireland 1660–1760* (Oxford: Oxford University Press, 1992).

Curtin, N.J., *The United Irishmen: popular politics in Ulster and Dublin, 1791–98* (Oxford: Oxford University Press, 1994).

[Drennan, W.], *A letter to Edmund Burke ... containing some reflections on patriotism, party-spirit, and the union of free nations* (Dublin: William Hallhead, 1780).

Duchal, J., *A sermon on occasion of the much lamented death of the late Reverend Mr John Abernethy* (Belfast: James Blow, 1741).

Elliott, M., *Wolfe Tone: prophet of Irish Independence* (New Haven: Yale University Press, 1989).
   Francis Hutcheson on Human Nature, ed. T. Mautner (Cambridge: Cambridge University Press, 1993).

Gillespie, R., 'The Presbyterian revolution in Ulster, 1660–1690', in W.J. Sheils and Diana Wood (eds.), *The churches, Ireland and the Irish, Studies in Church History 25* (Oxford: Blackwell, 1989), pp. 159–70.

Green, E.R.R., 'The "strange humours" that drove the Scotch-Irish to America, 1729', *William and Mary Quarterly*, 3rd series, 12 (1955), 113–23.

Griffin, P., *The people with no name: Ireland's Ulster Scots, America's Scots Irish, and the creation of a British Atlantic World, 1689–1764* (Princeton: Princeton University Press, 2001).

Harris, J.A., 'Religion in Hutcheson's moral philosophy', *Journal of the History of Philosophy* 46:2 (2008), 205–22.

Herlihy, K. (ed.), *The politics of Irish dissent 1650–1800* (Dublin: Irish Academic Press, 1997).

Hilton, B., *A mad, bad, and dangerous people? England 1783–1846* (Oxford: Oxford University Press, 2006).

His Grace Charles Duke of Grafton, and His Excellency Henry Earl of Gallway, Lords Justices General and General Governors of Ireland: their speech to both Houses of Parliament [Dublin: Andrew Crooke, 1715].

Historical collections relative to the town of Belfast, ed. H. Joy (Belfast: John Berwick, 1817).

Holmes, A.R., 'Tradition and Enlightenment: conversion and assurance of salvation in Ulster Presbyterianism, 1700–1859' in M. Brown et al. (eds.), *Converts and conversion in Ireland, 1650–1850* (Dublin: Four Courts Press, 2005), pp. 129–56.

The shaping of Ulster Presbyterian belief and practice, 1770–1840 (Oxford: Oxford University Press, 2006).

Hutcheson, F., *A system of moral philosophy*, 2 vols. (Glasgow: R. and A. Foulis, 1755).

Journals of the House of Lords, 8 vols. (Dublin: William Sleater, 1779–1800).

Kidd, C., 'Subscription, the Scottish Enlightenment and the moderate interpretation of history', *Journal of Ecclesiastical History*, 55:3 (2004), 502–19.

Kirkpatrick, J., *God's dominion over kings and other magistrates* (Belfast: James Blow, 1714).

London-Derry Journal, 1775.

Maclaine, A., *A sermon preached at Antrim, Dec. 18, 1745, being the National Fast* (Dublin: A. Reilly, 1746).

Malcome, J., *Personal perswasion no foundation for religious obedience* (Belfast: Robert Gardner, 1720).

McBride, I.R., *Scripture politics: Ulster Presbyterians and Irish radicalism in the late eighteenth century* (Oxford: Oxford University Press, 1998).

Eighteenth century Ireland: the isle of slaves (Dublin: Gill & Macmillan, 2009).

McSkimmin, S., *Annals of Ulster: or Ireland fifty years ago* (Belfast: John Henderson, 1849).

Miller, D.W., 'Presbyterianism and "modernization" in Ulster', *Past and Present*, 80 (1978), 66–90.

'Religious commotions in the Scottish diaspora: a transatlantic perspective on "evangelicalism" in a mainline denomination' in D.A. Wilson and M.G. Spencer (eds.), *Ulster Presbyterians in the Atlantic world: religion, politics and identity* (Dublin: Four Courts Press, 2006), pp. 22–38.

Moore, J., 'Evangelical Calvinists versus the Hutcheson circle: debating the faith in Scotland, 1738–1739' in A. Dunan-Page and C. Prunier (eds.), *Debating the faith: religion and letter writing in Great Britain, 1550–1800* (Dordrecht: Springer, 2013), pp. 177–93.

Northern Star, 1795–6.

Pocock, J.G.A., 'Clergy and commerce: the conservative Enlightenment in England' in R. Ajello (ed.), *L'Età dei Lumi: studi storici sul settecento Europeo in onore di Franco Venturi*, 2 vols. (Naples: Jovene, 1985), pp. 523–62.

'Enthusiasm: the antiself of Enlightenment', *Huntington Library Quarterly*, 60:1–2 (1997), 7–28.

Pringle, F., *The Gospel Ministry, an ordinance of Christ; and the duty of ministers and people* (n.p., 1796).

The Works of Thomas Reid, D.D., ed. William Hamilton, 2nd edn (Edinburgh: McLachlan, Stewart, 1849).

Sloan, D., *The Scottish Enlightenment and the American college ideal* (New York: Teachers College Press, 1971).

Stavely, W., *War proclaimed, and victory ensured; or, The Lamb's conquests illustrated* (Belfast: Thomas Storey, 1795).

Stewart, D., *The Seceders in Ireland with annals of their congregations* (Belfast: Presbyterian Historical Society, 1950).

Strain, R.M.W., *Belfast and its Charitable Society* (Oxford: Oxford University Press, 1961).

The insolence of the Dissenters against the Established Church (London: J. Baker and T. Warner, 1716).

The life of Theobald Wolfe Tone, ed. T. Bartlett (Dublin: Lilliput Press, 1998).

Whan, R., *The Presbyterians of Ulster, 1680–1730* (Woodbridge: The Boydell Press, 2013).

Wiles, M., *Archetypal heresy: Arianism through the centuries* (Oxford: Oxford University Press, 1996).

Wills, G., *Inventing America: Jefferson's Declaration of Independence* (New York: Doubleday, 1978).

13 Protestantism in the Nineteenth Century: Revival and Crisis

Andrew R. Holmes

Acheson, A., *A history of the Church of Ireland 1691–2001*, 2nd edn (Dublin: The Columba Press / SPCK, 2002).

Brown, S.J., *The national Churches of England, Ireland, and Scotland 1801–46* (Oxford: Oxford University Press, 2001).

Providence and Empire: religion, politics and society in the United Kingdom, 1815–1914 (Harlow: Pearson Longman, 2008).

Connolly, S.J., *Religion and society in nineteenth-century Ireland* (Dundalk: Economic Social History Society of Ireland, 1985).

Fitzpatrick, D., *Descendancy: Irish Protestant histories since 1795* (Cambridge: Cambridge University Press, 2014).

Hall, J., and G.H. Stuart, *The American Evangelists, D.L. Moody and Ira D. Sankey, in Great Britain and Ireland* (New York: Dodd and Mead, 1875).

Hempton, D., *Methodism: empire of the spirit* (New Haven: Yale University Press, 2005).

Hempton, D., and M. Hill, *Evangelical Protestantism in Ulster society 1740–1890* (London: Routledge, 1992).

Hill, M., 'Gender, culture and "the spiritual empire": the Irish Protestant female missionary experience', *Women's History Review*, 16 (2007), 203–26.

Holmes, A.R., 'The experience and understanding of religious revival in Ulster Presbyterianism, *c.* 1800–1930, *Irish Historical Studies*, 34 (2004–5), 361–85.

'Biblical authority and the impact of Higher Criticism in Irish Presbyterianism, *c.* 1850–1930', *Church History*, 75 (2006), 343–73.

The shaping of Ulster Presbyterian belief and practice, 1770–1840 (Oxford: Oxford University Press, 2006).

Bibliography

'The shaping of Irish Presbyterian attitudes to mission, 1790–1840', *Journal of Ecclesiastical History*, 57:4 (2006), 711–37.

'Ulster Presbyterianism as a popular religious culture, 1750–1860' in K. Cooper and J. Gregory (eds.), *Elite and popular religion: studies in church history* (Woodbridge: Boydell and Brewer, 2006), pp. 315–26.

'Covenanter politics: evangelicalism, political liberalism and Ulster Presbyterians, 1798–1914', *English Historical Review*, 125 (2010), 340–69.

'The Ulster revival of 1859: causes, controversies and consequences', *Journal of Ecclesiastical History*, 63 (2012), 488–515.

'Religion, anti-slavery, and identity: Irish Presbyterians, the United States, and transatlantic evangelicalism, *c.* 1820–1914', *Irish Historical Studies*, 39 (2014–15), 378–98.

Holmes, J., *Religious revivals in Britain and Ireland 1859–1905* (Dublin: Irish Academic Press, 2000).

Holmes, R.F.G., *Henry Cooke* (Belfast: Christian Journals, 1981).

   Our Irish Presbyterian heritage (Belfast: Publications Committee of the Presbyterian Church in Ireland, 1985).

Jackson, A., *Ireland 1798–1998: war, peace and beyond* (Malden: Wiley-Blackwell, 2010).

Jones, G., 'Darwinism in Ireland' in D. Attis (ed.), *Science and Irish culture*, vol. I (Dublin: Royal Dublin Society, 2004), pp. 115–37.

Levistone Cooney, D., *The Methodists in Ireland: a short history* (Dublin: The Columba Press, 2004).

Livingstone, D.N., *Dealing with Darwin: place, politics, and rhetoric in religious engagements with evolution* (Baltimore, MD: Johns Hopkins University Press, 2014).

Magee, W., *A charge delivered at his primary visitation: in St. Patrick's Cathedral, Dublin, on Thursday the 24th of October, 1822* (Dublin: Richard Coyne, 1822).

McBride, I.R., *Scripture politics: Ulster Presbyterians and Irish Radicalism in the late eighteenth century* (Oxford: Clarendon Press, 1998).

Ridden, J., 'The forgotten history of the Protestant crusade: religious liberalism in Ireland', *Journal of Religious History*, 31 (2007), 78–102.

Salmon, G., *The evidences of the work of the holy spirit: a sermon preached in St Stephen's Church, Dublin, on Sunday, July 3, 1859 . . . with an appendix on the revival movement in the north of Ireland*, 3rd edn (Dublin, 1859).

Stanley, B., 'Christian missions, antislavery and the claims of humanity, c.1813–1873' in S. Gilley and B. Stanley (eds.), *World Christianities, c.1815–c.1914: The Cambridge history of Christianity*, vol. VIII (Cambridge: Cambridge University Press, 2006), pp. 443–57.

Whelan, I., *The Bible War in Ireland: the 'Second Reformation' and the polarization of Protestant–Catholic Relations, 1800–1840* (Dublin: Lilliput Press, 2005).

Yates, N., *The religious condition of Ireland 1770–1850* (Oxford: Oxford University Press, 2006).

14 Language and Literacy in the Eighteenth and Nineteenth Centuries

Aidan Doyle

Batia, T.K., and W.C. Ritchie (eds.), *The handbook of bilingualism* (Oxford: Blackwell, 2004).

Caerwen Williams, E., and P.K. Ford, *The Irish literary tradition* (Cardiff: University of Wales Press, 1992).

Callahan, J., 'The Irish language in Pennsylvania' in T.W. Ihde (ed.), *The Irish language in the United States: a historical, sociolinguistic and applied linguistic survey* (Westport, CT: Bergin and Garvey, 1994), pp. 18–26.

Cullen, L., 'Patrons, teachers and literacy in Irish: 1700–1850' in M. Daly and D. Dickson (eds.), *The origins of popular literacy in Ireland: changes and educational development 1700–1920* (Dublin: Department of Modern History, TCD, 1990), pp. 15–44.

de Brún, P. (ed.), 'Bíoblóir á chosaint féin', *Éigse*, 23 (1988), 80–2.

Scriptural instruction in the vernacular: the Irish Society and its teachers, 1818–27 (Dublin: Dublin Institute for Advanced Studies, 2009).

de Fréine, S., *The great silence: the study of a relationship between language and nationality* (Baile Atha Cliath: Foilseacháin Náisiúnta Teoranta, 1965).

Denvir, G., 'Literature in Irish, 1800–1890: from the Act of Union to the Gaelic League' in M. Kelleher and P. O'Leary (eds.), *The Cambridge history of Irish literature*, 2 vols. (Cambridge: Cambridge University Press, 2006), vol. I, pp. 544–98.

Dillon, C., 'English, Irish and the south Ulster poets and scribes' in J. Kelly and C. Mac Murchaidh (eds.), *Irish and English: essays on the Irish and English cultural frontier, 1600–1900* (Dublin: Four Courts Press, 2012), pp. 141–61.

Dolan, T., 'Translating Irelands: the English language in the Irish context' in M. Cronin and C. Ó Cuilleanáin (eds.), *The languages of Ireland* (Dublin: Four Courts Press, 2003), pp. 78–92.

Doyle, A., *A history of the Irish language: from the Norman Invasion to Independence* (Oxford: Oxford University Press, 2015).

'A sociolinguistic analysis of a national language: Irish in the nineteenth century' in A. Havinga and N. Langer, *Invisible languages in the nineteenth century* (Berne: Peter Lang, 2015), pp. 117–34.

'The "decline" of the Irish language in the eighteenth and nineteenth centuries: a new interpretation', *Studia Hibernica*, 41 (2015), 165–76.

Filppula, M., *The grammar of Irish English: language in Hibernian style* (London: Routledge, 1999).

Filppula, M., et al., *English and Celtic in contact* (London: Routledge, 2008).

Fitzgerald, G., 'Estimates for baronies of minimum level of Irish-speaking amongst successive decennial cohorts: 1771–1781 to 1861–1871', *Proceedings of the Royal Irish Academy*, 84C (1984), 117–55.

Havinga, A., and N. Langer (eds.), *Invisible languages in the nineteenth century* (Berne: Peter Lang, 2015).

Herity, M. (ed.), *Ordnance Survey letters: Meath* (Dublin: Four Masters Press, 2001).

Ihde, T.W. (ed.), *The Irish language in the United States: a historical, sociolinguistic and applied linguistic survey* (Westport, CT: Bergin and Garvey, 1994).

Kallen, J., 'Irish as an American ethnic language' in Ihde (ed.), *The Irish language in the United States: a historical, sociolinguistic and applied linguistic survey* (Westport, CT: Bergin and Garvey, 1994), pp. 27–40.

'Irish English: context and contacts' in J. Kallen (ed.), *Focus on Ireland* (Amsterdam: John Benjamins, 1997), pp. 1–33.

Kelly, J., 'Irish Protestants and the Irish language in the eighteenth century' in J. Kelly and C. Mac Murchaidh (eds.), *Irish and English: Essays on the Irish and English Cultural Frontier, 1600–1900* (Dublin: Four Courts Press, 2012), pp. 189–217.

Educational print and the emergence of mass education in Ireland, c.1650 – c.1830' in J. Kelly and S. Hegarty (eds.), *New perspectives on the history of education in Ireland and Europe, 1700–1900* (Dublin: Four Courts Press, 2017), pp. 34–71.

Kelly, J., and C. Mac Murchaidh, 'Introduction: establishing the context' in J. Kelly and C. Mac Murchaidh, *Irish and English: essays on the Irish and English cultural frontier, 1600–1900* (Dublin: Four Courts Press, 2012), pp. 15–42.

Mac Mathúna, L., *Béarla sa Ghaeilge – cabhair choigríche: an códmheascadh Gaeilge/Béarla i litríocht na Gaeilge 1600–1900* (Baile Atha Cliath: An Clóchomhar, 2007).

'Verisimilitude or subversion? Probing the interaction of English and Irish in selected warrants and macaronic verse in the eighteenth century' in J. Kelly and C. Mac Murchaidh (eds.), *Irish and English: essays on the Irish and English cultural frontier, 1600–1900* (Dublin: Four Courts Press, 2012), pp. 116–40.

Mac Murchaidh, C., 'The Catholic Church and the Irish language' in J. Kelly and C. Mac Murchaidh, *Irish and English: essays on the Irish and English cultural frontier, 1600–1900* (Dublin: Four Courts Press, 2012), pp. 162–88.

Ní Chonghaile, D., '"Sagart gan iomrádh": an tAthair Domhnall Ó Morchadha (1858–1935) agus amhráin Pennsylvania' in R. Nic Congáil et al. (eds.), *Litríocht na Gaeilge ar fud an domhain* I (Baile Atha Cliath: LeabhairComhar, 2015), pp. 191–214.

Ní Mhunghaile, L., 'Bilingualism, print culture in Irish and the public sphere' in J. Kelly and C. Mac Murchaidh, *Irish and English: essays on the Irish and English cultural frontier, 1600–1900* (Dublin: Four Courts Press, 2012), pp. 218–42.

Ní Urdail, M., *The scribe in eighteenth- and nineteenth-century Ireland: motivations and milieu* (Munster: Nodus Publikationen, 2000).

Nic Craith, M., *Malartú teanga: an Ghaeilge i gCorcaigh sa naoú haois déag* (Baile Atha Cliath: Cumann Eorpach Léann na hÉireann, 1993).

'Legacy and loss: the Great Silence and its aftermath' in J. Crowley et al. (eds.), *Atlas of the Great Irish Famine* (Cork: Cork University Press, 2012).

Ó Ciosáin, N., *Print and popular culture in Ireland 1757–1850* (Dublin: Lilliput Press, 1997).

'Print and Irish, 1570–1900: an exception among the Celtic languages', *Radharc*, 5–7 (2004–6), 73–106.

'The print culture of the Celtic languages, 1700–1900', *Cultural and Social History*, 10:3 (2013), 347–67.

Ó Cuív, B., *Irish dialects and Irish-speaking districts* (Dublin: Dublin Institute for Advanced Studies, 1951).

'Irish language and literature, 1691–1845' in T.W. Moody and W.E. Vaughan (eds.), *A new history of Ireland*, vol. III (Oxford: Oxford University Press, 1986), pp. 509–45.

Ó Huallacháin, C., *The Irish and Irish* (Dublin: Assisi Press, 1994).

Ó Macháin, P., 'Imirce agus filleadh lámhscríbhinní na nGael' in R. Nic Congáil et al. (eds.), *Litríocht na Gaeilge ar fud an domhain* I (Baile Atha Cliath: LeabhairComhar, 2015), pp. 109–54.

Ó Muirithe, D., *An t-Amhrán Macarónach* (Baile Atha Cliath: An Clóchomhar, 1980).

Ó Murchú, M., 'Language and society in nineteenth-century Ireland' in G. Jenkins (ed.), *Language and community in the nineteenth century* (Cardiff: University of Wales Press, 1998), pp. 341–68.

Ó Tuathaigh, G., *Ireland before the Famine 1798–1848* (Dublin: Gill & Macmillan, 1972).

'Gaelic Ireland, popular politics and Daniel O'Connell', *Journal of the Galway Archaeological and Historical Society*, 34 (1974), 21–34.

Odlin, T., 'Bilingualism and substrate influence: a look at clefts and reflexives' in J. Kallen (ed.), *Focus on Ireland* (Amsterdam: John Benjamins, 1997), pp. 35–50.

Sharpe, R., 'Tadhg Gaelach Ó Súilleabháin's *Pious miscellany*: editions of the Munster best-seller in the early nineteenth century', *Proceedings of the Royal Irish Academy*, 114C (2014), 235–93.

Smyth, W., *Map-making, landscapes and memory* (Cork: Cork University Press, 2006).

Swift, J., 'A dialogue in Hibernian style between A and B' in *The prose writings of Jonathan Swift*, vol. IV, ed. H. Davis and L. Landa (Oxford: Blackwell, 1973).

Tighe, W., *Statistical observations relative to the County of Kilkenny, made in the years 1800–1801* (Dublin: Graisberry and Campbell, 1802).

Ua Duinnín, P. (ed.), *Amhráin Eoghain Ruaidh Uí Shúilleabháin* (Baile Atha Cliath: Connradh na Gaedhilge, 1901).

Wall, M., 'The decline of the Irish language' in B. Ó Cuív (ed.), *A view of the Irish language* (Dublin: The Stationery Office, 1969), pp. 81–90.

Williams, N., *Riocard Bairéad – Amhráin* (Baile Atha Cliath: An Clóchomhar, 1978).

'Gaelic texts and English script' in M. Caball and A. Carpenter (eds.), *Oral and print cultures in Ireland 1600–1900* (Dublin: Four Courts Press, 2010), pp. 85–101.

Wolbersen, H., 'The decline of the South Jutish in Angeln: a historical case of transformation into the modern age around 1800' in A. Havinga and N. Langer, *Invisible languages in the nineteenth century* (Berne: Peter Lang, 2015), pp. 149–172.

Wolf, N.M., *An Irish-Speaking island: state, religion, community, and the linguistic landscape in Ireland, 1770–1870* (Madison: The University of Wisconsin Press, 2014).

15 Futures Past: Enlightenment and Antiquarianism in the Eighteenth Century

Michael Brown and Lesa Ní Mhunghaile

Berkeley, G., *Principles of human knowledge* in George Berkeley, *Philosophical works*, ed. M. Ayers (London: Everyman, 1993).

Berman, D., 'The Irish Counter-Enlightenment' in R. Kearney (ed.), *The Irish mind: exploring intellectual traditions* (Dublin: Wolfhound Press, 1985), pp. 119–40.

'The Irish pragmatist' in C. Fauske (ed.), *Archbishop William King and the Anglican Irish context, 1688–1729* (Dublin: Four Courts Press, 2004), pp. 123–34.

'David Hume on the 1641 Rebellion in Ireland', *Studies*, 258 (1976), 101–12.

Brown, M., *Francis Hutcheson in Dublin, 1719–1730: the crucible of his thought* (Dublin: Four Courts Press, 2002).

A political biography of John Toland (London: Pickering and Chatto, 2012).

The Irish Enlightenment (Cambridge, MA: Harvard University Press, 2016).

Burke, E., *Writings and speeches,* vol. II: *Party, parliament and the American crisis, 1766–1774* (Oxford: Clarendon Press, 1981).

Philosophical enquiry into the origin of our ideas of the sublime and beautiful, ed. A. Phillips (Oxford: Oxford University Press, 1990).

Writings and speeches, vol. VI: India: the launching of the Warren Hastings impeachment, 1786–1788 (Oxford: Clarendon Press, 1991).

Writings and speeches of Edmund Burke, vol. IX: I: The Revolutionary War, 1794–1797; II Ireland (Oxford: Clarendon Press, 1991).

Writings and speeches, vol. III: Party, parliament and the American War, 1774–1780 (Oxford: Clarendon Press, 1996).

Reflections on the Revolution in France, ed. J.C.D. Clark (Stanford, CA: Stanford University Press, 2001).

Champion, J., *The pillars of priestcraft shaken: the Church of England and its enemies, 1660–1730* (Cambridge: Cambridge University Press, 1992).

Cox, R., *Hibernia Anglicana, or, the history of Ireland, from the Conquest thereof by the English, to this present time with an introductory discourse touching the ancient state of that kingdom,* 2 vols. (London, 1689).

Cunningham, B., *The world of Geoffrey Keating: history, myth and religion in seventeenth-century Ireland* (Dublin: Four Courts Press, 2000).

Dobbs, A., *An essay on the trade and improvement of Ireland* (Dublin: J. Smith, 1729).

Fagan, P., *Catholics in a Protestant country: the papist constituency in eighteenth-century Dublin* (Dublin: Four Courts Press, 1988).

Fauske, C., *A political biography of William King* (London: Pickering and Chatto, 2011).

Ferguson, A., *An essay on the history of civil society* (Edinburgh: A. Kincaid and J. Bell, 1767).

Gibbons, L., and K. O'Conor (eds.), *Charles O'Conor of Ballinagare: life and works* (Dublin: Four Courts Press, 2015).

Harrison, A., *Ag Cruinniú Meala* (Dublin: An Clóchomhar Tta, 1988).

The Dean's friend: Anthony Raymond 1675–1726, Jonathan Swift and the Irish language (Dublin: de Burca Publishers, 1999).

Hayton, D., 'Anglo-Irish attitudes: changing perceptions of national identity among the Protestant Ascendancy in Ireland, ca. 1690–1750', *Studies in Eighteenth-Century Culture,* 17 (1987), 145–57.

Hudson, N., '"Oral tradition": the evolution of an eighteenth-century concept' in A. Ribeiro and J. Basker (eds.), *Tradition in transition: women writers, marginal texts, and the eighteenth-century canon* (Oxford: Clarendon Press, 1996), pp. 161–76.

Israel, J., *Radical Enlightenment: philosophy and the making of modernity, 1650–1750* (Oxford: Oxford University Press, 2001).

Johnson, S., *A journey to the Western Isles of Scotland* (London: W. Strahan, 1775).

Kelly, J., 'Jonathan Swift and the Irish economy in the 1720s', *Eighteenth-Century Ireland,* 6 (1991), 7–36.

'"A wild capuchin of Cork": Arthur O'Leary (1729–1802)' in G. Moran (ed.), *Radical Irish priests, 1660–1970* (Dublin: Four Courts Press, 1998), pp. 39–61.

'Irish Protestants and the Irish language in the eighteenth century' in J. Kelly and C. Mac Murchaidh (eds.), *Irish and English: essays on the Irish linguistic and cultural frontier, 1600–1900* (Dublin: Four Courts Press, 2012), pp. 189–217.

Kidd, C., *British identities before nationalism: ethnicity and nationhood in the Atlantic world 1600–1800* (Cambridge: Cambridge University Press, 1999).

King, W., *Europe's deliverance from France and slavery* (Dublin: Tim Goodvin, 1691).

The state of the Protestants of Ireland under the late King James' Government (London: Samuel Roycroft, 1691).

Essay on the origin of evil, trans. Edmund Law (London: R. Knaplock, 1731).

Ledwich, E., *Antiquities of Ireland* (Dublin: Arthur Grueber, 1790).

Leerssen, J., *Mere Irish and Fíor-Ghael: studies in the idea of Irish nationality* (Cork: Cork University Press, 1996).

Remembrance and imagination: patterns in the historical and literary representation of Ireland in the nineteenth century (Cork: Cork University Press, 1996).

Leighton, C.D.A., 'The enlightened religion of Robert Clayton', *Studia Hibernica*, 29 (1995–7), 157–84.

Livesey, J., *Civil society and empire: Ireland and Scotland in the eighteenth-century Atlantic world* (New Haven: Yale University Press, 2009).

Lock, F.P., *Edmund Burke, vol. II: 1784–1797* (Oxford: Oxford University Press, 2006).

Lyons, C., 'Sylvester O'Halloran's General history (1778): Irish historiography and the late eighteenth-century British Empire', PhD thesis, National University of Ireland, Galway, 2011.

Mac Craith, M., 'Literature in Irish, c.1550–1690: from the Elizabethan settlement to the Battle of the Boyne' in M. Kelleher and P. O'Leary (eds.), *The Cambridge history of Irish literature*, 2 vols. (Cambridge: Cambridge University Press, 2006), vol. I, pp. 191–231.

Mac Mathúna, L., 'Getting to grips with innovation and genre diversification in the work of the Ó Neachtain circle in early eighteenth-century Dublin', *Eighteenth-Century Ireland*, 27 (2012), 53–83.

Madden, S., *A letter to the Dublin Society on the improving their fund* (Dublin: R. Reilly, 1739).

Mautner, T. (ed.), *Francis Hutcheson: two texts on human nature* (Cambridge: Cambridge University Press, 1993).

McGuinness, P. et al. (eds.), *John Toland's Christianity not mysterious: text, associated works and critical essays* (Dublin: Lilliput Press, 1997).

Mirala, P., '"A large mob calling themselves Freemasons": masonic parades in Ulster' in E. Magennis and P. Jupp (eds.), *Crowds in Ireland, c.1720–1920* (London: Palgrave Macmillan, 2000), pp. 117–38.

Freemasonry in Ulster, 1733–1813 (Dublin: Four Courts Press, 2007).

Morley, V., *Ó Chéitinn go Raiftearaí* (Dublin: Coiscéim, 2011).

Ní Mhunghaile, L. (ed.), *Charlotte Brooke's Reliques of Irish poetry* (Dublin: Irish Manuscripts Commission, 2009).

Ré Órga na nGael: Joseph Cooper Walker 1760–1810 (Indreabhán: Cló Iar-Chonnacht, 2013).

'"An Solamh sochmadh": Seon Mac Solaidh agus ciorcal Neachtain' in L. Mac Mathúna and R. Uí Chollatáin (eds.), *Saothrú na Gaeilge scríofa i suímh uirbeacha na hÉireann, 1700–1850* (Dublin: Four Courts Press, 2016), pp. 74–95.

Ó Catháin, D., 'Dermot O'Connor, translator of Keating', *Eighteenth-Century Ireland*, 2 (1987), 67–87.

O'Connor, D., *The general history of Ireland . . . collected by the learned Geoffrey Keating, D.D. faithfully translated from the original Irish language* (London: B. Creake, and Dublin: James Carson, 1723).

O'Conor, C., *Dissertations on the ancient history of Ireland* (Dublin: James Hoey, 1753).

O'Flaherty, E., 'Burke and the Irish constitution' in S.P. Donlan (ed.), *Edmund Burke's Irish identities* (Dublin: Irish Academic Press, 2006), pp. 102–17.

O'Flaherty, R., *Ogygia* (London: R. Everingham, 1685).

O'Halloran, C., '"The island of saints and scholars": views of the early church and sectarian politics in late-eighteenth-century Ireland', *Eighteenth-Century Ireland*, 5 (1990), 7–20.

Golden ages and barbarous nations (Cork: Cork University Press, 2004).

'"A Revolution in our moral and civil affairs": Charles O'Conor and the creation of a community of scholars in late eighteenth-century Ireland' in L. Gibbons and K. O'Conor (eds.), *Charles O'Conor of Ballinagare: life and works* (Dublin: Four Courts Press, 2015), pp. 81–96.

O'Halloran, S., *An introduction to the study of the history and antiquities of Ireland* (Dublin: Thomas Ewing, 1772).

A general history of Ireland, 2 vols. (London: A. Hamilton, 1778).

O'Leary, A., *Miscellaneous tracts*, 2nd edn (Dublin: Thomas McDonnel, 1781).

Pocock, J.G.A., 'The political economy of Burke's analysis of the French Revolution' in Pocock, *Virtue, commerce and history: essays on political thought and history, chiefly in the eighteenth century* (Cambridge: Cambridge University Press, 1985), pp. 193–212.

Rubel, M., *Savage and barbarian: historical attitudes in the criticism of Homer and Ossian in Britain, 1760–1800* (Amsterdam: North-Holland, 1978).

Stafford, F., *The sublime savage: James Macpherson and the poems of Ossian* (Edinburgh: Edinburgh University Press, 1988).

Sullivan, R.E., *John Toland and the Deist Controversy: a study in adaptations* (Cambridge, MA: Harvard University Press, 1982).

Swift, J., *Major works*, ed. A. Ross and D. Wooley (Oxford: Oxford University Press, 2003).

Toland, J., *Tetradymus* (London: J. Brotherstow, 1720).

Vallancey, C., *An essay on the antiquity of the Irish language: being a collation of the Irish with the Punic language* (Dublin: S. Powell, 1772).

Walsh, P., *A prospect of the state of Ireland* (London: Johanna Broom, 1682).

16 Art and Architecture in the Long Eighteenth Century

Christine Casey

Manuscript

Haliday MS 4B: Royal Irish Academy
Wide Street Commissioners minutes, DCLA/WSC/Mins: Dublin City Archives

Electronic

Dictionary of Irish Architects 1720–1940, Irish Architectural Archive, at www.dia.ie/architects/view.

The National Inventory of Architectural Heritage survey at www.buildingsofireland.ie.

Printed

Baker, M., 'The making of portrait busts in the mid-eighteenth century: Roubiliac, Scheemakers and Trinity College, Dublin', *Burlington Magazine*, 137:12 (1995), 821–31.

Barnard, T., *Making the grand figure: lives and possessions in Ireland, 1641–1770* (New Haven: Yale University Press, 2004).

Bennet, S., *Cultivating the human faculties: James Barry (1741–1806) and the Society of Arts* (Bethlehem, PA: Lehigh University Press, 2009).

Bennett, D., *Irish Georgian silver* (London: Cassell, 1972).

Brett, C., *Court houses and market houses of the province of Ulster* (Belfast: Ulster Architectural Heritage Society, 1973).

Butler, R., 'Westminster, the Irish Grand Juries and the political context for Assize Court building, 1800–1850', History of Art Postgraduate Research Seminar, Trinity College Dublin, 12 March 2014.

Byrne, H., 'The speculative building activities of Simon Vierpyl', *Bulletin of the Irish Georgian Society*, 37 (1995), 31–5.

Calderón, L., and K. Dechant, 'New light on Hugh Montgomerie, Richard Castle and Number 85 Saint Stephen's Green' in C. Casey (ed.), *The eighteenth-century Dublin town house: form, function and finance* (Dublin: Four Courts Press, 2010), pp. 174–96.

Casey, C., 'Court houses, market houses and townhalls of Leinster', MA thesis, University College Dublin, 1982.

'Books and builders: a bibliographical approach to Irish eighteenth-century architecture', PhD thesis, University of Dublin, 1991.

'Newly discovered building accounts for Charlemont House and the Casino at Marino', *Apollo*, 140:448 (June 1999), 42–50.

The buildings of Ireland, vol. III: *Dublin* (New Haven: Yale University Press, 2005).

'A Palladian palazzo in Ireland's capital', *Country Life*, 204: 50 (8 Dec. 2010), 44–50.

'Grand Tour: the passage of migrant craftsmen from Lake Lugano to County Kildare' in R. Gillespie and R. Foster (eds.), *Irish provincial cultures in the long eighteenth century: making the middling sort* (Dublin: Four Courts Press, 2010), pp. 157–74.

Casey, C., and A. Rowan, *The buildings of Ireland, vol. II: North-Leinster* (Harmondsworth: Penguin, 1993).

Clark, M., *The Dublin Civic Portraiture Collection: patronage, politics and patriotism, 1603–2013* (Dublin: Four Courts Press, 2016).

Clark, M., and A. Smeaton (eds.), *The Georgian squares of Dublin: an architectural history* (Dublin: Dublin City Council, 2006).

Colvin, H., and M. Craig, *Architectural drawings in the library of Elton Hall* (Oxford: Roxburghe Club, 1964).

Cornforth, J., *Early Georgian interiors* (New Haven: Yale University Press, 2004).

Cowhey, A., 'Dublin cabinetmakers and their clientele 1800–1841', PhD thesis, University College Dublin, 2007.

Craig, M., *The volunteer earl: being the life and times of James Caulfeild, the first Earl of Charlemont* (London: Cresset Press, 1948).

Dublin 1660–1860: the shaping of a city (London: Cresset Press, 1952).

The architecture of Ireland (London and Dublin: Batsford and Eason & Son, 1982).

'The quest of Sir Edward Lovett Pearce', *Irish Arts Review Yearbook 1996,* 12 (1996), 27–34.

Craig, M., and D. FitzGerald, Knight of Glin, 'Castletown, County Kildare', *Country Life,* 145:3760 (1969), 722–6; 3761 (1969), 798–802.

Crookshank, A., and the Knight of Glin, *The painters of Ireland 1660–1920* (London: Barrie and Jenkins, 1979).

Ireland's painters 1600–1940 (New Haven: Yale University Press, 2002).

Cullen, F., *Visual politics: the representation of Ireland 1750–1930* (Cork: Cork University Press, 1997).

The Irish face: redefining the Irish portrait (London: National Portrait Gallery, 2004).

Curran, C.P., *Dublin decorative plasterwork of the seventeenth and eighteenth centuries* (London: Alec Tiranti, 1967).

Dunne, T. (ed.), *James Barry 1741–1806: 'The Great Historical Painter'* (Cork: Crawford Art Gallery and Gandon Editions, 2005).

Dunne, T., and W.L. Pressly (eds.), *James Barry, 1741–1806: history painter* (Farnham: Ashgate, 2010).

Figgis, N. (ed.), *Art and architecture of Ireland,* vol. II: *Painting 1600–1900* (New Haven: Yale University Press, 2014).

FitzGerald, A., 'Cosmopolitan commerce: the Dublin goldsmith Robert Calderwood', *Apollo,* 162:523 (Sept. 2005), 46–50.

'The production and consumption of goldsmiths' work in eighteenth-century Dublin', PhD thesis, Royal College of Art, London, 2005.

FitzGerald, B. (ed.), *Correspondence of Emily, Duchess of Leinster (1731–1814),* 3 vols. (Dublin: Stationery Office, 1949–57).

Fraser, M., 'Public building and colonial policy in Dublin, 1760–1800', *Architectural History,* 27 (1985), 102–23.

Gilchrist, A., 'The greatest traveller in eighteenth-century Ireland', *Bulletin of the Irish Georgian Society,* 3 (1960), 7–8.

Glin, Knight of, and J. Peill, *Irish furniture* (New Haven: Yale University Press, 2007).

Gough, M., 'The Dublin Wide Streets Commissioners (1758–1851): an early modern planning authority', *Pleanáil: Journal of the Irish Planning Institute,* 11 (1992–3), 126–55.

Griffin, D.J., 'An architectural history of Castletown' in *Castletown: decorative arts* (Dublin: OPW, 2011), pp. 29–46.

Griffin, D.J., and C. Pegum, *Leinster House* (Dublin: OPW, 2000).

Gunnis, R., *Dictionary of British sculptors 1660–1851,* 2nd edn (London: Abbey Library, 1968).

Harris, E., 'Thomas Wright and Viscount Limerick at Tollymore Park', *Irish Architectural and Decorative Studies,* 16 (2013), 50.

Harris, J., *Sir William Chambers, Knight of the Polar Star* (London: Zwemmer, 1970).

Hayes, M., 'Anglo-Irish architectural exchange in the early eighteenth century: patrons, practitioners and pieds-à-terre', PhD thesis, Trinity College Dublin, 2015.

Hill, J., *The building of Limerick* (Cork: Mercier Press, 1991).

Jôekalda, K., 'What has become of the New Art History?', *Journal of Art Historiography,* 9 (2013), 1–7.

Johnston-Liik, E.M., *History of the Irish Parliament 1692–1800: commons, constituencies and statutes,* 6 vols. (Belfast: Ulster Historical Foundation, 2002).

Kelly, J., 'Francis Wheatley: his Irish paintings' in A.M. Dalsimer (ed.), *Visualizing Ireland: national identity and the pictorial tradition* (London: Faber & Faber, 1993), pp. 145–63.

Laffan, W. (ed.), *The cries of Dublin* (Tralee: Churchill House Press, 2003).

Laffan, W., and C. Monkhouse (eds.), *Ireland: crossroads of art and design 1690–1840* (Chicago: The Art Institute, 2015).

Laffan, W., and K. Mulligan, *Russborough: a great Irish house, its families and collections* (Russborough: Alfred Beit Foundation, 2014).

Loeber, R., et al. (eds.), *Art and architecture of Ireland*, vol. iv: *Architecture 1600–2000* (New Haven: Yale University Press, 2014).

Logan, J., ' "Dropped into this kingdom from the clouds": the Irish career of Davis Dukart, architect and engineer, 1761–1781', *Irish Architectural and Decorative Studies*, 10 (2007), 34–89.

Lucey, C., ' "Made in the new taste": domestic neoclassicism and the Dublin building industry, 1765–1801', PhD thesis, University College Dublin, 2009.

'Classicism or commerce? The town house interior as commodity' in C. Casey (ed.), *The eighteenth-century Dublin town house: form, function and finance* (Dublin: Four Courts Press, 2010), pp. 236–48.

'The scale of plasterwork production in the metropolitan centres of Britain and Ireland' in C. Casey and C. Lucey (eds.), *Decorative plasterwork in Ireland and Europe* (Dublin: Four Courts Press, 2012), pp. 194–218.

Madden, G., 'Rathfarnham Castle', *Irish Arts Review*, 4:1 (1987), 22–6.

Malcomson, A.P.W., *Nathaniel Clements (1705–77): politics, fashion and architecture in mid-eighteenth-century Ireland* (Dublin: Four Courts Press, 2015).

'Manuscript autobiography of Pole Cosby', *Journal of the Kildare Archaeological Society*, 5 (1906–08), 79–99, 165–84, 253–73, 311–24, 423–36.

Marshall, C., and P. Murray (eds.), *Art and architecture of Ireland*, vol. v: *Twentieth century* (New Haven: Yale University Press, 2014), pp. 207–12.

Marson, P., *Belmore: the Lowry Corrys of Castle Coole 1646–1913* (Belfast: Ulster Historical Foundation, 2007).

McCarthy, M., *Lord Charlemont and his circle: essays in honour of Michael Wynne* (Dublin: Four Courts Press, 2001).

McCullough, N. (ed.), *A vision of the city: Dublin and the Wide Streets Commissioners* (Dublin: Dublin Corporation, 1991).

McDonnell, J., *Irish eighteenth-century stuccowork and its European sources* (Dublin: National Gallery of Ireland, 1991).

Ecclesiastical art of the Penal Era (Maynooth: St Patrick's College, 1995).

'The art of the sculptor-*stuccatore*: Bartholomew Cramillion in Dublin and Brussels 1755–72', *Apollo*, 156:487 (Sept. 2002), 41–9.

McEvansoneya, P., 'Royal monuments and civic ritual in eighteenth-century Dublin' in C. Chastel-Rousseau (ed.), *Reading the royal monument in eighteenth-century Europe* (Farnham: Ashgate, 2011), pp. 173–94.

McKenna, M., 'Castletown: the British context', BA thesis, Trinity College Dublin, 2014.

McParland, E., 'Francis Johnston, architect, 1760–1829', *Irish Georgian Society Bulletin*, 12:3–4 (1969), 61–139.

'James Gandon and the Royal Exchange competition 1768–69', *Journal of the Royal Society of Antiquaries of Ireland*, 102 (1972), 58–72.

'The Wide Streets Commissioners: their importance for Dublin architecture in the late 18th–early 19th century', *Irish Georgian Society Bulletin*, 15:1 (1972), 1–32.

'An academic palazzo in Ireland – the Provost's House, Trinity College, Dublin' parts 1 and 2, *Country Life*, 160:4137 (14 Oct. 1976), 1034–7; 160:4138 (21 Oct. 1976), 1106–9.

'Rathfarnham Castle, Co. Dublin', *Country Life*, 172:4438 (9 Sept. 1982), 734–7.

James Gandon: Vitruvius Hibernicus (London: Zwemmer, 1985).

'Strategy in the planning of Dublin, 1750–1800' in P. Butel and L.M. Cullen (eds.), *Cities and merchants: French and Irish perspectives on urban development, 1500–1900* (Dublin: Trinity College, Department of Modern History, 1986), pp. 97–107.

'Edward Lovett Pearce and the parliament house in Dublin', *Burlington Magazine*, 131:1031 (1989), 91–100.

'Eclecticism: the provincial's advantage', *Irish Arts Review Yearbook 1991–1992*, 210–13.

'Sir Thomas Hewett and the new Junta for Architecture' in Giles Worsley (ed.), *The role of the amateur architect* (London: Georgian Group, 1994), pp. 21–6.

Public architecture in Ireland, 1680–1760 (New Haven: Yale University Press, 2001).

Mulligan, K.V., *The buildings of Ireland*, vol. iv: *South Ulster* (New Haven: Yale University Press, 2013).

Murphy, P. (ed.), *Art and architecture of Ireland*, vol. iii: *Sculpture 1600–2000* (New Haven: Yale University Press, 2014).

O'Connor, C., *The pleasing hours: James Caulfeild, first Earl of Charlemont 1728–1799: traveller, connoisseur and patron of the arts* (Cork: Collins Press, 1999).

O'Connor Drury, M., 'Conversations with Wittgenstein' in R. Rhees (ed.), *Recollections of Wittgenstein* (Oxford: Oxford University Press, 1984), pp. 76–171.

O'Kane, F., *Ireland and the picturesque: design, landscape painting and tourism 1700–1840* (New Haven: Yale University Press, 2013).

Palumbo-Fossati, C., *Gli stuccatori ticinesi Lafranchini in Inghilterra e in Irlanda nel secolo xviii* (Lugano: Fondazione Ticino Nostro, 1982).

Pointon, M., *Hanging the head: portraiture and social formation in eighteenth-century England* (New Haven: Paul Mellon Centre for Studies in British Art, 1998).

Potterton, H., *Irish church monuments 1570–1880* (Belfast: Ulster Architectural Heritage Society, 1975).

Pressly, W.L., *The life and art of James Barry* (New Haven: Yale University Press, 1981).

James Barry's murals at the Royal Society of Arts: envisioning a new public art (Cork: Cork University Press, 2014).

Robinson, J.M., *James Wyatt (1746–1813): architect of George III* (New Haven: Yale University Press, 2012).

Rodger, R., 'Recording the fabric of great cities', Survey of London, English Heritage, London, 10 May 2010.

Roscoe, I., E. Hardy and M.G. Sullivan, *A biographical dictionary of sculptors in Britain 1660–1751* (New Haven: Yale University Press, 2009).

Stanford, W.B., and E. Finopoulos (eds.), *The travels of Lord Charlemont in Greece & Turkey, 1749* (London: Trigraph for the A.G. Leventis Foundation, 1984).

Strickland, W.G., *A dictionary of Irish artists*, 2 vols. (reprint, Shannon: Irish University Press, 1968).

Taylor, E., 'Silver for a countess's levee: the Kildare toilet service', *Irish Arts Review*, 14 (1998), 115–25.

Thomas Bell, T., *An essay on the origin and progress of Gothic architecture with reference to the ancient history and present state of the remains of such architecture in Ireland, to which* was awarded the prize proposed by the Royal Irish Academy for the best essay on that subject (Dublin and London: W.F. Wakeman and Baldwin and Cradock, 1829).

Thorpe, R., 'Thomas Cooley before the Dublin Royal Exchange', *Irish Architectural and Decorative Studies*, 8 (2005), 71–85.

Turpin, J., *John Hogan: Irish neoclassical sculptor in Rome 1800–1858* (Blackrock: Irish Academic Press, 1982).

Usher, R., *Protestant Dublin, 1660–1760: architecture and iconography* (Basingstoke: Palgrave Macmillan, 2012).

Waldré U., and C. Lynch, 'Vincenzo Waldré (Faenza 1740–Dublino 1814): un artista versatile in Inghilterra ed Irlanda', *Torricellianan, Bolletino della Società de Scienze e Lettere, Faenza*, 60 (October 2010), 79–216.

Walsh, P., *The making of the Irish Protestant Ascendancy: the life of William Conolly, 1662–1729* (Woodbridge: The Boydell Press, 2010).

Weber, S. (ed.), *William Kent: designing Georgian Britain* (New Haven: Yale University Press, 2013).

Whaley, J., *Germany and the Holy Roman Empire*, vol. II: *From the Peace of Westphalia to the Dissolution of the Reich 1648–1806* (Oxford: Oxford University Press, 2012).

Worsley, G., 'Castletown, County Kildare', *Country Life*, 188:11 (17 March 1994), 52–7.

17 Civil Society, *c.*1700–*c.*1850

Martyn J. Powell

American Turf Register and Sporting Magazine, 1839.

Anglo-Celt, 1868.

Belfast News-Letter, 1790, 1807, 1811, 1824.

Berman, S., 'Civil society and the collapse of the Weimar Republic', *World Politics*, 49:3 (1997), 401–29.

Bermeo, N., 'Civil society after democracy: some conclusions' in N. Bermeo and P. Nord (eds.), *Civil society before democracy: lessons from nineteenth-century Europe* (Lanham, MD: Rowman and Littlefield, 2000), pp. 237–60.

   Ordinary people in extraordinary times (Princeton: Princeton University Press, 2003).

Bermeo, N., and P. Nord, *Civil society before democracy: lessons from nineteenth-century Europe* (Lanham, MD: Rowman and Littlefield, 2000).

Clark, P., *British clubs and societies, 1580–1800: the origins of an associational world* (Oxford: Oxford University Press, 2000).

Comerford, R.V., *The Fenians in Context: Irish Politics and Society 1848–82* (Dublin: Wolfhound Press, 1985).

Cormier, J., and P. Couton, 'Civil society, mobilization and communal violence: Quebec and Ireland, 1890–1920', *Sociological Quarterly*, 45:3 (2004), 487–508.

D'Arcy, F., 'Labour, nationality and religion in nineteenth-century Ireland: the case of Thaddeus O'Malley', *Old Limerick Journal*, 31 (1994), 11–14.

de Tocqueville, A., *Democracy in America*, trans. G. Lawrence (New York: Anchor, 1969).

Dublin Penny Journal, 1833.

Dudley, R., *The Irish lottery, 1780–1801* (Dublin: Four Courts Press, 2005).

Freeman's Journal, 1820–1, 1830, 1832–3, 1839, 1840–1, 1844–9, 1851–2.

Giugni, M., D. McAdam and C. Tilly, *How social movements matter* (Minneapolis: University of Minnesota Press, 1999).

Habermas, J., *The structural transformation of the public sphere*, trans. Thomas Burger (Cambridge, MA: MIT Press, 1989).

Hibernian Journal, 1776.

Irish Examiner, 1848.

Kelly, J., 'Elite political clubs, 1770–1800' in J. Kelly and M.J. Powell (eds.), *Clubs and societies in eighteenth-century Ireland* (Dublin: Four Courts Press, 2010), pp. 264–89.

Kelly, J., 'The Bar Club, 1787–93: a dining club case study' in J. Kelly and M.J. Powell (eds.), *Clubs and societies in eighteenth-century Ireland* (Dublin: Four Courts Press, 2010), pp. 373–91.

Kelly, J., and M.J. Powell (eds.), *Clubs and societies in eighteenth-century Ireland* (Dublin: Four Courts Press, 2010).

Kingon, S.T., 'Ulster opposition to Catholic emancipation, 1828–9', *Irish Historical Studies*, 34 (2004–5), 137–55.

Lennon, C. (ed.), *Confraternities and sodalities in Ireland: charity, church and sociability* (Blackrock: Columba Press, 2012).

Limerick Chronicle, 1779.

Londonderry Journal, 1776.

Malcolm, E., *Ireland sober, Ireland free: drink and temperance in nineteenth-century Ireland* (Syracuse, NY: Syracuse University Press, 1986).

Mirala, P., 'Masonic sociability and its limitations: the case of Ireland' in J. Kelly and M.J. Powell (eds.), *Clubs and societies in eighteenth-century Ireland* (Dublin: Four Courts Press, 2010), pp. 315–31.

Nation, 1845–8, 1873.

Neswald, E., 'Science, sociability and the improvement of Ireland: the Galway Mechanics' Institute, 1826–51', *British Journal for the History of Science*, 29:4 (2006), 503–34.

O'Dowd, M., 'O'Connell and the lady patriots: women and O'Connellite politics, 1824–1845' in A. Blackstock and E. Magennis (eds.), *Politics and political culture in Britain and Ireland, 1750–1850* (Belfast: Ulster Historical Foundation, 2007), pp. 283–303.

Owens, G.M., 'Popular mobilisation and the rising of 1848: the clubs of the Irish Confederation' in L.M. Geary (ed.), *Rebellion and remembrance in modern Ireland* (Dublin: Four Courts Press, 2001), pp. 51–63.

Porter, R., *Enlightenment: Britain and the creation of the modern world* (London: Allen Lane, 2000).

Powell, M.J., 'Political toasting in eighteenth-century Ireland', *History*, 91:304 (2006), 508–29.

'The Aldermen of Skinner's Alley: ultra-Protestantism before the Orange Order' in J. Kelly and M.J. Powell (eds.), *Clubs and societies in eighteenth-century Ireland* (Dublin: Four Courts Press, 2010), pp. 203–23.

'Ireland's urban houghers: moral economy and popular protest in the late eighteenth century' in M. Brown and S. Donlan (eds.), *The laws and other legalities of Ireland, 1689–1850* (Farnham: Ashgate, 2011), pp. 231–54.

Puttnam, R., *Bowling alone: the collapse and revival of American community* (New York: Simon and Schuster, 2001).

Ryan, David, *Blasphemers and blackguards: the Irish Hellfire Clubs* (Dublin: Irish Academic Press, 2012).

Senior, H., ''The place of Fenianism in the Irish Republican tradition', *Irish University Review*, 4:3 (1967), 250–9.

Smyth, J., *The men of no property: Irish radicals and popular politics in the late eighteenth century* (Basingstoke: Macmillan, 1992).

Sporting Magazine, September 1844.

18 Sport and Recreation in the Eighteenth and Nineteenth Centuries

James Kelly

Manuscript

'Charles Abbot's tour of Ireland, 1792', ed. C.J. Woods (unpublished edition of Abbot papers, 30/9 ff. 1–19: The National Archives)

Pembroke Estate papers, 97/46/1/2/5/73: National Archives of Ireland

Sneyd papers, T/3229: Public Record Office of Northern Ireland

Printed

Barnard, T., 'Reading in eighteenth-century Ireland: public and private pleasures' in B. Cunningham and M. Kennedy (eds.), *The Experience of Reading: Irish Historical Perspectives* (Dublin: Economic and Social History Society, 1999), pp. 60–77.

  Making the grand figure: lives and possessions in Ireland, 1641–1770 (New Haven: Yale University Press, 2004).

Belfast News Letter, 1756, 1847.

Bergin, J., and E. Kinsella, 'Hurling in London (1733–1818) and New York (1781–2)', *Archivium Hibernicum*, 68 (2015), 139–67.

Borgonovo, J., 'Politics as leisure: brass bands in Cork, 1845–1918' in L. Lane and W. Murphy (eds.), *Leisure and the Irish in the nineteenth century* (Liverpool: Liverpool University Press, 2016), pp. 23–40.

Bourke, E. (ed.), *Poor Green Erin: German travel writers' narratives on Ireland from before the 1798 Rising to after the Great Famine*, 2nd edn (Frankfurt: Lang, 2013).

Cole, R.C., *Irish booksellers and English writers, 1740–1800* (London: Mansell, 1986).

Connolly, S.J., *Priests and people in pre-Famine Ireland, 1780–1845* (Dublin: Gill & Macmillan, 1982).

  'Ag deanamh *commanding*: elite responses to popular culture, 1660–1850' in J.S. Donnelly and K.A. Miller (eds.), *Irish popular culture, 1650–1850* (Dublin: Irish Academic Press, 1998), pp. 1–29.

Cork Examiner, 1869.

Cork General Advertiser, 1777.

Curtis, L.P., 'Stopping the hunt, 1881–1882: an aspect of the Irish Land War' in C.H.E. Philpin (ed.), *Nationalism and popular protest in Ireland* (Cambridge: Cambridge University Press, 1987), pp. 349–402.

Deeney, T., *History of Ballyarnett Racecourse and the Derry/Londonderry Races* (Ballyarnett: Ballyarnett Press, 2012).

Donnelly, J.S., and K.A. Miller (eds.), *Irish popular culture, 1650–1850* (Dublin: Irish Academic Press, 1998).

Dublin Evening Journal, 1778.

Dublin Intelligence, 1731.

Dublin Morning Post, 1790–91.

Exshaw's Gentleman's and London Magazine, January 1773.

Freeman's Journal, 1773, 1791, 1795, 1837–80.

Greene, J.C., *Theatre in Dublin, 1745–1820: a calendar of performances*, 6 vols. (Bethlehem, PA: Lehigh University Press, 2011).

Theatre in Dublin, 1745–1820: a history, 2 vols. (Bethlehem, PA: Lehigh University Press, 2011).

Greene, J.C., and G.L.H. Clark, *The Dublin stage, 1720–1745: a calendar of plays, entertainments and afterpieces* (Bethlehem, PA: Lehigh University Press, 1993).

Griffin, B., *Cycling in Victorian Ireland* (Dublin: Irish Academic Press, 2006).

Harris, B., 'The Patriot clubs of the 1750s' in J. Kelly and M.J. Powell (eds.), *Clubs and societies in eighteenth-century Ireland* (Dublin: Four Courts Press, 2010), pp. 224–43.

Hayton, D.W., and A.R. Holmes (eds.), *Ourselves alone: religion, society and politics in the eighteenth and nineteenth centuries* (Dublin: Four Courts Press, 2016),

Hibernian Chronicle (Cork), 1771–86.

Hibernian Journal, 1794.

Hibernian Magazine, 1771.

Hibernian Morning Post, 1775.

Hoppen, K.T., *The mid-Victorian generation, 1846–86* (Oxford: Oxford University Press, 1998).

Hoyle, E., *The polite gamester: containing short treatises on the games of whist, quadrille, backgammon, piquet and chess . . .* (Dublin: Ewing, 1745).

Irish Historic Towns Atlas, 3 vols. (Dublin: Royal Irish Academy, 1996–2012).

Jennings, M.L., and G.M. Ashford (eds.), *The letters of Katherine Conolly, 1707–47* (Dublin: Irish Manuscripts Commission, forthcoming).

Kelly, J., 'Elite political clubs, 1770–1800' in J. Kelly and M.J. Powell (eds.), *Clubs and societies in eighteenth-century Ireland* (Dublin: Four Courts Press, 2010), pp. 264–89.

'The Bar Club, 1787–93: a dining club case study' in J. Kelly and M.J. Powell (eds.), *Clubs and societies in eighteenth-century Ireland* (Dublin: Four Courts Press, 2010), pp. 373–92.

Sport in Ireland, 1600–1840 (Dublin: Four Courts Press, 2014).

'The consumption and sociable use of alcohol in eighteenth-century Ireland', *Proceedings of the Royal Irish Academy*, 115C (2015), 219–55.

Kelly, J., and M.J. Powell (eds.), *Clubs and societies in eighteenth-century Ireland* (Dublin: Four Courts Press, 2010).

Kennedy, M., 'Women and reading in eighteenth-century Ireland' in B. Cunningham and M. Kennedy (eds.), *The experience of reading: Irish historical perspectives* (Dublin: Economic and Social History Society, 1999), pp. 78–98.

Kerry Examiner, 1843.

Kohl, J.G., *Ireland: Dublin, the Shannon, Limerick, Cork and the Kilkenny Races . . .* (London: Chapman and Hall, 1844).

Lane, L., and Murphy, W. (eds.), *Leisure and the Irish in the nineteenth century* (Liverpool: Liverpool University Press, 2016).

Leinster Express, 1870.

Leinster Independent, 1836.

Limerick Chronicle, 1771–2.

Loeber R., and M. Stouthamer-Loeber (eds.), 'Dublin and its vicinity in 1797', *Irish Geography*, 35:2 (2002), 133–55.

Morash, C., *A history of Irish theatre, 1601–2000* (Cambridge: Cambridge University Press, 2002).

Ó Crualaoich, G., 'The merry wake', in J.S. Donnelly and K.A. Miller (eds.), *Irish popular culture, 1650–1850* (Dublin: Irish Academic Press, 1998), pp. 173–200.

Ó Giollain, D., 'The pattern', in J.S. Donnelly and K.A. Miller (eds.), *Irish popular culture, 1650–1850* (Dublin: Irish Academic Press, 1998), pp. 201–21.

Ó Maitiu, S., *The Humours of Donnybrook: Dublin's famous fair and its suppression* (Dublin: Irish Academic Press, 1995).

Ozanam, J., *Recreations for gentlemen and ladies: being ingenious sports and pastimes . . .*, 4th edn (Dublin, 1790).

Plumb, J.H., 'The commercialization of leisure' in N. McKendrick, J. Brewer and J.H. Plumb, *The birth of a consumer society: the commercialization of eighteenth-century England* (London: Hutchinson, 1983), pp. 265–85.

Powell, M.J., 'Political toasting in eighteenth-century Ireland', *History*, 91 (2006), 508–29.

' "Beef, claret and communication": convivial clubs in the public sphere, 1750–1800' in J. Kelly and M.J. Powell (eds.), *Clubs and societies in eighteenth-century Ireland* (Dublin: Four Courts Press, 2010), pp. 353–72.

'Hunting clubs and societies' in Kelly and Powell (eds.), *Clubs and societies in eighteenth-century Ireland* (Dublin: Four Courts Press, 2010), pp. 392–408.

'The Society of Free Citizens and other popular political clubs' in J. Kelly and M.J. Powell (eds.), *Clubs and societies in eighteenth-century Ireland* (Dublin: Four Courts Press, 2010), pp. 244–63.

Pue's Occurrences, 1732, 1734.

Ramsey's Waterford Chronicle, 1787.

Rouse, P., *Sport and Ireland: a history* (Oxford: Oxford University Press, 2015).

Rule, J., *The labouring classes in early industrial England, 1750–1850* (Harlow: Longman, 1986).

Tuam Herald, 1868.

Walker's Hibernian Magazine, 1778, 1780.

Watters, E.R., *Infinite variety: Dan Lowrey's Music Hall, 1879–1897* (Dublin: Gill & Macmillan, 1975).

Young, A., *Tour in Ireland*, 2 vols. (London: G. Bell and Sons, 1892).

19 Bourgeois Ireland, or, on the Benefits of Keeping One's Hands Clean

Ciaran O'Neill

Manuscript

Larcom papers, MS 7511: National Library of Ireland

Printed

Ackroyd, M., et al., *Advancing with the army: medicine, the professions, and social mobility in the British Isles 1790–1850* (Oxford: Oxford University Press , 2006).

Adelman, J., 'Communities of science: the Queen's Colleges and scientific culture in provincial Ireland, 1845–1875', PhD thesis, NUI Galway, 2006.

'Animal knowledge: zoology and classification in nineteenth-century Dublin', *Field Day Review*, 5 (2009), 109–21.

Akenson, D.H., *Ireland, Sweden and the great European migration, 1814–1914* (Montreal: McGill-Queen's University Press, 2011).

Andrews, J.H., *A paper landscape: the Ordnance Survey in nineteenth-century Ireland* (Oxford: Oxford University Press, 1964).

Bailey, C., *Irish London: middle-class migration in the global eighteenth century* (Liverpool: Liverpool University Press, 2013).

Baker, S., *Picturing the beast: animals, identity, and representation* (Chicago: University of Illinois Press, 1993).

Barnard, T., *A new anatomy of Ireland: the Irish Protestants 1649–1770* (New Haven: Yale University Press, 2003).

Bayly, C., *The birth of the modern world 1780–1914: global connections and comparisons* (Oxford: Blackwell, 2004).

Bielenberg, A., 'Late Victorian elite formation and philanthropy: the making of Edward Guinness', *Studia Hibernica*, 32 (2002), 133–54.

Bonsall, P., *The Irish RMs: the resident magistrates in the British administration of Ireland* (Dublin: Four Courts Press, 1997).

Bright, K., *The Royal Dublin Society 1815–45* (Dublin: Four Courts Press, 2004).

Byrne, M., *Tullamore: a portrait* (Tullamore: Esker Press, 2010).

Campbell, F., *The Irish Establishment 1879–1914* (Oxford: Oxford University Press, 2009).

Charle, C., *Les élites de la République 1880–1900* (Paris: Fayard, 1987).

Connolly, S.J. (ed.), *Belfast 400: people, place and history* (Liverpool: Liverpool University Press, 2012).

Corfield, P., *The impact of English towns 1700–1800* (Oxford: Oxford University Press, 1982).

Cowie, H., *Exhibiting animals in nineteenth-century Britain: empathy, education and entertainment* (Basingstoke: Palgrave, 2014).

Crawford, W.H., 'The Belfast middle classes in the late eighteenth century' in D. Dickson et al. (eds.), *The United Irishmen: republicanism, radicalism and rebellion* (Dublin: Lilliput Press, 1993), pp. 62–73.

Crossman, V., *Local government in nineteenth-century Ireland* (Belfast: Institute of Irish Studies, 1994).

Cullen, C., 'The Museum of Irish Industry, Robert Kane and education for all in the Dublin of the 1850s and 1860s', *History of Education*, 38:1 (2009), 99–113.

Davidoff, L., and C. Hall, *Family fortunes: men and women of the English middle classes 1780–1850* (London: Routledge, 2002).

Dickson, D., *Old world colony: Cork and south Munster, 1630–1830* (Cork: Cork University Press, 2005).

Dublin: the making of a capital city (London: Profile, 2014).

Dickson, D., J. Pyz and C. Shepard (eds.), *Irish classrooms and British Empire: imperial contexts in the origins of modern education* (Dublin: Four Courts Press, 2012).

Elias, N., *The civilizing process* (New York: Urizen Books, 1978, original 1939).

Fagan, P., *Catholics in a Protestant country: the papist constituency in eighteenth-century Dublin* (Dublin: Four Courts Press, 1998).

Farmar, T., *Privileged lives: a social history of middle-class Ireland 1882–1989* (Dublin: A. and A. Farmar, 2012).

Feingold, W.L., 'The tenants' movement to capture the Irish Poor Law Boards, 1877–1886', *Albion*, 7:3 (1975), 216–31.

Foster, R.F., *Vivid faces: the revolutionary generation in Ireland 1890–1923* (London: Penguin, 2014).

Galavan, S., 'Building Victorian Dublin: Meade & Son and the expansion of the city' in C. O'Neill (ed.), *Irish elites in the nineteenth century* (Dublin: Four Courts Press, 2013), pp. 51–67.

Gamble, N.E., 'The business community and trade of Belfast 1767–1800', PhD thesis, University of Dublin, 1978.

Geoghegan, P.M., *King Dan: the rise of Daniel O'Connell, 1775–1829* (Dublin: Gill & Macmillan, 2008).

Gibson, W., *Rambles in Europe in 1839: with sketches of prominent surgeons, physicians, medical schools, hospitals, literary personages, scenery, etc.* (Philadelphia: Lea and Blanchard, 1841).

Goldsmith, O., *The deserted village* (London: W. Griffin, 1770).

Grace, P., *The middle class of Callan, Co. Kilkenny, 1825–45* (Dublin: Four Courts Press, 2015).

Gray, P., *The making of the Irish Poor Law, 1815–43* (Manchester: Manchester University Press 2009).

Gunn, S., *The public culture of the Victorian middle class: ritual and authority in the English industrial city 1840–1914* (Manchester: Manchester University Press, 2007).

Harrison, C., *The bourgeois citizen in nineteenth-century France: gender, sociability, and the uses of emulation* (Oxford: Clarendon Press, 1999).

Hart, J., 'Nineteenth-century social reform: a Tory interpretation of history', *Past and Present*, 31 (1965), 39–61.

Hatfield, M., 'Games for boys: masculinity, boyhood, and play in Ireland, 1890–1939' in R. Barr, S. Brady and J. McGaughey (eds.), *Ireland and masculinities in history: from the sixteenth century to the present* (Basingstoke: Palgrave, 2016).

Hearn, M., *Below stairs: domestic service remembered in Dublin and beyond 1880–1922* (Dublin: Lilliput Press, 1993).

Herson, J., *Divergent paths: family histories of Irish emigrants in Britain 1820–1920* (Manchester: Manchester University Press, 2015).

Hickson, C.R., and J.D. Turner, 'The rise and decline of the Irish stock market, 1865–1913', *European Review of Economic History*, 9 (2005), 3–33.

Jenkins, W.A., *Between raid and rebellion: the Irish in Buffalo and Toronto, 1867–1916* (Montreal: McGill-Queen's University Press, 2013).

Joyce, P., *The state of freedom: a social history of the British state since 1800* (Cambridge: Cambridge University Press, 2013).

Kelly, J., *Sport in Ireland 1600–1840* (Dublin: Four Courts Press, 2014).

Kelly, L., *Irish women in medicine, c.1880s–1920s: origins, education and careers* (Manchester: Manchester University Press, 2012).

Kenny, C., 'The exclusion of Catholics from the legal profession in Ireland, 1537–1829', *Irish Historical Studies*, 25 (1987), 337–57.

Kete, K., *The beast in the boudoir: petkeeping in nineteenth-century Paris* (Berkeley: University of California Press, 1994).

Kirkpatrick, K., and B. Farago (eds.), *Animals in Irish literature and culture* (Basingstoke: Palgrave, 2014).

Kocka, J., *Industrial culture and bourgeois society: business, labor, and bureaucracy in modern Germany* (New York: Bergahn, 1999).

Kocka, J., and A. Mitchell, *Bourgeois society in nineteenth-century Europe* (Oxford: Berg, 1993).

Lamont, M., and M. Fournier, *Cultivating differences: symbolic boundaries and the making of inequality* (Chicago: University of Chicago Press, 1992).

Lane, F. (ed.), *Politics, society and the middle class in modern Ireland* (Basingstoke: Palgrave, 2010).

Larcom, T., 'Memoir of the professional life of the late Captain Drummond' in *Papers on subjects connected with the duties of the Corps of Royal Engineers*, 4 (1840), pp. ix–xxiv.

Light, A., *Mrs Woolf and the servants: the hidden heart of domestic service* (London: Fig Tree, 2007).

MacDonagh, O., *The Inspector General: Sir Jeremiah Fitzpatrick and the politics of social reform, 1783–1802* (London: Croom Helm, 1981).

Magray, M.P., *The transforming power of the nuns: women, religion, and cultural change in Ireland, 1750–1900* (Oxford: Oxford University Press, 1998).

Maza, S.C., *The myth of the French bourgeoisie: an essay on the social imaginary, 1750–1850* (Cambridge, MA: Harvard University Press, 2003).

McDowell, R.B., *The Irish Administration, 1801–1914* (London: Routledge and Kegan Paul, 1964).

Meaney, G., M. O'Dowd and B. Whelan (eds.), *Reading the Irish woman: studies in cultural encounter and exchange, 1714–1960* (Liverpool: Liverpool University Press, 2013).

Moretti, F., *The bourgeois: between history and literature* (London: Verso, 2013).

Morris, R.J., *Class, sect and party: the making of the British middle class, Leeds 1820–50* (Manchester: Manchester University Press, 1990).

Moulton, M., *Ireland and the Irish in inter-war England* (Cambridge: Cambridge University Press, 2014).

Munck, T., *Seventeenth-century Europe: state, conflict and social order in Europe 1598–1700*, 2nd edn (Basingstoke: Palgrave Macmillan, 2005).

Murphy, J.H. (ed.), *Evangelicals and Catholics in nineteenth-century Ireland* (Dublin: Four Courts Press, 2004).

Murphy, W., *Political imprisonment and the Irish, 1912–1921* (Oxford: Oxford University Press, 2014).

Newsome, D., *The Victorian world picture* (London: Fontana, 1998).

Nolan, B., *Oonagh Keogh: a celebration* (Dublin: Irish Stock Exchange, 2014).

O'Brien, J.B., *The Catholic middle classes in pre-Famine Cork*. The O'Donnell Lecture, 1979 (Dublin: National University of Ireland, 1980).

O'Neill, C. (ed.), *Irish elites in the nineteenth century* (Dublin: Four Courts Press, 2013).
  Catholics of consequence: transnational education, social mobility and the Irish Catholic elite (Oxford: Oxford University Press, 2014).

Pašeta, S., *Nationalist women in Ireland, 1900–1918* (Cambridge: Cambridge University Press, 2013).

Purdue, O., *Belfast: the emerging city 1850–1914* (Dublin: Irish Academic Press, 2013).

Rains, S., *Commodity culture and social class in Dublin, 1850–1916* (Dublin: Irish Academic Press, 2010).
  '"Do you ring? Or are you rung for?" Mass media, class, and social aspiration in Edwardian Ireland', *New Hibernia Review*, 14:3 (2014), 17–35.

Read, D., *The English provinces c.1760–1960: a study in influence* (London: Edward Arnold, 1964).

Ricardo López, A., and B. Weinstein (eds.), *The making of the middle class: toward a transnational history* (Durham, NC: Duke University Press, 2012).

Rich, R., *Bourgeois consumption: food, space and identity in London and Paris, 1850–1914* (Manchester: Manchester University Press, 2011).

Rouse, P., *Sport and Ireland: a history* (Oxford: Oxford University Press, 2015).

Shovlin, F., ' "Endless stories about the Distillery": Joyce, death and whiskey', *Joyce Studies Annual* (2007), 134–58.

Siegel, J., *Modernity and bourgeois life: society, politics, and culture in England, France and Germany since 1750* (Cambridge: Cambridge University Press, 2012).

Smith, A., *The wealth of nations*, 2 vols. (London: John Dent & Sons, 1901, original 1776).

Sutherland, G.M., *In search of the new woman: middle-class women and work in Britain 1870–1914* (Cambridge: Cambridge University Press, 2015).

Tiersten, L., *Marianne in the market: envisioning consumer society in fin-de-siècle France* (Los Angeles: University of California Press, 2001).

Walker, S.P., ' "Men of small standing"? Locating accountants in English society during the mid-nineteenth century', *European Accounting Review*, 11:2 (2002), 377–99.

Wright, J., *The natural leaders and their world: politics, culture and society in Belfast, c.1801–1832* (Liverpool: Liverpool University Press, 2012).

Young, G.M., *Portrait of an age*, 2nd edn (London: Phoenix Press, 2002).

20 The Growth of the State in the Nineteenth Century

Virginia Crossman

Manuscript

Anglesey papers, D/619: Public Record Office of Northern Ireland

Balbriggan Petty Sessions Order Book, CSPS, 1/350: National Archives of Ireland

Memoirs of Head Constable Robert Dunlop, T/2815/1: Public Record Office of Northern Ireland

Monteagle papers, MS 548: National Library of Ireland

Official Papers (MA), 145/8: National Archives of Ireland

Peel papers, Add. MS 40313–36: British Library

Printed

Akenson, D.H., 'Pre-university education 1782–1870' in W.E. Vaughan (ed.), *A New History of Ireland*, vol. v: *Ireland under the Union 1801–70* (Oxford: Oxford University Press, 1989), pp. 523–37.

Bartlett, T., 'From Irish state to British Empire: reflections on state-building in Ireland, 1690–1830', *Études Irlandaises*, 20:1 (1995), 23–37.

Campbell, F., *The Irish Establishment 1879–1914* (Oxford: Oxford University Press, 2009).

 'The social composition of the senior officers of the Royal Irish Constabulary, 1881–1911', *Irish Historical Studies*, 36 (2009), 522–41.

Carroll, P., 'Science, power, bodies: the mobilization of nature as state formation', *Journal of Historical Sociology*, 9 (1996), 139–67.

Comerford, R.V., *Inventing the nation: Ireland* (London: Arnold, 2003).

'The British state and the education of Irish Catholics 1850–1921' in J. Tomiak et al. (eds), *Schooling, educational policy and ethnic identity* (London: Institute of Education, 1991), pp. 15–25.

Cousins, M., 'The Irish parliament and relief of the poor: the 1772 legislation establishing houses of industry', *Eighteenth-Century Ireland*, 28 (2013), 95–115.

Crossman, V., *Local government in nineteenth-century Ireland* (Belfast: Institute of Irish Studies, 1994).

Politics, law and order in nineteenth-century Ireland (Dublin: Gill & Macmillan, 1996).

Politics, pauperism and power in late nineteenth-century Ireland (Manchester: Manchester University Press, 2006).

Poverty and the Poor Law in Ireland 1850–1914 (Liverpool: Liverpool University Press, 2013).

de Beaumont, G.A. de la Bonniere, *Ireland, social, political and religious*, ed. W.C. Taylor, 2 vols. (London: R. Bentley, 1839).

Dickson, D., 'In search of the old Irish poor law' in R. Mitchison and P. Roebuck (eds.), *Economy and society in Scotland and Ireland* (Edinburgh: John Donald, 1988), pp. 149–59.

Feingold, W.L., *The revolt of the tenantry: the transformation of local government in Ireland 1872–1886* (Boston, MA: Northeastern University Press, 1984).

Geary, L.M., *Medicine and charity in Ireland 1718–1851* (Dublin: UCD Press, 2004).

Gray, P., *The making of the Irish Poor Law 1815–43* (Manchester: Manchester University Press, 2009).

Hutton, C., 'Publishing the Irish cultural revival 1891–1922' in C. Hutton and P. Walsh (eds.), *The Oxford history of the Irish book, vol. V* (Oxford: Oxford University Press, 2011), pp. 17–42.

Innes, J., 'What would a "Four Nations" approach to study of eighteenth-century British social policy entail?' in S.J. Connolly (ed.), *Kingdoms united? Great Britain and Ireland since 1500: integration and diversity* (Dublin: Four Courts Press, 1998), pp. 181–99.

Kelly, J., 'Defending the established order: Richard Woodward Bishop of Cloyne (1726–94)' in J. Kelly, John McCafferty and I. McGrath (eds.), *Parliament, politics and power: essays on Irish history 1660–1850* (Dublin: UCD Press, 2009), pp. 143–74.

Kilcommins, S., I. O'Donnell, E. O'Sullivan and B. Vaughan, *Crime, punishment and the search for order in Ireland* (Dublin: IPA, 2004).

Lewis, G.C., *On local disturbances in Ireland, and on the Irish church question* (London: B. Fellowes, 1836).

Lowe, W.J., and E. Malcolm, 'The domestication of the Royal Irish Constabulary', *Irish Economic and Social History*, 19 (1992), 27–48.

MacDonagh, O., *The Inspector General: Sir Jeremiah Fitzpatrick and social reform, 1783–1802* (London: Croom Helm, 1981).

'Ideas and institutions, 1830–45' in W.E. Vaughan (ed.), *A new history of Ireland, vol. v: Ireland under the Union 1801–70* (Oxford: Oxford University Press, 1989), pp. 193–217.

Malcolm, E., *The Irish policeman 1822–1922: a life* (Dublin: Four Courts Press, 2006).

Malcolm, E., and G. Jones, 'Introduction: an anatomy of Irish medical history' in E. Malcolm and G. Jones (eds.), *Medicine, disease and the state in Ireland, 1650–1940* (Cork: Cork University Press, 1999), pp. 1–17.

McDowell, R.B., *The Irish Administration 1801–1914* (London: Routledge and Kegan Paul, 1964).

'Administration and the public services, 1800–70' in W.E. Vaughan (ed.), *A new history of Ireland,* vol. v: *Ireland under the Union 1801–70* (Oxford: Oxford University Press, 1989), pp. 538–61.

Murphy, I., 'Primary education' in P.J. Corish (ed.), *History of Irish Catholicism: the Church since Emancipation* (Dublin: Gill & Macmillan, 1971), pp. 1–52.

Ó Ciosáin, N., *Ireland in official print culture 1800–1850* (Oxford: Oxford University Press, 2014).

Palmer, S.H., 'The Irish police experiment: the beginnings of modern police in the British Isles 1785–95', *Social Science Quarterly*, 56:3 (1975), 410–24.

Police and protest in England and Ireland, 1780–1850 (Cambridge: Cambridge University Press, 1988).

Poor Inquiry (Ireland): Second Report of the Commissioners for Inquiring into the Condition of the Poorer Classes in Ireland, Parliamentary Papers, 1837 (68), Appendix 5.

Report of the Select Committee on Irish Miscellaneous Estimates, Parliamentary Papers 1829 (342).

Ridden, J., 'Irish reform between the 1798 Rebellion and the Great Famine' in R.A. Burns and J. Innes (eds.), *Rethinking the age of reform* (Cambridge: Cambridge University Press, 2003), pp. 271–94.

Second Annual Report of the Commissioners for Administering the Laws for Relief of the Poor in Ireland, under the Medical Charities Act, Parliamentary Papers, 1854 [1759].

Sixth Annual Report of the Poor Law Commissioners, Parliamentary Papers, 1840 (245).

Sneddon, A., 'State intervention and provincial health care: the county infirmary system in late eighteenth-century Ulster', *Irish Historical Studies*, 38 (2012), 5–21.

Standing Rules and Regulations for the government and guidance of the Constabulary Force in Ireland; as approved by his excellency the Earl of Mulgrave, Lord Lieutenant General and General Governor of Ireland (Dublin: G. and J. Grierson, 1837).

Vaughan, W.E. (ed.), *A new history of Ireland,* vol. v: *Ireland under the Union 1801–70* (Oxford: Oxford University Press, 1989).

Wilde, W.R., *Irish popular superstitions* (Dublin: J. McGlashen, 1852).

21 The Irish in Europe in the Eighteenth Century, 1691–1815

Liam Chambers

Manuscript

Archives du Collège des Irlandais, Paris, MS B2.g.1; MS C1.d13; MS C3.a3
Archives du Ministère des Affaires Étrangères, Affaires Diverses Politiques, 10
Archives of San Clemente, Rome, Codex II, volume 2

Printed

Barnard, T.C., *Making the grand figure: lives and possessions in Ireland, 1641–1770* (New Haven: Yale University Press, 2004).

Bartlett, T., ' "Ormuzd abroad … Ahriman at home": some early historians of the "Wild Geese" in French service, 1840–1950' in J. Conroy (ed.), *Franco-Irish connections: essays, memoirs and poems* (Dublin: Four Courts Press, 2009), pp. 15–30.

Beaurepaire, P.-Y., *L'autre et le frère: l'étranger et la Franc-maçonnerie en France au XVIIIe siècle* (Paris: H. Champion, 1998).

Begadon, C., 'Laity and clergy in the Catholic renewal of Dublin, c.1750–1830', PhD thesis, National University of Ireland, Maynooth, 2009.

Bergin, J., 'Irish Catholics and their networks in eighteenth-century London', *Eighteenth-Century Life*, 39:1 (2015), 66–102.

Binasco, M., and V. Orschel, 'Prosopography of Irish students admitted to the Irish College, Rome, 1628–1798', *Archivium Hibernicum*, 66 (2013), 16–62.

Bracken, D., 'Piracy and poverty: aspects of the Irish Jacobite experience in France, 1691–1720' in T. O'Connor (ed.), *The Irish in Europe, 1580–1815* (Dublin: Four Courts Press, 2001), pp. 127–42.

Brockliss, L.W.B., 'Étudiants de médicine des Îles Britanniques inscrits en France sous l'ancien régime' in P. Ferté and C. Barrera (eds.), *Étudiants de l'exil: migrations internationals et universités refuges (XVIe–XXe s.)* (Toulouse: Presses Universitaires du Mirail, 2009), pp. 81–104.

'Medicine, religion and social mobility in eighteenth- and early nineteenth-century Ireland' in J. Kelly and F. Clark (eds.), *Ireland and medicine in the seventeenth and eighteenth centuries* (Farnham: Ashgate, 2010), pp. 73–108.

'The Irish colleges on the continent and the creation of an educated clergy' in T. O'Connor and M.A. Lyons (eds.), *The Ulster Earls and Baroque Europe: refashioning Irish identities, 1600–1800* (Dublin: Four Courts Press, 2010), pp. 142–65.

Brockliss, L.W.B., and P. Ferté, 'Irish clerics in France in the seventeenth and eighteenth centuries: a statistical study', *Proceedings of the Royal Irish Academy*, 87c (1987), 527–72.

'A prosopography of Irish clerics in the universities of Paris and Toulouse', *Archivium Hibernicum,* 58 (2004), 7–166.

Byrne, A., 'Irish soldiers in Russia, 1690–1812: a re-assessment', *Irish Sword*, 28 (2011), 43–58.

Canny, N., 'Ireland and Continental Europe, c.1600–c.1750' in A. Jackson (ed.), *The Oxford handbook of modern Irish history* (Oxford: Oxford University Press, 2014), pp. 333–53.

Chambers, L., 'Rivalry and reform in the Irish College Paris, 1676–1775' in T. O'Connor and M.A. Lyons (eds.), *Irish communities in early modern Europe* (Dublin: Four Courts Press, 2006), pp. 103–29.

'Irish fondations and boursiers in early modern Paris, 1682–1793', *Irish Economic and Social History*, 35 (2008), 1–22.

'Revolutionary and refractory? The Irish Colleges in Paris and the French Revolution', *Journal of Irish and Scottish Studies*, 2:1 (2008), 29–51.

'Irish Catholics and Aristotelian scholastic philosophy in early modern France, c.1600–c.1750' in J. McEvoy and M. Dunne (eds.), *The Irish contribution to European scholastic thought* (Dublin: Four Courts Press, 2009), pp. 212–30.

'Les confessions au carrefour: Catholiques et Protestants irlandais à Spa au XVIIIe siècle' in D. Droixhe (ed.), *Spa, carrefour de l'Europe des Lumières: les hôtes de la cité thermale au XVIIIe siècle* (Paris: Hermann, 2013), pp. 35–65.

'Patrick Boyle, the Irish Colleges and the historiography of Irish Catholicism', *Studies in Church History*, 49 (2013), 317–29.

Chambers, L., and T. O'Connor (eds.), *College communities abroad: education, migration and Catholicism in early modern Europe* (Manchester: Manchester University Press, 2017).

Clarke de Dromantin, Patrick, *Les réfugiés Jacobites dans la France du XVIIIe siècle* (Bordeaux: Presses Universitaires de Bordeaux, 2005).

Coolahan, M.L., 'Archipelagic identities in Europe: Irish nuns in English convents' in C. Bowden and J.E. Kelly (eds.), *The English convents in exile, 1600–1800: communities, culture and identity* (Farnham: Ashgate, 2013), pp. 211–28.

Corp, E., *A court in exile: the Stuarts in France, 1689–1718* (Cambridge: Cambridge University Press, 2004).

Coudray, P.-L., '"Irlandois de nation": Irish soldiers in Angers as an illustration of Franco-Irish relationships in the seventeenth and eighteenth centuries' in N. Genet-Rouffiac and D. Murphy (eds.), *Franco-Irish military connections, 1590–1945* (Dublin: Four Courts Press, 2009), pp. 94–108.

Crespo Solana, A. (ed.), *Communidades transnacionales: colonias de mercaderes extranjeros en el mundo Atlántico, 1500–1830* (Madrid: Doce Calles, 2010).

'The Irish merchant communities of Bordeaux, La Rochelle and Cognac in the eighteenth century' in P. Butel and L.M. Cullen (eds.), *Négoce et industrie en France et en Irlande aux XVIII et XIX siècles* (Paris: Éditions du Centre National de la Recherche Scientifique, 1980), pp. 51–63.

'The Irish diaspora of the seventeenth and eighteenth centuries' in N. Canny (ed.), *Europeans on the move: studies on European migration, 1500–1800* (Oxford: Oxford University Press, 1994), pp. 113–49.

The Irish brandy houses of eighteenth-century France (Dublin: Irish Academic Press, 2000).

'Apotheosis and crisis: the Irish diaspora in the age of Choiseul' in T. O'Connor and M.A. Lyons (eds.), *Irish communities in early modern Europe* (Dublin: Four Courts Press, 2006), pp. 6–31.

'The two George Fitzgeralds of London, 1718–1759' in D. Dickson, J. Parmentier and J. Ohlmeyer (eds.), *Irish and Scottish mercantile networks in Europe and overseas in the seventeenth and eighteenth centuries* (Ghent: Academia Press, 2007), pp. 251–70.

'Choiseul's Irish circle and the Irish community: the end of the *ancien régime*', *Eighteenth-Century Ireland*, 24 (2009), 62–83.

Cullen, L., J. Shovlin and T. Truxes (eds.), *The Bordeaux–Dublin letters, 1757: correspondence of an Irish community abroad* (Oxford: Oxford University Press, 2013).

de Ridder-Symoens, H., 'Mobility' in H. de Ridder-Symoens (ed.), *A history of the university in Europe, vol. II: Universities in early modern Europe, 1500–1800* (Cambridge: Cambridge University Press, 1996), pp. 416–48.

del Carmen Lario, M., 'The Irish traders of eighteenth-century Cadiz' in D. Dickson, J. Parmentier and J. Ohlmeyer (eds.), *Irish and Scottish mercantile networks in Europe and overseas in the seventeenth and eighteenth centuries* (Ghent: Academia Press, 2007), pp. 207–26.

Dickson, D., 'Famine and economic change in eighteenth-century Ireland' in A. Jackson (ed.), *The Oxford handbook of Irish history* (Oxford: Oxford University Press, 2014), pp. 422–38.

Dickson, D., J. Parmentier and J. Ohlmeyer (eds.), *Irish and Scottish mercantile networks in Europe and overseas in the seventeenth and eighteenth centuries* (Ghent: Academia Press, 2007).

Downey, D.M., 'Wild geese and the double headed eagle: Irish integration in Austria, c.1630–c.1918' in P. Leifer and E. Sagarra (eds.), *Austro-Irish links through the centuries* (Vienna: Diplomatic Academy of Vienna, 2002), pp. 41–57.

'Beneath the harp and the Burgundian cross: Irish regiments in the Spanish Bourbon army, 1700–1818' in H. O'Donnell (ed.), *Presencia irlandesa en la milicia española* (Revista Internacional de Historia Militar 92) (Madrid: Ministerio de Defensa, 2014), pp. 83–105.

Fenning, H., *The undoing of the friars of Ireland: a study of the novitiate question in the eighteenth century* (Louvain: Publications Universitaires de Louvain, 1972).

The Irish Dominican Province, 1698–1797 (Dublin: Dominican Publications, 1990), pp. 19–23.

Ferté, P., 'Étudiants et professeurs irlandais dans les universités de Toulouse et de Cahors (XVIIe–XVIIIe siècles): les limites de la mission irlandaise' in T. O'Connor and M.A. Lyons (eds.), *Irish communities in early modern Europe* (Dublin: Four Courts Press, 2006), pp. 69–84.

Figgis, N., 'Irish artists in Rome in the eighteenth century' in W. Laffan (ed.), *The sublime and the beautiful: Irish art, 1700–1830* (London: Pyms Gallery, 2001), pp. 18–27.

Garland, J., 'Irish officers in the Neapolitan service', *Irish Genealogist*, 5 (1979), 728–9.

'Irish officers in the Bavarian service during the War of the Spanish Succession', *Irish Sword*, 14 (1981), 240–55.

Genet-Rouffiac, Nathalie, *Le grand exil: les Jacobites en France, 1688–1715* (Mercuès: Service Historique de la Défense, 2007).

Harris, P.R. (ed.), *Douai College documents, 1639–1794* (St Albans: Catholic Record Society, 1972).

Hernán, E. García and Ó. Recio Morales (eds.), *Extranjeros en el ejército: militares irlandeses en la sociedad Española, 1580–1818* (Madrid: Ministerio de Defensa, 2007).

Le grand dictionnaire historique, ou le mélange curieux de l'histoire sacrée et profane, 10 vols. (Paris: Les Libraires Associés, 1759), vol. VI, pp. 405–33.

Livesey, J., *Civil society and empire: Ireland and Scotland in the eighteenth-century Atlantic world* (New Haven: Yale University Press, 2009).

Lyons, M.A., '"Digne de compassion": female dependants of Irish Jacobite soldiers in France, c.1692–c.1730', *Eighteenth-Century Ireland*, 23 (2008), 55–75.

MacCana, P., *Collège des Irlandais, Paris and Irish studies* (Dublin: Dublin Institute for Advanced Studies, 2001).

MacGeoghegan, J., *Histoire de l'Irlande ancienne et moderne,* 3 vols. (Paris: Antoine Boudet, 1758–62; Amsterdam: n.p., 1763).

McDonnell, H., 'Some documents relating to the involvement of the Irish Brigade in the Rebellion of 1745', *Irish Sword*, 16 (1984–6), 3–21.

McMahon, J., 'The silent century, 1698–1829' in E. Bhreathnach, J. McMahon and J. McCafferty (eds.), *The Irish Franciscans, 1534–1990* (Dublin: Four Courts Press, 2009), pp. 77–101.

Mijers, E., 'Irish students in the Netherlands, 1650–1750', *Archivium Hibernicum*, 59 (2005), 66–78.

Murdoch, S., 'Irish entrepreneurs and Sweden in the first half of the eighteenth century' in T. O'Connor and M.A. Lyons (eds.), *Irish communities in early modern Europe* (Dublin: Four Courts Press, 2006), pp. 348–66.

Murphy, A.E., *Richard Cantillon: entrepreneur and economist,* 2nd edn (Oxford: Oxford University Press, 1989).

Murtagh, H., 'Irish soldiers abroad, 1600–1800' in T. Bartlett and K. Jeffery (ed.), *A military history of Ireland* (Cambridge: Cambridge University Press, 1996), pp. 294–314.

Nilis, J., 'Irish students at Leuven University, 1548–1797', *Archivium Hibernicum*, 60 (2006–7), 1–304.

Nolan, P., *The Irish dames of Ypres* (Dublin: Browne and Nolan, 1908).

Ó Buachalla, B., *Aisling Ghéar: na Stíobhartaigh agus an tAos Léinn, 1603–1788* (Baile Átha Cliath: An Clóchomhar, 1996).

Ó Ciardha, É., *Ireland and the Jacobite cause, 1685–1766* (Dublin: Four Courts Press, 2002).

Ó Ciosáin, É., 'Irish soldiers and regiments in the French service before 1690' in N. Genet-Rouffiac and D. Murphy (eds.), *Franco-Irish military connections, 1590–1945* (Dublin: Four Courts Press, 2009), pp. 15–31.

Ó Conaill, C., 'The Irish regiments in France: an overview of the presence of Irish soldiers in the French service, 1716–1791' in E. Maher and G. Neville (eds.), *France–Ireland: anatomy of a relationship* (Frankfurt: Peter Lang, 2004), pp. 327–42.

' "Ruddy cheeks and strapping thighs": an analysis of the ordinary soldiers in the ranks of the Irish regiments of eighteenth-century France', *Irish Sword*, 34:98 (2005), 411–25.

Ó hAnnracháin, E., 'Irish veterans at the Hôtel Royal des Invalides (1692–1769)', *Irish Sword*, 31:83 (1999), 5–39.

'The Duke of Parma's company of Irish Guards, 1702–1733', *Irish Sword*, 29 (2014), 362–85.

O'Callaghan, J.C., *History of the Irish Brigades in the service of France* (Glasgow: Cameron and Ferguson, 1870).

O'Connor, P., 'Irish clerics and Jacobites in early eighteenth-century Paris, 1700–30' in T. O'Connor (ed.), *The Irish in Europe, 1580–1815* (Dublin: Four Courts Press, 2001), pp. 175–90.

O'Connor, T., *An Irish Theologian in Enlightenment France: Luke Joseph Hooke, 1714–96* (Dublin: Four Courts Press, 1995).

(ed.), *The Irish in Europe, 1580–1815* (Dublin: Four Courts Press, 2001).

O'Connor, T., and M.A. Lyons (eds.), *Irish communities in early modern Europe* (Dublin: Four Courts Press, 2006).

Strangers to citizens: the Irish in Europe, 1600–1800 (Dublin: Wordwell Books, 2008).

O'Neill Teixeira, P., 'The Lisbon Irish in the 18th century' in I. Pérez Tostado and E. García Hernan (eds.), *Irlanda y el Atlántico Ibérico: molividad, participación e intercambio cultural (1580–1823)* (Valencia: Albatros Ediciones, 2010), pp. 253–66.

Parmentier, J., 'The Irish connection: the Irish merchant community in Ostend and Bruges during the late seventeenth and eighteenth centuries', *Eighteenth-Century Ireland*, 20 (2005), 31–54.

'The Ray dynasty: Irish mercantile empire builders in Ostend, 1690–1790' in T. O'Connor and M.A. Lyons (eds.), *Irish communities in early modern Europe* (Dublin: Four Courts Press, 2006), pp. 367–82.

Pfister, C., 'Dunkerque et l'Irlande, 1690–1790' in D. Dickson, J. Parmentier and J. Ohlmeyer (eds.), *Irish and Scottish mercantile networks in Europe and overseas in the seventeenth and eighteenth centuries* (Ghent: Academia Press, 2007), pp. 93–114.

Power, O., 'The 18th century sugar and slave trade at St Croix, Danish West Indies' in P. Tostado and E. García Hernan (eds.), *Irlanda y el Atlántico Ibérico: molividad, participación e intercambio cultural (1580–1823)* (Valencia: Albatros Ediciones, 2010), pp. 51–7.

Rapport, M., *Nationality and citizenship in Revolutionary France: the treatment of foreigners, 1789–1799* (Oxford: Oxford University Press, 2000).

Recio Morales, O., 'Los estudios Irlandeses y el Atlántico Ibérico (siglos XVI–XVIII): una selección bibliográfica' in P. Tostado and E. García Hernan (eds.), *Irlanda y el Atlántico Ibérico: molividad, participación e intercambio cultural (1580–1823)* (Valencia: Albatros Ediciones, 2010), pp. 323–35.

Ireland and the Spanish Empire, 1600–1825 (Dublin: Four Courts Press, 2010).

Richard-Maupillier, F., 'The Irish in the regiments of Duke Leopold of Lorraine, 1698–1729', *Archivium Hibernicum*, 67 (2014), 285–312.

Rowlands, G., *An army in exile: Louis XIV and the Irish forces of James II in France, 1691–1698* (London: Royal Stuart Society, 2001).

'Foreign service in the age of absolute monarchy: Louis XIV and his *forces étrangères*', *War in History*, 17:2 (2010), 141–65.

Saupin, G., 'Les réseaux commerciaux des Irlandais de Nantes sous le règne de Louis XIV' in D. Dickson, J. Parmentier and J. Ohlmeyer (eds.), *Irish and Scottish mercantile networks in Europe and overseas in the seventeenth and eighteenth centuries* (Ghent: Academia Press, 2007), pp. 115–46.

Scott, S., 'The French Revolution and the Irish regiments in France' in H. Gough and D. Dickson (eds.), *Ireland and the French Revolution* (Dublin: Irish Academic Press, 1990), pp. 14–27.

Simms, J.G., 'The Irish on the continent, 1691–1800' in T.W. Moody and W.E. Vaughan (eds.), A new history of Ireland, vol. IV: *Eighteenth-century Ireland* (Oxford: Oxford University Press, 1986), pp. 629–56.

St John, J., *Letters from France to a gentleman in the south of Ireland*, 2 vols. (Dublin: P. Byrne, 1788).

Swords, L., *The green cockade: the Irish in the French Revolution, 1789–1815* (Dublin: Glendale, 1989).

'Irish material in the files of Jean Fromont, notary at Paris', *Collectanea Hibernica*, 34–5 (1992–3), 77–115; 36–7 (1994–5), 85–139.

Téllez Alarcia, D., 'Política y familia en el grupo irlandés de XVIII: ¿un partido irlandés en la Corte?' in E. García Hernán and Ó. Recio Morales (eds.), *Extranjeros en el ejército: militares Irlandeses en la sociedad Española, 1580–1818* (Madrid: Ministerio de Defensa, 2007), pp. 255–67.

Tostado, I. Pérez and E. García Hernan (eds.), *Irlanda y el Atlántico Ibérico: molividad, participación e intercambio cultural (1580–1823)* (Valencia: Albatros Ediciones, 2010).

Villar Garcia, M. Begona (ed.), *La emigración Irlandesa en el siglo XVIII* (Malaga: Universidad de Málaga, 2000).

Villar Garcia, M. Begona, 'Irish migration and exiles in Spain: refugees, soldiers, traders and statesmen' in T. O'Connor and M.A. Lyons (eds.), *Irish communities in early modern Europe* (Dublin: Four Courts Press, 2006), pp. 172–99.

White, M., 'The role of Irish doctors in eighteenth-century Spanish medicine' in D.M. Downey and J. Crespo MacLennan (eds.), *Spanish–Irish relations through the ages* (Dublin: Four Courts Press, 2008), pp. 149–74.

Wilson, P.H., 'The German "soldier trade" of the seventeenth and eighteenth centuries: a reassessment', *International History Review*, 19 (1996), 757–92.

'The politics of military recruitment in eighteenth-century Germany', *English Historical Review*, 117 (2002), 536–68.

22 'Irish' Migration to America in the Eighteenth Century? Or the Strange Case for the 'Scots/Irish'

Patrick Griffin

Akenson, D., *If the Irish ran the world: Montserrat, 1630–1730* (Montreal: McGill-Queen's University Press, 1997).

Appleby, J., *The relentless revolution: a history of capitalism* (New York: Norton, 2011).

Bailyn, B., *The peopling of British North America: an introduction* (New York: Knopf, 1986).

Voyagers to the West: a passage in the peopling of America on the eve of the Revolution (New York: Knopf, 1986).

Bankhurst, B., *Ulster Presbyterians and the Scots Irish diaspora, 1750–1764* (Basingstoke: Palgrave Macmillan, 2013).

Boston Newsletter, 1759.

Bric, M.J., *Ireland, Philadelphia and the re-invention of America, 1760–1800* (Dublin: Four Courts Press, 2008).

Canny, N. (ed.), *Europeans on the move: studies on European migration* (Oxford: Oxford University Press, 1994).

Canny, N., and P. Morgan (eds.), *The Oxford handbook of the Atlantic world, c.1450–c.1850* (Oxford: Oxford University Press, 2011).

Cotlar, S., *Tom Paine's America: the rise and fall of Transatlantic radicalism in the early Republic* (Charlottesville: University of Virginia Press, 2011).

Cullen, L.M., 'The Irish Diaspora', in N. Canny (ed.), *Europeans on the move: studies on European migration* (Oxford: Oxford University Press, 1994), pp. 113–49.

Devine, T., *Scotland's Empire and the shaping of the Americas* (Washington, DC: Smithsonian Books, 2004).

To the ends of the earth: Scotland's global diaspora 1750–2010 (Washington, DC: Smithsonian Books, 2011).

Dickson, R.J., *Ulster emigration to colonial America* (London: Routledge, 1966).

Doyle, D., *Ireland, Irishmen, and Revolutionary America, 1760–1820* (Cork: Mercier Press, 1981).

Fischer, D.H., *Albion's seed: four British folkways in America* (Oxford: Oxford University Press, 1989).

Fitzpatrick, R., and K. McNally, *God's frontiersmen: the Scots-Irish epic* (Chatswood, New South Wales: Peribo, 1989).

Fogleman, A., 'From slaves, convicts, and servants to free passengers: the transformation of immigration in the era of the American Revolution', *Journal of American History*, 85:1 (1998), pp. 43–76.

Glasgow, M., *The Scotch Irish in Northern Ireland and the American colonies* (New York: G.P. Putnam's Sons, 1936).

Gleason, D. (ed.), *The Irish in the Atlantic world* (Columbia: University of South Carolina Press, 2013).

Griffin, P., *The people with no name: Ireland's Ulster Scots, America's Scots Irish, and the creation of a British Atlantic world, 1689–1764* (Princeton: Princeton University Press, 2001).

'The two migrations myth, the Scotch Irish, and Irish American experience' in A. H. Wyndham (ed.), *Re-Imagining Ireland: how a storied island is transforming its politics, economy, religious life, and culture for the 21st century* (Charlottesville: University of Virginia Press, 2006).

American Leviathan: empire, nation, and revolutionary frontier (New York: Hill and Wang, 2007).

'Irish migration to the colonial south: a plea for a forgotten topic' in B. Giemza (ed.), *Rethinking the Irish in the American South: beyond rounders and reelers* (Jackson: University Press of Mississippi, 2013), pp. 51–74.

Hofstra, W. (ed.), *Ulster to America: the Scots-Irish migration experience, 1680–1830* (Knoxville: University of Tennessee Press, 2012).

Jones, M., 'The Scotch-Irish in British America' in B. Bailyn and P. Morgan (eds.), *Strangers within the realm: cultural margins of the first British Empire* (Chapel Hill: University of North Carolina Press, 1991), pp. 284–313.

Kelly, J., "The resumption of emigration from Ireland after the American War of Independence, 1784–87", *Studia Hibernica, 24* (1984–88), 61–89.

Kenny, K., *The American Irish: a history* (New York: Longman, 2000).

Peaceable kingdom lost: the Paxton Boys and the destruction of William Penn's holy experiment (Oxford: Oxford University Press, 2009).

Kirkham, G., 'Ulster emigration to North America, 1680–1720' in H.T. Blethen and C.W. Wood (eds.), *Ulster and North America: Transatlantic perspectives on the Scotch-Irish* (Tuscaloosa: University of Alabama Press, 1997), pp. 76–117.

Leyburn, J., *The Scotch Irish: a social history* (Chapel Hill: University of North Carolina Press, 1962).

MacMaster, R., *Scotch-Irish merchants in colonial America* (Belfast: Ulster Historical Foundation, 2009).

McCoy, D., *The elusive republic: political economy in Jeffersonian America* (Chapel Hill: University of North Carolina Press, 1996).

McWhiney, G., *Cracker culture: Celtic ways in the Old South* (Tuscaloosa: University of Alabama Press, 1988).

Merrell, J., *Into the American woods: negotiators on the Pennsylvania frontier* (New York: Norton, 2000).

Merritt, J., *At the crossroads: Indians and Empires on a mid-Atlantic frontier, 1700–1763* (Chapel Hill: University of North Carolina Press, 2003).

Miller, K., *Emigrants and exiles: Ireland and the Irish exodus to North America* (Oxford: Oxford University Press, 1985).

'"Scotch Irish," "Black Irish" and "Real Irish": emigrants and identities in the Old South' in A. Bielenberg (ed.), *The Irish diaspora* (New York: Longman, 2000), pp. 139–57.

'"Scotch-Irish myths" and "Irish" identities in eighteenth- and nineteenth-century America' in C. Fanning (ed.), *New perspectives on the Irish diaspora* (Carbondale: Southern Illinois University Press, 2000), pp. 75–92.

'Ulster Presbyterians and the "two traditions" in Ireland and America' in T. Brotherstone, A. Clark and K. Whelan (eds.), *These fissured isles: Ireland, Scotland and the making of modern Britain 1798–1848* (Edinburgh: John Donald, 2005), pp. 260–77.

Ireland and Irish America: culture, class, and Transatlantic migration (Dublin: Field Day Publications, 2008).

Miller, K., A. Schrier, B. Boling and D. Doyle, *Irish immigrants in the Land of Canaan: letters and memoirs from colonial and Revolutionary America, 1675–1815* (Oxford: Oxford University Press, 2003).

Montgomery, M., 'Searching for security: backcountry Carolina, 1760s–1780s' in W. Hofstra (ed.), *Ulster to America: the Scots-Irish migration experience, 1680–1830* (Knoxville: University of Tennessee Press, 2012), pp. 147–64.

O'Toole, F., *White savage: William Johnson and the invention of America* (New York: Farrar, Straus, and Giroux 2005).

Quinn, D.B., *Ireland and America: their early associations 1500–1640* (Liverpool: Liverpool University Press, 1991).

Schmidt, L.E., *Holy fairs: Scottish communions and American revivals in the early modern period* (Princeton: Princeton University Press, 1989).

Smout, T.C., N.C. Landsman and T.M. Devine, 'Scottish emigration in the seventeenth and eighteenth centuries' in N. Canny (ed.), *Europeans on the move: studies on European migration* (Oxford: Oxford University Press, 1994), pp. 76–112.

The Massachusetts Gazette, and Boston News-Letter, 1764.

The Pennsylvania Gazette, 1747–76.

The Virginia Gazette, 1776.

Vann, B., *In search of Ulster-Scots land: the birth and geotheological imagings of a Transatlantic people, 1603–1703* (Columbia: University of South Carolina Press, 2008).

Way, P., *Common labour workers and the digging of North American canals, 1780–1860* (Cambridge: Cambridge University Press, 1993).

Webb, J., *Born fighting: how the Scots-Irish shaped America* (New York: Broadway Books, 2004).

Wilson, D., *United Irishmen, United States: immigrant radicals in the early Republic* (Ithaca, NY: Cornell University Press, 1998).

Wilson, D.A., and G. Morton (eds.), *Irish and Scottish encounters with indigenous peoples: Canada, the United States, New Zealand, and Australia* (Montreal: McGill-Queen's University Press, 2013).

Wokeck, M., *Trade in strangers: the beginnings of mass migration to North America* (University Park: Pennsylvania State University Press, 1999).

23 Ireland and the Empire in the Nineteenth Century

Barry Crosbie

Manuscript

R. Evans papers, MS E 404: Oriental and India Office Collections, British Library.

Printed

Akenson, D.H., *The Irish education experiment: the national system of education in the nineteenth century* (London: Routledge, 2012).

Andrews, J.H., *A paper landscape: the Ordnance Survey in nineteenth-century Ireland* (Oxford: Oxford University Press, 1975).

Bairner, A., 'Ireland, sport and empire' in K. Jeffery (ed.), *An Irish empire? Aspects of Ireland and the British Empire* (Manchester: Manchester University Press, 1996), pp. 57–77.

Ballantyne, T., 'The sinews of empire: Ireland, India and the construction of British colonial knowledge' in T. McDonough (ed.), *Was Ireland a Colony? Economics, politics and culture in nineteenth-century Ireland* (Dublin: Irish Academic Press, 2005), pp. 145–61.

Barr, C., '"Imperium in imperio": Irish episcopal imperialism in the nineteenth century', *English Historical Review*, 123 (2008), 611–50.

Barr, C., and H.M. Carey (eds.), *Religion and greater Ireland: Christianity and Irish global networks, 1750–1950* (Montreal: McGill-Queen's University Press, 2015).

Bartlett, T., and K. Jeffery (eds.), *A military history of Ireland* (Cambridge: Cambridge University Press, 1997).

Bayly, C.A., 'The British and indigenous peoples, 1760–1860: power, perception and identity' in M. Daunton and R. Halpern (eds.), *Empire and others: British encounters with indigenous peoples, 1600–1850* (Philadelphia: University of Pennsylvania Press, 1999), pp. 19–41.

'Ircland, India and the Empire: *c.*1780–1914', *Transactions of the Royal Historical Society,* 6th series, 10 (2000), 377–97.

Bubb, A., 'The life of the Irish soldier in India: representations and self-representations', *Modern Asian Studies,* 46:4 (2012), 769–813.

Carey, H.M., *God's Empire: religion and colonialism in the British World, c.1800–1908* (Cambridge: Cambridge University Press, 2011).

Cleary, J., 'Amongst empires: a short history of Ireland and empire studies in international context', *Eire-Ireland,* 42:1 and 2 (2007), 11–47.

Crosbie, B., *Irish imperial networks: migration, social communication and exchange in nineteenth-century India* (Cambridge: Cambridge University Press, 2012).

Crosbie, B., and M. Hampton (eds.), *The cultural construction of the British world* (Manchester: Manchester University Press, 2015), pp. 1–23.

Devine, T.M., *Scotland's empire: the origins of the global diaspora* (London: Penguin, 2012).

Dickson, D., J. Pyz and C. Shepard (eds.), *Irish classrooms and British Empire: imperial contexts in the origins of modern education* (Dublin: Four Courts Press, 2012).

Doherty, G.M., *The Irish Ordnance Survey: history, culture and memory* (Dublin: Four Courts Press, 2004).

Dooley, T., *The decline of the big house in Ireland* (Dublin: Wolfhound Press, 2001).

Edney, M.H., *Mapping an empire: the geographical construction of British India, 1765–1843* (Chicago: University of Chicago Press, 1999).

Fitzpatrick, D., 'Ireland and empire' in A. Porter (ed.), *The Oxford history of the British Empire, vol. III: The nineteenth century* (Oxford: Oxford University Press, 1999), pp. 494–521.

Heffernan, P., *An Irish doctor's memories* (Dublin: Clonmore & Reynolds, 1958).

Hoey, W., *A monograph on trade and manufactures in northern India* (Lucknow: American Methodist Mission Press, 1880).

Howe, S., *Ireland and empire: colonial legacies in Irish history and culture* (Oxford: Oxford University Press, 2002).

Howell, P., and D. Lambert, 'Sir John Pope Hennessy and colonial government: humanitarianism and the translation of slavery in the imperial network' in D. Lambert and A. Lester (eds.), *Colonial lives across the British Empire: imperial careering in the long nineteenth century* (Cambridge: Cambridge University Press, 2006), pp. 228–57.

Hunt, T., *Sport and society in Victorian Ireland: the case of Westmeath* (Cork: Cork University Press, 2007).

Jackson, A., 'Ireland, the Union and the Empire, 1800–1960' in K. Kenny (ed.), *Ireland and the British Empire,* The Oxford History of the British Empire Companion Series (Oxford: Oxford University Press, 2004), pp. 123–53.

The two Unions: Ireland, Scotland and the survival of the United Kingdom, 1707–2007 (Oxford: Oxford University Press, 2015).

Jeffery, K. (ed.), *An Irish empire? Aspects of Ireland and the British Empire* (Manchester: Manchester University Press, 1996).

Jones, G., ' "Strike out boldly for the prizes that are available to you": medical emigration from Ireland, 1860–1905', *Medical History*, 54 (2010), 55–74.

Kehoe, S. Karly, 'Accessing empire: Irish surgeons and the Royal Navy, 1840–1880', *Social History of Medicine*, 26:2 (2012), 204–24.

Kenny, K., 'The Irish in the Empire' in K. Kenny (ed.), *Ireland and the British Empire*, Oxford History of the British Empire companion series (Oxford: Oxford University Press, 2004), pp. 90–123.

Laidlaw, Z., 'Richard Bourke: Irish liberalism tempered by empire' in D. Lambert and A. Lester (eds.), *Colonial lives across the British Empire: imperial careering in the long nineteenth century* (Cambridge: Cambridge University Press, 2006), pp. 113–44.

Lowe, K., and E. McLaughlin, 'Sir John Pope-Hennessy and the "native race craze": colonial government in Hong Kong, 1877–1882', *Journal of Imperial and Commonwealth History*, 20 (1992), 223–47.

MacDonagh, O., *Ireland* (Englewood Cliffs, NJ: Prentice Hall, 1968).

MacKenzie, J.M., 'Irish, Scottish, Welsh and English worlds? A four-nation approach to the history of the British Empire', *History Compass*, 6:5 (2008), 1244–63.

   The Scots in South Africa: ethnicity, identity, gender and race, 1772–1914 (Manchester: Manchester University Press, 2012).

Magee, G.B., and A.S. Thompson, *Empire and globalisation: networks of people, goods and capital in the British world, c.1850–1914* (Cambridge: Cambridge University Press, 2010).

McCarthy, A., *Scottishness and Irishness in New Zealand since 1840* (Manchester: Manchester University Press, 2005).

McDevitt, P., *May the best man win: sport, masculinity and nationalism in Great Britain and the Empire, 1880–1935* (Basingstoke: Palgrave Macmillan, 2004).

McDonough, T., *Was Ireland a colony? Economics, politics and culture in nineteenth-century Ireland* (Dublin: Irish Academic Press, 2005).

McDowell, R.B., 'Ireland in the eighteenth-century British Empire' in J.G. Barry (ed.), *Historical Studies IX* (Belfast: Blackstaff Press, 1974), pp. 57–63.

Ó Cadhla, S., and É. Ó Cuív, *Civilising Ireland: Ordnance Survey, 1824–1842: ethnography, cartography, translation* (Dublin: Irish Academic Press, 2007).

O'Leary, P., *Servants of Empire: the Irish in Punjab, 1881–1921* (Manchester: Manchester University Press, 2011).

O'Malley, K., *Ireland, India and Empire: Indo-Irish radical connections, 1919–1964* (Manchester: Manchester University Press, 2008).

O'Neill, C., *Catholics of consequence: transnational education, social mobility, and the Irish Catholic elite, 1850–1900* (Oxford: Oxford University Press, 2014).

O'Shea, H., *Ireland and the end of the British Empire: the Republic and its role in the Cyprus emergency* (New York: I.B. Taurus, 2015).

O'Sullivan, K., *Ireland, Africa and the end of empire: small state identity in the Cold War, 1955–1975* (Manchester: Manchester University Press, 2014).

Pope-Hennessy, J., *Verandah: some episodes in the Crown Colonies, 1867–1889* (London: George Allen and Unwin, 1964).

Proudfoot, L., and D. Hall, *Imperial spaces: placing the Irish and Scots in colonial Australia* (Manchester: Manchester University Press, 2011).

Ridden, J., 'Making good citizens: national identity, religion and liberalism among the Irish elite, c.1800–1850', PhD thesis, King's College London, 1998.

Rouse, P., *Sport and Ireland: a history* (Oxford: Oxford University Press, 2015).

Shepard, C., ' "I have a notion to go off to India": Colonel Alexander Porter and Irish recruitment to the Indian Medical Service', *Irish Economic and Social History*, 41 (2014), 36–52.

Silvestri, M., *Ireland and India: nationalism, empire and memory* (Basingstoke: Palgrave Macmillan, 2009).

Sinclair, G., *At the end of the line: colonial policing and the imperial endgame, 1945–1980* (Manchester: Manchester University Press, 2006).

Thompson, A., *Britain's experience of empire in the twentieth century*, Oxford History of the British Empire Companion Series (Oxford: Oxford University Press, 2011).

Whelehan, N., *The dynamiters: Irish nationalism and political violence in the wider world, 1867–1900* (Cambridge: Cambridge University Press, 2012).

Wright, J., ' "The Belfast Chameleon": Ulster, Ceylon and the imperial career of Sir James Emerson Tennent', *Britain and the World*, 6:2 (2013), 192–219.

24 The Great Famine, 1845–1850

Peter Gray

Manuscript

Clarendon deposit, Irish, box 43: Bodleian Library, Oxford

Graham papers, Bundle 95B: British Library

Hickleton papers: Borthwick Institute, York

Russell papers, PRO 30/22/6A: The National Archives

Printed

Beames, M., 'Rural conflict in pre-Famine Ireland: peasant assassinations in Tipperary 1837–47', *Past and Present*, 81 (1978), pp. 75–91.

Bourke, A., *'The visitation of God'? The potato and the Great Irish Famine* (Dublin: Lilliput Press, 1993).

Butt, I., *The rate in aid: a letter to the Rt. Hon. the Earl of Roden* (Dublin: J. McGlashan, 1849).

Connolly, S.J., 'The Great Famine and Irish politics' in C. Póirtéir (ed.), *The Great Irish Famine* (Dublin: Mercier Press, 1995), pp. 34–49.

Coogan, T.P., *The Famine plot: England's role in Ireland's greatest tragedy* (New York: Palgrave Macmillan, 2012).

Crawford, E.M., *Counting the people: a survey of the Irish censuses, 1813–1911* (Dublin: Four Courts Press, 2003).

Crawford, W.S., *Depopulation not necessary*, 2nd edn (London: Gilpin, 1850).

Crowley, J., W.J. Smyth and M. Murphy (eds.), *Atlas of the Great Irish Famine, 1845–52* (Cork: Cork University Press, 2012).

Daily News, 1847.

Daly, M., *The Famine in Ireland* (Dundalk: Dublin Historical Society, 1986).

Dickson, D., 'The 1740–41 famine', in J. Crowley, W.J. Smyth and M. Murphy (eds.), *Atlas of the Great Irish Famine, 1845–52* (Cork: Cork University Press, 2012), pp. 23–7.

Donnelly, J.S., ' "Irish property must pay for Irish poverty": British public opinion and the Great Irish Famine' in C. Morash and R. Hayes (eds.), *Fearful realities: new perspectives on the Famine* (Blackrock: Irish Academic Press, 1996), pp. 60–76.

'The construction of the memory of the Famine in Ireland and the Irish diaspora, 1850–1900', *Eire-Ireland*, 31 (1996), 26–61.

The Great Irish Potato Famine (Stroud: Sutton, 2001).

Freeman's Journal, 1848.

Geary, L., 'Famine, fever and the bloody flux' in C. Póirtéir (ed.), *The Great Irish Famine* (Cork: Mercier Press, 1995), pp. 86–103.

Medicine and charity in Ireland, 1718–1851 (Dublin: UCD Press, 2004).

Gray, P., *Famine, land and politics: British government and Irish society, 1843–50* (Dublin: Irish Academic Press, 1999).

'National humiliation and the great hunger: fast and famine in 1847', *Irish Historical Studies*, 21 (2000), 193–216.

The making of the Irish Poor Law, 1815–43 (Manchester: Manchester University Press, 2009).

'Accounting for catastrophe: William Wilde, the 1851 Irish census and the Great Famine' in M. De Nie and S. Farrell (eds.), *Power and popular culture in modern Ireland* (Dublin: Irish Academic Press, 2010), pp. 50–66.

'A "people's viceroyalty"? Popularity, theatre and executive politics 1835–47' in P. Gray and O. Purdue (eds.), *The Irish Lord Lieutenancy c.1541–1922* (Dublin: UCD Press, 2012), pp. 158–78.

'"The Great British Famine of 1845–50"? Ireland, the UK and peripherality in famine relief and philanthropy' in D. Curran, L. Luciuk and A. Newby (eds.), *Famines in European economic history: the last great European famines reconsidered* (London: Routledge, 2015), pp. 83–96.

Greville, C.C.F., *The Greville Memoirs (second part): a journal of the reign of Queen Victoria from 1837 to 1852*, 3 vols. (London: Longmans, Green and Co., 1885).

Haines, R., *Charles Trevelyan and the Great Irish Famine* (Dublin: Four Courts Press, 2004).

Hansard's Parliamentary Debates, 3rd series.

Hatton, H.E., *The largest amount of good: Quaker relief in Ireland 1654–1921* (Montreal: McGill-Queen's University Press, 1993).

Hilton, B., 'Peel: a reappraisal', *Historical Journal*, 22 (1979), 585–614.

Illustrated London News, 1847.

Jordan, D.E., *Land and popular politics in Ireland: County Mayo from the Plantation to the Land War* (Cambridge: Cambridge University Press, 1994).

Kelly, J., 'Coping with crisis: the response to the famine of 1740–41', *Eighteenth-Century Ireland*, 27 (2012), 99–122.

Kennedy, L., *Unhappy the land: the most oppressed people ever, the Irish?* (Sallins: Merrion Press, 2015).

Kerr, D.A., *'A nation of beggars'? Priests, people and politics in Famine Ireland 1846–1852* (Oxford: Clarendon Press, 1994).

Kinealy, C., *Repeal and revolution: 1848 in Ireland* (Manchester: Manchester University Press, 2009).

Charity and the Great Hunger in Ireland (London: Bloomsbury, 2013).

MacDonagh, O., *The emancipist: Daniel O'Connell, 1830–47* (London: Weidenfeld and Nicolson, 1989).

McDowell, R.B., 'Administration and the public services 1800–70' in W.E. Vaughan (ed.), *A new history of Ireland*, vol. v: Ireland under the Union I (1801–70) (Oxford: Oxford University Press, 1989), pp. 538–61.

Mokyr, J., *Why Ireland starved* (London: Unwin, 1983).

Mokyr, J., and C. Ó Gráda, 'Poor and getting poorer? Living standards in Ireland before the Famine', *Economic History Review*, 2nd series, 61 (1988), 209–35.

Murphy, M.O., *Compassionate stranger: Asenath Nicholson and the Great Irish Famine* (Syracuse, NY: Syracuse University Press, 2015).

Nally, D., *Human encumbrances: political violence and the Great Irish Famine* (South Bend, IN: University of Notre Dame Press, 2011).

'The colonial dimensions of the Great Irish Famine' in J. Crowley, W.J. Smyth and M. Murphy (eds.), *Atlas of the Great Irish Famine, 1845–52* (Cork: Cork University Press, 2012), pp. 64–74.

Neal, F., *Black '47: Britain and the Famine Irish* (Basingstoke: Macmillan, 1998).

Nicholson, A., *Annals of the Famine in Ireland* [1850], ed. M. Murphy (Dublin: Lilliput Press, 1998).

Ó Gráda, C., *Ireland before and after the Famine: explorations in economic history, 1800–1925* (Manchester: Manchester University Press, 1988).

'Poverty, population and agriculture, 1801–45' in W.E. Vaughan (ed.), *A new history of Ireland*, vol. v: *Ireland under the Union 1801–70* (Oxford: Oxford University Press, 1989), pp. 108–36.

Ireland: a new economic history, 1780–1939 (Oxford: Oxford University Press, 1994).

The Great Irish Famine (Cambridge: Cambridge University Press, 1995).

Black '47 and beyond: the Great Irish Famine in history, economy and memory (Princeton: Princeton University Press, 1999).

'The Great Famine and other famines', in *Ireland's Great Famine: interdisciplinary perspectives* (Dublin: UCD Press, 2006), pp. 196–216.

'Mortality and the Great Famine' in J. Crowley, W.J. Smyth and M. Murphy (eds.), *Atlas of the Great Irish Famine, 1845–52* (Cork: Cork University Press, 2012), pp. 170–9.

O'Neill, T.P., 'Famine evictions' in C. King (ed.), *Famine, land and culture in Ireland* (Dublin: UCD Press, 2000), pp. 29–70.

O'Rourke, K., 'Did the Great Famine matter?', *Journal of Economic History*, 51 (1991), 1–22.

[O'Sullivan, S.], 'Land Commission in Ireland', *Dublin University Magazine*, 25 (May 1845).

Quinn, J., *John Mitchel* (Dublin: UCD Press, 2009).

Ridgway, C. (ed.), *The Morpeth Roll: Ireland identified in 1841* (Dublin: Four Courts Press, 2013).

Sarbaugh, T.J., 'A moral spectacle: American relief and the Famine 1845–9', *Eire-Ireland*, 15 (1980), 6–14.

Sim, D., *A Union forever: the Irish question in US foreign relations in the Victorian age* (Ithaca, NY: Cornell University Press, 2013).

Smyth, W.J., 'The longue durée – imperial Britain and colonial Ireland' in J. Crowley, W.J. Smyth and M. Murphy (eds.), *Atlas of the Great Irish Famine, 1845–52* (Cork: Cork University Press, 2012), pp. 46–63.

' "Variations in vulnerability": understanding where and why people died' in J. Crowley, W.J. Smyth and M. Murphy (eds.), *Atlas of the Great Irish Famine, 1845–52* (Cork: Cork University Press, 2012), pp. 180–97.

Solar, P., 'The Great Famine was no ordinary subsistence crisis' in E.M. Crawford (ed.), *Famine: the Irish experience 900–1900* (Edinburgh: John Donald, 1989), pp. 112–29.

The Times, 1845–7.

Trevelyan, C.E., *The Irish Crisis* (London: Longman, Brown, Green and Longmans, 1848).

Vaughan, W.E. (ed.), *A new history of Ireland,* vol. v: Ireland under the Union, 1801–70 (Oxford: Clarendon Press, 1989).

Walker, B.M., 'Villain, victim or prophet: William Gregory and the Great Famine', *Irish Historical Studies,* 38 (2012–13), 579–99.

Whelan, I., 'Edward Nangle and the Achill Mission, 1834–1852' in R. Gillespie and G. Moran (eds.), *"A Various County": Essays in Mayo History 1500–1900* (Westport: Foilseacháin Náisiúnta Teoranta, 1987), pp. 113–34.

Whelan, I., 'The stigma of souperism', in C. Póirtéir (ed.), *The Great Irish Famine* (Cork: Mercier Press, 1995), pp. 135–54.

25 Irish Emigration, *c.*1845–1900

Kevin Kenny

Akenson, D.H., 'An agnostic view of the historiography of the Irish-Americans', *Labour/ Le Travail,* 14 (Fall 1984), 123–59.

The Irish diaspora: a primer (Toronto: P.D. Meany, 1993).

Ireland, Sweden and the great European migration, 1815–1914 (Liverpool: Liverpool University Press, 2011).

Anbinder, T., 'Lord Palmerston and the Irish Famine migration', *Historical Journal,* 44 (2001), 441–69.

'From Famine to Five Points: Lord Lansdowne's Irish tenants encounter North America's most notorious slum', *American Historical Review,* 107 (2002), 351–87.

Belchem, J., 'Nationalism, republicanism and exile: Irish emigrants and the revolutions of 1848', *Past and Present,* 146 (1995), 103–35.

Bielenberg, A. (ed.), *The Irish diaspora* (Harlow: Longman, 2000).

Blessing, P.J., 'Irish' in S. Thernstrom (ed.), *The Harvard encyclopedia of American ethnic groups* (Cambridge, MA: Belknap Press of Harvard University Press, 1980), p. 528

'Irish emigration to the United States, 1800–1920: an overview' in P.J. Drudy (ed.), *Irish in America: emigration, assimilation, and impact* (Cambridge: Cambridge University Press, 1985), pp. 11–37.

Boyer, G.R., T.J. Hatton and K. O'Rourke, 'The impact of emigration on real wages in Ireland, 1850–1914' in T.J. Hatton and J.G. Williamson (eds.), *Migration and the international labor market, 1850–1939* (New York: Routledge, 1994), pp. 221–39.

Brown, T.N., *Irish-American nationalism, 1870–1890* (Philadelphia: Lippincott, 1966).

Brundage, D., *Irish nationalists in America: the politics of exile, 1798–1998* (Oxford: Oxford University Press, 2016).

Burchell, R.A., *The San Francisco Irish, 1848–1880* (Manchester: Manchester University Press, 1979).

Campbell, M., *Ireland's new worlds: immigrants, politics, and society in the United States and Australia, 1815–1922* (Madison: University of Wisconsin Press, 2008).

Connell, K.H., 'Peasant marriage in Ireland after the Great Famine', *Past and Present,* 12 (1957), 76–91.

'Peasant marriage in Ireland: its structure and development since the Famine', *Economic History Review,* 2nd series, 14 (1962), 502–23.

Cousens, S.H., 'Regional death rates in Ireland during the Great Famine, from 1846 to 1851', *Population Studies,* 14 (1960), 55–74.

'The regional pattern of emigration during the Great Irish Famine, 1846–51', *Transactions and Papers (Institute of British Geographers),* 28 (1960), 119–34.

'Emigration and demographic change in Ireland, 1851–1861', *Economic History Review,* 14 (1961), 275–88.

'The regional variations in population changes in Ireland, 1861–1881', *Economic History Review*, 17 (1964), 301–21.

Crowley, J., W.J. Smyth and M. Murphy (eds.), *Atlas of the Great Irish Famine, 1845–50* (Cork: Cork University Press, 2012).

Davis, G., *The Irish in Britain, 1815–1914* (Dublin: Gill & Macmillan, 1991).

Diner, H., *Erin's daughters in America: Irish immigrant women in the nineteenth century* (Baltimore: Johns Hopkins University Press, 1983).

Doan, R., 'Green gold to the emerald shores: Irish immigration to the United States and Transatlantic monetary aid, 1854–1923', PhD thesis, Temple University, 1998.

Donnelly, Jr. J.S., *The Great Irish Potato Famine* (Stroud: Sutton, 2001).

Doyle, D.N., 'The Irish as urban pioneers in the United States, 1850–1870', *Journal of American Ethnic History*, 10 (Fall 1990–Winter 1991), 36–59.

'The remaking of Irish-America, 1845–80' in W.E. Vaughan (ed.), A new history of Ireland, vol. VI: *Ireland under the Union 1870–1921* (Oxford: Oxford University Press, 1996), pp. 725–63.

Emmons, D.M., *The Butte Irish: class and ethnicity in an American mining town, 1875–1925* (Urbana: University of Illinois Press, 1989).

Fitzpatrick, D., *Irish emigration 1801–1921* (Dundalk: Economic and Social History Society of Ireland, 1984).

'Emigration, 1801–70' in W.E. Vaughan (ed.), *A new history of Ireland*, vol. V: *Ireland under the Union 1801–70* (Oxford: Oxford University Press, 1989), pp. 562–622.

(ed.), *Oceans of consolation: personal accounts of Irish migration to Australia* (Ithaca, NY: Cornell University Press, 1994).

'Emigration, 1871–1921' in W.E. Vaughan (ed.), *A new history of Ireland*, vol. VI: *Ireland under the Union 1870–1921* (Oxford: Oxford University Press, 1996), pp. 606–52.

Foner, E., 'Class, ethnicity, and radicalism in the Gilded Age: the Land League and Irish-America' in E. Foner, *Politics and ideology in the age of the Civil War* (Oxford: Oxford University Press, 1980), pp. 150–200.

Fraser, L., *To Tara via Holyhead: Irish Catholic immigrants in nineteenth-century Christchurch* (Auckland: Auckland University Press, 1997).

Gray, P., *The Irish Famine* (New York: Harry N. Abrams, 1995).

'Famine relief policy in comparative perspective: Ireland, Scotland, and Northwest Europe, 1845–1849', *Éire-Ireland*, 32:1 (1997), 86–108.

Famine, land, and politics: British government and Irish society, 1843–1850 (Dublin: Irish Academic Press, 2001).

Guinnane, T.W., *The vanishing Irish: households, migration, and the rural economy in Ireland, 1850–1914* (Princeton: Princeton University Press, 1997).

Haines, R., *Charles Treveylan and the great Irish Famine* (Dublin: Four Courts Press, 2004).

Hatton, T.J., and J.G. Williamson, 'After the Famine: emigration from Ireland, 1850–1913', *Journal of Economic History*, 53 (1993), 575–600.

The age of mass migration: causes and economic impact (Oxford: Oxford University Press, 1998).

Jackson, P., 'Women in nineteenth-century Irish emigration', *International Migration Review*, 18 (1984), 1004–20.

Kennedy, R.E., *The Irish: emigration, marriage, and fertility* (Berkeley: University of California Press, 1973).

Kenny, K., *Making sense of the Molly Maguires* (Oxford: Oxford University Press, 1998).

The American Irish: a history (New York: Longman, 2000).

'The Irish in the Empire' in K. Kenny (ed.), *Ireland and the British Empire,* The Oxford History of the British Empire Companion Series (Oxford: Oxford University Press, 2004), pp. 90–122.

Lynch-Brennan, M., *The Irish Bridget: Irish immigrant women in domestic service in America, 1840–1930* (Syracuse, NY: Syracuse University Press, 2009).

MacDonagh, O., 'The Irish Famine emigration to the United States', *Perspectives in American History*, 10 (1976), 357–446.

MacKay, D., *Flight from famine: the coming of the Irish to Canada* (Toronto: McClelland and Stewart, 1990).

MacRaild, D.M., *The Irish diaspora in Britain, 1750–1939*, 2nd edn (New York: St. Martin's Press, 2011).

McCarthy, A., *Irish migrants in New Zealand, 1840–1937: 'the desired haven'* (Rochester, NY: The Boydell Press, 2005).

Miller, K.A., *Emigrants and exiles: Ireland and the Irish exodus to North America* (Oxford: Oxford University Press, 1985).

Miller, K., with B. Boling and D.N. Doyle, 'Emigrants and exiles: Irish cultures and Irish emigration to North America, 1790–1922', *Irish Historical Studies*, 22 (1980–1), 97–125.

Mitchel, J., *The last conquest of Ireland (perhaps)*, ed. P. Maume (Dublin: UCD Press, 2005).

Moran, G., *Sending out Ireland's poor: assisted emigration to North America in the nineteenth century* (Dublin: Four Courts Press, 2013).

Nelson, B., *Irish nationalists and the making of the Irish race* (Princeton: Princeton University Press, 2012).

Nolan, J., *Ourselves alone: women's emigration from Ireland, 1885–1920* (Lexington: University Press of Kentucky, 1989).

Ó Cuív, B., *Irish dialects and Irish-speaking districts: three lectures* (Dublin: Dublin Institute for Advanced Studies, 1980).

Ó Gráda, C., 'Seasonal migration and post-Famine adjustment in the west of Ireland', *Studia Hibernica*, 13 (1973), 48–76.

O'Farrell, P., *The Irish in Australia* (Kensington, NSW: University of New South Wales Press, 1987).

'Irish in Australia and New Zealand, 1801–70' in W.E. Vaughan (ed.), *A new history of Ireland, vol. V: Ireland under the Union 1801–70* (Oxford: Oxford University Press, 1989), pp. 661–81.

'Irish in Australia and New Zealand, 1870–1990' in W.E. Vaughan (ed.), *A new history of Ireland*, vol. VI: Ireland under the Union 1870–1921 (Oxford: Oxford University Press, 1996), pp. 703–24.

O'Gallagher, M., *Grosse Île: gateway to Canada, 1832–1937* (St. Foy, Quebec: Carraig Books, 1984).

O'Neil, T.M., 'Miners in migration: the case of nineteenth-century Irish and Irish-American copper miners', *Éire-Ireland*, 36 (Spring/Summer 2001), 124–40.

Quigley, M., 'Grosse Île: Canada's Famine memorial', *Éire-Ireland*, 32 (Spring 1997), 7–19.

Scally, R.J., *The end of hidden Ireland: rebellion, famine, and emigration* (Oxford: Oxford University Press, 1995).

Schrier, A., *Ireland and the American migration, 1850–1900* (Minneapolis: University of Minnesota Press, 1958).

Trevelyan, C., *The Irish crisis* (London: Longman, Brown, Green and Longmans, 1848).

Ueda, R., *Postwar immigrant America: a social history* (New York: Bedford/St. Martin's, 1994).

Walsh, B.M., 'A perspective on Irish population patterns', *Éire-Ireland*, 4 (1969), 3–21.

'Marriage rates and population pressure: Ireland, 1871 and 1911', *Economic History Review*, 23 (1970), 148–62.

Walsh, V.A., ' "A fanatic heart": the cause of Irish-American nationalism in Pittsburgh during the Gilded Age', *Journal of Social History*, 15 (1981), 187–204.

Whelehan, N., *The dynamiters: Irish nationalism and political violence in the wider world, 1867–1900* (Cambridge: Cambridge University Press, 2012).

Wilson, D., *The Irish in Canada* (Ottawa: Canadian Historical Association, 1989).

26 Post-Famine Politics, 1850–1879

Douglas Kanter

Manuscript

Acton papers, Add. MS 8119: Cambridge University Library

Butt papers, MS 8692: National Library of Ireland

Carlingford papers, DD/SH/61: Somerset Record Office

Dufferin papers, D/1070: Public Record Office of Northern Ireland

Gavan Duffy papers, MS 7404: National Library of Ireland

New Kirby papers: Irish College Rome

Smith O'Brien papers, MS 446: National Library of Ireland

Printed

Barr, C., 'An Irish dimension to a British *Kulturkampf* ?', *Journal of Ecclesiastical History*, 36 (2005), 473–95.

'Giuseppe Mazzini and Irish nationalism, 1845–70' in C.A. Bayly and E.F. Biagini (eds.), *Giuseppe Mazzini and the globalisation of democratic nationalism, 1830–1920* (Oxford: Oxford University Press, 2008), pp. 133–42.

Bew, J., *The glory of being Britons: civic Unionism in nineteenth-century Belfast* (Dublin: Irish Academic Press, 2009).

Bew, P., *Ireland: the politics of enmity, 1789–2006* (Oxford: Oxford University Press, 2007).

Enigma: a new life of Charles Stewart Parnell (Dublin: Gill & Macmillan, 2011).

Butt, I., *Irish federalism! Its meaning, its objects, and its hopes*, 3rd edn (Dublin: John Falconer, 1871).

The Celt, 1858.

Comerford, R.V., 'Churchmen, tenants, and independent opposition, 1850–56' in W.E. Vaughan (ed.), *A new history of Ireland*, vol. v: *Ireland under the Union 1801–70* (Oxford: Oxford University Press, 1989), pp. 396–414.

The Fenians in context: Irish politics and society, 1848–82, 2nd edn (Dublin: Wolfhound Press, 1998).

'Fenianism: the scope and limitations of a concept' in F. McGarry and J. McConnell (eds.), *The black hand of Republicanism: Fenianism in modern Ireland* (Dublin: Irish Academic Press, 2009), pp. 179–89.

Farrell, S., 'Recapturing the flag: the campaign to repeal the Party Processions Act, 1860–1872', *Éire-Ireland*, 32 (1997), 52–78.

Freeman's Journal, 1850, 1852.

Golden, J.J., 'The Protestant influence on the origins of Irish home rule, 1861–1871', *English Historical Review*, 128 (2013), 1483–1516.

Gray, P., 'Famine and land, 1845–80' in A. Jackson (ed.), *The Oxford handbook of modern Irish history* (Oxford: Oxford University Press, 2014), pp. 544–61.

Hall, G.R., *Ulster Liberalism, 1778–1876* (Dublin: Four Courts Press, 2011).

Hansard, 3rd series.

Holmes, A.R., 'Covenanter politics: evangelicalism, political liberalism and Ulster Presbyterians, 1798–1914', *English Historical Review*, 125 (2010), 340–69.

Hoppen, K.T., 'Tories, Catholics, and the general election of 1859', *Historical Journal*, 13 (1970), 48–67.

Elections, politics, and society in Ireland, 1832–1885 (Oxford: Oxford University Press, 1984).

'Gladstone, Salisbury and the end of Irish assimilation' in M.E. Daly and K.T. Hoppen (eds.), *Gladstone: Ireland and beyond* (Dublin: Four Courts Press, 2011), pp. 45–63.

Horgan, D.T., 'The Irish Catholic Whigs in parliament, 1847–74', PhD thesis, University of Minnesota, 1975.

Jackson, A., *Home Rule: an Irish history, 1800–2000* (Oxford: Oxford University Press, 2003).

The two Unions: Ireland, Scotland, and the survival of the United Kingdom, 1707–2007 (Oxford: Oxford University Press, 2012).

Keogh, R.A., ' "Nothing is so bad for the Irish as Ireland alone": William Keogh and Catholic loyalty', *Irish Historical Studies*, 38 (2012–13), 230–48.

Knowlton, S.R., *Popular politics and the Irish Catholic Church: the rise and fall of the Independent Irish Party, 1850–1859* (New York: Garland, 1991).

Larkin, E., *The making of the Roman Catholic Church in Ireland, 1850–1860* (Chapel Hill: University of North Carolina Press, 1980).

The consolidation of the Roman Catholic Church in Ireland, 1860–1870 (Chapel Hill: University of North Carolina Press, 1987).

The Roman Catholic Church and the Home Rule movement in Ireland, 1870–1874 (Chapel Hill: University of North Carolina Press, 1990).

The Roman Catholic Church and the emergence of the modern Irish political system, 1874–1878 (Dublin: Four Courts Press, 1996).

Legg, M.-L., *Newspapers and nationalism: the Irish provincial press, 1850–1892* (Dublin: Four Courts Press, 1999).

Murphy, J.H., *Abject loyalty: nationalism and monarchy in Ireland during the reign of Queen Victoria* (Washington, DC: Catholic University of America Press, 2001).

Ireland's Czar: Gladstonian government and the lord lieutenancies of the red Earl Spencer, 1868–86 (Dublin: UCD Press, 2014).

Nation, 1855, 1869.

O'Day, A., *Irish Home Rule, 1867–1921* (Manchester: Manchester University Press, 1998).

Potter, M., *William Monsell of Tervoe, 1812–1894: Catholic Unionist, Anglo-Irishman* (Dublin: Irish Academic Press, 2009).

Ramón, M., *A provisional dictator: James Stephens and the Fenian movement* (Dublin: UCD Press, 2007).

Reid, C.W., ' "An experiment in constructive unionism": Isaac Butt, Home Rule and federalist political thought during the 1870s', *English Historical Review*, 129 (2014), 332–61.

Shields, A., *The Irish Conservative Party, 1852–1868: land, politics and religion* (Dublin: Irish Academic Press, 2007).

Spence, J., 'Isaac Butt, Irish nationality and the conditional defence of the Union, 1833–70' in D.G. Boyce and A. O'Day (eds.), *Defenders of the Union: a survey of British and Irish unionism since 1801* (London: Routledge, 2001), pp. 65–89.

Sullivan, A.M., *New Ireland*, 2 vols. (London: Sampson Low, Marston, Searle, and Rivington, 1877).

Thornley, D., *Isaac Butt and Home Rule* (London: MacGibbon and Kee, 1964).

The Times, 1867.

Townend, P.A., 'Between two worlds: Irish nationalists and imperial crisis, 1878–1880', *Past and Present*, 194 (2007), 139–74.

Vincent, J. (ed.), *Disraeli, Derby and the Conservative Party: journals and memoirs of Edward Henry, Lord Stanley, 1849–1869* (Hassocks: Harvester Press, 1978).

Walker, B.M., 'The Irish electorate, 1868–1915', *Irish Historical Studies*, 18 (1973), 359–406.

(ed.), *Parliamentary election results in Ireland, 1801–1922* (Dublin: Royal Irish Academy, 1978).

Warren, A., 'Disraeli, the Conservatives and the government of Ireland: part 2, 1868–1881', *Parliamentary History*, 28 (1999), 145–67.

'Palmerston, the Whigs and the government of Ireland, 1855–1866' in D. Brown and M. Taylor (eds.), *Palmerston studies II* (Southampton: Hartley Institute, 2007), 95–126.

27 Afterword

Toby Barnard

Akenson, D.H., *The Irish education experiment: the national system of education in the nineteenth century* (London: Routledge, 1970).

Bailey, C., 'From innovation to emulation: London's Benevolent Society of St. Patrick, 1783–1800', *Eighteenth-Century Ireland,* 27 (2012), 162–84.

Irish London: middle-class migration in the global eighteenth century (Liverpool: Liverpool University Press, 2013).

Barnard, T., 'Sir John Gilbert' in M. Clark, Y. Desmond and N.P. Hardiman (eds.), *Sir John T. Gilbert, 1829–1898: historian, archivist and librarian* (Dublin: Dublin Corporation, 1999), pp. 92–110.

'Considering the inconsiderable: electors, patrons and Irish elections, 1659–1761' in D.W. Hayton (ed.), *The Irish Parliament in the eighteenth century: the long apprenticeship* (Edinburgh: Edinburgh University Press, 2001), pp. 107–27.

A new anatomy of Ireland: the Irish Protestants, 1641–1770 (New Haven: Yale University Press, 2003).

'Scholars and antiquarians: the clergy and learning, 1600–2000' in T. Barnard and W.G. Neely (eds.), *The clergy of the Church of Ireland, 1000–2000: messengers, watchmen and stewards* (Dublin: Four Courts Press, 2006), pp. 231–58.

'The eighteenth-century parish' in E. FitzPatrick and R. Gillespie (eds.), *The parish in medieval and early modern Ireland: community, territory and building* (Dublin: Four Courts Press, 2006), pp. 297–324.

'Churchwardens' accounts and the confessional state in Ireland, *c.*1660–1800' in V. Hitchman and A. Foster (eds.), *Views from the parish: churchwardens' accounts c.1500– c.1800* (Cambridge: Scholars Press, 2015), pp. 109–20.

'Delusions of grandeur? "Big" houses in eighteenth-century Ireland', *Eighteenth-Century Ireland*, 30 (2015), pp. 124–49.

'Educating eighteenth-century Ulster' in D.W. Hayton and A. Holmes (eds.), *Ourselves alone? Religion, society and politics in eighteenth- and nineteenth-century Ireland* (Dublin: Four Courts Press, 2016), pp. 104–25.

Brought to book: print in Ireland, 1680–1784 (Dublin: Four Courts Press, 2017).

Bartlett, T., 'Review article – *A new history of Ireland*', *Past and Present*, 116 (1987), 206–19.

Begadon, C., 'The renewal of Catholic religious culture in eighteenth-century Dublin' in J. Bergin et al. (eds.), *New perspectives on the Penal Laws* (Dublin: Eighteenth-Century Ireland Society, 2011), pp. 227–47.

Bergin, J., 'The Irish Catholic interest at the London Inns of Court, 1671–1800', *Eighteenth-Century Ireland*, 24 (2009), pp. 36–61.

'Irish Catholics and their networks in London', *Eighteenth-Century Life*, 39 (2015), 66–102.

Bourke, R., *Empire and revolution: the political life of Edmund Burke* (Princeton: Princeton University Press, 2015).

Breatnach, R.A., 'The end of a tradition: a survey of eighteenth-century Gaelic literature', *Studia Hibernica*, 1 (1961), 128–50.

Broderick, D., *The first toll roads: Ireland's turnpike roads 1729–1858* (Cork: Collins Press, 2002).

Brown, M., *The Irish Enlightenment* (Cambridge, MA: Harvard University Press, 2016).

Brown, M., and S.P. Donlan (eds.), *The laws and other legalities of Ireland 1689–1850* (Farnham: Ashgate, 2011).

Butler, S., *Irish tales*, ed. I.C. Ross, A. Douglas and A. Markey (Dublin: Four Courts Press, 2010).

Chaigneau, W., *The history of Jack Connor*, ed. I.C. Ross (Dublin: Four Courts Press, 2013).

Comerford, R.V., and J. Kelly (eds.), *Associational culture in Ireland and abroad* (Dublin: Irish Academic Press, 2010).

Connolly, S.J., *Religion, law and power: the making of Protestant Ireland, 1660–1760* (Oxford: Oxford University Press, 1992).

Divided kingdom: Ireland 1630–1800 (Oxford: Oxford University Press, 2008).

Crawford, J., *The Church of Ireland in Victorian Dublin* (Dublin: Four Courts Press, 2005).

Crosbie, B., *Irish imperial networks: migration, social communication and exchange in nineteenth-century India* (Cambridge: Cambridge University Press, 2012).

Cullen, L.M., J. Shovlin and T.M. Truxes (eds.), *The Bordeaux–Dublin letters, 1757: correspondence of an Irish Community abroad* (Oxford: Oxford University Press, 2013).

Davis, W., *The diary of an Offaly schoolboy, 1858–9*, ed. S. Robinson (Tullamore: Esker Press, 2010).

Dickson, D., *New foundations: Ireland 1660–1800*, 2nd edn (Dublin: Irish Academic Press, 2000).

Dictionary of Irish biography, ed. J.I. McGuire and James Quinn, 9 vols. (Cambridge: Cambridge University Press, 2009).

Dorian, H., *The outer edge of Ulster: a memoir of social life in nineteenth-century Donegal*, ed. B. Mac Suibhne and D. Dickson (Dublin: Lilliput Press, 2000).

Doyle, A., *A history of the Irish language from the Norman Invasion to Independence* (Oxford: Oxford University Press, 2015).

'The "decline" of the Irish language in the eighteenth and nineteenth centuries: a new interpretation', *Studia Hibernica*, 41 (2015), 117–34.

Fagan, P., *Catholics in a Protestant country: the papist constituency in eighteenth-century Dublin* (Dublin: Four Courts Press, 1998).

FitzPatrick, E., and R. Gillespie (eds.), *The parish in medieval and early modern Ireland: community, territory and building* (Dublin: Four Courts Press, 2006).

Garnham, N., *The courts, crime and the criminal law in Ireland, 1692–1760* (Dublin: Irish Academic Press, 1996).

'How violent was eighteenth-century Ireland?' *Irish Historical Studies*, 30 (1997), 377–92.

The militia in eighteenth-century Ireland (Woodbridge: The Boydell Press, 2012).

Gibbons, L., and K. O'Conor (eds.), *Charles O'Conor of Ballinagare: life and works* (Dublin: Four Courts Press, 2015).

Gillen, U., 'Monarchy, republic and empire: Irish public opinion and France, c.1787–1804', DPhil thesis, Oxford University, 2005.

Gillespie, R., *Seventeenth-century Ireland* (Dublin: Gill & Macmillan, 2006).

Greene, J.C., *Theatre in Dublin, 1745–1820: a history*, 2 vols. (Bethlehem, PA: Lehigh University Press, 2011).

Gribbon, H.D., 'The Irish Linen Board, 1711–1828' in L.M. Cullen and T.C. Smout (eds.), *Comparative aspects of Scottish and Irish economic and social history, 1600–1900* (Edinburgh: John Donald [1977]), pp. 77–87.

Hamilton, H.D., *The cries of Dublin, 1760*, ed. W. Laffan (Tralee: Churchill House Press, 2003).

Hayton, D.W. (ed.), *The Irish Parliament in the eighteenth century: the long apprenticeship* (Edinburgh: Edinburgh University Press, 2001).

Ruling Ireland, 1685–1742: politicians and parties (Woodbridge: The Boydell Press, 2004).

The Anglo-Irish experience, c.1680–1730: religion, identity and patriotism (Woodbridge: The Boydell Press, 2012).

Hayton, D.W., J. Kelly and J. Bergin (eds.), *The eighteenth-century composite state: representative institutions in Ireland and Europe, 1689–1800* (Basingstoke: Palgrave Macmillan, 2010).

Higgins, P., *A nation of politicians: gender, patriotism and political culture in late eighteenth-century Ireland* (Madison: University of Wisconsin Press, 2010).

Hill, J.R., *From patriots to unionists: Dublin civic politics and Irish Protestant patriotism, 1660–1840* (Oxford: Oxford University Press, 1997).

Holmes, A.R., *The shaping of Ulster Presbyterian belief and practice, 1770–1840* (Oxford: Oxford University Press, 2006).

Johnston-Liik, E.M., *History of the Irish parliament, 1692–1800*, 6 vols. (Belfast: Ulster Historical Foundation, 2002).

Kelly, J., 'Conservative Protestant thought in later eighteenth-century Ireland' in S.J. Connolly (ed.), *Political ideas in eighteenth-century Ireland* (Dublin: Four Courts Press, 2000), pp. 185–220.

'Defending the established order: Richard Woodward, bishop of Cloyne (1726–94)' in J. Kelly, J. McCafferty and C.I. McGrath (eds.), *People, politics and power: essays in Irish history 1660–1850* (Dublin: UCD Press, 2009), pp. 143–74.

Sir Richard Musgrave 1746–1818: ultra-Protestant ideologue (Dublin: Four Courts Press, 2009).

Kelly, J., and M.J. Powell (eds.), *Clubs and societies in eighteenth-century Ireland* (Dublin: Four Courts Press, 2010).

Kelly, J., *'The Downfall of Hagan': Sligo Ribbonism in 1842* (Dublin: Four Courts Press, 2008).

Lario, M., 'Irish traders in eighteenth-century Cadiz' in D. Dickson, J. Parmentier and J. Ohlmeyer (eds.), *Irish and Scottish mercantile networks in Europe and overseas in the seventeenth and eighteenth centuries* (Ghent: Academia Press, 2007), pp. 211–30.

Lario de Oñate, M., 'Irish integration in the eighteenth century maritime mercantile city of Cadiz' in O. Recio Morales (ed.), *Redes de nación y espacios de poder: la comunidad Irlandesa en España y la América Española, 1600–1825./Power strategies: Spain and Ireland 1600–1825* (Valencia: Albatros Ediciones, 2012), pp. 183–90.

Leerssen, J., *Hidden Ireland, public sphere* (Galway: Arlen Press, 2002).

Legg, M.L. (ed.), *The Synge letters: Bishop Edward Synge to his daughter, Alicia, Roscommon to London, 1746–1752* (Dublin: Irish Manuscripts Commission, 1996).

(ed.), *The diary of Nicholas Peacock 1740–1751* (Dublin: Four Courts Press, 2005).

Leighton, C.D.A., *Catholicism in a Protestant kingdom: a study of the Irish ancien régime* (Dublin: Gill & Macmillan, 1994).

Lennon, C. (ed.), *Confraternities and sodalities in Ireland: charity, devotion and sociability* (Dublin: Columba Press, 2012).

Livesey, J., *Civil society and empire: Ireland and Scotland in the eighteenth-century Atlantic world* (New Haven: Yale University Press, 2009).

Loeber, R., and M. Loeber, *A guide to Irish fiction, 1650–1900* (Dublin: Four Courts Press, 2006).

Lyttleton, J., and T. O'Keeffe (eds.), *The manor in medieval and early modern Ireland* (Dublin: Four Courts Press, 2005).

Magennis, E., 'Coal, corn and canals: parliament and the dispersal of public moneys, 1693–1772' in D.W. Hayton (ed.), *The Irish Parliament in the eighteenth century: the long apprenticeship* (Edinburgh: Edinburgh University Press, 2001), pp. 71–86.

Malcomson, A.P.W., *Archbishop Charles Agar: churchmanship and politics in Ireland, 1760–1810* (Dublin; Four Courts Press, 2002).

Nathaniel Clements: government and the governing elite in Ireland, 1725–75 (Dublin: Four Courts Press, 2005).

John Foster (1740–1828): the politics of improvement and prosperity (Dublin: Four Courts Press, 2011).

McBride, I., *Eighteenth-century Ireland* (Dublin: Gill & Macmillan, 2009).

McCarthy, M. (ed.), *Lord Charlemont and his circle* (Dublin: Four Courts Press, 2001).

McDonnell, J., 'Art and patronage in the penal era' in Maynooth College, *Ecclesiastical art of the penal era* (Maynooth: St Patrick's College, 1995).

McGrath, C.I., *The making of the eighteenth-century Irish constitution: government, parliament and the revenue, 1692–1714* (Dublin: Four Courts Press, 2000).

McGrath, M. (ed.), *Cinnlae Amhlaoibh Uí Shúileabháin/The diary of Humphrey O'Sullivan,* 4 vols. (London: Irish Texts Society, 1936–7).

McNally, P., *Parties, patriots and undertakers: parliamentary politics in early Hanoverian Ireland* (Dublin: Four Courts Press, 1997).

Moody, T.W., and W.E. Vaughan (eds.), *A new history of Ireland, vol. IV: Ireland 1690–1800* (Oxford: Oxford University Press, 1986).

Morley, V., *Irish opinion and the American Revolution, 1760–1783* (Cambridge: Cambridge University Press, 2002).

Murphy, M., and M. Stout (eds.), *Agriculture and settlement in Ireland* (Dublin: Four Courts Press, 2015).

Murphy, S., 'The Dublin anti-union riot of 3 December 1759' in G. O'Brien (ed.), *Parliament, politics and people: essays in eighteenth-century Irish history* (Dublin: Irish Academic Press, 1989), pp. 49–68.

Murray, D., *Romanticism, nationalism and Irish Antiquarian Societies, 1840–80* (Maynooth: Maynooth University, 2000).

Musgrave, R., *Memoirs of the Irish rebellion of 1798*, 4th edn (Fort Wayne, IN: Round Tower Press, 1995).

Musielak, R., *Charlemont's Marino: portrait of a landscape* (Dublin: Office of Public Works, [2014]).

Ní Mhungaile, L., 'Bilingualism, print culture in Irish and the public sphere, 1700–c.1830' in J. Kelly and C. Mac Murchaidh (eds.), *Irish and English: essays on the English linguistic and cultural frontier, 1600–1900* (Dublin: Four Courts Press, 2012), pp. 218–42.

Ó Ciosáin, N., *Ireland in official print culture 1800–1850: a new reading of the Poor Inquiry* (Oxford: Oxford University Press, 2014).

Ó Floinn, R. (ed.), *Franciscan faith: sacred art in Ireland, AD 1600–1750* (Dublin: Wordwell, 2011).

O'Connor, C., *The pleasing hours: James Caulfeild, first Earl of Charlemont, 1728–99: traveller, connoisseur and patron of the arts in Ireland* (Cork: Collins Press, 1999).

O'Neill, C., *Catholics of consequence: transnational education, social mobility and the Catholic elite, 1850–1900* (Oxford: Oxford University Press, 2014).

Power, O., 'The "quadripartite concern" of St. Croix: an Irish Catholic experiment in the Danish West Indies' in D.T. Gleeson (ed.), *The Irish in the Atlantic world* (Columbia: University of South Carolina Press, 2010), pp. 213–28.

'Friend, foe or family? Catholic creoles, French Huguenots, Scottish dissenters: aspects of the Irish diaspora at St Cruz, Danish West Indies, c.1760' in N. Whelehan (ed.), *Transnational perspectives on modern Irish history* (London: Routledge, 2015), pp. 30–44.

Power, T.P., 'Publishing and sectarian tension in South Munster in the 1760s', *Eighteenth-Century Ireland*, 19 (2004), 75–110.

Ross, I.C., '"One of the principal nations in Europe": the representation of Ireland in Sarah Butler's *Irish tales*', *Eighteenth-Century Fiction*, 7 (1994), 1–16.

'Novels, chapbooks, folklore: the several lives of William Chaigneau's Jack Connor, now Conyers: or, John Connor, alias Jack the Bachelor, the famous Irish bucker', *Eighteenth-Century Ireland*, 30 (2015), 60–90.

Small, S., *Political thought in Ireland: republicanism, patriotism and radicalism* (Oxford: Oxford University Press, 2002).

Smyth, J., *The men of no property: Irish radicals and popular politics in the late eighteenth century* (Basingstoke: Macmillan, 1992).

Vaughan, W.E., *Murder trials in Ireland, 1836–1914* (Dublin: Four Courts Press, 2009).

Walsh, P., *The making of the Irish Protestant Ascendancy: the life of William Conolly, 1662–1729* (Woodbridge: The Boydell Press, 2010).

'The Irish fiscal state, 1690–1769', *Historical Journal*, 56 (2013), 629–56.

'Enforcing the fiscal state: the army, the revenue and the Irish experience of the fiscal-military state' in A. Graham and P. Walsh (eds.), *The British fiscal-military states, 1660–c.1783* (London: Routledge, 2016), pp. 48–65.

Wolf, N.M., *An Irish-speaking island: state, religion, community and the linguistic landscape in Ireland, 1770–1870* (Madison: University of Wisconsin Press, 2014).

Wright, J., *The 'natural leaders' and their world: politics, culture and society in Belfast, c.1801–1832* (Liverpool: Liverpool University Press, 2012).

Index

THE CAMBRIDGE HISTORY OF

Ireland

General Editor – Thomas Bartlett

'These four volumes stand as an intellectual riposte to those who doubt the vital importance of the study of history in our universities and in our society.'

MICHAEL D. HIGGINS, PRESIDENT OF IRELAND

'mammoth ... inspiring ... marvellously satisfying.'

THE IRISH TIMES

'Bursting with provocative, intelligent analysis and accessible narratives.'

DIARMAID FERRITER, BEST OF 2018, *IRISH INDEPENDENT*

'Only one word will do: awesome.'

ANDREW LYNCH, *SUNDAY BUSINESS POST*

'Magnificent.'

EAMON DUFFY, *THE TABLET*

'An essential starting point for anyone who wants seriously to understand the Irish past, present and future.'

PATRICK WALSH, *HISTORY TODAY*

'...an achievement for which the hundred and more contributors, the four editors and especially their chief, Thomas Bartlett, deserve the very highest praise.'

IRISH HISTORICAL STUDIES

CAMBRIDGE
UNIVERSITY PRESS
www.cambridge.org

ISBN 978-1-107-53559-6

9 781107 535596